Germany

Hamburg &
the North
p643

Lower Saxony
& Bremen
p505

Berlin
p54

Around
Berlin
p124

Cologne &
Northern Rhineland
p462

Central
Germany
p526

Saxony
p140

Frankfurt &
Southern Rhineland
p370

Stuttgart & the
Black Forest
p306

Bavaria
p227

Munich
p182

THIS EDITION WRITTEN AND RESEARCHED BY

Andrea Schulte-Peevers,
Kerry Christiani, Marc Di Duca, Catherine Le Nevez,
Tom Masters, Ryan Ver Berkmoes, Benedict Walker

Contents

BLACK FOREST P328

PRETZELS P45

Contents

Contents

BURG KATZ P439

Welcome to Germany

Prepare for a roller coaster of feasts, treats and temptations as you take in Germany's soul-stirring scenery, spirit-lifting culture, big-city beauties, romantic palaces and half-timbered towns.

Bewitching Scenery

There's something undeniably artistic in the way Germany's scenery unfolds – the corrugated, dune-fringed coasts of the north; the moody forests, romantic river valleys and vast vineyards of the centre; and the off-the-charts splendour of the Alps, carved into rugged glory by glaciers and the elements. All are integral parts of a magical natural matrix that's bound to give your camera batteries a workout. Get off the highway and into the great outdoors to soak up the epic landscapes that make each delicious, slow, winding mile so precious.

Pleasures of Civilisation

You'll encounter history in towns where streets were laid out long before Columbus set sail, and in castles that loom above prim, half-timbered villages. The great cities – Berlin, Munich and Hamburg among them – come in more flavours than a jar of jelly beans but will all wow you with a cultural kaleidoscope that spans the arc from art museums and high-brow opera to naughty cabaret and underground clubs. And wherever you go, Romanesque, Gothic and baroque classics rub rafters with architectural creations from modern masters such as Daniel Libeskind, David Chipperfield and Frank Gehry.

Gastronomic Delights

Experiencing Germany through its food and drink will add a rich layer to your memories (and possibly your belly!). You'll quickly discover that the local food is so much more than sausages, pretzels, schnitzel and roast pork accompanied by big mugs of foamy beer. Beyond the clichés awaits a cornucopia of regional and seasonal palate-teasers. Share the German people's obsession with white asparagus in springtime, chanterelle mushrooms in summer and game in autumn. Sample not only the famous beer but also world-class wines, most notably the noble Riesling.

High on History

Few countries have had as much impact on the world as Germany, which has given us the Hanseatic League, the Reformation and, yes, Hitler and the Holocaust, but also the printing press, the automobile, aspirin and MP3 technology. It is the birthplace of Martin Luther, Albert Einstein and Karl Marx, of Goethe, Beethoven, the Brothers Grimm and other heavyweights who have left their mark on human history. You can stand in a Roman amphitheatre, sleep in a medieval castle and walk along remnants of the Berlin Wall – in Germany the past is very much present wherever you go.

Why I Love Germany

By Andrea Schulte-Peevers, Author

Truth be told, I had to leave my home country of Germany to learn to love it. From my new perch in Los Angeles, I returned time and again, crisscrossing the land on my travels between the wind-caressed North Sea and the jagged Alpine peaks. I've cycled through romantic river valleys, sampled the best beer and wine, partied to techno till sunrise and stood in awe before sites that have shaped the course of history. After 15 years of discoveries, I could no longer resist the temptations of this gorgeous, complex and forever changing country, and decamped to Berlin for good. I haven't looked back.

For more about our writers, see page 816

Above: Rural view near Berchtesgaden (p245)

Germany

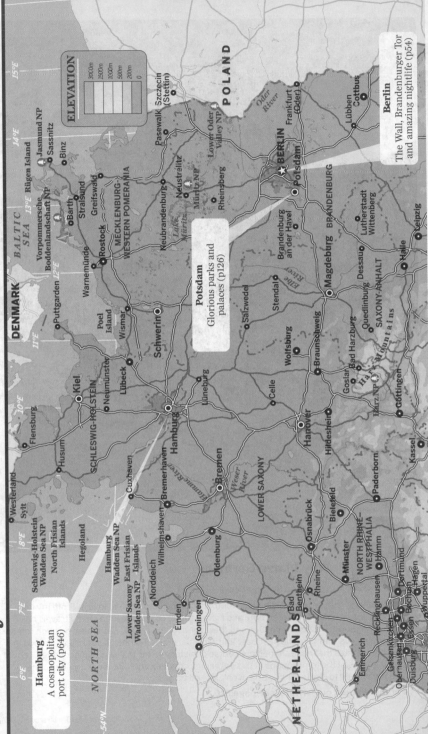

Hamburg
A cosmopolitan port city (p646)

Potsdam
Glorious parks and palaces (p126)

Berlin
The Wall, Brandenburger Tor and amazing nightlife (p54)

ELEVATION

| 3000m |
| 1500m |
| 1000m |
| 500m |
| 200m |
| 0 |

100 km
50 miles

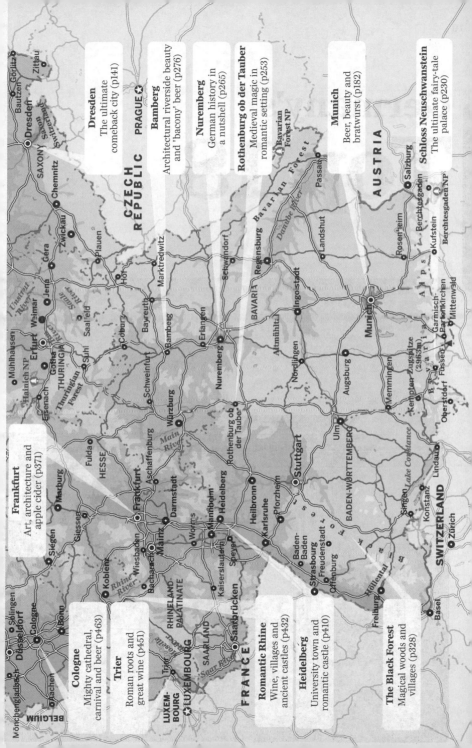

Dresden
The ultimate comeback city (p141)

Bamberg
Architectural riverside beauty and 'bacony' beer (p276)

Nuremberg
German history in a nutshell (p265)

Rothenburg ob der Tauber
Medieval magic in romantic setting (p253)

Munich
Beer, beauty and bratwurst (p182)

Schloss Neuschwanstein
The ultimate fairy-tale palace (p230)

Frankfurt
Art, architecture and apple cider (p371)

Cologne
Mighty cathedral, carnival and beer (p463)

Trier
Roman roots and great wine (p451)

Romantic Rhine
Wine, villages and ancient castles (p432)

Heidelberg
University town and romantic castle (p410)

The Black Forest
Magical woods and villages (p328)

Germany's
Top 18

Berlin

1 The glamour and grit of Berlin (p54) are bound to mesmerise anyone keen on exploring its vibrant culture, edgy architecture, fabulous food, intense parties and palpable history. Over a quarter-century after the Wall's collapse, the German capital is increasingly grown up without relinquishing its indie spirit and penchant for creative improvisation. There's haute cuisine in a former brewery, all-night parties in power stations and world-class art in a WWII bunker. Visit major historical sites – the Reichstag, Brandenburger Tor and Checkpoint Charlie among them – then feast on a smorgasbord of culture in myriad museums. Brandenburger Tor (p59)

Munich

2 If you're looking for Alpine clichés, Munich (p182) will hand them to you in one chic and compact package. But the Bavarian capital also has plenty of unexpected trump cards under its often bright-blue skies. Folklore and age-old traditions exist side by side with sleek BMWs, designer boutiques and high-powered industry. The city's museums showcase everything from artistic masterpieces to technological treasures and Oktoberfest history, while its music and cultural scenes are second only to Berlin's. BMW Welt (p204)

RICOWDE/GETTY IMAGES ©

MICHAEL THALER/SHUTTERSTOCK ©

RICHARD I'ANSON/GETTY IMAGES ©

DANIEL SCHOENEN/LOOK-FOTO/GETTY IMAGES ©

Heidelberg

3 The 19th-century romantics found sublime beauty and spiritual inspiration in Germany's oldest university town (p410) and so, in his way, did Mark Twain, who was beguiled by the ruins of the hillside castle. Generations of students have attended lectures, sung lustily with beer steins in hand, carved their names into tavern tables and, occasionally, been sent to the student jail. All of this has left its mark on the modern-day city, where age-old traditions endure alongside world-class research, innovative cultural events and a sometimes raucous nightlife scene.

The Black Forest

4 Mist, snow or shine, the deep, dark Black Forest (p328) is just beautiful. If it's back-to-nature moments you're after, this sylvan slice of southwestern Germany is the place to linger. Every valley reveals new surprises: half-timbered villages looking every inch the fairy-tale fantasy, thunderous waterfalls, and cuckoo clocks the size of houses. Breathe in the cold, sappy air, drive roller-coaster roads to middle-of-nowhere lakes, have your cake, walk it off on trail after gorgeously wooded trail, then hide away in a heavy-lidded farmhouse. Hear that? Silence. What a wonderful thing.

Schloss Neuschwanstein

5 Commissioned by Bavaria's most celebrated (and loopiest) 19th-century monarch, King Ludwig II, Neuschwanstein palace (p230) rises from the mysterious Alpine forests like a bedtime-storybook illustration. Inside, the make-believe continues, with chambers and halls reflecting Ludwig's obsession with the mythical Teutonic past – and his admiration of composer Wagner – in a confection that puts even the flashiest *palazzo* in the shade. It's said to have inspired Walt's castle at Disney World; now it inspires tourist masses along the Romantic Road, which culminates at its gates.

LEXAN/SHUTTERSTOCK ©

H & D ZIELSKE/LOOK-FOTO/GETTY IMAGES ©

PHOTO BY BRIAN T EVANS/GETTY IMAGES ©

Trier

6 There was a time when Trier (p451) was the capital of western Europe. OK, that time was 2000 years ago, when emperor Constantine ruled the fading Roman Empire from here. But nowhere has the Roman legacy survived as beautifully and tangibly as in this charming town with its ancient amphitheatre, thermal baths and famous Porta Nigra city gate. Of course Unesco noticed... Today, Germany's oldest city is as unhurried as the Moselle River it sits on, within a grape toss of the country's finest – and steepest – vineyards.

Nuremberg

7 Capital of Franconia, an independent region until 1806, Nuremberg (p265) may conjure visions of Nazi rallies and grisly war trials, but there's so much more to this energetic city. Dürer hailed from the Altstadt; his house is now a museum. Germany's first railway trundled from here to neighbouring Fürth, leaving a trail of choo-choo heritage. And Germany's toy capital has heaps of things for kids to enjoy. When you're done with sightseeing, the local beer is as dark as the coffee and best employed to chase down Nuremberg's delicious finger-sized bratwurst. Frauenkirche (p266)

German Food & Drink

8 If you crave traditional German comfort food, you'll certainly find plenty of places to indulge in a meat-potato-cabbage diet. These days, though, 'typical' German fare is lighter, healthier, creative and prepared with seasonal and locally sourced ingredients. The cities especially brim with organic eateries, gourmet kitchens, vegan bistros and a UN worth of ethnic restaurants. Talented chefs have been racking up the Michelin stars, especially in the Black Forest. And then there's German beer and bread. Is there any other country that does either better? Pretzels

Dresden

9 The apocalypse came on a cold February night in 1945. Hours of carpet bombing reduced Germany's 'Florence on the Elbe' (p141) to a smouldering pile of bricks. Dresden's comeback is nothing short of a miracle. Reconstructed architectural jewels pair with stunning art collections that justify the city's place in the pantheon of European cultural capitals. Add to that an energetic pub quarter, Daniel Libeskind's redesigned Military History Museum and a tiara of villas and palaces and you've got one enticing package of discovery. Semperoper (p146)

The Romantic Rhine

10 As the mighty Rhine flows from Rüdesheim to Koblenz (p432), the landscape's unique face-off between rock and water creates a magical mix of the wild (churning whirlpools, dramatic cliffs), the agricultural (near-vertical vineyards), the medieval (hilltop castles, half-timbered hamlets), the legendary (Loreley) and the modern (in the 19th-century sense: barges, ferries, passenger steamers and trains). Trails take you through vineyards and forests, up to panoramic viewpoints and massive stone fortresses. Burg Katz (p439)

Picturesque Towns & Villages

11 Germany's pot-pourri of villages is rich and irresistible, and needs to be appreciated gradually. Take your time as you come upon hushed hamlets and half-timbered beauties radiant with geranium-festooned windows in places such as Schiltach (p340). Follow cobbled lanes worn smooth by centuries of horses' hooves, wagon wheels and shoe leather to bustling marketplaces lorded over by lofty church spires. Stay overnight for a hearty supper in a country inn and you've got the whole fairy-tale experience.

Oktoberfest

12 Anyone with a taste for beer knows that the daddy of all beer festivals, Oktoberfest (p207), takes place annually in Munich. The world's favourite suds fest actually begins in mid-September and runs for 16 ethanol-fuelled days on the Theresienwiese (Theresa's Meadow), with troops of crimson-faced oompah bands entertaining revellers; armies of traditionally garbed locals and foreigners guzzling their way through seven million litres of lager; and entire farms of chickens hitting the grill. So find your favourite tent and raise your 1L stein. *'Ozapft ist's!'* (The tap is in!).

11

MICHAEL TAYLOR/GETTY IMAGES ©

ALLAN BAXTER/GETTY IMAGES ©

Cologne Cathedral

13 At unexpected moments you see it: Cologne's cathedral (Kölner Dom; p463), the city's twin-towered icon, looming over an urban vista and the timeless course of the Rhine River. And why shouldn't it? This perfectly formed testament to faith and conviction was started in 1248 and consecrated six centuries later. You can feel the echoes of the passage of time as you sit in its soaring stained glass–lit and artwork-filled interior. Climb a tower for views of the surrounding city that are like no others.

Hamburg

14 Anyone who thinks Germany doesn't have round-the-clock delights hasn't been to Hamburg (p646). This ancient, wealthy city on the Elbe River traces it roots back to the Hanseatic League and beyond. By day you can tour its magnificent port, explore its history in restored quarters and discover shops selling goods you didn't think were sold. By night, some of Europe's best music clubs pull in the punters, and diversions for virtually every other taste are plentiful as well. And then, another Hamburg day begins.

Bamberg

15 Often overlooked by travellers but actually one of Germany's most attractive towns, Bamberg (p276) is a medieval and baroque masterwork chock-full of Unesco-listed townhouses that were mercifully spared the destruction of WWII. Half of the Altstadt's beauty comes from its location straddling two waterways, the River Regnitz and the Rhine-Main-Danube Canal. Away from the urban eye candy, lower-brow entertainment is provided by Bamberg's numerous brew-pubs that cook up the town's unique *Rauchbier* (smoked beer) – some say it tastes a bit like bacon.

Potsdam

16 Your camera will have a love affair with the marvellous palaces, idyllic parks, stunning views, and inspired architecture of Potsdam (p126). Just across the Glienicke 'spy bridge' from Berlin, Brandenburg's state capital was catapulted to prominence by King Frederick the Great. His giddily rococo Sanssouci palace is the glorious crown of this Unesco-recognised cultural tapestry that synthesises 18th-century artistic trends from around Europe in one stupendous masterpiece. A day spent here is sure to charm and enlighten you. Neues Palais, Park Sanssouci (p126)

Rothenburg ob der Tauber

17 With its jumble of neatly restored half-timbered houses enclosed by sturdy ramparts, Rothenburg ob der Tauber (p253) lays on the medieval cuteness with a trowel. (One might even say it's too cute for its own good, if the deluges of day-trippers are any indication.) The trick is to experience this historic wonderland at its most magical: early or late in the day, when the last coaches have hit the road and you can soak up the romance all by yourself on gentle strolls along moonlit cobbled lanes.

Frankfurt

18 Germany's financial capital, Frankfurt (p371) may first appear all buttoned up, but behind the corporate demeanour lurks a city brimming with cultural, culinary and shopping diversions. The best way to discover the city's soul is to head away from the high-rises. Join locals in the grassy parkland along the Main River, grab an espresso at an old-time cafe, go museum-hopping along the riverbank and sip tart *Ebbelwei* (apple cider) while tucking into hearty local fare at a wood-panelled tavern.

ZOOM-ZOOM/GETTY IMAGES ©

PETER ADAMS/GETTY IMAGES ©

PLAN YOUR TRIP GERMANY'S TOP 18

Need to Know

For more information, see Survival Guide (p765)

Currency
Euro (€)

Language
German

Visas
Generally not required for tourist stays up to 90 days (or at all for EU nationals); some nationalities need a Schengen Visa (p775).

Money
ATMs widely available in cities and towns, rarely in villages. Cash is king almost everywhere; credit cards are not widely accepted.

Mobile Phones
Mobile phones operate on GSM900/1800. If you have a European or Australian phone, save money by slipping in a German SIM card.

Time
Central European Time (GMT/UTC plus one hour)

When to Go

Warm to hot summers, mild winters
Warm to hot summers, cold winters
Mild summers, cold winters
Cold climate

Hamburg
GO May–Sep

Berlin
GO May, Jun, Sep & Oct

Frankfurt
GO May–Sep

Munich
GO Apr, May, Sep & Oct

Freiburg
GO Apr–Oct

High Season
(Jul & Aug)

➡ Busy roads and long lines at key sights

➡ Vacancies at a premium and higher prices in seaside and mountain resorts

➡ Festivals celebrate everything from music to wine and sailing to samba

Shoulder Season (Apr–Jun, Sep–Oct)

➡ Smaller crowds and lower prices, except on public holidays

➡ Blooming flowers in spring; radiant foliage in autumn

➡ Sunny, temperate weather ideal for outdoor pursuits

Low Season
(Nov–Mar)

➡ No queues but shorter hours at key sights; some may close for the season

➡ Theatre, concert and opera season in full swing

➡ Ski resorts busiest in January and February

Useful Websites

Lonely Planet (www.lonelyplanet.com/germany) Hotel bookings, traveller forum and more.

German National Tourist Office (www.germany.travel)

Facts About Germany (www.tatsachen-ueber-deutschland.de/en) Reference tool on all aspects of German society.

Deutschland Online (www.magazine-deutschland.de) Insightful features on culture, business and politics.

Online German course (www.deutsch-lernen.com)

Important Numbers

Germany country code	☏49
International access code	☏00
Ambulance, fire brigade	☏112
Police	☏110

Exchange Rates

Australia	A$1	€0.64
Canada	C$1	€0.68
Japan	¥100	€0.73
New Zealand	NZ$1	€0.59
UK	UK£1	€1.36
US	US$1	€0.89

For current exchange rates, see www.xe.com.

Daily Costs

Budget: Less than €100

➡ Hostel, camping or private room: €15–30

➡ Up to €8 per meal or self-cater

➡ Take advantage of Happy Hours and free or low-cost museums and entertainment

Midrange: €100–200

➡ Private apartment or double room: €60–100

➡ Three-course dinner at nice restaurant: €30–40

➡ Couple of beers in a pub or beer garden: €8

Top End: More than €200

➡ Fancy loft apartment or double in top-end hotel: from €150

➡ Sit-down lunch, dinner at top-rated restaurant: €100

➡ Concert or opera tickets: €50–150

Opening Hours

The following are typical opening hours in Germany, although these may vary seasonally and between cities and villages. For specifics, see individual listings. Where hours vary across the year, we've provided those applicable in high season.

Banks 9am to 4pm Monday to Friday, extended hours usually on Tuesday and Thursday, some open Saturday

Bars 6pm to 1am

Cafes 8am to 8pm

Clubs 11pm to early morning hours

Post offices 9am to 6pm Monday to Friday, 9am to 1pm Saturday

Restaurants 11am to 11pm (food service often stops at 9pm in rural areas)

Major stores and supermarkets 9.30am to 8pm Monday to Saturday (shorter hours outside city centres)

Arriving in Germany

Frankfurt Airport (p396) S-Bahn train lines S8 and S9 link the airport with the city centre in 15 minutes several times hourly for €4.55. Taxis make the trip in 20 to 30 minutes and average €30.

Munich Airport (p223) The S1 and S8 trains link the airport with the city centre in 40 minutes (€10.80). The Lufthansa Airport Bus (€10.50) departs every 20 minutes and takes about the same time as the train. A taxi costs about €60.

Getting Around

Germans are whizzes at moving people around, and the public transport network is one of the best in Europe. The best ways of getting around the country are by car and by train.

Train Extensive network of long-distance and regional trains with frequent departures; fairly expensive but numerous deals available.

Car Useful for travelling at your own pace or for visiting regions with no or minimal public transport. Cars can be hired in every town and city. Drive on the right.

Bus Cheaper and slower than trains and with a growing long-haul network. Regional bus services fill the gaps in areas not served by rail.

Air Only useful for longer distances, eg Hamburg to Munich or Berlin to Munich.

For much more on **getting around**, see p780

First Time Germany

For more information, see Survival Guide (p765)

Checklist

➡ Make sure your passport is valid for at least four months past your planned date of departure from Germany

➡ Make advance bookings for major events, travel, accommodation and popular sights

➡ Check the airline baggage restrictions

➡ Alert your credit-/debit-card company that you'll be travelling to Germany

➡ Organise travel insurance (p771)

➡ Check if your mobile/cell phone (p774) will work in Germany and the cost of roaming

➡ Find out what you need to hire a car (p782)

What to Pack

➡ Good walking shoes

➡ Travel adapter plug

➡ Umbrella/raincoat

➡ Bathing suit

➡ Sunhat and sunglasses

➡ Pocket knife

➡ Curiosity and a sense of humour

Top Tips for Your Trip

➡ As much fun as it is to speed along the autobahn, be sure to get onto some country roads to sample Germany's often stunning scenery.

➡ Go local. A destination's spirit is best revealed by walking around a neighbourhood, people-watching in a park, using public transport or simply being curious about local food and drink.

➡ Don't be shy about chatting up strangers. Most Germans speak at least a few words of English and are happy to help.

What to Wear

Basically, anything goes. If you want to blend in, remember that Hamburg, Stuttgart, Frankfurt and Munich are considerably more fashion-conscious than, say, Berlin, Cologne or Dresden. Since the weather is unpredictable, even in summer, bring layers of clothing. A waterproof coat and sturdy shoes are a good idea for all-weather sightseeing. Winters can get fiercely cold, so pack gloves, a hat, and a heavy coat and boots. For evening wear, smart casual is the norm, but upmarket places may insist on shoes (not trainers) and trousers or dresses instead of jeans. Jackets and ties are only required in casinos and at the most formal establishments.

Sleeping

Outside of high season, holidays and major trade shows, it's generally not necessary to book your accommodation in advance.

➡ **Hotels** Range from mum-and-dad joints to restored castles and international chains.

➡ **Hostels** Both indie hostels and those belonging to Hostelling International are plentiful.

➡ **Gasthaus/Gasthof** Country inns, often in lovely locations, offer cultural immersion and a restaurant.

➡ **Pensionen** The German version of B&Bs is prevalent in rural areas and good value.

➡ **Furnished flats** For maximum space and privacy. Airbnb and Wimdu are the major peer-to-peer agencies.

Money

Germany is still largely a cash-based society and credit-card use is not common. International hotel chains, high-end restaurants, department stores and fancy boutiques usually accept credit cards, but always make it a habit to enquire first, just to be on the safe side. Mastercard and Visa are more widely accepted than American Express and Diner's Club. ATMs are ubiquitous in towns and cities but not usually in rural areas. Be wary of those not affiliated with major banks as they charge exorbitant transaction fees. ATMs do not recognise pins with more than four digits.

For more information, see p772.

Black forest gateau

Bargaining

Gentle haggling is common at flea markets; in all other instances you're expected to pay the stated price. In hotels, you may get a better rate if you're staying more than one night.

Tipping

➡ **Hotels** €1 per bag is standard. It's also nice to leave a little cash for the room cleaners, say €1 or €2 per day.

➡ **Restaurants** Restaurant bills always include *Bedienung* (service charge), but most people add 5% or 10% unless the service was truly abhorrent.

➡ **Bars** About 5%, rounded to nearest euro. For drinks brought to your table, tip as for restaurants.

➡ **Taxis** Tip about 10%, rounded to the nearest euro.

➡ **Toilet attendants** Loose change.

Etiquette

Germany is a fairly formal society; the following tips will help you avoid faux pas.

➡ **Greetings** Shake hands and say *'Guten Morgen'* (before noon), *'Guten Tag'* (between noon and 6pm) or *'Guten Abend'* (after 6pm). Use the formal *'Sie'* (you) with strangers and only switch to the informal *'du'* and first names if invited to do so. With friends and children, use first names and *'du'*.

➡ **Asking for Help** Germans use the same word – *'Entschuldigung'* – to say 'excuse me' (to attract attention) and 'sorry' (to apologise).

➡ **Eating & Drinking** At the table, say *'Guten Appetit'* before digging in. Germans hold the fork in the left hand and the knife in the right hand. To signal that you have finished eating, lay your knife and fork parallel across your plate. If drinking wine, the proper toast is *'Zum Wohl'*; with beer it's *'Prost'*.

Language

It is perfectly possible to travel in Germany without speaking a word of German, but life gets easier if you master a few basic phrases. People are more likely to speak English in big cities, the western part of the country and in tourist hotspots. Things get a little trickier in rural areas, especially in the former East Germany.

For more on language, see p789.

What's New

New Unesco sites

Hercules towering over a baroque park and palace at Wilhelmshöhe (p534) in Kassel and the red-brick warren of warehouses of the Speicherstadt (p651) in Hamburg became Unesco sites in 2013 and 2015, respectively.

Berliner Stadtschloss

The reconstruction of the Prussian royal city palace in central Berlin got underway in June 2013 and is expected to be completed as the Humboldtforum museum and cultural centre in 2019.

Nationalpark Schwarzwald

A 100 sq km mosaic of moors, glacial lakes and conifer forest became the Black Forest National Park in 2014, making it the 15th in Germany. (p333)

Long-distance coaches

Thanks to the lifting of a 1931 law prohibiting domestic long-distance coach travel, new low-cost bus companies now crisscross Germany.

Europäisches Hansemuseum, Lübeck

This beautifully curated new museum trains the spotlight on the rise and fall of the Hanseatic League, the European trading alliance that lasted nearly 600 years. (p674)

Rüstkammer Dresden

Step into the world of medieval knights with this shiny collection of armour displayed in the Riesensaal (Giant's Hall) at Dresden's Residenzschloss. (p278)

Grimmwelt, Kassel

Kassel, on the Fairytale Road, reopened its Brothers Grimm museum in September 2015 with a playful and interactive exhibit on the impact the brothers had on German language, literature and society. (p535)

Richard Wagner museums in Bayreuth & Leipzig

Bayreuth's Wagner museum (p280) is in the composer's former villa, and a new extension reopened in 2015 with exhibits about his life, times and work. There's also a new museum in his birth city of Leipzig (p161).

Dommuseum Hildesheim

Reopened in April 2015 after a five-year makeover, this engaging museum showcases 1000 years of church history in the cloisters of the Unesco-listed Mariendom. (p613)

Food trends

The global street food phenomenon has arrived in German cities, especially in Berlin. Gourmet burgers are big, as are vegan and vegetarian restaurants. The craft beer movement is also making inroads in this mother-country of beer.

For more recommendations and reviews, see lonelyplanet.com/germany

If You Like...

Churches & Cathedrals

More than places of worship, churches and cathedrals are also great architectural monuments, often filled with priceless treasure reflecting artistic acumen through the ages.

Kölner Dom The riverside twin spires of Germany's largest cathedral dominate Cologne's skyline. (p463)

Aachener Dom Some 30 German kings were crowned where Charlemagne lies buried in an elaborate gilded shrine. (p487)

Schlosskirche Protestant reformer Martin Luther is buried in Lutherstadt-Wittenberg, in the church where he pinned his 95 theses in 1517. (p580)

Wieskirche Rising from an Alpine meadow where a miracle-working Jesus statue was found, the Wieskirche represents the pinnacle of rococo exuberance. (p233)

Frauenkirche This harmoniously proportioned church in Dresden rose from the ashes of WWII when its spitting-image replica reopened in 2005. (p142)

Castles & Palaces

Germany's castles are a legacy of the feudal system that saw the country divided into hundreds of fiefdoms until its 1871 unification.

Schloss Neuschwanstein Thick woods cradle Germany's most famous palace, the inspiration for Disney's *Sleeping Beauty* castle. (p230)

Wartburg Protestant reformer Martin Luther translated the New Testament into German while in hiding at this medieval castle in Eisenach. (p555)

Schloss Heidelberg Although destroyed repeatedly throughout the centuries, there's still a majesty surrounding this red-sandstone hilltop Gothic pile. (p410)

Burg Hohenzollern Every bit the fairy-tale castle, the ancestral seat of the Prussian ruling family rises dramatically from an exposed crag near Tübingen. (p321)

Romantic Rhine Castles More than a dozen medieval robber-baron hangouts straddle craggy hilltops along this fabled river stretch. (p432)

Schloss Sanssouci Prussian king Frederick the Great sought solace amid the intimate splendour of his Potsdam summer palace. (p126)

Enchanting Towns

There's no simpler pleasure than strolling around a charismatic village laced with time-worn lanes, peppered with ancient churches and anchored by a fountain-studded square.

Quedlinburg Drift around this medieval warren of cobbled lanes lined by more than 1400 half-timbered houses. (p574)

Lindau Lovely Lindau has a 9th-century pedigree and a to-die-for location on an island in Lake Constance. (p368)

Bacharach Plunge into the Middle Ages in this pint-sized Moselle town flanked by vineyards and lorded over by a mighty castle. (p436)

Schiltach Cuddled by the Kinzig Valley, this romantic Black Forest town oozes history from every flower-festooned facade. (p340)

Baden-Baden Relaxation is taken very seriously in this classy spa town in the Black Forest foothills. (p328)

Görlitz Germany's easternmost town is so pristinely preserved that it's often used as a film location. (p175)

Celle A radiantly old-world gem with colourfully painted and ornately carved half-timbered buildings. (p609)

WWII Sites

Shudder at the atrocities committed by the Nazis, then honour those who gave their lives to rid the world of the Third Reich at these original sites.

Berchtesgaden Learn how this breathtaking Alpine town became Hitler's southern headquarters at the Dokumentation Obersalzberg (p245), then exorcise Nazi ghosts on the trip up to the 'Eagle's Nest' (p245).

Concentration Camps The darkest side of WWII is commemorated in camps at Bergen-Belsen (p611), Buchenwald (p553), Dachau (p224), Mittelbau Dora (p579), Sachsenhausen (p133) and Neuengamme (p671).

Remagen The pivotal capture of the Bridge at Remagen by American troops in March 1945 is poignantly remembered in the Friedensmuseum. (p484)

Peenemünde The deadly V2 rocket was developed in a research facility on Usedom Island, now the Historisch-Technisches Informationszentrum. (p714)

Nuremberg See the site of Nazi mass rallies at the Reichsparteitagsgelände (p267), then visit the courtroom where the Nuremberg Trials took place in 1945 (p266).

Laboe In this town on Kiel Firth, you can clamber around WWII-era U-Boat 995, which is similar to the one featured in the 1981 movie *Das Boot*. (p683)

Jewish Sites

Jewish history in Germany is often equated with the Holocaust, but even the Nazis could not wipe out 1600 years of Jewish life and cultural contributions to this country.

Top: Cable car ascending the Nebelhorn, Oberstdorf (p240)
Bottom: Half-timbered houses in Quedlinburg (p574)

Holocaust Memorial Peter Eisenman poignantly captures the horror of the Holocaust with this vast undulating maze of tomblike plinths in Berlin. (p59)

Jüdisches Museum Daniel Libeskind's extraordinary zinc-clad building in Berlin is a powerful metaphor for this eye-opening chronicle of Jewish life in Germany. (p75)

Judenhof Visit the Rhine city of Speyer to see the oldest, largest and best preserved Mikwe (ritual bath) north of the Alps. (p420)

Frankfurt am Main Two museums (p378 & p379) and a cemetery (p379) trace Jewish life, while the Wall of Names (p379) keeps alive the memory of 11,000 Frankfurt Jews murdered during the Holocaust.

Stolpersteine The cobblestone-sized brass 'stumbling blocks' embedded in pavements throughout Germany mark the last residence of Jews deported by the Nazis. (p69)

Train Journeys

Slow travel was never more fun than aboard Germany's historic trains, some of them more than 100 years old and pulled by steam locomotives.

Zugspitzbahn Have your breath quite literally taken away on this pulse-quickening journey up Germany's tallest mountain; it starts in Garmisch-Partenkirchen. (p236)

Molli Schmalspurbahn Since 1886 this pint-sized train has been shuttling visitors through gorgeous scenery from Bad Doberan to coastal Heiligendamm. (p702)

Harzer Schmalspurbahnen The mother lode for fans of narrow-gauge trains traverses the Harz Mountains on three scenic routes, including one up the legendary Mt Brocken. (p573)

Lössnitzgrundbahn The most scenic approach to Moritzburg Castle is aboard this historic steam train chugging between Radebeul and Radeburg, near Dresden. (p157)

Chiemseebahn Dating from 1887, this is the world's oldest narrow-gauge steam train. (p244)

Wine Tasting

Whether at estate tastings, vineyard hikes, cellar tours or wine festivals, an immersion in German wine culture should be part of any itinerary.

Rheingau Sample the renowned rieslings in this celebrated region around Rüdesheim on the short stretch where the Rhine flows west to east. (p433)

Kaiserstuhl Lots of sun and fertile soil create ideal growing conditions for fruity Spätburger (Pinot noir) and Grauburgunder (Pinot gris). (p352)

Deutsche Weinstrasse Winding through the Palatinate, the bucolic German Wine Route is famous for its muscular rieslings and robust Dornfelder reds. (p427)

Moselle With a wine-growing tradition rooted in Roman times, this meandering region grows light-bodied whites that want to be drunk young. (p444)

Mittelrhein Wine tasting in this region is as much about the romantic Rhine Gorge setting as it is about the wonderful vintages. (p432)

Freyburg This lovely town on Thuringia's Saale River is the home of Rotkappchen, Germany's largest producer of sparkling wine. (p565)

Historisches Museum der Pfalz Dating back 1700 years, the world's oldest wine is among the fascinating exhibits at this well-curated museum in Speyer. (p420)

Great Outdoors

Germany is an all-seasons outdoor playground, so whatever your adrenaline fix, you'll find it here.

Black Forest Fir-cloaked hills, steep gorges, misty waterfalls and sweeping viewpoints await those who hit the trail in this fabled region. (p328)

Spreewald Leave the crowds behind as you dip your paddles into this timeless warren of gentle waterways near Berlin. (p134)

Altmühltal Radweg Pull up at a pebbled beach for a picnic after pedalling past craggy rock formations carved by this serene river in northern Bavaria. (p287)

Saxon Switzerland Rock hounds can test their mettle with hundreds of climbs on soul-stirring sandstone cliffs and rockscapes. (p158)

Zugspitze Only seasoned mountaineers should make the breathtaking ascent to the 'roof' of Germany. (p236)

Oberstdorf Whether you're into downhill, cross-country or boarding, this pretty ski region has a piste with your name on it. (p240)

Spa Time

Soothe achy bones or simply take a day to relax in one of Germany's many sumptuous day spas, many fed by naturally heated mineral water.

Friedrichsbad Taking the waters doesn't get more regal than at this 19th-century Roman-Irish bath in Baden-Baden. (p330)

Alpamare Plunge down Germany's longest water slide at Bad Tölz' family-friendly water complex, complete with wave pool and saunas. (p242)

Bade:haus Norderney Indulge in Thalassotherapy at Europe's oldest seawater wave pool in grand Bauhaus style. (p641)

Meersburg Therme Relax in thermal waters, sweat it out in replica stone-age huts and take in the fabulous scenery at this waterfront spa on Lake Constance. (p364)

Kaiser-Friedrich-Therme Work out the kinks in pools fed by naturally heated mineral water in this baronial spa in Wiesbaden. (p399)

Carolus Thermal Baths Bliss out in oriental pools and enjoy honey rubs and deep-tissue massages in Aachen's elegant bathing temple. (p489)

Islands

For an authentic experience off the usual tourist track, catch a boat to these off-shore escapes.

Rügen Germany's largest island has charmed visitors since the 19th century with its sandy beaches, white chalk cliffs and historic resorts. (p709)

Mainau Be enchanted by the profusion of tulips, dahlias, roses and orchids in this garden island

owned by a member of the Swedish royal family. (p363)

Sylt Big wind and waves translate into world-class windsurfing on this glamorous North Sea island. (p688)

Hiddensee For a genuine sense of happy isolation visit this car-free Baltic island in the winter. (p713)

Herreninsel This island in the Chiemsee is home to the grandest of Ludwig's II palaces, Schloss Herrenchiemsee, a tribute to French Sun King Louis XIV. (p243)

Norderney This is the most accessible of the East Frisian islands with more than enough soft white sand for everyone. (p640)

German Flavours

Sure, there are pizzas and hamburgers everywhere, but for a true taste of Germany try one of these traditional dishes.

Bratwurst Nuremberg's finger-sized links, grilled and served in a bun or with sauerkraut, are top dogs in Germany. (p274)

Pork knuckle A Munich beer hall like the Augustiner-Grossgaststätte is the perfect place for tackling this classic gut-buster. (p742)

Doner kebab It was a Turkish immigrant in Berlin who first came up with the idea of tucking spit-roasted slivered meat into a pita bread along with salad and a garlicky sauce. (p742)

Spätzle This noodle dish hails from the Stuttgart region and is often smothered in cheese or topped with lentils. (p313)

Black forest gateau Enjoy a slice of this creamy liqueur-drenched sponge cake symphony at Café Schäfer in Triberg, where it was invented. (p353)

Haute cuisine The country's greatest density of Michelin-starred restaurants is in Baden-Württemberg, including two three-star temples in Baiersbronn. (p42)

Souvenirs

Even in the age of global commerce, Germany has some unmatched treasures.

Käthe Wohlfahrt Weihnachts-dorf In this museum-like shop in Rothenburg ob der Tauber you can stock up on Christmas angels, ornaments and nut-crackers year-round. (p256)

Ampelmann The endearing fellow on East Germany's pe-destrian traffic light has evolved into its own brand, with multiple stores in Berlin. (p120)

Woodcarvings Carved wood sculptures are a special-ity throughout the Alpine regions, but the workshops in Oberammergau are especially renowned. (p235)

Glass Fans of the fragile can pick up exquisite hand-blown vases, glasses and bowls from traditional artisans in the Bavar-ian Forest. (p304)

Marzipan Some of the world's best marzipan hails from Niede-regger in the northern German town of Lübeck. (p680)

Porcelain Precious porcelain is the hallmark of Meissen, the cradle of European porcelain manufacturing. (p157)

Month by Month

January

Except in the ski resorts, the Germans have the country pretty much to themselves this month. Short and cold days make this a good time to enjoy in-depth explorations of museums and churches.

🏃 Mountain Madness

Grab your skis or snowboard and hit the slopes in resorts that range from glamorous Garmisch-Partenkirchen (p236) to the family-friendly Bavarian Forest (p304). No matter whether you're a black diamond daredevil or Sesame Street novice, there's a piste with your name on it.

February

It's not as sweltering as Rio, but the German Carnival is still a good excuse for a party. Ski resorts are busiest thanks to school holidays, so make reservations.

☆ Berlin Film Festival

Stars, directors and critics sashay down the red carpet for two weeks of screenings and glamour parties at the Berlinale, one of Europe's most prestigious celluloid festivals. (p94)

🎭 Karneval/Fasching

The pre-Lenten season is celebrated with costumed street partying, parades, satirical shows and general revelry. The biggest parties are along the Rhine in Düsseldorf, Cologne and Mainz, but the Black Forest and Munich also have their own traditions.

March

Days start getting longer and the first inkling of spring is in the air. Fresh herring hits the menus, especially along the coastal regions, and dishes prepared with *Bärlauch* (wild garlic) are all the rage.

🔒 CeBIT

Geeks, suits and the merely tech-curious converge on Hanover's fairground for the world's largest digital trade fair. (p603)

April

No matter if you stopped believing in the Easter Bunny long ago, there's no escaping him in Germany in April. Meanwhile, nothing epitomises the arrival of spring more than the first crop of white asparagus. Germans go nuts for it.

🎭 Walpurgisnacht

The pagan Witches' Sabbath festival on 30 April sees Harz villages roaring to life as young and old dress up as witches and warlocks and parade through the streets singing and dancing.

◉ Maifest

Villagers celebrate the end of winter on 30 April by chopping down a tree for a Maypole (*Maibaum*), painting, carving and decorating it, and staging a merry revelry with traditional costumes, singing and dancing.

May

Often surprisingly warm and sunny, this is one of the loveliest months, perfect for ringing in beer-garden season. There are lots of public holidays, which Germans turn into extended weekends or miniholidays, resulting in busy roads and lodging shortages.

🎎 Hafengeburtstag

Hamburg lets its hair down in early May at this raucous three-day harbourside festival with a fun fair, music and merriment. (p659)

🎎 Karneval der Kulturen

Hundreds of thousands of revellers celebrate Berlin's multicultural tapestry with parties, exotic nosh and a fun parade of flamboyantly dressed dancers, DJs, artists and musicians shimmying through the streets of Kreuzberg. (p95)

☉ Labour Day

The first day of May is a public holiday in Germany, with some cities hosting political demonstrations for workers' rights. In Berlin, protests have taken on a violent nature in the past, although now it's mostly a big street fair.

☉ Muttertag

Mothers are honoured on the second Sunday of May, much to the delight of florists, sweet shops and greeting-card companies.

Make restaurant reservations far in advance.

🎎 Wave-Gotik-Treffen

Thousands of Goths paint the town black as they descend upon Leipzig during the long Whitsuntide/Pentecost weekend, in what is billed as the world's largest Goth gathering. (p168)

June

Germany's festival pace quickens, while gourmets can rejoice in the bounty of fresh, local produce in the markets. Life moves outdoors as the summer solstice means the sun doesn't set until around 9.30pm.

☉ Vatertag

Father's Day, now also known as *Männertag* (Men's Day), is essentially an excuse for men to get liquored up with the blessing of the missus. It's always on Ascension Day.

🎎 Africa Festival

Europe's largest festival of African music and culture attracts around 100,000 people to Würzburg and features concerts, foods and crafts. (p251)

🏃 Kieler Woche

More than three million salty types flock to the Baltic Sea each year when Kiel hosts the world's biggest boat party, with hundreds of regattas, ship parades, historic vessels and non-stop weeklong partying. (p682)

🍷 Christopher Street Day

No matter your sexual persuasion, come out and paint the town pink at major gay-pride celebrations in Berlin, Cologne and Hamburg.

☆ Bachfest

This nine-day music festival in Leipzig celebrates not only the work of Johann Sebastian Bach but also the music of other major composers. (p168)

🏃 Stocherkahnrennen

Tübingen's traditional punting boat race pits rivalling student fraternities against each other in a hilarious and wacky costumed spectacle on the Neckar River. (p318)

July

School's out for the summer and peak travelling season begins, so you'd better be the gregarious type. Prebook accommodation whether you're headed to the mountains or the coast. It won't be the Med, but swimming is now possible in lakes, rivers, and the Baltic and North Seas.

☆ Samba Festival

This orgy of song and dance in Coburg attracts around 100 bands and 3000 performers from a dozen nations, and up to 200,000 visitors. (p283)

☆ Schleswig-Holstein Music Festival

Leading international musicians and promising young artists perform during this festival, in castles, churches, warehouses and animal barns throughout Germany's northernmost state. Held from mid-July until August.

August

August tends to be Germany's hottest month but days are often cooled by afternoon thunderstorms. It's the season for *Pfifferlinge* (chanterelle mushrooms) and fresh berries, which you can pick in the forests.

Shooting Festivals

More than a million Germans (mostly men) belong to shooting clubs and show off their skills at marksmen's festivals. The biggest one is in Hanover; the oldest, in Düsseldorf.

Wine Festivals

With grapes ripening to a plump sweetness, the wine festival season starts, with tastings, folkloric parades, fireworks and the election of local and regional wine queens. The Dürkheimer Wurstmarkt (www.duerkheimer-wurstmarkt.de) is one of the biggest and most famous. (p431)

Kinderzeche

Dinkelsbühl, on the Romantic Road, hosts this 10-day festival featuring children performing in historical re-enactments, along with a pageant and the usual merriment. (p258)

Wagner Festival

German high society descends upon Bayreuth to practise the art of listening at epic productions of Wagner operas staged in a custom-built festival hall. Mere mortals must hope to score tickets via a lottery system. (p286)

Museumsuferfest

Some three million culture vultures descend upon Frankfurt's Museum Embankment in late August to nose around museums, shop for global crafts and enjoy concerts and dance performances along the Main River. (p382)

Stuttgarter Sommerfest

More than half a million people come out to Stuttgart's Schlossplatz and Eckensee Lake for this chic four-day festival with open-air concerts, entertainment and culinary treats. (p311)

September

Often a great month weather-wise – sunny but not too hot. The main travel season is over but September is still busy thanks to lots of wine and autumn festivals. Trees may start turning into a riot of colour towards the end of the month.

Berlin Marathon

You can sweat it out with the other 50,000 runners or just cheer 'em on during Germany's biggest street race, which has seen nine world records set since 1977. (p95)

Erntedankfest

Rural towns celebrate the harvest with decorated church altars, *Erntedank-* *zug* (processions) and villagers dressed in folkloric garments.

Oktoberfest

Munich's legendary beer-swilling party. Enough said. (p207)

Cannstatter Volksfest

Stuttgart's answer to Oktoberfest, this beer-guzzling bash lifts spirits with oompah bands, carnival rides and fireworks. (p311)

October

Children are back in school and most people at work as days get shorter, colder and wetter. Trade-fair season kicks into high gear, affecting lodging prices and availability in Frankfurt, Cologne, Berlin, Hamburg and other cities. Tourist offices, museums and attractions start keeping shorter hours. Some close down for the winter season.

Frankfurt Book Fair

Bookworms invade Frankfurt for the world's largest book fair, with 7300 exhibitors from more than a hundred countries. (p374)

November

This can be a dreary month mainly spent indoors. However, queues at tourist sights are short, and theatre, concert, opera and other cultural events are plentiful. Bring warm clothes and rain gear.

✳ St Martinstag

This festival, held on 10-11 November, honours the 4th-century St Martin, known for his humility and generosity, with a lantern procession and a re-enactment of the famous scene where he cuts his coat in half to share with a beggar. This is followed by a big feast of stuffed roast goose.

December

Cold and sun-deprived days are brightened by Advent, the four weeks of festivities preceding Christmas that are celebrated with enchanting markets, illuminated streets, Advent calendars, candle-festooned wreaths, home-baked cookies and other rituals. The ski resorts usually get their first dusting of snow.

◎ Nikolaustag

On the eve of 5 December, German children put their boots outside the door hoping that St Nick will fill them with sweets and small toys overnight. Ill-behaved children, though, may find only a prickly rod left behind by St Nick's helper, Knecht Ruprecht.

🔒 Christmas Markets

Mulled wine, spicy gingerbread cookies, shimmering ornaments – these and lots more are typical features of German Christmas markets, held from late November until late December. The Christkindlesmarkt held in Nuremberg is especially famous. (p270)

✳ Silvester

New Year's Eve is called 'Silvester' in honour of the 4th-century pope under whom the Romans adopted Christianity as their official religion. The new year is greeted with fireworks launched by thousands of amateur pyromaniacs.

Itineraries

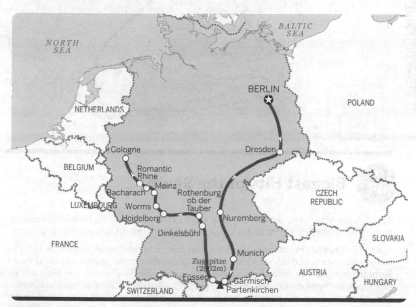

2 WEEKS: Top of the Pops

Bookended by great cities, this road trip is a fine introduction for first-timers that lets you sample the best of German culture, character, architecture and landscapes.

Kick off in **Berlin** to sample its top-notch museums, old and bold architecture and nice-to-naughty nightlife. Next, head to show-stopping **Dresden**, sitting proud and pretty in its baroque splendour on the Elbe River. Push south to **Nuremberg**, with its evocative walled medieval centre, and on to **Munich** to wrap up a day of palace- and museum-hopping with an evening in a beer garden. Drive to **Garmisch-Partenkirchen** to breathe the fresh Alpine air on an exhilarating train-and-cable-car trip up the **Zugspitze**, then get up early the next day to beat the crowds swarming 'Mad' King Ludwig II's Schloss Neuschwanstein in **Füssen**. In the afternoon, point the compass north for the Romantic Road, possibly overnighting in **Dinkelsbühl** or **Rothenburg ob der Tauber**. Next, cut west to historic **Heidelberg**, with its romantically ruined fortress, then north to **Worms** and **Mainz** with their majestic Romanesque cathedrals. After a night in enchanting **Bacharach**, follow the **Romantic Rhine** through fairy-tale scenery before winding up in cosmopolitan **Cologne** for church-hopping, great art and rustic beer halls.

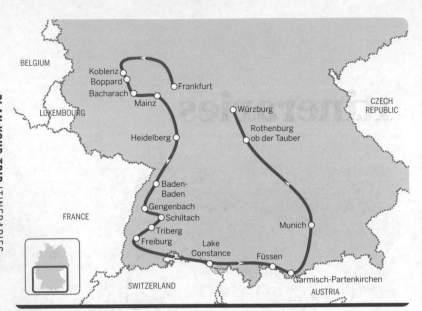

2 WEEKS

Biggest Hits of the South

This driving route links the most storied stops in Germany's south, including majestic mountains, legendary rivers, historic towns, half-timbered villages and lordly palaces.

Start in **Frankfurt**, where you can soak up culture in world-class museums, cider in traditional taverns and skyline views from the Main river promenade. Steer northwest to **Koblenz**, the gateway to the Romantic Rhine, a scene-stealing combo of steeply terraced vineyards, medieval castles and higgledy-piggledy villages. Say hello to the legendary Loreley as you follow the western river bank south, perhaps stopping in postcard-pretty **Boppard** and fairy-tale-like **Bacharach**, or fancying yourself knight or damsel for a night in a luxurious castle hotel. The next morning, make a quick stop in **Mainz**, where Johannes Gutenberg ushered in the information age by inventing moveable printing type.

Next, follow in the footsteps of Mark Twain in bewitching **Heidelberg**, Germany's oldest university town, where you shouldn't miss a tour of the imposing hilltop castle. Take a day's break from culture in **Baden-Baden**, the legendary spa resort where royals, celebrities, politicians and mere mortals have for centuries frolicked in elegant bathing temples. From here go cuckoo for the Black Forest, an intoxicating mosaic of forest-cloaked hills, glacial lakes, snug valleys and half-timbered villages such as **Gengenbach**, **Schiltach** and **Triberg**. Build in at least half a day in student-flavoured **Freiburg**, with its imposing minster; it's the place to enjoy crisp local wine alfresco amid tangled cobbled lanes.

From here cut east to the vast **Lake Constance** and follow its scenic northern shore, perhaps stopping in pretty **Meersburg**, at the prehistoric *Pfahlbauten* (pile dwellings) or in **Friedrichshafen**, the birthplace of the Zeppelin airship. Consider overnighting in lovely **Lindau**, a teensy, alley-laced island. You're now in Bavaria, en route to the fabled Schloss Neuschwanstein in **Füssen** and on to **Garmisch-Partenkirchen**, where a train-and-cable-car combo delivers you to the top of the Zugspitze, Germany's highest Alpine peak. Come back down to earth in a beer hall in **Munich** before wrapping up your journey with a couple of days on the Romantic Road. Essential stops include **Rothenburg ob der Tauber** and **Würzburg**, from where it's a quick drive back to Frankfurt.

 Tour de Germany

With a month at your disposal, this epic trip offers the mother lode of soul-stirring land-scapes and villages but also lets you experience urban edginess in Germany's top cities. It's best done by car but a train-and-bus combo is also an option.

Base yourself in **Berlin** for a few days and add a one-day excursion to park-and-palace-filled **Potsdam**. Kayak or canoe around the canal-laced **Spreewald** before embarking on a quick detour to **Görlitz** on the Polish border, one of Germany's best-preserved small towns. Set aside two days to get acquainted with the cultural riches of **Dresden**, then continue on to **Weimar** and **Erfurt** to walk in the footsteps of Germany's greatest intellects.

Spend the next three days exploring a trio of evocative medieval gems: compact **Bamberg** with its romantic old town; the powerhouse of **Nuremberg** that is also (in) famous for its Third Reich legacy; and **Regensburg**, a lively university town founded by the Romans and studded with medieval townhouses overlooking the coursing Danube. Wend your way towards Munich via the enchanting **Altmühltal Nature Park**, best savoured slowly, on foot, by bike or by boat.

Make a study of **Munich** for a few days, perhaps folding day trips up the **Zugspitze** and to King Ludwig II's **Schloss Neuschwanstein** into your itinerary. Continue west to Lake Constance, where stops should include enchanting **Lindau** and picture-perfect **Meersburg**. Revel in the youthful spirit of ancient **Freiburg** for a day, then steer north for scenic drives through the Black Forest, ending in **Baden-Baden** for the night. Relax in the town's thermal spas before moving on to **Heidelberg**, with its ancient student taverns and charismatic ruined castle. Cut across the Rhine to **Speyer** for a spin around its Romanesque cathedral, then compare it to its upriver cousins in **Worms** and **Mainz**.

You're in the heart of wine country now, so sample the local tipple in idyllic villages like **Bacharach** or **Boppard** as you follow the Romantic Rhine north through dramatic castle-studded scenery. Your grand tour culminates in **Cologne**; its magnificent cathedral will come into view long before you've reached town. Great museums, Romanesque churches and Rhenish *joie de vivre* will easily keep you entertained for a day or two.

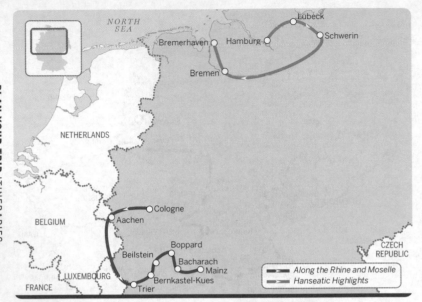

NORTH SEA

NETHERLANDS

BELGIUM

LUXEMBOURG

FRANCE

CZECH REPUBLIC

Lübeck
Schwerin
Hamburg
Bremerhaven
Bremen

Cologne
Aachen
Boppard
Beilstein
Bacharach
Mainz
Bernkastel-Kues
Trier

Along the Rhine and Moselle
Hanseatic Highlights

Along the Rhine & Moselle

1 WEEK

This scenic journey folds grand architecture, absorbing history, world-class art and fine wine into one enticing package.

Start in **Cologne**, where you can stand in awe of the twin-spired Kölner Dom, explore engaging museums dedicated to chocolate, contemporary art or sports and spend an evening guzzling *Kölsch* beer in a Rhenish tavern. Head to **Aachen** to walk in the footsteps of Charlemagne and munch on a crunchy *Printen* cookie, then travel back in time another few centuries in storied **Trier**. More than 2000 years old, it's home to some of the finest Roman monuments north of the Alps. The following day, mosey along the Moselle River, which runs its serene, serpentine course past steep vineyards to meet the Rhine at Koblenz. En route, swoon over crisp riesling in half-timbered **Bernkastel-Kues** or fairy-tale **Beilstein**, then compare it with wines grown in the slate-rich Rhine soil. Follow the Rhine south as it sweeps past picture-postcard villages like **Boppard** and **Bacharach**, craggy cliffs crowned by medieval castles, and near-vertical vineyards. Wrap up in **Mainz** with its grand cathedral and fabulous museum dedicated to moveable type inventor and local boy Johannes Gutenberg.

Hanseatic Highlights

1 WEEK

This itinerary hops around northern Germany to delightful cities shaped by the sea and a long mercantile tradition rooted in the medieval Hanseatic League. You can drive it, but thanks to fast and direct connections, it's just as easily done by train.

Kick-off in cosmopolitan **Hamburg**, a maritime city that cradles an elegant historic centre, a converted docklands quarter, the red-brick Speicherstadt (warehouse district) and a gloriously seedy party and red-light district under its self-confident mantle. Venture on to enchanting **Lübeck**, where the landmark Holsten Gate is a shutterbug favourite. Try the delicious local marzipan before heading to pastoral **Schwerin**, a cultural hub hemmed in by crystalline lakes. Sitting pretty on an island in one of them is the much-photographed, golden-domed Schloss Schwerin. Carry on to **Bremen**, the northern terminus of the 'Fairy-Tale Road'. After greeting the statue of the Town Musicians, check out Expressionist architecture, mummified corpses and the Beck's brewery before partying till dawn in Das Viertel. Steer north to **Bremerhaven**, the port of dreams for millions hoping for a better life in the New World. The superb German Emigration Centre tells their story.

Plan Your Trip

Germany Outdoors

No matter what kind of activity gets you off the couch, you can pursue it in Germany. There's plenty to do year-round – hiking among spring wildflowers, swimming in a lake warmed by the summer sun, cycling through a kaleidoscope of autumn foliage or celebrating winter by schussing through deep powder. Wherever you go, you'll find outfitters and local operators eager to gear you up.

Hiking & Mountaineering

Wanderlust? Germans coined the word. And their passion for *Wandern* (walking) is unrivalled. High-altitude treks in the Bavarian Alps, Black Forest hikes over wooded hill and dale, Rhineland vineyard strolls – this country will soon have you itching to grab your boots and stride its 200,000km of well-signposted trails, some traversing national and nature parks or biosphere reserves.

Local tourist offices can help you find a route to match your fitness and time frame, and can supply you with maps and tips. Many offer multiday 'hiking without luggage' packages that include accommodation and luggage transfer between hotels.

The Bavarian Alps are Germany's mountaineering heartland, whether for day treks or multiday hut-to-hut hikes. Before heading out, seek local advice and instruction on routes, equipment and weather, as trails can be narrow, steep and have icy patches, even in summer.

The Deutscher Alpenverein (www.alpenverein.de) is a goldmine of information and maintains hundreds of Alpine huts, where you can spend the night and get a meal.

Best Outdoor Activities

Best Skiing
Bavarian Alps (p230) A holy grail for downhill and cross-country skiers, with titanic peaks, groomed slopes and an impeccable snow record.

Best Hiking
Black Forest (p333) Mile after pine-scented mile of trails weaving through forests, mist-enshrouded valleys and half-timbered villages, freshly minted for a fairy tale.

Best Climbing
Saxon Switzerland (p158) Some 1100 exhilarating peaks and scenery that moves the soul in this sandstone wonderland.

Best Canoeing
Lake Constance (p357) Kayak over to Switzerland or Austria and glimpse the Alps on the horizon as you paddle.

Best Cycling
Altmühltal Radweg (p286) A 'Best of Bavaria' bike ride, taking in river bends and dense forests, ragged limestone cliffs and castle-topped villages.

Local DAV chapters also organise courses and guided treks. Membership can yield a 30% to 50% discount on huts, and other benefits.

Rock Climbing

Clambering around steep rock faces is popular in the crag-riddled heights of central and southern Germany. Rock hounds test their mettle on limestone cliffs in Bavaria's Altmühltal Nature Park, with climbs from grades 1 to 10. Another *klettern* (climbing) hot spot, particularly among free climbers, is Saxon Switzerland, with 1100 climbing peaks, routes graded 1 to 11, and exhilarating views over bizarre sandstone rock formations. Most towns have climbing walls where you can limber up. For information see www.dav-felsinfo.de, www.klettern.de or www.climbing.de.

Best Walks For...

Alpine trekkers Colossal mountains and jewel-coloured lakes in the Berchtesgaden National Park (p246).

Family ramblers Partnachklamm and red-squirrel-spotting on the trail shadowing Triberger Wasserfälle (p353), at 163m Germany's highest waterfall.

Beach combers Bracing sea air atop the wild limestone cliffs of Rügen's **Stubbenkammer**

(Nationalparks Jasmund; www.nationalpark-jasmund.de) and dune walking on Sylt (p688).

Serious mountaineers The rooftop of Germany at 2962m; the tough ascent and phenomenal four-country views making Zugspitze (p236) breathtaking in every sense of the word.

Long-distance hikers Bavaria's beautiful 200km Altmühltal Panoramaweg (p336), the wild and woody 169km Rennsteig (p558) or the 280km Westweg (p336), the ultimate Black Forest walk.

Wine lovers Vine-strewn hills in the Rhine Valley (p432) and sipping pinots along the Kaiserstuhl's 15km Winzerweg (p352).

Birdwatchers Storks, geese and cranes in the Naturpark Elbufer-Drawehn, or ospreys, white-tailed eagles and kingfishers in the Müritz National Park (p699).

Escapists The fir-cloaked hills of the Black Forest and the Bavarian Forest National Park (p304).

Rock fans The rockscapes of Saxon Switzerland and limestone cliffs in Naturpark Obere Donau (p358).

Cycling

Strap on your helmet! Germany is superb cycling territory, whether you're off on a leisurely spin along the beach, a downhill ride in the Alps or a multiday freewheeling adventure. Local tourist offices can give you advice on day trips and you can rent city, mountain and electro-bikes in most towns.

The country is also criss-crossed by more than 200 well-signposted long-distance trails covering 70,000km – ideal for *Radwandern* (bike touring). Routes combine lightly travelled back roads, forestry tracks and paved highways with dedicated bike lanes. Many traverse nature reserves, meander along rivers or venture into steep mountain terrain.

The national cycling organisation Allgemeiner Deutscher Fahrrad Club (ADFC; www.adfc.de) produces the best maps for on-the-road navigation. These indicate inclines, track conditions, repair shops and UTM grid coordinates for GPS users. ADFC also offers a useful directory called Bett & Bike (www.bettundbike.de; available online or in bookshops) that lists bicycle-friendly hotels, inns and hostels.

RESOURCES
....

➡ **German National Tourist Office** (www.germany.travel) Inspiration on walking and cycling throughout Germany.

➡ **Kompass** (www.kompass.de) A reliable series of 1:25,000 scale walking maps and information on trails.

➡ **Tourentipp** (www.tourentipp. de) Weather forecasts, hut info and walks organised by region.

➡ **Wanderbares Deutschland** (www.wanderbares-deutschland. de) Dozens of walking trails, with a handy interactive map.

➡ **Wandern ohne Gepäck** (www.wandern-ohne-gepaeck-deutschland.de) The 'hiking without luggage' specialists.

Cycling on the Elberadweg (p584)

Top Long-Distance Cycling Routes

Altmühltal Radweg (160km) Rothenburg ob der Tauber to Beilngries, following the river through the Altmühltal Nature Park; easy to moderate

Elberadweg (860km) Elbe River from Saxon Switzerland to Hamburg through wine country, heath and marshland, past Dresden, Dessau and Wittenberg

Donauradweg (434km) Neu-Ulm to Passau; delightful, easy to moderate riverside trip

Bodensee-Königssee Radweg (418km) Lindau to Berchtesgaden; moderate route along the foot of the Alps with magnificent views

Romantische Strasse (359km) Würzburg to Füssen; easy to moderate and one of the nicest ways to explore this famous holiday route; busy during summer

Winter Sports

Modern lifts, primed ski runs from easy-peasy blues to death-wish blacks, cross-country trails through untouched nature, log huts, steaming mulled wine, hearty dinners by crackling fires: these are the hallmarks of a German skiing holiday.

The Bavarian Alps, only an hour's drive south of Munich, offer the best downhill slopes and most reliable snow conditions. The most famous and ritzy resort is Garmisch-Partenkirchen, which hosted the FIS Alpine Skiing World Championship in 2011 and is just a snowball's throw from Zugspitze. It has 60km of slopes, mostly geared towards intermediates. Picture-book-pretty Oberstdorf in the Allgäu Alps forms the heart of the Oberstdorf-Kleinwalsertal ski region, which has 125km of slopes. It's good for boarders, with snow parks and a half-pipe to play on, and cross-country skiers come to glide along 75km of classic and 55km of skating tracks. For low-key skiing and stunning scenery, there is Berchtesgaden and Mittenwald, presided over by the jagged Karwendel range. Can't or won't ski? All resorts offer snowy fun from tobogganing and ice skating to snow-shoeing and winter walking.

Elsewhere in the country, the mountains may not soar as high, but prices are cheaper and the atmosphere is less frenetic. The

RIVERBOAT ROMANCE
....

Put your feet up and watch the great outdoors drift past on a riverboat cruise along some of Germany's greatest rivers from Easter to October.

High on the list is the Romantic Rhine, where boats drift past vine-covered hills, cliffs crowned with robber-knight castles and picturesque villages. Or combine wine-tasting with a mini cruise along the Moselle between Koblenz and Trier, each bend in the river revealing vine-draped loveliness.

In Berlin you can mix sightseeing with a meander along the Spree, in Hamburg the Elbe, in Passau the Danube, and in Stuttgart the Neckar. For a taste of history, hop aboard a paddle-wheel steam boat in Dresden or a punt in Tübingen.

Bavarian Forest and the Black Forest have the most reliable snow levels, with moderate downhill action on the Grosser Arber and Feldberg mountains, as well as abundant *Langlaufloipen* (cross-country trails) where you can shuffle through frozen woods in quiet exhilaration.

At higher elevations, the season generally runs from late November or early December to March. Rates for skis, boots and poles cost around €25/15 for downhill/cross-country gear hire. Group ski/snowboard lessons cost around €45 per day.

Water Sports

Germany's lakes, rivers, canals and coasts offer plenty of water-based action, though the swimming season is relatively short (June to September) and water temperatures rarely climb above 21°C.

Slip into a canoe or kayak to absorb the natural rhythm of the waterways threading through the lushly wooded Spreewald and Bavaria's Altmühltal Nature Park. The lake-dotted wilderness of the Müritz National Park is great for paddle-and-camp trips. Or paddle across Lake Constance to Switzerland and Austria with the Alps on the horizon. The season runs from around April to October and a one-/two-person canoe or kayak cost around €25/30 per day.

Stiff breezes and big waves draw sailors, surfers, windsurfers and kite surfers to the North Sea and Baltic coasts. Sylt on the North Sea and Rügen on the Baltic have some of the country's top conditions and schools for water-based activities.

Plan Your Trip
Eat & Drink Like a Local

'Keep it simple, local and seasonal' is the ethos in Germany, a rising star in Europe's kitchen. Food is bound to play a big part in your travels here. You'll never forget that first creamy forkful of real black forest gateau, tangy rieslings sipped in Rhineland wineries and seafood savoured on Baltic beaches.

Food Experiences

Cheap Eats

Some of your best German food experiences are likely to be the snack-on-the-hoof variety. At street stalls you'll get versed in German *Wurst* (sausage) and chomp your way around the globe, often with change from a €5 note. In Berlin and other cities, street food includes Greek, Italian, Mexican, Middle Eastern and Chinese bites. The *Imbiss* fast-food stall is a ubiquitous phenomenon, allowing you to eat on the run.

Germany's Turkish population invented the modern doner kebab *(Döner)*. Most kebab joints also do vegetarian versions. In the briny north, snack on fish (usually herring) sandwiches.

Top Five Snacks

➡ **Curry 36** (p105) The *Currywurst* (curried sausage) crown goes to this curb-side joint in Kreuzberg.

➡ **Rosenthaler Grill- und Schlemmerbuffet** (p106) Oscar-worthy doner kebabs in Berlin.

➡ **Bratwursthäusle** (p274) Finger-sized Nuremberg bratwurst – spiced and super-crisp.

➡ **Gosch** (p690) Fast-fish outlet, with exceptional smoked fish, in Sylt.

➡ **Die Kichererbse** (p321) Finger-licking, real-deal falafel in Tübingen.

The Year in Food

Spring (Mar–May)

During *Spargelzeit* Germans go wild for asparagus. *Bärlauch* (wild garlic) is bountiful and Baltic towns celebrate the humble herring.

Summer (Jun–Aug)

Pfifferlinge (chanterelle mushrooms) and a feast of forest berries trumpet summer's arrival. Beer gardens brim with folk lapping up the warm weather, and folksy wine festivals are in full swing.

Autumn (Sep–Oct)

Autumn days are rich and earthy, with game, wild mushrooms and pumpkins aplenty. At Oktoberfest in September, 6.9 million party-goers wash down entire farms of pigs, oxen and chickens with *Mass* (litres) of beer.

Winter (Nov–Feb)

'Tis the season for gingerbread and mulled wine at Christmas. Munich throws festivals for pre-Lenten *Starkbier* (strong beer), the malty 7.5% brews monks once dubbed *flüssiges Brot* (liquid bread).

WHAT'S HOT

➡ Asian fusion

➡ Creative vegan and vegetarian food

➡ Locavore (locally produced) and seasonal food

➡ Street food and food trucks

➡ Craft beer

➡ Gourmet burgers

➡ Cocktail bars, rooftop bars, wine bars

➡ Modern German cuisine

Going Gourmet

Germany has been redeeming itself gastronomically over the past decade. In top kitchens across the country, chefs are putting an imaginative spin on tried-and-trusted specialities in a wave referred to as *neue Deutsche Küche* (new German cuisine).

To see Germany's meteoric rise in the Michelin world, look no further than the Black Forest village of Baiersbronn, where master chefs Harald Wohlfahrt (Schwarzwaldstube) and Peter Lumpp (Restaurant Bareiss) have both been awarded the coveted three Michelin stars. They are no exception: Berlin alone had 15 Michelin-starred restaurants, including five with two stars, in 2015 – and other cities are swiftly following suit.

Besides Michelin and Gault Millau, Germany has its own ratings and guides, including **Der Feinschmecker** (www.der-feinschmecker.de), **Aral's Schlemmer Atlas** (www.schlemmer-atlas.de) and **Marcellino's Restaurant Report** (www.marcellinos.de).

Meals of a Lifetime

From fine dining to hearty German grub served with a dollop of history, whet your appetite with our pick of the best.

➡ **La Soupe Populaire** (p107) Tim Raue heads up this industro-chic gourmet haunt in a converted Berlin brewery, adding a pinch of creativity to German soul food.

➡ **Söl'ring** (p691) In a dune setting in Sylt, with crashing surf as the backbeat, Johannes King's kitchen wows with stunning renditions of seasonal produce and seafood.

➡ **Schwarzwaldstube** (p341) Harald Wohlfahrt cooks French with precision and panache at this three Michelin-starred Black Forest hideaway in Baiersbronn.

➡ **Zur Herrenmühle** (p417) Dine under 300-year-old wooden beams at this 1690 flour mill turned elegant country-style restaurant in Heidelberg.

➡ **Esszimmer** (p215) Bobby Bräuer helms this Michelin-starred Mediterranean number at BMW World. It's Munich's finest.

Cookery Courses

Germany's fledgling cookery school scene has spread its wings in recent years, and there's a sprinkling of places where you can learn some culinary magic. Expect to pay between €140 and €240 for a day at the stove, usually including lunch and recipes to take home.

At Schwarzwaldstube (p341), classes revolve around a theme such as cooking with asparagus or making pasta. For a more traditional focus, join the kings of Knödel for an English-language dumpling-making workshop at **Wirtshaus in der Au** (☏089-448 14 00; http://wirtshausinderau.de; Lilienstrasse 51) in Munich. Or search for regional courses to suit you. Check out www.kochschule.de and www.die-kochschulen.de (both in German).

Local Specialities

Drift to the Baltic and North Sea coasts for pickled herrings with oomph and sweet-sour *Mecklenburger Rippenbraten* (rolled pork stuffed with lemons, apples, plums and raisins). Hamburg locals love their eels and *Labskaus* (minced beef, potato and beetroot, served with a fried egg and gherkins), while Bavarians match excellent beer with gut-busting platters of pork knuckles and *Klösse* (dumplings). Then there's Saxony and Thuringia for lentil and potato soups, the Black Forest for its trout, ham and famous gateau, and rural Swabia for culinary one-offs such as *Spätzle* (noodle-dumpling hybrids) and *Maultaschen* (ravioli's Teutonic relative). Traditional fare, such as *Eisbein* (salt-cured ham hock with sauerkraut) and *Bouletten* (meatballs), never goes out of fashion in Berlin.

Almost every town in Germany has a weekly *Bauernmarkt* (farmers market).

ANANDOART/SHUTTERSTOCK ©

Top: Feasting at
Oktoberfest

Bottom: Bavarian
sausages

KARL ALLGAEUER/SHUTTERSTOCK ©

DOS & DON'TS

➡ Do say 'Guten Appetit' (good appetite) before eating, and 'Prost!' when drinking a toast.

➡ Do offer to help wash up afterwards – locals tend to be quite punctilious about housework.

➡ Do specify if you don't want your restaurant dishes slathered in mayonnaise, Quark (type of cheese) or dressing. Germans are generous in this department.

➡ Don't expect a glass of tap water at a restaurant or cafe; although things are changing, especially in cities, it's still an uncommon request that may not be understood or honoured.

➡ Don't plonk yourself down at the Stammtisch table. Empty or not, these are reserved for regulars only.

This is the place to bag local fruit and veg, cheese, wurst, fish, preserves, herbs and sometimes homegrown wine and schnapps. Biomärkte (organic markets and supermarkets) can also be found in most towns and cities.

Dare to Try

Feeling daring? Why not give some of Germany's more unusual dishes a whirl.

➡ **Sauere Kuttlen/Nierle/Lüngerl** (sour tripe/kidneys/lung) No Baden-Württemberg beer fest would be complete without these offal faves, simmered in vinegar or wine, bay, laurel, juniper and spices.

➡ **Handkäs mit Musik** (hand cheese with music) Hesse's pongy sour-milk cheese, rolled by hand and marinated in oil and vinegar with onions. A sure-fire recipe for flatulence – hence the music!

➡ **Saumagen** Rhineland-Palatinate brings you stuffed pig stomach (reminiscent of haggis). Eat it with sauerkraut and sautéed potatoes.

➡ **Labskaus** Every Hamburg seafarer worth his salt adores this mishmash of corned beef, beetroot, potatoes, onions and occasionally herring, topped with a fried egg and served with gherkins.

➡ **Bubespitzle** Otherwise known as Schupfnudeln, this Swabian dish's ingredients are innocuous: potato noodles tossed in butter, served with sauerkraut and speck (cured ham). But the name (literally, 'little boys' penises') certainly isn't.

At the Table

When to Eat

Though city folk might just grab a coffee en route to the office, Frühstück (breakfast) is a traditionally sweet and savoury smorgasbord of bread, cheese, salami, wurst, preserves, yoghurt and muesli. At weekends, it's a more leisurely, family-oriented affair. Many cafes have embraced the brunch trend, serving all-you-can eat buffets with fresh rolls, eggs, smoked fish, fruit salad and even Prosecco.

While the older generation may still sit down for Mittagessen at noon sharp, the focus on lunch as the main meal of the day is waning thanks to a shift in work patterns. Many restaurants still tout a fixed lunch menu (Mittagsmenü or Tagesmenü), which can be an affordable way of dining at upscale restaurants.

Dinner is served in homes at around 7pm. For those who have already eaten heartily at midday, there is Abendbrot, bread with cold cuts. Outside the cities, with their late-night dining scenes, Germans head to restaurants earlier than elsewhere in Europe, and many kitchens in rural areas stop serving at around 9pm. At home, meals are relaxed and require few airs and graces beyond the obligatory 'Guten Appetit' (good appetite), exchanged before eating.

Where to Eat

➡ **Gaststätten & Gasthöfe** Rural inns with a laid-back feel, local crowd and solid menu of gutbürgerliche Küche (home cooking).

➡ **Eiscafé** Italian-style cafes, where you can grab an ice cream or cappuccino and head outside to slurp and sip.

➡ **Stehcafé** A stand-up cafe for coffee and snacks at speed and on the cheap.

➡ **Cafe-Konditorei** A traditional cake shop and cafe.

➡ **Ratskeller** Atmospheric town-hall basement restaurant, generally frequented more by tourists than locals nowadays.

➡ **Bierkeller & Weinkeller** The emphasis is on beer and wine respectively, with a little food (sausages, pretzels, cold cuts) on the side.

➡ **Imbiss** Handy speed-feed stops for savoury fodder, such as wurst-in-a-bun, kebabs or pizza.

➡ **Apfelweinwirtschaft** Frankfurt's historic *Ebbelwei* (apple wine) taverns. Warm, woody and serving good honest regional fare.

➡ **Biergarten** Beer garden – often with tree shade and a meaty menu.

Roll out the Barrel

Up and down this hop-crazy country you will find buzzing microbreweries and brewpubs, cavernous beer halls and chestnut-shaded beer gardens that invite you to linger, quaff a cold one and raise a toast – *Prost!*

Some of the best are in Bavaria, home to Ingolstadt of 1516 Beer Purity Law fame. Munich offers a taste of Oktoberfest year-round in historic beer halls, where you can hoist a *Mass* litre of *Weizen* and sway to oompah bands, and in leafy beer gardens perfect for imbibing and chomping on *Brez'n* (warm pretzels) and *Weisswurst* (herb-veal-pork sausage). This festive spirit spills into other Bavarian cities such as Regensburg, and Bamberg (which runs a five-brewery tour), and into villages where monks brew potent dark beers as they have for eons. Cologne is another German beer stronghold, famous for straw-gold *Kölsch* served in skinny glasses called *Stangen*.

Breweries offering a peek behind the scenes include Hamburg's Holsten breweries (www.holsten-pilsener.de), Bremen's Beck's (p622) and Jever's Friesisches Brauhaus zu Jever (p636).

Kaffee und Kuchen

Anyone who has spent any length of time in Germany knows the reverence bestowed on the 3pm weekend ritual of *Kaffee und Kuchen* (coffee and cake). More than just a chance to devour delectable cakes and tortes, Germans see it as a social event. You'll find *Cafe-Konditoreien* (cafe-cake shops) pretty much everywhere – in castles, in the middle of the forest, even plopped on top of mountains. Track down the best by asking sweet-toothed locals where the cake is *hausgemacht* (homemade).

While coffee in Germany is not as strong as that served in France or Italy, you can expect a decent cup. All the usual varieties are on offer, including cappuccinos and lattes, although you still frequently see French-style bowls of milky coffee *(Milchkaffee)*. Order a *Kanne* (pot) or *Tasse* (cup) of *Kaffee* (coffee) and what you will get is filter coffee, usually with a portion of *Kaffeesahne* (condensed milk).

East Frisians in Bremen and Lower Saxony are the country's biggest consumers of tea, and have dozens of their own varieties, which they traditionally drink with cream and *Kluntje* (rock sugar). Tea frequently comes as a glass or pot of hot water, with the tea bag served to the side.

Dining Tips

One early-20th-century German book of manners that we have seen exhorts dinner guests not to use their knives to carve their initials into the table of their hosts! Things have moved on somewhat since those days. With good manners now automatic, there's little need to panic at the dinner table, although a few tips might come in handy for first-time visitors.

➡ **On the menu** English menus are prevalent in big cities, but the more rural and remote you travel, the less common they become. Most places will have a waiter or waitress who can translate, but it helps to learn a few phrases of German.

➡ **Paying the bill** Sometimes the person who invites will pay, but generally Germans go Dutch and split the bill evenly. This might mean everyone chipping in at the end of a meal or asking to pay separately (*getrennte Rechnung*). Buying rounds in bars British-style is not usually the done thing, though Germans might buy each other the odd drink. In bars and beer halls, table service is still quite common and waiting staff often come around to *abkassieren* (cash up).

➡ **Table reservations** If you want to dine at trendy or Michelin-starred restaurants, it is wise to make reservations at least a week in advance. Most Gasthöfe, Gaststätten, cafes and beer halls should be able to squeeze you in at a moment's notice.

➡ **Tipping** A service charge is not included in the bill. Tipping is quite an individual matter, but most Germans will tip between 5% and 10% in restaurants, and simply round to the nearest euro in cafes and bars. Do whatever you're comfortable with, given the service and setting. Give any tip directly to the server when paying your bill. Say either the amount you want to pay, or 'Stimmt so' if you don't want change.

Plan Your Trip
Travel with Children

Travelling to Germany with tots can be child's play, especially if you keep a light schedule and involve them in trip planning. Plus, kids are a great excuse if you secretly yearn to ride roller coasters or dip into the fairy-tale landscapes of Brothers Grimm.

Best Regions for Kids

Stuttgart & the Black Forest (p306)

Fairy-tale forest trails, farm stays and outdoor activities galore. Zip across to the Lake Constance for kayaking, swimming and cycling, Triberg for its whopping cuckoo clocks and Europa-Park to race around Europe in miniature.

Bavaria (p227)

Discover storybook Germany, with its Christmas-card mountain scenery and high-on-a-hill Schloss Neuschwanstein, the blueprint for Disney's *Sleeping Beauty* castle. Find diversions aplenty in Munich and sight-packed Nuremberg – one of Germany's most engaging cities for kiddies.

Central Germany (p526)

Hike in the mythical Harz Mountains and the Thuringian Forest and enjoy happy-ever-after moments along the 600km Fairy-Tale Road, taking in castles, hamlets and other stops that inspired the tales of Brothers Grimm.

Hamburg & the North (p643)

Go for Lübeck's puppet theatre, pearly white beaches and candy-striped lighthouses on the Baltic and North Sea coasts. Müritz National Park is fabulous for paddle-and-camp trips, and Sylt for boat trips to seal colonies.

Germany for Children

Travelling to Germany with kids in tow? You're in for a treat. Kids will already have seen in bedtime picture books many of the things that make the country so special: enchanting palaces and legend-shrouded castles lifted high by mountaintops; medieval towns and half-timbered villages that take you back several centuries; islands and meandering rivers; and deep, dark forests that fire little imaginations. This is the birthplace of the Brothers Grimm and their unforgettable fairy tales. Follow the Fairy-Tale Road to see Sleeping Beauty's castle and dance to the tune of the Pied Piper in the town of Hamelin.

Cities also have much to keep the little ones amused, with interactive museums, imaginative playgrounds, puppet shows, outdoor pools and zoos.

Tourist offices can point you to children's attractions, child-care facilities and English-speaking pediatricians. If you need a babysitter, ask staff at your hotel for a referral.

Breastfeeding in public is practised, although most women are discreet about it. Restaurants are rarely equipped with nappy-change facilities, but some fast-food places have a fold-down change table in the women's toilet.

Outdoor Activities

The great outdoors yields endless variety in Germany. Tourist offices can recommend well-marked walking trails suitable for families, including those pushing strollers, or can hook you up with a local guide. Ask about kid-geared activities like geocaching, animal-spotting safaris and nature walks.

Water rats will love frolicking on Germany's beaches, which are clean and usually devoid of big surf and dangerous undercurrents. Water temperatures rarely exceed 21°C (70°F), though lakes tend to be a bit warmer. Many have an inexpensive *Strandbad* (lido) with change rooms, playgrounds, splash zones, slides, ping-pong tables, restaurants or boat rentals. Kayaking is active fun for children from the age of seven, and short excursions or multiday paddle-and-camp trips are available.

Cycling is big in Germany, with safe, well-signposted routes running along lakes and coastlines, through forests and up into the hills. The vast majority of bike rental outlets have children's bikes and can recommend kid-friendly tours.

All ski resorts have ski schools with English-speaking instructors that initiate kids in the art of the snow plough in group or private lessons. Families with kids under 10 may find smaller resorts in the Bavarian Forest or Black Forest easier to navigate and better value than bigger Alpine resorts like Garmisch-Partenkirchen. All of them, of course, have plenty of off-piste fun as well: snow-shoeing, sledding, walking and ice skating.

Museums

Germany is full of child-friendly museums that play to young imaginations or impart knowledge in interactive and engaging ways. Open-air museums like the Schwarzwälder Freilichtmuseum in the Black Forest or the Freilandmuseum Lehde in the Spreewald are fun places to learn about traditional culture. Cologne has the Schokoladen Museum (Chocolate Museum), Nuremberg the Spielzeugmuseum (Toy Museum) and Munich the Deutsches Museum (German Museum). Berlin is a sure-fire kid-pleaser with its Museum für Naturkunde, home to the stuffed polar bear Knut and Jurassic giants in the dino hall, and hands-on science and technology wizardry at the Deutsches Technikmuseum. Kid-oriented audioguides (in German and English) are becoming more widely available. Staff also run tot-geared activities, although these are usually in German.

Theme Parks

There's plenty of fun and thrills in theme parks. The country's biggest is Europa-Park near Freiburg, which has gentle rides for young children, white-knuckle coasters for teens and its own mousy mascot, the Euromaus. For fishy encounters, seek out one of the country's eight SeaLife aquariums with touch tanks, fish feedings and activities. The Legoland amusement park in Ulm has shows, rides and a miniature world built from millions of Lego bricks, while Ravensburger Spieleland is like a board game come to life; there's also an indoor one in Berlin. Older kids may be drawn to movie-themed parks, such as Filmpark Babelsberg in Potsdam, for stunt shows, behind-the-scenes tours and potential actor-sightings.

Dining Out

As long as they're not running wild, children are generally welcome in German restaurants, especially in informal cafes, bistros, pizzerias or Gaststatten (inns). High chairs are common and the server may even bring a damp cloth at the end of your meal to wipe sticky little fingers.

Many less formal restaurants offer a limited *Kindermenü* (children's menu) or *Kinderteller* (children's meals). Dishes generally loved by children include *Schnitzel mit Pommes* (schnitzel with fries), *Bratwurst* (sausage), *Nudeln mit Tomatensosse* (pasta with tomato sauce), *Spätzle* (egg-based mini-dumpling-like noodles) or the German version of mac 'n' cheese, *Käsespätzle. Maultaschen*, a spin on ravioli, may also go down well. Pizzerias are cheap, ubiquitous and most will be happy to customise pizzas.

Germany is fabulous snack territory. Larger malls have food courts, self-service cafeterias are often found in department stores and farmers markets also have food stalls. The most popular snacks on the run are bratwurst in a bun and doner kebab (sliced meat in a pita pocket with salad and sauce). And there's no shortage of international fast food chains. Note that you have to pay extra for ketchup.

Baby food, infant formulas, soy and cow's milk, and nappies (diapers) are widely available in supermarkets and chemists (drugstores).

Drinks

Tap water is clean and fine to drink, although most cafes and restaurants are reluctant to serve it. In that case, order a *Mineralwasser* (mineral water), either *mit Sprudel* (fizzy) or *ohne Sprudel* (flat). Mixing juices and fizzy mineral water (*Schorle*) is refreshing and popular.

Children's Discounts

Many museums, monuments and attractions are free to anyone under 18, but the cut-off age varies. In general, you can assume kids under five don't pay at all. Most places also offer family tickets.

Children qualify for discounts on public transport and tours, where they usually pay half price, and sometimes less. Some hotels, including many international chains, have discounted rates for kids or don't charge extra if they're under a cer-

tain age (varying from three to 16) and stay in their parents' room without extra bedding. The *Kurtaxe* (tourist tax) you pay in most resorts gets you a *Gästekarte* (guest card) for free local transport and entry to museums, pools and attractions.

Children's Highlights
Outdoor Activities

➡ **Black Forest** (p328) Go down to these seemingly never-ending woods for hiking, cycling, skiing, sledding and snow-shoeing.

➡ **Spreewald** (p134) Navigate the channels and canals of this Unesco biosphere reserve by canoe, kayak or punt.

➡ **Sylt** (p688) This wave-lashed island in the North Sea is ideal for surfing, windsurfing or horse riding.

➡ **Bavarian Alps** (p230) Have Heidi moments striking out on foot or take to the slopes in winter.

➡ **Lake Constance** (p357) A family magnet, where you can walk, pedal, kayak or boat it over to Switzerland and Austria.

➡ **Rügen** (p709) Sheltered Baltic Sea beaches and family rambles along limestone cliffs and through enchanting beech forests.

Amusement Parks

➡ **Europa-Park** (p352) Huge Europe-themed amusement park with whizzy rides and a mouse mascot.

➡ **Märchengarten** (p317) Low-key fairy-tale-themed park for tots in Ludwigsburg.

➡ **Steinwasen Park** (p348) Forest park near Freiburg with rides, Alpine animals and a hanging bridge.

➡ **Ravensburger Spieleland** (p367) Board-game-inspired park with giant rubber duck races and speed cow milking.

➡ **Feenweltchen** (Fairy World; adult/concession/family €6/5/14.50, combination ticket with grottoes €12/10.50/29; ⊙9am-6pm May-Oct) A magical world of elves, fairies and sprites attached to a colourful grotto in Saalfeld.

➡ **Playmobil** (p273) In Nuremberg, tots love the life-sized versions of these toys.

TOP FIVE GERMAN READS FOR KIDS

➡ **The Robber Hotzenplotz** (Otfried Preussler, 1963) A rambunctious picture book about a thief, set in a small town in southern Germany.

➡ **Candy Bombers** (Robert Elmer, 2006) Tale of two teenagers struggling to survive in post-WWII Berlin (from age nine).

➡ **Momo** (Michael Ende, 1973) A tale about time involving an orphan girl who lives in a ruined amphitheatre at the edge of an unnamed city.

➡ **The Original Folk and Fairy Tales of the Brothers Grimm** (Jacob Grimm & Wilhelm Grimm, 1812 & 1815) This classic contains 156 of the Grimm's folk and fairy tales – from 'Rapunzel' to 'Hansel and Gretel' and 'The Frog King'.

➡ **The Never-Ending Story** (Michael Ende, 1979) German novel about a boy who reads a magical book that plunges him into a fantasy world.

Planes, Trains & Automobiles

Also see If You Like... Train Journeys (p27) for fun narrow-gauge train rides.

➡ **Nürburgring** (www.nuerburgring.de) Legendary car racing track.

➡ **Technik Museum** (p420) A Boeing 747, 1960s U-boat and Soviet space shuttle await inspection in Speyer.

➡ **Deutsches Technikmuseum** (p78) Giant shrine to technology in Berlin.

➡ **Phaeno** (p618) Scientific exhibits and experiments in Wolfsburg's cutting-edge building by Zaha Hadid.

➡ **Miniatur Wunderland** (p651) In Hamburg, one of the world's largest model railways.

➡ **Deutsche Bahn Museum** (p266) Choo-choo themed attractions including Children's Railway World, Nuremberg.

Planning

Accommodation

Many hotels have family rooms with three or four beds, large doubles with a sofa-bed or adjoining rooms with a connecting door. Practically all can provide cots, though sometimes for a small extra charge. In some properties, smaller children (generally under 12) stay free or are given a discount.

Farm stays (*Urlaub auf dem Bauernhof*) are popular with families and offer a low-key, inexpensive experience. A variation on the theme are *Heuhotels* (hay hotels), which offer the option of literally sleeping in a barn on a bed of hay. See www.heuhotels. de for details. Camping is also huge, but in summer the most popular sites book out far in advance.

Hostelling International-affiliated hostels (DJH hostels) have family rooms and activities, but independent hostels tend to have more of a party vibe and don't always welcome children.

Getting Around

Children under 12 or smaller than 1.5m (59 inches) must ride in the back seat in cars (taxis included) and use a car seat or booster that's appropriate for their weight. Only children older than 12 and over 1.5m tall may ride in front. Car seats are occa-sionally provided free by rental companies but must be reserved.

Train is a great way to get around Germany. Children under 15 travel free if accompanied by at least one parent or grandparent, but names of children aged between six and 14 must be registered on your ticket at time of purchase. Children under six always travel free and without a ticket.

The superfast ICE trains have compartments for families with small children (*Kleinkindabteil*) that are equipped with tables, stroller storage, an electrical outlet (for warming bottles) and, sometimes, a change table. Book these early.

Seat reservations for families (*Familienreservierung*) cost a flat €8 for two adults and up to three children.

Useful Websites

➡ **Familienurlaub in Deutschland** (www. familienfreundlich.de) Hotels, tips, route planners and more.

➡ **German National Tourist Office** (www. germany.travel) Popular family sights and destinations.

➡ **Urlaub auf dem Bauernhof** (www. bauernhofurlaub.de) Over 5000 farm-stay properties throughout Germany.

Regions at a Glance

Berlin

Art & Culture
Nightlife
History

Museums & Galleries

From art deco to agriculture, sex to sugar, and diamonds to dinosaurs, there is hardly a theme not covered in Berlin's nearly 200 museums, most famously in the tantalising treasures of Museum Island.

Party Till You Drop

Berlin is the spiritual home of the 'lost weekend'. Kick off a night on the razzle in a bar or pub, catch tomorrow's headline acts in an indie-music venue, then dance till dawn or beyond in clubs helmed by DJ royalty.

Historic Sights

In Berlin the past is always present. Its legendary sights take you back to the era of Prussian glory, the dark ages of the Third Reich, the tense period of the Cold War and the euphoria of reunification.

p54

Around Berlin

Palaces
Watery Fun
History

A Taste of Royalty

Schloss Sanssouci is the jewel among Potsdam's palaces, but the nearby Neues Palais, Marmorpalais and Schloss Cecilienhof are other fabled and fanciful addresses.

Aquatic Adventures

Tour Potsdam's palaces by boat, take a punt to a Sorb village in the emerald-green Spreewald or kayak around Brandenburg an der Havel. This region is best experienced from the water.

Momentous Moments

Visit seminal sites of the 20th century, such as one of Germany's first concentration camps, the palace where Allied leaders decided the country's post-WWII fate, and a sinister KGB prison.

p124

Saxony

Museums
Palaces
Art & Culture

Iconic Collections

Dresden's wealth of paintings, porcelain, armour, sculptures and other priceless collections is truly stunning. If time is tight, focus on the whimsical objects in the unmissable Green Vault.

Palace Envy

Style, grandeur and artistry combine in Saxony's grand palaces, such as the Elbe-fronting Schloss Pillnitz, the moated Moritzburg and the hulking Albrechtsburg.

Artistic Legacies

Saxony's landscapes have long tugged at the hearts of artists such as Canaletto and Caspar David Friedrich, while Bach, Schumann and Wagner have shaped its musical heritage. Walk in their footsteps in Leipzig, Zwickau and Dresden.

p140

Munich

Art & Culture
Beer
Sports

Classy Canvasses

Feast your eyes on a who's who of creative hotshots of the past 800 years – from Dürer to Degas to Dalí – in the triumphal trio of Pinakothek museums.

Bottoms Up

The Hofbräuhaus may be the world's most famous pub, but you'll find lots of cheer and beer throughout Munich. On balmy nights, clink mugs below the chestnut trees in a convivial beer garden.

Arenas & Athletes

The Olympiapark has hosted top athletes, and not just since the 1972 Olympic Games. Soccer fans are drawn to the Allianz Arena, home base of Germany's most famous soccer team, FC Bayern München.

p182

Bavaria

Churches
Villages
Activities

Baroque Beauties

If you want to 'go for baroque', you've hit the mother lode in Bavaria. The Wieskirche in Steingaden and the Würzburg Residenz are among many resplendent examples.

Medieval Villages

Proving that good things come in small packages, Bavaria's medieval villages are endowed with timeless beauty, palpable romance and a sense of history spilling from every nook and cranny.

Outdoor Fun

Each season offers its own delights – hiking among spring wildflowers, swimming in an Alpine lake warmed by the summer sun, cycling beneath gorgeous autumn foliage or schussing through deep winter snow.

p227

Stuttgart & the Black Forest

Food
Hiking
Cars

Gourmet Haven

Black forest gateau, brook trout, smoked ham, *Maultaschen*, *Spätzle* – foodies, eat your hearts out in this culinary paradise with Germany's greatest density of Michelin-starred chefs.

Trail Blazing

No matter if it's a short hike to a waterfall or a multiday trek from village to village, in the Black Forest you'll be treated to a rich tapestry of natural beauty combined with timeless traditions.

Motor City

Connect with Germany's storied car culture by visiting the architecturally stunning Mercedes-Benz Museum and futuristic Porsche Museum in Stuttgart.

p306

Frankfurt & the Southern Rhineland

Wine
Castles
City Life

Grape Delights

Nope, Germany is not all about beer. Put some zing in your step sampling crisp whites and velvety reds in the top wine-growing areas that hug the Moselle River and Rhine.

Romantic Castles

Few buildings speak more to the imagination than craggy medieval stone castles. From Heidelberg and the Romantic Rhine to the Palatinate, this region delivers them in abundance.

Urban delights

The business of Frankfurt may be business, but this 'Mainhattan' is no buttoned-up metropolis, as you'll quickly discover in its apple-wine taverns, fine museums and fashionable shopping areas.

p370

Cologne & the Northern Rhineland

History
City Life
Off-beat Culture

Historic Cities

Hunt for history and connect with the Romans in Xanten and Cologne, pay your respects to Charlemagne in Aachen and applaud Münster and Osnabrück where the epic Thirty Years' War ended.

Rhenish Style

Break for *a Kölsch* between marvelling at Cologne's magnificent cathedral, sampling its stunning portfolio of museums or taking a cruise on the Rhine.

Industrial Artistry

It takes ingenuity to recycle dormant industrial sites into something exciting. In the Ruhrgebiet you can see art in a gas tank, sip martinis in a boiler house or listen to Mozart in a compressor hall.

p462

Central Germany

Drives
History
Outdoors

Fairy-Tale Drive

Keep an eye out for witches, goblins and 'sleeping beauties' as you follow in the footsteps of the Brothers Grimm along the Fairy-Tale Road.

Poets & Thinkers

A keystone of German culture, this region gave birth to Martin Luther and the Reformation, inspired dramatists Goethe and Schiller, launched the Bauhaus design movement and pioneered optical precision technology.

Harz Ramble

Forest trails beckon in the Harz Mountains, including the trek up myth-laden Mt Brocken. Stop also in half-timbered Quedlinburg, explore mining history in Goslar and hurtle along on a century-old narrow-gauge steam train.

p526

Lower Saxony & Bremen

Outdoors
City Life
Gardens

Island Walks

Sure, you can walk around an island, but have you ever walked *to* an island? You can do so across the tidal flats in the Wadden Sea National Park in East Frisia.

Hanse Meets Hi-Tech

A major trading town since the Middle Ages, Bremen now wows with a charming historic centre, a hip nightlife quarter, a vast container port and a poignant emigration museum.

Glorious Gardens

A touch of Versailles is what you'll find at Hanover's Herrenhäuser Gärten, a manicured jumble of gardens accented with whimsical art by Niki de Saint Phalle.

p595

Hamburg & the North

Islands
Architecture
City Life

Remote Shores

There's almost something otherworldly about Germany's islands, from glamourous Sylt to family-friendly Usedom. Hit the surf, cycle among the dunes or relax on a white sandy beach.

Hanseatic Beauties

Savour the red-brick splendour of charismatic Lübeck, Wismar, Stralsund and Greifswald, all Baltic towns with a pedigree going back to the Hanseatic League.

Happening Hamburg

In the 'gateway to the world', discover the sublime (Kunsthalle), the naughty (the Reeperbahn red-light district), the historic (St Nikolai), the futuristic (HafenCity), the posh (Alster Lakes) and the raucous (Fischmarkt).

p643

On the Road

Berlin

POP 3.56 MILLION / ☑ 030

Best Places to Eat

➡ La Soupe Populaire (p107)

➡ Zenkichi (p104)

➡ Cafe Jacques (p105)

➡ Restaurant am Steinplatz (p109)

➡ Burgermeister (p105)

Best Places to Stay

➡ Circus Hotel (p96)

➡ Michelberger Hotel (p100)

➡ Mandala Hotel (p97)

➡ Das Stue (p97)

➡ Grand Hostel Berlin (p97)

Why Go?

Berlin is a bon vivant, passionately feasting on the smorgasbord of life, never taking things – or itself – too seriously. Its unique blend of glamour and grit is bound to mesmerise anyone keen to connect with its vibrant culture, superb museums, fabulous food, intense parties and tangible history. When it comes to creativity, the sky's the limit in Berlin. Since the fall of the Wall, the city has become a giant lab of cultural experimentation thanks to an abundance of space, cheap rent and a free-wheeling spirit that nurtures and encourages new ideas. All this trendiness is a triumph for a city that's long been in the cross hairs of history: Berlin staged a revolution, was headquarters to the Nazis, bombed to bits, divided in two and finally reunited – and that was just in the 20th century! Must-sees or aimless explorations – this city delivers it all in one exciting and memorable package.

When to Go

Spring and autumn are generally best for visiting Berlin as the weather is the most stable and cultural events of all stripes are in full swing. Summers essentially bring a population exchange as locals leave town for hotter climes and tourists, especially from southern Europe, flock to Berlin to escape the heat. This is the time of outdoor anything: concerts, festivals, beer gardens, parties, beach bars, cinema. Winters are cold and dark and life moves indoors, except during Christmas market season in December.

History

By German standards, Berlin entered onto the stage rather late and puttered along in relative obscurity for centuries. Founded in the 13th century as a trading post, it achieved a modicum of prominence after coming under the rule of the powerful Hohenzollern clan from southern Germany in 1411. It managed to cling to power until the abolition of the monarchy in 1918.

In 1701 Elector Friedrich III was elevated to King Friedrich I, making Berlin a royal residence. The promotion significantly shaped the city, which blossomed under Friedrich I's grandson, Frederick the Great, who sought greatness as much on the battlefield as through building and embracing the ideals of the Enlightenment. The best bits of Unter den Linden date back to his reign, when Berlin blossomed into a cultural centre that some even called 'Athens on the Spree'.

As throughout northern Europe, the Industrial Revolution began its march on Berlin in the 19th century, vastly expanding the city's population growth and spawning a new working class. Berlin boomed politically, economically and culturally, especially after becoming capital of the German Reich in 1871. By 1900 the population had reached two million.

World War I stifled Berlin's momentum, while the 1920s were marred by instability, corruption and inflation. Berliners responded like there was no tomorrow and made their city as much a den of decadence as a cauldron of creativity. Artists of all stripes flocked to this city of cabaret, Dada and jazz.

Hitler's rise to power put an instant damper on the fun as the dark ages of the Third Reich descended upon the world. Berlin suffered heavy bombing in WWII and a crushing invasion of 1.5 million Soviet soldiers during the final Battle of Berlin in April 1945. Few original Nazi-era sights remain, but memorials and museums keep the horror in focus.

After WWII, Germany fell into the cross hairs of the Cold War; a country divided ideologically and literally by a fortified border and the infamous Berlin Wall, whose construction began in 1961. Just how differently the two Germanys developed is still palpable in Berlin, expressed not only through Wall remnants but through vastly different urban planning and architectural styles.

Since reunification, Berlin has again become a hotbed of creativity, with unbridled nightlife, an explosive art scene and booming fashion and design industries. Sure, problems persist – empty city coffers, high unemployment, the delayed Berlin Brandenburg Airport, to name a few – but Berlin's allure to tourists and newcomers from around the world remains unabated. It's a city that dances to its own tune, where individualism triumphs over conformity and brilliant ideas are celebrated. Few people who live here don't love it. Few people who visit will ever forget it.

◉ Sights

Berlin is a sprawling city split into 12 official *Bezirke* (districts; for example Mitte, Prenzlauer Berg and Kreuzberg), which are subdivided into individual neighbourhoods (*Kieze*). Finding your bearings in Berlin is fairly easy. Key sights such as the Reichstag, the Brandenburger Tor and the famous Museumsinsel cluster in the walkable historic city centre – Mitte – which also cradles the Scheunenviertel, a maze-like hipster quarter around Hackescher Markt. North of Mitte, residential Prenzlauer Berg entices with pastel-coloured town houses, indie boutiques, cosy cafes and a fun flea market, while to the south loom the contemporary high-rises of Potsdamer Platz. Further south, gritty but cool Kreuzberg and Neukölln are party central, as is student-flavoured Friedrichshain east across the Spree River and home to the East Side Gallery stretch of the Berlin Wall. Western Berlin's hub is Charlottenburg, with great shopping and a famous Prussian royal palace.

◉ Reichstag & Unter den Linden

With the mother lode of key sights clustered within a walkable area, this part of Berlin should be your first port of call. Book ahead for access to the Reichstag dome, then pick up Unter den Linden just past the Brandenburger Tor. You'll quickly notice that these

> ❶ **PLANNING AHEAD**

➡ **Two months** Book online tickets to the Philharmonie, Staatsoper and Sammlung Boros

➡ **One month** Make online reservations for the Reichstag dome, the Neues Museum and the Pergamonmuseum

➡ **Two weeks** Reserve a table at trendy or Michelin-starred restaurants, especially for Friday and Saturday nights

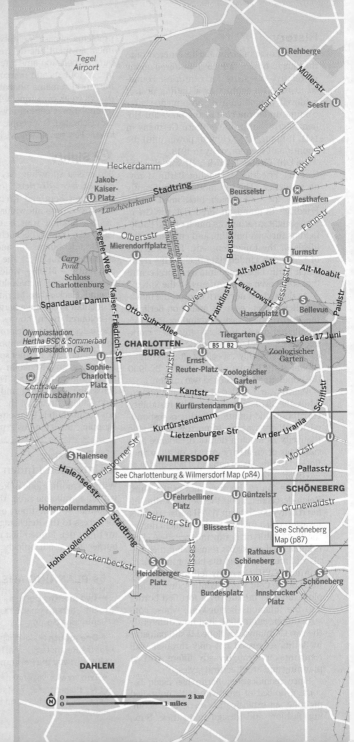

Berlin Highlights

❶ Marvelling at Queen Nefertiti, the Ishtar Gate and many more ancient treasures on **Museumsinsel** (p61)

❷ Letting the sights drift by while sipping a cool drink on the deck of a **river boat** (p91)

❸ Checking out sexy bods while chilling and bronzing on the **Badeschiff** (p94), a cargo barge turned lifestyle pool

❹ Putting together the distinctive Berlin look by scouring the local-designer boutiques of the **Scheunenviertel** (p118)

❺ Getting high on the knock-out views from the **Reichstag** (p58) roof or the **Fernsehturm** (p66), Germany's tallest structure

❻ Hobnobbing with **Kreuzberg** hipsters for a night of tabloid-worthy drinking and debauchery (p111)

❼ Looking for traces of the elusive Berlin Wall at the **Gedenkstätte Berliner Mauer** (p72)

❽ Treasure hunting and karaoke crooning in the **Mauerpark** (p81)

❾ Getting a dose of asphalt-free exercise in the vast **Tiergarten** (p74) park

❿ Flashing back to Roaring Twenties glamour at **Chamäleon Varieté** (p117)

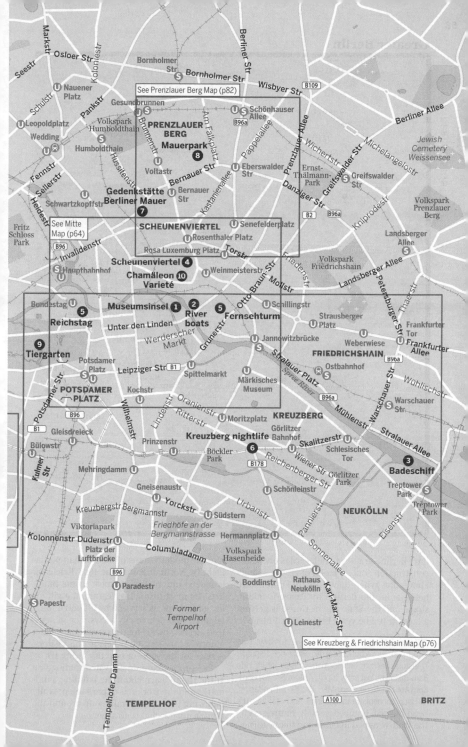

Greater Berlin

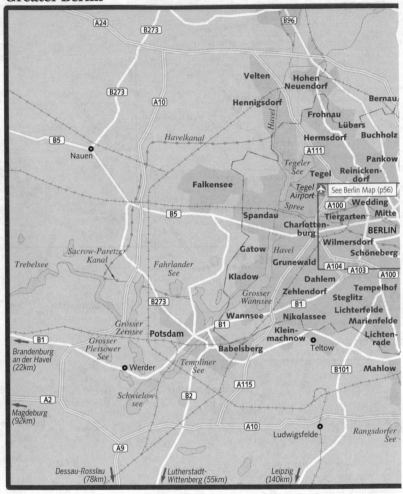

days Berlin's grandest boulevard is one giant construction zone. A ballet of cranes swings above sites where new U-Bahn stations are being built, the Berlin City Palace is taking shape and the State Opera House is getting a facelift. It'll be years before all is finished.

★ Reichstag   HISTORIC BUILDING
(Map p64; www.bundestag.de; Platz der Republik 1, Vistors' Service: Scheidemannstrasse; ⏰ lift ride 8am-midnight, last entry 10pm, Visitors' Service 8am-8pm Apr-Oct, to 6pm Nov-Mar; 🚌 100, S Bundestag, R Hauptbahnhof, Brandenburger Tor) FREE It's been burned, bombed, rebuilt, buttressed by the Wall, wrapped in fabric and finally turned

into the modern home of the German parliament by Norman Foster: the 1894 Reichstag is indeed one of Berlin's most iconic buildings. Its most distinctive feature, the glittering glass dome, is serviced by lift and affords fabulous 360-degree city views. For guaranteed access, make free reservations online; otherwise, try scoring tickets at the Visitors' Service for the same or next day. Bring ID.

Pick up a free auto-activated audioguide at the top to learn about the building, landmarks and the workings of parliament while following the ramp spiralling up around the dome's mirror-clad central cone.

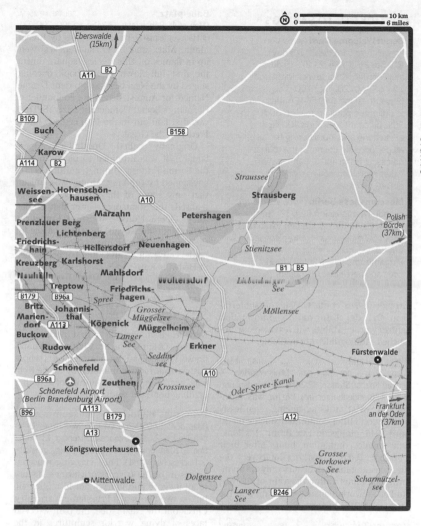

★ Brandenburger Tor & Pariser Platz
LANDMARK

(Map p64; Pariser Platz; ⊙24hr; Ⓢ Brandenburger Tor, Ⓡ Brandenburger Tor) **FREE** A symbol of division during the Cold War, the landmark Brandenburg Gate now epitomises German reunification. Carl Gotthard Langhans found inspiration in Athens' Acropolis for the elegant triumphal arch, completed in 1791 as the royal city gate. It stands sentinel over Pariser Platz, a harmoniously proportioned square once again framed by banks as well as the US, British and French embassies, just as it was during its 19th-century heyday.

Holocaust Memorial
MEMORIAL

(Memorial to the Murdered European Jews; Map p64; ☎030-2639 4336; www.stiftung-denkmal. de; Cora-Berliner-Strasse 1; audioguide adult/concession €4/2; ⊙field 24hr, information centre 10am-8pm Tue-Sun Apr-Sep, to 7pm Oct-Mar, last entry 45min before closing; Ⓢ Brandenburger Tor, Ⓡ Brandenburger Tor) **FREE** Inaugurated in 2005, this football-field-sized memorial by American architect Peter Eisenman consists of 2711 sarcophagi-like concrete columns rising in sombre silence from undulating ground. You're free to access this maze at any point and make your individual journey

BERLIN SIGHTS

ℹ TICKETS TO SAVINGS

Berlin Welcome Card (www.berlin-welcomecard.de; 2/3/5 days €19.50/26.70/34.50, 2/3/5 days incl Potsdam & up to 3 children under 15yr €21.50/28.70/39.50, 3 days incl Museum Island €40.50) Entitles you to unlimited public transport and up to 50% discount to around 200 sights, attractions and tours during the selected period. Sold online, at the tourist offices, U-Bahn and S-Bahn station ticket vending machines, on buses and at BVG offices.

Museumspass Berlin (www.visitberlin.de; adult/concession €24/12) Buys admission to the permanent exhibits of about 50 museums for three consecutive days, including big draws like the Pergamonmuseum. Sold at tourist offices and participating museums.

through it. For context, visit the subterranean **Ort der Information** (Information Centre) whose exhibits will leave no one untouched. Audioguides are available.

Hitler's Bunker   HISTORIC SITE

(Map p64; cnr In den Ministergärten & Gertrud-Kolmar-Strasse; ⊘24hr; Ⓢ Brandenburger Tor, Ⓡ Brandenburger Tor) Berlin was burning and Soviet tanks advancing relentlessly when Adolf Hitler committed suicide on 30 April 1945, alongside Eva Braun, his longtime female companion, hours after their marriage. Today, a parking lot covers the site, revealing its dark history only via an information panel with a diagram of the vast bunker network, construction data and the site's post-WWII history.

Madame Tussauds   MUSEUM

(Map p64; ☏01806-545 800; www.madametussauds.com/berlin; Unter den Linden 74; adult/child 3-14 €23.50/18.50; ⊘10am-7pm, to 8pm Aug, last admission 1hr before closing; Ⓠ100, Ⓢ Brandenburger Tor, Ⓡ Brandenburger Tor) At this legendary wax museum the world's biggest pop stars, Hollywood legends, sports heroes and historical icons stand very still for you to snap their picture. Sure, it's an expensive haven of kitsch and camp, but where else can you have a candlelit dinner with George Clooney? Avoid wait times and save money by buying tickets online.

Bebelplatz   SQUARE, MEMORIAL

(Map p64; Bebelplatz; ⊘24hr; 🚇100, 200, TXL, Ⓢ Hausvogteiplatz) In 1933, books by Brecht, Mann, Marx and other 'subversives' went up in flames on this treeless square during the first full-blown public book burning, staged by the Nazi German Student League. Named for August Bebel, the co-founder of Germany's Social Democratic Party (SPD), it was first laid out in the 18th century under Frederick the Great.

Originally called Opernplatz (Opera Square), it was intended to be the hub of the Forum Fridericianum, a cultural centre envisioned by the king. Money woes meant that only some of the buildings could be realised: the Staatsoper Unter den Linden (State Opera House), the Alte Königliche Bibliothek (Old Royal Library), a palace for the king's brother Heinrich (now the Humboldt University) and the copper-domed St-Hedwigs-Kathedrale.

Neue Wache   MEMORIAL

(Map p64; Unter den Linden 4; ⊘10am-6pm; 🚇100, 200, TXL) **FREE** This columned, temple-like neoclassical structure (1818) was Karl Friedrich Schinkel's first Berlin commission. Originally a Prussian royal guardhouse, it is now an antiwar memorial whose austere interior is dominated by Käthe Kollwitz' heart-wrenching sculpture of a mother cradling her dead soldier son.

Deutsches Historisches Museum   MUSEUM

(Map p64; ☏030-203 040; www.dhm.de; Unter den Linden 2; adult/concession/under 18 €8/4/free; ⊘10am-6pm; 🚇100, 200, Ⓢ Hausvogteiplatz, Ⓡ Hackescher Markt) This engaging museum zeroes in on 1500 years of German history in all its gore and glory – not in a nutshell, but on two floors of a Prussian-era armoury. Check out the Nazi globe, the pain-wrecked faces of dying warrior sculptures in the courtyard, and the temporary exhibits in the boldly modern annex designed by IM Pei.

⊙ Friedrichstrasse

Friedrichstrasse bisects Unter den Linden and runs north into the 'East End' theatre district and south to Checkpoint Charlie past upscale shopping and Gendarmenmarkt, Berlin's most beautiful square.

Checkpoint Charlie   HISTORIC SITE

(Map p76; cnr Zimmerstrasse & Friedrichstrasse; ⊘24hr; Ⓢ Kochstrasse, Stadtmitte) Checkpoint Charlie was the principal gateway for foreigners and diplomats between the two Berlins from 1961 to 1990. The only direct Cold War–era confrontation between the US and the Soviet Union took place right here when tanks faced off shortly after the Wall went up, nearly triggering a third world war. Alas, this potent symbol of the Cold War has degenerated into a tacky tourist trap, although the free open-air exhibit illustrating Cold War milestones is one redeeming aspect.

Mauermuseum MUSEUM
(Haus am Checkpoint Charlie; Map p76; ☑ 030-253 7250; www.mauermuseum.de; Friedrichstrasse 43-45; adult/concession €12.50/9.50, audioguide €3.50; ⊙ 9am-10pm; Ⓢ Kochstrasse) The Cold War years, especially the history and horror of the Berlin Wall, are engagingly, if haphazardly, documented in this privately run tourist magnet. Open since 1961, the aging exhibit is still strong when it comes to telling the stories of escape attempts to the West. Original devices used in the process, including a hot-air balloon, a one-person submarine and a BMW Isetta, are crowd favourites.

Friedrichstadtpassagen ARCHITECTURE
(Map p64; Friedrichstrasse, btwn Französische Strasse & Mohrenstrasse; ⊙ 10am-8pm Mon-Sat; Ⓢ Französische Strasse, Stadtmitte) Even if you're not part of the Gucci and Prada brigade, the architectural wow factor of this trio of shopping complexes (called *Quartiere*), linked by a subterranean passageway, is undeniable. Highlights are Jean Nouvel's shimmering glass funnel inside the Galeries Lafayette, the dazzlingly patterned art-deco-style Quartier 206 and John Chamberlain's tower made from crushed cars in Quartier 205.

★**Gendarmenmarkt** SQUARE
(Map p64; ⊙ 24hr; Ⓢ Französische Strasse, Stadtmitte) Berlin's most graceful square is bookended by the domed 18th-century German and French cathedrals and punctuated by a grandly porticoed concert hall, the Konzerthaus. It was named for the Gens d'Armes, an 18th-century Prussian regiment consisting of French Huguenot immigrants whose story is chronicled in a museum inside the French cathedral. Climb the tower here for grand views of historic Berlin.

Tränenpalast MUSEUM
(Map p64; ☑ 030-4677 7790; www.hdg.de; Reichstagufer 17; ⊙ 9am-7pm Tue-Fri, 10am-6pm Sat & Sun; Ⓢ Friedrichstrasse, Ⓡ Friedrichstrasse) FREE During the Cold War, tears flowed copiously in this glass-and-steel border-crossing pavilion where East Berliners had to bid adieu to family visiting from West Germany – hence its moniker 'Palace of Tears'. The exhibit uses original objects (including the claustrophobic passport control booths and a border auto-firing system), photographs and historical footage to document the division's social impact on the daily lives of Germans on both sides of the border.

◉ **Museumsinsel**

On Museumsinsel (Museum Island) you can walk through ancient Babylon, meet an Egyptian queen or be mesmerised by Monet. The Unesco-recognised cluster of five museums is Berlin's most important treasure trove of 6000 years of art, artefacts, sculpture and architecture from Europe and beyond. Under the aegis of British architect David Chipperfield the complex is being put through a major update and restructure expected to be completed in 2025. Read about the masterplan at www.museumsinsel-berlin.de.

★**Pergamonmuseum** MUSEUM
(Map p64; ☑ 030-266 424 242; www.smb.museum; Bodestrasse 1-3; adult/concession €12/6; ⊙ 10am-6pm, to 8pm Thu; ☒ 100, Ⓡ Hackescher Markt, Friedrichstrasse) Opening a fascinating window onto the ancient world, this palatial three-wing complex unites a rich feast of classical sculpture and monumental architecture from Greece, Rome, Babylon and the Middle East, including the radiant-blue Ishtar Gate from Babylon, the Roman Market Gate of Miletus and the Caliph's Palace of Mshatta. Renovations put the namesake Pergamon Altar off limits until 2019. Budget at least two hours for this amazing place and be sure to pick up the free and excellent audioguide.

★**Neues Museum** MUSEUM
(New Museum; Map p64; ☑ 030-266 424 242; www.smb.museum; Bodestrasse 1-3; adult/concession €12/6; ⊙ 10am-6pm, to 8pm Thu; ☒ 100, 200, Ⓡ Hackescher Markt) David Chipperfield's

---

ⓘ **MUSEUM ISLAND TIPS**

➡ If you're going to see more than one Museumsinsel collection, it pays to get a day pass valid for one-time admission at all five for €18 (concession €9).

➡ Skip the queues by buying timed tickets online, which also nets a small discount.

The Berlin Wall

The construction of the Berlin Wall was a unique event in human history, not only for physically bisecting a city but by becoming a dividing line between competing ideologies and political systems. It's this global impact and universal legacy that continue to fascinate people more than a quarter century after its triumphant tear-down. Fortunately, plenty of original Wall segments and other vestiges remain, along with museums and memorials, to help fathom the realities and challenges of daily life in Berlin during the Cold War.

Our illustration points out the top highlights you can visit to learn about different aspects of these often tense decades. The best place to start is at the **Gedenkstätte Berliner Mauer ❶** for an excellent introduction to what the inner-city border actually looked liked and what it meant to live in its shadow. Reflect upon what you've learned while relaxing on the former death strip that is now the **Mauerpark ❷** before heading to the emotionally charged exhibit at the **Tränenpalast ❸**, an actual border crossing

Brandenburg Gate

People around the world cheered as East and West Berliners partied together atop the Berlin Wall in front of the iconic city gate which today is a photogenic symbol of united Germany.

Tränenpalast

This modernist 1962 glass-and-steel border pavilion was dubbed 'Palace of Tears' because of the many tearful farewells that took place outside the building as East Germans and their western visitors had to say goodbye.

Potsdamer Platz

Nowhere was the death strip as wide as on the former no-man's-land around Potsdamer Platz from which sprouted a new postmodern city quarter in the 1990s. A tiny section of the Berlin Wall serves as a reminder.

Checkpoint Charlie

Only diplomats and foreigners were allowed to use this border crossing. Weeks after the Wall was built, US and Soviet tanks faced off here in one of the hottest moments of the Cold War.

Bernauer Strasse

Chausseestr

Unter den Linden

Leipziger Str

pavilion. Relive the euphoria of the Wall's demise at the **Brandenburg Gate** ❹, then marvel at the revival of **Potsdamer Platz** ❺ that was nothing but death strip wasteland until the 1990s. The Wall's geopolitical significance is the focus at **Checkpoint Charlie** ❻, which saw some of the tensest moments of the Cold War. Wrap up with finding your favourite mural motif at the **East Side Gallery** ❼.

It's possible to explore these sights by using a combination of walking and public transport, although a bike ride is actually the best method for getting a sense of the former Wall's erratic flow through the central city.

FAST FACTS

» **Beginning of construction:** 13 August 1961
» **Total length:** 155km
» **Height:** 3.6m
» **Weight of each segment:** 2.6 tonnes
» **Number of watchtowers:** 300

Mauerpark
Famous for its flea market and karaoke, this popular park actually occupies a converted section of death strip. A 30m segment of surviving Wall is now an official practice ground for budding graffiti artists.

❷

remnants of the Wall →

DAVID PEEVERS/GETTY IMAGES ©

JOHN FREEMAN/GETTY IMAGES ©

Gedenkstätte Berliner Mauer
Germany's central memorial to the Berlin Wall and its victims exposes the complexity and barbaric nature of the border installation along a 1.4km stretch of the barrier's course.

Alexanderplatz

Alexander Str

East Side Gallery
Paralleling the Spree for 1.3km, this is the longest Wall vestige. After its collapse, more than a hundred international artists expressed their feelings about this historic moment in a series of colourful murals.

MEIN GOTT. HILF MIR. DIESE TÖDLICHE LIEBE ZU ÜBERLEBEN

DMITRY VRUBEL/

Engelbecken

❼

Mitte

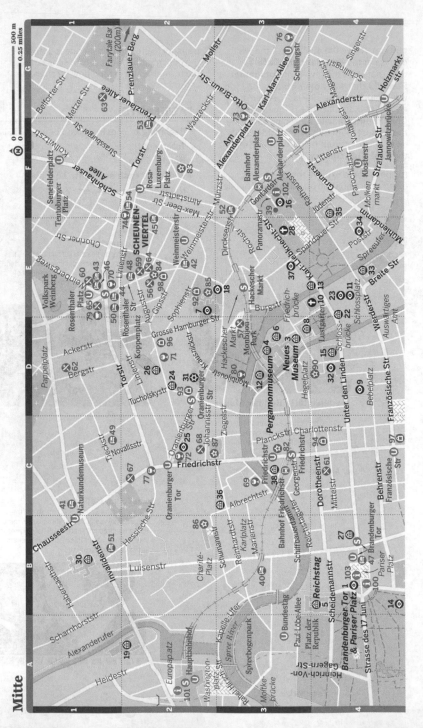

reconstruction of the bombed-out Neues Museum is now the residence of Queen Nefertiti, the show-stopper of the Egyptian Museum that also features mummies, sculptures and sarcophagi. Pride of place of the Museum of Pre- and Early History in the same building goes to Trojan antiquities, a Neanderthal skull and the 3000-year-old 'Berliner Goldhut', a golden conical hat. Skip the queue by buying your timed ticket online.

Altes Museum
MUSEUM

(Old Museum; Map p64; ☑ 030-266 424 242; www.smb.museum; Am Lustgarten; adult/concession €10/5; ☺10am-6pm Tue, Wed & Fri-Sun, to 8pm Thu, closed Mon; ☐100, 200, ☒Friedrichstrasse, Hackescher Markt) A curtain of fluted columns gives way to the Pantheon-inspired rotunda of the grand neoclassical Old Museum, which harbours a prized antiquities collection. In the downstairs galleries, sculptures, vases, tomb reliefs and jewellery shed light on various facets of life in ancient Greece, while upstairs the focus is on the Etruscans and Romans. Top draws include the Praying Boy bronze sculpture, Roman silver vessels, an 'erotic cabinet' (over 18 only!) and portraits of Caesar and Cleopatra.

Alte Nationalgalerie
MUSEUM

(Old National Gallery; Map p64; ☑ 030-266 424 242; www.smb.museum; Bodestrasse 1-3; adult/concession €10/5; ☺10am-6pm Tue, Wed & Fri-Sun, to 8pm Thu, closed Mon; ☐100, 200, ☒Hackescher Markt) The Greek temple-style Old National Gallery is a three-storey showcase of 19th-century European art. To get a sense of the period's virtuosity, pay special attention to the moody landscapes by Romantic heart-throb Caspar David Friedrich, the epic canvases by Franz Krüger and Adolf Menzel glorifying Prussia, the Gothic fantasies of Karl Friedrich Schinkel, and the sprinkling of French and German impressionists.

Bodemuseum
MUSEUM

(Map p64; ☑ 030-266 424 242; www.smb.museum; cnr Am Kupfergraben & Monbijoubrücke; adult/concession €12/6; ☺10am-6pm Tue, Wed & Fri-Sun, to 8pm Thu, closed Mon; ☒Hackescher Markt, Friedrichstrasse) On the northern tip of Museumsinsel, this palatial edifice houses a comprehensive collection of European sculpture from the early Middle Ages to the 18th century, including priceless masterpieces by Tilman Riemenschneider, Donatello and Giovanni Pisano. Other rooms harbour a precious coin collection and a smattering

Mitte

of Byzantine art, including sarcophagi and ivory carvings.

Berliner Dom CHURCH

(Berlin Cathedral; Map p64; ☎030-2026 9136; www.berlinerdom.de; Am Lustgarten; adult/concession/under 18 €7/5/free; ⏰9am-8pm Apr-Oct, to 7pm Nov-Mar; 🚌100, 200, 🚆Hackescher Markt) Pompous yet majestic, the Italian Renaissance–style former royal court church (1905) does triple duty as house of worship, museum and concert hall. Inside it's gilt to the hilt and outfitted with a lavish marble-and-onyx altar, a 7269-pipe Sauer organ and elaborate royal sarcophagi. Climb up the 267 steps to the gallery for glorious city views.

Alexanderplatz & Around

A major shopping hub in eastern Berlin, Alexanderplatz ('Alex' for short) was named in honour of Tsar Alexander I on his 1805 visit to Berlin. Despite post-reunification attempts to temper the 1960s socialist look, the square remains an amorphous beast, cluttered with big stores, a hotel and a fountain. Confusingly bifurcated by roads, train and tram tracks, the area's main redeeming feature is the needle-like TV Tower.

Fernsehturm LANDMARK

(TV Tower; Map p64; ☎030-247 575 875; www.tv-turm.de; Panoramastrasse 1a; adult/child €13/8.50, timed ticket adult/child €19.50/12; ⏰9am-midnight Mar-Oct, 10am-midnight Nov-Feb; [S]Alexanderplatz, 🚆Alexanderplatz) Germany's tallest structure, the TV Tower has been soaring 368m high since 1969 and is as iconic to Berlin as the Eiffel Tower is to Paris. Views are stunning on clear days from the panorama level at 203m or the upstairs restaurant, which makes one revolution per hour.

To skip the line, buy a timed ticket (called a 'Fast View') online.

Marienkirche   CHURCH
(Map p64; www.marienkirche-berlin.de; Karl-Liebknecht-Strasse 8; ⊙10am-6pm; 🚌100, 200, 🚉Hackescher Markt, Alexanderplatz) This Gothic brick gem has welcomed worshippers since the 13th century, making it one of Berlin's oldest surviving churches. A faded *Dance of Death* fresco in the vestibule, inspired by a 15th-century plague, leads to a relatively plain interior enlivened by elaborate epitaphs and a baroque alabaster pulpit by Andreas Schlüter (1703).

Check the schedule for organ concerts and English-language services.

Rotes Rathaus   HISTORIC BUILDING
(Map p64; Rathausstrasse 15; ⊙closed to the public; Ⓢ Alexanderplatz, Klosterstrasse, 🚉Alexanderplatz) The hulking Rotes Rathaus is the office

of Berlin's senate and governing mayor. The structure blends Italian Renaissance elements with northern German brick architecture and is framed by a terracotta frieze that illustrates Berlin milestones until 1871.

Sealife Berlin   AQUARIUM
(Map p64; ☎0180-666 690 101; www.visitsealife.com; Spandauer Strasse 3; adult/child €18/14.50; ⊙10am-7pm, last admission 6pm; 🚌100, 200, 🚉Hackescher Markt, Alexanderplatz) Sharks dart, moray eels lurk and spider crabs scuttle in this rambling aquarium; other crowd favourites include smile-inducing seahorses, ethereal jellyfish and Ophira the Octopus. Visits conclude with a slow lift ride through the Aquadom, a 25m-high cylindrical tropical fish tank. Check the website for online savings.

DDR Museum   MUSEUM
(GDR Museum; Map p64; ☎030-847 123 731; www.ddr-museum.de; Karl-Liebknecht-Strasse 1; adult/

BERLIN CITY PALACE: BACK TO THE FUTURE

Berlin has its Prussian-era royal city palace back. Well, almost. After two decades of debate and bickering, construction of the behemoth finally got underway on Schlossplatz, opposite Museum Island, in July 2013. A mere two years later, the city celebrated the topping out ceremony: the shell was done, dome and all.

Although the facade will eventually look like the city palace where Prussia's rulers made their home until 1918, the structure will actually be known as the **Humboldt-Forum** (Berlin City Palace; Map p64; Schlossplatz; 🚌100, 200). Its modern interior will be a nexus for science, education and intercultural dialogue, and will shelter the precious non-European art collections currently on view at the Museum of Ethnology and the Museum of Asian Art in the suburb of Dahlem. To turn the vision into reality, the city hired none other than Neil MacGregor, previously the director of the British Museum in London.

The historic palace was barely damaged in WWII, but was blown up by East Germany's government in 1950 for ideological reasons. In its stead they built the so-called Palast der Republik (Palace of the Republic) which doubled as the seat of the GDR parliament and a cultural venue. Riddled with asbestos, it had its date with the wrecking ball in 2006.

The Stadtschloss 2.0 comes with a projected price tag of €620 million, with most of the bill footed by the federal government. The design by Italian architect Franco Stella has three sides of the facade looking like a baroque blast from the past and thus visually completing the historic ensemble of Museum Island, Berlin Cathedral and New Royal Stables. The name, by the way, honours the philosopher and university founder Wilhelm von Humboldt and his explorer brother Alexander.

If all goes to plan, the Humboldt-Forum could open as early as 2019. In the meantime, exhibits inside the **Humboldt-Box** (Map p64; ☎0180-503 0707; www.humboldt-box.com; Schlossplatz; 🕙10am-7pm Apr-Sep, to 6pm Nov-Mar; 🚌100, 200, [S] Hausvogteiplatz) [FREE], including a fantastically detailed model of the historic city centre, open a window on the project's evolution, scope and scale.

concession €7/4; 🕙10am-8pm, to 10pm Sat; 👪; 🚌100, 200, 🚆Hackescher Markt) This interactive museum does an entertaining job at pulling back the iron curtain on an extinct society. You'll learn how, under socialism, kids were put through collective potty training, engineers earned little more than farmers, and everyone, it seems, went on nudist holidays. A highlight is a simulated ride in a Trabi.

The more sinister sides of daily life are also addressed, including the chronic supply shortages and surveillance by the Stasi (secret police).

Nikolaiviertel NEIGHBOURHOOD

(Map p64; btwn Rathausstrasse, Breite Strasse, Spandauer Strasse & Mühlendamm; [S] Klosterstrasse) [FREE] Commissioned by the East German government in celebration of Berlin's 750th birthday, the twee Nicholas Quarter is a half-hearted attempt at re-creating the city's medieval birthplace around its oldest surviving building, the 1230 Nikolaikirche. The maze of cobbled lanes is worth a quick stroll while several olde-worlde-style restaurants provide sustenance.

Märkisches Museum MUSEUM

(Map p64; ☎030-2400 2162; www.stadtmuseum.de; Köllnischer Park 5; adult/concession/under 18 €5/3/free; 🕙10am-6pm Tue-Sun; [S] Märkisches Museum) This old-school history museum is a rewarding stop for anyone keen on learning how the medieval trading village of Berlin-Cölln evolved into today's metropolis. The exhibits take you on a virtual walk through the city's streets and quarters, from the medieval Klosterviertel to the socialist Stalinallee boulevard. Paintings and sculpture, artefacts, furniture and objects from daily life illustrate the urban evolution, while scale models help visually demonstrate the city's physical growth.

👁 Scheunenviertel

With its boutique-lined lanes and charming courtyards, including the Hackesche Höfe, the Scheunenviertel is fashionista central and teems with hip bars and restaurants. Come face to face with the quarter's Jewish roots on a visit of the Neue Synagoge, then check out the bleeding-edge art galleries along Auguststrasse and Linienstrasse.

Hackesche Höfe HISTORIC SITE

(Map p64; ☎030-2809 8010; www.hackesche-hoefe.com; enter from Rosenthaler Strasse 40/41 or Sophienstrasse 6; [S] Weinmeisterstrasse, 🚋M1, 🚆Hackescher Markt) [FREE] The Hackesche Höfe is the largest and most famous of the courtyard ensembles peppered throughout the Scheunenviertel. Built in 1907, the eight interlinked Höfe reopened in 1996 with a congenial mix of cafes, galleries, boutiques and entertainment venues. The main entrance on Rosenthaler Strasse leads to **Court I**, prettily festooned with art nouveau tiles, while Court VII segues to the romantic **Rosenhöfe** with a sunken rose garden and tendril-like balustrades.

Neue Synagoge SYNAGOGUE

(Map p64; ☎030-8802 8300; www.centrumjudaicum.de; Oranienburger Strasse 28-30; adult/concession €5/4; ⏰10am-6pm Mon-Fri, 10am-7pm Sun, closes 3pm Fri & 6pm Sun Oct-Mar; [S] Oranienburger Tor, 🚆Oranienburger Strasse) The gleaming gold dome of the Neue Synagoge is the most visible symbol of Berlin's revitalised Jewish community. The 1866 original was Germany's largest synagogue but its modern incarnation is not so much a house of worship (although prayer services do take place), as a museum and place of remembrance called Centrum Judaicum. The dome can be climbed (€3/2.50).

Kunsthaus Tacheles LANDMARK

(Map p64; Oranienburger Strasse 54-56; ⏰closed; [S] Oranienburger Tor, 🚆Oranienburger Strasse) The graffiti-slathered empty hulk on Oranienburger Strasse is all that's left of the Kunsthaus Tacheles, which for over 20 years was one of Berlin's most beloved alternative art and cultural spaces.

Jüdische Mädchenschule HISTORIC BUILDING

(Map p64; www.maedchenschule.org; Auguststrasse 11-13; ⏰hours vary; [S] Oranienburger Tor, 🚋M1, 🚆Oranienburger Strasse) [FREE] A 1920s former Jewish Girls' School reopened in 2012 as a cultural and culinary centre in a sensitively restored New Objectivity structure by Alexander Beer. Two galleries – **CWC** and **Michael Fuchs** – and the **Museum The Kennedys** have set up shop in the former classrooms, while the ground floor has the Jewish deli **Mogg & Melzer** (Map p64; ☎030-330 060 770; www.moggandmelzer.com; Auguststrasse 11-13; mains €7-15; ⏰8am-late Mon-Fri, 10am-late Sat & Sun; 🚋M1, 🚆Oranienburger Strasse) and the Michelin-starred Pauly Saal (p104).

KW Institute for Contemporary Art GALLERY

(Map p64, ☎030 243 4590; www.kw-berlin.de; Auguststrasse 69; adult/concession €6/4; ⏰noon- 7pm, to 9pm Tue; [S] Oranienburger Strasse, 🚋M1, 🚆Oranienburger Tor) In an old margarine factory, non-profit KW helped

TRACES OF JEWISH LIFE IN THE SCHEUNENVIERTEL

Jewish history is omnipresent in the Scheunenviertel, Berlin's traditional Jewish quarter. The great Enlightenment philosopher Moses Mendelssohn was among the 12,000 people buried in the **Alter Jüdischer Friedhof** (Map p64; Grosse Hamburger Strasse; 🚋M1, 🚆Hackescher Markt), one of the city's oldest Jewish cemeteries.

Street-art-decorated **Haus Schwarzenberg**, next to the Hackesche Höfe, harbours three small museums dealing with the fate of Jews under the Nazis: the **Museum Blindenwerkstatt Otto Weidt** (Map p64; ☎030-2859 9407; www.museum-blindenwerkstatt.de; 1st courtyard left, Rosenthaler Strasse 39; ⏰10am-8pm; 🚋M1, 🚆Hackescher Markt) [FREE] documents how broom and brush maker Otto Weidt saved many of his blind and deaf Jewish workers from the Nazis; the **Anne Frank Zentrum** (Map p64; ☎030-288 865 600; www.annefrank.de; Rosenthaler Strasse 39; adult/concession €5/3; ⏰10am-6pm Tue-Sun; [S] Weinmeisterstrasse, 🚆Hackescher Markt) uses artefacts and photographs to tell the extraordinary story of the famous German-Jewish girl who died at Bergen-Belsen concentration camp; and the **Gedenkstätte Stille Helden** ('Silent Heroes' Memorial Exhibit; Map p64; ☎030-2345 7919; www.gedenkstaette-stille-helden.de; Rosenthaler Strasse 39; ⏰10am-8pm; 🚋M1, 🚆Hackescher Markt) [FREE] zeroes in on ordinary Germans who found the courage to hide and help their Jewish neighbours.

Also keep your eyes on the ground to spot small, engraved brass paving stones outside house entrances. Part of a nationwide project initiated by Berlin-born artist Gunter Demnig, these so-called **Stolpersteine** (stumbling blocks) are essentially mini-memorials and are engraved with the names of the people (usually Jews) who lived in the building before being killed by the Nazis.

Museumsinsel

Navigating around this five-museum treasure repository can be a little daunting, so we've put together this itinerary to help you find the must-see highlights while maximising your time and energy. You'll need a minimum of four hours and an 'area ticket' for entry to all museums.

Start in the Altes Museum by admiring the roll call of antique gods guarded by a perky bronze statue called the **Praying Boy** ❶, the poster child of a prized collection of antiquities. Next up, head to the Neues Museum for your audience with **Queen Nefertiti** ❷, the star of the Egyptian collection atop the grand central staircase. One more floor up, don't miss the dazzling Bronze Age **Berliner Goldhut** ❸ (room 305). Leaving the Neues Museum, turn left for the Pergamonmuseum. With the namesake altar off limits until 2019, the first major sight you'll see is the **Ishtar Gate** ❹. Upstairs, pick your way through the Islamic collection, past carpets, prayer niches and a caliph's palace to the intricately painted **Aleppo Room** ❺. Jump ahead to the 19th century at the Alte Nationalgalerie to zero in on paintings by **Caspar David Friedrich** ❻ on the 3rd floor and precious sculptures such as Schadow's **Statue of Two Princesses** ❼ on the ground floor. Wrap up your explorations at the Bodemuseum, reached in a five-minute walk. Admire the foyer with its equestrian statue of Friedrich Wilhelm, then feast your eyes on European sculpture without missing masterpieces by **Tilman Riemenschneider** ❽ in room 212.

FAST FACTS

» **Oldest object:** 700,000-year-old Paleolithic hand axe at Neues Museum

» **Newest object:** piece of barbed wire from Berlin Wall at Neues Museum

» **Oldest museum:** Altes Museum, 1830

» **Most popular museum in Germany:** Pergamonmuseum (1.26 million visitors)

» **Total Museumsinsel visitors (2013):** 2.92 million

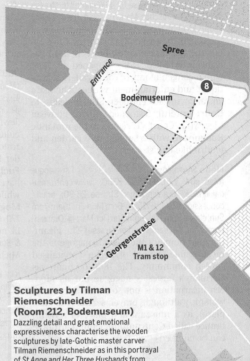

Spree

Entrance

Bodemuseum ❽

Georgenstrasse

M1 & 12 Tram stop

Dorotheenstrasse

M1 & 12 Tram stop

Unter den Linden

Sculptures by Tilman Riemenschneider (Room 212, Bodemuseum)

Dazzling detail and great emotional expressiveness characterise the wooden sculptures by late-Gothic master carver Tilman Riemenschneider as in this portrayal of *St Anne and Her Three Husbands* from around 1510.

INGO JEZIERSKI/ALAMY ©

Bust of Queen Nefertiti (Room 210, Neues Museum)

In the north dome, fall in love with Berlin's most beautiful woman, the 3330-year-old Egyptian queen Nefertiti, she of the long graceful neck and timeless good looks – despite the odd wrinkle and missing eye.

JEAN-PIERRE LESCOURRET/GETTY IMAGES ©

TIBOR BOGNAR/GETTY IMAGES ©

Aleppo Room (Room 16, Pergamonmuseum)

A highlight of the Museum of Islamic Art, this richly painted, wood-panelled reception room from a Christian merchant's home in 17th-century Aleppo, Syria, combines Islamic floral and geometric motifs with courtly scenes and Christian themes.

Ishtar Gate (Room 9, Pergamonmuseum)

Draw breath as you enter the 2600-year-old city gate to Babylon with soaring walls sheathed in radiant blue glazed bricks and adorned with ochre reliefs of strutting lions, bulls and dragons representing Babylonian gods.

PAOLO CORDELLI/GETTY IMAGES ©

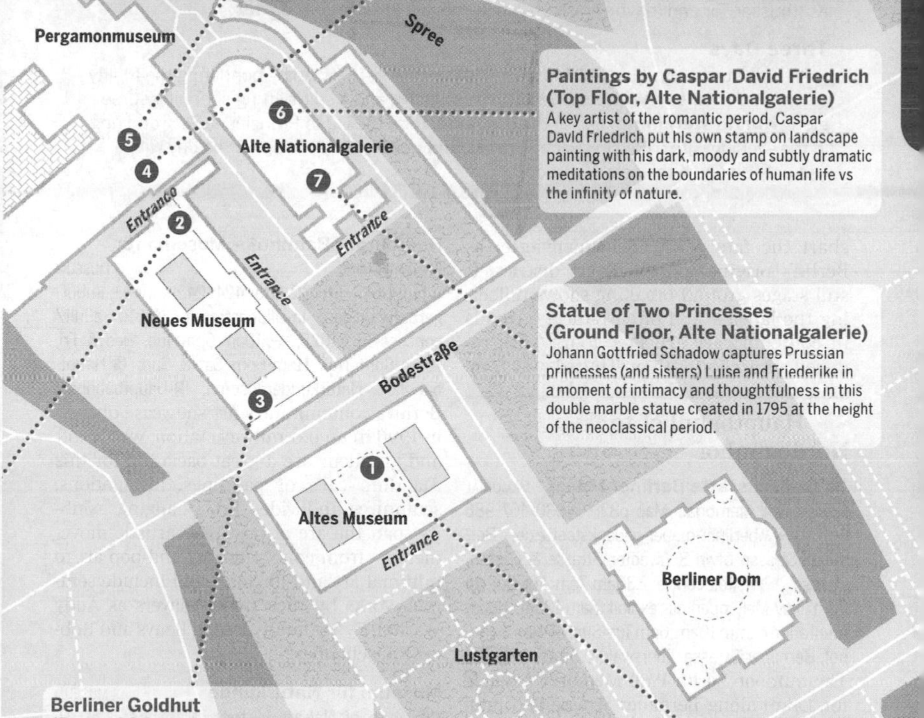
Spree
Pergamonmuseum
5
4
6
Alte Nationalgalerie
7
Entrance
2
Entrance
Entrance
Neues Museum
Bodestraße
3
1
Altes Museum
Entrance
Berliner Dom
Lustgarten

Paintings by Caspar David Friedrich (Top Floor, Alte Nationalgalerie)

A key artist of the romantic period, Caspar David Friedrich put his own stamp on landscape painting with his dark, moody and subtly dramatic meditations on the boundaries of human life vs the infinity of nature.

Statue of Two Princesses (Ground Floor, Alte Nationalgalerie)

Johann Gottfried Schadow captures Prussian princesses (and sisters) Luise and Friederike in a moment of intimacy and thoughtfulness in this double marble statue created in 1795 at the height of the neoclassical period.

Berliner Goldhut (Room 305, Neues Museum)

Marvel at the Bronze Age artistry of the Berlin Gold Hat, a ceremonial gold cone embossed with ornamental bands believed to have been used in predicting the best times for planting and harvesting.

ANDREAS RENTZ/GETTY IMAGES ©

Praying Boy (Room 5, Altes Museum)

The top draw at the Old Museum is the *Praying Boy*, ancient Greece's 'Next Top Model'. The life-size bronze statue of a young male nude is the epitome of physical perfection and was cast around 300 BC in Rhodes.

OHELIA2/CREATIVE COMMONS ©

BERLIN IN...

One Day

Book ahead for an early time slot on the lift to the **Reichstag** dome, then snap a picture of the **Brandenburger Tor** before stumbling around the **Holocaust Memorial** and admiring the contemporary architecture of **Potsdamer Platz**. Ponder Cold War madness at **Checkpoint Charlie**, then head to **Museumsinsel** to admire Queen Nefertiti and the Ishtar Gate. Finish up with a night of mirth and gaiety in the Scheunenviertel.

Two Days

Kick off day two coming to grips with what life was like in divided Berlin at the **Gedenkstätte Berliner Mauer**. Intensify the experience at the **DDR Museum** and on a walk along the **East Side Gallery**. Spend the afternoon soaking up the urban spirit of Kreuzberg with its sassy shops and street art, grab dinner along the canal, drinks around Kottbusser Tor and maybe finish up with a concert at **Lido** or **Magnet**.

Three Days

Day three starts royally at **Schloss Charlottenburg**, followed by pondering the futility of war at the **Kaiser-Wilhelm-Gedächtniskirche** and a spirit-lifting shopping spree along **Kurfürstendamm** and at the **KaDeWe**. Ride the U2 to Prenzlauer Berg and ring in the evening with a cold Pilsner at **Prater Biergarten**, then wrap up the day with a leisurely dinner in the neighbourhood.

---

chart the fate of the Scheunenviertel as Berlin's original post-Wall art district. It still stages ground-breaking shows reflecting the latest – and often radical – trends in contemporary art. Free tours (with reduced admission) run on Thursday at 7pm.

👁 Hauptbahnhof to Nordbahnhof

★ **Gedenkstätte Berliner Mauer**   MEMORIAL
(Berlin Wall Memorial; Map p82; ☑030-467 986 666; www.berliner-mauer-gedenkstaette.de; Bernauer Strasse btwn Schwedter Strasse & Gartenstrasse; ☺visitor centre 9.30am-7pm Apr-Oct, to 6pm Nov-Mar, open-air exhibit 8am-10pm, documentation centre 10am-6pm Tue-Sun; ⓡNordbahnhof, Bernauer Strasse, Eberswalder Strasse) FREE
The outdoor Berlin Wall Memorial extends for 1.4km along Bernauer Strasse and integrates an original section of Wall, vestiges of the border installations and escape tunnels, a chapel and a monument. Multimedia stations, panels, excavations and a Documentation Centre provide context and explain what the border fortifications looked like and how they shaped the everyday lives of people on both sides of it. There's a great view from the centre's viewing platform.

Hamburger Bahnhof – Museum für Gegenwart   MUSEUM

(Map p64; ☑030-266 424 242; www.hamburgerbahnhof.de; Invalidenstrasse 50-51; adult/concession €10/5; ☺10am-6pm Tue, Wed & Fri, 10am-8pm Thu, 11am-6pm Sat & Sun; ⑤Hauptbahnhof, Naturkundemuseum, ⓡHauptbahnhof)
Berlin's contemporary art showcase opened in 1996 in an old railway station, whose loft and grandeur are a great backdrop for this Aladdin's cave of paintings, installations, sculptures and video art. Changing exhibits span the arc of post-1950 artistic movements – from conceptual art and pop art to minimal art and Fluxus – and include seminal works by such major players as Andy Warhol, Cy Twombly, Joseph Beuys and Robert Rauschenberg.

Museum für Naturkunde   MUSEUM

(Museum of Natural History; Map p64; ☑030-2093 8591; www.naturkundemuseum-berlin.de; Invalidenstrasse 43; adult/concession incl audioguide €6/3.50; ☺9.30am-6pm Tue-Fri, 10am-6pm Sat & Sun; ⑤Naturkundemuseum) Fossils and minerals don't quicken your pulse? Well, how about the world's largest mounted dino skeleton? The 13m-high *Brachiosaurus branchai* is joined by a dozen other Jurassic buddies, some of which are brought to virtual flesh-and-bone life with the help of clever 'Juraskopes'. Other crowd favourites include

Knut, the world's most famous dead polar bear, and an ultrarare archaeopteryx.

Sammlung Boros
GALLERY

(Boros Collection; Map p64; ☑ 030-2759 4065; www.sammlung-boros.de; Reinhardtstrasse 20; adult/concession €12/6; ☉ tours 3-6.30pm Thu, 10am-6.30pm Fri, 10am-4.30pm Sat & Sun; ⑤ Oranienburger Tor, Friedrichstrasse, ⑭ M1, ⑭ Friedrichstrasse) This Nazi-era bunker shelters one of Berlin's finest private contemporary art collections. Advertising guru Christian Boros acquired the behemoth in 2003 and converted it into a shining beacon of art. Book online (weeks, if not months, ahead) to join a guided tour (also in English) of works by such hot shots as Wolfgang Tilmanns, Olafur Eliasson and Ai Weiwei, and to pick up fascinating nuggets about the building's past incarnations as a tropical-fruit warehouse and techno and fetish club.

⊙ Potsdamer Platz, Kulturforum & Tiergarten

Potsdamer Platz, built from scratch in the 1990s from terrain once bifurcated by the Berlin Wall, is essentially a showcase of urban renewal. Some of the world's finest architects, including Renzo Piano, Richard Rodgers and Helmut Jahn, collaborated on this modern reinterpretation of the historic square, which was Berlin's central traffic, entertainment and commercial hub until WWII sucked all life out of the area.

The new Potsdamer Platz is divided into three slices: **DaimlerCity** with a large mall, public art and high-profile entertainment venues; the flashy **Sony Center** anchored by a plaza dramatically canopied by a glass roof; and the comparatively subdued **Beisheim Center**, which was inspired by American skyscraper design.

A visit to Potsdamer Platz is easily combined with the **Kulturforum**, a cluster of world-class art museums and the eye-catching Berliner Philharmonie (p116), the city's most famous concert hall. And if your head is spinning after all that cultural stimulus, the leafy paths of the glorious **Tiergarten**, one of the world's largest city parks, will likely prove a restorative antidote. For a walking tour of Tiergarten, see p93.

Sony Center
BUILDING

(Map p76; Potsdamer Strasse; ⊟ 200, ⑤ Potsdamer Platz, ⑭ Potsdamer Platz) Designed by Helmut Jahn, the visually dramatic Sony Center is fronted by a 26-floor, glass-and-steel tower and integrates rare relics from Potsdamer Platz' prewar era, such as the opulent Kaisersaal. The heart of the Sony Center, though, is a central plaza canopied by a tent-like glass roof with supporting beams radiating out like bicycle spokes. The plaza and its many cafes lend themselves to hanging out and people-watching.

Museum für Film und Fernsehen
MUSEUM

(Map p76; ☑ 030-300 9030; www.deutsche-kinemathek.de; Potsdamer Strasse 2; adult/concession €7/4.50; ☉ 10am-6pm Tue, Wed & Thu-Sun, to 8pm Thu, closed Mon; ⊟ 200, ⑤ Potsdamer Platz, ⑭ Potsdamer Platz) Germany's film history gets the star treatment at this engaging museum. Explore galleries dedicated to pioneers such as Fritz Lang, ground-breaking movies such as Leni Riefenstahl's Nazi-era *Olympia* and legendary divas such as Marlene Dietrich. The TV exhibit has more niche appeal but is still fun if you want to know what *Star Trek* sounds like in German.

Legoland Discovery Centre
AMUSEMENT PARK

(Map p76; ☑ 01806 6669 0110; www.legolanddiscoverycentre.de/berlin; Potsdamer Strasse 4; admission €14-18.50, depending on admission time; ☉ 10am-7pm, last admission 5pm; ⊟ 200, ⑤ Potsdamer Platz, ⑭ Potsdamer Platz) Geared towards the elementary school set, this cute indoor amusement park features a 4D cinema, a Lego factory and Dragon Castle 'slowlercoaster ride'. Check online for deals.

★ Gemäldegalerie
GALLERY

(Gallery of Old Masters; Map p76; ☑ 030-266 424 242; www.smb.museum/gg; Matthäikirchplatz 8; adult/concession €10/5; ☉ 10am-6pm Tue, Wed & Fri, 10am-8pm Thu, 11am-6pm Sat & Sun; ⊟ M29, M41, 200, ⑤ Potsdamer Platz, ⑭ Potsdamer Platz) The principal Kulturforum museum boasts one of the world's finest and most comprehensive collections of European art from the 13th to the 18th centuries. Wear comfy shoes when exploring the 72 galleries: a walk past masterpieces by Rembrandt, Dürer, Hals, Vermeer, Gainsborough and many more Old Masters covers almost 2km.

Kunstgewerbemuseum
MUSEUM

(Museum of Decorative Arts; Map p76; ☑ 030-266 424 242; www.smb.museum; Matthäikirchplatz; adult/concession/under 18 €8/4/free; ☉ 10am-6pm Tue-Fri, 11am-6pm Sat & Sun; ⊟ 200, ⑤ Potsdamer Platz, ⑭ Potsdamer Platz) This prized collection of European design, fashion and decorative arts from the Middle Ages to today is part of the Kulturforum museum cluster. Feast your eyes on exquisitely ornate reliquaries, portable altars, chests, leather wallpaper as well as Jugendstil and Bauhaus classics by Henry van de Velde and Wilhelm Wagenfeld. Pride of place goes to the new Fashion Gallery with classic designer outfits and accessories from the past 150 years.

Gedenkstätte Deutscher Widerstand
MEMORIAL

(German Resistance Memorial Center; Map p76; ☑030-2699 5000; www.gdw-berlin.de; Stauffenbergstrasse 13-14, enter via courtyard; ☉9am-6pm Mon-Wed & Fri, 9am-8pm Thu, 10am-6pm Sat & Sun; 🚌M29, M41, Ⓢ Potsdamer Platz, Kurfürstenstrasse, Ⓡ Potsdamer Platz) **FREE** This important exhibit on German Nazi resistance occupies the very rooms where high-ranking officers led by Claus Schenk Graf von Stauffenberg plotted the assassination attempt on Hitler on 20 July 1944. There's a memorial in the courtyard where the main conspirators were shot right after the failed coup, a story poignantly retold in the 2008 movie *Valkyrie*.

OTHER KULTURFORUM MUSEUMS

In addition to the Gemäldegalerie and the Kunstgewerbemuseum, the Kulturforum encompasses three other top museums: the **Kupferstichkabinett** (Museum of Prints and Drawings; Map p76; ☑030-266 424 242; www.smb.museum/kk; Matthäikirchplatz; adult/concession €6/3; ☉10am-6pm Tue-Fri, 11am-6pm Sat & Sun; 🚌200, M41, M29, Ⓢ Potsdamer Platz, Ⓡ Potsdamer Platz) with prints and drawings since the 14th century; the **Musikinstrumenten-Museum** (Musical Instruments Museum; Map p76; ☑030-254 810; www.mim-berlin.de; Tiergartenstrasse 1, enter via Ben-Gurion-Strasse; adult/concession €6/3; ☉9am-5pm Tue, Wed & Fri, 9am-8pm Thu, 10am-5pm Sat & Sun; 🚌200, Ⓢ Potsdamer Platz, Ⓡ Potsdamer Platz) with rare historical instruments; and the **Neue Nationalgalerie**, which at time of research was closed for renovation until at least 2018. A combined ticket for same-day admission to the permanent collection to the four open museums costs €12 (concession €6). Buying tickets online yields a small discount.

Bauhaus Archiv
MUSEUM

(Map p84; ☑030-254 0020; www.bauhaus.de; Klingelhöferstrasse 14; adult/concession incl audioguide Wed-Fri €7/4, Sat-Mon €8/5; ☉10am-5pm Wed-Mon; 🚌100, Ⓢ Nollendorfplatz) Founded in 1919, the Bauhaus was a seminal school of avant-garde architecture, design and art. This avant-garde building, designed by its founder Walter Gropius, presents paintings, drawings, sculptures, models and other objects and documents by such famous artist-teachers as Klee, Feininger and Kandinsky. There's a good cafe and gift shop. A building expansion is planned to open in 2019.

Tiergarten
PARK

(Map p84; 🚌100, 200, Ⓢ Brandenburger Tor, Ⓡ Potsdamer Platz, Brandenburger Tor) **FREE** Berlin's rulers used to hunt boar and pheasants in the rambling Tiergarten until garden architect Peter Lenné landscaped the grounds in the 18th century. Today, one of the world's largest urban parks is popular for strolling, jogging, picnicking, Frisbee tossing and, yes, nude sunbathing and gay cruising (especially around the Löwenbrücke). It is bisected by a major artery, the Strasse des 17 Juni. Walking across the entire park takes about an hour, but even a shorter stroll has its rewards.

Martin-Gropius-Bau
GALLERY

(Map p76; ☑030-254 860; www.gropiusbau.de; Niederkirchner Strasse 7; cost varies, free under 16; ☉10am-7pm Wed-Mon; 🚌M41, Ⓢ Potsdamer Platz, Ⓡ Potsdamer Platz) With its mosaics, terracotta reliefs and airy atrium, this Italian Renaissance-style exhibit space named for its architect (Bauhaus founder Walter Gropius' great-uncle) is a celebrated venue for high-calibre travelling shows. Whether it's a David Bowie retrospective, the latest works of Ai Weiwei or an ethnological exhibit on the mysteries of Angkor Wat, it's bound to be well curated and utterly fascinating.

Topographie des Terrors
MUSEUM

(Topography of Terror; Map p76; ☑030-2548 0950; www.topographie.de; Niederkirchner Strasse 8; ☉10am-8pm, grounds close at dusk or 8pm at latest; 🚹; Ⓢ Potsdamer Platz, Ⓡ Potsdamer Platz) **FREE** In the same spot where once stood the most feared institutions of Nazi Germany (including the Gestapo headquarters and the SS central command), this compelling exhibit chronicles the stages of terror and persecution, puts a face on the perpetrators and details the impact these brutal institutions had on all of Europe. A second exhibit outside zeroes in on how life changed for

Berlin and its people after the Nazis made it their capital.

To complement the exhibits, a self-guided tour of the historic grounds takes you past 15 information stations with photos, documents and 3D graphics as well as a 200m stretch of the Berlin Wall.

Dalí – Die Ausstellung   GALLERY
(Map p76; ☑0700-3254 2375; www.daliberlin.de; Leipziger Platz 7; adult/concession €12.50/9.50; ◎noon-8pm Mon-Sat, 10am-8pm Sun; ☒200, Ⓢ Potsdamer Platz, ⓇPotsdamer Platz) If you only know Salvador Dalí as the painter of melting watches, burning giraffes and other surrealist imagery, this private collection will likely open new perspectives on the man. Here, the focus is on his graphics, illustrations, sculptures, drawings and films, with highlights including etchings on the theme of Tristan and Isolde, epic sculptures such as *Surrealist Angel* as well as the *Don Quixote* lithographs.

◉ Kreuzberg & Northern Neukölln

Kreuzberg gets its street cred from being delightfully edgy, wacky and, most of all, unpredictable. While the western half around Bergmannstrasse has an upmarket, genteel air, eastern Kreuzberg (still nicknamed SO36 after its pre-reunification postal code) is a multicultural mosaic, a bubbly hodgepodge of tousled students, aspiring creatives, shisha-smoking Turks and Arabs, and international life artists. Spend a day searching for great street art, soaking up the multi-culti vibe, scarfing a shawarma, browsing vintage stores and hanging by the river or canal, then find out why Kreuzberg is also known as a night crawler's paradise.

All that hipness has spilled across the Landwehrkanal to the northern part of Neukölln. Once known for its crime and poor schools, the district has catapulted from ghetto-gritty to funkytown-hip in no time. At least partly thanks to an influx of young, creative neo-Berliners (including many from Italy, Spain and Australia), the quarter sees trash-trendy bars, performance spaces and galleries coming online almost daily. If you need a break, head over to the vast Tempelhofer Park, an urban playground on a former airfield.

Jüdisches Museum   MUSEUM
(Jewish Museum; Map p76; ☑030-2599 3300; www.jmberlin.de; Lindenstrasse 9-14; adult/

VIEW FROM THE TOP
....
Panoramapunkt (Map p76; ☑030-2593 7080; www.panoramapunkt.de; Potsdamer Platz 1; adult/concession €6.50/5, without wait €10.50/8; ◎10am-8pm Apr-Oct, to 6pm Nov-Mar, last entry 30min before closing; ☒M41, 200, Ⓢ Potsdamer Platz, ⓇPotsdamer Platz) Europe's fastest lift, Panoramapunkt yo-yos up and down the red-brick postmodern Kollhoff Tower. From the bi-level viewing platform at a lofty 100m, you can pinpoint the sights, make a java stop in the 1930s-style cafe, enjoy the sunset from the terrace and check out the exhibit that peels back the layers of the history of the quarter.

concession €8/3, audioguide €3; ◎10am-8pm, to 10pm Mon, last entry 1hr before closing; Ⓢ Hallesches Tor, Kochstrasse) In a landmark building by American-Polish architect Daniel Libeskind, Berlin's Jewish Museum offers a chronicle of the trials and triumphs in 2000 years of Jewish life in Germany. The exhibit smoothly navigates all major periods, from the Middle Ages via the Enlightenment to the community's post-1990 renaissance. Find out about Jewish cultural contributions, holiday traditions, the difficult road to emancipation and outstanding individuals (eg Moses Mendelssohn, Levi Strauss) and the fates of ordinary people.

Berlinische Galerie   GALLERY
(Berlin Museum of Modern Art, Photography & Architecture; Map p76; ☑030-7890 2600; www.berlinischegalerie.de; Alte Jakobstrasse 124-128; adult/concession/under 18 €8/5/free; ◎10am-6pm Wed-Mon; Ⓢ Kochstrasse, Hallesches Tor) This newly renovated gallery in a stark, whitewashed bi-level space of a converted glass warehouse is a superb spot for taking stock of what Berlin's art scene has been up to since 1870. Temporary exhibits occupy the ground floor from where two floating stairways lead upstairs to selections from the permanent collection, which is especially strong when it comes to Dada, New Objectivity, Eastern Europe avant-garde and art created during the city's division.

Jüdisches Museum ticket holders qualify for reduced admission on the same day and the following two days, and vice versa.

BERLIN SIGHTS

Kreuzberg & Friedrichshain

A map of the Kreuzberg & Friedrichshain area of Berlin with the following labels:

MUSEUMSINSEL

Bahnhof Friedrichstr
Friedrichstr
Scheidemannstr
Dorotheenstr
Karl-Liebknecht-Str
Klosterstr
Pariser Platz
Strasse des 17 Juni
Behrenstr
Französische Str
Breite Str
Tiergartentunnel
B5
Bellevueallee
Holocaust Memorial
Französische Str
Hausvogteiplatz
Märkisches Museum
Tiergarten
Ebertstr
Wilhelmstr
Stadtmitte
B1
Gemäldegalerie
Bellevuestr
Mohrenstr
Leipziger Str
Spittelmarkt
Tiergartenstr
16
20 24
Potsdamer Platz
Krausenstr
32
Amrumstr
2 14
82
Schützenstr
Axel-Springer-Str
15
Potsdamer Str
39 22
9
31
7
Zimmerstr
19
Sebastianstr
Stallschreiberstr
11
Sigismundstr
Niederkirchner Str
Kochstr
Rudi-Dutschke-Str
Oranienstr
Moritzplatz
18 26
Kochstr
Markgrafenstr
Lindenstr
5
73
74
Linkstr
Köthener Str
Reichpietschufer
42
Anhalter Str
Ritterstr
Alexandrinenstr
Prinzenstr
38
Stauffenbergstr
B1
Mendelssohn-Bartholdy-Park
Anhalter Bahnhof
Stresemannstr
78
12
Alte Jakobstr
Gitschiner Str
Gitschiner Str
Schwules Museum (300m)
Franz-Klühs-Str
Böckler Park
Gleisdreieck
Trebbiner Str
Möckernstr
Möckernbrücke
Mehringplatz
Prinzenstr
Urbanhafen
10
Tempelhofer Ufer
Landwehrkanal
Wilmsstr
34
Halleches Tor
Blücherstr
Blücher Platz
Urbanstr
Obentrautstr
Mehringdamm
46
Baruther Str
Zossener Str
Gneisenaustr
Blücherstr
Körtestr
Yorckstr
Yorckstr
35
Gneisenaustr
Gneisenaustr
Südstern
Yorckstr
Yorckstr
Hagelberger Str
36
Friesenstr
Alter St-Matthäus-Kirchhof
Katzbachstr
Kreuzbergstr
4
Marheineke platz
Bergmannstr
Friedhöfe an der Bergmannstrasse
Zülichauer Str
83
Arndtstr
Viktoriapark
Methfesselstr
Fidicinstr
Jüterboger Str
Kolonnenstr
Dudenstr
Schwiebusser Str
Platz der Luftbrücke
Platz der Luftbrücke
Columbiadamm
Loewenhardtdamm
Boelckestr
Wolffring
B96
Former Tempelhof Airport
Garnisonsfriedhof
General-Pape-Str
Gontermannstr
Bäumerplan
Adolf-Scheidt-Platz
Paradestr
Paradestr
25
Tempelhofer Damm
Papestr
TEMPELHOF
Tempelhof

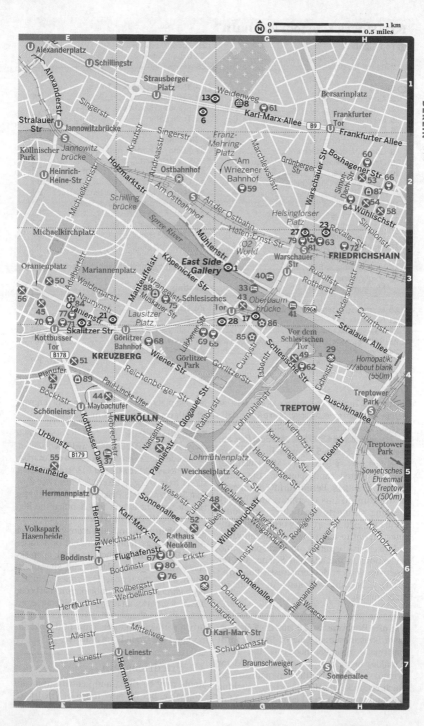

Kreuzberg & Friedrichshain

Deutsches Technikmuseum   MUSEUM
(German Museum of Technology; Map p76; ☑ 030-902 540; www.sdtb.de; Trebbiner Strasse 9; adult/concession/under 18 €8/4/free, after 3pm free, audioguide €2/1; ⏰ 9am-5.30pm Tue-Fri, 10am-6pm Sat & Sun; ⛢; ⓢ Gleisdreieck, Möckernbrücke) A roof-mounted 'candy bomber' (the plane used in the 1948 Berlin Airlift) is merely the overture to this enormous and hugely engaging shrine to technology. Standouts among the exhibits are the world's first computer, an entire hall of vintage locomotives and extensive exhibits on aerospace and navigation. At the adjacent Science Center Spectrum (enter Möckernstrasse 26, same ticket) kids can participate in hands-on experiments.

Bergmannkiez   NEIGHBOURHOOD
(Map p76; Bergmannstrasse & around; ⓢ Mehringdamm, Gneisenaustrasse) One of Berlin's most charismatic neighbourhoods is the Bergmannkiez in western Kreuzberg, named for its main shopping strip, the Bergmannstrasse, which is chock-a-block with people-watching cafes and quirky shops. It culminates in Mar-heinekeplatz, punctuated by a newly renovated 19th-century gourmet market hall.

Tempelhofer Park   PARK
(Map p76; ☑ 030-200 037 441; www.thf-berlin.de; enter via Oderstrasse, Tempelhofer Damm or Columbiadamm; tours adult/concession €13/9; ⏰ sunrise to sunset, tours in English 1.30pm & 3.30pm Wed & Fri, 3pm Sat, 2pm Sun; ⓢ Paradestrasse, Boddinstrasse, Leinestrasse) The airport that handled the Berlin Airlift of 1948–49 has been repurposed as a giant urban park and adventure playground. Also known as Tempelhofer Feld or Tempelhofer Freiheit, it's a noncommercial, open-sky space where cyclists, bladers and kite-surfers whisk along the tarmac. Fun zones include a beer garden near Columbiadamm, barbecue areas, dog parks, an artsy minigolf course, art installations, abandoned aeroplanes and an urban gardening project. Tours of the old airport and the grounds are available.

◎ Friedrichshain

Rents may be rising and gentrification unstoppable, but for now, much of Friedrichshain, in former East Berlin, is still the domain of students, artists and eccentrics. There are few stand-out sights, but the boutique- and cafe-lined streets around Boxhagener Platz will repay those happy to wander and soak up the scene. After dark, Friedrichshain morphs into a hugely popular bar-stumbling and high-energy party zone.

★ **East Side Gallery** LANDMARK
(Map p76; www.eastsidegallery-berlin.de; Mühlenstrasse btwn Oberbaumbrücke & Ostbahnhof;

TREPTOWER PARK & THE SOVIET WAR MEMORIAL

Treptower Park, southeast of Kreuzberg, is an easy escape from the urban bustle with a patchwork of forest, lawns, a lake, an observatory and beer gardens. In summer, **Stern und Kreisschiffahrt** (p91) operates cruises from landing docks just south of the Treptower Park S-Bahn station.

The park's main sight is the gargantuan **Sowjetisches Ehrenmal Treptow** (Soviet War Memorial; Treptower Park; ⏰24hr; 🚇Treptower Park) FREE, built atop the graves of 5000 Soviet soldiers killed in the 1945 Battle of Berlin. Inaugurated in 1949, it's a bombastic and sobering testament to the immensity of Russia's wartime losses.

Coming from the S-Bahn station, you'll first be greeted by a **statue of a grieving Mother Russia** followed by kneeling soldiers flanking the gateway to the memorial itself; the red marble used here was supposedly scavenged from Hitler's ruined chancellery. Views open up to an enormous sunken lawn lined by **sarcophagi** representing the then 16 Soviet republics, each decorated with war scenes and Stalin quotations. The epic composition reaches a crescendo at the **mausoleum**, topped by a 13m statue of a Russian soldier clutching a child, his sword resting on a shattered swastika. The socialist-realism mosaic within the plinth shows grateful Soviets honouring the fallen.

ℹ STREET ART & WHERE TO FIND IT

Graffiti and street art have been part of Berlin's creative DNA since the 1970s. Since the fall of the Wall in 1989, though, the German capital has evolved into a hub, drawing international heavyweights such as Blu, JR, Os Gemeos, Romero and ROA along with local talent such as Alias, El Bocho and XOOOOX.

There's street art and graffiti pretty much everywhere, but some of the best work is still to be found in Kreuzberg. The area around U-Bahn station Schlesisches Tor has some house-wall-size classics, including **Leviathan** (Map p76; Falckensteinstrasse 48; ⓢ Schlesisches Tor) by Blu and **Yellow Man** (Map p76; Oppelner Strasse; ⓢ Schlesisches Tor) by the Brazilian twins Os Gemeos. Skalitzer Strasse is also a fertile hunting ground with Victor Ash's **Astronaut** (Map p76; Mariannenstrasse; ⓢ Kottbusser Tor) and ROA's **Nature Morte** (Map p76; cnr Oranienstrasse & Manteuffelstrasse; ⓢ Görlitzer Bahnhof) being highlights.

Friedrichshain, across the Spree River, has the **East Side Gallery** (p79), of course, as well as some interesting stuff on the RAW Gelände along Revaler Strasse, especially at the **Urban Spree** (Map p76; www.urbanspree.com; Revaler Strasse 99; ⊙ noon-11pm; ⓢ Warschauer Strasse, ⓡ Warschauer Strasse) bar and gallery. In Mitte, there's plenty to discover in the courtyard of **Haus Schwarzenberg** (Map p64; www.haus-schwarzenberg.org; Rosenthaler Strasse 39; ⓡ M1, ⓡ Hackescher Markt). Prenzlauer Berg has the **Mauerpark**, where budding artists may legally polish their skills along a section of the Berlin Wall.

⊙ 24hr; ⓢ Warschauer Strasse, ⓡ Ostbahnhof, Warschauer Strasse) **FREE** The year was 1989. After 28 years, the Berlin Wall, that grim and grey divider of humanity, finally met its maker. Most of it was quickly dismantled, but along Mühlenstrasse, paralleling the Spree, a 1.3km stretch became the East Side Gallery, the world's largest open-air mural collection. In more than 100 paintings, dozens of international artists translated the era's global euphoria and optimism into a mix of political statements, drug-induced musings and truly artistic visions.

Birgit Kinder's *Test the Best,* showing a Trabi bursting through the Wall; *The Mortal Kiss* by Dimitri Vrubel, which has Erich Honecker and Leonid Brezhnev locking lips; and Thierry Noir's bright cartoon faces are all shutterbug favourites.

Karl-Marx-Allee
STREET

(Map p76; ⓢ Strausberger Platz, Weberwiese, Frankfurter Tor) It's easy to feel like Gulliver in the Land of Brobdingnag when walking down monumental Karl-Marx-Allee, one of Berlin's most impressive GDR-era relics. Built between 1952 and 1960, the 90m-wide boulevard runs for 2.3km between Alexanderplatz and Frankfurter Tor and is a fabulous showcase of East German architecture. A considerable source of national pride back then, it provided modern flats for comrades and served as a backdrop for military parades.

Café Sibylle
HISTORIC SITE

(Map p76; ☏ 030-2935 2203; www.cafe-sibylle.de; Karl-Marx-Allee 72; exhibit free; ⊙ 10am-8pm, rooftop 1-5pm Mon, Wed & Fri; ⓢ Weberwiese, Strausberger Platz) Open since 1953, this was once one of East Berlin's most popular cafes and still makes for a delightfully retro coffee break. It also features a small exhibit charting the milestones of Karl-Marx-Allee from its inception to today.

The exhibit features portraits and biographies of the architects of KMA, alongside posters, toys and other items from socialist times. There's even a piece of Stalin's moustache scavenged from the nearby statue that was torn down in 1961.

Computerspielemuseum
MUSEUM

(Map p76; ☏ 030-6098 8577; www.computerspielemuseum.de; Karl-Marx-Allee 93a; adult/concession €8/5; ⊙ 10am-8pm; ⓢ Weberwiese) This well-curated museum takes you on a fascinating trip down computer-game memory lane while putting the industry's evolution into historical and cultural context. Colourful and engaging, it features interactive stations amid hundreds of original exhibits, including an ultra-rare 1972 Pong arcade machine and its twisted modern cousin, the 'PainStation' (must be over 18 to play...).

RAW Gelände
ARTS CENTRE

(Map p76; www.raw-tempel.de; along Revaler Strasse; ⓢ Warschauer Strasse, ⓡ Warschauer Strasse, Ostkreuz) This jumble of derelict buildings is one of the last subcultural compounds in central Berlin. Founded in 1867 as a train repair station ('Reichsbahn-Ausbesserungs-Werk', aka RAW), it remained in operation until 1994. Since 1999, the graffiti-slathered grounds have been a thriving offbeat sociocultural centre for creatives of all stripes, and also harbour clubs, bars, an indoor skate park, a swimming pool club and a bunker-turned-climbing-wall.

Prenzlauer Berg

Splendidly well-groomed Prenzlauer Berg is one of Berlin's most pleasant residential neighbourhoods and a joy to explore on foot. On Sundays, the world descends on its Mauerpark for flea markets, outdoor karaoke and chilling in the sun. The eastern end of the Gedenkstätte Berliner Mauer (p72) is close to the park – a visit here is essential to understanding how the Berlin Wall shaped the city.

Mauerpark PARK
(Map p82; www.mauerpark.info; btwn Bernauer Strasse, Schwedter Strasse & Gleimstrasse; [S] Eberswalder Strasse, [🚋] M1) With its wimpy trees and anaemic lawn, Mauerpark is hardly your typical leafy oasis, especially given that it was forged from a section of Cold War–era death strip (a short stretch of Berlin Wall survives). It's this mystique combined with an unassuming vibe and a hugely popular Sunday flea market and karaoke show that has endeared the place to locals and visitors alike.

Kulturbrauerei HISTORIC BUILDING
(Map p82; ☎030-4431 5152; www.kulturbrauerei.de; Schönhauser Allee 36; [S] Eberswalder Strasse, [🚋] M1) The fanciful red-and-yellow brick buildings of this 19th-century brewery have been recycled into a cultural powerhouse with a small village's worth of venues, from concert and theatre halls to restaurants, nightclubs, stores and a multiscreen cinema. From spring to autumn there's a Sunday street food market as well.

Museum in der Kulturbrauerei MUSEUM
(Map p82; ☎030-467 777 911; www.hdg.de/berlin/museum-in-der-kulturbrauerei; Knaackstrasse 97; 🕐10am-6pm Tue, Wed & Fri-Sun, to 8pm Thu; [S] Eberswalder Strasse, [🚋] M1, 12) [FREE] This exhibit uses original documents and objects (including a camper-style Trabi car) to teach the rest of us about daily life in

WORTH A TRIP

THE STASI: FEAR & LOATHING IN EASTERN BERLIN

In East Germany, the walls had ears. Modelled after the Soviet KGB, the Ministerium für Staatssicherheit (Ministry of State Security, 'Stasi' for short) was founded in 1950. It was secret police, central intelligence agency and bureau of criminal investigation all rolled into one. Called the 'shield and sword' of the SED, the sole East German party, it put millions of its own citizens under surveillance in order to suppress internal opposition. The Stasi grew steadily in power and size and, by the end, had 91,000 official full-time employees and 189,000 'unofficial' informants. The latter were regular folks recruited to spy on their co-workers, friends, family and neighbours.

The original Stasi HQ now harbours an **exhibit** (☎030-553 6854; www.stasimuseum.de; Haus 1, Ruschestrasse 103; adult/concession €6/4.50; 🕐10am-6pm Mon-Fri, noon-6pm Sat & Sun; [S] Magdalenenstrasse) that provides an overview of the structure, methods and effects of the organisation. Marvel at cunningly low-tech surveillance devices (hidden in watering cans, rocks, even neckties), a prisoner transport van with tiny, lightless cells and the obsessively neat offices of Stasi chief Erich Mielke. Other rooms introduce the ideology, rituals and institutions of GDR society. Panelling is partly in English.

Victims of Stasi persecution often ended up in the grim **Stasi Prison** (Gedenkstätte Hohenschönhausen; ☎030-9860 8230; http://en.stiftung-hsh.de; Genslerstrasse 66; adult/concession €5/2.50; 🕐tours in English 11.30am Apr-Oct, plus 2.30pm year-round, in German hourly 10am-4pm Apr-Oct, 11am-3pm Mon-Fri, 10am-4pm Sat & Sun Nov-Mar; [🚋] M5 to Freienwalder Strasse), now a memorial site officially called Gedenkstätte Hohenschönhausen. Tours reveal the full extent of the terror and cruelty perpetrated upon suspected regime opponents, many of them utterly innocent. If you've seen the Academy Award–winning movie *The Lives of Others*, you'll recognise many of the original settings. To get here, take tram M5 from Alexanderplatz to Freienwalder Strasse, then walk 10 minutes along Freienwalder Strasse.

Prenzlauer Berg

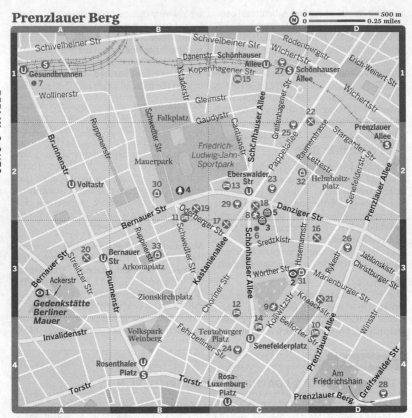

East Germany. Four themed sections juxtapose the lofty aspirations of the socialist state with the sobering realities of material shortages, surveillance and oppression. Case studies show the different paths individuals took to deal with their living conditions

Kollwitzplatz   SQUARE

(Map p82; [♿]; [S] Senefelderplatz) Triangular Kollwitzplatz is the epicentre of Prenzlauer Berg gentrification. To pick up on the local vibe, linger with macchiato mamas and media daddies in a street cafe or join them at the organic farmers market (p120). The park in the square's centre is tot heaven with three playgrounds plus a bronze sculpture of the artist Käthe Kollwitz for clambering on.

◉ City West & Charlottenburg

The glittering heart of West Berlin during the Cold War, Charlottenburg is nirvana for shopaholics, royal groupies and culture lov-

ers. On its main artery – Kurfürstendamm – fashionable boutiques mix it up with high-street chains and department stores, including the famous KaDeWe. Eclipsed by historic Mitte and other eastern districts after reunification, Charlottenburg is finally reclaiming some of the limelight, especially in the area around Zoo Station coined City West. Recent developments include the Waldorf Astoria the rejuvenated Zoopalast cinema and the Bikini Berlin (p119) concept mall.

★ Schloss Charlottenburg   PALACE

([☎] 030-320 910; www.spsg.de; Spandauer Damm 10-22; day pass to all 4 buildings adult/concession €17/13; [☉] hours vary by building; [🚌] M45, 109, 309, [S] Richard-Wagner-Platz, Sophie-Charlotte-Platz) Charlottenburg Palace is one of the few sites in Berlin that still reflects the one-time grandeur of the Hohenzollern clan that ruled the region from 1415 to 1918. Originally a petite summer retreat, it grew into an exquisite ba-

Prenzlauer Berg

roque pile with opulent private apartments, richly festooned festival halls, collections of precious porcelain and paintings by French 18th-century masters. It's lovely in summer when you can fold a stroll in the palace park into a day of peeking at royal treasures.

Museum Berggruen GALLERY
(📞030-266 424 242; www.smb.museum/mb; Schlossstrasse 1; adult/concession €10/5; ⊙10am-6pm Tue-Fri, 11am-6pm Sat & Sun; 🚊M45, 109, 309, 🚇Richard-Wagner-Platz, Sophie-Charlotte-Platz) Fans of classical modern art will be in their element at this delightful museum. Picasso is especially well represented with paintings, drawings and sculptures from all major creative phases. Elsewhere it's off to Paul Klee's emotional world, Matisse's paper cut-outs, Giacometti's elongated sculptures and a sprinkling of African art that inspired both Klee and Picasso.

Sammlung Scharf-Gerstenberg GALLERY
(📞030-266 424 242; www.smb.museum/ssg; Schlossstrasse 70; adult/concession €10/5; ⊙10am-6pm Tue-Fri, 11am-6pm Sat & Sun; 🚇Sophie-Charlotte-Platz, then bus 309, 🚇Richard-Wagner-Platz, then bus 145) This gallery in the 19th-century former royal stables across from Schloss Charlottenburg showcases a complete survey of surrealist art, with large bodies of work by René Magritte and Max Ernst alongside dreamscapes by Dalí and Dubuffet. Standouts among their 18th-century forerunners include Goya's spooky etchings and the creepy dungeon scenes by Italian engraver Giovanni Battista Piranesi.

Bröhan Museum MUSEUM
(📞030-3269 0600; www.broehan-museum.de; Schlossstrasse 1a; adult/concession/under 18 €8/5/free; ⊙10am-6pm Tue-Sun; 🚊M45, 109, 309, 🚇Sophie-Charlotte-Platz, Richard-Wagner-Platz) This private museum trains the spotlight on art nouveau, art deco and functionalism, all decorative styles in vogue between 1889 and 1939 and considered the midwives of modern design. Highlights include fully furnished and decorated period rooms by Hector Guimard and Peter Behrens, a Berlin Secession picture gallery and a section dedicated to Henry van de Velde.

ℹ **TOP TIPS FOR VISITING SCHLOSS CHARLOTTENBURG**

➡ Unless you have bought an online day pass, arrive early to avoid long queues, especially on weekends and in summer.

➡ Visit Wednesday to Sunday, when all palace buildings are open.

➡ A palace visit is easily combined with a spin around the trio of adjacent art museums.

Charlottenburg & Wilmersdorf

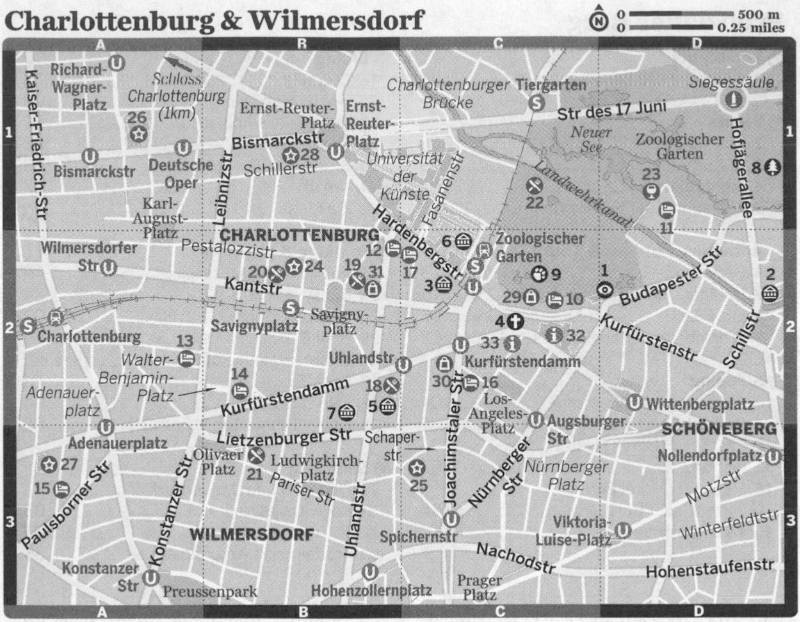

Story of Berlin MUSEUM

(Map p84; ☎030-8872 0100; www.story-of-berlin.de; Kurfürstendamm 207-208, enter via Ku'damm Karree mall; adult/concession €12/9; ⏰10am-8pm, last admission 6pm; [S]Uhlandstrasse) This multimedia museum breaks down 800 years of Berlin history into bite-size chunks that are easy to swallow but substantial enough to be satisfying. Each of the 23 rooms uses sound, light, technology and original objects to zero in on a specific theme or epoch in the city's history, from its founding in 1237 to the fall of the Berlin Wall. A creepily fascinating highlight is a tour (also in English) of a still functional atomic bunker beneath the building.

Käthe-Kollwitz-Museum MUSEUM

(Map p84; ☎030-882 5210; www.kaethe-kollwitz.de; Fasanenstrasse 24; adult/concession €6/3, audioguide €3; ⏰11am-6pm; [S]Uhlandstrasse) This museum in a charming villa is devoted to German artist Käthe Kollwitz (1867–1945), whose social and political awareness lent a tortured power to her lithographs, graphics, woodcuts, sculptures and drawings. Highlights include the antihunger lithograph *Brot!* (Bread!, 1924) and the woodcut series *Krieg* (War, 1922–23).

Kaiser-Wilhelm-Gedächtniskirche CHURCH

(Kaiser Wilhelm Memorial Church; Map p84; ☎030-218 5023; www.gedaechtniskirche.com; Breitscheidplatz; ⏰church 9am-7pm, memorial hall 10am-6pm Mon-Fri, 10am-5.30pm Sat, noon-5.30pm Sun; 🚌100, [S]Zoologischer Garten, Kurfürstendamm, 🚆Zoologischer Garten) [FREE] The bombed-out tower of this landmark church, consecrated in 1895, serves as an antiwar memorial, standing quiet and dignified amid the roaring traffic. The adjacent octagonal hall of worship, added in 1961, has amazing midnight-blue glass walls and a giant 'floating' Jesus.

Zoo Berlin ZOO

(Map p84; ☎030-254 010; www.zoo-berlin.de; Hardenbergplatz 8; adult/child €13/6.50, with aquarium €20/10; ⏰9am-6.30pm mid-Mar–Oct, 9am-5pm Nov–mid-Mar; 🚌100, 200, [S]Zoologischer Garten, 🚆Zoologischer Garten) Berlin's zoo holds a triple record as Germany's oldest, most species-rich and most popular animal park. It was established in 1844 under King Friedrich Wilhelm IV, who not only donated the land but also pheasants and other animals from the royal family's private reserve on the Pfaueninsel. The menagerie includes 20,000 critters representing 1500 species, including orangutans, koalas, rhinos, giraffes and penguins.

Charlottenburg & Wilmersdorf

Enter via the Lion's Gate on Hardenberg-platz or the Elephant Gate on Budapester Strasse.

Aquarium Berlin   AQUARIUM
(Map p84; ☎030-254 010; www.aquarium-berlin.
de; Budapester Strasse 32; adult/child €13/6.50,
with zoo €20/10; ☉9am-6pm; Ⓢ Zoologischer
Garten, Ⓡ Zoologischer Garten) Three floors of
exotic fish, amphibians and reptiles await
at this endearingly old-fashioned aquarium
with its darkened halls and glowing tanks.
Some of the specimens in the famous Croc-
odile Hall could be the stuff of nightmares,
but dancing jellyfish, iridescent poison frogs
and a real-life 'Nemo' should bring smiles to
young and old.

Museum für Fotografie   MUSEUM
(Map p84; ☎030-266 424 242; www.smb.muse-
um/mf; Jebensstrasse 2; adult/concession €10/5;
☉10am-6pm Tue, Wed & Fri, 10am-8pm Thu, 11am-
6pm Sat & Sun; Ⓢ Zoologischer Garten, Ⓡ Zoologischer Garten) The artistic legacy of Helmut
Newton (1920–2004), the Berlin-born enfant
terrible of fashion and lifestyle photography,
is given centre stage at Berlin's Photography
Museum in a converted Prussian officers'
casino behind Bahnhof Zoo. On the top
floor, the gloriously restored barrel-vaulted
Kaisersaal (Emperor's Hall) forms a grand

backdrop for changing high-calibre photography exhibits drawn from the archive of
the State Art Library.

C/O Berlin   GALLERY
(Map p84; ☎030-284 441 662; www.co-berlin.org;
Hardenbergstrasse 22-24; adult/concession/un-
der 18 €10/5/free; ☉11am-8pm; Ⓢ Zoologischer
Garten, Ⓡ Zoologischer Garten) The nonprofit
C/O Berlin is a cutting-edge exhibition and
event space for contemporary photography
ensconced in the iconic Amerika Haus. Built
in the 1950s, it served as a US culture and
information centre during the Cold War.
Previous exhibits have showcased the work
of Annie Leibovitz, Martin Parr, Nan Goldin,
Anton Corbijn and other members of the
shutterbug elite.

◉ Schöneberg

Schöneberg flaunts a mellow middle-class
identity but has a radical pedigree rooted
in the squatter days of the '80s. Handsome
19th-century town houses line many of
its quiet and leafy side streets, which are
squeezed tight with boho cafes and indie boutiques. It's a charismatic neighbourhood perfect for exploring on foot, ideally by starting
at Nollendorfplatz U-Bahn station and heading south to ethnic-flavoured Hauptstrasse,

WORTH A TRIP

OLYMPIASTADION

Olympiastadion (☑ 030-2500 2322; www.olympiastadion-berlin.de; Olympischer Platz 3; self-guided tour adult/concession €7/5.50, guided tour €11/9.50, Hertha BSC tour €12/10.50; ☺ 9am-7pm Apr-Jul, Sep & Oct, 9am-8pm Aug, 10am-4pm Nov-Mar; ⑤ Olympiastadion, ⑧ Olympiastadion) Built for the 1936 Olympic Games, Berlin's coliseum-style Olympiastadion was completely revamped for the 2006 FIFA World Cup and now sports a spidery oval roof, snazzy VIP boxes and top-notch sound, lighting and projection systems. On non-event days (call ahead to check) you can explore the stadium on your own (audioguide €4) or join a guided tour for access to the locker rooms, warm-up areas and VIP areas.

via Maassenstrasse, Goltzstrasse and Akazienstrasse (1.5km walk). On Saturday, a lively farmers' market takes over Winterfeldtplatz.

Nollendorfplatz is also the gateway to Berlin's historic gay quarter along Motzstrasse and Fuggerstrasse. One local gal who liked to party with the 'boyz' back in the 1920s was Marlene Dietrich. She's buried not far from Rathaus Schöneberg, the town hall where John F Kennedy gave his morale-boosting 'Ich bin ein Berliner!' speech back in 1963. In the late '70s, David Bowie and Iggy Pop shared a flat at Hauptstrasse 155.

◉ Southwestern Berlin

Much of Berlin's southwest is covered by forest, rivers and lakes. Besides the **Freie Universität** (☑ 030-8381; www.fu-berlin.de; Habelschwerdter Allee 45; ⓤ Thielplatz), which is one of Germany's 11 'elite' universities, and the **Botanischer Garten** (☑ 030-8385 0100; www.bgbm.org; Königin-Luise-Strasse 6-8; adult/concession €6/3; ☺ garden 9am-dusk, museum 10am-6pm; ⑤ Dahlem-Dorf, ⑧ Botanischer Garten), you'll find several excellent museums in the district.

Museen Dahlem   MUSEUM
(☑ 030-266 424 242; www.smb.museum; Lansstrasse 8; adult/concession/under 18 €9/4/free; ☺ 10am-5pm Tue-Fri, 11am-6pm Sat & Sun, Junior Museum 11am-6pm Sat & Sun; ⑤ Dahlem-Dorf) Unless some mad scientist invents a magic time-travel-teleporter machine, the three collections of art and objects from around

the globe within the Museen Dahlem are your best bet for exploring the world in a few hours.

Highlights of the **Museum of Ethnology** include masks and musical instruments in the Africa exhibit, and outriggers and traditional huts in the South Seas hall. Among prime works in the **Museum of Asian Art** are the Japanese tearoom and a 16th-century Chinese imperial throne. At the **Museum of European Cultures** exhibits range from Swedish armoires to a Venetian gondola.

AlliiertenMuseum   MUSEUM
(Allied Museum; ☑ 030-818 1990; www.alliiertenmuseum.de; Clayallee 135; ☺ 10am-6pm Tue-Sun; ⑤ Oskar-Helene-Heim) **FREE** The original Checkpoint Charlie guard cabin, a Berlin Airlift plane and a reconstructed spy tunnel are among the dramatic exhibits at the Allied Museum, which documents the history and challenges faced by the Western Allies during the Cold War. There's also a survey of events leading to the collapse of communism and the fall of the Berlin Wall. An original piece of the Wall sits in the yard.

Brücke-Museum   GALLERY
(☑ 030-831 2029; www.bruecke-museum.de; Bussardsteig 9; adult/concession €6/4; ☺ 11am-5pm, closed Tue; ⑤ Oskar-Helene-Heim, then bus 115 to Pücklerstrasse) In 1905 Karl Schmidt-Rottluff, Erich Heckel and Ernst Ludwig Kirchner founded Germany's first modern-artist group, called Die Brücke (The Bridge). Rejecting traditional techniques taught in the academies, they experimented with bright, emotional colours and warped perspectives that paved the way for German expressionism and modern art in general. Schmitt-Rottluff's personal collection forms the core of this lovely presentation of expressionist art.

Haus der Wannsee-Konferenz MEMORIAL SITE
(☑ 030-805 0010; www.ghwk.de; Am Grossen Wannsee 56-58; ☺ 10am-6pm; ⑧ Wannsee, then bus 114) **FREE** In January 1942 a group of 15 high-ranking Nazi officials met in a stately villa near Lake Wannsee to hammer out the details of the 'Final Solution': the systematic deportation and murder of European Jews in Eastern Europe. Today, this exhibit commemorates this sinister meeting and its ramifications in the very room where discussions took place.

Liebermann-Villa am Wannsee   MUSEUM
(☑ 030-8058 5900; www.liebermann-villa.de; Colomierstrasse 3; adult/concession €7/4, audi-

oguide €3; 🕐10am-6pm Wed, Fri & Sat, 10am-7pm Thu & Sun Apr-Sep, 11am-5pm Wed-Mon Oct-Mar; 🚆Wannsee, then bus 114) This lovely villa was the summer home of Berlin Secession founder Max Liebermann from 1909 until his death in 1935. Liebermann loved the lyricism of nature and often painted the gardens as seen through the window of his barrel-vaulted upstairs studio.

Activities

Cycling

Berlin is flat and bike-friendly, with special bike lanes and quiet side streets for stress-free riding. There are even eye-level miniature traffic lights at intersections. Still, it pays to keep your wits about you (and preferably with a helmet on) when negotiating city streets. Getting a tyre caught in the tram tracks is particularly nasty.

Of course it's far more relaxing to pedal around leafy suburbs. The Grunewald forest, for instance, with its many lakes, is a great getaway. Or follow the course of the former Berlin Wall along the marked Berliner Mauerweg. The websites www.bbbike.de and www.mvz-info.de are handy for route planning.

Bicycles *(Fahrräder)* may be taken aboard designated U-Bahn and S-Bahn cars (usually the last ones; look for the bicycle logo) as well as on night buses (Sunday to Thursday only) and trams. You need a separate bicycle ticket called a *Fahrradkarte*. Taking a bike on regional trains (RE, RB) costs €3.30 per trip or €6 per day.

Many hostels and hotels have guest bicycles, often for free or a nominal fee. If not, rental stations are practically at every corner. These include not only the expected (bike shops, petrol stations) but also convenience stores, cafes and even clothing boutiques.

Prices start at €6 per day, although €10 or €12 is more typical and the definition of 'day' can mean anything from eight hours to 24 hours. A cash or credit-card deposit and/or photo ID is usually required.

Recommended outfits are **Fahrradstation** (☎0180-510 8000; www.fashrradstation.de), **Prenzlberger Orange Bikes** (Map p82; ☎030-4435 6852; www.orange-bikes.de; Kollwitzstrasse 37, Prenzlauer Berg; per 24hr €7; 🕐noon-6pm Apr-Nov; [S]Senefelderplatz) and **Lila Bike** (Map p82; ☎0176 9957 9089; www.berlin-citytours-by-bike.de; Schönhauser Allee 41; first 24hr €8, additional 24hr €5; 🕐10am-3pm & 4-8pm Mon-Sat, 1-3pm & 4-8pm Sun Apr-Oct, to 6pm Nov-Mar; [S]Eberswalder Strasse, 🚋M1, 12). Be sure to book ahead (online or by phone), especially in summer.

Running

Berlin has great running terrain in its many parks. Flat and spread out, the Tiergarten (p74) is among the most popular and convenient, although the Grunewald in southwest Berlin is even prettier. The trip around the scenic Schlachtensee (in Grunewald) is 5km. The Schloss Charlottenburg (p82) park is also good for a nice, easy trot. More challenging is Volkspark Friedrichshain, which has stairs, hills and even a fitness trail.

Schöneberg

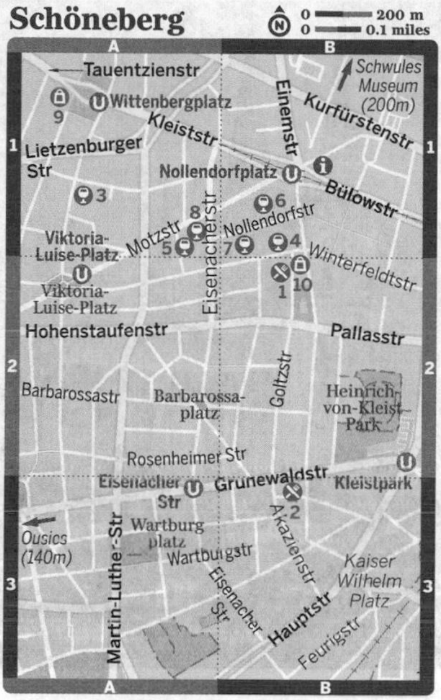

Schöneberg

Eating

1 Habibi B2
2 Martha's B3

Drinking & Nightlife

3 Connection Club A1
4 Green Door B1
5 Hafen A1
6 Heile Welt B1
7 Stagger Lee B1
8 Tom's Bar A1

Shopping

9 KaDeWe A1
10 Markt am Winterfeldtplatz B2

1. Kölner Dom 2. Allianz Arena
3. Schloss Neuschwanstein 4. Jüdisches Museum

YURI TURKOV/SHUTTERSTOCK ©

Architectural Icons

From Roman amphitheatres to glass-and-steel skyscrapers, Germany abounds with fine architecture representing a rainbow of styles and reflecting the era and culture in which it was built. Marvel at architects' vision, builders' ingenuity, changes in taste and innovations in materials and technology as you discover Instagram-worthy landmarks wherever you go.

Schloss Neuschwanstein

Bavarian King Ludwig II was not quite of this world and neither is his most sugary palace, a turreted mirage rising from the thickly forested Alpine foothills. Germany's most photographed castle reflects the king's obsession with Teutonic mythology and medieval grandeur, inspired by the operas of Richard Wagner. (p230)

Kölner Dom

The blueprint for the mighty Cologne cathedral was drafted in the 13th century, but it took more than 600 years to complete this spirit-lifting masterpiece with its filigree twin towers, luminous stained-glass windows and priceless artwork. (p463)

Jüdisches Museum, Berlin

Berlin's Jewish Museum by Daniel Libeskind is essentially a 3D metaphor for the tortured history of the Jewish people. Its zigzag outline symbolises a broken Star of David, while on the inside three intersecting walkways – called axes – represent the fates of Jews during the Nazi years. (p75)

Allianz Arena, Munich

Germany's winningest football (soccer) team, the FC Bayern München, plays home games in this breathtaking stadium designed by the Swiss firm of Herzog & de Meuron (2006). Its most striking feature is the facade, which consists of 2784 shimmering white, diamond-shaped pillows that can be illuminated in different colours. (p205)

Swimming

Berlin has lots of indoor and outdoor public pools. For the full list, see www.berlinerbaed-erbetriebe.de. Opening hours vary widely by day, time and pool, so check online or call ahead. Many facilities also have saunas.

Sommerbad Olympiastadion SWIMMING
(☑030-66631152; www.berlinerbaeder.de/baeder/sommerbad-olympiastadion; Osttor, Olympischer Platz 3; adult/concession €4/2.50; ⊙7am-8pm May–mid-Sep; Ⓢ Olympiastadion, Ⓡ Olympiastadion) Do your laps in the 50m pool built for the 1936 Olympic athletes.

THE BERLIN WALL

It's more than a tad ironic that Berlin's most popular tourist attraction is one that no longer exists. For 28 years the Berlin Wall, the most potent symbol of the Cold War, divided not only a city but the world.

Construction Shortly after midnight on 13 August 1961, East German soldiers and police began rolling out miles of barbed wire that would soon be replaced with prefab concrete slabs. The Berlin Wall was a desperate measure launched by the German Democratic Republic (GDR; East Germany) government to stop the sustained brain-and-brawn drain the country had experienced since its 1949 founding. Some 3.6 million people had already left for West Germany, putting the GDR on the brink of economic and political collapse.

The Physical Border Euphemistically called 'Anti-Fascist Protection Barrier', the Berlin Wall was continually reinforced and refined. In the end, it was a complex border-security system consisting not of one, but two, walls: the main wall abutting the border with West Berlin and the so-called hinterland security wall. In between was the 'death strip', riddled with trenches, floodlights, patrol roads, attack dogs, electrified alarm fences and watchtowers staffed by guards with shoot-to-kill orders. Nearly 100,000 GDR citizens tried to escape, some using ingenious contraptions such as homemade hot-air balloons or U-boats. Hundreds also died in the process.

The End The Wall's demise in 1989 came as unexpectedly as its construction. Once again the GDR was losing its people in droves, this time via Hungary, which had opened its borders with Austria. Thus emboldened, East Germans took to the streets, culminating in a gathering of 500,000 people on Alexanderplatz in early November. Something had to give. It did on 9 November 1989 when a GDR spokesperson (mistakenly, it later turned out) announced during a press conference that all travel restrictions to the West would be lifted. Immediately. Amid scenes of wild partying, the two Berlins came together again.

How to explore the Wall Today, only about 2km of the Berlin Wall still stands, the longest being the 1.3km-long East Side Gallery (p79). The best place to study up on the barrier and its impact on Berlin is the Gedenkstätte Berliner Mauer (p72), but there are several other ways to connect with this horrid if fascinating chapter of Berlin's past.

➜ Take a guided walking or bicycle tour along the Wall, for instance with Fat Tire Bike Tours (p91) or Berlin on Bike (p91).

➜ Follow the **double row of cobblestones** set into the pavement that guides you along 5.7km of the Wall's course.

➜ Look for the 30 information panels of the **Berlin Wall History Mile** (www.berlin.de/mauer/geschichtsmeile/index.en.html) that draw attention, in four languages, to specific events that took place at each location.

➜ Follow all or part of the 160km-long **Berliner Mauerweg** (Berlin Wall Trail), a signposted walking and cycling path with information panels set up along the former border fortifications.

➜ A brilliant source for tracking down smaller traces of the Wall, such as lamps, patrol paths, perimeter fences and switchboxes, is the **Memorial Landscape Berlin Wall** (www.berlin-wall-map.com), an interactive Geographic Information System (GIS).

Strandbad Wannsee SWIMMING
(☎ 030-803 5450; www.berlinerbaeder.de/baeder/strandbad-wannsee; Wannseebadweg 25; adult/concession €5.50/3.50; ⏲ 10am-7pm Mon-Fri, 9am-8pm Sat & Sun Apr-Sep; [R] Nikolassee) This lakeside public pool has delighted water rats for over a century. On hot days, its 1200m-long sandy beach can get very busy. Besides swimming, you can rent boats, play volleyball, basketball or table tennis or grab a snack or drink. Hours may vary slightly; check the website for specifics.

The Strandbad is about 1.3km northwest of the S-Bahn station Nikolassee. Walk north on Borussenstrasse, then turn left onto Wannseebadweg.

Stadtbad Neukölln SWIMMING
(Map p76; ☎ 030-682 4980; www.berlinerbaeder.de/baeder/stadtbad-neukoelln; Ganghoferstrasse 3; adult/concession €5.50/3.50; ⏲ hours vary; [S] Rathaus Neukölln, Karl-Marx-Strasse) This gorgeous bathing temple from 1914 wows swimmers with mosaics, frescoes, marble and brass. There are two pools (20m and 25m) and a Russian-Roman bath with sauna. Mondays are reserved for women only.

Tours

Bus

You'll see them everywhere around town: colourful buses (in summer, often open-top double-deckers) that tick off all the key sights on two-hour loops with basic taped commentary in eight languages. You're free to get off and back on at any of the stops. Buses depart roughly every 15 or 30 minutes between 10am and 5pm or 6pm daily; tickets cost from €10 to €20 (half-price for teens, free for children). Traditional tours (where you stay on the bus), combination boat/bus tours, as well as trips to Potsdam, Dresden and the Spreewald are also available. Look for flyers in hotel lobbies or in tourist offices.

Bicycle

Tour companies listed here operate various English-language tours.

Berlin on Bike BICYCLE TOUR
(Map p82; ☎ 030-4373 9999; www.berlinonbike.de; Knaackstrasse 97, Kulturbrauerei, Court 4; tours incl bike €19, concession €17; [S] Eberswalder Strasse) This well-established company runs a busy schedule of general city tours (Berlin's Best) and Berlin Wall tours in English, as well as half a dozen themed tours (including Streetart Berlin, Nightseeing and Future Berlin) in German only (in English on request). Reservations recommended.

Fat Tire Bike Tours BICYCLE TOUR
(Map p64; ☎ 030-2404 7991; www.fattirebiketours.com/berlin; Panoramastrasse 1a; adult/concession incl bicycle €26/24; [S] Alexanderplatz, [R] Alexanderplatz) Has classic city, Nazi and Berlin Wall tours as well as a fascinating 'Raw: Berlin Exposed' tour that gets under the city's urban, subcultural skin, as well as a trip to Potsdam. Tours leave from the TV Tower main entrance. E-bike tours are available. Reservations recommended (and, for some tours, required).

Boat

A lovely way to experience Berlin on a warm day is from the deck of a boat cruising along the city's rivers, canals and lakes. Tours range from one-hour spins around the historic centre (from €11) to longer trips to Schloss Charlottenburg and beyond (from €15). Most offer live commentary in English and German. **Stern und Kreisschiffahrt** (☎ 030-536 3600; www.sternundkreis.de; tours from €12; ⏲ Mar-Dec) and **Reederei Riedel** (☎ 030-6796 1470; www.reederei-riedel.de; tours from €12; ⏲ Mar-Dec) are among the main operators. The main season runs from April to mid-October, with a limited schedule in November, December and March.

Walking

Several English-language walking-tour companies run introductory spins that take in both blockbuster and offbeat sights, plus themed tours (eg Third Reich, Cold War, Sachsenhausen, Potsdam). Guides are fluent English speakers, well-informed, sharp-witted and keen to answer your questions. Tours don't require reservations – just show up at one of the meeting points. Since these can change at the drop of a hat, we have not listed them here. Please contact the companies directly.

[i] BUS TOUR ON THE CHEAP

Get a crash course in 'Berlinology' by hopping on the upper deck of bus 100 or 200 at Zoo Station or Alexanderplatz and letting the landmarks whoosh by for the price of a standard bus ticket (€2.70, day pass €6.90). Bus 100 goes via the Tiergarten, 200 via Potsdamer Platz. Without traffic, trips take about 30 minutes.

BERLIN FOR CHILDREN

Travelling to Berlin with tots can be child's play, especially if you keep a light schedule and involve the kids in the day-to-day planning. There's plenty to see and do to keep youngsters entertained, from zoos to kid-oriented museums. Parks with imaginative playgrounds abound in all neighbourhoods.

If the 20,000 furry, feathered and finned friends at the Zoo Berlin (p84) fail to enchant the little ones, there's always the enormous adventure playground. The crocodiles and jellyfish next door at the Aquarium Berlin (p85) rarely fail to make a lasting impression either. Finny friends take centre stage at SeaLife Berlin (p67) – its smaller size makes it suitable for the kindergarten set, as does the affiliated Legoland Discovery Centre (p73)

Kid-friendly museums include the Museum für Naturkunde (p72), with its giant dinosaur skeletons, and the Deutsches Technikmuseum (p78), with its planes, trains and automobiles and hands-on science centre.

Older kids might get a kick out of the interactive computer games at the Computerspielemuseum (p80) or the Cold War spy and escape exhibits at the Mauermuseum (p61). Follow a visit here with a trip around Berlin's 'Wild East' in a quaint GDR-era car on a Trabi Safari (p94). And you'll score big-time with your music-loving teens if you take them on the Berlin Music Tours (p94).

Baby food, infant formula, soy and cow's milk, disposable nappies (diapers) and the like are widely available at chemists (drugstores) and in supermarkets. Breastfeeding in public is practised, although most women are discreet about it. Restaurants sometimes have a special children's menu or can prepare simple dishes, even if they're not listed. In good weather, picnics in the park or by the Spree River or Landwehr canal are a sunny option.

Many museums, monuments and attractions are free to anyone under 18, but the cut-off might also be age 12 or 14. On public transport, children under six travel free and those between six and 14 pay the reduced (*ermässigt*) fare. Many stations have lifts (elevators).

If you need an English-speaking babysitter, ask at your hotel or contact Babysitter Express (www.babysitter-express.de) or Welcome Kids (www.welcome-kids.de).

Alternative Berlin Tours   WALKING TOUR
(☑ 0162 819 8264; www.alternativeberlin.com; tours €10-20) Pay-what-you-wish subculture tours that get beneath the skin of the city, plus a street-art workshop, an alternative pub crawl, the surreal 'Twilight Tour', an eco-tour and a food-and-drink tour.

Original Berlin Walks   WALKING TOUR
(☑ 030-301 9194; www.berlinwalks.de; adult €12-15, concession €10-12) Berlin's longest-running English-language walking tour company does one general and various themed city tours (Third Reich, Jewish Life, Berlin Wall) as well as trips out to Sachsenhausen concentration camp and Potsdam.

Brewer's Berlin Tours   WALKING TOUR
(☑ 0177 388 1537; www.brewersberlintours.com; adult/concession €15/12) Local experts run an epic all-day Best of Berlin tour and a shorter donation-based Berlin Free Tour as well as a Craft Beer and Breweries tour with tastings (€35) and an excursion to Potsdam.

Insider Tour Berlin   WALKING TOUR
(☑ 030-692 3149; www.insidertour.com; tours €12-15, concession €10-12) Insightful general and themed tours of Berlin (eg Cold War, Third Reich, Jewish Berlin), plus day trips to Dresden (€49) and Potsdam, and a pub crawl.

New Berlin Tours   WALKING TOUR
(www.newberlintours.com; adult €12-15, concession €10-13) Entertaining and informative city spins by the pioneers of the donation-based 'free tour' and the pub crawl. Also offers tours to Sachsenhausen concentration camp, themed tours (Red Berlin, Third Reich, Alternative Berlin) and a trip to Potsdam.

Speciality Tours

Berlinagenten   GUIDED TOUR
(☑ 030-4372 0701; www.berlinagenten.com) Get a handle on all facets of Berlin's urban lifestyle with an insider private guide who opens doors to hot and/or secret bars, boutiques, restaurants, clubs, private homes and sights. Dozens of culinary, cultural and lifestyle

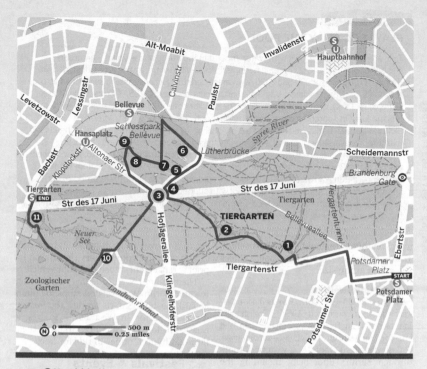

City Walk
A Leisurely Tiergarten Meander

START POTSDAMER PLATZ
END TIERGARTEN S-BAHN STATION
LENGTH 5KM; TWO HOURS

A ramble around Tiergarten delivers a relaxing respite from the sightseeing track. From Potsdamer Platz, make your way to **1 Luiseninsel**, an enchanting gated garden dotted with statues and seasonal flower beds. Not far away is **2 Rousseauinsel**, a memorial to 18th-century French philosopher Jean-Jacques ('Back to Nature') Rousseau. It was modelled after his actual burial site near Paris and placed on a teensy island in a sweet little pond.

At the heart of the park, engulfed by traffic, the imposing **3 Siegessäule** (Victory Column) is crowned by a gilded statue of the goddess Victoria and commemorates Prussian military triumphs enforced by Iron Chancellor Otto von Bismarck. Nearby, the **4 Bismarck Denkmal**, a monument to the man, shows him flanked by statues of Atlas (with the world on his back), Siegfried (wielding a sword) and Germania (stomping a panther).

Following Spreeweg north takes you past the oval **5 Bundespräsidialamt**, the offices of the German president, to his residence in **6 Schloss Bellevue**, a former royal palace. Follow the path along the Spree, then turn left into the **7 Englischer Garten** (English Garden) created in the '50s in commemoration of the 1948 Berlin Airlift. At its heart, overlooking a pretty pond, the reed-thatched **8 Teehaus im Englischen Garten** has beer, international fare and free summer concerts. Afterwards, check out the latest art exhibit at nearby **9 Akademie der Künste** (Academy of Arts), on the edge of the Hansaviertel. This modernist quarter was created during a 1957 building exhibition that drew the world's top architects, including Walter Gropius, Alvar Aalto and Le Corbusier.

Walk south through the park, crossing Altonaer Strasse and Strasse des 17 Juni, to arrive at Neuer See with **10 Café am Neuen See** (p111) at its south end. Stroll north along Landwehrkanal via **11 Gaslaternenmuseum**, an open-air collection of historic gas lanterns, and finish up at Tiergarten S-Bahn station.

DON'T MISS

PLAY IT COOL BY THE POOL

Take an old river barge, fill it with water, moor it in the Spree and – voila! – an urban lifestyle pool is born. In summer, a hedonistic Ibiza-vibe reigns at the artist-designed **Badeschiff** (Map p76; 030-533 2030; www.arena-berlin.de; Eichenstrasse 4; summer adult/concession €5/3; 8am-midnight May-Sep, shorter hours in winter; 265, Schlesische Strasse, Treptower Park), with bods bronzing in the sand or cooling off in the water and a bar to fuel the fun. On scorching days, come before noon or risk a long wait. After-dark action includes parties, bands, movies and simply chilling. In winter, an ethereally glowing plastic membrane covers the pool and a deliciously toasty chill zone with saunas and bar.

In 2015, the Badeschiff got competition from **Haubentaucher** (Map p76; www.haubentaucher.berlin; Revaler Strasse 99, Gate 1; admission varies, usually under €5; from 10am, weather permitting; Warschauer Strasse, Warschauer Strasse), another combo of bar, lounge, club, event space and, yes, a pool with sundeck and small beach. The urban chill-zone with industrial charm and Med-flair is part of the graffiti-festooned RAW Gelände, the cluster of party venues along Revaler Strasse.

tours on offer, including the best-selling 'Gastro Rallye' for the ultimate foodie. Prices depend on group size.

Berliner Unterwelten GUIDED TOUR
(Map p82; 030-4991 0517; www.berliner-unterwelten.de; adult/concession €11/9; English tours 1pm Mon & 11am Thu-Mon year-round, 11am Wed Mar-Nov, 1pm Wed-Sun Apr-Oct; Gesundbrunnen, Gesundbrunnen) Operates a variety of tours through Berlin's underbelly, including the 90-minute 'Dark Worlds' tour of a WWII underground bunker that has you picking your way past heavy steel doors, hospital beds and filter systems. Buy tickets at the kiosk next to the south exit of the Gesundbrunnen U-Bahn station (outside Kaufland).

Berlin Music Tours BUS TOUR, WALKING TOUR
(030-3087 5633; www.musictours-berlin.com; bus/walking tours in German €29/12; bus tour 12.30pm Sat, walking tour 2pm Sun) BMT's multimedia bus tour gives you the lowdown on four decades of Berlin's music history – from Bowie to U2 and Rammstein, cult clubs to the Love Parade – along with the scoop on who's rocking the city right now. Also available: music walking tours; tours of the Hansa recording studios; tours on Bowie, Depeche Mode and U2; and private minibus tours. See website for dates and reservations.

English tours on request (price depends on group size).

Trabi Safari CAR TOUR
(Map p76; 030-2759 2273; www.trabi-safari.de; Zimmerstrasse 97; per person from €34; Kochstrasse) Catch the *Good Bye, Lenin!* vibe on tours of Berlin's classic sights or the 'Wild East' with you driving or riding as a passen-ger in a convoy of GDR-made Trabant cars (Trabi) with live commentary (in English by prior arrangement) piped into your vehicle.

The two-hour Wall Ride has you steering towards Berlin Wall–related stops, or jump aboard Mustang Safaris around the former American sector in West Berlin in, yes, a classic Mustang. Drivers need to bring their licence. Children under 15 ride for free.

Festivals & Events

Berlin is very much a party town with a busy year-round calendar of concerts, street parties, mega sports events, trade shows and festivals celebrating everything from film to fetish, music to movies, travel to fashion. Berlin's **tourist office** (Map p64; 030-250 025; www.visitberlin.de; Brandenburger Tor, south gate, Pariser Platz; 9.30am-7pm Apr-Oct, to 6pm Nov-Mar; Brandenburger Tor, Brandenburger Tor) website has a searchable events calendar and can also help you book tickets. To get you planning, we've listed a few highlights:

January & February

Berlin Fashion Week FASHION
(www.berlin-fashionweek.de) Twice a year, in January and in July, international fashion folk descend on the city to present or assess next season's threads. See the website for public events.

Berlinale FILM
(www.berlinale.de) The world's stars and starlets, directors and critics invade in February for Berlin's glamorous international film festival.

May & June

Karneval der Kulturen STREET FAIR
(☎030 6097 7022; www.karneval-berlin.de) Exuberant three-day festival in the streets of Kreuzberg culminating in a parade of costumed dancers, singers, DJs and musicians. Pentecost weekend in May or June.

Christopher Street Day GAY, LESBIAN
(www.csd-berlin.de) People of every sexual orientation paint the town pink at one of Europe's biggest gay-pride parades and parties held in late June.

July & August

Internationales Berliner Bierfestival BEER
(www.bierfestival-berlin.de) [FREE] Who needs Oktoberfest when you can have the 'world's longest beer garden'? Pick your poison from over 300 breweries from nearly 100 countries along 2km of Karl-Marx-Allee.

September & October

Berlin Marathon SPORT
(www.berlin-marathon.com; ⏲Sep) Sweat it out with the other 40,000 runners or just cheer 'em on during one of the world's biggest and most prestigious street races.

November & December

Jazzfest Berlin MUSIC FESTIVAL
(www.jazzfest-berlin.de) This top-rated jazz festival doo-wops through the city with performances by fresh and big-time talent in November.

Christmas Markets CHRISTMAS MARKET
(www.visitberlin.de) Pick up shimmering ornaments or indulge in potent mulled wine at dozens of Yuletide markets held throughout the city from late November to late December.

Sleeping

Berlin offers the gamut of places to unpack your suitcase. Just about every international chain now has a flagship in the German capital, but more interesting options that better reflect the city's verve and spirit abound. You can sleep in a former bank, boat or factory, in the home of a silent-movie diva, in a 'flying bed', or even a coffin. Standards are high but fierce competition has kept prices low compared to other capital cities. Seasonal room-rate variations are rare but prices spike during major trade shows, festivals and public holidays.

Berlin's hostel scene is as vibrant as ever and consists of both classic backpacker hostels with large dorms and a communal spirit to modern 'flashpacker' crash pads catering to wallet-watching city-breakers. Also increasingly popular are hostel-hotel hybrids with hotel-like amenities. You'll find them in all districts, but especially in Kreuzberg and Friedrichshain – putting you within stumbling distance of bars and clubs.

For style-minded budget travellers who've outgrown hostels, there's now an increasing number of inexpensive designer hotels with chic interiors but small rooms and minimal amenities. Design-lovers with deeper pockets can choose from lifestyle and boutique hotels as well as *Kunsthotels* (art hotels), which are designed by artists and/or liberally sprinkled with original art.

Nostalgic types seeking Old Berlin flavour should check into a charismatic B&B, called *Hotel-Pension* or simply *Pension*. They're a dying breed, but for now there's still a fair number, especially in Charlottenburg.

As is the current trend, furnished flats are a popular – and economical – alternative to hotels in Berlin.

To minimise travel time, pick a place close to a U-Bahn or S-Bahn station and avoid those too far outside the S-Bahn ring.

Mitte

Circus Hostel HOSTEL €
(Map p64; ☎030-2000 3939; www.circus-berlin.de; Weinbergsweg 1a; dm €19-31, s/d from €46/58; [@][wifi]; [S]Rosenthaler Platz) Clean, cheerfully painted rooms, abundant shared facilities, helpful staff and a great location are among the factors that have kept Circus at the top of the hostel heap for about two decades. The cafe serves inexpensive breakfasts, drinks and snacks, while the basement bar has parties, events and its own craft brewery.

Motel One Berlin-Alexanderplatz HOTEL €
(Map p64; ☎030-2005 4080; www.motel-one.de; Dircksenstrasse 36; d from €73; [P][❄][@][wifi]; [S]Alexanderplatz, [R]Alexanderplatz) If you value location over luxury, this budget designer chain makes for an excellent crash pad. Smallish rooms come with up-to-the-minute touches (granite counters, massage showerheads, air-con) that are normally the staples of posher players. Arne Jacobsen's turquoise egg chairs add hipness to the lobby. Check

the website for the other eight Berlin locations. Optional breakfast is €9.50.

Wombat's Berlin
HOSTEL €

(Map p64; ☑ 030-8471 0820; www.wombats-hostels.com; Alte Schönhauser Strasse 2; dm €13-24, d €58-78; @ 🖥; Ⓢ Rosa-Luxemburg-Platz) Sociable and central, Wombat's gets hostelling right. From backpack-sized in-room lockers to individual reading lamps and a guest kitchen with dishwasher, the attention to detail here is impressive. Spacious en-suite rooms are as much part of the deal as free linen and a welcome drink, best enjoyed with fellow party pilgrims at sunset on the rooftop.
Optional breakfast buffet €3.90.

★ Circus Hotel
HOTEL €€

(Map p64; ☑ 030-2000 3939; www.circus-berlin.de; Rosenthaler Strasse 1; d €85-120, apt €120-190; @ 🖥; Ⓢ Rosenthaler Platz) At this superb budget boutique hotel, none of the mod rooms are alike, but all feature upbeat colours, thoughtful design touches, sleek oak floors and quality beds. Baths have walk-in rain showers. Unexpected perks include a roof terrace with summertime yoga, bike rentals and a fabulous breakfast buffet (€9) served until 1pm. Simply good value all-round.

Hotel Amano
HOTEL €€

(Map p64; ☑ 030-809 4150; www.amanogroup.de; Auguststrasse 43; d €70-165, apt €90-185; Ⓟ ✳ @ 🖥; Ⓢ Rosenthaler Platz) This sleek budget designer hotel has public areas dressed in brushed-copper walls and cocoa-hued banquettes, and efficiently styled rooms, where white furniture teams up with oak floors and natural-toned fabrics to create crisp cosiness. For space-cravers there are apartments in three sizes and with kitchens. Optional breakfast buffet for €15.

There's a popular bar, which opens up a branch on the rooftop in summer.

Adina Apartment Hotel Berlin Checkpoint Charlie
APARTMENT €€

(Map p76; ☑ 030-200 7670; www.tfehotels.com/de/brands/adina-apartment-hotels; Krausenstrasse 35-36; d from €100, 1-bedroom apt from €145; Ⓟ ✳ @ 🖥 ⊠; Ⓢ Stadtmitte, Spittelmarkt) Adina's contemporary one- and two-bedroom apartments with full kitchens are tailor-made for cost-conscious families, anyone in need of elbow room, and self-caterers (a supermarket is a minute away). Regular hotel rooms without kitchens are also available. Staff are accommodating and the pool and sauna are great for combating post-flight fatigue. See the website for other Adina properties in town. Optional breakfast is €19.

Mani Hotel
BOUTIQUE HOTEL €€

(Map p64; ☑ 030-5302 8080; www.hotel-mani.com; Torstrasse 136; d €75-180; Ⓟ 🖥; Ⓢ Rosenthaler Platz) Cocooned behind an elegant black facade on trendy Torstrasse, Mani flaunts an uncluttered urban feel and sleek rooms that pack plenty of creature comforts into a compact frame. The downstairs restaurant wows cool-hunters with its French-Israeli fare. Optional breakfast buffet is €15.

Arte Luise Kunsthotel
BOUTIQUE HOTEL €€

(Map p64; ☑ 030-284 480; www.luise-berlin.com; Luisenstrasse 19; d €89-169, with shared bathroom €49-84; ✳ @ 🖥; Ⓢ Friedrichstrasse, Ⓡ Friedrichstrasse) At this 'gallery with rooms', each unit is designed by different artists, who receive royalties whenever it's rented. They're all wonderfully imaginative, but we're especially fond of No 107 with its giant bed, and the boudoir-red 'Cabaret' (No 206). Cash-strapped art fans should enquire about the smaller, bathless rooms. Avoid those facing the train tracks. Optional breakfast available for €13.

Hotel Honigmond
BOUTIQUE HOTEL €€

(Map p64; ☑ 030-284 4550; www.honigmond-berlin.de; Tieckstrasse 12; d incl breakfast €110-193; Ⓟ @ 🖥; Ⓢ Oranienburger Tor) This delightful hotel scores a perfect 10 on our 'charm-o-meter', not for being particularly lavish, but for its friendly yet elegant ambience. The restaurant is a local favourite and rooms sparkle in colonial-style glory. The nicest are in the new wing and flaunt their historic features – ornate stucco ceilings, frescoes, parquet floors – to maximum effect.

Boutique Hotel i31
BOUTIQUE HOTEL €€

(Map p64; ☑ 030-338 4000; www.hotel-i31.de; Invalidenstrasse 31; r €90-167; Ⓟ ✳ 🖥; Ⓢ Naturkundemuseum) This contemporary contender has modern rooms in soothing colours and various relaxation zones, including a sauna, a sunny terrace and a small garden with sun loungers. Nice touch: the minibar with free soft drinks. For a little more space and luxury (Molton Brown amenities, for example) book a 'comfort room' on the upper floors. Breakfast buffet: €16.50.

Flower's Boardinghouse Mitte
APARTMENT €€

(Map p64; ☑ 030-2804 5306; www.flowersberlin.de; Mulackstrasse 1; apt from €93; ⊙ reception 9am-6pm; 🖥; Ⓢ Weinmeisterstrasse, Rosa-Luxemburg-Platz) Self-caterers won't miss many comforts of home in these breezy apartments in three sizes – L, XL and XXL – the last being a split-level unit with fabulous views over the rooftops. Units come with open kitchens and TV/DVD; rates include a small breakfast (rolls, coffee, tea) you pick up at reception.

Soho House Berlin BOUTIQUE HOTEL €€€
(Map p64; ☎030-405 0440; www.sohohouseberlin.com; Torstrasse 1; d €110-580, apt €220-700; [P] ❄ 📶 🏊; [S] Rosa-Luxemburg-Platz) The Berlin edition of the eponymous members' club and celeb-fave doubles as a hotel. The vintage-eclectic rooms vary dramatically in size and amenities, but may include Jamboxes, huge flat-screen TVs and freestanding tubs. Staying here also buys access to members-only areas such as the restaurant, the rooftop pool/bar and a small movie theatre.

Casa Camper BOUTIQUE HOTEL €€€
(Map p64; ☎030-2000 3410; www.casacamper.com; Weinmeisterstrasse 1; r/ste incl breakfast from €175/300; [P] ❄ 📶; [S] Weinmeisterstrasse) Catalan shoemaker Camper has translated its concept of chic yet sensible footwear into this style-pit for trend-conscious global nomads. Minimalist-mod rooms come with day-lit bathrooms and beds that invite hitting the snooze button. Minibars are eschewed for a top-floor lounge with stellar views and free 24/7 hot and cold snacks and drinks

Hotel Adlon Kempinski LUXURY HOTEL €€€
(Map p64; ☎030-226 10; www.kempinski.com; Unter den Linden 77, Pariser Platz; r from €260; ❄ [@] 📶 🏊; [S] Brandenburger Tor, 🚆 Brandenburger Tor) The Adlon has been Berlin's most high-profile defender of the grand tradition since 1907. The striking lobby is a mere overture to the full symphony of luxury awaiting in spacious, amenity-laden rooms and suites with timelessly regal decor. An Ayurvedic spa, a two-Michelin-star restaurant and a nightclub add 21st-century spice.

🛏 Potsdamer Platz & Tiergarten

Scandic Berlin Potsdamer Platz HOTEL €€
(Map p76; ☎030-700 7790; www.scandichotels.com; Gabriele-Tergit-Promenade 19; d €90-170; [P] ❄ [@] 📶; [S] Mendelssohn-Bartholdy-Park) 🍃 This Scandinavian import gets kudos for its central location and spacious blond-wood rooms with big bathrooms as well as for going the extra mile when it comes to being green. Distinctive features include the eighth-floor gym-with-a-view, honey from the rooftop beehive and free bikes. Optional (partly organic) breakfast is €9.

★**Das Stue** BOUTIQUE HOTEL €€€
(Map p84; ☎030-311 7220; www.das-stue.com; Drakestrasse 1; r from €200; ❄ 📶 🏊; 🚌100, 106, 200) This charismatic refuge from the urban bustle flaunts understated grandeur and has the Tiergarten park as a front yard. A grand foyer with sweeping staircases and an artsy chandelier leads the way to a hip bar, a Michelin-starred restaurant and rooms dressed in earth tones. The sleek spa has a pool, sauna and top-notch massages. Optional breakfast is €25.

★**Mandala Hotel** HOTEL €€€
(Map p76; ☎030-590 050 000; www.themandala.de; Potsdamer Strasse 3; ste from €180; [P] ❄ [@] 📶; [S] Potsdamer Platz, 🚆 Potsdamer Platz) How 'suite' it is to be staying at this sophisticated yet unfussy cocoon. Understated, zeitgeist-compatible rooms come in 10 sizes (40 to 200 sq metres) and are equipped with a kitchenette, walk-in closets and spacious desks in case you're here to ink that deal. Day spa and 24/7 fitness centre for relaxation, plus onsite two-Michelin-star restaurant.

🛏 Kreuzberg

Hüttenpalast HOSTEL €
(Map p76; ☎030-3730 5806; www.huettenpalast.de; Hobrechtstrasse 66; d campervans & cabins/hotel from €69/74; 🕐check-in 8am-6pm or by arrangement; 📶; [S] Hermannplatz) This indoor camping ground in an old vacuum-cleaner factory is an unusual place to hang your hat, even by Berlin standards. Sure, it has hotel-style rooms with private bath, but who wants those when you can sleep in a romantic wooden hut with rooftop terrace or in a snug vintage caravan? The little garden invites socialising.

★**Grand Hostel Berlin** HOSTEL €
(Map p76; ☎030-2009 5450; www.grandhostel-berlin.de; Tempelhofer Ufer 14; dm from €14, d without/with bathroom €44/58; [@] 📶; [S] Möckernbrücke) Afternoon tea in the library bar? Check. Rooms with stucco-ornamented ceilings? Got 'em. Canal views? Yup. OK, the Grand Hostel may be no five-star hotel, but it is one of Berlin's most supremely comfortable and atmospheric hostels. Ensconced in a fully renovated 1870s building are private rooms and dorms with quality single beds (linen costs €3.60) and large lockers.

GAY & LESBIAN BERLIN

Berlin's legendary liberalism has spawned one of the world's biggest and most diverse GLBT playgrounds. Anything goes in 'Homopolis' (and we *do* mean anything!), from the highbrow to the hands-on, the bourgeois to the bizarre, the mainstream to the flamboyant.

Berlin's gayscape ranges from mellow cafes, campy bars and cinemas to saunas, cruising areas, clubs with dark rooms and all-out sex venues. As elsewhere, gay men have more options for having fun, but grrrls – from lipstick lesbians to hippie chicks to bad-ass dykes – won't feel left out. Except for the most hard-core sex places, gay spots also get their share of opposite-sex and straight patrons.

The closest that Berlin comes to a 'gay village' is Schöneberg (Motzstrasse and Fuggerstrasse especially), where the rainbow flag has proudly flown since the 1920s. Institutions such as Tom's, Connection and Hafen still pull in the punters and there's also plenty of action for the leather and fetish set. Current hipster central is Kreuzberg, especially around Kottbusser Tor. Mehringdamm also has a concentration of gay venues. Friedrichshain has such key clubs as Berghain/Panorama Bar (p114) and the hands-on **Lab. oratory** (Map p76; www.lab-oratory.de; Am Wriezener Bahnhof; ☉ Thu-Mon; ⓡ Ostbahnhof). In Prenzlauer Berg, gay-geared locales include a few popular cruising dens and fun stations for the fetish set.

Information

Mann-O-Meter (Map p87; ☎ 030-216 8008; www.mann-o-meter.de; Bülowstrasse 106; ☉ 5-10pm Mon-Fri, 4-8pm Sat & Sun; Ⓢ Nollendorfplatz) Gay information centre. Also operates a hotline to report attacks on gays.

Out in Berlin (www.out-in-berlin.com) Up-to-date free English/German booklet available online and often at tourist offices.

Siegessäule (www.siegessaeule.de) The free mag and website is Berlin's lesbigay 'bible'.

Festivals

In mid-June, huge crowds paint the town pink during the **Lesbisch-Schwules Strassenfest** (Lesbigay Street Festival; www.stadtfest.berlin/en; Ⓢ Nollendorfplatz) in Schöneberg, which basically serves as a warm-up for **Christopher Street Day** (p95) later that month.

Sights

In a former print shop near Schöneberg, the nonprofit **Schwules Museum** (Gay Museum; ☎ 030-6959 9050; www.schwulesmuseum.de; Lützowstrasse 73; adult/concession €7.50/4; ☉ 2-6pm Mon, Wed-Fri & Sun, 2-7pm Sat, 2-8pm Thu; ⓡ M29, Ⓢ Nollendorfplatz, Kurfürstenstrasse) is one of the largest and most important cultural institutions documenting LGBTIQ culture around the world, albeit with a special focus on Berlin and Germany.

The **Denkmal für die im Nationalsozialismus verfolgten Homosexuellen** (Memorial to the Homosexuals Persecuted under the Nazi Regime; Map p64; www.stiftung-denkmal. de; Ebertstrasse; ☉ 24hr; Ⓢ Brandenburger Tor, Potsdamer Platz, ⓡ Brandenburger Tor, Potsdamer Platz) trains the spotlight on the persecution and suffering of Europe's gay community under the Nazis. The freestanding, 4m-high, off-kilter concrete cube was designed by Danish-Norwegian artists Michael Elmgreen and Ingar Dragset. A looped video plays through a warped, narrow window.

Bars

Heile Welt (Map p87; ☎ 030-2191 7507; Motzstrasse 5; ☉ from 6pm; Ⓢ Nollendorfplatz) Chic yet loungy, Schöneberg's 'Perfect World' gets high marks for its communicative vibe, high flirt factor and handsome laddies. It's a great whistle-stop before launching into a raunchy night but gets packed in its own right as the moon rises higher in the sky.

Tom's Bar (Map p87; ☎ 030-213 4570; www.tomsbar.de; Motzstrasse 19; ☉ 10pm-6am; Ⓢ Nollendorfplatz) Erotic artist Tom of Finland inspired the name of this cruisy, been-here-forever Schöneberg bar and labyrinthine darkroom. On Mondays drinks are two-for-one.

Himmelreich (Map p76; ☎030-2936 9292; www.himmelreich-berlin.de; Simon-Dach-Strasse 36; ⊙6pm-2am Mon-Thu, to 4am Fri, 2pm-4am Sat, 2pm-2am Sun; ⑤Warschauer Strasse, ⓡWarschauer Strasse) Friedrichshain party animals are fed at this red-hued cocktail lounge where Tuesdays are women-only and on Wednesdays drinks are two-for-one.

Roses (Map p76; ☎030-615 6570; Oranienstrasse 187; ⊙9pm-late; ⑤Kottbusser Tor) At this Kreuzberg palace of camp and kitsch, with pink furry walls Barbie would love, drinks are cheap and the bartenders pour with a generous elbow, making this a packed – and polysexual – pit stop during hard-partying nights.

Zum Schmutzigen Hobby (Map p76; www.ninaqueer.com; Revaler Strasse 99, RAW Gelände, Gate 2; ⊙from 7pm; ⑤Warschauer Strasse, ⓡWarschauer Strasse) Although founder and trash-drag deity Nina Queer has moved on to other pastures, this living-room-sized, deliciously kitsch party den is still swarmed nightly.

Hafen (Map p87; ☎030-211 4118; www.hafen-berlin.de; Motzstrasse 19; ⊙from 8pm; ⑤Nollendorfplatz) The all-comer Harbour has been a friendly stop to dock in Schöneberg for more than two decades. There are DJs, parties, drinking and flirting, plus Hendryk's hilarious Monday quiz night (in English on the first Monday of the month).

Clubs & Parties

Some of the best queer club nights are independent of the venues they use and may move around, although most have some temporary residency. Always check the websites or the listings mags for the latest scoop.

SchwuZ (Map p76; ☎030-5770 2270; www.schwuz.de; Rollbergstrasse 26; ⊙Thu-Sat; ☒104, 167, ⑤Rathaus Neukölln) Even after relocating, this long-running queer party institution is the go-to spot for high-energy flirting and dancing. Different sounds nightly, so check what's on before heading out. Good for easing into the gay party scene.

Connection Club (Map p87; ☎030-218 1432; www.connectionclub.de; Fuggerstrasse 33; ⊙Fri & Sat; ⑤Wittenbergplatz) This legendary men-only party den with Berlin's largest darkroom was a techno pioneer way back in the '80s and still hasn't lost its grip on the scene.

Homopatik (://about blank, Markgrafendamm 24; ⊙3rd Fri of the month; ⓡOstkreuz) Get lost on the multiple dark dance floors and in the idyllic garden when this hipster party for gays and friends takes over ://about blank in Friedrichshain. Every third Friday of the month.

Klub International (Map p64; www.klub-international.com; Kino International, Karl-Marx-Allee 33; ⊙from 11pm first Sat of month) Up to 1500 boyz to men come out to a glamorous GDR-era cinema to work three sizzling dance floors where Berlin's finest trash queen DJanes spin a sound cocktail of house, nu rave and pop.

Chantals House of Shame (Map p82; www.facebook.com/ChantalsHouseofShame?sk=wall; Bassy Club, Schönhauser Allee 176a; ⊙from 11pm Thu; ⑤Senefelderplatz) Trash diva Chantal's louche lair is a beloved institution, as much for the glam factor as for the over-the-top transvestite shows and the hotties who love 'em.

GMF (www.gmf-berlin.de; ⊙11pm Sun) Berlin's premier Sunday club is known for excessive SM (standing and modelling) with lots of smooth surfaces – and that goes for both the crowd and the setting. Predominantly boyz, but girls OK. Check website for latest location.

Irrenhaus (Map p76; www.ninaqueer.com; Comet Club, Falckensteinstrasse 47; ⊙3rd Sat of the month; ⓤSchlesisches Tor) The name means 'insane asylum' and that's no joke. Party hostess with the mostest, trash queen Nina Queer puts on nutty, naughty shows at Comet Club that are not for the faint-of-heart. Expect the best. Fear the worst. Mixed.

Café Fatal (p113) All comers descend on SO36 for the ultimate rainbow tea dance that goes from 'strictly ballroom' to 'dirty dancing' in a flash. If you can't tell a waltz from a cha cha, come at 7pm for free dance lessons.

CITY TAX

Value-added tax (VAT; 7%) has long been included in room rates, but since 1 January 2014 an additional 5% 'City Tax' is payable on the net room rates, ie excluding VAT and fees for amenities and services such as mini-bar, sauna or spa. The tax is added to the hotel bill. Business travellers are exempt if they can prove the purpose of their trip (eg with a letter from the company or a bill issued to the employer). Rates quoted in this book do not include the tax.

Hotel Sarotti-Höfe HOTEL €€
(Map p76; ☎030-6003 1680; www.hotel-sarotti-hoefe.de; Mehringdamm 55; d €100-180; [P] @ 📶; [S] Mehringdamm) You'll have sweet dreams in this 19th-century ex-chocolate factory whose courtyard-cloistered rooms are quiet despite being smack dab in the bustling Bergmannstrasse quarter. Rooms exude elegant yesteryear flair with rich earth-toned fabrics and dark-wood furniture. The nicest (deluxe category) come with private terrace. Check-in is at the onsite Cafe Sarotti-Höfe (breakfast buffet €12).

Hotel Riehmers Hofgarten HOTEL €€
(Map p76; ☎030-7809 8800; www.riehmers-hofgarten.de; Yorckstrasse 83; s/d from €98/131, apt €175; 📶; [S] Mehringdamm) Take a romantic 19th-century building, add contemporary art, stir in a few zeitgeist touches such as iPod docks and you'll get one winning cocktail of a hotel. Richmers' high-ceilinged rooms are modern but not stark; if you're noise-sensitive, get a (slightly pricier) courtyard-facing room. Assets include in-room tea and coffee facilities and a gourmet restaurant. Breakfast buffet €9.

Friedrichshain

Eastern Comfort Hostelboat HOSTEL €
(Map p76; ☎030-6676 3806; www.eastern-comfort.com; Mühlenstrasse 73-77; dm €16, d €50-78; ⏲reception 8am-midnight; @ 📶; [S] Warschauer Strasse, [R] Warschauer Strasse) Let the Spree River murmur you to sleep while you're snugly ensconced in this two-boat floating hostel right by the East Side Gallery. Cabins are carpeted and trimmed in wood, but sweetly snug (except for 'first-class'); most have their own shower and toilet. The party zones of Kreuzberg and Friedrichshain are handily within staggering distance.

Optional breakfast is €6. Linen is €5, or bring your own.

★ Michelberger Hotel HOTEL €€
(Map p76; ☎030-2977 8590; www.michelbergerhotel.com; Warschauer Strasse 39; d €84-190; 📶; [S] Warschauer Strasse, [R] Warschauer Strasse) The ultimate in creative crash pads, Michelsberger perfectly encapsulates Berlin's offbeat DIY spirit without being self-consciously cool. Rooms don't hide their factory pedigree, but are comfortable and come in sizes suitable for lovebirds, families or rock bands. Staff are friendly and clued-in, and the restaurant is popular with both guests and locals.

Almodóvar Hotel HOTEL €€
(☎030-692 097 080; www.almodovarhotel.de; Boxhagener Strasse 83; d €94-130; 🚌240, 🚋M13, [R] Ostkreuz) A certified 'biohotel', Almodóvar is perfect for those wanting to keep their healthy ways while travelling. A yoga mat is a standard amenity in the 60 rooms dressed in crisp white, red and black, while the locavore restaurant turns out vegan, raw food, lactose- and gluten-free dishes and the spa offers Ayurvedic treatments. Breakfast is €14.

nhow HOTEL €€
(Map p76; ☎030-290 2990; www.nhow-hotels.com/berlin; Stralauer Allee 3; d €125-215; [P] ❄ 📶; [S] Warschauer Strasse, [R] Warschauer Strasse) This riverside behemoth bills itself as a music and lifestyle hotel and underscores the point by having two onsite recording studios. The look is definitely dynamic, what with a sideways tower jutting out over the Spree and Karim Rashid's digi-pop-pink design that would make Barbie proud.

Worth a little extra: a room with a river view. Optional breakfast is €24.

Prenzlauer Berg

★ EastSeven Berlin Hostel HOSTEL €
(Map p82; ☎030-9362 2240; www.eastseven.de; Schwedter Strasse 7; dm €23-25, d €62; @ 📶; [S] Senefelderplatz) Staff at this personable, delightful hostel close to hip hang-outs and public transport go out of their way to make all feel welcome. Make new friends at garden barbecues, spaghetti dinners or chilling in the lounge, then retreat to comfy pine beds in brightly painted dorms with lockers, or a private room. Baths are shared, linen is free and breakfast is €3.

Meininger Hotel Berlin
Prenzlauer Berg
HOSTEL, HOTEL €

(Map p82; ☑ 030-9832 1074; www.meininger-ho-tels.com; Schönhauser Allee 19; dm from €18, d from €54; @ ⬆; Ⓢ Senefelderplatz) This popular hostel-hotel combo draws school groups, flashpackers and business types, which makes for an interesting guest mix. A lift whisks you to mod and spacious en-suite rooms and dorms with quality furnishings, flat-screen TVs and handy blackout blinds to combat jet-lag (or hangovers). It's close to bars, markets and transport. Breakfast is €6.90.

Check the website for other Meininger locations.

Linnen
GUESTHOUSE €€

(Map p82; ☑ 030-4737 2440; www.linnenberlin. com; Eberswalder Strasse 35; d €88-169; ⬆; Ⓢ Eberswalder Strasse) This little 'boutique inn' brims with charisma and character in each of its five homey (and TV-less) rooms. No 4, for instance, gets forest-cabin flair from wooden walls decorated with bird feeders, while No 1 has a four-poster bed and balcony. The onsite café serves breakfast, sandwiches and cakes.

★ Ackselhaus &
Blue Home
BOUTIQUE HOTEL €€

(Map p82; ☑ 030-4433 7633; www.ackselhaus. do; Belforter Strasse 21; ste/apt incl breakfast from €120/150; @ ⬆; Ⓢ Senefelderplatz, 🚊 M10) At this charismatic retreat in a 19th-century building you'll sleep in large, classily decorated themed rooms (eg Africa, Rome, Maritime), each with thoughtfully picked special features: a freestanding tub, perhaps, a four-poster bed or Chinese antiques. Many face the enchanting courtyard garden. The breakfast buffet is served – beneath crystal chandeliers – until 11am (until 12.30pm at weekends).

🛏 City West, Charlottenburg & Schöneberg

★ 25hours Hotel Bikini Berlin
HOTEL €€

(Map p84; ☑ 030-120 2210; www.25hours-hotels. com; Budapester Strasse 40; r €85-289; ❄ @ ⬆; Ⓢ Zoologischer Garten, 🚊 Zoologischer Garten) The 'urban jungle' theme of this hip lifestyle outpost in the iconic 1950s Bikini Haus reflects its location between the city's zoo and main shopping district. Rooms are stylish, if a tad compact, with the nicer ones facing the animal park. Quirk factors include an onsite

bakery, hammocks in the public areas and a sauna with zoo view.

The rooftop bar and restaurant are popular with locals as well.

Hotel Askanischer Hof
HOTEL €€

(Map p84; ☑ 030-881 8033; www.askanischer-hof. de; Kurfürstendamm 53; d incl breakfast €80-160; ⬆; Ⓢ Adenauerplatz) If you're after character and vintage flair, you'll find heaps of both at this 17-room jewel with a Roaring Twenties pedigree. An ornate oak door leads to a quiet oasis where no two rooms are alike, but all are filled with antiques, lace curtains, frilly chandeliers and time-worn oriental rugs. The quaint Old Berlin charms make a popular setting for fashion shoots.

Propeller Island City Lodge
GUESTHOUSE €€

(Map p84; ☑ 8am-noon 030-891 9016; www. propeller-island.de; Albrecht-Achilles-Strasse 58; d €79-1150; ⬆; Ⓢ Adenauerplatz) A novel by the master of imagination, Jules Verne, inspired this hotel's name, and indeed every single room here is a journey to a unique, surreal and slightly wicked world. To be stranded on Propeller Island may have you waking up on the ceiling, in a prison cell or inside a kaleidoscope.

Artist-composer-owner Lars Stroschen designed and crafted all the furniture and fixtures, creating sinks from metal beer barrels, taps (faucets) from heater valves and table bases from tree trunks. Don't expect TV, room service or pillow treats.

Hotel Art Nouveau
B&B €€

(Map p84; ☑ 030-327 7440; www.hotelartnouveau. de; Leibnizstrasse 59; d €96-176; 🅿 @ ⬆; Ⓢ Adenauerplatz) A quaint birdcage lift drops you off with belle époque flourish at this arty B&B where rooms skimp neither on space nor charisma and offer a blend of youthful flair and tradition. The well-travelled owners are fluent English-speakers with a knack for creating a home-away-from-home ambience. Bonus points for the superb beds, the breakfast buffet (€9) and the honour bar.

Wyndham Berlin Excelsior Hotel
HOTEL €€

(Map p84; ☑ 030-303 1550; www.hotel-excelsior.de; Hardenbergstrasse 14; d €80-123; ❄ ⬆; Ⓢ Zoologischer Garten, 🚊 Zoologischer Garten) This progressively designed outpost, with a living-room-style lobby complete with library and fireplace, should suit buttoned-up business types as much as couples on a getaway. White and chocolate dominate the modern rooms; the 'superior' category includes wi-fi

FURNISHED APARTMENTS

For self-caterers, independent types, the budget-conscious, families and anyone in need of plenty of privacy, a short-term furnished-flat rental may well be the cat's pyjamas. Plenty of options have been popping up lately, but these are our favourites:

Brilliant Apartments (Map p82; ☑ 030-8061 4796; www.brilliant-apartments.de; Oderberger Strasse 38; apt from €93; ☜; Ⓢ Eberswalder Strasse) The name is the game in these 11 stylish and modern units with full kitchens that sleep from one to six people. They are located on Oderberger Strasse and Rykestrasse, both hip drags in Prenzlauer Berg that put you close to everything.

Gorki Apartments (Map p64; ☑ 030-4849 6480; www.gorkiapartments.dc; Weinbergsweg 25; apt €115-215; ☜; Ⓢ Rosenthaler Platz, ☐ M1, 12) Idiosyncratic modern furniture and decor meet retro touches such as sparkling parquet floors and stucco ornamentation in these 34 spacious, super-central lifestyle apartments with kitchens.

Miniloft Berlin (Map p64; ☑ 030-847 1090; www.miniloft.com; Hessische Strasse 5; apt €125-165; ☜; Ⓢ Naturkundemuseum) Architect-designed lofts in an energy-efficient building, some with south-facing panorama windows, others with cosy alcoves, all outfitted with modern designer furniture and kitchenettes.

T&C Apartments (Map p82; ☑ 030-405 046 612; www.tc-apartments-berlin.de; Kopenhagener Strasse 72; studio apt from €45; Ⓢ Schönhauser Allee) Huge selection of stylish, hand-picked, one- to four-room apartments in Mitte, Prenzlauer Berg, Tiergarten and Schöneberg; headquarters located in Prenzlauer Berg.

ÏMA Loft Apartments (Map p76; ☑ 030-6162 8913; www.imalofts.com; Ritterstrasse 12-14; apt €55-200; ☜; Ⓢ Moritzplatz) These uncluttered, contemporary apartments are part of the ÏMA Design Village, an old factory shared by design studios and a dance and theatre academy. They sleep from one to four.

Berlin Lofts (☑ 0151 2121 9126; www.berlinlofts.com; Stephanstrasse 60; studio from €44, apt from €127; ◍☜; Ⓢ Westhafen, Birkenstrasse, Ⓡ Westhafen) Rents huge lofts in handsomely converted historic buildings, including an old smithy and a bi-level horse barn. The area, alas, is not nearly as hip, although public-transport connections are decent. Trivia bonus: Kommune 1, Germany's first politically motivated student commune, formed in 1967, once lived in one of the apartments.

and spa access. The Franke restaurant gets high marks for its innovative brasserie fare.

★ **Hotel am Steinplatz** BOUTIQUE HOTEL €€€
(Map p84; ☑ 030-554 4440; www.hotelsteinplatz.com; Steinplatz 4; r €135-165; ❿❄◍☜; Ⓢ Ernst-Reuter-Platz) Vladimir Nabokov and Romy Schneider were among the guests of the original Hotel am Steinplatz, which got a second lease on life in 2013, a century after it first opened. Rooms in this elegant art-deco jewel reinterpret the 1920s in contemporary style with fantastic lamps, iPod docks and black-and-white bathrooms. Classy bar and restaurant, to boot.

Sofitel Berlin Kurfürstendamm HOTEL €€€
(Map p84; ☑ 030-800 9990; www.sofitel-berlin-kurfuerstendamm.com/en; Augsburger Strasse 41; d €103-190; ❿❄◍☜; Ⓢ Kurfürstendamm) Renowned Berlin architect Jan Kleihues pulled out all the stops to create this award-winning

alchemy of art, architecture and design. A sophisticated but unfussy ambience accented by tasteful contemporary art as well as supremely comfortable XL-sized rooms with sitting areas and walk-in closet make this French-flavoured refuge a perfect launch pad for urban explorers. Great restaurant, too.

✕ Eating

If you crave traditional comfort food, you'll certainly find plenty of places to indulge in roast pork knuckles, smoked pork chops or calves liver in Berlin. These days, though, typical local fare is lighter, healthier, more creative and more likely to come from gourmet kitchens, organic eateries and a United Nations worth of ethnic restaurants. The most exciting newcomers can usually be found in Mitte and Kreuzberg.

Eschewing tradition, a growing league of chefs has jumped on the locavore bandwagon and lets local, farm-fresh and often organic ingredients steer a seasonally calibrated menu. The Michelin testers too have confirmed that Berlin is ripe for the culinary big time by awarding their coveted stars to 13 chefs.

If there ever was a snack food with cult status, the humble *Currywurst* is it. A slivered, subtly spiced pork sausage swimming in tomato sauce and dusted with curry powder, it's as iconic as the Brandenburg Gate. A legacy of Berlin's vast Turkish community is the doner kebab, served in a pita with salad and sauce.

Berlin's multicultural tapestry has brought the world's foods to town, from Austrian schnitzel to Zambian zebra steaks. Sushi is hugely popular and Mexican and Korean restaurants have of late been proliferating. Reflecting the trend towards tasty and healthy food is the abundance of Asian eateries, especially Thai and Vietnamese.

Vegan restaurants have also been sprouting quicker than alfalfa, as have 'bio' cafes where dishes are prepared from organic and locally sourced ingredients. Also popular is 'guerrilla dining': secret supper parties held in private homes for short periods or at irregular intervals and often accessible by invitation only.

✕ Mitte

District Môt
VIETNAMESE €

(Map p64; ☑ 030-2008 9284; www.districtmot. com; Rosenthaler Strasse 62; dishes €8-19; ☺ noon-1am Sun-Thu, to 2am Fri & Sat; Ⓢ Rosenthaler Platz, Ⓜ M1) At this colourful mock-Saigon street-food parlour, patrons squat on tiny plastic stools around wooden tables where rolls of toilet paper irreverently stand in for paper napkins. The small-plate menu mixes the familiar (steamy *pho* noodle soup, papaya salad) with the adventurous (stewed eel, deep-fried silk worms).

House of Small Wonder
INTERNATIONAL €

(Map p64; ☑ 030-2758 2877; www.houseofsmall wonder.de; Johannisstrasse 20; mains €7.50-10; ☺ 9am-5pm Mon-Fri, 10am-5pm Sat & Sun; ☞; Ⓢ Oranienburger Tor, Ⓡ Oranienburger Strasse, Friedrichstrasse) A steep spiralling staircase leads up to this whimsical brunch and lunch cafe where plants are potted in birdcages and the ceiling is made of opaque glass panels. The menu features comfort food inspired by American, Japanese and European tastes and includes sandwiches, home-baked goods and such eccentric mains as Okinawan Taco Rice.

Gelateria Giorgio Lombardi
CAFE €

(Map p64; ☑ 030-5056 6195; Weinbergsweg 5; per scoop €1.80; ☺ 9am-10pm Mon-Thu, to midnight Fri, 10am-midnight Sat, 10am-10pm Sun; Ⓢ Rosenthaler Platz, Ⓜ M1, 12) There's good ice cream and then there's Giorgio Lombardi's *gelato*, made fresh daily in the tiny onsite show lab with nothing but natural, seasonal, quality ingredients. One taste of the chocolate sorbet and you're hooked! A full cafe, it also serves cappuccino, homemade cakes and tiramisu as well as a sinfully rich hot chocolate and crusty panini.

Ishin – Mittelstrasse
JAPANESE €€

(Map p64; ☑ 030-2067 4829; www.ishin.de; Mittelstrasse 24; sushi platter €8-19.50, bowl €5-13; ☺ 11am-10pm Mon-Sat; Ⓢ Friedrichstrasse, Ⓡ Friedrichstrasse) Look beyond the cafeteria-style decor to sushi glory for minimal prices. Combination platters are ample and affordable, especially during happy hour (all day Wednesday and Saturday, until 4pm on other days). If you're not in the mood for raw fish, tuck into a steaming rice bowl topped with meat and/or veg. Nice touch: the unlimited free green tea.

Muret La Barba
ITALIAN €€

(Map p64; ☑ 030-2809 7212; www.muretla-barba.de; Rosenthaler Strasse 61; mains €9-19; ☺ 10am-midnight Mon-Fri, noon-midnight Sat & Sun; Ⓢ Rosenthaler Platz, Ⓜ M1) This wine shop–bar-restaurant combo oozes the kind of rustic authenticity that instantly transports cognoscenti to Italy. The food is hearty, inventive and made with top ingredients imported from the motherland. All wine is available by the glass or by the bottle (corkage fee €9.50).

Chèn Chè
VIETNAMESE €€

(Map p64; ☑ 030-2888 4282; www.chenche-berlin.de; Rosenthaler Strasse 13; dishes €7-11; ☺ noon-midnight; ☞; Ⓢ Rosenthaler Platz, Ⓜ M1) Settle down in the charming Zen garden or beneath the hexagonal chandelier of this exotic Vietnamese teahouse and pick from the small menu of steaming *pho* (soups), curries and noodle dishes served in traditional clay pots. Exquisite tea selection and small store.

Augustiner am Gendarmenmarkt
GERMAN €€

(Map p64; ☑ 030-2045 4020; www.augustiner-braeu-berlin.de; Charlottenstrasse 55; mains €6-19; ☺ 10am-2am; Ⓢ Französische Strasse) Tourists, concert-goers and hearty-food lovers rub shoulders at rustic tables in this surprisingly authentic Bavarian beer hall. Soak up the down-to-earth vibe right along with a mug of full-bodied Augustiner brew. Sausages, roast pork and pretzels provide rib-sticking sustenance, but there's also plenty of lighter (even meat-free) fare as well as good-value lunch specials.

★ Zenkichi
JAPANESE €€€

(Map p64; ☑ 030-2463 0810; www.zenkichi.de; Johannisstrasse 20; omakase €75, small plates €4.50-17; ☉ 6-11pm Tue-Sat; Ⓢ Oranienburger Tor, Friedrichstrasse, Ⓡ Friedrichstrasse) Tokyo meets Berlin at this lantern-lit basement izakaya serving authentic gourmet Japanese fare and supreme sake in cozy booths shielded by wooden bamboo blinds for extra privacy. Opt for the seasonally changing eight-course *omakase* (chef's) menu or put together your own selection from the small-plate à la carte menu.

Dae Mon
KOREAN €€€

(Map p64; ☑ 030-2630 4811; http://dae-mon.com; Monbijouplatz 11; small plates €6-28; ☉ 6-11pm Mon-Sat; Ⓜ M1, Ⓡ Hackescher Markt) This gourmet Korean restaurant with show kitchen is a treat for both palate and eyes. The dimly lit, black-on-black decor and sleek glass plates beautifully show off the contemporary small-plate compositions featuring primo ingredients such as lobster, king crab and kobe beef.

Katz Orange
INTERNATIONAL €€€

(Map p64; ☑ 030-983 208 430; www.katzorange. com; Bergstrasse 22; mains €18-26; ☉ 6-11pm; Ⓢ Rosenthaler Platz, Ⓜ M8) With its gourmet organic farm-to-table menu, stylish country flair and swift and smiling servers, the 'Orange Cat' hits a gastro grand slam. It will have you purring for Duroc pork that's been slow-roasted for 12 hours giving extra-rich flavour. The setting in a castle-like former brewery is stunning, especially in summer when the patio opens.

Weinbar Rutz
GERMAN €€€

(Map p64; ☑ 030-2462 8760; www.rutz-weinbar.de; Chausseestrasse 8; bar mains €16-23.50, 3-/4-course menu €44/54; ☉ 4-11pm Tue-Sat; Ⓢ Oranienburger Tor) Below his high-concept gourmet temple, Michelin-starred Marco Müller operates a more down-to-earth wine bar where the menu has a distinct earthy and carnivorous bent. Many of the meats and sausages are sourced from Berlin and surrounds. Finish up with a Berlin cheesecake with bramble-berries, walnuts and elderberry ice cream.

Pauly Saal
GERMAN €€€

(Map p64; ☑ 030-3300 6070; www.paulysaal. com; Auguststrasse 11-13; 2-/3-/4-course lunch €34/46/59, 4-/7-course dinner €68/97; ☉ noon-2pm & 6-9.30pm, bar to 2.30am Tue-Sat; Ⓢ Oranienburger Tor, Ⓜ M1, Ⓡ Oranienburger Strasse) Regionally hunted and gathered ingredients fused with exotic flavours steer the light and contemporary menu at this Michelin-starred restaurant. Set in the high-ceilinged gym of a Bauhaus-era former Jewish girls' school, the epicurean hotspot gets 1920s glam from Murano chandeliers and such eye-catching art work as Cosima von Bonin's giant red rocket.

On balmy days, sit beneath the old school yard's leafy trees.

✖ Potsdamer Platz & Tiergarten

Vapiano
ITALIAN €

(Map p64; ☑ 030-2300 5005; www.vapiano.de; Potsdamer Platz 5; mains €5.50-10; ☉ 10am-1am Mon-Sat, 10am-midnight Sun; Ⓜ 200, Ⓢ Potsdamer Platz, Ⓡ Potsdamer Platz) Matteo Thun's jazzy decor is a great foil for the tasty Italian fare at this successful German self-service chain. Mix-and-match pastas, creative salads and crusty pizzas are all prepared right before your eyes, and there's fresh basil on the table. Your order is recorded on a chip card and paid for upon leaving.

Desbrosses
FRENCH €€€

(Map p64; ☑ 030-337 775 402; www.desbrosses.de; Ritz-Carlton Berlin, Potsdamer Platz 3; mains €14-29; ☉ 6.30am-2.30pm Mon-Sat, to 3.30pm Sun, 5.30-11pm daily; ☎; Ⓜ 200, Ⓢ Potsdamer Platz, Ⓡ Potsdamer Platz) The original 1875 brasserie at the Ritz-Carlton was moved here from southern France and is anchored by an open kitchen where toqued chefs turn out French country classics, regional specials and vegan dishes. For a treat, book ahead for the legendary Sunday brunch (12.30pm to 3.30pm September to June; €98) with bottomless Champagne.

Facil
INTERNATIONAL €€€

(Map p76; ☑ 030-590 051 234; www.facil. de; 5th fl, Mandala Hotel, Potsdamer Strasse 3; 1-/2-/3-course lunch €19/34/45, 4-8 course dinner €108-185; ☉ noon-3pm & 7-11pm Mon-Fri; Ⓜ 200, Ⓢ Potsdamer Platz, Ⓡ Potsdamer Platz) With two Michelin stars to his name, Michael Kempf's fare is hugely innovative yet deliciously devoid of unnecessary flights of fancy. Enjoy it while draped in a sleek Donghia chair and surrounded by a bamboo garden. The glass ceiling can be retracted for al fresco dining in fine weather. Budget-minded gourmets take advantage of the lunchtime menu.

✕ Kreuzberg & Northern Neukölln

★ Burgermeister
AMERICAN €

(Map p76; ☑ 030-2388 3840; www.burgermeister. berlin; Oberbaumstrasse 8; burgers €3-4.50; ☺ 11am-3am Sun-Thu, to 4am Fri & Sat; ⑤ Schlesisches Tor) It's green, ornate, a century old and...it used to be a toilet. Now it's a burger joint beneath the elevated U-Bahn tracks. Get in line for the plump all-beef patties (try the Meisterburger with fried onions, bacon and barbecue sauce) paired with cheese fries and such homemade dips as peanut or mango curry.

Masaniello
ITALIAN €

(Map p76; ☑ 030-692 6657; www.masaniello.de; Hasenheide 20; pizza €6-9.50; ☺ noon-midnight; ⑤ Hermannplatz) Tables are almost too small for the wagon-wheel-size certified Neapolitan pizzas tickled by wood fire at this low-key pizzeria, whose spacious flowery terrace transports you to the boot on a balmy summer night. A vegan fave is the Pizza Contadina with eggplant, peppers, zucchini, mushrooms and artichokes.

Curry 36
GERMAN €

(Map p76; ☑ 030-251 7368; www.curry36.de; Mehringdamm 36; snacks €2-6; ☺ 9am-5am; ⑤ Mehringdamm) Day after day, night after night, a motley crowd – cops, cabbies, queens, office jockeys, savvy tourists etc – wait their turn at this top-ranked Currywurst purveyor that's been frying 'em up since 1981.

★ Cafe Jacques
INTERNATIONAL €€

(Map p76; ☑ 030-694 1048; Maybachufer 14; mains €12-20; ☺ 6pm-late; ⑤ Schönleinstrasse) A favourite with off-duty chefs and loyal foodies, Jacques infallibly charms with flattering candlelight, arty-elegant decor and fantastic wine. It's the perfect date spot but, quite frankly, you only have to be in love with good food to appreciate the French- and North African–inspired blackboard menu. Fish and meat are always tops and the pasta is homemade. Reservations essential.

Max und Moritz
GERMAN €€

(Map p76; ☑ 030-6951 5911; www.maxundmoritz-berlin.de; Oranienstrasse 162; mains €9.50-17; ☺ 5pm-midnight; ⑤ Moritzplatz) The patina of yesteryear hangs over this ode-to-old-school brewpub named for the cheeky Wilhelm Busch cartoon characters. Since 1902 it has packed hungry diners and drinkers into its rustic tile-and-stucco ornamented rooms for sudsy home brews and granny-style Berlin fare. A menu favourite is the *Kutschergulasch* (goulash cooked with beer).

Defne
TURKISH €€

(Map p76; ☑ 030-8179 7111; www.defne-restaurant.de; Planufer 92c; mains €8-20; ☺ 4pm-1am Apr-Sep, 5pm-1am Oct- Mar; ⑤ Kottbusser Tor, Schönleinstrasse) If you thought Turkish cuisine stopped at the doner kebab, canal-side Defne will teach you otherwise. The appetiser platter alone elicits intense cravings (fabulous walnut-chilli paste!), but inventive mains such as *ali nacik* (sliced lamb with puréed eggplant and yoghurt) also warrant repeat visits. Lovely summer terrace.

Cevicheria
PERUVIAN €€

(Map p76; ☑ 030-5562 4038; cevicheria-berlin.com; Dresdener Strasse 120; ceviche €8-18; ☺ noon-11pm Mon-Fri, 2-11pm Sat; ⑤ Kottbusser Tor, Moritzplatz) With this little joint, the global culinary craze for ceviche, Peru's national dish, has finally reached Berlin. Fish, shrimp, scallops, octopus or any combination thereof are marinated in lime and combined with coriander, onions and spices. Leave room for a 'Lima sigh', a dessert made from sweetened condensed milk and topped with meringue.

Freischwimmer
INTERNATIONAL €€

(Map p76; ☑ 030-6107 4309; www.freischwimmer-berlin.com; Vor dem Schlesischen Tor 2a; mains €8.50-20; ☺ noon-late Mon-Fri, 10am-late Sat & Sun; ⑤ Schlesisches Tor, ⓡ Treptower Park) In fine weather, few places are more idyllic than this rustic 1930s boathouse turned canal-side chill zone. The menu runs from meat and fish cooked on a lava rock grill to crisp salads, *Flammekuche* (French pizza) and seasonal specials. It's also a popular Sunday brunch spot (€12.90). Kayak and boat rentals available.

Henne
GERMAN €€

(Map p76; ☑ 030-614 7730; www.henne-berlin.de; Leuschnerdamm 25; half chicken €8.30; ☺ 6pm-midnight Tue-Sat, 5pm-midnight Sun; ⓜ M29, 140, 147, ⑤ Moritzplatz, Kottbusser Tor) This Old Berlin institution operates on the KISS (keep it simple, stupid!) principle: milk-fed chicken spun on the rotisserie for moist yet crispy perfection. That's all it's been serving for over a century, alongside tangy potato and white cabbage salads. Eat

ROSENTHALER PLATZ: SNACK CENTRAL

For feeding hunger pangs on the quick and cheap, choices could not be greater than the area around Rosenthaler Platz. Here's our personal hit list:

➡ **Rosenthaler Grill- und Schlemmerbuffet** (☎030-283 2153; Torstrasse 125; dishes €2.80-7) for Oscar-worthy doner kebabs

➡ **Rosenburger** (Map p64; ☎030-2408 3037; Brunnenstrasse 196; burgers €3-6; ⏰11am-3am Sun-Thu, to 5am Fri & Sat; [S] Rosenthaler Platz, 🚋M1, 12) for freshly made organic burgers

➡ **Côcô** (Map p64; ☎030-2463 0595; www.co-co.net; Rosenthaler Strasse 2; sandwiches €5-6.50; ⏰11am-10pm Mon-Thu, to 11pm Fri & Sat, noon-10pm Sun; [S] Rosenthaler Platz, 🚋M1, 12) for bulging *bánh mì* (Vietnamese sandwiches)

in the garden or in the cosy 1907 dining room that's resisted the tides of time. Reservations essential.

Sauvage Paleothek PALEO €€
(Map p76; ☎030-5316 7547; www.sauvageberlin.com; Pflügerstrasse 25; small plates €3-9; ⏰6-11pm Tue-Sun; [S] Hermannplatz) Berlin's first paleo restaurant opened in 2011 in a former brothel and has since spawned a fancier cousin in Prenzlauer Berg. Put together a stone-age meal from the constantly changing menu of animal- and plant-based paleo tapas. Typical choices: bone marrow on toast or pollock ceviche.

It also doubles as a meeting place for the paleo community and offers a library and cooking courses (in English).

Industry Standard FRENCH €€€
(Map p76; ☎030-6272 7732; www.industry-standard.de; Sonnenallee 83; small plates €9-15; ⏰6-11pm Wed-Sun; 🚌M41, [S] Rathaus Neukölln) The concept of bistronomy, ie casual fine dining, has not exactly made a splash in Berlin, but Industry Standard has set out to change that. In a deliberated improvised setting, it serves soulful simple food rooted in French cooking and put together in unexpected ways with top-notch ingredients. Signature dishes: beef tartar and bone marrow on toast.

eins44 FRENCH €€€
(Map p76; ☎030-6298 1212; www.eins44.com; Elbestrasse 28/29; mains lunch €6-8, dinner €22-25, 3-/4-/5-course meal €41/51/61; ⏰noon-3pm Tue-Fri, 7pm-midnight Tue-Sat; 🚌M41, 104, 167, [S] Hermannplatz) This fine-dining outpost in a late-19th-century distillery specialises in Franco-German cuisine from old-fashioned to postmodern. Metal lamps, tiles and heavy wooden tables create industrial charm enhanced by large black-and-white photos. Lunches are mellow, dinners trendy. The entrance is in the second courtyard.

Horváth AUSTRIAN €€€
(Map p76; ☎030-6128 9992; www.restaurant-horvath.de; Paul-Lincke-Ufer 44a; 4-/6-/8-/10-course menu €63/83/103/119; ⏰6-11pm Wed-Sun; [S] Kottbusser Tor) At his canal-side restaurant, Michelin-starred Sebastian Frank performs culinary alchemy with European classic dishes, fearlessly combining textures, flavours and ingredients. To truly test his talents, order the 10-course small-plate dinner. Despite the fanciful cuisine, the ambience in the elegantly rustic dining room remains relaxed. Nice summer terrace.

🍴 Friedrichshain

Lemon Leaf ASIAN €
(Map p76; ☎030-2900 9428; www.lemonleaf.de; Grünberger Strasse 69; mains €6-9; ⏰noon-midnight; 🌱; [S] Frankfurter Tor) Cheap and cheerful, this place is always swarmed by loyal locals, and for good reason: light, inventive and fresh, the Vietnamese menu has few false notes. Intriguing choice: the sweet-sour Indochine salad with banana blossoms.

Spätzle & Knödel GERMAN €€
(Map p76; ☎030-2757 1151; www.spaetzleknoedel.de; Wühlischstrasse 20; mains €7-14; ⏰5-11pm; [S] Samariterstrasse) This elbows-on-the-table gastropub is a great place to get your southern German comfort food fix, from roast pork with dark-beer gravy, goulash with red cabbage and of course the eponymous *Spätzle* (German mac 'n' cheese) and *Knödel* (dumplings). Bonus: Bavarian Riegele, Maisel and Weihenstephan beers on tap.

Schalander GERMAN €€
(☎030-8961 7073; www.schalander-berlin.de; Bänschstrasse 91; snacks €4-10, mains €9-17; ⏰4pm-late Mon-Fri, 3pm-late Sat, noon-late Sun; 📶; [S] Samariterstrasse, 🚋Frankfurter Allee) See the pub action reflected in the very shiny steel vats that churn out the full-bodied Pilsner, *Dunkel* (dark) and *Weizen* (wheat) at this old-school gastropub far off the tourist track. The menu is big on beer-hall-type

meaty mains along with *Flammkuche* (Alsatian pizza). For an unusual finish, order the wheat beer crème brûlée.

Lisboa Bar PORTUGUESE €€

(Map p76; ☎030-9362 1978; www.lisboa-bar-berlin.de; Krossener Strasse 20; tapas €3-10; ⏰11am-midnight; [S] Warschauer Strasse, Samariterstrasse, 🚋M13, 🚆Warschauer Strasse) The hearty tapas at this cosy Portuguese outpost are an excellent base for a dedicated neighbourhood pub crawl. Try the *pasteis de bacalhau* (fish dumplings), brandy shrimp or chicken in hot piri-piri sauce, or any of the weekly specials.

🍴 Prenzlauer Berg

Zia Maria ITALIAN €

(Map p82; www.zia-maria.de; Pappelallee 32a; pizza slices €1.50-3.50; ⏰noon-11.30pm; [S] Schönhauser Allee, 🚋12, 🚆Schönhauser Allee) Pizza kitchen-cum-gallery gets a big thumbs up for its freshly made crispy-crust pies with classic and eclectic toppings, including wafer-thin prosciutto, nutmeg-laced artichokes and pungent Italian sausage. Two slices are enough to fill up most.

Konnopke's Imbiss GERMAN €

(Map p82; ☎030-442 7765; www.konnopke-imbiss.de; Schönhauser Allee 44a; sausages €1.40-1.90; ⏰9am-8pm Mon-Fri, 11.30am-8pm Sat; [S] Eberswalder Strasse, 🚋M1, M10) Brave the inevitable queue at this famous sausage kitchen, ensconced in the same spot below the elevated U-Bahn track since 1930, but now equipped with a heated pavilion and an English menu. The 'secret' sauce topping their classic *Currywurst* comes in a four-part heat scale from mild to wild.

Habba Habba MIDDLE EASTERN €

(Map p82; ☎030-3674 5726; www.habba-habba.de; Kastanienallee 15; dishes €4-9; ⏰10am-10pm; 🌿; 🚋M1, 12, 🚆Eberswalder Strasse) This tiny Imbiss makes the best wraps in town for our money, especially the one stuffed with tangy pomegranate-marinated chicken and nutty buckwheat dressed in a minty yoghurt sauce. One bite and you're hooked. Also served as low-carb bowls and as vegetarian and vegan versions.

Chutnify INDIAN €

(Map p82; ☎030-4401 0795; www.chutnify.com; Sredzkistrasse 43; mains €6.50-8.50; ⏰noon-10pm Tue-Sun; [S] Eberswalder Strasse, 🚆Prenzlauer Allee) South Indian crêpes called dosas, filled with everything from potato masala to marinated pork and tandoori chicken, are the ammo at Aparna Aurora's little restaurant with its brick-wall-lined and cheerfully decorated dining room and spacious sidewalk terrace. Among the starters, the *bhelpuri* (an Indian street snack made from puffed rice, tomato and peanuts) is a stand-out.

★**La Soupe Populaire** GERMAN €€

(Map p64; ☎030-4431 9680; www.lasoupepopulaire.de; Prenzlauer Allee 242; mains €14-21; ⏰noon-2.30pm & 5.30-10.10pm Thu-Sat; [S] Senefelder Platz, 🚋M2) Helmed by local top toque Tim Raue, this industrial-chic gastro destination inside a defunct 19th-century brewery embraces the soulful goodness of German home-cooking. The star of the regular menu is Raue's riff on *Königsberger Klopse* (veal meatballs in caper sauce) but there's also a separate one inspired by changing art exhibits in the hall overlooked by the dining room.

Umami VIETNAMESE €€

(Map p82; ☎030-2886 0626; www.umami-restaurant.de; Knaackstrasse 16-18; mains €7.50-15; ⏰noon-11.30pm; [S] Senefelderplatz, 🚋M2) A mellow 1950s lounge-vibe and an inspired menu of Indochine home cooking divided into 'regular' and 'vegetarian' choices are the main draws of this corner restaurant. Top picks include the Deep Gold Beef with fresh mango strips and the Monk's Lunch featuring lemongrass-marinated seitan in caramelised soy-sauce. For drinks, there's exotic coffees, teas, fruit juices and cocktails.

Studio Tim Raue INTERNATIONAL €€

(Map p82; ☎030-4431 0950; http://factoryberlin.com/studio; Rheinsberger Strasse 76/77; lunch under €10, 4-10 course dinner €48-88; ⏰noon-2pm & 6.30-9.30pm Tue-Sat; [S] Bernauer Strasse) Decked out in eclectic vintage decor, the fourth outpost of Berlin kitchenmeister Tim Raue is part of Factory Berlin, a start-up tech campus that counts Mozilla and Soundcloud among its residents. The cooking is just as innovative, especially at dinnertime when the changing menu draws inspiration from the cuisines of the world. Budget gourmets should come for lunch.

Oderquelle GERMAN €€

(Map p82; ☎030-4400 8080; www.oderquelle.de; Oderberger Strasse 27; mains €10-20; ⏰6-11pm Mon-Sat, from noon Sun; [S] Eberswalder Strasse, 🚋M1, 12) It's always fun to pop by this woodsy resto and see what's inspired the chef today.

Most likely, it will be a well-crafted German meal, perhaps with a slight Mediterranean nuance. On the standard menu, the crispy *Flammkuche* (Alsatian pizza) is a reliable standby. Best seat: on the footpath so you can keep an eye on the parade of passers-by.

✖ City West & Charlottenburg

Good Friends   CHINESE €€

(Map p84; ☑ 030-313 2659; www.goodfriends-berlin.de; Kantstrasse 30; mains €7-32; ☺ noon-1am; ⓡ Savignyplatz) Good Friends is widely considered Berlin's best Cantonese restaurant. The ducks dangling in the window are the mere overture to a menu long enough to confuse Confucius and including plenty of authentic homestyle dishes. If sea cucumber with fish belly prove too challenging, you can always fall back on sweet-and-sour pork or fried rice with shrimp.

Café-Restaurant Wintergarten
im Literaturhaus   INTERNATIONAL €€

(Map p84; ☑ 030-882 5414; www.literaturhaus-berlin.de/wintergarten-cafe-restaurant.html; Fasanenstrasse 23; mains €8-16; ☺ 9am-midnight; Ⓢ Uhlandstrasse) The hustle and bustle of Ku'damm is only a block away from this genteel art nouveau villa with attached literary salon and bookstore. Tuck into seasonal bistro cuisine amid elegant Old Berlin flair in the gracefully stucco-ornamented rooms

or, if weather permits, in the idyllic garden. Breakfast is served until 2pm.

Neni   INTERNATIONAL €€

(Map p84; ☑ 030-120 221 200; www.neni.at/berlin; Budapester Strasse 40; mains €6-26; ☺ noon-11pm Mon-Fri, 12.30-11pm Sat & Sun; ◨ 100, 200, Ⓢ Bahnhof Zoologischer Garten, ⓡ Bahnhof Zoologischer Garten) This always-busy greenhouse-style dining hall at the 25hours Hotel Bikini Berlin presents a spirited menu inspired by the cuisines of such varied countries as Morocco, Israel and Austria. Grilled scallops, pulled chicken salad, felafel and reportedly the city's best hummus all make appearances. Views of the Berlin zoo and the city roofs from the 10th floor are a bonus.

Brauhaus Lemke   GERMAN €€

(☑ 030-3087 8979; www.brauhaus-lemke.com; Luisenplatz 1; mains €7-18; ☺ noon-midnight; ◨ M45, 109, 309, Ⓢ Richard-Wagner-Platz) This congenial tourist-geared beer hall serves soul-sustaining German fare alongside its homemade brews, including pils, wheat and seasonal specials. In summer the terrace tables with view of Charlottenburg Palace are much in demand.

Mr Hai Kabuki   JAPANESE €€

(Map p84; ☑ 030-8862 8136; www.mrhai.de; Olivaer Platz 9; platters from €14.50; ☺ noon-midnight; ◨ M19, 109, Ⓢ Adenauerplatz, Uhlandstrasse) Purists can stick to classic nigiri and maki but most regulars flock to Mr Hai for more unconventional sushi morsels, composed like

---

MOBILE KITCHEN CRAZE

The street food and food-truck phenomenon has finally taken Berlin by storm. The colourful mobile kitchens can be spotted throughout the city, usually at parties, events or open-air markets, with exact dates and locations posted on their Facebook pages.

The trend began making a splash back in 2013 with such pioneers as the indoor **Street Food Thursday** (www.markthalleneun.de/maerkte/street-food-thursday) at Markthalle Neun in Kreuzberg and the pop-up **Bite Club** (www.biteclub.de), **Burgers & Hip Hop** (www.facebook.com/burgersandhiphop), Beer & Beef and Thai & Techno parties. Burgers & Beef has since made occasional appearances at Prince Charles club in Kreuzberg, while Bite Club has established a biweekly summer residency on the Spree near the Badeschiff. In the meantime, several other culinary entrepreneurs have also jumped on the bandwagon.

On Sundays, **Village Market** (www.neueheimat.com) sets up trucks and stalls at Neue Heimat on the RAW grounds along Revaler Strasse in Friedrichshain. Luring everyone from bleary-eyed clubbers to hip families, it has a relaxed daytime party vibe with DJs, art projects and sometimes live jazz. If you're in Prenzlauer Berg, head to **Street Food auf Achse** (www.streetfoodaufachse.de) in the Kulturbrauerei, a platform for around 40 mobile kitchens in a 19th-century red-brick brewery turned cultural complex.

Note that these events only take place in the warmer months (usually May to September) and seem to come and go at the drop of a hat. Always check the websites before setting out.

little works of art. Creations feature kimchi, pumpkin or cream cheese or are flambéed and deep-fried. There's also a convincing selection of sake cocktails, including the Geisha with cassis, martini and lemon juice.

Dicke Wirtin
GERMAN €€

(Map p84; ☑030-312 4952; www.dicke-wirtin.de; Carmerstrasse 9; mains €6-16.50; ⊗11am-late; ⓡSavignyplatz) Old Berlin charm oozes from every nook and cranny of this been-here-forever pub which pours nine draught beers (including the superb Kloster Andechs) and nearly three dozen homemade schnapps varieties. Hearty local and German fare, such as smoked pork chop, beef liver and breaded schnitzel, keeps brains balanced. Bargain lunches, too.

Schleusenkrug
GERMAN €€

(Map p84; ☑030-313 9909; www.schleusenkrug.de; Müller-Breslau-Strasse; mains €8-15; ⊗10am-midnight May-Sep, to 7pm Oct-Apr; ⓢZoologischer Garten, ⓡZoologischer Garten) Sitting pretty on the edge of the Tiergarten, next to a Landwehrkanal lock, Schleusenkrug truly comes into its own during beer garden season. People from all walks of life hunker over big mugs and comfort food – from grilled sausages to *Flammkuche* (Alsatian pizza) and weekly specials. Breakfast is served until 3pm.

★Restaurant am Steinplatz
GERMAN €€€

(Map p84; ☑030-554 4440; www.marriott.de; Steinplatz 4; mains €17-26, 3-/4-course dinner €39/49; ⊗noon-2.30pm & 6.30-10.30pm; ☐M45, ⓢErnst-Reuter-Platz, Bahnhof Zoologischer Garten, ⓡBahnhof Zoologischer Garten) The 1920s gets a 21st-century makeover both in the kitchen and the decor at this stylish outpost. The dining room is anchored by an open kitchen where veteran chef Marcus Zimmer feeds regional products and herbs from his own garden into classic Berlin recipes. Even rustic beer-hall dishes such as *Eisbein* (boiled pork knuckle) are imaginatively reinterpreted and beautifully plated.

Restaurant Faubourg
FRENCH €€€

(Map p84; ☑030-800 999 7700; www.sofitel-berlin-kurfurstendamm.com; Augsburger Strasse 41; mains €20-38; ⊗noon-11pm; ⓢKurfürstendamm) Superb French-inspired dishes prepared either in classic or contemporary style, a stunning Bauhaus-style setting with original art and extravagant copper lamps as well as Germany's youngest sommelier make the Faubourg a standout among Berlin's hotel restaurants.

SCHÖNEBERG
Habibi
MIDDLE EASTERN €

(Map p87; ☑030-215 3332; Goltzstrasse 24; snacks €2.50-5; ⊗11am-3am Sun-Thu, to 5pm Fri & Sat; ⓢNollendorfplatz) *Habibi* means 'my beloved' and the object of obsession in this cheerfully painted, been-here-forever snack place is soul-sustaining felafel, best paired with a freshly pressed carrot juice. The shawarma is another good choice and great for restoring brain balance after a night on the razzle.

Ousies
GREEK €€

(☑030-216 7957; www.taverna-ousies.de; Grunewaldstrasse 54; dishes €4.40-19.50; ⊗5-10.30pm; ⓢBayerischer Platz) You'll be as exuberant as Zorba at this popular *ouzeria,* the Greek equivalent of a tapas bar. Ideally assemble a posse of friends and sample a variety of tantalising dishes, from *spalia* (stewed lamb shoulder) to *loukaniko* (homemade farmers' sausage) and grilled meats. The stone floor, warm lighting and wooden tables help conjure up a Greek holiday feeling.

Martha's
INTERNATIONAL €€€

(Map p87; ☑030-7800 6665; http://marthas.berlin; Grunewaldstrasse 81; mains €17-29.50; ⊗6-10.30pm Tue-Sun, bar 6pm-late; ⓢEisenacher Strasse) At his first solo venture, Michael Schmuck creates sophisticated yet affordable cuisine that follows the seasons while pushing the boundaries of culinary globalism. Such flavour combinations as pikeperch with poached oyster and Yuzu are fairly typical. The casually elegant dining space, with its stucco-ornamented ceiling and sleek backlit bar, invites lingering long after the last forkful.

Drinking & Nightlife

Berlin is a great place for boozers. From cosy pubs, riverside beach bars, chestnut-shaded beer gardens, underground dives, DJ bars, snazzy hotel lounges and designer cocktail temples, you're rarely far from a good time. Kreuzberg and Friedrichshain are currently the edgiest bar-hopping grounds, with swanky Mitte and Charlottenburg being more suited for date nights than dedicated late nights. The line between cafe and bar is often blurred, with many places changing stripes as the hands move around the clock.

Bars and cafes don't usually charge admission unless there is live music or some other event going on (and often not even then). Some bars add a euro or two to your first drink as a 'tip for the DJ'. Clubs charge

TRENDY TORSTRASSE

Though loud, ho-hum and heavily trafficked, Torstrasse is booming, and not just since Brangelina were rumoured to have bought a flat nearby. With surprising speed, this main thoroughfare has turned into a funkytown strip where trendy eats pop up with the frequency of fruit-fly births, gritty-glam bars pack in night crawlers and indie and design boutiques lure the style-savvy.

anywhere from a couple of euros to €15; sometimes admission is free during the first hour after opening. In terms of dress code, most of Berlin's clubs are quite relaxed. In general, individual style almost always beats high heels and Armani, and if your attitude is right, age rarely matters either.

 Mitte

Strandbar Mitte
BAR

(Map p64; 030-2838 5588; www.strandbar-mitte. de; Monbijoustrasse 3; 10am-late May-Sep; M1, Oranienburger Strasse) With a full-on view of the Bodemuseum, palm trees and a relaxed ambience, Germany's first beach bar (since 2002) is great for balancing a surfeit of sightseeing with a reviving drink and thin-crust pizza. At night, there's dancing under the stars with tango, cha cha, swing and salsa.

Larry
BAR

(Map p64; www.larryberlin.de; Chausseestrasse 131; Oranienburger Tor) Larry is a breath of fresh air among the chi-chi cocktail bars on Torstrasse and surrounds. This is a small, keep-it-real place with a crowd and drinks' menu to match. Cool retro sounds enliven the two rooms, each decorated with vintage slot machines and a 1977 pinball machine.

Butcher's
BAR

(Map p64; www.butcher-berlin.de; Torstrasse 116; 8.30pm-late Tue-Sat; Rosenthaler Platz, M1) Channeling PDT in New York, this furtive libation station in a former butchershop is entered via a red British phone booth tucked into a sausage parlour called Fleischerei. Drinks are expertly mixed and the ambience is refined, even if meat hooks, a leather bar and blood-red light play upon the place's early incarnation.

Mein Haus am See
CAFE, BAR

(Map p64; 030-2759 0873; www.mein-haus-am-see.blogspol.de, Brunnenstrasse 197/198; 24hr; Rosenthaler Platz, M1) This 'House by the Lake' is nowhere near anything liquid, unless you count the massive amount of beverages consumed at this multitasking all-hours cafe-bar, gallery, performance space and club. Plop down onto grandma's sofa for intimate chats or grab a seat on the staircase for stadium-style hipster-watching.

Berliner Republik
PUB

(Map p64; 030-3087 2293; www.die-berliner-republik.de; Schiffbauerdamm 8; 10am-6am; Friedrichstrasse, Friedrichstrasse) Just as in a mini-stock exchange, the price of beer (18 varieties on tap!) fluctuates with demand after 5pm at this riverside pub. Everyone goes Pavlovian when a heavy brass bell rings, signalling rock-bottom prices. In summer, seats on the terrace are the most coveted.

G&T Bar
BAR

(Map p64; www.amanogroup.de; Friedrichstrasse 113; 8pm-late; Oranienburger Tor, M1) In classic Berlin style, Germany's first drinking salon devoted to gin-based libations is appropriately dressed in Tanqueray green and tucked into the back of a courtyard off busy Friedrichstrasse. Here, even a basic gin and tonic is elevated to a complex cocktail concoction thanks to richly nuanced tea infusions that turn it into a so-called GT&T.

Lost in Grub Street
BAR

(Map p64; 030-2060 3780; http://lostingrubstreet.de; Jägerstrasse 34; from 6pm; Hausvogteiplatz) This cocktail bar packs a punch, so to speak. The focus here is on 'Big Bowls': huge stainless steel vessels filled with potent punch for classy and convivial sharing. If that's not your thing, opt for a 'short drink', creative cocktails made from such unusual cocktail ingredients as chocolate, carrot or jalapeños.

Clärchens Ballhaus
CLUB

(Map p64; 030-282 9295; www.ballhaus.de; Auguststrasse 24; 11am-late, dancing from 9pm or 9.30pm; M1, Oranienburger Strasse) Yesteryear is right now at this late, great 19th-century dance hall where groovers and grannies hoof it across the parquet without even a touch of irony. There are different sounds nightly – salsa to swing, tango to disco – and a live band on Saturday.

Pizza and German staples provide sustenance all day long (in summer in the pretty garden; pizza €5.50 to €11.50, mains €6.50 to €18). Dance lessons, dinners and classical Sunday afternoon concerts are held upstairs amid the stylishly faded grandeur of the *Spiegelsaal* (Mirror Hall).

Tresor CLUB

(Map p64; www.tresorberlin.com; Köpenicker Strasse 70; ⏲Mon, Wed, Fri & Sat; [S] Heinrich-Heine-Strasse) One of Berlin's original techno labels and dance temples, Tresor has all the right ingredients for success: the industrial maze of a derelict power station, awesome sound and still a fairly respectable DJ line-up. Look for the namesake vault in the basement at the end of a 30m-long tunnel. The door is relatively easy.

KitKatClub CLUB

(Map p64; www.kitkatclub.de; Köpenicker Strasse 76, enter via Brückenstrasse; ⏲Fri-Mon; [S] Heinrich-Heine-Strasse) This 'kitty' is naughty, sexy and decadent, listens to hip hop and house, and fancies leather and lace, vinyl and whips. Berlin's most (in)famous erotic nightclub hides out at Sage Club with its four dance floors, shimmering pool and fire-breathing dragon. The website has dress code tips.

Kaffee Burger CLUB

(Map p64; www.kaffeeburger.de; Torstrasse 60; [S] Rosa-Luxemburg-Platz) Nothing to do with either coffee or meat patties, this sweaty cult club with lovingly faded Commie-era decor is a fun-for-all concert and party pen with a sound policy that swings from indie and electro to *klezmer* punk without missing a beat. Also has readings and poetry slams.

House of Weekend CLUB

(Map p64; ☎reservations 030-3397 8804; www.houseofweekend.berlin; Am Alexanderplatz 5; ⏲roof garden from 7pm weather permitting, studio floor from 11pm; [S] Alexanderplatz, 🚆Alexanderplatz) In summer, the House of Weekend wows with sundowners, private cabanas and 360° views from its sophisticated rooftop terrace. After 11pm, the cadre of shiny happy people moves down to the 15th floor for hot-stepping electro with the occasional excursion into hip hop and dubstep courtesy of top local and visiting DJs.

🍷 Potsdamer Platz & Tiergarten

Café am Neuen See BEER GARDEN

(Map p84; ☎030-254 4930; www.cafeamneuensee.de; Lichtensteinallee 2; ⏲9am-11pm, beer garden from 11am Mon-Fri, from 10am Sat & Sun; 🚌200, [S] Zoologischer Garten, Tiergarten, 🚆Zoologischer Garten) Next to an idyllic pond in the southwestern section of Tiergarten, this restaurant gets jammed year-round for its sumptuous breakfast, pizza and seasonal fare, but really comes into its own during beer garden season. Enjoy a micro-vacation from the city bustle over a cold one or take your sweetie on a spin in a row boat.

Curtain Club BAR

(Map p64; ☎030-337 776 196; www.ritzcarlton.de; Ritz-Carlton Berlin, Potsdamer Strasse 3; ⏲from 6pm; 🚌200, [S] Potsdamer Platz, 🚆Potsdamer Platz) At 6pm sharp, a real former beefeater (Tower of London guard) ceremoniously pulls back the curtains on this clubby Ritz-Carlton bar, presided over by cocktail-meister Arnd Heissen. The martini selection is certainly impressive, but Heissen's true calling is perfume-inspired cocktails such as Hypnôse featuring rose-blossom vodka, lemon, viola, passion fruit and vanilla.

Solar BAR

(Map p76; ☎0163 765 2700; www.solar-berlin.de; Stresemannstrasse 76; ⏲6pm-2am Sun-Thu, to 4am Fri & Sat; 🚆Anhalter Bahnhof) Watch the city light up from this 17th-floor glass-walled sky lounge above a posh restaurant (mains €17 to €34). With its dim lighting, soft black leather couches and breathtaking views, it's a great spot for a date or sunset drinks. Even getting there aboard an exterior glass lift is half the fun. The entrance is behind the Pit Stop auto shop.

🍷 Kreuzberg & Northern Neukölln

★ Schwarze Traube COCKTAIL BAR

(Map p76; ☎030-2313 5569; www.schwarzetraube.de; Wrangelstrasse 24; ⏲7pm-2am Sun-Thu, to 5pm Fri & Sat; [S] Görlitzer Bahnhof) Mixologist Atalay Aktas was Germany's Best Bartender of 2013 and this pint-sized drinking parlour is where he and his staff create their magic potions. Since there's no menu, each drink is calibrated to the taste and mood of each patron using premium spirits, expertise and a dash of psychology.

Hopfenreich PUB

(Map p76; ☎030-8806 1080; www.facebook.com/hopfenreichberlin; Sorauer Strasse 31; ⏲4pm-2am Mon-Thu, to 3am Fri-Sun; [S] Schlesisches Tor) Berlin's first dedicated craft beer bar has 14 ales, IPAs and other brews from around the world on tap, including local labels Heidenpeters and Hops & Barley, plus around three dozen bottled varieties. It's all served in a cosy corner pub near the Schlesische Strasse party mile. Tastings, tap takeovers and guest brewers keep things in flux.

Würgeengel BAR

(Map p76; ☎030-615 5560; www.wuergeengel.de; Dresdener Strasse 122; ⏲7pm-late; [S]Kottbusser Tor) For a swish night out, point the compass to Würgeengel, a stylish art deco–style bar with lots of chandeliers and shiny black surfaces. It's always busy but especially so after the final credits roll at the adjacent Babylon cinema.

Locke Müller COCKTAIL BAR

(Map p76; ☎0176 2430 2393; www.lockemueller.de; Spreewaldplatz 14; ⏲7.30pm-4.30am; [S]Görlitzer Bahnhof) This pretense-free, retro-smart bar is named for a fictitious local boxer whose image graces a wall along with dozens of old parking tickets. The dedicated bartenders are not shy about applying their classic training to boundary-pushing experimental concotions, but can also please those with more conventional inclinations.

Twinpigs BAR

(Map p76; Boddinstrasse 57a; ⏲4pm-3am Tue-Sun; [S]Rathaus Neukölln) Deftly mixed cocktails – both classic and with a twist – as well as craft beer by local purveyors Heidenpeters and Rollberger characterise the drinks menu at this elegantly woodsy hangout. The vibe is mellow and the sound levels are conversation-friendly during the week. DJs get the crowd dancing on weekends.

Klunkerkranich BAR

(Map p76; www.klunkerkranich.de; Karl-Marx-Strasse 66; ⏲10am-1.30am Mon-Sat, noon-1.30am Sun, weather permitting; [S]Rathaus Neukölln) During the warmer months, this club-garden-bar combo opens up on the rooftop parking deck of the Neukölln Arcaden shopping mall. They do breakfast, light lunches and tapas, but it is mostly a fab place for sundowners while chilling to local DJs or bands. Get there via the lifts behind the 'Bibliothek/Post' entrance of Karl-Marx-Strasse (5th floor).

Monarch Bar BAR

(Map p76; www.kottimonarch.de; Skalitzer Strasse 134; ⏲from 9pm Tue-Sat; [S]Kottbusser Tor) Behind a long window front, eye level with the elevated U-Bahn tracks, Monarch is an ingenious blend of trashy sophistication, an international crowd, strong drinks and danceable tunes beyond the mainstream. Enter via the signless steel door adjacent to the doner kebab shop. Smoking OK.

Madame Claude PUB

(Map p76; ☎030-8411 0859; www.madameclaude.de; Lübbener Strasse 19; ⏲from 7pm; [S]Schlesisches Tor, Görlitzer Bahnhof) Gravity is upended at this David Lynchian booze burrow where the furniture dangles from the ceiling and the moulding is on the floor. There are concerts, DJs and events every night, including eXperimondays, Wednesday's music quiz night and open-mike Sundays. The name honours a famous French prostitute – *très apropos* given the place's bordello pedigree.

Möbel Olfe PUB

(Map p76; ☎030-2327 4690; www.moebel-olfe.de; Reichenberger Strasse 177; ⏲from 6pm Tue-Sun; [S]Kottbusser Tor) An old furniture store has been recast as a pleasantly trashy and always-busy drinking den with cheap Polish beer and a friendly crowd that's usually mixed but goes predominantly gay on Thursdays and girl on Tuesdays. Enter via Dresdener Strasse.

Club der Visionäre CLUB

(Map p76; ☎030-6951 8942; www.clubdervisionaere.com; Am Flutgraben 1; ⏲2pm-late Mon-Fri, noon-late Sat & Sun; [S]Schlesisches Tor, [R]Treptower Park) It's cold beer, crispy pizza and fine electro at this summertime chill and party playground in an old canal-side boatshed. Park yourself beneath the weeping willows, stake out some turf on the upstairs deck or hit the tiny dance floor. To keep the party going year-round, CDV expanded to the Hoppetosse boat moored nearby in the Spree in 2015.

Ritter Butzke CLUB

(Map p76; www.ritterbutzke.de; Ritterstrasse 24; ⏲Thu-Sat; [S]Moritzplatz) Ritter Butzke is a former bathroom fittings factory turned Kreuzberg party circuit fixture. Wrinkle-free hipsters hit the four floors for high-quality electronic music spun by both DJ legends and the latest sound spinners of the deep house and techno scenes.

Prince Charles CLUB

(Map p76; ☎030-200 950 933; www.princecharlesberlin.com; Prinzenstrasse 85F; ⏲from 7pm Wed-Sat; [S]Moritzplatz) Prince Charles is a stylish mix of club and bar ensconced in a former pool and overlooked by a kitschy-cute fish mural. Electro, techno and house rule the turntables. The venue also hosts concerts, gay parties and the 'Burgers & Hip Hop' street food party. In summer, the action spills into the courtyard.

SO36 CLUB
(Map p76; ☎030-6140 1306; www.so36.de; Oranienstrasse 190; ⏰nightly; [S] Kottbusser Tor) This legendary club began as an artist squat in the early 1970s and soon evolved into Berlin's seminal punk venue, known for wild concerts by the Dead Kennedys, Die Ärzte and Einstürzende Neubauten. The crowd depends on the night's program: electro party, punk concert, lesbigay tea dance, night flea market – anything goes.

Watergate CLUB
(Map p76; ☎030-6128 0394; www.water-gate.de; Falckensteinstrasse 49a; ⏰from midnight Wed, Fri & Sat; [S] Schlesisches Tor) For a short night's journey into day, check into this high-octane riverside club with two floors, panoramic windows and a floating terrace overlooking the Oberbaumbrücke and Universal Music. Top DJs keep electro-hungry hipsters hot and sweaty till way past sunrise. Long queues, tight door.

Friedrichshain

★Neue Heimat BAR
(Map p76; www.neueheimat.com; Revaler Strasse 99, enter near Dirschauer Strasse; ⏰6pm-4am Thu-Sat, noon-2am Sun; [S] Warschauer Strasse, 🚋M13, 🚋Warschauer Strasse) The Neue Heimat is a true chameleon: bar, club, concert venue, gallery and creative event space and Sunday street food market, all taking place in two industrial halls with outdoor areas on the RAW Gelände party compound. No matter what's on the schedule, though, you'll always be able to get a drink.

★Briefmarken Weine WINE BAR
(Map p76; ☎030 4202 5292; www.briefmarken-weine.de; Karl-Marx-Allee 99; ⏰7pm-midnight; [S] Weberwiese) For *dolce vita* right on socialist Karl-Marx-Allee, head to this charmingly nostalgic Italian wine bar ensconced in a former stamp shop. The original wooden cabinetry now holds a handpicked selection of bottles from Italy while old black-and-white movies are projected onto walls with faded wallpaper. For eats, there's a daily pasta and quality cheeses, prosciutto and salami.

Fairytale Bar COCKTAIL BAR
(Map p82; ☎0170 219 5155; Am Friedrichshain 24; ⏰6.30pm-2.30am Wed-Sat; 🚌200, 🚋M4) Once upon a time there was a bar in Berlin that whisked you into a magical world with bewitchingly costumed staff, mirrors that turned your eyes square and a menu that looked like a pop-up fairytale book. Get lost in this expressionist riff on *Alice in Wonderland* with such fanciful cocktails as Black Knight or Frog Prince.

Booze Bar BAR
(Map p76; ☎030-9559 1145; www.facebook.com/booze.bar.berlin; Boxhagener Strasse 105; ⏰7pm-2am Mon-Thu, to 5pm Fri & Sat, to 1am Sun; [S] Samariterstrasse) Sink into comfy lounge sofas, surrounded by warmly lit brick walls and a photograph of actor Terence Hill, a cigarette coolly stuck between his lips. The ambience is relaxed and the classic drinks finely crafted by a young team. DJs hit the decks from Wednesday to Saturday.

Jigger, Beaker & Glass COCKTAIL BAR
(Map p76; ☎0157 5675 5726; www.facebook.com/jiggerbeakerglass; Gärtnerstrasse 15; ⏰7pm-3am Wed-Sun; [S] Samariter Strasse) Named for a 1930s book of cocktail recipes collected by American author Charles H Baker on his travels, this dimly lit drinking den dishes out primarily Prohibition-era cocktails. The two owners, both well-known Berlin barmeisters, like to get creative with such out-there ingredients as sesame-oil-infused rum, pickle juice or bacon-flavoured gin, usually with convincing results.

Hops & Barley PUB
(Map p76; ☎030-2936 7534; www.hopsandbarley-berlin.de; Wühlischstrasse 22/23; ⏰from 5pm Mon-Fri, from 3pm Sat & Sun; [S] Warschauer Strasse, Samariterstrasse, 🚋Warschauer Strasse, Ostkreuz) Conversation flows as freely as the unfiltered Pilsner, malty *Dunkel* (dark) and fruity *Weizen* (wheat) produced right at one of Berlin's oldest craft breweries inside a former butcher's shop. For variety, the brewmeisters also produce weekly blackboard specials and potent cider. Two beamers project soccer games.

Crack Bellmer BAR, CLUB
(Map p76; www.crackbellmer.de; RAW Gelände, enter near Simon-Dach-Strasse; ⏰from 7pm; [S] Warschauer Strasse, 🚋M13, 🚋Warschauer Strasse) Behind the requisite street-art-festooned facade awaits an industrial-chic space with vintage sofas, lofty ceilings and chandeliers. Popular for pre-party warm-ups, post-party night caps and any time in between, including the Sunday afternoon swing tea dance.

PARTY MILES

➤ **Torstrasse, Mitte** A globe-spanning roster of shiny, happy hipsters populates the shabby-chic drinking dens lining this noisy thoroughfare.

➤ **Oranienburger Strasse, Mitte** Hopscotch around sex workers and pub crawlers to find the few remaining thirst parlours worth your money.

➤ **Kottbusser Tor/Oranienstrasse, Kreuzberg** Grunge-tastic area perfect for dedicated drink-a-thons with alternative flair.

➤ **Schlesische Strasse, Kreuzberg** Freestyle strip where you could kick off with cocktails at Badeschiff, catch a band at Magnet Club and dance till sunrise at Watergate or Club der Visionäre.

➤ **Skalitzer Strasse, Kreuzberg** Eclectic, more local-flavoured street with some quality cocktail bars just off it.

➤ **Weserstrasse, Neukölln** The main party drag in this hipster hood is packed with an eclectic mix of pubs and bars, from trashy to stylish.

➤ **RAW Gelände, Friedrichshain** The skinny-jeanster set invades the gritty clubs and bars along this 'techno strip' set up in a former train repair station.

➤ **Simon-Dach-Strasse, Friedrichshain** If you need a cheap buzz, head to this well-trodden booze strip popular with field-tripping school groups and stag parties.

Berghain/Panorama Bar   CLUB
(Map p76; www.berghain.de; Am Wriezener Bahnhof; ⊙ midnight Fri to Mon morning; ⬛ Ostbahnhof) Only world-class spinmasters heat up this hedonistic bass junkie hellhole inside a labyrinthine ex-power plant. Hard-edged minimal techno dominates the ex-turbine hall (Berghain) while house dominates at Panorama Bar one floor up. Strict door, no cameras. Check the website for midweek concerts and record-release parties at the main venue and the adjacent **Kantine am Berghain** (Map p76; ✆ 030-2936 0210; www.berghain.de; Am Wriezener Bahnhof; ⊙ hours vary; ⬛ Ostbahnhof).

://about blank   CLUB
(www.aboutparty.net; Markgrafendamm 24c; ⊙ varies, always Fri & Sat; ⬛ Ostkreuz) At this industrial-flavoured party pen with garden, a steady line-up of top DJs feeds a diverse bunch of revellers dance-worthy electronic gruel during intense club nights that usually segue into the morning and beyond. Run by a collective, the venue also hosts cultural and political events.

Suicide Circus   CLUB
(Map p76; www.suicide-berlin.com; Revaler Strasse 99; ⊙ always Fri & Sat, other days vary; ⬛ Warschauer Strasse, ⬛ Warschauer Strasse) Tousled hipsters hungry for an eclectic electro shower invade this gritty dancing den equipped with a top-notch sound system that occasionally brings DJ royalty behind the decks.

In summer, watch the stars fade on the outdoor floor.

🍺 Prenzlauer Berg

Prater Biergarten   BEER GARDEN
(Map p82; ✆ 030-448 5688; www.pratergarten.de; Kastanienallee 7-9; ⊙ noon-late Apr-Sep, weather permitting; Ⓢ Eberswalder Strasse) Berlin's oldest beer garden has seen beer-soaked nights since 1837 and is still a charismatic spot for guzzling a custom-brewed Prater Pilsner beneath the ancient chestnut trees (self-service). Kids can romp around the small play area.

In foul weather, and in winter, the adjacent beer hall is a fine place to sample classic Berlin dishes (mains €8 to €20).

Le Croco Bleu   COCKTAIL BAR
(Map p64; ✆ 0151 5824 7804; www.lecrocobleu.com; Prenzlauer Allee 242; ⊙ 6pm-late Thu-Sat; Ⓢ Rosa-Luxemburg-Strasse, Senefelder Platz, ⬛ M2) Berlin cocktail luminary Gregor Scholl's newest 'laboratory' occupies the machine room of a defunct 19th-century brewery. Amid stuffed animals, mushroom tables and other whimsical Hansel-and-Gretel decor, you get to enjoy extravagant twists on time-tested classics. Fairy Floss – a Sazerac topped with absinthe-laced cotton candy – never fails to elicit oohs and aahs.

Becketts Kopf COCKTAIL BAR
(Map p82; ☎030-9900 5188; www.becketts-kopf.de; Pappelallee 64; 🕐8pm-late; [S]Schönhauser Allee, 🚋12, 🚆Schönhauser Allee) Past Samuel Beckett's portrait, the art of cocktail-making is taken very seriously. Settle into a heavy armchair in the warmly lit lounge and take your sweet time to peruse the extensive – and poetic – drinks menu. All the classics are accounted for, of course, but it's the seasonal special concoctions that truly stimulate the senses.

Bryk Bar COCKTAIL BAR
(Map p82; ☎030-3810 0165; www.bryk-bar.com; Rykestrasse 18; 🕐noon-2am Sun-Thu, to 3am Fri & Sat; [S]Eberswalder Strasse) Both vintage and industrial elements contribute to the unhurried, dapper ambience at this darkly lit non-smoking bar. Cocktails are potent, deftly mixed and bear conversation-inspiring names such as 'Oily Bondage for Beginners' and 'Holy Shit – Is that Mary?' (their Bloody Mary capped with celery foam).

Deck 5 BAR
(Map p82; www.freiluftrebellen.de; Schönhauser Allee 80; 🕐noon-midnight, usually Apr-Sep, weather permitting; [S]Schönhauser Allee, 🚋M1, 🚆Schönhauser Allee) Soak up the rays and the grand city views at this beach bar in the sky while sinking your toes into tonnes of sand on the top parking deck of the Schönhauser Arkaden mall. To get there, take the lift from within the mall or walk up a never-ending flight of stairs from Greifenhagener Strasse.

Bassy CLUB
(Map p82; ☎030-3744 8020; www.bassy-club.de; Schönhauser Allee 176a; 🕐9pm-late; [S]Senefelderplatz) Most punters here have a post-Woodstock birth date, but happily ride the retro wave at this trashy-charming concert and party den dedicated 'strictly' to pre-1969 sounds – surf music, rockabilly, swing and country among them. Concerts, burlesque cabaret and the infamous Chantals House of Shame (p99) gay party on Thursdays beef up the schedule. Dress…creatively.

August Fengler BAR, CLUB
(Map p82; www.augustfengler.de; Lychener Strasse 11; 🕐7pm-4am; [S]Eberswalder Strasse, 🚋M1) With its flirty vibe, tiny dance floor and foosball in the cellar, this local institution scores a trifecta on key ingredients for a good night out. Wallet-friendly drinks prices and a pretence-free crowd don't hurt either. Music-wise anything goes, from new wave, rock and latin to soul, indie and ska.

🍷 Charlottenburg & Schöneberg

Monkey Bar BAR
(Map p84; ☎030-120 221 210; www.25hours-hotel.com; Budapester Strasse 40; 🕐noon-1am Sun-Thu, to 2am Fri & Sat; 📶; 🚌100, 200, [S]Bahnhof Zoologischer Garten, 🚆Bahnhof Zoologischer Garten) On the 10th floor of the 25hours Hotel Bikini Berlin, this 'urban jungle' hotspot delivers fabulous views of the city and the Berlin Zoo – in summer from a sweeping terrace. Drinks-wise, the list gives prominent nods to tiki concoctions and gin-based cocktail sorcery.

Stagger Lee COCKTAIL BAR
(Map p87; ☎030-2903 6158; www.staggerlee.de; Nollendorfstrasse 27; 🕐7pm-2am; [S]Nollendorfplatz) Belly up to the polished wooden bar or plop down on chocolate-hued Chesterfield sofas at this sophisticated cocktail saloon, which mixes and pours the tried and true, with a base of rye, bourbon and tequila. The name channels a famous 19th-century St Louis murderer immortalised in song by everyone from Nick Cave to The Clash.

Green Door COCKTAIL BAR
(Map p87; ☎030-215 2515; www.greendoor.de; Winterfeldtstrasse 50; 🕐6pm-3am Sun-Thu, to 4am Fri & Sat; [S]Nollendorfplatz) A long line of renowned mixologists has presided over this softly lit bar behind the eponymous green door – a nod to Prohibition-era speakeasies. Amid walls sheathed in gingham and '70s swirls, you can choose from over 500 cocktails, including some potent house concoctions.

☆ Entertainment

Sometimes it seems as though Berliners are the lotus eaters of Germany, people who love nothing better than a good time. Pack some

MUSICAL LUNCHES

Give your feet a rest and your ears a workout during the free lunchtime chamber music concerts held in the foyer of the Berliner Philharmonie every Tuesday at 1pm between early September and mid-June. A cafe serves refreshments and light lunches.

stamina if you want to join them. With no curfew, this is a notoriously late city, where bars stay packed from dusk to dawn, and some clubs don't hit their stride until 6am.

Zitty and *Tip* are the most widely read of the biweekly German-language listings magazines available at newsstands. Party-oriented *030* is a decent freezine. For up-to-the-minute happenings, also check www.sugarhigh.de and www.ronorp.net. The English-language monthly *Ex-Berliner* also has some information.

Credit-card bookings by telephone or online through a venue's box office are now fairly common, although many only take reservations and then make you pick up tickets in person. Ticket agencies (*Theaterkasse*) are commonly found in shopping malls and charge sometimes-steep service fees. The main online agency is www.eventim.de. Hekticket (www.hekticket.de) sells half-price tickets after 2pm for select same-day performances online and in person at its outlets near Zoo Station and Alexanderplatz. For indie concerts and events, the best agency is **Koka 36** (Map p76; ☎030-6110 1313; www.koka36.de; Oranienstrasse 29; ⏲9am-7pm Mon-Fri, 10am-4pm Sat; [S] Kottbusser Tor) in Kreuzberg.

Live Music

Lido LIVE MUSIC

(Map p76; ☎030-6956 6840; www.lido-berlin.de; Cuvrystrasse 7; [S] Schlesisches Tor) A 1950s cinema has been recycled into a rock-indie-electro-pop mecca with mosh-pit electricity and a crowd that cares more about the music than about looking good. Global DJs and talented upwardly mobile live noise-makers pull in the punters. Holds legendary Balkan-beats parties every few weeks.

Astra Kulturhaus LIVE MUSIC

(Map p76; ☎tickets 030-611 0133; www.astra-berlin.de; Revaler Strasse 99; [S] Warschauer Strasse, [R] Warschauer Strasse) With space for 1500, Astra is one of the bigger indie venues in town, yet often fills up easily, and not just when international headliners hit the stage. The party roster lures punters with electro swing, indie rock, electro and other sounds across the spectrum. Bonus: the sweet '50s East Berlin decor.

Magnet Club LIVE MUSIC

(Map p76; www.magnet-club.de; Falckensteinstrasse 48; [S] Schlesisches Tor) This indie and alt-sound bastion is known for bookers with an astronomer's ability to detect stars in the making. After the last riff, the crowd hits the dance floor to – depending on the night – rock, trash, hip hop, metal or punk.

A-Trane JAZZ

(Map p84; ☎030-313 2550; www.a-trane.de; Bleibtreustrasse 1; ⏲8pm-1am Sun-Thu, 8pm-late Fri & Sat; [R] Savignyplatz) Herbie Hancock and Diana Krall have graced the stage of this intimate jazz club, but mostly it's emerging talent bringing their A-game to the A-Trane. Entry is free on Monday when local boy Andreas Schmidt shows off his skills, and after 12.30am on Saturday for the late-night jam session.

b-Flat LIVE MUSIC

(Map p64; ☎030-283 3123; www.b-flat-berlin.de; Rosenthaler Strasse 13; ⏲8pm-late Sun-Thu, 9pm-late Fri & Sat; [S] Rosenthaler Platz, 🚋M1) Cool cats of all ages come out to this intimate venue for jazz and acoustic music, where the audience sits within spitting distance of the performers. Mal Waldron, Randy Brecker and even Mikis Theodorakis have graced its stage. Wednesday's free jam session often brings down the house.

Classical & Opera

Berliner Philharmonie CLASSICAL MUSIC

(Map p76; ☎tickets 030-254 888 999; www.berliner-philharmoniker.de; Herbert-von-Karajan-Strasse 1; 🚌200, [S] Potsdamer Platz, [R] Potsdamer Platz) This world-famous concert hall has supreme acoustics and, thanks to Hans Scharoun's clever terraced vineyard design, not a bad seat in the house. It's the home turf of the Berliner Philharmoniker, who will be led by Sir Simon Rattle until 2018

> **DON'T MISS**
>
> **BEARPIT KARAOKE**
>
> Roughly from late spring to autumn, Berlin's greatest free entertainment kicks off on Sundays around 3pm when Joe Hatchiban sets up his custom-made mobile karaoke unit in the Mauerpark's amphitheatre. As many as 2000 people cram onto the stone seats to cheer and clap for eager crooners ranging from giggling 11 year olds to Broadway-calibre belters. Give generously when Joe passes the coffee can, for this show must go on forever. For more information, go to www.bearpitkaraoke.com.

when Russia-born Kirill Petrenko will pick up the baton as music director. Chamber music concerts take place at the adjacent Kammermusiksaal.

Konzerthaus Berlin CLASSICAL MUSIC
(Map p64; ☑ tickets 030-203 092 101; www.konzerthaus.de; Gendarmenmarkt 2; Ⓢ Stadtmitte, Französische Strasse) This top-ranked concert hall – a Schinkel design from 1821 – counts the Konzerthausorchester Berlin as its 'house band', but also hosts international soloists, thematic concert cycles, children's events and concerts by the Rundfunk-Sinfonieorchester Berlin. Guided tours (€6, in German) at 1pm on Saturdays.

Staatsoper im Schiller Theater OPERA
(Map p84; ☑ information 030-2035 4438, tickets 030-2035 4555; www.staatsoper-berlin.de; Bismarckstrasse 110; Ⓢ Ernst-Reuter-Platz) Point your highbrow compass towards the Daniel Barenboim–led Staatsoper, Berlin's top opera company. While its historic digs on Unter den Linden are getting a facelift, the high-calibre productions are staged at the Schiller Theater in Charlottenburg. All operas are sung in their original language.

Deutsche Oper Berlin OPERA
(Map p84; ☑ 030-3438 4343; www.deutscheoperberlin.de; Bismarckstrasse 35; Ⓢ Deutsche Oper) The German Opera was founded by local citizens in 1912 as a counterpoint to the royal opera (today's Staatsoper) on Unter den Linden. The original building was destroyed in WWII and rebuilt by 1961 as a huge, modernist venue with seating for nearly 1900 opera aficionados. It boasts a repertory of around 70 operas, all sung in their original language.

Cabaret & Varieté

Admiralspalast PERFORMING ARTS
(Map p64; ☑ tickets 030-2250 7000; www.admiralspalast.de; Friedrichstrasse 101; Ⓢ Friedrichstrasse, 🚇 M1, 🚌 Friedrichstrasse) This beautifully restored 1920s 'palace' stages crowd-pleasing international plays, concerts and comedy shows in its glamorous historic main hall. More intimate programs are presented on the smaller studio stage on the 4th floor. Most performances are suitable for non-German speakers, but do check ahead.

Bar Jeder Vernunft CABARET
(Map p84; ☑ 030-883 1582; www.bar-jeder-vernunft.de; Schaperstrasse 24; Ⓢ Spichernstrasse) Life's still a cabaret at this intimate 1912 mirrored art nouveau tent, which puts on sophisti-

cated song-and-dance shows, comedy and *chanson* nightly. Seating is in upholstered booths or at little cafe tables, both with waiter service.

Chamäleon Varieté CABARET
(Map p64; ☑ 030-400 0590; www.chamaeleonberlin.com; Rosenthaler Strasse 40/41; 🚇 M1, 🚌 Hackescher Markt) A marriage of art-nouveau charms and high-tech theatre trappings, this intimate 1920s-style venue in an old ballroom hosts classy variety shows – comedy, juggling acts and singing – often in sassy, sexy and unconventional fashion.

Table service is offered before the show and during intermission.

Friedrichstadt-Palast CABARET
(Map p64; ☑ 030-2326 2326; www.palast.berlin; Friedrichstrasse 107; Ⓢ Oranienburger Tor, 🚇 M1) Europe's largest revue theatre has a tradition going back to the 1920s and is famous for glitzy-glam Vegas-style productions with leggy showgirls, a high-tech stage, mind-boggling special effects and abundant artistry.

Cinemas

The following venues all screen English-language films. In summer, watching movies al fresco in a *Freiluftkino* (outdoor cinema) is a venerable tradition. Check the listings mags for what's on where.

Arsenal CINEMA
(Map p76; ☑ 030-2695 5100; www.arsenal-berlin.de; Sony Center, Potsdamer Strasse 2; 🚌 200, Ⓢ Potsdamer Platz, 🚌 Potsdamer Platz) The antithesis of popcorn culture, this artsy twin-screen cinema features a bold global flick schedule that hopscotches from Japanese satire to Brazilian comedy and German road movies. Many films have English subtitles.

SHOPPING BY NEIGHBOURHOOD

➡ **Scheunenviertel** Hipster central with edgy international labels alongside local fashions and accessories in chic boutiques.

➡ **Friedrichstrasse/Gendarmenmarkt** Material-girl heaven with lots of hip big-ticket designer labels and exclusive concept stores.

➡ **Prenzlauer Berg** (eg Kastanienallee, Stargarder Strasse, around Kollwitzplatz) Berlin-made fashions, niche boutiques, anything for children and a fabulous flea market.

➡ **CityWest & Charlottenburg** Mainstream on Kurfürstendamm, indie boutiques in the side streets, concept stores at Bikini Berlin, homewares on Kantstrasse.

➡ **Kreuzberg & Neukölln** Vintage fashion and streetwear along with music and accessories, all in indie boutiques. Hubs include Oranienstrasse and Bergmannstrasse.

➡ **Schöneberg** Well-edited lifestyle boutiques for grown-up good-life lovers.

➡ **Friedrichshain** Wühlischstrasse and around for sassy fashions by small local labels.

Babylon CINEMA

(Map p64; ☎030-242 5969; www.babylonberlin.de; Rosa-Luxemburg-Strasse 30; [S] Rosa-Luxemburg-Platz) This top-rated indie screens a well-curated potpourri of cinematic expression, from new German films and international art-house flicks to themed retrospectives and other stuff you'd never catch at the multiplex. For silent movies, the original theatre organ is put through its paces. Also hosts occasional readings and concerts.

It's in a fabulous protected 1920s building by New Objectivity wizard Hans Poelzig.

Cinestar Original im Sony Center CINEMA

(Map p76; ☎030-2606 6400; www.cinestar.de; Potsdamer Strasse 4, Sony Center; [S] Potsdamer Platz, [U] Potsdamer Platz) A favourite among English-speaking expats and Germans, this state-of-the-art cinema with nine screens, comfy seats and the top technology shows the latest Hollywood blockbusters in 2D and 3D, all in English, all the time.

Theatre

Most plays are performed in German, naturally, but of late several of the major stages have started using English surtitles in some of their productions, including those listed here.

English Theatre Berlin THEATRE

(Map p76; ☎030-691 1211; www.etberlin.de; Fidicinstrasse 40; [S] Platz der Luftbrücke) Berlin's oldest English-language theatre puts on an engaging roster of in-house productions, plays by international visiting troupes, concerts, comedy, dance and cabaret.

Deutsches Theater THEATRE

(Map p64; ☎030-2844 1225; www.deutschestheater.de; Schumannstrasse 13a; [S] Oranienburger Tor) Steered by the seminal Max Reinhardt from 1905 until 1932, the DT is still among Germany's top stages. Now under artistic director Ulrich Khuon, the repertory includes both classical and bold new plays that usually reflect the issues and big themes of today. Plays are also performed in the adjacent *Kammerspiele* and at the 80-seat Box&Bar.

Schaubühne THEATRE

(Map p84; ☎030-890 023; www.schaubuehne.de; Kurfürstendamm 153; [S] Adenauerplatz) In a converted 1920s expressionist cinema by Erich Mendelsohn, this is western Berlin's main stage for experimental, contemporary theatre, often with a critical and analytical look at current social and political issues. The cast of dedicated actors is led by director Thomas Ostermeier. Some performances feature English surtitles.

Maxim Gorki Theater THEATRE

(Map p64; ☎030-2022 1115; www.gorki.de; Am Festungsgraben 2; 🚌100, 200, [S] Friedrichstrasse, [U] Friedrichstrasse) Artistic director Shermin Langhoff has made the smallest of Berlin's four state-funded theatres the dedicated home of the so-called 'post-migrant theatre'. Productions look at the lives of second- and third-generation Germans and examine such issues as integration, identity, transition and discrimination. All performances have English surtitles.

Sport

Hertha BSC SPECTATOR SPORT

(☎tickets 030-300 928 1892; www.herthabsc.de; tickets €15-96) Many Berliners live and die by the fortunes of the local soccer team, Hertha

BSC, which has seen its shares of ups and downs in recent years, but has mostly managed to stay in the *Bundesliga* (premier league). Home games are played at the Olympic Stadium (p86). Tickets are usually still available on game day.

Shopping

Berlin's main shopping boulevard is Kurfürstendamm and its extension Tauentzienstrasse, which are chock-a-bloc with the usual high-street chains. You'll find more of the same in malls such as **Alexa** (Map p64; ☎030-269 3400; www.alexacentre.com; Grunerstrasse 20; 🕒10am-9pm Mon-Sat; [S] Alexanderplatz, 🚇Alexanderplatz) near Alexanderplatz and LP 12 Mall of Berlin near Potsdamer Platz. Getting the most out of shopping in Berlin, though, means venturing off the high street and into the *Kieze* (neighbourhoods) for local flavour. Each comes with its own identity and mix of stores calibrated to the needs, tastes and bank accounts of local residents.

Big shops in the centre are open from 10am to 8pm or 9pm. Local boutiques keep flexible hours, usually opening at 11am or noon and closing at 7pm, or even 4pm or earlier on Saturday. Many of the latter do not accept credit cards.

★Markthalle Neun MARKET

(Map p76; ☎030-6107 3473; www.markthalleneun.de; Eisenbahnstrasse 42/43; 🕒5-10pm Thu, 10am-8pm Tue & Fri, 10am-6pm Sat; [S] Görlitzer Bahnhof) This delightful 1891 market hall with its iron-beam-supported ceiling was saved by dedicated locals in 2009. On market days, local and regional producers present their wares, while during Street Food Thursday a couple of dozen international amateur or semipro chefs set up their stalls to serve delicious snacks from around the world. There's even an onsite craft brewery, Heidenpeters.

Bikini Berlin SHOPPING MALL

(Map p84; www.bikiniberlin.de; Budapester Strasse 38-50; 🕒10am-8pm Mon-Sat; 🚌100, 200, [S] Zoologischer Garten, 🚇Zoologischer Garten) Germany's first concept mall opened in 2014 in a spectacularly rehabilitated 1950s architectural icon nicknamed 'Bikini' because of its design: a 200m-long upper and lower section separated by an open floor, now chastely covered by a glass facade. Inside are three floors of urban indie boutiques and short-lease pop-up 'boxes' that offer a platform for up-and-coming designers.

LP12 Mall of Berlin SHOPPING MALL

(Map p64; www.mallofberlin.de; Leipziger Platz 12; 🕒10am-9pm Mon-Sat; 🚌200, [S] Potsdamer Platz, 🚇Potsdamer Platz) This spanking new retail quarter is tailor-made for black-belt mall rats. More than 270 stores vie for your shopping euros, including flagship stores by Karl Lagerfeld, Hugo Boss, Liebeskind, Muji and other international high-end brands alongside the usual high-street chains like Mango and H&M.

FLEA MARKETS

➡ **Mauerpark** (Map p82; www.mauerparkmarkt.de; Bernauer Strasse 63-64; 🕒9am-6pm Sun; [S] Eberwalder Strasse, 🚊M1, M10) The mother of all flea markets may be quite overrun but is still a good show with lots of local designers, plus regular folks cleaning out their closets.

➡ **Arkonaplatz** (Map p82; www.troedelmarkt-arkonaplatz.de; Arkonaplatz; 🕒10am-4pm Sun; [S] Bernauer Strasse, 🚊M1, M10) Smallish and not so frantic, this is still an essential stop for retro fans, including vestiges from East Germany.

➡ **Boxhagener Platz** (Map p76; Boxhagener Platz; 🕒10am-6pm Sun; [S] Warschauer Strasse, Samariter Strasse, 🚇Warschauer Strasse) Popular treasure-hunting grounds with plenty of entertainment, cafes and people-watching.

➡ **Nowkoelln Flowmarkt** (Map p76; www.nowkoelln.de; Maybachufer; 🕒10am-6pm 2nd & 4th Sun of month; [S] Kottbusser Tor, Schönleinstrasse) Idyllic canal-side location, secondhand bargains galore and handmade threads and jewellery.

➡ **RAW Flohmarkt** (Map p76; www.raw-flohmarkt-berlin.de; Revaler Strasse 99, RAW Gelände; 🕒9am-7pm Sun; [S] Warschauer Strasse, 🚇Warschauer Strasse) True bargains still abound at this nicely trashy market on the grounds of a railway-repair station turned party zone.

Dussmann – Das Kulturkaufhaus BOOKS, MUSIC
(Map p64; ☎030-2025 1111; www.kulturkaufhaus.de; Friedrichstrasse 90; ⏲9am-midnight Mon-Fri, to 11.30pm Sat; [S] Friedrichstrasse, 🚆 Friedrichstrasse) It's easy to lose track of time in this cultural playground with wall-to-wall books, DVDs and CDs, leaving no genre unaccounted for. Bonus points for the free reading-glass rentals, downstairs cafe and performance space used for concerts, political discussions and high-profile book readings and signings.

Fassbender & Rausch FOOD
(Map p64; ☎030-757 882 440; www.fassbender-rausch.com; Charlottenstrasse 60; ⏲10am-8pm Mon-Sat, 11am-8pm Sun; [S] Stadtmitte) If the Aztecs thought of chocolate as the elixir of the gods, then this emporium of truffles and pralines must be heaven. Bonus: the chocolate volcano and giant replicas of Berlin landmarks. The upstairs cafe-restaurant has views of Gendarmenmarkt and serves sinful drinking chocolates and cakes as well as dishes prepared and seasoned with cocoa.

Markt am Winterfeldtplatz MARKET
(Map p87; Winterfeldtplatz; ⏲8am-2pm Wed, 8am-4pm Sat; [S] Nollendorfplatz) If it's Wednesday or Saturday morning, you're in luck because ho-hum Winterfeldtplatz erupts with farm-fresh fare. Along with seasonal produce, you'll find handmade cheeses, cured meats, tubs spilling over with olives, local honey and plenty more foodie staples and surprises. The Saturday edition also has artsy-craftsy stalls.

Kollwitzplatzmarkt MARKET
(Map p82; Kollwitzstrasse; ⏲noon-7pm Thu, 9am-4pm Sat; [S] Senefelderplatz) Berlin's poshest farmers market has everything you need to put together a gourmet picnic or meal. Velvety gorgonzolas, juniper-berry smoked ham, crusty sourdough bread and homemade pesto are among the exquisite morsels scooped up by well-heeled locals. The Saturday edition also features handicrafts.

KaDeWe DEPARTMENT STORE
(Map p87; ☎030-212 10; www.kadewe.de; Tauentzienstrasse 21-24; ⏲10am-8pm Mon-Thu, 10am-9pm Fri, 9.30am-8pm Sat; [S] Wittenbergplatz) Just past the centennial mark, this venerable department store has an assortment so vast that a pirate-style campaign is the best way to plunder its bounty. If pushed for time, hurry up to the legendary 6th-floor gourmet food hall. The name, by the way, stands for *Kaufhaus des Westens* (department store of the West).

Galeries Lafayette DEPARTMENT STORE
(Map p64; ☎030-209 480; www.galerieslafayette.de; Friedrichstrasse 76-78; ⏲10am-8pm Mon-Sat; [S] Französische Strasse) Stop by the Berlin branch of the exquisite French fashion emporium if only to check out the show-stealing interior (designed by Jean Nouvel, no less), centred on a huge glass cone shimmering with kaleidoscopic intensity. Around it wrap three circular floors filled with fancy fashions, fragrances and accessories, while glorious gourmet treats await in the basement food hall.

Ampelmann Galerie SOUVENIRS
(Map p64; ☎030-4472 6438; www.ampelmann.de; Court V, Hackesche Höfe, Rosenthaler Strasse 40/41; ⏲9.30am-9pm Mon-Sat, 10.30am-7pm Sun; [S] Weinmeisterstrasse, 🚋M1, 🚆 Hackescher Markt) It took a vociferous grassroots campaign to save the little Ampelmann, the endearing fellow on East German pedestrian traffic lights. Now the beloved cult figure and global brand graces an entire store worth of T-shirts, fridge magnets, pasta, onesies, umbrellas and other knick-knacks.

Check the website for additional branches around town.

★ **Türkischer Markt** MARKET
(Turkish Market; Map p76; www.tuerkenmarkt.de; Maybachufer; ⏲11am-6.30pm Tue & Fri; [S] Schönleinstrasse, Kottbusser Tor) At this lively canal-side market thrifty hipsters mix it up with Turkish-Germans and pram-pushing mums. Stock up on olives, creamy cheese spreads, crusty flatbreads and mountains of fruit and vegetables, all at bargain prices. In good weather, market-goers gather for impromptu concerts towards the eastern end of the strip.

Käthe Wohlfahrt HANDICRAFTS
(Map p84; ☎09861-4090; http://wohlfahrt.com/en/christmas-stores/berlin; Kurfürstendamm 225-226; ⏲10am-8pm Mon-Fri, 10am-8pm Sat, 1-6pm Sun; [S] Kurfürstendamm) With its mind-boggling assortment of traditional German Yuletide decorations and ornaments, this shop lets you celebrate Christmas year-round. It's accessed via a ramp that spirals around an 8m-high Christmas tree.

Galerie Eigen+Art ARTS
(Map p64; ☎030-280 6605; www.eigen-art.com; Auguststrasse 26; ⏲11am-6pm Tue-Sat; 🚆 Oranienburger Strasse) This key gallery for all sorts of contemporary art – from painting to

performance – is led by Gerd Harry Lybke, who has a knack for shepherding tomorrow's red-hot artist to international fame. Neo Rauch, Martin Eder and Carsten Nicolai have all been taken under his wing.

Stilwerk HOMEWARES
(Map p84; www.stilwerk.de/berlin; Kantstrasse 17; ⏰10am-7pm Mon-Sat; [R] Savignyplatz) This four-storey temple of good taste will have devotees of the finer things itching to redecorate. Everything you could possibly want for home and hearth is here – from tactile key rings to glossy grand pianos and vintage lamps – plus many international design brands (eg Bang & Olufsen, Vitra, Ligne Roset and Niessing).

Kauf Dich Glücklich FASHION
(Map p64; ☎030-2887 8817; www.kaufdichgluecklich-shop.de; Rosenthaler Strasse 17; ⏰11am-8pm Mon-Sat; [S] Weinmeisterstrasse, Rosenthaler Platz) What began as a waffle cafe and vintage shop has turned into a small emporium of indie fashion boutiques with this branch being the flagship. It's a prettily arranged and eclectic mix of reasonably priced accessories, music and clothing for him and her from the own-brand KDG-collection and other handpicked, mostly Scandinavian and Berlin, labels.

Bonbonmacherei FOOD
(Map p64; ☎030-4405 5243; www.bonbonmacherei.de; Oranienburger Strasse 32, Heckmann Höfe; ⏰noon-8pm Wed-Sat Sep-Jun; 🚊M1, [R] Oranienburger Strasse) The aroma of peppermint and liquorice wafts through this old-fashioned basement candy kitchen whose owners use antique equipment and time-tested recipes to churn out such tasty treats as their signature leaf-shaped Berliner Maiblätter.

Hard Wax MUSIC
(Map p76; ☎030-6113 0111; www.hardwax.com; Paul-Lincke-Ufer 44a, 3rd fl, door A, 2nd courtyard; ⏰noon-8pm Mon-Sat; [S] Kottbusser Tor) This well-hidden outpost has been on the cutting edge of electronic music for about two decades and is a must-stop for fans of techno, house, minimal, dubstep and whatever permutation comes along next.

Ta(u)sche ACCESSORIES
(Map p82; ☎030-4030 1770; www.tausche.de; Raumerstrasse 8; ⏰10am-8pm Mon-Fri, to 6pm Sat; [S] Eberswalder Strasse) Heike Braun and Antje Strubels now sell their ingenious messenger-style bags around the world, but this is the store where it all began. Bags come in 11 sizes with exchangeable flaps that zip off and on in seconds. There's a huge range of flaps to match your mood or outfit, plus various inserts, depending on whether you need to lug a laptop, a camera or nappies (diapers).

[i] Information

EMERGENCY & MEDICAL SERVICES

➡ In an emergency call ☎110 for the police and ☎112 for the fire brigade or an ambulance.

➡ Many doctors in private practice are English-speaking but do ask ahead. The most central hospital with a 24-hour emergency room is the renowned **Charité Mitte** (☎030-450 50; www.charite.de; Luisenstrasse 65 (emergency room), Charitéplatz 1 (general entrance); ⏰24hr; 🚌147, [S] Oranienburger Tor)

TOURIST INFORMATION

The city tourist board, **Visit Berlin** (www.visitberlin.de), has info desks at both airports and also operates five walk-in offices and a **call centre** (☎030-2500 2333; ⏰9am-7pm Mon-Fri, 10am-6pm Sat, 10am-2pm Sun) with multilingual staff who field general questions and can make hotel and ticket bookings.

Brandenburger Tor (Map p64; Brandenburger Tor, south wing, Pariser Platz; ⏰9.30am-7pm Apr-Oct, to 6pm Nov-Mar; [S] Brandenburger Tor, [R] Brandenburger Tor)

Rankestrasse (Map p84; cnr Rankestrasse & Kurfürstendamm; ⏰10am-6pm Apr-Oct, to 4pm Nov-Mar; [S] Kurfürstendamm)

Hauptbahnhof (Map p64; Hauptbahnhof, Europaplatz entrance, ground fl; ⏰8am-10pm; [S] Hauptbahnhof, [R] Hauptbahnhof)

Europa Center (Map p84; Tauentzienstrasse 9, Europa Center, ground fl; ⏰10am-8pm Mon-Sat; [S] Kurfürstendamm)

TV Tower (Map p64; Panoramastrasse 1a, TV Tower, ground fl; ⏰10am-6pm Apr-Oct, to 4pm Nov-Mar; 🚌100, 200, [S] Alexanderplatz, [R] Alexanderplatz)

USEFUL WEBSITES

➡ **Museumsportal** (www.museumsportal.de) Gateway to Berlin's museums and galleries.

➡ **Berlin Galleries Art Map** (www.berliner-galerien.de) A comprehensive overview of the latest commercial gallery shows.

➡ **Tip Berlin** (www.tip-berlin.de) & **Zitty Berlin** (www.zitty.de) Listings magazines.

➡ **Resident Advisor** (www.residentadvisor.net) Lists the latests clubs and parties.

➡ **Exberliner** (www.exberliner.com) Online version of monthly English-language city magazine.

ℹ TICKETS & PASSES

➡ The transport network is divided into fare zones A, B and C with tickets available for zones AB, BC or ABC. One ticket is valid for travel on all forms of public transportation.

➡ Most trips within Berlin require an AB ticket, valid for two hours (interruptions and transfers allowed but not round-trips). Notable exceptions include trips to Potsdam and Schönefeld airport, where the ABC tariff applies.

➡ Children aged six to 14 qualify for reduced (*ermässigt*) rates, while kids under six travel free.

➡ Tickets are available from bus drivers, vending machines at U- or S-Bahn stations (English instructions available), vending machines aboard trams and from station offices and news kiosks sporting the yellow BVG logo. Some vending machines accept debit cards. Bus drivers and tram vending machines only take cash.

➡ Don't buy from scammers selling used tickets at station exits. Not only is it illegal, but tickets may also be forged or expired.

➡ All tickets, except those bought from bus drivers and on trams, must be stamped before boarding. Anyone caught without a validated ticket escapes only with a red face and a €40 fine, payable on the spot.

➡ If you're taking more than two trips in a day, a day pass (*Tageskarte*) will save you money. It's valid for unlimited rides on all forms of public transport until 3am the following day. The group day pass (*Kleingruppen-Tageskarte*) is valid for up to five people travelling together.

➡ For short trips, buy the *Kurzstrecke*, which is good for three stops on the U-Bahn and S-Bahn or six on any bus or tram; no changes allowed.

ℹ Getting There & Away

AIR

Most visitors arrive in Berlin by air. Until the opening of the new Berlin Brandenburg Airport, flights continue to land at the city's Tegel and Schönefeld airports.

BUS

➡ Berlin is served by a large number of long-haul bus companies, including Berlinlinienbus, Postbus and Mein Fernbus, from throughout Germany. Check www.buslinensuche.de (also in English) for details.

➡ Most long-haul buses arrive at the **Zentraler Omnibusbahnhof** (ZOB; www.iob-berlin.de; Masurenallee 4-6; Ⓢ Kaiserdamm, Ⓡ Messe/ ICC Nord) near the trade-fair grounds in far western Berlin. The U2 U-Bahn line links to the city centre. Some bus operators also stop at Alexanderplatz and other points around town.

CAR

The A10 ring road links Berlin with other German and foreign cities, including: the A11 to Szczecin (Stettin) in Poland; the A12 to Frankfurt an der Oder; the A13 to Dresden; the A9 to Leipzig, Nuremberg and Munich; the A2 to Hanover and the Ruhrgebiet cities; and the A24 to Hamburg.

TRAIN

➡ Berlin has several train stations, but most services converge at the Hauptbahnhof (main train station) in the city centre, just north of the Reichstag and Brandenburger Tor. From here, the U-Bahn, S-Bahn, trams and buses provide links to all parts of town. Taxi ranks are located outside the north exit (Europaplatz) and the south exit (Washingtonplatz).

➡ Buy tickets in the *Reisezentrum* (travel centre) located between tracks 14 and 15 on the first upper level (OG1), online at www.bahn. de and, for shorter distances, at station vending machines.

➡ The left-luggage office (€5 per piece, per 24 hours) is behind the Reisebank currency exchange on level OG1, opposite the Reise-zentrum. Self-service lockers are hidden on the lower level of the parking garage, accessible near the Kaiser's supermarket on the first lower floor.

➡ Other services include a 24-hour pharmacy, a tourist office and other stores open daily from 8am to 10pm.

ℹ Getting Around

TO/FROM THE AIRPORTS
Berlin Brandenburg Airport

At the time of writing, a tentative opening date of late 2017 for Berlin's new central airport had been announced but, given repeated delays over the past years, it's anybody's guess whether this new deadline will be met. Check www.berlin-air-port.de for the latest.

Schönefeld

The airport train station is about 400m from the terminals. Free shuttle buses run every 10 minutes; walking takes five to 10 minutes.

Airport-Express Regular Deutsche Bahn regional trains, identified as RE7 and RB14 in timetables, go to central Berlin twice hourly (€3.30, 30 minutes).

S-Bahn The S9 runs every 20 minutes and is handy for Friedrichshain or Prenzlauer Berg. For the Messe (trade-fair grounds), take the S45 to Südkreuz and change to the S41. Tickets cost €3.30.

Taxi A cab ride to, say, Alexanderplatz averages €40 and take 40 minutes to an hour.

Tegel

Bus TXL to Alexanderplatz (€2.70, 40 minutes) via Haupbahnhof every 10 minutes. X9 for Kurfürstendamm and Zoo Station (€2.70, 20 minutes).

U-Bahn Closest U-Bahn station is Jakob-Kaiser-Platz, served by bus 109 and X9. From here, the U7 goes straight to Schöneberg and Kreuzberg (€2.70).

BICYCLE

➡ Bicycles are handy both for in-depth explorations of local neighbourhoods and for getting across town.

➡ Many hostels and hotels have bikes for guest use, often for free or a nominal fee. Also, rental stations can be found at practically every corner; these include not only the expected (bike shops, petrol stations), but also convenience stores, cafes and even clothing boutiques.

➡ Prices start at €6 per day, although the definition of 'day' can mean anything from eight hours to 24 hours. A cash or credit-card deposit and/or photo ID is usually required.

➡ Bicycles may be taken aboard designated U-Bahn and S-Bahn carriages (usually the last ones, look for the bicycle logo) as well as on trams, regional trains (RE, RB) and night buses (Sunday to Thursday only). You need to get a separate ticket called a *Fahrradkarte* (bicycle ticket, €1.80).

➡ The websites www.bbbike.de and www.vmz-info.de are handy for route planning.

CAR & MOTORCYCLE

Driving in Berlin is more hassle than it's worth, especially since parking is hard to find and expensive (about €1 to €2 per hour), so we highly recommend you make use of the excellent public-transport system instead. Central Berlin (defined as the area bounded by the S-Bahn circle line) is a restricted low-emission zone, which means all cars entering it need an *Umweltplakette* (emission sticker).

PUBLIC TRANSPORT

Berlin's public-transport system is run by **BVG** (www.bvg.de) and consists of the U-Bahn (underground or subway), S-Bahn (light rail), buses

ⓘ SHORT CAB TRIPS

A great way to cover short distances quickly is the *Kurzstreckentarif* (short-trip rate), which lets up to four people ride a cab for up to 2km for a mere €4. This only works if you flag down a moving taxi and tell the driver you want a '*Kurzstrecke*' before he or she has activated the regular meter. If you want to continue past 2km, regular rates apply to the entire trip. Passengers love it, but cabbies don't, and there's been talk about getting rid of the tariff altogether.

and trams. For trip planning and general information, check the website.

Bus

➡ Buses are slow but useful for sightseeing on the cheap (especially lines 100 and 200). They run frequently between 4.30am and 12.30am.

➡ Night buses (N1, N2 etc) take over in the interim while MetroBuses (M19, M41 etc) operate 24/7.

S-Bahn

S-Bahn trains (S1, S2, etc) don't run as frequently as the U-Bahn but make fewer stops and thus are useful for covering longer distances. They run from 4am until 1am and all night on Friday, Saturday and public holidays.

Tram

Trams only operate in the eastern districts. Those designated M1, M2 etc run 24/7.

U-Bahn

The U-Bahn is the quickest way of getting around Berlin. Lines (U1, U2 etc) operate from 4am until about 12.30am and throughout the night on Friday, Saturday and public holidays (all lines except U4 and U55). From Sunday to Thursday, buses take over the night runs.

TAXI

➡ You can order a **taxi** (🖉 44 33 11, 030-20 20 20) by phone, flag one down or pick one up at a rank. At night, cars often line up outside theatres, clubs and other venues.

➡ Flag fall is €3.40, then it's €1.79 per kilometre up to 7km and €1.28 for each additional kilometre. There's a surcharge of €1.50 if paying by credit or debit card, but none for night trips. Bulky luggage that does not fit into the trunk may be charged at €1 per piece.

➡ Tip about 10%.

Around Berlin

Best Places to Eat

➡ Maison Charlotte (p132)

➡ Edelmond Fisch- und Steakhaus (p135)

➡ Restaurant Altes Gärtnerhaus (p135)

➡ Schmiede 9 (p132)

Best Places to Stay

➡ Hotel Villa Monte Vino (p132)

➡ Schlosshotel Lübbenau (p137)

➡ Pension Zum Birnbaum (p138)

➡ Pension am Alten Bauernhafen (p137)

Why Go?

Berlin is fabulous, and you'll certainly want to spend quite a bit of time there, but don't forget to earmark a day (or two or three) for the surrounding state of Brandenburg. A land shaped by lakes, canals and waterways, large swathes of it are protected as biosphere preserves and nature parks, creating a delightful escape from the urban hustle for Berliners and visitors alike. Culture lovers, too, will be rewarded. Headlining the list of discoveries is the drop-dead-gorgeous park and palace of Sanssouci (the 'German Versailles') in Potsdam, a jewel box of a summer retreat built by King Frederick the Great and a mere half-hour train ride from central Berlin. Nowhere is Brandenburg's watery heritage more evident than in the Spreewald, one of Germany's most unique landscapes and home to the indigenous Sorb ethnic minority, who cling to their ancient customs and traditions in handsome remote hamlets. A sobering antidote to all that cultural and natural splendour – and no less important or memorable – is the Nazi-era concentration camp at Sachsenhausen, north of Berlin.

When to Go

Water characterises much of the countryside around Berlin, meaning that you will want to visit between spring and autumn when you can experience the region at its best by taking a boat trip or hiring a kayak. Of course you won't be alone, especially on blue-sky weekends, during the summer school holidays and around public holidays. Potsdam, too, is best visited midweek during summer, but its palaces and museum actually make a fine destination year-round. Sachsenhausen is, by definition, of timeless appeal.

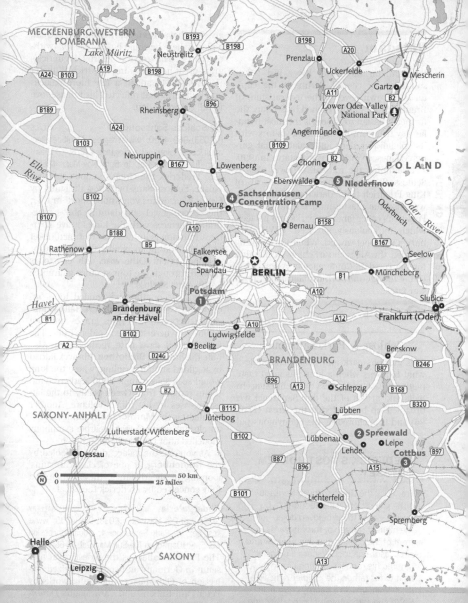

Around Berlin Highlights

1 Reliving the majesty that once surrounded **Schloss Sanssouci** (p126) and other Potsdam palaces

2 Communing with nature while punting around the web of waterways in the enchanting **Spreewald** (p134)

3 Getting into the mind of an eccentric aristocratic garden artist at **Park & Schloss Branitz** (p136) in Cottbus

4 Preparing for goosebumps as you confront the ghosts of **Sachsenhausen concentration camp** (p133)

5 Rubbing your eyes in disbelief at huge barges travelling in a massive **ship lift** (p139) at Niederfinow

Potsdam

📞 0331 / POP 152,000

Potsdam, on the Havel River just 25km southwest of central Berlin, is the capital and crown jewel of the federal state of Brandenburg. Easily reached by S-Bahn, the former Prussian royal seat is the most popular day trip from Berlin, luring visitors with its splendid gardens and palaces that garnered Unesco World Heritage status in 1990.

Headlining the roll call of royal pads is Schloss Sanssouci, the private retreat of King Friedrich II (Frederick the Great), who was also the mastermind behind many of Potsdam's other fabulous parks and palaces, which miraculously survived WWII with nary a shrapnel wound. When the shooting stopped, the Allies chose Schloss Cecilienhof for the Potsdam Conference of August 1945 to lay the groundwork for Germany's postwar fate.

⊙ Sights

⊙ Schloss & Park Sanssouci

This glorious park and palace ensemble is what happens when a king has good taste, plenty of cash and access to the finest architects and artists of the day. Sanssouci was dreamed up by Frederick the Great (1712–86) and is anchored by the eponymous pal-

---

FREDERICK'S POSTMORTEM ODYSSEY

Frederick the Great so loved Sanssouci, he gave specific instructions to be buried – next to his beloved dogs – on the highest terrace of the vineyards in front of the palace. Alas, his nephew and successor Friedrich Wilhem II blithely ignored his request, putting him instead next to his father, the 'Soldier King' Friedrich Wilhelm I, in a nearby church. In WWII, the sarcophagi of both father and son were moved by German soldiers for safekeeping and, after the war, ended up in the ancestral Hohenzollern castle in southern Germany. Only after reunification, in 1991, did Frederick the Great get his final wish, being reburied in the exact spot he'd personally picked out more than 250 years before. It's marked by a simple gravestone.

---

ace, which was his favourite summer retreat, a place where he could be 'sans souci' (without cares). His grave is nearby. Frederick's great-great nephew, King Friedrich Wilhelm IV (1795–1861), added a few more palaces and buildings that reflected his intense love for all things Italian.

★ Schloss Sanssouci   PALACE

(📞 0331-969 4200; www.spsg.de; Maulbeerallee; adult/concession incl audioguide €12/8; ⊙ 10am-6pm Tue-Sun Apr-Oct, to 5pm Nov-Mar; 🚌 650, 695) Frederick the Great's famous summer palace, Schloss Sanssouci, was designed by Georg Wenzeslaus von Knobelsdorff in 1747; the rococo jewel sits daintily above vine-draped terraces with the king's grave nearby. Admission is limited and by timed ticket only; book online to avoid wait times and/or disappointment. Otherwise, only city tours booked through the tourist office guarantee entry to the Schloss.

Standouts on the audioguided tours include the **Konzertsaal** (Concert Hall), whimsically decorated with vines, grapes and even a cobweb where sculpted spiders frolic. The king himself gave flute recitals here. Also note the intimate **Bibliothek** (library), lidded by a gilded sunburst ceiling, where the king would seek solace amid 2000 leather-bound tomes ranging from Greek poetry to the latest releases by his friend Voltaire. Another highlight is the **Marmorsaal** (Marble Room), an elegant white Carrara marble symphony modelled after the Pantheon in Rome.

As you exit the palace, don't be fooled by the **Ruinenberg**, a pile of classical 'ruins' looming in the distance: they're merely a folly conceived by Frederick the Great.

Bildergalerie   GALLERY

(Gallery of Old Masters; 📞 0331-969 4200; www.spsg.de; Im Park Sanssouci 4; adult/concession €6/5; ⊙ 10am-6pm Tue-Sun May-Oct; 🚌 650, 695) The Picture Gallery is the oldest royal museum in Germany and shelters a prized collection of Old Masters, including works by Peter Paul Rubens and Caravaggio's *Doubting Thomas*.

The interior of the elongated hall, with its gilded barrel-vaulted ceiling and patterned marble floors, is perhaps just as impressive as the mostly large-scale paintings that cover practically every inch of wall space.

Neue Kammern   PALACE

(New Chambers; 📞 0331-969 4200; www.spsg.de; Park Sanssouci; adult/concession incl tour or

🛈 TIPS FOR VISITING SANSSOUCI

➡ Admission to Schloss Sanssouci is by timed ticket only. Book online to pick your favourite time slot and skip the line.

➡ The palaces all have different opening hours and admission prices. Most are closed on Monday, some are open weekends only and minor ones are closed in winter.

➡ Ticket sanssouci+, a one-day pass to all Potsdam palaces, is €19 (concession €14) and sold at all buildings, the tourist offices and online. There's also a €3 day fee for taking pictures (Fotoerlaubnis) inside the palaces.

➡ Park Sanssouci is open from dawn till dusk year-round. Admission is free, but there are machines by the entrance where you can make a voluntary donation of €2.

➡ The palaces are fairly well spaced – it's almost 2km between the Neues Palais and Schloss Sanssouci. Take your sweet time wandering the meandering paths to discover your favourite spots.

➡ Cycling is officially permitted along Ökonomieweg and Maulbeerallee, which is also the route followed by bus 695, the main line to the park from the Hauptbahnhof.

➡ Picnicking is permitted throughout the park and there are also two restaurants: **Drachenhaus** (☑ 0331-505 3808; www.drachenhaus.de; Maulbeerallee 4; mains €8-23; ☺11am-8pm or later Apr-Oct, to 6pm Tue-Sun Nov, Dec & Mar, 11am-6pm Sat & Sun Jan & Feb) and **Potsdam Historische Mühle** (☑ 0331-281 493; www.moevenpick-restaurants.com; Zur Historischen Mühle 2; mains €10-18; ☺8am-10pm)

audioguide €4/3; ☺10am-6pm Tue-Sun Apr-Oct; 🚌650, 696) The New Chambers were originally an orangery and later a guesthouse. The rococo interior drips in opulence, most notably in the **Ovidsaal**, a grand ballroom with a gilded relief, and in the **Jasper Hall**, drenched in precious stones and lidded by a Venus fresco.

Historische Mühle HISTORIC BUILDING

(Historical Mill; ☑ 0331-550 6851; www.spsg.de; Maulbeerallee 5; adult/concession €3/2; ☺10am-6pm daily Apr-Oct, 10am-4pm Sat & Sun Nov & Jan-Mar; 🚌650, 695) This 18th-century Dutch-style windmill contains exhibits about historic and contemporary mill technology and offers a close-up of the grinding mechanism and a top-floor viewing platform.

According to legend, Frederick the Great ordered its owner to demolish the original mill because of the noise. However, when the miller refused and threatened to go to court, the king acquiesced.

★ Chinesisches Haus HISTORIC BUILDING

(Chinese House; ☑ 0331-969 4200; www.spsg. de; Am Grünen Gitter; adult/concession €3/2; ☺10am-6pm Tue-Sun May-Oct; 🚌605, 606 to Schloss Charlottenhof; 🚊91 to Schloss Charlottenhof) The 18th-century fad for the Far East is poignantly reflected in the Chinese House. The cloverleaf-shaped shutterbug favourite sports an enchanting exterior of exotically dressed gilded figures shown sipping tea, dancing and playing musical instruments amid palm-shaped pillars. Inside is a precious collection of Chinese and Meissen porcelain.

Neues Palais PALACE

(New Palace; ☑ 0331-969 4200; www.spsg.de; Am Neuen Palais; adult/concession incl tour or audioguide €8/6; ☺10am-6pm Wed-Mon Apr-Oct, to 5pm Nov-Mar; 🚌605 or 695 to Neues Palais, 🚆Potsdam Charlottenhof) The final palace commissioned by Frederick the Great, the Neues Palais has made-to-impress dimensions, a central dome and a lavish exterior capped with a parade of sandstone figures. The interior attests to the high level of artistry and craftsmanship of the 18th century. It's an opulent symphony of ceiling frescoes, gilded stucco ornamentation, ornately carved wainscoting and fanciful wall coverings alongside paintings (by Antoine Pesne, for example) and richly crafted furniture.

The palace was built in only six years, largely to demonstrate the undiminished power of the Prussian state following the bloody Seven Years War (1756–63). The king himself rarely camped out here, preferring the intimacy of Schloss Sanssouci and using it for representational purposes only. Only the last German Kaiser, Wilhelm II, used it as a residence until 1918.

Potsdam

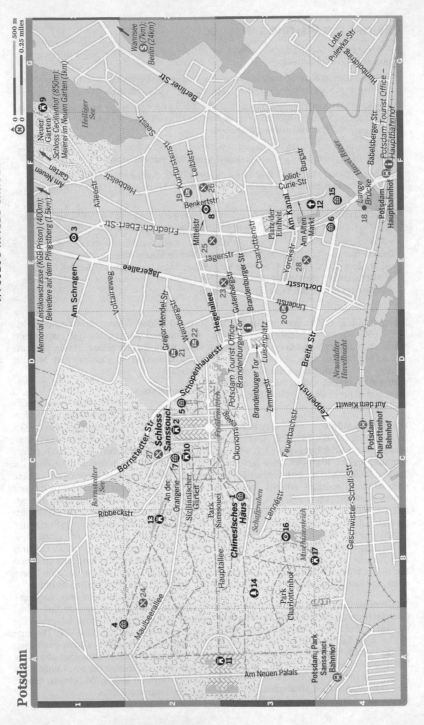

Memorial Leistikowstrasse (KGB Prison) (400m); Belvedere auf dem Pfingstberg (1.5km)

Neuer Garten
Schloss Cecilienhof (850m); Meierei im Neuen Garten (1km)

Wannsee S (7km); Berlin (24km)

Am Neuen Garten

Heiliger See

Seestr

Berliner Str

Lotte-Pulewka-Str

Humboldtring

Babelsberger Str

Potsdam Tourist Office – Hauptbahnhof

Potsdam Hauptbahnhof

Havel River

Lange Brücke

Joliot-Curie-Str

Burgstr

Am Alten Markt

Am Kanal

Platz der Einheit

Charlottenstr

Yorckstr

Dortusstr

Lindenstr

Breite Str

Zeppelinstr

Auf dem Kiewitt

Neustädter Havelbucht

Potsdam Charlottenhof Bahnhof

Geschwister-Scholl-Str

Feuerbachstr

Luisenplatz

Zimmerstr

Brandenburger Tor

Brandenburger Tor

Potsdam Tourist Office-Brandenburger Tor

Okonomie weg

Lennéstr

Schafgraben

Park Sanssouci

Chinesisches Haus

Sizilianischer Garten

An der Orangerie

Ribbeckstr

Bornstedter See

Bornstedter Str

Schloss Sanssouci

Schopenhauerstr

Hegelallee

Gutenbergstr

Brandenburger Str

Weinbergstr

Gregor-Mendel-Str

Am Schragen

Jägerallee

Voltaireweg

Friedrich-Ebert-Str

Hebbelstr

Alleestr

Kurfürstenstr

Leiblstr

Benkertstr

Mittelstr

Jägerstr

Charlottenstr

Am Neuen Palais

Hauptallee

Park Charlottenhof

Maulbeerallee

Mühlenteich

Potsdam; Park Sanssouci Bahnhof

Potsdam

Since the massive structure has been undergoing gradual restoration for years, not all rooms may be accessible. Among the most impressive are the rococo **Grottensaal** (Grotto Hall), the **Marmorsaal** (Marble Hall) and the **Unteres Fürstenquartier**, an especially elaborately styled guest apartment whose dining room walls are sheathed in richly red silk damask with gold-braided trim.

The pair of lavish buildings behind the Schloss is called the **Communs**. It originally housed the palace servants and kitchens and is now part of Potsdam University.

Orangerieschloss
PALACE

(Orangery Palace; ☑ 0331-969 4200; www.spsg.de; An der Orangerie 3-5; adult/concession €4/3; ☺ 10am-6pm Tue-Sun May-Oct) Modelled after an Italian Renaissance villa, the 300m-long Orangery Palace (1864) was Friedrich Wilhelm IV's favourite building project. Its highlight is the **Raffaelsaal**, which brims with 19th-century copies of the famous painter's masterpieces. The greenhouses are still used for storing potted plants in winter. Note that some sections may be closed while the building is undergoing long-term restoration.

Belvedere auf dem Klausberg
HISTORIC BUILDING

(☑ 0331-969 4206; www.spsg.de; An der Orangerie 1; admission €2; ☺ 10am-6pm Sat & Sun May-Oct) Frederick the Great's final building project was this temple-like Belvedere, modelled on Nero's palace in Rome. The panorama of park, lakes and Potsdam is predictably fabulous from up here. The upstairs hall has an impressive frescoed dome, oak parquet and fanciful stucco marble.

Park Charlottenhof
PARK

Laid out by Peter Lenné for Friedrich Wilhelm IV, Park Charlottenhof segues imperceptibly from Park Sanssouci but gets far fewer visitors. Buildings here reflect the king's passion for Italy. The small neoclassical **Schloss Charlottenhof** (☑ 0331-969 4200; www.spsg. de; Geschwister-Scholl-Strasse 34a; tour adult/concession €4/3; ☺ tours 10am-6pm Tue-Sun May-Oct), for instance, was modelled after a Roman villa. It was designed by Karl Friedrich Schinkel who, aided by his student Ludwig Persius, also dreamed up the nearby **Römische Bäder** (Roman Baths; ☑ 0331-969 4200; www.spsg.de; adult/concession €5/4; ☺ 10am-6pm Tue-Sun May–Oct), a picturesque cluster of Italian country villas. A same-day combination ticket is €8 (concession €6).

◉ Altstadt

Although much of Potsdam's historic town centre fell victim to WWII bombing and socialist town planning, it's been nicely restored and is worth a leisurely stroll. A landmark is the baroque **Brandenburger Tor** (Brandenburg Gate), a triumphal arch built to commemorate Frederick the Great's 1770 victory in the Seven Years' War. It's the gateway to pedestrianised Brandenburger Strasse, the main commercial drag, which links with the scenic Holländisches Viertel (Dutch Quarter).

Holländisches Viertel NEIGHBOURHOOD
(Dutch Quarter; www.hollaendisches-viertel.net; Mittelstrasse) This picturesque cluster of 134 gabled red-brick houses was built around 1730 for Dutch workers invited to Potsdam by Friedrich Wilhelm I. The entire district has been done up beautifully and brims with galleries, boutiques, cafes and restaurants; Mittelstrasse is especially scenic. Further up Friedrich-Ebert-Strasse is the **Nauener Tor** (Nauen Gate, 1755), a fanciful city gate.

Potsdamer Stadtschloss (Landtag Brandenburg) HISTORIC BUILDING
(Potsdam City Palace; ☑0331-966 1253; www.stadtschloss-potsdam.org; Alter Markt; ☺usually 10am-5pm Mon-Fri) **FREE** Potsdam's newest landmark is the replica of the 18th-century Prussian City Palace that was partly destroyed in WWII and completely removed by East German town planners in 1960. It reopened in October 2013 as the new home of the Brandenburg state parliament. Of the original building, only the ornate Fortuna Portal remains and now forms the main entrance to the compound, sections of which (including the rooftop terrace) are open to the public.

Nikolaikirche CHURCH
(☑0331-270 8602; www.nikolai-potsdam.de; Alter Markt 1; tower €5; ☺9am-7pm Mon-Sat, 11.30am-7pm Sun Apr-Oct, to 5pm Nov-Mar) In Potsdam's historic centre, around the Alter Markt (old market), the great patina-green dome of Karl Friedrich Schinkel's neoclassical Nikolaikirche (1850) is complemented by a 16m-high obelisk festooned with imagery of famous local architects, including Schinkel. The tower can be climbed.

◉ Neuer Garten & Around

North of the Potsdam old town, the winding lakeside Neuer Garten (New Garden) is laid out in natural English style on the western shore of the Heiliger See, and is a fine park in which to relax. A couple of palaces provide cultural diversions.

Marmorpalais PALACE
(Marble Palace; ☑0331-969 4550; www.spsg.de; Im Neuen Garten 10; tour adult/concession €5/4; ☺10am-6pm Tue-Sun May-Oct, 10am-4pm Sat & Sun Nov-Mar; ▣603) The neoclassical Marble Palace was built in 1792 as a summer residence for Friedrich Wilhelm II by Carl Gotthard Langhans (of Berlin's Brandenburg Gate fame) and has a stunning interior marked by a grand central staircase, marble fireplaces, stucco ceilings and lots of precious Wedgwood porcelain. The most fanciful room is the Turkish-tent-style **Orientalisches Kabinett** (Oriental Cabinet).

Schloss Cecilienhof PALACE
(☑0331-969 4520; www.spsg.de; Im Neuen Garten 11; tours adult/concession €6/5; ☺10am-6pm Tue-Sun Apr-Oct, to 5pm Nov-Mar; ▣603) This English-style country palace was completed in 1917 for crown prince Wilhelm and his wife Cecilie, but is most famous for hosting the 1945 Potsdam Conference where Stalin, Truman and Churchill (replaced by his successor Clement Atlee) hammered out Ger-

---

POTSDAM'S CELLULOID LEGACY

Film buffs will know that Potsdam is famous not merely for its palaces but also for being the birthplace of European film production. For it was here, in the suburb of Babelsberg, about 4km west of the city centre, that the venerable **UFA Studio** was founded in 1912. A few years later, it was already producing such seminal flicks as *Metropolis* and *Blue Angel*. Continuing as DEFA in GDR times, the dream factory was resurrected as **Studio Babelsberg** after reunification and has since produced or co-produced such international blockbusters as *Inglorious Basterds*, *The Grand Budapest Hotel* and *The Hunger Games*.

There are two ways to plug into the Potsdam film experience. In town, the handsome baroque royal stables now house the **Filmmuseum Potsdam** (☑0331-271 8112; www.filmmuseum-potsdam.de; Breite Strasse 1a; adult/concession €4.50/3.50; ☺10am-6pm Tue-Sun), which presents an engaging romp through German movie history with an emphasis on the DEFA period. In Babelsberg, next to the actual film studios, **Filmpark Babelsberg** (☑0331-721 2750; www.filmpark-babelsberg.de; Grossbeerenstrasse 200; adult/concession/child €21/17/14; ☺10am-6pm Apr-Oct; ▣601, 690, ▤Medienstadt Babelsberg) is a movie-themed amusement park with stunt shows, animal shows, outdoor movie sets and a studio tour with stops at the prop room, the costume department and workshops.

many's postwar fate. The conference room, with its giant round table, looks as though the delegates just left.

⊙ Alexandrowka & Pfingstberg

North of the Altstadt, Potsdam slopes up to the Pfingstberg past a Russian colony, a Russian Orthodox church and a Jewish cemetery.

Alexandrowka NEIGHBOURHOOD
(📞 0331-817 0203; www.alexandrowka.de; Russische Kolonie 1; museum adult/concession/under 14 €3.50/3/free; ⊙ museum 10am-6pm Tue-Sun; 🚌 92 or 96 from Hauptbahnhof) One of Potsdam's most unusual neighbourhoods, Alexandrowka is a Russian colony that was a gift from Friedrich Wilhelm III to his close friend Tsar Alexander in 1820. The first residents were the singers of a Russian military choir who had much delighted the king. Descendants of the original settlers still live in the chalet-like wooden houses surrounded by gardens and orchards. Learn more at the pretty little museum with nearby garden cafe.

Karl Friedrich Schinkel designed the Russian Orthodox church, called **Alexander-Newski-Gedächtniskirche**, just north of the colony.

Belvedere auf dem Pfingstberg PALACE
(📞 0331-2005 7930; www.pfingstberg.de; Pfingstberg; adult/concession €4/3; ⊙ 10am-6pm Apr-Oct, 10am-4pm Sat & Sun Mar & Nov; 🚌 92 or 96 from Hauptbahnhof) FREE For splendid views over Potsdam and surrounds, ascend the spiralling wrought-iron staircases of the twin-towered Belvedere palace commissioned by Friedrich Wilhelm IV and modelled on an Italian Renaissance–style villa. The 1801 **Pomonatempel** just below it was Karl Friedrich Schinkel's very first architectural commission.

Memorial Leistikowstrasse
(KGB Prison) MEMORIAL
(📞 0331-201 1540; www.gedenkstaette-leistikowstrasse.de; Leistikowstrasse 1; ⊙ 2-6pm Tue-Sun) FREE Now a memorial site, Potsdam's central remand prison for Soviet Counter Intelligence – colloquially known as KGB prison – is a particularly sinister Cold War relic. All sorts of (real or alleged) crimes could land you here, including espionage, desertion, insubordination or Nazi complicity. Using letters, documents, photographs, personal items and taped interviews, exhibits outline the fate of individuals. Prisoners were often abused and tortured until they

confessed, then tried in closed sessions without legal representation and usually sent straight to the Gulag or the executioner.

In the creepy basement cells you can still see messages inmates scratched into the walls. The building remained a prison until 1980, was then used for equipment storage and was only vacated in 1994 as one of the last Soviet military outposts in Germany.

The prison was part of Military Station 7, a top-secret walled town where ranking members of the Soviet military lived and worked. Locals had only a vague idea what went on behind these walls. For a self-guided tour of the entire compound, pick up a map at the memorial.

☞ Tours

Schiffahrt in Potsdam BOAT
(📞 0331-275 9210; www.schiffahrt-in-potsdam.de; Lange Brücke 6; ⊙ 10am-7pm Apr-Oct) A relaxing way to enjoy Potsdam is from the deck of a cruise boat. The most popular trip is the 90-minute *Schlösserundfahrt* palace cruise (€14), but there's also a two-hour tour to Lake Wannsee (€15) and a three-hour trip around several Havel lakes (€16). Boats depart from the docks near Lange Brücke.

🛏 Sleeping

Most people visit Potsdam on a day trip from Berlin. At night, the town gets very quiet. The tourist office (p132) books private rooms and hotels in person, by phone or online.

★ Hotel Villa Monte Vino   HOTEL €€

(☑ 0331-201 3339; www.hotelvillamontevino.de; Gregor-Mendel-Strasse 27; d incl breakfast from €125; P 🛜) This charming 1890 villa, complete with dreamy garden and Rapunzel tower, is a superb find tucked into the leafy hillside above Schloss Sanssouci. Run by passionate owners, it harmoniously blends historic and modern touches and even has a small gym and sauna. Rooms don't skimp on space and are sheathed in soothing earth tones.

Hotel am Grossen Waisenhaus   HOTEL €€

(☑ 0331-601 0780; www.hotelwaisenhaus.de; Lindenstrasse 28/29; d incl breakfast €80-157; P 🛜) This classy entry occupies an erstwhile 18th-century baroque barracks for married soldiers that also went through a stint as an orphanage hospital (as reflected in the name). Historical quirks combine with carefully designed contemporary features in three room categories, all with sparkling plank floors. Generous breakfast.

Remise Blumberg   PENSION €€

(☑ 0331-280 3231; www.pension-blumberg.de; Weinbergstrasse 26; d incl breakfast €90-100; P 🛜) In this quiet eight-room gem, you'll have plenty of space to stretch out in comfortably furnished units with small kitchens. Greet the day with an excellent breakfast (complete with sparkling wine), which, in fine weather, is served in the secluded courtyard. Other thoughtful extras include extra-thick mattresses, bike rentals and free public-transport passes.

Das Kleine Apartmenthotel
im Holländerhaus   APARTMENTS €€

(☑ 0331-279 110; www.hollaenderhaus.potsdam. de; Kurfürstenstrasse 15; apt €100-200, breakfast €14; P @ 🛜) This delightful place combines the charm of a 1733 Dutch Quarter building with an edgy, creative design scheme. Wood, steel and bold colour splashes give the 12 good-sized apartments with kitchens a contemporary look. The leafy courtyard is a good unwinding spot.

✖ Eating & Drinking

Hafthorn   GASTROPUB €

(☑ 0331-280 0820; www.hafthorn.de; Friedrich-Ebert-Strasse 90; dishes €5-9; ⊙ from 6pm; 🚃 695) Check your pretensions at the door of this cheerily charming pub, the home of quirky metal lamps, big burgers and sudsy Bohemian beer. An all-ages crowd shares laughter inside this former bakery and, in summer, along candlelit benches in the beer garden.

Maison Charlotte   FRENCH €€

(☑ 0331-280 5450; www.maison-charlotte.de; Mittelstrasse 20; Flammkuchen €8-12.50, 3-/4-course menu €39-47; ⊙ noon-11pm) There's a rustic lyricism to the French country cuisine in this darling Dutch Quarter bistro, no matter whether your appetite runs towards a simple *Flammkuchen* (Alsatian pizza), Breton fish soup or a multi-course menu. Budget *bon vivants* come for the daily lunch special: €7.50, including a glass of wine.

Schmiede 9   GERMAN €€

(☑ 0331-6264 8440; www.kutschstall.de; Am Neuen Markt 9a; mains €12-19; ⊙ 10am-5pm Sun-Tue, 10am-10pm Wed-Sat) A restored smithy in a half-timbered house forms the backdrop for this upbeat cafe and restaurant where a small army of chefs prepares modern regional fare in a show kitchen. The lunch specials are a bargain at around €7 and the Sunday brunch comes with childcare.

Brasserie zu Gutenberg   FRENCH €€

(☑ 0331-7403 6878; www.brasserie-zu-gutenberg. de; Jägerstrasse 10, cnr Gutenbergstrasse; mains €8.50-22; ⊙ noon-midnight) This charming little brasserie with dark-wood tables and chocolate-brown banquettes is great for a quick bite of quiche and coffee or for a hearty meal, perhaps featuring the signature *coq au vin* and a glass of fine Bordeaux.

Meierei im Neuen Garten   GERMAN €€

(☑ 0331-704 3211; www.meierei-potsdam.de; Im Neuen Garten 10; mains €5-13; ⊙ noon-10pm Tue-Fri, 11am-10pm Sat & Sun; 🚃 603 to Höhenstrasse) The Berlin Wall once ran right past this brewpub that's especially lovely in summer when you can count the boats sailing on the Jungfernsee from your beer-garden table. The hearty dishes are a perfect match for the delicious *Helles* (pale lager) and seasonal suds brewed on the premises.

❶ Information

Potsdam Tourist Office – Hauptbahnhof

(☑ 0331-2755 8899; www.potsdam-tourism. com; Inside the main train station; ⊙ 9.30am-8pm Mon-Sat May-Oct, to 6pm Mon-Sat Nov-Apr, 10am-4pm Sun year-round) There's another office at Brandenburger Tor (☑ 0331-2755 8899; www.potsdam-tourism.com; Brandenburger Strasse 3; ⊙ 10am-6pm Mon-Sat, 10am-4pm Sun Apr-Oct, shorter hours Sat & Sun Nov-Mar; 🚃 605, 631, 650).

ⓘ Getting There & Away

CAR
Drivers coming from Berlin should take the A100 to the A115.

TRAIN
Regional trains leaving from Berlin-Hauptbahnhof and Zoologischer Garten take about 25 minutes to reach Potsdam-Hauptbahnhof; some continue on to Potsdam-Charlottenhof and Potsdam-Sanssouci, which are actually closer to Park Sanssouci. The S7 from central Berlin makes the trip in about 40 minutes. You need a ticket covering zones ABC (€3.30) for either service.

ⓘ Getting Around

BICYCLE
Potsdam per Pedales (☑ 0331-748 0057; www.potsdam-per-pedales.de; Potsdam Hauptbahnhof, platform 6/7; adult/concession per day €10.50/8; ☺ 9.30am-7pm Apr-Oct; ⊞ Potsdam Hauptbahnhof) This outfit right on the station platform rents out quality bicycles and offers guided and self-guided bike tours. If you want to see more of Potsdam than Sanssouci Park, a bike is ideal.

PUBLIC TRANSPORT
Buses and trams operate throughout Potsdam. Buses for Sanssouci leave from right outside Potsdam Hauptbahnhof. Bus 605, 695 and X15 also make frequent departures to the park.

Sachsenhausen Concentration Camp

Gedenkstätte und Museum Sachsenhausen MEMORIAL
(☑ 03301-200 200; www.stiftung-bg.de; Strasse der Nationen 22; ☺ 8.30am-6pm mid-Mar–mid-Oct, to 4.30pm mid-Oct–mid-Mar, museums closed Mon; ⓡ S1 to Oranienburg) **FREE** About 35km north of Berlin, Sachsenhausen was built by prisoners and opened in 1936 as a prototype for other camps. By 1945, some 200,000 people passed through its sinister gates, most of them political opponents, gypsies, Jews and POWs. By 1945, tens of thousands had died here from hunger, exhaustion, illness, exposure, medical experiments and executions. A tour of the memorial site with its remaining buildings and exhibits will leave no one untouched.

Unless you're on a guided tour, pick up a leaflet (€0.50) or, better yet, an audioguide (€3, including leaflet) at the visitor centre to get a better grasp of this huge site. Avoid visiting on a Monday when all indoor exhibits are closed.

The approach to the camp takes you past photographs taken just before the camp's liberation in April 1945. Just beyond the perimeter, the **Neues Museum** (New Museum) has exhibits on Sachsenhausen's precursor, the nearby Oranienburg concentration camp, and on the history of the memorial site.

Proceed to **Tower A**, the entrance gate, cynically labelled, as at Auschwitz, Arbeit Macht Frei (Work Sets You Free). Beyond here is the roll-call area, with barracks and other buildings fanning out beyond. Off to the right, two restored barracks illustrate the abysmal living conditions prisoners endured. **Barrack 38** has an exhibit on Jewish inmates, while **Barrack 39** graphically portrays daily life at the camp. The prison, where famous inmates included Hitler's would-be assassin Georg Elser and the minister Martin Niemöller, is next door. Exhibits in the **infirmary barracks** on the other side of the roll-call area illustrate the camp's poor medical care and the horrific medical experiments performed on prisoners.

Towards the centre, the **Prisoners' Kitchen** chronicles key moments in the camp's history. Exhibits include instruments of torture, the original gallows that stood in the roll-call area and, in the cellar, heart-wrenching artwork scratched into the wall by prisoners.

The most sickening displays, though, are about the extermination area called **Station Z**, which was separated from the rest of the grounds and consisted of an execution trench, a crematorium and a gas chamber. The most notorious mass executions took place in autumn 1941, when over 10,000 Soviet POWs were executed here in the course of four weeks.

In April 1945, the Nazis evacuated the camp in advance of the Red Army. Thousands of prisoners succumbed during this so-called 'death march', whose victims are commemorated by a plaque as you approach the camp (at the corner of Strasse der Einheit and Strasse der Nationen).

After the war, the Soviets held some 60,000 German POWs in what was now **Speziallager No 7** (Special Camp No 7); about 12,000 died of malnutrition and disease before it was dissolved in 1950. There are exhibits about this period in a new building and two original camp barracks in the far right corner of the grounds.

After 1950, Soviet and East German military used the grounds for another decade until the camp became a memorial site in 1961.

Note that no food is available at the memorial site, although a vending machine in the Neues Museum dispenses hot drinks. There are cafes, bakeries and small markets outside Oranienburg train station.

ᐅ Tours

Most Berlin-based tour companies offer guided tours (p91) of Sachsenhausen.

Friends of Sachsenhausen WALKING TOUR
(www.stiftung-bg.de/foerderverein; adult/concession €14/12; ⊙10.20am Tue, Thu & Sun) The non-profit Friends of Sachsenhausen runs guided four-hour tours to the memorial from the historic traffic light on Potsdamer Platz in central Berlin. Guides have been trained by the memorial foundation.

ⓘ Getting There & Away

The S1 makes the trip thrice hourly from central Berlin (eg Friedrichstrasse station) to Oranienburg (€3.30, 45 minutes). Hourly regional RE5 and RB12 trains leaving from Hauptbahnhof are faster (€3.30, 25 minutes). The camp is about 2km from the Oranienburg train station. Turn right onto Stralsunder Strasse, right on Bernauer Strasse, left on Strasse der Einheit and right on Strasse der Nationen. Alternatively, bus 804 makes hourly trips.

Spreewald

The Spreewald, a unique lacework of channels and canals hemmed in by forest, is the closest thing Berlin has to a backyard garden. Visitors come to this Unesco biosphere reserve in droves to hike, fish and punt, canoe or kayak on its extensive network of waterways. Lübben and Lübbenau, the main tourist towns, often drown beneath the tides of visitors vying for rides aboard a *Kahn* (shallow punt boat) steered by ferrymen in traditional garb and once the only way of getting around in these parts. To truly appreciate the Spreewald's unique charms, hire your own canoe or kayak or get yourself onto a walking trail.

The Spreewald is also famous for being the home of the Sorb ethnic minority and for producing over 40,000 tonnes of gherkins every year!

ⓘ Getting There & Around

Hourly RE regional trains depart central from Berlin (eg Hauptbahnhof) for Lübben (€9.80, 57 minutes) and Lübbenau (€11.50, 63 minutes) en route to Cottbus (€14.30, 1½ hours). The towns are also linked by a 13km trail along the Spree. Cyclists can explore the region by following a section of the 260km Gurkenradweg (Cucumber Trail). There's a **bike rental station** (☑ 035603-158 790; Lübben train station; bikes per day €8-17; ⊙ call ahead) at the Lübben train station. Book ahead.

Lübben

☑ 03546 / POP 13,700

Tidy Lübben has a history going back to the 12th century. Activity centres on the Schloss and the adjacent harbour area, both about 1.5km east of the train station. To get there, follow Bahnhofstrasse, turn left on Logenstrasse and continue to Ernst-von-Houwald-Damm, where you'll also find the **tourist office** (☑ 03546-3090; www.luebben.de; Ernst-von-Houwald-Damm 15; ⊙10am-6pm Mon-Fri, 9.30am-6pm Sat & Sun Apr-Oct, 10am-4pm Mon-Fri Nov-Mar). En route, you'll pass the Paul-Gerhardt-Kirche, where 17th-century poet and hymn writer Paul Gerhardt is buried. The Markt and Hauptstrasse are two blocks north.

◉ Sights & Activities

Museum Schloss Lübben MUSEUM
(☑ 03546-187 478; www.museum-luebben.de; Ernst-von-Houwald-Damm 14; adult/concession €4.50/2.50; ⊙10am-5pm Tue-Sun Apr-Oct, 10am-4pm Wed-Fri, 1-5pm Sat & Sun Nov-Mar) The prettiest building in town is the petite Schloss, now home to a nicely curated regional history museum. Exhibit highlights include an interactive town model and a 2m-long medieval executioner's sword. Follow up with a (free) wander around the **Schlossinsel**, an artificial archipelago with gardens, a leafy maze, playgrounds, cafes and a harbour area where you can board punts for leisurely tours.

Bootsverleih Gebauer BOAT RENTAL
(☑ 03546-7194; www.spreewald-bootsverleih.de; Lindenstrasse 18; single kayak 2hr/day €9/19, bicycle per day €12) Rents out canoes, kayaks and row boats from one to four people as well as bicycles.

🍴 Sleeping & Eating

Hotel Lindengarten HOTEL €€
(☑ 03546-4172; www.spreewald-luebben.de; Treppendorfer Dorfstrasse 15; d incl breakfast €81-90;

P) This family-run hotel has bright and airy rooms, upbeat flair and a nice restaurant serving local dishes. Free pick-ups from the station can be arranged.

Edelmond Fisch- und Steakhaus GERMAN €€
(📋 03546-179 4257; www.restaurant-edelmond-lübben.de; Ernst-von-Houwald-Damm 14; mains €8-17; ⊙ 11am-11pm Tue-Sun) For a culinary treat, book a table in the elegant palace restaurant, where classic dishes are given a regional spin and the menu also features fresh fish and dry-aged steaks. It's affiliated with Edelmond, a regional purveyor of organic artisanal chocolates. In summer, you can sit in the romantic garden.

Restaurant Altes
Gärtnerhaus MEDITERRANEAN €€
(📋 03546-186 956; www.ladencafe-luebben.de; Ernst-von-Houwald-Damm 6; mains €7-14; ⊙ 5-10pm Mon, noon-10pm Tue-Sun) This lovingly decorated little cottage with living-room charm and a small beer garden is a popular stop, be it just for coffee and a slice of homemade cake or for a full meal of tasty Mediterranean or regional dishes, including fish. It's in the former palace gardener's house.

Goldener Löwe GERMAN €€
(📋 03546-7309; www.goldenerloewe-luebben.de; Hauptstrasse 14; mains €8-12; ⊙ 11am-10pm) Lübben's oldest restaurant is an ambience-laden purveyor of German dishes, including a fish platter featuring local eel, perch and carp. In summer, enjoy your meal in the beer garden. It also has a few rooms for rent (doubles €65), in case you feel like dawdling.

Lübbenau
📋 03542 / POP 16,100
Poet Theodor Fontane called Lübbenau the 'secret capital' of the Spreewald and, indeed, it is a pretty little town, even when deluged by day trippers. Its entire economy seems built on tourism and no matter where you go, a forest of signs points to hotels, restaurants and other businesses, making navigating a snap. Wander away from the harbour and main street to escape the crowds. The **tourist office** (📋 03542-887 040; www.luebbenau spree-wald.com; Ehm-Welk-Strasse 15; ⊙ 10am-6pm Mon-Fri, to 4pm Sat & Sun) is near the baroque Nikolaikirche church in the town centre, about 600m north of the train station.

◉ Sights

★ Freilandmuseum Lehde MUSEUM
(Open-Air Museum Lehde; 📋 03542-2472; www.museum-osl.de; Lehde; adult/concession €5/3.50; ⊙ 10am-6pm Apr-Sep, to 5pm Oct) In the protected village of Lehde, this cluster of historic Sorb farm buildings gives you a good sense of what rural life in the Spreewald

---

THE SORBS

The Spreewald is part of the area inhabited by the Sorbs, one of four officially recognised German national minorities (the others being Danes, Frisians and Roma/Sinti), with its own language, customs and traditions. This intriguing group, numbering around 60,000, descends from the Slavic Wends, who settled between the Elbe and Oder Rivers in the 5th century in an area called Lusatia (Łužica in Sorbian).

After Lusatia was conquered by the German King Heinrich I in 929, the Sorbs lost their political independence and, for centuries, were subjected to relentless Christianisation and Germanisation. In 1815, their land was partitioned into Lower Sorbia, centred on the Spreewald and Cottbus (Chóśebuz), which went to Prussia, while Upper Sorbia, around Bautzen (Budyšin), went to Saxony. The Upper Sorbian dialect, closely related to Czech, enjoyed a certain prestige in Saxony, but the Kingdom of Prussia tried to suppress Lower Sorbian, which is similar to Polish.

Sorbian groups banded together under a head organisation called Domowina in 1912 in order to fight for the group's rights and interests. The Nazis outlawed the organisation and banned their culture and language. In GDR times, Sorbs enjoyed protected status but were also forced to vacate large parts of their land to make room for coal-mining operations. In reunited Germany, Sorbs receive subsidies from state and federal governments (around €17 million in 2015) to keep their culture alive. Colourful Sorbian festivals such as the *Vogelhochzeit* (Birds' Wedding) on 25 January and a symbolic witch-burning on 30 April attract great media attention and huge numbers of tourists. In 2008, Stanislaw Tillich became the first Sorb to be elected governor of Saxony.

For further information, contact the **Sorbisches Institut** (www.serbski-institut.de).

PARK & SCHLOSS BRANITZ

Park & Schloss Branitz (📞 0355-751 50; www.pueckler-museum.de; Robinienweg 5; park free, Schloss adult/concession €5.50/4; ☉10am-6pm daily Apr-Oct, 11am-4pm Tue-Sun Nov-Mar; 🚌 10 to Branitz Schloss) A highlight of a visit to Cottbus, about 35km southeast of Lübbenau, is this palace-and-park ensemble, which stems from the feverish brow of Prince Hermann von Pückler-Muskau (1785–1871) – aristocrat, writer, lady's man, eccentric and one of Germany's most formidable garden architects. From 1845 until his death, he turned his bleak ancestral family estate into an arcadian English-style park – shaping hills, moving trees, digging canals and lakes and building pyramid-shaped tumuli, one of which serves as his burial place.

For an introduction to this brilliant, if kooky, man, swing by the multimedia exhibit in the **Gutshof** (adult/concession €4.50/3.50; ☉10am-5pm Apr-Oct), then see how his fascination for the exotic translated into his living space on a spin around the Schloss itself. Highlights in this late-baroque confection by Gottfried Semper (of Dresden opera fame) include such 'souvenirs' as 3000-year-old Egyptian burial urns and rooms clad in wallpaper patterned like oriental carpets. Temporary exhibits are housed in the **Marstall** (adult/concession €3.50/2.50; ☉11am-5pm May-Sep).

A combined ticket (adult/concession €10/7) is available, providing access to all three sites.

Trains to Lübben and Lübbenau continue on to Cottbus. Bus 10 makes the 4km trip from Cottbus train station to the park at least hourly (€1.50, 25 minutes).

was like a century ago. Wander among the reed-covered buildings, stop at a punt-builder's workshop, meet local folk dressed in colourful Sorb costumes or discover the secrets of the famous Spreewald gherkin.

A popular two-hour boat tour (€10) goes out to Lehde from Lübbenau, but you can escape the crowds by taking a 30-minute walk instead. The route through the forest follows the Leiper Weg, which was the first road built in the Spreewald in 1935–6.

Spreewald-Museum Lübbenau MUSEUM (📞 03542-2472; www.museum-osl.de; Topfmarkt 12; adult/concession €5/3.50; ☉10am-6pm Tue-Sun Apr-Oct, noon-4pm Tue-Sun Nov-Mar) Take a trip down the Spreewald memory lane at this regional-history museum imaginatively set up like an historic department store. Stops include a grocery, a bakery, a furrier and shoemaker as well as a clothing store featuring traditional Sorb garb. A modern annex houses the locomotive and a passenger car of the *Spreewaldbahn*, a narrow-gauge train that connected local villages from 1898 until 1970.

Haus für Mensch und Natur MUSEUM (📞 03542-892 10; Schulstrasse 9; ☉10am-5pm Tue-Sun Apr-Oct) **FREE** An old school building now houses the Spreewald Biosphere Reserve information centre where you can learn all about the region's natural development, marvel at its incredible plant and animal diversity

and test your eco-IQ at a computer game. It's right next to the tourist office.

Bootsverleih Richter BOAT RENTAL (📞 03542-3764; www.bootsverleih-richter.de; Dammstrasse 76a; single kayak per person 2hr/day €7/15-18; ☉9am-6pm late-Mar–mid-Oct) Active types won't have trouble hiring canoes or kayaks from several outfitters, including this dynamic operation with a huge fleet of well-maintained boats. Staff can help you put together tours of various lengths.

👉 Tours

Several operators offer pretty much the same **punt boat tours**, from a two-hour trip to Lehde to a day-long excursion through alder forests, past old mills and historic inns, serving lunch and refreshments. Crowds can be heavy, especially on summer weekends and on public holidays.

Grosser Hafen Lübbenau BOATING (📞 03542-2225; www.grosser-kahnhafen.de; Dammstrasse 77a; boat tours €10-25; ☉from 10am) This is the largest local outfit with punt boats departing continuously from 10am. No reservations are necessary.

🛏 Sleeping & Eating

Check with the tourist office about private rooms (from €17) or simply walk about town and look for signs saying *Gästezimmer*.

Pension am Alten Bauernhafen PENSION €
(☎ 03542-2930; www.am-alten-bauernhafen.de; Stottoff 5; d incl breakfast from €50; P) Charmingly decorated, with large rooms and a fantastic waterfront location, this family-run B&B is in a quiet side street, yet in the heart of the historic centre. Many of the breakfast items are sourced from the owner couple's own organic garden.

Brauhaus & Pension Babben PENSION €
(☎ 03542-2126; www.babben-bier.de; Brauhausgasse 2; d incl breakfast €55-60, apt from €55; ⏲ brewpub from 5pm Apr-Oct) This family-owned brewery has made a mean Pilsner and seasonal beers since 1928, all of them unfiltered, unpasteurised and therefore always fresh. The menu features casual pub eats; upstairs is a handful of cosy rooms that are simply but functionally furnished. There's also a few holiday apartments here and across the street that sleep up to four.

Hotel Nordic Spreewald HOTEL €€
(☎ 03542-424 41; www.hotel-nordic-spreewald.de; Hauptstrasse 33, Ortsteil Zerkwitz; d incl breakfast €80-102; P 📶) The charming owners of this adorable oasis, about 3km outside the historic centre, often go the extra mile to make their guests happy. Feast on the bountiful breakfast buffet, then rent a bike or e-bike to explore the surrounds, surf the Web while putting your feet up in the garden or retreat to squeaky-clean rooms with sitting areas and flat-screen TVs.

Schlosshotel Lübbenau HOTEL €€
(☎ 03542-8730; www.schloss-luebbenau.de; Schlossbezirk 6; d €100-170; P 📶) Lübbenau's poshest digs occupy the local palace, idyllically surrounded by a tranquil park. Rooms don't scrimp on space, are warmly furnished in natural colours and come with sitting areas and parquet floors. The prettily tiled basement spa is a great spot for unwinding with a steam or massage, and there are two restaurants serving Mediterranean and regional cuisine, respectively.

Brandenburg an der Havel

☎ 03381 / POP 71,300

The pretty town of Brandenburg an der Havel, some 50km west of Berlin, was shaped by water. Set amid a pastoral landscape of lakes, rivers and canals, its historic centre is peppered with stately examples of medieval Gothic red-brick architecture. First settled by Slavs in the 6th century, Brandenburg was a bishopric in the early Middle Ages and the regional capital until the 15th century. Today it's an easy day trip from Berlin or lovely base for exploring the region by bicycle or boat.

Sights & Activities

Brandenburg is split into three sections – the Neustadt, the Altstadt and the Dominsel – each on its own island in the Havel River.

Dom zu Brandenburg & Museum CHURCH
(☎ 03381-211 2223; www.dom-brandenburg.de; Burghof 10; adult/concession €5/3; ⏲ 10am-5pm Mon-Sat, 11.30am-5pm Sun Apr-Oct, to 4pm Nov-Mar) FREE Founded more than 850 years ago, this predominantly Gothic church brims with treasures. Note the carved 14th-century Bohemian Altar in the south transept, the vaulted and painted *Bunte Kapelle* (Coloured Chapel) in the north transept and the medieval stained glass in the choir. The museum has outstanding medieval vestments and a so-called *Hungertuch* (hunger blanket, 1290) with embroidered medallions depicting the life of Jesus.

Archäologisches Landesmuseum Brandenburg MUSEUM
(☎ 03381-410 4112; www.landesmuseum-brandenburg.de; Neustädtische Heidestrasse 28; adult/concession €5/3.50; ⏲ 10am-5pm Tue-Sun) The beautiful Gothic red-brick St Pauli monastery has risen from ruins and now forms an atmospheric backdrop for nine rooms brimming with Brandenburg's archaeological collection, including rare Stone Age textiles, Bronze Age gold rings, Germanic tools and medieval coins.

Katharinenkirche CHURCH
(☎ 03381-521 162; Katharinenkirchplatz 2; ⏲ 11am-3pm Mon-Sat, 1-4pm Sun) FREE This vast Gothic brick church has a lavishly detailed and decorated facade. See if you can spot your favourite biblical characters on the medieval *Meadow of Heaven* ceiling fresco.

Tours

Nordstern Reederei (☎ 03381-226 960; www.nordstern-reederei.de; tours €10-16; ⏲ Apr-Oct) and **Fahrgastschiff Havelfee** (☎ 03381-522 331; www.fgs-havelfee.de; tours €9-15; ⏲ Apr-Oct) both operate boat tours around the Havel lakes from landing stages near the Jahrtausendbrücke.

🛏 Sleeping

Pension Zum Birnbaum PENSION €
(☑ 03381-527 50; www.pension-zum-birnbaum.de; Mittelstrasse 1; d incl breakfast €65-70; P 🕏) A singing host, breakfast under a pear tree and handsomely furnished and modern, if snug, rooms recommend this little 19th-century inn that places you close to the train station and the Neustadt.

Sorat Hotel Brandenburg HOTEL €€
(☑ 03381-5970; www.sorat-hotels.com/brandenburg; Altstädtischer Markt 1; d from €93, breakfast €10; P ✳ 🕏) You'll sleep well in these bright, modern rooms rendered in cheerful reds and yellows and in pretty surroundings right by the town hall. Facilities include bike rentals and a small gym for keeping fit, a pretty good restaurant for sustenance and a sauna for winding down at the end of the day.

🍴 Eating

Cafébar Brückenhäuschen CAFE €
(☑ 03381-229 048; www.cafebar-kanu.de; Ritterstrasse 76; snacks €2.50-6.50; ⊘ 8.30am-6.30pm Mon-Fri, from 9.30am Sat & Sun) This kiosk right by the Jahrtausendbrücke is a top address for coffee and homemade cake (try the nut tarts). In fine weather you can relax canalside in beach chairs or rent a canoe (per two hours €10, per day €28).

Fisch am Mühlendamm SEAFOOD €
(☑ 03381-796 360; Mühlendamm 1; from €2; ⊘ 9am-8pm Mon-Sat) For a quick fish snack, pop into this little shack along Mühlendamm overlooking the water.

Restaurant an der Dominsel GERMAN €€
(☑ 03381-891 807; www.restaurant-dominsel.de; Neustädtische Fischerstrasse 14; mains €9-22; ⊘ 11am-midnight) Built around vestiges of the medieval town wall, this restaurant specialises in regional food, especially fish dishes, but what you'll probably remember most are the fabulous Dom views. It's right by the Mühlentorturm.

ℹ Information

Tourist Office (☑ 03381-796 360; www.stg-brandenburg.de; Neustädtischer Markt 3; ⊘ 9am-8pm Mon-Sat) Brandenburg's tourist office can help with maps, information and hotel rooms.

ℹ Getting There & Around

Regional trains link Brandenburg twice hourly with all major stations in central Berlin, including the Hauptbahnhof (€6.80, 45 minutes), and with Potsdam (€5.60, 30 minutes). From the station, it's about a 1.2km walk via Geschwister-Scholl-Strasse and St-Annen-Strasse to the Neustädtischer Markt. Trams 2 and 6 will get you there as well in about five minutes. Free parking is available at the corner of Grillendamm and Krakauer Strasse, just north of the Dom.

Frankfurt (Oder)

☑ 0335 / POP 58,000

Germany's 'other' Frankfurt, on the Oder River 90km east of Berlin, was practically wiped off the map in the final days of WWII and never recovered its one-time grandeur as a medieval trading centre and university town. It didn't help that the city was split in two after the war, with the eastern suburb across the river becoming the Polish town of Słubice. The GDR era imposed a decidedly unflattering Stalinist look, but the scenic river setting, a few architectural gems and the proximity to Poland (cheaper vodka and cigarettes, for all you hedonists) make fairly compelling excuses to pop by.

⊙ Sights

Marienkirche CHURCH
(☑ 0335-224 42; www.st-marien-ffo.de; Oberkirchplatz; ⊘ 10am-6pm May-Sep, to 4pm Oct-Apr) Looming above Marktplatz is the crenulated tower of the Church of St Mary, a huge red-brick Gothic hall church. Ruined by war and socialist-era disregard, it boasts a proud new roof and fantastic medieval stained-glass windows, which were squirrelled away as war booty in Russia until 2007. Today the church hosts events, concerts and exhibits.

Museum Junge Kunst MUSEUM
(☑ 0335-552 4150; www.museum-junge-kunst.de; Marktplatz 1 & Carl-Philipp-Emanuel-Bach-Strasse 11; adult/concession €6/4.20; ⊘ 11am-5pm Tue-Sun) Art created in the GDR rarely gets much attention these days, which is what makes this museum so special. Its 11,000 works rank among the world's finest and most comprehensive collections of East German art. Changing exhibits are presented in two locations – the Rathaus (town hall) and the riverside PackHof – and may include paintings by Werner Tübke, sculpture by Gustav Seitz and installations by Via Lewandowsky.

Kleist-Museum MUSEUM
(☑ 0335-387 2210; www.kleist-museum.de; Faberstrasse 6-7; adult/concession €5/3; ⊘ 10am-

6pm Tue-Sun) Heinrich von Kleist, one of Germany's key poets and dramatists of the Romantic Age, was born in Frankfurt (Oder) in 1777. A pilgrimage stop for literature fans, this sensitively curated exhibit in an old garrison school on the river walk chronicles the life, works and importance of the man who committed suicide, along with his lover, at age 34.

Take a walking tour in the footsteps of Kleist; ask for the free Kleist-Route pamphlet.

🛏 Sleeping & Eating

Hotel zur Alten Oder   HOTEL €
(☑ 0335-556 220; www.zuraltenoder.de; Fischerstrasse 32; d incl breakfast from €68; P 🐾) No two rooms are alike in this little hotel in a historic building, but all are drenched in bold colours, simply but charmingly furnished and sporting a country-style look. Breakfasts are lavish affairs that should tide you over into the early afternoon.

Turm 24   GERMAN €€
(☑ 0335-504 517; www.turm24.de; Logenstrasse 8; mains €10.50-23; ⊙ 11.30am-10pm Tue-Sun) Some locals joke that the best thing about this smart restaurant on the 24th floor of the Oderturm is that you can't see the Oderturm. Perhaps. But the panoramic views from up here are indeed fabulous and the German food is solid, with selections including regional fish and game along with steaks, salads and pasta dishes.

ℹ Information

Tourist Office (☑ 0335-610 0800; www.tourismus-ffo.de; Grosse Oderstrasse 29; ⊙ 10am-6pm Mon-Fri, 10am-2pm Sat) The local tourist office can provide information about both Frankfurt and Slubice on the Polish side of the Oder.

ℹ Getting There & Around

Regional trains leave Berlin-Hauptbahnhof half-hourly (€9.80, 1¼ hours). The central Marktplatz is about 1km northeast of the train station.

Chorin & Niederfinow

About 60km northeast of Berlin, in the heart of the Unesco Biosphere Reserve Schorfhei-

de-Chorin, **Kloster Chorin** (Chorin Monastery; ☑ 033366-703 77; www.kloster-chorin.org; Amt Chorin 11a; adult/concession €4/2.50; ⊙ 9am-6pm Apr-Oct, 10am-4pm Nov-Mar) is a romantically ruined monastery near a little lake and surrounded by a lush park. Built by Cistercian monks over six decades starting in 1273, it is widely considered one of the finest red-brick Gothic structures in northern Germany. It's an enchanting setting for concerts, theatre, markets and festivals, including the **Choriner Musiksommer** (☑ 03334-818 472; www.musiksommer-chorin.de; ⊙ Jun-Aug) classical concert series.

About 20km southeast of Chorin, the tiny village of Niederfinow is famous for its spectacular ship lift, the **Schiffshebewerk Niederfinow** (Ship's Lift; ☑ 033362-215; www.schiffshebewerk-niederfinow.info; Hebewerkstrasse 52; adult/concession €2/1; ⊙ 9am-6pm mid-Mar–mid-Oct, to 4pm mid-Oct–Dec & mid-Feb–mid-Mar), which links the Oder River and the Oder Havel Canal. This remarkable feat of engineering was completed in 1934 and measures 60m high, 27m wide and 94m long. Cargo barges sail into a sort of giant bathtub, which is then raised or lowered 36m, water and all. Visitors can enjoy the ride aboard tourist boats operated by **Fahrgastschifffahrt Neumann** (☑ 03334-244 05; www.schiffshebewerk-niederfinow.info/neumann; adult/child €7/4; ⊙ 11am, 1pm & 3pm late Mar-Oct).

To accommodate larger and multiple boats, an even more massive **modern ship lift** has been taking shape adjacent to the historic one. It is expected to be operational in 2016. A boat-shaped information centre has details about this ambitious project.

Regional trains make hourly trips to Chorin from Berlin-Hauptbahnhof (€8.40, 45 minutes) and are often met by bus 912 to the monastery. Alternatively, it's a 2.5km walk along a marked trail through the woods. There's a **bike rental shop** (☑ 033366-537 00; www.fahrradverleih-chorin.de; Chorin train station; per 8hr €9.80) in the train station. Seeing the monastery in the morning, then cycling over to the ship lift and back would make a nice day trip. To go directly to the Niederfinow ship lift, get off at Eberswalde and switch to bus 912 right there (€6.80, 1¼ hours).

Saxony

POP 4 MILLION / AREA 18,413 SQ KM

Best Places to Eat

➡ Restaurant Genuss-Atelier (p152)

➡ Vino e Cultura (p178)

➡ Restaurant Vincenz Richter (p158)

➡ Stadtpfeiffer (p171)

➡ Auerbachs Keller (p171)

Best Places to Stay

➡ Hotel Börse (p178)

➡ Steigenberger Grandhotel Handelshof (p170)

➡ Hotel Schloss Eckberg (p151)

➡ Burg Altrathen (p159)

➡ Ferdinands Homestay (p160)

Why Go?

Saxony has an enormous amount to to offer anyone interested in history, music, art, mountain scenery, castles and cobbled-street market towns, and its warm and welcoming people, stellar opera houses and deeply entrenched love of culture will win over anyone who takes the time to explore this often-overlooked corner of Germany.

Many heavyweights have shaped Saxony's cultural landscape: Bach, Canaletto, Goethe, Luther and Wagner among them, while Dresden's Semperoper and Leipzig's Gewandhaus have for centuries been among the world's finest musical venues. Today both of Saxony's biggest cities also offer impressive (and great value) music, art and entertainment activities, which ensure a steady flow of young creatives from all over Germany and beyond.

Many visitors skip Saxony and head straight to Berlin for their fix of Eastern Germany, missing Saxony's unique charms and character (not to mention an entirely different history). If you take the time to come here, you'll quickly understand how multifaceted, progressive and fascinating Saxony can be.

When to Go

The cities are fun in the summer when life moves outdoors, festivals are in full swing and you can boat or cycle along the Elbe River. Thanks to lots of world-class museums and performance venues, Dresden is also a fine destination in winter, especially in December during the famous Christmas market (Striezelmarkt). Avoid Leipzig during the springtime trade-fair crunch, especially in March and April. The Bachfest in June draws scores of visitors. The trails and rock walls in Saxon Switzerland are busiest in summer and autumn, particularly at the weekend.

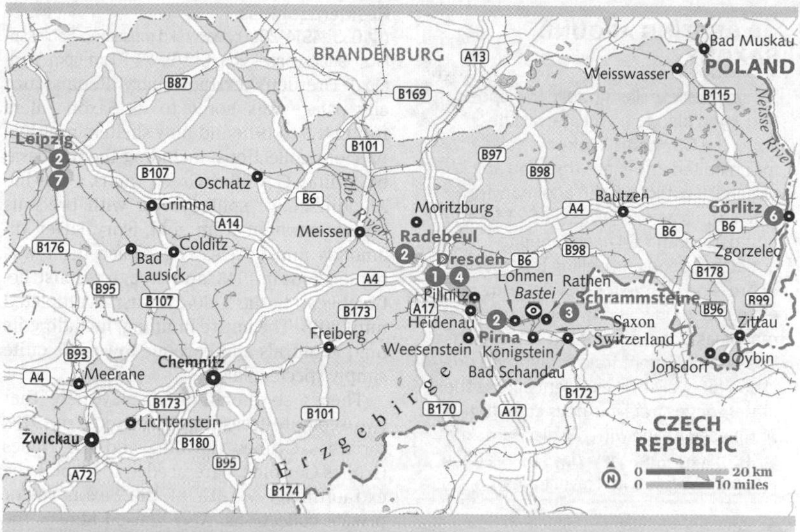

Saxony Highlights

[1] Taking in the stunning baroque silhouette of Dresden's Altstadt, with the remarkable **Residenzschloss** (p142) and **Frauenkirche** (p142)

[2] Travelling back in time to the GDR at museums in **Leipzig** (p164), **Pirna** (p156) and **Radebeul** (p156)

[3] Clambering up the **Schrammsteine** (p161) for gobsmacking panoramas of the Saxon Switzerland and the Elbe

[4] Donning sunglasses to view the dazzling treasures at Dresden's **Grünes Gewölbe** (p142)

[5] Marvelling at the architecture of **Görlitz** (p176), one of Germany's most attractive cities

[6] Treating your ears to a concert at Leipzig's storied **Gewandhausorchester** (p172)

DRESDEN

☎0351 / POP 512,000

There are few city silhouettes more striking than Dresden's. The classic view from the Elbe's northern bank takes in spires, towers and domes belonging to palaces, churches and stately buildings, and indeed it's hard to believe that the city was all but wiped off the map by Allied bombings in 1945.

Dresden's cultural heyday came under the 18th-century reign of Augustus the Strong (August der Starke) and his son Augustus III, who produced many of Dresden's iconic buildings, including the Zwinger and the Frauenkirche. While the devastating 1945 allied firestorm levelled most of these treasures, their contents were safely removed before the bombings and now take pride of place in Dresden's rebuilt museums.

The city has had a few tough years of late, however. In 2014, a populist protest movement called PEGIDA (Patriotic Europeans Against the Islamisation of the West) was founded here and quickly became a nationwide phenomenon. But although the city, once known as the 'Florence of the North', gave birth to this anti-Islamic movement, the overwhelming majority of Dresden's residents do not agree with its message. It's hard to find a single museum, cultural institute or university here that isn't bedecked with large signs declaring support for multiculturalism, welcoming migrants and generally subverting the PEGIDA message, which itself seems to have lost public support in the intervening period. Dresden and its surroundings may have been nicknamed 'the valley of the clueless' under communism (due to locals not being able to pick up West German TV), but its public institutions now proclaim themselves *'für ein weltoffenes Dresden'* ('for a Dresden open to the world'). Take some time to get to know this fascinating, contradictory city.

ℹ️ GETTING AROUND SAXONY

Saxony has excellent public transport, and if you plan to travel all over the state, the **Sachsen-Ticket** is valid for unlimited 2nd-class travel on any regional Deutsche Bahn and many privately run trains. The cost is €23 for the first person and €4 each for up to four additional people travelling together. There is no charge for bicycles. Buy tickets online or in stations from vending machines or ticket counters. Elsewhere, buses supplement train routes, and provision for cyclists is excellent across the state. Longer train journeys can often be purchased online with big discounts if you book at least a few days beforehand and are flexibile with travel times.

👁 Sights

Key sights cluster in the compact Altstadt on the Elbe's south bank, about 1km from the Hauptbahnhof via Prager Strasse, the main pedestrianised shopping strip. From here, Augustusbrücke leads across the river to the Neustadt, with its own major train station (Dresden-Neustadt) and the main pub and party quarter in the Äussere Neustadt (Outer Neustadt).

👁 Altstadt

Frauenkirche   CHURCH
(www.frauenkirche-dresden.de;   Neumarkt;   audioguide €2.50, cupola adult/student €8/5 ; ⊙10am-noon & 1-6pm) **FREE** The domed Frauenkirche – Dresden's most beloved symbol – has literally risen from the city's ashes. The original graced its skyline for two centuries before collapsing after the February 1945 bombing, and was rebuilt from a pile of rubble between 1994 and 2005. A spitting image of the original, it may not bear the gravitas of age but that only slightly detracts from its festive beauty inside and out. The altar, reassembled from nearly 2000 fragments, is especially striking.

The cuploa can be climbed. The galleried interior is a wonderful place for concerts, meditations and services. Check the website for the current schedule or stop by the Frauenkirche tourist office, which screens a documentary about the church's history.

Residenzschloss   PALACE
(📞0351-4914 2000; www.skd.museum; Schlossplatz; adult/concession €12/9; ⊙10am-6pm Wed-Mon) Dresden's extraordinary Renaissance city palace was home to its Saxon rulers from 1485 to 1918 and now shelters multiple precious collections, including the unmissable Grünes Gewölbe (Green Vault), a real-life Aladdin's Cave spilling over with precious objects wrought from gold, ivory, silver, diamonds and jewels. The palace itself was bombed out in 1945, and though reconstruction began in the 1960s, it wasn't completed until 2013. The entire building, including its unique murals and baroque towers, is quite simply spectacular.

There's so much on display here that two separate treasure chambers – the Historisches Grünes Gewölbe and the Neues Grünes Gewölbe – are needed to display the extraordinary wealth of the Saxon rulers' private collections. Also housed here is the Kupferstich-Kabinett, which counts around half a million prints and drawings by 20,000 artists (including Dürer, Rembrandt and Michelangelo) in its possession. Numismatists might want to drop by the Münzkabinett (Coin Cabinet) in the palace tower for a small array of historic coins and medals.

The Türckische Cammer (Turkish Chamber), one of the richest collections of Ottoman art outside Turkey, is also here. A huge three-mast tent made of gold and silk is one standout among many. The new Riesensaal (Giant's Hall) houses a spectacular collection of armour, including re-creations of several jousting tournaments. You can easily spend several hours exploring the various collections here. Tickets to the Residenzschloss are good for all these collections except for the Historisches Grünes Gewölbe, which need to be purchased separately and have timed entrance.

⭐ **Historisches Grünes Gewölbe**   MUSEUM
(Historic Green Vault; 📞0351-4914 2000; www.skd. museum; Residenzschloss; admission incl audioguide €14; ⊙10am-6pm Wed-Mon) The Historic Green Vault displays some 3000 precious items in the same fashion as during the time of August der Starke, namely on shelves and tables without glass protection in a series of increasingly lavish rooms. Admission is by timed ticket only, and only a limited number of visitors per hour may pass through the 'dust lock'. Get advance tickets online or by phone since only 40% are sold at the palace box office for same-day admission.

Neues Grünes Gewölbe   MUSEUM
(New Green Vault; ☑ 0351-4914 2000; www.skd.museum; Residenzschloss; adult/under 17yr incl audioguide €14/free; ☺10am-6pm Wed-Mon) The New Green Vault presents some 1000 objects in 10 modern rooms. Key sights include a frigate fashioned from ivory with wafer-thin sails, a cherry pit with 185 faces carved into it and an exotic ensemble of 132 gem-studded figurines representing a royal court in India. The artistry of each item is dazzling. To avoid the worst crush of people, visit during lunchtime.

Katholische Hofkirche   CHURCH
(Schlossplatz; ☺9am-5pm Mon-Thu, 1-5pm Fri, 10am-5pm Sat, noon-4pm Sun) **FREE** The Katholische Hofkirche (also called Dresden Cathedral) makes up an integral part of the baroque ensemble crowning the Altstadt, and is one of Dresden's most dazzling buildings. Built between 1739 and 1751 by Gaetano Chiaveri as a Catholic rival to the Protestant Frauenkirche, its detailed and exuberant exterior is extraordinarily impressive, while its rather bare interior is enlivened by the gilded altar, pulpit and organ. Destroyed in WWII, it was rebuilt in the 1980s.

★Zwinger   PALACE
(☑ 0351-4914 2000; www.der-dresdner-zwinger.de; Theaterplatz 1; ☺10am-6pm Tue-Sun) **FREE** A collaboration between the architect Matthäus Pöppelmann and the sculptor Balthasar Permoser, the Zwinger was built between 1710 and 1728 on the orders of Augustus the Strong, who wanted something similar to Louis XIV's palace at Versailles for himself. Primarily a party palace for royals, the Zwinger has ornate portals that lead into the vast fountain-studded courtyard, which is framed by buildings lavishly festooned with evocative sculpture. Today it houses three superb museums within its baroque walls.

Atop the western pavilion stands a tense-looking Atlas. Opposite him is a carillon of 40 Meissen porcelain bells, which tinkle every 15 minutes. Entry to the magnificent courtyard is free, but all three museums are ticketed. The Gemäldegalerie Alte Meister (Old Masters Gallery) and Porzellansammlung (Porcelain Collection) are unmissable, while the historic scientific instruments at the Mathematisch-Physikalischer Salon are perhaps more for the scientifically minded.

➡ ★Gemäldegalerie Alte Meister
(www.skd.museum; Zwinger, Theaterplatz 1; adult/student €10/7.50, audioguide €3; ☺10am-6pm Tue-Sun) This astounding collection of Eu-

ropean art from the 16th to 18th centuries boasts an incredible number of masterpieces, including Rafael's famous *Sistine Madonna,* which dominates the enormous main hall on the ground floor, as well as works by Titian, Tintoretto, Holbein, Dürer and Cranach, whose *Paradise* (1530) is particularly arresting. Upstairs you'll find an exquisite display of Rembrandt, Boticelli, Veronese, Van Dyck, Vermeer, Brueghel and Poussin. Finally, don't miss Canaletto's sumptuous portrayals of 18th century Dresden on the top floor.

➡ Porzellansammlung
(www.skd.museum; Zwinger, Theaterplatz 1; adult/student €10/7.50) Housed in two gorgeously converted curving galleries, this extraordinary collection ranges from Chinese porcelain from the 17th and 18th centuries to that produced in Meissen, as the European art of making 'white gold' was perfected under August the Strong. The fabulous Tiersaal (animal hall) is the ultimate highlight, where you can see hundreds of animals rendered in porcelain, although the full-on crucifixion scene is quite a show stopper in itself as well.

➡ Mathematisch-
Physikalischer Salon
(www.skd.museum; Zwinger, Theaterplatz 1; adult/student/under 17yr €6/4.50/free; ☺10am-6pm Tue-Sun) This wonderful collection of scientific implements dating from the early 16th century on will delight anyone interested in the history of science and the Enlightenment, with its telescopes, barometers and dozens of other early instruments. A free audioguide puts the collection into context.

★Albertinum   MUSEUM
(☑ 0351-4914 2000; www.skd.museum; enter from Brühlsche Terrasse or Georg-Treu-Platz 2; adult/concession/under 17yr €10/7.50/free; ☺10am-6pm Tue-Sun; ℗) After massive renovations following severe 2002 flood damage, the Renaissance-era former arsenal became the stunning home of the Galerie Neue Meister (New Masters Gallery), which displays an arc of paintings by some of the great names in art from the 18th century onwards. Caspar David Friedrich and Claude Monet's landscapes compete with the abstract visions of Marc Chagall and Gerhard Richter, all in gorgeous rooms orbiting a light-filled courtyard. There's also a superb sculpture collection spread over the lower floors.

Dresden

SAXONY

500 m
0.25 miles

Lobtauer Str
29

Nordstr

Radeberger Str

Genuss-Ate iler
(1km);
Hotel Schloss
Eckberg (2km)

Forststr

Bischofsweg

Alaunplatz

32

Kamenzer Str

Prossnitzstr

13

Holzhofgasse

49

11

40

48

Görlitzer Str

26
51

58
36
47
43
50 38
42

55 35
62
59

56
37

25

Forsteistr

Jordanstr

Kunsthofpassage

Louisenstr

Böhmische Str

17

44 54

Rothenburger Str

Bautzner Str

Hoyerswerdaer Str

Elbe River

Käthe- Kollwitz-Ufer

Albertbrücke

Pfeifferharinstr

Protenhauerstr

53

Glacisstr

Alaunstr

Hospitalstr

Carolabrücke

Wigardstr

Katharinenstr

52

Dammweg

Militärhistorisches Museum
Dresden (1.5km)

Königsbrücker Str

D.-Friedrich-Wolf-Str

Elna-Berger-Str

31
46

Dresden-
Neustadt

Lössnitzstr

Schlesischer
Platz

Schlesischer
Platz

Grossenhainer Str

Gothaer Str

Leipziger Str

Albertplatz

21

Theresienstr

61

Nieritzstr

28

Königstr

NEUSTADT

6

Metzer Str

Rittelstr

Hainstr

Arnoldstr

Neustädter
Markt

Albertstr

Köpckestr

Neustädter Str

Hauptstr

Rähnitzgasse

27

Palaisplatz

Grosse Meissner Str

Augustusbrücke

Terrassenufer

16

Devrientstr

Marienbrücke

Ostra-Allee

Am
Schiesshaus

23

45

Dresden
Mitte

33

Schützengasse

18

Magdeburger Str

Trabi
Safari (1km)

Weisseritzstr

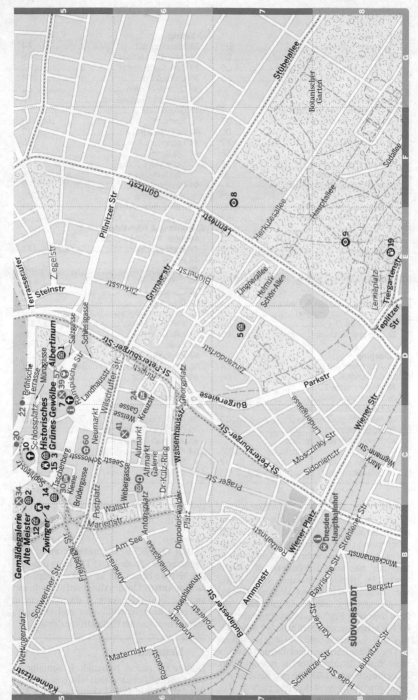

SAXONY

Stübelallee

Botanischer Garten

Gützstr

Lennéstr

Herkulesallee

Hauptallee

Südallee

Pillnitzer Str

Grunaer str

Blüherstr

Zirkusstr

8

9

19

Terrasserufer

Steinstr

Z egelstr

Lingnerallee

Helmut Schön-Alle?

Lennéplatz

Tiergartenstr

Teplitzer Str

Brühlsche Terrasse

Albertinum

Salzgasse

Schiessgasse

St.-Petersburger-Str

5

22

Historisches Grünes Gewölbe

Münzgasse

Rampische Str

Landhausstr

Wilsdruffer Str

Georgplatz

Bürgerwiese

Zinzendorfst

Parkstr

Wiener Str

7 39 57

1

Schlossplatz

20

10

Neumarkt

Weisse Gasse

Kreuzstr

24

41

Waisenhausstr

St.-Petersburger-Str

Lindengasse

Mosczinsky Str

Sidonienstr

Marschallstr

Wismann-Str

Schlossst

15 3

Taschenberg

Seesch Schlossst

60

Altmarkt

Altmarkt Galerie

Dr.-Külz-Ring

Prager Str

Reitbahnstr

Kleine Brüdergasse

Webergasse

Antonsplatz

Gemäldegalerie Alte Meister

34

2

Alte Meister

12

4

14

Zwinger

Schweriner Str

Freiberger Str

Annenstr

Marienstr

Postplatz

Wallstr

Am See

Dippoldiswalder Platz

Ammonstr

Budapester Str

Wiener Platz

Dresden Hauptbahnhof

Winckelmannstr

Bayrische Str

Strehlener Str

Wettingerplatz

Könneritztr

Littegasse

Josephinenstr

Polierstr

Annenstr

Rosenstr

Maternistr

Budapester Str

Schweizer Str

Hohe Str

Kaitzer Str

Leubnitzer Str

Bergstr

SÜDVORSTADT

Dresden

Semperoper   HISTORIC BUILDING
(☏0351-320 7360; www.semperoper-erleben.
de; Theaterplatz 2; tour adult/concession €10/6;
☉hours vary) One of Germany's most famous
opera houses, the Semperoper opened in
1841 and has hosted premieres of famous
works by Richard Strauss, Carl Maria
von Weber and Richard Wagner. Guided
45-minute tours operate almost daily (the
3pm tour is in English); exact times depend
on the rehearsal and performance schedule.
Buy advance tickets online to skip the queue.

The original Semperoper burned down a
mere three decades after its inauguration.
After reopening in 1878, the neo-Renaissance
jewel entered its most dazzling period. Alas,
WWII put an end to the fun and it wasn't until 1985 that music again filled the grand hall.

Yenidze   ARCHITECTURE
(☏0351-490 5990; www.kuppelrestaurant.de; Weis-
seritzstrasse 3; ☉noon-11pm) The huge mosque-
like Yenidze began life in 1909 as a cigarette
factory with a chimney disguised as a minaret
and a stained-glass dome. Today it's home to
offices, a ho-hum restaurant and Dresden's
highest beer garden (beneath the dome).

◎ Neustadt

Despite its name, Neustadt is actually an
older part of Dresden that was considerably
less damaged in WWII than the Altstadt. It

consists of the gentrified Innere Neustadt, with Hauptstrasse as its main artery, and the still delightfully wacky Äussere (Outer) Neustadt pub district north of Albertplatz.

★ Militärhistorisches Museum Dresden
MUSEUM

(☎ 0351-823 2803; www.mhmbw.de; Olbrichtplatz 2; adult/concession €5/3; ⊗ 10am-6pm Thu-Tue, to 9pm Mon; 🚋 7 or 8 to Stauffenbergallee) Even devout pacifists will be awed by this engaging museum that reopened in 2011 in a 19th-century arsenal bisected by a bold glass-and-steel wedge designed by Daniel Libeskind. Exhibits have been updated for the 21st century, so don't expect a roll call of military victories or parade of weapons. Instead, you'll find a progressive – and often artistic – look at the roots and ramifications of war and aggression.

Exhibits in the Libeskind wedge focus on women in the war, animals in the war, war-themed toys, the economy of war and the suffering brought on by war. The historical wing presents a chronology of German wars from the Middle Ages to the 20th century. Standouts among the countless intriguing objects are a 1975 Soyuz landing capsule, a V2 rocket, and personal items of concentration camp victims. Allow at least two hours to do this amazing museum justice.

Kunsthofpassage
ARCHITECTURE

(enter from Alaunstrasse 70 or Görlitzer Strasse 23; ⊗ 24hr) **FREE** Take a web of grimy courtyards, a load of paint and a bunch of visionary Dresden artists and out comes the Kunsthofpassage, one of the most refreshingly artistic spaces in the Neustadt. Each courtyard has its own charm, but favourites include the Court of the Elements, where 'music' is created by water running down interlinked rain pipes affixed to a turquoise facade, and the Court of the Animals, where monkeys leap above the head of a giant giraffe.

Pfunds Molkerei
ARCHITECTURE

(☎ 0351 808 080; www.pfunds.de; Bautzner Strasse 79; ⊗ 10am-6pm Mon-Sat, 10am-3pm Sun) **FREE** The Guinness-certified 'world's most beautiful dairy shop' was founded in 1880 and is a riot of hand-painted tiles and enamelled sculpture, all handmade by Villeroy & Boch. The shop sells replica tiles, wines, cheeses and other milk products. Not surprisingly, the upstairs cafe-restaurant has a strong lactose theme. Slip in between coach tours for a less shuffling look round.

Dreikönigskirche
CHURCH

(☎ 0351-812 4102; www.hdk-dkk.de; Hauptstrasse 23; tower adult/concession €3/2; ⊗ 11.30am-4pm Tue, 11am-5pm Wed-Sat, 11.30am-5pm Sun May-Oct) Designed by Zwinger architect Pöppelmann, the most eye-catching feature of the Dreikönigskirche is the baroque altar that was ruined in 1945 and left as a memorial. Also note the 12m-long Renaissance-era Dance of Death sandstone relief opposite the altar, beneath the organ. The 88m-high tower can be scaled for some panoramic views.

⊙ Grosser Garten & Around

Grosser Garten
GARDENS

(www.grosser-garten-dresden.de; Hauptallee 5; ⊗ 24hr) **FREE** The aptly named Grosser Garten (Great Garden) is a relaxing refuge during the warmer months. A visitor magnet here is the modernised **Zoo Dresden** (☎ 0351-478 060; www.zoo-dresden.de; Tiergartenstrasse 1; adult/child €12/4; ⊗ 8.30am-6.30pm Apr-Oct, 8.30am-4.30pm Nov-Mar) in the southwest corner, where crowds gravitate towards the Africa Hall and the lion enclosure. In the northwest corner is the architecturally distinguished transparent **Gläserne Manufaktur** (Transparent Factory; ☎ 0351-420 4411; www.glaesernemanufaktur.de; cnr Lennéstrasse & Stübelallee; building free, tours adult/concession €5/3; ⊗ 8.30am-7pm Mon-Fri, 9am-6pm Sat & Sun), where you can observe how the Volkswagen luxury model 'Phaeton' is being constructed. Right next to it is the free **Botanischer Garten** (botanical garden).

Deutsches Hygiene-Museum
MUSEUM

(☎ 0351-484 6400; www.dhmd.de; Lingnerplatz 1; adult/student/under 16 €7/3/free, valid on 2 consecutive days; ⊗ 10am-6pm Tue-Sun; 👣) Not an institution dedicated to the history of cleaning products, the German Hygiene Museum is, in fact, all about human beings. The permanent exhibit uses intriguing objects, interpretive panelling, installations and interactive stations to examine the human body in its social, cultural, historical and scientific contexts. Living and dying, eating and drinking, sex and beauty are all addressed. The **Children's Museum** in the basement takes four to 12-year-olds on an interactive romp through the mysteries of the five senses.

☞ Tours

NightWalk Dresden
WALKING TOURS

(☎ 0172-781 5007; www.nightwalk-dresden.de; Albertplatz; tours €15; ⊗ tour 9pm) See street art,

ℹ DRESDEN-CARDS

The excellent Dresden-Card (www.dresden.de/dresdencard) provides free public transport as well as sweeping sightseeing discounts. Various cards are available from the Tourist Office (p155). The one-day **Dresden-City-Card** (single/family €10/15) is good for transport and discounts to 90 sights, attractions, tours and other participating venues. The two-day version (€35/65) delivers free admission to all state museums with the exception of the Historisches Grüne Gewölbe, and discounts on many others.The **Dresden-Regio-Card** (€40/60 for 3 days) includes all this plus discounts to 40 additional sights. All in all, they're excellent value and guarantee big savings if you plan to visit several museums in Dresden.

learn about what life was like in East Germany and visit fun pubs and bars in the Outer Neustadt on this super fun tour. Night-Walk also have the exclusive rights to take visitors to the slaughterhouse where Kurt Vonnegut survived the bombing of Dresden in 1945 and which he later immortalised in *Slaughterhouse-Five* (p153).

Sächsische Dampfschiffahrt   BOAT TOUR
(☑ 0331-866 090; www.saechsische-dampfschif-fahrt.de) From April to October, steamers plough up the Elbe several times daily between Dresden and Bad Schandau, stopping in Rathen, Königstein and other towns. The entire round trip takes 5½ hours and costs €25 (concession €18). You can do the entire trip or hop aboard along the way, and there are a number of other specialist cruises available, including downstream to Meissen.

Grosse Stadtrundfahrt   BUS TOUR
(☑ 0351-899 5650; www.stadtrundfahrt.com; Theaterplatz; day pass adult/concession €20/18; ☺ 9.30am-10pm Apr-Oct, to 8pm Nov-Mar) Narrated hop-on, hop-off tour with 22 stops and optional short guided tours ticks off all major sights. Buses leave every 15 to 30 minutes.

Trabi Safari   CAR TOUR
(☑ 0351-8990 0110; www.trabi-safari.de; Bremer Strasse 35; per person €34-60) Get behind the wheel of the ultimate GDR-mobile for this 1½-hour guided drive around the city, taking in sights from all eras. The price depends on the number of people in the car: four people to a car is the best value.

✪ Festivals & Events

Internationales Dixieland Festival   MUSIC FESTIVAL
(www.dixieland.de) Bands from around the world descend on Dresden for one week in May.

Dresdener Musikfestspiele   MUSIC FESTIVAL
(www.musikfestspiele.com) Held mid-May to June, with mostly classical music.

Bunte Republik Neustadt   STREET FESTIVAL
(www.brn-dresden.de) The Outer Neustadt celebrates its alternative roots on the third June weekend with lots of music, food and wacky merriment.

Striezelmarkt   CHRISTMAS MARKET
During December, sample the famous Dresdener Stollen (fruit cake) at one of Germany's oldest and best Christmas markets.

🛏 Sleeping

Dresden's hotels can be horrendously expensive, with rates among the highest in Germany. Thankfully there are plenty of cheap beds available at the city's superb hostels.

🛏 Altstadt

Hotel Bülow Residenz   HOTEL €
(☑ 0351-800 3291; www.buelow-residenz.de; Rähnitzgasse 19; d from €69; P ❋ ☜) This place occupies one of Dresden's oldest town houses and is a class act, from the welcome drink to the spacious gold-and-crimson-hued rooms baronially cloaked in antiques, paintings and porcelain. Days get off to a breezy start with a lavish breakfast in the glass-covered courtyard atrium. You can get excellent deals by booking ahead online: walk-ins are far pricier.

Aparthotel am Zwinger   APARTMENT €
(☑ 0351-8990 0100; www.aparthotel-zwinger.de; Maxstrasse 3; apt €60-130; ☺ reception 7am-10pm Mon-Fri, 9.30am-6pm Sat & Sun, or by arrangement; P @ ☜) This excellent option has bright, functional and spacious apartments with kitchens that even come equipped with Nespresso machines. Units are spread over several buildings, but all are super-central and quiet. Access to the buffet breakfast costs €10, and it's a good option unless you're self-catering, as the neighbourhood is pretty low on breakfast options.

★ **Gewandhaus Hotel**　BOUTIQUE HOTEL €€
(📞0351-4949 3636; www.gewandhaus-hotel.de; Ringstrasse 1; d from €133; P✳@🛜🏊) Fresh from a total renovation and rebirth as a boutique hotel, the stunning Gewandhaus, an 18th-century trading house of tailors and fabric merchants that burned down in 1945, now has sleek public areas, beautiful and bright rooms, and a breakfast that sets a high bar for anything else offered in the city.

Hotel Taschenbergpalais Kempinski　HOTEL €€€
(📞0351-491　20; www.kempinski-dresden.de; Taschenberg 3; r €130-256; ✳@🛜🏊) You might never get around to sightseeing when staying at this swank 18th-century mansion where luxury is taken very seriously. Checking in here buys views over the Zwinger from rakishly handsome rooms that beautifully bridge the traditional and the contemporary with rich royal blue colours and marble bathrooms with Bulgari toiletries. In winter, the courtyard turns into an ice rink.

🛏 **Neustadt**

Kangaroo-Stop　HOSTEL €
(📞0351-314　3455; www.kangaroo-stop.de; Erna-Berger-Strasse 8-10; dm €14.50 18.50, d €46, linen €2; P@🛜) With an Australian theme throughout, this superb hostel is spread over two buildings: one for backies, the other for families. Some rooms have sinks, but other facilities are shared. Strike up new friendships in the kitchen-diner and communal areas, then mine the knowledgeable owner for the insider scoop on the city. Add on breakfast for €6 per person.

Hostel Louise 20　HOSTEL €
(📞0351-889 4894; www.louise20.de; Louisenstrasse 20; dm/s/d/apt from €16/32/42/106; 😊@🛜) Right in the heart of the Outer Neustadt, this friendly and well-run hostel is an obvious choice for travellers wanting to hang out and take in the spirit of alternative Dresden. Dorms are simple, but clean and comfortable, each with lockers for security and shared bathrooms. Larger apartments are great for groups (up to eight people).

Lollis Homestay　HOSTEL €
(📞0351-810 8458; www.lollishome.de; Görlitzer Strasse 34; dm €15-20, d €46-52, linen €2, breakfast €4; @🛜) This is a textbook backpacker hostel: friendly, communicative, casual and with neatly designed themed rooms (Cinema, Desert, Giants), including a rather gimmicky double where you live out that *Good Bye, Lenin!* vibe by bedding down in a real GDR-era Trabi car. Bikes, tea and coffee are free, and the communal room and kitchen are conducive to meeting fellow travellers.

Hostel Mondpalast　HOSTEL €
(📞0351-563 4050; www.mondpalast.de; Louisenstrasse 77; dm €15-22, d €56, linen €2; @🛜) A funky location in the thick of the Äussere Neustadt is the main draw of this out-of-this-world hostel-bar-cafe (with cheap drinks). Each funky and playful room is designed to reflect a sign of the zodiac. Bonus points for the bike rentals and the well-equipped kitchen. Breakfast is €7.

Hotel Martha Dresden　HOTEL €€
(📞0351-817　60; www.hotel-martha-dresden. de; Nieritzstrasse 11; s €76-89, d €113-121, apt €138; 🛜) Big windows, wooden floors and Biedermeier-inspired furnishings combine with an attractive winter garden and a smiley welcome to make a great option with easy access to the sights across the river. The hotel is wheelchair-accessible. Breakfast is €10; bike rental is available.

Hotel Privat　HOTEL €€
(📞0351-811 770; www.das-nichtraucher-hotel.de; Forststrasse 22; s/d €78/99; P@) This small,

---

DRESDEN & WWII

Between 13 and 15 February 1945, British and American planes unleashed 3900 tonnes of explosives on Dresden in four huge air raids. Bombs and incendiary shells whipped up a mammoth firestorm, and ashes rained down on villages 35km away. When the blazes had died down and the dust settled, tens of thousands of Dresdners had lost their lives and 20 sq km of this once elegant baroque city lay in smouldering ruins.

Historians still argue over whether this constituted a war crime committed by the Allies on an innocent civilian population. Some claim that with the Red Army at the gates of Berlin, the war was effectively won, and the Allies gained little military advantage from the destruction of Dresden. Others have said that as the last urban centre in the east of the country left intact, Dresden could have provided shelter for German troops returning from the east and was a viable target.

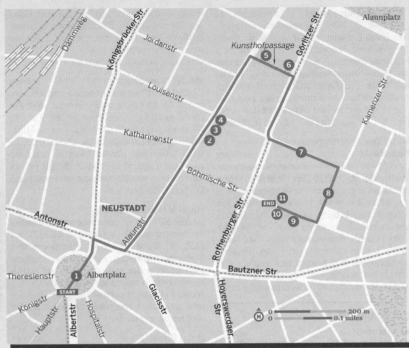

City Walk
Street Art in the Outer Neustadt

START ALBERTPLATZ
FINISH BÖHMISCHE STRASSE
LENGTH 2KM; ONE TO 1½ HOURS

If you're finished feasting your eyes on Dresden's baroque beauties, it's time for a dose of real life in the colourful, alt-flavoured Äussere (Outer) Neustadt.

Start your tour on ❶ **Albertplatz**, perhaps casting at the two fountains representing turbulent and still waters, then plunge into the depth of the Outer Neustadt via Alaunstrasse. Soon on your right is ❷ **Die Scheune** (p154), Dresden's oldest youth club, which has been going strong since 1951. Stop to admire the latest artistic outpourings on the officially designated ❸ **Graffiti Wall** just before Katy's Garage, then rub your eyes in disbelief at the ❹ **17m-long bicycle**, an art installation by Dutch artist Wouter Mijland. Keep going on Alaunstrasse to the whimsical ❺ **Kunsthofpassage** (p147), a cluster of five interlinked artist-designed courtyards. Give your camera a workout, then grab a yummy ice cream at ❻ **Neumanns Tiki** (p154), family-owned since 1966, then turn right onto Görlitzer Strasse. Make a note to come back in the evening to join the other 'lost kids' in the 'Bermuda Triangle' of densely clustered ❼ **bars and pubs** around Louisenstrasse, then make your way down gritty Martin-Luther-Strasse, home to some especially fine ❽ **street art**. Next up is the Outer Neustadt's most intriguing lane, Böhmische Strasse, home to not only art squat-turned-gastropub ❾ **Raskolnikoff** (p152) but also to the intriguing ❿ **Ukradena Galerie**, Dresden's smallest gallery (its name means 'stolen gallery' in Czech). Part of an experimental street art project, it's really just a small display case affixed to a wall with a different artist installing a new exhibit every week – see if you can make the vernissage (preview) of the new piece each Sunday at 6pm! Across the street, you can add your own wisdom (in chalk) to a ⓫ **long blackboard** intended to combat illegal graffiti.

family-run hotel in a quiet residential district a short wander from the Neustadt's bars has plenty of easy Saxon charm. There are 30 decent-sized rooms, some with alcoves and balconies, and a complete and utter ban on any kind of smoking (see website name!). A good option for peace and quiet within easy reach of fun.

★ Hotel Schloss Eckberg HOTEL €€€

(☑ 0351-80 990; www.schloss-eckberg.de; Bautzner Strasse 134; d Kavaliershaus/Schloss from €135/210; P ✿ @) This romantic castle set in its own riverside park east of the Neustadt is a breathtaking place to stay. Rooms in the Schloss itself are pricier and have oodles of historic flair, but staying in the modern Kavaliershaus lets you enjoy almost as many amenities and the same dreamy setting. The downside: you may not want to see Dresden itself at all.

✕ Eating

✕ Altstadt

brennNessel VEGETARIAN €€

(☑ 0351-494 3319; www.brennnessel-dresden.de; Schützengasse 18; mains €9-15; ⊘ 11am-midnight) This fearfully popular, largely vegetarian gastropub in a miraculously surviving 350-year-old building is an oasis in the otherwise empty and anodyne streets of the Altstadt. Indeed, reserve for lunch if you'd like to eat outside in the charming, sun-dappled courtyard as it's something of a favourite hang-out for off-duty Semperoper musicians and nearby office workers.

There's a huge menu, with daily changing specials, meat options and a vegan menu.

Ladencafé Aha INTERNATIONAL €€

(☑ 0351-496 0673; www.ladencafe.de; Kreuzstrasse 7; mains €8-16; ⊘ 9am-midnight; ✐ ✚) Dine outside on the pavement in front of the impressive Kreuzkirche, or retire to the cosy interior of this charming vegetarian-leaning health food cafe. There's a great menu, full of fresh regional produce and plenty of meat-free options, and its individualism makes it a far cry from the other identikit Altstadt eating options. There's a kids' play area.

Cafe Alte Meister INTERNATIONAL €€

(☑ 0351-481 0426; www.altemeister.net; Theaterplatz 1a; mains €10-25; ⊘ 10am-1am) If you've worked up an appetite or need a break from museum-hopping, retreat to this elegant filling station for creative and seasonal bistro fare in its artsy interior or on the terrace. At night, the ambience is a bit more formal.

Grand Café SAXON €€

(☑ 0351-496 2444; www.coselpalais-dresden.de; An der Frauenkirche 12; mains €9-19; ⊘ 10am-midnight) The imaginative mains (try roasted pike perch on crispy Dijon mustard rösti with lemon and vegetables) and sumptuous cakes are good, but they act more as appetisers for the gold-trimmed baroque Coselpalais, which houses the cafe and makes for a stylish (if slightly formal) refuelling stop.

Sophienkeller SAXON €€

(☑ 0351-497 260; www.sophienkeller-dresden.de; Taschenberg 3; mains €10-15; ⊘ 11am-1am) The 1730s theme with waitresses trussed up in period garb may be a bit overcooked but the local specialities certainly aren't. Most of it is rib-sticking fare, like the boneless half duck with red cabbage or the spit-roasted suckling pig. Wash it down with a mug of dark Bohemian Krušovice. Great ambience amid vaulted ceilings in the Taschenbergpalais building.

Zum Schiesshaus SAXON €€

(☑ 0351-484 5990; www.zum-schiesshaus.de; Am Schiesshaus 19; mains €10-25; ⊘ 11am-1am) If you're yearning for something traditional, meaty and quintessentially Saxon, then this is the place for you. Oozing old world atmosphere despite having been destroyed in both the Thirty Year War and WWII, this former medieval shooting range has been rebuilt and now caters for those wanting a hearty meal washed down with plenty of local beer.

✕ Neustadt

Cafe Continental CAFE, INTERNATIONAL €

(☑ 0351-272 1722; www.cafe-continental-dresden.de; Görlitzer Strasse 1; dishes €4-15; ⊘ 24hr) If the greenly lit openings behind the bar remind you of aquariums, you've hit the nail on the head, for buzzy 'Conti' was a pet store back in GDR days. Today, it's a great place to hit no matter the hour for anything from cappuccino and cocktails to homemade cakes or a full meal. Breakfast is served until 4pm.

Dampfschwein INTERNATIONAL €

(www.dampfschwein.de; Louisenstrasse 26; mains €5-7; ⊘ 11.30am-10pm Mon-Thu, to midnight Fri & Sat, 1-10pm Sun) Finally that hipster favourite, pulled pork (slow cooked pork that becomes so soft it can be easily torn into shreds), has made it to Dresden's hippest street. Fill

SAXONY DRESDEN

freshly baked buns with delicious stacks of pork, add some barbecue or apple sauce and some spicy cheese and bam! – one of Dresden's best fast food options.

Curry & Co   GERMAN €
(☑ 0351-209 3154; www.curryundco.com; Louisenstrasse 62; sausages €2.50-3.30; ⊙ 11am-10pm Sun-Wed, to midnight Thu, to 2am Fri & Sat) This upbeat outfit has elevated the lowly *Currywurst* to an art form and is busy day and night. Choose from smoked, all-beef, chicken or vegan varieties, and pair your pick with your favourite homemade sauce, from mild curry to hot chilli-onion. Don't skip the fries.

England, England   BRITISH €
(www.englandengland.de; Martin-Luther-Strasse 25; snacks €2.50-5; ⊙ noon-7pm Tue-Fri, 10am-7pm Sat & Sun) This recent arrival in Dresden seeks to provide a little corner of England in the Saxon capital, where the tea is milky, breakfast (on Sundays only) is calorific and the treats (do not miss the courgette and lemon cream cake) as sugary as you'll find back in Albion.

Kochbox   BURGERS €
(☑ 0351-796 7138; Görlitzer Strasse 3; dishes €3-6; ⊙ 5pm-3am) This little joint gets howling in the wee hours when starving night-owls invade in hopes of restoring balance to the brain with fist-sized burgers made from fresh (not frozen) meat.

★Restaurant Genuss-Atelier   GERMAN €€
(☑ 0351-2502 8337; www.genuss-atelier.net; Bautzner Strasse 149; mains €16-20; ⊙ noon-11pm Wed-Sun; 🚊 11 to Waldschlösschen) Lighting up Dresden's culinary scene of late is this fantastic place that's well worth the trip on the 11 tram. The creative menu is streets ahead of most offerings elsewhere, although the best way to experience the 'Pleasure-Atelier' is to book a surprise menu (three/four/five courses €35/45/55) and let the chefs show off their craft. Reservations essential.

★Raskolnikoff   INTERNATIONAL €€
(☑ 0351-804 5706; www.raskolnikoff.de; Böhmische Strasse 34; mains €10-15; ⊙ 11am-2am Mon-Fri, 9am-2am Sat & Sun) An artist squat before the Wall came down, Raskolnikoff now brims with grown-up artsy-bohemian flair, especially in the sweet little garden at the back, complete with bizarre water feature. The seasonally calibrated menu showcases the fruits of regional terroir in globally inspired dishes, and the beer is brewed locally.

Breakfast is served until 2pm, with an excellent brunch (€14.90) on Sundays.

Upstairs are seven handsomely done-up rooms (single/double €47/64) and one studio with kitchenette (€57/74).

★Little India   INDIAN €€
(☑ 0351-3232 6400; www.littleindia-dresden.de; Louisenstrasse 48; mains €10-15; ⊙ 11am-2.30pm & 5-11pm Tue-Sun; 🍴) Bright, minimalist and informal, this fantastic Indian restaurant is a world away from most in Dresden, and its popularity is obvious (be prepared to wait for a table when it's busy). The menu is large (and available in English!) and includes superb tandoori dishes and an entire vegetarian section, as well as standard chicken, lamb and pork mains. The naan is heavenly.

La Casina Rosa   ITALIAN €€
(☑ 0351-801 4848; www.la-casina-rosa.de; Alaunstrasse 93; mains €7-10; ⊙ noon-3pm Tue-Wed & Fri-Sat, 6-11pm Mon-Sat) Everybody feels like family at this neighbourhood-adored trattoria with its warren of cosy rooms (plus small summer garden out the back) and feisty pasta and pizza, plus seasonally inspired specials. Menu stars include the richly flavoured tagliatelle with porcini, veal, cherry tomatoes and thyme, and the 'piccola Capri' pizza topped with shrimp, zucchini and rucula. Reservations are a good idea.

PlanWirtschaft   INTERNATIONAL €€
(☑ 0351-801 3187; Louisenstrasse 20; mains €9-15; ⊙ 7.30am-1am) The winning formula has stayed the same at this long-time favourite that has just undergone a facelift: fresh ingredients sourced from local suppliers, a menu that dazzles with inventiveness and smiley staff that makes even first-timers feel at home. Sit inside the cafe, the romantic garden or the cosy brick cellar. Brunch is a definite highlight.

Lila Sosse   MODERN GERMAN €€
(☑ 0351-803 6723; www.lilasosse.de; Alaunstrasse 70, Kunsthofpassage; appetisers €3.50-9.50, mains €13-15) This jumping joint puts a new spin on modern German cooking by serving intriguing appetisers in glass preserve jars. You're free to order just a couple (the fennel-orange salad and carp with capers are recommended) or, if your tummy needs silencing, pair them with a meaty main and dessert. Reservations essential. It's part of the charming Kunsthofpassage courtyard complex.

Drinking & Nightlife

 Altstadt

Karl May Bar   BAR
(☑ 0351-491 20; www.kempinski.com; Taschenberg 3; ☺ 6pm-2am) Cocktail connoisseurs gravitate to this sophisticated bar inside the Taschenbergpalais hotel. Sink into a heavy burgundy-coloured leather chair to sip tried-and-true classics, or sample one of the 100 whiskies at the curved, dark wood bar. Live music Friday and Saturday, happy hour 6pm to 8pm.

Twist Sky Bar   BAR
(☑ 0351-795 150; Salzgasse 4; ☺ 8pm-2am) Yes it may be inside the rather faceless Hotel Innside, part of the Melia chain, but this 6th-floor cocktail lounge gives you incredible views of the next-door Frauenkirche dome, while the classic and contemporary cocktails are no let-down. Expect a rather staid crowd of business types and visitors.

Fährgarten Johannstadt   BEER GARDEN
(☑ 0351-459 6262; www.faehrgarten.de; Käthe-Kollwitz-Ufer 23b; ☺ 10am-1am Apr-Oct) One of Dresden's most popular drinking spots, this riverfront beer garden has superb Elbe views, pulls great ales and does a mean barbecue.

Neustadt

If you're up for a night on the razzle, head out to the Äussere Neustadt, which is chock-a-block with cafes and bars. Alaunstrasse, Louisenstrasse and Görlitzer Strasse are where it's happening. Indeed, at the corner of Louisenstrasse and Görlitzer Strasse, people just plonk themselves down on the pavement come the late afternoon and drink in big seated groups...who needs bars?

Bottoms Up   BAR
(Martin-Luther-Strasse 31; ☺ 5pm-5am Mon-Fri, 10am-5am Sat & Sun) This is one of Neustadt's most popular and happening bars. There's an outside beer garden, cider on tap, choices of beers ranging from fancy Belgian to local German, and a cosy interior that gets packed at night. The weekend brunch is excellent.

Lebowski Bar   BAR
(www.dudes-bar.de; Görlitzer Strasse 5; ☺ 7pm-5am Sun-Thu, to 7am Fri & Sat) When everything else is closed, 'dudes' can still toast the sunrise with a White Russian while the eponymous cult movie reels off in the background. It's nearly always busy with a welcoming crowd.

Lloyd's   CAFE, BAR
(☑ 0351-501 8775; www.lloyds-cafe-bar.de; Martin-Luther-Strasse 17; ☺ 8am-1am) In a quiet corner of the Neustadt, Lloyd's oozes flair thanks to stylish cream-coloured leather furniture, huge mirrors and fanciful chandeliers. It's a solid pit stop from breakfast to that last expertly poured cocktail; it even does a respectable afternoon tea and cake by the fireplace.

Louisengarten   BEER GARDEN
(www.biergarten-dresden.de; Louisenstrasse 43; ☺ 4pm-1am Sun-Thu, 3pm-2am Fri & Sat) This boho-flavoured beer garden takes the go-local concept to the limit. Wind down the day with beer (Lenin's Hanf, aka Lenin's Hemp) supplied by the nearby Neustädter Hausbrauerei and grilled meats courtesy of the butcher down the street.

Combo   CAFE
(Louisenstrasse 66; ☺ 9am-2am) Laid-back to the point of toppling, this '70s-retro cafe has enormous windows that fold back when the heat is on, 1960s airport furniture and great coffee served with a side of water and two gummy bears.

Café 100
PUB

(☑ 0351-273 5010; www.cafe100.de; Alaunstrasse 100; ⏱ 8pm-late) One of the first pubs in the Neustadt to open after the Wende, Café 100 does double duty as a studenty pub on the ground floor and a candle-lit wine bar in the cavernous cellar. Jazz fans invade during the twice-monthly jam sessions.

Neumanns Tiki
BAR

(☑ 0351-810 3837; Görlitzer Strasse 21; ⏱ 11am-1am) This legendary Polynesian-style parlour has been plying locals with divine homemade ice cream since 1966, but is also a go-to place for colourful, umbrella-crowned cocktails.

Altes Wettbüro
CLUB

(www.altes-wettbuero.de; Antonstrasse 8; ⏱ from 4pm Tue-Sat) Once a casino (its name means 'the old betting office'), this place is today better employed as a place for the Neustadt's young, mixed and alternative crowd to dance to a varied music selection, including live acts; there are even film showings. There's a beer garden with great food as well.

Club Koralle
CLUB

(www.club-koralle.de; Rothenburger Strasse 30; ⏱ 10pm-6am Fri & Sat) This underground institution is where a young crowd searching for electronic music comes to dance each weekend. It's small and can get sweaty down there, but it's a lot of fun with an alternative vibe and some of the best local DJ talent.

Downtown
CLUB

(☑ 0351-811 5592; www.downtown-dresden.de; Katharinenstrasse 11-13; ⏱ 10pm-late Fri & Sat) This iconic old factory is home to one of Dresden's most popular clubs, a mainstream affair that packs in a young and up-for-it crowd with three floors of dance action, including a main floor with hits of the '80s and '90s (you have been warned), an Electro Lounge and a loft floor with R'n'B sounds.

Boy's
GAY BAR

(☑ 0351-563 3630; www.boys-dresden.de; Alaunstrasse 80; ⏱ 8pm-3am Sun-Thu, to 5am Fri & Sat) This is Dresden's standard-issue gay bar, and it's a lively place that draws a mixed-age crowd and hosts busy parties on Friday and Saturday.

☆ Entertainment

The finest all-round listings guide to Dresden is *SAX* (www.cybersax.de), sold at newsstands. Regular freebies include *Blitz* (www.blitz-world.de) and *Kneipensurfer* (www.kneipensurfer.de). Each has an extensive internet presence. Print versions can be picked up at tourist offices, cafes, pubs and hostels.

Semperoper Dresden
OPERA

(☑ 0351-491 1705; www.semperoper.de; Theaterplatz 2; ⏱ ticket office 10am-6pm Mon-Fri, 10am-5pm Sat & Sun) Dresden's famous opera house is the home of the Sächsische Staatsoper Dresden, which puts on brilliant performances that usually sell out. Tickets are sold by phone, in person and online.

Dresdner Philharmonie
CLASSICAL MUSIC

(☑ 0351-486 6866; www.dresdnerphilharmonie.de) While its permanent home, the Kulturpalast, is getting a facelift and is due to reopen in 2016, Dresden's renowned orchestra performs at venues around town. The website has all the dates and details. Buy tickets by phone or online.

★ Die Scheune
LIVE MUSIC

(☑ 0351-3235 5640; www.scheune.org; Alaunstrasse 36-40) Generations of young folks have memories of the 'Barn', which started out as a mainstream GDR-era youth club before turning into an offbeat culture centre with almost daily concerts, cabaret, parties or performances. The cafe serves Indian food, there's a beer garden and the weekend brunch is epic.

Blue Note
JAZZ

(☑ 0351-801 4275; www.jazzdepartment.com; Görlitzer Strasse 2b; ⏱ 8pm-5am) Small, smoky and smooth, this converted space has concerts featuring regional talent almost nightly (usually jazz, but also blues and rock), then turns into a night-owl magnet until the wee hours. Many concerts are free. The drinks menu features beer from around the world and a mind-boggling selection of single malt whiskies.

Katy's Garage
LIVE MUSIC

(www.katysgarage.de; Alaunstrasse 48; ⏱ 8pm-5am Mon-Sat) This institution can be found at the junction of the Neustadt's two most happening streets. As the name suggests, this cavernous party pit is set in a former tyre shop with matching decor and even drinks named after car parts. It's part beer garden, part restaurant, part bar, part cinema, part live music venue and all Dresden.

Jazzclub Tonne
LIVE MUSIC

(☑ 0351-802 6017; www.jazzclubtonne.de; Königstrasse 15; ⏱ 8pm-2am) Cool cats of all ages comes out to this legendary Dresden jazz joint for good music from local and international talent.

ℹ Information

Krankenhaus Dresden-Friedrichstadt
(☑0351-4800; www.khdf.de; Friedrichstrasse 41; ⊗24hr) Central hospital with 24-hour emergency room.

Post Office Altmarkt-Galerie
(Altmarkt-Galerie; ⊗9.30am-9pm Mon-Sat) Enter from Wallstrasse.

Post Office Neustadt (Königsbrücker Strasse 21-29; ⊗9am-7pm Mon-Fri, 10am-1pm Sat) The main post office in the Neustadt.

Tourist Office – Frauenkirche (☑0351-501 501; www.dresden.de; QF Passage, Neumarkt 2; ⊗10am-7pm Mon-Fri, to 6pm Sat, to 3pm Sun) Go to the basement of the shopping mall to find the city's most central tourist office. Helpful English-speaking staff can give you advice, book rooms and tours, rent out audioguides and sell the excellent value Dresden Cards (p148).

Tourist Office – Hauptbahnhof (☑0351-501 501; www.dresden.de; main train station, Wiener Platz; ⊗8am-8pm) Small office inside the main train station.

ℹ Getting There & Away

AIR

Dresden International (DRS; www.dresden-airport.de) has flights to many German cities and destinations such as London, Barcelona, Vienna and Zurich.

CAR

Dresden is connected to Leipzig via the A14/A4, to Berlin via the A13/A113, and to Saxon Switzerland and the Czech Republic via the B172 south. All major international car rental companies have outlets at the airport.

TRAIN

Fast trains make the trip to Dresden from Berlin-Hauptbahnhof in two hours (€40) and Leipzig in 1¼ hours (€24.50). The S1 local train runs half-hourly to Meissen (€6.40, 40 minutes) and Bad Schandau in Saxon Switzerland (€6.40, 45 minutes).

ℹ Getting Around

TO/FROM THE AIRPORT

Dresden airport is about 9km north of the city centre. The S2 train links the airport with the city centre several times hourly (€2.20). Taxis are about €20.

BICYCLE

As a flat and spacious city, Dresden is perfect for cycling. Ask at your hotel or hostel about

bike rentals. **Roll On** (☑0152-2267 3460; www.rollondresden.de; Königsbrücker Strasse 4a/Albertplatz; bike/scooter per day from €10/23; ⊗10am-1pm & 4-7pm Mon-Fri, 10am-1pm Sat, 10am-noon Sun) in the Neustadt also rents out motorised scooters.

PUBLIC TRANSPORT

Buses and trams are run by **Dresdner Verkehrsbetriebe** (DVB; ☑0351-857 1011; www.dvb.de/en). Fares within town cost €2.20, and a day pass €6. Buy tickets from vending machines at stops or aboard trams, and remember to validate them in the machines provided.

TAXI

There are taxi ranks at the Hauptbahnhof and Neustadt station, or ring ☑0351-211 211.

AROUND DRESDEN

Dresden is surrounded by a trio of fabulous castles as well as the porcelain town of Meissen. If you only have time for one castle, then Schloss Pillnitz has the best garden, Schloss Moritzburg has the most interesting interiors and Schloss Weesenstein the most romantic location. Alternatively, Meissen offers a castle, cathedral and its immense porcelain heritage. All four places are easily reached by public transport.

Schloss & Park Pillnitz

Schloss & Park Pillnitz   PALACE
(☑0351-261 3260; www.schlosspillnitz.de; August-Böckstiegel-Strasse 2; park only adult/concession €2/1, park, museums & greenhouses €8/6; ⊗park 9am-6pm, museums 10am-6pm Tue-Sun May-Oct) Baroque has gone exotic at Schloss Pillnitz, a delightful pleasure palace, festooned with fanciful Chinese flourishes. This is where the Saxon rulers once lived it up during long hot Dresden summers. Explore the wonderful gardens, then study the history of the palace and life at court in the Schlossmuseum. Two other buildings, the Wasserpalais and the Bergpalais, house the Kunstgewerbemuseum, which is filled with fancy furniture and knick-knacks from the Saxon court, including Augustus the Strong's throne.

Tickets are also good for the two greenhouses (February to April only). Pillnitz is dreamily wedged in between vineyards and the Elbe, some 14km upriver from central Dresden. Drivers need to take the B6 (Bautzner Landstrasse) to Pillnitzer Landstrasse. Otherwise, take tram 6 from

WORTH A TRIP

GDR MUSEUMS NEAR DRESDEN

Not far from Dresden, in Radebeul and Pirna, two museums offer a fascinating glimpse into an extinct society. And no, were not talking Neanderthals or ancient Greeks. We're talking the GDR, the 'other' Germany that ceased to exist with reunification in 1990. Along with the former country's demise came the disappearance of many of its products, traditions and institutions that had shaped daily life for 40 years. A bafflingly eclectic collection of this socialist-era flotsam and jetsam – including flags and posters, typewriters and radios, uniforms and furniture, dolls and detergents – has been assembled in these two 'time capsules'.

DDR Museum Pirna (☑ 03501-774 842; www.ddr-museum-pirna.de; Rottwerndorferstrasse 45; adult/children €7/6; ⊙ 10am-6pm Tue-Sun Apr-Oct, 10am-5pm Tue-Thu, Sat & Sun Nov-Mar) In a former army barracks, you can snoop around a furnished apartment, sit in a classroom with a portrait of GDR leader Walter Ulbricht glowering down at you, or find out how much a Junge Pioniere youth organisation uniform cost. Thousands of objects are creatively arranged and while most are self-explanatory, others would benefit from informational text.

To get here, take the S1 from Dresden's Hauptbahnhof to Pirna, walk five minutes to the central bus station (ZOB) and hop on local bus N for 'Geibeltbad/Freizeitzentrum' (€4, 35 minutes).

Zeitreise DDR Museum Radebeul (☑ 0351-835 1780; www.ddr-museum-dresden.de; Wasastrasse 50; adult/concession €8.50/7.50; ⊙ 10am-6pm Tue-Sun) Large and well organised, each of the four floors here is dedicated to a particular theme, such as work, daily life and state institutions. This is rounded off by a fabulous collection of Trabi cars, Simson motorbikes and other vehicles. A timeline charts milestones in Cold War history and there's a restaurant serving GDR-era cuisine.

The Zeitreise Museum is reached by taking tram 4 to Wasastrasse; from the Antonstrasse/Leipziger Strasse stop in Dresden-Neustadt (€4), it will take about 20 minutes.

Dresden-Neustadt, then catch bus 63 at Schillerplatz to Pillnitzer Platz. The loveliest approach is by steamer operated by **Sächsische Dampfschiffahrt** (☑ 03521-866 090; www.saechsische-dampfschiffahrt.de; one-way adult/concession €13/10), which makes the trip from Dresden's Terrassenufer in 90 minutes.

Schloss Weesenstein

Schloss Weesenstein PALACE
(☑ 035027-6260; www.schloss-weesenstein.de; Am Schlossberg 1, Müglitztal; adult/concession €6/3, audioguide €2; ⊙ 9am-6pm daily Apr-Oct, 10am-5pm Tue-Sun Feb, Mar, Nov & Dec, 10am-5pm Sat & Sun Jan) A magnificent sight on a rocky crag high above the Müglitz River, Schloss Weesenstein is an amazing alchemy of styles, blending medieval roots with Renaissance and baroque embellishments. This resulted in an architectural curiosity where the banquet halls ended up beneath the roof, the horse stables on the 5th floor and the residential quarters in the cellar.

The palace owes its distinctive looks to the noble Bünau family who dabbled with it for 12 generations from 1406 until 1772. In the 19th century, it became the private retreat of King Johann of Saxony, who distinguished himself not only as a ruler but also as a philosopher and translator of Dante into German. Lavishly furnished and decorated period rooms on the ground floor contain an exhibit about the man and life at court. In keeping with the topsy-turvy architecture, the permanent exhibit takes you on a reverse journey through Saxon history, ending with the Middle Ages.

There are several restaurants, including a cafe in the former palace prison, a traditional brewpub and the upmarket Königliche Schlossküche. After filling your belly, you can take a digestive saunter in the lovely baroque park.

Schloss Weesenstein is about 16km southeast of Dresden. From Dresden Hauptbahnhof take the S1 and change to the SB72 in Heidenau (€6, 25 minutes). Weesenstein train station is about 500m south of the castle – follow the road up the hill. By car, take the A17 to Pirna, then head towards Glashütte and follow the signs to the Schloss.

Schloss Moritzburg

Schloss Moritzburg PALACE
(☑035207-8730; www.schloss-moritzburg.de; Schlossallee; adult/concession €7/3.50, audioguide €2; ☉10am-5.30pm daily Apr-Oct, 10am-4.30pm Sat-Sun Mar) An impossibly romantic vision in yellow and white surrounded by an enormous moat-like lake and a park that is at turns both wild and formal, baroque Schloss Moritzburg was the preferred hunting palace of the Saxon rulers and the site of some rather lavish post-hunting parties under August the Strong. No surprise then that antlers are the main decorative feature in halls sheathed in rich leather wall covering, some painted with mythological scenes.

Prized trophies include the antlers of an extinct species of giant stag and bizarrely misshapen ones in the Hall of Monstrosities. Much prettier is the legendary Federzimmer (Feather Room) downstairs whose centrepiece is a bed made from over a million colourful duck, pheasant and peacock feathers.

Moritzburg is about 14km north of Dresden. Buses 326 and 457 make regular trips from Dresden-Neustadt train station (€4.20, 30 minutes). For a more atmospheric approach, take the S1 train to Radebeul-Ost (€4.20, 15 minutes) and from there the 1884 narrow-gauge *Lössnitzgrundbahn* (www.loessnitzgrundbahn.de; €6.70, 30 minutes) to the palace.

Meissen

☑03521 / POP 27,000
Straddling the Elbe around 25km upstream from Dresden, Meissen is the cradle of European porcelain manufacturing and still hitches its tourism appeal to the world-famous china first cooked up in its imposing castle in 1710. But even those left unmoved by August the Strong's 'white gold' will find the impressive position of the town, dominated by its soaring Gothic cathedral, fairytale-like castle and wonderful Elbe valley views compelling.

◉ Sights

Erlebniswelt Haus Meissen MUSEUM
(☑03521-468 208; www.meissen.com; Talstrasse 9; adult/concession €9/5; ☉9am-6pm May-Oct, 9am-5pm Nov-Apr) Next to the historic porcelain factory south of the Altstadt, this museum is *the* place to witness the astonishing artistry and craftsmanship that makes Meissen porcelain unique. Visits start with a 30-minute group tour (with English audioguide) of four studios where artists demonstrate the vase throwing, plate painting, figure moulding and glazing processes. This gives you a better appreciation for the ensuing collections of historic and contemporary porcelain, which can be enjoyed at your own speed afterwards.

The museum is hugely popular and often totally overrun by coach tours. As entry is timed and only in groups, you may have to wait a while during high season.

Albrechtsburg CASTLE, MUSEUM
(☑03521-470 70; www.albrechtsburg-meissen.de; Domplatz 1; adult/concession incl audioguide €8/4; ☉10am-6pm Mar-Oct, 10am-5pm Nov-Feb) Lording it over Meissen, the 15th-century Albrechtsburg was the first German castle constructed for residential purposes, but is more famous as the birthplace of European porcelain. An exhibit on the 2nd floor chronicles how it all began; a nifty touch terminal even lets you 'invent' your own porcelain.

It took a group of scientists led by Walther von Tschirnhaus and Johann Friedrich Böttger three years to discover the secret formula of the 'white gold', a feat achieved by the Chinese thousands of years earlier. Production began in the castle in 1710 and only moved to a custom-built factory in 1863. The invention's importance for Saxony can't be overstated, bringing enormous wealth and prestige to the Saxon electors (princes).

The palace is distinguished by several architectural innovations, most notably a curvilinear staircase and an eye-popping cell vaulting in the Great Hall, swathed in epic murals depicting scenes from the history of the palace and its builders, Elector Ernst of Saxony and his brother Albrecht.

Markt SQUARE
The handsome Markt is flanked by colourfully painted historic town houses along with the **Rathaus** (1472) and the Gothic **Frauenkirche** (☑03521-453 832; Markt; tower adult/concession €2/1; ☉usually 10am-5pm Apr-Oct). Its carillon is the world's oldest made from porcelain and chimes a different ditty six times daily. Climb the tower for fine red-roof views of the Altstadt.

Dom CHURCH
(☑03521-452 490; www.dom-zu-meissen.de; Domplatz 7; adult/concession €4/2.50; ☉9am-6pm Apr-Oct, 10am-4pm Nov-Mar) Meissen's dome, a high-Gothic masterpiece begun in 1250, does

not impress as much by its size as by the wealth of its interior decorations. Stained-glass windows showing scenes from the Old and New Testaments create an ethereal backdrop for the delicately carved statues in the choir, presumed to be the work of the famous Master of Naumburg. The altar triptych is attributed to Lucas Cranach the Elder. Tower tours (adult/concession €6/4.50) are offered several times daily from April to October.

🛏 Sleeping

Hotel Goldener Löwe
HOTEL €€

(☑ 03521-411 10; www.welcome-hotels.com; Heinrichsplatz 6; r from €66, breakfast €12; P @ 🛜) Everything works like a well-oiled machine behind the cheerful yellow facade of this 17th-century inn near the Markt. Rooms are a harmonious blend of antique-style furnishings with modern touches. Wind down the day at the restaurant or enjoy a glass of local wine in the tavern.

Herberge Orange
HOSTEL €

(☑ 03521-454 334; www.herberge-orange.de; Siebeneichener Strasse 34; dm/d €14/30, breakfast €5; P) This friendly, family-run riverside hostel is 1.5km south of the Markt, and is the best budget accommodation in Meissen. Add €2 per day for bed sheets and towel.

✗ Eating

★ Restaurant Vincenz Richter
GERMAN €€

(☑ 03521-453 285; www.vincenz-richter.de; An der Frauenkirche 12; mains €15-20; ⊙ noon-11pm Mon-Sat, to 6pm Sun; 🌢) Despite the historic guns and armour, the romance factor is high at this 16th-century inn thanks to attentive service, classy interpretations of classic Saxon dishes, and crisp whites from the Richters' own wine estate. Terrace tables have a view of Markt.

Domkeller
GERMAN €€

(☑ 03521-457 676; www.domkeller-meissen.com; Domplatz 9; mains €9-18; ⊙ 11.30am-11pm) High above Meissen, this atmospheric tavern outside the cathedral has been in the hearty food and drink business since 1470. Standouts on the Saxon menu include a beer goulash served in a hollowed-out bread bowl and the meat skewer that's flambéed at the table. The terrace has staggering views – get here early at lunchtime to secure a place.

ℹ Information

Tourist Office (☑ 03521-419 40; www.tourist-info-meissen.de; Markt 3; ⊙ 10am-6pm Mon-Fri, 10am-4pm Sat & Sun Apr-Oct, 10am-5pm Mon-Fri, 10am-3pm Sat Nov, Dec, Feb & Mar)

ℹ Getting There & Around

BOAT

Sächsische Dampfschiffahrt (☑ 03521-866 090; www.saechsische-dampfschiffahrt.de; one way/return €16/21.50; ⊙ May-Sep) Steam boats depart from the Terrassenufer in Dresden. Boats return upstream to Dresden at 2.45pm but take over three hours to make the trip. Many people opt to go from Dresden by boat and then return by train.

BUS

Stadtrundfahrt Meissen (☑ 03521-741 631; www.vg-meissen.de; day pass adult/concession €5/3.50; ⊙ 9.30am-6pm Apr-Oct) Hop-on, hop-off minibus links all major sights along two intersecting routes.

TRAIN

From Dresden, take the half-hourly S1 (€6, 40 minutes) to Meissen. For the porcelain factory, get off at Meissen-Triebischtal.

SAXON SWITZERLAND

About 40km south of Dresden, Saxon Switzerland (Sächsische Schweiz, aka Elbsandsteingebirge or Elbe Sandstone Mountains) embraces a unique and evocative landscape. This is wonderfully rugged country where nature has chiselled porous rock into bizarre columns, battered cliffs, tabletop mountains and deep valleys. The Elbe courses through thick forest, past villages and mighty hilltop castles. No wonder such fabled beauty was a big hit with 19th-century Romantic artists, including the painter Caspar David Friedrich. In 1990 about a third of the area became Saxony's first and only national park Saxon Switzerland National Park (Nationalpark Sächsische Schweiz). The glories continue on the Czech side of the border in the Bohemian-Switzerland National Park.

The main towns are dotted along the Elbe: Rathen with the famous Bastei rock formations, Königstein with its humungous fortress, and Bad Schandau, the 'capital' of Saxon Switzerland and its main commercial hub.

You could tick off the area's highlights on a long day trip from Dresden, but to truly experience the magic of Saxon Switzerland, stay overnight and enjoy a couple of good walks. In addition to hiking, this is one of Germany's premier rock-climbing destinations, offering over 15,000 routes. Cyclists can follow the lovely Elberadweg. If you don't want to go it alone, hook up with **Hobbit Hikes** (☑ 0173-380 0675; www.hobbit-hikes.de) for guided nature walks, hikes and climbs.

❶ Getting There & Around

BOAT
From April to October, steamers (p148) plough up the Elbe several times daily between Dresden and Bad Schandau.

BUS
Frank Nuhn Freizeit und Tourismus (☑ 035021-99080; www.frank-nuhn-freizeit-und-tourismus.de) From mid-April to October, a bus service shuttles between Königstein, Bad Schandau and the Bastei four times daily (€3 per ride). Buy tickets from the driver.

CAR
Towns are linked to Dresden and each other by the B172; coming from Dresden, it's faster to take the A17 and pick up the B172 in Pirna. There are only three bridges across the Elbe: two in Pirna and one in Bad Schandau. Passenger ferries (bicycles allowed) cross the Elbe in Stadt Wehlen, Rathen and Königstein, though only the ferry in Rathen is very regular.

TRAIN
The Dresden S1 S-Bahn line connects Bad Schandau, Königstein and Rathen with Dresden, Pirna, Radebeul and Meissen every 30 minutes. Bad Schandau is also a stop on long-distance EC trains travelling between Hamburg and Vienna.

Bastei & Rathen

The Bastei is a stunning rock formation nearly 200m above the Elbe and the village of Rathen. It's a wonderland of fluted pinnacles and offers panoramic views of the surrounding forests, cliffs and the Elbe River below. The much-photographed Basteibrücke, a sandstone bridge built in 1851, leads through the rocks to the remnants of a partly reconstructed medieval castle, the **Felsenburg Neurathen** (adult/concession €2/1; ☺ 9am-6pm), which is open for touring.

The Bastei is the most popular spot in the national park, so crowds are guaranteed unless you get here before 10am or after 4pm. Weekends and any day in the summer will be very crowded. An easy way to escape the crowd is by hitting the trail. A 5km loop leads from the car park to the Schwedenlöcher, a hideout where local troops dodged the advancing Swedes during the Thirty Years' War (1618–48).

🛏 Sleeping

★ Burg Altrathen   HOTEL €
(☑ 035024-7600; www.burg-altrathen.de; Am Grünbach 10-11; d €70-100; ❀ 🐾 🛜) This charmingly located hotel is inside an impressive mock castle on a hilltop above Rathen. There are romantically decked-out rooms, a great restaurant and a terrace with stellar Elbe views. The welcome is warm, and if the hotel itself is booked up, you can always try for a room at the sister Burgpension (€35 to €40 per person) just down the road.

Villa Zeissig   GUESTHOUSE €
(☑ 035024-70 205; www.villa-zeissig.de; Zum Grünbach 3-4; s/d €49/52; 🅿 🛜) On the hillside above Rathen's main street, this charming alpine-style chalet has several modern and spacious rooms with balconies. It's a short clamber up a staircase from the road.

❶ Getting There & Away

The nearest train station is in Rathen, where you need to catch the ferry across the Elbe, then follow a sweat-raising 30-minute trail to the top of the Bastei. Drivers can leave their car in the big car park near the train station. There's also a car park on the Bastei-side of the Elbe. Drive to Pirna, then follow the Basteistrasse (S167/164) to Lohmen, then catch the S165 (direction Hohenstein) and follow the signs. If you arrive early (before 10am), you should be able to snag a spot in the inner Bastei car park (€7 all day), from where it's only a 10-minute walk to the viewpoints. Otherwise, you need to park in the outer car park (€3 all day) about 3km away and either catch a shuttle bus (€1 each way) or walk.

Königstein

The charming village of Königstein has a cutesy town centre, a gorgeous location on the banks of the Elbe and is crowned by a massive citadel built on a tabletop mountain some 260m above. It's an excellent base for walkers, with most of the best walking in the national park within easy striking distance.

◉ Sights & Activities

Festung Königstein   FORTRESS
(☑ 035021-646 07; www.festung-koenigstein.de; adult/concession Apr-Oct €10/7, Nov-Mar €8/6, audioguide €3; ☺ 9am-6pm Apr-Oct, to 5pm Nov-Mar; 🚼) Festung Königstein is the largest intact fortress in Germany, and is so imposing and formidable that no one in history has ever even bothered to attack it, let alone conquer it. Begun in the 13th century, it was

WHAT'S IN A NAME?

With its highest peak rising to just 723m, Saxon Switzerland ain't exactly the Alps. So how did the region get its name? Credit belongs to the Swiss. During the 18th century, the area's romantic scenery, with its needle-nose pinnacles and craggy cliffs, lured countless artists from around the world. Among them was the Swiss landscape artist Adrian Zingg and his friend, the portraitist Anton Graff, who had been hired to teach at Dresden's prestigious art academy. Both felt that the landscape very much resembled their homeland (the Swiss Jura) and voila, the phrase 'Saxon Switzerland' was born. Travel writers picked it up and so it remains to this day.

repeatedly enlarged and is now a veritable textbook of military architecture, with 30 buildings spread across 9.5 hectares.

Inside, the main highlight is the In Lapide Regis, a superb permanent exhibition that tells the dramatic story of the fortress. Elsewhere within the sprawling fortress complex you can visit the Brunnenhaus, with its seemingly bottomless well, see an array of German weaponry, and enter the Georgenburg, once Saxony's most feared prison, whose famous inmates included Meissen porcelain inventor Johann Friedrich Böttger.

During WWII, the fortress served as a POW camp and a refuge for priceless art treasures from Dresden. Another draw is the widescreen view deep into the national park and across to the Lilienstein tabletop mountain.

🛏 Sleeping & Eating

⭐**Ferdinands
Homestay**   HOSTEL, CAMPGROUND €
(☑035022-547 75; www.ferdinandshomestay.de; Halbestadt 51; dm €14, d €30-40, tent site €2.50-5.50, campsite per person €6, breakfast €6.50; ☺Apr-Oct; ℙ😊) Ferdinands Homestay is a small and friendly riverside hostel and campsite combo in a secluded, remote spot on the northern bank of the Elbe, with some lovely river views. Booking ahead at weekends and during the summer months is always a good idea, as it's by far the best value in town.

Kleine Einkehr   SAXON
(☑035021-67 539; www.kleine-einkehr.de; Elbhäuserweg 23; mains €8-14; ☺noon-8pm Fri-Wed May-

Oct, noon-8pm Sat & Sun Nov-Apr) A wonderful 2km riverside walk from Königstein proper (cross under the railway line and then hook a left onto the river embankment) takes you to this popular family-run Saxon restaurant with outdoor tables and hearty traditional fare.

ℹ Information

The **Tourist Office** (☑035021-68261; www.koenigstein-sachsen.de; Pirnaer Strasse 2; ☺9am-9pm daily May-Sep, 9am-6pm daily Apr & Oct, 9am-6pm Mon-Fri, 9am-1pm Sat & Sun Nov-Mar) is on the town's main squre. English-speaking staff can help with accommodation, tours and hiking maps. There's no bridge across the Elbe here, but there is a ferry (€1) that goes back and forth until 11pm.

From April to October, the **Festungsexpress** (☑035021-990 80; www.frank-nuhn-freizeit-und-tourismus.de; one-way/return €5/3; ☺9am-4pm May-Oct, from 10am Apr) tourist train makes the steep climb half-hourly from Reissiger Platz in Königstein to the fortress. Alternatively it's a strenuous 30- to 45-minute climb from the bottom. The nearest car park is off the B172 (exit Festung), from where it's a 10-minute walk to the fortress.

Bad Schandau

☑035022 / POP 3500

The little spa town of Bad Schandau sits right on the Elbe and is the unofficial capital of Saxon Switzerland. Most hotels, supermarkets and restaurants are here, and it's also a central base for hikes.

◎ Sights & Activities

Personenaufzug   LIFT
(adult/concession return €2.80/2.20; ☺9am-6pm Apr & Oct, 9am-8pm May-Sep) This ancient lift, which dates from 1905, whisks you up a 50m-high tower for views and access to a footbridge linking to a pretty forest path that runs into the national park. It's on the road out of town, towards the Czech border.

Nationalparkzentrum   MUSEUM
(☑035022-502 40; www.lanu.de; Dresdner Strasse 2b; adult/concession €4/3; ☺9am-6pm, closed Jan & Mon Nov-Mar) The National Park Centre has ho-hum exhibitions on flora, fauna and how the sandstone formations were shaped, but the evocative visuals of the 17-minute introductory movie almost justify the admission price, if you're not actually planning to explore the mountains yourself.

Schrammsteinaussicht HIKING

The rugged Schrammsteine is the densest rock labyrinth in the national park and popular with rock hounds. A moderate to strenuous trail leads to a fantastic viewpoint of the rocks, the Elbe Valley and the national park. The first 20 minutes up the steep Obrigensteig are tough, but then the trail levels out and leads through fabulous rock formations. The final 'ascent' is straight up the rocks via a one-way network of steel stairs and ladders.

No technical skills are required, although you should be fairly surefooted. On your descent, follow the Mittelweg to the Elbleitenweg back to the Obrigensteig.

Kirnitzschtalbahn TRAM

(www.ovps.de; Kirnitzschtalstrasse 8; adult/concession €5/2.50, day pass €8/4; ⊘9.30am-7.30pm Apr-Oct) This solar-powered tram quaintly trundles 7km northeast along the Kirnitzsch River to Beuthenfall. The Lichtenhainer waterfall is just a 500m walk away and a good spot to begin a hike among the sandstone cliffs.

🛏 Sleeping

Lindenhof HOTEL €€

(☑035022-4890; www.lindenhof-bad-schandau. de; Rudolf-Sendig-Strasse 11; s/d €69/114; 🅿🛜) The Lindenhof is in the centre of Bad Schandau and is a popular choice for weekenders wanting urban comfort within easy reach of the mountains. There's also a good traditional restaurant on site.

ℹ Information

Tourist Office (☑035022-900 30; www. bad-schandau.de; Marktplatz 12; ⊘9am-9pm daily May-Sep, 9am-6pm daily Apr & Oct, 9am-6pm Mon-Fri, 9am-1pm Sat & Sun Nov-Mar, closed Wed Jan & Feb; 🖳) Bad Schandau's tourist office can be found on the town's main square and has lots of information and interactive displays, and can help with booking accommodation and hiking trips.

LEIPZIG & WESTERN SAXONY

Leipzig

☑0341 / POP 532,000

Hypezig! cry the papers, The New Berlin, says just about everybody. Yes, Leipzig is Saxony's coolest city, a playground for nomadic young creatives who have been displaced even by

---

SPOTLIGHT ON RICHARD WAGNER

Leipzig's musical legacy is also hitched to the ground-breaking – and controversial – 19th-century composer Richard Wagner, who first saw the light of day on 22 May 1813 in a Leipzig town house on Brühl St and later studied at the Alte Nikolaischule (Old St Nicholas School). It was in this city where he began his musical education and wrote his first compositions. Leipzig celebrated Wagner's bicentennial in 2013 with the opening of the **Richard-Wagner-Museum** (Map p168; www.richard-wagner-leipzig.de; adult/student €3/1.50; ⊘noon-5pm Tue-Thu, Sat & Sun) in his old school on the Nikolaikirchhof. The interesting display focuses on Wagner's formative years in Leipzig from 1813 to 1834. An annual Richard Wagner Festival is held in late May each year, with public performances of his operas taking place in front of Opera House.

---

the fast-gentrifying German capital, but it's also a city of enormous history, a trade-fair mecca and solidly in the sights of music lovers due to its intrinsic connection to the lives and work of Bach, Mendelssohn and Wagner.

To this day, one of the world's top classical bands (the Gewandhausorchester) and oldest and finest boys' choirs (the 800-year-old Thomanerchor) continue to delight audiences. When it comes to art, the neo-realistic New Leipzig School has stirred up the international art world with such protagonists as Neo Rauch and Tilo Baumgärtel for well over 10 years.

Leipzig became known as the *Stadt der Helden* (City of Heroes) for its leading role in the 1989 'Peaceful Revolution', when its residents organised protests against the communist regime in May of that year; by October, hundreds of thousands were taking to the streets and a few years later, the Cold War was history.

Don't hurry your visit here: while you can easily do the sights in a day or two, to really experience the place stay for longer, and acquaint yourself with Leipzig's less obvious areas: drink beer on the Karli, go antique shopping in Plagwitz or hang out with the punks in Connewitz.

Greater Leipzig

Hans-Driesch-Str

Goyastr

William-Zipperer-Str

Prießnitzstr

Geog-Schwarz-Str

Paul-Küstner-Str

Rietschelstr

Friesenstr

Cottaweg

Red Bull Arena

Am Sportforum

Großmannstr

Uhlandstr

Spittastr

Calvisiusstr

Erich-Köhn-Str

Angerstr

Heinickstr

Sportforum

Jahnallee

Merseburger str

Angerstraße, Straßenbahnhof

Zeppelinbrücke

Weiße Elster

Karl-Ferlemann-Str

Demmeringstr

Lindenauer Markt

Kuhturmstr

Lützner Str

Lütznerstr

Palmengarten

Mainzer str

Am Elsterwehr

Kathe-Kollwitz-Str

Lindenau, Bushof

Endersstr

Aurelienstr

Gutsmuthsstr

Helmholtzstr

Merseburger str

Josephstr

Birkenstr

Felsenkeller

Karl-Heine-str

Nonnenstraße

Kulturpark

Klingerweg

Karl-Heine-/Gießerstraße

17

16

10

Karl-Heine-/Merseburger Straße

Rudolpin-Sack-Str

Forststr

Gleisstr

Kleine Luppe

Klingerweg

Anton-Brückener-Allee

Leipzig-Plagwitz

Weißenfelser Str

Elsterpassage

Karl-Heine-Kanal

Nonnenstr

Holbeinstraße

Spinnerei Str

9

Bahnhof Plagwitz

Industriestr

Eduardstr

Industriestr

Holbeinstr

Köhnenritzstraße

Alte Salzstr

7

Naumburger str

Markranstädter str

Markranstädter Straße

Stieglitzstr

Stieglitzstraße

Klingenstr

Gießerstr

Wachsmuthstr

Zschochersche Str

Einsteinstr

Erich-Zeigner-Allee

Holbeinstr

Rochlitzstr

Schnorrstr

Die Nonne

Limburgerstr

Antonien-/Gießerstraße

Antonienstr

Adler

Antonienstr

Rödelstraße

Rödelstr

Oeserstr

Schleußiger Weg

Wigandstr

Hirzelstr

Baumannstr

Altranstädter str

Kantatenweg

Paußnitzstr

Panitzstr

Ruststr

Schwartzestraße

Silbermannstr

Hoyerstr

Elsterflutbett

Schwartzestr

Agricolastr

Kulkwitzer str

Campestr

Hüfferstr

Leipziger Ratsholz

Kötzschauer Straße

Kurt-Kresse-Str

Volkspark

Marpergerstr

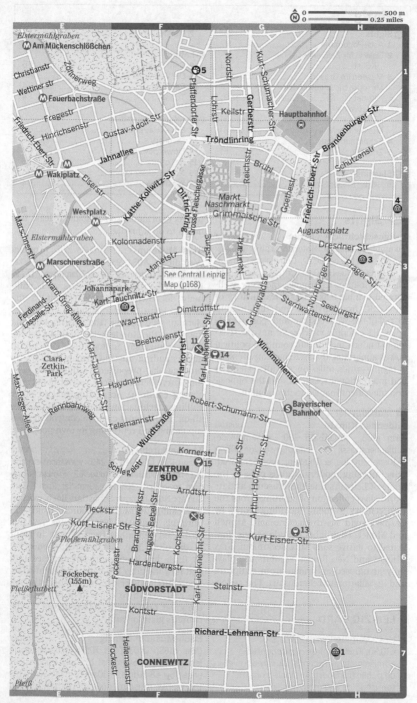

SAXONY

0 — 500 m
0 — 0.25 miles

Elstermühlgraben
Am Mückenschlößchen

Christianstr
Wettiner str
Zöllnerweg
Feuerbachstraße
Fregestr
Friedrich-Ebert-Str
Hinrichstr
Gustav-Adolf-Str
Jahnallee
Wakiplatz
Elsterstr
Westplatz
Käthe-Kollwitz-Str
Elstermühlgraben
Kolonnadenstr
Marschnerstr
Marschnerstraße
Manetstr
Johannapark
Karl-Tauchnitz-Str
2
Wachterstr
Ferdinand-Lassalle-Str
Edward-Grieg-Allee
Beethovenstr
Clara-Zetkin-Park
Karl-Tauchnitz-Str
Haydnstr
Max-Reger-Allee
Rennbahnweg
Telemannstr
Wundtstraße
Schlegelstr

Pfaffendorfer Str
5
Löhrstr
Nordstr
Keilstr
Gerberstr
Kurt-Schumacher-Str
Hauptbahnhof
Brandenburger Str
Tröndlinring
Schützenstr
Reichsstr
Brühl
Dittrichring
Grosse Fleischergasse
Markt
Naschmarkt
Grimmaische Str
Goethestr
Friedrich-Ebert-Str
4
Augustusplatz
Dresdner Str
3
Prager Str
Burgstr
Neumarkt
Grünewaldstr
Sternwartenstr
Seeburgstr
Nürnberger Str

See Central Leipzig
Map (p168)

Dimitroffstr
12
11
Karl-Liebknecht-Str
14
Harkortstr
Windmühlenstr

Robert-Schumann-Str
Bayerischer
Bahnhof
S

Kornerstr
15
ZENTRUM
SÜD
Arndtstr
Göringstr
Arthur-Hoffmann-Str

Fleckstr
Brandvorwerkstr
August-Bebel-Str
Kurt-Eisner-Str
8
Kochstr
Kurt-Eisner-Str
13

Pleißemühlgraben
Hardenbergstr
Karl-Liebknecht-Str

Fockeberg
(155m)
SÜDVORSTADT
Steinstr

Kontstr
Fockestr

Pleißeflutbett

Richard-Lehmann-Str

Heilemannstr
Fockestr
CONNEWITZ
1
7

Pleiße

Leipzig

SAXONY LEIPZIG

⊙ Sights

Zeitgeschichtliches Forum   MUSEUM
(Forum of Contemporary History; Map p168; ☑ 0341-222 00; www.hdg.de/leipzig; Grimmaische Strasse 6; ⊙ 9am-6pm Tue-Fri, 10am-6pm Sat & Sun) **FREE**
This fascinating, enormous and very well-curated exhibit tells the political history of the GDR, from division and dictatorship to fall-of-the-Wall ecstasy and post-*Wende* blues. It's essential viewing for anyone seeking to understand the late country's political power apparatus, the systematic oppression of regime critics, milestones in inter-German and international relations, and the opposition movement that led to its downfall.

★ Museum der
Bildenden Künste   MUSEUM
(Map p168; ☑ 0341-216 990; www.mdbk.de; Katharinenstrasse 10; adult/concession €5/4; ⊙ 10am-6pm Tue & Thu-Sun, noon-8pm Wed) This imposing modernist glass cube is the home of Leipzig's fine arts museum and its world-class collection of paintings from the 15th century to today, including works by Caspar David Friedrich, Cranach, Munch and Monet. Highlights include rooms dedicated to native sons Max Beckmann, Max Klinger and Neo Rauch. Exhibits are playfully juxtaposed and range from sculpture and installation to religious art. The collec-

LEIPZIG CARD

Use a **Leipzig Card** (1/3 days €10.90/21.90) for free or discounted admission to attractions, plus free travel on public transport. Available from the tourist office and most hotels.

tion is enormous, so set aside at least two hours to do it justice.

Stasi Museum   MUSEUM
(Map p168; ☑ 0341-961 2443; www.runde-ecke-leipzig.de; Dittrichring 24; ⊙ 10am-6pm) **FREE**
In the GDR the walls had ears, as is chillingly documented in this exhibit in the former Leipzig headquarters of the East German secret police (the Stasi), a building known as the Runde Ecke (Round Corner). English-language audioguides (€4) aid in understanding the all-German displays on propaganda, preposterous disguises, cunning surveillance devices, recruitment (even among children), scent storage and other chilling machinations that reveal the GDR's all-out zeal when it came to controlling, manipulating and repressing its own people.

Thomaskirche   CHURCH
(Map p168; ☑ 0341-222 240; www.thomaskirche.org; Thomaskirchhof 18; tower €2; ⊙ church 9am-6pm, tower 1pm, 2pm & 4.30pm Sat, 2pm & 3pm Sun Apr-Nov) Johann Sebastian Bach worked as a cantor in the Thomaskirche from 1723 until his death in 1750, and his remains lie buried beneath a bronze plate in front of the altar. The Thomanerchor, once led by Bach, has been going strong since 1212 and now includes 100 boys aged eight to 18. The church tower can be climbed, though the real reason to come here is to absorb the great man's legacy, often played on the church's giant organ.

Bach-Museum Leipzig   MUSEUM
(Map p168; ☑ 0341-913 70; www.bachmuseumleipzig.de; Thomaskirchhof 16; adult/concession/under 16yr €8/6/free; ⊙ 10am-6pm Tue-Sun) This interactive museum does more than tell you

CHURCH OF PEACE

Nikolaikirche (Church of St Nicholas; Map p168; www.nikolaikirche-leipzig.de; Nikolaikirchhof 3; ☺10am-6pm Mon-Sat, services 9.30am Sun) The Church of St Nicholas has Romanesque and Gothic roots but since 1797 has sported a striking neoclassical interior with palm-like pillars and cream-coloured pews. The design is certainly gorgeous but the church is most famous for playing a key role in the nonviolent movement that led to the downfall of the East German government. As early as 1982 it hosted 'peace prayers' every Monday at 5pm (still held today), which over time inspired and empowered local citizens to confront the injustices plaguing their country.

Starting in September 1989, the prayers were followed by candle-light demonstrations, which reached their peak on 9 October when 70,000 citizens took to the streets. The military, police and secret police stood ready to suppress the protests, as they had so violently done only two days earlier. But the order never came. The GDR leadership had capitulated. A singular palm-topped column outside the church commemorates this peaceful revolution.

about the life and accomplishments of Johann Sebastian Bach. Learn how to date a Bach manuscript, listen to baroque instruments or treat your ears to any composition he ever wrote. The 'treasure room' downstairs displays rare original manuscripts.

Museen im Grassi MUSEUM
(Map p162; www.grassimuseum.de; Johannisplatz 5-11; combined ticket adult/concession €15/12; ☺10am-6pm Tue-Sun) The university-run Museen im Grassi harbours three fantastic collections that are often overlooked, despite being a five-minute walk from Augustusplatz. At the stellar **Musikinstrumenten-Museum** (Map p162; ☎0341-973 0750; adult/concession €6/3, audioguide €1) you can discover music from five centuries in rarity-filled exhibits and an interactive sound laboratory. The **Museum für Völkerkunde** (Ethnological Museum; Map p162; ☎0341-973 1900; adult/concession €8/6) takes you on an eye-opening journey through the cultures of the world. The **Museum für Angewandte Kunst** (Museum of Applied Arts; Map p162; ☎0341-222 9100; adult/concession €8/5.50) has an excellent art nouveau and art deco furniture, porcelain, glass and ceramics collection.

Völkerschlachtdenkmal MONUMENT
(☎0341-241 6870; www.stadtgeschichtliches-museum-leipzig.de; Strasse des 18 Oktober 100; adult/child €8/6; ☺10am-6pm Apr-Oct, to 4pm Nov-Mar; ☐2 or 15 to Völkerschlachtdenkmal) Half a million soldiers fought – and one in five died – in the epic 1813 battle that led to the decisive victory of Prussian, Austrian and Russian forces over Napoleon's army. Built a century later near the killing fields, the Monument to the Battle of the Nations is a 91m colossus,

towering sombrely like something straight out of Gotham City. Views from the top are monumental. If you need to bone up on your history, swing by the integrated Forum 1813 exhibit within the monument complex first.

Asisi Panometer GALLERY
(Map p162; ☎0341-355 5340; www.asisi.de; Richard-Lehmann-Strasse 114; adult/concession €11.50/10; ☺10am-5pm Tue-Fri, 10am-6pm Sat & Sun; ☐16 to Richard-Lehmann/Zwickauer Strasse) The happy marriage of a *pan*orama and a gas*ometer* (a giant gas tank) is a panometer. The unusual concept is the brainchild of Berlin-based artist Yadegar Asisi, who uses paper and pencil and computer technology to create bafflingly detailed monumental scenes drawn from nature or history. Each work is about 100m long and 30m high.

Zoo Leipzig ZOO
(Map p162; ☎0341-593 3385; www.zoo-leipzig. de; Pfaffendorfer Strasse 29; adult/concession €18.50/15; ☺9am-7pm May-Sep, 9am-6pm Apr & Oct, 9am-5pm Nov-Mar; ☐12 to Zoo) One of Germany's most progressive, Leipzig Zoo's stand out attraction is Gondwanaland, a jungly wonderland of 17,000 plants and 300 exotic animals. Rare and endangered species such as Komodo dragons and pigmy hippos roam around spacious enclosures in a climate-controlled hall amid fragrant tropical plants. Explore by following a jungle path, a treetop trail or by drifting along in a boat.

Stadtgeschichtliches Museum MUSEUM
(City History Museum; Map p168; ☎0341-965 130; www.stadtgeschichtliches-museum-leipzig. de; Markt 1; adult/concession €6/4; ☺10am-6pm Tue-Sun) Leipzig's beautiful Renaissance town

hall is an atmospheric setting to recount the twists and turns of the city's history from its roots as a key medieval trading town to the present, including stops at the Battle of the Nations and the 1989 peaceful revolution. A nearby modern extension, the **Neubau** (Map p168; Böttchergässchen 3; adult/concession €6/4; ☺10am-6pm Tue-Sun) presents quality temporary exhibits, and is included on the combined ticket (adult/concession €10/8).

Galerie für Zeitgenössische Kunst   GALLERY
(Map p162; ☎140 8126; www.gfzk-leipzig.de; Karl-Tauchnitz-Strasse 9-11; adult/concession per space €5/3, both spaces €8/4, Wed free; ☺2-7pm Tue-Fri, noon-6pm Sat & Sun) Contemporary art in all media is the speciality of this gallery, presented in temporary exhibits in a minimalist container-like space and a late-19th-century villa.

Schumann-Haus   MUSEUM
(Map p162; ☎0341-393 9620; www.schumann-verein.de; Inselstrasse 18; adult/concession €3/2; ☺2-6pm Wed-Fri, 10am-6pm Sat & Sun) The 'Spring Symphony' is among the works Robert Schumann composed in this house where he and his wife, pianist Clara Wieck, spent their first four years of marriage. A small exhibit provides background on the personal life and achievements of this famous musical couple.

ℹ️ LEIPZIGER NOTENSPUR

Bach, Mendelssohn-Bartholdy, Schumann, Wagner, Mahler and Grieg are among the many world-famous musicians who've left their mark on Leipzig, a legacy that to this day is upheld by the illustrious Gewandhaus Orchestra and the St Thomas Boys' Choir. You can walk in the footsteps of these greats by following the 5km Leipziger Notenspur (Leipzig Music Trail) to the places where they lived and worked. At each of the 23 stops, there are information panels in English and German and phone numbers you can call to listen to music or additional commentary. There's even a far longer 40km route designed to be followed by bike riders through further-flung areas of musical interest around Leipzig's suburbs. For details or to download a map, see www.notenspur-leipzig.de.

Mendelssohn-Haus   MUSEUM
(Map p168; ☎0341-127 0294; www.mendelssohn-stiftung.de; Goldschmidtstrasse 12; adult/concession incl audioguide €7.50/6; ☺10am-6pm) A key figure of the Romantic age, Felix Mendelssohn-Bartholdy was appointed music director of the Leipzig Gewandhausorchester in 1835 and held the position until shortly before his sudden death at age 38. Learn more in this intimate exhibit in the Biedermeier-furnished apartment where he lived with his family until his death in 1847. There are frequent evening recitals of Mendelssohn's work here (tickets €15).

Augustusplatz   SQUARE
(Map p168) Massive Augustusplatz may look nondescript at best, and foreboding at worst, but it is actually flanked by some of Leipzig's most famous buildings, including the **Gewandhaus** and the **opera house**. On its western front, the 11-story **Kroch-Haus** was Leipzig's first high-rise and is topped by a clock and two buff sentries. More eyecatching is the glass-fronted **Paulinum**, the university church and new campus building, which is being constructed on the same spot as the medieval Paulinerkirche that was demolished in 1968 by GDR authorities. Delays to the construction have plagued the project, but it should be open in 2016. The boldly modern structure is by Dutch architect Erick van Egeraat.

City-Hochhaus   LANDMARK
(Map p168; lift €3; ☺terrace 9am-midnight Mon-Thu, to 1pm Fri & Sat, to 11pm Sun) For sweeping city views, ride the lift to the 29th floor of the modernist City-Hochhaus; there's a restaurant there.

🚩 Tours

Leipzig Erleben   WALKING TOUR
(☎0341-7104 280; www.leipzig-erleben.com) Runs two daily 2½-hour combination walking/bus tours in German and English departing from the tourist office. If booked separately, the walking tour is €5, the bus tour €10. Bike tours and thematic tours are also available, including Jewish Leipzig and architecture tours.

Trabi Erleben   CAR TOUR
(☎0341-1409 0922; www.trabi-stadtrundfahrt.de; per person €28-40) Explore Leipzig from behind the steering wheel or as a passenger in a GDR-built Trabi on a 90-minute self-drive

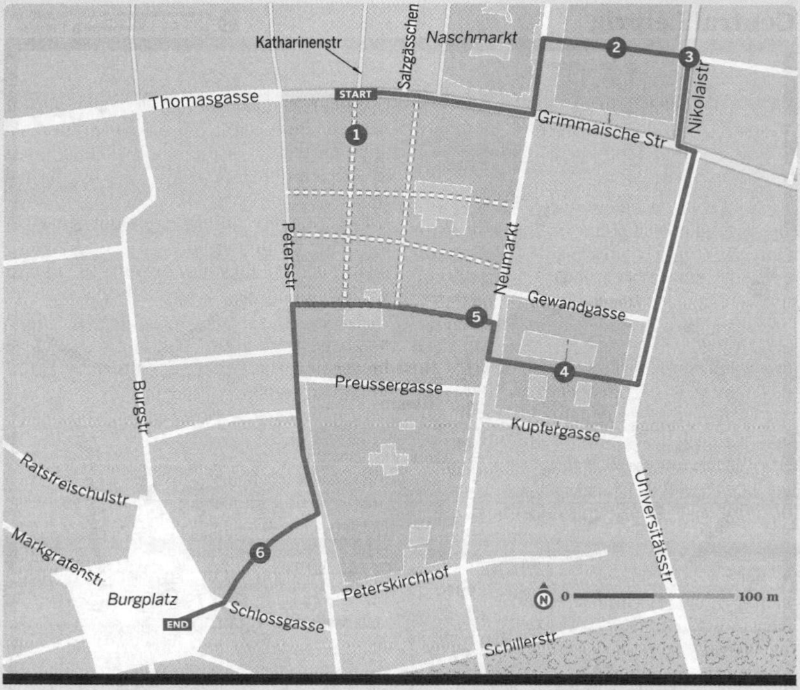

Walking Tour
Leipzig's Top Trading Palaces

START GRIMMAISCHE STRASSE
FINISH BURGPLATZ
LENGTH 1KM; ONE HOUR

Leipzig's 500-year pedigree as a trading hub is reflected in its many historic arcades, courtyards and trade-fair palaces dotted around the city centre. Today the often grand buildings harbour boutiques, cafes and restaurants alongside offices and apartments on the upper floors.

The most famous arcade is the 1914 1 **Mädlerpassage**, a lavish mix of neo-Renaissance and art nouveau and home to Auerbachs Keller, the restaurant featured in Goethe's *Faust*. In fact, touching the foot of the Faust statue near the Grimmaische Strasse exit is supposed to bring you good luck.

Make your way to Reichsstrasse and the gorgeously restored 1908 2 **Speck's Hof**, whose light-flooded atriums are decorated with murals, tiles and paintings by local artists Moritz Götze, Bruno Griesel and Johannes Grützke. Exit onto Nikolaistrasse via the attached 3 **Hansa-Haus**, past a water-filled copy of a 3500-year-old Ming Dynasty sound bowl. Wet your hands and run them over the two pommels to make the water fizz.

Follow Nikolaistrasse down to Universitätsstrasse and the 1893 4 **Städtisches Kaufhaus**. It's on the site of Leipzig's first cloth exchange (Gewandhaus) and the original concert hall of the Gewandhaus Orchestra, which was torn down to make room for this neo-baroque complex.

Exit onto Neumarkt and immediately enter the 5 **Messehofpassage**, which was the first post-WWII trade building to be completed in 1950. Remodelled a few years ago, the mushroom-shaped column near the Peterstrasse exit is the only vestige of the old arcade.

Turn left on Peterstrasse and head down to the 6 **Petersbogen**, an elegantly curving glass-covered arcade from 2001 that replaced the Juridicum Passage, which was destroyed in WWII. Before that, Leipzig's esteemed law school stood in this place for 500 years.

Central Leipzig

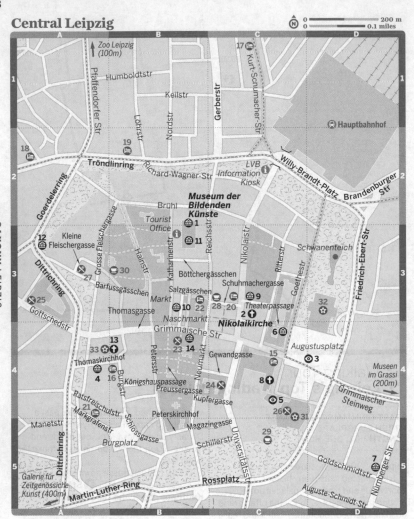

putt-putt with live commentary piped into your vehicle. Prior reservation required; prices depend on the number of people.

🎭 Festivals & Events

Leipziger Buchmesse BOOK FAIR
(www.leipziger-buchmesse.de) One of the highlights of Leipzig's annual events calendar; held in late March. The second biggest in the country after Frankfurt.

Wave-Gotik-Treffen FESTIVAL
(www.wave-gotik-treffen.de) On Whitsuntide (mid- to late May or early to mid-June),

a black tide descends on Leipzig for the Wave-Gotik-Treffen, the world's largest goth festival, with a pagan village, a medieval market and lots of dark music. This is a fun time to visit the city, though you might feel a bit out of place without a black bridal veil.

Bachfest MUSIC FESTIVAL
(Bach Festival; www.bach-leipzig.de) The 10-day Bach Festival takes place in late May or early June and attracts huge numbers of fans from around the world.

Central Leipzig

SAXONY LEIPZIG

🛏 Sleeping

★ Meisterzimmer
BOUTIQUE HOTEL €

(Map p162; ☎0341-3067 7099; www.meisterzim
mer.de; Spinnereistrasse 7; r from €75) Somewhere
between a hotel and a thoroughly designer
Airbnb loft, this selection of minimalist but
supremely style-conscious rooms is inside a
massive converted factory that is now home
to half of Leipzig's creative industries. If you
don't enjoy public areas in hotels, but love
a light-bathed converted factory, this is the
place for you. Booking ahead is essential.

To get here, take the S-Bahn to
Leipzig-Plagwitz.

Hostel Sleepy Lion
HOSTEL €

(Map p168; ☎0341-993 9480; www.hostel-
leipzig.de; Jacobstrasse 1; dm/s/d/apt from
€13.50/40.50/49/60, linen €2.50, breakfast €4;
@🖳🛜) This top-rated hostel gets our thumbs
up with its clean and cheerfully painted en-
suite rooms, a super-central location and
clued-in staff. Every budget can be catered
for in dorms sleeping four to 10, as well as
private rooms and spacious 4th floor apartments with killer views. The kitchen is very
basic, however, and not really suitable for
self-caterers.

Hostel Blauer Stern
HOSTEL €

(Map p162; ☎0341-4927 6166; www.hostel-
blauerstern.de; Lindenauer Markt 20; dm/s/d/tr/q

€18/25/35/45/50; 🛜) If you're interested in
exploring Leipzig's alternative scene, then
this is a great option, in the western district
of Plagwitz, a fast up-and-coming, young and
arty slice of town. The thoughtfully decorated rooms all have an East German retro style,
and big weekly discounts can make them a
steal. Take tram 7 or 15 from Hauptbahnhof.

Motel One
HOTEL €

(Map p168; ☎0341-337 4370; www.motel-one.
de; Nikolaistrasse 23; d from €79; 🅿🖳🛜) The
older of two Motel One outposts in Leipzig
has a five-star location opposite the Nikolaikirche and also gets most other things right,
from the smart lobby-lounge to the snug but
smartly designed rooms. No surprise that it's
often booked out. Breakfast costs €7.50.

Central Globetrotter
HOTEL €

(Map p168; ☎0341-149 8960; www.globetrot
ter-leipzig.de; Kurt-Schumacher-Strasse 41; dm
€12.50-18, d €44, linen €2.50; @🛜) This low-key
hostel adjacent to the train station has basic
but clean four- to eight-bed dorms and private rooms (some with facilities) spread over
three floors reached via a creaky wooden
staircase. There are lockers in the corridors
and gender-segregated, communal showers.

Hotel Fürstenhof
HOTEL €€

(Map p168; ☎0341-1400; www.hotelfuerstenhof-
leipzig.com; Tröndlinring 8; d from €135; 🖳@🛜🏊)

The grande dame of the Leipzig hotel scene, with a 200-year-old pedigree, this understated place is the haunt of a low-key, old money crowd. It has updated old-world flair, impeccable service, a gourmet restaurant and an oh-so-soothing grotto-style pool and spa – and it is just a short wander from most of the sights.

Abito Suites APARTMENT €€
(Map p168; 0341-985 2788; www.abito.de; Grimmaische Strasse 16; ste €125-155;) This excellent option offers self-contained suites with some awesome views right in the heart of Leipzig. Spacious and modern luxury units feature Italian designer furniture, purple and gold accents and such lifestyle essentials as Illy espresso machines and a free minibar. There's no reception: check-in is via an automated system, so book ahead.

Quartier M APARTMENT €€
(Map p168; 0341-2133 8800; www.apartment-leipzig.de; Markgrafenstrasse 10; apt €75-110;) The building oozes old-world flair but the roomy apartments with full kitchens are state-of-the-art and pack plenty of modern design cachet. Some units come with balcony or terrace. Rates drop significantly for stays over seven days; located above an organic supermarket.

arcona Living Bach14 HOTEL, STUDIO €€
(Map p168; 0341-496 140; http://bach14.arcona.de; Thomaskirchhof 13/14; d from €115;) In this musically themed marvel, you'll sleep sweetly in sleek rooms decorated with sound-sculpture lamps, Bach manuscript wallpaper and colours ranging from subdued olive to perky raspberry. The quietest rooms are in the garden wing, while those in the historic front section have views of the famous Thomanerkirche.

★**Steigenberger Grandhotel Handelshof** HOTEL €€€
(Map p168; 0341-350 5810; www.steigenberger.com/Leipzig; Salzgässchen 6; r from €169;) Behind the imposing historic facade of a 1909 municipal trading hall, this exclusive boutique luxury joint outclasses most of Leipzig's hotels with its super-central location, charmingly efficient team and modern rooms dressed in crisp white-silver-purple colours and complete with high ceilings and marble bathrooms. The stylish bilevel spa is the perfect bliss-out station.

✗ Eating

★**Reisladen** INTERNATIONAL €
(Map p162; Karl-Heine-Strasse 49; mains €3.50-4.50; 11.30am-2.30pm;) If you're exploring funky Plagwitz, then this lunch-only joint will surely be top of your list for a wonderfully good value, healthy and tasty lunch. Normally with a line out the door, this local establishment has daily changing specials of rice dishes that can be taken away or eaten in; it's a great choice for vegetarians and vegans.

★**Tobagi** KOREAN €€
(Map p162; Riemannstrasse 52; mains €8-11; 6-11pm) This totally unsassuming Korean place just off the Karli is a study in the advantages of not judging a book by its cover. Meet the eccentric and often cantankerous Korean owner before settling down for a superb meal of traditional dishes, including wonderful *bulgogi* (marinated grilled beef), rich *bibimbap* (rice mixed with egg, vegetables, chilli peppers, sliced meat and soybean paste) and an excellent spinach salad.

Die Versorger CAFE €
(Map p162; www.die-versorger.com; Spinnereistrasse 7; mains €4-9; 8.30am-6pm Mon-Fri, 10am-7pm Sat) This charming garden cafe within Plagwitz's converted Baumwollspinnerei factory complex is also about the only place to have lunch nearby. Stop in for healthy and daily changing specials, a variety of wraps, sandwiches, salads and soups.

Macis INTERNATIONAL €€
(Map p168; 0341-2228 7520; www.macis-leipzig.de; Markgrafenstrasse 10; mains lunch €15-22, dinner €17-28; 8am-2.30pm & 5.30-10.30pm Mon-Sat) At this inspired port of call affiliated with the adjacent baker and organic supermarket, only regionally sourced ingredients find their destiny in such internationally inspired dishes as lamb ragout, green haddock curry and black squid risotto.

Telegraph CAFE €€
(Map p168; 0341-149 4990; www.cafe-telegraph.de; Dittrichring 18-20; mains €7-15; 8am-midnight;) Leipzig goes cosmopolitan at this elegantly high-ceilinged cafe with curved booths and wooden tables, a bilingual menu and a stack of international mags and dailies. It's a popular breakfast spot, available until a hangover-friendly 3pm. The menu is heavy on Austrian classics, and the omelette is simply fantastic.

Pilot
CAFE, INTERNATIONAL €€

(Map p168; ☎0341-126 8117; www.enk-leipzig.
de; Bosestrasse 1; mains €7-20; ☺9am-late; 🛜)
This retro-styled and quite charming establishment draws a bohemian crowd with its
rustic menu, back-to-basic Saxon dishes and
a splash of more contemporary specials and
fresh salads. Its extensive drinks selection,
including rich espresso from Trieste and a
long tea list, is a further draw.

Cafe Pushkin
CAFE, PUB €€

(Map p162; ☎0341-392 0105; www.cafepushkin.de; Karl-Liebknecht-Strasse 74; mains €5-12;
☺9am-late) This charming old pub on the
Südvorstadt's super cool Karli is a bit of local
institution. The selection of burgers, nachos
and sausages won't blow you away, but it's
good comfort food in a friendly and somewhat eccentric atmosphere. It's also a great
breakfast spot following a night out here.

★Auerbachs Keller
GERMAN €€€

(Map p168; ☎0341-216 100; www.auer-
bachs-keller-leipzig.de; Mädlerpassage, Grimmaische Strasse 2-4; mains Keller €10-27, Weinstuben
€33-35; ☺Keller noon-11pm daily, Weinstuben
6-11pm Mon-Sat) Founded in 1525, Auerbachs
Keller is one of Germany's best-known restaurants. It's cosy and touristy but the food's
actually quite good and the setting memorable. There are two sections: the vaulted
Grosser Keller for hearty Saxonian dishes
and the four historic rooms of the Historische Weinstuben for upmarket German
fare. Reservations highly advised.

In Goethe's *Faust*, Part I, Mephistoph-
eles and Faust carouse here with students
before riding off on a barrel. The scene is
depicted on a carved tree trunk in what is
now the Goethezimmer (Goethe Room),
where the great writer allegedly came for
'inspiration'.

Stadtpfeiffer
INTERNATIONAL €€€

(Map p168; ☎0341-217 8920; www.stadtpfeiffer.
de; Augustusplatz 8; 4-/6-course menu €108/128;
☺6-11pm Tue-Sat) Petra and Detlef Schlegel
give deceptively simple sounding dishes the
star treatment and so it was only natural
when they were the first in Leipzig to get
the Michelin nod. Pairing punctilious craftsmanship with bottomless imagination, they
create such exquisitely calibrated dishes as
smoked Arctic char with foie gras or warm
chocolate cake with lavender ice cream. It's
a relaxed spot inside the Gewandhaus concert hall.

Max Enk
MODERN GERMAN €€€

(Map p168; ☎0341-9999 7638; www.max-enk.de;
Städtisches Kaufhaus, Neumarkt 9-19; mains €20-
28, 5-course menu €65; ☺noon-2pm & 6pm-1am
Mon-Fri, noon-1am Sat, 11.30am-4pm Sun) People
share laughs over hand-picked wines and
plates of elegant comfort food kicked into
high gear at this sleek outpost. The Wiener
schnitzel is excellent, the quality meats are
grilled to perfection and the weekday multi-
course lunches are a steal.

🍷 Drinking & Nightlife

Leipzig is Saxony's liveliest city, with a particularly wide selection of bars, pubs and
clubs and an impressive underground scene
for a place of its size. There are several areas of Leipzig particularly noted for their
going-out options: in the city centre there's
the boisterous Drallewatsch pub strip on
narrow Barfussgässchen, as well as the more
upmarket theatre district around Gottsched-
strasse. But the cooler, younger crowds tend
to gravitate towards the Südvorstadt's long
Karl-Liebknecht-Strasse (aka Südmeile) and
Plagwitz's pub-and-restaurant-packed Karl-
Heine-Strasse. The best listings magazine is
Kreuzer (www.kreuzer-leipzig.de).

★Distillery
CLUB

(Map p162; ☎0341-3559 7410; www.distillery.de;
Kurt-Eisner-Strasse 91; ☺from 11.30pm Fri & Sat;
🚋9 to Kurt-Eisner/A-Hoffmann-Strasse) One of the
oldest techno clubs in eastern Germany, Distillery has been going for over 20 years and remains among the best. With an unpretentious
crowd, cool location, decent drinks prices and
occasional star DJs (Ellen Allien, Carl Craig,
Richie Hawtin), its popularity is easy to understand. As well as techno, there's also house,
drum'n'bass and hip hop to be had here.

Westwerk
CLUB

(Map p162; www.westwerk-leipzig.de; Karl-Heine-
Strasse 85-93; ☺8pm-3am Mon-Thu, to 5am Fri &
Sat) Trendy Plagwitz's signature club is inside an impressive factory conversion and
is a very chilled hang-out during the week,
when the cool crowd plays table tennis and
kicker (fussball) or checks out the 'mini art
gallery', which is essentially an odd dark
room the size of a photo booth. Weekends
see the dance floor packed.

Flowerpower
PUB

(Map p162; ☎0341-961 3441; www.flower-power.
de; Riemannstrasse 42; ☺7pm-11am; 🛜) It's party time any time at this dark, long-running

psychedelic flashback to the '60s (cool pinball machines). Admission is always free and the music tends to be older than the international and up-for-it crowd. If you've run out of party options on a Tuesday morning, this is the destination for you.

Noch Besser Leben PUB
(Map p162; www.nochbesserleben.com; Merseburger Strasse 25; ☺7.30pm-4am) Despite the address, this locally beloved bar can be found on Plagwitz's main drag, Karl-Heine-Strasse, and is a great, if smoky, spot to join a cool local crowd drinking an impressive selection of beer. It has a communal, friendly atmosphere, for which only the German word *gemütlich* (approximately translated as cosy) will do.

Conne Island CLUB
(www.conne-island.de; Koburger Strasse 3; ☺4-10pm Mon-Sat, to 8pm Sun; ⊞9 to Koburger Brücke) Run by a collective, this cult location has defined Leipzig nightlife for ages with concerts and club nights that feed the gamut of musical appetites – punk to indie, techno to hip hop. It's in the punkish-anarchist enclave of Connewitz.

Moritzbastei CAFE, BAR
(Map p168; ✆0341-702 590; www.moritzbastei.de; Universitätsstrasse 9; ☺10am-late Mon-Fri, noon-late Sat; ☏) This legendary (sub)cultural centre in a warren of cellars of the old city fortifications keeps an all-ages crowd happy with parties (almost nightly), concerts, art and readings. It harbours stylish cocktail and wine bars as well as a daytime cafe (dishes €2 to €5) that serves delicious coffee, along with healthy and wallet-friendly fare. Summer terrace, too.

Beyer Haus PUB
(Map p162; Ernst-Schneller-Strasse 6; ☺7pm-2am Mon-Sat, to midnight Sun) Just off the Karli, this large but extremely cosy pub is popular with a studenty, alternative crowd who come here to drink beer under the two enormous glass chandeliers and to enjoy the odd live musical performances. Friendly fun.

naTo PUB
(Map p162; ✆0341-391 5539; www.nato-leipzig.de; Karl-Liebknecht-Strasse 46; ☺7-11pm) The mother of Leipzig's alternative-music pub-clubs, with jazz, experimental and indie sounds alongside films and theatre. Great outdoor seating in summer.

Café Riquet CAFE
(Map p168; ✆0341-961 0000; www.riquethaus.de; Schuhmachergässchen 1; ☺9am-8pm) Two bronze elephants guard the entrance to this Viennese-style coffeehouse in a superb art nouveau building topped by a Asian-style turret. Good for a stylish coffee-and-cake break.

Zum Arabischen Coffe Baum CAFE
(Map p168; ✆0341-961 0060; www.coffe-baum.de; Kleine Fleischergasse 4; mains €8-18; ☺11am-midnight) One of Europe's oldest coffeehouses, this cosy multifloor warren has been open since 1720. It's an atmospheric, if rather touristy, spot to try the famous local treat called Leipziger Lerche (lark) – a marzipan-filled shortcrust pastry. Other mouthwatering cakes, light meals and alcohol are also available. The small, free 'museum' has over 500 coffee-related objects.

☆ Entertainment

Gewandhausorchester CLASSICAL MUSIC
(Map p168; ✆0341-127 0280; www.gewandhausorchester.de; Augustusplatz 8) Led by Ricardo Chailly since 2005, the Gewandhaus is one of Europe's finest and oldest civic orchestras. With a tradition harking back to 1743, it became an orchestra of European renown a century later under music director Felix Mendelssohn-Bartholdy. Tickets are available by email, phone and in person.

Thomanerchor CLASSICAL MUSIC
(Map p168; ✆0341-984 4211; www.thomaskirche.org; Thomaskirchhof 18; tickets €2) Leipzig's famous boys' choir performs Bach motets and cantatas at 6pm on Friday and 3pm on Saturday at the Thomaskirche (p164) and also sings during Sunday services at 9.30am. Special concerts take place throughout the year. Performances are usually filled to capacity, so try to be there when doors open 45 minutes before concerts begin.

Oper Leipzig OPERA
(Map p168; ✆0341-126 1261; www.oper-leipzig.de; Augustusplatz 12) Leipzig's Opernhaus (opera house) has a 300-year-old tradition, though the building only went up in the 1950s. The program is an eclectic mix of classics and contemporary works; the Gewandhausorchester provides the music. Buy tickets online, by phone or in person.

ℹ Information

The main post office is in the Hauptbahnhof.

Tourist Office (Map p168; ☎ 0341-710 4260, room referral 0341-710 4255; www.leipzig. travel; Katharinenstrasse 8; ⊙ 9.30am-6pm Mon-Fri, to 4pm Sat, to 3pm Sun) Room referral, ticket sales, maps and general information. Also sells the Leipzig Card (one/three days €10.90/21.90).

❶ Getting There & Away

AIR

Leipzig-Halle Airport (www.leipzig-halle-airport. de) is about 21km west of Leipzig. It has domestic and international flights connecting it with many German cities as well as London and Paris.

CAR

Leipzig lies just south of the A14 Halle-Dresden autobahn and 15km east of the A9, which links Berlin to Nuremberg. All major international car hire agencies can be found at the airport, as well as several more at the Hauptbahnhof.

TRAIN

Deutsche Bahn has frequent services to Frankfurt (€76, 3¾ hours), Dresden (€24.50, 1¼ hours) and Berlin (€47, 1¼ hours), though all of these can be had for considerably less by booking online several days in advance.

❶ Getting Around

PUBLIC TRANSPORT

Buses and trams are run by **LVB** (☎ 194 49; www.lvb.de), which operates an **information kiosk** (Map p168; Willy-Brandt-Platz; ⊙ 8am-8pm Mon-Fri, 8am-4pm Sat) outside the Hauptbahnhof. The central tram station is here as well. There's also a second LVG information kiosk on **Markgrafenstrasse** (Markgrafenstrasse 2; ⊙ 8am-8pm Mon-Sat). Single tickets cost €1.80 for up to four stops and €2.40 for longer trips; day passes are €6.50. The S-Bahn is run by Deutsche Bahn, but the ticketing system is integrated, so LVB tickets are valid on S-Bahn services within Leipzig itself.

TAXI

Taxis are expensive here. Flagfall is €3.50, and each kilometre €2.50.

Chemnitz

☎ 0371 / POP 242,000

Like most of eastern Germany's cities, Chemnitz had to reinvent itself post-*Wende*, and has done so with some measure of success. Known from 1953 to 1990 as Karl-Marx-Stadt, the GDR gave it a Stalinist makeover, and smokestack industries once earned it the nickname of 'Saxon Manches-

ter'. Such scars don't heal easily but Chemnitz has done a remarkable job, at least in its revitalised city centre that is now a pedestrianised glass-and-steel shopping and entertainment district.It doesn't draw many travellers, but some excellent museums and a friendly and progressive feel might tempt some to stop by.

◉ Sights

Chemnitz's compact and largely pedestrianised centre is a pleasing mix of historic and modern centred on Markt. The dominant building is the stately 15th-century **Altes Rathaus** (Old Town Hall) whose distinctive tower sports an ornate Renaissance portal and a carillon with cute little figures re-enacting town history at 11am, 4pm and 7pm. The old town hall segues into the **Neues Rathaus** (New Town Hall, 1911) whose imposing size is best appreciated from Neumarkt, which is also flanked by the **Galerie Roter Turm**. This modern shopping mall with a pleasing terracotta facade was designed by architectural top dog Hans Kollhoff. The equally esteemed Helmut Jahn dreamed up the adjacent glass-and-steel **Galeria Kaufhof** department store.

SAXONY CHEMNITZ

CHEMNITZ'S SCHLOSSBERG

About 1.3 km north of Chemnitz's centre is the Schlossteich, an idyllic park-ringed pond with a music pavilion for summer concerts. As well as being a lovely place for a wander, there are two other standout attractions here. To get here, take Bus 76 from the city centre and get off at Schlossberg.

Schlosskirche (☎ 0371-369 550; http://schloss.kirche chemnitz.info; Schlossplatz 7; ⊙ 2.30-5.30pm weekends & holidays) This 12th-century Benedictine monastery has been recast into a weighty Gothic hall church and houses Hans Witten's intriguing sculpture *Christ at the Column* (1515).

Schlossbergmuseum (☎ 0371-488 4501; www.schlossbergmuseum.de; Schlossberg 12; adult/concession €6/4; ⊙ 11am-6pm Tue-Sun) This late-Gothic monastery houses the Schlossbergmuseum, whose vaulted interior is a rich backdrop for Saxon 15th- and 16th-century sculpture.

Kunstsammlungen Chemnitz   MUSEUM

(Chemnitz Art Museum; ☑0371-488 4424; www.
kunstsammlungen-chemnitz.de; Theaterplatz 1;
adult/concession €6/4; ⊙11am-6pm Tue-Sun)
Flanking Chemnitz' most beautiful square,
the historic Theaterplatz, this lovely art museum stages large-scale temporary exhibits
sometimes drawn from its own collection of
paintings, sculpture, graphics, textiles and
crafts. Special strengths include Romantic
Age painters (Caspar David Friedrich, Ludwig Richter) and sculptures by Degas, Rodin
and Baselitz. The neo-baroque opera house,
the St Petrikirche and a hotel complete the
ensemble around Theaterplatz.

★ Museum Gunzenhauser   GALLERY

(☑0371-488 7024; www.kunstsammlungen-chem
nitz.de; Falkeplatz; adult/concession €7/4.50;
⊙11am-6pm Tue-Sun) A former 1930 bank
building, built in austere New Objectivity
style, is now a gallery of 20th-century art,
most famous for its expressionist works
by such key artists as Max Beckmann, Ernst Ludwig Kirchner and local boy Karl
Schmidt-Rottluff. Pride of place, though,
goes to a career-spanning collection of
works by Otto Dix on the 3rd floor. It's a superb collection and shouldn't be missed by
modern art lovers.

Karl Marx Monument   MONUMENT

(cnr Strasse der Nationen & Brückenstrasse)
Things have rather turned against the founder of communism since this 7m-high bronze
head (one that catches the German philosopher on a very bad hair day) was erected
in 1971. Behind Marx there's a huge frieze
exhorting 'Workers of the world, unite!' in
several languages. Attempts to remove the
monument after the end of communism
were resisted by locals, however, and Marx's
head remains a symbol of the city today.

DAStietz   MUSEUM

(☑0371-488 4397; ww.dastietz.de; Moritzstrasse
20) Beautifully renovated, this former 1913
department store now houses the city library
as well as the Neue Sächsische Galerie
(☑0371-367 6680; www.neue-saechsische-galerie.
de; adult/child €3/free; ⊙11am-5pm Thu-Mon,
11am-7pm Tue), which presents contemporary Saxon art, and the Museum für
Naturkunde (Natural History Museum; ☑0371-
488 4551; www.naturkunde-chemnitz.de; adult/
concession €4/2.50; ⊙10am-5pm Mon, Tue, Thu &
Fri, 10am-6pm Sat & Sun), whose most interesting exhibit, the Versteinerter Wald (petrified

forest), can be admired for free in the atrium; some of the stony trunks are 290 million years old.

Henry Van de Velde Museum   MUSEUM

(☑0371-488 4424; www.kunstsammlungen-chem
nitz.de; Parkstrasse 58; adult/child €3/free;
⊙10am-6pm Wed & Fri-Sun) Around 2.5km
south of the centre, this small but choice
museum occupies the 1903 Villa Esche,
which was Belgian artist Van de Velde's first
commission in Germany. The dining room
and music salon have been restored as period rooms, while upstairs you'll find a small
collection of crafts and furniture. Take tram
4 to Haydnstrasse.

🛏 Sleeping

Biendo Hotel   HOTEL €

(☑0371-433 1920; www.biendo-hotel.de; Strasse
der Nationen 12; s/d from €44/55; P🛜) This
fantastic midrange place is affordable
enough for nearly all visitors. On the 5th
and 6th floor of a GDR-era office building,
centrally located Biendo pitches itself somewhere between business and boutique hotel,
with small but good-value rooms that enjoy
contemporary furnishings and sweeping
city views. The breakfast (€8), served in the
light-bathed breakfast room, is worth it.

DJH Hostel   HOSTEL €

(☑0371-2780 9897; www.chemnitz-city.jugend
herberge.de; Getreidemarkt 6; dm incl breakfast
under/over 27yr €22/25.50; ⊙reception 8-11am
& 4-10pm; P@) If you like your hostel with
a dash of quirk and history, this industrial-
flavoured contender in a former converting
station in the town centre should fit the bill.
En suite dorms sleep three to eight.

Hotel an der Oper   HOTEL €€

(☑0371-6810; www.hoteloper-chemnitz.de; Strasse
der Nationen 56; s/d from €75/110; P✳🛜) With
front-row views of the historic opera house,
this renovated hotel spells comfort in soothing, good-sized rooms furnished in vanilla
and chocolate hues. The chic cocktail bar
has an impressive whisky selection, while
the Scala restaurant has top-notch food and
sumptuous views onto Theaterplatz.

🍴 Eating

Kellerhaus   GERMAN €€

(☑0371-335 1677; www.kellerhaus-chemnitz.de;
Schlossberg 2; mains €10-20; ⊙11am-10.30pm)
For a first-rate culinary journey at mod-
erate prices, it's well worth heading a bit

ESCAPE TO COLDITZ

Schloss Colditz (☎ 034381-437 77; www.schloss-colditz.com; Schlossgasse 1; adult/concession museum €4/3, tour €8.50/7; ☺ museum 10am-5pm Apr-Oct, to 4pm Nov-Mar, tours 10.30am, 1pm & 3pm) The very name Colditz is enough to send goosebumps down many people's spines, and so it might come as a surprise that the famous WWII-era high security prison for Allied officers is not as instantaneously recognisable to most Germans, who grew up without the string of books and films this iconic prison has inspired. A Renaissance castle straddling a crag above sleepy Colditz, some 46km southeast of Leipzig, Schloss Colditz has seen stints as a hunting lodge, a poorhouse and even a psychiatric hospital.

But its notoriety stems from its years as Oflag IVC, where the Nazis imprisoned officers who had already escaped from less secure camps and been recaptured, including a nephew of Winston Churchill.

As you would expect, some 300 prisoners here made further attempts to escape and 31 actually managed to flee. The would-be escapees were often aided by ingenious self-made gadgetry, including a glider fashioned from wood and bed sheets, and a homemade sewing machine for making fake German uniforms. Most astounding, perhaps, is a 44m-long tunnel below the chapel that French officers dug in 1941-–42, before the Germans caught them. You can see some of these contraptions, along with lots of photographs, in the small but fascinating Fluchtmuseum (Escape Museum) within the castle.

On weekdays bus 690 makes the trip from Leipzig Hauptbahnhof to Colditz and back several times daily (€7, two hours). For specific timetables, see www.mdv.de.

away from the town centre to this half-timbered charmer at the foot of the historic Schlossberg quarter. Sit in the cosy cellar, the low-ceilinged main dining room or on the terrace.

Ratskeller   GERMAN €€
(☎ 0371-694 9875; www.ratskeller-chemnitz. de; Markt 1; mains €7-18; ☺ 11am-midnight) The rustic, olde-worlde setting amid gorgeously painted vaulted ceilings just couldn't get any more charming, and this vast subterranean hall serves up decent German fare until late by local standards. In summer you can also eat outside on the Markt.

Cafe Michaelis   INTERNATIONAL €€
(☎ 0371-2733 7985; www.michaelis-chemnitz.de; Am Düsseldorfer Platz 11; mains €11-22; ☺ 9am-10pm Mon-Thu, to 11pm Fri & Sat, 10am-9pm Sun) A century-old Chemnitz coffeehouse tradition, Cafe Michaelis nevertheless enjoys a modern look thanks to a recent makover yet remains famous for its mindboggling selection of truly mouthwatering cakes. If you don't have a sweet tooth, opt for a crisp salad, homemade pasta or meaty main from the extensive menu. Big terrace in summer.

ℹ️ Information

Main Post Office (Strasse der Nationen 2-4; ☺ 9am-7pm Mon-Fri, 9am-2pm Sat)

Tourist Office (☎ 0371 690 680; www.chemnitz-tourismus.de; Markt 1; ☺ 9am-7pm Mon-Fri, 9am-4pm Sat, 11am-1pm Sun)

ℹ️ Getting There & Around

LOCAL TRANSPORT
All trams and buses pass through the city-centre Zentralhaltestelle (central stop). Single tickets are €2 and a day pass is €4.

TRAIN
Chemnitz is linked by direct train to Dresden (€15, one hour), Leipzig (€15, one hour) and Zwickau (€6.20, 30 minutes).

EASTERN SAXONY

Görlitz

☑ 03581 / POP 54,000

Görlitz, Germany's most Eastern city, is also Saxony's most magical town, a dreamy coalescence of fabulous architecture, idyllic cobbled streets and and intriguing history. Having miraculously escaped destruction during WWII, Görlitz offers the visitor some nearly 4200 heritage buildings and is a veritable encyclopedia of European architectural styles, from the Renaissance to the 19th century.

Ironically, even though the Iron Curtain lifted decades ago, Görlitz is still a divided city. After WWII it was split in two when the Allies declared the Neisse River as the boundary between Germany and Poland. Görlitz' former eastern flank is now the Polish town of Zgorzelec, easily reached via a footbridge across the river (indeed, it's hard to tell you've even left Germany). In recent years, Görlitz has enjoyed a mini boom and is popular with visitors both for its wonderful history and excellent eating and sleeping options.

◎ Sights

Görlitz' sights cluster in the Altstadt, reached from the train station via Berliner Strasse or Jakobstrasse. It is organised around several squares, most notably the large Obermarkt and the smaller, cuter Untermarkt. From the latter, Neissstrasse leads down to the river and the footbridge to Zgorzelec.

◎ Obermarkt & Southern Altstadt

Reichenbacher Turm   VIEWPOINT
(www.museum-goerlitz.de; Platz des 17 Juni; adult/concession €3/2; ◎10am-5pm Tue-Sun May-Oct) Climb the 165 steps to the top of this tower,

---

DON'T MISS

GÖRLITZ'S HOLY REPLICA

Heiliges Grab (☑ 03581-315 864; http://kulturstiftung.kkvsol.net; Heilig-Grab-Strasse 79; admission €2; ◎10am-6pm Mon-Sat, 11am-6pm Sun Apr-Sep, to 4pm Nov-Feb, to 5pm Mar & Oct) The Heiliges Grab is a close replica of the Holy Sepulchre in Jerusalem as it looked in the Middle Ages during the time of the crusades. Among these crusaders was local boy Georg Emmerich, who made the trip primarily in atonement for knocking up the neighbour's daughter. Absolved from his sins, he returned, became the town mayor and, in 1480, instigated the construction of the Heiliges Grab.

It is part of a larger ensemble that also includes a double chapel and a salvation house, and marks the final stop in the via dolorosa (Station of the Cross) pilgrimage path that starts at the west portal of the Peterskirche and runs via Nikolaistrasse, Bogstrasse and Steinweg.

---

inhabited by a watchman until 1904. En route, exhibits on the purpose of such watchmen (eg keeping an eye out for fire or advancing marauders) provide a modest excuse to catch your breath. There's another tower a short walk south on Marienplatz, called **Dicker Turm** (Fat Tower), thanks to its 6m-thick walls.

Dreifaltigkeitskirche   CHURCH
(Klosterplatz 21; audioguide €2; ◎10am-6pm Mon-Sat, 11am-6pm Sun Apr-Oct, to 4pm Nov-Mar) Dominating Obermarkt, this 15th-century former Franciscan monastery church is packed with medieval masterpieces, most notably the baroque high altar and the late Gothic 'Golden Mary' altar.

Art Nouveau Department Store   ARCHITECTURE
(Marienplatz) This architectural stunner is centred on a galleried atrium accented with wooden balustrades, floating staircases and palatial chandeliers and lidded by an ornately patterned glass ceiling. It is currently undergoing renovation and is due to reopen as a department store in 2016, but until it does you can still peer in through the windows.

Another art nouveau delicacy is the nearby Strassburg Passage, a light-flooded shopping arcade connecting Berliner Strasse and Jacobstrasse.

◎ Untermarkt & Eastern Altstadt

Barockhaus   MUSEUM
(☑ 03581-671 355; www.museum-goerlitz.de; Neissstrasse 30; adult/concession €5/3.50; ◎10am-5pm Tue-Sat) This museum will fascinate anyone with a taste for the odd with its curiously broad exhibits. Wealthy merchant Johann Christian Ameiss translated his wealth into this magnificent baroque residence that later became the seat of a prestigious science society. On the 1st floor, family rooms with period furnishings lead to smaller cabinets brimming with baroque porcelain, art, glass, silver and other precious objects. Exhibits on the upper floor highlight society members' diverse research interests – ranging from physics and archaeology to music.

Schlesisches Museum zu Görlitz   MUSEUM
(☑ 03581-879 10; www.schlesisches-museum.de; Brüderstrasse 8, adult/concession incl audioguide €5/3; ◎10am-6pm Tue-Sun) The splendid Schönhof, a 1526 Renaissance residence, forms the atmospheric backdrop to this comprehensive exhibit on the culture and history of Silesia, a region that's often found

ZWICKAU: SAXONY'S AUTO HERITAGE

Zwickau, a pleasant but otherwise unremarkable town in southwest Saxony, is famous for its contribution to the German automobile history, being both the birthplace of the Audi brand (in 1910) and the rather less celebrated yet still highly iconic GDR-era Trabant (from 1957). The car industry has been shaped here by one man in particular: August Horch (1868–1951). The first Horch cars rolled onto the road in 1904 and quickly became the queen among luxury vehicles, besting even Mercedes Benz. Horch later founded Audi, which remains one of the world's leading luxury car manufacturers today.

In the excellent **August Horch Museum** (☑ 0375-2717 3812; www.horch-museum.de; Audistrasse 7; adult/concession €6/4, audioguide €1.50; ⊙ 9.30am-5pm Tue-Sun), within the original early-20th-century Audi factory, gleaming and imaginatively presented exhibits range from old-timer gems like the 1911 Horch Phaeton to the latest Audi R8. And, of course, there are plenty of Trabants (three million were produced in town here until 1990) and other Eastern European cars. You can walk around an early petrol station, inspect Audi founder August Horch's original wood-panelled office, stroll down a 1930s streetscape and even learn how Trabants were made.

The museum is about 2km north of the Altstadt; take tram 4 to Kurt-Eisner-Strasse. Zwickau can easily be visited on a day trip, and there's no reason to stay overnight. There are direct train links to Leipzig (€17.90, two hours), Chemnitz (€6.20, 45 minutes) and Dresden (€25.50, two hours).

itself in the cross-hairs of political power players and repeatedly changed borders and identity over the past thousand years. Fine art, fabulous glass and ceramics and objects from daily life complement the historical displays spread over 17 themed rooms in the historic main building and a modern annex.

Signage is only in German and Polish, meaning that the free audioguide is useful.

Rathaus
HISTORIC BUILDING

(Untermarkt) Görlitz' town hall takes up the entire western side of Untermarkt, but the oldest and most noteworthy section is the tower building with the curving Renaissance staircase fronted by a sculpture of the goddess Justitia. Take a moment to observe the lower of the two tower clocks and you'll notice that the helmeted soldier in the middle briefly drops his chin every minute.

Flüsterbogen
HISTORIC BUILDING

On the north side of Untermarkt, you can whisper sweet nothings to your sweetie via the reverberating stone arch in the entranceway at No 22. The Renaissance **Ratsapotheke** (pharmacy) at No 24 is easily recognised by its spidery sundial, another of Görlitz' architectural masterpieces.

Peterskirche
CHURCH

(⊙10am-6pm Mon-Sat, 11.45am-6pm Sun) Crowning Görlitz' skyline, this Gothic church is especially famous for its Sonnenorgel (Sun Organ), fashioned by Silesian-Italian Euge-

nio Casparini in 1703. It boasts 88 registers and 6095 pipes and derives its name from the 17 circular sunshields integrated into the organ case. The church tower can be climbed (€2) but views are only so-so.

🛏 Sleeping

⭐ **Pension Miejski**
PENSION €

(☑ in Poland 888 579 253; www.pensjonat-miejski.pl; Nowomiejjska 1, Zgorzelec; s/d/tr/apt €33/38/48/55; P ☺ 🛜) Cross the footbridge onto the Polish side of the Neisse River, turn right and wander up the hill and you'll find this superb value-for-money option. There are eight impeccably maintained and spacious rooms done up in warm colours. Fast wi-fi, coffee and parking are all free, though book ahead for the latter as there are limited spaces.

Pension Goldene Feder
PENSION €

(☑ 03581-400 403; www.pension-goerlitz.de; Handwerk 12; d €55-70; P 🛜) A winner for fans of retro touches such as writing paper, quill and ink in your room, the 'Golden Feather' harmoniously mixes modern and vintage furnishings with art created by friends of the owner couple. Breakfast includes fruit and eggs from the family farm.

DJH Hostel
HOSTEL €

(☑ 03581-649 0700; www.goerlitz-city.jugendherberge.de; Peterstrasse 15; dm incl breakfast under/over 27yr €25.50/29.50; ⊙ check-in 4-9pm Apr-Sep, 5-8pm Oct-Mar; @🛜) This vast and

WORTH A TRIP

BAD MUSKAU

Squeezed against the border with Poland, drowsy Bad Muskau is a tiny spa-village with one big attraction. Unesco-listed **Muskauer Park** (☑035771-631 00; www.muskauer-park. de; Neues Schloss; park free, exhibit adult/concession €7/3.50, tower €4/2; ☺ exhibit 10am-6pm Apr-Oct) is the verdant masterpiece of 19th-century celebrity landscape gardener Prince Hermann von Pückler, who inherited his family estate in 1811. 'Prince Pickle', as the English dubbed him, toiled on the park for nearly 30 years but never completed his 'painting with plants' because debt forced him to sell the estate in 1844. He nevertheless set the bar high for landscapers to follow, even compiling a meticulous instruction manual on landscaping techniques. The park and town suffered enormously when the last major battle of WWII was fought on its grounds in early 1945. In the same year, the park was divided between Germany and Poland when the River Neisse, which bisects von Pückler's creation, became the new border.

A stroll around the landscaped park will eventually take you to its main building, the Neues Schloss, home of the **tourist office** (☑035771-631 00; ☺10am-6pm Apr-Oct, to 5pm Nov-Mar) in the west wing and to Pückler!, an interactive, push-button caper through the action-packed life of the park's flamboyant mastermind. Take in views of the park from the top of the palace tower.

At a whopping 560 hectares, the folly-peppered park is too large to be fully explored on foot. Bike hire (€5 per day) is available at the well-signposted Schlossvorwerk, a leafy courtyard where you'll also find a cafe, gift shops and luggage lockers.

Bad Muskau is about 55km north of Görlitz. Coming by train, take an Ostdeutsche Eisenbahn train to Weisswasser (€7.80, 50 minutes), then change to bus 250 to Kirchplatz (€3, 20 minutes). The park entrance is a short signposted walk away. Alternatively, it's possible on certain days from April to October to take a picturesque steamtrain ride from Weisswasser (€6.90 return) on the **Waldeisenbahn Muskau** (www.waldeisenbahn.de).

modern hostel behind a historic facade is squarely aimed at groups. While it does boast an excellent Altstadt location, plenty of public and outdoor space and shiny en suite rooms sleeping two to six, it's nevertheless rather charmless and impersonal. Families will appreciate the private apartments (from €35 including breakfast).

★ **Hotel Börse**   HOTEL €€
(☑03581-764 20; www.boerse-goerlitz.de; Untermarkt 16; s/d from €75/113; P @ ⚶) Four-poster beds, sparkling glass chandeliers, marble bathrooms, patterned parquet floors and elegant antiques are the hallmarks of this stylish hotel in an 18th-century palais. With its absolutely perfect location, old-world atmosphere and surprisingly affordable rates, this is our best bet for a comfortable and memorable stay in Görlitz.

Rooms in the affiliated **Gästehaus am Flüsterbogen** (s/d €60/85) sport a similarly subtle romantic style but are a tad bigger. For a more contemporary feel, book into the nearby **Herberge zum 6. Gebot** (s/d €55/69), which translates as 'Inn of the 6th Commandment' (that would be the one about adultery). As a sweet touch of irony, rooms are named

for such famous philanderers as Henry VIII and Casanova. Check-in and breakfast are all at the Hotel Börse.

Romantik Hotel Tuchmacher   HOTEL €€
(☑03581-473 10; www.tuchmacher.de; Peterstrasse 8; s/d/ste €102/132/188; P ⚶) In the most coveted rooms at this posh Renaissance charmer near the Peterskirche you'll be sleeping beneath richly painted baroque ceilings, but others are just as nice with warm hues and classical furnishings. Roast in the hot tub or sauna before toasting the day over a sophisticated meal in the on-site restaurant.

✗ Eating

★ **Vino e Cultura**   ITALIAN €€
(☑03581-879 6850; www.vinoecultura.de; Untermarkt 2; mains €10-20; ☺3-11pm Tue-Fri, noon-11pm Sat & Sun) The vaulted space right on historic Untermarkt has been glitzily converted and is now easily Görlitz's prime foodie destination. The menu, courtesy of the clearly ambitious French chef, is adventurous (try monkfish with paprika chutney or duck breast with caramelised apricots), the staff is charming and the entire place a great leap forward for the local eating scene.

Filetto   ITALIAN €€

(📞03581-421 131; Peterstrasse 1; mains €8-20; 🕐6-11pm daily, noon-3pm & 6-11pm Sat & Sun; 📶) This warm and friendly place in the heart of the old town has an Italian-leaning menu that is focused heavily on steaks and a simple list of French wines. It's cosy and oozes history (the building dates from 1530 and was once the town apothecary); it's a good idea to reserve a table in the evenings.

Restaurant Lucie Schulte   INTERNATIONAL €€

(📞03581-410 260; Untermarkt 22; mains €12-23; 🕐noon-3pm & 6-11pm) In the romantic courtyard of the Flüsterbogen building, you'll find this upmarket place that is popular with locals and visitors alike. Despite the formal setting, there's room for some creativity: unusual flavour pairings and an impressive international wine list are what set the menu apart from many others in town.

St Jonathan   SAXON, MEDITERRANEAN €€

(📞03581-421 082; www.goerlitz-restaurant.de; Peterstrasse 16; mains €8-23; 🕐noon-3pm Tue-Sun, 6-11pm daily) In a gorgeously attired dining space and atmospheric historic setting, St Jon-

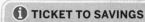

🛈 TICKET TO SAVINGS

Combination tickets to see both the large and the small Lenten veil are €8 per adult (€5 concession). Tickets include English-language audioguides.

athan offers delicious pasta, huge steaks and traditional regional dishes at linen-bedecked tables beneath a painted vaulted ceiling. For a romantic and unusual experience, book the table for two inside the fireplace.

🛈 Information

Banks with ATMs are scattered throughout but are especially numerous around Postplatz, which is also where you'll find the main post office.

Görlitz Tourist Office (📞03581-475 70; www. goerlitz.de; Obermarkt 32; 🕐9am-6pm Mon-Fri, to 5pm Sat, to 4pm Sun May-Oct, 9.30am-6pm Mon-Fri, to 2.30pm Sa & Sun Nov-Apr) The main tourist office offers lots of information and has English-speaking staff.

I-Vent Private Tourist Office (📞03581-421 362; www.goerlitz-tourismus.de; Obermarkt 33; 🕐9am-6pm Mon-Fri, 9.30am-5pm Sat,

SAXONY GÖRLITZ

WORTH A TRIP

BAUTZEN: MUSTARD, PRISONS & SORBS

Rising high above the Spree River, with no fewer than 17 towers and much of the town fortification still ringing the Altstadt, Bautzen hasn't changed much for centuries. While its old town is now ringed by a fairly unremarkable modern city, Bautzen is actually known across Germany for three things: its famous mustard, its two infamous prisons and its Slavic-speaking Sorbs, a protected (and endangered) ethnic minority group within Germany. Budyšin, as the Sorb language calls it, is home to several Sorb cultural institutions, and public signage is bilingual, though you'll be lucky to hear the language spoken. You can learn all about Sorbian culture at the **Sorbisches Museum** (📞03591-270 8700; www.sorbisches-museum.de; Ortenburg 3-5; adult/concession €3.50/2; 🕐10am-6pm Tue-Sun), and even try excellent Sorbian dishes at **Wjelbik** (📞03591-420 60; www.wjelbik. de; Kornstrasse 7; mains €10-20; 🕐lunch & dinner Tue-Sat, lunch Sun) nearby.

It seems incongruous that this pretty, historical town has been known as *Gefängnisstadt* (prison town) for over a century. Its two prisons – Bautzen I and Bautzen II – were built in 1904 and 1906, respectively. Bautzen I is still in use, and was used by both the Nazis and the communists in the past. Bautzen II became a notorious Stasi prison in the 1950s and was controlled by the GDR Ministry of State Security. More than 2700 regime critics, would-be escapees and those who aided them, purported spies for the West and other political prisoners were incarcerated here from 1956 to 1989. You can learn about the prison's history at the **Gedenkstätte Bautzen** (📞03591-404 74; www. gedenkstae tte-bautzen.de; Weigangstrasse 8a; 🕐10am-4pm Mon-Thu, 10am-8pm Fri, 10am-6pm Sat & Sun) **FREE**.

Finally, the city's unique mustard heritage can be seen all over Bautzen in numerous specialist shops, though perhaps it's best explored at **Bautzner Senfstube** (📞03591-598 015; www.senf-stube.de; Schlossstrasse 3; mains €8-15; 🕐11am-10pm), where the main menu offers dishes prepared with the product. Bautzen can be easily reached on a day trip by train from Dresden (€12, 45 minutes) or Görlitz (€8.20, 30 minutes).

WORTH A TRIP

CHOO-CHOO TRAIN TO THE MOUNTAINS

South of Zittau, the Zittauer Gebirge is the smallest low-mountain range in Europe. With its idyllic gorges, thick forests and whimsical rock formations, it's great for hiking and clearing your head. You can drive or take the bus, but getting there is much more fun aboard the narrow-gauge **Zittauer Schmalspurbahn** (☑03583-540 540; www.soeg-zit tau.de; return trip €15), which has been steaming through the trees since 1890. Historic locomotives depart year-round from an tiny timber station in front of Zittau's train station up to the sleepy resort villages of Oybin and Jonsdorf, splitting at Bertsdorf. The largest and nicest town is **Oybin**, which wraps around a beehive-shaped hill topped by a romantically ruined castle and monastery. Trains also stop at the **Teufelsmühle** (Devil's Mill), built for silver miners in the 17th century, from where a trail leads up to the **Töpfer**, a photogenic 582m-high mountain whose evocative sandstone formations have been nicknamed 'tortoise' or 'breeding hen'.

9.30am-3pm Sun Apr-Oct, 9am-6pm Mon-Fri, 9.30am-3pm Sat Nov-Mar) A privately run tourist office representing both Görlitz and Zgorzelec.

❶ Getting There & Away

Trains run regularly between Görlitz and Dresden (€21.70, one to 1½ hours) via Bautzen (€8.90, 30 minutes). For Berlin (from €44.30, three hours), change in Cottbus. Trains also run to Zittau (€6.10, 40 minutes). The train station is south of the old town; take Berliner Strasse to get there.

Zittau

☑03583 / POP 27,550

In the far southeast corner of Saxony, cradled by Poland and the Czech Republic, Zittau makes for an easy day trip from Dresden or Görlitz. Its largely baroque Altstadt came through WWII mostly intact, though Cold War–era neglect is still evident in places. The town is a major stop for religious pilgrims thanks to two precious late-medieval Lenten veils that are ultra-rare and stunning pieces of artistry. By contrast, the newest attraction is the bright and whimsical Pop-Art Quarter, one of the largest of its kind in Germany.

◉ Sights

Sights cluster around the Markt, which is about 1km south of the Hauptbahnhof via Bahnhofstrasse and Bautzener Strasse. With its baroque fountain, stately town houses and imposing Italian palazzo–style Rathaus (town hall) by Prussian master builder Karl Friedrich Schinkel, it exudes a touch of light-hearted Mediterranean flair.

Museum Kirche
zum Heiligen Kreuz   MUSEUM
(☑03583-500 8920; www.zittauer-fastentuecher. de; Frauenstrasse 23; adult/concession €5/3; ⊙10am-5pm daily Apr-Oct, 10am-5pm Tue-Sun Nov-Mar) This former church holds Zittau's most famous attraction, the 1472 Grosses Zittauer Fastentuch (Large Zittau Lenten Veil). The house-sized painted linen cloth shows a complete illustrated Bible in 90-odd scenes – Genesis to the Last Judgement. Its original purpose was to conceal the altar from the congregation during Lent. Ask for the accompanying voiceover to be played in English.

Also note the morbidly charming tombstones in the church cemetery.

Kulturhistorisches Museum
Franziskanerkloster   MUSEUM
(☑03583-554 790; www.zittauer-fastentuecher.de; Klosterstrasse 3; adult/concession €5/3; ⊙10am-5pm daily Apr-Oct, closed Mon Nov-Mar) The star exhibit at this museum is the 1573 Kleines Zittauer Fastentuch (Small Zittau Lenten Veil), which depicts the crucifixion scene framed by 40 symbols of the Passion of Christ, and is one of only seven such veils that have survived. The rest of the museum chronicles regional history.

Pop-Art-Viertel   NEIGHBOURHOOD
(www.mandauerglanz.de; btwn Grüne Strasse & Rosenstrasse) A rather more contemporary Zittau attraction is this once drab cluster of GDR-era buildings that have been transformed into a colourful and fanciful living quarter dreamed up by Berlin artist Sergej Alexander Dott. Giant sheep clambering around bright orange facades, and centaurs and angels standing guard over a pedestrianised walkway spanned by a massive double helix are just some highlights.

Salzhaus   HISTORIC BUILDING
(www.salzhaus-zittau.de; Neustadt; ⊗8am-6.30pm)
Overlooking fountain-studded Neustadt
square, the weighty Salzhaus was originally
a 16th-century salt storage house and now
brims with market stalls, shops, restaurants
and the public library.

Johanniskirche   CHURCH
(☑03583-510 933; www.johanniskirche-zittau.
de; Johannisplatz 1; tower adult/concession €2/1;
⊗noon-6pm Mon-Fri, 10am-4pm Sat & Sun Apr-
Oct, 10am-4.30pm Mon-Fri, 10am-4pm Sat & Sun
Nov-Mar) Zittau's grand Church of St John
has medieval roots, but the current version
was designed by celebrated Prussian architect Karl Friedrich Schinkel who added
the wooden coffered ceiling, the neo-Gothic north tower and the baptismal font. It
was consecrated in 1837. The south tower
can be climbed for sweeping views of the
mountains.

🛏 Sleeping & Eating

Hotel Dreiländereck   HOTEL €€
(☑03583-5550; www.hotel-dle.de; Bautzener
Strasse 9; s/d €73/95; ℗⊚) This one-time
brewery on Zittau's pedestrianised commercial strip is a solid pick, with an old-school
style; the green and gold colour schemes
aren't to everyone's taste. The contemporary
brasserie (mains €9 to €18) has vaulted ceilings and a large terrace.

★Dornspachhaus   GERMAN €€
(☑03583-795 883; www.dornspachhaus.de;
Bautzener Strasse 2; mains €7-18; ⊗11.30am-2pm
& 5.30-9.30pm) Zittau's oldest eatery dates

from 1533 and oozes history. But it's not
just a tourist piece: it also serves delicious
regional cuisine and has a lovely courtyard.
A speciality is the Bohemian goulash, a
creamy blend of slivered pork, pickles and
mushrooms served in a bowl of bread, while
during apsaragus season you're spoiled for
choice.

Seeger Schänke   GERMAN €€
(☑03583-510 980; www.seeger-schaenke.de; Innere Weberstrasse 38; mains €10-14; ⊗11am-2pm
Mon-Fri, 6-10pm daily) 'Seeger' is local dialect
for 'clock', which explains the abundance of
time pieces decorating this rustic pub that's
often so crowded in the evenings that you
have to wait for a table. There's a pleasant
courtyard out the back, which is a great
place for lunch in the sunshine during the
summer months.

ℹ Information

Tourist Office (☑03583-752 200; www.zittau.
eu; Markt 1; ⊗9am-6pm Mon-Fri, 9am-1pm Sat
year-round, 10am-noon Sun May-Oct) You'll find
the tourist office inside the Rathaus.

ℹ Getting There & Away

ODEG trains run to Görlitz (€7.30, 35 minutes),
while Deutsche Bahn operates direct services to
Dresden (€21.50, 1½ hours). Going to Bautzen
requires a change in Görlitz (€8.70, 1½ hours).

SAXONY ZITTAU

Munich

Includes →

Best Places to Eat

→ Fraunhofer (p213)

→ Königsquelle (p212)

→ Tantris (p214)

→ Prinz Myshkin (p212)

→ Esszimmer (p215)

Best Places to Drink

→ Alter Simpl (p217)

→ Augustiner Bräustuben (p219)

→ Hofbräuhaus (p216)

→ Hirschgarten (p218)

→ Baader Café (p217)

Why Go?

The natural habitat of well-heeled power dressers and Lederhosen-clad thigh-slappers, Mediterranean-style street cafes and Mitteleuropa beer halls, highbrow art and high-tech industry, Germany's unofficial southern capital is a flourishing success story that revels in its own contradictions. If you're looking for Alpine clichés, they're all here, but the Bavarian metropolis has many an unexpected card down its Dirndl.

But whatever else this city is, it's popular. Statistics show Munich is enticing more visitors than ever, especially in summer and during Oktoberfest, when the entire planet seems to arrive to toast the town.

Munich's walkable centre retains a small-town air but holds some world-class sights, especially art galleries and museums. Throw in royal Bavarian heritage, an entire suburb of Olympic legacy and a kitbag of dark tourism, and it's clear why southern Germany's metropolis is such a favourite among those who seek out the past but like to hit the town once they're done.

When to Go

Lovers of German beer will find true happiness in Munich's beer halls during Stark Bier Zeit (strong beer season). This popular festival takes place for three weeks in February or March and is the time to sup the strong ale monks once brewed to sustain themselves through the Lenten fast.

September to October is the best time to amble in the Englischer Garten (English Garden) as its trees fire off an autumnal salute.

In December, pretty Marienplatz at the city's heart fills with Christmassy stalls, lights and enough yuletide cheer to share among its international gaggle of shoppers.

History

It was Benedictine monks, drawn by fertile farmland and the closeness to Catholic Italy, who settled in what is now Munich. The city derives its name from the medieval *Munichen* (monks). In 1158 the Imperial Diet in Augsburg sanctioned the rule of Heinrich der Löwe, and Munich the city was born.

In 1240 the city passed to the House of Wittelsbach, which would govern Munich (and Bavaria) until the 20th century. Munich prospered as a salt-trading centre but was hit hard by plague in 1349. The epidemic subsided only after 150 years, whereupon the relieved *Schäffler* (coopers) initiated a ritualistic dance to remind burghers of their good fortune. The Schäfflertanz is performed every seven years but is re-enacted daily by the little figures on the city's Glockenspiel (carillon) on Marienplatz.

By the 19th century an explosion of monument building gave Munich its spectacular architecture and wide Italianate avenues. Things got out of hand after King Ludwig II ascended the throne in 1864, as spending for his grandiose projects (such as Schloss Neuschwanstein south of Munich) bankrupted the royal house and threatened the government's coffers. Ironically, today they are the biggest money-spinners of Bavaria's tourism industry.

Munich has seen many turbulent times, but the 20th century was particularly bumpy. WWI practically starved the city to death, while the Nazis first rose to prominence here and WWII nearly wiped Munich off the map.

The 1972 Olympic Games began as a celebration of a new democratic Germany but ended in tragedy when 17 people were killed in a terrorist hostage-taking incident. In 2006 the city won a brighter place in sporting history when it hosted the opening game of the FIFA World Cup.

Today Munich's claim to being the 'secret capital' of Germany is well founded. The city is recognised for its high living standards – with more millionaires per capita than any other German city except Hamburg – and for haute couture that rivals that of Paris and Milan. Having celebrated its 850th birthday just short of a decade ago, this great metropolis is striding affluently forward into the 21st century.

◉ Sights

Munich's major sights cluster around the Altstadt, with the main museum district just north of the Residenz. However, it will take another day or two to explore bohemian Schwabing, the sprawling Englischer Garten, and trendy Haidhausen to the east. Northwest of the Altstadt you'll find cosmopolitan Neuhausen, the Olympiapark and another of Munich's royal highlights – Schloss Nymphenburg.

◉ Altstadt

Marienplatz   SQUARE
(Map p188; ⓢ Marienplatz; ⓤ Marienplatz) The epicentral heart and soul of the Altstadt, Marienplatz is a popular gathering spot and packs a lot of personality into a compact frame. It's anchored by the **Mariensäule** (Mary's Column; Map p188), built in 1638 to celebrate victory over Swedish forces during the Thirty Years' War. This is the busiest spot in all Munich, with throngs of tourists swarming across its expanse from early morning till late at night.

Neues Rathaus   HISTORIC BUILDING
(New Town Hall; Map p188; Marienplatz; ⓤ Marienplatz, ⓢ Marienplatz) The soot-blackened façade of the neo-Gothic Neues Rathaus is festooned with gargoyles, statues and a dragon scaling the turrets; the tourist office is on the ground floor. For pinpointing Munich's landmarks without losing your breath, catch the lift up the 85m-tall **tower** (adult/concession €2.50/1; ⊙ 10am-7pm daily).

The **Glockenspiel** (⊙ 11am, noon, 5pm & 9pm) has 43 bells and 32 figures that perform two historical events. The top half tells the story of a tournament held in 1568 to celebrate the marriage of Duke Wilhelm V to Renata of Lothringen, while the bottom half portrays the Schäfflertanz (cooper's dance).

Frauenkirche   CHURCH
(Church of Our Lady; Map p188; www.muenchner-dom.de; Frauenplatz 1; ⊙ 7am-7pm Sat-Wed, to 8.30pm Thu, to 6pm Fri; ⓢ Marienplatz) The landmark Frauenkirche, built between 1468 and 1488, is Munich's spiritual heart and the Mt Everest among its churches. No other building in the central city may stand taller than its onion-domed twin towers, which reach a skyscraping 99m. The south tower can be climbed but was under urgent renovation at the time of writing.

Munich Highlights

1 Raising a 1L stein of *Bier* at an authentic beer hall, such as the **Augustiner Bräustuben** (p219)

2 Feeling your brow growing higher among the world-class art collections at the **Alte Pinakothek** (p194)

3 Revelling in the blingfest that is the **Schatzkammer der Residenz** (p193)

4 Squeezing Alpine style into Lederhosen or a Dirndl at a

folk-costume emporium, such as **Holareidulijö** (p221)

6 Enjoying a brunch of traditional *Weisswurst* (veal sausage), a pretzel and a *Weissbier* (wheat beer) at **Weisses Brauhaus** (p213)

7 Watching daredevil surfers negotiate an urban wave on the artificial stream in the **Englischer Garten** (p197)

5 Getting under the high-octane hood of **BMW Welt** (p204)

The church sustained severe bomb damage in WWII; its reconstruction is a soaring passage of light but otherwise fairly spartan. Of note are the epic cenotaph (empty tomb) of Ludwig the Bavarian, just past the entrance, and the bronze plaques of Pope Benedict XVI and his predecessor John Paul II, affixed to nearby pillars.

Asamkirche   CHURCH
(Map p188; Sendlinger Strasse 32; ⊙9am-6pm Sat-Thu, 1-6pm Fri; 🚇Sendlinger Tor, ⓤSendlinger Tor) **FREE** Though pocket sized, the late-baroque Asamkirche, built in 1746, is as rich and epic as a giant's treasure chest. Its creators, the brothers Cosmas Damian Asam and Egid Quirin Asam, dug deep into their considerable talent box to swathe every inch of wall space with gilt garlands and docile cherubs, false marble and oversized barley twist columns.

The crowning glory is the ceiling fresco illustrating the life of St John Nepomuk, to whom the church is dedicated (lie down on your back on a pew to fully appreciate the complicated perspective). The brothers lived next door and this was originally their private chapel; the main altar could be seen through a window from their home.

St Peterskirche   CHURCH
(Church of St Peter; Map p188; Rindermarkt 1; church free, tower adult/concession €2/1; ⊙tower 9am-6pm Mon-Fri, from 10am Sat & Sun; ⓤMarienplatz, ⓢMarienplatz) Some 306 steps divide you from the best view of central Munich from the 92m tower of St Peterskirche, Munich's oldest church (1150). Inside awaits a virtual textbook of art through the centuries. Worth a closer peek are the Gothic St-Martin-Altar, the baroque ceiling fresco by Johann Baptist Zimmermann and rococo sculptures by Ignaz Günther.

Viktualienmarkt   MARKET
(Map p188; ⊙Mon-Fri & morning Sat; ⓤMarienplatz, ⓢMarienplatz) Fresh fruit and vegetables, piles of artisan cheeses, tubs of exotic olives, hams and jams, chanterelles and truffles – Viktualienmarkt is a feast of flavours and one of central Europe's finest gourmet markets.

The market moved here in 1807 when it outgrew the Marienplatz and many of the stalls have been run by generations of the same family. Put together a picnic and head for the market's very own beer garden for an al fresco lunch with a brew and to watch the traders in action.

Heiliggeistkirche   CHURCH
(Church of the Holy Spirit; Map p188; Im Tal 77; ⊙7am-6pm; ⓤMarienplatz, ⓢMarienplatz) Gothic at its core, this baroque church on the edge of the Viktualienmarkt has fantastic ceiling frescoes created by the Asam brothers in 1720, depicting the foundation of a hospice that once stood next door. The hospice was demolished to make way for the new Viktualienmarkt.

Münchner Stadtmuseum   MUSEUM
(City Museum; Map p188; www.muenchner-stadt museum.de; St-Jakobs-Platz 1; adult/concession/child €6/3.50/free, audioguide free; ⊙10am-6pm Tue-Sun; ⓤMarienplatz, ⓢMarienplatz) Installed for the city's 850th birthday (2008), the Münchner Stadtmuseum's Typisch München (Typical Munich) exhibition – taking up the whole of a rambling building – tells Munich's story in an imaginative, uncluttered and engaging way. Exhibits in each section represent something quintessential about the city; a booklet/audioguide relates the tale behind them, thus condensing a long and tangled history into easily digestible themes.

Set out in chronological order, the exhibition kicks off with the founding monks and ends in the postwar-boom decades. The first of five sections, Old Munich, contains a scale model of the city in the late 16th century (one of five commissioned by Duke Albrecht V; the Bayerisches Nationalmuseum (p200) displays the others), but the highlight here is the *The Morris Dancers*, a series of statuettes gyrating like 15th-century ravers. It's one of the most valuable works owned by the city.

Next comes New Munich, which charts the Bavarian capital's 18th- and 19th-century transformation into prestigious royal capital and the making of the modern city. The *Canaletto View* gives an idea in oil paint of how Munich looked in the mid-18th century, before the Wittelsbachs (the German noble family that ruled Bavaria) launched their makeover. The section also takes a fascinating look at the origins of Oktoberfest and Munich's cuisine, as well as the phenomenon of the 'Munich Beauty' – Munich's womenfolk are regarded as Germany's most attractive.

City of Munich examines the weird and wonderful late 19th and early 20th centuries, a period known for Jugenstil architecture and design, Richard Wagner and avant-garde rumblings in Schwabing. Munich became the 'city of art and beer', a title many are likely to agree it still holds today.

The fourth hall, Revue, becomes a little obscure but basically deals with the aftermath of WWI and the rise of the Nazis. The lead-up to war and the city's suffering during WWII occupy the Feuchtwangersaal, where a photo of a very determined Chamberlain stands next to the other signatories to the Munich Agreement. This is followed by a couple of fascinating rooms that paint a portrait of the modern city, including nostalgic TV footage from the last 40 years.

Though the Typical Munich exhibition touches on the period, the rise of the Nazis has been rightly left as a powerful separate exhibition called Nationalsozialismus in München. This occupies an eerily windowless annexe.

Jüdisches Museum
MUSEUM

(Jewish Museum; Map p188; www.juedisches-museum-muenchen.de; St-Jakobs-Platz 16; adult/child €6/3; ☺10am-6pm Tue-Sun; ⓢSendlinger Tor, ⓤSendlinger Tor) Coming to terms with its Nazi past has not historically been a priority in Munich, which is why the opening of the Jewish Museum in 2007 was hailed as a milestone. The permanent exhibition offers an insight into Jewish history, life and culture in the city. The Holocaust is dealt with, but the focus is clearly on contemporary Jewish culture.

The museum is part of the Jewish complex on St-Jakobs-Platz that also includes a community centre with a restaurant and a bunker-like synagogue that's rarely open to the public. Munich has the second-largest Jewish population in Germany after Berlin's: around 9300 people.

Michaelskirche
CHURCH

(Church of St Michael; Map p188; Kaufingerstrasse 52; crypt admission €2; ☺crypt 9.30am-4.30pm Mon-Fri, to 2.30pm Sat & Sun; ⓢKarlsplatz, ⓤKarlsplatz) It stands quiet and dignified amid the retail frenzy out on Kaufingerstrasse, but to fans of Ludwig II, the Michaelskirche is the ultimate place of pilgrimage. Its dank crypt is the final resting place of the Mad King, whose humble tomb is usually drowned in flowers.

Completed in 1597, St Michael's was the largest Renaissance church north of the Alps when it was built. It boasts an impressive unsupported barrel-vaulted ceiling, and the massive bronze statue between the two entrances shows the archangel finishing off a dragon-like creature, a classic Counter Reformation-era symbol of Catholicism triumphing over Protestantism. The building has been fully renovated in recent years and has never looked more impressive.

Altes Rathaus
HISTORIC BUILDING

(Old Town Hall; Map p188; Marienplatz; ⓤMarienplatz, ⓢMarienplatz) The eastern side of Marienplatz is dominated by the Altes Rathaus. Lightning got the better of the medieval original in 1460 and WWII bombs levelled its successor, so what you see is really the third incarnation of the building designed by Jörg von Halspach of Frauenkirche fame. On 9 November 1938 Joseph Goebbels gave a hate-filled speech here that launched the nationwide *Kristallnacht* pogroms.

Today the church houses the adorable Spielzeugmuseum (Toy Museum; Map p188; www.toymuseum.de; Marienplatz 15; adult/child €4/1; ☺10am-5.30pm; ⓢMarienplatz, ⓤMarienplatz), with its huge collection of rare and precious toys from Europe and the US.

Bier & Oktoberfestmuseum
MUSEUM

(Beer & Oktoberfest Museum; Map p188; www.bier-und-oktoberfestmuseum.de; Sterneckerstrasse 2; adult/concession €4/2.50; ☺1-6pm Tue-Sat; ⓢIsartor, ⓢIsartor) Head to this popular museum to learn all about Bavarian suds and the world's most famous booze-up. The four floors heave with old brewing

MUNICH SIGHTS

MUNICH'S BEST MUSEUMS

Munich has almost 50 museums, some so vast and containing so many exhibits you could spend a whole day shuffling through a single institution. Gallery fatigue strikes many a visitor and it's easy to get your *pinakotheks* in a twist. Here we list Munich's best museums – be selective and take your time.

Curious kids KinderReich at the Deutsches Museum (p200)

Petrol heads BMW Welt (p204)

Tech types Deutsches Museum (p200)

Design devotees Pinakothek der Moderne (p195)

Dino hunters Paläontologisches Museum (p205)

Sovereign stalkers Residenzmuseum (p192)

Art-ficionados Alte Pinakothek (p194)

History seekers Bayerisches Nationalmuseum (p200)

Central Munich

200 m
0.1 miles

Königinstr

Von-der-Tann-Str

Karl-Scharnagl-Ring

Galeriestr

Hofgarten

8

94

59

Marstallplatz

Maximilianstr

88

44

Hildegardstr

Neuturmstr

91

Am Platz

75

36

Ludwigstr

82

12

7

21

Residenzmuseum

92

90

19

Pfisterstr

2

Sparkassenstr

Münzstr

Ludwigstr

Ledererstr

Odeonsplatz

101

14

1

Max
Joseph-
Platz

Residenzstr

83

Castles &
Altenhofstr
46

Burgstr

Jägerstr

23

9

Theatinerstr

Salvatorstr

100

Museums Infopoint

20

95

i

15

MAXVORSTADT

Brienner Str

Oskar-von-Miller-Ring

17

43

57

Kardinal-Faulhaber-Str

Maffeistr

Schäfflerstr

99

Marienplatz

Tourist Office –
Marienplatz

10

Maximiliansplatz

27

Promenadeplatz

Löwengrube

Frauenplatz

Kaufingerstr

Brienner Str

Ottostr

Sonnenstr

Lenbachplatz

81

Maxburgstr

16

66

Neuhauser Str

Altheimer Eck

Karolinenplatz

Barer Str

Karlstr

37

Sonnenstr

Karlsplatz

74

Herzogspitalstr

Brienner Str

Karlstr

Arcisstr

4

Alter
Botanischer
Garten

Elisenstr

Palace
of Justice

35

Karlsplatz

103

K

26

Schützenstr

73

Zweigstr

34

39

Hauptbahnhof
(100m);

25

Adolf-Kolping-Str

86

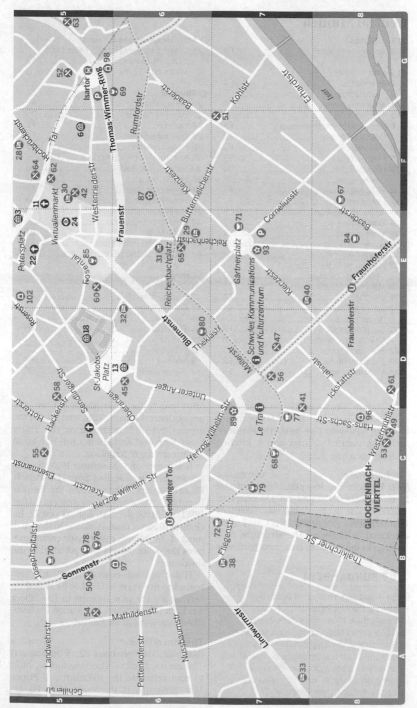

MUNICH

Central Munich

vats, historic photos and some of the earliest Oktoberfest regalia. The 14th-century building has some fine medieval features, including painted ceilings and a kitchen with an open fire.

Feldherrnhalle HISTORIC BUILDING
(Field Marshalls' Hall; Map p188; Residenzstrasse 1; Ⓤ Odeonsplatz) Corking up Odeonsplatz' southern side is Friedrich von Gärnter's Feldherrnhalle, modelled on the Loggia dei Lanzi in Florence. The structure pays homage to the Bavarian army and positively

---

ⓘ SUNDAY BEST

Save yourself a bailout of euros by visiting the Alte Pinakothek, Neue Pinakothek, Pinakothek der Moderne, Bayerisches Nationalmuseum, Museum Brandhorst, the Glyptothek, Archäologische Staatssammlung and several other less-visited museums and galleries on a Sunday, when admission to each is reduced to a symbolic €1.

---

drips with testosterone; check out the statues of General Johann Tilly, who kicked the Swedes out of Munich during the Thirty Years' War; and Karl Philipp von Wrede, an ally-turned-foe of Napoleon.

It was here on 9 November 1923 that police stopped the so-called Beer Hall Putsch, Hitler's attempt to bring down the Weimar Republic (Germany's government after WWI). A fierce skirmish left 20 people, including 16 Nazis, dead. A plaque in the pavement of the square's eastern side commemorates the police officers who perished in the incident.

Hitler was subsequently tried and sentenced to five years in jail, but he ended up serving a mere nine months in Landsberg am Lech prison, where he penned his hate-filled manifesto, *Mein Kampf*.

Theatinerkirche CHURCH
(Map p188; Theatinerstrasse 22; Ⓢ Odeonsplatz) The mustard-yellow Theatinerkirche, built to commemorate the 1662 birth of Prince Max Emanuel, is the work of Swiss ar-

chitect Enrico Zuccalli. Also known as St Kajetan's, it's a voluptuous design with two massive twin towers flanking a giant cupola. Inside, an ornate dome lords over the Fürstengruft (royal crypt), the final destination of several Wittelsbach rulers, including King Maximilian II (1811–64). The building was receiving much-needed renovation at the time of research but was still open to the public.

Alter Hof
PALACE

(Map p188; Burgstrasse 8; Ⓢ Marienplatz, Ⓤ Marienplatz) Alter Hof was the starter home of the Wittelsbach family and has its origins in the 12th century. The Bavarian rulers moved out of this central palace as long ago as the 15th century. Visitors can only see the central courtyard, where the bay window on the southern facade was nicknamed Monkey Tower in honour of a valiant ape that saved an infant Ludwig the Bavarian from the clutches of a ferocious market pig. Local lore at its most bizarre.

Münzhof
ARCHITECTURE

(Map p188; Hofgraben 4; Ⓤ Marienplatz, Ⓢ Marienplatz) The former Münzhof (mint) has a pretty courtyard, remarkable for its three-storey Renaissance arcades dating from 1567. An inscription on the western side of the building reads Moneta Regis (Money Rules), particularly apt words for this well-heeled part of Europe. The building now houses the agency charged with protecting Bavaria's many historical monuments.

◉ Residenz & Around

The Residenz is a suitably grand palace that reflects the splendour and power of the Wittelsbach clan, the Bavarian rulers who lived here from 1385 to 1918. The edifice dwarfs Max-Joseph-Platz along with the grandiose Nationaltheater (p220), home to the Bavarian State Opera. Its museums are among the jewels in Munich's cultural crown and are an unmissable part of the Bavarian experience.

Four giant bronze **lion statues** (Map p188; Residenzstrasse; Ⓤ Odeonsplatz) guard the

Schwabing & the Englischer Garten

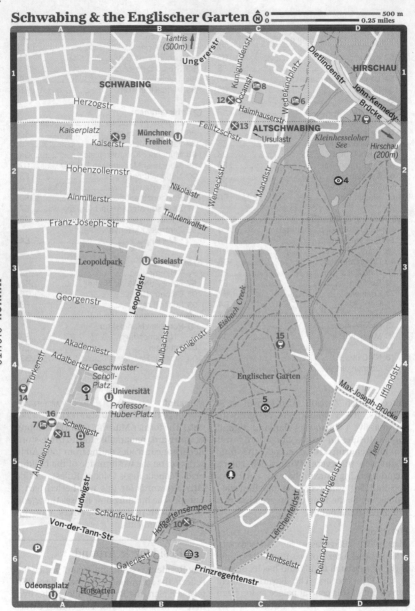

entrance to the palace, supported by pedestals festooned with a half-human, half-animal face. Note the creatures' remarkably shiny noses. If you wait a moment, you'll see the reason for the sheen: scores of people walk by and casually rub one or all four noses. It's supposed to bring wealth and good luck.

★ **Residenzmuseum** MUSEUM
(Map p188; ☑ 089-290 671; www.residenz-muenchen. de; Residenzstrasse 1; adult/concession/under 18yr

Schwabing & the Englischer Garten

€.7/6/free; ⊙ 9am-6pm Apr–mid-Oct, 10am-5pm mid-Oct–Mar, last entry 1hr before closing; Ⓤ Odeonsplatz) Home to Bavaria's Wittelsbach rulers from 1508 until WWI, the Residenz is Munich's number one attraction. The amazing treasures, as well as all the trappings of their lifestyles over the centuries, are on display at the Residenzmuseum, which takes up around half of the palace. Allow at least two hours to see everything at a gallop.

Tours are in the company of a rather long-winded audioguide (free), and gone are the days when the building was divided into morning and afternoon sections, all of which means a lot of ground to cover in one go. It's worth fast forwarding a bit to where the prescribed route splits into short and long tours, taking the long route for the most spectacular interiors. Approximately 90 rooms are open to the public at any one time, but as renovation work is ongoing, closures are inevitable and you may not see all the highlights.

When wandering the Residenz, don't forget that only 50 sq metres of the building's roof remained intact at the end of WWII. Most of what you see today is a painstaking postwar reconstruction.

The tours kick off at the Grottenhof (Grotto Court), home of the wonderful Perseusbrunnen (Perseus Fountain), with its namesake holding the dripping head of Medusa. Next door is the famous Antiquarium, a barrel-vaulted hall smothered in frescoes and built to house the Wittelsbachs' enormous antique collection. It's widely regarded as the finest Renaissance interior north of the Alps.

Further along the tour route, the neo-Byzantine Hofkirche was built for Ludwig I in 1826. After WWII only the red-brick walls were left; it reopened as an atmospheric concert venue in 2003.

Upstairs are the Kurfürstenzimmer (Electors Rooms), with some stunning Italian portraits and a passage lined with two dozen views of Italy, painted by local romantic artist Carl Rottmann. Also up here are François Cuvilliés' Reiche Zimmer (Rich Rooms), a six-room extravaganza of exuberant rococo carried out by the top stucco and fresco artists of the day; they're a definite highlight. More rococo magic awaits in the Ahnengallery (Ancestors Gallery), with 121 portraits of the rulers of Bavaria in chronological order.

The Hofkapelle, reserved for the ruler and his family, fades quickly in the memory when you see the exquisite Reichekapelle, with its blue and gilt ceiling, inlaid marble and 16th-century organ. Considered the finest rococo interiors in southern Germany, another spot to linger is the Steinzimmer (Stone Rooms), the emperor's quarters, awash in intricately patterned and coloured marble.

Schatzkammer der Residenz MUSEUM

(Residence Treasury; Map p188; Residenzstrasse 1; adult/concession/under 18yr €7/6/free; ⊙ 9am-6pm Apr–mid-Oct, 10am-5pm mid-Oct–Mar, last entry 1hr before closing; Ⓤ Odeonsplatz) The Residenzmuseum entrance also leads to the Schatzkammer der Residenz, a veritable banker's bonus worth of jewel-encrusted bling of yesteryear, from golden toothpicks to finely crafted swords, and miniatures in ivory to gold-entombed cosmetics trunks. The 1250 incredibly intricate and attractive items on display come in every precious material you could imagine, including lapis lazuli, crystal, coral and amber.

Definite highlights are the Bavarian crown insignia and the ruby-and-diamond-encrusted jewellery of Queen Therese (1792–1854).

MUNICH SIGHTS

MAXIMILIANSTRASSE

It's pricey and pretentious, but no trip to Munich would be complete without a wander along Maximilianstrasse, one of the city's swishest boulevards. Starting at Max-Joseph-Platz, it's a 1km-long ribbon of style where well-heeled shoppers browse for Breguet and Prada and bored bodyguards loiter by Bentleys and Rolls Royces. Recently it's also become a haunt for Munich's many beggars. Several of the city's finest theatrical venues, including the Nationaltheater, the Kammerspiele and the GOP Varieté Theater, are also here.

Built between 1852 and 1875, Maximilianstrasse was essentially an ego trip for King Max II. He harnessed the skills of architect Friedrich von Bürklein to create a unique stylistic hotchpotch ranging from Bavarian rustic to Italian Renaissance and English Gothic. It even became known as the Maximilianic Style. That's the king gazing down upon his boulevard – engulfed by roaring traffic – from his perch at the centre of the strip. Clinging to the base are four rather stern-looking children holding the coats of arms of Bavaria, Franconia, Swabia and the Palatinate.

Cuvilliés-Theater THEATRE
(Map p188; Residenzstrasse 1; adult/concession/under 18yr €3.50/2.50/free; ⊘2-6pm Mon-Sat, 9am-6pm Sun Apr-Jul & Sep–mid-Oct, 9am-6pm daily Aug, 2-5pm Mon-Sat, 10am-5pm Sun Nov-Mar; ⒽNationaltheater) Commissioned by Maximilian III in the mid-18th century, François Cuvilliés fashioned one of Europe's finest rococo theatres. Famous for hosting the premiere of Mozart's opera *Idomeneo,* the theatre was restored to its former glory by means of a restoration in the mid-noughties, and its stage once again hosts high-brow musical and operatic performances.

Access is limited to the auditorium, where you can take a seat and admire the four tiers of *loggia* (galleries), dripping with rococo embellishment, at your leisure.

Monument to the Victims of National Socialism MONUMENT
(Map p188; Brienner Strasse; ⓤOdeonsplatz) This striking monument is made up of four Ts holding up a block-like cage in which an eternal flame flutters in remembrance of those who died at the hands of the Nazis due to their political beliefs, race, religion, sexual orientation or disability. Moved to this spot in 2014, it's a sternly simple reminder of Munich's not-so-distant past.

Hofgarten GARDENS
(Map p188; ⓤOdeonsplatz) Office workers catching some rays during their lunch break, stylish mothers pushing prams, seniors on bikes, a gaggle of chatty nuns – everybody comes to the Hofgarten. The formal court gardens, with fountains, radiant flower beds, lime tree–lined gravel paths and benches galore, sit just north of the

Residenz. Paths converge at the **Dianatempel** (Map p188), a striking octagonal pavilion honouring the Roman goddess of the hunt. Enter the gardens from Odeonsplatz.

⊙ Maxvorstadt, Schwabing & the Englischer Garten

Visitors spending even just a few hours in the city are likely to find themselves in Maxvorstadt at some point, as the district is home to Munich's Kunstareal (art district), an entire neighbourhood of top-drawer museums.

Alte Pinakothek MUSEUM
(Map p198; ☑089-238 0526; www.pinakothek.de; Barer Strasse 27; adult/child €4/2, Sun €1, audioguide €4.50; ⊘10am-8pm Tue, to 6pm Wed-Sun; ⒼPinakotheken, ⒽPinakotheken) Munich's main repository of Old European Masters is crammed with all the major players that decorated canvases between the 14th and 18th centuries. This neoclassical temple was masterminded by Leo von Klenze and is a delicacy even if you can't tell your Rembrandt from your Rubens. The collection is world famous for its exceptional quality and depth, especially when it comes to German masters.

The oldest works are altar paintings, among which Michael Pacher's *Four Church Fathers* and Lucas Cranach the Elder's *Crucifixion* (1503), an emotional rendition of the suffering Jesus, stand out.

A key room is the Dürersaal upstairs. Here hangs Albrecht Dürer's famous Christ-like *Self-Portrait* (1500), showing the gaze of an artist brimming with self-confidence. His final major work, *The Four Apostles,* depicts

John, Peter, Paul and Mark as rather humble men, in keeping with post-Reformation ideas. Compare this to Matthias Grünewald's *Sts Erasmus and Maurice*, which shows the saints dressed in rich robes like kings.

For a secular theme, inspect Albrecht Altdorfer's *Battle of Alexander the Great* (1529), which captures in dizzying detail a 6th-century war pitting Greeks against Persians.

There's a choice bunch of works by Dutch masters, including an altarpiece by Rogier van der Weyden called *The Adoration of the Magi*, plus *The Seven Joys of Mary* by Hans Memling, *Danae* by Jan Gossaert and *The Land of Cockayne* by Pieter Bruegel the Elder. At 6m in height, Rubens' epic *Last Judgment* is so big that Klenze custom-designed the hall for it. A memorable portrait is *Hélène Fourment* (1631), a youthful beauty who was the ageing Rubens' second wife.

The Italians are represented by Botticelli, Rafael, Titian and many others, while the French collection includes paintings by Nicolas Poussin, Claude Lorrain and François Boucher. Among the Spaniards are such heavy hitters as El Greco, Murillo and Velázquez.

The Alte Pinakothek is under much-needed renovation until mid-2018, with parts of the building taking turns to close while work is carried out.

Pinakothek der Moderne
MUSEUM
(Map p198; ☑089-2380 5360; www.pinakothek.de; Barer Strasse 40; adult/child €10/7, Sun €1; ☉10am-6pm Tue, Wed & Fri-Sun, to 8pm Thu; ▣ Pinakotheken, ▣Pinakotheken) Germany's largest modern-art museum unites four significant collections under a single roof: 20th-century art, applied design from the 19th century to today, a graphics collection and an architecture museum. It's housed in a spectacular building by Stephan Braunfels, whose four-storey interior centres on a vast eye-like dome through which soft natural light filters throughout the blanched white galleries.

The State Gallery of Modern Art has some exemplary modern classics by Picasso, Klee, Dalí and Kandinsky and many lesser-known works that will be new to most visitors. More recent big shots include Georg Baselitz, Andy Warhol, Cy Twombly, Dan Flavin and the late enfant terrible Joseph Beuys.

In a world obsessed by retro style, the New Collection is the busiest section of the museum. Housed in the basement, it focuses on applied design from the industrial revolution via art nouveau and Bauhaus to today. VW Beetles, Eames chairs and early Apple Macs stand alongside more obscure interwar items that wouldn't be out of place in a Kraftwerk video. There's lots of 1960s furniture, the latest spool tape recorders and an exhibition of the weirdest jewellery you'll ever see.

The State Graphics Collection boasts 400,000 pieces of art on paper, including drawings, prints and engravings by such craftsmen as Leonardo da Vinci and Paul Cézanne. Because of the light-sensitive nature of these works, only a tiny fraction of the collection is shown at any given time.

Finally, there's the Architecture Museum, with entire studios of drawings, blueprints, photographs and models by such top practitioners as baroque architect Balthasar Neumann, Bauhaus maven Le Corbusier and 1920s expressionist Erich Mendelsohn.

Neue Pinakothek
MUSEUM
(Map p198; ☑089-2380 5195; www.pinakothek.de; Barer Strasse 29; adult/child €7/5, Sun €1; ☉10am-6pm Thu-Mon, to 8pm Wed; ▣ Pinakotheken, ▣Pinakotheken) The Neue Pinakothek harbours a well-respected collection of 19th- and early-20th-century paintings and sculpture, from rococo to *Jugendstil* (art nouveau). All the world-famous household names get wall space here, including crowd-pleasing French impressionists such as Monet, Cézanne and Degas as well as Van Gogh, whose boldly pigmented *Sunflowers* (1888) radiates cheer.

Perhaps the most memorable canvases, though, are by Romantic painter Caspar David Friedrich, who specialised in emotionally charged, brooding landscapes.

There are also several works by Gauguin, including *Breton Peasant Women* (1894), and Manet, including *Breakfast in the Studio* (1869). Turner gets a look-in with his dramatically sublime *Ostende* (1844).

Local painters represented in the exhibition include Carl Spitzweg and Wilhelm von Kobell of the Dachau School and Munich society painters such as Wilhelm von Kaulbach, Franz Lenbach and Karl von Piloty. Another focus is work by the Deutschrömer (German Romans), a group of neoclassicists centred on Johann Koch, who stuck mainly to Italian landscapes.

Museum Brandhorst
GALLERY
(Map p198; www.museum-brandhorst.de; Theresienstrasse 35a; adult/child €7/5, Sun €1; ☉10am-6pm Tue, Wed & Fri-Sun, to 8pm Thu; ▣ Maxvorstadt/Sammlung Brandhorst, ▣Pinakotheken) A

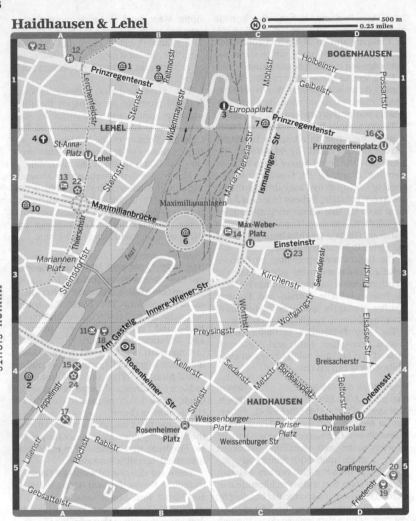

Haidhausen & Lehel

big, bold and aptly abstract building, clad entirely in vividly multihued ceramic tubes, the Brandhorst jostled its way into the Munich Kunstareal in a punk blaze of colour mid-2009. Its walls, its floor and occasionally its ceiling provide space for some of the most challenging art in the city, among it some instantly recognisable 20th-century images by Andy Warhol, whose work dominates the collection.

Pop art's 1960s poster boy pops up throughout the gallery and even has an entire room dedicated to pieces such as

his punkish *Self-Portrait* (1986), *Marilyn* (1962) and *Triple Elvis* (1963).

The other prevailing artist at the Brandhorst is the lesser-known Cy Twombly. His arrestingly spectacular splash-and-dribble canvases are a bit of an acquired taste, but this is the place to acquire it if ever there was one.

Elsewhere Dan Flavin floodlights various corners with his eye-watering light installations and other big names such as Mario Merz, Alex Katz and Sigmar Polke also make an appearance. Damien Hirst gets a look-in here and there.

Haidhausen & Lehel

Lenbachhaus MUSEUM
(Municipal Gallery; Map p198; ☑ 089-2333 2000; www.lenbachhaus.de; Luisenstrasse 33; adult/concession incl audioguide €10/5; ☺10am-9pm Tue, to 6pm Wed-Sun; ⬛Königsplatz, ⓤKönigsplatz) Reopened in 2013 to rave reviews after a four-year renovation that saw the addition of a new wing by noted architect Norman Foster, this glorious gallery is once again the go-to place to admire the vibrant canvases of Kandinsky, Franz Marc, Paul Klee and other members of ground-breaking modernist group Der Blaue Reiter (The Blue Rider), founded in Munich in 1911.

Contemporary art is another focal point. An eyecatcher is a glass-and-steel sculpture by Olafur Eliasson in the soaring new atrium. Many other big names are also represented, including Gerhard Richter, Sigmar Polke, Anselm Kiefer, Andy Warhol, Dan Flavin, Richard Serra and Jenny Holzer.

Tickets are also valid for special exhibits at the nearby Kunstbau, a 120m-long tunnel above the Königsplatz U-Bahn station.

Glyptothek MUSEUM
(Map p198; www.antike-am-koenigsplatz.mwn.de; Königsplatz 3; adult/concession €6/4, Sun €1; ☺10am-5pm Fri-Sun, Tue & Wed, to 8pm Thu; ⬛Königsplatz, ⓤKönigsplatz) If you're a fan of classical art or simply enjoy the sight of naked guys without noses (or other pertinent body parts), make a beeline for the Glyptothek. One of Munich's oldest museums, it's a feast of art and sculpture from ancient Greece and Rome amassed by Ludwig I between 1806 and 1830, and it opens a surprisingly naughty window onto the ancient world. Tickets for the museum are also valid for the Antikensammlungen.

Museum Reich der Kristalle MUSEUM
(Map p198; Theresienstrasse 41; adult/concession €4/2; ☺1-5pm Tue-Sun; ⬛Maxvorstadt/Sammlung Brandhorst, ⬛Pinakotheken) If diamonds are your best friends, head to the Museum Reich der Kristalle, with its Fort Knox-worthy collection of gemstones and crystals, including a giant Russian emerald and meteorite fragments from Kansas.

Antikensammlungen MUSEUM
(Map p188; www.antike-am-koenigsplatz.mwn.de; Königsplatz 1; adult/concession €6/4, Sun €1; ☺10am-5pm Fri-Sun, Tue & Wed, to 8pm Wed; ⬛Königsplatz, ⓤKönigsplatz) This old-school museum is an engaging showcase of exquisite Greek, Roman and Etruscan antiquities. The collection of Greek vases, each artistically decorated with gods and heroes, wars and weddings, is particularly outstanding. Other galleries present gold and silver jewellery and ornaments, figurines made from terracotta and more precious bronze, and super-fragile glass drinking vessels. Tickets for the museum are also valid for the Glyptothek.

Englischer Garten PARK
(Map p192; ⓤUniversität) The sprawling English Garden is among Europe's biggest city parks – it even rivals London's Hyde Park

Nymphenburg, Neuhausen & Olympiapark

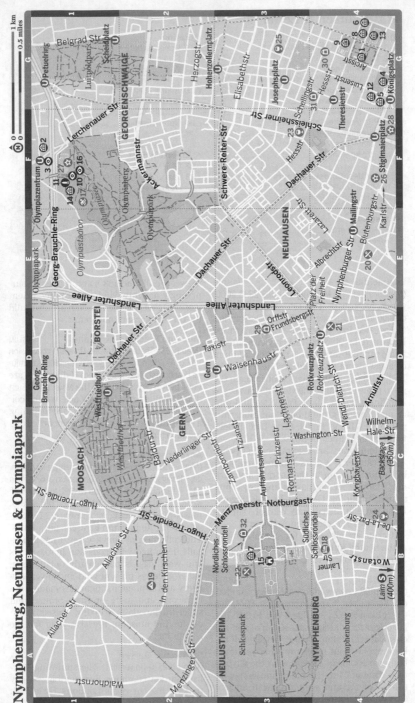

Nymphenburg, Neuhausen & Olympiapark

and New York's Central Park for size – and is a popular playground for locals and visitors alike. Stretching north from Prinzregentenstrasse for about 5km, it was commissioned by Elector Karl Theodor in 1789 and designed by Benjamin Thompson, an American-born scientist working as an adviser to the Bavarian government.

Paths wander through dark stands of mature oak and maple before emerging into sunlit meadows of lush grass. Locals are mindful of the park's popularity and tolerate the close quarters of cyclists, walkers and joggers. Street musicians dodge balls kicked by children and students sprawl on the grass to chat about missed lectures.

Sooner or later you'll find your way to the **Kleinhesseloher See** (Map p192), a lovely lake at the centre of the park. Work up a sweat while taking a spin around three little islands, then quaff a well-earned foamy one at the **Seehaus beer garden** (Map p192; Kleinhesselohe 3; 🚲; Ⓢ Münchner Freiheit).

Several historic follies lend the park a playful charm. The wholly unexpected **Chinesischer Turm** (Chinese Tower; Map p192; ☑089-383 8730; www.chinaturm.de; Englischer Garten 3; ⊙10am-11pm; ⊜ Chinesischer Turm, ⊜ Tivolistrasse), now at the heart of Munich's oldest beer garden, was built in the 18th century during a pan-European craze for all things oriental. Further south, at the top of a gentle hill, stands the heavily photographed **Monopteros** (Map p192) (1838), a small Greek temple whose ledges are often knee-to-knee with dangling legs belonging to people admiring the view of the Munich skyline.

Another hint of Asia awaits further south at the **Japanisches Teehaus** (Japanese Teahouse; Map p192; Englischer Garten), built for the 1972 Olympics by an idyllic duck pond. The best time to come is for

---

NO WAVE GOODBYE

At the southern tip of the Englischer Garten you'll see scores of people leaning over a bridge to cheer on wetsuit-clad daredevils as they 'hang 10' on an artificially created wave at **Surfing in the Eisbach** (Map p196; Prinzregentenstrasse; ⊜ Nationalmuseum/ Haus der Kunst) . It's only a single wave, but it's a damn fine one. The surfers are such an attraction that the tourist office includes them in its brochures.

A few years ago park authorities attempted to ban this watery entertainment, but a successful campaign by surfers saw plans to turn the wave off shelved.

To find out more about Munich's urban surfers, see www.eisbachwelle.de.

an authentic tea ceremony celebrated by a Japanese tea master.

Bayerisches Nationalmuseum MUSEUM
(Map p196; www.bayerisches-nationalmuseum.de; Prinzregentenstrasse 3; adult/concession €7/6, Sun €1; ⊙ 10am-5pm Tue, Wed & Fri-Sun, to 8pm Thu; 🚋 Nationalmuseum/Haus Der Kunst, 🚋 Nationalmuseum/Haus Der Kunst) Picture the classic 19th-century museum, a palatial neoclassical edifice overflowing with exotic treasure and thought-provoking works of art, a repository for a nation's history, a grand purpose-built display case for royal trinkets, church baubles and state-owned rarities – this is the Bavarian National Museum, a good old-fashioned institution for no-nonsense museum lovers. As the collection fills 40 rooms over three floors, there's a lot to get through here, so be prepared for at least two hours' legwork.

Most visitors start on the 1st floor, where hall after hall is packed with baroque, mannerist and Renaissance sculpture, ecclesiastical treasures (check out all those wobbly Gothic 'S' figures), Renaissance clothing and one-off pieces such as the 1000-year-old St Kunigunde's chest fashioned in mammoth ivory and gold. Climb to the 2nd floor to move up in history to the rococo, *Jugendstil* and modern periods, represented by priceless collections of Nymphenburg and Meissen porcelain, Tiffany glass, Augsburg silver and precious items used by the Bavarian royal family. Also up here is a huge circular model of Munich in the first half of the 19th century, shortly after it was transformed into a capital fit for a kingdom.

It's easy to miss, but the building's basement also holds an evocatively displayed collection of Krippen (nativity scenes), some with a Cecil B DeMille–style cast of thousands. Retold in paper, wood and resin, there are Christmas-story scenes here from Bohemia, Moravia and Tyrol, but the biggest contingent hails from Naples. Also here is the excellent museum shop.

◉ Haidhausen & Lehel

Deutsches Museum MUSEUM
(Map p196; 🕿 089-217 9333; www.deutsches-museum.de; Museumsinsel 1; adult/child €11/4; ⊙ 9am-5pm; 🚋 Deutsches Museum) If you're one of those people for whom science is an unfathomable turn-off, a visit to the Deutsches Museum might just show you that physics and engineering are more fun than you thought. Spending a few hours in this temple to technology is an eye-opening journey of discovery and the exhibitions and demonstrations will certainly be a hit with young, sponge-like minds.

There are tons of interactive displays (including glass blowing and paper making), live demonstrations and experiments, model coal and salt mines, and engaging sections on cave paintings, geodesy, microelectronics and astronomy. In fact, it can be pretty overwhelming after a while, so it's best to prioritise what you want to see.

The place to entertain children aged three to eight is the fabulous KinderReich, where 1000 activities, from a kid-size mouse wheel to interactive water fun, await. Get the littlies to climb all over a fire engine, build things with giant Lego, construct a waterway with canals and locks, or bang on a drum all day in a – thankfully – soundproof instrument room. Note that KinderReich closes at 4.30pm.

Sammlung Schack MUSEUM
(Map p196; www.sammlung-schack.de; Prinzregentenstrasse 9; adult/concession €4/3; ⊙ 10am-6pm Wed-Sun; 🚋 Reitmorstrasse/Sammlung Schack) Count Adolf Friedrich von Schack (1815–94) was a great fan of 19th-century Romantic painters such as Böcklin, Feuerbach and von Schwind. His collection is housed in the former Prussian embassy, now the Schack-Galerie. A tour of the intimate space is like an escape into the idealised fantasy worlds created by these artists.

Haus der Kunst MUSEUM
(House of Art; Map p192; www.hausderkunst.de; Prinzregentenstrasse 1; adult/concession €12/10; ⊙ 10am-8pm Fri-Wed, to 10pm Thu; 🚋 Nationalmuseum/Haus Der Kunst, 🚋 Nationalmuseum/Haus Der Kunst) This stern art deco edifice was built in 1937 to showcase Nazi art, but now the Haus der Kunst presents works by exactly the artists whom the Nazis rejected and deemed degenerate. Temporary shows focus on contemporary art and design.

Staatliches Museum für Völkerkunde MUSEUM
(State Museum of Ethnology; Map p196; www.voelkerkundemuseum-muenchen.de; Maximilianstrasse 42, adult/concession €5/4, Sun €1; ⊙ 9.30am-5.30pm Tue-Sun; 🚋 Maxmonument) With a bonanza of art and objects from Africa, India, the Americas, the Middle East and Polynesia, the State Museum of Ethnology has one of the most prestigious and

THE WHITE ROSE

Open resistance to the Nazis was rare during the Third Reich; after 1933, intimidation and the instant 'justice' of the Gestapo and SS served as powerful disincentives. One of the few groups to rebel was the ill-fated Weisse Rose (White Rose), led by Munich University students Hans and Sophie Scholl.

The nonviolent White Rose began operating in 1942, its members stealing out at night to smear 'Freedom!' and 'Down with Hitler!' on the city's walls. Soon they were printing anti-Nazi leaflets on the mass extermination of the Jews and other Nazi atrocities. One read: 'We shall not be silent – we are your guilty conscience. The White Rose will not leave you in peace'.

In February 1943, Hans and Sophie were caught distributing leaflets at the university. Together with their best friend, Christoph Probst, the Scholls were arrested and charged with treason. After a summary trial, all three were found guilty and beheaded the same afternoon. Their extraordinary courage inspired the award-winning film *Sophie Scholl – Die Letzten Tage* (Sophie Scholl – The Final Days; 2005).

A memorial exhibit to the White Rose, **DenkStätte** (Map p192; Geschwister-Scholl-Platz 1; ⊙10am-4pm Mon-Fri, noon-3pm Sat ; U Universität) FREE is within the Ludwig-Maximilian-Universität.

complete ethnological collections anywhere. Sculpture from West and Central Africa is particularly impressive, as are Peruvian ceramics, Indian jewellery, mummy parts, and artefacts from the days of Captain Cook.

Klosterkirche St Anna im Lehel CHURCH
(Map p196; St-Anna-Platz 21; ⊙6am-7pm; 🚊Lehel, U Lehel) The Asamkirche may be more sumptuous, but the Klosterkirche St Anna im Lehel is actually a collaboration of the top dogs of the rococo. Johann Michael Fischer designed the building, and Cosmas Damian Asam painted the stunning ceiling fresco and altar.

Maximilianeum HISTORIC BUILDING
(Map p196; Max-Planck-Strasse 1; 🚊Maximilianeum) Maximilianstrasse culminates in the glorious Maximilianeum, completed in 1874, a decade after Max II's sudden death. It's an imposing structure, drawn like a theatre curtain across a hilltop, and bedecked with mosaics, paintings and other artistic objects. It's framed by an undulating park called the Maximiliananlagen, which is a haven for cyclists in summer and tobogganists in winter.

Kulturzentrum Gasteig CULTURAL CENTRE
(Gasteig Culture Centre; Map p196; ☑089-480 980; www.gasteig.de; Rosenheimer Strasse 5; ⊙8am-11pm; 🚊Am Gasteig) One of Munich's top cultural venues, the Kulturzentrum Gasteig caused quite a controversy a generation ago due to its postmodern, boxy, glass-and-brick design. The complex harbours four concert halls, including the 2400-seat Philharmonie, the permanent home of the Münchner Philharmoniker.

◉ Bogenhausen

Museum Villa Stuck MUSEUM
(Map p196; www.villastuck.de; Prinzregentenstrasse 60; adult/concession €9/4.50; ⊙11am-6pm Tue-Sun; 🚊Friedensengel/Villa Stuck) Franz von Stuck was a leading light in Munich's art scene around the turn of the 20th century and his residence is one of the finest *Jugendstil* homes you'll ever see. Stuck came up with the intricate design, which forges tapestries, patterned floors, coffered ceilings and other elements into a harmonious work of art. Today his pad is open as a museum with changing exhibitions.

Friedensengel STATUE
(Map p196; 🚊Friedensengel/Villa Stuck) Just east of the Isar River, the *Friedensengel* (Angel of Peace) statue stands guard from its perch atop a 23m-high column. It commemorates the 1871 Treaty of Versailles, which ended the Franco-Prussian War, and the base contains some shimmering golden Roman-style mosaics.

Prinzregententheater THEATRE
(Map p196; ☑089-218 502; www.prinzregenten theater.de; Prinzregentenplatz 12; S Prinzregentenplatz) One of Bogenhausen's main landmarks is the Prinzregententheater. Its dramatic mix of art nouveau and neoclassical styles was conceived under Prince Regent Luitpold as a festival house for Richard Wagner operas.

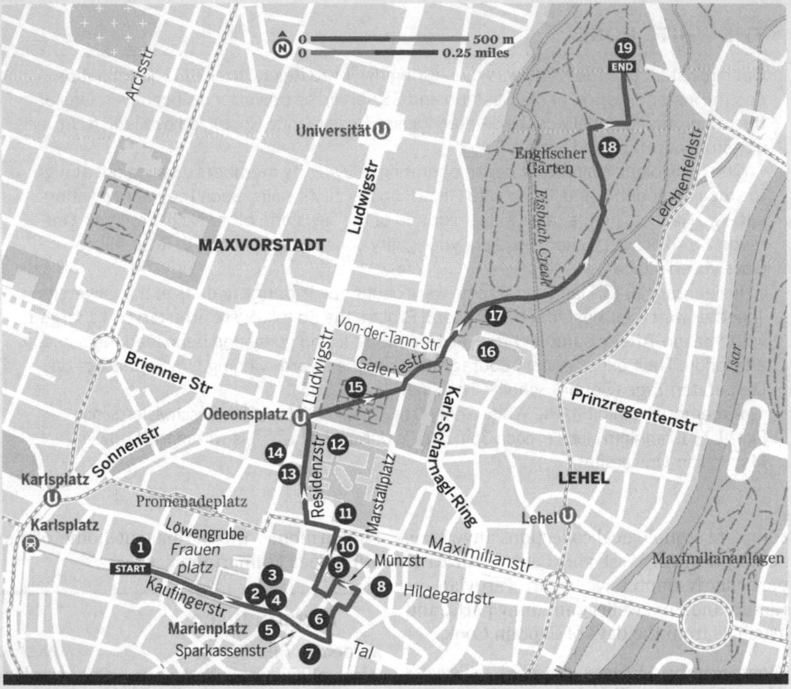

City Walk
Munich's Altstadt

START MICHAELSKIRCHE
END CHINESISCHER TURM
LENGTH 5KM, 2½ HOURS

This circuit takes in the key sights in Munich's historic centre. Commence at [1] **Michaelskirche** (p187), final resting place of King Ludwig II. Proceed east along the main shopping drag, passing by Munich's landmark Frauenkirche. The way opens into Marienplatz, punctuated by the [2] **Mariensäule** (p183) in front of the neo-Gothic [3] **Neues Rathaus** (p183). The [4] **Fischbrunnen** gushes peacefully near the entrance. The steeple of [5] **St Peterskirche** (p186) affords a great vista of the old town, including the [6] **Altes Rathaus** (p187). To see Asam frescoes, peek inside the [7] **Heiliggeistkirche** (p186).

Head east on Im Tal, taking a left into Maderbräustrasse to Orlandostrasse, site of the [8] **Hofbräuhaus** (p216), Munich's most (in)famous beer hall. Then go west on Münzstrasse, left into Sparkassenstrasse and then into the alley Ledererstrasse. At Burgstrasse, turn right into the courtyard of the [9] **Alter Hof** (p191), the Wittelsbachs' early residence in Munich. Exit north and proceed along Hofgraben, past the former [10] **Münzhof** (p191). The street opens into Maximilianstrasse and Max-Joseph-Platz, address of the grand [11] **Nationaltheater** (p220) and fine opera. The [12] **Residenz** (p192) was the seat of the Wittelsbach rulers for over four centuries.

Stroll north on Residenzstrasse to reach Odeonsplatz, site of the Nazis' first lunge at power. Here looms the [13] **Feldherrnhalle** (p190), a hulking shrine to war heroes. The mustard-yellow [14] **Theatinerkirche** (p190) contains the Wittelsbachs' family crypt. Head into green territory from here, starting with the neoclassical [15] **Hofgarten** (p194). Cross it diagonally and go through the underpass to enter the Englischer Garten. Proceed past the [16] **Haus der Kunst** (p200). The route winds past the ceremonial [17] **Japanisches Teehaus** (p199). A little hill with a classical folly, the [18] **Monopteros** (p199), completes the leisurely scene. At the end, take a seat in the beer garden alongside the multitiered [19] **Chinesischer Turm** (p199).

☉ Westend & Theresienwiese

Theresienwiese   PARK
(Map p208; U Theresienwiese) The huge There-sienwiese (Theresa Meadow), better known as Wies'n, southwest of the Altstadt, is the site of the Oktoberfest. At the western end of the 'meadow' is the **Ruhmeshalle** (Hall of Fame; Map p208; Theresienhöhe 16; U Theresien-wiese) FREE guarding solemn statues of Ba-varian leaders, as well as the **Bavariastatue** (Statue of Bavaria; Map p208; Theresienhöhe 16; adult/concession €3.50/2.50; ☉9am-6pm Apr–mid-Oct, to 8pm during Oktoberfest; U Theresien wiese), an 18m-high Amazon in the Statue of Liberty tradition, oak wreath in her hand and lion at her feet.

This iron lady has a cunning design that makes her seem solid, but actually you can climb her via the knee joint up to the head for a great view of the Oktoberfest. At other times, views are not particularly inspiring.

Verkehrszentrum   MUSEUM
(Map p208; www.deutsches-museum.de/verkehrszentrum; Theresienhöhe 14a; adult/con-cession €6/3; ☉9am-5pm; S Theresienwiese) Sheltered in a historic trade-fair complex, the Verkehrszentrum features some fas-cinating exhibits, with hands-on displays about pioneering research and famous in-ventions, plus cars, boats and trains, and the history of car racing. Another section shows off the Deutsches Museum's entire vehicle collection, from the first motorcars to high-speed ICE (inter-city express) trains.

☉ Olympiapark & Around

Olympiapark   STADIUM
(Olympic Park; Map p198; www.olympiapark.de; stadium adult/child €3/2, stadium tour adult/con-cession €7.50/5; ☉stadium tours 11am, 1pm & 4pm Apr-Oct; U Olympiazentrum) The area to the north of the city where soldiers once parad-ed and the world's first Zeppelin landed in 1909 found a new role in the 1960s as the Olympiapark. Built for the 1972 Olympic Summer Games, it has quite a small-scale feel and some may be amazed that the games could once have been held at such a petite venue.

The complex draws people year-round with concerts, festivals and sporting events, and its swimming hall and ice-skating rink are open to the public.

A good first stop is the Info-Pavilion, which has information, maps, tour tickets

---

OKTOBERFEST

It all started as an elaborate wedding toast – and turned into the world's biggest collec-tive booze-up. In October 1810 the future king, Bavarian Crown Prince Ludwig I, married Princess Therese and the newlyweds threw an enormous party at the city gates, com-plete with a horse race. The next year Ludwig's fun-loving subjects came back for more. The festival was extended and, to fend off autumn, was moved forward to September. As the years rolled on, the racehorses were dropped and sometimes the party had to be cancelled, but the institution called Oktoberfest was here to stay.

Nearly two centuries later, this 16-day extravaganza draws more than six million vis-itors a year to celebrate a marriage of good cheer and outright debauchery. A special dark, strong beer (Wies'nbier) is brewed for the occasion, and Müncheners spend the day at the office in Lederhosen and Dirndl in order to hit the festival right after work. No admission fee is charged, but most of the fun costs something.

On the meadow called Theresienwiese (Wies'n for short), a temporary city is erected, consisting of beer tents, amusements and rides – just what drinkers need after several frothy ones! The action kicks off with the Brewer's Parade at 11am on the first day of the festival. The parade begins at Sonnenstrasse and winds its way to the fairgrounds via Schwanthalerstrasse. At noon, the lord mayor stands before the thirsty crowds at Theresienwiese and, with due pomp, slams a wooden tap into a cask of beer. As the beer gushes out, the mayor exclaims, O'zapft ist's! (It's tapped!). The next day resembles the opening of the Olympics, as a young woman on horseback leads a parade of costumed participants from all over the world.

Hotels book out very quickly and prices skyrocket, so reserve accommodation as early as you can (a year in advance). The festival is a 15-minute walk southwest of the Hauptbahnhof, and is served by its own U-Bahn station, Theresienwiese. Trams and bus-es have signs reading Zur Festwiese (literally 'to the Festival Meadow').

DON'T MISS

BMW PLANT TOURS

If you like cars, be sure not to miss a tour of BMW's state-of-the-art plant. **BMW Plant Tours** (📞089-125 016 001; www.bmw-welt.com; adult/concession €8/5; ☻9am-6.15pm Mon-Fri; Ⓤ Petuelring) in English and German last 2½ hours and take in the entire production process. Booking well ahead is essential, especially in summer.

and a model of the complex. Staff also rent out MP3 players for a self-guided audio tour.

Olympiapark has two famous eye-catchers: the 290m **Olympiaturm** (Olympic Tower; Map p198; adult/child €5.50/3.50; ☻9am-midnight; Ⓤ Olympiazentrum) and the warped Olympiastadion. Germans have a soft spot for the latter because it was on this hallowed turf in 1974 that the national soccer team – led by 'the Kaiser' Franz Beckenbauer – won the FIFA World Cup.

When the sky is clear, you'll quite literally have Munich at your feet against the breathtaking backdrop of the Alps from the top of the Olympiaturm.

BMW Welt   NOTABLE BUILDING

(BMW World; Map p198; 📞089-125 016 001; www.bmw-welt.de; Am Olympiapark 1; tours adult/child €7/5; ☻7.30am-midnight; Ⓤ Olympiazentrum) **FREE** Next to the Olympiapark, the glass-and-steel, double-cone tornado spiraling down from a dark cloud the size of an aircraft carrier holds BMW Welt, truly a petrol head's dream. Apart from its role as a prestigious car pick-up centre, this king of showrooms acts as a shop window for BMW's latest models and a show space for the company as a whole.

Straddle a powerful motorbike, marvel at technology-packed saloons and estates (no tyre kicking, please), browse the 'lifestyle' shop or take the 80-minute guided tour. On the Junior Campus, kids learn about mobility, fancy themselves car engineers and even get to design their own vehicle in workshops. Hang around long enough and you're sure to see motorbike stunts on the staircases and other petrol-fuelled antics.

BMW Museum   MUSEUM

(Map p198; www.bmw-welt.de; Am Olympiapark 2; adult/concession €10/7; ☻10am-6pm Tue-Sun; Ⓤ Olympiazentrum) This silver bowl-shaped museum comprises seven themed 'houses'

that examine the development of BMW's product line and include sections on motorcycles and motor racing. Even if you can't tell a head gasket from a crankshaft, the interior design – with its curvy retro feel, futuristic bridges, squares and huge backlit wall screens – is reason enough to visit.

The museum is linked to two more architecturally stunning buildings: the BMW headquarters (closed to the public) and the BMW Welt showroom.

Rock Museum   MUSEUM

(Map p198; www.rockmuseum.de; Besucherplattform des Münchner Olympiaturms; adult/child €4.50/3.50; ☻9am-midnight; Ⓤ Olympiazentrum) Your lift ticket to the Olympiaturm also buys access to the small if quirky Rock Museum. Ozzie Osbourne's signed guitar, a poem penned by Jim Morrison and Britney Spears' glitter jeans jostle for space with letters, photos and concert tickets, all the result of three decades of collecting by a pair of rock fans.

👁 Outer Districts

Schloss Nymphenburg   PALACE

(Map p198; www.schloss-nymphenburg.de; adult/concession €6/5; ☻9am-6pm Apr–mid-Oct, 10am-4pm mid-Oct–Mar; 🚊Schloss Nymphenburg) This commanding palace and its lavish gardens sprawl around 5km northwest of the Altstadt. Begun in 1664 as a villa for Electress Adelaide of Savoy, the stately pile was extended over the next century to create the royal family's summer residence. Franz Duke of Bavaria, head of the once royal Wittelsbach family, still occupies an apartment here.

The main palace building consists of a large villa and two wings of creaking parquet floors and sumptuous period rooms. Right at the beginning of the self-guided tour comes the high point of the entire *Schloss*, the **Schönheitengalerie**, housed in the former apartments of Queen Caroline. Some 38 portraits of attractive females chosen by an admiring King Ludwig I peer prettily from the walls. The most famous image is of Helene Sedlmayr, the daughter of a shoemaker, wearing a lavish frock the king gave her for the sitting. You'll also find Ludwig's beautiful, but notorious, lover Lola Montez, as well as 19th-century gossip-column celebrity Lady Jane Ellenborough and English beauty Lady Jane Erskin.

Further along the tour route comes the Queen's Bedroom, which still contains the sleigh bed on which Ludwig II was born, and the King's Chamber, resplendent with three-dimensional ceiling frescoes.

Also in the main building is the **Marstall-museum**, displaying royal coaches and riding gear. This includes Ludwig II's fairy tale–like rococo sleigh, ingeniously fitted with oil lamps for his crazed nocturnal outings. Upstairs is the world's largest collection of porcelain made by the famous Nymphenburger Manufaktur. Also known as the Sammlung Bäuml, it presents the entire product palette from the company's founding in 1747 until 1930.

The sprawling park behind Schloss Nymphenburg is a favourite spot with Münchners and visitors for strolling, jogging or whiling away a lazy afternoon. It's laid out in grand English style and accented with water features, including a large lake, a cascade and a canal, popular for feeding swans and for ice skating and ice curling when it freezes over in winter.

The park's chief folly, the **Amalienburg**, is a small hunting lodge dripping with crystal and gilt decoration; don't miss the amazing **Spiegelsaal** (hall of mirrors). The two-storey Pagodenburg was built in the early 18th century as a Chinese teahouse and is swathed in ceramic tiles depicting landscapes, figures and floral ornamentation. The Badenburg is a sauna and bathing house that still has its original heating system. Finally, the **Magdalenenklause** was built as a mock hermitage in faux-ruined style.

Allianz Arena STADIUM
(☎tours 089-6993 1222; www.allianz-arena.de; Werner-Heisenberg-Allee 25, Fröttmaning; tour

MUNICH FOR CHILDREN

(Tiny) hands down, Munich is a great city for children, with plenty of activities to please even the most attention span–challenged tots. There are plenty of parks for romping around, swimming pools and lakes for cooling off, and family-friendly beer gardens with children's playgrounds for making new friends.

Deutsches Museum (p200) Many of the city's museums have special kid-oriented programs, but the highly interactive KinderReich at the Deutches Museum specifically lures the single-digit set.

Tierpark Hellabrunn (p206) Petting baby goats, feeding pelicans, watching falcons and hawks perform or even riding a camel should make for some unforgettable memories at the city zoo.

SeaLife München (Map p198; www.visitsealife.com; Willi-Daume-Platz 1; adult/child gate prices €16.95/13.50; ⏲10am-7pm; [S]Olympiazentrum) For a fishy immersion, head to this new attraction in the Olympiapark.

Paläontologisches Museum (Palaeontological Museum; Map p198; www.palmuc.de; Richard-Wagner-Strasse 10; admission free; ⏲8am-4pm Mon-Thu, to 2pm Fri; 🚋Königsplatz, [U]Königsplatz) [FREE] Dino fans will gravitate here.

Museum Mensch und Natur (Museum of Humankind & Nature; Map p198; www.mmn-muenchen.de; Schloss Nymphenburg; adult/child €3/2; ⏲9am-5pm Tue, Wed & Fri, to 8pm Thu, 10am-6pm Sat & Sun; 🚋Schloss Nymphenburg) Budding scientists will find plenty to marvel at in this museum within the Schloss Nymphenburg.

Spielzeugmuseum (p187) The Spielzeugmuseum is of the look-but-don't-touch variety, but kids might still get a kick out of seeing what toys grandma used to pester for.

Münchner Marionettentheater (Map p188; ☎089-265 712; www.muema-theater.de; Blumenstrasse 32; ⏲3pm Wed-Sun, 8pm Sat) The adorable singing and dancing marionettes performing here have enthralled generations of wee ones.

Münchner Theater für Kinder (Map p198; ☎089-594 545; www.mtfk.de; Dachauer Strasse 46) This theatre offers budding thespians a chance to enjoy fairy tales and children's classics in the style of *Pinocchio* and German children's classic *Max & Moritz*.

Brauseschwein (Map p198; Frundsbergstrasse 52; ⏲10am-1pm & 3pm-6.30pm Mon-Fri, 11am-2pm Sat) This wacky toy shop near Schloss Nymphenburg sells everything from penny candy to joke articles and wooden trains.

adult/child €10/6.50; ⏲ tours in English 1pm; [U] Fröttmaning) Sporting and architecture fans alike should take a side trip to the northern suburb of Fröttmaning to see the ultraslick €340-million Allianz Arena, Munich's dramatic football stadium. The 75-minute stadium tours are hugely popular (no tours on match days). Tickets can be booked online.

Nicknamed the life belt and the rubber boat, the stadium has walls made of inflatable cushions that can be individually lit to match the colours of the host team (red for 1 FC Bayern, blue for TSV 1860, and white for the national side).

Tierpark Hellabrunn ZOO
(Hellabrunn Zoo; ☎ 089-625 080; www.tierpark-hellabrunn.de; Tierparkstrasse 30; adult/child €14/5; ⏲ 9am-6pm Apr-Sep, to 5pm Oct-Mar; 🚌 52 from Marienplatz, 🚋 Tiroler Platz, [U] Thalkirchen) Some 6km south of the city centre, Tierpark Hellabrunn has 5000 furry, feathered and finned friends that rarely fail to enthral the little ones. The zoo was one of the first to organise animals by continent, with enclosures aiming to mimic natural habitats as closely as possible.

Activities

Boating

A lovely spot to take your sweetheart for a spin is on the Kleinhesseloher See (p199) in the Englischer Garten. Rowing or pedal boats cost around €8 per half-hour for up to four people. Boats may also be hired at the Olympiapark (p203).

Cycling

Munich is an excellent place for cycling, particularly along the Isar River. Some 1200km of cycle paths within the city limits make it one of Europe's friendliest places for two-wheelers.

Swimming

Bathing in the Isar River isn't advisable, due to strong and unpredictable currents (especially in the Englischer Garten), though many locals do. Better to head out of town to one of the many nearby swimming lakes, including the popular **Feringasee** (by car, take the S8 to Unterföhring, then follow signs), where the party never stops on hot summer days; the pretty **Feldmochinger See**, which is framed by gentle mounds and has a special area for wheelchair-bound bathers (by car, take the S1 to Feldmoching); and the **Unterföhringer See** (🚗 S8, bicyclevia the Isarradweg), which has warm water and is easily reached by bicycle via the Isarradweg or via the S8 to Unterföhring.

The best public swimming-pool options, both indoors, are the **Olympia Schwimmhalle** (Map p198; www.swm.de; Coubertinplatz 1; 3hr pass adult/concession €4.60/3.40; ⏲ 7am-11pm; [S] Olympiazentrum), where Mark Spitz famously won seven gold medals in 1972, and the spectacular **Müller'sches Volksbad** (Map p196; www.swm.de; Rosenheimer Strasse 1; adult/child €4.30/3.30; ⏲ 7.30am-11pm; 🚋 Am Gasteig), where you can swim in art-nouveau splendour.

Tours

For a budget tour of Munich's high-brow collections, try **bus 100 Museenlinie**, which runs from the Hauptbahnhof to the Ostbahnhof (east station) via 21 of the city's museums and galleries, including all the big hitters. As this is an ordinary bus route, the tour costs no more than a public-transport ticket.

★ **Radius Tours & Bike Rental** TOUR
(Map p208; ☎ 089-543 487 7720; www.radiustours.com; Arnulfstrasse 3; [S] Hauptbahnhof, 🚋 Hauptbahnhof, [U] Hauptbahnhof) Entertaining and informative English-language tours include the two-hour Discover Munich walk (€13), the fascinating 2½-hour Hitler and the Third Reich tour (€15), and the three-hour Bavarian Beer tour (€29.50). The company also runs popular excursions to Neuschwanstein, Salzburg and Dachau and has hundreds of bikes for hire (€14.50 per day).

Mike's Bike Tours BICYCLE TOUR
(Map p188; ☎ 089-2554 3987; www.mikesbiketours.com; Bräuhaus Strasse 10; tours from €30; [S] Marienplatz, [U] Marienplatz) This outfit runs various guided bike tours of the city as well as a couple of other themed excursions. The standard tour is around four hours long (with a one-hour beer-garden break; lunch is not included); the deluxe tour goes for seven hours and covers 16km.

New Europe Munich WALKING TOUR
(www.newmunichtours.com; ⏲ tours 10am, 10.45am & 2pm; [S] Marienplatz, [U] Marienplatz) Departing from Marienplatz, these English-language walking tours tick off all Munich's central landmarks in three hours. Guides are well informed and fun, though they are under pressure at the end of the tour to get as much as they can in tips. The

company also runs (paid) tours to Dachau (€22) and Neuschwanstein (€37).

Grayline Hop-On-Hop-Off Tours　BUS TOUR
(www.grayline.com/Munich; adult/child €15/10; ⊙ hourly) This tour-bus company offers a choice of three tours, from one-hour high-lights to the 2½-hour grand tour, as well as excursions to Ludwig II's castles, the Romantic Road, Dachau, Berchtesgaden, Zugspitze and Salzburg. All tours can be booked online and the buses are new. The **main departure point** (Map p188; Ⓢ Hauptbahnhof, Ⓤ Hauptbahnhof) is outside the Karstadt department store opposite the Hauptbahnhof.

✦ Festivals & Events

Munich always has something to celebrate. For details, check www.muenchen-tourist.de.

Fasching　CARNIVAL
Beginning on 7 January and ending on Ash Wednesday, this carnival involves all kinds of merriment, such as costume parades and fancy-dress balls.

Starkbierzeit　BEER
Salvator, Optimator, Unimator, Maximator and Triumphator are not the names of gladiators but potent *doppelbock* brews de-kegged only between Shrovetide and Easter. Many of Bavaria's breweries take part.

Frühlingsfest　BEER
(www.fruehlingsfest-muenchen.de) This mini-Oktoberfest kicks off the outdoor-festival season with two weeks of beer tents and attractions starting in mid-April.

Maidult　CULTURAL
The first of three dult fairs (traditional fairs with rides and food) held on the Mariahilf-platz. Starts on the Saturday preceding 1 May.

Filmfest München　FILM
(www.filmfest-muenchen.de) This festival presents intriguing and often high-calibre fare by newbies and masters from around the world.

Tollwood Festival　CULTURAL
(www.tollwood.de) Major world-culture festival with concerts, theatre, circus, readings and other fun events held from late June to late July. Also throughout December on the Theresienwiese.

Christopher Street Day　GAY & LESBIAN
(www.csd-munich.de) Gay festival and parade culminating in a big street party on Marien-platz. Usually held on the second weekend in July.

Jakobidult　CULTURAL
The second dult festival (traditional fair with rides and food) of the year starts on the Saturday following 25 July and continues for one week.

Opernfestspiele　MUSIC
(Opera Festival; www.muenchner-opern-festspiele.de) The Bavarian State Opera brings in top-notch talent from around the world for this month-long festival, which takes place at numerous venues around the city throughout July.

Oktoberfest　BEER
(www.oktoberfest.de) Legendary beer-swilling party running from mid-September to the first Sunday in October. Held on the Theresienwiese.

Munich Marathon　SPORTS
(www.muenchenmarathon.de) More than 10,000 runners from around the world take to the streets in mid-October, finishing after just over 42km at the Olympiastadion.

Christkindlmarkt　CHRISTMAS MARKET
(www.christkindlmarkt.de; ⊙ late Nov-Christmas Eve) Traditional Christmas market on Marienplatz.

🛏 Sleeping

Room rates in Munich tend to be high, and they skyrocket during the Oktoberfest. Book well ahead. Budget travellers are spoilt for choice around the Hauptbahnhof, where the majority of hostels congregate, while the Altstadt has the most top-end hotels. Hostels are widespread but tend to be big, professionally run affairs that lack atmosphere.

🛏 Altstadt & Around

Hotel Blauer Bock　HOTEL €€
(Map p188; ☑ 089-231 780; www.hotelblauerbock.de; Sebastiansplatz 9; s/d from €47/79; ☏; Ⓤ Marienplatz, Ⓢ Marienplatz) A pretzel's throw from the Viktualienmarkt, this simple hotel has cunningly slipped through the net of Altstadt gentrification to become one of the city centre's best deals. The cheapest, unmodernised rooms have shared facilities, the updated en-suite chambers are of a 21st-century vintage, and all are quiet, despite the location. Superb restaurant.

Westend & Theresienwiese

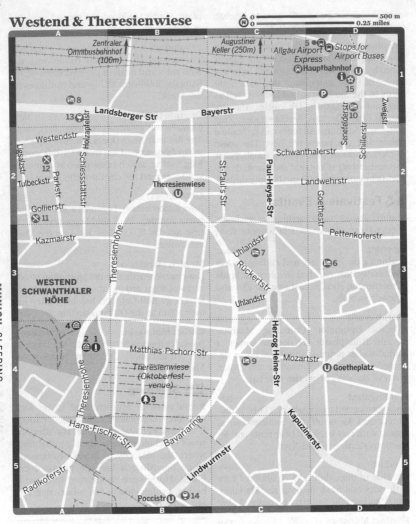

Westend & Theresienwiese

⊚ Sights
1 Bavariastatue	A4
2 Ruhmeshalle	A4
3 Theresienwiese	B4
4 Verkehrszentrum	A4

⊛ Activities, Courses & Tours
5 Radius Tours & Bike Rental	D1

⊜ Sleeping
6 Hotel Mariandl	D3
7 Hotel Uhland	C3
8 Meininger's	A1

9 Pension Westfalia	C4
10 Wombats City Hostel Munich	D1

⊗ Eating
11 Bodhi	A2
12 Marais	A2

⊜ Drinking & Nightlife
13 Augustiner Bräustuben	A1
14 Substanz	B5

✪ Entertainment
15 München Ticket	D1

Hotel am Viktualienmarkt   HOTEL €€
(Map p188; ☑089-231 1090; www.hotel-am-vik-tualienmarkt.de; Utzschneiderstrasse 14; s/d from €59/129; ☎; ⓤMarienplatz, ⓢMarienplatz) Elke and her daughter Stephanie run this good-value property with panache and a sunny attitude. The best of the up-to-date 26 rooms have wooden floors and framed poster art. All this, plus the city-centre location, makes it a superb deal.

Hotel am Markt   HOTEL €€
(Map p188; ☑089-225 014; www.hotel-am-markt.eu; Heiliggeiststrasse 6; d from €112; ☎; ⓢMarienplatz, ⓤMarienplatz) As super central as you could wish, this slender, medieval-style hotel occupies a gabled and turreted building overlooking the Viktualienmarkt. Bedrooms are midrange business standard, some with cheap flatpack, others with vaguely antique-style furniture. Bathrooms are also a mixed bag, but the general standard is good. There's a restaurant on site.

★Bayerischer Hof   HOTEL €€€
(Map p188; ☑089-21 200; www.bayerischerhof.de; Promenadeplatz 2-6; r €250-450; ✖☎✖; ⓑTheatinerstrasse) Around since 1841, this is one of the grande dames of Munich hotels. Rooms come in a number of styles, from busy Laura Ashley to minimalist cosmopolitan. The super-central location and pool come in addition to impeccably regimented staff. Marble, antiques and oil paintings abound, and you can dine till you burst at any of the five fabulous restaurants.

Cortiina   HOTEL €€€
(Map p188; ☑089-242 2490; www.cortiina.com; Ledererstrasse 8; s €120-269, d €150-309; ✖✖☎; ⓤMarienplatz, ⓢMarienplatz) Tiptoeing between hip and haute, this hotel scores best with trendy, design-minded travellers. The street-level lounge usually buzzes with cocktail-swigging belles and beaus, but all traces of hustle evaporate the moment you step into your minimalist, feng shui–inspired room. Breakfast is an unappetising €22.50 extra.

Hotel Mandarin Oriental Munich HOTEL €€€
(Map p188; ☑089-290 980; www.mandarin oriental.com; Neuturmstrasse 1; d from €625; ✖✖⊗ ☎✖; ⓤMarienplatz, ⓢMarienplatz) These magnificent neo-Renaissance digs lure the world's glamorous, rich, powerful and famous with opulently understated rooms and top-notch service. Paul McCartney, Bill Clinton and Prince Charles have crumpled the sheets here. Service is polite almost to a fault, but – incredibly – breakfast and internet access are extra.

Gärtnerplatzviertel & Glockenbachviertel

Pension Gärtnerplatz   GUESTHOUSE €€
(Map p188; ☑089-202 5170; www.pensiongaert nerplatz.de; Klenzestrasse 45; s/d €82/130; ☎; ⓤFraunhoferstrasse) Flee the urban hullabaloo to an Alpine fantasy land where rooms entice with carved wood, painted bedsteads, woollen rugs and crisp, quality bedding. In one room a portrait of Ludwig II watches you as you slumber; breakfasts are honestly organic.

Deutsche Eiche   HOTEL €€
(Map p188; ☑089-231 1660; www.deutsche-eiche.com; Reichenbachstrasse 13; s/d from €99/159; ☎; ⓑReichenbachplatz) The rainbow flag flutters alongside the usual national pennants outside this traditionally gay outpost that invites style junkies of all sexual orientations to enjoy the slick rooms and first-class restaurant. There's a sauna on the premises.

Around the Hauptbahnhof

Wombats City Hostel Munich   HOSTEL €
(Map p208; ☑089-5998 9180; www.wombats-hostels.com; Senefelderstrasse 1; dm €23-32, d €84; ℗◉☎; ⓑHauptbahnhof, ⓤHauptbahnhof) Munich's top hostel is a professionally run affair with a whopping 300 dorm beds plus private rooms. Dorms are painted in cheerful pastels and outfitted with wooden floors, ensuite facilities, sturdy lockers and comfy pine bunks, all in a central location near the train station. A free welcome drink awaits in the bar. Buffet breakfast costs €4.30.

Meininger's   HOSTEL, HOTEL €
(Map p208; ☑089-5499 8023; www.meininger-hostels.de; Landsbergerstrasse 20; dm/s/d without breakfast from €16/50/66; ☎; ⓑHolzapfelstrasse) About 800m west of the Hauptbahnhof, this energetic hostel-hotel has basic, clean, bright rooms with big dorms divided into two for a bit of privacy. Room rates vary wildly depending on the date, events taking place in Munich, and occupancy. Breakfast is an extra €6.90; bike hire costs from €8 per day.

Hotel Cocoon   DESIGN HOTEL €€
(Map p188; ☑089-5999 3907; www.hotel-cocoon.de; Lindwurmstrasse 35; s/d from €69/89; ⊖☎; ⓑSendlinger Tor, ⓤSendlinger Tor) Fans of

retro design will strike gold in this central lifestyle hotel. Things kick off in reception, with its faux-'70s veneer and dangling '60s ball chairs, and continue in the rooms. All are identical, decorated in retro oranges and greens and equipped with LCD TV, iPod dock and a 'laptop cabin'. Breakfast costs €9.

The glass showers stand in the sleeping area, with only a kitschy Alpine-meadow scene veiling life's vitals.

Hotel Eder
HOTEL €€

(Map p188; ☏089-554 660; www.hotel eder. de; Zweigstrasse 8; s €55-180, d €65-230; ☺ ☎; ☒Hauptbahnhof, ☒Hauptbahnhof, ☒Hauptbahnhof) A slice of small-town Bavaria teleported to the slightly seedy area south of the Hauptbahnhof, this rustic oasis has its chequered curtains, carved-wood chairs and Sisi/Ludwig II portraits firmly in place for those who didn't come all this way for the cocktails. The unevenly sized rooms are slightly vanilla, but when rates are midrange to low, this is a nifty deal.

Hotelissimo Haberstock
HOTEL €€

(Map p188; ☏089-557 855; www.hotelissimo.com; Schillerstrasse 4; s/d from €74/104; ☎; ☒Hauptbahnhof, ☒Hauptbahnhof, ☒Hauptbahnhof) The cheery decor at this value-for-money pick reflects the vision of the owners, a husband-and-wife team with a feel for colour, fabrics and design. Easy-on-the-eye gold, brown and cream tones dominate the good-sized rooms on the lower floors, while upper ones radiate a bolder, Mediterranean palette.

Hotel Müller
HOTEL €€

(Map p188; ☏089-232 3860; www.hotel-mueller-muenchen.de; Fliegenstrasse 4; s/d from €79/109; ☎; ☒Sendlinger Tor) This friendly hotel has big, bright, business-standard rooms and a good price-to-quality ratio, with five-star breakfasts and polite staff. Despite the city-centre location, the side-street position is pretty quiet.

Hotel Königshof
HOTEL €€€

(Map p188; ☏089-55 1360; www.koenigshof-hotel. de; Karlsplatz 25; d from €190; ☒ ☎; ☒Karlsplatz, ☒Karlsplatz, ☒Karlsplatz) Over-the-top luxury and obsessive attention to detail make the 'King's Court' a real treat. Rooms range from better-than-average business standard to sumptuous belle époque–style quarters. A Michelin-starred restaurant and a stylish bar are on the premises, and some of the rooms have views of busy Karlsplatz (Stachus), giving the place a heart-of-the-action feel.

Anna Hotel
DESIGN HOTEL €€€

(Map p188; ☏089-599 940; www.geisel-privathotels.de; Schützenstrasse 1; s €160-215, d €175-235; ☒ ☎; ☒Karlsplatz, ☒Karlsplatz, ☒Karlsplatz) Urban sophisticates love this well-positioned designer den, where you can retire to rooms dressed in sensuous Donghia furniture and regal colours or tempered by teakwood, marble and mosaics and offering a more minimalist feel. The swanky restaurant-bar is a hive of dining activity.

🛏 Schwabing

La Maison
DESIGN HOTEL €€

(Map p192; ☏089-3303 5550; www.hotel-la-maison.com; Occamstrasse 24; s/d from €110/125; ☒ ☒ ☎; ☒Münchner Freiheit) Discerningly retro and immaculate in shades of imperial purple and uber-cool grey, this sassy number wows, its rooms flaunting heated oak floors, jet-black washbasins and starkly contrasting design throughout – though the operators can't resist putting a pack of gummy bears on the expertly ruffed pillows! Cool bar on ground level.

Gästehaus Englischer Garten
GUESTHOUSE €€

(Map p192; ☏089-383 9410; www.hotelenglischergarten.de; Liebergesellstrasse 8; s €75-205, d €87-205; ☒ ☒ ☎; ☒Münchner Freiheit) Cosily inserted into a 200-year-old ivy-clad mill, this small guesthouse on the edge of the Englischer Garten offers a Bavarian version of the British B&B experience. Not all rooms are en suite, but the breakfast is generous and there's cycle hire (€12 per day).

Hotel Marienbad
HOTEL €€

(Map p188; ☏089-595 585; www.hotelmarienbad.de; Barer Strasse 11; s €55-135, d €120-155; ☎; ☒Ottostrasse) Back in the 19th century, Wagner, Puccini and Rilke shacked up at the Marienbad, which once ranked among Munich's finest hotels. The place is still friendly and well maintained, and the 30 rooms flaunt an endearing jumble of styles, from playful art nouveau to floral country Bavarian to campy 1960s utilitarian. Amenities, fortunately, are of more recent vintage.

Hotel Hauser
HOTEL €€

(Map p192; ☏089-286 6750; www.hotel-hauser. de; Schellingstrasse 11; s €80-165, d €118-225; ☎; ☒Universität) The ageing woody rooms here date back to the optimistic days of the economic miracle (the 1950s) but are pristinely maintained, if small. Unexpected extras include a sauna and solarium.

Nymphenburg, Neuhausen & Around

Tent CAMPGROUND €
(Map p198; ☑089-141 4300; www.the-tent.com; In den Kirschen 30; tent bunks/floor space €10.50/7.50, campsites from €11; ☉ Jun-Nov; ☺ Botanischer Garten) A kilometre north of Schloss Nymphenburg, this youth-oriented camping ground has classic tent pitches as well as a 160-bunk main tent with floor space and foam mats for shoestring nomads. It's by far the cheapest sleep in town during the Oktoberfest.

★ **Hotel Laimer Hof** HOTEL €€
(Map p198; ☑089-178 0380; www.laimerhof.de; Laimer Strasse 40; s/d from €65/75; P @ ☎; ☺ Romanplatz) Just a five-minute amble from Schloss Nymphenburg, this superbly tranquil refuge is run by a friendly team who take time to get to know their guests. No two of the 23 rooms are alike, but all boast antique touches, oriental carpets and golden beds. Free bike rental, and coffee and tea in the lobby. Breakfast costs €10.

Haidhausen & Lehel

Hotel Ritzi HOTEL €€€
(Map p196; ☑089-414 240 890; www.hotel-ritzi.de; Maria-Theresia-Strasse 2a; s/d from €100/149; ☎; ☺ Maximilaneum) At this charming art hotel next to a little park, creaky wooden stairs (no lift) lead to rooms that transport you to the Caribbean, Africa, Morocco and other exotic lands. But it's the *Jugendstil* features of the building that really impress, as does the much-praised restaurant downstairs, with its Sunday brunch and well-chosen wine list.

Hotel Opéra HOTEL €€€
(Map p196; ☑089-210 4940; www.hotel-opera.de; St-Anna-Strasse 10; d from €230; ❀ ☎; ☺ Maxmonument, ☑ Lehel) Like the gates to heaven, a white double door opens at the touch of a tiny brass button at the Hotel Opéra. Beyond awaits a smart, petite cocoon of quiet sophistication with peaches-and-cream marble floors, a chandelier scavenged from the Vatican and uniquely decorated rooms.

Westend & Theresienwiese

Pension Westfalia B&B €
(Map p208; ☑089-530 377; www.pension-westfalia.de; Mozartstrasse 23; s/d from €38/50; ☎; ☑ Goetheplatz) Literally a stumble away from the Oktoberfest meadow, this stately four-storey villa conceals a cosy, family-run guesthouse that makes a serene base for sightseeing (outside the beer fest). Rooms are reached by lift; the cheaper ones have corridor facilities.

Hotel Mariandl HOTEL €€
(Map p208; ☑089-552 9100; www.mariandl.com; Goethestrasse 51; s €68-98, d €88-128; ☎; ☺ Sendlinger Tor, ☑ Sendlinger Tor) If you like your history laced with quirkiness, you'll find both aplenty in this rambling neo-Gothic mansion. It's an utterly charming place where rooms convincingly capture the *Jugendstil* period with hand-selected antiques and ornamented ceilings. Breakfast is served until 4pm in the Vienna-style downstairs cafe, which also hosts frequent live jazz or classical-music nights.

Hotel Uhland HOTEL €€
(Map p208; ☑089-543 350; www.hotel-uhland.de; Uhlandstrasse 1; s/d incl breakfast from €75/95; P ☎; ☑ Theresienwiese) The Uhland is an enduring favourite with regulars who like their hotel to feel like a home away from home. Free parking, a breakfast buffet with organic products, and minibar drinks that won't dent your budget are just some of the thoughtful features. Rooms have extra-large waterbeds.

✗ Eating

Munich's food was once described by Viennese actor Helmut Qualtinger as 'garnish for the beer', and while that may still ring true in traditional beer halls and eateries, where the menu rarely ventures beyond the roast-pork-and-sausage routine, elsewhere Munich can claim to have southern Germany's most exciting restaurant scene. There's lots of innovation going on in Munich's kitchens, where the best dishes make use of fresh regional, seasonal and organic ingredients. The Bavarian capital is also the best place between Vienna and Paris for a spot of internationally flavoured dining, especially when it comes to Italian, Afghan and Turkish food, and even vegetarians can look forward to something other than noodles and salads. The latest craze is for burgers: if you do plump for this non-traditional fare, at least go for the 100%-Bavarian-beef version.

✗ Altstadt & Around

Küche am Tor GERMAN, ITALIAN €
(Map p188; Lueg Ins Land 1; mains around €8.50; ☉ noon-5pm Mon-Fri; ☑; ☺ Isartor, ☑ Isartor)

No-nonsense, blink-and-you'd-miss-it lunch stop for local office workers with a comfortingly short menu of mostly German fare, but containing little Mediterranean touches such as pesto, tuna and *salsiccia* (Italian sausage).

Hans im Glück BURGERS €

(Map p188; Sonnenstrasse 24; burgers €8; ⏲11am-midnight Mon-Thu, to 2am Fri & Sat; 🚋Karlsplatz, [S]Karlsplatz, [U]Karlsplatz) Plugging into Munich's current obsession with the burger, this new joint in the old post office building serves a juicy selection of meat in buns amid a forest of real birch trunks that grow straight out of the floor. Takeaway and veggie versions available.

Schmalznudel CAFE €

(Cafe Frischhut; Map p188; Prälat-Zistl-Strasse 8; pastries €1.70; ⏲8am-6pm; [U]Marienplatz, [S]Marienplatz) This incredibly popular institution serves just four traditional pastries, one of which, the *Schmalznudel* (an oily type of doughnut), gives the place its local nickname. Every baked goodie you munch here is crisp and fragrant, as they're always fresh off the hotplate. They're best eaten with a steaming pot of coffee on a winter's day.

Königsquelle EUROPEAN €€

(Map p188; ☎089-220 071; www.koenigsquelle.com; Baaderplatz 2; mains €9-21; ⏲5pm-1am Sun-Fri, from 7pm Sat; 🚋Isartor, 🚋Isartor) This Munich institution is well loved for its attentive service, expertly prepared food and dark, well-stocked hardwood bar containing what must be the Bavarian capital's best selection of malt whiskies. The hardly decipherable handwritten menu hovers somewhere mid-Alps, with anything from schnitzel to linguine and goat's cheese to cannelloni to choose from.

Refettorio ITALIAN €€

(Map p188; ☎089-2280 1680; www.refettoriomuenchen.de; Marstallplatz 3; mains €11.50-28.50; ⏲noon-midnight Tue-Fri, 10am-midnight Sat, 10am-6pm Sun; 📶; 🚋Nationaltheater) The latest recruit to Munich's army of Italian eateries is this colourful, fresh-feeling and utterly 21st-century place near the opera and the Residenztheater. Every table and chair is a different colour, Greek mosaics hang at strategic points and bits of art are dotted like pepperoni on a pizza. The menu is expertly executed and commendably brief.

Fedora ITALIAN €€

(Map p188; www.fedorabar.de; Ledererstrasse 3; mains around €12, pizzas €10-15; ⏲10am-1am Mon-Thu, to 2am Fri & Sat, 4pm-midnight Sun; [U]Marienplatz, [S]Marienplatz) Occupying the vaulted spaces of the 13th-century Zerwirkgewölbe, this Italian job named after the famous hat does a decent pizza and has an open kitchen where you can watch cooks load it up. Tables bearing chequered tablecloths spread out from a big bar, and there's plenty of sunny street-side seating.

Conviva INTERNATIONAL €€

(Map p188; www.conviva-muenchen.de; Hildegardstrasse 1; 3-course lunch €8-10, dinner mains €10-15; ⏲11am-1am Mon-Sat, from 5pm Sun; 🌿; 🚋Kammerspiele) The industrially exposed interior and barely dressed tables mean nothing distracts from the great food at this theatre restaurant. The daily-changing menus make the most of local seasonal ingredients and are reassuringly short.

Prinz Myshkin VEGETARIAN €€

(Map p188; ☎089-265 596; www.prinzmyshkin.com; Hackenstrasse 2; mains €10-19; ⏲11am-12.30am; 🌿; [U]Marienplatz, [S]Marienplatz) This place is proof, if any were needed, that the vegetarian experience has left the sandals, beards and lentils era. Occupying a former brewery, Munich's premier meat-free dining spot is an vaulted and open-plan but intimate space. Health-conscious eaters come to savour imaginative dishes such as curry-orange-carrot soup, unexpectedly good curries and 'wellness desserts'.

Bratwurstherzl FRANCONIAN €€

(Map p188; Dreifaltigkeitsplatz 1; mains €7-16; ⏲10am-11pm Mon-Sat; [U]Marienplatz, [S]Marienplatz) Cosy panelling and an ancient vaulted brick ceiling set the tone of this Old Munich tavern with a Franconian focus. Homemade organic sausages are grilled to perfection on an open beechwood fire and served on heart-shaped pewter plates. They're best enjoyed with a cold one from the Hacker-Pschorr brewery.

OskarMaria INTERNATIONAL €€

(Map p188; www.oskarmaria.com; Salvatorplatz 1; mains €8-26; ⏲10am-midnight Mon-Sat, to 7pm Sun; [U]Odeonsplatz) The cafe at the Literaturhaus cultural centre is a commendably stylish spot, with bookishly high ceilings, rows of small central European cafe tables and sprightly waiters. The highbrow atmosphere will be appreciated by those who prefer their eateries (virtually) tourist free and the menu features international staples plus several Bavarian favourites.

Cafe Luitpold
CAFE €€

(Map p188; www.cafe-luitpold.de; Briennerstrasse 11; mains €11-20; ☺8am-7pm Mon, to 11pm Tue-Sat, 9am-7pm Sun; ⓊOdeonsplatz) A cluster of pillarbox-red street-side tables and chairs announces you've arrived at this stylish but not uber-cool retreat. It offers a choice of three spaces: a lively bar, a less boisterous columned cafe and a cool palm-leaved atrium. Good for a daytime coffee-and-cake halt or a full evening blowout with all the trimmings.

Weisses Brauhaus
BAVARIAN €€

(Map p188; ☑089-290 1380; www.weisses-brau haus.de; Tal 7; mains €7-20; ⓊMarienplatz, ⓈMarienplatz) One of Munich's classic beer halls, in the evenings this place is charged with red-faced, ale-infused hilarity, with Alpine whoops accompanying the rabble-rousing oompah band. The *Weisswurst* (veal sausage) here sets the standard for the rest to aspire to; sluice down a pair with the unsurpassed Schneider *Weissbier*. It's understandably very popular and reservations are recommended after 7pm.

Tegernseer Tal
BAVARIAN €€

(Map p188; Tal 8; mains €9-20; ☺9.30am-1am Sun-Wed, to 3am Thu-Sat; ☎; ⓊMarienplatz, ⓈMarienplatz) A blond-wood interior illuminated by a huge skylight makes this a bright alternative to Munich's dark-panelled taverns. And with Alpine Tegernseer beer on tap and an imaginative menu of regional food, this is generally a lighter, calmer beer-hall experience with a less raucous ambience.

Einstein
JEWISH €€

(Map p188; St-Jakobs-Platz 18; mains €10-19; ☺noon-3pm & 6pm-midnight Sat-Thu, 12.30-3pm Fri; ⓇMarienplatz, ⓊMarienplatz) Reflected in the plate-glass windows of the Jewish Museum, this is the only kosher eatery in the city centre. The ID and bag search entry process is worth it for the restaurant's uncluttered lines, smartly laid tables, soothing ambience and menu of well-crafted Israeli dishes.

Lemar
AFGHANI €€

(Map p188; ☑089-2694 9454; Brunnstrasse 4; mains €12.50-15; ☺6-11pm; ⓇSendlinger Tor, ⓊSendlinger Tor) Lemar provides an excellent introduction to this little-known but tasty cuisine, serving scrumptious Afghan dishes such as spicy lentil soup, chicken kebabs, fried basmati rice with raisins and pistachios, and *mantu* (pasta balls filled with meat and yoghurt). Rave reviews from all who eat in the authentic cushion-strewn dining space mean bookings may be necessary.

Galleria
ITALIAN €€€

(Map p188; ☑089-297 995; www.ristorante-galleria.de; Sparkassenstrasse 11; 2/3 courses €16/25; ☺noon-2.30pm & 6-11pm; ⓈMarienplatz, ⓊMarienplatz) Munich has a multitude of Italian eateries, but Galleria is a cut above the rest. The compact interior hits you first, a multihued, eclectic mix of contemporary art and tightly packed tables. The menu has a few surprises, such as turbot with lentil curry and coconut foam. Reservations are pretty much essential in the evening.

✖ Gärtnerplatzviertel & Glockenbachviertel

Götterspeise
CAFE €

(Map p188; Jahnstrasse 30; snacks from €3; ☺8am-7pm Mon-Fri, 9am-6pm Sat; ⓇMüllerstrasse) The name of this cafe translates as 'food of the gods' and the food in question is that most addictive of treats, chocolate. Here it comes in many forms, both liquid and solid, but there are also teas, coffees and cakes and little smokers' perches outside for Germany's many puffing chocoholics.

Wiener Cafe
CAFE €

(Map p188; cnr Reichenbachstrasse & Rumford-strasse; snacks €1.50-5; ☺8.30am-6pm Mon-Fri, 8am-5pm Sat; ⓇReichenbachplatz) The only cool thing about this delightfully old-fashioned central European coffeehouse is the marble table tops.

★ Fraunhofer
BAVARIAN €€

(Map p188; ☑089-266 460; www.fraunhofertheat er.de; Fraunhoferstrasse 9; mains €7-25; ☺4.30pm-1am Mon-Fri, 10am-1am Sat; ☎; ⓇMüllerstrasse) With its screechy parquet floors, stuccoed ceilings, wood panelling and virtually no trace that the last century even happened, this wonderfully characterful inn is perfect for exploring the region with a fork. The menu is a seasonally adapted checklist of southern German favourites but also features at least a dozen vegetarian dishes and the odd exotic ingredient.

The tiny theatre at the back stages great shows and was among the venues that pioneered a modern style of *Volksmusik* (folk music) back in the '70s and '80s.

Bamyan
AFGHANI €€

(Map p188; www.bamyan.de; Hans-Sachs-Strasse 3; mains €8-16; ☺3pm-1am Mon-Sat, from 6pm Sun; ⓇMüllerstrasse) The terms 'happy hour', 'cocktail' and 'chilled vibe' don't often go together with the word 'Afghan', but that's exactly the combination you get at this exotic hang-out, named after the Buddha statues infamously destroyed by the Taliban in 2001. Central Asian soups, kebabs, rice and lamb dishes and big salads are eaten at handmade tables inlaid with ornate metalwork.

MC Müller BURGERS €€
(Map p188; www.mcmueller.org; cnr Müllerstrasse & Fraunhoferstrasse; burgers €7.20-15.50; ⊙ 6pm-2am Mon-Thu, to 4am Fri & Sat; ﷺ Müllerstrasse) Retro '60s looks and triple duty as bar, DJ lounge and burger joint until the wee hours.

Sushi & Soul SUSHI €€
(Map p188; Klenzestrasse 21; mains €12-20; ⊙ 6pm-1am; ﷺ Reichenbachplatz) This popular sushi joint serves up piscine morsels and creative cocktails to a Japanese-pop soundtrack.

La Bouche FRENCH €€€
(Map p188; ✆ 089-265 626; www.restaurant-la-bouche.de; Jahnstrasse 30; mains €14.50-30; ⊙ noon-3pm Mon-Fri, 6pm-midnight Mon-Sat; Ⓤ Fraunhoferstrasse) Expect good Gallic goings-on at this French-inspired port of call, where tables are squished as tight as lovers and the accent is on imaginative but gimmick-free fare, such as truffle ravioli, veal liver with caramelised apple, and plenty of fish. It's much bigger than first meets the eye: there's a second room at the back.

🍴 Schwabing & Maxvorstadt

Pommes Boutique FAST FOOD €
(Map p192; Amalienstrasse 46; fries €3.20; ⊙ 10am-10pm Mon-Sat, noon-8pm Sun; Ⓤ Universität) This funky lunch halt serves cheap-as-chips Belgian-style fries made from organic potatoes, 30-odd finger-licking dips to dunk them in and *Currywurst* to die for.

Chopan AFGHANI €€
(Map p198; Elvirastrasse 18A; mains €7-17.50; ⊙ 6pm-midnight; Ⓤ Maillingerstrasse) Munich has a huge Afghan community, whose most respected eatery is this much-lauded restaurant done out Central Asian caravanserai style with rich fabrics, multihued glass lanterns and geometric patterns. In this culinary Aladdin's cave you'll discover an exotic menu of lamb, lentils, rice, spinach and flatbread in various combinations, but there are no alcoholic beverages to see things on their way.

Potting Shed BURGERS €€
(Map p192; Occamstrasse 11; mains €6-17; ⊙ from 6pm; Ⓤ Münchner Freiheit) This relaxed hangout serves tapas, gourmet burgers and cocktails to an easy-going evening crowd. The burger menu whisks you round the globe, but it's the house speciality, the 'Potting Shed Special', involving an organic beef burger flambéed in whisky, that catches the eye on the simple but well-concocted menu.

Ruff's Burger BURGERS €€
(Map p192; Occamstrasse 4; burgers €7-15; ⊙ 11.30am-11pm Mon-Wed, to midnight Thu-Sat, to 10pm Sun; Ⓤ Münchner Freiheit) Munich's obsession with putting a fried bit of meat between two buns continues at this Schwabing joint, where the burgers are 100% Bavarian beef – except, of course, for the token veggie version. Erdinger and Tegernseer beer and mostly outdoor seating.

★ Tantris INTERNATIONAL €€€
(✆ 089-361 9590; www.tantris.de; Johann-Fichte-Strasse 7; menu from €80; ⊙ noon-3pm & 6.30pm-1am Tue-Sat; 🐾; Ⓤ Dietlindenstrasse) Tantris means 'the search for perfection' and here, at one of Germany's most famous restaurants, they're not far off it. The interior design is full-bodied '70s – all postbox reds, truffle blacks and illuminated yellows – with sublime food and service sometimes as unobtrusive as it is efficient. The wine cellar is probably Germany's best. Reservations are essential.

Cochinchina ASIAN €€€
(Map p192; ✆ 089-3898 9577; www.cochinchina.de; Kaiserstrasse 28; mains around €20; ⊙ 11.30am-2.30pm & 6pm-midnight; Ⓤ Münchner Freiheit) Bearing an old name for southern Vietnam, this cosmopolitan Asiatic fusion restaurant is Munich's top place for Vietnamese and Chinese concoctions, consumed in a dark, dramatically exotic space devoted to the firefly and splashed with the odd bit of colour in the shape of Chinese vases and lamps. The traditional *pho* soup is southern Germany's best.

🍴 Nymphenburg, Neuhausen & Around

Eiscafé Sarcletti GELATERIA €
(Map p198; www.sarcletti.de; Nymphenburger Strasse 155; ⊙ 9am-11.30pm May-Aug, slightly shorter hours Sep-Apr; ﷺ Volkartstrasse) Ice-cream addicts have been getting their gelato fix at this Munich institution since 1879. Choose from more than 50 mouth-watering flavours, from not-so-plain vanilla to coconut milk and lime.

Schlosscafé Im Palmenhaus
CAFE €€

(Map p198; www.palmenhaus.de; Schloss Nymphenburg 43; mains €9-15; ⊙11am-6pm Tue-Fri, from 10am Sat & Sun; 🚊Schloss Nymphenburg) The glass-fronted 1820 palm house where Ludwig II used to keep his exotic house plants warm in winter is now a high-ceilinged and pleasantly scented cafe serving soups, salads, sandwiches and other light meals. It's just behind Schloss Nymphenburg.

Esszimmer
MEDITERRANEAN €€€

(Map p198; ☑089-358 991 814; www.bmw-welt. com; BMW Welt, Am Olympiapark 1; 4/5 courses €90/110; ⊙from 4pm Tue-Sat; ⓧ🐾; Ⓤ Olympiazentrum) It took Bobby Bräuer, head chef at the gourmet restaurant at BMW World, just two years to gain his first Michelin star. Munich's top dining spot is the place to sample high-octane French and Mediterranean morsels, served in a trendily dark and veneered dining room above the i8s and 7 Series. Life in the gastronomic fast lane.

✕ Haidhausen & Lehel

Wirtshaus in der Au
BAVARIAN €€

(Map p196; ☑089-448 1400; Lilienstrasse 51; mains €10-16; ⊙5pm-midnight Mon-Fri, from 10am Sat & Sun; 🚊Deutsches Museum) This Bavarian tavern's simple slogan is 'Beer and dumplings since 1901', and it's that time-honoured staple (the dumpling) that's the speciality here (the tavern even runs a dumpling-making course in English). Once a brewery, the space-rich dining area has chunky tiled floors, a lofty ceiling and a crackling fireplace in winter. When spring springs, the beer garden fills.

Dreigroschenkeller
BAVARIAN €€

(Map p196; Lilienstrasse 2; mains €10-19; ⊙5pm-1am Sun-Thu, to 3am Fri & Sat; 🚊Deutsches Museum) A cosy and labyrinthine brick-cellar pub with rooms – based upon Bertolt Brecht's *Die Dreigroschenoper* (The Threepenny Opera) – ranging from a prison cell to a red satiny salon. There are nine types of beer to choose from and an extensive menu of hearty international and Bavarian favourites.

Vegelangelo
VEGETARIAN €€

(Map p188; ☑089-2880 6836; www.vegelangelo.de; Thomas-Wimmer-Ring 16; mains €10-19, set menu €24-30; ⊙noon-2pm Tue-Thu, 6pm-late Mon-Sat; 🗷; 🚊Isartor, Ⓢ Isartor) Reservations are compulsory at this petite vegie spot, where Indian odds and ends, a piano and a small Victorian fireplace distract little from the superb meat-free cooking, all of which can be converted to suit vegans. There's a set-menu-only policy Friday and Saturday. No prams allowed.

Swagat
INDIAN €€

(Map p196; Prinzregentenplatz 13; mains €10.50-22.50; ⊙11.30am-2.30pm & 5.30pm-1am; 🗷; 🚊Prinzregentenplatz, Ⓤ Prinzregentenplatz) Swagat fills every nook of an intimate cellar space with Indian fabrics, cavorting Hindu gods and snow-white tablecloths. The curry is as hot as Bavarians can take it, and there's plenty to please non-carnivores.

✕ Westend

★Marais
CAFE €

(Map p208; Parkstrasse 2; dishes €5-13; ⊙8am-8pm Tue-Sat, 10am-6pm Sun; 🗷; 🚊Holzapfelstrasse) Is it a junk shop, a cafe or a sewing shop? Well, Westend's oddest coffeehouse is in fact all three, and everything you see in this converted haberdashery – the knick-knacks, the cakes and the antique chair you're sitting on – is for sale.

Bodhi
VEGAN €€

(Map p208; Ligsalzstrasse 23; mains €10-17; ⊙from 5pm Mon-Fri, from noon Sat, 10am-2pm Sun; 🗷; Ⓤ Schwanthalerhöhe) This new vegan restaurant has an uncluttered, wood-rich interior where health-conscious diners feast on meat-and-dairy-free pastas, burgers, salads, soya steaks and tofu-based dishes. Whether those same wellness fanatics swill it all down with the large selection of cocktails and whisky, we'll never know.

La Vecchia Masseria
ITALIAN €€

(Map p188; Mathildenstrasse 3; mains €9-18, pizzas €7-8.50; ⊙11.30am-12.30am; 🚊Sendlinger Tor, Ⓢ Sendlinger Tor) One of Munich's longest-established Italian *osterie*, this earthy, rurally themed place has chunky wood tables, antique tin buckets, baskets and clothing irons, all conjuring up the ambience of an Apennine farmhouse. There's a small beer garden out the front, but this only operates until 9.30pm.

🍷 Drinking & Nightlife

Munich is a great place for boozers. Raucous beer halls, snazzy hotel lounges, chestnut-canopied beer gardens, hipster DJ bars, designer cocktail temples – the variety is so huge that finding a party den to match your mood is not exactly a tall order. Generally speaking, student-flavoured places abound in

Maxvorstadt and Schwabing, while traditional beer halls and taverns cluster in the Altstadt; Haidhausen attracts trendy types, and the Gärtnerplatzviertel and Glockenbachviertel are alive with gay bars and hipster haunts.

No matter where you are, you won't be far from an enticing cafe to get a java-infused pick-me-up. Many also serve light fare and delicious (often homemade) cakes and are great places to linger, chat, write postcards or simply watch people on parade.

Bavaria's brews are best sampled in a venerable *Bierkeller* (beer hall) or *Biergarten* (beer garden). People come primarily to drink, although food is usually served. In beer gardens you are usually allowed to bring your own picnic as long as you sit at tables without tablecloths and order something to drink. Sometimes there's a resident brass band pumping oompah music. And don't even think about sitting at a *Stammtisch* (a table reserved for regulars; look for a brass plaque or some other sign)! Beer gardens are, for the most part, very family friendly, with play areas and kids' menus.

Munich has a thriving club scene, so no matter whether your musical tastes run to disco or dance hall, house or punk, techno or punk-folk, you'll find a place to get those feet moving. To get the latest from the scene, peruse the listings mags or sift through the myriad flyers in shops, cafes and bars. This being Munich, expect pretty strict doors at most venues. Dance floors rarely heat up before 1am, so showing up early may increase your chances of getting in without suffering the indignities of a ridiculous wait and possible rejection. If you look under 30, bring ID. Cover charges rarely exceed €15.

Altstadt & Around

Hofbräuhaus BEER HALL

(Map p188; ☎089-290 136 100; www.hofbraeuhaus.de; Am Platzl 9; 1L beer €8, mains €10-20; 🕒9am-11.30pm; 🚋Kammerspiele, [S] Marienplatz, [U] Marienplatz) Every visitor to Munich should make a pilgrimage to this mothership of all beer halls, if only once. There is a range of spaces in which to do your mass lifting: the horse chestnut–shaded garden, the main hall next to the oompah band, tables opposite the industrial-scale kitchen and quieter corners.

Harry Klein CLUB

(Map p188; www.harrykleinclub.de; Sonnenstrasse 8; 🕒from 11pm; 🚋Karlsplatz, [S] Karlsplatz, [U] Karlsplatz) Follow the gold-lined passageway off Sonnenstrasse to what some regard as one of the best *Elektro-clubs* in the world. Nights here are an amazing alchemy of electro sound and visuals, with live video art projected onto the walls Kraftwerk style blending to awe-inspiring effect with the music.

MilchundBar CLUB

(Map p188; www.milchundbar.de; Sonnenstrasse 27; 🚋Sendlinger Tor, [U] Sendlinger Tor) This relative newcomer is one of the hottest addresses in the city centre for those who like to spend the hours between supper and breakfast boogieing to an eclectic mix of nostalgia hits during the week and top DJs at the weekends.

Rote Sonne CLUB

(Map p188; www.rote-sonne.com; Maximiliansplatz 5; 🕒from 11pm Thu-Sun; 🚋Lenbachplatz) Named for a 1969 Munich cult movie starring It-Girl Uschi Obermaier, the Red Sun is a fiery nirvana for fans of electronic sounds. A global roster of DJs keeps the wooden dance floor packed and sweaty until the sun rises.

Viktualienmarkt BEER GARDEN

(Map p188; Viktualienmarkt 6; 🕒9am-10pm; [U] Marienplatz, [S] Marienplatz) After a day of sightseeing or stocking up on tasty nibbles at the Viktualienmarkt, find a table at this chestnut-shaded beer garden, a Munich institution since 1807. The breweries take turns serving here, so you never know what's on tap.

Schumann's Bar BAR

(Map p188; ☎089-229 060; www.schumanns.de; Odeonsplatz 6-7; 🕒8am-3am Mon-Fri, 6pm-3am Sat & Sun; [S] Odeonsplatz) Urbane and sophisticated, Schumann's shakes up Munich's nightlife with libational flights of fancy in an impressive range of concoctions. It's also good for weekday breakfasts.

Braunauer Hof PUB

(Map p188; Frauenstrasse 42; 🕒11.30am-11pm Mon-Sat; 🚋Isartor, [S] Isartor) Near the Isartor, drinkers can choose between the traditional Bavarian interior or the beer garden out the back that enjoys a surprisingly tranquil setting despite its city-centre location. Most come for the Paulaner beer of an eve, but the €8.50 lunch menu is good value for money.

Stereo Cafe CAFE

(Map p188; www.stereocafe.de; Residenzstrasse 25; 🕒10am-8pm Mon-Sat; 🚋Theatinerstrasse) Right opposite the Residenz, with bar stools looking out of huge windows at its western flank, this light, airy, vaguely Portuguese place (port, *pastel de nata,* Atlantic fish dishes) is a real gem and a nice spot for a pre-theatre aperitif or mid-sightseeing/shopping time-out. It's accessed through the downstairs men's-accessory emporium.

Café Cord
CAFE

(Map p188; ☑089-5454 0780; www.cafe-cord. tv; Sonnenstrasse 19; mains €10-20; ⊙11am-1am Mon-Sat; 🛜; 🚉Karlsplatz, 🅂Karlsplatz, 🆄Karlsplatz) Set back from busy Sonnenstrasse in a modern precinct, clean-cut Cord is good stop for a light lunch or coffee or an ideal first pit stop before a long night on the club circuit. In summer, the delicious global fare tastes best on the romantic, twinkly courtyard.

Heart
CLUB

(Map p188; www.h-e-a-r-t.me; Lenbachplatz 2a; 🚉Lenbachplatz) Exclusive dine-dance-flirt club ensconced somewhat fittingly in the old stock exchange and aimed at well-heeled over-25s who like their beef tartar served at 5am. Dress to impress for the cool, well-illuminated, mirror-ceilinged hall and other impressively designed chill spaces.

🍸 Gärtnerplatzviertel & Glockenbackviertel

Baader Café
CAFE

(Map p188; Baaderstrasse 47; ⊙9.30am-1am; 🛜; 🚉Fraunhoferstrasse) Around since the mid-'80s, this literary think-and-drink place lures all sorts, from short skirts to tweed jackets, who linger over daytime coffees and nighttime cocktails. It's normally packed, even on winter Wednesday mornings, and is popular for Sunday brunch.

Trachtenvogl
CAFE

(Map p188; Reichenbachstrasse 47; ⊙10am-1am Sun-Thu, to 2am Fri & Sat; 🛜; 🚉Fraunhoferstrasse) At night you'll have to shoehorn your way into this buzzy lair favoured by a chatty, boozy crowd of scenesters, artists and students. Daytimes are mellower – all the better to sample its hot-chocolate menu and check out the incongruous collection of cuckoo clocks and antlers, left over from the days when this was a traditional garment shop.

Del Fiori
CAFE

(Map p188; Gärtnerplatz 1; ⊙10am-midnight; 🛜; 🚉Reichenbachplatz) Come to this buzzing Italian coffeehouse for the outdoor seating on the Gärtnerplatz, where there's standing room only from the first rays of late winter to the last of autumn. Great people-watching possibilities all day long.

Schwabing & Maxvorstadt

★ Alter Simpl
PUB

(Map p192; www.eggerlokale.de; Türkenstrasse 57; ⊙11am-3am Mon-Fri, to 4am Sat & Sun; 🚉Schellingstrasse) Thomas Mann and Hermann Hesse used to knock 'em back at this well-scuffed and wood-panelled thirst parlour. A bookish ambience still pervades, making this an apt spot to curl up with a weighty tome over a few Irish ales. The curious name is an abbreviation of the satirical magazine *Simplicissimus.*

Hirschau
BEER GARDEN

(Gysslingstrasse 15; ⊙11.30am-11pm Mon-Fri, from 10am Sat & Sun; 🆄Dietlindenstrasse) This monster beer garden can seat 1700 quaffers and hosts live music almost every day in the summer months. Dispatch the kids to the excellent playground and adjacent minigolf course while you indulge in some tankard caressing.

Salon Иркутск
BAR

(Map p198; www.salonirkutsk.de; Isabellastrasse 4; ⊙5pm-late; 🆄Josephsplatz) Escape the sugary cocktails and belly-inflating suds to one of Munich's more cultured watering holes, which touts itself as a Franco-Slavic evening bistro. You'll soon see this is no place to get slammed on Russian ethanol or cheap Gallic plonk – Monday is piano night, Wednesday is French evening and the green-painted, wood-panelled interior hosts exhibitions of local art.

Black Bean
CAFE

(Map p192; Amalienstrasse 44; ⊙7am-7pm Mon-Fri, from 8am Sat & Sun; 🛜; 🆄Universität) If you thought the only decent brew Bavarians could mash was beer, train your Arabica radar to this regional retort to Starbucks. The organic coffee gets tops marks, as do the muffins.

Eat the Rich
BAR

(Map p198; www.eattherich.de; Hessstrasse 90; ⊙7pm-1am Wed & Thu, to 4am Fri & Sat; 🆄Theresienstrasse) Strong cocktails served in half-litre glasses quickly loosen inhibitions at this sizzling nightspot, a great place to crash when the party's winding down everywhere else. Food is served till 3am on weekends.

News Bar
CAFE

(Map p192; www.newsbarmunich.de; Amalienstrasse 55; ⊙10am-midnight Sun-Thu, to 1am Fri &

Sat; 🕿; Ⓤ Universität) From tousled students to young managers and greying professors, everybody loves their news, especially at this stylish cafe that sells international papers and mags. It's an ideal breakfast spot before embarking on a day of Pinakothek museum hopping.

🍷 Nymphenburg, Neuhausen & Around

Hirschgarten　　　　　BEER GARDEN
(Map p198; www.hirschgarten.de; Hirschgarten 1; ⊙11.30am-1am; 🚃 Kriemhildenstrasse, Ⓢ Laim) The Everest of Munich beer gardens can accommodate up to 8000 Augustiner lovers but still manages to feel airy and uncluttered. It's in a lovely spot in a former royal hunting preserve and rubs up against a deer enclosure and a carousel. Steer here after visiting Schloss Nymphenburg – it's only a short walk south of the palace.

Augustiner Keller　　　　BEER GARDEN
(Arnulfstrasse 52; ⊙10am-1am Apr-Oct; 🚗; 🚃 Hopfenstrasse) Every year this leafy 5000-seat beer garden, about 500m west of the Hauptbahnhof, buzzes with fairy-lit thirst-quenching activity from the first sign that spring may have *gesprungen*. The ancient chestnuts are thick enough to seek refuge under when it rains,

---

OUT & ABOUT IN MUNICH

Munich's gay and lesbian scene is the liveliest in Bavaria but tame compared to that of Berlin, Cologne or Amsterdam. The rainbow flag flies especially proudly along Müllerstrasse and the adjoining Glockenbachviertel and Gärtnerplatzviertel. To plug into the scene, keep an eye out for freebie mags *Our Munich* and *Sergej*, which contain up-to-date listings and news about the community and gay-friendly establishments around town. Another source of info is www.gaytouristoffice.com.

Sub (Map p188; 🖫 089-856 346 400; www.subonline.org; Müllerstrasse 14; ⊙7-11pm Sun-Thu, to midnight Fri & Sat; 🚃 Müllerstrasse) is a one-stop service and information agency; lesbians can also turn to **Le Tra** (Map p188; 🖫 089-725 4272; www.letra.de; Angertorstrasse 3; ⊙2.30-5pm Mon & Wed, 10.30am-1pm Tue; 🚃 Müllerstrasse).

The main street parties of the year are Christopher Street Day (p207), held on Marienplatz on the second weekend in July, and the Schwules Strassenfest (www.schwules-strassenfest.de), held in mid-August along Hans-Sachs-Strasse in the Glockenbachviertel. During Oktoberfest, lesbigay folks invade the Bräurosl beer tent on the first Sunday and Fischer-Vroni on the second Monday.

Bars & Clubs

Ochsengarten (Map p188; www.ochsengarten.de; Müllerstrasse 47; 🚃 Müllerstrasse) The first bar to open in the Bavarian capital where to get in you have to be clad in leather, rubber, lycra, neopren or any other kinky attire you can think of. Gay men only.

Edelheiss (Map p188; www.edelheiss.de; Pestalozzistrasse 6; 🚃 Sendlinger Tor, Ⓤ Sendlinger Tor) A laid-back cafe by day, Edelheiss has vibrant party nights.

Nil (Map p188; www.cafenil.com; Hans-Sachs-Strasse 2; meals €3.50-8; ⊙3pm-3am; 🚃 Müllerstrasse) A construct in wood and marble with a vaguely Egyptian theme, this chilled-out cafe-bar is open till 3am and is a good place to crash after the party has stopped elsewhere.

NY Club (Map p188; www.nyclub.de; Sonnenstrasse 25; ⊙Fri & Sat; 🚃 Sendlinger Tor, Ⓤ Sendlinger Tor) After a complete revamp, it's again 'Raining Men' at Munich's hottest gay dance temple, where you can party away with Ibiza-style abandon on the cool, backlit main floor.

Bau (Map p188; www.bau-munich.de; Müllerstrasse 41; 🚃 Müllerstrasse) Bi-level bar that's partly central for manly men, with plenty of leather, Levi's and uniforms on show. Foam parties take place in the small cellar darkroom.

Prosecco (Map p188; www.prosecco-munich.de; Theklatstrasse 1; 🚃 Müllerstrasse) Fun venue for dancing, cruising and drinking that attracts a mixed bunch of party people with quirky decor and a cheesy mix of music (mostly '80s and charts).

or else lug your mug to the actual beer cellar. Small playground.

Haidhausen & Lehel

Biergarten Muffatwerk
BEER GARDEN
(Map p196; www.muffatwerk.de; Zellstrasse 4; ☺from noon; 🚇Am Gasteig) Think of this one as a progressive beer garden with reggae instead of oompah, civilised imbibing instead of brainless guzzling, organic meats, fish and vegetables on the grill, and the option of chilling in lounge chairs. Opening hours are open-ended, meaning some very late finishes.

P1
CLUB
(Map p196; www.p1-club.de; Prinzregentenstrasse 1; 🚇Nationalmuseum/Haus der Kunst) If you make it past the notorious face control at Munich's premier late spot, you'll encounter a crowd of Bundesliga reserve players, Q-list celebs and quite a few Russian speakers too busy seeing and being seen to actually have a good time. But it's all part of the fun, and the decor and summer terrace have their appeal.

Kultfabrik
CLUB
(Map p196; www.kultfabrik.de; Grafingerstrasse 6; 🚇Ostbahnhof) This former dumpling factory on the wrong side of the Ostbahnhof has more than a dozen, mostly mainstream, venues as well as numerous fast-food eateries, making it the best place in Munich to *carpe noctem* if you like that sort of thing.

Optimolwerke
CLUB
(Map p196; www.optimolwerke.de; Friedenstrasse 10; 🚇Ostbahnhof) Just behind Kultfabrik, Optimol is another clubber's nirvana, with around 10 venues after dark. Latin lovers flock to **Do Brasil**, while **Die Burg** keeps the party hits and classics booming till 6am.

Westend

★Augustiner Bräustuben
BEER HALL
(Map p208; ☎089-507 047; www.braeustuben. de; Landsberger Strasse 19; ☺10am-midnight; 🚇Holzapfelstrasse) Depending on the wind, an aroma of hops envelops you as you approach this traditional beer hall inside the Augustiner brewery. The Bavarian fare is superb, especially the *Schweinshaxe* (pork knuckle). Due to the location the atmosphere in the evenings is slightly more authentic than that of its city-centre cousins, with fewer tourists at the long tables.

Backstage
CLUB
(www.backstage.eu; Reitknechtstrasse 6; 🚇Hirschgarten) Refreshingly non-mainstream, this groovetastic club has a chilled night beer garden and a shape-shifting line-up of punk, nu metal, hip hop, dance hall and other alternative sounds, both canned and live.

Substanz
CLUB
(Map p208; www.substanz-club.de; Ruppertstrasse 28; 🚇Poccistrasse) About as alternative as things get in Munich, this low-key, beery lair gets feet moving with house to indie to soul and brings out the city's edgy wordsmiths for regular poetry slams. Also hosts unusual events for a club, such as vinyl flea markets and soccer tournaments.

☆ Entertainment

Tickets to cultural and sporting events are available at venue box offices and official ticket outlets, such as **Zentraler Kartenvorverkauf** (Map p188; ☎089-5450 6060; www. zkv-muenchen.de; Marienplatz; ☺9am-8pm Mon-Sat; 🚇Marienplatz). Outlets are also good for online bookings, as is **München Ticket** (Map p208; ☎089-5481 8181; www.muenchenticket.de; Bahnhofplatz 2; ☺10am-8pm Mon-Sat; 🚇Hauptbahnhof), which shares premises with the tourist office at the Hauptbahnhof.

Websites useful for tuning into the local scene include www.munig.com, www. munichx.de, www.ganz-muenchen.de and www.muenchengehtaus.com. All are in German but are not too hard to navigate with some basic language skills. *In München* (www.in-muenchen.de), a freebie mag available at bars, restaurants and shops, is the most detailed print source for what's on in Munich. *Munich Found* (www.munichfound.de) is an English-language magazine geared towards expats and visitors. For glossy weekly lifestyle and entertainment news, consult *Prinz München* (http://prinz. de/muenchen/).

Cinemas

For show information check any of the listings publications. Movies presented in their original language are denoted in listings by the acronym OF (*Originalfassung*) or OV (*Originalversion*); those with German subtitles are marked OmU (*Original mit Untertiteln*).

Museum-Lichtspiele
CINEMA
(Map p196; ☎089-482 403; www.museum-lichtspiele.de; Lilienstrasse 2; 🚇Deutsches Museum) Cult cinema with wacky interior and

ℹ CITY TOUR CARD

The Munich City Tour Card (www.citytourcard-muenchen.com; 1/3 days €10.90/20.90) includes all public transport in the *Innenraum* (Munich city – zones 1 to 4, marked white on transport maps) and discounts of between 10% and 50% for over 50 attractions, tours, eateries and theatres. These include the Residenz Musuem (p192), the BMW Museum (p204) and the Bier & Oktoberfestmuseum (p187). It's available at some hotels, tourist offices, Munich public transport authority (MVV) offices and U-Bahn, S-Bahn and DB vending machines.

screenings of the *Rocky Horror Picture Show* (11pm Friday and Saturday nights). Shows English-language movies.

Cinema
CINEMA
(Map p198; ☑089-555 255; www.cinema-muenchen.de; Nymphenburger Strasse 31; Ⓤ Stiglmaierplatz) Cult cinema with all films in English, all the time.

Classical & Opera

Bayerische Staatsoper OPERA
(Bavarian State Opera; Map p188; ☑089-218 501; www.staatsoper.de; Max-Joseph-Platz 2; ☒ Nationaltheater) One of the world's best opera companies, the Bavarian State Opera performs to sell-out crowds at the **Nationaltheater** (Map p188; www.staatstheater.bayern.de; Max-Joseph-Platz 2; ☒ Nationaltheater) in the Residenz and puts the emphasis on Mozart, Strauss and Wagner. In summer it hosts the prestigious Opernfestspiele (p207). The opera's house band is the Bayerisches Staatsorchester, in business since 1523 and thus Munich's oldest orchestra.

Münchner Philharmoniker CLASSICAL MUSIC
(Map p196; ☑089-480 985 500; www.mphil.de; Rosenheimer Strasse 5; ⊙mid-Sep–Jun; ☒ Am Gasteig) Munich's premier orchestra regularly performs at the Gasteig Cultural Centre (p201). Book tickets early, as performances usually sell out.

BR-Symphonieorchester CLASSICAL MUSIC
(www.br-so.com) Charismatic Lithuanian maestro Mariss Jansons has rejuvenated this orchestra's playlist and often performs with its choir at such venues as the Gasteig (p201) and the Prinzregententheater (p201).

Staatstheater am Gärtnerplatz CLASSICAL MUSIC
(Map p188; ☑089-2185 1960; www.gaertner platz-theater.de; Gärtnerplatz 3; ☒ Reichenbachplatz) Spruced up for its 150th birthday in November 2015, this grand theatre specialises in light opera, musicals and dance.

Jazz

Jazzclub Unterfahrt im Einstein LIVE MUSIC
(Map p196; ☑089-448 2794; www.unterfahrt.de; Einsteinstrasse 42; Ⓤ Max-Weber-Platz) Join a diverse crowd at this long-established, intimate club for a mixed bag of acts ranging from old bebop to edgy experimental. The Sunday open-jam session is legendary.

Jazzbar Vogler JAZZ
(Map p188; www.jazzbar-vogler.com; Rumfordstrasse 17; ☒ Reichenbachplatz) This intimate watering hole brings some of Munich's baddest cats to the stage. You never know who'll show up for Monday's jam session, and Tuesday to Thursday are live piano nights, but the main acts are on Friday and Saturday.

Theatre

Bayerisches Staatsschauspiel THEATRE
(☑089-2185 1940; www.residenztheater.de) This leading ensemble has a bit of a conservative streak but still manages to find relevance for today's mad, mad world in works by Shakespeare, Schiller and other tried-and-true playwrights. Performances are in the **Residenztheater** (Map p188; Max-Joseph-Platz 2; ☒ Nationaltheater), the **Theater im Marstall** (Map p188; Marstallplatz 4; ☒ Kammerspiele) and the now fully renovated Cuvilliés-Theater (p194).

Münchner Kammerspiele THEATRE
(Map p188; ☑089-2339 6600; www.muenchner-kammerspiele.de; Maximilianstrasse 26; ☒ Kammerspiele) A venerable theatre with an edgy, slightly populist bent, the Kammerspiele delivers provocative interpretations of the classics as well as works by contemporary playwrights. Performances are in a beautifully refurbished art nouveau theatre at Maximilianstrasse 26 and in the **Neues Haus** (Map p188; Falckenbergstrasse 1), a new glass cube nearby.

Deutsches Theater THEATRE
(Map p188; ☑089-5523 4444; www.deutsches-theater.de; Schwanthalerstrasse 13; Ⓤ Hauptbahnhof, Ⓢ Hauptbahnhof) Munich's answer to London's West End hosts touring

road shows such as *The Rocky Horror Show*, *Spamalot* and *Mamma Mia*.

GOP Varieté Theater   THEATER
(Map p196; ☑089-210 288 444; www.variete.de; Maximilianstrasse 47; ⓐMaxmonument) Hosts a real jumble of acts and shows, from magicians to light comedies to musicals.

Spectator Sports

FC Bayern München   FOOTBALL
(☑089-6993 1333; www.fcbayern.de; Allianz Arena, Werner-Heisenberg-Allee 25, Fröttmaning; ⓤFröttmaning) Germany's most successful team both domestically and on a European level plays home games the impressive Allianz Arena, built for the 2006 World Cup. Tickets can be ordered online.

EHC München   ICE HOCKEY
(Map p198; www.ehc-muenchen.de; Olympia Eishalle, Olympiapark; ⓤOlympiazentrum) It's not one of Germany's premier ice-hockey outfits, but EHC München's games at the Olympic ice rink are exciting spectacles nonetheless, plus the team features several Canadian and American players.

🛍 Shopping

Munich is a fun and sophisticated place to shop that goes far beyond chains and department stores. If you want those, head to Neuhauser Strasse and Kaufingerstrasse. Southeast of there, Sendlinger Strasse has smaller and somewhat more individual stores, including a few resale and vintage emporia.

To truly unchain yourself, though, you need to hit the Gärtnerplatzviertel and Glockenbachviertel, the bastion of well-curated indie stores and local designer boutiques. Hans-Sachs-Strasse and Reichenbachstrasse are especially worth visiting. Maxvorstadt, especially Türkenstrasse, also has an interesting line-up of stores with merchandise you certainly won't find back home.

Globetrotter   OUTDOOR EQUIPMENT
(Map p188; www.globetrotter.de; Isartorplatz 8-10; ⊙10am-8pm Mon-Sat; ⓤIsartor, ⓢIsartor) Munich's premier outdoor and travel stockist is worth a browse even if you've never pulled on a pair of hiking boots. The basement boasts a lake for testing out kayaks and there's a cafe, a travel agent and even a branch of the Alpenverein, as well as every travel and outdoor accessory you could possibly need.

Manufactum   HOMEWARES
(Map p188; www.manufactum.de; Dienerstrasse 12; ⊙9.30am-7pm Mon-Sat; ⓢMarienplatz, ⓐMarienplatz) Anyone with an admiration for top-quality design from Germany and further afield should make a beeline for this store. Last-a-lifetime household items compete for shelf space with retro toys, Bauhaus lamps and times-gone-by stationery. The stock changes according to the season.

Munich Readery   BOOKS
(Map p198; www.readery.de; Augustenstrasse 104; ⊙11am-8pm Mon-Fri, 10am-6pm Sat; ⓤTheresienstrasse) With Germany's biggest collection of secondhand English-language titles, the Readery is the place to go in Bavaria for holiday reading matter. The shop holds events such as author readings and there's a monthly book club. See the website for details.

Holareidulijö   CLOTHING
(Map p198; www.holareidulijoe.com; Schellingstrasse 81; ⊙noon-6.30pm Tue-Fri, 10am-1pm Sat; ⓐSchellingstrasse) Munich's only secondhand traditional-clothing store (the name is a phonetic yodel) is worth a look even if you don't intend buying. Apparently, wearing hand-me-down Lederhosen greatly reduces the risk of chafing.

Words' Worth Books   BOOKS
(Map p192; www.wordsworth.de; Schellingstrasse 3; ⊙9am-8pm Mon-Fri, 10am-4pm Sat; ⓐSchellingstrasse) You'll find tons of English-language books, from secondhand novels to the latest bestsellers, at this excellent and long-established bookstore.

Porzellan Manufaktur Nymphenburg   CERAMICS
(Map p198; www.nymphenburg.com; Nördliches Schlossrondell 8; ⊙10am-5pm Mon-Fri; ⓐSchloss Nymphenburg) Traditional and contemporary porcelain masterpieces by the royal manufacturer. Also in the Altstadt at Odeonsplatz 1 (Map p188; ☑089-282 428; Odeonsplatz 1; ⊙10am-6.30pm Mon-Fri, to 4pm Sat; ⓤOdeonsplatz).

7 Himmel   CLOTHING
(Map p188; Hans-Sachs-Strasse 17; ⊙11am-7pm Mon-Fri, 10am-6pm Sat; ⓐMüllerstrasse) Female cool-hunters will be in seventh heaven (a translation of the boutique's name) when browsing the assortment of fashions and accessories by hip indie labels sold at surprisingly reasonable prices.

Flohmarkt Riem
MARKET

(www.flohmarkt-riem.com; Willy-Brandt-Platz; ⊕6am-4pm Sat; ⓤMessestadt-Ost) Play urban archaeologist and sift through heaps of junk to unearth the odd treasure at Bavaria's largest flea market. It's located outside the city centre by the trade-fair grounds in Riem. Take the U2 to Messestadt-Ost.

Schuster
OUTDOOR EQUIPMENT, SPORTS

(Map p188; Rosenstrasse 1-5; ⊕10am-8pm Mon-Sat; ⓢMarienplatz, ⓤMarienplatz) Get tooled up for the Alps at this sports megastore boasting seven shiny floors of equipment, including cycling, skiing, travel and camping paraphernalia.

Loden-Frey
CLOTHING

(Map p188; www.lodenfrey.com; Maffeistrasse 5-7; ⊕10am-8pm Mon-Sat; ⓖTheatinerstrasse) The famous cloth producer stocks a wide range of Bavarian wear and other top-end clothes. The Lederhosen and Dirndl outfits are a cut above the discount night-out versions and prices are accordingly high.

Foto-Video-Media Sauter
ELECTRONICS

(Map p188; Sonnenstrasse 26; ⊕9.30am-8pm Mon-Fri, to 7pm Sat; ⓤSendlinger Tor) The largest camera and video shop in town.

Stachus Passagen
MALL

(Map p188; www.stachus-passagen.de; Karlsplatz/Stachus; ⊕9.30am-8pm Mon-Sat; ⓖKarlsplatz, ⓢKarlsplatz, ⓤKarlsplatz) Europe's biggest underground shopping mall, with 36 escalators and 250,000 shoppers a day wandering its 58 mainstream shops.

ℹ Information

DANGERS & ANNOYANCES
During Oktoberfest crime and staggering drunks are major problems, especially around the Hauptbahnhof. It's no joke: drunks in a crowd trying to make their way home can get violent, and there are around 100 cases of assault every year. Leave early or stay cautious – if not sober – yourself.

Strong and unpredictable currents make cooling off in the Eisbach creek in the Englischer Garten more dangerous than it looks. Exercise extreme caution; there have been deaths.

Even the most verdant öko-warrior might interrupt his/her yoghurt pot of rainwater to agree with you that fast-moving bikes in central Munich are a menace. Make sure you don't wander onto bike lanes, especially when waiting to cross the road and when alighting from buses and trams.

INTERNET ACCESS
As across the rest of Europe, internet cafes are generally a thing of the past. Wi-fi is widespread though rarely free. Most public libraries offer internet access to non-residents. Check www.muenchner-stadtbibliothek.de (in German) for details.

MEDICAL SERVICES
The US and UK consulates can provide lists of English-speaking doctors.

Ärztlicher Hausbesuchdienst (☏089-555 566; www.ahd-hausbesuch.de) Doctor home and hotel visits.

Bereitschaftsdienst der Münchner Ärzte (☏089-116 117; ⊕24hr) Evening and weekend nonemergency medical services; English-speaking doctors.

Chirurgische Klinik (☏089-856 931 234; www.chkmb.de; Nussbaumstrasse 20; ⓤSendlinger Tor) Emergency room.

Emergency dentist (☏089-7233 093)

Emergency pharmacy (www.apotheken.de) Online referrals to the nearest open pharmacy. Most pharmacies have employees who speak passable English, but there are several designated international pharmacies with staff fluent in English, including **Ludwigs-Apotheke** (Neuhauser Strasse 11; ⊕8am-6.30pm Mon-Fri, 8.30am-1pm Sat; ⓤMarienplatz) and **Guten Tag Apotheke** (Bahnhofplatz 2; ⊕7am-8pm Mon-Fri, from 8am Sat; ⓖHauptbahnhof, ⓤHauptbahnhof, ⓢHauptbahnhof).

Schwabing Hospital (☏089-30 680; Kölner Platz 1; ⓤScheidplatz) Accident and Emergency.

MONEY
ATMs abound in the city centre, though not all take every type of card.

Reisebank (Bahnhofplatz 2; ⊕7am-10pm; ⓖHauptbahnhof, ⓤHauptbahnhof, ⓢHauptbahnhof) Best place to change and withdraw money at the Hauptbahnhof.

POST
Post office (Map p188; Sattlerstrasse 1; ⊕9am-6pm Mon-Fri, to 12.30pm Sat; ⓤMarienplatz, ⓢMarienplatz) For additional branches, search www.deutschepost.de.

TOURIST INFORMATION
Tourist Office – Marienplatz (Map p188; ☏089-2339 6500; www.muenchen.de; Marienplatz 2; ⊕10am-8pm Mon-Fri, to 4pm Sat, to 2pm Sun Apr-Dec, closed Sun Jan-Mar; ⓤMarienplatz, ⓢMarienplatz) There's another branch at the Hauptbahnhof (Map p208; ☏089-2339 6500; www.muenchen.de; Bahnhofplatz 2; ⊕9am-8pm Mon-Sat, 10am-6pm Sun; ⓖHauptbahnhof, ⓤHauptbahnhof, ⓢHauptbahnhof).

Castles & Museums Infopoint (Map p188; ☑ 089-2101 4050; www.infopoint-museen-bayern.de; Alter Hof 1; ⊙10am-6pm Mon-Sat; Ⓤ Marienplatz, Ⓢ Marienplatz) Central information point for museums and palaces throughout Bavaria.

ⓘ Getting There & Away

AIR

Munich Airport (☑ 089-975 00; www.munich-airport.de), also known as Flughafen Franz-Josef Strauss, is second in importance only to Frankfurt for international and domestic connections. The main carrier is Lufthansa, but there are over 80 other companies operating from the airport's two runways, from major carriers such as British Airways and Emirates to minor operations such as Luxair and Air Malta.

Only one major airline from the UK doesn't use Munich's main airport – Ryanair flies into Memmingen's **Allgäu Airport** (FMM; ☑ 08331-984 2000; www.allgaeu-airport.de), 125km to the west.

BUS

Europabus links Munich to the Romantic Road. For times and fares for this service and all other national and international coaches, contact **Sindbad** (☑ 089-5454 8989; www.sindbad-gmbh.de; Hackerbrücke 4-6 (ZOB); Ⓢ Hackerbrücke).

The bold new **Zentraler Omnibusbahnhof** (Central Bus Station, ZOB; www.muenchen-zob.de; Arnulfstrasse 21; Ⓢ Hackerbrücke) located next to the Hackerbrücke S-Bahn station handles the vast majority of international and domestic coach services. There's a Eurolines/Touring office, a supermarket and various eateries on the 1st floor; buses depart from ground level.

The main operator out of the ZOB is now low-cost coach company **Meinfernbus/Flixbus** (☑ 0180 515 9915; www.meinfernbus.de; Zentraler Omnibusbahnhof, Arnulfstrasse 21), which links Munich to countless destinations across Germany and beyond.

A special Deutsche Bahn express coach leaves for Prague (€61, five hours, four daily) from the ZOB.

CAR & MOTORCYCLE

Munich has autobahns radiating in all directions. Take the A9 to Nuremberg, the A8 to Salzburg, the A95 to Garmisch-Partenkirchen and the A8 to Ulm or Stuttgart.

Naturally, Munich Airport has branches of all major car-hire companies. Book ahead online for the best rates.

TRAIN

Train connections from Munich to destinations in Bavaria are excellent and there are also numerous services to more distant cities within Germany and around Europe. All services leave from the Hauptbahnhof (Central Station).

Staffed by native English speakers, **Euraide** (www.euraide.de; Desk 1, Reisezentrum, Hauptbahnhof; ⊙10am-7pm Mon-Fri Mar-Apr & Aug-Dec, to 8pm May-Jul; ◨ Hauptbahnhof, Ⓤ Hauptbahnhof, Ⓢ Hauptbahnhof) is a friendly agency based at the Hauptbahnhof that sells all DB products, makes reservations and can create personalised rail tours of Germany and beyond.

Connections from Munich:

➡ **Augsburg** €13.30 to €20.50, 30 minutes, three hourly

➡ **Baden-Baden** €87, four hours, hourly (change in Mannheim)

➡ **Berlin** €130, 6½ hours, hourly

➡ **Cologne** €142, 4½ hours, hourly

➡ **Frankfurt** €101, 3¼ hours, hourly

➡ **Freiburg** €93, 4½ hours, hourly (change in Mannheim)

➡ **Nuremberg** €19 to €55, one hour to one hour 40 minutes, twice hourly

➡ **Paris** from €142, six hours, daily

➡ **Prague** €74, 6¼ hours, three daily

➡ **Regensberg** €27.50, 1¾ hours, hourly

➡ **Vienna** €93, 4½ hours, every two hours

➡ **Würzburg** €71, two hours, twice hourly

➡ **Zürich** €83, 4¼ hours, three daily

ⓘ Getting Around

Central Munich is compact enough to explore on foot. The outlying suburbs are easily reachable by public transport, which is extensive and efficient, if showing its age slightly.

TO/FROM THE AIRPORT

Munich's airport is about 30km northeast of the city and linked by S-Bahn (S1 and S8) to the Hauptbahnhof. The trip costs €10.80, takes about 40 minutes and runs every 20 minutes almost 24 hours a day.

The Lufthansa Airport Bus shuttles at 20-minute intervals between the airport and Arnulfstrasse, next to the Hauptbahnhof, between 5.15am and 7.55pm. The trip takes about 45 minutes and costs €10.50 (return €17).

If you've booked a flight from Munich's 'other' airport at Memmingen (around 125km to the west), the **Allgäu Airport Express** (Map p208; www.aaexpress.de; single €17, €12 if prebooked online) also leaves from Arnulfstrasse at the Hauptbahnhof, making the trip up to seven times a day. The journey takes one hour 40 minutes and the fare is €13 (return €19.50).

A taxi from Munich Airport to the Altstadt costs €50 to €70.

CAR & MOTORCYCLE

Driving in central Munich can be a nightmare; many streets are one way or pedestrian only, ticket enforcement is Orwellian and parking is a nightmare. Car parks (indicated on the tourist-office map) charge about €1.70 to €2.20 per hour.

PUBLIC TRANSPORT

Munich's efficient public-transport system is composed of buses, trams, the U-Bahn and the S-Bahn. It's operated by MVV (www.mvv-muenchen.de), which maintains offices in the U-Bahn stations at Marienplatz, the Hauptbahnhof, Sendlinger Tor, the Ostbahnhof and Poccistrasse. Staff hand out free network maps and timetables, sell tickets and answer questions. Automated trip planning in English is best done online. The U-Bahn and S-Bahn run almost 24 hours a day, with perhaps a short gap between 2am and 4am. Night buses and trams operate in the city centre.

Tickets & Fares

The city-of-Munich region is divided into four zones, with most places of visitor interest (except Dachau and the airport) conveniently clustering within the white *Innenraum* (inner zone).

Short rides (*Kurzstrecke*; four bus or tram stops, or two U-Bahn or S-Bahn stops) cost

€1.40; longer trips cost €2.70. Children aged between six and 14 pay a flat €1.30 regardless of the length of the trip. Day passes are €6.20 for individuals and €11.70 for up to five people travelling together; a weekly pass called an IsarCard costs €14.10. Bikes cost €2.60 to take aboard and may only be taken on U-Bahn and S-Bahn trains, but not during the 6am to 9am and 4pm to 6pm rush hours.

Bus drivers sell single tickets and day passes, but tickets for the U-Bahn and S-Bahn and other passes must be purchased from vending machines at stations or MVV offices. Tram tickets are available from vending machines aboard. Most tickets must be stamped (validated) at station platform entrances and aboard buses and trams before use. The fine for getting caught without a valid ticket is €40.

TAXI

Taxis cost €3.50 at flag fall plus €1.50 to €1.80 per kilometre and are not much more convenient than public transport. Luggage is charged at €1.20 per piece. Ring a taxi on ☑ 216 10 or ☑ 194 10. Taxi ranks are indicated on the city's tourist map.

AROUND MUNICH

Dachau

KZ-Gedenkstätte Dachau   MEMORIAL (Dachau Concentration Camp Memorial Site; ☑ 08131-669 970; www.kz-gedenkstaette-dachau. de; Peter-Roth-Strasse 2a, Dachau; museum admission free; ⊙ 9am-5pm Tue-Sun) Officially called the KZ-Gedenkstätte Dachau, this was the Nazis' first concentration camp, built by Heinrich Himmler in March 1933 to house political prisoners. All in all, it 'processed' more than 200,000 inmates, killing at least 43,000, and is now a haunting memorial. Expect to spend two to three hours here to fully absorb the exhibits. Note that children aged under 12 may find the experience too disturbing.

The place to start is the visitors centre, which houses a bookshop, a cafe and a tour-booking desk where you can pick up an audioguide (€3). It's on your left as you enter the main gate. Two-and-a-half-hour tours (€3) also run from here from Tuesday to Sunday at 11am and 1pm (extra tours run at 12.15pm on Sunday between August and September).

You pass into the compound itself through the Jourhaus, originally the only entrance. Set in wrought iron, the infamous,

Around Munich Ⓝ 0 —— 10 km / 0 —— 5 miles

MUNICH DACHAU

chilling slogan *Arbeit Macht Frei* (Work Sets You Free) hits you at the gate.

The museum is at the southern end of the camp. Here, a 22-minute English-language documentary runs at 10am, 11.30am, 12.30pm, 2pm and 3pm and uses mostly post-liberation footage to outline what took place here. Either side of the small cinema extends an exhibition relating the camp's harrowing story, from a relatively orderly prison for religious inmates, leftists and criminals to an overcrowded concentration camp racked by typhus, and its eventual liberation by the US Army in April 1945.

Disturbing displays include photographs of the camp, its officers and prisoners (all male until 1944), and of horrifying 'scientific experiments' carried out by Nazi doctors. Other exhibits include a whipping block, a chart showing the system of prisoner categories (Jews, homosexuals, Jehovah's Witnesses, Poles, Roma and other 'asocial' people) and documents on the persecution of 'degenerate' authors banned by the party. There's also a lot of information on the rise of the Nazis and other concentration camps around Europe, a scale model of the camp at its greatest extent and numerous uniforms and everyday objects belonging to inmates and guards.

Outside, in the former roll-call square, is the International Memorial (1968), inscribed in English, French, Yiddish, German and Russian, which reads 'Never Again'. Behind the exhibit building, the bunker was the notorious camp prison where inmates were tortured. Executions took place in the prison yard.

Inmates were housed in large barracks, now demolished, which used to line the main road north of the roll-call square. In the camp's northwestern corner is the crematorium and gas chamber, disguised as a shower room but never used. Several religious shrines, including a timber Russian Orthodox church, stand nearby.

Dachau is about 16km northwest of central Munich. The S2 makes the trip from Munich Hauptbahnhof to the station in Dachau in 21 minutes. You'll need a two-zone ticket (€5.20). Here change to frequent bus 726 (direction Saubachsiedlung) to get to the camp. Show your stamped ticket to the driver. By car, follow Dachauer Strasse straight out to Dachau and follow the KZ-Gedenkstätte signs.

Schleissheim

When you've exhausted all possibilities in central Munich, the northern suburb of Schleissheim is well worth the short S-Bahn trip for its three elegant palaces and a high-flying aviation museum – a great way to entertain the kids on a rainy afternoon.

To get to Schleissheim, take the S1 (direction Freising) to Oberschleissheim (€5.20), then walk along Mittenheimer Strasse for about 15 minutes towards the palaces. On weekdays only, bus 292 goes to the Mittenheimer Strasse stop.

By car, take Leopoldstrasse north until it becomes Ingolstädter Strasse. Then take the A99 to the Neuherberg exit, at the southern end of the airstrip.

⊙ Sights

Neues Schloss Schleissheim   PALACE
(New Palace; www.schloesser-schleissheim.de; Max-Emanuel-Platz 1, adult/concession €4.50/3.50, all 3 palaces €8/6; ☉9am-6pm Apr-Sep, 10am-4pm Oct-Mar, closed Mon year-round; ☒Mittenheimer Strasse) The crown jewel of Schleissheim's palatial trio is the Neues Schloss Schleissheim. This pompous pile was dreamed up by Prince-Elector Max Emanuel in 1701 in anticipation of his promotion to emperor. It never came. Instead he was forced into exile for over a decade and didn't get back to building until 1715. Cash-flow problems required the scaling back of the original plans, but given the palace's huge dimensions and opulent interior, it's hard to imagine where exactly the cuts fell.

Some of the finest artists of the baroque era were called in to create such eye-pleasing sights as the ceremonial staircase, the Victory Hall and the Grand Gallery. There are outstanding pieces of period furniture, including the elector's four-poster bed, and intricately inlaid tables, and a particularly impressive ceiling fresco by Cosmas Damian Asam.

The palace is home to the Staatsgalerie (State Gallery), a selection of European baroque art drawn from the Bavarian State Collection, including works by such masters as Peter Paul Rubens, Anthony van Dyck and Carlo Saraceni. The most impressive room here is the Grand Galerie.

Flugwerft Schleissheim   MUSEUM
(www.deutsches-museum.de/flugwerft; Ferdinand-Schulz-Allee; adult/child €6/3; ☉9am-5pm;

⊠Mittenheimerstrasse) The Flugwerft Schleissheim, the aviation branch of the Deutsches Museum, makes for a nice change of pace and aesthetics from Schleissheim's regal palaces. Spirits will soar at the sight of the lethal Soviet MiG-21 fighter jet, the Vietnam-era F-4E Phantom and a replica of Otto Lilienthal's 1894 glider, with a revolutionary wing shaped like Batman's cape. Kids can climb into an original cockpit, land a plane and even get their pilot's licence.

Altes Schloss Schleissheim　PALACE
(www.schloesser-schleissheim.de; Maximilianshof 1; adult/concession €3/2, all 3 palaces €8/6; ☻9am-6pm Apr-Sep, 10am-4pm Oct-Mar, closed Mon year-round; ⊠Mittenheimer Strasse) The Altes Schloss Schleissheim is a mere shadow of its Renaissance self, having been altered and refashioned in the intervening centuries. It houses paintings and sculpture depicting religious culture and festivals all over the world, including an impressive collection of more than 100 nativity scenes.

Schloss Lustheim　PALACE
(www.schloesser-schleissheim.de; adult/concession €3.50/2.50, all 3 palaces €8/6; ☻9am-6pm Apr-Sep, 10am-4pm Oct-Mar, closed Mon year-round; ⊠Mittenheimer Strasse) While construction of Prince-Elector Max Emanuel's Neues Schloss Schleissheim was going on, the elector and his retinue resided in the fanciful hunting palace of Schloss Lustheim, on a little island in the eastern Schlosspark. It now provides an elegant setting for porcelain masterpieces from Meissen.

Starnberg

Around 25km southwest of Munich, glittering Lake Starnberg (Starnberger See) was once the haunt of Bavaria's royal family but now provides a bit of easily accessible R and R for anyone looking to escape the hustle of the Bavarian capital.

At the northern end of the lake, the affluent, century-old town of Starnberg is the northern gateway to the lake district but lacks any lasting allure, meaning most visitors head straight on to other towns or sites along the lake's edge. The train station is just steps from the lake's shore, where you'll find cruise-boat landing docks, pedal-boat hire and lots of strolling day-trippers. Besides

Lake Starnberg, the area comprises the Ammersee and the much smaller Pilsensee, Wörthsee and Wesslinger See. Naturally, the region attracts water-sports enthusiasts, but it also has enough history to satisfy those who enjoy exploring the past.

◉ Sights

Berg　VILLAGE
(Starnberger See) Those on the King Ludwig II trail should make a beeline for this tiny village on the eastern shore of Lake Starnberg. It was here that he famously (and mysteriously) drowned along with his doctor in just a few feet of water. The spot where his body was found is marked with a large, solumn cross backed by a *Votivkapelle* (Memorial Chapel). Berg is 5km from Starnberg and can be reached on foot in around an hour.

Museum Starnberger See　MUSEUM
(www.museum-starnberger-see.de; Possenhofener Strasse 5, Starnberg; adult/child €3/2; ☻10am-5pm Tue-Sun) You may have to duck your head when touring this 400-year-old farmhouse that offers a glimpse of life on the lake as it once was. It also boasts a precious Ignaz Günther sculpture in the little chapel. The modern extension showcases a fancy royal barge and a section on its construction.

❶ Information

Starnberger Fünf-Seen-Land Tourist Office
(☑ 08151-906 00; www.sta5.de; Wittelsbacherstrasse 2c, Starnberg; ☻8am-6pm Mon-Fri year round, 9am-1pm Sat May–mid-Oct) Just north of Starnberg's Bahnhofsplatz, this tourist office has a free room-finding service and offers trip planning to other lake towns. The website has links to all tourist offices in the local communities.

❶ Getting There & Around

Starnberg is a half-hour ride on the S6 train from Munich Hauptbahnhof (€5.20).

From Easter to mid-October **Bayerische-Seen-Schifffahrt** (www.seenschifffahrt.de) runs boat services from Starnberg to other lakeside towns as well as offering longer cruises. Boats dock behind the S-Bahn station in Starnberg.

If you'd rather get around the lake under your own steam, Bike It hires out two-wheelers. **Paul Dechant** (☑ 08151 121 06; Hauptstrasse 20), near the S-Bahn station, hires out rowing, pedal and electric-powered boats from €15 per hour.

Bavaria

POP 12.6 MILLION

Best Places to Eat

➡ Albrecht Dürer Stube (p274)

➡ Le Ciel (p247)

➡ Bürgerspital Weinstube (p252)

➡ Mittermeier (p256)

➡ August (p263)

Best Places to Stay

➡ Hotel Herrnschlösschen (p256)

➡ Petit Hotel Orphée (p291)

➡ Dom Hotel (p263)

➡ Hotel Deutscher Kaiser (p271)

➡ Elements Hotel (p291)

Why Go?

From the cloud-shredding Alps to the fertile Danube plain, the Free State of Bavaria is a place that keeps its clichéd promises. Story-book castles bequeathed by an oddball king poke through dark forest, cowbells tinkle in flower-filled meadows, the thwack of palm on lederhosen accompanies the clump of frothy stein on timber bench, and medieval walled towns go about their time-warped business.

But diverse Bavaria offers much more than the chocolate-box idyll. Learn about Bavaria's state-of-the-art motor industry in Ingolstadt, discover its Nazi past in Nuremberg and Berchtesgaden, sip world-class wines in Würzburg, get on the Wagner trail in Bayreuth or seek out countless kiddy attractions across the state. Destinations are often described as possessing 'something for everyone', but in Bavaria's case this is no exaggeration.

And, whatever you do in Germany's southeast, every occasion is infused with that untranslatable feel-good air of *Gemütlichkeit* (coziness) that makes exploring the region such an easygoing experience.

When to Go

A winter journey along an off-season, tourist-free Romantic Road really sees the snow-bound route live up to its name. Come the spring, tuck into some seasonal fare as Bavaria goes crazy for asparagus during *Spargelzeit* (from late March). The summer months are all about the beer garden, and this is obviously the best time to savour the region's unsurpassed brews in the balmy, fairy-lit air. Autumn is the time to experience the dreamy haze of the Bavarian Forest and the bustle of Bavaria's cities, revived after the summer's time-out.

Bavaria Highlights

1 Indulging your romantic fantasies at fairy-tale **Schloss Neuschwanstein** (p230)

2 Rack-and-pinioning your way to the top of the **Zugspitze** (p236), Germany's highest peak

3 Perching at the Eagle's Nest in **Berchtesgaden** (p246) to enjoy show-stopping Alpine vistas

4 Striking a trail through the tranquil wilds of the **Bavarian Forest National Park** (p304)

5 Going full circle around the town walls of quaint **Dinkelsbühl** (p257)

6 Messing around on the waters of the achingly picturesque **Königssee** (p245)

7 Revisiting Bavaria's Nazi past in **Nuremberg** (p265)

8 Going frothy at the mouth in the hundreds of superb **beer gardens, breweries and brewpubs** across the region

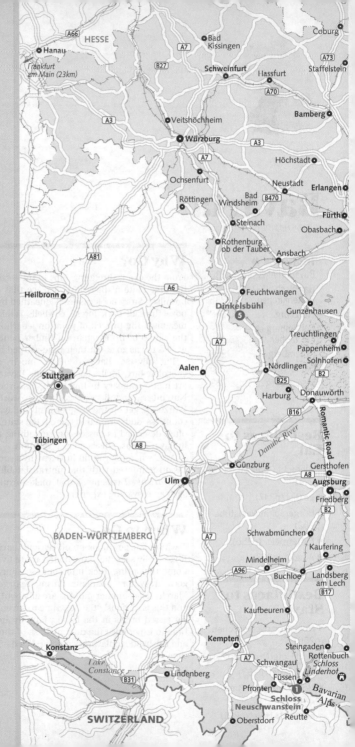

History

For centuries Bavaria was ruled as a duchy in the Holy Roman Empire, a patchwork of nations that extended from Italy to the North Sea. In the early 19th century, a conquering Napoleon annexed Bavaria, elevated it to the rank of kingdom and doubled its size. The fledgling nation became the object of power struggles between Prussia and Austria and, in 1871, was brought into the German Reich by Bismarck.

Bavaria was the only German state that refused to ratify the Basic Law (Germany's near constitution) following WWII. Instead, Bavaria's leaders opted to return to its pre-war status as a 'free state', and drafted their own constitution. Almost ever since, the *Land* (state) has been ruled by the Christlich-Soziale Union (CSU), the arch-conservative party that is peculiar to Bavaria. Its dominance of the politics of a single *Land* is unique in postwar Germany, having ruled for all but five of the last 50 years without the need to form a coalition with anyone else. Its sister party, the CDU, operates in the rest of the country by mutual agreement.

ℹ Getting There & Around

Munich is Bavaria's main transport hub, second only to Frankfurt in flight and rail connections. Rail is the best way to reach Munich from other parts of Germany, and the best means of getting from the Bavarian capital to other parts of Bavaria. Air links within Bavaria are much less extensive.

Without your own set of wheels in Eastern Bavaria and the Alps, you'll have to rely on bus services, which peter out in the evenings and at weekends. Trips along the Romantic Road can be done by tour bus, although again a car is a better idea. Several long-distance cycling routes cross Bavaria and the region's cities are some of the most cycle-friendly in the world, so getting around on two wheels could not be easier.

If you're travelling in a group, or can assemble one (as some people do pre-departure), you can make enormous savings with the Bayern-Ticket (€23, plus €5 per additional passenger). This allows up to five adults unlimited travel on one weekday from 9am to 3am, or from midnight to 3am the next day on weekends. The single version, costing €23, is also a good deal and means that all fares in Bavaria are basically capped at that price, as long as you don't leave before 9am. Both are good for 2nd-class rail travel across Bavaria (regional trains only, no ICs or ICEs), as well as most public transport.

BAVARIAN ALPS

Stretching west from Germany's remote southeastern corner to the Allgäu region near Lake Constance, the Bavarian Alps (Bayerische Alpen) form a stunningly beautiful natural divide along the Austrian border. Ranges further south may be higher, but these mountains shoot up from the foothills so abruptly that the impact is all the more dramatic.

The region is pocked with quaint frescoed villages, spas and health retreats, and possibilities for skiing, snowboarding, hiking, canoeing and paragliding – much of it year-round. The ski season lasts from about late December until April, while summer activities stretch from late May to November.

One of the largest resorts in the area is Garmisch-Partenkirchen, one of urban Bavaria's favourite getaways. Berchtesgaden, Füssen and Oberstdorf are also good bases.

ℹ Getting Around

There are few direct train routes between main centres, meaning buses are the most efficient method of public transport in the Alpine area. If you're driving, sometimes a short cut via Austria works out to be quicker (such as between Garmisch-Partenkirchen and Füssen or Oberstdorf).

Füssen

📱 08362 / POP 14,600

Nestled at the foot of the Alps, tourist-busy Füssen is the southern climax of the Romantic Road, with the nearby castles of Neuschwanstein and Hohenschwangau the highlight of many a southern Germany trip. But having 'done' the country's most popular tourist route and seen Ludwig II's fantasy palaces, there are other reasons to linger longer in the area. The town of Füssen is worth half a day's exploration and, from here, you can easily escape the crowds into a landscape of gentle hiking trails and Alpine vistas.

◉ Sights

★ Schloss Neuschwanstein   CASTLE
(📱 tickets 08362-930 830; www.neuschwanstein. de; Neuschwansteinstrasse 20; adult/concession €12/11, incl Hohenschwangau €23/21; ⊙ 9am-6pm Apr mid Oct, 10am-4pm mid-Oct–Mar) Appearing through the mountaintops like a mirage, Schloss Neuschwanstein was the model for Disney's *Sleeping Beauty* castle. King Ludwig II planned this fairy-tale pile

himself, with the help of a stage designer rather than an architect. He envisioned it as a giant stage on which to recreate the world of Germanic mythology, inspired by the operatic works of his friend Richard Wagner. The most impressive room is the **Sänger-saal** (Minstrels' Hall), whose frescos depict scenes from the opera *Tannhäuser*.

Built as a romantic medieval castle, work started in 1869 and, like so many of Ludwig's grand schemes, was never finished. For all the coffer-depleting sums spent on it, the king spent just over 170 days in residence.

Completed sections include Ludwig's Tristan and Isolde–themed bedroom, dominated by a huge Gothic-style bed crowned with intricately carved cathedral-like spires; a gaudy artificial grotto (another allusion to *Tannhäuser*); and the Byzantine-style **Thronsaal** (Throne Room) with an incredible mosaic floor containing over two million stones. The painting opposite the (throne-less) throne platform depicts another castle dreamed up by Ludwig that was never built. Almost every window provides tour-halting views across the plain below.

The tour ends with a 20-minute film on the castle and its creator, and there's a reasonably priced cafe and the inevitable gift shops.

For the postcard view of Neuschwanstein and the plains beyond, walk 10 minutes up to **Marienbrücke** (Mary's Bridge), which spans the spectacular Pöllat Gorge over a waterfall just above the castle. It's said Ludwig enjoyed coming up here after dark to watch the candlelight radiating from the Sängersaal.

Schloss Hohenschwangau CASTLE
(☏08362-930 830; www.hohenschwangau.de; Alpseestrasse 30; adult/concession €12/11, incl Neuschwanstein €23/21; ☉8am-5.30pm Apr–mid-Oct, 9am-3.30pm mid-Oct–Mar) King Ludwig II grew up at the sun-yellow Schloss Hohenschwangau and later enjoyed summers here until his death in 1886. His father, Maximilian II, built this palace in a neo-Gothic style atop 12th-century ruins left by Schwangau knights. Far less showy than Neuschwanstein, Hohenschwangau has a distinctly lived-in feel where every piece of furniture is a used original. After his father died, Ludwig's main alteration was having stars, illuminated with hidden oil lamps, painted on the ceiling of his bedroom.

It was at Hohenschwangau where Ludwig first met Richard Wagner. The **Hohenstaufensaal** features a square piano where the hard-up composer would entertain Ludwig with excerpts from his latest oeuvre. Some

ⓘ CASTLE TICKETS & TOURS

Schloss Neuschwanstein and Schloss Hohenschwangau can only be visited on guided tours (in German or English), which last about 35 minutes each (Hohenschwangau is first). Strictly timed tickets are available from the **Ticket Centre** (☏08362-930 830; www.hohenschwangau.de; Alpseestrasse 12; ☉8am-5.30pm Apr–mid-Oct, 9am-3.30pm mid-Oct–Mar) at the foot of the castles. In summer, come as early as 8am to ensure you get in that day.

Enough time is left between tours for the steep 30- to 40-minute walk between the castles. Alternatively, you can take a horse-drawn carriage, which is only marginally quicker.

Tickets for the **Museum of the Bavarian Kings** (p232) can be bought at the Ticket Centre and at the museum.

All Munich's tour companies run day excursions out to the castles.

rooms have frescos from German mythology, including the story of the Swan Knight, *Lohengrin*. The swan theme runs throughout.

Hohes Schloss CASTLE, GALLERY
(Magnusplatz 10; adult/concession €6/4; ☉galleries 11am-5pm Tue-Sun Apr-Oct, 1-4pm Fri-Sun Nov-Mar) The Hohes Schloss, a late-Gothic confection and one-time retreat of the bishops of Augsburg, lords it over Füssen's compact historical centre. The north wing of the palace contains the **Staatsgalerie** (State Gallery), with regional paintings and sculpture from the 15th and 16th centuries. The **Städtische Gemäldegalerie** (City Paintings Gallery) below is a showcase of 19th-century artists.

The inner courtyard is a masterpiece of illusionary architecture dating back to 1499; you'll do a double take before realising that the gables, oriels and windows are not quite as they seem.

Museum Füssen MUSEUM
(Lechhalde 3; adult/concession €6/4; ☉11am-5pm Tue-Sun Apr-Oct, 1-4pm Fri-Sun Nov-Mar) Below the Hohes Schloss, and integrated into the former Abbey of St Mang, this museum highlights Füssen's heyday as a 16th-century violin-making centre. You can also view the abbey's festive baroque rooms, Romanesque cloister and the St Anna Kapelle (AD 830) with its famous 'Dance of Death' paintings.

BAVARIA FÜSSEN

MUSEUM OF THE BAVARIAN KINGS

Museum der Bayerischen Könige (Museum of the Bavarian Kings; www.museumderbayerischenkoenige.de; Alpseestrasse 27; adult/concession €9.50/8; ◉10am-6pm) Palace-fatigued visitors often head straight for the bus stop, coach park or nearest beer after a tour of the castles, most overlooking this worthwhile museum, installed in a former lakeside hotel 400m from the castle ticket office (heading towards Alpsee lake). The architecturally stunning museum is packed with historical background on Bavaria's first family and well worth the extra legwork.

The big-window views across the stunningly beautiful lake (a great picnic spot) to the Alps are almost as stunning as the Wittelsbach bling on show, including Ludwig II's famous blue-and-gold robe.

A detailed audioguide is included in the ticket price.

Tegelbergbahn　　　　CABLE CAR
(www.tegelbergbahn.de; one-way/return €12.40/19.40; ◉9am-5pm) For fabulous views of the Alps and the Forggensee, take this cable car to the top of the Tegelberg (1730m), a prime launching point for hang-gliders and parasailers. From here it's a wonderful hike down to the castles (two to three hours; follow the signs to Königsschlösser). To get to the valley station, take RVO bus 73 or 78 (www.rvo-bus.de) from Füssen Bahnhof.

🛏 Sleeping

Accommodation in the area is surprisingly good value and the tourist office can help track down private rooms from as low as €30 per person.

Old Kings Hostel　　　　HOSTEL €
(☑08362-883 7385; www.oldkingshostel.com; Franziskanergasse 2; dm €22, d €52-58) This new design hostel tucked away in the mesh of lanes in the old town has two dorms and three doubles, all with a different quirky, but not overplayed, theme. Kitchen, continental breakfast (€5), laundry service and local beer are all available and the whole place is kept very neat and tidy.

Steakhaus　　　　GUESTHOUSE €
(☑08362-509 883; www.steakhouse-fuessen.de; Tiroler Strasse 31; s/d €30/74; ℗ 🖥) These budget rooms above a restaurant a 10-minute walk south of Füssen town centre, towards the border with Austria, will win no prizes for decor or character, but the location at the Lechfall gorge, with uncluttered views of the Alps, River Lech and surrounding forests, is pure magic.

★Hotel Sonne　　　　DESIGN HOTEL €€
(☑08362-9080; www.hotel-sonne.de; Prinzregentenplatz 1; s/d from €89/109; ℗ 🖥) Although traditional looking from outside, this Altstadt favourite offers an unexpected design-hotel experience within. Themed rooms feature everything from swooping bed canopies to big-print wallpaper, huge pieces of wall art to sumptious fabrics. The public spaces are littered with pieces of art, period costumes and design features – the overall effect is impressive and unusual for this part of Germany.

Altstadthotel Zum Hechten　　　　HOTEL €€
(☑08362-916 00; www.hotel-hechten.com; Ritterstrasse 6; s €59-69, d €94-100; ℗ 🖥) This is one of Füssen's oldest hotels and one of its friendliest. Public areas are traditional in style, while the bedrooms are bright and modern with beautifully patterned parquet floors, a large bed and sunny colours. The small but classy spa is great for relaxing after a day on the trail.

Fantasia　　　　DESIGN HOTEL €€
(☑08362-9080; www.hotel-fantasia.de; Ottostrasse 1; s €39-79, d €49-99; @🖥) This late-19th-century former holiday home for nuns and monks has been converted into a quirky design-hotel. The lounge is straight out of a design magazine; the rooms are slightly less wild, but still boast huge ceiling prints of Neuschwanstein Castle and idiosyncratic furniture. There's a pleasant garden in which to unwind after a hard day's sightseeing.

🍴 Eating

Vinzenzmurr　　　　BAVARIAN €
(Reichenstrasse 35; all dishes under €6; ◉8am-6pm Mon-Fri, to 1pm Sat) Füssen branch of the Munich butcher and self-service canteen offering no-nonsense portions of *Leberkäse* (meatloaf) in a bun, goulash soup, *Saures Lüngerl* (goat or beef lung with dumplings), bratwurst and schnitzel as well as something for those crazy vegetarians. No coffee or desserts.

Beim Olivenbauer AUSTRIAN, ITALIAN €€
(Ottostrasse 7; mains €6.50-16; ⊙11.30am-11.30pm) The Tyrol meets the Allgäu at this fun eatery, its interior a jumble of Doric columns, mismatched tables and chairs, multi-hued paint and assorted rural knick-knackery. Treat yourself to a wheel of pizza and a glass of Austrian wine, or go local with a plate of *Maultaschen* (pork and spinach ravioli) and a mug of local beer.

There's a kids corner and a sunny beer garden too. Takeaway pizza service available.

Zum Hechten BAVARIAN €€
(Ritterstrasse 6; mains €8-19; ⊙10am-10pm) Füssen's best hotel restaurant keeps things regional with a menu of Allgäu staples like schnitzel and noodles, Bavarian pork-themed favourites, and local specialities such as venison goulash from the Ammertal. Post-meal, relax in the wood-panelled dining room caressing a König Ludwig Dunkel, one of Germany's best dark beers, brewed by the current head of the Wittelsbach family.

Zum Franziskaner BAVARIAN €€
(Kemptener Strasse 1; mains €6-19.50; ⊙noon-11pm) This revamped restaurant specialises in *Schweinshaxe* (pork knuckle) and schnitzel, prepared in more varieties than you can shake a haunch at. There's some choice for noncarnivores such as *Käsespätzle* (rolled cheese noodles) and salads, and when the sun shines the outdoor seating shares the pavement with the 'foot-washing' statue.

ℹ Information

Tourist Office (☑08362-938 50; www.fuessen.de; Kaiser-Maximilian-Platz; ⊙9am-6pm Mon-Fri, 10am-2pm Sat, 10am-noon Sun) Can help find rooms.

ℹ Getting There & Away

BUS
The **Deutsche Touring** (www.touring.de, www.romantic-road.com), the Romantic Road Coach (p248), leaves from outside Füssen train station at 8am. It arrives in Füssen at 8.30pm.

TRAIN
If you want to do the castles in a single day from Munich, you'll need to start early. The first train leaves Munich at 5.53am (€26.20; change in Buchloe), reaching Füssen at 7.52am. Otherwise, direct trains leave Munich once every two hours throughout the day.

ℹ Getting Around

The brand-new train and bus stations are just a short stroll from the historical centre. The castles are around 3.5km away across the River Lech, so in theory are reachable on foot.

BUS
RVO buses 78 and 73 (www.rvo-bus.de) serve the castles from Füssen Bahnhof (€4.40 return, eight minutes, at least hourly). Tickets from the driver.

TAXI
Taxis to the castles are €10 each way and can be picked up at Füssen Bahnhof.

Wieskirche

Wieskirche CHURCH
(☑08862-932 930; www.wieskirche.de; ⊙8am-8pm Apr-Oct, to 5pm Nov-Mar) FREE Located in the village of Wies, just off the B17 between Füssen and Schongau, the Wieskirche is one of Bavaria's best-known baroque churches and a Unesco-listed heritage site. About a million visitors a year flock to see its pride and joy, the monumental work of the legendary artist-brothers, Dominikus and Johann Baptist Zimmermann.

In 1730, a farmer in Steingaden, about 30km northeast of Füssen, witnessed the miracle in his Christ statue shedding tears. Pilgrims poured into the town in such numbers over the next decade that the local abbot commissioned a new church to house the weepy work. Inside the almost circular structure, eight snow-white pillars are topped by gold capital stones and swirling decorations. The unsupported dome must have seemed like God's work in the mid-17th century, its surface adorned with a pastel ceiling fresco celebrating Christ's resurrection.

From Füssen, regional RVO bus 73 (www.rvo-bus.de) makes the journey four times daily. The Romantic Road Coach (p248) also stops here long enough in both directions to enable a brief look round and then get back on. By car, take the B17 northeast and turn right (east) at Steingaden.

Schloss Linderhof

Schloss Linderhof CASTLE
(www.schlosslinderhof.de; adult/concession €8.50/7.50; ⊙9am-6pm Apr-mid-Oct, 10am-4pm mid-Oct–Mar) A pocket-sized trove of weird treasures, Schloss Linderhof was Ludwig II's smallest but most sumptuous palace, and

the only one he lived to see fully completed. Finished in 1878, the palace hugs a steep hillside in a fantasy landscape of French gardens, fountains and follies. The reclusive king used the palace as a retreat and hardly ever received visitors here. Linderhof was inspired by Versailles and dedicated to Louis XIV, the French 'sun king'.

Linderhof's myth-laden, jewel-encrusted rooms are a monument to the king's excesses that so unsettled the governors in Munich. The **private bedroom** is the largest, heavily ornamented and anchored by an enormous 108-candle crystal chandelier weighing 500kg. An artificial waterfall, built to cool the room in summer, cascades just outside the window. The **dining room** reflects the king's fetish for privacy and inventions. The king ate from a mechanised dining board, whimsically labelled 'Table, Lay Yourself', that sank through the floor so that his servants could replenish it without being seen.

Created by the famous court gardener Carl von Effner, the gardens and outbuildings, open April to October, are as fascinating as the castle itself. The highlight here is the oriental-style **Moorish Kiosk**, where Ludwig, dressed in oriental garb, would preside over nightly entertainment from a peacock throne. Underwater light dances on the stalactites at the **Venus Grotto**, an artificial cave inspired

LUDWIG II, THE FAIRY-TALE KING

Every year on 13 June, a stirring ceremony takes place in Berg, on the eastern shore of Lake Starnberg. A small boat quietly glides towards a cross just offshore and a plain wreath is fastened to its front. The sound of a single trumpet cuts the silence as the boat returns from this solemn ritual in honour of the most beloved king ever to rule Bavaria: Ludwig II.

The cross marks the spot where Ludwig died under mysterious circumstances in 1886. His early death capped the life of a man at odds with the harsh realities of a modern world no longer in need of a romantic and idealistic monarch.

Prinz Otto Ludwig Friedrich Wilhelm was a sensitive soul, fascinated by romantic epics, architecture and music, but his parents, Maximilian II and Marie, took little interest in his musings and he suffered a lonely and joyless childhood. In 1864, at 18 years old, the prince became king. He was briefly engaged to the sister of Elisabeth (Sisi), the Austrian empress, but, as a rule, he preferred the company of men. He also worshipped composer Richard Wagner, whose Bayreuth opera house was built with Ludwig's funds.

Ludwig was an enthusiastic leader initially, but Bavaria's days as a sovereign state were numbered, and he became a puppet king after the creation of the German Reich in 1871 (which had its advantages, as Bismarck gave Ludwig a hefty allowance). Ludwig withdrew completely to drink, draw up castle plans and view concerts and operas in private. His obsession with French culture and the Sun King, Louis XIV, inspired the fantastical palaces of **Neuschwanstein** (p230), **Linderhof** (p233) and **Herrenchiemsee** (p243) – lavish projects that spelt his undoing.

Contrary to popular belief, it was only Ludwig's purse – and not the state treasury – that was being bankrupted. However, by 1886 his ever-growing mountain of debt and erratic behaviour had put him at odds with his cabinet. The king, it seemed, needed to be 'managed'.

In January 1886, several ministers and relatives arranged a hasty psychiatric test that diagnosed Ludwig as mentally unfit to rule (this was made easier by the fact that his brother had been declared insane years earlier). That June, he was removed to Schloss Berg on Lake Starnberg. A few days later the dejected bachelor and his doctor took a Sunday evening lakeside walk and were found several hours later, drowned in just a few feet of water.

No one knows with certainty what happened that night. There was no eyewitness nor any proper criminal investigation. The circumstantial evidence was conflicting and incomplete. Reports and documents were tampered with, destroyed or lost. Conspiracy theories abound. That summer the authorities opened Neuschwanstein to the public to help pay off Ludwig's huge debts. King Ludwig II was dead, but the myth, and a tourist industry, had been born.

by a stage set for Wagner's *Tannhäuser*. Now sadly empty, Ludwig's fantastic conch-shaped boat is moored by the shore.

Linderhof is about 13km west of Oberammergau and 26km northwest of Garmisch-Partenkirchen. Bus 9622 travels to Linderhof from Oberammergau nine times a day. If coming from Garmisch-Partenkirchen change in Ettal or Oberammergau. The last service from Linderhof is just before 6pm but, if you miss it, the 13km vista-rich hike back to Oberammergau is an easygoing amble along the valley floor through shady woodland.

Oberammergau

08822 / POP 5100

Quietly quaint Oberammergau occupies a wide valley surrounded by the dark forests and snow-dusted peaks of the Ammergauer Alps. The centre is packed with traditional painted houses, woodcarving shops and awestruck tourists who come here to learn about the town's world-famous Passion Play. It's also a great budget base for hikes and cross-country skiing trips into easily accessible Alpine back country.

Sights & Activities

Passionstheater   THEATRE
(08822-945 8833; www.passionstheater.de; Othmar-Weis-Strasse 1; combined tour & Oberammergau Museum entry adult/concession €8/7; ⊙ tours 10am & 2pm in German, 11pm in English Apr-Oct & Dec) The Passionstheater, where the Passion Play is performed, can be visited as part of a guided tour. The tour provides ample background on the play's history and also lets you peek at the costumes and sets.

Ask at the tourist office about music, plays and opera performances that take place here over the summer.

Pilatushaus   NOTABLE BUILDING
(Ludwig-Thoma-Strasse 10; ⊙ 1-5pm Tue-Sat mid-May–mid-Oct) FREE Aside from the Passion Play, Oberammergau's other claim to fame is its Lüftmalerei, the eye-popping house facades painted in an illusionist style. The pick of the crop is the amazing Pilatushaus, whose painted columns snap into 3-D as you approach. It contains a gallery and several workshops.

Oberammergau Museum   MUSEUM
(08822-941 36; www.oberammergaumuseum.de; Dorfstrasse 8; combined museum entry & Passiontheater tour adult/concession €8/7; ⊙ 10am–

5pm Tue-Sun Apr-Oct) This is one of the best places to view exquisite examples of Oberammergau's famously intricate woodcarving art. The village has a long tradition of craftspeople producing anything from an entire nativity scene in a single walnut shell to a life-size Virgin Mary. If you get the urge to take some home, plenty of specialist shops around town sell pricey pieces.

Festivals & Events

Passion Play   THEATRE
(www.passionplay-oberammergau.com) A blend of opera, ritual and Hollywood epic, the Passion Play has been performed every year ending in a zero (plus some extra years for a variety of reasons) since the late 17th century as a collective thank-you from the villagers for being spared the plague.

Half the village takes part, sewing amazing costumes and growing hair and beards for their roles (no wigs or false hair allowed). The next performances will take place between May and October 2020, but tours of the Passionstheater enable you to take a peek at the costumes and sets anytime.

The next performances will take place between May and October 2020, but tours of the Passionstheater enable you to take a peek at the costumes and sets anytime. The theatre doesn't lie dormant in the decade between Passion Plays – ask at the tourist office about music, plays and opera performances that take place here over the summer.

Sleeping & Eating

DJH Hostel   HOSTEL €
(08822-4114; www.oberammergau.jugendherberge.de; Malensteinweg 10; dm from €22.90) This hostel provides immaculate en suite rooms, a guest kitchen and a filling Alpine breakfast.

Gästehaus Richter   B&B €
(08822-935 765; www.gaestehaus-richter.de; Welfengasse 2; s/d €39/70;) The best deal in Oberammergau, this family-run guesthouse offers well-maintained rooms with some traditional Alpine elements, a guest kitchen and a hearty breakfast.

Hotel Turmwirt   HOTEL €€
(08822-926 00; www.turmwirt.de; Ettalerstrasse 2; s/d from €75/99;) This recently updated hotel next to the church has pristine business-standard rooms, some with Alpine views from the balconies and bits of woodcarving art throughout.

ⓘ ALPINE GUEST CARDS

Overnight anywhere in Garmisch-Partenkirchen and Oberammergau and your hotel or guesthouse should issue you with a free *Gästekarte*, which gives free bus travel anywhere between Garmisch-Partenkirchen and Füssen as well as many other discounts.

Mundart   BAVARIAN €€
(⌷08822-949 7565; www.restaurant-mundart.de; Bahnhofstrasse 12; mains €11.60-17.90; ⊘11am-11pm Wed-Sun; 🖘) Mouth-wateringly light, 21st-century versions of Bavarian classics await at this trendy, baby-blue and grey themed restaurant near the train station. The menu is reassuringly brief, prices reasonable and the service the best in the village. Always a choice of dishes for noncarnivores.

ⓘ Information

Tourist Office (⌷08822-922 740; www.ammergauer-alpen.de; Eugen-Papst-Strasse 9a; ⊘9am-6pm Mon-Fri, 9am-1pm Sat & Sun, closed Sat & Sun Nov-Mar) The tourist office can help find accommodation.

ⓘ Getting There & Around

Hourly trains connect Munich with Oberammergau (change at Murnau; €19.80, 1¾ hours). Hourly RVO bus 9606 goes direct to Garmisch-Partenkirchen via Ettal; change at Echelsbacher Brücke for Füssen.

Ettal

Kloster Ettal   MONASTERY
(www.kloster-ettal.de; Kaiser-Ludwig-Platz 1; ⊘8.30am-noon & 1.15-5.45pm Mon-Sat, 9-10.45am & 2.30-5.30pm Sun) FREE Ettal would be just another bend in the road were it not for this famous monastery. The highlight here is the sugary rococo basilica housing the monks' prized possession, a marble Madonna brought from Rome by Ludwig der Bayer in 1330. However, some might argue that the real high point is sampling the monastically distilled Ettaler Klosterlikör, an equally sugary herbal digestif.

Ettal is 5km south of Oberammergau, an easy hike along the Ammer River. Otherwise take bus 9606 from Garmisch-Partenkirchen or Oberammergau.

Garmisch-Partenkirchen
⌷08821 / POP 26,000

An incredibly popular hang-out for outdoorsy types, skiing fans and day trippers from Munich, the double-barrelled resort of Garmisch-Partenkirchen is blessed with a fabled setting a snowball's throw from the Alps. To say you 'wintered in Garmisch' still has an aristocratic ring, and the area offers some of the best skiing in the land, including runs on Germany's highest peak, the Zugspitze (2964m).

The towns of Garmisch and Partenkirchen were merged for the 1936 Winter Olympics and, to this day, host international skiing events. Each retains its own distinct character: Garmisch has a more 21st-century feel, while Partenkirchen has retained its oldworld Alpine village vibe.

Garmisch-Partenkirchen also makes a handy base for excursions to Ludwig II's palaces, including nearby Schloss Linderhof (p233) and the lesser-known Jagdschloss Schachen, as well as Oberammergau (p235) and even, at a push, Neuschwanstein (p230) and Hohenschwangau (p231) castles.

⊙ Sights

Zugspitze   MOUNTAIN
(www.zugspitze.de; return adult/child €51/29.50; ⊘train 8.15am-2.15pm) On good days, views from Germany's rooftop extend into four countries. The round trip starts in Garmisch aboard a cogwheel train (Zahnradbahn) that chugs along the mountain base to the Eibsee, an idyllic forest lake. From here, the Eibsee-Seilbahn, a super-steep cable car, swings to the top at 2962m. When you're done admiring the views, the Gletscherbahn cable car takes you to the Zugspitze glacier at 2600m, from where the cogwheel train heads back to Garmisch.

The trip to the Zugspitze summit is as memorable as it is popular; beat the crowds by starting early in the day and, if possible, skip weekends altogether.

Partnachklamm   CANYON
(www.partnachklamm.eu; adult/concession €4/2.50; ⊘8am-6pm) A top attraction around Garmisch is this narrow and dramatically beautiful 700m-long gorge with walls rising up to 80m. The trail hewn into the rock is especially spectacular in winter when you can walk beneath curtains of icicles and frozen waterfalls.

Around Garmisch-Partenkirchen

Jagdschloss Schachen   CASTLE
(☑ 08822-920 30; adult/concession €4.50/3.50;
⊙ tours 11am, 1pm, 2pm & 3pm Jun-Sep) A popular hiking route is to King Ludwig II's hunting lodge, Jagdschloss Schachen, which can
be reached via the Partnachklamm in about
a four-hour hike (10km). A plain wooden hut
from the outside, the interior is surprisingly
magnificent; the **Moorish Room** is something straight out of *Arabian Nights*.

🏃 Activities

Garmisch has two big ski fields: the Zugspitze plateau (2964m) and the Classic Ski
Area (Alpspitze, 2628m; Hausberg, 1340m;
Kreuzeck, 1651m; day pass per adult/child
€39.50/23). Local buses serve all the valley
stations. Cross-country ski trails run along
the main valleys, including a long section
from Garmisch to Mittenwald. If you're a beginner, expect to pay around €60 per day for

group ski lessons, around €45 per hour for
private instruction.

The area around Garmisch-Partenkirchen
is also prime hiking and mountaineering
territory. The tourist office's website has a
superbly interactive tour-planning facility to
help you plot your way through the peaks on
foot, and many brochures and maps are also
available with route suggestions for all levels. Qualified Alpine guides are also on hand
at the tourist office between 4pm and 6pm
Monday and Thursday to answer questions
and provide all kinds of information. Hiking
to the Zugspitze summit is only possible in
summer and is only recommended for those
with experience in mountaineering.

Skischule   SKIING
(Map p239; ☑ 08821-4931; www.skischule-gap.de;
Am Hausberg 8) Ski hire and courses.

ℹ TOP SNOW

A **Top Snow Card** (two days, adult/child €82.50/43.50) covers all the slopes around Garmisch as well as over the border in the Tyrol (an incredible 207km of pistes and 89 ski lifts).

Alpensport Total   SKIING
(Map p239; ☑ 08821-1425; www.alpensporttotal.de; Marienplatz 18) Winter ski school and hire centre that organises other outdoor activities in the warmer months.

Bergsteigerschule Zugspitze   HIKING
(☑ 08821-589 99; www.bergsteigerschule-zugspitze.de; Am Kreuzeckbahnhof 12a) A mountaineering school, offering guided hikes and courses. Located at the lower station of the Alpspitzbahn, southwest of the town.

Deutscher Alpenverein   HIKING
(Map p239; ☑ 08821-2701; www.alpenverein-gapa.de; Carl-Reiser-Strasse 2; ◷ 2-6pm Mon & Tue, 10am-noon & 4-7pm Wed & Thu, 8am-1pm Fri) The German Alpine Club offers guided hikes and courses and its website is a mine of detailed, expertly updated local information, albeit in German only.

🛏 Sleeping

The tourist office operates a 24-hour outdoor room-reservation noticeboard.

Hostel 2962   HOSTEL €
(Map p239; ☑ 08821-909 2674; www.hostel2962-garmisch.com; Partnachauenstrasse 3; dm/d from €20/60; ☎) Touted as a hostel, the somewhat vibe-less 2962 is essentially a typical Garmisch hotel with seven dorms, but a good choice nonetheless. If you can get into one of the four- or five-bed rooms, it's the cheapest sleep in town. Breakfast is an extra €6 if you stay in a dorm.

DJH Hostel   HOSTEL €
(☑ 08821-967 050; www.garmisch.jugendherberge.de; Jochstrasse 10; dm from €24.90; P @ ☎) The standards at this smart, immaculately maintained hostel are as good as at some chain hotels. Rooms have Ikea-style furnishings and fruity colour schemes, and there are indoor and outdoor climbing walls if the Alps are not enough. Located 4.5km north of the town. Arrange a free transfer from the train station.

Hotel Garmischer Hof   HOTEL €€
(Map p239; ☑ 08821-9110; www.garmischer-hof.de; Chamonixstrasse 10; s €59-80, d €98-138;

☎ ⊠) In the ownership of the Seiwald family since 1928, many a climber, skier and Alpine adventurer has creased the sheets at this welcoming inn. Rooms are elegant and cosy with some traditional Alpine touches, the buffet breakfast is served in the vaulted cafe-restaurant, and there's a spa and sauna providing après-ski relief.

Gasthof zum Rassen   HOTEL €€
(☑ 08821-2089; www.gasthof-rassen.de; Ludwigstrasse 45; s €32-53, d €52-90; P ☎) This beautifully frescoed 14th-century building is home to a great option in this price bracket, where the simply furnished, contemporary rooms contrast with the traditionally frilly styling of the communal areas. The cavernous event hall, formerly a brewery, houses Bavaria's oldest folk theatre.

Reindl's Partenkirchner Hof   HOTEL €€€
(Map p239; ☑ 08821-943 870; www.reindls.de; Bahnhofstrasse 15; d incl breakfast €140-230; P @ ☎) Though Reindl's doesn't look like five stars from the outside, this elegant luxury hotel is stacked with perks, a wine bar and a top-notch gourmet restaurant. Rooms are studies in folk-themed elegance and some enjoy gobsmacking mountain views.

🍴 Eating

Hobi's   BAKERY €
(Map p239; Zugspitzstrasse 2; snacks €2-5.50; ◷ 5.45am-12.30pm & 2.30-5.30pm Mon-Fri, 5.45am-noon Sat, 6.30-11am Sun; ☎) G-P's best bakery piles the cakes and sandwiches high and ladles out soup throughout the day. Lots of seats and good wi-fi.

★ Gasthof Fraundorfer   BAVARIAN €€
(www.gasthof-fraundorfer.de; Ludwigstrasse 24; mains €8-19; ◷ 7am-midnight Thu-Mon, from 5pm Wed) If you came to the Alps to experience yodelling, knee slapping and red-faced locals in lederhosen, you just arrived at the right address. Steins of frothing ale fuel the increasingly raucous atmosphere as the evening progresses and monster portions of plattered pig meat push belt buckles to the limit. Decor ranges from baroque cherubs to hunting trophies and the 'Sports Corner'. Unmissable.

Zum Wildschütz   BAVARIAN €€
(Map p239; Bankgasse 9; mains €9-20; ◷ 11.30am-10pm) The best place in town for fresh venison, rabbit, wild boar and other seasonal game dishes, this place is, not surprisingly, popular with hunters. The Tyrolean and south Bavarian takes on schnitzel aren't bad

Garmisch-Partenkirchen

either. If you prefer your victuals critter free, look elsewhere.

Zirbel
PUB FOOD €€

(Map p239; Promenadestrasse 2; mains €8-20; ⊙5pm 1am) Slightly away from the tourists and guarded by a grumpy-looking wood-carved bear, this popular, low-beamed and rustically themed pub serves noodle dishes, salads and schnitzel, all swilled down with Hofbräu beer. Sadly, only open in the evenings.

Bräustüberl
GERMAN €€

(Map p239; ☑ 08821-2312; www.braeustue-berl-garmisch.de; Fürstenstrasse 23; mains €6-19; ⊙10am-1am) This quintessentially Bavarian tavern is the place to cosy up with some lo-cal nosh, served by dirndl-trussed waitress-es, while the enormous enamel coal-burning stove revives chilled extremities. Live music and theatre take place in the upstairs hall.

Hofbräustüberl
BAVARIAN, YUGOSLAV €€

(Map p239; Chamonixstrasse 2; mains €11-20; ⊙11.30am-3pm & 5-11pm) Balkan spice meets south German heartiness at this Bavarian-Yugoslav restaurant right in the thick of things. Despite the seemingly echt-Bayern (authentic Bavarian) name, the long menu is a mixed bag of Alps and Adriat-ic, the interior understated and quite formal, the service top-notch. The Yugoslav wines are a rare treat.

Colosseo
ITALIAN €€

(Map p239; Klammstrasse 7; pizzas €4-9, other mains €5-20; ⊙11.30am-2.30pm & 5-11.30pm) If you fancy an Alpine take on *la dolce vita,* with mountain views and a bit of faux ar-chaeology thrown in, this much-lauded pas-

Garmisch-Partenkirchen

⊕ Activities, Courses & Tours
1 Alpensport Total	A2
2 Deutscher Alpenverein	C1
3 Fahrrad Ostler	A2
4 Skischule	A2

⊜ Sleeping
5 Hostel 2962	C2
6 Hotel Garmischer Hof	B1
7 Reindl's Partenkirchner Hof	D2

⊗ Eating
8 Bräustüberl	A1
9 Colosseo	B2
Hobi's	(see 1)
10 Hofbräustüberl	B1
11 Zirbel	A2
12 Zum Wildschütz	A2

ta and pizza parlour with a mammoth menu is the place to head.

❶ Information

Mountain Rescue (☑ 08821-3611, 112; www.bergwacht-bayern.de; Auenstrasse 7) Mountain rescue station.

Post Office (Map p239; Bahnhofstrasse 31)

Tourist Office (Map p239; ☑ 08821-180 700; www.gapa.de; Richard-Strauss-Platz 2; ⊙9am-6pm Mon-Sat, 10am-noon Sun) Friendly staff hands out maps, brochures and advice.

❶ Getting There & Around

Garmisch-Partenkirchen has hourly connections from Munich (€20.70, one hour 20 minutes); special packages, available from Munich Haupt-bahnhof, combine the return trip with a Zug-spitze day ski pass (around €50).

RVO bus 9606 (www.rvo-bus.de) leaves at 9.40am, reaching the Füssen castles at Neuschwanstein and Hohenschwangau two hours later. On the way back take the 4.13pm bus 9651 and change onto the 9606 at Echelsbacher Brücke or take the direct service at 5.18pm. The 9606 also runs hourly to Oberammergau (40 minutes).

The A95 from Munich is the direct road route. The most central parking is at the Kongresshaus (next to the tourist office).

Bus tickets cost €1.50 for journeys in town. For bike hire, try **Fahrrad Ostler** (Map p239; ☑ 08821-3362; Kreuzstrasse 1; per day/week from €10/40).

Mittenwald

☑ 08823 / POP 7300

Nestled in a cul-de-sac under snowcapped peaks, sleepily alluring Mittenwald, 20km southeast of Garmisch-Partenkirchen, is the most natural spot imaginable for a resort. Known far and wide for its master violin makers, the citizens of this drowsy village seem almost bemused by its popularity. The air is ridiculously clean, and on the main street the loudest noise is a babbling brook.

The **tourist office** (☑ 08823-339 81; mittenwald.de; Dammkarstrasse 3; ⊗ 8.30am-6pm Mon-Fri, 9am-noon Sat, 10am-noon Sun mid-May–mid-Oct, shorter hours rest of the year) has details of excellent hiking and cycling routes. Popular hikes with cable-car access will take you up the grandaddy Alpspitze (2628m), as well as the Wank, Mt Karwendel and the Wettersteinspitze. Return tickets to Karwendel, which boasts Germany's second-highest cable-car route, cost €26.50 per adult and $16.50 per child return.

The Karwendel ski field has one of the longest runs (7km) in Germany, but it is primarily for freestyle pros. All-day ski passes to the nearby Kranzberg ski fields, the best all-round option, cost €27 per adult and €20 per child. For equipment hire and ski/snowboard instruction contact the **Erste Skischule Mittenwald** (☑ 08823-3582; www.skischule-mittenwald.de; Bahnhofsplatz 14).

The only classic off-piste sight in town is the **Geigenbaumuseum** (www.geigenbau-museum-mittenwald.de; Ballenhausgasse 3; adult/concession €4.50/3.50; ⊗ 11am-4pm Tue-Sun), a collection of over 200 locally crafted violins and the tools used to fashion them. It's also the venue for occasional concerts.

Behind a pretty facade, **Hotel-Gasthof Alpenrose** (☑ 08823-927 00; www.alpenrose-mitten-

wald.de; Obermarkt 1; s €30-59, d €77-97) has cosy, old-style rooms, a restaurant and live Bavarian music almost nightly. A short walk from the Obermarkt, **Gaststätte Römerschanz** (Innsbrucker Strasse 30; mains €7-17; ⊗ 10am-midnight Wed-Mon) has Mittenwald's tastiest food.

Mittenwald is served by trains from Garmisch-Partenkirchen (€4.40, 20 minutes, hourly), Munich (€24.20, 1¾ hours, hourly) and Innsbruck (€10.10, one hour, seven daily), across the border in Austria. Otherwise RVO bus 9608 connects Mittenwald with Garmisch-Partenkirchen (30 minutes) several times a day.

Oberstdorf

☑ 08322 / POP 9570

Spectacularly situated in the western Alps, the Allgäu region feels a long, long way from the rest of Bavaria, both in its cuisine (more *Spätzle* than dumplings) and the dialect, which is closer to the Swabian of Baden-Württemberg. The Allgäu's chief draw is the car-free resort of Oberstdorf, a major skiing centre a short hop from Austria.

🏃 Activities

Oberstdorf is almost ringed by towering peaks and offers some top-draw hiking. Skiers value the resort for its friendliness, lower prices and less-crowded pistes. The village is surrounded by 70km of well-maintained cross-country trails and three ski fields: the Nebelhorn, Fellhorn/Kanzelwand and Söllereck. For ski hire and tuition, try **Alpin Skischule** (☑ 08322-952 90; www.alpinskischule.de; Am Bahnhofplatz 1a) opposite the train station or **Erste Skischule Oberstdorf** (☑ 08322-3110; www.skischule-oberstdorf.de; Freiherr-von-Brutscher-Strasse 4).

Gaisalpseen   HIKING
(single/return €31.50/24.50; ⊗ 9am-5pm daily) For an exhilarating day walk, ride the Nebelhorn cable car to the upper station, then hike down via the Gaisalpseen, two lovely alpine lakes (six hours).

Eissportzentrum Oberstdorf   ICE SKATING
(☑ 08322-700 510; www.eissportzentrum-oberstdorf.de/; Rossbichlstrasse 2-6) The Eissportzentrum Oberstdorf, behind the Nebelhorn cable-car station, is the biggest ice-skating complex in Germany, with three separate rinks.

🛏 Sleeping

Oberstdorf is chock-full with private guesthouses, but owners are usually reluctant to rent rooms for just a single night, even in the quieter shoulder seasons.

DJH Hostel
HOSTEL €

(☏ 08322-987 50; www.oberstdorf.jugendherberge. de; Kornau 8; dm €28.90; 🛜) A relaxed, 200-bed chalet-hostel with commanding views of the Allgäu Alps. Take bus 1 from the bus station in front of the Hauptbahnhof to the Reute stop; it's in the suburb of Kornau, near the Söllereck chairlift.

Haus Edelweiss
APARTMENTS €€

(☏ 08322-959 60; www.edelweiss.de; Freibergstrasse 7; apt from €107; P⊜🛜) As crisp and sparkling as freshly fallen alpine snow, this new apartment hotel just a couple of blocks from the tourist office has 19 pristine, self-contained flats with fully equipped kitchens, ideal for stays of three nights or more. Generally the longer you tarry, the fewer euros per night you spend.

Weinklause
GUESTHOUSE €€

(☏ 08322-969 30; www.weinklause.de; Prinzenstrasse 10; s €73, d €110-172; P🛜) Willing to take one-nighters at the drop of a felt hat, this superb lodge offers all kinds of rooms and apartments, some with kitchenettes, others with jaw-dropping, spectacular alpine views. A generous breakfast is served in the restaurant, which comes to life most nights with local live music.

✖ Eating & Drinking

Weinstube am Frohmarkt
TYROLEAN €€

(☏ 08322-3988; www.weinstube-oberstdorf.de; Am Frohmarkt 2; mains €10-19; ⊙5pm-midnight Mon-Sat) 'Where did Bavaria go?' you might exclaim at this intimate wine bar, where the musty-sweet aroma of wine, cheese and Tyrolean cured ham scents the air. Rub shoulders with locals downstairs over a plate of wild boar or Tessin-style turkey steak, or retreat upstairs for a quiet nip of wine.

Nordi Stüble
SWABIAN €€

(☏ 08322-7641; cnr Walserstrasse & Luitpoldstrasse; mains €9-20; ⊙11am-10pm Mon-Sat) Family owned and run, this intimate neighbourhood eatery, a small wood-panelled dining room bedecked in rural junk of yesteryear, is the place to enjoy local takes on schnitzel and *Maultaschen*. All dishes are prepared fresh, so be prepared to wait; a Stuttgart Dinkelacker beer is the way to wash it all down.

Oberstdorfer Dampfbierbrauerei
BREWERY

(www.dampfbierbrauerei.de; Bahnhofplatz 8; ⊙11am-1am) Knock back a few 'steamy ales' at Germany's southernmost brewery, right next to the train station.

ℹ Information

Tourist Office (☏ 08322-7000; www.oberstdorf.de; Prinzregenten-Platz 1; ⊙9am-5pm Mon-Fri, 9.30am-noon Sat) The tourist office and its branch office (Bahnhofplatz; ⊙10am-5pm daily) run a room-finding service.

ℹ Getting There & Away

There are at least five direct trains daily from Munich (€32.70, 2½ hours), otherwise change in Buchloe. The train station is a short walk north of the town centre on Bahnhofstrasse.

Andechs

Kloster Andechs
MONASTERY

(☏ 08152-376 253; www.andechs.de; admission free; ⊙8am-6pm Mon-Fri, 9am-6pm Sat, 9.45am-6pm Sun) Founded in the 10th century, the gorgeous hilltop monastery of Andechs has long been a place of pilgrimage, though today more visitors come to slurp the Benedictines' fabled ales.

The church owns two relics of enormous importance: branches that are thought to come from Christ's crown of thorns, and a victory cross of Charlemagne, whose army overran much of Western Europe in the 9th century. In the Holy Chapel, the votive candles, some of them over 1m tall, are among Germany's oldest. The remains of Carl Orff, the composer of *Carmina Burana*, are interred here as well.

Outside, soak up the magnificent views of the purple-grey Alps and forested hills before plunging into the nearby **Bräustüberl** (⊙10am-8pm), the monks' beer hall and garden. There are seven varieties of beer on offer, from the rich and velvety Doppelbock dark to the fruity unfiltered *Weissbier* (wheat beer). The place is incredibly popular and, on summer weekends, you may have to join a queue of day trippers at the door to get in.

The easiest way to reach Andechs from Munich is to take the S8 to Herrsching (49 minutes), then change to bus 951 or the private Ammersee-Reisen bus (€2.20, nine times daily). Alternatively, it's a pleasant 4km hike south from Herrsching through the protected woodland of the Kiental.

BAVARIA ANDECHS

Bad Tölz

📞 08041 / POP 18.000

Situated some 40km south of central Munich, Bad Tölz is a pretty spa town straddling the Isar River. The town's gentle inclines provide a delightful spot for its attractive, frescoed houses and the quaint shops of the old town. At weekends thousands flock here from Munich to enjoy the town's famous, ultramodern swimming complex, Alpine slide and hiking trips along the river. Bad Tölz is also the gateway to the Tölzer Land region and its emerald-green lakes, the Walchensee and the Kochelsee.

◉ Sights & Activities

Cobblestoned and car-free, Marktstrasse is flanked by statuesque town houses with ornate overhanging eaves that look twice as high on the sloping street.

Kalvarienberg LANDMARK

Above the town, on Kalvarienberg, looms Bad Tölz' landmark, the twin-towered Kalvarienbergkirche (Cavalry Church). This enormous baroque structure stands side by side with the petite Leonhardikapelle (Leonhardi Chapel; 1718), the destination of the town's well-known Leonhardi pilgrimage.

Stadtmuseum MUSEUM

(📞 08041-793 5156; Marktstrasse 48; adult/concession €2/1.50; ⊙10am-5pm Tue-Sun) The Stadtmuseum touches on practically all aspects of local culture and history, with a fine collection of painted armoires (the so-called Tölzer Kasten), a 2m-tall, single-stringed *Nonnengeige* (marine trumpet), examples of traditional glass painting and a cart used in the Leonhardifahrt.

Alpamare SPA

(📞 08041-509 999; www.alpamare.de; Ludwigstrasse 14; day pass adult/child €35/25; ⊙9.30am-10pm) In the spa section of town, west of the Isar River, you'll find the fantastic water complex Alpamare, Europe's first covered aquapark. This huge centre has heated indoor and outdoor mineral pools, a wave and surfing pool, a series of wicked water slides (including Germany's longest, the 330m-long Alpabob-Wildwasser), saunas, solariums and its own hotel. Bus 9570 from the train station stops 100m away.

Blomberg HIKING

Southwest of Bad Tölz, the Blomberg (1248m) is a family-friendly mountain that has a natural toboggan track in winter, plus easy hiking and a fun Alpine slide in summer. Unless you're walking, getting up the hill involves, weather permitting, a chairlift ride aboard the **Blombergbahn** (www.blombergbahn.de; top station adult/child return €9.50/4; ⊙11am-4pm Sat & Sun).

Over 1km long, the fibreglass Alpine toboggan track snakes down the mountain from the middle station. You zip down at up to 50km/h through the 17 hairpin bends on little wheeled bobsleds with a joystick to control braking. A long-sleeved shirt and jeans will provide a little protection. Riding up to the midway station and sliding down costs €5 per adult (€4 concession), with discounts for multiple trips.

To reach Blomberg, take RVO bus 9612 from the train station to the Blombergbahn stop.

✹ Festivals & Events

Leonhardifahrt RELIGIOUS L

(www.bad-toelz.de) Every year on 6 November, residents pay homage to the patron saint of horses, Leonhard. The famous Leonhardifahrt is a pilgrimage up to the Leonhardi chapel on Kalvarienberg, where townsfolk dress up in traditional costume and ride dozens of garlanded horse carts to the strains of brass bands.

🛏 Sleeping & Eating

Posthotel Kolberbräu HOTEL €€

(📞 08041-768 80; www.kolberbraeu.de; Marktstrasse 29; s/d from €55/96; 🛜) Very well appointed 30-room inn amid the bustle of the main street, with hefty timber furniture, a classic Bavarian restaurant and a tradition going back over four centuries.

Gasthof Zantl BAVARIAN €€

(www.gasthof-zantl.de; Salzstrasse 31; mains €8-18; ⊙11.30am-2.30pm & 5pm-late, closed Thu) One of Bad Tölz' oldest buildings, this convivial tavern has a predictably pork-heavy menu, with ingredients sourced from local villages as much as possible. There's a sunny beer garden out front.

ℹ Information

Tourist Office (📞 08041-793 5156; www.bad-toelz.de; Marktstrasse 48; ⊙10am-5pm Tue-Sun)

ⓘ Getting There & Away

The private **Bayerische Oberlandbahn** (BOB; ☑ 08024-99/ 171; www.bayerischeoberland-bahn.de) runs at least hourly trains between Bad Tölz and Munich Hauptbahnhof (€12.50, 50 minutes). Alternatively, take the S2 from central Munich to Holzkirchen, then change to the BOB. In Holzkirchen make sure you board the Bad Tölz–bound portion of the train. The BOB/ Alpamare KombiTicket (adult/child €39/28) entitles the holder to return 2nd class travel to/ from Munich, bus travel from the train station to Alpamare and entry to Alpamare for four hours.

Chiemsee

☑ 08051

Most foreign visitors arrive at the shores of the Bavarian Sea – as Chiemsee is affection-ately known – in search of King Ludwig II's Schloss Herrenchiemsee. This is Bavaria's biggest lake (if you don't count Bodensee which is only partially in the state) and its natural beauty and water sports make the area popular with de-stressing city dwellers, and many affluent Munich residents own weekend retreats by its shimmering waters.

The towns of Prien am Chiemsee and, about 5km south, Bernau am Chiemsee (both on the Munich–Salzburg rail line) are good bases for exploring the lake. Of the two towns, Prien is by far the larger and liveli-er. If you're day tripping to Herrenchiemsee, conveniently interconnecting transport is available. To explore further, you'll probably need a set of wheels.

◎ Sights

Schloss Herrenchiemsee CASTLE
(☑ 08051-688 70; www.herren-chiemsee.de; adult/ concession €10/9; ☺ tours 9am-6pm Apr-Oct, 9.40am-4.15pm Nov-Mar) An island just 1.5km across the Chiemsee from Prien, Herreninsel, is home to Ludwig II's Versailles-inspired cas-tle. Begun in 1878, it was never intended as a residence, but as a homage to absolutist mon-archy, as epitomised by Ludwig's hero, Louis XIV. Ludwig spent only 10 days here and even then was rarely seen, preferring to read at night and sleep all day. The palace is typical of Ludwig's creations, the product of his roman-tic obsessions and unfettered imagination.

Ludwig splurged more money on this pal-ace than on Neuschwanstein and Linderhof combined, but when cash ran out in 1885, one year before his death, 50 rooms remained unfinished. Those that were completed outdo each other in opulence. The vast **Gesand-tentreppe** (Ambassador Staircase), a double staircase leading to a frescoed gallery and topped by a glass roof, is the first visual knock-out on the guided tour, but that fades in com-parison to the stunning **Grosse Spiegel-galerie** (Great Hall of Mirrors). This tunnel of light runs the length of the garden (98m, or 10m longer than that in Versailles). It sports 52 candelabra and 33 great glass chandeliers with 7000 candles, which took 70 servants half an hour to light. In late July it becomes a wonderful venue for classical concerts.

The **Paradeschlafzimmer** (State Bed-room) features a canopied bed that perch-es altar-like on a pedestal behind a golden balustrade. This was the heart of the pal-ace, where morning and evening audiences were held. But it's the king's bedroom, the **Kleines Blaues Schlafzimmer** (Little Blue Bedroom), that really takes the cake. The decoration is sickly sweet, encrusted with gilded stucco and wildly extravagant carv-ings. The room is bathed in a soft blue light emanating from a glass globe at the foot of the bed. It supposedly took 18 months for a technician to perfect the lamp to the king's satisfaction.

Admission to the palace also entitles you to a spin around the **König-Ludwig II-Museum**, where you can see the king's christening and coronation robes, more blueprints of megalomaniac buildings and his death mask.

To reach the palace, take the hourly or half-hourly ferry from Prien-Stock (€7.60 re-turn, 15 to 20 minutes) or from Bernau-Felden (€7.90, 25 minutes, May to October). From the boat landing on Herreninsel, it's about a 20-minute walk through pretty gardens to the palace. Palace tours, offered in German or English, last 30 minutes.

Fraueninsel ISLAND
A third of this tiny island is occupied by **Frauenwörth Abbey** (www.frauenwoerth.de) **FREE**, founded in the late 8th century, mak-ing it one of the oldest abbeys in Bavaria. The 10th-century church, whose free-standing campanile sports a distinctive onion-dome top (11th century), is worth a visit. Opposite the church is the AD 860 Carolingian **Torh-alle** (admission €2; ☺ 10am-6pm May-Oct). It houses medieval objets d'art, sculpture and changing exhibitions of regional paintings from the 18th to the 20th centuries.

Return ferry fare, including a stop at Herreninsel, is €8.60 from Prien-Stock and €8.90 from Bernau-Felden.

🏃 Activities

The swimming beaches at Chieming and Gstadt (both free) are the easiest to reach, on the lake's eastern and northern shores respectively. A variety of boats are available for hire at many beaches, for €13 to €25 per hour. In Prien, **Bootsverleih Stöffl** (www. stoeffl.de; Strandpromenade) is possibly the best company to turn to.

Prienavera   SWIMMING
(☑ 08051-609 570; www.prienavera.de; Seestrasse 120; 4hr pass adult/child €11/6, day pass €13/7; ☺10am-10pm Mon-Fri, 9am-10pm Sat & Sun) The futuristic-looking glass roof by the harbour in Prien-Stock shelters Prienavera, a popular pool complex with a wellness area, water slides and a restaurant.

🛌 Sleeping

Panorama Camping Harras   CAMPGROUND €
(☑ 08051-904 613; www.camping-harras.de; Harrasser Strasse 135; per person/tent/car from €5.90/4.60/3) This camping ground is scenically located on a peninsula with its own private beach, and catamaran and surfboard hire. The restaurant has a delightful lakeside terrace.

Hotel Bonnschlössl   HOTEL €€
(☑ 08051-961 400; www.bonnschloessl.de; Ferdinand-Bonn-Strasse 2, Bernau; s €51-64, d €88-111; 🛜) Built in 1477, this pocket-size 21-room palace hotel with faux turrets once belonged to the Bavarian royal court. Rooms are stylish, if slightly overfurnished, and there's a wonderful terrace with a rambling garden. There's a small spa area, a library and a lobby bar, but no restaurant.

Hotel Garni Möwe   HOTEL €€
(☑ 08051-5004; www.hotel-garni-moewe.de; Seestrasse 111, Prien; d €59-128; 🛜🏊) This traditional Bavarian hotel right on the lakefront is excellent value, especially the loft rooms. It has its own bike and boat hire, plus a fitness centre, and the large garden is perfect for travellers with children.

Luitpold am See   HOTEL €€
(☑ 08051-609 100; www.herrenchiemsee-schloss-hotel.de; Seestrasse 101, Prien; s €57-79, d €112-150; 🛜) Right on the lake shore in Prien, the 54 rooms at this excellent choice offer a good price to standard ratio, with their pristine bathrooms, wood-rich furnishings and pretty views. There's an onsite restaurant and *Konditorei* (cafe-bakery) and reception can help out with travel arrangements, tours and such.

🍴 Eating

Alter Wirt   BAVARIAN €€
(Kirchplatz 9, Bernau; mains €9.50-17.50; ☺11am-11pm Tue-Sun) This massive half-timbered inn with five centuries of history, situated on Bernau's main street, plates up south German meat blocks and international standards to a mix of locals and tourists. For dessert why not try 'Hot Love' (*Heisse Liebe*) – vanilla and chocolate ice cream with hot raspberry sauce and cream.

Badehaus   BAVARIAN €€
(☑ 08051-970 300; Rathausstrasse 11; mains €7-18; ☺10am-late) Near the Chiemsee Info-Center and the lake shore, this fancy restaurant, contemporary beer hall and garden has quirky decor and gourmet-style fare priced for all wallet capacities. The Jazzkeller beneath the complex puts on regular jam sessions and other musical events in the evenings.

Westernacher am See   MODERN BAVARIAN €€
(☑ 08051-4722; www.westernacher-chiemsee.de; Seestrasse 115, Prien; mains €7.90-19.50) This lakeside dining haven has a multiple personality, with a cosy restaurant, cocktail bar, cafe, beer garden and glassed-in winter terrace. The long menu is an eclectic affair combining pizzas, Bavarian favourites, Italian pasta, Thai curries and Chiemsee fish dishes.

ℹ️ Information

Bernau Tourist Office (☑ 08051-986 80; www.bernau-am-chiemsee.de; Aschauer Strasse 10; ☺8.30am-6pm Mon-Fri, 9am-noon Sat, shorter hours mid-Sep–Jun)

Chiemsee Tourist Office (☑ 08051-965 550; www.chiemsee-alpenland.de; Felden 10; ☺10am-12.30pm & 1.30-6.30pm Mon-Fri) On the southern lake shore, near the Bernau-Felden autobahn exit.

Prien Tourist Office (☑ 08051-690 50; www.tourismus.prien.de; Alte Rathausstrasse 11; ☺8.30am-5pm Mon-Fri, to 4pm Sat, closed Sat Oct-Apr)

ℹ️ Getting There & Around

Meridian trains run hourly from Munich to Prien (€17.90, 55 minutes) and Bernau (€19.80, one hour). Hourly RVO bus 9505 connects the two lake towns.

Local buses run from Prien Bahnhof to the harbour in Stock. You can also take the historic **Chiemseebahn** (www.chiemsee-schifffahrt.de; one-way/return €2.70/3.70), the world's oldest narrow-gauge steam train (1887).

Chiemsee Schifffahrt (☑ 08051-6090; www.chiemsee-schifffahrt.de; Seestrasse 108) operates half-hourly to hourly ferries from Prien with stops at Herreninsel, Fraueninsel, Seebruck and Chieming on a schedule that changes seasonally. You can circumnavigate the entire lake and make all these stops (getting off and catching the next ferry that comes your way) for €12.20. Children aged six to 15 get a 50% discount.

Chiemgauer Radhaus (⊘08051-4631; Bahnhofsplatz 6) and **Chiemgau Biking** (⊘08051-961 4973; www.chiemgau-biking.de; Chiemseestrasse 84) hire out mountain bikes for between €12 and €22 per day.

Berchtesgaden

⊘08652 / POP 7800

Wedged into Austria and framed by six formidable mountain ranges, the Berchtesgadener Land is a drop-dead-gorgeous corner of Bavaria steeped in myths and legends. Local lore has it that angels given the task of distributing the earth's wonders were startled by God's order to get a move on and dropped them all here. These most definitely included the Watzmann (2713m), Germany's second-highest mountain, and the pristine Königssee, perhaps Germany's most photogenic body of water.

Much of the area is protected by law within the Berchtesgaden National Park, which was declared a 'biosphere reserve' by Unesco in 1990. The village of Berchtesgaden is the obvious base for hiking circuits into the park.

Away from the trails, the main draws are the mountaintop Eagle's Nest, a lodge built for Hitler and now a major dark-tourism destination, and Dokumentation Obersalzberg, a museum that chronicles the region's sinister Nazi past.

◉ Sights

Eagle's Nest HISTORIC SITE
(Kehlsteinhaus; ⊘08652-2969; www.kehlsteinhaus.de; Obersalzberg; adult/child €16.10/9.30; ⊘buses 7.40am-4pm mid-May–Oct) The Eagle's Nest was built as a mountaintop retreat for Hitler, and gifted to him on his 50th birthday. It took some 3000 workers only two years to carve the precipitous 6km-long mountain road, cut a 124m-long tunnel and a brass-panelled lift through the rock, and build the lodge itself (now a restaurant). It can only be reached by special shuttle bus from the Kehlsteinhaus bus station.

On clear days, views from the top are breathtaking. If you're not driving, bus 838 makes the trip to the shuttle bus stop from

the Berchtesgaden Hauptbahnhof every half-hour.

At the mountain station, you'll be asked to book a spot on a return bus. Allow at least two hours to get through lines, explore the lodge and the mountaintop, and perhaps have a bite to eat. Don't panic if you miss your bus – just go back to the mountain station kiosk and rebook.

Königssee LAKE
Crossing the serenely picturesque Königssee makes for some unforgettable memories and once-in-a-lifetime photo opportunities. Cradled by steep mountain walls some 5km south of Berchtesgaden, the emerald-green Königssee is Germany's highest lake (603m), with drinkably pure waters shimmering into fjordlike depths. Bus 841/842 makes the trip out here from the Berchtesgaden train station roughly every hour.

Escape the hubbub of the bustling lakeside tourist village of Schönau by taking an electric **boat tour** (⊘08652-963 696; www.seenschifffahrt.de; Schönau; return boat adult/child €13.90/7; ⊘boats 8am-5.15pm May–mid-Oct) to **St Bartholomä**, a quaint onion-domed chapel on the western shore. At some point, the boat will stop while the captain plays a horn towards the Echo Wall – the sound will bounce seven times. From St Bartholomä, an easy trail leads to the wondrous **Eiskapelle** (ice chapel) in about one hour.

You can also skip the crowds by meandering along the lake shore. It's a nice and easy 3.5km return walk to the secluded **Malerwinkel** (Painter's Corner), a lookout famed for its picturesque vantage point.

Dokumentation Obersalzberg MUSEUM
(⊘08652-947 960; www.obersalzberg.de; Salzbergstrasse 41, Obersalzberg; adult/concession €3/free, audioguide €2; ⊘9am-5pm daily Apr-Oct, 10am-3pm Tue-Sun Nov-Mar, last entry 1hr before closing) In 1933 the quiet mountain village of Obersalzberg (3km from Berchtesgaden) became the second seat of Nazi power after Berlin, a dark period that's given the full historical treatment at this excellent exhibit. It documents the forced takeover of the area, the construction of the compound and the daily life of the Nazi elite. All facets of Nazi terror are dealt with, including Hitler's near-mythical appeal, his racial politics, the resistance movement, foreign policy and the death camps.

A section of the underground bunker network is open for perusal. Hourly bus 838 from Berchtesgaden train station will get you there.

BAVARIA BERCHTESGADEN

Salzbergwerk
HISTORIC SITE

(www.salzzeitreise.de; Bergwerkstrasse 83; adult/child €16/9.50; ⊙9am-5pm May-Oct, 11am-3pm Nov-Apr) Once a major producer of 'white gold', Berchtesgaden has thrown open its salt mines for fun-filled 90-minute tours. Kids especially love donning miners' garb and whooshing down a wooden slide into the depths of the mine. Down below, highlights include mysteriously glowing salt grottoes and crossing a 100m-long subterranean salt lake on a wooden raft. Take hourly bus 848 from Berchtesgaden train station.

🏃 Activities

Berchtesgaden National Park
NATIONAL PARK

(www.nationalpark-berchtesgaden.de) The wilds of this 210-sq-km park offer some of the best hiking in Germany. A good introduction is a 2km trail up from St Bartholomä beside the Königssee to the notorious Watzmann-Ostwand, where scores of mountaineers have met their deaths. Another popular hike goes from the southern end of the Königssee to the Obersee.

For details of routes visit the **national park office** (Haus der Berge; ☑08652-979 0600; Hanielstrasse 7; ⊙9am-5pm), or buy a copy of the *Berchtesgadener Land* (sheet 794) map in the Kompass series.

Jenner-Königssee Area
SKIING

(www.jennerbahn.de; daily pass €31.70) The Jenner-Königssee area at Königssee is the biggest and most varied of five local ski fields. For equipment hire and courses, try **Skischule Treff-Aktiv** (☑08652-667 10; www.skischule-treffaktiv.de; Jennerbahnstrasse 19).

Watzmann Therme
SPA

(☑08652-946 40; www.watzmann-therme.de; Bergwerkstrasse 54; 2hr/4hr/day €10.50/13.90/15.50; ⊙10am-10pm Sun-Thu, to midnight Fri & Sat) The Watzman Therme is Berchtesgaden's thermal wellness complex, with several indoor and outdoor pools and various hydrotherapeutic treatment stations, a sauna and inspiring Alpine views.

👉 Tours

Eagle's Nest Tours
TOUR

(☑08652-649 71; www.eagles-nest-tours.com; adult/child €53/35; ⊙1.15pm mid May-Oct) This highly reputable outfit offers a fascinating overview of Berchtesgaden's Nazi legacy. Guests are taken not only to the Eagle's Nest but around the Obersalzberg area and into the underground bunker system. The four-hour English-language tour departs from the tourist office, across the roundabout opposite the train station. Booking ahead is advisable in July and August.

🛏 Sleeping

DJH Hostel
HOSTEL €

(☑08652-943 70; www.berchtesgaden.jugendherberge.de; Struberberg 6; dm from €22.90; 🛜) This 265-bed hostel is situated in the suburb of Strub, and has great views of Mt Watzmann. It's a 25-minute walk from the Hauptbahnhof or a short hop on bus 839.

KS Hostel Berchtesgaden
HOSTEL €

(☑08652-979 8420; www.hostel-berchtesgaden.de; Bahnhofplatz 4; s/d/dm €26/52/22; 🛜) This basic hostel above a Burger King is actually attached to the railway station, making it good for arrival and departure as well as for accessing buses to the sights. Rooms are spartan but there are no bunks to climb up into and you get 10% off a burger downstairs.

Hotel Krone
HOTEL €€

(☑08652-946 00; www.hotel-krone-berchtesgaden.de; Am Rad 5; s €47-56, d €78-112) Ambling distance from the town centre, this family-run gem provides almost unrivalled views of the valley and the Alps beyond. The wood-rich cabin-style rooms are generously cut affairs, with carved ceilings, niches and bedsteads all in fragrant pine. Take breakfast on the suntrap terrace for a memorable start to the day.

Hotel Bavaria
HOTEL €€

(☑08652-966 10; www.hotelbavaria.net; Sunklergässchen 11; s/d €60/115; 🅿) In the same family for over a century, this well-run hotel offers a romantic vision of Alpine life with rooms bedecked in frilly curtains, canopied beds, heart-shaped mirrors and knotty wood galore. Five of the pricier rooms have private whirlpools. Breakfast is a gourmet affair, with sparkling wine and both hot and cold delectables.

Hotel Vier Jahreszeiten
HOTEL €€

(☑08652-9520; www.hotel-vierjahreszeiten-berchtesgaden.de; Maximilianstrasse 20; s €50-69, d €79-94; 🅿🛜♨) For a taste of Berchtesgaden's storied past, stay at this traditional lodge where Bavarian royalty once crumpled the sheets. Rooms have been updated in the last decade and south-facing (more-expensive) rooms offer dramatic mountain views. After a day's sightseeing, dinner in the hunting lodge-style Hubertusstube restaurant is a real treat.

✗ Eating

Gaststätte St Bartholomä BAVARIAN €€
(☑ 08652-964 937; www.bartholomae-wirt.de; St Bartholomä; mains €7-16; ☺ open according to the boat tour timetable) Perched on the shore of the Königssee, and accessible by boat tour (p245), this is a tourist haunt that actually serves delicious food made with ingredients picked, plucked and hunted from the surrounding forests and the lake. Savour generous platters of venison in mushroom sauce with dumplings and red sauerkraut in the large beer garden or indoors.

Bräustübl BAVARIAN €€
(☑ 08652-976 724; www.braeustueberl-berchtesgaden.de; Bräuhausstrasse 13; mains €6.80-16; ☺ 10am-1am) Past the vaulted entrance painted in Bavaria's white and blue diamonds this cosy beer hall-beer garden is run by the local brewery. Expect a carnivorous feast with such favourite rib-stickers as pork roast and the house speciality: breaded calf's head (tastes better than it sounds). On Friday and Saturday, an oompah band launches into knee-slapping action.

Le Ciel INTERNATIONAL €€€
(☑ 08652-975 50; www.restaurant-leciel.de; Hintereck 1; mains €30-40; ☺ 6.30-10.30pm Wed-Sat) Don't let the Hotel InterConti location turn you off: Le Ciel really is as heavenly as its French name suggests and it has the Michelin star to prove it. Testers were especially impressed by Ulrich Heimann's knack for spinning regional ingredients into inspired gourmet compositions. Service is smooth and the circular dining room is magical. Only 32 seats, so book ahead if you can.

❶ Information

Post Office (Franziskanerplatz 2)
Tourist Office (☑ 08652-896 70; www.berchtesgaden.com; Königsseer Strasse; ☺ 8.30am-6pm Mon-Fri, 9am-5pm Sat, 9am-3pm Sun, reduced hours mid-Oct–Mar) Near the train station, this very helpful office has detailed information on the entire Berchtesgaden region.

❶ Getting There & Around

Travelling from Munich by train involves a change from Meridian to BLB (Berchtesgadener Land Bahn) trains at Freilassing (€33.80, 2½ hours, at least hourly connections). The best option between Berchtesgaden and Salzburg is RVO bus 840 (45 minutes), which leaves from the train station in both towns roughly hourly.

Berchtesgaden is south of the Munich–Salzburg A8 autobahn.

The train station in Berchtesgaden is around 15 minutes' walk from the village centre. The Eagle's Nest, Königssee and Dokumentation Obersalzberg all require trips by bus if you don't have your own transport. Seeing all the sights in a day without your own transport is virtually impossible.

THE ROMANTIC ROAD

From the vineyards of Würzburg to the foot of the Alps, the almost 400km-long Romantic Road (Romantische Strasse) draws two million visitors every year, making it by far the most popular of Germany's holiday routes. This well-trodden trail cuts through a cultural and historical cross-section of southern Germany as it traverses Franconia and clips Baden-Württemberg in the north before plunging into Bavaria proper to end at Ludwig II's crazy castles. Expect lots of Japanese signs and menus, tourist coaches and kitsch galore, but also a fair wedge of *Gemütlichkeit* and geniune hospitality from those who earn their living on this most romantic of routes.

❶ Information

The Romantic Road runs north–south through western Bavaria, covering 385km between Würzburg and Füssen near the Austrian border. It passes through more than two dozen cities and towns, including Rothenburg ob der Tauber, Dinkelsbühl and Augsburg.

❶ Getting There & Away

Though Frankfurt is the most popular gateway for the Romantic Road, Munich is a good choice as well, especially if you decide to take the bus.

With its gentle gradients and bucolic flavour between towns, the Romantic Road is ideal for the holidaying cyclist. Bikes can be hired at many train stations; tourist offices keep lists of bicycle-friendly hotels that permit storage, or check out **Bett und Bike** (www.bettundbike.de) predeparture.

Direct trains run from Munich to Füssen (€26.20, two hours) at the southern end of the Romantic Road every two hours, more often if you change in Buchloe. Rothenburg is linked by train to Würzburg (€13.30, one hour), Munich (from €40.60, three hours), Augsburg (€32.40, 2½ hours) and Nuremberg (€22, 1¼ to two hours), with at least one change needed in Steinach to reach any destination.

❶ Getting Around

It is possible to do this route using train connections and local buses, but the going is complicated, tedious and slow on weekdays, virtually impossible at weekends. The ideal way to travel is by car, though many foreign travellers prefer to take Deutsche Touring's **Romantic Road Coach** (www.romanticroadcoach.de), which can get incredibly crowded in summer. From April to October the special coach runs daily in each direction between Frankfurt and Füssen (for Neuschwanstein); the entire journey takes around 12 hours. There's no charge for breaking the journey and continuing the next day.

Tickets are available for short segments of the trip, and reservations are only necessary during peak-season weekends. Reservations can be made through travel agents, **Deutsche Touring** (www.touring.de, www.romantic-road.com) and Deutsche Bahn's Reisezentrum offices in the train stations. If you stayed on the coach all the way from Frankfurt to Füssen (a pointless exercise), the total fare would be €110. The average fare from one stop to the next is around €5.

Coaches can accommodate bicycles but you must give three working days' notice. Students, children, pensioners and rail-pass holders qualify for discounts of between 10% and 50%.

For detailed schedules and prices, see www.romanticroadcoach.de.

Würzburg

☑ 0931 / POP 133,800

'If I could choose my place of birth, I would consider Würzburg', wrote author Hermann Hesse, and it's not difficult to see why. This scenic town straddles the Main River and is renowned for its art, architecture and delicate wines. A large student population guarantees a lively scene, and plenty of hip nightlife pulsates through its cobbled streets.

Würzburg was a Franconian duchy when, in 686, three Irish missionaries tried to persuade Duke Gosbert to convert to Christianity, and ditch his wife. Gosbert was mulling it over when his wife had the three bumped off. When the murders were discovered decades later, the martyrs became saints and Würzburg was made a pilgrimage city, and, in 742, a bishopric.

For centuries the resident prince-bishops wielded enormous power and wealth, and the city grew in opulence under their rule. Their crowning glory is the Residenz, one of the finest baroque structures in Germany and a Unesco World Heritage Site.

Decimated in WWII when 90% of the city centre was flattened, the authorities originally planned to leave the ruins as a reminder of the horrors of war. But a valiant rebuilding project saw the city restored almost to its pre-war glory.

◎ Sights

★**Würzburg Residenz** PALACE
(www.residenz-wuerzburg.de; Balthasar-Neumann-Promenade; adult/concession/under 18yr €7.50/6.50/free; ◎9am-6pm Apr-Oct, 10am-4.30pm Nov-Mar, 45-min English tours 11am & 3pm, also 4.30pm Apr-Oct) The vast Unesco-listed Residenz, built by 18th-century architect Balthasar Neumann as the home of the local prince-bishops, is one of Germany's most important and beautiful baroque palaces. Top billing goes to the brilliant zigzagging **Treppenhaus** (Staircase), lidded by what still is the world's largest fresco, a masterpiece by Giovanni Battista Tiepolo depicting

---

HITLER'S MOUNTAIN RETREAT

Of all the German towns tainted by the Third Reich, Berchtesgaden has a burden heavier than most. Hitler fell in love with nearby Obersalzberg in the 1920s and bought a small country home, later enlarged into the imposing Berghof.

After seizing power in 1933, Hitler established a part-time headquarters here and brought much of the party brass with him. They bought, or often confiscated, large tracts of land and tore down farmhouses to erect a 2m-high barbed-wire fence. Obersalzberg was sealed off as the fortified southern headquarters of the NSDAP (National Socialist German Workers' Party). In 1938, British prime minister Neville Chamberlain visited for negotiations (later continued in Munich) which led to the infamous promise of 'peace in our time' at the expense of Czechoslovakia's Sudetenland.

Little is left of Hitler's Alpine fortress today. In the final days of WWII, the Royal Air Force levelled much of Obersalzberg, though the Eagle's Nest, Hitler's mountaintop eyrie, was left strangely unscathed. The historical twists and turns are dissected at the impressive **Dokumentation Obersalzberg** (p245).

allegories of the four then-known continents (Europe, Africa, America and Asia).

The structure was commissioned in 1720 by prince-bishop Johann Philipp Franz von Schönborn, who was unhappy with his old-fashioned digs up in Marienberg Fortress, and took almost 60 years to complete. Today the 360 rooms are home to government institutions, university faculties and a museum, but the grandest 40 have been restored for visitors to admire.

Besides the Grand Staircase, feast your eyes on the ice-white stucco-adorned **Weisser Saal** (White Hall) before entering the **Kaisersaal** (Imperial Hall), canopied by another impressive Tiepolo fresco. Other stunners include the gilded stucco **Spiegelkabinett** (Mirror Hall), covered with a unique mirror-like glass painted with figural, floral and animal motifs (accessible by tour only).

In the residence's south wing, the **Hofkirche** (Court Church) is another Neumann and Tiepolo co-production. Its marble columns, gold leaf and profusion of angels match the Residenz in splendour and proportions.

Entered via frilly wrought-iron gates, the **Hofgarten** (Court Garden; ⊘ until dusk; admission free) is a smooth blend of French- and English-style landscaping teeming with whimsical sculptures of children, mostly by court sculptor Peter Wagner. Concerts, festivals and special events take place here during the warmer months.

The complex also houses collections of antiques, paintings and drawings in the Martin-von-Wagner Museum (no relation to Peter) and, handily, a winery in the atmospheric cellar, the **Staatlicher Hofkeller Würzburg**, that is open for tours with tasting.

Festung Marienberg
FORTRESS

(tour adult/concession €3.50/2.50; ⊘ tours 11am, 2pm, 3pm & 4pm Tue-Sun, also 10am & 1pm Sat & Sun mid-Mar–Oct, 11am, 2pm & 3pm Sat & Sun Nov–mid-Mar) Enjoy panoramic city and vineyard views from this hulking fortress whose construction was initiated around 1200 by the local prince-bishops who governed here until 1719. Dramatically illuminated at night, the structure was only penetrated once, by Swedish troops during the Thirty Years' War, in 1631. Inside, the **Fürstenbaumuseum** (closed November to mid-March) sheds light on its former residents' pompous lifestyle, while the **Mainfränkisches Museum** presents city history and works by local late-Gothic master carver Tilmann Riemenschneider and other famous artists.

The fortress is a pleasant 25-minute walk uphill through the vineyards from the Alte Mainbrücke via the Tellsteige trail.

Neumünster
CHURCH

(Schönbornstrasse; ⊘ 6am-6.30pm Mon-Sat, from 8am Sun) In the Altstadt, this satisfyingly symmetrical church stands on the site where three ill-fated Irish missionaries who tried to convert Duke Gosbert to Christianity in 686 met their maker. Romanesque at its core, it was given a thorough baroque restyle by the Zimmermann brothers and is typical of their work. The interior has busts of the three martyrs (Kilian, Colonan and Totnan) on the high altar, and the tomb of St Kilian lurks in the well-lit crypt.

Dom St Kilian
CHURCH

(www.dom-wuerzburg.de; Domstrasse 40; ⊘ 8am-7pm Mon-Sat, 8am-8pm Sun) **FREE** Würzburg's highly unusual cathedral has a Romanesque core that has been altered many times over the centuries. Recently renovated, the elaborate stucco work of the chancel contrasts starkly with the bare whitewash of the austere Romanesque nave which is capped with a ceiling that wouldn't look out of place in a 1960s bus station.

The whole mishmash creates quite an impression and is possibly Germany's oddest cathedral interior. The **Schönbornkapelle** by Balthasar Neumann returns a little baroque order to things.

Museum Am Dom
ART MUSEUM

(www.museum-am-dom.de; Kiliansplatz; adult/concession €3.50/2.50; ⊘ 10am-6pm Tue-Sun Apr-Oct, to 5pm Nov-Mar) Housed in a beautiful building by the cathedral, this worthwhile museum displays collections of modern art on Christian themes. Works of international renown by Joseph Beuys, Otto Dix and Käthe Kollwitz are on show, as well as masterpieces of the Romantic, Gothic and baroque periods.

Museum im Kulturspeicher
ART MUSEUM

(☑ 0931-322 250; www.kulturspeicher.de; Veitshöchheimer Strasse 5; adult/concession €3.50/2; ⊘ 1-6pm Tue, 11am-6pm Wed & Fri-Sun, 11am-7pm Thu) In a born-again historic granary right on the Main River, you'll find this absorbing art museum with choice artworks from the 19th to the 21st centuries. The emphasis is on German impressionism, neo-realism and contemporary art, but the building also houses the post-1945 constructivist works of the Peter C Ruppert collection, a challenging assembly of computer art, sculpture, paintings and photographs.

Würzburg

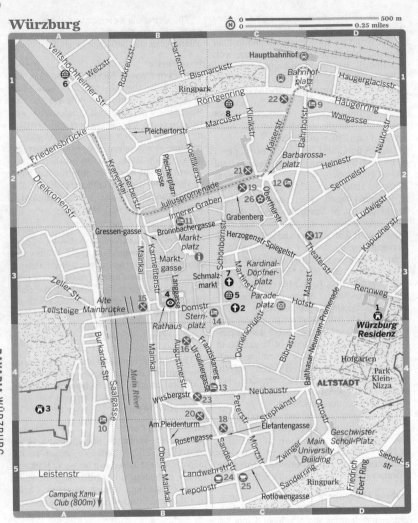

Grafeneckart
MEMORIAL

(Domstrasse) FREE Adjoining the Rathaus, the 1659-built Grafeneckart houses a scale model of the WWII bombing, which starkly depicts the extent of the damage to the city following the night of 16 March 1945, when 1000 tonnes of explosives were dropped on the city and 5000 citizens lost their lives in just 20 minutes. Viewing it before you climb up to the fortress overlooking the city gives you an appreciation of Würzburg's astonishing recovery.

Röntgen Gedächtnisstätte
MUSEUM

(www.wilhelmconradroentgen.de; Röntgenring 8; ⊙8am-8pm Mon-Fri, 8am-6pm Sat) FREE Win-
ner of the very first Nobel Prize in 1901, Wilhelm Conrad Röntgen discovered X-rays in 1895; his preserved laboratory forms the heart of this small exhibition which is complemented by a film on Röntgen's life and work in English.

🎊 Festivals & Events

Mozart Fest
MUSIC

(☎0931-372 336; www.mozartfest-wuerzburg.de; ⊙mid-May–mid-Jun) Germany's oldest Mozart festival takes place at the Residenz.

Africa Festival CULTURAL
(📞0931-150 60; www.africafestival.org; ⊙early Jun) Held on the meadows northwest of the river at Mainwiesen, complete with markets, food stalls and, if it rains, lots of mud.

Hoffest am Stein WINE, MUSIC
(www.hoffest-am-stein.de; ⊙early Jul) Wine and music festival held in the first half of July at the Weingut am Stein.

🛏 Sleeping

Babelfish HOSTEL €
(📞0931-304 0430; www.babelfish-hostel.de; Haugerring 2; dm €17-23, s/d €45/70) With a name inspired by a creature in Douglas Adams' novel *The Hitchhiker's Guide to the Galaxy*, this uncluttered and spotlessly clean hostel has 74 beds spread over two floors and a sunny rooftop terrace. The communal areas are an inviting place to down a few beers in the evening and there's a well-equipped guest kitchen.

Breakfast is €4.90 extra; reception is open 8am to midnight.

DJH Hostel HOSTEL €
(📞0931-467 7860; www.wuerzburg.jugendherberge.de; Fred-Joseph-Platz 2; dm from €25.90) At the foot of the fortress, this well-equipped, wheelchair-friendly hostel has room for over 230 snoozers in three- to eight-bed dorms.

Camping Kanu Club CAMPGROUND €
(📞0931-725 36; www.kc-wuerzburg.de; Mergentheimer Strasse 13b; per person/tent €4/3) The closest camping ground to the town centre. Take tram 3 or 5 to the Judenbühlweg stop, which is on its doorstep.

Hotel Rebstock HOTEL €€
(📞0931-309 30; www.rebstock.com; Neubaustrasse 7; s/d from €92/113; ❄@🛜) Würzburg's top digs, in a squarely renovated rococo town house, has 70 unique, stylishly finished rooms with the gamut of amenities, impeccable service and an Altstadt location. A pillow selection and supercomfy 'gel' beds should ease you into slumberland, perhaps after a fine meal in the dramatic bistro or the slick Michelin-star restaurant.

Hotel Zum Winzermännle HOTEL €€
(📞0931-541 56; www.winzermaennle.de; Domstrasse 32; s €60-79, d €90-110; P🛜) This family-run converted winery is a feel-good retreat in the city's pedestrianised heart. Rooms are well-furnished if a little on the old-fashioned side; some among those fac-

Würzburg

ing the quiet courtyard have balconies. Communal areas are bright and often seasonally decorated. Breakfast costs €7.

Hotel Poppular HOTEL €€
(📞0931-322 770; www.hotelpoppular.de; Textorstrasse 17; r €72-100; P🛜) Relatively basic, city-centre hotel above a wine restaurant where rooms have a vague Scandinavian feel and are immaculately kept. An excellent deal for the location within suitcase-dragging distance of the Hauptbahnhof and often massively discounted on popular booking websites. For walkers-in: reception closes at 10pm.

Hotel Dortmunder Hof HOTEL €€
(📞0931-561 63; www.dortmunder-hof.de; Innerer Graben 22; s €42-65, d €76-100) This bike-friendly hotel occupies a brightly renovated building with spotless, en-suite rooms with cable TV. Parking can be arranged close by, and there's live music in the cellar bar.

✗ Eating

For a town of its size, Würzburg has an enticing selection of wine taverns, beer gardens, cafes and restaurants, with plenty of student hang-outs among them.

Uni-Café   CAFE €
(Neubaustrasse 2; snacks €3-9; ☺8am-1am) Hugely popular cafe strung over two levels, with a student-priced, daily-changing menu of burgers and salads plus a buzzy bar.

Eva's   VEGETARIAN €
(Sanderstrasse 2a; dishes from €4; ☺8.30am-4pm Mon-Fri;✈) Come here for wholesome lactose-, meat- and gluten-free snacks and other healthy fare at simple wooden tables. Also runs the adjacent specialist grocery.

Denn's Bio Bistro   HEALTH FOOD €
(Juliuspromenade 64; dishes €2-6; ☺9am-8pm Mon-Sat) Order healthy organic sandwiches, quiche, pizza, soup, cakes and other snacks at this self-service bistro then feel all those nutrients being absorbed as you browse the attached organic supermarket.

Capri & Blaue Grotto   ITALIAN €
(Elefantengasse 1; pizzas €5.90-8.30, other mains €6.90-10.90; ☺11.30am-2pm & 6-10.30pm) This outpost of the *bel paese* has been plating up pronto pasta and pizza since 1952 – it was in fact Germany's first ever pizzeria.

Starback   BAKERY €
(Kaiserstrasse 33; snacks from €0.79; ☺7am-7pm Mon-Fri, to 6pm Sat) No German-language skills are required to put together a budget breakfast or lunch at this no-frills self-service bakery opposite the train station.

★Bürgerspital
Weinstube   WINE RESTAURANT €€
(☎0931-352 880; Theaterstrasse 19; mains €13-24; ☺10am-11pm) If you are going to eat out just once in Würzburg, the aromatic and cosy nooks of this labyrinthine medieval place probably provide the top local experience. Choose from a broad selection of Franconian wines (some of Germany's best) and wonderful regional dishes and snacks, including *Mostsuppe* (a tasty wine soup).

Backöfele   FRANCONIAN €€
(☎0931-590 59; www.backoefele.de; Ursulinergasse 2; mains €7-19.50; ☺noon-midnight Mon-Thu, to 1am Fri & Sat, to 11pm Sun) This old-timey warren has been serving hearty Franconian food for nearly 50 years. Find a table in the cobbled courtyard or one of four historic rooms,

each candlelit and uniquely furnished with local flair. Featuring schnitzel, snails, bratwurst in wine, wine soup with cinnamon croutons, grilled meat and other local faves, the menu makes for mouth-watering reading. Bookings recommended.

Juliusspital   WINE RESTAURANT €€
(Juliuspromenade 19; mains €11-22; ☺10am-midnight) This attractive *Weinstube* (traditional wine tavern) features fabulous Franconian fish and even better wines. Ambient lighting, scurrying waiters and walls occupied by oil paintings make this the place to head to for a special do.

Alte Mainmühle   FRANCONIAN €€
(☎0931-167 77; www.alte-mainmuehle.de; Mainkai 1; mains €8-23; ☺9.30am-midnight) Accessed straight from the old bridge, tourists and locals alike cram into this old mill to savour modern twists on Franconian classics (including popular river fish). In summer the double terrace beckons – the upper one delivers pretty views of the bridge and Marienberg Fortress; in winter retreat to the snug timber dining room. Year round, guests spill out onto the bridge itself, wine glass in hand.

♟ Drinking & Entertainment

For more options, grab a copy of the monthly listing magazine *Frizz* (in German). Look out for posters and flyers advertising big-name concerts that take place on the Residenzplatz.

Kult   CAFE, BAR
(Landwehrstrasse 10; ☺6pm-1am Mon, from 10am Tue-Sun) Enjoy a tailor-made breakfast, munch a cheap lunch or party into the wee hours at Würzburg's hippest cafe. The unpretentious interior, with its salvaged tables and old beige benches, hosts regular fancy-dress parties, table-football tournaments and other offbeat events. DJs take over at weekends.

MUCK   CAFE, BAR
(www.cafe-muck.de; Sanderstrasse 29; ☺Sun-Thu 9am-1am, Fri & Sat till late) One of the earliest openers in town, and serving a hangover-busting breakfast, this long-established cafe morphs into something of an informal party after nightfall.

Standard   LIVE MUSIC
(Oberthürstrasse 11a; ☺noon-1am Mon-Thu, to 2am Fri & Sat, 10am-late Sun) Soulful jazz spins beneath a corrugated-iron ceiling and stainless-steel fans, while bands and DJs play a

couple of times or more a week in a second, dimly lit downstairs bar.

❶ Information

Post Office (Paradeplatz 4)

Tourist Office (☑ 0931-372 398; www.wuerzburg.de; Marktplatz 9; ⊙10am-5pm Mon-Fri, 10am-2pm Sat & Sun, closed Sun Nov-Apr) Within the attractive Falkenhaus this efficient office can help you with room reservations and tour bookings.

❶ Getting There & Away

BUS

The Romantic Road Coach (p248) stops at the main bus station next to the Hauptbahnhof, and at the Residenzplatz. Budget coach company **Meinfernbus** (www.meinfernbus.de) links Würzburg with numerous destinations across Germany and beyond including both Nuremberg and Munich.

TRAIN

Train connections from Würzburg:

➡ **Bamberg** €20.70, one hour, twice hourly

➡ **Frankfurt** €30 to €35, one hour, hourly

➡ **Nuremberg** €20.90 to €29, one hour, twice hourly

➡ **Rothenburg ob der Tauber** Change in Steinach; €13.30, one hour, hourly

❶ Getting Around

The most useful service is bus 9 which shuttles roughly hourly between the Residenz and the Festung Marienberg. Otherwise Würzburg can be easily tackled on foot.

Rothenburg ob der Tauber

☑ 09861 / POP 10,900

A medieval gem, Rothenburg ob der Tauber (meaning 'above the Tauber River') is a top tourist stop along the Romantic Road. With its web of cobbled lanes, higgledy-piggledy houses and towered walls, the town is the fairy-tale Germany the hordes of tourists came to see. Urban conservation orders here are the strictest in Germany – and at times it feels like a medieval theme park – but all's forgiven in the evenings, when the yellow lamplight casts its spell long after the last tour buses have left.

◉ Sights

Jakobskirche CHURCH
(Church of St Jacob; Klingengasse 1; adult/concession €2.50/1.50; ⊙9am-5.15pm Mon-Sat,

10.45am-5.15pm Sun) One of the few places of worship in Bavaria to charge admission, Rothenburg's Lutheran parish church was begun in the 14th century and finished in the 15th. The building sports some wonderfully aged stained-glass windows, but the top attraction is Tilman Riemenschneider's **Heilig Blut Altar** (Altar of the Holy Blood). The gilded cross above the main scene depicting the Last Supper incorporates Rothenburg's most treasured reliquary – a rock crystal capsule said to contain three drops of Christ's blood.

Mittelalterliches Kriminalmuseum MUSEUM
(Medieval Crime & Punishment Museum; www.kriminalmuseum.eu; Burggasse 3; adult/concessions €5/3.50; ⊙10am-6pm May-Oct, shorter hours Nov-Apr) Medieval implements of torture and punishment are on show at this gruesomely fascinating museum. Exhibits include chastity belts, masks of disgrace for gossips, a cage for cheating bakers, a neck brace for quarrelsome women and a beer-barrel pen for drunks. You can even snap a selfie in the stocks!

Deutsches Weihnachtsmuseum MUSEUM
(Christmas Museum; ☑ 09861-409 365; www.weihnachtsmuseum.de; Herrngasse 1; adult/child/family €4/2.50/7; ⊙10am-5pm daily Easter-Christmas, shorter hours Jan–Easter) If you're glad Christmas comes but once every 365 days, then stay well clear of the Käthe Wohlfahrt Weihnachtsdorf (p256), a Yuletide superstore that also houses this Christmas Museum. This repository of all things 'Ho! Ho! Ho!' traces the development of various Christmas customs and decorations, and includes a display of 150 Santa figures, plus lots of retro baubles and tinsel – particularly surreal in mid-July when the mercury outside is pushing 30°C.

Not as big a hit with younger kids as you might predict, as they can't get their hands on anything.

Stadtmauer HISTORIC SITE
(Town Wall) With time and fresh legs, a 2.5km circular walk around the unbroken ring of town walls gives a sense of the importance medieval man placed on defending his settlement. A great lookout point is the eastern tower, the **Röderturm** (Rödergasse; adult/child €1.50/1; ⊙9am-5pm Mar-Nov), but for the most impressive views head to the west side of town, where a sweeping view of the Tauber Valley includes the Doppelbrücke, a double-decker bridge.

Rothenburg ob der Tauber

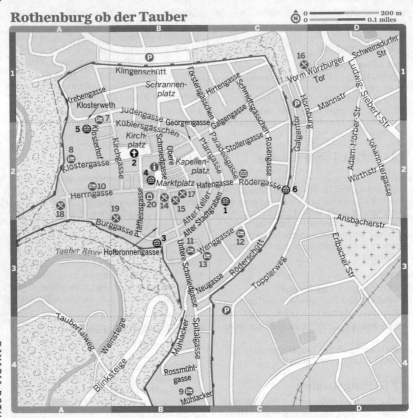

Alt-Rothenburger Handwerkerhaus
HISTORIC BUILDING

(Alter Stadtgraben 26; adult/concession €3/2.50; 11am-5pm Mon-Fri, from 10am Sat & Sun Easter-Oct, 2-4pm daily Dec) Hidden down a little alley is the Alt-Rothenburger Handwerkerhaus, where numerous artisans – including coopers, weavers, cobblers and potters – have their workshops today, and mostly have had for the house's more than 700-year existence. It's half museum, half active workplace and you can easily spend an hour or so watching the craftsmen at work.

Reichsstadtmuseum
MUSEUM

(www.reichsstadtmuseum.rothenburg.de; Klosterhof 5; adult/concession €4.50/3.50; 9.30am-5.30pm Apr-Oct, 1-4pm Nov-Mar) Highlights of the Reichsstadtmuseum, housed in a former Dominican convent, include the *Rothenburger Passion* (1494), a cycle of 12 panels by Martinus Schwarz, and the oldest convent kitchen in Germany, as well as weap-

ons and armour. Outside the main entrance (on your right as you're facing the museum), you'll see a spinning barrel, where the nuns distributed bread to the poor – and where women would leave babies they couldn't afford to keep.

For a serene break between sightseeing, head to the **Klostergarten** (Monastery Garden) behind the museum (enter from Klosterhof).

Rathausturm
HISTORIC BUILDING

(Town Hall Tower; Marktplatz; adult/concession €2/0.50; 9.30am-12.30pm & 1-5pm daily Apr-Oct, 10.30am-2pm & 2.30-6pm daily Dec, noon-3pm Sat & Sun rest of year) The Rathaus on Marktplatz was begun in Gothic style in the 14th century and was completed during the Renaissance. Climb the 220 steps of the medieval town hall to the viewing platform of the Rathausturm to be rewarded with widescreen views of the Tauber.

Rothenburg ob der Tauber

☞ Tours

The tourist office runs 90-minute walking tours (€7; in English) at 2pm from April to October. Every evening a lantern-toting *Nachtwächter* (Night Watchman) dressed in traditional costume leads an entertaining tour of the Altstadt; English tours (€7) meet at the Rathaus just before 8pm.

⚜ Festivals & Events

Historisches Festspiel 'Der Meistertrunk'　　　　THEATRE
(www.meistertrunk.de; ⊗ late May) Takes place on Whitsuntide, with parades, dances and a medieval market. The highlight is the re-enactment of the mythical *Meistertrunk* story. The *Meistertrunk* play itself is performed three more times: once during the Reichsstadt-Festtage (early September), when the city's history is re-enacted in the streets, and twice during the Rothenburger Herbst, an autumn celebration (October).

Historischer Schäfertanz　　　　DANCE
(Historical Shepherds' Dance; www.schaefertanz-rothenburg.de; Marktplatz) Featuring colourfully dressed couples; takes places on Marktplatz several times between April and October.

Christmas Market　　　　MARKET
Rothenburg's Christmas market is one of the most romantic in Germany. It's set out around the central Marktplatz during Advent.

🛏 Sleeping

DJH Hostel　　　　HOSTEL €
(☑ 09861-941 60; www.rothenburg.jugendherberge.de; Mühlacker 1; dm from €25.40; 🛜) Rothenburg's youth hostel occupies two enormous old buildings in the south of town.

It's agreeably renovated and extremely well equipped, but you can hear the screams of noisy school groups from outside.

Hotel Raidel　　　　HOTEL €
(☑ 09861-3115; www.gaestehaus-raidel.de; Wenggasse 3; s/d €45/69; 🛜) With 500-year-old exposed beams studded with wooden nails, antiques throughout and a welcoming owner, as well as musical instruments for the guests to play, this is the place to check in if you're craving some genuine romance on the Romantic Road. Rates include breakfast.

Pension Birgit　　　　B&B €
(☑ 09861-6107; www.birgit-pension.de; Wenggasse 16; s/d from €30/40; 🛜) Basic owner-run pension that offers Rothenburg's cheapest rooms in an epicentral location. Rates include a modest buffet breakfast.

Kreuzerhof Hotel Garni　　　　GUESTHOUSE €
(☑ 09861-3424; www.kreuzerhof-rothenburg.de; Millergasse 2-6; s €45-52, d €62-78; 🛜) Away from the tourist swarms, this quiet family-run B&B has charming, randomly furnished rooms with antique touches in a medieval town house and annexe. There's free tea and coffee and the generous breakfast is an energy-boosting set-up for the day.

★ Burg-Hotel　　　　HOTEL €€
(☑ 09861-948 90; www.burghotel.eu; Klostergasse 1-3; s €100-135, d €125-195; P ⊖ ❋ 🛜) Each of the 17 elegantly furnished guest rooms at this boutique hotel built into the town walls has its own private sitting area. The lower floors shelter a decadent spa with tanning beds, saunas and rainforest showers, and a cellar with a Steinway piano; while phenomenal valley views unfurl from the breakfast room and stone terrace.

SNOWBALLS

Diller's Schneeballen (Hofbronnengasse 16; ⊙10am-6pm) Rothenburg's most obvious speciality is Schneeballen, ribbons of dough loosely shaped into balls, deep-fried then coated in icing sugar, chocolate and other dentist's foes. Some 27 different types are produced at Diller's Schneeballen.

A more limited range is available all over town.

The owners have recently taken over the hotel across the road where there are 14 more modern rooms and a restaurant.

Altfränkische Weinstube HOTEL €€
(☑09861-6404; www.altfraenkische.de; Klosterhof 7; d €75-118; ✿) This characterful 650-year-old inn has eight wonderfully romantic rural-style rooms with exposed half-timber, bathtubs and most with four-poster or canopied beds. From 6pm onwards, the tavern serves up sound regional fare (mains €8.80 to €15.50) with a dollop of medieval cheer.

★**Hotel Herrnschlösschen** HOTEL €€€
(☑09861-873 890; www.herrnschloesschen.de; Herrngasse 20; r from €210) The most recent addition to Rothenburg's hotel stock has breathed life back into a 900-year-old mansion. The whole place is a blend of ancient and new, with Gothic arches leaping over faux-retro furniture and ageing oak preventing ceilings from crashing down onto chic 21st-century beds. The hotel's restaurant has established itself as one of the town's most innovative dining spots.

 Eating

TobinGo KEBAB €
(Hafengasse 2; mains €3.50-8; ⊙10am-10pm) You can't say you've been to Bavaria until you've consumed a kebab in a twee medieval setting.

Zur Höll FRANCONIAN €€
(☑09861-4229; www.hoell.rothenburg.de; Burggasse 8; mains €6.80-20; ⊙5-11pm) This medieval wine tavern is in the town's oldest original building, with sections dating back to the year 900. The menu of regional specialities is limited but refined, though it's the superb selection of Franconian wines that people really come for.

Gasthof Goldener Greifen FRANCONIAN €€
(☑09861-2281; www.gasthof-greifen-rothenburg.de; Obere Schmiedgasse 5; mains €8-17; ⊙11am-9.30pm) Erstwhile home of Heinrich Toppler, one of Rothenburg's most famous medieval mayors (the dining room was his office), the 700-year-old Golden Griffin is the locals' choice in the touristy centre serving a hearty menu of Franconian favourites in an austere semi-medieval setting and out back in the sunny and secluded garden.

Mittermeier BAVARIAN, INTERNATIONAL €€
(☑09861-945 430; www.villamittermeier.de; Vorm Würzburger Tor 7; mains €12-19; ⊙6-10.30pm Tue-Sat; ℗✿) Supporters of the slow food movement and deserved holders of a Michelin Bib Gourmand, this hotel restaurant pairs punctilious craftsmanship with top-notch ingredients, sourced regionally whenever possible. There are five different dining areas including a black-and-white tiled 'temple', an alfresco terrace and a barrel-shaped wine cellar. The wine list is one of the best in Franconia.

Weinstube zum Pulverer FRANCONIAN €€
(☑09861-976 182; Herrngasse 31; mains €5-16.50; ⊙5pm-late Mon & Wed-Fri, from noon Sat & Sun, closed Tue) The ornately carved timber chairs in this ancient wood-panelled wine bar (allegedly Rothenburg's oldest) are works of art. Its simple but filling dishes, like soup in a bowl made of bread, gourmet sandwiches and cakes, are equally artistic. There's also a piano for postprandial self-expression.

🛍 **Shopping**

**Käthe Wohlfahrt
Weihnachtsdorf** CHRISTMAS DECORATIONS
(www.wohlfahrt.com; Herrngasse 1; ⊙9am-6pm) With its mind-boggling assortment of Yuletide decorations and ornaments, this huge shop lets you celebrate Christmas every day of the year. Many of the items are handcrafted with amazing skill and imagination; prices are correspondingly high.

ℹ **Information**

Post Office (Rödergasse 11)

Tourist Office (☑09861-404 800; www.tourismus.rothenburg.de; Marktplatz 2; ⊙9am-6pm Mon-Fri, 10am-5pm Sat & Sun May-Oct, 9am-5pm Mon-Fri, 10am-1pm Sat Nov-Mar) Helpful office offering free internet access.

ⓘ Getting There & Away

BUS
The Romantic Road Coach (p248) stops in the main bus park at the Hauptbahnhof and on the more central Schrannenplatz.

CAR
The A7 autobahn runs right past town.

TRAIN
You can go anywhere by train from Rothenburg, as long as it's Steinach. Change there for services to Würzburg (€13.30, one hour and 10 minutes). Travel to and from Munich (from €31, three hours) can involve up to three different trains.

ⓘ Getting Around
The city has five car parks right outside the walls. The town centre is essentially closed to nonresident vehicles, though hotel guests are exempt.

Dinkelsbühl

☑ 09851 / POP 11,300

Some 40km south of Rothenburg, immaculately preserved Dinkelsbühl proudly traces its roots to a royal residence founded by Carolingian kings in the 8th century. Saved from destruction in the Thirty Years' War and ignored by WWII bombers, this is arguably the Romantic Road's quaintest and most authentically medieval halt. For a good overall impression of the town, walk along the fortified walls with their 18 towers and four gates.

◉ Sights

Haus der Geschichte
MUSEUM

(Altrathausplatz 14; adult/child €4/2; ⊗9am-6pm Mon-Fri, 10am-5pm Sat & Sun May-Oct, 10am-5pm daily Nov-Apr) Dinkelsbühl's history comes under the microscope at the Haus der Geschichte, which occupies the old town hall. There's an interesting section on the Thirty Years' War and a gallery with paintings depicting Dinkelsbühl at the turn of the century. Audioguides are included in the ticket price.

Münster St Georg
CHURCH

(Marktplatz 1) Standing sentry over the heart of Dinkelsbühl is one of southern Germany's purest late-Gothic hall churches. Rather austere from the outside, the interior stuns with an incredible fan-vaulted ceiling. A curiosity is the **Pretzl Window** donated by the bakers' guild; it's located in the upper section of the last window in the right aisle.

Museum of the 3rd Dimension
MUSEUM

(☑ 09851-6336; www.3d-museum.de; Nördlinger Tor; adult/concession/under 12yr €10/8/6; ⊗11am-5pm daily Apr-Oct, 11am-5pm Sat & Sun Nov-Mar) Located just outside the easternmost town gate, this is an engaging place to entertain young minds, bored with the Romantic Road's medieval pageant. Inside there are three floors of holographic images, stereoscopes and attention-grabbing 3-D imagery. The you-gotta-be-kidding admission includes a pair of red-green-tinted specs.

BOTTOMS UP FOR FREEDOM

In 1631 the Thirty Years' War – pitching Catholics against Protestants – reached the gates of Rothenburg ob der Tauber. Catholic General Tilly and 60,000 of his troops besieged the Protestant market town and demanded its surrender. The town resisted but couldn't stave off the onslaught of marauding soldiers, and the mayor and other town dignitaries were captured and sentenced to death.

And that's about where the story ends and the legend begins. As the tale goes, Rothenburg's town council tried to sate Tilly's bloodthirstiness by presenting him with a 3L pitcher of wine. Tilly, after taking a sip or two, presented the men with an unusual challenge, saying 'If one of you has the courage to step forward and down this mug of wine in one gulp, then I shall spare the town and the lives of the councilmen!' Mayor Georg Nusch accepted – and succeeded! And that's why you can still wander through Rothenburg's wonderful medieval lanes today.

It's pretty much accepted that Tilly was really placated with hard cash. Nevertheless, local poet Adam Hörber couldn't resist turning the tale of the Meistertrunk into a play, which, since 1881, has been performed every Whitsuntide (Pentecost), the seventh Sunday after Easter. It's also re-enacted several times daily by the clock figures on the tourist office building.

BAVARIA DINKELSBÜHL

✲✲ Festivals & Events

Kinderzeche
HISTORY, MUSIC
(www.kinderzeche.de; ⏀Jul) In the third week of July, the 10-day Kinderzeche celebrates how, during the Thirty Years' War, the town's children persuaded the invading Swedish troops to spare Dinkelsbühl from a ransacking. The festivities include a pageant, re-enactments in the festival hall, lots of music and other merriment.

🛏 Sleeping

DJH Hostel
HOSTEL €
(☑09851-9509; www.dinkelsbuehl.jugendherberge. de; Koppengasse 10; dm from €22.50; 🛜) Undergoing a complete refit at the time of research, Dinkelsbühl's hostel in the western part of the Altstadt occupies a beautiful 15th-century granary.

Campingpark 'Romantische Strasse'
CAMPGROUND €
(☑09851-7817; www.campingplatz-dinkelsbuehl. de; Kobeltsmühle 6; per tent/person €9.30/4.40) This camping ground is set on the shores of a swimmable lake 1.5km northeast of the Wörnitz Tor.

★ Dinkelsbühler Kunst-Stuben
GUESTHOUSE €€
(☑09851-6750; www.kunst-stuben.de; Segringer Strasse 52; s €60, d €80-85, ste €90; ⏀◉🛜) Personal attention and charm by the bucketload make this guesthouse, situated near the westernmost gate (Segringer Tor), one of the best on the entire Romantic Road. Furniture (including the four-posters) is all handmade by Voglauer, the cosy library is perfect for curling up in with a good read, and the suite is a matchless deal for travelling families. The artist owner will show his Asia travel films if enough guests are interested.

Gasthof Goldenes Lamm
HOTEL €€
(☑09851-6441; www.goldenes.de; Lange Gasse 26-28; s €55-70, d €80-105; ℗🛜) Run by the same family for four generations, this stress-free, bike-friendly oasis has pleasant rooms at the top of a creaky staircase, and a funky rooftop garden deck with plump sofas. The attached wood-panelled restaurant plates up Franconian-Swabian specialities, including a vegetarian selection.

Deutsches Haus
HOTEL €€
(☑09851-6058; www.deutsches-haus.net; Weinmarkt 3; s €80-99, d €116-129; 🛜) Concealed behind the town's most ornate and out-of-kilter facade, the 19 elegant rooms at this central inn opposite the Münster St Georg flaunt antique touches and big 21st-century bathrooms. Downstairs Dinkelbühl's haughtiest restaurant serves game and fish prepared according to age old recipes.

🍴 Eating

Haus Appelberg
FRANCONIAN, INTERNATIONAL €€
(☑09851-582 838; www.haus-appelberg.de; Nördlinger Strasse 40; dishes €6-11; ⏀6pm-midnight Mon-Sat) At this 40-cover wine restaurant, the owners double up as cooks to keep tables supplied with traditional dishes such as local fish, Franconian sausages and *Maultaschen*. On warm days swap the rustic interior for the secluded terrace, a fine spot for some evening idling over a Franconian white.

The eight rooms upstairs are of a very high standard and boast traditional antique touches.

Weib's Brauhaus
PUB FOOD €€
(Untere Schmiedgasse 13; mains €5.70-14.60; ⏀11am-1am Thu-Mon, 6pm-1am Wed; 🍴) A female brewmaster presides over the copper vats at this half-timbered pub-restaurant, which has a good-time vibe thanks to its friendly crowd of regulars. Many dishes are made with the house brew, including the popular *Weib's Töpfle* ('woman's pot') – pork in beer sauce with croquettes.

ℹ Information

Tourist Office
(☑09851-902 440; www. dinkelsbuehl.de; Altrathausplatz 14; ⏀9am-6pm Mon-Fri, 10am-5pm Sat & Sun May-Oct, 10am-5pm daily Nov-Apr)

ℹ Getting There & Away

Despite a railway line cutting through the town, Dinkelsbühl is not served by passenger trains. Regional bus 501 to Nördlingen (50 minutes, eight daily) stops at the new ZOB Schwedenwiese bus station. Reaching Rothenburg is a real test of patience without your own car. Change from bus 805 to a train in Ansbach, then change trains in Steinach. The Europabus stops right in the Altstadt at Schweinemarkt.

Nördlingen

☑09081 / POP 19,400

Charmingly medieval, Nördlingen sees fewer tourists than its better-known neighbours and manages to retain an air of authenticity, which is a relief after some of the Romantic

Road's kitschy extremes. The town lies within the Ries Basin, a massive impact crater gouged out by a meteorite more than 15 million years ago. The crater – some 25km in diameter – is one of the best preserved on earth, and has been declared a special 'geopark'. Nördlingen's 14th-century walls, all original, mimic the crater's rim and are almost perfectly circular.

Incidentally, if you've seen the 1970s film *Willy Wonka and the Chocolate Factory*, you've already looked down upon Nördlingen from a glass elevator.

◎ Sights

You can circumnavigate the entire town in around an hour by taking the sentry walk (free) on top of the walls all the way.

St Georgskirche CHURCH
(tower adult/child €3/1.80; ⊙ tower 9am-6pm daily, to 7pm Jul & Aug, to 5pm Nov-Mar) Dominating the heart of town, the immense late-Gothic St Georgskirche got its baroque mantle in the 18th century. To truly appreciate Nördlingen's circular shape and the dished-out crater in which it lies, scramble up the 350 steps of the church's 90m-tall Daniel Tower.

Bayerisches Eisenbahnmuseum MUSEUM
(www.bayerisches-eisenbahnmuseum.de; Am Hohen Weg 6a; adult/child €6/3; ⊙ noon-4pm Tue-Sat, 10am-5pm Sun May-Sep, noon-4pm Sat, 10am-5pm Sun Oct-Mar) Half museum, half junkyard retirement home for old locos, this trainspotter's paradise occupies a disused engine depot across the tracks from the train station (no access from the platforms). The museum runs steam and old diesel trains up to Dinkelsbühl, Feuchtwangen and Gunzenhausen several times a year; see the website for details.

Rieskrater Museum MUSEUM
(Eugene-Shoemaker-Platz 1; adult/concession €4.50/2.50, ticket also valid for Stadtmuseum; ⊙ 10am-4.30pm Tue-Sun, closed noon-1.30pm Nov-Apr) Situated in an ancient barn, this unique museum explores the formation of meteorite craters and the consequences of such violent collisions with Earth. Rocks, including a genuine moon rock (on permanent loan from NASA), fossils and other geological displays shed light on the mystery of meteors.

Stadtmuseum MUSEUM
(Vordere Gerbergasse 1; adult/concession €4.50/2.50, ticket also valid for Rieskrater Museum; ⊙ 1.30-4.30pm Tue-Sun Mar-early Nov) Nördlingen's worthwhile municipal museum covers an ambitious sweep of human existence on the planet, from the early Stone Age to 20th-century art, via the Battle of Nördlingen during the Thirty Years' War, Roman endeavours in the area and the town's once-bustling mercantile life.

Stadtmauermuseum MUSEUM
(Löpsinger Torturm; adult/concession €2/1.40; ⊙ 10am-4.30pm Tue-Sun Apr-Oct) Head up the spiral staircase of the Löpsinger Torturm for an engaging exhibition on the history of the town's defences, an apt place to kick off a circuit of the walls.

🛌 Sleeping & Eating

Hotel Altreuter HOTEL €
(☑ 09081-4319; www.hotel-altreuter.de; Marktplatz 11; s/d from €36/52) Perched above a busy cafe and bakery, the bog-standard rooms here are of the could-be-anywhere type, but the epicentral location cannot be beaten. Bathrooms are private and breakfast is served downstairs in the cafe.

Jugend & Familengästehaus GUESTHOUSE €
(JUFA; ☑ 09081-290 8390; www.jufa.eu; Bleichgraben 3a; d €50; ℗ @ 🕾) Located just outside the town walls, this shiny, 186-bed hostel-guesthouse is spacious and clean-cut. There are two- to four-bed rooms, ideal for couples or families, and facilities include bicycle hire and a cafe with internet terminals. Unless you are travelling with an entire handball team in tow, dorms are off limits to individual travellers, no matter how hard you plead.

Kaiserhof Hotel Sonne HOTEL €€
(☑ 09081-5067; www.kaiserhof-hotel-sonne.de; Marktplatz 3; s €55-75, d €80-120; ℗ 🕾) Right on the main square, Nördlingen's top digs once hosted crowned heads and their entourages, but have quietly gone to seed in recent years. However, rooms are still packed with character, mixing modern comforts with traditional charm, and the atmospheric regional restaurant downstairs is still worth a shot.

La Fontana ITALIAN €
(Bei den Kornschrannen 2; mains around €8; ⊙ 11am-11pm) Nördlingen's most popular restaurant is this large Italian pizza-pasta place occupying the terracotta Kornschrannen as well as tumbling tables out onto Schrannenstrasse. The menu is long, the service swift and when the sun is shining there's no lovelier spot to fill the hole.

Cafe-buch.de
CAFE €

(Weinmarkt 4; snacks from €2; ⊙10am-6pm Mon-Sat, from 11am Sun) That winning combination of coffee, cakes and secondhand books makes this new cafe a pleasing mid-stroll halt for literary types. No English is spoken.

Café Radlos
CAFE €€

(www.café-radlos.de; Löpsinger Strasse 8; mains €6.50-10; ⊙5pm-1am Mon-Fri, from noon Sat & Sun; 🖃🖉) More than just a place to tuck into tasty pizzas and pastas, this convivially random cafe, Nördlingen's coolest haunt, parades cherry-red walls that showcase local art and photography exhibits. Kids have their own toy-filled corner, while you relax with board games, soak up the sunshine in the beer garden, or surf the web.

ℹ Information

Geopark Ries Information Centre (www.geopark-ries.de; Eugene-Shoemaker-Platz; ⊙10am-4.30pm Tue-Sun) Free exhibition on the Ries crater.

Tourist Office (📋 09081-841 16; www.noerdlingen.de; Marktplatz 2; ⊙9.30am-6pm Mon-Thu, to 4.30pm Fri, 10am-2pm Sat Easter-Oct, plus 10am-2pm Sun Jul & Aug, closed Sat & Sun rest of year) Staff sell the Nördlinger TouristCard (€9.95) that saves you around €8 if you visit everything in town.

ℹ Getting There & Away

BUS

The Europabus stops at the Rathaus. Bus 501 runs to Dinkelsbühl from the new bus station (50 minutes, eight daily).

TRAIN

Train journeys to and from Munich (€26.80, two hours) and Augsburg (€15.70, 1¼ hours) require a change in Donauwörth.

Donauwörth

📋 0906 / POP 18,550

Sitting pretty at the confluence of the Danube and Wörnitz rivers, Donauwörth rose from its humble beginnings as a 5th-century fishing village to its zenith as a Free Imperial City in 1301. Three medieval gates and five town wall towers still guard it today, and faithful rebuilding – after WWII had destroyed 75% of the medieval old town – means steep-roofed houses in a rainbow of colours still line its main street, Reichstrasse.

Reichstrasse is around 10 minutes' walk north of the train station. Turn right onto Bahnhofstrasse and cross the bridge onto Ried Island.

◉ Sights

Liebfraukirche
CHURCH

(Reichstrasse) At the western end of Reichstrasse rises this 15th-century Gothic church with original frescos and a curiously sloping floor that drops 120cm. Swabia's largest church bell (6550kg) swings in the belfry.

Käthe-Kruse-Puppenmuseum
MUSEUM

(www.kaethe-kruse.de; Pflegstrasse 21a; adult/child €2.50/1.50; ⊙11am-6pm Tue-Sun May-Sep, 2-5pm Thu-Sun Oct-Apr) This nostalgia-inducing museum fills a former monastery with old dolls and dollhouses by world-renowned designer Käthe Kruse (1883–1968).

Rathaus
HISTORIC BUILDING

(Rathausgasse) Work on the landmark town hall began in 1236, but it has seen many alterations and additions over the centuries. At 11am and 4pm daily, the carillon on the ornamented step gable plays a composition by local legend Werner Egk (1901–83) from his opera *Die Zaubergeige* (The Magic Violin). The building also houses the tourist office.

Heilig-Kreuz-Kirche
CHURCH

(Heilig-Kreuz-Strasse) Overlooking the grassy banks of the shallow River Wörnitz, this soaring baroque confection has for centuries lured the faithful to pray before a chip of wood, said to come from the Holy Cross, installed in the ornate-ceilinged **Gnadenkappelle** (Grace Chapel).

🛏 Sleeping & Eating

Drei Kronen
HOTEL €€

(📋 09851-706 170; www.hotel3kronen.com; Bahnhofstrasse 25; s/d €82/115; 🅿🖃) Situated opposite the train station a little way along Bahnhofstrasse, the 'Three Crowns' has the town's most comfortable rooms and a lamplit restaurant. The reception is, inconveniently, closed in the evenings and all weekend, but staff are around in the restaurant.

Posthotel Traube
BAVARIAN €€

(Kapellstrasse 14-16; mains €5.50-17; ⊙11am-2pm & 5-10pm Mon-Fri & Sun, closed Sat) Choose from a cafe, coffee house, restaurant or beer garden at this friendly, multitasking hotel where Mozart stayed as a boy in 1777. The schnitzel, cordon bleu and local carp in beer sauce are where your forefinger should land on the menu.

Cafe Rafaello
ITALIAN €€

(Fischerplatz 1; mains €6-24.50; ⊘10am-midnight daily) On Ried Island, this Italian job specialising in seafood uses Apennines kitsch to recreate *La Dolce Vita* to southern German tastes. The endless menu has something for everyone.

❶ Information

Tourist Office (☑09851-789 151; www.donauwoerth.de; Rathausgasse 1; ⊘9am-noon & 1-6pm Mon-Fri, 3-5pm Sat & Sun May-Sep, shorter hours Mon-Fri, closed Sat & Sun Oct-Apr)

❶ Getting There & Away

BUS
The Romantic Road Coach (p248) stops by the Liebfraukirche.

CAR & MOTORCYCLE
Donauwörth is at the crossroads of the B2, B16 and B25 roads.

TRAIN
Train connections from Donauwörth:
➡ **Augsburg** €6.60, 30 minutes, twice hourly
➡ **Harburg** €3.70, 11 minutes, twice hourly
➡ **Ingolstadt** €12.10, 45 minutes, hourly
➡ **Nördlingen** €6.10, 30 minutes, hourly

Augsburg

☑0821 / POP 276,500

The largest city on the Romantic Road (and Bavaria's third largest), Augsburg is also one of Germany's oldest, founded by the stepchildren of Roman emperor Augustus over 2000 years ago. As an independent city state from the 13th century, it was also one of Germany's wealthiest, free to raise its own taxes, with public coffers bulging on the proceeds of the textile trade. Banking families such as the Fuggers and the Welsers even bankrolled entire countries and helped out the odd skint monarch. However, from the 16th century, religious strife and economic decline plagued the city. Augsburg finally joined the Kingdom of Bavaria in 1806.

Shaped by Romans, medieval artisans, bankers, traders and, more recently, industry and technology, this attractive city of spires and cobbles is an easy day trip from Munich or an engaging stop on the Romantic Road, though one with a grittier, less quaint atmosphere than others along the route.

◉ Sights

Fuggerei
HISTORIC SITE

(www.fugger.de; Jakober Strasse; adult/concession €4/3; ⊘8am-8pm Apr-Sep, 9am-6pm Oct-Mar) The legacy of Jakob Fugger 'The Rich' lives on at Augsburg's Catholic welfare settlement, the Fuggerei, which is the oldest of its kind in existence.

Around 200 people live here today and their rent remains frozen at 1 Rhenish guilder (now €0.88) per year, plus utilities and three daily prayers. Residents wave to you as you wander through the car-free lanes of this gated community flanked by its 52 pin-neat houses (containing 140 apartments) and little gardens.

To see how residents lived before running water and central heating, one of the apartments now houses the **Fuggereimuseum** (Mittlere Gasse 14; admission incl with entry to the Fuggerei; ⊘9am-8pm Mar-Oct, 9am-6pm Nov-Apr), while there's a modern apartment open for public viewing at Ochsengasse 51. Interpretive panels are in German but you can ask for an information leaflet in English or download it from the website before you arrive.

Rathausplatz
SQUARE

The heart of Augsburg's Altstadt, this large, pedestrianised square is anchored by the **Augustusbrunnen**, a fountain honouring the Roman emperor; its four figures represent the Lech River and the Wertach, Singold and Brunnenbach Brooks.

Rising above the square are the twin onion-domed spires of the Renaissance **Rathaus**, built by Elias Holl from 1615 to 1620 and crowned by a 4m-tall pine cone, the city's emblem (also an ancient fertility symbol). Upstairs is the **Goldener Saal** (Golden Hall; Rathausplatz; adult/concession €2.50/1; ⊘10am-6pm), a huge banquet hall with an amazing gilded and frescoed coffered ceiling.

For panoramic views over Rathausplatz and the city, climb to the top of the **Perlachturm** (Rathausplatz; adult/concession €2/1; ⊘10am-6pm daily Apr-Nov), a former guard tower, and also an Elias Holl creation.

St Anna Kirche
CHURCH

(Im Annahof 2, off Annastrasse; ⊘noon-5pm Mon, 10am-12.30pm & 3-5pm Tue-Sat, 10am-12.30pm & 3-4pm Sun) Often regarded as the first Renaissance church in Germany, the rather plain-looking (and well-hidden) St Anna Kirche is accessed via a set of cloisters lined with tombstones. The church contains a bevy of treasures, as well as the sumptuous

BAVARIA AUGSBURG

WORTH A TRIP

HARBURG

Looming over the Wörnitz River, the medieval covered parapets, towers, turrets, keep and red-tiled roofs of the 12th-century **Schloss Harburg** (www.burg-harburg.de; adult/child €5/3; ⊙10am-5pm Tue-Sun mid-Mar–Oct) are so perfectly preserved they almost seem like a film set. Tours tell the building's long tale and evoke the ghosts that are said to use the castle as a hang-out.

From the castle, the walk to Harburg's cute, half-timbered **Altstadt** takes around 10 minutes, slightly more the other way as you're heading uphill. A fabulous panorama of the village and castle can be admired from the 1702 **Stone Bridge** spanning the Wörnitz.

The Europabus stops in the village (outside the Gasthof Grüner Baum) but not at the castle. Hourly trains run to Nördlingen (€4.40, 19 minutes) and Donauwörth (€3.70, 11 minutes). The train station is about a 30-minute walk from the castle. Harburg is on the B25 road.

Fuggerkapelle, where Jacob Fugger and some of his relatives lie buried, and the lavishly frescoed **Goldschmiedekapelle** (Goldsmiths' Chapel; 1420) – under renovation at the time of research.

The church played an important role during the Reformation. In 1518 Martin Luther, in town to defend his beliefs before the papal legate, stayed at what was then a Carmelite monastery. His rooms have been turned into the **Lutherstiege**, a recently revamped exhibition about the Reformation and Luther's life.

Maximilianmuseum   MUSEUM

(☑0821-324 4102; www.kunstsammlungen-museen.augsburg.de; Philippine-Welser-Strasse 24; adult/concession €7/5.50; ⊙10am-5pm Tue-Sun) The Maximilianmuseum occupies two patrician town houses joined by a statue-studded courtyard covered by a glass-and-steel roof. Highlights include a fabulous collection of Elias Holl's original wooden models for his architectural creations, and a collection of gold and silver coins that can be viewed through sliding magnifying glass panels. However, the real highlights here are the expertly curated temporary exhibitions on a variety of Bavarian themes.

Bertolt-Brecht-Haus   MUSEUM

(☑0821-324 2779; Auf dem Rain 7; adult/concession €2.50/2; ⊙10am-5pm Tue-Sun) Opened in 1998 to celebrate Brecht's 100th birthday, this house museum is the birthplace of the famous playwright and poet, where he lived from 1898 to 1900 before moving across town. Among the displays are old theatre posters and a great series of life-size chronological photos, as well as his mother's bedroom. The building is due for a revamp in 2016 so may be closed for some time.

Dom Mariä Heimsuchung   CHURCH

(Hoher Weg; ⊙7am-6pm) Augsburg's cathedral has its origins in the 10th century but was Gothicised and enlarged in the 14th and 15th centuries. The star treasures here are the so-called 'Prophets' Windows'. Depicting David, Daniel, Jonah, Hosea and Moses, they are among the oldest figurative stained-glass windows in Germany, dating from the 12th century. Look out for four paintings by Hans Holbein the Elder, including one of Jesus' circumcision.

Jüdisches Kulturmuseum   MUSEUM

(☑0821-513 658; www.jkmas.de; Halderstrasse 6-8; adult/concession €4/2; ⊙9am-6pm Tue-Thu, to 4pm Fri, 10am-5pm Sun) About 300m east of the main train station, as you head towards the Altstadt, you'll come to the Synagoge Augsburg, an art-nouveau temple built between 1914 and 1917 and housing a worthwhile Jewish museum. Exhibitions here focus on Jewish life in the region, presenting religious artefacts collected from defunct synagogues across Swabia.

🛏 Sleeping

Augsburg is a good alternative base for Oktoberfest, though hotel owners pump up their prices just as much as their Munich counterparts.

Übernacht   HOSTEL €

(☑0821-4554 2828; www.uebernacht-hostel.de; Karlstrasse 4; dm/d from €19/42; 🛜) Professionally run, 21st-century operation spread over three floors of an office block with a wide selection of bright dorms, doubles and apartments, some en suite, some with shared facilities. Amenities are hotel standard and there's a superb kitchen for guest use. Book ahead in summer and during Oktoberfest.

Gästehaus SLEPS   GUESTHOUSE €

(☑0821-780 8890; www.sleps.de; Unterer Graben 6; s €42-49 d €59-69; 🛜) The SLEPS is simply the singles and doubles at Augsburg's youth hostel *(Jugendherberge)*, rebranded as a guesthouse. Rooms still have that whiff of institutional occupation about them but are bright, clean and quiet. For these prices the decent buffet breakfast is a real bonus.

★ Dom Hotel
HOTEL €€

(☎ 0821-343 930; www.domhotel-augsburg.de; Frauentorstrasse 8; s €70-150, d €95-190; 🅿 ❄ @ 🛜 🏊) Augsburg's top choice packs a 500-year-old former bishop's guesthouse (Martin Luther and Kaiser Maxmilian I stayed here) with 57 rooms, all different but sharing a stylishly understated air and pristine upkeep; some have cathedral views. However, the big pluses here are the large swimming pool, fitness centre and solarium. Parking is an extra €6.

Hotel am Rathaus
HOTEL €€

(☎ 0821-346 490; www.hotel-am-rathaus-augsburg.de; Am Hinteren Perlachberg 1; s €69-98, d €105-145; 🛜) Just steps from Rathausplatz and Maximilianstrasse, this central boutique hotel hires out 31 rooms with freshly neutral decor and a sunny little breakfast room. Attracts a business-oriented clientele, so watch out for special weekend deals (almost a third off normal rates).

Steigenberger Drei Mohren Hotel
HOTEL €€€

(☎ 0821-503 60; www.augsburg.steigenberger.de; Maximilianstrasse 40; r €125-280; 🅿 ❄ ✳ @ 🛜) A proud Leopold Mozart stayed here with his prodigious offspring in 1766 and it remains Augsburg's oldest and grandest hotel. The punctiliously maintained rooms are the last word in soothing design and come with marble bathrooms and original art.

Dine in house at Maximilians, a great place to swing by for Sunday brunch.

✖ Eating

In the evening, Maximilianstrasse is the place to tarry, with cafes tumbling out onto the pavements and Augsburg's young and beautiful watching the world go by.

Barfüsser Café
CAFE €

(☎ 0821-450 4966; Barfüsserstrasse 10; snacks €2-7; ⊗ 11am-6pm Mon, Tue, Thu & Fri, from 9am Wed & Sat) Follow a short flight of steps down from the street through a covered passageway to uncover this pretty snack stop by a little canal. It's run by a team of staff with disabilities, for whom it provides work opportunities as part of a community project, and serves delectable homemade cakes, pastries, salads and light lunches. Tram 1 stops outside.

Anno 1578
CAFE €

(Fuggerplatz 9; mains €4.50-10; ⊗ 9am-7pm Mon-Sat; 🛜) Munch on blockbuster breakfasts, lunchtime burgers and sandwiches, or just pop by for a cappuccino or ice cream at this trendy cafe under ancient neon-uplit vaulting. The central table, a huge chunk of timber, is a great place to meet locals and other travellers.

Die Extra Veganten
VEGAN €

(Frauentorstrasse 4; mains €5-7; ⊗ 11am-7pm Tue-Sat; ✖) Modestly proportioned, 15-seat vegan cafe near the cathedral offering owner-prepared meat- and dairy-free wraps, kebabs, salads, *Käsespätzle* (egg noodles), cakes and smoothies. The name is a good example of German humour.

Bauerntanz
GERMAN €€

(Bauerntanzgässchen 1; mains €7-17; ⊗ 11am-11.30pm) Belly-satisfying helpings of creative Swabian and Bavarian food – *Spätzle* (noodles) and more *Spätzle* – are plated up by friendly staff at this prim Alpine tavern with lace curtains, hefty timber interior and chequered fabrics. When the sun makes an appearance, everyone bails for the outdoor seating.

Bayerisches Haus am Dom
BAVARIAN €€

(☎ 0821-349 7990; Johannisgasse 4; mains €7.20-16.50; ⊗ 11am-midnight Mon-Sat, to 11pm Sun) Enjoy an elbow massage from the locals at chunky timber benches, while refuelling on Bavarian and Swabian dishes, cheap lunch options (€6.50) or a sandwich served by dirndl-clad waitresses. Erdinger and Andechser are the frothy double act that stimulates nightly frivolity in the beer garden.

August
INTERNATIONAL €€€

(☎ 0821-352 79; Frauentorstrasse 27; dinner €130; ⊗ from 7pm Wed-Sat) Most Augsburgers have little inkling their city possesses two Michelin stars, both of which belong to chef Christian Grünwald. Treat yourself to some of Bavaria's most innovative cooking in the minimalist dining room, though with just 16 covers, reservations are essential.

⊖ Drinking

Elements
CAFE

(Frauentorstrasse 2) Knock back a cocktail or five at this trendy cafe-bistro which attracts the beautiful people of an eve. Weekend breakfast is ideal for those who rise at the crack of lunchtime.

Thing BEER GARDEN

(Vorderer Lech 45) Augsburg's coolest beer garden sports totem poles and often gets crowded in the evenings. Serves great burgers and beer.

☆ Entertainment

Augsburger Puppenkiste THEATRE
(☑ 0821-450 3450; www.augsburger-puppenkiste.de; Spitalgasse 15) The celebrated puppet theatre holds performances of modern and classic fairy tales that even non–German speakers will enjoy. Advance bookings are essential.

❶ Information

Post Office (Halderstrasse 29) At the Hauptbahnhof.
Tourist Office (☑ 0821-502 0723; www.augsburg-tourismus.de; Rathausplatz; ❀ 9am-6pm Mon-Fri, 10am-5pm Sat, 10am-3pm Sun) Doubles as citizen's advice point, so staff can be slightly distracted.

❶ Getting There & Away

BUS
The Romantic Road Coach (p248) stops at the Hauptbahnhof and the Rathaus. Low-cost coach company **Meinfernbus** (www.meinfernbus.de) runs to Munich 11 times a day (one hour).

CAR & MOTORCYCLE
Augsburg is just off the A8 northwest of Munich.

TRAIN
Augsburg rail connections:
➔ **Füssen** €20.90, two hours, every two hours or change in Buchloe
➔ **Munich** €13.30 to €20, 30 to 45 minutes, three hourly
➔ **Nuremberg** €27.50, one to two hours, hourly
➔ **Ulm** €17.90 to €24, 45 minutes to one hour, three hourly

❶ Getting Around

From the train station take tram 3, 4 or 6 (€1.30) to the central interchange at Königsplatz where all Augsburg's tram routes converge.

Landsberg am Lech

☑ 08191 / POP 28,100

Lovely Landsberg am Lech is often overlooked by Romantic Road trippers on their town-hopping way between Füssen to the south and Augsburg to the north. But it's for this very absence of tourists and a less commercial ambience that this walled town on the River Lech is worth a halt, if only brief.

Landsberg can claim to be the town where one of the German language's best-selling books was written. It was during Hitler's 264 days of incarceration in a Landsberg jail, following the 1923 beer-hall putsch, that he penned his hate-filled *Mein Kampf*, a book that sold an estimated seven million copies when published. The jail later held Nazi war criminals and is still in use.

◉ Sights

Landsberg's hefty medieval defensive walls are punctuated by some beefy gates, the most impressive of which are the 1425 **Bayertor** to the east and the Renaissance-styled **Sandauer Tor** to the north. The tall **Schmalztor** was left centrally stranded when the fortifications were moved further out and still overlooks the main square and the 500 listed buildings within the town walls.

Stadtpfarrkirche Mariä Himmelfahrt CHURCH
(Georg-Hellmair-Platz) This huge 15th-century church was built by Matthäus von Ensingen, architect of Bern Cathedral. The barrel nave is stuccoed to baroque perfection, while a cast of saints populates columns and alcoves above the pews. Gothic-era stained glass casts rainbow hues on the church's most valuable work of art, the 15th-century *Madonna with Child* by local sculptor Lorenz Luidl.

Johanniskirche CHURCH
(Vorderer Anger) If you've already seen the Wieskirche (p233) to the south, you'll instantly recognise this small baroque church as a creation by the same architect, Dominikus Zimmermann, who lived in Landsberg and even served as its mayor.

Heilig-Kreuz-Kirche CHURCH
(Von-Helfenstein-Gasse) Head uphill from the Schmalztor to view this beautiful baroque Jesuit church, the interior a hallucination in broodily dark gilding and glorious ceiling decoration.

Neues Stadtmuseum MUSEUM
(www.museum-landsberg.de; Von-Helfenstein-Gasse 426; adult/concession €3.50/2; ❀ 2-5pm Tue-Fri, from 11am Sat & Sun May-Jan, closed Feb-Apr) Housed in a former Jesuit school, Landsberg's municipal museum chronicles the area's past from prehistory to the 20th century, and displays numerous works of local art, both religious and secular in nature.

🛏 Sleeping & Eating

Stadthotel Augsburger Hof　　　HOTEL €€
(☑08191-969 596; www.stadthotel-landsberg.de; Schlossergasse 378; s €40-65, d €80; 🅿🐶🛜) The 14 en-suite rooms at this highly recommended traditional inn are a superb deal, and have chunky pine beds and well-maintained bathrooms throughout. The owners and staff are a friendly bunch, and the breakfast is a filling set-up for the day. Cycle hire and cycle friendly.

Lechgarten　　　BAVARIAN €€
(www.lechgarten.de; Hubert-von-Herkomer-Strasse 73; mains €5-11; ⊙4-11pm Mon-Fri, 10am-11pm Sat & Sun Apr-Oct) Lansberg's top beer garden on the tree-shaded banks of the River Lech has 250 seats, beer from Andechs Monastery and hearty beer-garden fare. Live music summer weekends, pretty river views any time.

Schafbräu　　　INTERNATIONAL €€
(Hinterer Anger 338; mains €6-16; ⊙11.30am-11pm) This cosy Bavarian-styled tavern has an international menu that leans firmly towards southern Europe. If you don't feel like moving far afterwards, there are rooms to rent upstairs.

ⓘ Information

Tourist Office (☑08191-128 246; www.landsberg.de; Rathaus, Hauptplatz 152; ⊙9am-6pm Mon-Fri May-Oct, 11am-5pm Sat & Sun Apr-Oct, shorter hours Mon-Fri, closed Sat & Sun Nov-Mar)

ⓘ Getting There & Away

BUS
The Romantic Road Coach (p248) makes an epicentral stop on the Hauptplatz.

TRAIN
Landsberg has the following rail connections:
➡ **Augsburg** €8.10, 50 minutes, hourly
➡ **Füssen** Change at Kaufering; €15.70, 1½ hours, every two hours
➡ **Munich** Change at Kaufering; €13.30, 50 minutes, twice hourly

NUREMBERG & FRANCONIA

Somewhere between Ingolstadt and Nuremberg, Bavaria's accent mellows, the oompah bands play that little bit quieter and wine competes with beer as the local tipple. This is Franconia (Franken) and, as every local will tell you, Franconians, who inhabit the wooded hills and the banks of the Main River in Bavaria's northern reaches, are a breed apart from their brash and extrovert cousins to the south.

In the northwest, the region's winegrowers produce some exceptional whites, sold in a distinctive teardrop-shaped bottle called the *Bocksbeutel*. For outdoor enthusiasts, the Altmühltal Nature Park offers wonderful hiking, biking and canoeing. But it is Franconia's old royalty and incredible cities – Nuremberg, Bamberg and Coburg – that draw the biggest crowds.

Nuremberg

☑0911 / POP 510,600

Nuremberg (Nürnberg), Bavaria's second-largest city and the unofficial capital of Franconia, is an energetic place where the nightlife is intense and the beer is as dark as coffee. As one of Bavaria's biggest draws it is alive with visitors year-round, but especially during the spectacular Christmas market.

For centuries, Nuremberg was the undeclared capital of the Holy Roman Empire and the preferred residence of most German kings, who kept their crown jewels here. Rich and stuffed with architectural wonders, it was also a magnet for famous artists, though the most famous of all, Albrecht Dürer, was actually born here. 'Nuremberg shines throughout Germany like a sun among the moon and stars,' gushed Martin Luther. By the 19th century, the city had become a powerhouse in Germany's industrial revolution.

The Nazis saw a perfect stage for their activities in working-class Nuremberg. It was here that the fanatical party rallies were held, the boycott of Jewish businesses began and the infamous Nuremberg Laws outlawing German citizenship for Jewish people were enacted. On 2 January 1945, Allied bombers reduced the city to landfill, killing 6000 people in the process.

After WWII the city was chosen as the site of the war crimes tribunal, now known as the Nuremberg Trials. Later, the painstaking reconstruction – using the original stone – of almost all the city's main buildings, including the castle and old churches in the Altstadt, returned the city to some of its former glory.

◉ Sights

Most major sights are within the Altstadt.

★ Kaiserburg   CASTLE

(Imperial Castle; ☑0911-244 6590; www.kaiser-burg-nuernberg.de; Auf der Burg; adult/concession incl Sinwell Tower €7/6, Palas & Museum €5.50/4.50; ⊙9am-6pm Apr-Sep, 10am-4pm Oct-Mar) This enormous castle complex above the Altstadt poignantly reflects Nuremberg's medieval might. The main attraction is a tour of the newly renovated **Palas** (residential wing) to see the lavish Knights' and Imperial Hall, a Romanesque double chapel and an exhibit on the inner workings of the Holy Roman Empire. This segues to the **Kaiserburg Museum**, which focuses on the castle's military and building history. Elsewhere, enjoy panoramic views from the **Sinwell Tower** or peer 48m down into the **Deep Well**.

For centuries the castle, which has origins in the 12th century, also sheltered the crown jewels (crown, sceptre, orb etc) of the Holy Roman Empire, which are now kept at Hofburg palace in Vienna. It also played a key role in the drawing up of Emperor Charles IV's Golden Bull, a document that changed the way Holy Roman Emperors were elected. The exhibition contains an original statue taken from Prague's Charles Bridge of Charles IV, who spent a lot of time in both Bohemia and Franconia during his reign.

★ Deutsche Bahn Museum   MUSEUM

(☑0800-3268 7386; www.db-museum.de; Lessingstrasse 6; adult/child €5/2.50; ⊙9am-5pm Tue-Fri, 10am-6pm Sat & Sun) Forget Dürer and Nazi rallies, Nuremberg is a railway town at heart. Germany's first passenger trains ran between here and Fürth, a fact reflected in the unmissable German Railways Museum which explores the history of Germany's legendary rail system. The huge exhibition which continues across the road is one of Nuremberg's top sights, especially if you have a soft spot for things that run on rails.

If you're with kids, head straight for KIBALA (Kinder-Bahnland – Children's Railway World), a recently refashioned part of the museum with lots of hands-on, interactive choo-choo-themed attractions. There's also a huge model railway, one of Germany's largest, set in motion every hour by a uniformed controller.

The main exhibition, charting almost two centuries of rail history, starts on the ground floor and continues with more recent exhibits on the 1st floor. Passing quickly through the historically inaccurate beginning (as every rail buff knows, the world's first railway was the Stockton–Darlington, not the Liverpool–Manchester), highlights include Germany's oldest railway carriage dating from 1835 and lots of interesting Deutsche Reichsbahn paraphernalia from East Germany.

However, the real meat of the show are the two halls of locos and rolling stock. The first hall contains Ludwig II's incredible rococo rail carriage, dubbed the 'Versailles of the rails', as well as Bismarck's considerably less ostentatious means of transport. There's also Germany's most famous steam loco, the Adler, built by the Stephensons in Newcastle-upon-Tyne for the Nuremberg–Fürth line. The second hall across the road from the main building houses some mammoth engines, some with their Nazi or Deutsche Reichsbahn insignia still in place.

Hauptmarkt   SQUARE

(Hauptmarkt) This bustling square in the heart of the Altstadt is the site of daily markets as well as the famous *Christkindlesmarkt* (Christmas Market). At the eastern end is the ornate Gothic **Frauenkirche** (church). Daily at noon crowds crane their necks to witness the clock's figures enact a spectacle called the *Männleinlaufen* (Little Men Dancing). Rising from the square like a Gothic spire is the sculpture-festooned **Schöner Brunnen** (Beautiful Fountain). Touch the golden ring in the ornate wrought-iron gate for good luck.

Memorium Nuremberg Trials   MEMORIAL

(☑0911-3217 9372; www.memorium-nuremberg.de; Bärenschanzstrasse 72; adult/concession incl audioguide €5/3; ⊙10am-6pm Wed-Mon) Göring, Hess, Speer and 21 other Nazi leaders were tried for crimes against peace and humanity by the Allies in **Schwurgerichtssaal 600** (Court Room 600) of this still-working courthouse. Today the room forms part of an engaging exhibit detailing the background, progression and impact of the trials using film, photographs, audiotape and even the original defendants' dock. To get here, take the U1 towards Bärenschanze and get off at Sielstrasse.

The initial and most famous trial, held from 20 November 1945 until 1 October 1946, resulted in three acquittals, 12 sentences to death by hanging, three life sentences and four long prison sentences. Hermann Göring, the Reich's field marshal, famously cheated the hangman by taking a cyanide capsule in his cell hours before his scheduled execution.

Although it's easy to assume that Nuremberg was chosen as a trial venue because of its role during the Nazi years, it was actually picked for practical reasons: the largely intact Palace of Justice was able to accommodate lawyers and staff from all four Allied nations.

Note that Court Room 600 is still used for trials and may be closed to visitors.

Reichsparteitagsgelände   HISTORIC SITE

(Luitpoldhain; ☑0911-231 5666; www.museen-nuernberg.de; Bayernstrasse 110; grounds free, documentation centre adult/concession incl audioguide €5/3; ☉grounds 24hr, documentation centre 9am-6pm Mon-Fri, 10am-6pm Sat & Sun) The infamous black-and-white images of ecstatic Nazi supporters hailing their Führer were taken here in Nuremberg. Much of the grounds were destroyed during Allied bombing raids, but enough remains to get a sense of the megalomania behind it, especially after visiting the excellent **Dokumentationszentrum** (Documentation Centre) served by tram 9 from the Hauptbahnhof.

In the north wing of the partly finished Kongresshalle (Congress Hall), the Documentation Centre examines various historical aspects, including the rise of the NSDAP, the Hitler cult, the party rallies and the Nuremberg Trials.

East of here is the **Zeppelinfeld**, where most of the big Nazi parades, rallies and events took place. It is fronted by a 350m-long grandstand, the Zeppelintribüne, where you can still stand on the very balcony from where Hitler incited the masses. It now hosts sporting events and rock concerts, though this rehabilitation has caused controversy.

The grounds are bisected by the 2km-long and 40m-wide **Grosse Strasse** (Great Road), which was planned as a military parade road. Zeppelinfeld, Kongresshalle and Grosse Strasse are all protected landmarks for being significant examples of Nazi architecture.

The Reichsparteitagsgelände is about 4km southeast of the city centre.

Germanisches Nationalmuseum   MUSEUM

(German National Museum; ☑0911-133 10; www.gnm.de; Kartäusergasse 1; adult/concession €8/5; ☉10am-6pm Tue & Thu-Sun, to 9pm Wed) Spanning prehistory to the early 20th century, this museum is the German-speaking world's biggest and most important museum of Teutonic culture. It features works by German painters and sculptors, an archaeological collection, arms and armour, musical and scientific instruments, and toys.

Highlights of the eclectic collection include Dürer's anatomically detailed *Hercules Slaying the Stymphalian Birds* and the world's oldest terrestrial globe and pocket watch as well as 20th-century design classics and baroque dollhouses.

Neues Museum   MUSEUM

(☑0911-240 269; www.nmn.de; Luitpoldstrasse 5; adult/child €4/3; ☉10am-6pm Fri-Wed, to 6pm Thu, closed Mon) The aptly named New Museum showcases contemporary art and design, with resident collections of paintings, sculpture, photography, video art and installations focusing on artists from Eastern Europe, as well as travelling shows. Equally stunning is the award-winning building itself, with a dramatic 100m curved glass facade that, literally and figuratively, reflects the stone town wall opposite.

Albrecht-Dürer-Haus   MUSEUM

(☑0911-231 2568; Albrecht-Dürer-Strasse 39; adult/concession €5/3; ☉10am-5pm Fri-Wed, to 8pm Thu) Dürer, Germany's most famous Renaissance draughtsman, lived and worked at Albrecht-Dürer-Haus from 1509 until his death in 1528. After a multimedia show, there's an audioguide tour of the four-storey house, which is narrated by 'Agnes', Dürer's wife. Highlights are the hands-on demonstrations in the recreated studio and print shop on the 3rd floor and, in the attic, a gallery featuring copies and originals of Dürer's work.

Altes Rathaus   HISTORIC BUILDING

(Rathausplatz 2) Beneath the Altes Rathaus (1616–22), a hulk of a building with lovely Renaissance-style interiors, you'll find the macabre **Mittelalterliche Lochgefängnisse** (Medieval Dungeons; ☑0911-231 2690; adult/concession €3.50/1.50; ☉tours 10am-4.30pm Tue-Sun). This 12-cell death row and torture chamber must be seen on a 30-minute guided tour (held every half-hour) and might easily put you off lunch.

Stadtmuseum Fembohaus   MUSEUM

(☑0911-231 2595; Burgstrasse 15; adult/child €5/3; ☉10am-5pm Tue-Fri, 10am-6pm Sat & Sun) Offering an entertaining overview of the city's history, highlights of the Stadtmuseum Fembohaus include the restored historic rooms of this 16th-century merchant's house. Also here, **Noricama** takes you on a flashy Hollywoodesque multimedia journey (in German and English) through Nuremberg's history.

Nuremberg

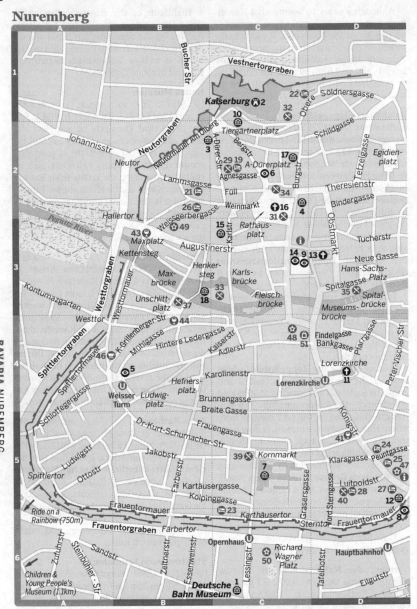

BAVARIA NUREMBERG

Jüdisches Museum Franken JEWISH. MUSEUM
(☎0911-770 577; www.juedisches-museum.org;
Königstrasse 89; adult/concession €3/2; ⏰10am–
5pm Wed-Sun, to 8pm Tue) A quick U-Bahn ride
away in the neighbouring town of Fürth is the
Jüdisches Museum Franken. Fürth once had
the largest Jewish congregation of any city in
southern Germany, and this museum, housed
in a handsomely restored building, chronicles
the history of Jewish life in the region from
the Middle Ages to today. To reach the museum, take the U1 to the Rathaus stop in Fürth.

tures and symbols; check out the ornate carvings over the **Bridal Doorway** to the north, showing the Wise and Foolish Virgins. Inside, the bronze shrine of St Sebald (Nuremberg's own saint) is a Gothic and Renaissance masterpiece that took its maker, Peter Vischer the Elder, and his two sons more than 11 years to complete (Vischer is in it, too, sporting a skullcap).

The church is free to enter, despite the misleading sign on the door.

Felsengänge HISTORIC SITE

(Underground Cellars; www.felsengaenge-nuernberg. de; Bergstrasse 19; tours adult/concession €6/5; ⓣtours 2.30pm daily, also 5.30pm Fri & Sat) Beneath the Albrecht Dürer Monument on Albrecht-Dürer-Platz are the chilly Felsengänge. Departing from the brewery shop at Bergstrasse 19, tours descend to this four-storey subterranean warren, which dates from the 14th century and once housed a brewery and a beer cellar. During WWII, it served as an air-raid shelter. Tours take a minimum of three people. Take a jacket against the chill.

Spielzeugmuseum MUSEUM

(Toy Museum; Karlstrasse 13-15; adult/child €5/3; ⓣ10am-5pm Tue-Fri, to 6pm Sat & Sun) Nuremberg has long been a centre of toy manufacturing, and the large Spielzeugmuseum presents toys in their infinite variety – from innocent hoops to blood-and-guts computer games, historical wooden and tin toys to Barbie et al. Kids and kids at heart will delight in the imaginatively designed play area.

Chekarussell Brunnen FOUNTAIN

(Am Weissen Turm) At the foot of the fortified Weisser Turm (White Tower; now the gateway to the U-Bahn station of the same name) stands this large and startlingly grotesque sculptural work depicting six interpretations of marriage (from first love to quarrel to death-do-us-part), all based on a verse by Hans Sachs, the medieval cobbler-poet. You soon realise why the artist faced a blizzard of criticism when the fountain was unveiled in 1984; it really is enough to put anyone off tying the knot.

Lorenzkirche CHURCH

(Lorenzplatz) Dark and atmospheric, the Lorenzkirche has dramatically downlit pillars, taupe stone columns, sooty ceilings and many artistic highlights. Check out the 15th-century tabernacle in the left aisle – the delicate carved strands wind up to the vaulted ceiling. Remarkable also are the stained

St Sebalduskirche CHURCH

(www.sebalduskirche.de; Albrecht-Dürer-Platz 1; ⓣ9.30am-4pm Jan-Mar, to 6pm Apr-Dec) Nuremberg's oldest church was built in rusty pink-veined sandstone in the 13th century. Its exterior is replete with religious sculp-

Nuremberg

glass (including a rose window 9m in diameter) and Veit Stoss' *Engelsgruss* (Annunciation), a wooden carving with life-size figures suspended above the high altar.

Handwerkerhof   MARKET
(www.handwerkerhof.de; Am Königstor; ⊙ 9am-6.30pm Mon-Fri, 10am-4pm Sat mid-Mar–Dec) FREE
A recreation of an old-world Nuremberg crafts quarter, the Handwerkerhof is a self-contained tourist trap by the Königstor. It's about as quaint as a hammer on your thumbnail, but if you're in the market for souvenirs you may find some decent merchandise (and the bratwurst aren't bad here either).

🧭 Tours

Old Town Walking Tours   WALKING TOUR
(www.nuernberg-tours.de; adult/child €9/free; ⊙ 1.30pm May-Oct) English-language Old Town walking tours are run by the tourist office – tours leave from the Hauptmarkt branch and take two hours.

Geschichte für Alle   CULTURAL TOUR
(☑ 0911-307 360; www.geschichte-fuer-alle.de; adult/concession €8/7) Intriguing range of themed English-language tours by a non-profit association. The 'Albrecht Dürer' and 'Life in Medieval Nuremberg' tours come highly recommended.

Nuremberg Tours   WALKING TOUR
(www.nurembergtours.com; adult/concession €19/17; ⊙ 11.15am Mon, Wed & Sat Apr-Oct) Four-hour walking and public transport tours taking in the city centre and the Reichsparteitagsgelände (p267). Groups meet at the entrance to the Hauptbahnhof.

✴ Festivals & Events

Christkindlesmarkt   CHRISTMAS MARKET
(www.christkindlesmarkt.de) From late November to Christmas Eve, the Hauptmarkt is taken over by the most famous Christkindlesmarkt in Germany. Yuletide shoppers descend on the 'Christmas City' from all over Europe to seek out unique gifts at the scores of colourful timber trinket stalls that fill the square.

The aroma of mulled wine and roast sausages permeates the chilly air, while special festive events take place across the city.

🛏 Sleeping

Accommodation gets tight and rates rocket during the Christmas market and the toy fair (trade only) in late January to early February. At other times, cheap rooms can be found, especially if you book ahead.

Five Reasons
HOSTEL €

(📋 0911-9928 6625; www.five-reasons.de; Frauentormauer 42; dm/d from €23/69; @🕾) Crisply appointed, newly renovated and rebranded 90-bed hostel with spotless dorms, the trendiest hostel bathrooms you are ever likely to encounter, pre-made beds, card keys, fully equipped kitchen, a small bar and very nice staff. Breakfast is an extra €3.10 to €5.80, depending on what option you choose. Overall a great place to lay your head.

DJH Hostel
HOSTEL €

(📋 0911-230 9360; www.nuernberg.jugendherberge.de; Burg 2; dm from €31.90) Open year round, this youth hostel is a real tripstopper with a standard of facilities many four-star hotels would envy. Fully revamped a few years ago, the old Kornhaus is a dramatic building itself, but now sports funky corridors, crisply maintained dorms with super-modern bathrooms, a canteen, bar and very helpful staff.

Be aware that in the summer months you can get a discounted single on popular booking sites for the price of a dorm bed in a four-bunk room here.

Probst-Garni Hotel
PENSION €

(📋 0911-203 433; www.hotel-garni-probst.de; Luitpoldstrasse 9; s/d €56/75; 🕾) A creaky lift from street level takes you up to this realistically priced, centrally located guesthouse, run for 70 years by three generations of Probsts. The 33 gracefully old-fashioned rooms are multi-hued and high-ceilinged but some are more renovated than others. Furniture in the breakfast room is family made.

Hotel Drei Linden
HOTEL €

(📋 0911-506 800; www.hotel-drei-linden-nuernberg.de; Äussere Sulzbacher Strasse 1-3; s/d €52/69; 🕾) A cheap-ish deal, rooms here are comfortable though not at all chic, and there's round-the-clock free tea and coffee. Breakfast is a whopping €9.50 extra. Located 1km east of the Altstadt; take tram 8 from the Hauptbahnhof to Deichlerstrasse.

Knaus-Campingpark
CAMPGROUND €

(📋 0911-981 2717; www.knauscamp.de; Hans-Kalb-Strasse 56; per tent/person €5.50/7.90; 🕾) A camping ground near the lakes in the Volkspark, southeast of the city centre. Take the U1 to Messezentrum, then walk about 1km.

Hotel Elch
HOTEL €€

(📋 0911-249 2980; www.hotel-elch.com; Irrerstrasse 9; s/d from €57/70; 🕾) Occupying a 14th-century, half-timbered house near the Kaiserburg, the Elch has seen big changes in recent years with a new boutique wing added and the reception and restaurant given a complete 21st-century makeover. The result is you now have a choice between fairy-tale 'historic' and slick 'boutique', the latter of which costs a bit more.

Hotel Deutscher Kaiser
HOTEL €€

(📋 0911-242 660; www.deutscher-kaiser-hotel.de; Königstrasse 55; s/d from €92/109; @🕾) Epicentral in its location, aristocratic in its design and service, this treat of a historic hotel has been in the same family since the turn of the 20th century. Climb the castle-like granite stairs to find rooms of understated simplicity, flaunting oversize beds, Italian porcelain, silk lampshades and real period furniture (Biedermeier and *Jugendstil*).

The club-like reading room with newspapers and magazines in German and English is a welcome extra and the breakfast room is a study in soothing, early morning elegance. Renovation work is ongoing.

Art & Business Hotel
HOTEL €€

(📋 0911-232 10; www.art-business-hotel.com; Gleissbühlstrasse 15; s/d from €74/105; 🕾) No need to be an artist or a businessperson to stay at this up-to-the-minute place, a short amble from the Hauptbahnhof. From the trendy bar to the latest in slate bathroom styling, design here is bold, but not overpoweringly so. From reception follow the wobbly carpet to your room, a well-maintained haven uninfected by traffic noise despite the city-centre frenzy outside.

Local Technicolor art and design brings cheer to the communal spaces and there's a small sculpture garden out back. Rates tumble at weekends.

Burghotel
HOTEL €€

(📋 0911-238 890; www.burghotel-nuernberg.de; Lammsgasse 3; s/d from €66/77; @🕾🖳) The mock-Gothic reception area and lantern-lit corridors (watch your head) indicate you're in for a slightly different hotel experience

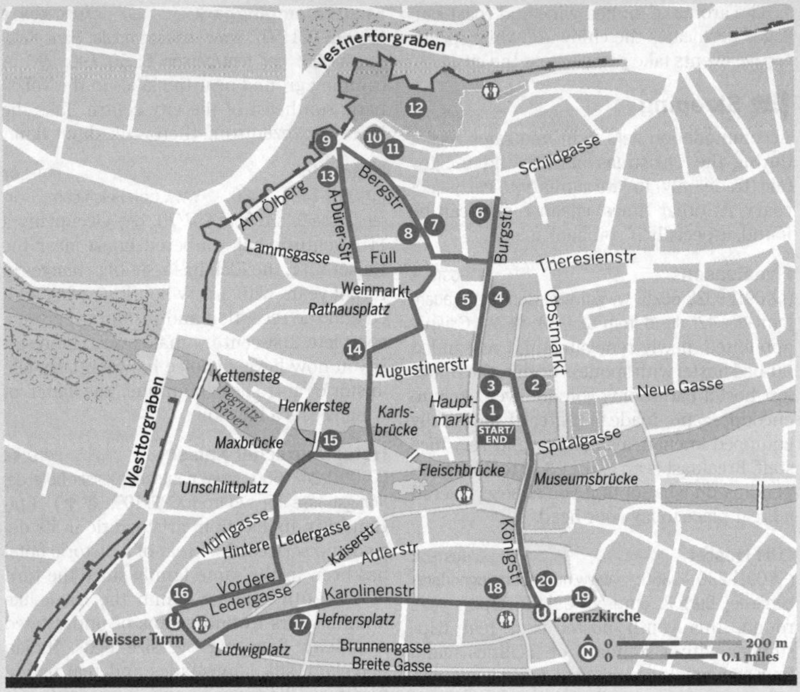

City Walk
Nuremberg Altstadt

START HAUPTMARKT
FINISH HAUPTMARKT
LENGTH 2.5KM, TWO HOURS

This circuit covers the historic centre's key sights over a leisurely 2.5km walk. The tour starts at the 1 **Hauptmarkt**, the main square. At the eastern end is the ornate Gothic 2 **Pfarrkirche Unsere Liebe Frau**. The 3 **Schöner Brunnen** (p266) rises up from the cobblestones like a buried cathedral. Walk north to the 4 **Altes Rathaus** (p267), the old town hall, with its medieval dungeons. Opposite stands the 13th-century 5 **St Sebalduskirche** (p269). Just up Burgstrasse is the 6 **Stadtmuseum Fembohaus** (p267). Backtrack south to Halbwachsengässchen and turn right into Albrecht-Dürer-Platz, with the 7 **Albrecht Dürer Monument**. Directly beneath are the 8 **Felsengänge** (p269), tunnels once used as an air-raid shelter.

Moving up Bergstrasse, you'll reach the massive 9 **Tiergärtnertor**, a 16th-century tower. Nearby is the half-timbered 10 **Pilatushaus**. A few steps east is the 11 **Historischer Kunstbunker**, where precious art was stored in WWII. Looming over the scene is the 12 **Kaiserburg** (p266). Go south to the 13 **Albrecht-Dürer-Haus** (p267). Continue south along Albrecht-Dürer-Strasse, turn left on Füll and skirt the back of Sebalduskirche to Karlsstrasse, where you'll reach the 14 **Spielzeugmuseum** (p269).

Cross the Karlsbrücke to enjoy a view of the 15 **Weinstadl**, an old wine depot overlooking the river. Continue across the Henkersteg and wend your way south to Vordere Ledergasse, which leads west to the amazing 16 **Ehekarussell Brunnen** (p269), with its shocking images of married life. Head east on Ludwigplatz past the 17 **Peter-Henlein-Brunnen**, with a statue of the first watchmaker, and proceed along Karolinenstrasse to reach the city's oldest house, 18 **Nassauer Haus** at No 2, and the massive 19 **Lorenzkirche** (p269). The 20 **Tugendbrunnen** (Fountain of the Seven Virtues) is on the north side of the church.

Continuing north up Königstrasse will return you to the Hauptmarkt, your starting point.

here. The small singles and doubles have strange '50s-style built-in timber furniture reminiscent of yesteryear train carriages, old-fashioned bedhead radios and chunky TVs, while some much larger 'comfort' rooms under the eaves have spacious sitting areas and more up-to-date amenities.

Apart from the medieval theme, the big draw here is the basement heated swimming pool, where all guests are free to make a splash.

Agneshof HOTEL €€
(☑0911-214 440; www.agneshof-nuernberg.de; Agnesgasse 10; s/d from €82/96; P🐾) Tranquilly located in the antiques quarter near the St Sebalduskirche, the Agneshof's public areas have a sophisticated, artsy touch. The 74 box-ticking rooms have whitewashed walls and '90s furniture; some at the top have views of the Kaiserburg. There's a state-of-the-art wellness centre, and a pretty summer courtyard garden strewn with deckchairs. Breakfast is a cheeky extra €7.

Hotel Victoria HOTEL €€
(☑0911-240 50; www.hotelvictoria.de; Königstrasse 80; s/d from €82/98; P@🐾) A hotel since 1896, the Victoria is a solid option with a central location. With its early-21st-century bathrooms and now ever so slightly dated decor, the price is about right. Popular with business travellers. Parking costs €12.

Hotel Drei Raben BOUTIQUE HOTEL €€€
(☑0911-274 380; www.hoteldreiraben.de; Königstrasse 63; d incl breakfast from €150; P✳🐾) The design of this classy charmer builds on the legend of the three ravens perched on the building's chimney stack, who tell stories from Nuremberg lore. Art and decor in the 'mythical theme' rooms reflect a particular tale, from the life of Albrecht Dürer to the first railway. Valet parking available (€15).

NUREMBERG FOR KIDS

No city in Bavaria has more for kids to see and do than Nuremberg. In fact, keeping the little 'uns entertained in the Franconian capital is child's play.

Museums

Children & Young People's Museum (☑0911 600 040; www.kindermuseum-nuernberg. de; Michael-Ende-Strasse 17; adult/family €7/19; ☺2-5.30pm Sat, 10am-5.30pm Sun Sep-Jun) Educational exhibitions and lots of hands-on fun – just a pity it's not open more often.

School Museum (☑0911-530 2574; Äussere Sulzbacher Strasse 62; adult/child €5/3; ☺9am-5pm Tue-Fri, 10am-6pm Sat & Sun) Recreated classroom plus school-related exhibits from the 17th century to the Third Reich.

Deutsche Bahn Museum (p266) Feeds the kids' obsession for choo-choos.

Play

Playground of the Senses (www.erfahrungsfeld.nuernberg.de; Untere Talgasse 8; adult/child €8/6.50; ☺9am-6pm Mon-Fri, 1-6pm Sat, 10am-6pm Sun May–mid-Sep) Some 80 hands-on 'stations' designed to educate children in the laws of nature, physics and the human body. Take the U2 or U3 to Wöhrder Wiese.

Toys

Playmobil (☑0911-9666 1700; www.playmobil-funpark.de; Brandstätterstrasse 2-10; admission €11; ☺9am-7pm May-Sep, 9am-6pm Oct) This theme park has life-size versions of the popular toys. It's located 9km west of the city centre in Zirndorf; take the S4 to Anwanden, then change to bus 151. Free admission if it's your birthday. Special 'Kleine Dürer' (Little Dürer; €2.99) figures are on sale here and at the tourist office.

Käthe Wohlfahrt Christmas shop (www.wohlfahrt.com; Königstrasse 8) The Nuremberg branch of this year-round Christmas shop.

Spielzeugmuseum (p269) Some 1400 sq metres of Matchbox, Barbie, Playmobil and Lego, plus a great play area.

Germanisches Nationalmuseum (p267) Has a toy section and holds ocassional tours for children.

✕ Eating

Café am Trödelmarkt
CAFE €

(Trödelmarkt 42; dishes €4-8.50; ☺9am 6pm Mon-Sat, 11am-6pm Sun) A gorgeous place on a sunny day, this multilevel waterfront cafe overlooks the covered Henkersteg bridge. It's especially popular for its continental breakfasts, and has fantastic cakes, as well as good blackboard lunchtime specials between 11am and 2pm.

Naturkostladen Lotos
ORGANIC, BUFFET €

(www.naturkostladen-lotos.de; Am Unschlittplatz 1; dishes €3-6; ☺9.30am-6pm Mon-Fri, to 4pm Sat; ✎) Unclog arteries and blast free radicals with a blitz of grain burgers, spinach soup or vegie pizza at this health-food shop. The fresh bread and cheese counter is a treasure chest of nutritious picnic supplies.

Suppdiwupp
CAFETERIA €

(Lorenzer Strasse 27; mains €3.50-7; ☺11am-6pm Mon-Thu, to 4pm Fri & Sat) This fragrantly spicy, recently revamped lunch halt has a weekly changing menu, outdoor seating and a choice of nonliquid mains (sandwiches, salads) if you don't fancy a bowl of broth. Very popular early afternoon so get there early.

Wurst Durst
GERMAN €

(Luitpoldstrasse 13; dishes €3-5; ☺11am-6pm Tue-Thu, to 5am Fri & Sat) Wedged between the facades of Luitpoldstrasse, this tiny snack bar offers munchies relief in the form of Belgian fries, sausages and trays of *Currywurst*.

Sushi Glas
SUSHI €

(Kornmarkt 5-7; sushi from €5; ☺noon-11pm Mon-Wed, noon-midnight Thu-Sat, 6-10pm Sun) Take a pew in this 21st-century sugar cube to watch the sushi chef deftly craft your order. When the mercury climbs high, enjoy your nigiri, sashimi and American sushi beneath the huge sunshades on the Kornmarkt.

★ Albrecht Dürer Stube
FRANCONIAN €€

(☑0911-227 209; www.albrecht-duerer-stube.de; cnr Albrecht-Dürer-Strasse & Agnesgasse; mains €7-15; ☺6pm-midnight Mon-Sat, 11.30am-2.30pm Fri & Sun) This unpretentious and intimate restaurant has a Dürer-inspired dining room, prettily laid tables, a ceramic stove keeping things toasty when they're not outside, and a menu of Nuremberg sausages, steaks, sea fish, seasonal specials, Franconian wine and *Landbier* (regional beer). There aren't many tables so booking ahead at weekends is recommended.

Goldenes Posthorn
FRANCONIAN €€

(☑0911-225 153; Glöckleinsgasse 2, cnr Sebalder Platz; mains €9-19; ☺11am-11pm; ✎) Push open the heavy copper door to find a real culinary treat that has hosted royals, artists and professors (including Albrecht Dürer) since 1498. You can't go wrong sticking with the miniature local sausages, but the pork shoulder and the house speciality – vinegar-marinated ox cheeks – are highly recommended as well.

Heilig-Geist-Spital
BAVARIAN €€

(☑0911-221 761; Spitalgasse 16; mains €7-17; ☺11.30am-11pm) Lots of dark carved wood, a herd of hunting trophies and a romantic candlelit half-light make this former hospital, suspended over the Pegnitz, one of the most atmospheric dining rooms in town. Sample the delicious, seasonally changing menu inside or out in the pretty courtyard, a real treat if you are looking for somewhere traditional to dine.

Bratwursthäusle
GERMAN €€

(http://die-nuernberger-bratwurst.de; Rathausplatz 1; meals €7.20-12.90; ☺10am-10pm Mon-Sat) Seared over a flaming beech-wood grill, the little links sold at this rustic inn arguably set the standard across the land. You can dine in the timbered restaurant or on the terrace with views of the Hauptmarkt. Service can be flustered at busy times.

Marientorzwinger
GERMAN €€

(Lorenzer Strasse 33; mains €7-17; ☺11.30am-1am) The last remaining *Zwinger* eatery (taverns built between the inner and outer walls when they relinquished their military use) in Nuremberg is an atmospheric place to chomp on a mixed bag of sturdy regional specials in the simple wood-panelled dining room or the leafy beer garden. Fürth-brewed Tucher is the ale of choice here.

Burgwächter
FRANCONIAN, INTERNATIONAL €€

(☑0911-222 126; Am Ölberg 10; mains €9-15; ☺11am-11pm; ✎) Refuel after a tour of the Kaiserburg with prime steaks, bratwurst with potato salad, and vegetarian-friendly Swabian filled pastas and salads, as you feast your eyes on the best terrace views from any Nuremberg eatery or drinking spot. With kiddies in tow, ask for *Kloss* (a simple dumpling with sauce).

American Diner
AMERICAN €€

(Gewerbemuseumsplatz 3; burgers €8-11; ☺11am-1am) For the juiciest burgers in town, head for this retro diner in the Cinecitta Cinema, Germany's biggest multiplex.

 Drinking

Kettensteg
BEER GARDEN

(www.restaurant-biergarten-kettensteg.de; Maxplatz 35; ☺11am-11pm) At the end of the chain bridge and in the shadow of the Halletor you'll find this classic Bavarian beer garden complete with its gravel floor, folding slatted chairs, fairylights, tree shade and river views. Zirndorfer, Lederer and Tucher beers are on tap and some of the food comes on heart-shaped plates.

Treibhaus
CAFE

(✆0911-223 041; Karl-Grillenberger-Strasse 28; light meals €5-10; ☺9am to last customer; 🖝) Off the path of most visitors, this bustling cafe is a Nuremberg institution and one of the most happening places in town. Set yourself down in the sun on a yellow director's chair out front or warm yourself with something strong around the huge zinc bar inside.

Kloster
PUB

(Obere Wörthstrasse 19; ☺5pm-1am) One of Nuremberg's best drinking dens is all dressed up as a monastery replete with ecclesiastic knick-knacks including coffins emerging from the walls. The monks here pray to the god of *Landbier* and won't be up at 5am for matins, that's for sure.

Cafe Katz
BAR

(Hans-Sachs-Platz 8; ☺11am-1am Sun-Thu, to 2am Fri & Sat) From the outside this place looks like a secondhand furniture shop, the vitrines packed with 1970s coffee tables, old school desks and 1980s high-back chairs. But the La Marzocco espresso machine gives the game away as this is one of Nuremberg's coolest cafes, a hip spot to see, be seen and enjoy a drink and/or a vegie or vegan meal on retro furnishings.

Barfüsser Brauhaus
BEER HALL

(Königstrasse 60; ☺11am-1am Mon-Fri, to 2am Sat) This beer hall deep below street level is a popular spot to hug a mug of site-brewed ale, bubbling frothily in the copper kettles that occupy the cavernous vaulted interior. The traditional trappings of the huge quaffing space clash oddly with the yellow polo shirts of the waiting staff, but that's our only criticism.

Meisengeige
BAR

(Am Laufer Schlagturm 3; ☺30min before start of film to midnight Sun-Wed, to 1am Thu, to 2am Fri & Sat) Art- and foreign-film cinema with attached pub; it's a conversation-inspiring spot for a drink even if you're not going to see a film.

☆ **Entertainment**

The excellent *Plärrer* (www.plaerrer.de), available at newsstands throughout the city and from the tourist office, is the best source of information on events around town.

Mata Hari Bar
LIVE MUSIC

(www.mataharibar.de; Weissgerbergasse 31; ☺from 8pm Wed-Sun) This bar with live music and DJ nights is a Nuremberg institution. After 9pm it's usually standing room only and the party goes on well into the early hours.

Hirsch
LIVE MUSIC

(✆0911-429 414; www.der-hirsch.de; Vogelweiherstrasse 66) This converted factory, 2.5km south of the Hauptbahnhof, hosts live alternative music almost daily, both big-name acts and local names. Take the U1 or U2 to Plärrer, then change to tram 4, alighting at Dianaplatz.

Staatstheater
THEATRE

(www.staatstheater-nuernberg.de; Richard-Wagner-Platz 2) Nuremberg's magnificent state theatre serves up an impressive mix of dramatic arts. The renovated art-nouveau opera house presents opera and ballet, while the Kammerspiele offers a varied program of classical and contemporary plays. The Nürnberger Philharmoniker also performs here.

Filmhaus
CINEMA

(✆0911-231 5823; www.kunstkulturquartier.de; Königstrasse 93) This small indie picture house shows foreign-language movies, reruns of cult German flicks and films for kids.

Loop Club
CLUB

(www.loopclub.de; Klingenhofstrasse 52) With three dance areas and a languid chill-out zone with lounge music, this place attracts a slightly more mature crowd, meaning '80s and '90s hits plus student nights. Take the U2 to Herrnhütte, turn right and it's a five-minute walk.

Mach1
CLUB

(✆0911-246 602; www.macheins.club; Kaiserstrasse 1-9; ☺Thu-Sat) This legendary dance temple has been around for decades, but still holds a spell over fashion victims. Don your best geek chic, line up and be mustered.

ℹ Information

Main Post Office (Bahnhofplatz 1)

ReiseBank (Hauptbahnhof)

Tourist Office (☑ 0911-233 60; www.touris-mus.nuernberg.de; Königstrasse 93; ⊘ 9am-7pm Mon-Sat, 10am-4pm Sun) Publishes the excellent *See & Enjoy* booklet, a comprehensive guide to the city.

Tourist Office (☑ 0911-233 60; www.touris-mus.nuernberg.de; Hauptmarkt 18; ⊘ 9am-6pm Mon-Sat year round, also 10am-4pm Sun Apr-Oct)

ℹ Getting There & Away

AIR

Nuremberg's **Albrecht Dürer Airport** (www.airport-nuernberg.de) 5km north of the centre, is served by regional and international carriers, including Ryanair, Lufthansa, Air Berlin and Air France.

BUS

Buses to destinations across Europe leave from the main bus station (ZOB) near the Hauptbahnhof. There's a Touring/Eurolines office nearby. **Meinfernbus** (www.mein-fernbus.de) links Nuremberg with countless destinations in Germany and beyond. Special Deutsche Bahn express coaches to Prague (€54, 3½ hours, nine daily) leave from outside the Hauptbahnhof.

TRAIN

Rail connections from Nuremberg:

→ **Berlin** €100, five hours, at least hourly
→ **Frankfurt** €55, 2½ hours, at least hourly
→ **Hamburg** €130, 4½ hours, nine daily
→ **Munich** €36 to €55, one hour, twice hourly
→ **Vienna** €103, five hours, every two hours

ℹ Getting Around

TO/FROM THE AIRPORT

U-Bahn 2 runs every few minutes from the Hauptbahnhof to the airport (€2.40, 13 minutes). A taxi to the airport will cost about €16.

ℹ NÜRNBERG + FÜRTH CARD

Available to those staying overnight in the two cities, the Nürnberg + Fürth Card (€25) is good for two days of public transport and admission to all museums and attractions in both cities. It can only be purchased from tourist offices or online from Nuremberg's official tourism website.

BICYCLE

Nuremberg has ample bike lanes along busy roads and the Altstadt is pretty bike friendly. For bike hire, try the excellent **Ride on a Rainbow** (☑ 0911-397 337; www.ride-on-a-rainbow.de; Adam-Kraft-Strasse 55; per day from €9).

PUBLIC TRANSPORT

The best transport around the Altstadt is at the end of your legs. Timed tickets on the VGN bus, tram and U-Bahn/S-Bahn networks cost from €1.80. A day pass costs €5.40. Passes bought on Saturday are valid all weekend.

Bamberg

☑ 0951 / POP 71,200

A disarmingly beautiful architectural masterpiece with an almost complete absence of modern eyesores, Bamberg's entire Altstadt is a Unesco World Heritage Site and one of Bavaria's unmissables. Generally regarded as one of Germany's most attractive settlements, the town is bisected by rivers and canals and was built by archbishops on seven hills, earning it the inevitable sobriquet of 'Franconian Rome'. Students inject some liveliness into its streets, pavement cafes, pubs and no fewer than 10 breweries cooking up Bamberg's famous smoked beer, but it's usually wide-eyed tourists who can be seen filing through its narrow medieval streets. The town can be tackled as a day trip from Nuremberg, but, to really do it justice and to experience the romantically lit streets once most visitors have left, consider an overnight stay.

◎ Sights

Bamberger Dom   CATHEDRAL
(www.erzbistum-bamberg.de; Domplatz; ⊘ 8am-6pm Apr-Oct, to 5pm Nov-Mar) **FREE** Beneath the quartet of spires, Bamberg's cathedral is packed with artistic treasures, most famously the life-size equestrian statue of the **Bamberger Reiter** (Bamberg Horseman), whose true identity remains a mystery. It overlooks the **tomb of cathedral founders**, Emperor Heinrich II and his wife Kunigunde, splendidly carved by Tilmann Riemenschneider. The **marble tomb of Clemens II** in the west choir is the only papal burial site north of the Alps. Nearby, the **Virgin Mary altar** by Veit Stoss also warrants closer inspection.

Founded by Heinrich II in 1004, the cathedral's current appearance dates to the early 13th century and is the outcome of a Romanesque-Gothic duel between church architects after the original and its immediate successor burnt down in the 12th century. The pillars have the original light hues of Franconian sandstone thanks to Ludwig I, who eradicated all postmedieval decoration in the early 19th century.

Altes Rathaus   HISTORIC BUILDING
(Old Town Hall; Obere Brücke; adult/concession €4.50/4; ⊘ 9.30am-4.30pm Tue-Sun) Like a ship in dry dock, Bamberg's 1462 Old Town Hall was built on an artifical island in the Regnitz River, allegedly because the local bishop had refused to give the town's citizens any land for its construction. Inside is a collection of precious porcelain, but even more enchanting are the richly detailed frescos adorning its facades – note the cherub's leg cheekily sticking out from the east facade.

Historisches Museum   MUSEUM
(⊘ 0951-519 0746; www.museum.bamberg.de; Domplatz 7; adult/concession €5/4.50; ⊘ 9am-5pm Tue-Sun May-Oct, occasionally open in winter for special exhibitions) Bamberg's main museum fills the Alte Hofhaltung (old court hall), a former prince-bishops' palace near the cathedral, with a mixed bag of exhibits. These include a model of the pilgrimage church Vierzehnheiligen and the Bamberger Götzen, ancient stone sculptures found in the region. Often of greater interest are the expertly curated special exhibitions, which examine aspects of the region's past in more detail.

Neue Residenz   PALACE
(New Residence; ⊘ 0951-519 390; Domplatz 8; adult/concession €4.50/3.50; ⊘ 9am-6pm Apr-Sep, 10am-4pm Oct-Mar) This splendid episcopal palace gives you an eyeful of the lavish lifestyle of Bamberg's prince-bishops who, between 1703 and 1802, occupied its 40-odd rooms that can only be seen on guided 45-minute tours (in German). Tickets are also good for the Bavarian State Gallery, with works by Lucas Cranach the Elder and other old masters. The baroque **Rose Garden** delivers fabulous views over Bamberg's sea of red-tiled roofs.

Fränkisches Brauereimuseum   MUSEUM
(⊘ 0951-530 16; www.brauereimuseum.de; Michaelsberg 10f; adult/concession €3.50/3; ⊘ 1-5pm Wed-Fri, 11am-5pm Sat & Sun Apr-Oct) Located in the Kloster St Michael, this comprehensive brewery museum exhibits over a thousand period mashing, boiling and bottling implements, as well as everything to do with local suds, such as beer mats,

tankards, enamel beer signs and lots of photos and documentation. If the displays have left you dry mouthed, quench your thirst in the small pub.

Kloster St Michael   MONASTERY
(Franziskanergasse 2; ⊘ 9am-6pm Apr-Oct) Above Domplatz, at the top of Michaelsberg, is the Benedictine Kloster St Michael, a former monastery and now an aged people's home. The monastery church is essential Bamberg viewing, both for its baroque art and the meticulous depictions of nearly 600 medicinal plants and flowers on the vaulted ceiling. The manicured garden terrace boasts a splendid city panorama.

☞ Tours

BierSchmecker Tour   WALKING TOUR
(www.bier.bamberg.info; adult €22) Possibly the most tempting tour of the amazingly varied offerings at the tourist office is the self-guided BierSchmecker Tour. The price includes entry to the Fränkisches Brauereimuseum (depending on the route taken), plus five beer vouchers valid in five pubs and breweries, an English information booklet, a route map and a souvenir stein.

🛌 Sleeping

Backpackers Bamberg   HOSTEL €
(⊘ 0951-222 1718; www.backpackersbamberg. de; Heiliggrabstrasse 4; dm €17-20, s/d €29/44; 🐾) Bamberg's backpacker hostel is a funky but well-kept affair, with clean dorms, a fully functional kitchen and a quiet, family-friendly atmosphere. Make sure you let staff know when you're arriving, as it's left unmanned for most of the day.

Located 400m north along Luitpoldstrasse from the Luitpoldbrücke.

Alt Bamberg   HOTEL €
(⊘ 0951-986 150; www.hotel-alt-bamberg. de; Habergasse 11; s/d from €45/65) Often heavily discounted on popular booking websites, the no-frills rooms at this well-located, old-school hotel are digs of choice for euro-watching nomads. Some rooms share showers, the breakfast is free and there's a well-respected Greek restaurant downstairs.

Campingplatz Insel   CAMPGROUND €
(⊘ 0951-563 20; www.campinginsel.de; Am Campingplatz 1; tents €4-8, adult/car €6/4) If rustling nylon is your abode of choice, this well-equipped site, in a tranquil spot right on the

river, is the sole camping option. Take bus 918 to Campingplatz.

Hotel Sankt Nepomuk   HOTEL €€

(☑0951-984 20; www.hotel-nepomuk.de; Obere Mühlbrücke 9; s/d from €90/130; P🖼) Aptly named after the patron saint of bridges, this is a classy establishment in a half-timbered former mill right on the Regnitz. It has a superb restaurant (mains €15 to €30) with a terrace and 24 new-fangled rooms of recent vintage. Breakfast is an extra €5.

Barockhotel am Dom   HOTEL €€

(☑0951-540 31; www.barockhotel.de; Vorderer Bach 4; s/d from €84/99; P🖼) The sugary facade, a sceptre's swipe from the Dom, gives a hint of the baroque heritage and original details within. The 19 rooms have sweeping views of the Dom or the roofs of the Altstadt, and breakfast is served in a 14th-century vault.

Hotel Residenzschloss   HOTEL €€

(☑0951-609 10; www.residenzschloss.com; Untere Sandstrasse 32; r from €92; P🖼) Bamberg's grandest digs occupy a palatial building formerly used as a hospital. But have no fear, as the swanky furnishings – from the Roman-style steam bath to the flashy piano bar – have little in common with institutional care. High-ceilinged rooms are business standard though display little historical charm. Take bus 916 from the ZOB.

✖ Eating & Drinking

Zum Sternla   FRANCONIAN €

(☑0951-287 50; Lange Strasse 46; mains €5-10; ⊗11am-11pm Tue-Sun) Bamberg's oldest *Wirtshaus* (inn; established 1380) bangs down bargain-priced staples including pork dishes, steaks, dumplings and sauerkraut, as well as specials, but it's a great, nontouristy place for a traditional *Brotzeit* (snack), or just a pretzel and a beer. The menu is helpfully translated from Franconian into German.

Klosterbräu   BREWERY €

(Obere Mühlbrücke 1-3; mains €7-12; ⊗11.30am-10pm Mon-Sat, to 9pm Sun) This beautiful half-timbered brewery is Bamberg's oldest. It draws *Stammgäste* (regulars) and tourists alike who wash down filling slabs of meat and dumplings with its excellent range of ales in the unpretentious dining room.

Messerschmidt   FRANCONIAN €€

(☑0951-297 800; Lange Strasse 41; mains €12-25; ⊗11am-10pm) This stylish gourmet eatery may be ensconced in the house where

aviation engineer Willy Messerschmidt was born, but there's nothing 'plane' about dining here. The place oozes old-world charm, with dark woods, white linens and traditionally formal service. Sharpen your molars on platters of roast duck and red cabbage out on the alfresco terrace overlooking a pretty park, or in the attached wine tavern.

Schlenkerla   GERMAN €€

(☑0951-560 60; www.schlenkerla.de; Dominikanerstrasse 6; mains €6.50-13; ⊗9.30am-11.30pm) Beneath wooden beams as dark as the superb *Rauchbier* poured straight from oak barrels, locals and visitors dig into scrumptious Franconian fare at this legendary flower-festooned tavern near the cathedral.

Kornblume   ORGANIC €€

(☑0951-917 1760; www.kornblume-bamberg.de; Kapellenstrasse 22; mains €7-22; ⊗5.30pm-midnight Wed-Mon, plus 11.30am-2pm Sun) Don't be deterred by the somewhat style-absent decor at this family-run place 1.5km east of the centre, as the tasty food is lovingly prepared and strict organic and ecofriendly principles impeccably upheld. The menu reads like a vegetarian's antioxidant bible, though the occasional meat dish also makes an appearance. Take bus 905 to Wunderburg.

Spezial-Keller   GERMAN €€

(☑0951-548 87; www.spezial-keller.de; Sternwartstrasse 8; dishes €6-13; ⊗3pm-late Tue-Fri, from noon Sat, from 10am Sun) The walk into the hills past the cathedral to this delightful beer garden is well worth it, both for the malty *Rauchbier* and the sweeping views of the Altstadt. In winter the action moves into the cosy tavern warmed by a traditional wood-burning tiled stove.

Ambräusianum   PUB FOOD €€

(☑0951-509 0262; Dominikanerstrasse 10; mains €10-14; ⊗11am-11pm Tue-Sat, 11am-9pm Sun) Bamberg's only brewpub does a killer *Weisswurst* breakfast – parsley-speckled veal sausage served with a big freshly baked pretzel and a *Weissbier* (wheat beer) – as well as schnitzel, pork knuckle and *Flammkuchen* (Alsatian pizza) that'll have you waddling out the door like a Christmas goose.

Torschuster   BAR

(Obere Karolinenstrasse 10; ⊗from 6pm Tue-Sun) Beers from all of Bamberg's breweries, a good selection of whisky, old enamel ad-

Bamberg

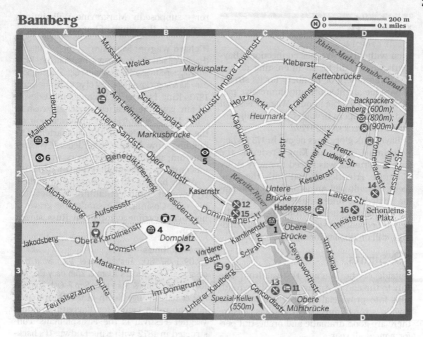

Bamberg

◎ Sights
1	Altes Rathaus	C2
2	Bamberger Dom	B3
3	Fränkisches Brauereimuseum	A2
4	Historisches Museum	B3
5	Klein Venedig	B2
6	Kloster St Michael	A2
7	Neue Residenz	B2

◎ Sleeping
8	Alt Bamberg	D2
9	Barockhotel am Dom	C3
10	Hotel Residenzschloss	A1
11	Hotel Sankt Nepomuk	C3

◎ Eating
12	Ambräusianum	C2
13	Klosterbräu	C3
14	Messerschmidt	D2
15	Schlenkerla	C2
16	Zum Sternla	D2

◎ Drinking & Nightlife
17	Torschuster	A3

vertising signs and in particular owner Thomas' eclectic vinyl collection make up one of Bamberg's best nights out and an after-dark antedote to medieval tavern life. Thomas' collection doesn't go much past the mid-eighties – make of that what you will.

ℹ Information

Post Office (Ludwigstrasse 25)
Tourist Office (☑ 0951-297 6200; www.bamberg.info; Geyersworthstrasse 5; ☺ 9.30am-6pm Mon-Fri, to 4pm Sat, to 2.30pm Sun) Staff sell the Bambergcard (€12), valid for three days of free bus rides and free museum entry.

ℹ Getting There & Around

BUS
Several buses, including 901, 902 and 931, connect the train station with the central bus station (ZOB). Bus 910 goes from the ZOB to Domplatz.

TRAIN
Bamberg has the following rail connections:
➡ **Berlin** €90, 4¼ hours, every two hours
➡ **Munich** €63, two hours, every two hours
➡ **Nuremberg** €21, 40 to 60 minutes, four hourly
➡ **Würzburg** €20.70, one hour, twice hourly

Bayreuth

📞 0921 / POP 71,600

Even without its Wagner connections, Bayreuth would still be an interesting detour from Nuremberg or Bamberg for its streets of baroque architecture and impressive palaces. But it's for the annual Wagner Festival that 60,000 opera devotees make a pilgrimage to this neck of the *Wald*.

Bayreuth's glory days began in 1735 when Wilhelmine, sister of King Frederick the Great of Prussia, was forced to marry stuffy Margrave Friedrich. Bored with the local scene, the cultured Anglo-oriented Wilhelmine invited the finest artists, poets, composers and architects in Europe to court. The period bequeathed some eye-catching buildings, still on display for all to see.

◎ Sights

Outside of the Wagner Festival from late July to the end of August, most of Bayreuth slips into provincial slumber, although the town's strong musical traditions ensure there are good dramatic and orchestral performances all year.

Markgräfliches Opernhaus   THEATRE

(Opernstrasse 14; adult/concession €2.50/2; ☺9am-6pm Apr-Sep, 10am-4pm Oct-Mar) Designed by Giuseppe Galli Bibiena, a famous 18th-century architect from Bologna, Bayreuth's opera house is one of Europe's most stunningly ornate baroque theatres. Germany's largest opera house until 1871, it has a lavish interior smothered in carved, gilded and marbled wood. However, Richard Wagner considered it too modest for his serious work and conducted here just once. The city has decided it's time this old dame had a facelift and until 2017 most of the building will be closed.

Neues Schloss   PALACE

(📞0921-759 690; Ludwigstrasse 21; adult/concession €5.50/4.50; ☺9am-6pm daily Apr-Sep, 10am-4pm Tue-Sun Oct-Mar) Opening into the vast Hofgarten, the Neues Schloss lies a short distance south of the main shopping street, Maxmilianstrasse. A riot of rococo style, the margrave's residence after 1753 features a vast collection of 18th-century Bayreuth porcelain. The annual VIP opening of the Wagner Festival is held in the Cedar Room. Also worth a look is the **Spiegelscherbenkabinett** (Broken Mirror Cabinet), which is lined with irregular shards of broken mirror – supposedly Margravine Wilhelmine's response to the vanity of her era.

Richard Wagner Museum   MUSEUM

(Haus Wahnfried; www.wagnermuseum.de; Richard-Wagner-Strasse 48; admission €8; ☺10am-6pm daily Jul & Aug, closed Mon rest of year) In the early 1870s King Ludwig II, Wagner's most devoted fan, gave the great composer the cash to build Haus Wahnfried, a mini-mansion on the northern edge of the Hofgarten. The building now houses the Richard Wagner Museum, which for three years was closed for complete renovation. It reopened in 2015.

At the back of the house is the unmarked, ivy-covered tomb containing Wagner and his wife Cosima. The sandstone grave of his loving canine companion Russ stands nearby.

Festspielhaus   THEATRE

(📞0921-787 80; Festspielhügel 1-2; adult/concession €7/5; ☺tours 10am & 2pm daily Dec-Apr, 10am, 11am, 2pm & 3pm May, Sep & Oct, 2pm Sat Nov, closed Jun-Aug) North of the Hauptbahnhof, the main venue for Bayreuth's annual Wagner Festival is the Festspielhaus, constructed in 1872 with King Ludwig II's backing. The structure was specially designed to accommodate Wagner's massive theatrical sets, with three storeys of mechanical works hidden below stage. It's still one of the largest opera venues in the world. To see inside you must join a guided tour. Take bus 305 to Am Festspielhaus.

Eremitage   PARK

Around 6km east of the centre lies the Eremitage, a lush park girding the **Altes Schloss** (📞0921-759 6937; adult/concession €4.50/3.50; ☺9am-6pm Apr-Sep), the summer residence that belonged to 18th-century Margrave Friedrich and his wife Wilhelmine. Visits to the palace are by guided tour only and take in the Chinese Mirror room where Countess Wilhelmine penned her memoirs.

Also in the park is horseshoe-shaped Neues Schloss (not to be confused with the one in town), which centres on the amazing mosaic Sun Temple with gilded Apollo sculpture. Take bus 302 from ZOH.

Maisel's Brauerei- & Büttnerei-Museum   BREWERY, MUSEUM

(📞0921-401 234; www.maisel.com/museum; Kulmbacher Strasse 40; tours adult/concession €5/3; ☺tours 2pm daily) For a fascinating look at the brewing process, head to this enormous museum next door to the brewery of one of Germany's top wheat-beer producers – Maisel. The 90-minute guided tour takes you into the bowels of the 19th-century plant, with atmospheric rooms filled with 4500 beer mugs and amusing artefacts. Visits conclude with a glass of sweet-cloudy *Weissbier*.

🛏 Sleeping

Don't even think of attempting a sleepover in Bayreuth during the Wagner Festival, as rooms are booked out months in advance and rates are doubled and even tripled.

Goldener Löwe
HOTEL €

(📞0921-746 06; www.goldener-loewe.de; Kulmbacher Strasse 30; s €35-56.50, d €73-92; P 🖢 🛎) Outside the summer months (rates increase considerably mid-July to end of August) this is a great little deal within easy walking distance of the sights. Rooms are tiny but impeccably kept, the Michelin-reviewed restaurant downstairs is tempting and there's free parking. The owners seem to have a bit of a jam fetish, every guest receiving a free jar.

DJH Hostel
HOSTEL €

(📞0921-764 380; www.bayreuth.jugendherberge. de; Universitätsstrasse 28; dm from €20.40) This excellent 140-bed hostel near the university has comfortable, fresh rooms, a relaxed atmosphere and heaps of guest facilities.

Hotel Goldener Hirsch
HOTEL €€

(📞0921-1504 4000; www.bayreuth-goldener-hirsch. de; Bahnhofstrasse 13; s €68-85, d €85-110; P 🖢 @ 🛎) Just across from the train station, the 'Golden Reindeer' looks a bit stuffy from the outside, but once indoors you'll discover crisp, well-maintained rooms with contemporary furniture and unscuffed, whitewashed walls. Some of the 40 rooms have baths. Parking is free.

Hotel Goldener Anker
HOTEL €€€

(📞0921-787 7740; www.anker-bayreuth.de; Opernstrasse 6; s €98-138, d €168-235; P 🖢 🛎) Bayreuth's top address just a few metres from the opera house oozes refined elegance, with many of the rooms decorated in heavy traditional style with swag curtains, dark woods and antique touches. There's a swanky restaurant at ground level, the service is impeccable and there is fresh fruit waiting for you on arrival.

🍴 Eating & Drinking

Kraftraum
CAFE €

(Sophienstrasse 16; mains €5.50-9; ⏰8am-1am Mon-Fri, from 9am Sat & Sun; 🖉) This vegetari-

KLEIN VENEDIG

Klein Venedig (Little Venice) A row of diminutive, half-timbered cottages once inhabited by fishermen and their families comprises Bamberg's Klein Venedig (Little Venice), which clasps the Regnitz's east bank between Markusbrücke and Untere Brücke. The little homes balance on poles set right into the water and are fronted by tiny gardens and terraces (wholly unlike Venice, but who cares).

Klein Venedig is well worth a stroll but looks at least as pretty from a distance, especially in summer when red geraniums spill from flower boxes. Good vantage points include the Untere Brücke near the Altes Rathaus, and Am Leinritt.

an eatery has plenty to tempt even the most committed meat eaters, including pastas, jacket potatoes, soups and huge salads. The retroish, shabby-chic interior empties on sunny days when everyone plumps for the alfresco seating out on the cobbles. Tempting weekend brunches (€13.50) always attract a large crowd.

Rosa Rosa
BISTRO €

(📞0921-685 02; Von-Römer-Strasse 2; mains €4-8; ⏰5pm-1am Mon-Fri, from 11am Sat, from 4pm Sun; 🖉) Join Bayreuth's chilled crowd at this bistro-cum-pub for belly-filling portions of salad, pasta and vegie fare, as well as seasonal dishes from the big specials board, or just a Frankenwälder beer in the evening. The poster-lined walls keep you up to date on the latest acts to hit town.

Hansl's Wood Oven Pizzeria
PIZZA €

(Friedrichstrasse 15; pizzas €4.60-9.10; ⏰10am-10.30pm) The best pizza in town is found at this tiny place tucked away in a corner of the square near the Stadthalle. There's next to no chance of a seat at mealtimes, so grab a takeaway. No debit/credit card payments.

Oskar
FRANCONIAN, BAVARIAN €€

(Maximilianstrasse 33; mains €7-15; ⏰8am-1am Mon-Sat, from 9am Sun) At the heart of the pedestrianised shopping boulevard, this multitasking, open-all-hours bar-cafe-restaurant is Bayreuth's busiest eatery. It's good for a busting Bavarian breakfast, a light lunch in the covered garden cafe, a full-on dinner feast in the dark-wood restaurant, or a *Landbier* and a couple of tasty Bayreuth bratwursts anytime you feel like it.

Torten Schmiede
CAFE

(Ludwigstrasse 10; ☺12.30-6pm Tue-Fri, 10am-6pm Sat) Bayreuth has lots of cafes, but with its car-boot sale of retro furniture, homemade cakes and 'street art' on the walls, this tiny halt is something that's a bit different. Enjoy your shot of caffeine and cake on a 1960s living room chair, or streetside on a mini chaise longue.

❶ Information

The **Bayreuth Card** (72hr €12.90) is good for unlimited trips on city buses, entry to eight museums and a two-hour guided city walk (in German). The card covers one adult and up to two children under 15.

Post Office (Hauptbahnhof)

Tourist Office (☑0921-885 88; www. bayreuth-tourismus.de; Opernstrasse 22; ☺9am-7pm Mon-Fri, 9am-4pm Sat all year, plus 10am-2pm Sun May-Oct) Has a train ticket booking desk and a worthwhile gift shop.

❶ Getting There & Away

Most rail journeys between Bayreuth and other towns in Bavaria require a change in Nuremberg.

➡ **Munich** Change in Nuremberg; €23 to €69, 2½ hours, hourly

➡ **Nuremberg** €21, one hour, at least hourly

➡ **Regensburg** Change in Nuremberg; €36, 2¼ hours, at least hourly

Coburg

☑09561 / POP 41,000

If marriage is diplomacy by another means, Coburg's rulers were surely masters of the art. Over four centuries, the princes and princesses of the house of Saxe-Coburg intrigued, romanced and ultimately wed themselves into the dynasties of Belgium, Bulgaria, Denmark, Portugal, Russia, Sweden and, most prominently, Great Britain. The crowning achievement came in 1857, when Albert of Saxe-Coburg-Gotha took his vows with first cousin Queen Victoria, founding the present British royal family. The British royals quietly adopted the less-German name of Windsor during WWI.

Coburg languished in the shadow of the Iron Curtain during the Cold War, all but closed in by East Germany on three sides, but since reunification the town has undergone a revival. Its proud Veste is one of Germany's finest medieval fortresses. What's

more, some sources contend that the original hot dog was invented here.

❍ Sights & Activities

Veste Coburg
FORTRESS, MUSEUM

(www.kunstsammlungen-coburg.de; adult/concession €6/3; ☺9.30am-5pm daily Apr-Oct, 1-4pm Tue-Sun Nov-Mar) Towering above Coburg's centre is a story-book medieval fortress, the Veste Coburg. With its triple ring of fortified walls, it's one of the most impressive fortresses in Germany though it attracts few foreign visitors. It houses the vast collection of the **Kunstsammlungen**, with works by star painters such as Rembrandt, Dürer and Cranach the Elder. The elaborate Jagdintarsien-Zimmer (Hunting Marquetry Room) is a superlative example of carved woodwork.

Protestant reformer Martin Luther, hoping to escape an imperial ban, sought refuge at the fortress in 1530. His former quarters have a writing desk and, in keeping with the Reformation, a rather plain bed.

Marktplatz
SQUARE

Coburg's epicentre is the magnificent Markt, a beautifully renovated square radiating a colourful, aristocratic charm. The fabulous Renaissance facades and ornate oriels of the **Stadthaus** (town house) and the **Rathaus** vie for attention, while a greening bronze of **Prince Albert**, looking rather more flamboyant and Teutonic medieval than the Brits are used to seeing Queen Victoria's husband, calmly surveys the scene.

Schloss Ehrenburg
CASTLE

(☑09561-808 832; www.sgvcoburg.de; Schlossplatz; adult/concession €4.50/3.50; ☺tours hourly 9am-5pm Tue-Sun Apr-Sep, 10am-4pm Tue-Sun Oct-Mar) The lavish Schloss Ehrenburg was once the town residence of the Coburg dukes. Prince Albert spent his childhood in this sumptuous, tapestry-lined palace, and his wife Queen Victoria stayed in a room with Germany's first flushing toilet (1860). The splendid **Riesensaal** (Hall of Giants) has a baroque ceiling supported by 28 statues of Atlas.

Coburger Puppenmuseum
MUSEUM

(www.coburger-puppenmuseum.de; Rückerstrasse 2-3; adult/child €4/2; ☺11am-4pm daily Apr-Oct, closed Mon Nov-Mar) Spanning 33 rooms, this delightfully old-fashioned museum displays a collection of 2000 dolls, dollhouses, miniature kitchens and chinaware, some from as far away as England and all dating from between

1800 and 1956. Aptly named 'Hallo Dolly', the stylish cafe next door is ideally situated for restoring calm after all those eerie glass eyes.

✨ Festivals & Events

Samba Festival
MUSIC

(www.samba-festival.de) Believe it or not, Coburg hosts Europe's largest Samba Festival every year in mid-July, an incongruous venue if ever there was one. This orgy of song and dance attracts almost 100 bands and up to 200,000 scantily clad, bum-wiggling visitors, many from the Portuguese-speaking world.

🛏 Sleeping & Eating

The best place to experience Coburg's famous 30cm-long sausages grilled over pinecone embers are the stands on Marktplatz.

Hotelpension Bärenturm
GUESTHOUSE €€

(☑ 09561-318 401; www.baerenturm-hotelpension. de; Untere Anlage 2; s €85, d €110-130; P 🛜) For those who prefer their complimentary pillow pack of gummy bears served with a touch of history, Coburg's most characterful digs started life as a defensive tower that was expanded in the early 19th century to house Prince Albert's private tutor. Each of the 15 rooms is a gem boasting squeaky parquet floors, antique-style furniture and regally high ceilings.

The Square
HOTEL €€

(☑ 09561-705 8520; www.hotelthesquare.com; Ketschengasse 1; s €69, d €79; P 🌀 @ 🛜) Right on the Marktplatz, what The Square lacks in character it more than makes up for in space and facilities. Each room has a kitchen, or corridor access to one, some have baths and the three large apartments cost the same as a double. You can also choose your view – the Prince Albert bronze out front or the pretty Stadtkirche out back.

Café Prinz Albert
CAFE €

(Ketschengasse 27; snacks & cakes €2-5; ⊙ 7.30am-6pm Mon-Fri, from 8am Sat) With a British royal theme throughout, this long-established cafe on newly renovated Albertsplatz is a good snack halt mid-sightseeing. The breakfast menu has a historical theme – the 'Martin Luther' (€2.90) is a sober, modest affair compared to the more lavish 'Prinz Albert' (€5.40).

Ratskeller
FRANCONIAN €

(Markt 1; mains €6-16.50; ⊙ 10am-midnight) Munch on regional dishes from Thuringia and Franconia while kicking back on well-padded leather benches under the heftily vaulted ceiling of Coburg's spectacular town hall.

Tie
VEGETARIAN €€€

(Leopoldstrasse 14; mains €9-19; ⊙ from 5pm Tue-Sun; 🌀) A five-minute walk east of the Marktplatz, this vegetarian restaurant serves up heavenly (if pricey) food crafted from fresh organic ingredients. Dishes range from vegetarian classics to Asian inspirations, with the odd fish or meat dish for the unconverted. Seasonally laid tables add colour to the simple decor.

ℹ Information

Tourist Office (☑ 09561-898 000; www. coburg-tourist.de; Herrngasse 4; ⊙ 9am-5pm Mon-Fri, 10am-2pm Sat & Sun) Helpful office where staff sell the CObook (€14.90), a five-day ticket good for 13 sights in Coburg and around as well as local public transport. English audioguides (€3.50) to the city are also available here.

ℹ Getting There & Away

Coburg has the following rail connections:
➡ **Bamberg** €12.10, one hour, hourly
➡ **Bayreuth** €17.90, 1½ hours, hourly
➡ **Nuremberg** €23.50, 1¾ hours, hourly

ℹ Getting Around

Veste-Express (one-way/return €3.50/4.50; ⊙ 10am-5pm Apr-Oct) This tourist train leaves the tourist office every 30 minutes for the Veste Coburg. Otherwise it's a steep, 3km climb.

Altmühltal Nature Park

The Altmühltal Nature Park is one of Germany's largest nature parks and covers some of Bavaria's most eye-pleasing terrain. The Altmühl River gently meanders through a region of little valleys and hills before joining the Rhine-Main Canal and eventually emptying into the Danube. Outdoor fun on well-marked hiking and biking trails is the main reason to head here, but the river is also ideal for canoeing. There's basic camping in designated spots along the river, and plenty of accommodation in the local area.

The park takes in 2900 sq km of land southwest of Regensburg, south of Nuremberg, east of Treuchtlingen and north of Eichstätt. The eastern boundaries of the park include the town of Kelheim.

284

H. & C. ZIELSKE /LOOK-FOTO/GETTY IMAGES ©

1. Rooftops in Celle 2. Old harbour in Wismar
3. Houses in Beilstein 4. Quedlinburg

JUERGEN SACK/GETTY IMAGES ©

Small-Town Charmers

Tourist-trail faves like Heidelberg, Rothenburg ob der Tauber and Oberammergau exude charm and quaintness from every crooked lane, cobbled stone or medieval facade. Alas, all too often they also drown in the sheer volume of visitors. If you crave beauty along with (relative) serenity, consider folding one of these much-lesser-known but no less lovely towns into your itinerary.

Quedlinburg

On the edge of the Harz Mountains, Quedlinburg is a symphony in half-timber whose original medieval layout is graced by over 1300 listed buildings. The first German king, Henry I, was buried in the hilltop Romanesque Stiftskirche St Servatius in 936. (p574)

Wismar

This Baltic seaside town was a Hanseatic League hot shot, and its historic wealth is still reflected in its distinctive silhouette, characterised by elaborately decorated red-brick Gothic town houses and churches. It's a delightful, lively place that's best enjoyed by kicking back over a beer by the harbour or in a cool cafe. (p703)

Celle

Compact Celle's old town teems with timber-framed houses boasting ornate, painted gables and is punctuated by a palace that blends Renaissance and baroque elements. In a lovely setting on the southern fringes of the Lüneburg Heath, Celle is a mere 40km northeast of Hanover. (p609)

Beilstein

Scoring high on the 'romance meter', pint-sized Beilstein on the Mosel is perfect for putting on the brakes during a busy itinerary. Take to the high ground on a vineyard trek to the requisite ruined hilltop castle, then soak up the fairy-tale flair along with a glass of wine in the cluster of higgledy-piggledy medieval houses. (p446)

North of the river, activities focus around the towns of Kipfenberg, Beilngries and Riedenburg.

🏃 Activities

Canoeing & Kayaking

The most beautiful section of the river is from Treuchtlingen or Pappenheim to Eichstätt or Kipfenberg, about a 60km stretch that you can do lazily in a kayak or canoe in two to three days. There are lots of little dams along the way, as well as some small rapids about 10km northwest of Dollnstein, so make sure you are up for little bits of portaging. Signs warn of impending doom, but locals say that, if you heed the warning to stay to the right, you'll be safe.

You can rent canoes and kayaks in just about every town along the river. Expect to pay about €15/25 per day for a one-/two-person boat, more for bigger ones. Staff will sometimes haul you and the boats to or from your embarkation point for a small charge.

You can get a full list of boat-hire outlets from the Informationszentrum Naturpark Altmühltal (p287).

San-Aktiv Tours   CANOEING
(📞 09831-4936; www.san-aktiv-tours.com; Otto-Dietrich-Strasse 3, Gunzenhausen) San-Aktiv Tours is the largest and best-organised of the canoe-hire companies in the park, with a network of vehicles to shuttle canoes, bicycles and people around the area. Trips through the park run from April to October, and you can canoe alone or join a group. Packages generally include the canoe, swim vests, maps, instructions and transfer back to the embarkation point.

Cycling & Hiking

With around 3000km of hiking trails and 800km of cycle trails criss-crossing the landscape, foot and pedal are the best ways to strike out into the park. Cycling trails are clearly labelled and have long rectangular brown signs bearing a bike symbol. The hiking-trail markers are yellow. The most popular cycling route is the Altmühltal Radweg, which runs parallel to the river for 166km. The Altmühltal-Panoramaweg stretching 200km between Gunzenhausen and Kelheim is a picturesque hiking route, which crosses the entire park from west to east.

You can rent bikes in almost every town within the park, and prices are more or less uniform. Most bike-hire agencies will also store bicycles. Ask for a list of bike-hire outlets at the Informationszentrum Naturpark Altmühltal.

Located in Eichstätt, **Kanuuh** (📞 08421-2110; www.kanuuh.de; Herzoggasse 3; €12/day) will bring the bikes to you, or take you and the bikes to anywhere in Altmühltal Nature Park for an extra fee.

Rock Climbing

The worn cliffs along the Altmühl River offer some appealing terrain for climbers of all skill levels. The medium-grade 45m-high rock face of Burgsteinfelsen, located between the towns of Dollnstein and Breitenfurt, has routes from the fourth to eighth climbing levels, with stunning views of the valley. The Dohlenfelsen face near the town of Wellheim has a simpler expanse that's more suitable for children. The Informationszentrum Naturpark Altmühltal can provide more details on the region's climbing options.

WAGNER FESTIVAL

Wagner Festival (www.bayreuther-festspiele.de) The Wagner Festival has been a summer fixture in Bayreuth for over 140 years and is generally regarded as the top Wagner event anywhere in the world. The festival lasts for 30 days (from late July to late August), with each performance attended by an audience of just over 1900. Demand is insane, with an estimated 500,000 fans vying for less than 60,000 tickets.

Until a few years ago all tickets were allocated in a shady lottery with preference given to 'patrons' and 'Wagner enthusiasts'. Ordinary, unconnected fans sometimes had to wait five to 10 years before 'winning' a seat. However, in a bid to introduce a bit more transparency into proceedings, the festival organisers recently decided to release the vast majority of tickets onto the open market in an online free-for-all. Every ticket is snapped up in seconds, a fact that has angered many a Wagner society. Alternatively, it is still possible to lay siege to the box office two and a half hours before performances begin in the hope of snapping up cheap returned tickets, but there's no guarantee you'll get in.

RICHARD WAGNER

With the backing of King Ludwig II, Richard Wagner (1813–83), the gifted, Leipzig-born composer and notoriously poor manager of money, turned Bayreuth into a mecca of opera and high-minded excess. Bayreuth profited from its luck and, it seems, is ever grateful.

For Wagner, listening to opera was meant to be work and he tested his listeners wherever possible. *Götterdämmerung, Parsifal, Tannhäuser* and *Tristan & Isolde* are grandiose pieces that will jolt any audience geared for light entertainment. Four days of *The Ring of the Nibelung* are good for limbering up.

After poring over Passau and a few other German cities, Wagner designed his own festival hall in Bayreuth. The unique acoustics are bounced up from a below-stage orchestra via reflecting boards onto the stage and into the house. The design took the body density of a packed house into account, still a remarkable achievement today.

Wagner was also a notorious womaniser, an infamous anti-Semite and a hardliner towards 'non-Europeans'. So extreme were these views that even Friedrich Nietzsche called Wagner's works 'inherently reactionary, and inhumane'. Wagner's works, and by extension Wagner himself, were embraced as a symbol of Aryan might by the Nazis and, even today, there is great debate among music lovers about the 'correctness' of supporting Wagner's music and the Wagner Festival in Bayreuth.

ℹ️ Information

The park's main information centre is in Eichstätt, a charmingly historic town at the southern end of the park that makes an excellent base for exploring.

Informationszentrum Naturpark Altmühltal (📞 08421-987 60; www.naturpark-altmuehltal. de; Notre Dame 1; ⏲ 9am-5pm Mon-Sat, 10am-5pm Sun Apr Oct, 8am-noon & 2-4pm Mon-Thu, 8am-noon Fri Nov-Mar) Has information on, and help with planning an itinerary around, Altmühltal Nature Park. The website has tonnes of information on every aspect of the park, including activities and accommodation.

ℹ️ Getting There & Around

There are bus and train connections between Eichstätt and all the major milestones along the river including, from west to east, Gunzenhausen, Treuchtlingen and Pappenheim.

BUS

From mid-April to October the FreizeitBus Altmühltal-Donautal takes passengers and their bikes around the park. Buses normally run three times a day. Route 1 runs from Regensburg and Kelheim to Riedenburg on weekends and holidays only. Route 2 travels between Eichstätt, Beilngries, Dietfurt and Riedenburg, with all-day service on weekends and holidays and restricted service on weekdays. All-day tickets, which cost €10.50 for passengers with bicycles and €7.50 for those without (or €23.50/17.50 per family with/without bicycles) are bought from the driver.

TRAIN

Hourly trains run between Eichstätt Bahnhof and Treuchtlingen (€6.10, 25 minutes), and between Treuchtlingen and Gunzenhausen (€4.50, 15 minutes). RE trains from Munich that run through Eichstätt Bahnhof also stop in Dollnstein, Solnhofen and Pappenheim.

Eichstätt

📞 08421 / POP 13,150

Hugging a tight bend in the Altmühl River, Eichstätt radiates a tranquil Mediterranean flair with cobbled streets meandering past elegantly Italianate buildings and leafy piazzas. Italian architects, notably Gabriel de Gabrieli and Maurizio Pedetti, rebuilt the town after Swedes razed the place during the Thirty Years' War (1618–48) and it came through WWII virtually without a graze. Since 1980 many of its baroque facades have played host to faculties belonging to Germany's sole Catholic university.

Eichstätt is pretty enough, but is really just a jumping-off and stocking-up point for flits into the wilds of Altmühltal Nature Park. You'll be chomping at the bit, eager to hit a trail or grab a paddle, if you stay more than a day.

👁️ Sights

Dom CHURCH
(www.bistum-eichstaett.de/dom; Domplatz; ⏲ 7.15am-7.30pm) Eichstätt's centre is dominated by the richly adorned Dom. Standout

features include an enormous 16th-century stained-glass window by Hans Holbein the Elder, and the carved sandstone Pappenheimer Altar (1489–97), depicting a pilgrimage from Pappenheim to Jerusalem. The seated statue is of St Willibald, the town's first bishop.

The adjoining **Domschatzmuseum** (Cathedral Treasury; ☑ 08421-507 42; Residenzplatz 7; adult/concession €3/1.50, Sun €1; ☺ 10.30am-5pm Wed-Fri, 10am-5pm Sat & Sun Apr-Nov) includes the robes of 8th-century English-born bishop St Willibald and baroque Gobelin tapestries.

Willibaldsburg
CASTLE

(☑ 08421-4730; Burgstrasse 19; adult/concession €4.50/3.50; ☺ 9am-6pm Tue-Sun Apr-Oct, 10am-4pm Tue-Sun Nov-Mar) The walk or drive up to the hilltop castle of Willibaldsburg (1355) is worth it for the views across the valley from the formally laid-out **Bastionsgarten**; many locals also head up here on sunny days for the nearby beer garden. The castle itself houses two museums, the most interesting of which is the Jura-Museum, specialising in fossils and containing a locally found archaeopteryx (the oldest-known fossil bird), as well as aquariums with living specimens of the fossilised animals.

Kloster St Walburga
CONVENT

(www.abtei-st-walburg.de; Westenstrasse) The final resting place of St Willibald's sister, the Kloster St Walburga is a popular local pilgrimage destination. Every year between mid-October and late February, water oozes from Walburga's relics in the underground chapel and drips down into a catchment. The nuns bottle diluted versions of the so-called *Walburgaöl* (Walburga oil) and give it away to the faithful.

A staircase from the lower chapel leads to an off-limits upper chapel where you can catch a glimpse through the grill of beautiful ex-voto tablets and other trinkets left as a thank-you to the saint. The main St Walburga Church above has a glorious rococo interior.

Fürstbischöfliche Residenz
PALACE

(Residenzplatz; admission €1; ☺ Mon-Fri 7.30am-noon, 2-4pm Mon-Wed, 2-5.30pm Thu) The prince-bishops lived it up at the baroque Residenz, built between 1725 and 1736 by Gabriel de Gabrieli. Inside, the stunning main staircase and a hall of mirrors stick in the mind. In the square outside rises a late 18th-century golden statue of the Madonna atop a 19m-high column.

🛏 Sleeping & Eating

Fuchs
HOTEL €

(☑ 08421-6789; www.hotel-fuchs.de; Ostenstrasse 8; s €45-65, d €72-80; ☎) This central, family-run hotel, with under-floor heating in the bathrooms, adjoins a cake shop with a sunny dining area. It's convenient to a launch ramp on the river where you can put in, and you can lock your canoe or kayak in the garage.

DJH Hostel
HOSTEL €

(☑ 08421-980 410; www.eichstaett.jugendherberge.de; Reichenaustrasse 15; dm from €19.90; ☎) This comfy, 122-bed youth hostel provides pretty views of the Altstadt. As you might expect, the hostel is very bike- and canoe-friendly.

Municipal Camping Ground
CAMPGROUND €

(☑ 08421-908 147; www.eichstaett.info/wohnmobilstellplatz; Pirkheimerstrasse; per campsite €8) This basic camping ground is on the northern bank of the Altmühl River, about 1km southeast of the town centre. It's open year-round, but closes for 10 days during the Volksfest (a mini-Oktoberfest) in late August and early September.

Hotel Adler
HOTEL €€

(☑ 08421-6767; www.adler-eichstaett.de; Marktplatz 22; s €58-67, d €80-106; ᴘ☎) A superb ambience reigns in this ornate 300-year-old building, Eichstätt's top digs. Sleeping quarters are bright and breezy and the generous breakfast buffet a proper set up for a day on the trail or river. Despite the posh feel, this hotel welcomes hiker and bikers.

Café im Paradeis
CAFE €€

(☑ 08421-3313; Marktplatz 9; mains €5-17; ☺ 8am-midnight) This open-all-hours spot on Markt is prime for people watching, wherever the hands of the clock may be. Recharge with a home-cooked meal or just a coffee, either in the olde-worlde antique-lined interior or out on the sunny terrace.

Trompete
BAVARIAN, ITALIAN €€

(www.braugasthof-trompete.de; Ostenstrasse 3; ☺ 7am-1am Mon-Fri, from 7.30am Sat & Sun) From breakfast to your last cocktail of the day, this friendly inn, just a short walk to the southeast of the centre, is a sure fire option at any time of day. The menu features some *echt*-Bavarian dishes such as *Ochsenbraten 'Altmühltaler Art'* (Altmühltaler roast beef) and *Krustenschäuferl* (roast pork with crispy skin) as well as Italian pizzas and pastas.

ℹ Information

Post Office (Domplatz 7)

Tourist Office (☑ 08421-600 1400; www.eich-stactt.de; Domplatz 8; ⊗9am-6pm Mon-Sat, 10am-1pm Sun Apr-Oct, 10am-noon & 2-4pm Mon-Thu, 10am-noon Fri Nov-Mar)

ℹ Getting There & Away

Eichstätt has two train stations. Mainline trains stop at the Bahnhof, 5km from the centre, from where coinciding diesel services shuttle to the Stadtbahnhof (town station). Trains run hourly between Ingolstadt and Eichstätt (€6.10, 25 minutes) and every two hours to Nuremberg (€19.80, 1½ hours).

REGENSBURG & THE DANUBE

The sparsely populated eastern reaches of Bavaria may live in the shadow of Bavaria's big-hitting attractions, but they hold many historical treasures to rival their neighbours. Top billing goes to Regensburg, a former capital, and one of Germany's prettiest and liveliest cities. From here the Danube gently winds its way to the Italianate city of Passau. Landshut was once the hereditary seat of the Wittelsbach family, and the region has also given the world a pope – Benedict XVI who was born in Marktl am Inn. Away from the towns, the Bavarian Forest broods in semi-undiscovered remoteness.

Eastern Bavaria was a seat of power in the Dark Ages, ruled by rich bishops at a time when Munich was but a modest trading post. A conquering Napoleon lumped Eastern Bavaria into river districts, and King Ludwig I sought to roll back these changes by recreating the boundaries of a glorified duchy from 1255. Though it brought a sense of renewed Bavarian identity, the area remained very much on the margins of things, giving rise to the odd and appealing mixture of ancient Roman cities, undulating farmland and rugged wilderness that it is today.

Regensburg

☑ 0941 / POP 140,300

A Roman settlement completed under Emperor Marcus Aurelius, Regensburg was the first capital of Bavaria, the residence of dukes, kings and bishops, and for 600 years a Free Imperial City. Two millennia of history bequeathed the city some of the region's finest architectural heritage, a fact recognised by Unesco in 2006. Though big on the historical wow factor, today's Regensburg is a laid-back and unpretentious sort of place, and a good springboard into the wider region.

◉ Sights

Schloss Thurn und Taxis CASTLE
(www.thurnundtaxis.de; Emmeramsplatz 5; tours adult/concession €13.50/11; ⊗tours hourly 10.30am-4.30pm late Mar-early Nov, to 3.30pm Sat & Sun Nov-Mar) In the 15th century, Franz von Taxis (1459-1517) assured his place in history by setting up the first European postal system, which remained a monopoly until the 19th century. In recognition of his services, the family was given the former Benedictine monastery St Emmeram, henceforth known as Schloss Thurn und Taxis. It was soon one of the most modern palaces in Europe, and featured such luxuries as flushing toilets, central heating and electricity. Tours include the Basilika St Emmeram.

The palace complex also contains the Schatzkammer (Treasury). The jewellery, porcelain and precious furnishings on display belonged, for many years, to the wealthiest dynasty in Germany. The fortune, administered by Prince Albert II, is still estimated at well over €1 billion.

Dom St Peter CHURCH
(www.bistum-regensburg.de; Domplatz; ⊗6.30am-7pm Jun-Sep, to 6pm Apr, May & Oct, to 5pm Nov-Mar) It takes a few seconds for your eyes to adjust to the dim interior of Regensburg's soaring landmark, the Dom St Peter, one of Bavaria's grandest Gothic cathedrals with stunning kaleidoscopic stained-glass windows and an opulent, silver-sheathed main altar.

The cathedral is home of the Domspatzen, a 1000-year-old boys' choir that accompanies the 10am Sunday service (only during the school year). The Domschatzmuseum (Cathedral Treasury) brims with monstrances, tapestries and other church treasures.

Altes Rathaus HISTORIC BUILDING
(Old Town Hall; Rathausplatz; adult/concession €7.50/4; ⊗tours in English 3pm Easter-Oct, 2pm Nov & Dec, in German every 30min) From 1663 to 1806, the Reichstag (imperial assembly) held its gatherings at Regensburg's old town, an important role commemorated by an exhibit in today's Reichstagsmuseum. Tours take in the lavish assembly hall and the original torture chambers in the cellar.

BAVARIA REGENSBURG

Buy tickets at the tourist office in the same building. Note that access is by tour only. Audioguides are available for English speakers in January and February.

Steinerne Brücke   BRIDGE

(Stone Bridge) An incredible feat of engineering for its day, Regensburg's 900-year-old Stone Bridge was at one time the only fortified crossing over the Danube. Damaged and neglected for centuries (especially by the buses that once used it) the entire expanse is currently under renovation. The design of the completed sections looks worryingly modern.

Golf Museum   MUSEUM

(www.golf-museum.com; Tändlergasse 3; adult/concession €7.50/5; ☺10am-6pm Mon-Sat) Claiming to be Europe's best golf museum (Scotland, home to the British Golf Museum, is strangely not counted as part of the continent), this unexpected repository of club, tee and score card (including one belonging to King George V of England) backswings its way through golf's illustrious past – interesting, even if you think a green fee is something to do with municipal recycling. The entrance is in an antiques shop.

Historisches Museum   MUSEUM

(Dachauplatz 2-4; adult/concession €5/2.50; ☺10am-4pm Tue-Sun) A medieval monastery provides a suitably atmospheric backdrop for the city's history museum. The collections plot the region's story from cave dweller to Roman, and medieval trader to 19th-century burgher.

Schottenkirche St Jakob   CHURCH

(Jakobstrasse 3) The sooty 12th-century main portal of the Schottenkirche St Jakob is considered one of the supreme examples of Romanesque architecture in Germany. Its reliefs and sculptures form an iconography that continues to baffle the experts. Sadly, it's protected from further pollution by an ageing glass structure that makes the whole thing an eyesore. However, this is more than made up for inside, where pure, tourist-free Romanesque austerity prevails.

Document Neupfarrplatz   HISTORIC SITE

(☑0941-507 3442; Neupfarrplatz; adult/concession €5/2.50; ☺tours 2.30pm Thu-Sat Sep-Jun, 2.30pm Thu-Mon Jul & Aug) Excavations in the mid-1990s revealed remains of Regensburg's once-thriving 16th-century Jewish quarter, along with Roman buildings, gold coins and a Nazi bunker. The subterranean Document Neupfarrplatz only provides access to a small portion of the excavated area, but tours feature a nifty multimedia presentation (in German) about the square's history. Back up above, on the square itself, a work by renowned Israeli artist Dani Karavan graces the site of the former synagogue.

Tickets are purchased from Tabak Götz at Neupfarrplatz 3.

Kepler-Gedächtnishaus   MUSEUM

(Kepler Memorial House; Keplerstrasse 5; adult/concession €2.20/1.10; ☺10.30am-4pm Sat & Sun) Disciples of astronomer and mathematician Johannes Kepler should visit the house he lived in while resident in Regensburg.

Alte Kapelle   CHURCH

(Alter Kornmarkt 8) South of the Dom, the humble exterior of the graceful Alte Kapelle belies the stunning interior with its rich rococo decorations. The core of the church, however, is about 1000 years old, although the vaulted ceilings were added in the Gothic period. The church is open only during services but you can always peek through the wrought-iron grill.

Roman Wall   HISTORIC SITE

The most tangible reminder of the ancient rectangular Castra Regina (Regen Fortress), where the name 'Regensburg' comes from, is the remaining Roman wall, which follows Unter den Schwibbögen and veers south onto Dr-Martin-Luther-Strasse. Dating from AD 179 the rough-hewn **Porta Praetoria** (Unter den Schwibbögen) arch is the tallest Roman structure in Bavaria and formed part of the city's defences for centuries.

MUSEUM OF BAVARIAN HISTORY

Regensburg is set to acquire a major attraction in 2018 – the Museum of Bavarian History. The architecturally striking building (other, less favourable, descriptions have been used) will be bolted together around 250m east of the Steinerne Brücke, altering the historical appearance of the river front. As well as the super-contemporary look of the structure, the wisdom of placing a major attraction in such a flood-prone location has been questioned.

☞ Tours

Schifffahrt Klinger BOAT TOUR
(☑0941-521 04; www.schifffahrtklinger.de; cruises adult/child from €8.50/3.50; ⊗Apr-late Oct) Offers short cruises on the Danube (50 minutes) and to the Walhalla monument.

Tourist Train Tours TRAIN
(depart Domplatz; adult/family €8/19; ⊗8 tours daily) Multilingual tourist train tours of the city centre take 45 minutes to complete a circuit from the south side of the cathedral. Fares include a free coffee at Haus Heuport.

✯ Festivals & Events

Dult FESTIVAL
Oktoberfest-style party with beer tents, carousel rides, entertainment and vendors on the Dultplatz, in May and late August or early September.

Weihnachtsmarkt CHRISTMAS MARKET
The Christmas market has stalls selling roasted almonds, gingerbread and traditional wooden toys. Held at Neupfarrplatz and Schloss Thurn und Taxis during December.

🛏 Sleeping

Regensburg has an unexpectedly wide choice of places to achieve REM, from blue-blooded antique-graced apartments to blood-red suites for fired-up honeymooners.

Brook Lane Hostel HOSTEL€
(☑0941-696 5521; www.hostel-regensburg.de; Obere Bachgasse 21; dm/s/d from €16/40/50, apt per person €55; 🖧) Regensburg's only backpacker hostel has its very own convenience store, which doubles up as reception, but isn't open 24 hours, so late landers should let staff know in advance. Dorms do the minimum required, but the apartments and doubles here are applaudable deals, especially if you're travelling in a twosome or more. Access to kitchens and washing machines throughout.

DJH Hostel HOSTEL€
(☑0941-466 2830; www.regensburg.jugendherberge.de; Wöhrdstrasse 60; dm from €25.40) Regensburg's 186-bed hostel occupies a beautiful old building on a large island about a 10-minute walk north of the Altstadt.

Hotel Am Peterstor HOTEL€
(☑0941-545 45; www.hotel-am-peterstor.de; Fröhliche-Türken-Strasse 12; s/d €40/50; ⊗reception 7-11am & 4-10.30pm; 🖧) The pale-grey decor might be grim, and the recepetion hours silly, but the location is great, the price is right and staff go out of their way to assist. Make sure you get a nonsmoking room, as some pong of secondhand smoke. Breakfast is an optional €5 extra. Payment on arrival.

★ Elements Hotel HOTEL€€
(☑0941-3819 8600; www.hotel-elements.de; Alter Kornmarkt 3; d from €105; 🖧) Four elements, four rooms, and what rooms they are! 'Fire' blazes in plush crimson; while 'Water' is a wellness suite with a Jacuzzi; 'Air' is playful and light and natural wood; and stone and leather reign in colonial-inspired 'Earth'. Breakfast costs an extra €15.

Extras such as in-room massages, candlelit dinner (€65) and breakfast in bed (€25) can be booked.

Petit Hotel Orphée HOTEL€€
(☑0941-596 020; www.hotel-orphee.de; Wahlenstrasse 1; s €35-125, d €75-165; 🖧) Behind a humble door lies a world of genuine charm, unexpected extras and ample attention to detail. The striped floors, wrought-iron beds, original sinks and common rooms with soft cushions and well-read books give the feel of a lovingly attended home.

Check-in and breakfast is nearby in the Cafe Orphée at Untere Bachgasse 8. Additional rooms are available above the cafe.

Hotel Goldenes Kreuz HOTEL€€
(☑0941-558 12; www.hotel-goldeneskreuz.de; Haidplatz 7; s €85-110, d €105-135; 🖧) Surely the best deal in town, each of the nine fairy-tale rooms bears the name of a crowned head and is fit for a kaiser. Huge mirrors, dark antique and Bauhaus furnishings, four-poster beds, chubby exposed beams and parquet flooring produce a stylishly aristocratic opus in leather, wood, crystal and fabric. Breakfast is in the house chapel.

Hotel Roter Hahn HOTEL€€
(☑0941-595 090; www.roter-hahn.com; Rote-Hahnen-Gasse 10; s €80-105, d €100-135; 🅿🖧) A bulky beamed ceiling and a glassed-in Roman stone well (staff appear to be oblivious of its provenance) greet you in the lobby of the 'Red Rooster', contrasting with streamlined rooms offering freshly maintained amenities. Parking costs €12; request a room on the 2nd floor to access the free wi-fi.

Zum Fröhlichen Türken HOTEL€€
(☑0941-536 51; www.hotel-zum-froehlichen-tuerken.de; Fröhliche-Türken-Strasse 11; s/d €62/89) With its comfortable, clean quarters, un-

Regensburg

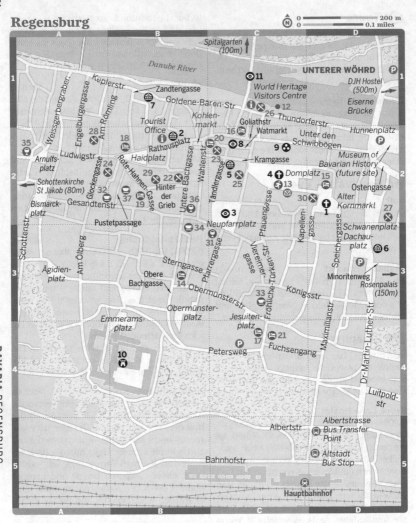

0   200 m
0   0.1 miles

Danube River

Spitalgarten
(100m)

UNTERER WÖHRD

DJH Hostel
(500m)
Eiserne
Brücke

Keplerstr
Zandtengasse
7
Goldene-Bären-Str
Kohlen-
markt
Tourist
Office 2
Rathausplatz
Haidplatz
18
28
35
Arnulfs-
platz
Ludwigstr
24
29 22
Rote-Hahnen-Gasse
32 37 19
Hinter
der
Grieb
36
Glockengasse
Gesandtenstr
Bismarck-
platz
Schottenkirche
St Jakob (80m)
Pustetpassage
Weissgerbergraben
Engelburgergasse
A E Römling
Schottenstr
Am Ölberg

World Heritage
Visitors Centre
11
26 12
Thundorferstr
Goliathstr
Watmarkt
16
20
8
9
Kramgasse
5
23
25
4 Domplatz
13
30
1
Alter
Kornmarkt
Museum of
Bavarian History
(future site)
Ostengasse
27
Hunnenplatz
Schwanenplatz
Dachau-
platz 6
Unter den
Schwibbögen

3
Neupfarrplatz
34
31
Pfarrergasse
Sterngasse
Ägidien-
platz
Obere
Bachgasse
14
Obermünsterstr
Obermünster-
platz
Emmerams-
platz
10
Petersweg
17 21
Fuchsengang
Jesuiten-
platz
33
Königsstr
Vareimer-
gasse
Prauengasse
HS-Türk-
Fröhliche-Türken-Str
Kapellen-
gasse
Speichergasse
Minoritenweg
Rosenpalais
(150m)
Maximilianstr
Dr-Martin-Luther-Str
Luitpold-
str

Albertstr
Albertstrasse
Bus Transfer
Point
Altstadt
Bus Stop
Bahnhofstr
Hauptbahnhof

stinting breakfast and mild-mannered staff, the 'Jolly Turk' will bring a smile to any price-conscious traveller's face. The pricier rooms have private bathrooms.

Goliath Hotel HOTEL €€€
(☑ 0941-200 0900; www.hotel-goliath.de; Goliath-strasse 10; s/d from €130/160; P ✱ ☎) Right in the heart of the city centre, the 41 rooms at the Goliath are all differently conceived and pristinely serviced. Some have little extras, such as bathroom–bedroom windows and big baths. It's funky, but doesn't go the whole

boutique hog and staff are surprisingly old school. Parking costs €12.

Eating

'In Regensburg we ate a magnificent lunch, had a divine musical entertainment, an English hostess and a wonderful Moselle wine,' wrote Mozart to his wife Constance in 1790. Available in Mozart's day, but better washed down with a local Kneitinger Pils, is the delectable bratwurst and *Händlmaier's Süsser Hausmachersenf* (a distinctive sweet mustard).

Regensburg

Spaghetteria Aquino

ITALIAN €

(www.spaghetteria-regensburg.de; Am Römling 12; dishes €5.50-10; ⊙11am-2.30pm & 5.30pm-midnight) Get carbed up at this former 17th-century chapel, where you can splatter six types of pasta with 24 types of sauce, and get out the door for the cost of a cocktail in Munich. The all-you-can-eat buffets (€5 to €6.50) are a cheap way to fill up at lunchtime and there are pizzas, salads and antipasti to choose from.

Historische Wurstkuchl

GERMAN €

(☑ 0941-466 210; www.wurstkuchl.de; Thundorferstrasse 3; 6 sausages €9; ⊙8am-7pm) Completely submerged several times by the Danube's fickle floods, this titchy eatery has been serving the city's traditional finger-size sausages, grilled over beech wood and dished up with sauerkraut and sweet grainy mustard, since 1135 and lays claim to being the world's oldest sausage kitchen.

Dampfnudel Uli

CAFE €

(Watmarkt 4; dishes €5-8; ⊙10.01am-6.01pm Wed-Fri, to 3.01pm Sat) This quirky, old-fashioned little noshery serves a mean *Dampfnudel* (steamed doughnut) with custard in a Gothic chamber lined with photos and beer steins (tankards) at the base of the Baumburger Tower.

★ Dicker Mann

BAVARIAN €€

(www.dicker-mann.de; Krebsgasse 6; mains €8-19; ⊙7am-midnight) Stylish, tranquil, very traditional inn and plating up all the staples of Bavarian sustenance, the 'Chubby Chappy' is one of the oldest restaurants in town, allegedly dating back to the 14th century. On a balmy eve, be sure to bag a table in the lovely beer garden out back.

★ Café Orphée

FRENCH €€

(Untere Bachgasse 8; mains €11-24; ⊙8am-1am) Claiming to be the Frenchiest bistro east of the Rhine – and it is as if you've been teleported to 1920s Paris – this visually pleasing, always bustling eatery, is bedecked in faded red velvet, dark wood and art nouveau posters. Light-lunch fare populates a handwritten menu of appetising Gallic favourites with slight Bavarian touches for sturdiness.

Haus Heuport

INTERNATIONAL €€

(Domplatz 7; mains €8.50-20.50; ⊙10am-midnight Mon-Fri, from 9am Sat & Sun; ☑) Enter an internal courtyard (flanked by stone blocks where medieval torches were once extinguished) and climb up the grand old wooden staircase to this space-rich Gothic dining hall for eye-to-eye views of the Dom St Peter and an internationally flavoured culinary celebration. The Sunday breakfast buffet runs to a hangover-busting 3pm. Always busy.

Vitus

FRENCH €€

(☑ 0941-526 46; Hinter der Grieb 8; mains €5.50-13.90; ⊙9am-11pm) Colourful canvases mix with ancient beamed ceilings at this bustling place serving provincial French food,

BAVARIA REGENSBURG

including delicious *Flammkuchen*, quiche, salads, meat and fish dishes, as well as a commendable number of meat-free options. Sit in the rustic bar area, the restaurant with linen-draped tables or the child-friendly cafe section.

Leerer Beutel
EUROPEAN €€

(☎0941-589 97; www.leerer-beutel.de; Bertoldstrasse 9; mains €10-23; ☺6pm-1am Mon, 11am-1am Tue-Sat, 11am-3pm Sun) Subscriber to the slow-food ethos, the cavernous restaurant at the eponymous cultural centre offers an imaginatively mixed menu of Bavarian, Tyrolean and Italian dishes, served indoors or out on the car-free cobbles. From Tuesday to Friday, clued-in locals invade for the two-course lunches for €6.50.

Weltenburger am Dom
BAVARIAN €€

(☎0941-586 1460; www.weltenburger-am-dom.de; Domplatz 3; dishes €8.40-17.90; ☺11am-11pm) Tightly packed gastropub with a mouth-watering menu card of huge gourmet burgers, sausage dishes, beer hall and garden favourites such as *Obazda* (cream cheese on pretzels) and *Sauerbraten* (marinated roast meat), dark beer goulash and a few token desserts. Make sure you are hungry before you come as portions are big.

Drinking

Spitalgarten
BEER GARDEN

(☎0941-847 74; www.spitalgarten.de; St Katharinenplatz 1; ☺9am-midnight) A veritable thicket of folding chairs and slatted tables by the Danube, this is one of the best places in town for some alfresco quaffing. It claims to have brewed beer (today's Spital) here since 1350, so it probably knows what it's doing by now.

Félix
CAFE

(Fröhliche-Türken-Strasse 6; ☺9am-2am Sun-Thu, 10am-3am Fri & Sat) Early birds breakfast, and after-dark trendoids leaf through the lengthy drinks menu behind the curvaceous neo-baroque frontage of this open-all-hours cafe with a welcoming air. You'd be lucky to get a seat here at lunchtime so arrive early.

Kneitinger
PUB

(Arnulfsplatz 3; ☺9am-midnight) This quintessential Bavarian brewpub is the place to go for some hearty home cooking, delicious house suds and outrageous oompah frolics. It's been in business since 1530.

Paletti
CAFE, BAR

(Gesandtenstrasse 6, Pustetpassage; ☺8am-1am Mon-Sat, from 4pm Sun) Tucked into a covered passageway off Gesandtenstrasse, this buzzy Italian cafe-bar that has not changed since the 1960s teleports you back to the postwar years of the *Wirtschaftswunder* (economic miracle).

Cafebar
CAFE, BAR

(Gesandtenstrasse 14; ☺8am-midnight Mon-Wed, to 1am Thu & Fri, 9am-1am Sat, 1pm-midnight Sun) This time-warped, tightly squeezed blast from the past in *Jugendstil* tile, cast iron and stained glass fills with newspaper-reading caffeine fans at first rays and ethanol fans after sundown.

Hemingway's
CAFE, BAR

(Obere Bachgasse 5; ☺9am-1am Sun-Thu, to 2am Fri & Sat) Black wood, big mirrors and lots of photos of Papa himself add to the cool atmosphere of this art-deco-style cafe-bar.

Augustiner
BEER GARDEN

(Neupfarrplatz 15; ☺10am-11.30pm) This popular fairy-lit beer garden and restaurant is ideally located in the heart of the city. Leave your beer-glass ring and pack away some traditional south German fare in the sprawling garden or cavernous interior.

Moritz
BAR

(Untere Bachgasse 15; ☺7.30am-1am Mon-Sat, from 9am Sun) Take some Gothic cross vaulting, paint it high-visibility tunnel orange, throw in some killer cocktails and invite the iPad crowd – and you've got Moritz!

ⓘ Information

Use the **Regensburg Card** (24/48hr €9/17) for free public transport and discounts at local attractions and businesses. Available at the tourist office.

Post Office (Domplatz) There's another branch next to the Hauptbahnhof.

Tourist Office (☎0941-507 4410; www.regensburg.de; Rathausplatz 4; ☺9am-6pm Mon-Fri, 9am-4pm Sat, 9.30am-4pm Sun Apr-Oct, closes 2.30pm Sun Nov-Mar; 🖥) In the historic

---

SCHINDLER'S PLAQUE

Oskar Schindler Plaque (Am Watmarkt 5) Oskar Schindler lived in Regensburg for years, and today one of his houses bears a plaque to his achievements, as commemorated in Steven Spielberg's epic dramatisation *Schindler's List*.

Altes Rathaus. Sells tickets, tours, rooms and an audioguide for self-guided tours.

World Heritage Visitors Centre (☑ 0941-507 4410; www.regensburg-welterbe.de; Weisse-Lamm-Gasse 1; ☉10am-7pm) Brand-new visitors centre by the Steinerne Brücke, focusing on the city's Unesco World Heritage Sites. Interesting interactive multimedia exhibits.

❶ Getting There & Away

CAR

Regensburg is about an hour's drive southeast of Nuremberg and northwest of Passau via the A3 autobahn. The A93 runs south to Munich.

TRAIN

Train connections from Regensburg:

➡ **Frankfurt am Main** €71, three hours, every two hours, change in Nuremberg or Würzburg

➡ **Landshut** €13.30, 40 minutes, hourly

➡ **Munich** €27.50, 1½ hours, hourly

➡ **Nuremberg** €20.70, one to two hours, hourly

➡ **Passau** From €24.20 to €29, one to two hours, hourly or change in Plattling

❶ Getting Around

BICYCLE

Bikehaus (☑ 0941-599 8808; www.bikehaus.de; Bahnhofstrasse 18; bikes per day €12; ☉10am-7pm Mon-Sat) At Bikehaus you can rent anything from kiddies bikes to fully saddled tourers and even a rickshaw for a novel city tour.

BUS

On weekdays the Altstadtbus (€1.10) somehow manages to squeeze its way through the narrow streets between the Hauptbahnhof and the Altstadt every 10 minutes between 9am and 7pm. The bus transfer point is one block north of the Hauptbahnhof, on Albertstrasse. Tickets for all city buses (except the Altstadtbus) cost €2.30 for journeys in the centre; an all-day ticket costs €5 at ticket machines; €3.80 at weekends when valid for both days.

CAR & MOTORCYCLE

The Steinerne Brücke and much of the Altstadt are closed to private vehicles. Car parks in the centre charge from €1.50 per hour and are well signposted.

Around Regensburg

Walhalla

Walhalla NOTABLE BUILDING
(www.walhalla-regensburg.de; adult/concession €4/3; ☉9am-5.45pm Apr-Sep, 10-11.45am & 1-3.45pm Oct-Mar) Modelled on the Parthenon in Athens, the Walhalla is a breathtaking Ludwig I monument dedicated to the giants of Germanic thought and deed. Marble steps seem to lead up forever from the banks of the Danube to this dazzling marble hall, with a gallery of 127 heroes in marble.

The collection includes a few dubious cases, such as astronomer Copernicus, born in a territory belonging to present-day Poland. The most recent addition (2009) is romantic poet Heinrich Heine, whose works were set to music by Strauss, Wagner and Brahms.

To get there take the Danube Valley country road (unnumbered) 10km east from Regensburg to the village of Donaustauf, then follow the signs. Alternatively, you can take a two-hour boat cruise with Schifffahrt Klinger (p291), which includes a one-hour stop at Walhalla, or take bus 5 from Regensburg Hauptbahnhof.

Ingolstadt

☑ 0841 / POP 129,100

Even by Bavaria's elevated standards, Danube-straddling Ingolstadt is astonishingly affluent. Auto manufacturer Audi has its headquarters here, flanked by a clutch of oil refineries on the outskirts, but industry has left few marks on the medieval centre, with its cobblestone streets and historic, if slightly over-renovated, buildings. Ingolstadt's museum-church has the largest flat fresco ever made, and few people may know that its old medical school figured in the literary birth of Frankenstein's monster, the monster by which all others are judged.

◉ Sights

Asamkirche Maria de Victoria CHURCH
(☑ 0841-305 1830; Neubaustrasse 11; adult/concession €2/1.50; ☉9am-noon & 12.30-5pm Tue-Sun Mar-Oct, 1-4pm Tue-Sun Nov-Feb) The Altstadt's crown jewel is the Asamkirche Maria de Victoria, a baroque masterpiece designed by brothers Cosmas Damian and Egid Quirin Asam between 1732 and 1736. The church's mesmerising trompe l'oeil ceiling, painted in just six weeks in 1735, is the world's largest fresco on a flat surface.

Visual illusions abound: stand on the little circle on the diamond tile near the door and look over your left shoulder at the archer with the flaming red turban – wherever you walk, the arrow points right at you. The fresco's Horn of Plenty, Moses' staff and the treasure chest also appear to dramatically alter as you move around the space.

Deutsches Medizinhistorisches Museum
MUSEUM

(German Museum of Medical History; ☑ 0841-305 2860; www.dmm-ingolstadt.de; Anatomiestrasse 18-20; adult/concession €5/2.50; ◷ 10am-5pm Tue-Sun) Located in the stately Alte Anatomie (Old Anatomy) at the university, this sometimes rather gory museum chronicles the evolution of medical science as well as the many (scary) instruments and techniques used. Unless you are, or have been, a medical student, pack a strong stomach for the visit.

The ground floor eases you into the exhibition with medical equipment such as birthing chairs, enema syringes, lancets used for bloodletting and other delightful paraphernalia guaranteed to make many go weak at the knees. Upstairs things get closer to the bone with displays of human skeletons, foetuses of conjoined twins, a pregnant uterus and a cyclops.

Neues Schloss
PALACE, MUSEUM

The ostentatious Neues Schloss (New Palace) was built for Duke Ludwig the Bearded in 1418. Fresh from a trip to wealth-laden France, Ludwig borrowed heavily from

THE BIRTH OF FRANKENSTEIN

Mary Shelley's *Frankenstein*, published in 1818, set a creepy precedent in the world of monster fantasies. The story is well known: young scientist Viktor Frankenstein travels to Ingolstadt to study medicine. He becomes obsessed with the idea of creating a human being and goes shopping for parts at the local cemetery. Unfortunately, his creature is a problem child and sets out to destroy its maker.

Shelley picked Ingolstadt because it was home to a prominent university and medical faculty. In the 19th century, a laboratory for scientists and medical doctors was housed in the Alte Anatomie (now the **Deutsches Medizinhistorisches Museum**). In the operating theatre, professors and their students carried out experiments on corpses and dead tissue, though perhaps one may have been inspired to work on something a bit scarier...

Gallic design and created a residence with 3m-thick walls, Gothic net vaulting and individually carved doorways. One guest who probably didn't appreciate its architectural merits was future French president Charles de Gaulle, held as prisoner of war here during WWI.

Today the building houses the **Bayerisches Armeemuseum** (Bavarian Military Museum; ☑ 0841-937 70; www.armeemuseum. de; Paradeplatz 4; adult/concession €3.50/3, Sun €2; ◷ 9am-5.30pm Tue-Fri, 10am-5.30pm Sat & Sun) with exhibits on long-forgotten battles, armaments dating back to the 14th century and legions of tin soldiers filling the rooms.

The second part of the museum is in the **Reduit Tilly** (adult/concession/child €3.50/3/ free, Sun €1; ◷ 9am-5.30pm Tue-Fri, 10am-5.30pm Sat & Sun) across the river. This 19th-century fortress has an undeniable aesthetic, having been designed by Ludwig I's chief architect. It was named after Johann Tilly – a field marshal of the Thirty Years' War who was known as the 'butcher of Magdeburg' – and features exhibits covering the history of WWI and post-WWI Germany.

The museum complex also houses the **Bayerisches Polizeimuseum** (Donaulände 1; adult/concession €3.50/3, Sun €1; ◷ 9am-5.30pm Tue-Fri, 10am-5.30pm Sat & Sun) which lives in the Turm Triva, built at the same time as the Reduit Tilly. Exhibitions trace the story of Bavarian police and their role in various episodes of history such as the Third Reich and the Cold War.

A combined ticket is available at each museum that covers entry to all three museums (adult/concession €7/5).

Museum Mobile
MUSEUM

(☑ 0800-283 4444; www.audi.de/foren; Ettinger Strasse 40; adult/child €4/free; ◷ 9am-6pm) This high-tech car museum is part of the Audi Forum complex. Exhibits on three floors chart Audi's humble beginnings in 1899 to its latest dream machines such as the R8. Some 50 cars and 20 motorbikes are on display, including prototypes that glide past visitors on an open lift. Bus 11 runs every 30 minutes from the Hauptbahnhof or central bus station (ZOB) to the Audi complex.

The two-hour tours of the **Audi factory** (☑ 0800-283 4444; adult/concession €7/3.50; ◷ Mon-Fri, 10.30am, 12.30pm & 2.30pm in German, 11.30am only in English) take you through the entire production process, from the metal press to the testing station.

Liebfrauenmünster CHURCH
(Kreuzstrasse; ⊙8am-6pm) Ingolstadt's biggest church was established by Duke Ludwig the Bearded in 1425 and enlarged over the next century. This classic Gothic hall church has a pair of strangely oblique square towers that flank the main entrance. Inside, subtle colours and a nave flooded with light intensify the magnificence of the high-lofted vaulting and the blossoming stonework of several side chapels.

The high altar by Hans Mielich (1560) has a rear panel depicting St Katharina debating with the professors at Ingolstadt's new university, ostensibly in a bid to convert the Protestant faculty to Catholicism – a poke at Luther's Reformation. At the rear of the church, there's a small Schatzkammer (treasury) displaying precious robes, goblets and monstrances belonging to the diocese.

Museum für Konkrete Kunst MUSEUM
(Museum of Concrete Art; ☑0841-305 1875; www.mkk-ingolstadt.de; Tränktorstrasse 6-8; adult/concession €3/1.50; ⊙10am-5pm Tue-Sun) This unique art museum showcases works and installations from the Concrete Movement, all of a bafflingly abstract nature. The movement was defined and dominated by interwar artists Max Bill and Theo van Doesburg whose works make up a large share of the collections.

Kreuztor HISTORIC BUILDING
(Kreuzstrasse) The Gothic Kreuztor (1385) was one of the four main gates into the city until the 19th century and its redbrick fairy-tale outline is now the emblem of Ingolstadt. This and the main gate within the Neues Schloss are all that remain of the erstwhile entrances into the medieval city, but the former fortifications, now flats, still encircle the centre.

Lechner Museum MUSEUM
(☑0841-305 2250; www.lechner-museum.de; Esplanade 9; adult/concession €3/1.50; ⊙11am-6pm Thu-Sun) This unusual art museum highlights works cast in steel, a medium that's more expressive than you might think. Exhibits are displayed in a striking glass-covered factory hall dating from 1953.

🛌 Sleeping

DJH Hostel HOSTEL €
(☑0841-305 1280; www.ingolstadt.jugendherberge.de; Friedhofstrasse 4; dm from €19.20) This beautiful, well-equipped and wheelchair-friendly hostel is in a renovated red-brick fortress (1828), about 150m west of the Kreuztor.

Enso Hotel HOTEL €€
(☑0841-885 590; www.enso-hotel.de; Bei der Arena 1; s/d from €99/129; 🅿🛜) Located just across the Danube from the city centre, the 176 business-standard rooms here come in bold dashes of lip-smacking red and soot black, with acres of retro faux veneer providing a funky feel. Traffic noise is barely audible despite the location at a busy intersection. Amenities include a commendable Italian restaurant-bar and a fitness room.

Hotel Anker HOTEL €€
(☑0841-300 50; www.hotel-restaurant-anker.de; Tränktorstrasse 1; s/d €64/94) Bright rooms, a touch of surrealist art and a commendably central location make this family-run hotel a good choice, although the lack of English is a slight downside. Try to avoid arriving at mealtimes, when staff are busy serving in the traditional restaurant downstairs.

Bayerischer Hof HOTEL €€
(☑0841-934 060; www.bayerischer-hof-ingolstadt.de; Münzbergstrasse 12; s €68-85, d €87-100) Located around a Bavarian eatery, the 34 rooms are a pretty good deal, and are filled with hardwood furniture, TVs and modern bathrooms. Rates come down at weekends and this is a good deal for lone travellers as almost half the rooms are singles.

Kult Hotel DESIGN HOTEL €€€
(☑0841-951 00; www.kult-hotel.de; Theodor-Heuss-Strasse 25; d €189; 🅿@🛜) The most eye-catching feature of rooms at this exciting design hotel, 2km northeast of the city centre, are the painted ceilings, each one a slightly saucy work of art. Otherwise fittings and furniture come sleek, room gadgets are the latest toys, and the restaurant constitutes a study in cool elegance.

🍴 Eating & Drinking

Local drinkers are proud that Germany's Beer Purity Law of 1516 was issued in Ingolstadt, the 500th anniversary of which the city celebrated in 2016. Herrnbräu, Nordbräu or Ingobräu are the excellent local brews.

For a quick bite head for the Viktualienmarkt, just off Rathausplatz, where fast-food stalls provide international flavour. Ingolstadt must have more Italian eateries per capita than any other Germany city!

BAVARIA INGOLSTADT

Zum Daniel
BAVARIAN €€

(☑0841-352 72; Roseneckstrasse 1; mains €8-17; ☺9am midnight Tue-Sun) Ingolstadt's oldest inn is a lovingly run, Michelin-reviewed local institution serving what many claim to be the town's best pork roast and seasonal specials.

Stella D'Oro
ITALIAN €€

(☑0841-794 3737; www.stelladoro.de; Griesbadgasse 2; mains €8.20-30.90; ☺11.30am-2.30pm & 5.30-11pm Mon-Sat) Ingolstadt has more Italian eateries than some Italian towns, so if you're going for *la dolce vita,* you might as well go for the best. The exquisite menu at this smart Italian job is divided into Terra (meat), Il Mare (fish), L'orot (vegetarian dishes) and Dolce (desserts) with the seafood a particularly refreshing change in meat-munching Bavaria.

Weissbräuhaus
PUB FOOD €€

(☑0841-328 90; Dollstrasse 3; mains €8.50-17.90; ☺11am-midnight) This modern beer hall serves standard Bavarian dishes, including the delicious *Weissbräupfändl* (pork fillet with homemade *Spätzle*). There's a beer garden with a charming fountain out back.

Kuchlbauer
PUB

(☑0841-335 512; www.biermuseum-ingolstadt.de; Schäffbräustrasse 11a; ☺11am-3pm & 5pm-1am) This unmissable brewpub, with oodles of brewing and rustic knick-knacks hanging from the walls and ceiling, really rocks (or should we say sways) when someone stokes up an accordion. Tipples include the house *Hefeweissbier* (unfiltered wheat beer) or you could try the Mass Goass, a 1L jug containing dark beer, cola and 4cL of cherry liqueur!

Neue Galerie Das MO
CAFE, BAR

(☑0841-339 60; Bergbräustrasse 7; ☺from 5pm) This trendy, evening-only place puts on occasional art exhibitions, but it's the walled beer garden in the shade of mature chestnut trees that punters really come for. The international menu offers everything from cheeseburgers to schnitzel and baked potatoes, and vegetarians are well catered for.

ⓘ Information

Post Office (Am Stein 8; ☺8.30am-6pm Mon-Fri, 9am-1pm Sat)

Sparkasse (Rathausplatz 6)

Tourist Office (☑0841-305 3005; www.ingolstadt-tourismus.de; Elisabethstrasse 3, Hauptbahnhof; ☺8.30am-6.30pm Mon-Fri, 9.30am-1pm Sat) The other branch is at Rathausplatz (☑0841-305 3030; Rathausplatz 2; ☺9am-6pm Mon-Fri, 10am-2pm Sat & Sun, shorter hours and closed Sun Nov Mar).

ⓘ Getting There & Away

When arriving by train from the north (from Eichstätt and Nuremberg), Ingolstadt Nord station is nearer to the historical centre than the Hauptbahnhof. Trains from the south arrive at the Hauptbahnhof. Ingolstadt has the following rail connections:

➡ **Munich** €17.90 to €28, one hour, twice hourly

➡ **Nuremberg** €20 to €31, 30 to 40 minutes, hourly

➡ **Regensburg** €15.70, two hours, twice hourly, change in Nuremberg

ⓘ Getting Around

Buses 10, 11 and 18 run every few minutes between the city centre and the Hauptbahnhof, 2.5km to the southeast.

Landshut

☑0871 / POP 66.200

A worthwhile halfway halt between Munich and Regensburg, or a place to kill half a day before a flight from nearby Munich Airport, Landshut (pronounced '*lants*-hoot') was the hereditary seat of the Wittelsbach family in the early 13th century, and capital of the Dukedom of Bavaria-Landshut for over a century. Apart from a brief episode as custodian of the Bavarian University two centuries ago, Landshuters have since been busy retreating into provincial obscurity, but the town's blue-blooded past is still echoed in its grand buildings, a historical pageant with a cast of thousands and one seriously tall church.

◉ Sights

Coming from the train station, you enter Landshut's historical core through the broken Gothic arch of the stocky **Ländtor**, virtually the only surviving chunk of the town's medieval defences. From here, Theaterstrasse brings you to the 600m-long **Altstadt**, one of Bavaria's most impressive medieval marketplaces. Pastel town houses lining its curving cobbled length hoist elaborate gables, every one a different bell-shaped or saw-toothed creation in brick and plaster.

Burg Trausnitz
CASTLE

(☑0871-924 110; www.burg-trausnitz.de; adult/concession €5.50/4.50; ☺tours 9am-6pm Apr-Sep, 10am-4pm Oct-Mar) Roosting high above the Altstadt is Burg Trausnitz, Landshut's star attraction. The 50-minute guided tour (in German with English text) takes you through the Gothic and Renaissance halls and chambers, ending at an alfresco party terrace with bird's-eye views of the town below. The tour includes the **Kunst- und Wunderkammer** (Room of Art and Curiosities), a typical Renaissance-era display of exotic curios assembled by the local dukes.

St Martin Church   CHURCH
(www.st.martin-landshut.de; Altstadt; ⊙7.30am-6pm Apr-Sep, to 5pm Oct-Mar) Rising in Gothic splendour at the southern end of the Altstadt is Landshut's record-breaking St Martin Church; its spire is the tallest brick structure in the world at 130.6m and took 55 years to build. It's by far Bavaria's tallest church with Regensburg's Dom a full 25m shorter.

Stadtresidenz   PALACE
(☑0871-924 110; Altstadt 79; adult/concession €3.50/2.50; ⊙tours in German hourly 9am-6pm Apr-Sep, 10am-4pm Oct-Mar, closed Mon) Gracing the Altstadt is the Stadtresidenz, a Renaissance palace built by Ludwig X which hosts temporary exhibitions on historical themes. Admission is by guided tour only.

★ Festivals & Events

Landshuter Hochzeit   MEDIEVAL
(www.landshuter-hochzeit.de) Every four years in July, the town hosts the Landshuter Hochzeit (next held in 2017 and 2021), one of Europe's biggest medieval bashes. It commemorates the marriage of Duke Georg der Reiche of Bavaria-Landshut to Princess Jadwiga of Poland in 1475.

🛏 Sleeping & Eating

DJH Hostel   HOSTEL €
(☑0871-234 49; www.landshut.jugendherberge.de; Richard-Schirrmann-Weg 6; dm from €21; ☞) This clean, well-run 100-bed hostel occupies an attractive old villa up by the castle, with views across town.

Goldene Sonne   HOTEL €€
(☑0871-925 30; www.goldenesonne.de; Neustadt 520; s/d from €70/90; ℗☞) True to its name, the 'Golden Sun' fills a magnificently gabled, six-storey town house with light. Rooms sport stylishly lofty ceilings, ornate mirrors, flat-screen TVs and renovated bathrooms. There's a fancy Bavarian restaurant on the premises.

Zur Insel   HOTEL €€
(☑0871-923 160; www.insel-landshut.de; Badstrasse 16; s €60-95, d €75-110; ☞) A good-value place to kip with 15 simple folksy rooms and a wood-panelled restaurant.

Augustiner an der St Martins Kirche   BAVARIAN €€
(www.landshut-augustiner.de; Kirchgasse 251; mains €7.90-18.90; ⊙10am-midnight) This dark wood tavern at the foot of the St Martin's spire is the best place in town to down a meat-dumpling combo, washed along with a frothy Munich wet one.

Alt Landshut   BAVARIAN €€
(Isarpromenade 3; mains €6-14; ⊙11am-11pm) Sunny days see locals linger over an Augustiner and some neighbourhood nosh outside by the Isar. In winter you can retreat to the simple whitewashed dining room.

❶ Information

Tourist Office (☑0871-922 050; www.landshut.de; Altstadt 315; ⊙9am-6pm Mon-Fri, 10am-4pm Sat Mar-Oct, 9am-5pm Mon-Fri, 10am-2pm Sat Nov-Feb)

❶ Getting There & Away

TO/FROM THE AIRPORT
The airport bus (€13, 35 minutes) leaves hourly from near the tourist office and the train station between 3am and 10pm.

TRAIN
Landshut is a fairly major stop on the Munich–Regensburg mainline.
➡ **Munich** €15.70, 45 minutes, twice hourly
➡ **Passau** €23.50, 1½ hours, hourly
➡ **Regensburg** €13.30, 40 minutes, at least hourly

Passau

☑0851 / POP 49,500

Water has quite literally shaped the picturesque town of Passau on the border with Austria. Its Altstadt is stacked atop a narrow peninsula that jabs its sharp end into the confluence of three rivers: the Danube, the Inn and the Ilz. The rivers brought wealth to Passau, which for centuries was an important trading centre, especially for Bohemian salt, Central Europe's 'white gold'. Christianity, meanwhile, generated prestige as Passau evolved into the largest bishopric in the Holy Roman Empire. The Altstadt remains pretty much as it was when the powerful

WORTH A TRIP

MARKTL AM INN

On a gentle bend in the Inn River, some 60km southwest of Passau, sits the drowsy settlement of Marktl am Inn. Few people outside of Germany (or indeed Bavaria) had heard of it before 19 April 2005, the day when its favourite son, Cardinal Joseph Ratzinger, was elected **Pope Benedict XVI**. Literally overnight the community was inundated with reporters, devotees and the plain curious, all seeking clues about the pontiff's life and times. Souvenirs like mitre-shaped cakes, *Papst-Bier* (Pope's Beer) and religious board games flooded the local shops.

The pope's **Geburtshaus** (✆ 08678-747 680; www.papsthaus.eu; Marktplatz 11; adult/concession €3.50/2.50; ⊙ 10am-noon & 2-6pm Tue-Fri, 10am-6pm Sat & Sun Easter-Oct) is the simple but pretty Bavarian home where Ratzinger was born in 1927 and lived for the first two years of his life before his family moved to Tittmoning. The exhibition kicks off with a film (in English) tracing the pontiff's early life, career and the symbols he selected for his papacy. You then head into the house proper, where exhibits expand on these themes. The modest room where Ratzinger came into the world is on the upper floor.

The **Heimatmuseum** (✆ 08678-8104; Marktplatz 2; adult/concession €2/1.50) is in possession of a golden chalice and a skullcap that was used by Ratzinger in his private chapel in Rome, but is only open to groups of five or more by prior arrangement; visitors should call the **tourist office** (✆ 08678-748 820; www.marktl.de; Marktplatz 1; ⊙ 10am-noon & 2-4pm daily) at least a day ahead to arrange entry. His baptismal font can be viewed at the **Pfarrkirche St Oswald** (Marktplatz 6), which is open for viewing except during church services.

With immaculate rooms and a superb restaurant, family-run **Pension Hummel** (✆ 08678-282; www.gasthof-hummel.de; Hauptstrasse 34; s/d €44/63), a few steps from the train station, is the best spot to get some shut-eye. Wash down no-nonsense Bavarian fare with a *Papst-Bier* at **Gasthaus Oberbräu** (✆ 08678-1040; Bahnhofstrasse 2; mains €6-11; ⊙ 10am-midnight).

Marktl is a very brief stop on an Inn-hugging branch line of the train service between Simbach and the junction at Mühldorf (€6.10, 20 minutes), from where there are regular direct connections to Munich, Passau and Landshut.

prince-bishops built its tight lanes, tunnels and archways with an Italiante flourish, but the western end (around Nibelungenplatz) has received a modern makeover with shopping malls centred on the hang-glider-shaped central bus station (ZOB).

Passau is a Danube river-cruise halt and is often bursting with day visitors. It's also the convergence point of several long-distance cycling routes.

⊙ Sights

Dom St Stephan   CHURCH
(www.bistum-passau.de; Domplatz; ⊙ 6.30am-7pm) There's been a church here since the late 5th century, but what you see today is much younger thanks to the fire of 1662, which ravaged much of the medieval town, including the cathedral. The rebuilding job went to a team of Italians, notably the architect Carlo Lurago and the stucco master Giovanni Battista Carlone. The result is a top-heavy baroque interior with a mob of saints and cherubs gazing down at the congregation from countless cornices and capitals.

The building's acoustics are perfect for its main attraction, the world's largest organ, which perches above the main entrance. This monster of a wind instrument contains an astonishing 17,974 pipes and it's an amazing acoustic experience to hear it in full puff. Half-hour organ recitals take place at noon daily Monday to Saturday (adult/child €4/2) and at 7.30pm on Thursday (adult/child €5/3) from May to October and for a week around Christmas. Show up at least 30 minutes early to ensure you get a seat.

Veste Oberhaus   FORTRESS
(www.oberhausmuseum.de; adult/concession €5/4; ⊙ 9am-5pm Mon-Fri, 10am-6pm Sat & Sun mid-Mar–mid-Nov) A 13th-century defensive fortress, built by the prince-bishops, Veste Oberhaus towers over Passau with patriarchal pomp. Not surprisingly, views of the city and into Austria are superb from up here.

Inside the bastion is the **Oberhausmuseum**, a regional history museum where you can uncover the mysteries of medieval cathedral building, learn what it took to become a knight and explore Passau's period as a centre of the salt trade. Displays are labelled in English.

Altes Rathaus   TOWN HALL
(Rathausplatz 2) An entrance in the side of the Altes Rathaus (Old Town Hall) flanking Schrottgasse takes you to the **Grosser Rathaussaal** (Great Assembly Room; adult/concession €2/1.50; ⊙10am-4pm), where large-scale paintings by 19th-century local artist Ferdinand Wagner show scenes from Passau's history with melodramatic flourish. You can also sneak into the adjacent Small Assembly Room for a peek at the ceiling fresco, which again features allegories of the three rivers.

The rest of the Rathaus is a grand Gothic affair topped by a 19th-century painted tower. A carillon chimes several times daily (hours are listed on the wall, alongside historical flood-level markers).

Passauer Glasmuseum   MUSEUM
(☑0851-350 71; www.glasmuseum.de; Hotel Wilder Mann, Am Rathausplatz; adult/concession €7/5; ⊙10am-5pm) Opened by Neil Armstrong, of all people, Passau's warren-like glass museum is filled with some 30,000 priceless pieces of glass and crystal from the baroque, classical, art-nouveau and art-deco periods. Much of what you see hails from the glassworks of Bohemia, but there are also works by Tiffany and famous Viennese producers. Be sure to pick up a floor plan as it's easy to get lost.

Dreiflusseck   LANDMARK
The very nib of the Altstadt peninsula, the point where the rivers merge, is known as the Dreiflusseck (Three River Corner). From the north the little Ilz sluices brackish water down from the peat-rich Bavarian Forest, meeting the cloudy brown of the Danube as it flows from the west and the pale snowmelt jade of the Inn from the south to create a murky tricolour. The effect is best observed from the ramparts of the Veste Oberhaus.

Museum Moderner Kunst   ART MUSEUM
(☑0851-383 8790; www.mmk-passau.de; Bräugasse 17; adult/concession €5/3; ⊙10am-6pm Tue-Sun) Gothic architecture contrasts with 20th- and 21st-century artworks at Passau's Modern Art Museum. The rump of the permanent exhibition is made up of cubist and Expressionist works by Georg Philipp Wörlen, who died in Passau in 1954 and whose architect son, Hanns Egon Wörlen, set up the museum in the 1980s. Temporary exhibitions normally showcase big-hitting German artists and native styles and personalities from the world of architecture.

Römermuseum   MUSEUM
(☑0851-347 69; Lederergasse 43; adult/concession €4/2; ⊙10am-4pm Tue-Sun Mar-mid-Nov) Roman Passau can be viewed from the ground up at this Roman fort museum. Civilian and military artefacts unearthed here and elsewhere in Eastern Bavaria are on show and the ruins of **Kastell Boiotro**, which stood here from AD 250 to 400, are still in situ; some of the towers are still inhabited. There's a castle-themed kids' playground nearby.

🏃 Activities

Wurm + Köck   BOAT TOUR
(☑0851-929 292; www.donauschiffahrt.de; Höllgasse 26) From March to early November, Wurm + Köck operates cruises to the Dreiflusseck from the docks near Rathausplatz, as well as a whole host of other sailings to places along the Danube. The most spectacular vessels in the fleet are the sparkling *Kristallschiff* (Crystal Ship), *Kristallkönigin* (Crystal Queen) and *Kristallprinzessin* (Crystal Princess), all three decorated inside and out with Swarovski crystals.

🛌 Sleeping

Pension Rössner   GUESTHOUSE €
(☑0851-931 350; www.pension-roessner.de; Bräugasse 19; s/d €35/60; P🗊) This immaculate place, in a restored mansion near the tip of the peninsula, offers great value for money and a friendly, cosy ambience. Each of the 16 rooms is uniquely decorated and many overlook the fortress. There's bike hire (€10 per day) and parking for €5 a day. Booking recommended.

Pension Vicus   GUESTHOUSE €
(☑0851-931 050; www.pension-vicus.de; Johann-Bergler-Strasse; s €38-44, d €62-69; P🗊) Bright, family-run pension on the south side of the Inn. Rooms have small kitchenettes and there's a supermarket next door. Breakfast is an extra €7. Take frequent bus 3 or 4 from the ZOB to the Johann-Bergler-Strasse stop.

DJH Hostel   HOSTEL €
(☑0851-493 780; www.passau.jugendherberge.de; Oberhaus 125; dm from €23.40) Beautifully renovated 127-bed hostel right in the fortress.

HendlHouseHotel HOTEL €

(☑0851-330 69; www.hendlhouse.com; Grosse Klingergasse 17; s/d €50/64; ☏) With their light, unfussy decor and well-tended bathrooms, the 15 pristine rooms at this Altstadt inn offer a high quality-to-price ratio. Buffet breakfast is served in the downstairs restaurant.

Camping Passau CAMPGROUND €

(☑0851-414 57; www.camping-passau.de; Halser Strasse 34; per person €9; ☺May-Sep) Tent-only camping ground idyllically set on the Ilz River, 15 minutes' walk from the Altstadt. Catch bus 1 or 2 to Ilzbrücke.

★**Hotel Schloss Ort** BOUTIQUE HOTEL €€

(☑0851-340 72; www.hotel-schloss-ort.de; Im Ort 11; s €68-121, d €97-184; P☏) This 800-year-old medieval palace by the Inn River conceals a tranquil boutique hotel, stylishly done out with polished timber floors, crisp white cotton sheets and wrought-iron bedsteads. Many of the 18 rooms enjoy river views and breakfast is served in the vaulted restaurant. Parking is an extra €4.

Hotel König HOTEL €€

(☑0851-3850; www.hotel-koenig.de; Untere Donaulände 1; s €69-90, d €89-130; P☏) This riverside property puts you smack in the heart of the Altstadt and near all the sights. The 41 timber-rich rooms – many of them enormous – are spread out over two buildings and most come with views of the Danube and fortress. One slight disadvantage is the lack of English. Parking is €10 a night.

Hotel Wilder Mann HOTEL €€

(☑0851-350 71; www.wilder-mann.com; Höllgasse 1; s €55-77, d €88-200; P☏) Sharing space with the Glasmuseum (p301), this historic hotel boasts former guests ranging from Empress Elisabeth (Sisi) of Austria to Yoko Ono. In the rooms, folksy painted furniture sits incongrously with 20th-century telephones and 21st-century TVs. The building is a warren of staircases, passageways and linking doors, so make sure you remember where your room is. Guests receive a miserly discount to the museum.

✗ Eating & Drinking

Cafe Greindl CAFE €

(www.greindl-passau.de; Willgasse 8, meals €6-10; ☺7am-6pm Mon-Sat, from 11am Sun) The affluent *Kaffee-und-Torte* society meet daily at this bright, flowery cafe that oozes Bavarian *Gemütlichkeit*. Declared one of Germany's best in 2014 by *Feinschmecker* magazine,

the early opening makes this a sure-fire breakfast option.

Café Kowalski CAFE €

(☑0851-2487; www.cafe-kowalski.de; Oberer Sand 1; dishes €4-11; ☺9.30am-1am Mon-Sat, from 10am Sun; ☏) Chat flows as freely as the wine and beer at this retro-furnished cafe, a kicker of a nightspot. The giant burgers, schnitzels and big breakfasts are best consumed on the terrace overlooking the Ilz River.

★**Heilig-Geist-Stifts-Schenke** BAVARIAN €€

(☑0851-2607; www.stiftskeller-passau.de; Heilig-Geist-Gasse 4; mains €10-20; ☺11am-11pm, closed Wed; ☏) Not only does this historical inn have a succession of walnut-panelled ceramic-stove-heated rooms, a candlelit cellar (from 6pm) and a vine-draped garden, but the food is equally inspired. Amid the river fish, steaks and seasonal dishes there are quite gourmet affairs such as beef fillet in flambéed cognac sauce. Help it all along with one of the many Austrian and German wines in stock.

Zum Grünen Baum ORGANIC €€

(☑0851-356 35; Höllgasse 7; mains €7.20-13.80; ☺10am-1am; ✓) Take a seat in the newly renovated interior to savour risottos, goulash, schnitzel and soups, prepared as far as possible using organic ingredients, which are locally sourced as far as possible. Cosy, friendly and tucked away in the atmospherically narrow lanes between the Danube and the Residenzplatz.

Diwan CAFE €€

(☑0851-490 3280; Niebelungenplatz 1, 9th fl, Stadtturm; mains €7-11; ☺9am-7pm Mon-Thu, to midnight Fri & Sat, 1-6pm Sun) Climb aboard the high-speed lift from street level to get to this trendy, high-perched cafe-lounge at the top of the Stadtturm, with by far the best views in town. From the tangled rattan and plush cappuccino-culture sofas you can see it all – the Dom St Stephan, the rivers, the Veste Oberhaus – while you tuck into the offerings of the changing seasonal menu.

Selly's Vegan Bar VEGAN €€

(Grosse Klingergasse 10; mains €8; ☺11am-2am Mon-Thu, to 4am Fri & Sat, closed Sun; ☏✓) Vegan cafe by day, slick drinking spot by night, the simple, 21st-century decor of this bar-restaurant is a world away from Bavaria's medieval inns. Burgers, curries, pastas and salads are served up meat- and dairy-free by the Czech owner.

STRAUBING

Some 30km southeast of Regensburg, Straubing enjoyed a brief heyday as part of a wonky alliance that formed the short-lived Duchy of Straubing-Holland. As a result, the centre is chock-a-block with historical buildings that opened new horizons in a small town. In August, the demand for folding benches soars during the **Gäubodenfest**, a 10-day blow-out that once brought together grain farmers in 1812, but now draws over 20,000 drinkers.

Lined with pastel-coloured houses from a variety of periods, the pedestrian square is lorded over by the Gothic **Stadtturm** (1316). It stands next to the richly gabled **Rathaus**, originally two merchant's homes but repackaged in neo-Gothic style in the 19th century. Just east of the tower is the gleaming golden **Dreifaltigkeitssäule** (Trinity Column), erected in 1709 as a nod to Catholic upheavals during the War of the Spanish Succession.

Straubing has about half a dozen historic churches. The most impressive is **St Jakobskirche** (Pfarrplatz), a late-Gothic hall church with original stained-glass windows; it was the recipient of a baroque makeover, courtesy of the frantically productive Asam brothers. The pair also designed the interior of the **Ursulinenkirche** (Burggasse), their final collaboration; its ceiling fresco depicts the martyrdom of St Ursula surrounded by allegorical representations of the four continents known at the time. Also worth a look is the nearby **Karmelitenkirche** (Hofstatt).

North of here is the former ducal residence **Herzogsschloss** (Schlossplatz), which overlooks the river. This rather austere 14th-century building was once the town's tax office.

One of Germany's most important repositories of Roman treasure is the intimate **Gäubodenmuseum** (☏ 09421-974 10; www.gaeubodenmuseum.de; Frauenhoferstrasse 23; adult/concession €4/3; ⊗ 10am-4pm Tue-Sun). Displays include imposing armour and masks for both soldiers and horses, probably plundered from a Roman store.

If you fancy staying over, the **tourist office** (☏ 09421-944 307; www.straubing.de; Theresienplatz 2; ⊗ 9am-5pm Mon-Wed & Fri, 9am-6pm Thu, 10am-2pm Sat) can find rooms.

Straubing has direct train connections to Regensburg (€10, 25 minutes, hourly). For Passau (€15.70, one hour and 10 minutes, hourly) and Munich (€23, two hours, hourly) change at Plattling or Neufahrn.

Andorfer Weissbräu   BEER GARDEN
(☏ 0851-754 444; Rennweg 2) High on a hill 1.5km north of the Altstadt, this rural beer garden attached to the Andorfer brewery serves filling Bavarian favourites, but the star of the show is the outstanding *Weizen* and *Weizenbock* (strong wheat beer) brewed metres away. Take bus 7 from the ZOB to Ries-Rennweg.

Caffè Bar Centrale   CAFE
(Rindermarkt 7) Venetian bar that has to spill out onto the cobbles of the Rindermarkt as it's so tiny inside. It may be small, but there's a huge drinks card and it's a fine place to head for a first or last drink. The Italian soundtrack fits nicely with the Italianate surroundings.

ⓘ Information

Post Office (Bahnhofstrasse 1; ⊗ 9.30am-8pm Mon-Sat)

Tourist Office (☏ 0851-955 980; www.tourism.passau.de; Rathausplatz 3; ⊗ 8.30am-6pm Mon-Fri, 9am-4pm Sat & Sun Easter–mid-Oct, shorter hours mid-Oct–Easter) Main tourist office in Passau, located in the Altstadt. There's another smaller office (Bahnhofstrasse 28; ⊗ 9am-5pm Mon-Fri, 10.30am-3.30pm Sat & Sun Easter-Sep, shorter hours Oct-Easter) opposite the Hauptbahnhof. Both branches of the tourist office sell the PassauCard (one day per adult/child €16/13.50, three days €30/22), valid for several attractions, unlimited use of public transport and a city river cruise.

ⓘ Getting There & Away

BUS

Buses leave at 7.45am and 4.25pm to the Czech border village of Železná Ruda (2½ hours), from where there are connections to Prague. **Meinfernbus** (www.meinfernbus.de) links Passau with Vienna, Berlin Regensburg and Nuremberg.

TRAIN

Rail connections from Passau:

➡ **Munich** €35.70, 2¼ hours, hourly (change in Mühldorf or Regensburg)

➡ **Nuremberg** €48, two hours, every two hours

➡ **Regensburg** €24.20 to €29, one hour, every two hours or change in Plattling

➡ **Vienna** €55, 2¾ hours, every two hours

❶ Getting Around

Central Passau is sufficiently compact to explore on foot. The CityBus links the Bahnhof with the Altstadt (€1) up to four times an hour. Longer trips within Passau cost €1.80; a day pass costs €4 (€5.50 for a family).

The walk up the hill to the Veste Oberhaus or the DJH Hostel, via Luitpoldbrücke and Ludwigsteig path, takes about 30 minutes. From April to October, a shuttle bus operates every 30 minutes from Rathausplatz (€1.80).

There are several public car parks near the train station, but only one in the Altstadt at Römerplatz (€0.60/8.40 per 30 minutes/day).

Bavarian Forest

Together with the Bohemian Forest on the Czech side of the border, the Bavarian Forest (Bayerischer Wald) forms the largest continuous woodland area in Europe. This inspiring landscape of peaceful rolling hills and rounded tree-covered peaks is interspersed with little-disturbed valleys and stretches of virgin woodland, providing a habitat for many species long since vanished from the rest of Central Europe. A large area is protected as the surprisingly wild and remote Bavarian Forest National Park (Nationalpark Bayerischer Wald).

Although incredibly good value, the region sees few international tourists and remains quite traditional. A centuries-old glassblowing industry is still active in many of the towns along the **Glasstrasse** (Glass Road), a 250km holiday route connecting Waldsassen with Passau. You can visit the studios, workshops, museums and shops, and stock up on traditional and contemporary designs.

The central town of Zwiesel is a natural base, but other settlements along the Waldbahn such as Frauenau and Grafenau are also good options if relying on public transport.

◉ Sights

Bavarian Forest National Park NATIONAL PARK
(Nationalpark Bayerischer Wald; www.nationalpark-bayerischer-wald.de) A paradise for outdoor fiends, the Bavarian Forest National Park extends for around 24,250 hectares along the Czech border, from Bayerisch Eisenstein in the north to Finsterau in the south. Its thick forest, most of it mountain spruce, is criss-crossed by hundreds of kilometres of marked hiking, cycling and cross-country skiing trails, some of which now link up with a similar network across the border. The region is home to deer, wild boar, fox, otter and countless bird species.

Around 1km northeast of the village of Neuschönau stands the **Hans-Eisenmann-Haus** (☑ 08558-96150; www.nationalpark-bayerischer-wald. de; Böhmstrasse 35; ⊙9am-6pm daily Apr-Oct, 9.30am-5pm daily Nov-Mar), the national park's main visitor centre. The free, but slightly dated, exhibition has hands-on displays designed to shed light on topics such as pollution and tree growth. There's also a children's discovery room, a shop and a library.

Glasmuseum MUSEUM
(☑ 09926-941 020; www.glasmuseum-frauenau. de; Am Museumspark 1, Frauenau; adult/concession €5/4.50; ⊙9am-5pm Tue-Sun) Frauenau's dazzlingly modern Glasmuseum covers four millennia of glassmaking history, starting with the ancient Egyptians and ending with modern glass art from around the world. Demonstrations and workshops for kids are regular features.

Museumsdorf Bayerischer Wald MUSEUM
(☑ 08504-8482; www.museumsdorf.com; Am Dreiburgensee, Tittling; adult/concession €6/4; ⊙9am-5pm Apr-Oct) Tittling, on the southern edge of the Bavarian Forest, is home to this 20-hectare open-air museum displaying 150 typical Bavarian Forest timber cottages and farmsteads from the 17th to the 19th centuries. Exhibitions inside the various buildings range from clothing and furniture to pottery and farming implements. Take frequent RBO bus 6124 to Tittling from Passau Hauptbahnhof.

Waldmuseum MUSEUM
(☑ 09922-503 706; www.waldmuseum.zwiesel. de; Kirchplatz 3; adult/concession €6/4; ⊙10am-5pm Wed-Mon) Housed in a former brewery, Zwiesel's 'Forest Museum' has exhibitions on local customs, flora and fauna, glassmaking and life in the forest.

🏃 Activities

Two long-distance hiking routes cut through the Bavarian Forest: the European Distance

Trails E6 (Baltic Sea to the Adriatic Sea) and E8 (North Sea to the Carpathian Mountains). There are mountain huts all along the way. Another popular hiking trail is the Gläserne Steig (Glass Trail) from Lam to Grafenau. Whatever route you're planning, maps produced by Kompass – sheets 185, 195 and 197 – are invaluable companions. They are available from tourist offices and the park visitor centre.

The Bavarian Forest has seven ski areas, but downhill skiing is low-key, even though the area's highest mountain, the Grosser Arber (1456m), occasionally hosts European and World Cup ski races. The major draw here is cross-country skiing, with 2000km of prepared routes through the ranges.

🛏 Sleeping

Accommodation in this region is a real bargain; Zwiesel and Grafenau have the best choices.

DJH Hostel   HOSTEL €
(☑ 08553-6000; www.waldhaeuser.jugendherberge. de; Herbergsweg 2, Neuschönau; dm from €21.90) The only hostel right in the Bavarian Forest National Park is an ideal base for hikers, bikers and cross-country skiers.

Ferienpark Arber   CAMPGROUND €
(☑ 09922-802 595; www.ferienpark-arber.de; Waldesruhweg 34, Zwiesel; per campsite €20.50) This convenient and well-equipped camping ground is about 500m north of Zwiesel train station.

★ Das Reiners   HOTEL €€
(☑ 08552-964 90; www.dasreiners.de; Grüb 20, Grafenau; s €66-75, d €112-190; ⓅⓈ🖂) Recently revamped and rebranded, this snazzily elegant hotel in Grafenau offers good value for the weary traveller. The stylish rooms are spacious and most have balconies. Guests are treated to a pool and sauna, and scrumptious buffet meals. Prices are for half-board.

Hotel Zur Waldbahn   HOTEL €€
(☑ 09922-8570; www.zurwaldbahn.de; Bahnhofplatz 2, Zwiesel; s €60-66, d €80-100; Ⓟ🖂) Opposite Zwiesel train station, many of the rooms at this characteristic inn, run by three generations of the same family, open to balconies with views over the town. The breakfast buffet is an especially generous spread and even includes homemade jams. The restaurant, serving traditional local fare, is the best in town.

❶ Information

Tourist Office (☑ 08552-962 343; www. grafenau.de; Rathausgasse 1, Grafenau; ⊙ 8am-5pm Mon-Thu, 8am-1pm Fri, 10-11.30am & 3-5pm Sat, 9.30-11.30am Sun)
Tourist Office (☑ 09922-840 523; www. zwiesel.de; Stadtplatz 27, Zwiesel; ⊙ 9am-noon & 1-4.30pm Mon-Fri)

❶ Getting There & Around

From Munich, Regensburg or Passau, Zwiesel is reached by rail via Plattling; most trains continue to Bayerisch Eisenstein on the Czech border, with connections to Prague. The scenic Waldbahn shuttles directly between Zwiesel and Bodenmais, and Zwiesel and Grafenau.

There's also a tight network of regional buses, though service can be infrequent. The Igel-Bus, operated by **Ostbayernbus** (www.ostbayernbus.de) navigates around the national park on five routes. A useful one is the Lusen-Bus (€5/12.50 per one/three days), which leaves from Grafenau Hauptbahnhof and travels to the Hans-Eisenmann-Haus, the DJH Hostel and the Lusen hiking area.

The best value is usually the Bayerwald-Ticket (€8), a day pass good for unlimited travel on bus and train across the forest area. It's available from the park visitor centre, stations and tourist offices throughout the area.

Stuttgart & the Black Forest

Best Places to Eat

➜ Valentin (p369)

➜ Olivo (p314)

➜ Kreuzblume (p347)

➜ Zur Forelle (p326)

➜ Weinstube im Baldreit (p332)

Best Places to Stay

➜ Hotel Scholl (p322)

➜ Hotel Schiefes Haus (p325)

➜ Weysses Rössle (p340)

➜ Die Reichstadt (p342)

➜ Parkhotel Wehrle (p353)

Why Go?

If one word could sum up Germany's southwesternmost region, it would be inventive. Baden-Würtemberg gave the world relativity (Einstein), DNA (Miescher) and the astronomical telescope (Kepler). It was here that Bosch invented the spark plug; Gottlieb Daimler the gas engine; and Count Ferdinand the zeppelin. And where would we be without black forest gateau, cuckoo clocks and the ultimate beer food, the pretzel?

Beyond the high-tech, urbanite pleasures of 21st-century Stuttgart lies a region still ripe for discovery. On the city fringes, country lanes roll into vineyards and lordly baroque palaces, spa towns and castles steeped in medieval myth. Swinging south, the Black Forest (*Schwarzwald* in German) looks every inch the Grimm fairy-tale blueprint. Hills rise sharply and wooded above church steeples, looming over half-timbered villages and a crochet of tightly woven valleys. It is a perfectly etched picture of sylvan beauty, a landscape refreshingly oblivious to time and trends.

When to Go

Snow dusts the heights from January to late February and pre-Lenten *Fasnacht* brings carnival shenanigans to the region's towns and villages. Enjoy cool forest hikes, riverside bike rides, splashy fun on Lake Constance and open-air festivals galore during summer. From late September to October the golden autumn days can be spent rambling in woods, mushrooming and snuggling up in Black Forest farmhouses.

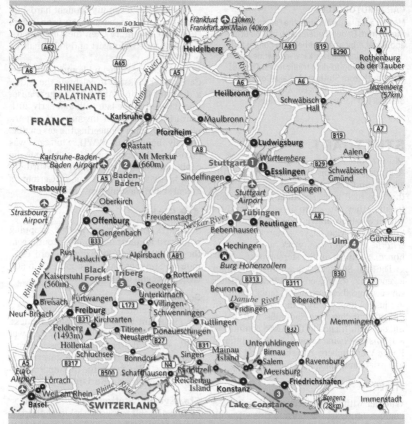

Stuttgart & the Black Forest Highlights

❶ Tuning into modern-day **Stuttgart** (p308)

❷ Wallowing in thermal waters and art nouveau grandeur in **Baden-Baden** (p328), belle of the Black Forest

❸ Hopping between borders on **Lake Constance** (p357), straddling

Switzerland, Germany and Austria

❹ Being amazed by Einstein's birthplace, **Ulm** (p323), crowned by the world's tallest cathedral steeple

❺ Going cuckoo for clocks, black forest gateau and waterfalls in **Triberg** (p353)

❻ Roaming hill, dale and kilometre after pristine kilometre of woodland in the **Black Forest** (p328)

❼ Cruising along the Neckar and living it up Goethe-style in postcard-pretty **Tübingen** (p318)

ℹ Getting There & Around

AIR

Flights to the region serve Stuttgart Airport (p316), a major hub for Germanwings; Karlsruhe-Baden-Baden airport (p333), a Ryanair base; and Basel-Mulhouse EuroAirport (p348), where easyJet operates.

BUS

Trains, trams and/or buses serve almost every town and village, though public transport across the Black Forest can be slow, and long-distance trips (for instance, Freiburg to Konstanz) may involve several changes. Plan your journey with the help of www.efa-bw.de and www.bahn.de.

CAR & MOTORCYCLE

Motorways blazing through the region include the A5 from Baden-Baden south to Freiburg and Basel, which can get hellishly congested due to ongoing roadworks; www.swr.de (in German) has up-to-date traffic news. The A81 runs south from Stuttgart to Lake Constance via Villingen-Schwenningen, while the A8 links Stuttgart to Karlsruhe, Ulm and Munich.

STUTTGART

📞 0711 / POP 600,000

Ask many Germans their opinion of Stuttgarters and they will go off on a tangent: they are road hogs, speeding along the autobahn; they are sharp-dressed executives with a Swabian drawl; they are tight-fisted homebodies who slave away to *schaffe, schaffe, Häusle baue* (work, work, build a house). So much for the stereotypes.

The real Stuttgart is less superficial than legend. True, some good-living locals like their cars fast and their restaurants fancy, but most are just as happy getting their boots dirty in the surrounding vine-clad hills and hanging out with friends in the rustic confines of a *Weinstube* (wine tavern). In the capital of Baden-Württemberg, city slickers and down-to-earth country kids walk hand in hand.

History

Whether with trusty steeds or turbocharged engines, Stuttgart was born to ride – founded as the stud farm Stuotgarten around AD 950. Progress was swift: by the 12th century Stuttgart was a trade centre, by the 13th century a blossoming city and by the early 14th century the seat of the Württemberg royal family. Count Eberhard im Bart added sheen to Swabian suburbia by introducing the *Kehrwoche* in 1492, the communal cleaning rota still revered today.

ⓘ BADEN-WÜRTTEMBERG TICKET

Available at all train stations and online (www.bahn.de), the great-value **Baden-Württemberg Ticket** allows unlimited 2nd-class travel on IRE, RE, RB, S-Bahn trains and buses in the region. The one-day ticket costs €23 for an individual, plus €5 per extra person. Children aged 15 and under travel for free when accompanied by an adult.

The early 16th century brought hardship, peasant wars, plague and Austrian rulers (1520–34). A century later, the Thirty Years' War devastated Stuttgart and killed half its population.

In 1818, King Wilhelm I launched the first Cannstatter Volksfest to celebrate the end of a dreadful famine. An age of industrialisation dawned in the late 19th and early 20th centuries, with Bosch inventing the spark plug and Daimler pioneering the gas engine. Heavily bombed in WWII, Stuttgart was painstakingly reconstructed and became the capital of the new state of Baden-Württemberg in 1953. Today it is one of Germany's greenest and most affluent cities.

⊙ Sights

Stuttgart's main artery is the shopping boulevard Königstrasse, running south from the Hauptbahnhof. Steep grades are common on Stuttgart's hillsides: more than 500 city streets end in *Stäffele* (staircases).

Schlossplatz   SQUARE

Stuttgart's central square is dominated by the exuberant three-winged Neues Schloss. Duke Karl Eugen von Württemberg's answer to Versailles, the baroque-neoclassical royal residence now houses state government ministries. A bronze statue of Emperor Wilhelm I graces nearby **Karlsplatz**.

Staatsgalerie Stuttgart   GALLERY

(📞 0711-470 400; www.staatsgalerie-stuttgart.de; Konrad-Adenauer-Strasse 30-32; adult/concession €7/5; ⊙ 10am-6pm Tue, Wed & Fri-Sun, to 8pm Thu) The neoclassical-meets-contemporary Staatsgalerie bears British architect James Stirling's curvy, colourful imprint. Alongside big-name exhibitions, the gallery harbours a representative collection of European art from the 14th to the 21st centuries as well as American post-WWII avantgardists.

Kunstmuseum Stuttgart   GALLERY

(📞 0711-2161 9600; www.kunstmuseum-stuttgart.de; Kleiner Schlossplatz 1; adult/concession €6/4; ⊙ 10am-6pm Tue-Thu, Sat & Sun, to 9pm Fri) Occupying a shimmering glass cube, this gallery presents high-calibre special exhibits alongside a permanent gallery filled with a prized collection of works by Otto Dix, Willi Baumeister and Alfred Höltzel. For a great view, head up to the Cube cafe.

Out front, the primary colours and geometric forms of Alexander Calder's mobile catch the eye.

Schlossgarten
GARDENS

The fountain-dotted **Mittlerer Schlossgarten** (Middle Palace Garden) draws thirsty crowds to its beer garden in summer. The **Unterer Schlossgarten** (Lower Palace Garden) is a ribbon of greenery rambling northeast to the Neckar River and the Rosensteinpark, home to the zoo. Sitting south, the **Oberer Schlossgarten** (Upper Palace Garden) is framed by eye-catching landmarks like the columned Staatstheater (p315) and the ultramodern **Landtag** (State Parliament), a glass rectangle housing the state parliament.

Turmforum
VIEWPOINT

(Hauptbahnhof; ⊙10am-6pm Mon-Thu & Sat & Sun, to 9pm Fri) FREE Some of the best views of Stuttgart are from the the top of the tower jutting out from the main train station. A free lift (elevator) deposits you right below the revolving Mercedes star. You also get a bird's-eye view of 'Stuttgart 21', a huge – and controversial – revamp of the main train station. Exhibits on floors 3, 5 and 7a explain the details.

Mercedes-Benz Museum
MUSEUM

(☑0711-173 0000; www.mercedes-benz-classic.com; Mercedesstrasse 100; adult/concession/under 15yr €8/4/free; ⊙9am-6pm Tue-Sun, last admission 5pm; ℝS1 to Neckarpark) A futuristic swirl on the cityscape, the Mercedes-Benz Museum takes a chronological spin through the Mercedes empire. Look out for legends like the 1885 Daimler Riding Car, the world's first gasoline-powered vehicle, and the record-breaking Lightning Benz that hit 228km/h at Daytona Beach in 1909.

Porsche Museum
MUSEUM

(☑0711-9112 0911; www.porsche.com/museum; Porscheplatz 1; adult/concession €8/4; ⊙9am-6pm Tue-Sun; ℝNeuwirtshaus) Like a pearly white spaceship preparing for lift-off, the barrier-free Porsche Museum is every little boy's dream. Groovy audioguides race you through the history of Porsche from its 1948 beginnings. Stop to glimpse the 911 GT1 that won Le Mans in 1998.

Landesmuseum Württemberg
MUSEUM

(www.landesmuseum-stuttgart.de; Schillerplatz 6; adult/concession €5.50/4.50; ⊙10am-5pm Tue-Sun) An archway leads to the turreted 10th-century Altes Schloss, where this museum features regional archaeology and architecture. The historic booty includes Celtic jewellery, neolithic pottery, diamond-encrusted crown jewels and rare artefacts. Time your visit to see, from the arcaded

GOING THE WHOLE HOG

Schweinemuseum (www.schweinemuseum.de; Schlachthofstrasse 2a; adult/concession €5.90/5; ⊙11am-7.30pm; Ⓤ Schlachthof) Billing itself as the world's biggest pig museum, the Schweinemuseum is one heck of a pigsty: 45,000 paintings, lucky trinkets, antiques, cartoons, piggy banks and a veritable mountain of cuddly toys cover the entire porcine spectrum. Since opening in 2010 in the city's 100-year-old former slaughterhouse, the kitsch-cool museum has drawn crowds to its exhibits spotlighting everything from pig worship to wild boar hunt rituals. In the adjacent beer garden (mains €12 to €19), you can pig out on schnitzel, pork knuckles and more.

courtyard, the rams above the clock tower lock horns on the hour.

Wilhelma Zoologisch-Botanischer Garten
ZOO

(www.wilhelma.de; Rosensteinpark; adult/concession €16/10, after 4pm & Nov-Feb €11/7; ⊙8.15am-dusk; Ⓤ Wilhelma) Wilhelma Zoologisch-Botanischer Garten is a quirky mix of zoo and botanical gardens. Kid magnets include semi-striped okapis, elephants, penguins and a petting farm. Greenhouses sheltering tree ferns, camellias and Amazonian species are among the botanical highlights. Sniff out the gigantic bloom of the malodorous titan arum in the Moorish Villa.

Württembergischer Kunstverein
GALLERY

(www.wkv-stuttgart.de; Schlossplatz 2; adult/concession €5/3; ⊙11am-6pm Tue-Sun, to 8pm Wed) Identified by its copper cupola, this gallery stages thought-provoking contemporary art exhibitions.

Schillerplatz
SQUARE

Cobbled Schillerplatz is where the poet-dramatist **Friedrich Schiller** is immortalised in bronze.

Stiftskirche
CHURCH

(Collegiate Church; Stiftstrasse 12; ⊙10am-7pm Mon & Thu, 10am-4pm Fri & Sat, 10am-6pm Sun) FREE Topped by two mismatched towers, this largely 15th-century church has Romanesque origins.

Stuttgart

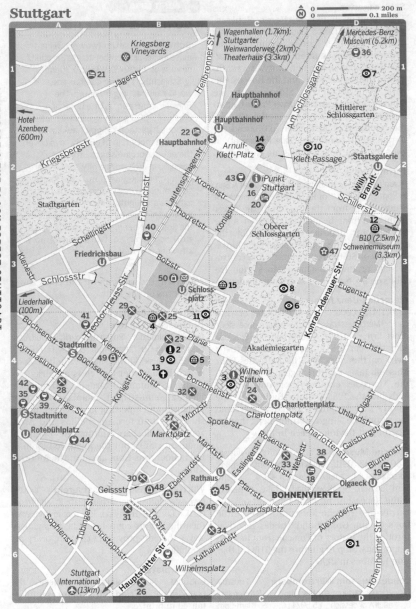

Tours

Pop into the tourist office for details on German-language guided tours, from vineyard ambles to after-work 'walk and wine' strolls.

CityTour Stuttgart BUS TOUR
(adult/concession €15/10; ☐10am-4pm) Departs roughly hourly from the tourist information and trundles past icons like Schlossplatz and the Mercedes-Benz Museum. Up to two

Stuttgart

children aged 14 and under go free when accompanied by an adult.

Neckar-Käpt'n   BOAT TOUR
(www.neckar-kaeptn.de; Ⓤ Wilhelma) From early May to late October, Neckar-Käpt'n runs cruises on the Neckar River, departing from its dock at Wilhelma in Bad Cannstatt on the U14.

✷ Festivals & Events

Sommerfest   MUSIC
(www.sommerfest-stuttgart.de) Riverside parties, open-air gigs and alfresco feasting are what this four-day August shindig is all about.

Weindorf   WINE
(www.stuttgarter-weindorf.de) A 10-day event where winemakers sell the year's vintages from hundreds of booths on Schlossplatz and the Oberer Schlossgarten. Begins on the last weekend in August.

Cannstatter Volksfest   BEER
(www.cannstatter-volksfest.de) Stuttgart's answer to Oktoberfest, this beer-guzzling bash, held over three consecutive weekends from late September to mid-October, lifts spirits with oompah music, fairground rides and fireworks.

Weihnachtsmarkt   CHRISTMAS MARKET
(www.stuttgarter-weihnachtsmarkt.de) One of Germany's biggest Christmas markets brings festive twinkle to Marktplatz, Schillerplatz and Schlossplatz from late November to 23 December.

🛏 Sleeping

Stuttgart is slowly upping the ante in slumberland but nondescript chains still reign supreme. Expect weekend discounts of 10% to 20% at hotels targeting business travellers. If you're seeking individual flair and a family welcome, stop by the tourist office for a list of private guesthouses and apartments.

DON'T MISS

BOHEMIAN BEANS

....

Bohnenviertel (Bean District; www.
bohnenviertel.net) To really slip under
Stuttgart's skin, mosey through one of
the city's lesser-known neighbourhoods.
Walk south to Hans-im-Glück Platz, centred on a fountain depicting the caged
Grimm's fairy-tale character Lucky Hans,
and you'll soon reach the boho-flavoured
Bohnenviertel, named after beans introduced in the 16th century. Back then
they were grown everywhere as the staple food of the poor tanners, dyers and
craftsmen who lived here.

A recent facelift has restored the
neighbourhood's cobbled lanes and
gabled houses, which harbour idiosyncratic galleries, workshops, bookshops,
wine taverns and cafes. The villagey
atmosphere is a refreshing tonic to the
big-city feel of central Stuttgart.

Hostel Alex 30   HOSTEL $

(☑0711-838 8950; www.alex30-hostel.de; Alexanderstrasse 30; dm €25-29, s/d €43/64; P🕏)
Fun-seekers on a budget should thrive at
this popular hostel within walking distance
of the city centre. Rooms are spick and span,
and the bar, sun deck and communal kitch-
en are ideal for swapping stories with fellow travellers. Light sleepers might want to
pack earplugs for thin walls and street noise.
Breakfast costs €8.

Hotel Azenberg   HOTEL $$

(☑0711-225 5040; www.hotelazenberg.de;
Seestrasse 114-116; s €75-120, d €85-135; P🕏🏊;
🚌43) This family-run choice has individually designed quarters with themes swinging
from English country manor to Picasso.
There's a pool, tree-shaded garden and mini
spa for relaxing moments. Take bus 43 from
Stadtmitte to Hölderlinstrasse.

City Hotel   HOTEL $$

(☑0711-210 810; www.cityhotel-stuttgart.de; Uhlandstrasse 18; s €87-95, d €101-119, incl breakfast;
P🕏) Eschew the anonymity of Stuttgart's
cookie-cutter chains for this intimate hotel
just off Charlottenplatz. Rooms are light, clean
and modern, if slightly lacklustre. Breakfast
on the terrace in summer is a bonus.

Ochsen Hotel   HISTORIC HOTEL $$

(☑0711-407 0500; www.ochsen-online.de; Ulmer
Strasse 323; s €89-140, d €119-170; P🕏; Ⓤ Insel-

strasse) It's worth going the extra mile to this
charismatic 18th-century hotel. Some of the
spacious, warm-hued rooms have whirlpool
tubs. The wood-panelled restaurant dishes
up appetising local fare.

Kronen Hotel   HOTEL $$$

(☑0711-225 10; www.kronenhotel-stuttgart.
de; Kronenstrasse 48; s €115-125, d €160-190;
P🕏@🕏) Right on the lap of Königstrasse,
this hotel outclasses most in Stuttgart with
its terrific location, good-natured staff,
well-appointed rooms and funkily lit sauna.
Breakfast is above par, with fresh fruit, egg
and bacon, smoked fish and pastries.

Steigenberger Graf Zeppelin   HOTEL $$$

(☑0711-204 80; www.stuttgart.steigenberger.de;
Arnulf-Klett-Platz 7; r €140-311; P🕏🕏🏊) While
its concrete facade won't bowl you over, inside is a different story. This five-star pad
facing the Hauptbahnhof is luxury all the
way with snazzy rooms, Zen-style spa and
Michelin-starred restaurant, Olivo (p314).

Der Zauberlehrling   BOUTIQUE HOTEL $$$

(☑0711-237 7770; www.zauberlehrling.de; Rosenstrasse 38; s €160-250, d €180-420; P🕏) The
dreamily styled rooms at the 'Sorcerer's Ap-
prentice' offer soothing quarters after a day
on the road. Each one interprets a different
theme (Mediterranean siesta, sunrise, 1001
Nights), through colour, furniture and features such as canopy beds, clawfoot tubs, tat-
ami mats or fireplaces. Breakfast costs €19.

Hotel am Schlossgarten   HOTEL $$$

(☑0711-202 60; www.hotelschlossgarten.com;
Schillerstrasse 23; r €142-220, ste €204-600;
P🕏🕏) Sidling up to the Schloss, this hotel
has handsome, park-facing rooms flaunting
the luxuries that justify the price tag. Book
a table at Michelin-starred Zirbelstube (tasting menus €109 to €139) for classy French
dining in subtly lit, pine-panelled surrounds.

🍴 Eating

Stuttgart has raised the bar in the kitchen,
with chefs putting an imaginative spin on local, seasonal ingredients. The city's half-doz-
en Michelin-starred restaurants prepare
cuisine with enough gourmet panache to
satisfy a food-literate crowd. For intimate
bistro-style dining, explore the backstreets
and the alleyways of Bohnenviertel.

Platzhirsch   INTERNATIONAL $

(☑0711-7616 2508; www.platzhirsch-stuttgart.
de; Geissstrasse 12; mains €6.20-11.80; ⊙11am-

2am) Combining a breath of country air with a pinch of urban cool, wood-panelled Platzhirsch has a good buzz and, in summer, a packed terrace. Dig into mains such as parmesan *Knödel* (dumplings) in thyme-honey sauce and saffron risotto with prawns. Lunch specials go for a wallet-friendly €6.80 to €7.80.

Forum Café
CAFE $

(Gymnasiumstrasse 21; snacks €4-7.50; ☺3-11.30pm Mon-Fri, noon-11.30pm Sat; ☑🖶) Wholesomely hip, kid-friendly cafe in the Forum Theatre, with yogi teas and organic snacks.

Stuttgarter Markthalle
MARKET $

(Market Hall; www.markthalle-stuttgart.de; Dorotheenstrasse 4; ☺7am-6.30pm Mon-Fri, 7am-5pm Sat) Olives, regional cheeses, spices, patisserie, fruit and veg, wine and tapas – you'll find it all under one roof at Stuttgart's art-nouveau market hall, which also has snack stands.

Food Market
MARKET $

(Marktplatz; ☺7.30am-1pm Tue, Thu & Sat) Self-caterers can pick up picnic fixings at the food market.

Reiskorn
INTERNATIONAL $$

(☑0711-664 7633; Torstrasse 27; mains €11-15.50; ☺5-10pm Sun-Thu, 5-11pm Fri, noon-11pm Sat; ☑) With an easygoing vibe and bamboo-green retro interior, this culinary globetrotter serves everything from aubergine schnitzel with feta cream to barramundi fillet in rice leaf with green curry. There are plenty of vegetarian and vegan choices.

Ochs'n'Willi
GERMAN $$

(☑0711-226 5191; www.ochsn-willi.de; Kleiner Schlossplatz 4; mains €11-28; ☺11am-11.30pm) A warm, woody hunter's cottage restaurant just this side of twee, Ochs'n'Willi delivers gutsy portions of Swabian and Bavarian fare. Dig into pork knuckles with lashings of dumplings and kraut, spot-on *Maultaschen* (pasta pockets) or rich, brothy *Gaisburger Marsch* (beef stew). There's a terrace for warm-weather dining.

Weinhaus Stetter
GERMAN $$

(☑0711-240 163; www.weinhaus-stetter.de; Rosenstrasse 32; snacks & mains €5-14.50; ☺3-11pm Mon-Fri, noon-3pm & 5.30-11pm Sat) This traditional wine tavern in the Bohnenviertel quarter serves up no-nonsense Swabian cooking, including flavoursome *Linsen und Saiten* (lentils with sausage) and beef roast with onion, in a convivial ambience. The attached wine shop sells 650 different vintages.

Weinstube Fröhlich
GERMAN $$

(☑0711-242 471; www.weinstube-froehlich.de; Leonhardstrasse 5; mains €14-32; ☺5.30pm-midnight Sun-Thu, 5.30pm-1am Fri & Sat) True, it's in the heart of the red-light district, but don't be put off. This softly lit, dark-wood-panelled restaurant is an atmospheric choice for well-executed Swabian fare (cheese-rich *Käsespätzle*, *Maultaschen* with potato salad, wild boar ragout) and regional wines.

Amadeus
INTERNATIONAL $$

(☑0711-292 678; Charlottenplatz 17; mains €10-26.50; ☺11.30am-11pm Mon-Fri, 9am-11pm Sat, 10am-9pm Sun) Once an 18th-century

---

SWABIAN MENU DECODER

As the Swabian saying goes: *Was der Bauer net kennt, frisst er net* (What the farmer doesn't know, he doesn't eat) – so find out before you dig in:

Bubespitzle Officially called *Schupfnudeln*, these short, thick potato noodles – vaguely reminiscent of gnocchi – are browned in butter and tossed with sauerkraut. Sounds appetising until you discover that *Bubespitzle* means 'little boys' penises'.

Gaisburger Marsch A strong beef stew served with potatoes and *Spätzle*.

Maultaschen Giant ravioli pockets, stuffed with leftover ground pork, spinach, onions and bread mush. The dish is nicknamed *Herrgottsbeschieserle* (God trickster) because it was a sly way to eat meat during Lent.

Saure Kuddle So who is for sour tripe? If you don't have the stomach, try potato-based, meat-free *saure Rädle* (sour wheels) instead.

Spätzle Stubby egg-based noodles. These are fried with onions and topped with cheese in the calorific treat *Käsespätzle*.

Zwiebelkuche Autumnal onion tart with bacon, cream and caraway seeds, which pairs nicely with *neuer Süsser* (new wine) or *Moschd* (cider).

DON'T MISS

THEODOR-HEUSS-STRASSE BAR CRAWL

Packed with clubs and hipper-than-thou lounges, Theodor-Heuss-Strasse is perfect for a late-night bar crawl.

7 Grad (Theodor-Heuss-Strasse 32; ☺7pm-3am Tue-Sat) DJs work the crowd into a sweat spinning house and electro at charcoal-black 7 Grad.

Barcode (Theodor-Heuss-Strasse 30; ☺11am-2am Mon-Thu, 11am-4pm Fri, 4pm-2am Sat) Barcode fuels the party with decadent cocktails in streamlined surrounds.

Rohbau (Theodor-Heuss-Strasse 26; ☺9pm-4am Fri & Sat) Rohbau pumps out '80s disco and rock in retro-cool surrounds.

Muttermilch (Theodor-Heuss-Strasse 23; ☺4pm-1am Wed & Thu, 4pm-5am Fri & Sat) Good-looking Stuttgarters dance to soul and funk at nouveau Alpine chic Muttermilch.

Ribingurūmu (Theodor-Heuss-Strasse 4; ☺4.30pm-2am Mon-Sat) A chilled-out crowd hangs out over jam-jar cocktails in Ribingurūmu, which exudes an 'old-skool' vibe with its vintage furnishings.

orphanage dishing up gruel, this chic, bustling restaurant now serves glorious Swabian food such as *Maultaschen* and riesling-laced *Kutteln* (tripe), as well as salads and international dishes from wok noodles to burritos. The terrace is a big draw in summer.

Alte Kanzlei GERMAN $$
(☑0711-294 457; Schillerplatz 5a; mains €11-24.50; ☺9.30am-midnight Mon-Thu, to 1am Fri & Sat, 9am-11pm Sun) Empty tables are rare as gold-dust at this convivial, high-ceilinged restaurant, with a terrace spilling out onto Schillerplatz. Feast on Swabian favourites like *Spanferkel* (roast suckling pig) and *Flädlesuppe* (pancake soup), washed down with regional tipples.

★**Olivo** MODERN EUROPEAN $$$
(☑0711-204 8277; www.olivo-restaurant.de; Arnulf-Klett-Platz 7; mains around €40, 4-course lunch/dinner €76/108; ☺noon-2pm & 6.30-10pm Wed-Fri, 6.30-10pm Tue & Sat) Young, sparky chef Nico Burkhardt works his stuff at Steigenberger's Michelin-starred restaurant. The minimalist-chic restaurant is lauded for exquisitely presented, French-inspired specialities such as Périgord goose liver with sheep's milk yoghurt, brioche crumble and woodruff, or beautifully cooked Breton turbot with ricotta and wild garlic.

Cube INTERNATIONAL $$$
(☑0711-280 4441; www.cube-restaurant.de; Kleiner Schlossplatz 1; 4-course lunch €29.80, mains €29-35; ☺10am-midnight Sun-Thu, 10am-2am Fri & Sat) The food is stellar but it actually plays second fiddle to the dazzling decor, refined ambience and stunning views at this glass-fronted cube atop the Kunstmuseum. Lunches are perky, fresh and international, while dinners feature more complex Pacific Rim-inspired cuisine. The lunch special is a steal at €8.90.

Délice MODERN EUROPEAN $$$
(☑0711-640 3222; www.restaurant-delice.de; Hauptstätter Strasse 61; 5-course tasting menu €98; ☺6.30pm-midnight Mon-Fri) Natural, integral flavours sing in specialities like medley of tuna with lemon vinaigrette and fried egg with parsnips and Périgord truffles at this vaulted Michelin-starred restaurant. The sommelier will talk you through the award-winning riesling selection.

🍷 Drinking & Nightlife

Ciba Mato LOUNGE
(www.ciba-mato.de; Wilhelmsplatz 11; ☺5pm-1am Mon-Thu, 5pm-3am Fri & Sat, 10am-1am Sun) There's more than a hint of Buddha Bar about this scarlet-walled, Asia-infused space. It's a slinky spot to sip a gingertini or pisco punch, or to hang out Bedouin-style in the shisha tent and nibble on fusion food. The terrace deck is a summertime magnet.

Sky Beach BAR
(www.skybeach.de; Königstrasse 6, top fl Galeria Kaufhof; ☺noon-12.30am Mon-Sat, 11am-midnight Sun Easter-Sep) When the sun comes out, Stuttgarters live it up at this urban beach, complete with sand, cabaña beds, DJs spinning mellow lounge beats and grandstand city views.

Biergarten im Schlossgarten BEER GARDEN
(www.biergarten-schlossgarten.de; ☺10.30am-1am May-Oct; 🐾) Toast to summer with beer and pretzels at Stuttgart's best-loved, 2000-seat beer garden in the green heart of the Schlossgarten. Regular live music on Sundays gets steins a-swinging.

Hüftengold CAFE
(Olgastrasse 44; ☺7am-midnight Mon-Fri, 9am-1am Sat, 10am-8pm Sun) Work on your own

Hüftengold (love handles) with cake and locally roasted coffee at this sylvan wonderland. The log stools and sheepskins create a wonderfully cosy vibe for brunch or evening chats by candlelight.

Zum Paulaner PUB
(Calwerstrasse 45; ⏰10am-midnight Sun-Thu, to 1am Fri & Sat) Freshly tapped Paulaner brews in a buzzy, tree-shaded beer garden.

Palast der Republik BEER GARDEN
(📞0711-226 4887; www.facebook.com/Palast-Stuttgart; Friedrichstrasse 27; ⏰11am-3am; Ⓤ Börsenplatz) The palace in question is more like a little kiosk, but that's not stopping everyone from students to bankers making this *the* local hotspot for chilling under the trees, cold beer in hand.

Wagenhallen CLUB
(www.wagenhallen.de; Innerer Nordbahnhof 1; Ⓤ Wagenhallen Nordbahnhof) Swim away from the mainstream at this post-industrial space 2km north of the centre, where club nights, gigs and workshops skip from Balkan-beat parties to poetry slams. There's a relaxed beer garden for summertime quaffing.

☆ Entertainment

For the low-down on events, grab a copy of German-language monthly *Lift Stuttgart* (www.lift-online.de) from the tourist office or news kiosks, or listings magazine *Prinz* (www.prinz.de/stuttgart.html). Events tickets can be purchased at the **i-Punkt desk** (📞0711-222 8243; Königstrasse 1a; ⏰9am-8pm Mon-Fri, 9am-6pm Sat, 11am-6pm Sun).

Liederhalle CONCERT VENUE
(📞0711-202 7710; www.liederhalle-stuttgart.de; Berliner Platz 1) Jimi Hendrix and Sting are among the stars who have performed at this culture and congress centre. The 1950s venue stages big-name classical and pop concerts, cabaret and comedy.

Staatstheater PERFORMING ARTS
(📞0711-202 090; www.staatstheater-stuttgart. de; Oberer Schlossgarten 6) Stuttgart's grandest theatre presents a top-drawer program of ballet, opera, theatre and classical music. The Stuttgart Ballet (www.stuttgart-ballet. de) is hailed as one of Europe's best.

Bix Jazzclub LIVE MUSIC
(📞0711-2384 0997; www.bix-stuttgart.de; Leonhardstrasse 28; ⏰7pm-2am Tue-Wed, 7pm-3am Thu-Sat) Suave chocolate-gold tones and soft lighting set the scene for first-rate jazz acts at Bix, swinging from big bands to soul and blues.

Kiste JAZZ
(www.kiste-stuttgart.de; Hauptstätter Strasse 35; ⏰6pm-1am Mon-Thu, to 2am Fri & Sat) Jampacked at weekends, this hole-in-the-wall bar is Stuttgart's leading jazz venue, with nightly concerts starting at 9pm or 10pm.

Theaterhaus THEATRE
(📞0711-402 0720; www.theaterhaus.com; Siemensstrasse 11; Ⓤ Maybachstrasse) Stages live rock, jazz and other music genres, plus theatre and comedy performances.

🔒 Shopping

Mooch around plane-tree-lined Königstrasse, Germany's longest shopping mile, for high-street brands and department stores, Calwer Strasse for boutiques, and Stiffstrasse for designer labels. The casual Bohnenviertel is the go-to quarter for antiques, art galleries, vintage garb and Stuttgart-made crafts and jewellery.

Tausche ACCESSORIES
(Eberhardstrasse 51; ⏰11am-7pm Mon-Fri, to 6pm Sat) Berlin's snazziest messenger bags have

---

DON'T MISS

THROUGH THE GRAPEVINE

Stuttgarter Weinwanderweg (www. stuttgarter-weinwanderweg.de) To taste the region's fruity Trollingers and citrusy rieslings, factor in a stroll through the vineyards surrounding Stuttgart. The Stuttgarter Weinwanderweg comprises several walking trails that thread through winegrowing villages. One begins at Pragsattel station (on the U5 or U6 line) and meanders northeast to Max-Eyth-See, affording fine views from Burgholzhofturm. Visit the website for alternative routes, maps and distances.

From October to March, look out for a broom above the door of *Besenwirtschaften* (Besa for short). Run by winegrowers, these rustic bolt-holes are atmospheric places to chat with locals while sampling the latest vintage and Swabian home cooking. Some operate every year but most don't. Check the Besen Kalender website (www.besen-kalender.de) during vintage season

winged their way south. Tausche's walls are a technicolour mosaic of exchangeable flaps: from *die blöde Kuh* (the silly cow) to Stuttgart's iconic Fernsehturm (TV Tower). Pick one to match your outfit and mood.

Brunnenhannes FASHION
(Geissstrasse 15; ⊘ 11am-7pm Tue-Fri, 11am-6pm Sat) Nothing to wear to Oktoberfest? Biker-meets-Bavaria Brunnenhannes has the solution, with lederhosen for strapping lads, dirndls for buxom dames and gingham lingerie that is half-kitsch, half-cool.

Feinkost Böhm FOOD & DRINK
(Kronprinzstrasse 6; ⊘ 10am-8pm Mon-Thu, 9am-8pm Fri & Sat) Böhm is a foodie one-stop shop with regional wine, beer, chocolate and preserves, and an appetising deli.

Königsbau Passagen SHOPPING CENTRE
Overlooking Schlossplatz is the classical, colonnaded Königsbau, reborn as an upmarket shopping mall, the Königsbau Passagen.

ⓘ Information

Königstrasse has many ATMs, including one in the tourist office.

Airport Tourist Office (☑ 0711-222 8100; ⊘ 8am-7pm Mon-Fri, 9am-1pm & 1.45-4.30pm Sat, 10am-1pm & 1.45-5.30pm Sun) The tourist office branch at Stuttgart International Airport is situated in Terminal 3, Level 2 (Arrivals).

Coffee Fellows (per 10min €0.50; ⊘ 8am-9pm; 🛜) Up the stairs opposite track 4 in the Hauptbahnhof. Free wi-fi.

iPunkt Stuttgart (☑ 0711-222 8100; www.stuttgart-tourist.de; Königstrasse 1a; ⊘ 9am-8pm Mon-Fri, 9am-6pm Sat, 10am-6pm Sun) The staff can help with room bookings (for a €3 fee) and public transport enquiries. Also has a list of vineyards open for tastings.

Klinikum Stuttgart (☑ 0711-278 01; Kriegsbergstrasse 60) The city's largest hospital.

Post Office (Bolzstrasse 3; ⊘ 10am-8pm Mon-Fri, 9am-4pm Sat) Just northwest of the Schlossplatz.

DISCOUNT CARDS

Get a **StuttCard** (24/48/72hr without VVS ticket €5/20/25, with VVS ticket €25/35/45) for free entry to most museums, plus discounts on events, activities and guided tours. Sold at the tourist office and some hotels.

Use **VVS 3-Day Ticket** (72hr inner city/metropolitan area €12/17) for unlimited use of public transport, available to guests with a hotel reservation.

ⓘ Getting There & Away

AIR

Stuttgart Airport (SGT; ☑ 0711-9480; www.stuttgart-airport.com) Stuttgart's airport, a major hub for Germanwings, is 13km south of the city. There are four terminals, all within easy walking distance of each other.

CAR & MOTORCYCLE

The A8 from Munich to Karlsruhe passes Stuttgart (often abbreviated to 'S' on highway signs), as does the A81 from Singen (near Lake Constance) to Heilbronn and Mannheim. Stuttgart is an Umweltzone (Green Zone; www.umwelt-plakette.de), where vehicles are graded according to their emissions levels. Expect to pay €6 to €10 for an *Umweltplakette* (environment sticker), which is obligatory in green zones and can be ordered online.

TRAIN

IC and ICE destinations include Berlin (€130 to €154, 5½ hours), Frankfurt (€47 to €63, 1¼ hours) and Munich (€53 to €57, 2¼ hours). There are frequent regional services to Tübingen (€13.30, one hour), Schwäbisch Hall (€17.90, 70 minutes) and Ulm (€19.80 to €26, one hour).

ⓘ Getting Around

TO/FROM THE AIRPORT

S2 and S3 trains take about 30 minutes from the airport to the Hauptbahnhof (€3.90).

BICYCLE

Rent a Bike (www.rentabike-stuttgart.de; Lautenschlagerstrasse 22; adult 6½hr/full day €12/18, concession €9/14) delivers and picks up bikes. Stuttgart has 50 **Call-a-Bike** (☑ 0700-0522 2222; www.callabike.de) stands. The first 30 minutes are free and rental costs €4.80 per hour thereafter (€15 per day). Visit the website for maps and details.

It's free to take your bike on *Stadtbahn* lines, except from 6am to 8.30am and 4pm to 6.30pm Monday to Friday. Bikes are allowed on S-Bahn trains (S1 to S6) but you need a *Kinderticket* (child's ticket) from 6am to 8.30am Monday to Friday. You can't take bikes on buses or the *Strassenbahn* (tramway).

CAR & MOTORCYCLE

Underground parking costs about €2.50 for the first hour and €2 for each subsequent hour. See www.parkinfo.com (in German) for a list of car parks. The Park & Ride ('P+R') options in Stuttgart's suburbs offer cheap parking; convenient lots include Degerloch Albstrasse (on the B27; take the U5 or U6 into town), which is 4km south of the centre; and Österfeld (on the A81; take the S1, S2 or S3 into the centre).

Avis, Budget, Europcar, Hertz, National and Sixt have offices at the airport (Terminal 2, Level 2). Europcar, Hertz and Avis have offices at the Hauptbahnhof.

PUBLIC TRANSPORT

From slowest to fastest, Stuttgart's VVS (www. vvs.de) public transport network consists of a *Zahnradbahn* (rack railway), buses, the *Strassenbahn* (tramway), *Stadtbahn* lines (light-rail lines beginning with U; underground in the city centre), S-Bahn lines (suburban rail lines S1 through to S6) and *Regionalbahn* lines (regional trains beginning with R). On Friday and Saturday there are night buses (beginning with N) with departures from Schlossplatz at 1.11am, 2.22am and 3.33am.

For travel within the city, single tickets are €2.30 and four-ride tickets (*Mehrfahrtenkarte*) cost €8.70. For short hops of three stops or less, a *Kurzstrecken* ticket (€1.20) suffices. A day pass, good for two zones (including, for instance, the Mercedes-Benz and Porsche Museums), is better value at €6.60 for one person and €11.50 for a group of between two and five.

TAXI

To order a taxi call ☑ 0711-551 0000.

AROUND STUTTGART

Max-Eyth-See

Max-Eyth-See   LAKE

When temperatures soar, Stuttgarters head to Max-Eyth-See for pedalo fun on the lake and picnicking beside the Neckar River. Murky water rules out swimming but there's a worthwhile bike path, which is part of the Neckar-Radweg (www.neckarradweg.de). The terraced vineyards rising above the river are scattered with Wengerter-Häuschen (tool sheds); some are more than 200 years old and are protected landmarks.

The lake is 9km northeast of Stuttgart Hauptbahnhof on the U14 line.

Grabkapelle Württemberg

Grabkapelle Württemberg   CHAPEL

When King Wilhelm I of Württemberg's beloved wife Katharina Pavlovna, daughter of a Russian tsar, died at the age of 30 in 1819, the king tore down the family castle and built this domed burial chapel. The king was also interred in the classical-style Russian Orthodox chapel decades later. Scenically

perched on a vine-strewn hill, the grounds afford long views down to the valley.

Grapkapelle Württemberg is 10km southeast of Stuttgart's centre. Take bus 61 from Stuttgart-Untertürkheim station, served by the S1.

Ludwigsburg

☑ 07141 / POP 87,740

This neat, cultured town is the childhood home of the dramatist Friedrich Schiller. Duke Eberhard Ludwig put it on the global map in the 18th century by erecting a chateau to out-pomp them all – the sublime, Versailles-inspired Residenzschloss. With its whimsical palaces and gardens, Ludwigsburg is baroque in overdrive and a flashback to when princes wore powdered wigs and lords went a-hunting.

Sights & Activities

★ **Residenzschloss**   PALACE

(www.schloss-ludwigsburg.de; tour adult/concession €7/3.50, museums incl audioguide €3.50/1.80; ⊙10am-5pm) Nicknamed the Swabian Versailles, the Residenzschloss is an extravagant 452-room baroque, rococo and Empire affair. The 90-minute chateau tours (in German) begin half-hourly; there's an English tour at 1.30pm.

The 18th-century feast continues with a spin of the staggeringly ornate Karl Eugen Apartment, and three museums showcasing everything from exquisite baroque paintings to fashion accessories and majolica.

Blühendes Barock   GARDENS

(Mömpelgardstrasse 28; adult/concession €8.50/ 4.20; ⊙gardens 7.30am-8.30pm, Märchengarten 9am-6pm, both closed early Nov–mid-Mar) Appealing in summer is a fragrant stroll amid the herbs, rhododendrons and gushing fountains of the Blühendes Barock gardens. Admission includes entry to the **Märchengarten** (adult/concession €8.50/4.20; ⊙9am-6pm), a fairy-tale theme park. Take the kids to see the witch with a Swabian cackle at the gingerbread house and admire your fairness in Snow White's magic mirror. Should you want Rapunzel to let down her hair at the tower, get practising: *Rapunzel, lass deinen Zopf herunter*. (The gold-tressed diva only understands well-pronounced German!)

Schloss Favorite   PALACE

(30min tour adult/concession €4/2; ⊙10am-noon & 1.30-5pm mid-Mar–Oct, 10am noon & 1.30 4pm

DON'T MISS

MESSING ABOUT ON THE RIVER

There's nothing like a languid paddle along the sun-dappled Neckar River in summer.

Bootsvermietung Märkle (Eberhards-brücke 1; ⊙11am-6pm Apr-Oct, to 9pm in summer) At Bootsvermietung Märkle, an hour of splashy fun in a rowboat, canoe, pedalo or 12-person Stocherkähne (punt) costs €6, €9, €12 and €48 respectively.

Punting (adult/child €6/3; ⊙1pm daily, plus 5pm Sat Apr-Oct) You can sign up at the tourist office for an hour's punting around the Neckarinsel, beginning at the Hölderlinturm.

Stocherkahnrennen (www.stocherkah-nrennen.com) Students in fancy dress do battle on the Neckar at June's hilarious Stocherkahnrennen punt race, where jostling, dunking and even snapping your rival's oar are permitted. The first team to reach the Neckarbrücke wins the race, the title and as much beer as they can sink. The losers have to down half a litre of cod-liver oil. Arrive early to snag a prime spot on Platanenallee.

Tue-Sun Nov–mid-Mar) Sitting in parkland, a five-minute walk north of the Residenz-schloss, is the petit baroque palace Schloss Favorite, graced with Empire-style furniture. Duke Eugen held glittering parties here.

❶ Information

Tourist Office (☑07141-910 2252; www.mik-ludwigsburg.de; Eberhardtstrasse 1; ⊙10am-6pm) Ludwigsburg's tourist office has excellent material in English on lodgings, festivals and events such as the baroque Christmas market.

❶ Getting There & Around

S-Bahn trains from Stuttgart serve the Haupt-bahnhof, 750m southwest of the centre. The Residenzschloss, on Schlossstrasse (the B27) lies 400m northeast of the central Marktplatz.

Stuttgart's S4 and S5 S-Bahn lines go directly to Ludwigsburg's Hauptbahnhof (€3.90, nine to 15 minutes), frequently linked to the chateau by buses 421, 425 and 427. On foot, the chateau is 1km from the train station.

There are two large car parks 500m south of the Residenzschloss, just off the B27.

Maulbronn

Kloster Maulbronn   MONASTERY
(Maulbronn Monastery; ☑07043-926 610; www.schloesser-und-gaerten.de; adult/concession/family €7/3.50/17.50; ⊙9am-5.30pm Mar-Oct, 9.30am-5pm Tue-Sun Nov-Feb) Billed as the best-preserved medieval monastery north of the Alps, the one-time Cistercian monastery Kloster Maul-bronn was founded by Alsatian monks in 1147. It was born again as a Protestant school in 1556 and designated a Unesco World Heritage Site in 1993. Its famous graduates include the astronomer Johannes Kepler. Aside from the Romanesque-Gothic portico in the monastery church and the weblike vaulting of the cloister, it's the insights into monastic life that make this place so culturally stimulating.

Maulbronn is 30km east of Karlsruhe and 33km northwest of Stuttgart, near the Pforzheim Ost exit on the A8. From Karlsru-he, take the S4 to Bretten Bahnhof and from there bus 700; from Stuttgart, take the train to Mühlacker and then bus 700.

SWABIAN ALPS & AROUND

Tübingen

☑07071 / POP 88,360
Liberal students and deeply traditional *Bur-schenschaften* (fraternities) singing ditties for beloved Germania, eco-warriors, artists and punks – all have a soft spot for this be-witchingly pretty Swabian city, where cobbled lanes lined with half-timbered town houses twist up to a turreted castle. It was here that Joseph Ratzinger, now Pope Benedict XVI, lectured on theology in the late 1960s; and here that Friedrich Hölderlin studied stan-zas, Johannes Kepler planetary motions, and Goethe the bottom of a beer glass.

The finest days unfold slowly in Tübingen: lingering in Altstadt cafes, punting on the plane-tree-lined Neckar River and pretending, as the students so diligently do, to work your brain cells in a chestnut-shaded beer garden.

◉ Sights & Activities

★**Schloss Hohentübingen**   CASTLE
(Burgsteige 11; ⊙7am-8pm) On its perch above Tübingen, this turreted 16th-century castle has a terrace overlooking the Neckar River,

the Altstadt's triangular rooftops and the vine-streaked hills beyond. An ornate Renaissance gate leads to the courtyard and the laboratory where Friedrich Miescher discovered DNA in 1869.

Museum Schloss Hohentübingen MUSEUM
(adult/concession €5/3; ⊙10am-5pm Wed-Sun, to 7pm Thu) Housed in Tübingen's hilltop castle, this archaeology museum hides the 35,000-year-old Vogelherd figurines, the world's oldest figurative artworks. These thumb-sized ivory carvings of mammoths and lions were unearthed in the Vogelherdhöhle caves in the Swabian Alps.

Am Markt SQUARE
Half-timbered town houses frame the Altstadt's main plaza Am Markt, a much-loved student hang-out. Rising above it is the 15th-century **Rathaus**, with a riotous baroque facade and an astronomical clock. Statues of four women representing the seasons grace the **Neptunbrunnen** (Am Markt) opposite. Keep an eye out for **No 15**, where a white window frame identifies a secret room where Jews hid in WWII.

Cottahaus LANDMARK
The Cottahaus is the one-time home of Johann Friedrich Cotta, who first published the works of Schiller and Goethe. A bit of a lad, Goethe conducted detailed research on Tübingen's pubs during his weeklong stay in 1797. The party-loving genius is commemorated by the plaque 'Hier wohnte Goethe' (Goethe lived here). On the wall of the grungy student digs next door is perhaps the more insightful sign 'Hier kotzte Goethe' (Goethe puked here).

Stiftskirche St Georg CHURCH
(Am Holzmarkt; ⊙9am-5pm) FREE The late-Gothic Stiftskirche shelters the tombs of the Württemberg dukes and some dazzling late-medieval stained-glass windows.

Platanenallee AREA
Steps lead down from Eberhardsbrücke bridge to Platanenallee, a leafy islet on the Neckar River canopied by sycamore trees, with views up to half-timbered houses in a fresco painter's palette of pastels and turreted villas nestled on the hillsides.

Hölderlinturm MUSEUM
(Bursagasse 6; adult/concession €2.50/1.50; ⊙10am-noon & 3-5pm Tue & Fri, 2-5pm Sat & Sun) You can see how the dreamy Neckar views from this silver-turreted tower fired the imagination of Romantic poet Friedrich Hölderlin, resident here from 1807 to 1843. It now contains a museum tracing his life and work.

Kunsthalle GALLERY
(www.kunsthalle-tuebingen.de; Philosophenweg 76; adult/concession €9/7; ⊙10am-6pm Tue-Sun) The streamlined Kunsthalle stages first-rate exhibitions of mostly contemporary art. During our visit, Beuys, Polke and Warhol were in the spotlight. Buses 5, 13 and 17 stop here.

Botanischer Garten GARDENS
(Hartmeyerstrasse 123; ⊙8am-4.45pm daily, to 6.45pm Sat & Sun in summer) FREE Greenfingered students tend to the Himalayan cedars, swamp cypresses and rhododendrons in the gardens and hothouses of the serene Botanischer Garten, 2km northwest of the centre. Take bus 5, 13, 15 or 17.

Wurmlinger Kapelle WALKING
(⊙chapel 10am-4pm May-Oct) A great hike is the Kreuzweg (way of the cross) to the 17th-century Wurmlinger Kapelle, 6km southwest of Tübingen. A footpath loops up through well-tended vineyards to the whitewashed pilgrimage chapel, where there are long views across the Ammer and Neckar valleys. The tourist office has leaflets (€1).

🛌 Sleeping

The tourist office has a free booklet listing private rooms, holiday homes, youth hostels and camping grounds in the area.

> **ⓘ DISCOUNT PASSES**
>
> Check into almost any hotel in Baden-Württemberg, pay the nominal Kurtaxe (holiday tax) and you automatically receive the money-saving **Gästekarte** (Guest Card), often entitling you to free entry to local swimming pools and attractions, plus hefty discounts on everything from bike hire and spas to ski lifts and boat trips. Versions with the **Konus** symbol offer free use of public transport.
>
> Most tourist offices in the Black Forest sell the three-day **SchwarzwaldCard** (adult/child €35/25) for admission to around 150 attractions in the Black Forest. Details on both cards are available at www.blackforest-tourism.com.

★ **Hotel am Schloss** HISTORIC HOTEL **$$**
(☑07071-929 40; www.hotelamschloss.de; Burg-steige 18; s €78, d €125-148, tr/q €225/290; P 🛜) So close to the castle you can almost touch it, this flower-bedecked hotel has dapper rooms ensconced in a 16th-century building. Rumour has it that Kepler was partial to the wine here; try a drop yourself before attempting the tongue twister above the bench outside: *dohoggeddiadiaemmer-dohogged* (the same people sit in the same spot). And a very nice spot it is, too.

Hotel La Casa HOTEL **$$**
(☑07071-946 66; www.lacasa-tuebingen.de; Hechinger Strasse 59; d €156-182; 🛜⛟) Tübin-gen's swishest hotel is a 15-minute stroll south of the Altstadt. Contemporary rooms designed with panache come with welcome tea, coffee and soft drinks. Breakfast is a smorgasbord of mostly organic goodies. The crowning glory is the top-floor spa with tremendous city views.

Hotel Hospiz GUESTHOUSE **$$**
(☑07071-9240; www.hotel-hospiz.de; Neckarhalde 2; s/d €70/110; 🛜) Huddled away in the Altstadt, this candy-floss-pink guesthouse has old-school, immaculately kept rooms, many looking across Tübingen's gables. Pastries, smoked fish and eggs are nice additions to the breakfast buffet. Parking costs an extra €7 per night.

✖ Eating

Kornblume VEGETARIAN **$**
(☑07071-527 08; Haaggasse 15; snacks & light meals €3-8; ☺8.30am-6pm Mon-Fri, 8.30am-3pm Sat; 🍽) Vegetarians and health-conscious locals squeeze into this hobbit-like cafe for wholesome soups, vitamin-rich juices and organic salads by the scoopful.

Samphat Thai THAI **$$**
(☑07071-566 7827; http://samphat-thai.de; Belth-lestrasse 13; mains €14-19; ☺5-11pm Tue-Sat, 11.30am-2pm & 5-11pm Sun) Slickly decorated in calming shades of lavender and violet, this sweet, petite Thai restaurant is the real deal. The smiley staff rustle up curries, noodles and wok dishes that are bang on the money and nicely presented. Veggie options are also available.

Mauganeschtle GERMAN **$$**
(☑07071-929 40; Burgsteige 18; mains €12-21.50; ☺noon-2.30pm & 7-10pm) It's a stiff climb up to this restaurant at Hotel am Schloss, but worth every step. Suspended above the rooftops of Tübingen, the terrace is a scenic spot for the house speciality, *Maultaschen,* with fillings like lamb, trout, porcini and veal.

Neckarmüller PUB FOOD **$$**
(☑07071-278 48; Gartenstrasse 4; mains €7.50-15; ☺10am-1am Mon-Sat, 10am-midnight Sun) Overlooking the Neckar, this cavernous microbrewery is a summertime magnet for its chestnut-shaded beer garden. Come for home brews by the metre and beer-laced dishes from (tasty) Swabian roast to (interesting) tripe stew.

Wurstküche GERMAN **$$**
(☑07071-927 50; Am Lustnauer Tor 8; mains €12.50-18.50; ☺11.30am-11pm Mon-Sat) The rustic, wood-panelled Wurstküche brims with locals quaffing wine and contentedly munching *Schupfnudeln* (potato noodles) and *Spanpferkel* (roast suckling pig).

WORTH A TRIP

NATURPARK SCHÖNBUCH

For back-to-nature hiking and cycling, make for this 156-sq-km **nature reserve** (www.naturpark-schoenbuch.de), 8km north of Tübingen. With a bit of luck birdwatchers might catch a glimpse of black woodpeckers and yellow-bellied toads.

The nature reserve's beech and oak woods fringe the village of **Bebenhausen** and its well-preserved **Cistercian Abbey** (www.kloster-bebenhausen.de; adult/concession €4.50/2.20, incl guided tour €6/3, audioguide €1; ☺9am-6pm Apr-Oct, 10am-noon & 1-5pm Nov-Mar, guided tours 2pm & 3pm Sat & Sun Apr-Oct). Founded in 1183 by Count Rudolph von Tübingen, the complex became a royal hunting retreat post-Reformation. A visit takes in the frescoed summer refectory, the Gothic abbey church and intricate star vaulting and half-timbered facades in the cloister.

Bebenhausen, 3km north of Tübingen, is the gateway to Naturpark Schönbuch. Buses run at least twice hourly (€2.30, 15 minutes).

🍷 Drinking

Weinhaus Beck   BAR
(Am Markt 1; ⊙9am-11pm) There's rarely an empty table at this wine tavern beside the Rathaus. It's a convivial place to enjoy a local tipple or coffee and cake.

Storchen   CAFE
(Ammergasse 3; ⊙3pm-1am, from 11am Sat) Mind your head climbing the stairs to this easygoing student hang-out, serving enormous mugs of milky coffee and cheap local brews under wooden beams.

Schwärzlocher Hof   BEER GARDEN
(Schwarzloch 1; ⊙11am-10pm Wed-Sun; 🐾) Scenically perched above the Ammer Valley, a 20-minute trudge west of town, this creaking farmhouse is famous for its beer garden and home-pressed *Most* (cider). Kids love the resident horses, rabbits and peacocks.

ℹ️ Information

Find ATMs around the Hauptbahnhof, Eberhardsbrücke and Am Markt.

Post Office (Belm Nonnenhaus 14; ⊙9am-7pm Mon-Fri, 9am-6pm Sat) In the Altstadt.

Tourist Office (☑07071-913 60; www.tuebingen-info.de; An der Neckarbrücke 1; ⊙9am-7pm Mon-Fri, 10am-4pm Sat, plus 11am-4pm Sun May-Sep) Tourist information.

ℹ️ Getting There & Around

Tübingen is an easy train ride from Stuttgart (€13.30, one hour, at least two per hour) and Villingen (€23.80, 1¾ to two hours, hourly).

The centre is a maze of one-way streets with residents-only parking, so head for a multistorey car park. To drive in Tübingen, you need to purchase an environmentally friendly *Umweltplakette* (emissions sticker).

Radlager (Lazarettgasse 19-21; ⊙9.30am-6.30pm Mon, Wed & Fri, 2-6.30pm Tue & Thu, 9.30am-2.30pm Sat) rents bikes for €10 per day.

Burg Hohenzollern

Burg Hohenzollern   CASTLE
(www.burg-hohenzollern.com; tour adult/concession €12/8, grounds admission without tour adult/concession €7/5; ⊙tour 10am-5.30pm mid-Mar–Oct, to 4.30pm Nov–mid-Mar) Rising dramatically from an exposed crag, with the medieval battlements and silver turrets often veiled in mist, Burg Hohenzollern is impressive from a distance, but up close it looks more contrived. Dating to 1867, this neo-Gothic castle

---

DON'T MISS

TOP SNACK SPOTS

Eating on the hoof? Try these informal nosh spots.

Die Kichererbse (Metzgergasse 2; snacks €3.50-5; ⊙11am-9pm Mon-Fri; 🖉) All hail the 'chickpea' for its scrummy falafel. Grab one of the few tables to chomp on a classic.

X (Kornhausstrasse 6; snacks €2.70-3.50; ⊙11am-1am) Hole-in-the-wall joint rustling up Tübingen's crispiest fries, bratwurst and burgers.

Wochenmarkt (Am Markt; ⊙7am-1pm Mon, Wed & Fri) Bag glossy fruit and veg, oven-fresh bread and local honey and herbs at Tübingen's farmers market.

Eiscafé San Marco (Nonnengasse 14; cone €1; ⊙8.30am-11pm Mon-Sat, 10.30am-11pm Sun) Italian-run, with hands-down the best gelati in town.

---

is the ancestral seat of the Hohenzollern family, the first and last monarchical rulers of the short-lived second German empire (1871–1918).

History fans should take a 35-minute German-language tour, which takes in towers, overblown salons replete with stained glass and frescos, and the dazzling Schatzkammer (treasury). The grounds command tremendous views over the Swabian Alps.

Frequent trains link Tübingen, 28km distant, with Hechingen, about 4km northwest of the castle.

Schwäbisch Hall

☑0791 / POP 37,140

Out on its rural lonesome near the Bavarian border, Schwäbisch Hall is an unsung gem. This medieval time capsule of higgledy-piggledy lanes, soaring half-timbered houses built high on the riches of salt, and covered bridges that criss-cross the Kocher River, is story-book stuff.

Buzzy cafes and first-rate museums add to the appeal of this town, known for its rare black-spotted pigs and the jangling piggy banks of its nationwide building society.

◉ Sights & Activities

A leisurely Altstadt saunter takes you along narrow alleys, among half-timbered hillside houses and up slopes overlooking the Kocher River. The islands and riverbank parks are great for picnics.

Am Markt SQUARE

Am Markt springs to life with a farmers market every Wednesday and Saturday morning. On the square, your gaze is drawn to the baroque-style **Rathaus** (Town Hall; Am Markt), festooned with coats of arms and cherubs, and to the terracotta-hued Widmanhaus at No 4, a remnant of a 13th-century Franciscan monastery. Steps lead spectacularly up to the late-Gothic **Kirche St Michael** (Am Markt; ⌚noon-5pm Mon, 10am-5pm Tue-Sat), which was built in place of the original three-aisled basilica. Note also the **Gotischer Fischbrunnen** (Am Markt; 1509), a large iron tub once used for storing fish before sale.

Neubau LANDMARK

Towering above Pfarrgasse is the steep-roofed, 16th-century Neubau, built as an arsenal and granary and now used as a theatre. Ascend the stone staircase for dreamy views over red-roofed houses to the former city fortifications, the covered Roter Steg bridge and the Henkerbrücke (Hangman's Bridge).

★**Kunsthalle Würth** GALLERY

(www.kunst.wuerth.com; Lange Strasse 35; ⌚10am-6pm daily, guided tours 11.30am & 2pm Sun) FREE The brainchild of industrialist Reinhold Würth, this contemporary gallery is housed in a striking limestone building that preserves part of a century-old brewery. Stellar temporary exhibitions have recently spotlighted the precious silver of London's Victoria & Albert Museum and Op Art kinetics. Guided tours (in German) and audioguides cost €6.

Hällisch-Fränkisches Museum MUSEUM

(adult/concession €2.50/2; ⌚10am-5pm Tue-Sun) This well-curated museum traces Schwäbisch Hall's history with its collection of shooting targets, Roman figurines, and rarities including an exquisite hand-painted wooden synagogue interior from 1738 and a 19th-century mouse guillotine.

Hohenloher Freilandmuseum MUSEUM

(Wackershofen; adult/concession €7/5; ⌚9am-6pm May-Sep, 10am-5pm Tue-Sun rest of year; 👪) One place you can be guaranteed of seeing a black-spotted pig is this open-air farming museum, a sure-fire hit with the kids with its traditional farmhouses, orchards and animals. It's 6km northwest of Schwäbisch Hall and served by bus 7.

Sleeping & Eating

★**Hotel Scholl** HOTEL $$

(☎0791-975 50; www.hotel-scholl.de; Klosterstrasse 2-4; s €79-109, d €124-169; 📶) A charming pick behind Am Markt, this family-run hotel has rustic-chic rooms with parquet floors, flat-screen TVs and granite or marble bathrooms. Most striking of all is the attic penthouse with its beams, free-standing shower and far-reaching views over town. Breakfast is a fine spread of cold cuts, fruit and cereals.

Der Adelshof HISTORIC HOTEL $$

(☎0791-758 90; www.hotel-adelshof.de; Am Markt 12; s €90-95, d €125-225, mains €15-34; P📶) This centuries-old pad is as posh as it gets in Schwäbisch Hall, with a wellness area and plush quarters, from the red-walled romance of the Chambre Rouge to the four-poster Turmzimmer. Its beamed Ratskeller knocks up spot-on local specialities, such as saddle of veal with mushrooms and pork tenderloin with lentils and *Spätzle* (egg noodles).

Entenbäck BISTRO $$

(☎0791-9782 9182; Steinerner Steg 1; mains €11.50-29; ⌚11am-2.30pm & 5-11pm Tue-Sat, 11am-8pm Sun) This inviting bistro receives high praise for its Swabian-meets-Mediterranean menu, from cream of riesling soup to duck-filled *Maultaschen* and roast beef with onions and *Spätzle*.

Brauerei-Ausschank Zum Löwen BREWPUB $$

(☎0791-204 1622; Mauerstrasse 17; mains €9-15.50; ⌚11.30am-2pm & 5.30-11pm Fri-Tue) Down by the river, this brewpub attracts a jovial bunch of locals who come for freshly tapped Haller Löwenbrauerei brews and hearty nosh-like pork cooked in beer-cumin sauce.

★**Rebers Pflug** INTERNATIONAL $$$

(☎0791-931 230; www.rebers-pflug.de; Weckriedener Strasse 2; mains €18.50-39, 4-course menu €59-78; ⌚6.30-9pm Mon & Tue, noon-2pm & 6-9pm Wed-Sat, 11.30am-2pm Sun) Hans-Harald Reber mans the stove at this 19th-century country house, one of Schwäbisch Hall's two Michelin-starred haunts. He puts his own imaginative spin on seasonal numbers such as local venison in a pumpernickel crust with sweet potato purée, asparagus and hazelnut *Spätzle*. Vegetarians are also well catered for. Dine in the chestnut-shaded garden in summer.

ℹ️ Information

Tourist Office (☎ 0791-751 246; www.schwaeb-ischhall.de; Am Markt 9; ⊙ 9am-6pm Mon-Fri, 10am-3pm Sat & Sun May-Sep, 9am-5pm Mon-Fri Oct-Apr) On the Altstadt's main square.

ℹ️ Getting There & Around

There are two train stations: trains from Stuttgart (€17.90, 1¼ hours, hourly) arrive at Hessental, on the right bank about 7km south of the centre and linked to the Altstadt by bus 1; trains from Heilbronn go to the left-bank Bahnhof Schwäbisch Hall, a short walk along Bahnhofstrasse from the centre.

Ulm

☎ 0731 / POP 122,800

Starting with the statistics, Ulm has the crookedest house (as listed in *Guinness World Records*) and one of the narrowest (4.5m wide), the world's oldest zoomorphic sculpture (aged 30,000 years) and tallest cathedral steeple (161.5m high), and is the birthplace of the physicist, Albert Einstein. Relatively speaking, of course.

This idiosyncratic city will win your affection with everyday encounters, particularly in summer as you pedal along the Danube, and the Fischerviertel's beer gardens hum with animated chatter. One *Helles* too many and you may decide to impress the locals by attempting the tongue twister: 'In Ulm, um Ulm, und um Ulm herum.'

⊙ Sights & Activities

Münster
CATHEDRAL

(www.ulmer-muenster.de; Münsterplatz; organ concerts adult/concession €8/4, tower adult/concession €5/3.50; ⊙ 9am-6.45pm, to 4.45pm in winter) FREE 'Ooh, it's so big'... First-time visitors gush as they strain their neck muscles gazing up at the Münster. It is. And rather beautiful. Celebrated for its 161.5m-high steeple, the world's tallest, this Goliath of cathedrals took a staggering 500 years to build from the first stone laid in 1377. Note the hallmarks on each stone, inscribed by cutters who were paid by the block. Those intent on cramming the Münster into one photo, filigree spire and all, should lie down on the cobbles.

Only by puffing up 768 spiral steps to the 143m-high viewing platform of the tower can you appreciate the Münster's dizzying height. There are terrific views of the Black Forest and, on cloud-free days, the Alps.

The Israelfenster, a stained-glass window above the west door, commemorates Jews killed during the Holocaust. The Gothic-style wooden pulpit canopy eliminates echoes during sermons. Biblical figures, and historical characters such as Pythagoras, embellish the 15th-century oak choir stalls. The Münster's regular organ concerts are a musical treat.

Marktplatz
SQUARE

Lording it over the Marktplatz, the 14th-century, step-gabled **Rathaus** sports an ornately painted Renaissance facade and a gilded astrological clock. Inside is a replica of Albrecht Berblinger's flying machine. In front is the **Fischkastenbrunnen** (Marktplatz), a fountain where fishmongers kept their catch alive on market days. The 36m-high glass pyramid behind the Rathaus is the city's main library, the **Zentralbibliothek** (Marktplatz), designed by Gottfried Böhm.

Stadtmauer
AREA

South of the Fischerviertel, along the Danube's north bank, runs the red-brick Stadtmauer (city wall), the height of which was reduced in the 19th century after Napoleon decided that a heavily fortified Ulm was against his best interests. Walk it for fine views over the river, the Altstadt and the colourful tile-roofed **Metzgerturm**, doing a Pisa by leaning 2m off-centre.

East of the Herdbrücke, the bridge to Neu-Ulm, a bronze **plaque** marks where Albrecht Berblinger, a tailor who invented a flying machine, attempted to fly over the Danube in 1811. The so-called 'Tailor of Ulm' made an embarrassing splash landing but his design was later shown to be workable (his failure was caused by a lack of thermals on that day).

Fischerviertel
AREA

The charming Fischerviertel, Ulm's old fishers' and tanners' quarter, is slightly southwest of the centre. Beautifully restored half-timbered houses huddle along the two channels of the Blau River. Harbouring art galleries, rustic restaurants, courtyards and the crookedest house in the world – as well as one of the narrowest – the cobbled lanes are ideal for a leisurely saunter.

Ulmer Museum
MUSEUM

(www.ulmer-museum.ulm.de; Marktplatz 9; adult/concession €5/3.50, Fri free; ⊙ 11am-5pm Tue-Sun, to 8pm Thu) This museum is a fascinating

Ulm

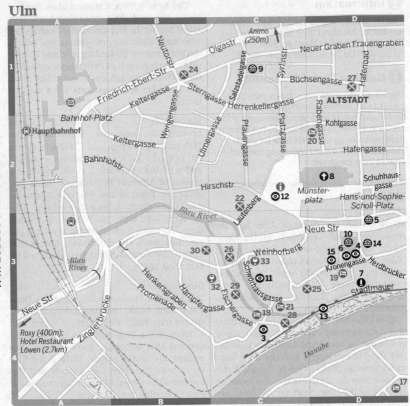

romp through ancient and modern art, history and archaeology. Standouts include the 20th-century Kurt Fried Collection, starring Klee, Picasso and Lichtenstein works. Archaeological highlights are tiny Upper Palaeolithic figurines, unearthed in caves in the Swabian Alps, including the 30,000-year-old ivory *Löwenmensch* (lion man), the world's oldest zoomorphic sculpture.

Kunsthalle Weishaupt   GALLERY
(www.kunsthalle-weishaupt.de; Hans-und-Sophie-Scholl-Platz 1; adult/concession €6/4; ⊙11am-5pm Tue-Sun, to 8pm Thu) The glass-fronted Kunsthalle Weishaupt contains the private collection of Siegfried Weishaupt. The accent is on modern and pop art, with bold paintings by Klein, Warhol and Haring.

Museum der Brotkultur   MUSEUM
(www.museum-brotkultur.de; Salzstadelgasse 10; adult/concession €4/3; ⊙10am-5pm) How grain grows, what makes a good dough and other bread-related mysteries are unravelled at the Museum of Bread Culture. The collection celebrates bread as the stuff of life over millennia and across cultures, displaying curios from mills to Egyptian corn mummies.

Stadthaus   LANDMARK
Designed by Richard Meier, the contemporary aesthetic of the concrete-and-glass Stadthaus is a dramatic contrast to the Münster. The American architect caused uproar by erecting a postmodern building alongside the city's Gothic giant, but the result is striking. The edifice stages exhibitions and events, and houses the tourist office and a cafe.

Schwörhaus   LANDMARK
(Oath House; Weinhof 12) On the third Monday of July, the mayor swears allegiance to the town's 1397 constitution from the 1st-floor loggia of the early-17th-century baroque Schwörhaus (Oath House), three blocks west of the Rathaus.

pricey Lego-themed amusement park, with shows, splashy rides and a miniature world built from 25 million Lego bricks. It's in Günzburg, 37km east of Ulm, just off the A8.

🛏 Sleeping

The tourist office lists apartments and guesthouses charging around €25 per person.

Brickstone Hostel HOSTEL **$**

(☎0731-708 2559; www.brickstone-hostel.de; Schützenstrasse 42; dm €18-22, s/d €30/44; 🛜) We love the homely vibe at this beautifully restored art-nouveau house in Neu-Ulm. The high-ceilinged rooms are kept spotless and backpacker perks include a self-catering kitchen with free coffee and tea, an honesty bar, bike rental and a cosy lounge with book exchange. Take bus 7 to Schützenstrasse from the Hauptbahnhof.

★ Hotel Schiefes Haus B&B **$$**

(☎0731-967 930; www.hotelschiefeshausulm.de; Schwörhausgasse 6; s €125, d €148-160; 🛜) There was a crooked man and he walked a crooked mile...presumably to the world's most crooked hotel. But fear not, ye of little wonkiness, this early-16th-century, half-timbered rarity is not about to topple into the Blau River. And up those creaking wooden stairs, in your snug, beamed room, you won't have to buckle yourself to the bed thanks to spirit levels and specially made height adjusters. If you're feeling *really* crooked, plump straight for room No 6.

Das Schmale Haus B&B **$$**

(☎0731-6027 2595; Fischergasse 27; s/d €119/149; 🅿) Measuring just 4.5m across, the half-timbered 'narrow house' is a one-off. The affable Heides have transformed this slender 16th-century pad into a gorgeous B&B, with exposed beams, downy bedding and wood floors in the three rooms.

Hotel Restaurant Löwen HOTEL **$$**

(☎0731-388 5880; www.hotel-loewen-ulm.de; Klosterhof 41; s €81-91, d €116-122; 🅿🛜) It's amazing what you can do with a former monastery and an eye for design. Exposed beams and stone add an historic edge to streamlined rooms with parquet floors and flat-screen TVs. The chestnut-canopied beer garden is a boon in summer. Take tram 1 from central Ulm to Söflingen.

Hotel Bäumle HISTORIC HOTEL **$$**

(☎0731-622 87; www.hotel-baeumle.de; Kohlgasse 6; s €70-82, d €98-112, tr €140; 🛜) Big on old-world

---

Einstein Fountain & Monument FOUNTAIN

A nod to Ulm's most famous son, Jürgen Goertz's fiendishly funny bronze fountain shows a wild-haired, tongue-poking-out Albert Einstein, who was born in Ulm but left when he was one year old. Standing in front of the 16th-century **Zeughaus**, the rocket-snail creation is a satirical play on humanity's attempts to manipulate evolution for its own self-interest. Nearby, at Zeughaus 14, is a single stone bearing the inscription *Ein Stein* (One Stone).

Einstein Memorial MEMORIAL

(Bahnhofstrasse) On Bahnhofstrasse sits Max Bill's memorial (1979) to the great physicist, a stack of red-granite pillars marking the spot where Einstein was born.

Legoland AMUSEMENT PARK

(www.legoland.de; adult/concession €41.50/37; ⊙10am-6pm late Mar-early Nov) A sure-fire kid-pleaser, Legoland Deutschland is a

Ulm

flair, the Bäumle can trace its history way back to 1522 and houses smart, immaculately kept rooms. Unless you class cathedral bells as 'noise', you're going to love the location. No lift.

Hotel am Rathaus & Hotel Reblaus HOTEL **$$**
(☑ 0731-968 490; www.rathausulm.de; Kronengasse 10; s €76-120, d €96-140, q €138-170, s/d without bathroom €64/76; 🛜) Just paces from the Rathaus, these twins ooze individual charm with flourishes like stucco and Biedermeier furnishings. Light sleepers take note: the walls are thin and the street can be noisy.

✕ Eating

Animo CAFE **$**
(☑ 0731-964 2937; www.cafe-animo.de; Syrlinstrasse 17; day specials around €7; ⊙ 7.30am-6pm Tue-Fri, 9am-6pm Sat & Sun; ☑) Snuggled away in a *Töpferei* (potter's workshop), Animo is a relaxed cafe, with excellent homemade cakes and vegetarian specials (creative salads, pasta, risotto and the like) – all served in beautifully detailed porcelain. Also hosts regular cultural events.

★ Zur Forelle GERMAN **$$**
(☑ 0731-639 24; Fischergasse 25; mains €12-25; ⊙ 11am-3pm & 5pm-midnight Mon-Fri, 11am-midnight Sat, 11am-10pm Sun) Since 1626, this low-ceilinged tavern has been convincing wayfarers (Einstein included) of the joys of seasonal Swabian cuisine. Ablaze with flowers in summer, this wood-panelled haunt by the Blau prides itself on its namesake *Forelle* (trout), kept fresh under the bridge.

Barfüsser PUB FOOD **$$**
(☑ 0731-602 1110; Lautenberg 1; mains €8-21; ⊙ 10am-1am Sun-Wed, to 2am Thu-Sat) Hearty fare like *Käsespätzle* (cheese noodles) and pork roast soak up the prize-winning beer, microbrewed in Neu-Ulm, at this brewpub. The lunch special goes for €6.90.

Gerberhaus MEDITERRANEAN **$$**
(☑ 0731-677 17; Weinhofberg 9; mains €10-22; ⊙ 11.30am-2.30pm & 5.30-10pm) This warm, inviting woodcutter's cottage hits the mark with its Med-inspired dishes. Plump for a river-facing table and sample clean, bright flavours like home-smoked salmon carpaccio and lemongrass crème brûlée. Day specials go for as little as €7.

Zunfthaus der Schiffleute GERMAN **$$**
(☑ 0731-175 5771; www.zunfthaus-ulm.com; Fischergasse 31; mains €11-28; ⊙ 11am-midnight) Looking proudly back on a 600-year tradition, this timber-framed restaurant sits by the river. The menu speaks of a chef who loves the region, with Swabian faves like *Katzagschroi* (beef, onions, egg and fried potatoes) and meaty one-pot *Schwäbisches Hochzeitssüppchen*.

Gaststätte Krone GERMAN **$$**
(☑ 0731-140 0874; www.krone-ulm.de; Kronengasse 4; mains €11-22.50; ⊙ 5pm-1am Mon-Fri, 10am-1am Sat & Sun; ☑) Going strong since 1320, Ulm's oldest inn is now a delightfully cosy, wood-panelled affair. The regional grub is second to none, whether you opt for *Rin-*

SPOT THE SPARROW

You can't move for *Spatzen* (sparrows) in the German language. You can eat like one (*essen wie ein Spatz*) and swear like one (*schimpfen wie ein Rohrspatz*); there are *Spatzenschleuder* (catapults), *Spätzles* (little darlings) and *Spatzenhirne* (bird brains). Nicknamed *Spatzen*, Ulm residents are, according to legend, indebted to the titchy bird for the construction of their fabulous Münster.

The story goes that the half-baked builders tried in vain to shove the wooden beams for the minster sideways through the city gate. They struggled, until a sparrow fluttered past with straw for its nest. Enlightened, the builders carried the beams lengthways, completed the job and placed a bronze statue of a sparrow at the top to honour the bird.

Today there are sparrows everywhere in Ulm: on postcards, in patisseries, at football matches (team SSV Ulm are dubbed die Spatzen) and, above all, in the colourful sculptures dotting the Altstadt.

derbrühe mit Flädle (beef broth with sliced pancakes) or *Linsen mit Saitenwürste* (lentils with poached sausages).

Zur Lochmühle   GERMAN $$
(☑ 0731-673 05; Gerbergasse 6; mains €9.50-22;) The watermill has been churning the Blau since 1356 at this rustic half-timbered pile. Plant yourself in the riverside beer garden for Swabian classics like crispy roast pork, *Schupfnudeln* and brook trout with lashings of potato salad.

Da Franco   ITALIAN $$$
(☑ 0731-305 85; Neuer Graben 23; mains €20-30; ⊙11am-midnight Tue-Sun) If you fancy a break from the norm, give this little Italian place a whirl. There is a seasonal touch to authentic dishes like swordfish with clams and veal escalope with asparagus, all cooked and presented with style.

Yamas   GREEK $$$
(☑ 0731-407 8614; Herrenkellergasse 29; mains €13.50-30, lunch specials €8.90-13.90; ⊙11.30am-3pm & 5pm-midnight Tue-Sun;) This classy Greek restaurant has a market-driven menu, lots of fresh seafood and a bulging wine cellar. Begin with some homemade dips and grilled octopus, before mains like sea bass with truffle mash and pork medallions with rosemary-thyme gravy.

🍸 Drinking & Entertainment

Naschkatze   CAFE
(http://cafenaschkatze.de; Marienstrasse 6, Neu-Ulm; ⊙8am-7pm Mon-Fri, 9am-6pm Sat, 10am-6pm Sun) Naschkatze, or 'sweet-toothed', is a fitting name for this vintage-cool cafe, where Ulmers come to lap up the retro vibe, coffee and homemade cakes.

Café im Stadthaus   CAFE
(Münsterplatz 50; ⊙8am-midnight Mon-Thu, 8am-1am Fri & Sat, 9am-midnight Sun) Go for coffee and linger for the mesmerising cathedral views at this glass cube.

Café im Kornhauskeller   CAFE
(Hafengasse 19; ⊙8am-midnight Mon-Sat, 9am-10pm Sun) Arty cafe with an inner courtyard for drinks, breakfast, light bites or ice cream.

Zur Zill   BAR
(Schwörhausgasse 19; ⊙10am-2am daily, to 4am Fri & Sat) Join a happy-go-lucky crowd for a cold beer or cocktail by the river.

Wilder Mann   PUB
(Fischergasse 2; ⊙11.30am-1am Mon-Thu, to 3am Fri-Sun) Service is a lucky dip and the food is mediocre, but by all means head to the people-watching terrace for a drink.

Roxy   CONCERT VENUE
(www.roxy.ulm.de; Schillerstrasse 1) This huge cultural venue, housed in a former industrial plant 1km south of the Hauptbahnhof, has a concert hall, cinema, disco, bar and special-event forum. Take tram line 1 to Ehinger Tor.

ℹ Information

Post Office (Bahnhofplatz 2; ⊙8.30am-6.30pm Mon-Fri, 9am-1pm Sat) To the left as you exit the Hauptbahnhof.

Tourist Office (☑ 0731-161 2830; www.tourismus.ulm.de; Münsterplatz 50, Stadthaus; ⊙9am-6pm Mon-Fri, 9am-4pm Sat, 11am-3pm Sun)

ℹ Getting There & Away

Ulm is about 90km southeast of Stuttgart and 150km west of Munich, near the intersection of the north–south A7 and the east–west A8.

ⓘ CITY SAVER

If you're planning on ticking off most of the major sights, consider investing in a good-value **UlmCard** (1/2 days €12/18), which covers public transport in Ulm and Neu-Ulm, a free city tour or rental of the itour audioguide, entry to all museums, plus numerous other discounts on tours, attractions and restaurants.

Ulm is well-served by ICE and EC trains; major destinations include Stuttgart (€19.80 to €26, 56 minutes to 1¼ hours, several hourly) and Munich (€30 to €38, 1¼ to two hours, several hourly).

ⓘ Getting Around

Ulm's ecofriendly trams run on renewable energy. There's a **local transport information counter** (www.swu-verkehr.de) in the tourist office. A single/day ticket for the bus and tram network in Ulm and Neu-Ulm costs €2.10/5.

Except in parking garages (€0.60 per 30 minutes), parking in the whole city centre is metered; many areas are limited to one hour (€1.80). There's a Park & Ride lot at Donaustadion, a stadium 1.5km northeast of the Münster and on tram line 1.

You can hire bikes from **Fahrradhandlung Ralf Reich** (📞 0731-211 79; Frauenstrasse 34; per day €9; ⏰ 9am-12.30pm & 2-6.30pm Mon-Fri, 9am-2pm Sat), a five-minute stroll northeast of the Münsterplatz. Bike paths shadow the Danube.

THE BLACK FOREST

Baden-Baden

📞 07221 / POP 54,500

Baden-Baden's air of old-world luxury and curative waters have attracted royals, the rich and celebrities over the years – Barack Obama and Bismarck, Queen Victoria and Victoria Beckham included. This Black Forest town boasts grand colonnaded buildings and whimsically turreted art-nouveau villas spread across the hillsides and framed by forested mountains.

The bon vivant spirit of France, just across the border, is tangible in the town's open-air cafes, chic boutiques and pristine gardens fringing the Oos River. And with its temple-like thermal baths – which put the *Baden* (bathe) in Baden – and palatial casino, the allure of this grand dame of German spa towns is as timeless as it is enduring.

◉ Sights

Trinkhalle   LANDMARK
(Pump Room; Kaiserallee 3; ⏰ 10am-5pm Mon-Sat, 2-5pm Sun) Standing proud above a manicured park, this neoclassical pump room was built in 1839 as an attractive addition to the Kurhaus. The 90m-long portico is embellished with 19th-century frescos of local legends. Baden-Baden's elixir of youth, some say, is the free curative mineral water that gushes from a faucet linked to the Friedrichsbad spring.

Kurhaus   LANDMARK
(www.kurhaus-baden-baden.de; Kaiserallee 1; tour €5) Corinthian columns and a frieze of mythical griffins grace the belle époque facade of the Kurhaus, which towers above well-groomed gardens. An alley of chestnut trees, flanked by two rows of boutiques, links the Kurhaus with Kaiserallee.

Casino   HISTORIC BUILDING
(www.casino-baden-baden.de; admission €5, guided tour €7; ⏰ 2pm-2am Sun-Thu, 2pm-3am Fri & Sat, guided tours 9.30-11.45am) The sublime casino seeks to emulate – indeed, outdo – the gilded splendour of Versailles. Marlene Dietrich called it 'the most beautiful casino in the world'. Gents must wear a jacket and tie. If you're not much of a gambler and want to simply marvel at the opulence, hook onto a 40-minute guided tour.

Museum Frieder Burda   GALLERY
(www.museum-frieder-burda.de; Lichtentaler Allee 8b; adult/concession €12/10; ⏰ 10am-6pm Tue-Sun) A Joan Miró sculpture guards the front of this architecturally innovative gallery, designed by Richard Meier. The star-studded collection of modern and contemporary art, featuring Picasso, Gerhard Richter and Jackson Pollock originals, is complemented by temporary exhibitions, such as recent ones spotlighting Neo-Expressionist Georg Baselitz and the striking light and shadow works of Heinz Mack.

Staatliche Kunsthalle   GALLERY
(www.kunsthalle-baden-baden.de; Lichtentaler Allee 8a; adult/concession €7/5, Fri free; ⏰ 10am-6pm Tue-Sun) Sidling up to the Museum Frieder Burda is this sky-lit gallery, which showcases rotating exhibitions of contempo-

Black Forest

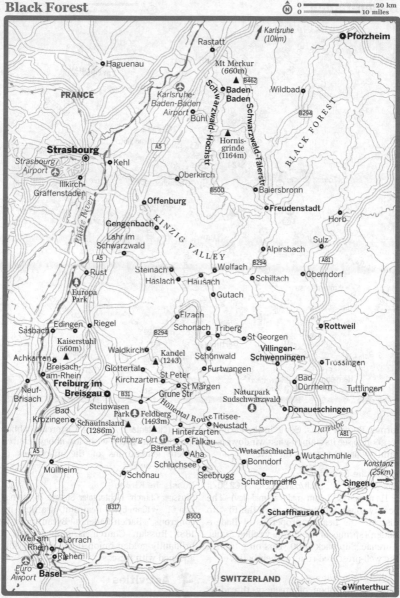

rary art in neoclassical surrounds. Recently it zoomed in on the highly experimental works of Czech artist Eva Kot'átková and the expressionistic painting of Beijing-based artist Li Songsong.

Stiftskirche CHURCH

(Marktplatz; ⊘8am-6pm) The centrepiece of cobbled Marktplatz is this pink church, a hotchpotch of Romanesque, late-Gothic and, to a lesser extent, baroque styles. Its foundations incorporate some ruins of the

Baden-Baden

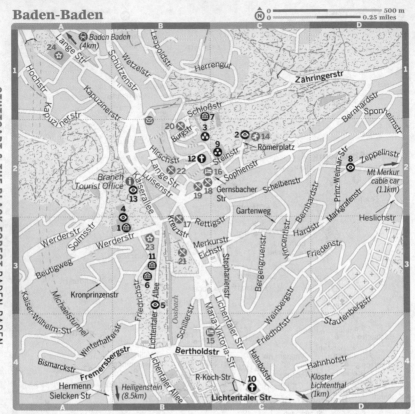

STUTTGART & THE BLACK FOREST BADEN-BADEN

former Roman baths. Come in the early afternoon to see its stained-glass windows cast rainbow patterns across the nave.

Römische Badruinen
RUIN

(Römerplatz; adult/concession €2.50/1; ⊙11am-noon & 3-4pm mid-Mar–mid-Nov) The beauty-conscious Romans were the first to discover the healing properties of Baden-Baden's springs in the city they called Aquae Aureliae. Slip back 2000 years on a tour of the well-preserved ruins of their baths.

Lichtentaler Allee
GARDENS

This 2.3km ribbon of greenery, threading from Goetheplatz to Kloster Lichtenthal, is quite a picture: studded with fountains and sculptures and carpeted with flowers (crocuses and daffodils in spring, magnolias, roses and azaleas in summer). Shadowing the sprightly Oosbach, its promenade and bridges are made for aimless ambling. The avenue concludes at the **Kloster Lichten-** thal (Lichtentaler Allee), a Cistercian abbey founded in 1245, with an abbey church where generations of the margraves of Baden lie buried.

Russische Kirche
CHURCH

(Russian Church; Lichtentaler Strasse 76; admission €1; ⊙10am-6pm) Beautiful, if a little incongrous, Baden-Baden's Byzantine-style 1882 Russian Church is topped with a brilliantly golden onion dome and lavishly adorned with frescos.

🏃 Activities

★Friedrichsbad
SPA

(⌨ 07221-275 920; www.carasana.de; Römerplatz 1; 3hr ticket €25, incl soap-&-brush massage €37; ⊙9am-10pm, last admission 7pm) If it's the body of Venus and the complexion of Cleopatra you desire, abandon modesty (and clothing) to wallow in thermal waters at this palatial 19th-century marble-and-mosaic-festooned

Baden-Baden

spa. As Mark Twain put it, 'after 10 minutes you forget time; after 20 minutes, the world', as you slip into the regime of steaming, scrubbing, hot-cold bathing and dunking in the Roman-Irish bath.

Caracalla Spa SPA
(☏07221-275 940; www.carasana.de; Römerplatz 11; 2/3/4hr €15/18/21; ☺8am-10pm, last admission 8pm) This modern, glass-fronted spa has a cluster of indoor and outdoor pools, grottos and surge channels, making the most of the mineral-rich spring water. For those who dare to bare, saunas range from the rustic 'forest' to the roasting 95°C 'fire' variety.

🛏 Sleeping

Baden-Baden is crammed with hotels, but bargains are rare. The tourist office has a room-reservation service, for a 10% fee.

Hotel am Markt HISTORIC HOTEL **$$**
(☏07221-270 40; www.hotel-am-markt-baden.de; Marktplatz 18; s €35-65, d €90-120; P⊛) Sitting pretty in front of the Stiftskirche, this 250-year-old hotel has 23 homely, well-kept rooms. It's quiet up here apart from your wake-up call of church bells, but then you wouldn't want to miss out on the great breakfast.

Heiligenstein HOTEL **$$**
(☏07221-961 40; www.hotel-heiligenstein.de; Heiligensteinstrasse 19a; s €87-91, d €119-124; P) It's worth going the extra mile (or seven) to this sweet hotel overlooking vineyards. Slick, earthy-hued rooms come with balconies and guests can put their feet up in the spa and

gardens. The highly regarded restaurant (mains €15 to €31) serves local, seasonally inspired fare, from freshly caught trout to venison with blackcurrant sauce and asparagus.

Rathausglöckel HOTEL **$$**
(☏07221-906 10; www.rathausgloeckel.de; Steinstrasse 7; s €80-100, d €115-139, ste €135-300; P⊛) Right in the thick of things, this family-run hotel occupies a 16th-century town house. The attractively renovated rooms (some with rooftop views) are dressed in muted tones with pine furniture – those on the 3rd floor command the best views over Baden-Baden's rooftops. Breakfast is a generous spread of fresh bread, fruit and pastries, homemade jam and bacon and eggs.

Hotel Belle Epoque LUXURY HOTEL **$$$**
(☏07221-300 660; www.hotel-belle-epoque.de; Maria-Viktoria-Strasse 2c; s €165-240, d €199-275,

---

DON'T MISS

TEN YEARS YOUNGER

Fettquelle (Römerplatz; ☺24hr) Rheumatism, arthritis, respiratory complaints, skin problems – all this and a host of other ailments can, apparently, be cured by Baden-Baden's mineral-rich spring water. If you'd rather drink the stuff than bathe in it, head to the Fettquelle fountain at the base of a flight of steps near Römerplatz, where you can fill your bottle for free. It might taste like lukewarm bath water but who cares if it makes you feel 10 years younger?

DON'T MISS

SILENT HEIGHTS

Escape the crowds and enjoy the view at these Baden-Baden lookouts.

Neues Schloss (Schlossstrasse) Vine-swathed steps lead from Marktplatz to the 15th-century Neues Schloss, the former residence of the Baden-Baden margraves, which is set to reopen as a luxury hotel in late 2017. The lookout affords far-reaching views over Baden-Baden's rooftops and spires to the Black Forest beyond.

Mt Merkur (funicular one-way/return €2/4; ⊙10am-10pm) Though modest in height, 668m Mt Merkur commands wide-screen views of Baden-Baden and the Murg Valley. It's a popular spot for paragliding, gentle hiking and family picnics. Buses 204 and 205 stop near the funicular, which has been trundling to the top since 1913.

Florentinerberg The Romans used to cool off here; check out the ruins of the original baths at the foot of the hill. Nowadays, the serene botanical gardens nurture wisteria, cypress trees, orange and lemon groves.

Paradies am Annaberg These Italianate gardens are the perfect spot to unwind, with their soothing fountains and waterfalls. There are fine views of the Altstadt and wooded hills from these heights. Bus 205 to Friedrichshöhe runs nearby.

ste €325-695; ☎) Nestling in manicured parkland, this neo-Renaissance villa is one of Baden-Baden's most characterful five-star pads. Antiques lend a dash of old-world opulence to the individually designed rooms. Rates include afternoon tea, with scones, cakes and fine brews served on the terrace or by the fireplace.

✖ Eating

Café König CAFE $
(Lichtentaler Strasse 12; cake €3.50-5; ⊙8.30am-6.30pm) Liszt and Tolstoy once sipped coffee at this venerable cafe, which has been doing a brisk trade in Baden-Baden's finest cakes, tortes, pralines and truffles for 250 years. Black forest gateau topped with clouds of cream, fresh berry tarts, moist nut cakes.

Kaffeehaus Baden-Baden CAFE $
(Gernsbacherstrasse 24; snacks €3-6; ⊙9.30am-6pm Mon-Fri, 10.30am-6pm Sat, 1-6pm Sun) The aroma of freshly roasted coffee fills this artsy cafe, a laid-back spot for espresso and a slice of tart. Its shop sells organic preserves and handmade ceramics.

★ Weinstube im Baldreit GERMAN $$
(☎07221-231 36; Küferstrasse 3; mains €12.50-19; ⊙5-10pm Tue-Sat) Tucked down cobbled lanes, this wine-cellar restaurant is tricky to find, but worth looking for. Baden-Alsatian fare such as *Flammkuchen* (Alsatian pizza) topped with Black Forest ham, Roquefort and pears is expertly matched with local wines. Eat in the ivy-swathed courtyard in summer, and the vaulted interior in winter.

La Casserole FRENCH $$
(☎07221-222 21; Gernsbacherstrasse 18; mains €12-18; ⊙5-11pm Mon, 11.30am-11pm Tue-Sat) Lace curtains, cheek-by-jowl tables and flickering candles create the classic bistro tableau at intimate La Casserole. Go for satisfying Alsatian specialities like beef cheeks braised in Pinot noir until tender, served with *Spätzle*.

La Provence FRENCH $$$
(☎07221-255 50; Schlossstrasse 20; mains €14-38, 3-course menu €31; ⊙5-11pm Tue-Fri, noon-11pm Sat & Sun) Housed in the Neues Schloss wine cellar, the vaulted ceilings, art-nouveau mirrors and sense of humour at La Provence complement the French cuisine. Specialities like garlicky escargots and chateaubriand with truffle are spot-on.

Rizzi INTERNATIONAL $$$
(☎07221-258 38; www.rizzi-baden-baden.de; Augaplatz 1; mains €18-48; ⊙noon-1am) A summertime favourite, this pink villa's tree-shaded patio is the place to sip excellent wines while tucking into choice steaks. Other menu faves include delicious burgers, homemade pastas and 'Rizzi-style sushi'.

☆ Entertainment

Festspielhaus CONCERT VENUE
(☎07221-301 3101; www.festspielhaus.de; Beim Alten Bahnhof 2, Robert-Schumann-Platz) Ensconced in an historic train station and fabled for its acoustics, the Festspielhaus is Europe's second biggest concert hall, seating 2500 theatre-goers, and a lavish tribute to

Baden-Baden's musical heritage. Under the direction of Andreas Mölich-Zebhauser, the grand venue hosts a world-class program of concerts, opera and ballet.

Baden-Badener Philharmonie　　ORCHESTRA
(☑07221-932 791; www.philharmonie.baden-baden.de; Solms-Strasse 1) The revered Baden-Badener Philharmonie frequently performs in the Kurhaus.

Baden-Baden Theater　　THEATRE
(☑07221-932 700; www.theater.baden-baden.de; Goetheplatz) The Baden-Baden Theater is a neo-baroque confection of white-and-red sandstone whose frilly interior looks like a miniature version of the Opéra-Garnier in Paris. It forms the gateway to Lichtentaler Allee and stages an eclectic line-up of German-language productions.

ℹ Information

Branch Tourist Office (Kaiserallee 3; ☉10am-5pm Mon-Sat, 2-5pm Sun) In the Trinkhalle. Sells events tickets.

Main Tourist Office (☑07221-275 200; www.baden-baden.com; Schwarzwaldstrasse 52; ☉9am-6pm Mon-Sat, 9am-1pm Sun) Situated 2km northwest of the centre. If you're driving from the northwest (from the A5) this place is on the way into town. Sells events tickets.

Post Office (Lange Strasse 44) Inside Kaufhaus Wagener.

ℹ Getting There & Away

Karlsruhe-Baden-Baden Airport (Baden Airpark; ☑07229-66 20 00; www.badenairpark.de), 15km west of Baden-Baden, serves destinations including London Stansted, Rome and Malaga by Ryanair.

Buses to Black Forest destinations depart from the bus station, next to the Bahnhof.

Baden-Baden is close to the A5 (Frankfurt–Basel autobahn) and is the northern starting point of the zigzagging Schwarzwald-Hochstrasse, which follows the B500.

Baden-Baden is on a major north–south rail corridor. Twice-hourly destinations include Freiburg (€21 to €41, 45 to 90 minutes) and Karlsruhe (€11 to €16, 15 to 30 minutes).

ℹ Getting Around

BUS

Local buses run by **Stadwerke Baden-Baden** (www.stadtwerke-baden-baden.de) cost €1.80/6 for a single/24-hour ticket. A day pass for up to five people is €9.80. Bus 201 (every 10 minutes) and other lines link the Bahnhof with Leopoldsplatz. Bus 205 runs roughly hourly between the Bahnhof and the airport, less frequently at weekends.

CAR & MOTORCYLE

The centre is mostly pedestrianised so it's best to park and walk. There is a free Park & Ride at the Bahnhof. Closer to the centre, the cheapest car park is at the Festspielhaus (€1 per hour). Michaelstunnel on the B500 routes traffic away from the centre, ducking underground west of the Festspielhaus and resurfacing just south of the Russische Kirche.

Karlsruhe

☑ 0721 / POP 295,000

When planning this radial city in 1715, the Margraves of Baden placed a mighty baroque palace smack in the middle – an urban layout so impressive it became the blueprint for Washington, DC.

Laid-back and cultured, Karlsruhe grows on you the longer you linger, with its rambling parks, museums crammed with futuristic

DON'T MISS

BLACK FOREST NATIONAL PARK

Nationalpark Schwarzwald (Black Forest National Park; ☑07449-9299 8444; www.schwarzwald-nationalpark.de; Schwarzwaldhochstrasse 2, Seebach; ☉10am-6pm Tue-Sun May-Sep, 10am-5pm Tue-Sun Oct-Apr) An outdoor wonderland of heather-speckled moors, glacial cirque lakes, deep valleys, mountains and near-untouched coniferous forest, the Black Forest National Park, which finally got the seal of approval (national park status) on 1 January 2014, is the Schwarzwald at its wildest and untamed best. Nature is left to its own devices in this 100-sq-km pocket of forest in the northern Black Forest, tucked between Baden-Baden and Freudenstadt and centred on the Schwarzwaldhochstrasse (Black Forest High Road) and the Murgtal valley and Mummelsee lake.

Hiking and cycling trails abound, as do discovery paths geared towards children. Stop by the information centre in Seebach for the low-down and to pick up maps. Details of guided tours and online maps are also available on the website.

gizmos and French Impressionist paintings. The suburbs dotted with art nouveau town houses are a reminder that France is just 15km away. Some 20,000 students keep the beer cheap and the vibe upbeat in the pubs, and the wheels of innovation in culture and technology turning.

◉ Sights & Activities

★ Schloss   PALACE

From the baroque-meets-neoclassical Schloss, Karlsruhe's 32 streets radiate like the spokes of a wheel. Karl Wilhelm Margrave of Baden-Durlach named his epicentral palace Karlsruhe (Karl's retreat) when founding the city in 1715. Destroyed during WWII, the grand palace was sensitively rebuilt. In warm weather, locals play pétanque on the fountain-strewn Schlossplatz parterre. The palace harbours the Badisches Landesmuseum (p334).

Edging north, the Schlossgarten is a popular student hang-out and a relaxed spot for walks and picnics.

Badisches Landesmuseum   MUSEUM

(www.landesmuseum.de; adult/concession €4/3, after 2pm Fri free; ☉10am-5pm Tue-Thu, 10am-6pm Fri-Sun) The treasure-trove Badisches Landesmuseum, inside the Schloss, shelters the jewel-encrusted crown of Baden's grand-ducal ruling family, and spoils of war from victorious battles against the Turks in the 17th century. Scale the tower for a better look at Karlsruhe's circular layout and for views stretching to the Black Forest.

Kunsthalle Karlsruhe   GALLERY

(www.kunsthalle-karlsruhe.de; Hans-Thoma-Strasse 2-6; adult/concession €12/9; ☉10am-6pm Tue-Sun) The outstanding State Art Gallery presents a world-class collection: from the canvases of late-Gothic German masters like Matthias Grünewald and Lucas Cranach the Elder to Impressionist paintings by Degas, Monet and Renoir. Step across to the Orangerie to view works by German artists like Georg Baselitz and Gerhard Richter.

Zentrum für Kunst und Medientechnologie   MUSEUM

(ZKM; www.zkm.de; Lorenzstrasse 19; entry to both museums €10/6.50, after 2pm Fri free; ☉10am-6pm Wed-Fri, 11am-6pm Sat & Sun) Set in an historic munitions factory, the ZKM is a mammoth exhibition and research complex fusing art and emerging electronic media technologies. The interactive Medienmuseum has media art displays, including a computer-generated 'legible city' and real-time bubble simulations. The Museum für Neue Kunst hosts first-rate temporary exhibitions of post-1960 art. Served by tram 2, the ZKM is 2km southwest of the Schloss and a similar distance northwest of the Hauptbahnhof.

Marktplatz   SQUARE

The grand neoclassical Marktplatz is dominated by the Ionic portico of the 19th-century Evangelische Stadtkirche and the dusky-pink Rathaus. The iconic red-stone pyramid is an incongruous tribute to Karl Wilhelm Margrave of Baden-Durlach and marks his tomb.

Museum beim Markt   MUSEUM

(Karl-Friedrich-Strasse 6; adult/concession €2/1; ☉11am-5pm Tue-Thu, 10am-6pm Fri-Sun) At the northern tip of Marktplatz, Museum beim Markt presents an intriguing stash of post-1900 applied arts, from art nouveau to Bauhaus.

Botanischer Garten   GARDENS

(Hans-Thoma-Strasse 6; garden admission free, greenhouses adult/concession €2/1; ☉10am-6pm) Lush with exotic foliage, the Botanischer Garten is speckled with greenhouses – one with a giant Victoria waterlily.

Museum in der Majolika   MUSEUM

(Ahaweg 6; adult/concession €2/1; ☉10am-1pm & 2-5pm Tue-Sun) A line of 1645 blue majolica tiles, called the Blaue Linie, connects the Schloss to the Museum in der Majolika, exhibiting glazed ceramics made in Karlsruhe since 1901.

🛏 Sleeping

Mainly geared towards corporate functions, Karlsruhe's hotels don't rank too highly on the charm-o-meter. Ask the tourist office for a list of private guesthouses.

Bed & Breakfast Karlsruhe   B&B $

(☎0157 850 730 50; www.bbkarlsruhe.de; Karlsstrasse 132a; dm/s/d €22/37/52) Artsy, individually decorated rooms, with a retro feel and paintings on the walls, make this one of Karlsruhe's most enticing budget picks. Bathrooms are shared, as is the kitchen. It's a 10-minute walk northwest of the Hauptbahnhof. The nearest tram stop is Kolpingplatz.

Hotel Rio   HOTEL $$

(☎0721-840 80; www.hotel-rio.de; Hans-Sachs-Strasse 2; s €70-108, d €86-125; Ⓟ🛜) Service can be brusque but this is still one of the best bets for spotless, contemporary quarters in Karlsruhe. Breakfast is worth the extra €6. Take the tram to Mühlburger Tor.

Acora Hotel HOTEL $$$
(☑0721-850 90; www.acora.de; Sophienstrasse 69-71; s €91-134, d €117-169; [P][🛜]) Chirpy staff make you feel right at home at this apartment-hotel, featuring bright, modern rooms equipped with kitchenettes.

✖ Eating & Drinking

Die Kippe PUB FOOD $
(Gottesauer Strasse 23; daily special €3.90; ⊙8am-1am, to 2am Fri & Sat) Every student has a tale about the 'dog end', named after the free tobacco behind the bar. Wallet-friendly daily specials skip from schnitzel to plaice with potato salad. There's live music a couple of times weekly, as well as bingo and quiz nights. The beer garden has a great buzz in summer. Take tram 1 or 2 to Durlacher Tor.

Casa do José PORTUGUESE $$
(☑0721-9143 8018; www.casadojose.de; Kriegsstrasse 92; mains €14-24; ⊙5-11pm Tue-Fri, 11.30am-11pm Sat & Sun) A slice of Portugal in the heart of Karlsruhe, Casa do José extends a heartfelt *bemvindo* (welcome). The look is modern rustic, with beams suspended above bistro tables in a light interior. *Petiscos* (Portuguese tapas) such as salt-cod fritters and fried garlic sausage are an appetising prelude to dishes like *cataplana de peixe e marisco* (paprika spiked fish and shellfish stew).

Vogelbräu PUB FOOD $$
(Kapellenstrasse 50; mains €6.50-13; ⊙10am-1am) Quaff a cold one with regulars by the copper vats or in the leafy beer garden of this microbrewery. The unfiltered house pils washes down hale and hearty food such as Berlin-style beef liver with mash and onions.

Oberländer Weinstuben GERMAN $$$
(☑0721-250 66; www.oberlaender-weinstube.de; Akademiestrasse 7; 3-course lunch/dinner €28/39, mains €18-26; ⊙noon-2pm & 6-10pm Tue-Sat) This highly atmospheric pick brings together an elegant wood-panelled tavern and a flowery courtyard. Fine wines marry perfectly with seasonal winners like stuffed ox-tail with spring leek and Pinot noir-shallot sauce – cooked with flair and served with finesse.

❶ Information

Hauptbahnhof Tourist Office (☑0721-3720 5383; www.karlsruhe-tourism.de; Bahnhofplatz 6; ⊙8.30am-6pm Mon-Fri, 9am-1pm Sat, 10am-1pm Sun) Across the street from the Hauptbahnhof. The iGuide (€7.50) is a self guided audiovisual walking tour of the centre lasting four hours. Also sells the Karlsruher WelcomeCard (24/48/72hr card €6.50/12.50/17.50) offering free or discounted entry to museums and other attractions.

Post Office (Poststrasse 3; ⊙9am-6.30pm Mon-Fri, 9am-1pm Sat) Just east of the Hauptbahnhof.

❶ Getting There & Away

Destinations well-served by train include Baden-Baden (€11 to €16, 15 to 30 minutes) and Freiburg (€27 to €36, one hour).

Karlsruhe is on the A5 (Frankfurt–Basel) and is the starting point of the A8 to Munich. There are Park & Ride options outside of the city centre; look for 'P+R' signs.

❶ Getting Around

The Hauptbahnhof is linked to the Marktplatz, 2km north, by tram and light-rail lines 2, 3, S1, S11, S4 and S41. Single tickets cost €2.30; a 24-Stunden-Karte (24-hour unlimited travel) costs €6 (€9.80 for up to five people).

A relaxed and ecofriendly way to explore Karlsruhe is by bike. Deutsche Bahn has Call-a-Bike stands across the city.

Freudenstadt

☑07441 / POP 23,550

Duke Friedrich I of Württemberg built a new capital here in 1599, which was bombed to bits in WWII. The upshot is that Freudenstadt's centre is underwhelming, though its magnificent setting in the Black Forest is anything but. Lovers of statistics will delight in ticking off Germany's biggest square (216m by 219m, for the record), dislocated by a T-junction of heavily trafficked roads.

Freudenstadt marks the southern end of the Schwarzwald-Hochstrasse and is a terminus for the gorgeous Schwarzwald-Tälerstrasse, which runs from Rastatt via Alpirsbach.

◉ Sights

Stadtkirche CHURCH
(⊙10am-5pm) In the southwest corner of Marktplatz looms the 17th-century red-sandstone Stadtkirche, with an ornate 12th-century Cluniac-style baptismal font, Gothic windows, Renaissance portals and baroque towers. The two naves are at right angles to each other, an unusual design by the geometrically minded duke.

DON'T MISS

A WALK IN THE BLACK FOREST

As locals will tell you, you need to hit the trails to really see the Black Forest. From gentle half-day strolls to multi-day treks, we've cherry-picked the region for a few of our favourites. Local tourist offices can help out with more info and maps, or check out the Schwarzwald Verein's free tour planner at www.wanderservice-schwarzwald.de.

It's also worth checking out the Schwarzwaldverein (www.schwarzwaldverein.de), whose well-marked paths criss-cross the darkest depths of the Black Forest.

Panoramaweg If you want to appreciate Baden-Baden and the northern Black Forest from its most photogenic angles, walk all or part of the 40km Panoramaweg, a high-level ridge trail weaving through orchards and woodlands past waterfalls and viewpoints.

Gütenbach-Simonswäldertal Gütenbach, 22km south of Triberg, is the trailhead for one of the Black Forest's most beautiful half-day hikes to Simonswäldertal, 13km distant. A forest trail threads to Balzer Herrgott, where a sandstone figure of Christ has grown into a tree. Walking downhill from here to Simonswälder Valley, fir-draped hills rise like a curtain before you.

Return by veering north to Teichsschlucht gorge, where a brook cascades through primeval forest lined with sheer cliffs and moss-strewn boulders. Head upstream to return to Gütenbach.

Westweg Up for an adventure? The 280km Westweg is a famous long-distance trail, marked with a red diamond, stretching from Pforzheim in the northern Black Forest to Basel in Switzerland. Highlights feature the steep Murg Valley, Titisee and 1493m Feldberg.

Wutachschlucht (www.wutachschlucht.de) This wild gorge, carved out by a fast-flowing river and flanked by near-vertical rock faces, lies near Bonndorf, close to the Swiss border and 15km east of Schluchsee. The best way to experience its unique microclimate, where you might spot orchids, ferns, rare butterflies and lizards, is on this 13km trail leading from Schattenmühle to Wutachmühle.

Feldberg Steig Orbiting the Black Forest's highest peak, 1493m Feldberg, this 12km walk traverses a nature reserve that's home to chamois and wildflowers. On clear days, the views of the Alps are glorious. It's possible to snowshoe part of this route in winter.

Martinskapelle A scenic and easygoing walk, this 10km loop begins at hilltop chapel Martinskapelle, 11km southwest of Triberg. The well-marked path wriggles through forest to tower-topped Brendturm (1149m) which affords views from Feldberg to the Vosges and the Alps on cloud-free days. Continue via Brendhäusle and Rosseck for a stunning vista of overlapping mountains and forest.

☆ Activities

The deep forested valleys on Freudenstadt's fringes are worth exploring. Scenic hiking trails include a 12km uphill walk to **Kniebis** on the Schwarzwald-Hochstrasse, where there are superb Kinzig Valley views. Ask the tourist office for details.

Jump on a mountain bike to tackle routes like the 85km **Kinzigtal-Radweg**, taking in dreamy landscapes and half-timbered villages, or the 60km **Murgtal-Radweg** over hill and dale to Rastatt. Both valleys have bike trails and it's possible to return to Freudenstadt by train.

Intersport Glaser   BICYCLE RENTAL
(Katharinenstrasse 8; bike rental per day €14-24; ☺9.30am-6.30pm Mon-Fri, 9.30am-4pm Sat) A

couple of blocks north of Marktplatz, this outlet hires mountain and electro bikes.

Panorama-Bad   SWIMMING
(www.panorama-bad.de; Ludwig-Jahn-Strasse 60; adult/concession 3hr pass €6.70/5.80; ☺9am-10pm Mon-Sat, 9am-8pm Sun) The glass-fronted Panorama-Bad is a relaxation magnet with pools, steam baths and saunas.

🛏 Sleeping & Eating

At the heart of Freudenstadt, the sprawling, arcaded Marktplatz harbours rows of shops and cafes with alfresco seating.

Camping Langenwald   CAMPGROUND $
(☎07441-2862; www.camping-langenwald.de; Strasburger Strasse 167; per person/tent €8/9; ☺Easter-Oct; ☀) With a solar-heated pool and

nature trail, this leafy site has impeccable eco credentials. It's served by bus 12 to Kniebis.

Warteck
HOTEL $$

(☑ 07441-919 20; www.warteck-freudenstadt.de; Stuttgarterstrasse 14; s €60-78, d €98-105; ⓟ 🛜) In the capable hands of the Glässel family since 1894, this hotel sports modern, gleamingly clean rooms. The real draw, however, is the wood-panelled restaurant (mains €14.50 to €39), serving market-fresh fare like beetroot tortellini and rack of venison with wild mushrooms.

Hotel Adler
HOTEL $$

(☑ 07441-915 20; www.adler-fds.de; Forststrasse 15-17; s €54.50-81, d €80-105; ⓟ 🛜) This family-run hotel near Marktplace has well-kept, recently renovated rooms and rents out e-bikes for €9/16 per half-/full day. The restaurant (mains €12 to €17) dishes up appetising regional grub such as *Zwiebelrostbraten* (roast beef with onions).

Turmbräu
GERMAN $$

(Marktplatz 64; mains €8-28; ☉ 11am-midnight, to 3am Fri & Sat) This lively microbrewery doubles as a beer garden. Pull up a chair in ye-olde barn to munch *Maultaschen* and guzzle Turmbräu brews – a 5L barrel costs €39.

🛈 Information

Tourist Office (☑ 07441-8640; www.freudenstadt.de; Marktplatz 64; ☉ 9am-6pm Mon-Fri, 10am-3pm Sat, 10am-1pm Sun; 🛜) Hotel reservations are free.

🛈 Getting There & Away

Freudenstadt's focal point is the Marktplatz on the B28. The town has two train stations: the Stadtbahnhof, five minutes' walk north of Marktplatz, and the Hauptbahnhof, 2km southeast of Marktplatz at the end of Bahnhofstrasse.

Trains on the Ortenau line, serving Offenburg and Strasbourg, depart hourly from the Hauptbahnhof and are covered by the 24-hour Europass. The pass represents excellent value at €11.50 for individuals and €18.40 for families. Trains go roughly hourly to Karlsruhe (€17.90, 1½ to two hours) from the Stadtbahnhof and Hauptbahnhof.

Kinzig Valley

Shaped like a horseshoe, the Kinzigtal (Kinzig Valley) begins south of Freudenstadt and shadows the babbling Kinzig River south to Schiltach, west to Haslach and north to Offenburg. Near Strasbourg, 95km downriver, the Kinzig is swallowed up by the mighty Rhine. The valley's inhabitants survived for centuries on mining and shipping goods by raft.

This Black Forest valley is astonishingly pretty, its hills brushed with thick larch and spruce forest and its half-timbered villages looking freshly minted for a fairy tale. For seasonal colour, come in autumn (foliage) or spring (fruit blossom).

🛈 Getting There & Away

The B294 follows the Kinzig from Freudenstadt to Haslach, from where the B33 leads north to Offenburg. If you're going south, pick up the B33 to Triberg and beyond in Hausach.

An hourly train line links Freudenstadt with Offenburg (€15.70, 1¼ hours), stopping in Alpirsbach (€3.65, 16 minutes), Schiltach (€6.10, 27 minutes), Hausach (€8.10, 42 minutes), Haslach (€10, 50 minutes) and Gengenbach (€13.30, one hour). From Hausach, trains run roughly hourly southeast to Triberg (€6.10, 20 minutes), Villingen (€12.10, 47 minutes) and Konstanz (€29.60, two hours).

Alpirsbach

☑ 07444 / POP 6580

Lore has it that Alpirsbach is named after a quaffing cleric who, when a glass of beer slipped clumsily from his hand and rolled into the river, exclaimed: *All Bier ist in den Bach!* (All the beer is in the stream!). A prophecy, it seems, as today Alpirsbacher Klosterbräu is brewed from pure spring water. Brewery tours (☑ 07441-670; www.alpirsbacher.com; Marktplatz 1; tours €7; ☉ 2.30pm) are in German, though guides may speak English. Two beers are thrown in for the price of a ticket.

A few paces north, you can watch chocolate being made and scoff delectable beer-filled pralines at **Schau-Confiserie Heinzelmann** (Ambrosius-Blarer-Platz 2; ☉ 9am-noon & 2-6pm Mon-Fri, to 5pm Sat).

All the more evocative for its lack of adornment, the 11th-century former Benedictine **Kloster Alpirsbach** (Klosterplatz 1; adult/concession €5/2.50; ☉ 10am-5.30pm Mon-Sat, 11am-5.30pm Sun) sits opposite. The monastery effectively conveys the simple, spiritual life in its flat-roofed church, spartan cells and Gothic cloister, which hosts candlelit concerts (www.kreuzgangkonzerte.de) from late June to early August. It's amazing what you can find under the floorboards,

Landscapes

Like a fine wine, Germany's landscapes want to be savoured. Remember this as you revel in the rustic grandeur of the Alps, sample the mellifluous meanderings of the Moselle or ramble in an enchanted forest that inspired fairy tales.

Bewitching Forests

1 Germany's ancient and inky forests captivate with enough drama and grace to convert even a dedicated loafer to the great outdoors. The Black Forest (p329) – fabled, fabulous and family friendly – is just one such green oasis exerting its siren call.

Coastal Charisma

2 Germany's coast is a tale of two seas. Undulating dunes hem the tranquil Baltic, punctuated by candy-striped lighthouses. Fierce and raw, the North Sea is dotted with scores of wind-whipped offshore islands, like glamorous Sylt (p688).

Sinuous Streams

3 Germany's rivers course vividly through the imagination, and none more so than the Romantic Rhine (p432). Rife with mythology, artist-inspiring scenery and legend-shrouded castles, its mystique will carve deeply into your memory.

Magic Mountains

4 The big-shouldered Bavarian Alps (p230) are Germany's 'upper storey'. Hike among fragrant pines in summer, through hamlets serenaded by the bells of onion-domed churches, or try snowshoeing through a winter wonderland.

Languorous Lakes

5 Germany's shimmering lakes are fantastic summer destinations. From sea-sized Lake Constance (p357) to pristine mountain pools and the 'land of a thousand lakes' (p699) in the north, you'll find plenty of ways to frolic in or out on the water.

Clockwise from top left
1. Hotzenwald in the Black Forest 2. Ellenbogen (p689). Sylt 3. The Rhine Valley 4. Bavarian Alps

as the museum reveals with its stash of 16th-century clothing, caricatures (of artistic scholars) and lines (of misbehaving ones).

The **tourist office** (☑ 07444-951 6281; www.stadt-alpirsbach.de; Krähenbadstrasse 2; ⊙ 9am-noon & 2-6pm Mon, 9am-noon & 2-5pm Tue & Thu, 9am-noon Wed, 9am-1pm & 2-5pm Fri, 10am-noon Sat) can supply hiking maps and, for cyclists, information on the 85km Kinzigtalradweg from Offenburg to Lossburg.

Schiltach

☑ 07836 / POP 3880

Sitting smugly at the foot of wooded hills and on the banks of the Kinzig and Schiltach Rivers, medieval Schiltach looks too perfect to be true. The meticulously restored half-timbered houses, which once belonged to tanners, merchants and raft builders, are a riot of crimson geraniums in summer.

◉ Sights & Activities

Because Schiltach is at the confluence of the Kinzig and Schiltach Rivers, logging was big business until the 19th century and huge rafts were built to ship timber as far as the Netherlands. The willow-fringed banks now attract grey herons and kids who come to splash in the shallow water when the sun's out.

Marktplatz   SQUARE
Centred on a trickling fountain, the sloping, triangular Marktplatz is Schiltach at its picture-book best. The frescos of its step-gabled, 16th-century Rathaus depict scenes from local history.

Schlossbergstrasse   STREET
Clamber south up Schlossbergstrasse, pausing to notice the plaques that denote the trades of one-time residents, such as the *Strumpfstricker* (stocking weaver) at No 6, and the sloping roofs where tanners once dried their skins. Up top there are views over Schiltach's red rooftops.

Museum am Markt   MUSEUM
(Marktplatz 13; ⊙ 11am-5pm Apr-Oct, Sat & Sun only Nov-Mar) FREE Museum am Markt is crammed with everything from antique spinning wheels to Biedermeier costumes. Highlights include the cobbler's workshop and an interactive display recounting the tale of the devilish Teufel von Schiltach.

Schüttesäge Museum   MUSEUM
(Gerbegasse; ⊙ 11am-5pm daily Apr-Oct, Sat & Sun only Nov-Mar) FREE The riverfront

Schüttesäge Museum focuses on Schiltach's rafting tradition with reconstructed workshops, a watermill generating hydroelectric power for many homes in the area and touchy-feely exhibits for kids, from different kinds of bark to forest animals.

🛏 Sleeping & Eating

Campingplatz Schiltach   CAMPGROUND $
(☑ 07836-7289; Bahnhofstrasse 6; per person/tent/car €5.50/3.50/3; ⊙ Apr-Oct) Beautifully positioned on the banks of the Kinzig, this campground has impeccable eco credentials and a playground and sandpit for kids.

★ **Weysses Rössle**   GUESTHOUSE $$
(☑ 07836-387; www.weysses-roessle.de; Schenkenzeller Strasse 42; s €55-59.50, d €78-96; P 🕸) Rosemarie and Ulrich continue the tradition of 19 generations in this 16th-century inn. Countrified rooms decorated with rosewood and floral fabrics also feature snazzy bathrooms and wi-fi. Its restaurant serves locally sourced, organic fare.

Zur Alten Brücke   GUESTHOUSE $$
(☑ 07836-2036; www.altebruecke.de; Schramberger Strasse 13; s/d/apt €60/90/110; P 🕸) You'll receive a warm welcome from Michael and Lisa at this riverside guesthouse. The pick of the bright, cheery rooms overlook the Schiltach. Michael cooks up seasonal, regional fare in the kitchen and there's a terrace for summer imbibing.

❶ Information

Tourist Office (☑ 07836-5850; www.schiltach.de; Marktplatz 6; ⊙ 9am-noon & 2-4pm Mon-Thu, 9am-noon Fri) The tourist office in the Rathaus can help find accommodation and offers free internet access. Hiking options are marked on an enamel sign just opposite.

Gutach

☑ 07831 / POP 2180

Worth the 4km detour south of the Kinzig Valley, the **Schwarzwälder Freilichtmuseum** (☑ 07831-935 60; www.vogtsbauernhof.org; adult/concession/child/family €9/8/5/25; ⊙ 9am-6pm late Mar-early Nov, to 7pm Aug, last entry 1hr before closing) spirals around the Vogtsbauernhof, an early-17th-century farmstead. Farmhouses shifted from their original locations have been painstakingly reconstructed, using techniques such as thatching and panelling, to create this authentic farming hamlet and preserve age-old Black Forest traditions.

WORTH A TRIP

REACH FOR THE STARS

Swinging along country lanes 6km north of Freudenstadt brings you to Baiersbronn. It looks like any other Black Forest town, snuggled among meadows and wooded hills. But on its fringes sit two of Germany's finest restaurants, both holders of the coveted three Michelin stars.

Schwarzwaldstube ([☑]07442-4920; www.traube-tonbach.de; Tonbachstrasse 237, Baiers-bronn-Tonbach; 5-/7-course menu €80/210, cookery courses around €170; ☉7pm-midnight Wed, noon-4.30pm & 7pm-midnight Thu-Sun) Schwarzwaldstube commands big forest views from its rustically elegant dining room. Here Harald Wohlfahrt performs culinary magic, while carefully sourcing and staying true to French cooking traditions. The tasting menu goes with the seasons, but you might begin with a palate-awakening variation of mackerel with cucumber-oyster relish, followed by saddle of venison with juniper crust and caramelised *chicorée* (chicory).

If you fancy getting behind the stove, sign up for one of the cookery classes, which revolve around a theme such as cooking with crustaceans, asparagus, goose or truffles, or techniques like pasta-making and preparing pâtés.

Restaurant Bareiss ([☑]07442-470; www.bareiss.com; Gärtenbühlweg 14, Baiersbronn-Mitteltal; lunch menu €95, dinner menus €168 210; ☉noon-2pm & 7-9.30pm Wed-Sun) Claus-Peter Lumpp has consistently won plaudits for his brilliantly composed, French-inflected menus at Restaurant Bareiss. On paper, dishes such as sautéed langoustine with almond cream and fried fillet of suckling calf and sweetbreads with chanterelles seem deceptively simple; on the plate they become things of beauty, rich in textures and aromas and presented with an artist's eye for detail.

Explore barns filled with wagons and horn sleds, *Rauchküchen* (kitchens for smoking fish and meat) and the Hippensep-penhof (1599), with its chapel and massive hipped roof constructed from 400 trees. It's a great place for families, with inquisitive farmyard animals to pet, artisans on hand to explain their crafts and frequent demonstrations, from sheep shearing to butter-making.

The self-controlled bobs of the **Schwarzwald Rodelbahn** (Black Forest Toboggan Run; Singersbach 4; adult/child €2.50/2; ☉10am-6pm Apr-early Nov), 1.5km north of Gutach, are faster than they look. Lay off the brakes for extra speed.

Haslach

[☑] 07832 / POP 6980

Back in the Kinzig Valley, Haslach's 17th-century former Capuchin monastery houses the **Schwarzwälder Trachtenmuseum** (Black Forest Costume Museum; www.trachtenmuseum-haslach.de.vu; Im Alten Kapuzinerkloster; adult/concession €2/1.50; ☉10am-12.30pm & 1.30-4pm Tue-Fri), showcasing flamboyant costumes and outrageous hats, the must-have accessories for the well-dressed Fräulein of the 1850s. Look out for the Black Forest *Bollenhut*, a straw bonnet topped with pompons

(red for unmarried women, black for married) and the *Schäppel,* a fragile-looking crown made from hundreds of beads and weighing up to 5kg.

Gengenbach

[☑] 07803 / POP 11,020

If ever a Black Forest town could be described as chocolate box, it would surely be Gengenbach, with its scrumptious Altstadt of half-timbered town houses framed by vineyards and orchards. It's fitting, then, that director Tim Burton made this the home of gluttonous Augustus Gloop in the 2005 blockbuster *Charlie and the Chocolate Factory* (though less so that he called it Düsseldorf).

☉ Sights & Activities

The best way to discover Gengenbach's historic centre is with a saunter through its narrow backstreets, such as the gently curving Engelgasse, off Hauptstrasse, lined with listed half-timbered houses draped in vines and bedecked with scarlet geraniums.

Between the town's two tower-topped gates sits the triangular Marktplatz, dominated by the Rathaus, an 18th-century pink-and-cream confection. The fountain bears a statue of a knight, a symbol of Gengenbach's medieval status as a Free Imperial City.

Amble east along Klosterstrasse to spy the former Benedictine monastery. The calm Kräutergarten is behind its walls.

The tourist office has info on the hour-long Weinpfad, a wine trail beginning in the Altstadt that threads through terraced vineyards to the Jakobskapelle, a 13th-century chapel commanding views that reach as far as Strasbourg on clear days. The free, lantern-lit Nachtwächterrundgang (night watchman's tour) starts at the Rathaus on Wednesday and Saturday at 10pm from May to July and at 9pm from August to October.

🛏 Sleeping & Eating

DJH Hostel
HOSTEL $

(🖂 07803-317 49; www.jugendherberge-schloss-ortenberg.de; Burgweg 21; dm €23-29) The Hogwarts gang would feel at home in the 12th-century Schloss Ortenberg, rebuilt in whimsical neo-Gothic style complete with lookout tower and wood-panelled dining hall. A staircase sweeps up to dorms with Kinzig Valley views. From Gengenbach station, take bus 7134 or 7160 to Ortenberg, and get off at the 'Schloss/Freudental' stop.

Pfeffermühle
B&B $$

(🖂 07803-933 50; www.pfeffermuehle-gengenbach.de; Oberdorfstrasse 24; s/d €54/84) In a snug half-timbered house dating to 1476, close to one of the Altstadt gate towers, this neat-and-tidy B&B is a bargain. Decorated with antique knick-knacks, the wood-panelled restaurant (mains €14 to €22) features

---

DON'T MISS

CHRISTMAS COUNTDOWN

Gengenbach Advent Calendar
Every December, Gengenbach rekindles childhood memories of opening tiny windows when the Rathaus morphs into the world's biggest advent calendar. At 6pm daily, one of 24 windows is opened to reveal a festive scene. In the past, the tableaux have been painted by well-known artists and children's-book illustrators such as Marc Chagall and Tomi Ungerer.

From late November to 23 December, a Christmas market brings extra yuletide sparkle, mulled wine and carols to the Marktplatz.

---

among the town's best, dishing out regional favourites like Black Forest trout and *Sauerbraten* (pot roast).

⭐ Die Reichstadt
BOUTIQUE HOTEL $$$

(🖂 07803-966 30; www.die-reichsstadt.de; Engelgasse 33; s €140-160, ste €190-210, 4-course half-board per person €35; 🅿 🛜) This boutique stunner on Engelgasse wings you to storybook heaven. Its 16th-century exterior conceals a pure, contemporary aesthetic, where clean lines, natural materials and subtle cream-caramel shades are enlivened with eye-catching details. A spa, sparkling wine on arrival, free fruit in your room and one of the top restaurants in town, with a season-driven menu, complete this pretty picture.

Holzofen-Bäckerei Klostermühle
BAKERY $

(Klosterstrasse 7; ⊙ 7am-6pm Mon-Fri, 7am-noon Sat) Opposite the Benedictine monastery, the stuck-in-time Holzofen-Bäckerei Klostermühle fills the lanes with wafts of freshly baked bread from its wood-fired oven. Buy a loaf to munch in the calm Kräutergarten.

ℹ Information

Tourist Office (🖂 07803-930 143; www.stadt-gengenbach.de; Im Winzerhof; ⊙ 9am-5pm Mon-Fri) The tourist office is in a courtyard just off Hauptstrasse.

Freiburg

🖂 0761 / POP 224.190

Sitting plump at the foot of the Black Forest's wooded slopes and vineyards, Freiburg is a sunny, cheerful university town, its medieval Altstadt a story-book tableau of gabled town houses, cobblestone lanes and cafe-rimmed plazas. Party-loving students spice up the local nightlife.

Blessed with 2000 hours of annual sunshine, this is Germany's warmest city. Indeed, while neighbouring hilltop villages are still shovelling snow, the trees in Freiburg are clouds of white blossom, and locals are already imbibing in canalside beer gardens. This eco-trailblazer has shrewdly tapped into that natural energy to generate nearly as much solar power as the whole of Britain, making it one of the country's greenest cities.

⊙ Sights

Freiburg's medieval past is tangible in backstreets like wisteria-draped Konviktstrasse and in the canalside Fischerau and Gerberau, the former fishing and tanning quarters. The Dreisam River runs along the Altstadt's southern edge.

Keep an eye out for the cheerful pavement mosaics in front of many shops – a cow is for a butcher, a pretzel for a baker, a diamond marks a jewellery shop, and so on.

★ **Freiburger Münster**   CATHEDRAL
(Freiburg Minster; ☑0761-202 790; www.freiburgermuenster.info; Münsterplatz; tower adult/concession €2/1.50; ⊙9.30am-5pm, tower 9.30am-4.45pm Mon-Sat, 1-5pm Sun) With its lacy spires, cheeky gargoyles and intricate entrance portal, Freiburg's 11th-century minster cuts an impressive figure above the central market square. It has dazzling kaleidoscopic stained-glass windows that were mostly financed by medieval guilds and a high altar with a masterful triptych by Dürer protégé Hans Baldung Grien. Square at the base, the tower becomes an octagon higher up and is crowned by a filigreed 116m-high spire. On clear days you can spy the Vosges Mountains in France.

Closer to the ground, near the main portal in fact, note the medieval wall measurements used to ensure that merchandise (eg loaves of bread) were of the requisite size.

Note that the cathedral is closed for visits during services (exact times are available at the info desk inside).

Augustinermuseum   MUSEUM
(☑0761-201 2531; Auginerplatz 1; adult/concession/under 18yr €6/4/free; ⊙10am-5pm Tue-Sun) Dip into the past as represented by artists working from the Middle Ages to the 19th century at this superb museum in a sensitively modernised monastery. The Sculpture Hall on the ground floor is especially impressive for its fine medieval sculpture and masterpieces by Renaissance artists Hans Baldung Grien and Lucas Cranach the Elder. Head upstairs for eye-level views of mounted gargoyles.

There is a cafe overlooking the cloister where you can sip a drink and soak up the monastic vibe. A €7/5 ticket includes temporary exhibitions and is valid for all museums in Freiburg.

Historisches Kaufhaus   HISTORIC BUILDING
(Münsterplatz) Facing the Münster's south side and embellished with polychrome tiled turrets is the arcaded brick-red Historisches Kaufhaus, an early-16th-century merchants' hall. The coats of arms on the oriels and

BEHOLD THE SUPER BOG

Duravit Design Centre (www.duravit.de; Werderstrasse 36; ⊙8am-6pm Mon-Fri, noon-4pm Sat) If giant cuckoo clocks and black forest gateau no longer thrill, how about a trip to the world's largest loo? Drive a couple of minutes south of Gutach on the B33 to Hornberg and there, in all its lavatorial glory, stands the titanic toilet dreamed up by Philippe Starck. Even if you have no interest in designer urinals or home jacuzzis, it's worth visiting the Duravit Design Centre for the tremendous view across the Black Forest from the 12m-high ceramic loo.

the four figures above the balcony symbolise Freiburg's allegiance to the House of Habsburg.

City Gates   GATE
(Kaiser-Joseph-Strasse) Freiburg has two intact medieval gates. The **Martinstor** (Martin's Gate) rises above Kaiser-Joseph-Strasse, while the 13th-century **Schwabentor**, on the Schwabenring, is a massive city gate with a mural of St George slaying the dragon and tram tracks running under its arches.

Schlossberg   VIEWPOINT
(Schlossbergring; cable car one way/return €3/5; ⊙9am-10pm, shorter hours in winter) The forested Schlossberg dominates Freiburg. Take the footpath opposite the Schwabentor, leading up through sun-dappled woods, or hitch a ride on the recently restored Schlossbergbahn cable car. For serious hikers, several trails begin here including those to St Peter (17km) and Kandel (25km).

The little peak is topped by the ice-cream-cone-shaped Aussichtsturm (lookout tower). From here, Freiburg spreads photogenically before you – the spire of the Münster soaring above a jumble of red gables, framed by the dark hills of the Black Forest.

Rathausplatz   SQUARE
(Town Hall Square) Join locals relaxing in a cafe by the fountain in chestnut-shaded Rathausplatz, Freiburg's prettiest square. Pull out your camera to snap pictures of the ox-blood-red 16th-century Altes Rathaus (Old Town Hall) with the tourist office, the step-gabled 19th-century Neues Rathaus

Freiburg

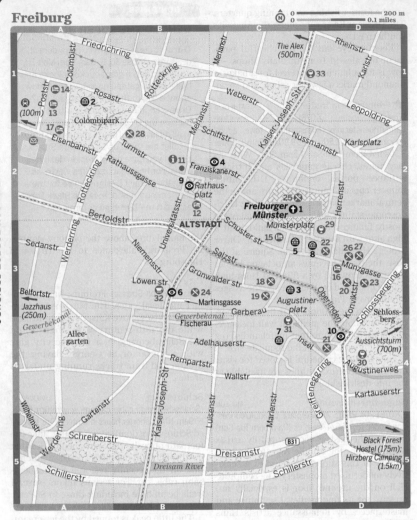

(New Town Hall) and the medieval Martins-kirche with its modern interior.

Haus zum Walfisch
LANDMARK

(House of the Whale; Franziskanerstrasse) The marvellously extravagant Haus zum Walfisch sports a late-Gothic oriel garnished with two impish gargoyles.

Archäologisches Museum
MUSEUM

(www.museen.freiburg.de; Rotteckring 5; adult/concession €3/2; ⊙10am-5pm Tue-Sun) In a sculpture-dotted park sits the neo-Gothic **Colombischlössle**. Built for the Countess of Colombi in 1859, the whimsical red-sandstone villa now harbours this archaeology-focused museum. From the skylit marble entrance, a cast-iron staircase ascends to a stash of finds from Celtic grave offerings to Roman artefacts.

Museum für Stadtgeschichte
MUSEUM

(Münsterplatz 30; adult/concession €3/2; ⊙10am-5pm Tue-Sun) The sculptor Christian Wentzinger's baroque town house, east of the Historisches Kaufhaus, now shelters this museum, spelling out in artefacts Freiburg's eventful past. Inside, a wrought-iron staircase guides the eye to an elaborate ceiling fresco.

Freiburg

Museum für Neue Kunst   GALLERY
(Marienstrasse 10; adult/concession €3/2; ☉10am-5pm Tue-Sun) Across the Gewerbekanal, this gallery highlights 20th-century Expressionist and abstract art, including emotive works by Oskar Kokoschka and Otto Dix.

⊂⊐ Tours

Freiburg Kultour   GUIDED TOUR
(www.freiburg-kultour.com; Rathausplatz 2-4; adult/concession €9/7; ☉10.30am Mon-Fri, 10am Sat in German, 11.30am Sat in English) Kultour offers 1½- to two-hour walking tours of the Altstadt and the Münster in German and English.

Fahrradtaxi   GUIDED TOUR
(☏0172-768 4370; www.fahrradtaxi-freiburg.de; An der Höhlgasse 5; ☉mid-Apr–Oct) Fahrradtaxi charges €7.50 for a 15-minute, two-person spin of the Altstadt in a pedicab. Call ahead or look for one on Rathausplatz or Münsterplatz.

⊨ Sleeping

Charismatic hotels abound in the Altstadt but it's wise to book ahead in summer. The tourist office offers a booking service (€3) and has a list of good-value private guesthouses.

Black Forest Hostel   HOSTEL $
(☏0761-881 7870; www.blackforest-hostel.de; Kartäuserstrasse 33; dm €17-27, s/d €35/58, linen €4; ☉reception 7am-1am; @) Boho budget digs with chilled common areas, a shared kitchen, bike rental and spacey stainless-steel showers. It's a five-minute walk from the town centre.

Hirzberg Camping   CAMPGROUND $
(☏0761-350 54; www.freiburg-camping.de; Kartäuserstrasse 99; campsites per adult/tent/car €8.80/4.70/2.70; P⊙) This year-round campground sits in a quiet woodland spot 1.5km east of Schwabentor. It has cooking facilities and bike rental. Take tram 1 to Musikhochschule.

The Alex   BOUTIQUE HOTEL $$
(☏0761-296 970; www.the-alex-hotel.de; Rheinstrasse 29; s €103-142, d €112-151; P❋⊙) This welcome newcomer to Freiburg's hotel scene has a clean, sleek aesthetic, with lots of plate glass, blonde wood, natural materials and a muted palette of colours. Besides contemporary-style rooms with rain showers, there's a bar, Winery29, where you can try locally produced wines.

Hotel Schwarzwälder Hof   HOTEL $$
(☏0761-380 30; www.schwarzwaelder-hof.com; Herrenstrasse 43; s €68-80, d €99-125; @) This bijou hotel has an unrivalled style-for-euro

ratio. A wrought-iron staircase sweeps up to snazzy rooms furnished in classic, modern or traditional style. Some have postcard views of the Altstadt.

Hotel am Rathaus HOTEL $$
(☑0761-296 160; www.am-rathaus.de; Rathausgasse 4-8; s €93-95, d €110-129; P🖤) Just steps away from the bustle of Rathausplatz, this neat-and-tidy hotel has spacious, neutral-toned rooms with homely touches like CD and DVD players; ask for a rear-facing room if you're a light sleeper.

Hotel Minerva HOTEL $$
(☑0761-386 490; www.minerva-freiburg.de; Poststrasse 8; s €65-95, d €130-155, tr €165; P🖤) All curvaceous windows and polished wood, this art nouveau charmer is five minutes' trudge from the Altstadt. The sleek, contemporary rooms feature free wi-fi. The sauna (€8) is another plus.

Hotel Barbara HISTORIC HOTEL $$
(☑0761-296 250; www.hotel-barbara.de; Poststrasse 4; s €80-94, d €110-151, apt €135-205; 🖤) A grandfather clock, curvy staircases and high ceilings give this art nouveau town house a nostalgic feel. It's a homely, family-run place with old-fashioned, pastel-hued rooms and homemade jams at breakfast.

Park Hotel Post HISTORIC HOTEL $$
(☑0761-385 480; www.park-hotel-post.de; Am Colombipark; s €109-159, d €139-199; P🖤) Slip back to the more graceful age of art nouveau at this refined pile overlooking Colombipark, with summery rooms decorated in blues and yellows. Attentive service and generous breakfasts sweeten the deal.

★Hotel Oberkirch HISTORIC HOTEL $$$
(☑0761-202 6868; www.hotel-oberkirch.de; Münsterplatz 22; s €75-104, d €154-174; P) Wake up to Münster views at this green-shuttered hotel. The country-style rooms feature floral wallpaper and half-canopies over the beds. Oberkirch has an intoxicating 250-year history; during a fire in WWII the hotelier doused the blaze with wine from his cellar. The dark-wood downstairs tavern (mains €13 to €23) does a roaring trade in hearty Badisch fare such as venison ragout with *Knödel* (dumplings).

✗ Eating

The Altstadt is stacked with cafes, wine taverns, brewpubs and restaurants, many spilling out onto pavement terraces. You can find cheap bites on Martinstor and Kartäuserstrasse.

Edo's Hummus Küche VEGETARIAN $
(http://thehummuscorner.com; Atrium Auginerplatz; light meals €2.50-8.50; ☺11.30am-9pm Mon-Sat; 🖤) Edo's pulls in the midday crowds by doing what it says on the tin – superb homemade hummus served with warm pitta, as well as lentil salad and falafel. The basic hummus plate for €4.30 is a meal in itself.

Chang THAI $
(Grünwälderstrasse 21; mains €6-9.50; ☺noon-11pm) Sweet little Thai place for inexpensive daily specials, from green curry to pad thai.

Münsterplatz Food Market MARKET $
(☺7.30am-1.30pm Mon-Fri, to 2pm Sat) Bag local goodies (honey, cheese, fruit and the like), or snack on a wurst-in-a-bun, topped with fried onions.

Markthalle MARKET $
(www.markthalle-freiburg.de; Martinsgasse 235; light meals €4-8; ☺8am-8pm Mon-Thu, to midnight Fri & Sat) Eat your way around the world – from curry to sushi, oysters to antipasti – at the food counters in this historic market hall, nicknamed 'Fressgässle'.

Rücker Käse und Wein DELI $
(Münzgasse 1; ☺10am-6.30pm Mon-Fri, 9am-3pm Sat) For wine and cheese.

Gasthaus zum Kranz GERMAN $$
(☑0761-217 1967; www.gasthauszumkranz.de; Herrenstrasse 40; mains €13-24; ☺11.30am-3pm & 5.30pm-midnight Mon-Sat, noon-3pm & 5.30pm-midnight Sun) There's always a good buzz at this quintessentially Badisch tavern. Pull up a chair at one of the wooden tables for well-prepared regional faves like roast suckling pig, *Maultaschen* and *Sauerbraten* (beef pot roast with vinegar, onions and peppercorns).

Englers Weinkrügle GERMAN $$
(☑0761-383 115; Konviktstrasse 12; mains €9-19; ☺11.30am-2pm & 5.30pm-midnight Tue-Sun) A warm, woody Baden-style *Weinstube* with wisteria growing out front and regional flavours on the menu. The trout in various guises (for instance, with riesling or almond-butter sauce) is delicious.

Enoteca Trattoria ITALIAN $$
(☑0761-389 9130; www.enoteca-freiburg.de; Schwabentorplatz 6; mains €16-30; ☺6pm-midnight Mon-Sat) This is the trattoria of the two Enoteca twins (the more formal restaurant is at

Gerberau 21). The chef here hits the mark with authentic Italian dishes such as Taleggio ravioli with Frascati sauce and glazed pear.

Martin's Bräu PUB FOOD $$
(www.martinsbräu-freiburg.de; Fressgässle 1; mains €9-18; ⊙11am-midnight, to 2am Fri & Sat) Homebrewed pilsners wash down meaty snacks from ox-tongue salad to half-metre bratwursts. Lunch is a snip at €5.50. It's off Kaiser-Joseph-Strasse.

★ **Kreuzblume** INTERNATIONAL $$$
(✆0761-311 94; www.hotel-kreuzblume.de; Konviktstrasse 31; 2-/3-/4-course dinner €32.50/39/47; ⊙6-10pm Wed-Sun) On a flower-festooned lane, this pocket-sized restaurant with clever backlighting and a menu fizzing with bright, sunny flavours attracts a rather food-literate clientele. Each dish combines just a few hand-picked ingredients in bold and tasty ways. Service is tops.

Zirbelstube FRENCH $$$
(✆0761-210 60; www.colombi.de; Rotteckring 16; mains €45-59; ⊙noon-2pm & 7pm-midnight Mon-Sat) Freiburg's bastion of fine dining is this candlelit restaurant, decorated in warm Swiss pine. Chefs of exacting standards allow each ingredient to shine in specialities like Black Forest chateaubriand with red wine jus and chanterelles and Breton turbot filet with artichoke-octopus salsa – all perfectly matched with quality wines.

Wolfshöhle MEDITERRANEAN $$$
(✆0761-303 03; Konviktstrasse 8; mains €21-36, 3-course lunch/dinner €33/54; ⊙6-10pm Mon, noon-2pm & 6-10pm Tue-Sat) With tables set up on a pretty square, Wolfshöhle is a summer-evening magnet. The menu whisks you off on a gastro tour of the Mediterranean, with well-executed dishes such as Iberian pork with wild-garlic purée and scampi with saffron-infused risotto.

🍷 Drinking & Entertainment

Freiburg's restless student population keep steins a-swinging in the beer gardens and bars and clubs pumping until the wee hours.

Schlappen CAFE, PUB
(Löwenstrasse 2; ⊙11am-1am Mon-Wed, to 2am Thu, to 3am Fri & Sat, 3pm-1am Sun) In historic digs and crammed with antiques and vintage theatre posters, this evergreen pub has made the magic happen for generations of students. Check out the skeleton in the men's toilet. Summer terrace.

COLD FEET OR WEDDED BLISS?

As you wander the Altstadt, watch out for the gurgling *Bächle*, streamlets once used to water livestock and extinguish fires. Today they provide welcome relief for hot feet on sweltering summer days. Just be aware that you could get more than you bargained for: legend has it that if you accidentally step into the *Bächle*, you'll marry a Freiburger or a Freiburgerin.

Alte Wache WINE BAR
(Münsterplatz 38; ⊙10am-9pm Mon-Sat) Right on the square, this 18th-century guardhouse serves local Müller-Thurgau and Pinot noir wines at the tasting tables. If they sharpen your appetite, you can order tapas on Thursdays.

Hausbrauerei Feierling BEER GARDEN
(Gerberau 46; ⊙11am-midnight, to 1am Fri & Sat Mar-Oct) This stream-side beer garden is a relaxed spot to quaff a cold one under the chestnut trees in summer. Pretzels and sausages (snacks €3 to €9.50) soak up the malty brews.

Greiffenegg-Schlössle BEER GARDEN
(Schlossbergring 3; ⊙11am-midnight Mar-Oct) All of Freiburg is at your feet from this chestnut-shaded beer garden atop Schlossberg. Perfect sunset spot.

Isle of Innisfree PUB
(Atrium Auginerplatz; ⊙6pm-midnight Mon-Thu, 5pm-2am Fri, 4pm-2am Sat, 7pm-midnight Sun) Find Guinness and the craic at this lively Irish watering hole, with a weekly line-up of quizzes, karaoke and live music.

White Rabbit Club CLUB
(www.white-rabbit-club.de; Leopoldring 1; ⊙9pm-3am Mon-Thu, 10pm-5am Fri & Sat) A student wonderland of cheap beers, DJs and gigs. Things get even curiouser at Wednesday night's open jam sessions.

Jazzhaus LIVE MUSIC
(✆0761-349 73; www.jazzhaus.de; Schnewlinstrasse 1) Under the brick arches of a wine cellar, this venue hosts first-rate jazz, rock and world-music concerts (€20 to €30) at 7pm or 8pm at least a couple of nights a week (see the website for details). It morphs into a club from 11pm to 3am on Friday and Saturday nights.

ℹ Information

Available at the tourist office, the three-day WelcomeKarte, covering all public transport and the Schauinslandbahn, costs €25/15 per adult/child.

Police Station (Rotteckring) Freiburg's police station.

Post Office (Eisenbahnstrasse 58-62; ⊙ 8.30am-6.30pm Mon-Fri, 9am-2pm Sat) Main post office.

Tourist Office (☎ 0761-388 1880; www. freiburg.de; Rathausplatz 2-4; ⊙ 8am-8pm Mon-Fri, 9.30am-5pm Sat, 10.30am-3.30pm Sun) Pick up the three-day WelcomeKarte at Freiburg's central tourist office.

ℹ Getting There & Around

AIR

Freiburg shares **EuroAirport** (BSL; ☑ in France 03 89 90 31 11; www.euroairport.com) with Basel (Switzerland) and Mulhouse (France). Low-cost airline easyJet flies from here to destinations including London, Berlin, Rome and Alicante.

BICYCLE

Bike paths run along the Dreisam River, leading westward to Breisach and then into France.

Freiburg Bikes (☎ 0761-202 3426; Wentzingerstrasse 15; city bike 4hr/day €8/16, mountain/e-bike per day €20/25; ⊙ 9.30am-1pm & 2-7pm Mon-Sat, 10am-1pm & 2-6pm Sun, shorter hours in winter), in a glass-enclosed pavilion across the bridge from the Hauptbahnhof, rents bikes and sells cycling maps.

BUS

The **airport bus** (☎ 0761-500 500; www.freiburger-reisedienst.de; one-way/return €26/42) goes hourly from Freiburg's bus station to EuroAirport.

Südbaden Bus (www.suedbadenbus.de) and **RVF** (www.rvf.de) operate bus and train links to towns and villages throughout the southern Black Forest. Single tickets for one/two/three zones cost €2.20/3.80/5.40; a 24-hour Regio24 ticket costs €5.50 for one person and €11 for two to five people.

Bus and tram travel within Freiburg is operated by **VAG** (www.vag-freiburg.de) and charged at the one-zone rate. Buy tickets from the vending machines or from the driver and validate upon boarding.

CAR & MOTORCYCLE

The Frankfurt–Basel A5 passes just west of Freiburg. The scenic B31 leads east through the Höllen Valley to Lake Constance. The B294 goes north into the Black Forest.

Car-hire agencies include **Europcar** (☎ 0761-515 100; Lörracher Strasse 10) and **Avis** (☎ 0761-197 19; St Georgener Strasse 7).

About 1.5km south of Martinstor, there's unmetered parking on some side streets (eg Türkenlouisstrasse). Otherwise, your best bet is to park at a free Park & Ride, such as the one al Bissierstrasse, a 10-minute ride from the centre on tram 1.

TRAIN

Freiburg is on a major north–south rail corridor, with frequent departures for destinations such as Basel (€19 to €24.20, 45 minutes) and Baden-Baden (€18.10 to €25.80, 45 minutes to one hour). Freiburg is also the western terminus of the Höllentalbahn to Donaueschingen via Neustadt (€5.40, 38 minutes, twice an hour). There's a local connection to Breisach (€5.40, 26 minutes, at least hourly).

Schauinsland

Freiburg seems tiny as you drift up above the city and into a tapestry of meadows and forest on the **Schauinslandbahn** (return adult/concession €12/11, one way €8.50/8; ⊙ 9am-5pm Oct-Jun, to 6pm Jul-Sep) to the 1284m **Schauinsland peak** (www.bergwelt-schauinsland.de). The lift provides a speedy link between Freiburg and the Black Forest highlands.

Up top there's a lookout tower commanding astounding views to the Rhine Valley and Alps, plus walking, cross-country and cycling trails that allow you to capture the scenery from many angles. Or you can bounce downhill on the 8km off-road **scooter track** (www.rollerstrecke.de; €22; ⊙ 2pm & 5pm Sun May-Jun, Sat & Sun Jul & Sep-Oct, Wed-Sun Aug), one of Europe's longest; it takes around an hour from top to bottom station. To reach Schauinslandbahn from Freiburg, take tram 2 to Günterstal and then bus 21 to Talstation.

On its quiet perch above the rippling hills of the Black Forest, **Die Halde** (☎ 07602-944 70; www.halde.com; Oberried-Hofsgrund; d €124-157, mains €16-26.50; [P][@][☎]) is a rustic-chic retreat, with an open fire crackling in the bar, calm rooms dressed in local wood and a glass-walled spa overlooking the valley. Martin Hegar cooks market-fresh dishes from trout to wild boar with panache in the wood-panelled restaurant.

Steinwasen Park

Steinwasen Park   AMUSEMENT PARK
(www.steinwasen-park.de; Steinwasen 1; adult/concession €23/19; ⊙ 9am-6pm late Mar-early Nov) Buried deep in the forest, the nature-focused Steinwasen Park is a big hit with families. A trail weaves past animal-friendly

enclosures, home to wild boar, ibex and burrowing marmots. One of the top attractions is a 218m-long hanging bridge, one of the world's longest. Steinwasen also has a bobsled run and a handful of whizzy rides such as Gletscherblitz and River Splash.

Todtnauer Wasserfall

Todtnauer Wasserfall   WATERFALL
(⊙ daylight hours) **FREE** Heading south on the Freiburg–Feldberg road, you'll glimpse the roaring Todtnauer Wasserfall. While the 97m falls are not as high as those in Triberg, they're every bit as spectacular – tumbling down sheer rock faces and illuminating the velvety hills with their brilliance. Hike the zigzagging 9km trail to Aftersteg for views over the cataract. Take care on paths in winter when the falls often freeze solid. The waterfall car park is on the L126.

St Peter

⌨ 07660 / POP 2550
The folk of the bucolic village of St Peter, on the southern slopes of Mt Kandel (1243m), are deeply committed to time-honoured traditions. On religious holidays, villagers still proudly don colourful, handmade Trachten (folkloric costumes).

The most outstanding landmark is the **Ehemaliges Benedikterkloster** (Former Benedictine Abbey; guided tours adult/concession €6/2; ⊙ tours 11.30am Sun, 11am Tue, 2.30pm Thu), a rococo jewel designed by Peter Thumb of Vorarlberg. Many of the period's top artists collaborated on the sumptuous interior of the twin-towered red-sandstone church, including Joseph Anton Feuchtmayer, who carved the gilded Zähringer duke statues affixed to pillars. Guided tours (in German) to the monastery complex include the rococo library.

The **tourist office** (⌨ 07660-910 224; www.st-peter-schwarzwald.de; Klosterhof 11; ⊙ 9am-noon & 3-5pm Mon-Fri) is under the archway leading to the Klosterhof (the abbey courtyard). A nearby information panel shows room availability.

By public transport, the best way to get from Freiburg to St Peter is to take the train to Kirchzarten (13 minutes, twice hourly) and then bus 7216 (23 minutes, twice hourly). St Peter is on the **Schwarzwald Panoramastrasse**, a 70km-long route from Waldkirch (17km northeast of Freiburg) to Feldberg with giddy mountain views.

Breisach

⌨ 07667 / POP 14,500
Rising above vineyards and the Rhine, Breisach is where the Black Forest spills into Alsace. Given its geographical and cultural proximity to France, it's little surprise that the locals share their neighbours' passion for a good bottle of plonk.

From the cobbled streets lined with pastel-painted houses you'd never guess that 85% of the town was flattened in WWII, so successful has been the reconstruction. Vauban's star-shaped French fortress-town of Neuf-Brisach (New Breisach), which made the Unesco World Heritage list in 2008, sits 4km west of Breisach.

◎ Sights & Activities

St Stephansmünster   CHURCH
(⊙ 9am-5pm Mon-Sat) High above the centre, the Romanesque and Gothic St Stephansmünster shelters a faded fresco cycle, Martin Schongauer's *The Last Judgment* (1491), and a magnificent altar triptych (1526) carved from linden wood. From the tree-shaded square outside, the Schänzletreppe leads down to Gutgesellentor, the gate where Pope John XXIII was scandalously caught fleeing the Council of Constance in 1415.

BFS   BOAT TOUR
(www.bfs-info.de; Rheinuferstrasse; ⊙ Apr-Sep) Boat excursions along the Rhine are run by BFS. A one-hour harbour tour costs €9.

⌸ Sleeping

DJH Hostel   HOSTEL $
(⌨ 07667-7665; www.jugendherberge-breisach.de; Rheinuferstrasse 12; dm 1st/subsequent night €30.40/27) On the banks of the Rhine, this hostel has first-rate facilities, including a barbecue hut, volleyball court and access to the swimming pool next door.

❶ Information

Tourist Office (⌨ 07667-940 155; http://tourismus.breisach.de; Marktplatz 16; ⊙ 9am-12.30pm & 1.30-6pm Mon-Fri, 10am-3pm Sat) The tourist office can advise on wine tasting and private rooms in the area.

❶ Getting There & Around

Breisach's train station, 500m southeast of Marktplatz, serves Freiburg (€5.40, 25 minutes, at least hourly) and towns in the Kaiserstuhl. Buses go to Colmar, 22km west.

Breisach is a terrific base for free-wheeling over borders. Great rides include crossing the Rhine to the delightful French town of Colmar, or pedalling through terraced vineyards to Freiburg. Hire wheels from **Funbike** (☑ 07667-7733; Metzgergasse 1; 1/3 days €10/25; ⊙ 9am-noon & 5-7pm) opposite the tourist office.

Feldberg

☑ 07655 / POP 1880

At 1493m Feldberg is the Black Forest's highest mountain, and one of the few places here with downhill skiing. The actual mountaintop is treeless and not particularly attractive but on clear days the view southward towards the Alps is mesmerising.

Feldberg is also the name given to a cluster of five villages, of which Altglashütten is the hub.

Around 9km west of Altglashütten is Feldberg-Ort, in the heart of the 42-sq-km nature reserve that covers much of the mountain. Most of the ski lifts are here, including the scenic Feldbergbahn chairlift to the Bismarckdenkmal (Bismarck monument).

✦ Activities

The Feldberg ski area comprises 28 lifts, all accessible with one ticket. Four groomed cross-country trails are also available. To hire skis, look out for the signs reading 'Skiverleih' or enquire at the tourist office.

Feldbergbahn   CABLE CAR, VIEWPOINT
(www.feldbergbahn.de; adult/concession return €9.50/6.60; ⊙ 9am-5pm Jul-Sep, 9am-4.30pm May, Jun & Oct) This cable car whisks you to the 1450m summit of Feldberg in minutes. The panorama unfolding at the top reaches across the patchwork meadows and woods of the Black Forest all the way to the Vosges, Swiss and French Alps on clear days.

Haus der Natur   HIKING
(☑ 07676-933 610; www.naturpark-suedschwarzwald.de; Dr-Pilet-Spur 4; ⊙ 10am-5pm) The eco-conscious Haus der Natur can advise on some of the area's great hiking opportunities, such as the rewarding 12km Feldberg–Steig (p336) to Feldberg summit. In winter, Feldberg's snowy heights are ideal for a stomp through twinkling woods. Strap on snowshoes to tackle the pretty 3km Seebuck-Trail or the more challenging 9km Gipfel-Trail. The Haus der Natur rents lightweight snowshoes for €10/5 per day for adults/children.

⌂ Sleeping

Naturfreundehaus   HOSTEL $
(☑ 07655-336; www.jugendherberge-feldberg.de; Am Baldenweger Buck; dm €15) ✦ In a Black Forest farmhouse a 30-minute walk from Feldberg's summit, this back-to-nature hostel uses renewable energy and serves fairtrade and organic produce at breakfast (€6). Surrounding views of wooded hills and comfy, pine-clad dorms make this a great spot for hiking in summer, and skiing and snowshoeing in winter.

Landhotel Sonneck   HOTEL $$
(☑ 07655-211; www.sonneck-feldberg.de; Schwarzenbachweg 5; d €96-116; ☎) Immaculate, light-filled rooms with pine furnishings and balconies are features at this hotel. The quaint restaurant (mains €8 to €15) dishes up hearty local fare.

ⓘ Information

Tourist Office (Kirchgasse 1; ⊙ 8am-noon & 1-5pm Mon-Fri) Altglashütten's Rathaus harbours the tourist office, with stacks of information on activities and Nordic walking poles for rent.

ⓘ Getting There & Away

Bärental and Altglashütten are stops on the Dreiseenbahn, linking Titisee with Seebrugg (Schluchsee). From the train station in Bärental, bus 7300 makes trips at least hourly to Feldberg-Ort (€2.20, 21 minutes).

From late December until the end of the season, shuttle buses run by Feldberg SBG link Feldberg and Titisee with the ski lifts (free with a lift ticket or Gästekarte).

If you're driving, take the B31 (Freiburg–Donaueschingen) to Titisee, then the B317. To get to Altglashütten, head down the B500 from Bärental.

Titisee-Neustadt

☑ 07651 / POP 11,860

Titisee is a cheerful summertime playground with a name that makes English-speaking travellers giggle. The shimmering blue-green glacial lake, ringed by forest, has everyone diving for their cameras.

✦ Activities

The forest trails around Titisee are hugely popular for Nordic walking, which, for the uninitiated, is walking briskly with poles to simultaneously exercise the upper body and legs. Snow transforms Titisee into a winter wonderland and a cross-country skiing magnet, with *Loipen* (tracks) threading through the hills and woods, including a 3km floodlit track for a starlit skate. The tourist office map highlights cross-country and Nordic walking trails in the area.

Seepromenade   WALKING, WATER SPORTS
Wander along the flowery Seestrasse promenade and you'll soon leave the crowds and made-in-China cuckoo clocks behind to find secluded bays ideal for swimming and picnicking. A lap of the lake is 7km. A laid-back way to appreciate its soothing beauty is to hire a rowing boat or pedalo at one of the set-ups along the lakefront; expect to pay around €6 per hour.

Strandbad Titisee   SWIMMING
(Strandbadstrasse 1; adult/concession €3.50/1.90; ☺9am-7pm May-Sep) This lakefront lido has a pool and children's pool, a slide, floating raft and a volleyball area, as well as lawns for sunbathing. You can also rent kayaks and stand-up paddle boards here for €10/18 per half/full hour.

Badeparadies   SPA
(www.badeparadies-schwarzwald.de; Am Badeparadies 1; 3hr €18, incl sauna complex €22; ☺10am-10pm Mon-Thu, 10am-11pm Fri, 9am-10pm Sat & Sun) This huge, glass-canopied leisure and wellness centre is a magnet year-round. You can lounge, cocktail in hand, by palm-fringed lagoons in Palmenoase, race down white-knuckle slides with gaggles of overexcited kids in Galaxy, or strip off in themed saunas with waterfalls and Black Forest views in the adults-only Wellnessoase.

🛏 Sleeping & Eating

Neubierhäusle   PENSION $
(☑07651-8230; www.neubierhaeusle.de; Neustädterstrasse 79; d €74-94, apt €134-174; P🐾) Big forest views, piny air and pastures on the doorstep – this farmhouse is the perfect country retreat. Dressed in local wood, the light-filled rooms are supremely comfy, while apartments have space for families. Your hosts lay on a hearty breakfast spread and you can help yourself to free tea and fruit. It's on the L156, 3km northeast of the station.

Action Forest Active Hotel   GUESTHOUSE $$
(☑07651-825 60; www.action-forest-hotel.de; Neustädter Strasse 41; s €60-75, d €100-130, tr €130-180, q €160-230; P🐾) You can't miss this green-fronted guesthouse, snuggled

up against the forest. It's run by a friendly family and contains spacious, light-filled rooms fitted out with country-style pine furnishings. It makes a great base for outdoorsy holidays, offering the whole shebang of activities – a climbing park, bike academy, winter sports school, guided hikes and stand-up paddle boarding.

Alemannenhof   HOTEL $$$
(☑07652-911 80; www.hotel-alemannenhof.de; Bruderhalde 21, Hinterzarten am Titisee; d €129-259; P🐾🌊) A pool, private beach and contemporary rooms with transparent shower stalls and balconies overlooking Titisee await at this farmhouse-style hotel. Opening onto a lakefront terrace, the all-pine restaurant (mains €22 to €34) serves regional cuisine with a twist, such as local beef with potato-rosemary purée and wild-garlic pasta.

❶ Information

Tourist Office (☑07652-1206 8120; www.titisee-neustadt.de; Strandbadstrasse 4; ☺9am-6pm Mon-Fri, 10am-1pm & 3-6pm Sat, 10am-1pm Sun) The tourist office in the Kurhaus, 500m southwest of the train station, stocks walking and cycling maps.

❶ Getting There & Around

Train routes include the twice-hourly Höllentalbahn to Freiburg (€5.40, 40 minutes) and hourly services to Donaueschingen (€10, 50 minutes), Feldberg (€2.20, 12 minutes) and Schluchsee (€2.20, 22 minutes).

From Titisee train station, there are frequent services on bus 7257 to Schluchsee (€2.20, 40 minutes) and bus 7300 to Feldberg–Bärental (€2.20, 13 minutes).

Ski-Hirt (☑07651-922 80; Titiseestrasse 28; ☺9am-6.30pm Mon-Fri, 9am-4pm Sat) rents reliable bikes and ski equipment, and can supply details on local cycling options.

Schluchsee
☑07656 / POP 2540
Photogenically poised above its namesake petrol-blue lake – the Black Forest's largest – and rimmed by forest, Schluchsee tempts you outdoors with pursuits such as swimming, windsurfing, hiking, cycling and, ahem, skinny-dipping from the secluded bays on the western shore. The otherwise sleepy resort jolts to life with sun-seekers in summer and cross-country skiers in winter.

KAISERSTUHL

Squeezed between the Black Forest and French Vosges, these low-lying volcanic hills in the Upper Rhine Valley yield highly quaffable wines, including fruity *Spätburgunder* (Pinot noir) and *Grauburgunder* (Pinot gris) varieties.

The grapes owe their quality to a unique microclimate, hailed as Germany's sunniest, and fertile loess (clay and silt) soil that retains heat during the night. Nature enthusiasts should look out for rarities like sand lizards, praying mantis and European bee-eaters.

The Breisach tourist office can advise on cellar tours, wine tastings, bike paths like the 55km **Kaiserstuhl-Tour** circuit, and trails such as the **Winzerweg** (Wine Growers' Trail), an intoxicating 15km hike from Achkarren to Riegel.

The Kaiserstuhlbahn does a loop around the Kaiserstuhl. Stops (where you may have to change trains) include Sasbach, Endingen, Riegel and Gottenheim.

Vitra Design Museum (www.design-museum.de; Charles-Eames-Strasse 1, Weil am Rhein; adult/concession €10/8, architectural tour €13/11; ⊙10am-6pm) Sharp angles contrast with graceful swirls on Frank Gehry's strikingly postmodern Vitra Design Museum. The blindingly white edifice hosts thought-provoking contemporary design exhibitions. Buildings on the nearby Vitra campus, designed by prominent architects like Nicholas Grimshaw, Zaha Hadid and Alvaro Siza, can be visited on a two-hour architectural tour, held in English at noon and 2pm daily.

Europa-Park (www.europapark.de; adult/concession €42.50/37; ⊙9am-6pm Apr-early Nov, to 8pm Aug–mid-Sep, 11am-7pm late Nov-early Jan) Germany's largest theme park, 35km north of Freiburg near Rust, is Europe in miniature. Get soaked fjord-rafting in Scandinavia before nipping across to England to race at Silverstone, or Greece to ride the water roller coaster Poseidon. Aside from white-knuckle thrills, Welt der Kinder amuses tots with labyrinths and Viking ships. When Mickey waltzed off to Paris, Europa-Park even got its own mousy mascot, Euromaus.

Shuttle buses (hourly in the morning) link Ringsheim train station, on the Freiburg–Offenburg line, with the park. By car, take the A5 exit to Rust (57b).

🏃 Activities

Aqua Fun Strandbad   SWIMMING
(Strandbadstrasse; adult/concession €4/2.70; ⊙9am-7pm Jun-Sep) Popular with families, this lakefront lido has a heated pool, water slide and rapid river, sandy beach and volleyball court.

T Toth   BOAT TOUR
(www.seerundfahrten.de) T Toth runs boat tours around Schluchsee, with stops in Aha, Seebrugg and the Strandbad. An hour-long round trip costs €9.50 (less for single stops). You can hire rowing boats and pedalos for €5/8 per half/full hour.

🛏 Sleeping & Eating

Decent beds are slim pickings in Schluchsee, though there are a few good-value pensions and farmstays – ask the tourist office.

Gasthof Hirschen   GUESTHOUSE $
(☎07656-989 40; www.hirschen-fischbach.de; Schluchseestrasse 9; s €49-51, d €74-92; P🐕) It's worth going the extra mile to this farmhouse prettily perched on a hillside in Fischbach, 4km north of Schluchsee. The simple, quiet rooms are a good-value base for summer hiking and modest winter skiing. There's also a sauna, playground and a restaurant (mains €13 to €21) dishing up regional fare.

Seehof   INTERNATIONAL $$
(☎07656-988 9965; Kirchsteige 4; mains €8-18; ⊙11.30am-10.30pm) An inviting spot for a bite to eat, with a terrace overlooking the lake, Seehof has a menu packed with local fish and meat mains, salads, pizzas and ice cream.

ℹ Information

The train tracks and the B500 shadow the lake's eastern shore between the lakefront and the Schluchsee's town centre. The lake's western shore is accessible only by bike or on foot.

Tourist Office (☎07652-1206 8500; www.schluchsee.de; Fischbacher Strasse 7, Haus des Gastes; ⊙8am-5pm Mon-Thu, 9am-5pm Fri) Situated 150m uphill from the church, with maps and info on activities and accommodation.

❶ Getting There & Around

Trains go hourly to Feldberg–Altglashütten (€2.10, 11 minutes) and Titisee (€2.10, 22 minutes). Bus 7257 links Schluchsee three or four times daily with the Neustadt and Titisee train stations (€2.10, 40 minutes).

City, mountain and e-bikes can be rented for €11/12/23 per day at **Müllers** (An der Staumauer 1; ⊙10am-6pm Apr-Oct). An hour's pedalo/rowing boat/motor boat hire costs €8/8/17.

Triberg

📳 07722 / POP 5000

Home to Germany's highest waterfall, heir to the original 1915 black forest gateau recipe and nesting ground of the world's biggest cuckoos, Triberg leaves visitors reeling with superlatives. It was here that in bleak winters past folk huddled in snowbound farmhouses to carve the clocks that would drive the world cuckoo, and here that in a flash of brilliance the waterfall was harnessed to power the country's first electric street lamps in 1884.

❷ Sights & Activities

★ **Triberger Wasserfälle** WATERFALL
(adult/concession/family €4/3.50/9.50; ⊙9am-7pm Mar-early Nov, 25-30 Dec) Niagara they ain't but Germany's highest waterfalls do exude their own wild romanticism. The Gutach River feeds the seven-tiered falls, which drop a total of 163m and are illuminated until 10pm.

A paved trail accesses the cascades. Pick up a bag of peanuts at the ticket counter to feed the tame squirrels.

1. Weltgrösste Kuckucksuhr LANDMARK
(First World's Largest Cuckoo Clock; 📳 07722-4689; www.1weltgroesstekuckucksuhr.de; Untertalstrasse 28, Schonach; adult/concession €1.20/0.60; ⊙9am-noon & 1-6pm) The 'world's oldest-largest cuckoo clock' kicked into gear in 1980 and took local clockmaker Joseph Dold three years to build by hand. A Dold family member is usually around to the explain the mechanism.

Haus der 1000 Uhren CLOCK MUSEUM
(www.hausder1000uhren.de; Hauptstrasse 79; ⊙9.30am-6pm summer, to 5.30pm winter) A glockenspiel bashes out melodies and a cuckoo greets his fans with a hopelessly croaky squawk on the hour at the kitschy House of 1000 Clocks, a wonderland of clocks from traditional to trendy. The latest

quartz models feature a sensor that sends the cuckoo to sleep after dark!

Sanitas Spa SPA
(📳 07722-860 20; www.sanitas-spa.de; Gartenstrasse 24; 2hr pass €15, half-day €26-30, full-day €45-50; ⊙9.30am-8pm) Fronted by wraparound windows overlooking Triberg's forested hills, Parkhotel Wehrle's day spa is gorgeous. This is a serene spot to wind down, with its spacily lit kidney-shaped pool, exquisitely tiled hammams, steam rooms, whirlpool and waterbed meditation room. Treatments vary from rhassoul clay wraps to reiki. Admission is cheaper on weekdays. Towel and robe hire is available for €8.

🛌 Sleeping & Eating

Kukucksnest B&B $
(📳 07722-869 487; Wallfahrtstrasse 15; d €64) Above the shop of master woodcarver Gerald Burger, is the beautiful nest he has carved for his guests, featuring blonde-wood rooms with flat-screen TVs. The *Wurzelsepp* (faces carved into fir tree roots) by the entrance supposedly ward off evil spirits.

★ **Parkhotel Wehrle** HISTORIC HOTEL $$$
(📳 07722-860 20; www.parkhotel-wehrle.de; Gartenstrasse 24; s €95-105, €145-179; 🅿🛜🌊) This 400-year-old hotel has a recommended integrated day spa. Often with a baroque or Biedermeier touch, quarters are roomy and beautifully furnished with antiques; the best have Duravit whirlpool tubs. Hemingway once waxed lyrical about the trout he ordered at the hotel's venerable **restaurant** (www.parkhotel-wehrle.de; Gartenstrasse 24; mains €13-32; ⊙6-9pm daily, noon-2pm Sun).

★ **Café Schäfer** CAFE $
(📳 07722-4465; www.cafe-schaefer-triberg.de; Hauptstrasse 33; cake €3-4; ⊙9am-6pm Mon, Tue, Thu & Fri, 8am-6pm Sat, 11am-6pm Sun) Confectioner Claus Schäfer uses the original 1915 recipe for black forest gateau to prepare this sinful treat that layers chocolate cake perfumed with cherry brandy, whipped cream and sour cherries and wraps it all in more cream and shaved chocolate. Trust us, it's worth the calories.

❶ Information

Triberg's main drag is the B500, which runs more or less parallel to the Gutach River. The town's focal point is the Marktplatz, a steep 1.2km uphill walk from the Bahnhof.

Triberg markets itself as Das Ferienland (The Holiday Region, www.dasferienland.de).

> **DON'T MISS**
>
> ## DRIVE TIME
>
> The Schwarzwald may be a forest but it sure is a big 'un and you'll need a car to reach its out-of-the-way corners.
>
> **Schwarzwald-Hochstrasse** (Black Forest Highway; www.schwarzwaldhochstrasse.de) Swoon over views of the mist-wreathed Vosges Mountains, heather-flecked forests and glacial lakes like Mummelsee on this high-altitude road, meandering 60km from Baden-Baden to Freudenstadt on the B500.
>
> **Badische Weinstrasse** (Baden Wine Road; www.deutsche-weinstrassen.de) From Baden-Baden south to Lörrach, this 160km route corkscrews through the red-wine vineyards of Ortenau, the Pinot noir of Kaiserstuhl and Tuniberg, and the white-wine vines of Markgräflerland.
>
> **Schwarzwald-Tälerstrasse** (Black Forest Valley Road) What scenery! Twisting 100km from Rastatt to Alpirsbach, this road dips into the forest-cloaked hills and half-timbered towns of the Murg and Kinzig valleys.
>
> **Deutsche Uhrenstrasse** (German Clock Road; www.deutscheuhrenstrasse.de) A 320km loop starting in Villingen-Schwenningen that revolves around the story of clockmaking in the Black Forest. Stops include Furtwangen and cuckoo-crazy Triberg.
>
> **Grüne Strasse** (Green Road; www.gruene-strasse.de) Linking the Black Forest with the Rhine Valley and French Vosges, this 160km route zips through Kirchzarten, Freiburg, Breisach, Colmar and Münster.

Tourist Office (☑ 07722-866 490; www.triberg.de; Wallfahrtstrasse 4; ◷ 9am-5pm Mon-Fri, 10am-5pm Sat & Sun) Inside the Schwarzwald-Museum. Stocks walking (€3), cross-country ski trail (€2) and mountain bike (€6.90) maps.

❶ Getting There & Away

The Schwarzwaldbahn train line loops southeast to Konstanz (€23.50, 1½ hours, hourly), and northwest to Offenburg (€12.10, 46 minutes, hourly).

Bus 7150 travels north through the Gutach and Kinzig Valleys to Offenburg; bus 7265 heads south to Villingen via St Georgen. Local buses operate between the Bahnhof and Marktplatz, and to the nearby town of Schonach (hourly).

Stöcklewaldturm

Triberg's waterfall is the trailhead for an attractive 6.5km walk to Stöcklewaldturm (1070m). A steady trudge through spruce forest and pastures brings you to this 19th-century **lookout tower** (admission €0.50; ◷ 10am-8pm Wed-Mon), where the 360-degree views stretch from the Swabian Alps to the snowcapped Alps. Footpaths head off in all directions from the summit, where the woodsy **cafe** (snacks €2.50-7; ◷ 10am-8pm Wed-Mon) is an inviting spot for a beer and snack or, in winter, hot chocolate. The car park on the L175 is a 10-minute stroll from the tower.

Martinskapelle

Named after the tiny chapel at the head of the Breg Valley, **Martinskapelle** attracts cross-country skiers in winter and hikers when the snow melts. The steep road up to the 1100m peak negotiates some pretty hairy switchbacks, swinging past wood-shingle farmhouses that cling to forested slopes.

To immerse yourself in the solace and wonderful views, stay the night at family-run **Höhengasthaus Kolmenhof** (☑ 07723-931 00; www.kolmenhof.de; An der Donauquelle; s/d €55/88; ☒☏☂☗). Sitting right at the main source of the Danube, the guesthouse has e-bike rental, a sauna for post-hiking or skiing relaxation and a rustic restaurant (mains €9 to €19). The speciality is fresh trout, served smoked, roasted in almond butter or poached in white wine.

Bus 7270 runs roughly hourly from the Marktplatz in Triberg to Escheck (€2.10, 20 minutes); from here it's a 4.5km walk to Martinskapelle. If you're driving, take the B500 from Triberg following signs to Schwarzenbach, Weissenbach and the K5730 to Martinskapelle.

Villingen-Schwenningen

☑ 07721 / POP 81.020

Villingen and Schwenningen trip simultaneously off the tongue, yet each town has its own flavour and history. Villingen once belonged to the Grand Duchy of Baden and Schwenningen to the duchy of Württemberg, conflicting allegiances that apparently can't be reconciled. Villingen, it must be said, is the more attractive of the twin towns.

Encircled by impenetrable walls that look as though they were built by the mythical local giant Romäus, Villingen's Altstadt is a late-medieval time capsule, with cobbled streets and handsome patrician houses. Though locals nickname it the *Städtle* (little town), the name seems inappropriate during February's mammoth weeklong *Fasnet* celebrations.

◎ Sights & Activities

Münster
CATHEDRAL

(Münsterplatz; ⊙9am-6pm) The main crowd-puller in Villingen's Altstadt is the red-sandstone, 12th-century Münster with its disparate spires: one overlaid with coloured tiles, the other spiky and festooned with gargoyles. The Romanesque portals with haut-relief doors depict dramatic biblical scenes.

Münsterplatz
SQUARE

The Münsterplatz is presided over by the step-gabled Altes Rathaus (Old Town Hall) and Klaus Ringwald's Münsterbrunnen, a bronze fountain and a tongue-in-cheek portrayal of characters that have shaped Villingen's history. The square throngs with activity on Wednesday and Saturday mornings when market stalls are piled high with local bread, meat, cheese, fruit and flowers.

Franziskaner Museum
MUSEUM

(Rietgasse 2; adult/concession €5/3; ⊙1-5pm Tue-Sat, 11am-5pm Sun) Next to the 13th-century Riettor and occupying a former Franciscan monastery, the Franziskaner Museum skips merrily through Villingen's history and heritage. Standouts include Celtic artefacts unearthed at Magdalenenberg, 30 minutes' walk south of Villingen's centre. Dating to 616 BC, the mystery-enshrouded site is one of the largest Hallstatt burial chambers ever discovered in Central Europe, and is shaded by a 1000-year-old oak tree.

Spitalgarten
GARDENS

Tucked behind the Franziskaner is the Spitalgarten, a park flanked by the original city walls. Here your gaze will be drawn to Romäusturm, a lofty 13th-century thieves' tower named after fabled local leviathan Remigius Mans (Romäus for short).

Kneippbad
SWIMMING

(Am Kneippbad 1; adult/child €4.20/2.80; ⊙6.30am-8pm Mon-Fri, 8am-8pm Sat & Sun mid-May–early Sep) If the sun's out, take a 3km walk northwest of the Altstadt to this forest lido, a family magnet with its outdoor pools, slides and volleyball courts.

🛏 Sleeping & Eating

Haus Bächle
GUESTHOUSE $

(⌨07721-597 29; Am Kneippbad 5; s/d €16/32; P) This half-timbered house overlooks the flowery Kurgarten. The tidy rooms are an absolute bargain and the Kneippbad is next door for early-morning swims.

Rindenmühle
HOTEL $$

(⌨07721-886 80; www.rindenmuehle.de; Am Kneippbad 9; s €78-105, d €120-145; P🐾) Next to the Kneippbad, this converted watermill houses one of Villingen's smartest hotels, with forest walks right on its doorstep. Rooms are slick and decorated in muted hues. In the restaurant (mains €26 to €36), Martin Weisser creates award-winning flavours using home-grown organic produce, including chickens, geese and herbs from his garden.

Zampolli
CAFE $

(Rietstrasse 33; ice-cream cone €1; ⊙9.30am-10.30pm Mon-Sat, 10.30am-10.30pm Sun Feb–mid-Nov) For an espresso or creamy gelati, head to this Italian-run cafe. By night, the pavement terrace facing Riettor is a laid-back spot for a drink.

Schlachthof
GERMAN $$

(⌨07721-878 7935; www.schlachthof-vs.de; Schlachthausstrasse 11; mains €11-22; ⊙11.45am-2pm & 6pm-midnight Tue-Fri, 6pm-midnight Sat, 11.45am-2pm Sun; 🚼) Wine-red walls, globe lights and wood panelling set the scene at this smart brasserie-style restaurant, a 10-minute stroll south of the Altstadt. The cooking is a regional-Mediterranean mix, with dishes such as chicken breast in rosemary butter with market veg and *Tafelspitz* (boiled beef). The €8.40 two-course lunch is a bargain.

❶ Information

Post Office (Bahnhofstrasse 6)

Villingen Tourist Office (⌨07721-822 525; www.tourismus-vs.de; Rietgasse 2; ⊙10am-5pm Mon-Sat, 11am-5pm Sun) In the Franziskaner Museum. You can pick up the itour audioguide in English; up to three hours costs €5. E-bikes are also available for rent for €10/20 per half/full day.

LOCAL KNOWLEDGE

CLAUS SCHÄFER, CONFECTIONER

Want to whip up your own black forest gateau back home? Claus Schäfer reveals how.

All About Cake Baking a black forest gateau isn't rocket science but it involves time, practice and top-quality ingredients. Eat the cake the day you make it, when it is freshest, and never freeze it or you will lose the aroma.

Secrets in the Mix Whip the cream until silky, blend in gelatine and two shots of quality kirsch. Mine comes from a local distillery and is 56% proof. The compote needs tangy cherries, sugar, cherry juice and a pinch of cinnamon. The bottom layer of sponge should be twice as thick as the other two, so it can support the compote without collapsing.

Finishing Touches These are important: spread the gateau with cream, then decorate with piped cream, cherries, chocolate shavings and a dusting of icing sugar.

Other Regional Flavours When in the Black Forest, try the fresh trout, smoked ham and *Kirschwasser* sold locally by farmers. The quality is higher and prices lower than elsewhere.

❶ Getting There & Around

Villingen's Bahnhof is on the scenic Schwarzwaldbahn train line from Konstanz (€19.80, 70 minutes) to Triberg (€6.10, 22 minutes) and Offenburg (€17.90, 70 minutes). Trains to Stuttgart (€27.90 to €29.50, 1¾ hours) involve a change in Rottweil, and to Freiburg (€19.80 to €29.60, two hours) a change in Donaueschingen.

From Villingen, buses 7265 and 7270 make regular trips north to Triberg. Frequent buses (eg line 1) link Villingen with Schwenningen.

Villingen-Schwenningen is just west of the A81 Stuttgart–Singen motorway and is also crossed by the B33 to Triberg and the B27 to Rottweil.

Rottweil

📞 0741 / POP 25,660

Baden-Württemberg's oldest town is the strapline of Roman-rooted Rottweil, founded in AD 73. But a torrent of bad press about the woofer with a nasty nip means that most folk readily associate the town with the Rottweiler, which was indeed bred here as a hardy butchers' dog until recently. Fear not, the Rottweiler locals are much tamer.

The sturdy 13th-century Schwarzes Tor is the gateway to Hauptstrasse and the well-preserved Altstadt, a cluster of redroofed, pastel-painted houses. Nearby at No 6, the curvaceous Hübschen Winkel will make you look twice with its 45-degree kink. Just west on Münsterplatz, the late Romanesque Münster-Heiliges-Kreuz features some striking Gothic stonework and ribbed vaulting. Equally worth a peek is the **Roman bath** (Hölderstrasse; ⊙ daylight hours) **FREE**, a

45m-by-42m bathing complex unearthed in 1967, about 1km south of the Altstadt.

The **tourist office** (📞 0741-494 280; www.rottweil.de; Hauptstrasse 21; ⊙ 9.30am-5.30pm Mon-Fri, 9.30am-12.30pm Sat) can advise on accommodation, tours and biking the Neckartal-Radweg.

Rottweil is just off the A81 Stuttgart–Singen motorway. Trains run at least hourly to Stuttgart (€22.70, 1½ hours) and Villingen (€3.40, 25 minutes).

Unterkirnach

📞 07721 / POP 2730

Nestled among velvety green hills, lowkey Unterkirnach appeals to families and outdoorsy types. Kids can slide and climb to their heart's content at the all-weather play centre **Spielscheune** (Schlossbergweg 4; admission €4.50; ⊙ 2-7pm Mon-Fri, 11am-7pm Sat & Sun), or toddle uphill to the **farm** to meet inquisitive goats and Highland cattle (feeding time is 3pm). In summer, the village is a great starting point for forest **hikes**, with 130km of marked walking trails, while in winter there are 50km of *Loipen* (cross-country ski tracks) and some terrific slopes to sledge.

Picturesquely perched above Unterkirnach, **Ackerloch Grillschopf** (www.ackerloch.de; Unteres Ackerloch; light meals €4-11; ⊙ 11.30am-midnight Wed-Mon) is a rickety barn, brimming with rustic warmth in winter and with a beer garden overlooking a broad valley in summer. Occasionally there is a suckling pig roasting on the spit and you can grill your own steaks and sausages on the barbecue.

Bus 61 runs roughly every hour between Unterkirnach and Villingen (€3.30, 18 minutes).

LAKE CONSTANCE

Nicknamed the *schwäbische Meer* (Swabian Sea), Lake Constance is Central Europe's third-largest lake and it straddles three countries: Germany, Austria and Switzerland. Formed by the Rhine Glacier during the last ice age and fed and drained by that same sprightly river today, this whopper of a lake measures 63km long by 14km wide and up to 250m deep. There is a certain novelty effect in the fact that this is the only place in the world where you can wake up in Germany, cycle across to Switzerland for lunch and make it to Austria in time for afternoon tea, strudel and snapshots of the Alps.

Taking in meadows and vineyards, orchards and wetlands, beaches and Alpine foothills, the lake's landscapes are like a 'greatest hits' of European scenery. Culture? It's all here, from baroque churches to Benedictine abbeys, Stone Age dwellings to Roman forts, and medieval castles to zeppelins.

Come in spring for blossoms and autumn for new wine, fewer crowds and top visibility when the warm *föhn* blows. Summers are crowded, but best for swimming and camping. Almost everything shuts from November to February, when fog descends and the first snowflakes dust the Alps.

ⓘ Getting There & Around

The most enjoyable way to cross the lake is by ferry. Konstanz is the main hub but Meersburg and Friedrichshafen also have plentiful ferry options.

Although most towns have a train station (Meersburg is an exception), in some cases buses provide the only land connections. **Euregio Bodensee** (www.euregiokarte.com), which groups all Lake Constance–area public transport, publishes a free *Fahrplan* with schedules for all train, bus and ferry services.

The **Euregio Bodensee Tageskarte** (www. euregiokarte.com; €18/24/31 for one/two/all zones) gets you all-day access to land transport around Lake Constance, including areas in Austria and Switzerland. It's sold at train stations and ferry docks. Children pay half price.

CAR FERRY

The roll-on roll-off **Konstanz–Meersburg car ferry** (www.sw.konstanz.de; car up to 4m incl driver/bicycle/pedestrian €9.30/5.20/2.80) runs 24 hours a day, except when high water levels prevent it from docking. The ferry runs every 15 minutes from 5.35am to 8.50pm, every 30 minutes from 8.50pm to midnight and every hour from midnight to 5.35am. The crossing, affording superb views from the top deck, takes 15 minutes.

DON'T MISS

CELEBRATE THE FIFTH SEASON

Boisterous and totally bonkers, the **Swabian-Alemannic Fasnacht** or *Fasnet* (not to be confused with Carnival) is a 500-year-old rite to banish winter and indulge in pre-Lenten feasting, parades, flirting and all-night drinkathons. Starting on Epiphany, festivities reach a crescendo the week before Ash Wednesday. Dress up to join the party, memorise a few sayings to dodge the witches, and catch the flying sausages – anything's possible, we swear. For *Fasnacht* at its traditional best, try the following:

Rottweil Fasnacht (www.narrenzunft.rottweil.de; Rottweil) At Monday's 8am *Narrensprung*, thousands of jester-like *Narros* in baroque masks ring through Baden-Württemberg's oldest town. Look out for the devil-like Federhannes and the Guller riding a cockerel.

Schramberg Fasnacht (www.narrenzunft-schramberg.de; Schramberg) Parade protagonists include the *hoorige Katz* (hairy cat) and the hopping Hans. Even more spectacular, however, is Da-Bach-Na-Fahrt, where characters hurtle down the river in wooden bathtubs.

Elzach Fasnacht (www.schuttig.info; Elzach) *Trallaho!* Wearing a hand-carved mask and a tricorn hat adorned with snail shells, *Schuttige* (ghoulish masked characters) dash through Elzach's streets cracking *Saublodere* (pig bladders) – dodge them unless you wish for many children! Sunday's torchlit parade and Shrove Tuesday's afternoon *Schutigumzug* are the must-sees.

WORTH A TRIP

NATURPARK OBERE DONAU

Upper Danube Valley Nature Reserve (www.naturpark-obere-donau.de) Theatrically set against limestone, cave-riddled cliffs, dappled with pine and beech woods that are burnished gold in autumn, and hugging the Danube's banks, the Upper Danube Valley Nature Reserve bombards you with rugged splendour. Stick to the autobahn, however, and you'll be none the wiser. To fully explore the nature reserve, slip into a bicycle saddle or walking boots, and hit the trail.

One of the finest stretches is between Fridingen and Beuron, a 12.5km ridge-top walk of three to four hours. The signposted, easy-to-navigate trail runs above ragged cliffs, affording eagle's-eye views of the meandering Danube, which has almost 2850km to go before emptying into the Black Sea. The vertigo-inducing outcrop of Laibfelsen is a great picnic spot. From here, the path dips in and out of woodlands and meadows flecked with purple thistles. In Beuron the big draw is the working Benedictine abbey, one of Germany's oldest, dating to 1077. The lavish stucco-and-fresco church is open to visitors. See the website www.beuron.de for more details.

Fridingen and Beuron lie on the L277, 45km east of Villingen.

The dock in Konstanz, served by local bus 1, is 4km northeast of the centre along Mainaustrasse. In Meersburg, car ferries leave from a dock 400m northwest of the old town.

PASSENGER FERRY

The most useful lines, run by German **BSB** (www.bsb-online.com) and Austrian **OBB** (www.bodenseeschifffahrt.at), link Konstanz with ports such as Meersburg (€5.90, 30 minutes), Friedrichshafen (€12.70, 1¾ hours), Lindau (€16.70, three hours) and Bregenz (€17.80, 3½ hours); children aged six to 15 years pay half-price. The website lists timetables in full.

Der Katamaran (www.der-katamaran.de; adult/6-14yr €10.20/5.10) is a sleek passenger service that takes 50 minutes to make the Konstanz–Friedrichshafen crossing (hourly from 6am to 7pm, plus hourly from 8pm to midnight on Fridays and Saturdays from mid-May to early October).

Konstanz

[☏] 07531 / POP 84,690

Sidling up to the Swiss border, bisected by the Rhine and outlined by the Alps, Konstanz sits prettily on the northwestern shore of Lake Constance. Roman emperors, medieval traders and the bishops of the 15th-century Council of Constance have all left their mark on this alley-woven town, mercifully spared from the WWII bombings that obliterated other German cities.

When the sun comes out, Konstanz is a feel-good university town with a lively buzz and upbeat bar scene, particularly in the cobbled Altstadt and the harbour where the voluptuous *Imperia* turns. In summer the

locals, nicknamed *Seehasen* (lake hares), head outdoors to the leafy promenade and enjoy lazy days in lakefront lidos.

⊙ Sights

★**Münster**   CATHEDRAL

(tower adult/child €2/1; ⊙10am-6pm Mon-Sat, 10am-6pm Sun, tower 10am-5pm Mon-Sat, 12.30-5.30pm Sun) Crowned by a filigreed spire and looking proudly back on 1000 years of history, the sandstone Münster was the church of the diocese of Konstanz until 1821. Its interior is an architectural potpourri of Romanesque, Gothic, Renaissance and baroque styles. Standouts include the 15th-century Schnegg, an ornate spiral staircase in the northern transept, to the left of which a door leads to the 1000-year-old crypt. From the crypt's polychrome chapel, you enter the sublime Gothic cloister.

On cloudless days, it's worth ascending the tower for broad views over the city and the lake.

Römersiedlung   RUIN

(Münsterplatz; tour €1; ⊙6pm Sun) The glass pyramid in front of the Münster shelters the Römersiedlung, the 3rd-century-AD remains of the Roman fort Constantia, which gave the city its name. You'll only get a sneak peek from above, so join one of the guided tours that begin at the tourist office for a touch of magic as a staircase opens from the cobbles and leads down to the ruins.

Rathaus   HISTORIC BUILDING

(City Hall; Kanzleistrasse) Slightly south of the Münster, the flamboyantly frescoed Renais-

Lake Constance

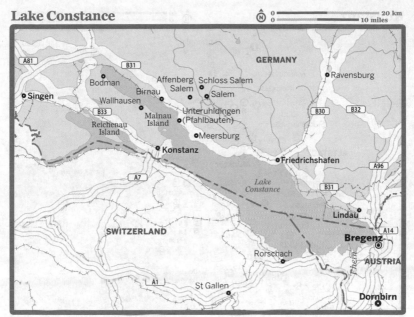

sance Rathaus occupies the former linen weavers' guildhall. Behind it you'll find a peaceful arcaded courtyard.

Niederburg
AREA
Best explored on foot, Konstanz' cobbled heart, Niederburg, stretches north from the Münster to the Rhine. The twisting lanes lined with half-timbered houses are the place to snoop around galleries and antique shops.

Rosgartenmuseum
MUSEUM
(www.rosgartenmuseum-konstanz.de; Rosgarten strasse 3-5; adult/concession €3/1.50, 1st Sun of the month & after 2pm Wed free; ⊘10am-6pm Tue-Fri, 10am-5pm Sat & Sun) The one-time butchers' guildhall now harbours the Rosgartenmuseum, spotlighting regional art and history, with an emphasis on medieval panel painting and sculpture.

Sea Life
AQUARIUM
(www.visitsealife.com/konstanz; Hafenstrasse 9; adult/child €17.50/12.95; ⊘10am-5pm) Running a dragnet through your wallet, the borderline kitsch Sea Life immerses you in an underwater world. Highlights include a shipwreck where you can handle starfish and get stingray close-ups, a shark tunnel, penguins, and a creepy corner blubbing with oddities like frogfish and, ugh, giant isopods.

Kloster Zoffingen
CONVENT
(Brückengasse 15) The 13th-century Kloster Zoffingen is Konstanz' only remaining convent, still in the hands of Dominican nuns.

Rheintorturm
TOWER
(Rhine Gate Tower; Rheinsteig) On the Rheinsteig is the medieval Rheintorturm, a defensive tower with a pyramid-shaped red-tile roof.

Pulverturm
TOWER
(Gunpowder Tower; Rheinsteig) About 200m west along the river is the squat 14th-century Pulverturm tower, with 2m-thick walls.

Domprobstei
HISTORIC BUILDING
(Rheingasse 20) The orange-red, baroque Domprobstei was once the residence of the cathedral provosts.

Konzilgebäude
HISTORIC BUILDING
(Council Building; Konzilstrasse) Look out for the white dormered Konzilgebäude, built in 1388, which served as a granary and warehouse before Pope Martin V was elected here in 1417. Today it's a conference and concert hall.

Zeppelin Monument
MONUMENT
(Stadtgarten) The Zeppelin Monument shows the airship inventor Count Ferdinand von Zeppelin in an Icarus-like pose. He was born in 1838 on the Insel islet.

Konstanz

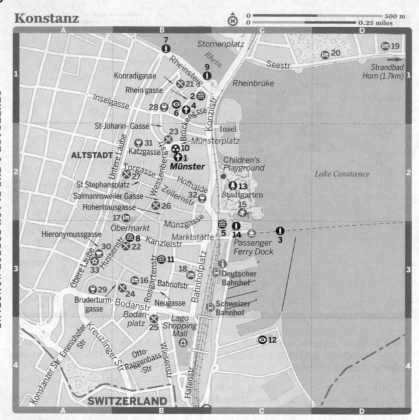

Stadtgarten
PARK

With its landscaped flower beds, plane trees and children's playground, the Stadtgarten is a fine place to kick back and enjoy dreamy views out over Lake Constance.

🏃 Activities

For some ozone-enriched summer fun, grab your bathers and head to the lake.

Strandbad Horn
BEACH

(Eichhornstrasse 100; ⊙mid-May–Sep) **FREE**
This lakefront beach, 4km northeast of the centre, has sunbathing lawns, a kiddie pool, playground, volleyball courts and even a naturist area.

La Canoa
CANOEING

(www.lacanoa.com; Robert-Bosch-Strasse 4; canoe/kayak 3hr €14/18, per day €21/27; ⊙10am-12.30pm & 2-6pm Tue-Fri, 10am-4pm Sat) La Canoa has canoe rental points in all major towns on the lake; see the website for details.

Bootsvermietung Konstanz
BOATING

(Stadtgarten; per hr €12-32; ⊙11am-7pm Easter–mid-Oct) This boat rental in the Stadtgarten has pedalos for trundling across the lake.

🛏 Sleeping

Rock up between November and mid-March and you may find some places closed. The tourist office has a free booking service and a list of private rooms.

Glückseligkeit Herberge
GUESTHOUSE $

(☎07531-902 2075; www.herberge-konstanz.de; Neugasse 20; s €30-50, d €50-70; 🛜) What a sweet deal this little guesthouse is. Housed in a period building in the Altstadt, it shelters petite but attractively decorated rooms. The attic room has direct access to the roof terrace, which peers over a jumble of rooftops to the cathedral spire. There's also a shared lounge, kitchen and patio. E-bikes are available for rental.

Konstanz

Hotel Barbarossa
HISTORIC HOTEL **$$**

(☑07531-128 990; www.barbarossa-hotel.com; Obermarkt 8-12; s €59-79, d €99-140; ☜) This 600-year-old patrician house features parquet-floored, individually decorated rooms, which are bright and appealing if a tad on the small side. The terrace has views over Konstanz' rooftops and spires.

Hotel Halm
HOTEL **$$**

(☑07531-1210; www.hotel-halm-konstanz.de; Bahnhofplatz 6; s €110-145, s €130-220; ☜) A joyous hop and skip from the lake and Altstadt, this late-19th-century pile has warm, elegantly furnished rooms with marble bathrooms; upgrade if you want a balcony with lake view. Skip the €17 breakfast and hit a nearby bakery instead.

Villa Barleben
HISTORIC HOTEL **$$$**

(☑07531-942 330; www.hotel-barleben.de; Seestrasse 15; s €75-165, d €95-255; ☜) Gregariously elegant, this 19th-century villa's sunny rooms and corridors are sprinkled with antiques and ethnic art. The rambling lakefront gardens are ideal for dozing in a *Strandkorb* (wicker beach lounger), G&T in hand, or enjoying lunch on the terrace.

Riva
BOUTIQUE HOTEL **$$$**

(☑07531-363 090; www.hotel-riva.de; Seestrasse 25; s €110-230, d €200-320; 🅿☜🕮) This ultra-chic contender has crisp white spaces, glass walls and a snail-like stairwell. Zenlike rooms with hardwood floors feature perks such as (like it!) free minibars. A rooftop pool, spa area and gym, and a gourmet restaurant and terrace overlooking the lake, seal the deal.

✖ Eating

Münsterplatz and Markstätte are peppered with pizzerias, snack bars and gelaterias. Watch out for rip-offs around Stadtgarten.

Voglhaus
CAFE **$**

(Wessenbergstrasse 8; light meals €5-8; ☉9am-6.30pm Mon-Sat, 11am-6pm Sun; ☑) Locals flock to the 'bird house' for its chilled vibe and contemporary wood-and-stone interior, warmed by an open fire in winter. Wood-oven bread with spreads, wholegrain

---

ⓘ BODENSEE ERLEBNISKARTE

The three-day **Bodensee Erlebniskarte** (adult/child €72/37, not incl ferries €40/20), available at area tourist and ferry offices from late March to mid-October, allows free travel on almost all boats and mountain cableways on and around Lake Constance (including its Austrian and Swiss shores). It also includes free entry to more than 160 tourist attractions and museums. There are also seven-day (adult/child €97/48) and 14-day (adult/child €140/70) versions.

ONE LAKE, TWO WHEELS, THREE COUNTRIES

Bodensee Radweg (www.boden-see-radweg.com) When the weather warms, there is no better way to explore Bodensee (Lake Constance) than with your bum in a saddle. The well-marked Bodensee Cycle Path is a 273km loop of Lake Constance, taking in vineyards, meadows, orchards, wetlands and historic towns. There are plenty of small beaches where you can stop for a refreshing dip in the lake. See the website for itineraries and maps. Bike hire is available in most towns for between €10 and €20 per day. While the entire route takes roughly a week, ferries and trains make it possible to cover shorter chunks, such as Friedrichshafen–Konstanz–Meersburg, in a weekend.

bagels, wraps and cupcakes pair nicely with smoothies and speciality coffees like Hansel and Gretel (with gingerbread syrup).

Zeitlos   GERMAN **$**
(☑ 07531-189 384; St Stephansplatz 25; snacks €4-10; ⊘ 10am-1am Mon-Fri, 10am-6pm Sat & Sun) Behind Stephanskirche, this beamed, stone-walled bistro overflows with regulars. It's a cosy spot for brunch or filling snacks like *Wurstsalat* (sausage salad) and *Maultaschen,* the local take on ravioli. Sit in the ivy-draped courtyard in summer. Gluten-free dishes are available.

Maximilian's   DELI **$**
(Hussenstrasse 9; cakes €2.50, lunch specials €7.90-12.80; ⊘ 10am-7pm Mon-Fri, 10am-6.30pm Sat) Fancy a picnic by the lake? Stop by this central deli for fresh bread, cheese, ham, wine and other goodies. It's also a snug spot for coffee and cake or light lunch specials.

La Bodega   TAPAS **$$**
(☑ 07531-277 88; Schreibergasse 40; tapas €5-10.50; ⊘ 5-11pm Tue-Sat) Squirrelled away in Nied-erburg, this candy-bright bodega with tiny terrace whips up tapas from *papas canarias* (Canarian potatoes) to stuffed calamari.

Münsterhof   GERMAN **$$**
(☑ 07531-363 8427; Münsterplatz 3; mains €9-22; ⊘ 11.30am-1am Sun-Thu, to 2am Fri, to 3am Sat; ☑ ⋒) Tables set up in front of the Münster, a slick bistro interior and a lunchtime buzz

have earned Münsterhof a loyal local following. Dishes from cordon bleu with pan fried potatoes to asparagus-filled *Maultaschen* in creamy chive sauce are substantial and satisfying. The €7.90 lunch is great value.

Tolle Knolle   INTERNATIONAL **$$**
(☑ 07531-175 75; Bodanplatz 9; mains €10-18; ⊘ 11am-11pm; ⋒) On a fountain-dotted square with alfresco seating, this art-slung restaurant lives up to its 'great potato' moniker. Potatoes come in various guises: with Wiener schnitzel, beer-battered fish and on the signature pizza.

San Martino   INTERNATIONAL **$$$**
(☑ 07531-284 5678; www.san-martino.net; Bruderturmgasse 3; mains €26-36, menus €56-115; ⊘ 11.30am-2pm & 5.30-10pm Tue-Sat) A class act, this Michelin-starred restaurant slumbers against the old city walls. Exposed stone, muted colours, soft light and bistro seating create an understated yet elegant feel. Jochen Fecht's beautifully cooked food has a seasonal touch – be it sesame-crusted yellowfin tuna with asparagus or wine-braised veal cheeks with creamy polenta. Vegans are also well catered for.

🍷 Drinking & Entertainment

A vibrant student population fuels Konstanz' after-dark scene. For the low-down, see www.party-news.de (in German). Head to the harbour for drinks with a lake view.

Klimperkasten   BAR
(Bodanstrasse 40; ⊘ 6pm-1am Mon-Thu, 6pm-2am Fri & Sat) Indie kids, garage and old-school fans all hail this retro cafe, which gets clubbier after dark when DJs work the decks. Occasionally hosts gigs.

Schwarze Katz   BAR
(Katzgasse 8; ⊘ 9.30am-midnight Tue-Sat, 9.30am-6pm Sun) With its relaxed mood, friendly crowd and reasonably priced drinks (including Black Forest Alpirsbacher beer), the Black Cat is a Konstanz favourite.

nikOlala   CAFE
(Hieronymusgasse 6; ⊘ 11am-6pm) A tiny pocket of vintage cool in the heart of the Altstadt, nikOlala brings together a craft shop and cafe. It's a nicely chilled spot for a coffee and *pastel de nata* (Portuguese custard tart) between sightseeing.

Brauhaus Johann Albrecht   PUB
(Konradigasse 2; ⊘ 11.30am-1pm) This step-gabled microbrewery is a relaxed haunt for

quaffing wheat beer or hoppy lager by the glass or metre. There's a terrace for summer imbibing.

Seekuh   PUB
(Konzilstrasse 1; ⊙5pm-1am Sun-Thu, 5pm-2am Fri & Sat) The rough and ready 'lake cow' is a Konstanz favourite for its beer garden, cheapish drinks and occasional gigs.

K9   CULTURAL CENTRE
(www.k9-kulturzentrum.de; Obere Laube 71) Once a medieval church, this is now Konstanz' most happening cultural venue, with a line-up skipping from salsa nights and film screenings to gigs, club nights and jive nights. See the website for schedules.

ℹ Information

ReiseBank (Hauptbahnhof; ⊙8am-6pm Mon-Fri, 8am-3pm Sat) Currency exchange, including Swiss francs.

Tourist Office (⊘07531-133 030; www.kon stanz-tourismus.de; Bahnhofplatz 43; ⊙9am-6.30pm Mon-Fri, 9am-4pm Sat, 10am-1pm Sun Apr-Oct, 9.30am-6pm Mon-Fri Nov-Mar) Just north of the train station. Inside you can pick up a walking-tour brochure (€1) and city map (€0.50); outside there's a hotel reservation board and free hotel telephone.

ℹ Getting There & Away

Konstanz is the main ferry hub for Lake Constance.

By car, Konstanz can be reached via the B33, which links up with the A81 to and from Stuttgart near Singen. Or you can take the B31 to Meersburg and then catch a car ferry.

Konstanz' Hauptbahnhof is the southern terminus of the scenic Schwarzwaldbahn, which trundles hourly through the Black Forest, linking Offenburg with towns such as Triberg and Villingen. To reach Lake Constance's northern shore, you usually have to change in Radolfzell. The Schweizer Bahnhof has connections to destinations throughout Switzerland.

ℹ Getting Around

The city centre is a traffic headache, especially on weekends. Your best bet is the free Park & Ride lot 3km northwest of the Altstadt, near the airfield on Byk-Gulden-Strasse, where your only outlay will be for a bus ticket.

Local buses (www.sw.konstanz.de) cost €2.30 for a single ticket; day passes are €4.50/7.80 for an individual/family. Bus 1 links the Meersburg car-ferry dock with the Altstadt. If you stay in Konstanz for at least two nights,

your hotelier will give you a Gästekarte entitling you to free local bus travel.

Bicycles can be hired from **Kultur-Rädle** (⊘07531-273 10; Bahnhofplatz 29; per day/week €13/70; ⊙9am-12.30pm & 2.30-6pm Mon-Fri, 10am-4pm Sat year-round, plus 10am-12.30pm Sun Easter-Sep), close to the tourist office.

Mainau Island

Mainau   GARDENS
(www.mainau.de; adult/concession €19/11 summer, €9.50/5.50 winter; ⊙10am-7pm late Mar-late Oct, 10am-5pm rest of year) Jutting out over the lake and bursting with flowers, the lusciously green islet of Mainau is a 45-hectare Mediterranean garden dreamed up by the Bernadotte family, relatives of the royal house of Sweden.

Around two million visitors flock here every year to admire sparkly lake and mountain views from the baroque castle and wander sequoia-shaded avenues and hothouses bristling with palms and orchids. Crowd-pullers include the **Butterfly House**, where hundreds of vivid butterflies flit amid the dewy foliage, an Italian Cascade integrating patterned flowers with waterfalls, and a petting zoo. Tulips and rhododendrons bloom in spring, hibiscus and roses in summer. Avoid weekends, when the gardens get crowded.

You can drive, walk or cycle to Mainau, 8km north of Konstanz. Take bus 4 from Konstanz' train station or hop aboard a passenger ferry.

Reichenau Island

Reichenau   ISLAND
(www.reichenau.de) In AD 724 a missionary named Pirmin founded a Benedictine monastery on Reichenau, a 4.5km-by-1.5km island (Lake Constance's largest) about 11km west of Konstanz. During its heyday, from 820 to 1050, the so-called Reichenauer School produced stunning illuminated manuscripts and vivid frescos. Today, three surviving churches provide silent testimony to Reichenau's Golden Age. Thanks to them, this fertile islet of orchards and wineries was declared a Unesco World Heritage Site in 2000.

Bring walking boots and binoculars to explore **Wollmatinger Ried**, a marshy nature reserve that attracts butterflies, migratory birds including kingfishers, grey herons and cuckoos, and even the odd beaver.

DON'T MISS

IMPERIA RULES

At the end of the pier, giving ferry passengers a come-hither look from her rotating pedestal, stands Imperia. Peter Lenk's 9m-high sculpture of a buxom prostitute, said to have plied her trade in the days of the Council of Constance, is immortalised in a novel by Honoré de Balzac. In her clutches are hilarious sculptures of a naked (and sagging) Pope Martin V and Holy Roman Emperor Sigismund, symbolising religious and imperial power.

A 2km-long tree-lined causeway connects the mainland with the island, which is served by bus 7372 from Konstanz. The Konstanz–Schaffhausen and Konstanz–Radolfzell ferries stop off at Reichenau.

Meersburg

🗷 07532 / POP 5630

Tumbling down vine-streaked slopes to Lake Constance and crowned by a perkily turreted medieval castle, Meersburg lives up to all those clichéd knights-in-armour, damsel-in-distress fantasies. And if its tangle of cobbled lanes and half-timbered houses filled with jovial banter doesn't sweep you off your feet, the local Pinot noir served in its cosy *Weinstuben* will.

⦿ Sights & Activities

Altes Schloss CASTLE

(adult/concession €9.50/6.50; ⊙9am-6.30pm Mar-Oct, 10am-6pm Nov-Feb) Looking across Lake Constance from its lofty perch, the Altes Schloss is an archetypal medieval stronghold, complete with keep, drawbridge, knights' hall and dungeons. Founded by Merovingian king Dagobert I in the 7th century, the fortress is among Germany's oldest, which is no mean feat in a country with a *lot* of old castles. The bishops of Konstanz used it as a summer residence between 1268 and 1803.

Neues Schloss CASTLE

(www.schloesser-und-gaerten.de; adult/concession €5/2.50; ⊙9am-6.30pm May-Oct, 11am-4pm Sat & Sun Nov-Apr) In 1710 Prince-Bishop Johann Franz Schenk von Stauffenberg, perhaps tired of the dinginess and rising damp, swapped the Altes Schloss for the dusky-pink, lavishly baroque Neues Schloss. A visit to the now state-owned palace takes in the extravagant bishops' apartments replete with stucco work and frescos, Bathasar Neumann's elegant staircase, and gardens with inspirational lake views.

Lakefront HARBOUR

Stroll the harbour for classic snaps of Lake Constance or to hire a pedalo. On the jetty, you can't miss – though the pious might prefer to – Peter Lenk's satirical Magische Säule (Magic Column). The sculpture is a hilarious satirical depiction of characters who have shaped Meersburg's history, including buxom wine-wench Wendelgart and poet Annette von Droste-Hülshoff (the seagull).

Meersburg Therme SPA

(🗷 07532-440 2850; www.meersburg-therme. de; Uferpromenade 12; thermal baths 2hr adult/concession €9/8.50, incl sauna 3hr €18/17.50; ⊙10am-10pm Mon-Thu, 10am-11pm Fri & Sat, 9am-10pm Sun) It's a five-minute walk east along the Uferpromenade to this lakefront spa, where the 34°C thermal waters, water jets and Swiss Alp views are soothing. Those who dare to bare all can skinny-dip in the lake and steam in saunas that are replicas of Unteruhldingen's Stone Age dwellings.

🛏 Sleeping & Eating

Meersburg goes with the seasons, with most places closing from November to Easter. Pick up a brochure listing good-value apartments and private rooms at the tourist office.

Characterful wine taverns line Unterstadtstrasse, while the lakefront Seepromenade has wall-to-wall pizzerias, cafes and gelaterias with alfresco seating.

Landhaus Ödenstein GUESTHOUSE $$

(🗷 07532-6142; www.oedenstein.de; Droste-Hülshoff-Weg 25; s €62-80, d €92-150; 🅿) Spectacularly plonked on a hill above vine-cloaked slopes, this family-run guesthouse has knockout views of Lake Constance and spotless, light-filled rooms with pine furnishings – the pick of which have balconies. A pretty garden, warm welcome and generous breakfasts sweeten the deal.

Gasthof zum Bären GUESTHOUSE $$

(🗷 07532-432 20; www.baeren-meersburg.de; Marktplatz 11; s €50, d €88-110; 🅿🖘) Straddling three 13th- to 17th-century buildings, this guesthouse near Obertor receives glowing reviews for its classic rooms, spruced up with stucco work, ornate wardrobes and lustrous wood; corner rooms No 13 and 23 are the most romantic.

The rustic tavern (mains €9 to €18) serves Lake Constance fare such as *Felchen* (whitefish).

Romantik Residenz
am See
BOUTIQUE HOTEL **$$$**
(☑ 07532-800 40; www.hotel-residenz-meersburg. com; Uferpromenade 11; s €87-122, d €150-288, apt €210-348;) Sitting with aplomb on the promenade, this romantic hotel is a class act. The higher you go, the better the view in the warm-hued rooms facing the vineyards or lake. In the hotel's Michelin-starred restaurant, **Casala** (Uferpromenade 11; tasting menus €78-146), chef Markus Philippi brings sophisticated Mediterranean cuisine to the table.

Valentino
PIZZA **$**
(☑ 07532-807 690; www.valentino-meersburg.de; Seepromenade 10; pizza €8-12; 11am-11pm) The pizzas and light, crisp *Flammkuchen* are the stars of the menu at this friendly Italian job. Nab a spot on the terrace when the sun's out.

Winzerstube zum Becher
GERMAN **$$**
(☑ 07532-9009; Höllgasse 4; mains €10.50-26; noon-2pm & 6-10pm Tue-Sun) Vines drape the facade of this wood-panelled bolt-hole, run by the same family since 1884. Home-grown Pinot noirs accompany Lake Constance classics such as whitefish in almond-butter sauce. The terrace affords Altes Schloss views.

Badische Weinstube
GERMAN **$$**
(☑ 07532-496 42; www.badische-weinstube.com; Unterstadtstrasse 17; mains €13-25; 5-11pm) Close to the lakefront, this wine tavern combines a mock-rustic interior with a pavement terrace. Try the homemade fish soup flavoured with saffron and garlic, followed, say, by Bodensee *Felchen* in almond butter or *Zwiebelrostbraten* (onion beef roast) with *Spätzle*.

❶ Information

Tourist Office (☑ 07532-440 400; www.meersburg.de; Kirchstrasse 4; 9am-12.30pm & 2-6pm Mon-Fri, 10am-3pm Sat, 10am-1pm Sun) Housed in a one-time Dominican monastery.

❶ Getting There & Away

Meersburg, which lacks a train station, is 18km west of Friedrichshafen.

From Monday to Friday, eight times a day, express bus 7394 makes the trip to Konstanz (€3.25, 40 minutes) and Friedrichshafen (€3.45, 26 minutes). Bus 7373 connects Meersburg with Ravensburg (€5.90, 40 minutes, four daily Mon-

day to Friday, two Saturday). Meersburg's main bus stop is next to the church.

❶ Getting Around

The best and only way to get around Meersburg is on foot. Even the large pay car park near the car-ferry port (€1.20 per hour) is often full in high season. You might find free parking north of the old town along Daisendorfer Strasse.

Hire bikes at **Hermann Dreher** (☑ 07532-5176; Stadtgraben 5; per day €5; rental 8am-noon), down the alley next to the tourist office.

Pfahlbauten

Pfahlbauten
ARCHAEOLOGICAL SITE
(Pile Dwellings; www.pfahlbauten.de; Strandpromenade 6, Unteruhldingen; adult/concession €9/6.50; 9am-6.30pm Apr-Sep, 9am-5pm Oct, 9am-5pm Sat & Sun Nov;) Awarded Unesco World Heritage status in 2011, the Pfahlbauten represent one of 11 prehistoric pile dwellings around the Alps. Based on the findings of local excavations, the carefully reconstructed dwellings catapult you back to the Stone and Bronze Ages, from 4000 to 850 BC. A spin of the lakefront complex takes in stilt dwellings that give an insight into the lives of farmers, fishermen and craftsmen. Kids love the hands-on activities from axe making to fire-starting using flints.

Birnau

Wallfahrtskirche Birnau
HISTORIC BUILDING
(Pilgrimage Church; Uhldingen-Mühlhofen; 7.30am-7pm, to 5.30pm in winter) The exuberant, powder-pink Birnau pilgrimage church is one of Lake Constance's architectural highlights. It was built by the rococo master Peter Thumb of Vorarlberg in 1746. The decor is so intricate and profuse you won't know where to look first. At some point your gaze will be drawn to the ceiling, where Gottfried Bernhard Göz worked his usual fresco magic.

Affenberg Salem

Affenberg Salem
ZOO
(www.affenberg-salem.de; adult/child €8.50/5.50; 9am-6pm Mar-Oct) No zoo-like cages, no circus antics, just happy Barbary macaques free to roam in a near-to-natural habitat: that's the concept behind conservation-oriented Affenberg Salem. Trails interweave the 20-hectare woodlands, where you can

feed tail-less monkeys one piece of special popcorn at a time, observe their behaviour (you scratch my back, I'll scratch yours...) and get primate close-ups at hourly feedings. The park is also home to storks; listen for bill clattering and look out for their nests near the entrance.

Schloss Salem

Schloss Salem PALACE
(www.salem.de; adult/concession €9/4.50; ☉9.30am-6pm Mon-Sat, 10.30am-6pm Sun Apr-Oct) Founded as a Cistercian monastery in 1134, the immense estate known as Schloss Salem was once the largest and richest of its kind in southern Germany. The Grand Duchy of Baden sold out to the state recently, but you can still picture the royals swanning around the hedge maze, gardens and extravagant rococo apartments dripping with stucco. The west wing shelters an elite boarding school, briefly attended by Prince Philip (Duke of Edinburgh and husband of Queen Elizabeth II).

Friedrichshafen

☑ 07541 / POP 59,000

Zeppelins, the cigar-shaped airships that first took flight in 1900 under the stewardship of high-flying Count Ferdinand von Zeppelin, will forever be associated with Friedrichshafen. An amble along the flowery lakefront promenade and a visit to the museum that celebrates the behemoth of the skies are the biggest draws of this industrial town, which was heavily bombed in WWII and rebuilt in the 1950s.

◉ Sights & Activities

★**Zeppelin Museum** MUSEUM
(www.zeppelin-museum.de; Seestrasse 22; adult/concession €8/4; ☉9am-5pm daily May-Oct, 10am-5pm Tue-Sun Nov-Apr) Near the eastern end of Friedrichshafen's lakefront promenade is the Zeppelin Museum, housed in the Bauhaus-style former Hafenbahnhof, built in 1932. The centrepiece is a full-scale mock-up of a 33m section of the *Hindenburg* (LZ 129), the largest airship ever built, measuring an incredible 245m long and outfitted as luxuriously as an ocean liner. The hydrogen-filled craft tragically burst into flames, killing 36, while landing in New Jersey in 1937.

Other exhibits provide technical and historical insights, including an original motor gondola from the famous Graf Zeppelin, which made 590 trips and travelled around the world in 21 days in 1929.

The top-floor art collection stars brutally realistic works by Otto Dix.

Lakefront AREA
A promenade runs through the lakefront, sculpture-dotted **Stadtgarten** park along Uferstrasse, a great spot for a picnic or stroll. Pedal and electric boats can be rented at the Gondelhafen (€9 to €23 per hour).

The western end of Friedrichshafen's promenade is anchored by the twin-onion-towered baroque **Schlosskirche**. It's the only accessible part of the Schloss and is still inhabited by the ducal family of Württemberg.

🛏 Sleeping & Eating

The tourist office has a free booking terminal. For lake-view snacks, hit Seestrasse's beer gardens, pizzerias and ice-cream parlours.

Gasthof Rebstock GUESTHOUSE $
(☑07541-950 1640; www.gasthof-rebstock-fn.de; Werastrasse 35; s/d/tr/q €65/80/95/110; 🛜) Geared up for cyclists and offering bike rental (€7 per day), this family-run hotel has a beer garden and humble but tidy rooms with pine furnishings. It's 750m northwest of the Stadtbahnhof.

Hotel Restaurant Maier HOTEL $$
(☑07541-4040; www.hotel-maier.de; Poststrasse 1-3, Friedrichshafen-Fischbach; s €59-95, d €89-160; 🅿🛜) The light-drenched rooms are immaculately kept at this family-run hotel, 5km west of Friedrichshafen and an eight-minute hop on the train. The mini spa invites relaxing moments, with its lake-facing terrace, steam room and sauna. Championing slow food, the wood-panelled restaurant is hailed far and wide for its regional food.

Brot, Kaffee, Wein CAFE $
(Karlstrasse 38; snacks €3-8; ☉8.30am-8pm Mon-Fri, 9am-8pm Sat, 9.30am-8pm Sun) Slick and monochrome, this deli-cafe has a lakeside terrace for lingering over a speciality coffee, breakfast, homemade ice cream or sourdough bread sandwich.

Beach Club TAPAS $
(Uferstrasse 1; snacks €6-8; ☉9am-midnight Apr-Oct) This lakefront shack is the place to unwind on the deck, mai tai in hand, admiring the *Klangschiff* sculpture and the not-so-distant Alps. Revive over tapas, salads and antipasti.

❶ Information

Post Office (Bahnhofplatz 1; ☉9am-6pm Mon-Fri, 9am-1pm Sat) To the right as you exit the Stadtbahnhof.

Tourist Office (✑07541-300 10; www.friedrichshafen.info; Bahnhofplatz 2; ☉9am-1pm & 2-6pm Mon-Fri, 9am-1pm Sat) On the square outside the Stadtbahnhof. Staff can book accommodation and zeppelin flights.

❶ Getting There & Around

There are ferry options, including a catamaran to Konstanz. Sailing times are posted on the waterfront just outside the Zeppelin Museum.

From Monday to Friday, seven times a day, express bus 7394 makes the trip to Konstanz (1¼ hours) via Meersburg (30 minutes). Birnau and Meersburg are also served almost hourly by bus 7395.

Friedrichshafen is on the Bodensee-Gürtelbahn train line, which runs along the lake's northern shore from Radolfzell to Lindau. There are also regular services on the Bodensee-Oberschwaben-Bahn to Ravensburg (€4.30, 20 minutes).

Ravensburg

✑0751 / POP 49,780

Ravensburg has puzzled the world for the past 125 years with its jigsaws and board games. The medieval Altstadt has toy-town appeal, studded with turrets, robber-knight towers and gabled patrician houses. For centuries dukes and wealthy merchants polished the cobbles of this Free Imperial City – now it's your turn.

◉ Sights & Activities

Marienplatz   SQUARE
The heart of Altstadt is the elongated, pedestrianised Marienplatz, framed by sturdy towers, like the round Grüner Turm, with its lustrous tiled roof, and frescoed patrician houses, such as the late-Gothic, step-gabled Waaghaus. The 15th-century **Lederhaus**, with its elaborate Renaissance facade, was once the domain of tanners and shoemakers.

Blaserturm   TOWER
(adult/concession €1.50/1; ☉11am-4pm early Apr-early Oct) The 51m-high Blaserturm is a part of the original fortifications and has superb views over the Altstadt from up top.

Liebfrauenkirche   CHURCH
(Church of Our Lady; Marienplatz) Rising high above Marienplatz, the weighty, late-Gothic Liebfrauenkirche conceals some fine examples of 15th-century stained glass and a gilt altar.

Ravensburger Spieleland   AMUSEMENT PARK
(www.spieleland.de; Mecklenbeuren; adult/concession €29/27; ☉10am-6pm Apr-Oct) Kids in tow? Take them to this board-game-inspired theme park, with attractions from giant rubber-duck racing and cow milking against the clock to rodeos and Alpine rafting. It's a 10-minute drive south of Ravensburg on the B467.

Museum Humpis   MUSEUM
(www.museum-humpis-quartier.de; Marktstrasse 45; adult/concession €4/2; ☉11am-6pm Tue-Sun, to 8pm Thu) Seven exceptional late-medieval houses set around a glass-covered courtyard shelter a permanent collection and rotating exhibitions focusing on Ravensburg's past as a trade centre. Free audioguides provide some background.

Mehlsack   TOWER
The all-white Mehlsack (Flour Sack) is a tower marking the Altstadt's southern edge. A steep staircase leads up to the **Veitsburg**, a quaint baroque castle, which now harbours the restaurant of the same name, with outlooks over Ravensburg's mosaic of red-tiled roofs.

⏑ Sleeping & Eating

Waldhorn   HISTORIC HOTEL $$
(✑0751-361 20; http://waldhorn.de; Marienplatz 15; s €75-125, d €135-150; 🖭) The Waldhorn creaks with history and its light, appealingly restored rooms make a great base for exploring the Altstadt. Lodged in the 15th-century vintners' guildhall, its wood-beamed restaurant (mains €12 to 25), Rebleuteshaus,

---

DON'T MISS

COME FLY WITH ME

Zeppelin NT (✑07541-590 00; www.zeppelinflug.de; 30/45/60/90/120-minute flights €200/295/395/565/745) Real airship fans will justify the splurge on a trip in a high-tech, 12-passenger Zeppelin NT. Shorter trips cover lake destinations such as Schloss Salem and Lindau, while longer ones drift across to Austria or Switzerland. Take-off and landing are in Friedrichshafen. The flights aren't cheap but not much can beat floating over Lake Constance with the Alps on the horizon, and so slowly that you can make the most of legendary photo ops.

turns out spot-on seasonal dishes like tender corn-fed chicken with herb gnocchi.

Gasthof Obertor GUESTHOUSE **$$**
(☑0751-366 70; www.hotelobertor.de; Marktstrasse 67; s €75-95, d €120-130; P 🐾) The affable Rimpps take pride in their lemon-fronted patrician house. It stands high above most Altstadt guesthouses, with spotless rooms, a sauna area and generous breakfasts.

Mohren INTERNATIONAL **$$**
(☑0751-1805 4310; www.mohren-ravensburg.de; Marktstrasse 61; mains €9-21.50; ⏰5pm-midnight Mon, 10.30am-2.30pm & 5.30pm-midnight Tue-Sat) Contemporary rustic best sums up Mohren, with its bright feel, exposed red brick and log piles. The slow food menu wings you from antipasti to steaks and Thai curries – all playfully presented and revealing the chef's pride in careful sourcing.

ℹ Information

Tourist Office (☑0751-828 00; www.ravensburg.de; Kirchstrasse 16; ⏰9am-5.30pm Mon-Fri, 10am-1pm Sat) A block northeast of Marienplatz.

ℹ Getting There & Away

The train station is six blocks west of the tourist office along Eisenbahnstrasse. Ravensburg is on the train line linking Friedrichshafen (€4.30, 20 minutes, at least twice hourly) with Ulm (€20.90, 1¼ hours, at least hourly) and Stuttgart (€36.20, 2½ hours, at least hourly).

Lindau

☑08382 / POP 24,800
Brochures rhapsodise about Lindau being Germany's 'Garden of Eden' and the 'Bavarian Riviera'. Paradise and southern France it ain't, but it is pretty special. Cradled in the southern crook of Lake Constance and almost dipping its toes into Austria, this is a good-looking, outgoing little town, with a candy-coloured postcard of an Altstadt, clear-day Alpine views and lakefront cafes that use every sunray to the max.

◎ Sights

Seepromenade AREA
In summer the harbourside promenade has a happy-go-lucky air, with its palms, bobbing boats and folk sunning themselves in pavement cafes.

Out at the harbour gates, looking across to the Alps, is Lindau's signature 36m-high

Neuer Leuchtturm (New Lighthouse; adult/concession €1.80/0.70; ⏰10am-7.30pm) and, just in case you forget which state you're in, a statue of the Bavarian lion. The square tile-roofed, 13th-century Mangturm (Old Lighthouse) guards the northern edge of the sheltered port.

Altes Rathaus LANDMARK
(Old Town Hall; Bismarckplatz) Lindau's biggest architectural stunner is the 15th-century step-gabled Altes Rathaus, a frescoed frenzy of cherubs, merry minstrels and galleons.

Stadtmuseum MUSEUM
(Marktplatz 6; adult/concession €7.50/3.50; ⏰10am-6pm) Lions and voluptuous dames dance across the trompe l'oeil facade of the flamboyantly baroque Haus zum Cavazzen, which contains this museum, showcasing a fine collection of furniture, weapons and paintings. The museum also showcases stellar temporary exhibitions, such as recent ones featuring works of Picasso, Chagall, Matisse and Emil Nolde.

Peterskirche CHURCH
(Schrannenplatz; ⏰daily) Looking back on a 1000-year history, this enigmatic church is now a war memorial, hiding exquisite time-faded frescos of the Passion of Christ by Hans Holbein the Elder. The cool, dimly lit interior is a quiet spot for contemplation. Next door is the turreted 14th-century Diebsturm, once a tiny jail.

🛏 Sleeping

Lindau virtually goes into hibernation from November to February, when many hotels close. Nip into the tourist office for a list of good-value holiday apartments.

Hotel Anker GUESTHOUSE **$$**
(☑08382-260 9844; www.anker-lindau.com; Bindergasse 15; s €55-69, d €99-169; 🐾) Shiny parquet floors, citrus colours and artwork have spruced up the charming and peaceful rooms at this central guesthouse, tucked down a cobbled lane. Rates include a hearty breakfast.

Hotel Garni-Brugger HISTORIC HOTEL **$$**
(☑08382-934 10; www.hotel-garni-brugger.de; Bei der Heidenmauer 11; s €60-88, d €94-130; 🐾) Our readers rave about this 18th-century hotel, with bright rooms done up in floral fabrics and pine. The family bends over backwards to please. Guests can unwind in

the little spa with steam room and sauna (€10) in the cooler months.

Alte Post
HOTEL **$$**

(☑08382-934 60; www.alte-post-lindau.de; Fischergasse 3; s €70-95, d €120-190) This 300-year-old coaching inn was once a stop on the Frankfurt–Milan mail run. Well-kept, light and spacious, the rooms are fitted out with chunky oak furnishings. Downstairs is a beer garden and a highly regarded restaurant (mains €12 to €23), with dishes like *Tafelspitz* (boiled beef) and *Maultaschen*, and local wines.

Reutemann & Seegarten
LUXURY HOTEL **$$$**

(☑08382-9150; www.reutemann-lindau.de; Ludwigstrasse 23; s €99-183, d €142-262; ☷☒) Wow, what a view! Facing the harbour, lighthouse and lion statue, this hotel has plush, spacious rooms done out in sunny shades, as well as a pool big enough to swim laps, a spa, gym and refined restaurant.

✖ Eating & Drinking

For a drink with a cool view, head to Seepromenade. The crowds on the main thoroughfare, Maximilianstrasse, can be dodged in nearby backstreets, where your euro will stretch further.

37°
CAFE **$**

(Bahnhofplatz 1; snacks €4-11; ☉10am-11pm Tue-Sun) Part boutique, part boho-chic cafe, 37° combines a high-ceilinged interior with a lake-facing pavement terrace. Pull up a candy-coloured chair for cold drinks and light bites such as tapas, quiche and soups.

Engelstube
GERMAN **$$**

(www.engel-lindau.de; mains €13-19; ☉11am-2pm & 5-11pm) Dark wood panelling keeps the vibe cosy at this smart wine tavern, which spills out onto a pavement terrace in summer. Regional dishes like Bodensee fish with herbs and roast Bavarian ox are cooked to a T.

★ Valentin
MEDITERRANEAN **$$$**

(☑08382-504 3740; In der Grub 28; mains €20-31, day specials €11.50-13.50; ☉noon-2pm & 6-10pm Wed-Mon) The chef carefully sources the local ingredients that go into his Med-style dishes at this sleek vaulted restaurant. Dishes like spinach and pecorino ravioli and locally caught trout with creamy lentils are beautifully cooked and presented.

Weinstube Frey
GERMAN **$$$**

(☑08382-947 9676; Maximilianstrasse 15; mains €16-22; ☉11.30am-10pm) This 500-year-old wood-panelled wine tavern oozes Bavarian charm with its cosy nooks. Dirndl-clad waitresses serve up regional wines and fare such as Lake Constance whitefish with market veg and *Zwiebelrostbraten*. Sit out on the terrace when the sun's out.

Marmor Saal
BAR

(Bahnhofplatz 1e; ☉10am-2am) The lakefront 'marble hall' once welcomed royalty and still has a feel of grandeur with its soaring columns, chandeliers and Biedermeier flourishes. Nowadays it's a relaxed cafe-bar with occasional live music and a chilled terrace.

ℹ Information

Post Office (Obere Schrannenplatz 4; ☉9am-6.30pm Mon-Fri, 9am-3pm Sat)

Tourist Office (☑08382-260 030; www.lindau.de; Alfred-Nobel-Platz 1; ☉10am-6pm Mon-Sat, 10am-1pm Sun, shorter hours in low season)

ℹ Getting There & Away

Lindau is on the B31 and connects to Munich by the A96. The precipitous Deutsche Alpenstrasse (German Alpine Rd), which winds giddily eastward to Berchtesgaden, begins here.

Lindau is at the eastern terminus of the train line, which goes along the lake's north shore via Friedrichshafen (€6.10, 20 minutes) westward to Radolfzell, and the southern terminus of the Südbahn to Ulm (€25.70, 1¾ hours) via Ravensburg (€10, 44 minutes).

ℹ Getting Around

The compact, walkable Insel (island), home to the town centre and harbour, is connected to the mainland by the Seebrücke, a road bridge at its northeastern tip, and by the Eisenbahndamm, a rail bridge open to cyclists and pedestrians. The Hauptbahnhof lies to the east of the island, a block south of the pedestrianised, shop-lined Maximilianstrasse.

Buses 1 and 2 link the Hauptbahnhof to the main bus hub, known as ZUP. A single ticket costs €2.10, a 24-hour pass is €5.40.

To get to the island by car follow the signs to 'Lindau-Insel'. It's easiest and cheapest to park at the large metered car park (€0.80 per hour) just before you cross the bridge to the island.

Bikes and tandems can be rented at **Unger's Fahrradverleih** (Inselgraben 14; per day bikes €6-12, tandems €18, electro bikes €20; ☉9am-1pm & 3-6pm Mon-Fri, 9am-1pm Sat & Sun).

Frankfurt & Southern Rhineland

Best Places to Eat

➡ Liller's Historische Schlossmühle (p452)

➡ Kalinski (p460)

➡ Restaurant 1832 (p428)

➡ Weinhotel Landsknecht (p439)

➡ Zu den 12 Aposteln (p387)

Best Places to Drink

➡ Kloster Machern (p453)

➡ Weinstube Spitzhäuschen (p450)

➡ Günderode Haus (p438)

➡ Zum Grünen Baum (p436)

➡ Baker Street (p460)

Why Go?

In this enchanting corner of Germany, the finer things in life take pride of place: good food, great wine, glorious walking and cycling, and exceptional art everywhere, from magnificent museums to quirky street sculptures.

Vineyards ribbon the steep-sided Romantic Rhine and Moselle Valleys, as well as the wisteria-draped German Wine Route, the country's warmest region. All three areas are strewn with hilltop castles, dark forests, and scores of snug wineries for sampling exquisite crisp whites.

History abounds here, from the preserved Roman amphitheatre and thermae in Germany's oldest city, Trier, to crooked half-timbered medieval villages, spectacular palaces, centres of learning like the ancient university city of Heidelberg and Goethe's birthplace, the finance and trade-fair hub of Frankfurt, and momentous industrial and engineering legacies such as the invention of the printing press in Mainz and the bicycle and automobile in Mannheim that continue to influence the world today.

When to Go

Frankfurt's attractions can be enjoyed at any time of the year, but you'll pay a fortune for accommodation if your visit coincides with a big trade fair. Nearby towns can provide a cheaper base, but you should still book *well* ahead.

The Moselle and the Rhine Valleys teem with visitors from May to August but are very quiet from November to March, although towns with Christmas markets are lively in December.

Along the German Wine Route, village wine festivals are held on weekends from March to mid-November.

FRANKFURT AM MAIN

☎ 069 / POP 709,395

Glinting with glass, steel and concrete skyscrapers, Frankfurt-on-the-Main (pronounced 'mine') is unlike any other German city. The focal point of a conurbation of 5.5 million inhabitants, 'Mainhattan' is a high-powered finance and business hub, home to one of the world's largest stock exchanges as well as the gleaming new headquarters of the European Central Bank. Frankfurt famously hosts some of the world's most important trade fairs, attracting thousands of business travellers. Its airport, the region's biggest employer, is the third-largest in Europe, handling over 57 million passengers per year.

Yet at its heart, Frankfurt is an unexpectedly traditional and charming city, with half-timbered buildings huddled in its quaint medieval Altstadt (old city), cosy apple wine taverns serving hearty regional food, village-like neighbourhoods filled with outdoor cafes, boutiques and street art, and beautiful parks, gardens and riverside paths. The city's cache of museums is second in Germany only to Berlin's, and its nightlife and entertainment scenes are bolstered by a spirited student population.

History

Around 2000 years ago Frankfurt was a site of Celtic and Germanic settlement and then, in the area known today as the Römerberg, a Roman garrison town.

Mentioned in historical documents as far back as AD 794, Frankfurt was an important centre of power in the Holy Roman Empire. With the election of Frederick I (Barbarossa) in 1152, the city became the customary site of the selection of German kings. International trade fairs – attracting business from the Mediterranean to the Baltic – were held here, beginning in the 12th century.

In 1372 Frankfurt became a 'free imperial city', a status it enjoyed almost uninterrupted until the Prussian takeover of 1866. A stock exchange began operating in Frankfurt in 1585, and it was here that the Rothschild banking family began its ascent in the 1760s.

Frankfurt has a strong Jewish history – in 1933, its 30,000-strong Jewish community, was Germany's second largest. Around town, you may see brass squares the size of a cobblestone embedded in the pavement. These *Stolpersteine* ('stumbling blocks') serve as memorials to Jews deported by the Nazis by marking their last place of residence.

About 80% of Frankfurt's medieval city centre was destroyed – and over 1000 people were killed – by Allied bombing raids in March 1944. The area around Römerberg has since been reconstructed.

Today, Frankfurt is a thriving, contemporary city still focused on trade fairs and finance.

Sights & Activities

Most of Frankfurt's museums are closed on Monday; exceptions include the Goethe-Haus, Senckenberg Museum and Explora.

Altstadt

The city's historic core centres on the Dom and the lively, tourist-mobbed Römerberg, a medieval public square ringed by reconstructed half-timbered buildings.

★Kaiserdom CATHEDRAL

(Imperial/Frankfurt Cathedral; Map p376; www.dom-frankfurt.de; Domplatz 14; tower adult/concession €3.50/1.50; ⏲ church 8am-8pm Mon-Thu, noon-8pm Fri, 9am-8pm Sat & Sun, tower 9am-6pm Apr-Oct, 11am-5pm Thu-Mon Nov-Mar; [S] Dom/Römer) Frankfurt's red-sandstone cathedral is dominated by a 95m-high Gothic **tower**, which can be climbed via 324 steps. Construction began in the 13th century; from 1356 to 1792, the Holy Roman Emperors were elected (and, after 1562, consecrated and crowned) in the **Wahlkapelle** at the end of the right aisle (look for the 'skull' altar). The cathedral was rebuilt both after an 1867 fire and after the bombings of 1944, which left it a burnt-out shell.

It's dedicated to the apostle St Bartholomew, hence its official name, Kaiserdom St Bartholomäus.

To the left as you enter the cathedral, the **Dommuseum** (Cathedral Museum; Map p376; www.dommuseum-frankfurt.de; museum adult/student €3/2, cathedral tours adult/student €4/2; ⏲ 10am-5pm Tue-Fri, 11am-5pm Sat, Sun & holidays, cathedral tours 3pm Tue-Sun except during weddings) has a small collection of precious liturgical objects and sells tickets for Dom tours (in German).

Frequent **concerts**, including organ recitals, take place here; schedules are listed on the Dom's website.

★Römerberg SQUARE

(Map p376; [S] Dom/Römer) The Römerberg is Frankfurt's old central square. Ornately gabled half timbered buildings, reconstructed

Frankfurt & Southern Rhineland Highlights

1 Floating past Frankfurt's medieval church spires, museum embankment and glittering skyscrapers aboard a **river cruise** (p382)

2 Catching a cable car uphill to head out on a **hike** (p437) through vineyards along the castle-studded Romantic Rhine Valley

3 Wandering the ruins and gardens of Heidelberg's romantic red-sandstone **Schloss** (p410)

4 Marvelling at the towering Romanesque **cathedral** (p402) in Mainz

5 Soaking in the steaming spring-fed pools of Wiesbaden's *Jugendstil* (art nouveau) **thermal baths** (p399)

6 Travelling back to the time of the gladiators at the remarkable Roman ruins in Germany's oldest city, **Trier** (p451)

7 **Cycling** (p444) along the gently winding, wine-tavern-lined Moselle Valley

8 Zooming around Germany's famed Formula One Grand Prix race track, the **HockenheimRing** (p422)

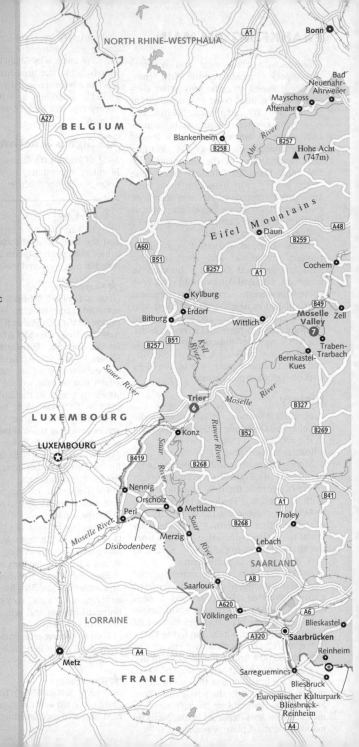

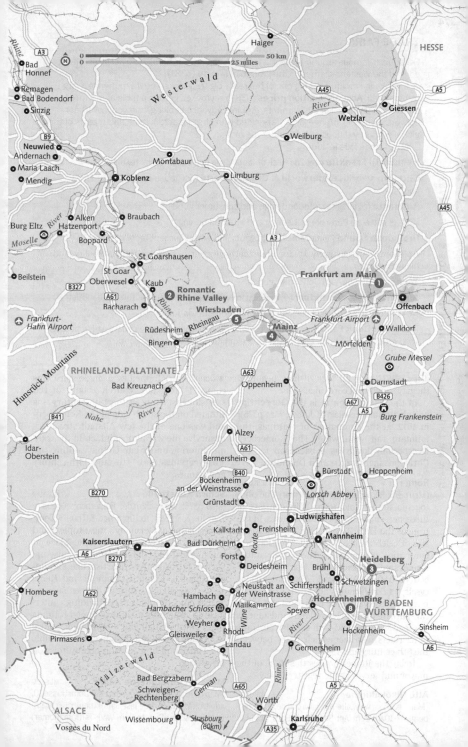

TRADE FAIRS

Frankfurt is famous around the world for its *Messen* (trade fairs), held at the southern edge of the Westend district on the ground of **Messe** (p381).

If you're in Frankfurt during one of the really big trade fairs, you'll experience a city transformed. **Accommodation prices** (p382) skyrocket, getting a table at many restaurants, even casual establishments, requires advance booking, and you'll overhear conversations – in strange jargon, sprinkled with obscure acronyms – about parts of the global economy that usually fly under the radar.

Major trade fairs include:

Heimtextil Frankfurt (⊘ 2nd week of Jan) Home and commercial textiles.

Christmasworld, Paperworld & Creativeworld (⊘ late Jan-early Feb) Consumer goods.

Ambiente (⊘ mid-Feb) Interior design and consumer goods.

ISH (⊘ mid-Mar) Bathrooms, heating and air-conditioning.

Prolight & Sound (⊘ early–mid-Apr) Events and entertainment technology.

Achema (⊘ mid-Jun every 3 years) Chemical engineering, environmental protection and biotechnology.

Tendence (⊘ late Aug) Consumer goods.

Automechanika Frankfurt (⊘ mid-Sep in even-numbered years) Automotive industry.

IAA (⊘ mid-late Sep in odd-numbered years) Automotive industry.

Frankfurt Book Fair (Frankfurter Buchmesse; www.buchmesse.de; ⊘ 5 days early/mid-Oct) The world's largest book fair draws 7000 exhibitors from over 100 countries.

after WWII, give an idea of how beautiful the city's medieval core once was.

In the square's centre is the **Gerechtigkeitsbrunnen** (Fountain of Justice; Map p376); in 1612, at the coronation of Matthias, the fountain ran with wine. The Römerberg is especially lovely as a backdrop for the Christmas market (p382) in December.

Römer   HISTORIC BUILDING
(Map p376; Römerberg; Ⓢ Dom/Römer) The photogenic Römer (old town hall) consists of three step-gabled 15th-century houses. In the time of the Holy Roman Empire, it was the site of celebrations during the election and coronation of emperors. The barrel-vaulted **Kaisersaal** (Emperor's Hall; Map p376; adult/child €2/0.50; ⊘ 10am-1pm & 2-5pm, closed during events; Ⓢ Dom/Römer), accessed from Limpurgerstrasse via a little courtyard and a spiral staircase made of carved red sandstone, is adorned with the mid-19th-century portraits of 52 rulers who made their mark between the 8th century and 1806.

Today the Römer houses the office of the mayor and serves as the registry office.

Alte Nikolaikirche   CHURCH
(Map p376; www.alte-nikolaikirche.de; Römerberg; ⊘ 10am-8pm Apr-Sep, 10am-6pm Oct-Mar;

Ⓢ Dom/Römer) Topped by a single spire, this compact Protestant church – built of red sandstone, starting in the 13th century – is situated on the south side of the Römerberg and was one of the few Altstadt structures to survive the war almost intact. In the tranquil interior, under late-Gothic vaulting, are stone carvings and 14th- and 15th-century gravestones.

Schirn Kunsthalle   MUSEUM
(Map p376; www.schirn.de; Römerberg; ⊘ 10am-7pm Tue & Fri-Sun, to 10pm Wed & Thu; Ⓢ Dom/Römer) Some of Germany's most topical and talked-about art exhibitions take place at this modern and contemporary art museum, such as retrospectives of artists like Kandinsky, Chagall, Kahlo, Giacometti and Klein, as well as digital art, and themes such as 'artists and prophets'. The building's interlocking structures include a domed rotunda main entrance hall and a 140m-long central exhibition building designed to resemble the Uffizi building in Florence. Admission prices vary.

Museum für Moderne Kunst   MUSEUM
(Map p376; www.mmk-frankfurt.de; Domstrasse 10; adult/child €12/6, free last Sat of month; ⊘ 10am-6pm Tue & Thu-Sun, to 8pm Wed; Ⓢ Dom/Römer)

The highly respected Museum of Modern Art – dubbed the 'slice of cake' because of its triangular footprint – focuses on European and American art from the 1960s to the present, with frequent temporary exhibits. The permanent collection (not always on display) includes works by Roy Lichtenstein, Claes Oldenburg and Joseph Beuys. Free tours in English on varying topics take place at 4pm every Saturday.

Historisches Museum MUSEUM
(Map p376; www.historisches-museum.frankfurt.de; Römerberg; adult/child €7/3.50; ⏲10am-5pm Tue & Thu-Sun, to 9pm Wed; [S] Dom/Römer) Established to showcase Frankfurt's long and fascinating history, Frankfurt's Historical Museum spent almost four decades in a concrete monstrosity that was demolished and is now in the process of being rebuilt. Parts reopened in May 2012; the rest should be operational by 2017.

Innenstadt

The Innenstadt (inner city), Frankfurt's financial, business and commercial heart, is bounded by the park-lined Main River to the south and elsewhere by a narrow, semicircular strip of parks. They follow the route of the city's medieval walls, torn down between 1806 and 1812.

Zeil AREA
(Map p376; [S] Hauptwache) The pedestrianised Zeil is lined by department stores, high-street chains and malls, including the architecturally striking **MyZeil** (Map p376; www.myzeil.de; Zeil 106; ⏲10am-8pm Mon-Wed, 10am-9pm Thu-Sat; [S] Hauptwache), with a mirrored vortex facade (head up to the 5th floor for a panorama from the observation deck).

Zeil is bookended by two squares called Konstablerwache and Hauptwache, both named after guardhouses of which only the one on Hauptwache (p387) survives (it's now an atmospheric cafe).

Riverfront Promenade PARK
(Map p376; [S] Willy-Brandt-Platz) Beautiful parkland runs along both banks of the Main River – perfect for strolling, running, cycling or a picnic. The most popular section is between the two pedestrian bridges, **Holbeinsteg** and **Eiserner Steg**.

Frankfurt Stock Exchange BUILDING
(Börse; Map p376; ☎069-2111 1515; http://deutsche-boerse.com; Börsenplatz; ⏲office 9am-5pm Mon-Fri, guided tour by reservation 10am, 11am & 2pm Mon-Fri; [S] Hauptwache) [FREE] The famous old Börse, built in 1843, is an impressively colonnaded neoclassical structure. The porch is decorated with allegorical statues of the five continents. You can see the all-electronic trading floor on a free tour (in German and English). Make reservations by phone, online or at Frankfurt's tourist office at least a day ahead and bring ID.

In the square out front, a sculpture entitled **Bulle und Bär** (Map p376) depicts a showdown between a bull and a bear in which the former clearly has the upper hoof.

Alte Oper OPERA HOUSE
(Map p376; Opernplatz 1; [S] Alte Oper) Inaugurated in 1880, the Italian Renaissance-style Alte Oper ('old opera house') anchors the western end of the Zeil-Fressgass pedestrian zone. Burnt out in 1944, it narrowly avoided being razed and replaced with 1960s cubes and was finally reconstructed between 1976 and 1981 to resemble the original, with statues of Goethe and Mozart gracing its ornate facade. Except for the mosaics in the lobby, the interior – closed except during concerts (p393) – is modern.

Main Tower VIEWPOINT
(Map p376; ☎069-3650 4878; www.maintower.de; Neue Mainzer Strasse 52-58; elevator adult/child €6.50/4.50; ⏲10am-9pm Sun-Thu, to 11pm Fri & Sat late Mar-late Oct, 10am-7pm Sun-Thu, to 9pm

[i] FRANKFURT MUSEUM TIPS

Most museums are free on the last Saturday of the month ('SaTourday'), when there are also special events and exhibitions for children (except in August and December). Museums that aren't free on the last Saturday of the month are the Deutsche Filmmuseum, Goethe-Haus, Museum for Communication, Senckenberg Natural History Museum and Palmengarten. Information is online at www.kultur-frankfurt.de.

The **Frankfurt Card** (one/two days €9.90/14.50, up to five people €20/29.50) offers museum discounts (and includes public transport). A great option for museum buffs, the **Museumsufer Ticket** (adult/child/family €18/10/28) gets you into 34 museums over two consecutive days. Pick it up from participating museums or from the tourist office.

Central Frankfurt

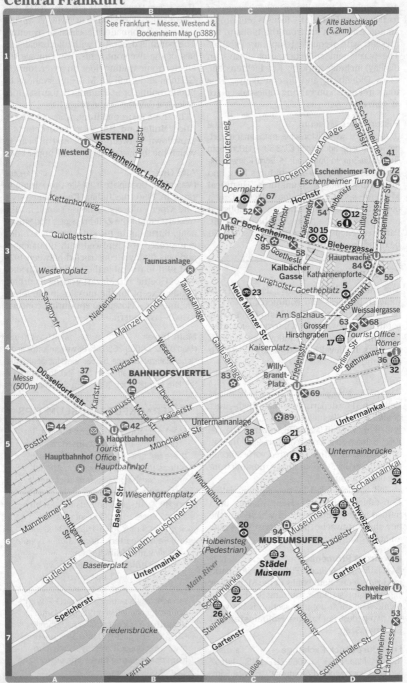

See Frankfurt – Messe, Westend & Bockenheim Map (p388)

Alte Batschkapp
(5.2km)

WESTEND
Westend
Bockenheimer Landstr
Liebigstr

Reuterweg

Bockenheimer Anlage

Eschersheimer Landstr

41

Eschenheimer Tor
Eschenheimer Turm
Eschenheimer Str
72

Kettenhofweg

Opernplatz
Hochstr
4
67
Talbenstr
54
Kaiserhofstr
Schillerstr
Grosse

Gulollettstr

52
Kleine Hochstr
Gr Bockenheimer Str
Alte Oper
30 15
6
12

85
Goethestr
58
Biebergasse
Hauptwache
84

Westendplatz

Taunusanlage
Taunusanlage

Kalbächer Gasse
Katharinenpforte
55

Savignystr

Niedenau

Mainzer Landstr

Neue Mainzer Str

Junghofstr
Goetheplatz
5
Rossmarkt
Weissalergasse

23

Am Salzhaus
63
68

Westendplatz

Wesertr

Gallusanlage

Grosser Hirschgraben
17
Tourist Office - Römer

Niddastr

Kaiserplatz
Friedenstr
Berliner Str
Bethmannstr
36
32

Düsseldorfer Str

Messe
(500m)

37
40

BAHNHOFSVIERTEL

47

83

Willy-Brandt-Platz
69

Karlstr

Taunusstr

Moselstr

Kaiserstr

Elbestr

89

Untermainanlage
Untermainkai
Untermainbrücke

44

42

Hauptbahnhof
Tourist Office - Hauptbahnhof
Münchener Str

38
21

31

24

Poststr

Hauptbahnhof

Schaumainkai

Mannheimer Str

Baseler Str

Wiesenhüttenplatz

43

Stuttgarter Str

Gutleutstr

Baselerplatz

Untermainkai

Wilhelm-Leuschner-Str

Windmühlstr

20

77
8
7

94
Museumsufer
MUSEUMSUFER
Städelstr

Schweizer Str

Holbeinsteg
(Pedestrian)

Main River

3
Städel Museum

Dürerstr

45

Speicherstr

Friedensbrücke

Schaumainkai

22

26

Steinlestr

Gartenstr

Gartenstr

Schweizer Platz

Holbeinstr

53

Schwanthaler Str

Oppenheimer Landstrasse

Kern-Kai

Allee

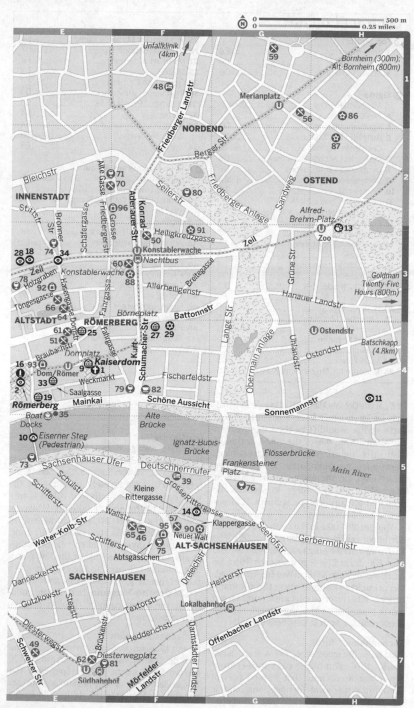

Central Frankfurt

Top Sights
1 Kaiserdom E4
2 Römerberg E4
3 Städel Museum C6

Sights
Alte Nikolaikirche .... (see 2)
4 Alte Oper C2
5 Apfelweinfestival D3
6 Bulle und Bär Statue D3
Christmas Market .... (see 2)
7 Deutsches Architekturmuseum D6
8 Deutsches Filmmuseum D6
9 Dommuseum E4
10 Eiserner Steg E5
11 European Central Bank Headquarters H4
12 Frankfurt Stock Exchange D3
13 Frankfurt Zoo H3
14 Frau Rauscher Brunnen F5
15 Fressgass D3
16 Gerechtigkeitsbrunnen E4
17 Goethe-Haus D4
18 Halligalli Kinderwelt E3
19 Historisches Museum E4
20 Holbeinsteg C6
21 Jüdisches Museum C5
Kaisersaal .... (see 32)
Kinder Museum .... (see 84)
22 Liebieghaus C7
23 Main Tower C3
24 Museum für Angewandte Kunst D5
25 Museum fur Moderne Kunst E4
26 Museum Giersch C7
27 Museum Judengasse F4
28 MyZeil E3
29 Old Jewish Cemetery F4
30 Rheingauer Weinmarkt D3
31 Riverfront Promenade C5
32 Römer D4
33 Schirn Kunsthalle E4
Wand der Namen .... (see 29)
34 Zeil E3

Activities, Courses & Tours
Kulturothek .... (see 64)
35 Primus Linie E4
36 Tourist Office Walking Tours D4

Sleeping
37 25hours Hotel by Levi's A4
38 Adina Apartment Hotel C5
39 DJH Hostel F5
40 Five Elements B4
41 Fleming's Hotel D2
42 Frankfurt Hostel B5
43 Hotel Excelsior B5
44 Hotel Hamburger Hof A5
45 Hotel Kautz D6
46 Hotel Royal F6
47 Steigenberger Frankfurter Hof D4
48 Villa Orange F1

Fri & Sat late Oct-late Mar, cocktail lounge 9pm-midnight Tue-Thu, to 1am Fri & Sat; [S] Alte Oper) Frankfurt's skyline wouldn't be the same without the Main Tower, one of the tallest and most distinctive high-rises in town. A great place to get a feel for 'Mainhattan' is 200m above street level, on the **observation platform** reached by lift in a mere 45 seconds. Be prepared for airport-type security. It closes during thunderstorms.

You can also take in the cityscape from the 53rd-floor **restaurant** (Map p376; ☎ 069-3650 4777; www.maintower-restaurant.de; 3-course menu lunch €30, dinner €79; 🕐 by reservation 6-9pm Tue & Sat, noon-2.30pm & 6-9pm Wed-Fri), or the adjacent **cocktail lounge**, where the minimum order is €25 (reservations are a good idea if you're planning on arriving after 6pm). The dress code for both is 'business casual'.

Eschenheimer Turm TOWER

(Map p376; [S] Eschenheimer Tor) A local landmark, this 47m-high, early-15th-century tower was a city gate that formed part of Frankfurt's medieval fortifications, and is one of the city's oldest surviving structures. The ground floor now houses a bar and restaurant.

Goethe-Haus HISTORIC BUILDING

(Map p376; www.goethehaus-frankfurt.de; Grosser Hirschgraben 23-25; adult/child €7/3, audioguide €3; 🕐 10am-6pm Mon-Sat, to 5.30pm Sun; [S] Willy-Brandt-Platz) Completely rebuilt after the war (only the cellar survived Allied bombing), the birthplace of Johann Wolfgang von Goethe (1749–1832) is furnished in the haute-bourgeois style of Goethe's time, based on an inventory taken when Goethe's family sold the place. One of the few pieces that actually belonged to the great man is a puppet theatre given to him at age four.

The **Goethe-Museum**, in the same building as the ticket counter, displays seminal paintings from Goethe's era.

Jüdisches Museum MUSEUM

(Jewish Museum; Map p376; www.juedischesmuseum.de; Untermainkai 14-15; adult/child €7/3.50, free last Sat of month; 🕐 10am-5pm Tue & Thu-Sun, to 8pm Wed; [S] Willy-Brandt-Platz) In the one-time residence of the Rothschild family, nine centuries of Jewish life in Frankfurt are explored with chronologically arranged artefacts, paintings (including a Matisse confiscated by the Nazis), photographs and documents. Exhibitions also cover religious practices, both in the synagogue and family rituals. Temporary exhibitions incur an extra charge.

Museum Judengasse   MUSEUM
(Map p376; www.juedischesmuseum.de; Kurt-Schumacher-Strasse 10; Ⓢ Konstablerwache) Most of Frankfurt's medieval Jewish ghetto, situated along narrow Judengasse (Jews' Street), was destroyed by a French bombardment in 1796, but you can get a sense of local Jewish life during the 15th to 18th centuries from the excavated remains of houses and ritual baths. Laws confining Frankfurt's Jews to the ghetto were repealed in 1811. Following renovations, the museum here is due to reopen in 2016.

Old Jewish Cemetery   JEWISH
(Map p376; Battonstrasse; ⊘ closed on Jewish holidays; Ⓢ Konstablerwache) About a third of the cemetery's original tombstones, dating from the 13th century to 1828, survived Nazi depredations; many still lean at crazy angles. Pick up the key at the Museum Judengasse; you'll be asked to leave ID as a deposit. Men are requested to wear a head covering.

The exterior of the cemetery's western wall is known as the **Wand der Namen** (Map p376) because it is studded with row upon row of metal cubes bearing the names of 11,000 Frankfurt Jews who died in the Holocaust. Visitors often place pebbles atop the cubes to indicate, in accordance with Jewish tradition, that the deceased is still remembered.

◉ **Sachsenhausen**

On the southern bank of the Main River, the Sachsenhausen neighbourhood stretches from the **Museumsufer** (Museum Embankment; www.museumsufer-frankfurt.de), Frankfurt's famed, riverside 'museum row', with 13 museums, to the buzzing restaurants and bars in the cobbled streets of Alt-

FRANKFURT FOR CHILDREN

Frankfurt is an easy and enjoyable place to travel if you've got the little ones along. The city has plenty of parks and playgrounds, several museums have child-friendly exhibits and restaurants welcome young 'uns.

Kid favourites include the fossils and dinosaurs at the **Senckenberg Museum** (p381); animals galore at the **Frankfurt Zoo** (p381); optical illusions at **Explora** (p381); and the **PalmenGarten's** (p381) parkland and fountains.

Attractions specifically designed for children:

Kinder Museum (Children's Museum; Map p376; http://kindermuseum.frankfurt.de; An der Hauptwache 15; adult/child €4/2; ⏲10am-6pm Tue-Sun, plus 10am-6pm Mon during school holidays; [S] Hauptwache) Kids aged six to 13 can engage with creative exhibitions at this dedicated children's museum, while littlies aged five and under can hang out in a fabulous playroom (admission free) off the lobby. It's situated at the entrance to the Hauptwache U-Bahn station, one storey below street level.

Halligalli Kinderwelt (Map p376; www.halligalli-myzeil.de; Zeil 106, 5th fl; adult/child 2-16yr/1-2yr €4/7.50/4.50, Fri-Sun €1 more; ⏲11am-8pm, reduced hours during Christmas; [S] Hauptwache) On the top floors of the **MyZeil** (p375) shopping mall, kids can bounce around a 1500-sq-metre indoor playground complex. It's an especially good option on rainy or chilly days.

Sachsenhausen (old Sachsenhausen) in the northeastern corner.

Sachsenhausen's periphery has a few U-Bahn and S-Bahn stations (Schweizer Platz, Südbahnhof and Lokalbahnhof) but for many areas trams provide the most convenient transport.

Museum für Angewandte Kunst MUSEUM
(Museum of Applied Arts; Map p376; www.museumangewandtekunst.de; Schaumainkai 17; adult/student €9/4.50; ⏲10am-6pm Tue & Thu-Sun, to 8pm Wed; 🚋16 Schweizerstrasse-Gartenstrasse) Beautiful furniture, textiles, metalwork, glass and ceramics from Europe (including *Jugendstil*/art nouveau) and Asia are displayed at Frankfurt's Museum of Applied Arts. It's set amid lush gardens; there's a smart cafe with outdoor seating.

Deutsches Filmmuseum MUSEUM
(Map p376; http://deutsches-filminstitut.de; Schaumainkai 41; adult/child €7/5; ⏲10am-6pm Tue & Thu-Sun, to 8pm Wed; 🚋16 Schweizerstrasse-Gartenstrasse) Permanent and changing exhibitions chart the history of cinema, how films are made, and specific genres and artists at this dynamic museum. Signs are in English and German; there's also an art-house cinema (p393) here.

Deutsches Architekturmuseum MUSEUM
(DAM; Map p376; www.dam-online.de; Schaumainkai 43; adult/child €9/4.50; ⏲11am-6pm Tue & Thu-Sun, to 8pm Wed; 🚋16 Schweizerstrasse-Gartenstrasse) Germany's architecture museum mounts three temporary exhibitions at a time, which often have a focus on a particular architect or firm. Not much relates to Frankfurt, though. Signs are in German and English.

★ **Städel Museum** MUSEUM
(Map p376; ☎069-605 098; www.staedelmuseum.de; Schaumainkai 63; adult/child €14/12; ⏲10am-7pm Tue, Wed, Sat & Sun, to 9pm Thu & Fri May-Jun & Sep, 10am-9pm daily Jul & Aug, 10am-6pm Tue, Wed, Sat & Sun, to 9pm Thu & Fri Oct-Apr; 🚋16 Otto-Hahn-Platz) Founded in 1815, this world-renowned art gallery has an outstanding collection of European art from masters including Dürer, Rembrandt, Rubens, Renoir, Picasso and Cézanne, dating from the Middle Ages to today. More contemporary works by artists including Francis Bacon and Gerhard Richter are showcased in a subterranean extension lit by circular skylights.

Liebieghaus MUSEUM
(Map p376; www.liebieghaus.de; Schaumainkai 71; adult/child €7/5; ⏲10am-6pm Tue, Wed, Sat & Sun, to 9pm Thu; 🚋16 Otto-Hahn-Plat 3) Inside a gorgeous 1890s villa, the Liebieghaus' superb sculpture collection encompasses Greek, Roman, Egyptian, medieval, Renaissance and baroque works, plus some items from East Asia. Special exhibitions (extra charges may apply) sometimes displace parts of the permanent collection.

Museum Giersch
MUSEUM

(Map p376; www.museum-giersch.de; Schaumainkai 83; adult/child €5/3; ⊙noon-7pm Tue-Thu, 10am-6pm Fri-Sun; ⓖ16 Gartenstrasse) Lesser-known Frankfurt-area artists from the 19th and early 20th centuries are the focus of the special exhibitions at this neoclassical riverside villa, with displays spanning painting, photography, sculpture and graphic art, along with architecture and applied art.

Frau Rauscher Brunnen
FOUNTAIN

(Map p376; Klappergasse; ⓖ14/18 Frankensteiner Platz) Inspired by a local song about apple wine, the Frau Rauscher Brunnen – a statue of a fierce-looking, apple wine jug-wielding woman – periodically spews a stream of water onto the footpath during the warmer months; when the street's busy, you'll often see pedestrians get drenched.

⊙ Messe, Westend & Bockenheim

Heading northwest from the Innenstadt along Bockenheimer Landstrasse brings you to the leafy Westend neighbourhood's parks and stately residential streets lined with grand 19th-century apartments and mansions.

At the area's southwestern edge is the Messe (trade fair grounds), which is frenetic during events but otherwise desolate. To the north lies the monumental IG-Farbenhaus, which anchors the new Westend campus of Goethe Universität (Frankfurt University).

Bockenheimer Landstrasse leads to Bockenheim, centred on the lively main shopping street, Leipziger Strasse.

Messe
CONFERENCE CENTRE

(Map p388; www.messefrankfurt.com; ⓡMesse) Spread out between 1km and 2km northwest of the Hauptbahnhof, Frankfurt's famous trade fair grounds are anchored by the iconic **MesseTurm** (Messe Tower; Map p388; www.messeturm.com), a 256m-high skyscraper nicknamed *der Bleistift* (the pencil) because its cylindrical core is topped by a 36m-high pyramid that makes its silhouette resemble a stubby pencil. The Messe grounds have absolutely nothing of interest to offer visitors except during trade fairs, which famously wreak periodic havoc on the local tourist economy.

PalmenGarten
PARK

(Map p388; www.palmengarten.de; Siesmayerstrasse 63; adult/child €7/2; ⊙9am-6pm Feb-Oct, to 4pm Nov-Jan; ⓢPalmengartenstrasse) Established in 1871, the botanical PalmenGarten (palm garden) is filled with historic tropical hothouses, rose gardens, playgrounds for kids, a pond with row boats (May to September) and a mini-gauge train. Open-air concerts take place here in summer. There's a second entrance on Palmengartenstrasse.

★Senckenberg Museum
MUSEUM

(Map p388; www.senckenberg.de; Senckenberganlage 25; adult/child €9/4.50, audioguide €3; ⊙9am-5pm Mon, Tue, Thu & Fri, to 8pm Wed, to 6pm Sat & Sun; ⓢBockenheimer Warte) Life-size dinosaur mock-ups guard the front of Frankfurt's natural history museum. Inside the early 1900s neo-baroque building, exhibits cover palaeontology (including fossils from the Grube Messel site; see p414), biology and geology. Most have English signs.

The museum is free to visitors from Frankfurt's twin cities, which include Birmingham (UK), Budapest, Cairo, Dubai, Guangzhou, Krakow, Lyon, Milan, Prague, Tel Aviv and Toronto.

⊙ Nordend & Bornheim

Quiet residential streets stretch northward from the Innenstadt, forming the Nordend neighbourhood and, to the northeast, Bornheim, with its lively pub zone.

Frankfurt's longest street, Berger Strasse, is the commercial heart of both Nordend and Bornheim. It's lined with eateries, cafes, wine bars, pubs and shops. The U4 U-Bahn line runs underneath.

Explora
MUSEUM

(☑069-788 888; www.exploramuseum.de; Glauburgplatz 1; adult/child €16/8; ⊙11am-6pm; ⓢGlauburgstrasse) Optical illusions and extraordinary images dazzle at this 'science centre', which survives without government subsidies. There's no information in English but visual highlights include stunning stereoscopic slides of insects and mammals; mind-boggling holograms; 3-D X-ray photos of flowers; and feels-like-you're-there 3-D photos of turn-of-the-20th-century Frankfurt, most of which was destroyed during WWII. Out front is a children's playground. It's 1.6km north of Konstablerwache.

⊙ Ostend

Frankfurt Zoo
ZOO

(Zoologisher Garten; Map p376; www.zoo-frankfurt.de; Bernhard-Grzimek-Allee 1; adult/child €10/5; ⊙9am-7pm late Mar-late Oct, 9am-5pm late Oct-late Mar; ⓢZoo) Dating from 1874, Frankfurt's

13-hectare zoo is home to 4500 animals and kid-friendly houses for primates, nocturnal creatures, birds and amphibians.

European Central Bank Headquarters BUILDING

(Map p376; www.ecb.europa.eu; Sonnemannstrasse 20; [S] Ostbahnhof) The European Central Bank (ECB) relocated in 2014 from Frankfurt's Eurotower into these striking 180m-high headquarters on the site of the city's former wholesale market. A visitor centre is planned to open here in 2016; check the website for updates.

☞ Tours

★ Primus Linie BOAT TOUR

(Map p376; www.primus-linie.de; Mainkai; adult/child one-way €8.95/4.95, full circuit €11.45/4.95; ⌚ hourly 11am-5pm Apr-Oct, hourly 11am-5pm Sat & Sun Mar, Nov & Dec; [S] Dom/Römer) Gliding past Frankfurt's landmarks aboard a boat is one of the most peaceful ways to see the city. Primus Linie runs 50-minute sightseeing cruises both upstream and down; for the best skyline views, take the full 100-minute circuit. It also hosts various dinner cruises and 'After Work Shipping' party cruises – schedules are posted online.

Tourist Office Walking Tours WALKING TOUR

(Map p376; www.frankfurt-tourismus.de; Römerberg 27; adult/child €14/6; ⌚ tours depart 2.30pm; [S] Dom/Römer) Two-hour walking tours of the city start every day at the Römer tourist office (no reservations needed). The tourist office also runs a variety of other walking tours, especially in summer, and has audiovisual iPod Touch and iPhone tours (four hours/all-day including rental €7.50/10).

Kulturothek WALKING TOUR

(Map p376; ☎ 069-281 010; www.kulturothek-frankfurt.de; An der Kleinmarkthalle 7-9; adult €8-19; [S] Hauptwache) Engaging tours (some in English) take in the city and its cultural institutions. Book ahead.

ⓘ APPLE WINE EXPRESS

Ebbelwei-Express (Apple Wine Express; www.ebbelwei-express.com; adult/child €8/3.50; ⌚ half-hourly 1.30-5.30pm Sat, Sun & public holidays Apr-Oct, reduced stops Nov-Mar) This loveable vintage tram's one-hour circuit takes in both banks of the Main between the zoo and the Messe. You can jump on at any of its 23 stops but you can't break your journey. Tickets include *Ebbelwei* (apple wine) or juice and pretzels.

Festivals & Events

Christopher Street Day GAY & LESBIAN

(www.csd-frankfurt.de; ⌚ Fri-Sun mid-Jul) Frankfurt's Christopher Street Day incorporates a colourful pride parade, as well as a *Strassenfest* (street festival) at Konstablerwache.

Apfelweinfestival WINE

(Map p376; www.frankfurt-tourismus.de; ⌚ mid-Aug; [S] Hauptwache) Frankfurt celebrates its famous *Apfelwein* (apple wine) with a 10-day festival on the Rossmarkt with live music and local-dialect poetry and storytelling. Stalls provide tastings and sell bottles, along with apple wine accoutrements such as a traditional ribbed glass or *Bembel* (blue-painted grey jug).

Museumsuferfest CULTURAL

(Museum Embankment Festival; www.museumsuferfest.de; ⌚ late Aug) Held on both banks of the Main, this huge two-day cultural festival held over the last weekend in August draws some three million people for discounted museum entry, tours, workshops, music and dance performances, stalls selling handicrafts, jewellery and clothing, and open-air art exhibitions. Each year has a different theme, such as 'Italy' or 'Indonesia'.

Rheingauer Weinmarkt WINE

(Rhine District Wine Festival; Map p376; ⌚ early–mid-Sep; [S] Alter Oper) More than 600 wines from the Rheingau wine-growing region are available to taste and buy from 30 stalls at this 10-day festival. It sets up around Grosse Bockenheimer Strasse in the pedestrianised Fressgass area.

Christmas Market MARKET

(Weihnachtsmarkt; Map p376; ⌚ 10am-9pm Mon-Sat, 11am-9pm Sun late Nov-23 Dec) Atmospherically set in the Altstadt, Frankfurt's Christmas market has choirs, ornament stalls, traditional foods and, of course, steaming-hot *Glühwein* (mulled wine).

Sleeping

Supply and demand reign supreme in Frankfurt's accommodation pricing. The city's hotels cater mainly to business travellers and so tend to drop rates on weekends (Friday, Saturday and Sunday nights), on public holidays and in July and August.

IG-FARBENHAUS – FROM NAZI INDUSTRIAL HQ TO BASTION OF HUMANISM

IG-Farbenhaus (Map p388; Grüneburgplatz 1; ⏲7am-10pm Mon-Sat; [S] Holzhausenstrasse) The monumental seven-storey-high IG-Farbenhaus was erected in 1931 as the headquarters of IG-Farben (pronounced 'ee geh far-behn'), the mammoth German chemicals conglomerate whose constituent companies included Agfa, BASF, Bayer and Hoechst. After Hitler came to power, Jewish scientists and executives were fired, and the company's products soon became central to the Nazi war effort.

Inside the Bauhaus-influenced building, you can check out an informative **historical exhibit** (in German and English).

From 1941 to 1944, staff based in this building kept the Final Solution running smoothly by carrying out the work of coordinating the production of the company's most notorious product, Zyklon-B, the cyanide-based killing agent used in the gas chambers of Auschwitz.

After the war, IG-Farbenhaus served briefly as the headquarters of General Dwight D Eisenhower, Supreme Commander of Allied Forces in Europe, and later as the headquarters of US occupation forces ('the Pentagon in Europe') and as a CIA bureau.

In 1995, with the Cold War over, US forces handed the building back to Germany's federal government. After refurbishment, it became the focal point of the new Westend campus of **Johann-Wolfgang-Goethe-Universität** (Frankfurt University, Map p388; www.uni-frankfurt.de) – and a bastion of the spirit of free inquiry and humanism that Nazism tried so hard to extinguish.

To get from floor to floor, you can hop (literally) onto one of the two **paternoster lifts**, whose open cabins keep cycling around like rosary beads. Signs warn that these historic elevators are not safe for children, pets and people wearing backpacks or skates.

About 50m from the southwest corner of the building (to the left as you approach the main entrance) stands the **Wollheim Memorial** (Map p388; www.wollheim-memorial.de; ⏲8am-6pm) in a little pavilion marked '107984' (Norbert Wollheim's prisoner number). Inside you can watch 24 video testimonials, a few in English, by survivors of IG Farben's corporate slave-labour camp, Buna/Monowitz (Auschwitz III). IG-Farben slave labourers who lived to write about their experiences include Primo Levi and Elie Wiesel.

Under the trees in front of IG-Farbenhaus, panels show **photographs** of German Jews, later sent to Buna/Monowitz, enjoying life in the years before the Holocaust, unaware of what was to come.

During major trade fairs (see p374), prices can triple or even quadruple, with very basic doubles going for €300 or more. The easiest way to find out if your trip coincides with one of the larger fairs is go to almost any hotel website and enter specific dates. Sky-high prices mean that you've got a big *Messe* on your hands.

To keep costs down during fairs, many travellers stay outside the city and commute using Frankfurt's fast, easy-to-use public transport system. In neighbouring cities such as Darmstadt, Wiesbaden and Mainz, which are an hour or less by S-Bahn from the trade fair grounds, prices rise much less dramatically than in Frankfurt itself. You'll still need to book well ahead.

The tourist office has a free hotel booking service. During trade fairs, it can also arrange private rooms (single/double from €60/85). At the airport, help with hotel reservations (including during trade fairs) is available from **Hotels & Tours** (☎069-6907 0402; https://hotels.frankfurt-airport.de; Terminal 1, Arrival Hall B, Frankfurt Aiport; ⏲7am-10pm).

You can find furnished rooms and apartments through a *Mitwohnzentrale* (accommodation finding service), such as www.city-residence.de and www.mitwohnzentrale.de.

🛏 Train Station Area

The Bahnhofsviertel (the area around the main train station, the Hauptbahnhof) has lots of moderately priced places to stay, few of them noteworthy but all of them just a short walk from most of the city's major sights. The Hauptbahnhof is a major S-Bahn (commuter rail), U-Bahn (metro/subway) and *Strassenbahn* (tram) hub, making it easy to reach both the airport and the Messe.

Be aware, however, that Frankfurt's extremely sleazy red-light area, a hang-out of drug addicts, is just east of the station, on and around Elbestrasse and Taunusstrasse.

Five Elements HOSTEL $
(Map p376; ☎ 069-2400 5885; www.5elementshostel.de; Moselstrasse 40; dm/s/d from €18/45/55; 📶; 🚉 Hauptbahnhof) The location mightn't be Frankfurt's most salubrious, but once you're inside the turn-of-the-20th-century gabled building it's a sanctuary of parquet floors, boldly coloured walls and designer furniture. Facilities include a laundry and 24-hour bar with a billiard table; breakfast costs €4.50. A private apartment sleeping up to four people with a private bathroom and kitchen costs €589 per week.

Frankfurt Hostel HOSTEL $
(Map p376; ☎ 069-247 5130; www.frankfurt-hostel.com; Kaiserstrasse 74, 3rd fl; dm €19-26, s/d from €49/59; @📶; 🚉 Hauptbahnhof) Reached via a pre-war marble-and-tile lobby and a mirrored lift, this lively, 200-bed hostel has a chill-out area for socialising, a small shared kitchen, squeaky wooden floors, free lockers and a free breakfast buffet. Dorm rooms, two of which are female-only, have three to 10 metal bunks.

Hotel Excelsior HOTEL $
(Map p376; ☎ 069-256 080; www.hotelexcelsior-frankfurt.de; Mannheimer Strasse 7-9; s/d from €53/69; [P]@📶; 🚉 Hauptbahnhof) The decor won't make you swoon but the excellent value just might, especially the freebies: minibar, breakfast, phone calls within Germany, and coffee, tea, fruit and cakes in the lobby. Its lift/elevator is slow, but handy if you're hauling luggage.

25hours Hotel by Levi's DESIGN HOTEL $$
(Map p376; ☎ 069-256 6770; www.25hours-hotels.com; Niddastrasse 58; d weekday/weekend from €149/89; [P]❄@📶; 🚉 Hauptbahnhof) Inspired by Levi's (yes, the jeans brand), this hipster haven has a rooftop terrace, free bike and Mini car rentals, and a Gibson Music Room for jamming on drums and guitars. Rooms are themed by decade, from the 1930s (calm colours) to the 1980s (tiger-print walls, optical-illusion carpets). Breakfast costs €18.

Hotel Hamburger Hof HOTEL $$
(Map p376; ☎ 069-2713 9690; www.hamburgerhof.com; Poststrasse 10-12; s/d weekday from €94/113, weekend €66/105; ❄@📶; 🚉 Hauptbahnhof) Directly across the road from the train station to the north (away from the grittiest part of the neighbourhood), this stylish three-star hotel has a spiffy white-and-maroon lobby and 62 comfortable rooms with contemporary furnishings and sparkling bathrooms.

Altstadt

The centre of the centre offers easy access to the Dom, the parks along the river and the Innenstadt, but properties here are limited and come at a premium.

Steigenberger Frankfurter Hof HISTORIC HOTEL $$$
(Map p376; ☎ 069-215 02; www.steigenberger.com; Am Kaiserplatz; d from €169; ❄@📶; [S] Willy-Brandt-Platz) Dating from 1876, this palatial hotel is a truly monumental place to rest your head. In addition to its 261 luxurious rooms and 42 even more luxurious suites, there are four gourmet restaurants, one of which has a Michelin star, a cigar lounge where 48 different kinds of rum are served fireside, a gym, a sun terrace and Frankfurt's largest spa.

Innenstadt

Staying in the inner city puts you close to the historic sites of the Altstadt, Frankfurt's tallest buildings, fine shopping and plenty of cultural venues, restaurants and nightlife, but it doesn't come cheap.

Fleming's Hotel HISTORIC HOTEL $$$
(Map p376; ☎ 069-427 2320; www.flemings-hotels.com; Eschenheimer Tor 2; d weekday/weekend from €168/134; ❄@📶; [S] Eschenheimer Tor) Classic 1950s elegance stretches from the stainless steel, neon and black-and-white marble of the lobby all the way up to the panoramic 7th-floor restaurant (p388), linked by a rare, hop-on-hop-off Paternoster lift/elevator. The 200 rooms are quietly luxurious, and some are huge. Amenities include a fitness room, sauna and steam bath.

Adina Apartment Hotel HOTEL $$$
(Map p376; ☎ 069-247 4740; www.adina.eu/adina-apartment-hotel-frankfurt; Wilhelm-Leuschner-Strasse 6; apt weekday/weekend from €197/143; [P]❄📶🏊; 🚋 11/12 Weserstrasse/Münchener Strasse) Handy for self-caterers and families, the spacious one- and two-bedroom apartments in this high-rise overlooking the Main River come with full kitchens and small balconies or roof terraces. Guests have free

use of the indoor pool but wi-fi is charged at €14.50 per 24 hours. Breakfast costs €21.

Sachsenhausen

A short stroll across the bridge from the city centre, the southern side of the river is brilliantly positioned for art along the Museumsufer and bars and taverns in Alt-Sachsenhausen.

Hotel Royal   HOTEL $
(Map p376; ☑069-460 920 600; www.hotel-royal-frankfurt.net; Wallstrasse 17; s/d/tr from €60/80/100; P 🖨; 🚇 Lokalbahnhof) Locations don't come better than the Royal's, a stone's throw from the bars of Alt-Sachsenhausen (weekends can be noisy – ask for a rear-facing room). It's an easy walk to the Museumsufer, the riverfront promenade and city centre. The rooms' decor is dated but they're comfortable and spotlessly clean, and service goes above and beyond. Limited parking costs €15.

DJH Hostel   HOSTEL $
(Map p376; ☑069-610 0150; www.jugendherberge-frankfurt.de; Deutschherrnufer 12; dm €19.50-31.50, s/d €43/75, 26 & under €38.50/66, f €76.50-90; @ 🖨; 🚇 14/18 Frankensteiner Platz) Advance bookings are advisable for Frankfurt's bustling, 432-bed *Jugendherberge*, situated within easy walking distance of the city centre and Alt Sachsenhausen's nightspots. Dorm rooms are single-sex; family rooms have three or four beds. There are washing machines, but no cooking facilities.

Hotel Kautz   HOTEL $$
(Map p376; ☑069-618 061; www.hotelkautz.de; Gartenstrasse 17; s/d/tr weekday from €85/99/115, weekend €69/79/99; 🖨; 🚇 Schweizer Platz) In the heart of Sachsenhausen's shopping district, this quiet, family-run hotel has 17 pretty rooms, a living-room-like lobby and a breakfast room decked out in white, pink and red. Breakfast costs €10. Reception is on the 1st floor; there's no lift/elevator.

Messe, Westend & Bockenheim

The area immediately surrounding the Messe is home to surprisingly few hotels, so even trade fair-goers who can afford Frankfurt's sky-high 'Messe rates' usually stay elsewhere in the centre, nearer to restaurants and other amenities.

Fairprice Apartments   APARTMENT $
(☑069-9739 2266; www.fairprice-frankfurt.com; Idsteiner Strasse 15; s/d from €66/75; ☺ reception 7am-10pm; 🚇 Galluswarte) The best deal in town, Fairprice keeps costs down by having no night staff (you can still access the property around the clock), no daily cleaning service and no breakfast. Its 91 stylish studio apartments have kitchenettes as well as good-sized bathrooms with powerful showers. It's 800m southwest of the Messe and 2km west of the Hauptbahnhof.

On-street parking is free.

★ Hotel Hessischer Hof   LUXURY HOTEL $$$
(Map p388; ☑069-754 00; www.hessischer-hof.de; Friedrich-Ebert-Anlage 40; d weekday/weekend from €249/160; P 🖨 🐾 @ 🖨; 🚇 Festhalle/Messe) Owned by the descendants of the Landgraves, Electors and Grand Dukes of the House of Hessen, this 1952-opened hotel is filled with over 1500 antiques from the family collections and renowned for its old-world luxury and superb service (some staff members have worked here for 40 years). Breakfast costs €32. There's a gym, roof terrace and late-night Jimmy's Bar (p392).

Hotel Palmenhof   HOTEL $$$
(Map p388; ☑069-753 0060; www.palmenhof.com; Bockenheimer Landstrasse 89-91; s €125-165, d €165-185, weekends s/d from €90/95; P 🖨; 🚇 Westend) In the heart of the leafy Westend, this art nouveau red-standstone establishment, constructed in 1890, offers 45 understated rooms with a mix of modern and classical furnishings. Breakfast costs €16.

Nordend & Bornheim

Northeast of the Innenstadt, this villagey part of town is a favourite destination for locals to enjoy a traditional Frankfurt-style meal, a mug of beer or a glass of apple wine.

★ Villa Orange   BOUTIQUE HOTEL $$
(Map p376; ☑069-405 840; www.villa-orange.de; Hebelstrasse 1; s/d weekday from €128/158, weekend from €95/119; P ❄ 🖨; 🚇 12/18 Friedberger Platz) 🌱 Offering a winning combination of tranquillity, modern German design and small-hotel comforts (such as a quiet corner library), this century-old, tangerine-coloured villa has 38 spacious rooms, some with free-standing baths and four-poster beds. Everything is organic – the sheets, the soap and the bountiful buffet breakfast.

Art-Hotel Robert Mayer   DESIGN HOTEL $$
(Map p388; 069-970 9100; www.arthotel-frankfurt.de; Robert Mayer Strasse 44; s/d weekday from €87/109, weekend from €62/84; ; 3/4 Nauheimer Strasse) Each of the 12 rooms at this beautiful 1905-built art nouveau hotel was designed by a different Frankfurt artist, with a mix of classical and contemporary styles. The age of the building means there's no lift/elevator, but limited underground parking is available (book ahead).

Ostend

The neighbourhoods east of the Innenstadt and the Nordend are known as the Ostend. Hanauer Landstrasse runs through the Osthafen ('eastern harbour') area.

Goldman
Twenty-Five Hours   BOUTIQUE HOTEL $$
(Goldman 25h; 069-4058 6890; www.25hours-hotel.com; Hanauer Landstrasse 127; d weekday/weekend from €155/105; ; 11 Osthafenplatz) The 49 original 22-sq-metre rooms at this hypercreative place were each designed by a local personality, while the 48 most recent rooms are inspired by New York's United Nations HQ. Amenities include free coffee, a top-notch Mediterranean restaurant and free bikes. Beehives on the roof produce house-brand honey.

✖ Eating

During trade fairs, getting a restaurant table generally requires making reservations a day or more ahead.

While you're in town, be sure to try Frankfurt's distinctive local specialities (see p390).

✖ Altstadt

Eateries immediately surrounding the Römerberg cater mainly to tourists, but nearby you'll find some very local – and atmospheric – dining options.

★**Kleinmarkthalle**   MARKET $
(Map p376; www.kleinmarkthalle.de; Hasengasse 5-7; 8am-6pm Mon-Fri, to 4pm Sat; Dom/Römer) ✐ Aromatic stalls inside this bustling traditional market hall sell artisan smoked sausages, cheeses, roasted nuts, breads, pretzels, loose-leaf teas, and pastries, cakes and chocolates, as well as fruit, vegetables, spices, fresh Italian pastas, Greek olives, meat, poultry and, downstairs, fish. It's unmissable for picnickers or self-caterers, or

anyone wanting to experience Frankfurt life. The upper-level wine bar opens to a terrace.

Bitter & Zart   CAFE $
(Map p376; www.bitterundzart.de; Braubachstrasse 14; dishes €4-7.20; 10am-7pm Mon-Sat, 11am-6pm Sun; Dom/Römer) Walk past the shelves piled high with chocolate pralines to order espresso, hot chocolate and luscious cakes like lemon cake, carrot cake and *Frankfurt Kränzen (butter-cream cake)*, with gluten-free options.

Karin   CAFE $
(Map p376; 069-295 217; www.cafekarin.de; Grosser Hirschgraben 28; mains €3.20-8.80; kitchen 9am-6pm Mon-Sat, 10am-6pm Sun, bar 9am-midnight Mon-Sat, 10am-7pm Sun; Hauptwache) Across from the Goethe-Haus, Karin serves German and international dishes and nine different breakfasts named for different Frankfurt neighbourhoods, from 'City' (croissant and marmalade) to 'Bornheim' (bread roll, salami, eggs and cheeses). Changing exhibits by local artists grace the walls. By night it morphs into a cool bar. Cash only.

Salzkammer   GERMAN $$
(Map p376; www.salzkammerffm.de; Weissadlergasse 15; mains €9-22; 11am-11pm Mon-Sat; Hauptwache) Warm timbers give this restaurant a cosy atmosphere, and it has a beautiful umbrella-shaded terrace, but it's the traditional German food that leaves a lasting impression, from Bavarian sausages with mustard and pretzels to three different sizes of schnitzel with lingonberry sauce and fried potatoes, beef broth with liver dumplings, and *Kaiserschmarrn* – caramelised, shredded pancakes with *Zwetschgenröster* (plum compote).

Fisch Franke   SEAFOOD $$
(Map p376; 069-296 261; www.fischfranke.de; Domstrasse 9; mains €12-26; 9am-9pm Mon-Fri, to 5pm Sat; Dom/Römer) In a large, light-filled space, 1920-established Fisch Franke serves superior fish dishes: ocean perch with new potatoes and green sauce, pollock with spinach and cheese sauce, langoustines with lemon butter, and its signature seafood chowder. Self-caterers should stop by the attached fishmonger and deli. It also runs cookery classes.

Mozart Café   CAFE $$
(Map p376; www.cafemozart-frankfurt.de; Töngesgasse 23-25; cakes €3-5.50, mains €8.50-18.50; 8am-9pm Mon-Sat, 9am-9pm Sun;

S Hauptwache) Take a seat on a red leather wing chair inside or at the Paris-cafe-style pavement tables to enjoy coffee and cake or a meal – the menu changes every few weeks depending on what's fresh at the markets.

✕ Innenstadt

The Innenstadt has some of Frankfurt's best dining options. The pedestrianised avenue linking the Alte Oper and the western end of the Zeil – officially called Kalbächer Gasse and Grosse Bockenheimer Strasse – is known affectionately as **'Fressgass'** (Munch Alley; Map p376; ⬚ Hauptwache) because of its gourmet shops and restaurants. Seating spills outside in warm weather.

★ Vevay   VEGETARIAN, VEGAN $
(Map p376; www.vevay.net; Neue Mainzerstrasse 20; dishes €5.50-11.50; ⊘ 9am-9pm Mon-Fri, 10am-9pm Sat; ⚬; S Willy-Brandt-Platz) 🍴 Even diehard carnivores might be converted after tucking into this stylish cafe's creative vegetarian and vegan dishes: tempeh with three-bean and coconut salad with mango and avocado salsa; oat and chickpea burger with quinoa and cucumber salad; rice noodle salad with tofu, snow peas and asparagus; and raw poppyseed chocolate cake. Bio-organic ingredients are primarily sourced from local farms.

You can also pick up dishes to take away in biodegradable packaging.

Ebert's Suppenstube   CAFE $
(Map p376; www.erbert-feinkost.de; Grosse Bockenheimer Strasse 31; dishes €2.50-6; ⊘ 11am-7pm Mon-Fri, to 6pm Sat; S Alte Oper) Soups made on the premises are the speciality of this terrific city-centre spot, with varieties like liver dumpling, lentil and local sausage, beef and ravioli, and vegetable. Other dishes include meatloaf, and pork loin served in a bread roll. There are tables indoors and out – and almost constant queues. Its butcher and deli are directly opposite.

Erzeugermarkt Konstablerwache   MARKET $
(Konstablerwache Farmers Market; Map p376; www.erzeugermarkt-konstablerwache.de; Konstablerwache; ⊘ 10am-8pm Thu, 8am-5pm Sat; S Konstablerwache) 🍴 This central farmers market is great to shop for wholesome picnic fare including fresh fruit and vegies, home-baked bread, delicious *Wurst* (sausages) and cheeses.

★ Zu den 12 Aposteln   GERMAN $$
(Map p376; ☎ 069-288 668; www.12aposteln-frankfurt.de; Rosenbergerstrasse 1; mains €9-24;

⊘ 11am-11pm; S Konstablerwache) Glowing with sepia-toned lamplight, the 12 Apostles has ground-floor and brick-cellar dining rooms serving wonderfully traditional German dishes: *Matjes* (herring) with sour cream, apple and fried onion; roast pork knuckle with pickled cabbage; Frankfurter schnitzel with *Grüne Sosse* (green sauce); and *Käsespätzle* (handmade cheese noodles with onions). It brews its own light and dark beers on the premises.

Outside there's a tree-shaded terrace.

Café Hauptwache   GERMAN $$
(Map p376; ☎ 069-2199 8627; http://web.cafe-hauptwache.de; An der Hauptwache 15; mains €10-26; ⊘ kitchen 10am-10pm Mon-Sat, noon-10pm Sun; S Hauptwache) One of Frankfurt's most beautiful buildings to have escaped WWII's destruction is this 1730-built baroque city guardhouse. A restaurant since 1904, it's enveloped by summer terraces and dwarfed by surrounding skyscrapers. Classical German fare includes grilled pork ribs with sauerkraut and mash, and potato soup with Frankfurt sausage.

Opern Cafe   CAFE $$
(Map p376; www.operncafe.com; Opernplatz 10; mains €14.50-23.50; ⊘ 9am-10pm Mon-Sat, 10am-10pm Sun; S Alte Oper) French-inspired mains like salmon tartare with avocado mousse or beef with Béarnaise sauce are the *pièces de résistance* of this little piece of Paris, but be sure to save room for desserts like chocolate soufflé or flambéed crêpe Suzette. Inside, the dining room has colourful light fittings made from hats; its outdoor terrace (heated in winter) overlooks the Alte Oper.

Brasserie   BISTRO $$
(Map p376; ☎ 069-9139 8634; Opernplatz 8; mains €13.50-32.50; ⊘ kitchen 11am-10pm; S Alte Oper) Sea bass with truffled leeks and spinach tagliatelle with scampi and lobster sauce are among the choices at this cosy little bistro. The front terrace has fabulous views of the Alte Oper and surrounding skyscrapers; inside, the small dining room is decorated with murals of the roaring 20s flapper era.

Ariston   GREEK $$
(Map p376; ☎ 069-9203 9950; www.ariston-restaurant.de; Heiligkreuzgasse 19; mezedes €5-10, mains €13.50-22.50; ⊘ 10.30am-midnight Mon-Sat, 5-11pm Sun; S Konstablerwache) Delicious Greek dishes, both traditional and creative, are served in an elegant corner dining room. Specialities include beef, lamb and wild-caught

Frankfurt – Messe, Westend & Bockenheim

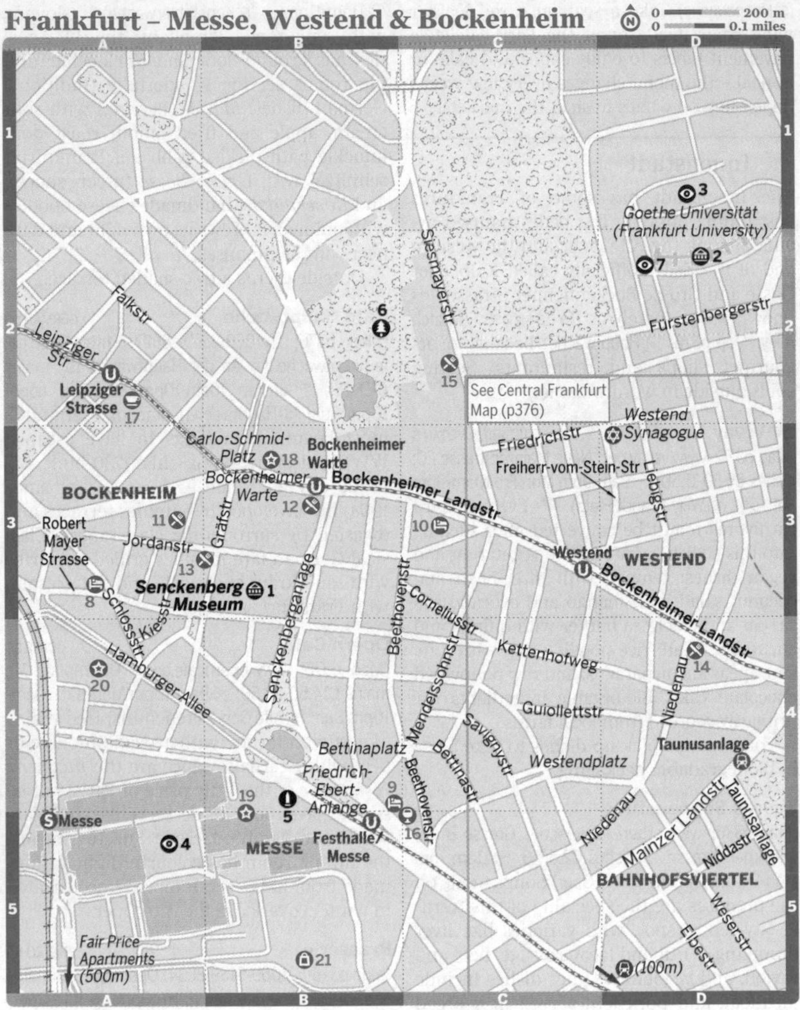

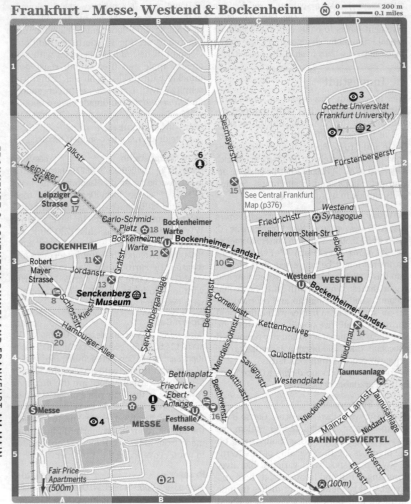

fish and, of course, *mezedes* (appetisers) such as fried baby octopus, *pitakia* (feta and sundried tomato-stuffed pita) and dolmades (rice-filled vine leaves). A two-/three-course business lunch costs €9.90/11.90.

Fleming's Club INTERNATIONAL **$$$**

(Map p376; ☎069-427 2320; www.flemings-hotels.com; Eschenheimer Tor 2; mains €18-38; 🕒6am-11pm; ❄📶; [S] Eschenheimer Tor) Stunning city views and equally stunning food await at this 7th-floor restaurant and bar, reached from the lobby of Fleming's Hotel via a Paternoster lift/elevator that will make you feel like you're in a 1930s movie. Start with dishes like lobster soup with pastis foam, followed by mains such as rib-eye steak with Béarnaise sauce and potato gratin.

Save room for desserts like Fleming's chocolate cup with double-chocolate ice cream, cookies, egg liqueur foam and strawberry coulis.

Buffalo STEAK **$$$**

(Map p376; ☎069-285 796; www.buffalo-steakhaus.de; Kaiserhofstrasse 18-20; mains €8.50-44.50; 🕒11.30am-11pm Mon-Sat; [S] Alte

Frankfurt – Messe, Westend & Bockenheim

Oper) Founded way back in 1973, this renowned steakhouse serves some of Frankfurt's most succulent sirloin, ternderloin and ribeye steaks, ranging from 180g to 400g, all shipped fresh from Argentina. There's an impressive international wine list. Unless you'll be dining from 3pm to 6pm, reservations are a must, daily all year. It's hidden down the stairs leading to tiny Zwingerstrasse.

✕ Sachsenhausen

Frankfurt's densest concentration of places to drink and eat is in Alt-Sachsenhausen. Head to bar- and eatery-packed streets such as Grosse Rittergasse, Kleine Rittergasse, Klappergasse and Wallstrasse. Seven blocks southwest, the southern end of shoplined Schweizer Strasse also has a string of restaurants.

Food Market   MARKET $
(Map p376; Diesterwegplatz; ☉8am-6pm Tue & Fri; ⓢSüdbahnhof) Colourful stalls sell fresh fruit and vegies, dark breads, cheeses, sausages and other picnic fare in front of the Südbahnhof.

★ Dauth-Schneider   GERMAN $$
(Map p376; ☑069-613 533; www.dauth-schneider. de; Neuer Wall 5; mains €8.30-14.50; ☉kitchen 11.30am-11.30pm; ⓡLokalbahnhof) With a history stretching back to 1849, this convivial tavern is not only a wonderful place to sample the local drop but also classic regional specialities like *Sulz Fleisch* (cold meat and jelly terrine), pork knuckle with sauerkraut,

Frankfurter schnitzel, sausages, and various tasting platters. Tables fill the tree-shaded terrace in summer.

Brasserie du Sud   FRENCH $$
(Map p376; ☑069-615 999; www.brasserie-du-sud. de; Oppenheimer Landstrasse 31; mains €18.50-23.50; ☉noon-11pm; ⓢSchweizer Platz) Split between an informal bistro and bar, a 40-seater restaurant and a wraparound, awning-shaded terrace (heated in winter, and open to 10pm in summer), Brasserie du Sud serves French Mediterranean dishes like saddle of lamb or duck breast with herb-gnocchi and cream of spinach in Pernod, complemented by superb wines.

Adolf Wagner   GERMAN $$
(Map p376; ☑069-612 565; www.apfelwein-wagner.com; Schweizer Strasse 71; mains €8.50-17.50; ☉11am-midnight; ⓢSchweizer Platz) Hang up your coat at one of the hooks along the wood-panelled wall of this 1931-opened apple wine tavern, take a seat at a long table and order something local from the menu – *Handkäse mit Musik* (hand-cheese with music) or *Frankfurter Grüne Sosse* (Frankfurt green sauce) along with a jug of *Apfelwein*.

Lobster   BISTRO $$
(Map p376; ☑069-612 920; www.lobster-weinbistrot.de; Wallstrasse 21; mains €15-30; ☉kitchen 6-10.30pm Mon-Sat; ⓡ14/18 Frankensteiner Platz) In a one-time grocery and milk shop from the 1950s, this cosy 'wine bistro' chalks its daily French-influenced meat and fish specials on the blackboards. Three dozen wines are available by the glass. There are just

FRANKFURT SPECIALITIES

Frankfurt's local delicacies are best experienced in the cosy surrounds of the city's traditional apple wine taverns.

➡ *Ebbelwei* (or *Ebbelwoi*; Frankfurt dialect for *Apfelwein*) Many Frankfurters derive great pleasure from savouring a glass of tangy, slightly carbonated apple wine with the alcohol content of a strong beer. Visitors, though, may find that the tart golden liquid, served straight up or *gespritzt* (with sparkling water), is something of an acquired taste (that doesn't resemble apples at all). It's traditionally served in a *Bembel*, a grey earthenware jug painted with cobalt-blue detailing.

➡ *Handkäse mit Musik* ('hand-cheese with music') The sort of dish you could only find in Germany, this opaque cheese marinated in oil and vinegar with chopped raw onions and cumin seeds is served with dark bread and butter. As you might imagine, this potent mixture tends to give one a healthy dose of wind – the release of which is the 'music'.

➡ *Frankfurter Grüne Sosse* (Frankfurt green sauce) Made from parsley, sorrel, dill, burnet, borage, chervil and chives mixed with boiled, sieved eggs and sour cream or yoghurt, this delicious green sauce is usually slathered on eggs, boiled potatoes or schnitzel.

---

seven tables, so reservations are a must, especially from Thursday to Saturday.

🍴 Messe, Westend & Bockenheim

Few places to eat are located right around the Messe as custom in this part of the city fluctuates so wildly, with throngs during fairs and scarcely a soul the rest of the time.

Near the Westend campus of Goethe Universität, you'll find restaurants along Feldbergstrasse, which is lined with impressive Wilhelmian-era buildings.

In Bockenheim, inexpensive eateries and ethnic take-aways line Leipziger Strasse. The streets southwest of Bockenheimer Warte have reasonably priced restaurants and bars.

Albatros   GERMAN $
(Map p388; www.cafe-albatros.de; Kiesstrasse 27; mains €4.50-9; ⊕kitchen 9am-9pm Mon-Sat, to 6pm Sun; 🖉; ⓢ16 Adalbertstrasse/Schlossstrasse) Plastered with anti-nuclear stickers and Green Party posters, with a patio out back, this old-time student favourite is especially popular for its sociable brunches, served on Sunday from 9am to 2.30pm (adults €11, children up to 12 €0.50 per year they've been alive).

Food Market   MARKET $
(Map p388; Bockenheimer Warte; ⊕8am-6pm Thu; ⓢBockenheimer Warte) Bockenheimer Warte's weekly market brims with fresh fruit, vegetables, cheeses, breads and, of course, stalls selling *Currywurst*.

Pielok   GERMAN $$
(Map p388; ☏069-776 468; www.restaurant-pielok.de; Jordanstrasse 3; mains lunch €6.90-10.80, dinner €11-23.50; ⊕kitchen 11.30am-2.30pm & 5.30-10.30pm Mon-Fri & during trade fairs Sun, 5.30-10.30pm Sat; ⓢ16 Adalbertstrasse/Schlossstrasse) Run by the same family since 1945, Pielok is frequented by loyal regulars, students and workers for its hearty *bürgerlich* (middle-class) German fare at reasonable prices. Think pork schnitzel with mushroom-cream sauce and *Spätzle* (noodles), or *Frankfurter Rippche* (ribs) with sauerkraut and brown bread. It has a lovely grape-shaded *Sommergarten* (summer garden).

Frankfurt & Friends   CAFE $$
(Map p388; www.frankfurtandfriends.de; Jordanstrasse 1; mains €8.50-22; ⊕noon-11pm Mon-Fri, 11am-11pm Sat & Sun; 🖉🖶; ⓢBockenheimer Warte) Nine different burgers (including a vegie burger, Frankfurt & Friends burger with bacon and cheese, and Tex-Mex burger with guacamole and jalapeño peppers) are among the choices at this minimalist cafe, along with gluten-free pastas. In the evening you can cook your own steak on sizzling 'hot rock' lavastone slabs.

There's an outside patio with warm, woolly blankets in winter.

Siesmayer   CAFE $$
(Map p388; www.palmengarten-gastronomie.de; Siesmayerstrasse 59; cakes €4-7.50, mains €11-24; ⊕8am-7pm; ⓢPalmengartenstrasse) Experience highly civilised Westend life at this el-

egant cafe/restaurant whose lovely patio is surrounded by the greenery of the Palmen-Garten. A glass case displays French-style pastries; meal options include soups and schnitzel. It's located on a street lined with 19th-century mansions.

Mon Amie Maxi
FRENCH $$$
(Map p388; ☎069-7140 2121; www.mook-group. de/monamiemaxi; Bockenheimer Landstrasse 31; mains €14-33; ☺noon-3pm & 6-10.30pm Sun-Fri, 10am-10.30pm Sat; ⓢAlte Oper) In a gorgeous belle époque–style space with bare boards, butter-coloured walls and an elevated front terrace, this grande dame specialises in seafood, including oysters (per half-dozen from €20) and sumptuous platters: Les Misérables (€33); Le Royal with a half-lobster (€90), and Le Maxi with a whole lobster (€130); and the monumental Le Mook with Alaskan king crab (€390).

French classics include escargot, foie gras, sole meunière, bouillabaisse and steak tartare.

🍴 Nordend & Bornheim

Offering a slice of everyday Frankfurt life, Berger Strasse is home to authentic and atmospheric bars and eateries, especially around Merianplatz. The stretch of Berger Strasse just north of Rendeler Strasse is known as Alt-Bornheim (old Bornheim).

Sandweg, which runs parallel to Berger Strasse, also has reasonably priced restaurants.

Café Kante
CAFE $
(Map p376; Kantstrasse 13; dishes €1.80-7.50; ☺7am-8pm; ⓢMerianplatz) The tantalising aromas of baking breads, cakes and croissants engulf you as you enter this tiny space filled with vintage bric-a-brac. Fantastic coffee too.

Eckhaus
GERMAN $$
(Map p376; ☎069-491 197; Bornheimer Landstrasse 45; mains €9.50-18; ☺kitchen 5-11pm Sun-Thu, to midnight Fri & Sat; ⓢMerianplatz) With smoke-stained walls and ancient floorboards, this cornerstone of the neighbourhood is as old-school as they come. Don't miss its hallmark *Kartoffelrösti* (shredded potato pancake).

🍷 Drinking & Nightlife

Frankfurt's lively drinking and nightlife scenes span snug traditional apple wine taverns, many of which are also great places to eat, to chic cocktail bars, raucous pubs and pumping clubs.

Dozens of bars spill onto the cobbled streets of Alt-Sachsenhausen, particularly around Kleine Rittergasse.

In summer, open-topped boat bars line up along the Main River's banks.

🍷 Altstadt

Naïv
BAR
(Map p376; www.naiv-frankfurt.de; Fahrgasse 4; ☺5pm-1am Mon-Fri, 10am-1am Sat, 10am-midnight Sun; ☐11/12 Börneplatz/Stolzestrasse) At any one time this airy, contemporary bar has between 30 to 50 craft beers from around the world – everywhere from Hawaii to Norway – in addition to three house beers (bio, cellar, and honey lager) and sophisticated street food–inspired fare. Even the slightest ray of sunshine sees the sprawling front terrace packed with locals.

Sugar Mama
CAFE
(Map p376; Kurt-Schumacher-Strasse 2; ☺10am-8pm; ☐11/12 Börneplatz/Stolzestrasse) Mismatched vintage furniture – '70s couches, rocking chairs, timber packing crates and cushioned cane armchairs – creates an outdoor lounge room on the pavement terrace fronting this hippie-chic cafe. Herbal teas range from lemon and ginger to lavender, rooibos, mint and peach; it also serves soy lattes, iced cappuccinos, and snacks such as quiches, cakes, brownies and cookies. Cash only.

Mantis
BAR
(Map p376; www.mantis-ffm.de; Katharinenpforte 6; ☺10am-1am Mon-Thu, to 2am Fri & Sat, noon-11pm Sun; ⓢHauptwache) Mantis' ground floor houses a buzzing, curvilinear glass-fronted bar and grill, with a huge range of wines and Champagnes, as well as cocktails like a Basil-Mint-Smash (basil, mint, gin, egg whites, lime juice, sugar and soda water) and a pricey but amazing Mantis Mai Tai with 23-year-old Guatemala Zacapa rum and apricot brandy.

The 1st-floor lounge bar opens to a roof garden.

🍷 Innenstadt

Apfelwein Klaus
TAVERN
(Map p376; www.apfelweinklaus.de; Kaiserhofstrasse 18; ☺5pm-midnight Mon-Sat; ⓢAlte Oper) Over 100 years old, this charming little stone vaulted cellar has communal benches where you can strike up a conversation with locals over a jug of apple wine and wonderful home-cooked Frankfurt specialities.

Barhundert COCKTAIL BAR

(Map p376; www.barhundert.de; Stiftstrasse 34; ⌚6pm 2am Mon & Tue, to 3am Wed & Thu, to 4am Fri & Sat; [S] Eschenheimer Tor) Cocktails at this elongated, neon-lit bar start from just €8 and include wild flavour combinations like Funky Monkey (green Chartreuse, gin and ginger beer), Green Lantern (green tea-infused tequila with grapes), Porn Star Martini (passionfruit, Champagne and vodka), and How I Met Your Father (gin, sugar, yoghurt liqueur and fresh mango).

Cave CLUB

(Map p376; http://the-cave.rocks; Brönnerstrasse 11; ⌚10pm-4am Tue & Thu, 10pm-6.30am Fri-Sun; [S] Eschenheimer Tor) At Frankfurt's number-one rock club, DJs (who take requests) feature alternative rock as well as punk and metal in two barrel-vaulted cellars. Things really get going around midnight. No dress code.

🍷 Sachsenhausen

Fichtekränzi TAVERN

(Map p376; www.fichtekraenzi.de; Wallstrasse 5; ⌚5pm-1am Mon-Sat, 4pm-1am Sun; 🚋14/18 Frankensteiner Platz) Founded in 1849, Fichtekränzi is an authentic apple wine tavern with wood-panelled walls, smoke-stained murals, long tables, long benches, a beer garden and a high-spirited atmosphere. Classic dishes include *Handkäse mit Musik,* schnitzel and apple strudel. Cash only.

Maincafé CAFE

(Map p376; http://maincafe.net; Schaumainkai 50; ⌚10am-2am Mar-late Oct; 🚋16 Otto-Hahn-Platz) Hidden away between the embankment and the water's edge, this cafe set in a grassy riverfront park with dazzling views of the city-centre skyline is an idyllic spot for a coffee, beer or glass of apple wine.

Südbahnhof CLUB

(Map p376; www.suedbahnhof.de; inside Südbahnhof; [S] Südbahnhof) This *Musik-Lokal,* inside the Südbahnhof S-Bahn station, is known for its '30-Plus' parties (€8, Saturday from 9pm to 3am), open to anyone who's been around for at least three decades. It often hosts dances for seniors (€4.50, Monday from 4pm to 8pm) and live music on Sunday afternoons.

Bootshaus Dreyer BAR

(Map p376; www.bootshaus-dreyer.de; Schaumainkai; ⌚11am-midnight Apr-Oct; 🚋16 Schweizerstrasse-Gartenstrasse) Festooned with geranium-filled flowerboxes, the top deck of this summertime boat bar is a sensational spot for an apple wine or beer on a balmy evening while watching the sun set over the dramatic skyline and the city lights reflecting on the river. To get even further out on the water, it also rents pedalboats (€12; weather permitting). Cash only.

🍷 Messe, Westend & Bockenheim

Kaffeerösterei Wissmüller CAFE

(Map p388; www.kaffeeroesterei-wissmueller.de; Leipziger Strasse 39; ⌚8am-6.30pm Mon-Fri, 9am-5pm Sat; [S] Leipziger Strasse) The pungent scent of freshly roasted coffee lures you through a covered alley and cobbled courtyard to this hidden spot. Kaffeerösterei Wissmüller has been roasting Stern ('star') coffee onsite since 1948, with beans sourced from 17 different countries including Brazil, Colombia, Kenya and Guatemala. Savour a cup at upturned barrels covered with hessian coffee sacks.

Jimmy's Bar BAR

(Map p388; www.hessischer-hof.de; Friedrich-Ebert-Anlage 40; ⌚8pm-4am; [S] Festhalle/Messe) Wood pannelling, leather armchairs, a live pianist from 10pm to 3am, and superior cocktails make this cigar bar in the basement of the Hotel Hessischer Hof a classy spot for night owls. Food is served until 3am.

🍷 Nordend & Bornheim

Odeon CLUB

(Map p376; http://the-odeon.de; Seilerstrasse 34; ⌚10pm-5am Mon & Thu-Sat, 6pm-2am Tue; [S] Konstablerwache) Noise levels aren't a problem at this spectacular club, which occupies an 1808 villa surrounded by manicured gardens with fountains, ponds and lounge chairs. Inside, the ground floor has a dance floor overlooked by a wraparound upper level balcony and candlelit lounge. Check the website for events, which include hip-hop on Mondays and '80s and '90s music every second Saturday.

☆ Entertainment

Frankfurt is a magnet for the entire Rhine-Main region, with a diverse range of cultural events. Thursday is a big night out for workers who commute to Frankfurt for the week and go 'home' on Friday.

Check nightlife events and cultural listings on the following websites:

➡ *Journal Frankfurt* (www.journal-frankfurt.de)

➡ *Prinz Frankfurt* (http://frankfurt.prinz.de)

➡ *Frizz* (www.frizz-frankfurt.de)

➡ *Strandgut* (www.strandgut.de)

Cabaret

Tigerpalast CABARET

(Map p376; ☎069-920 0220; www.tigerpalast.de; Heiligkreuzgasse 16-20; tickets €59.75-66.50; 🕐shows 7pm & 10pm Tue-Thu, 7.30pm & 10.30pm Fri & Sat, 4.30pm & 8pm Sun, closed mid-Jun–mid-Aug; [S]Konstablerwache) Hugely enjoyable even if you don't speak German, Tigerpalast is a top venue for cabaret and *Varieté* theatre, with programs that often include acrobats and circus and magic performances.

Mouson PERFORMING ARTS

(Künstlerhaus Mousonturm; Map p376; ☎069-405 8950; www.mousonturm.de; Waldschmidtstrasse 4; [S]Merianplatz) This rambling former soap factory serves as a forum for younger artists and hosts contemporary dance, theatre (sometimes in English) and cabaret, as well as concerts by up-and-coming bands. Schedules are posted online.

Cinemas

Listings are in the free *Kino Journal Frankfurt* (www.kinojournal-frankfurt.de), which comes out every Thursday and is available around town, including at the tourist office.

Kino im Filmmuseum CINEMA

(Map p376; ☎069-961 220 220; www.deutsches-filminstitut.de; Schaumainkai 41; adult/child €7/5; 🕐closed Mon; 🚋16 Schweizerstrasse/Gartenstrasse) This art cinema is attached to Frankfurt's cinema museum, the Deutsches Filmmuseum.

Orfeo's Erben CINEMA

(Map p388; ☎069-7076 9100; www.orfeos.de; Hamburger Allee 45; adult/child €10/7; 🚋17 Nauheimer Strasse) Orfeo's Erben screens non-dubbed art-house films (celluloid and digital).

Rock, Pop, Indie & Jazz

Batschkapp LIVE MUSIC

(www.batschkapp.de; Gwinnerstrasse 5; [S]Gwinnerstrasse) Since 1976, when it began staging live bands (rock, soul, et al), the legendary 'Batsch' has seen 'em come and go. Its new premises are in the Frankfurter Kulturzentrum, 8km northeast of the Hauptbahnhof; other concert venues include its former **Alte Batschkapp** ('old Batschkapp') premises at Maybachstrasse 24, 8km north of the Hauptbahnhof (S-Bahn Eschersheim), and **Nachtleben** (Map p376; Kurt-Schumacher-Strasse 45; 🕐10.30am-2am Mon-Wed, 10.30am-4am Thu-Sat, 7pm-2am Sun; [S]Konstablerwache).

Jazzkeller JAZZ

(Map p376; www.jazzkeller.com; Kleine Bockenheimer Strasse 18a; admission from €5; 🕐8pm-2am Tue-Thu, 10pm-3am Fri, 9pm-2am Sat, 8pm-1am Sun; [S]Alte Oper) Check out the walls for photos of jazz greats who've played at this great venue since it opened in 1952. Concerts begin at 9pm (8pm Sunday), except on DJ night (Friday) when there's dancing to Latin and funk. It's hidden away in a cellar across from Goethestrasse 27.

Mampf JAZZ

(Map p376; ☎069-448 674; www.mampf-jazz.de; Sandweg 64; 🕐6pm-1am Sun-Thu, 6pm-2am Fri & Sat; [S]Merianplatz) Cool jazz permeates this tiny, 1972-opened jazz-club/pub. Live concerts take place two or three times a week, often from 8.30pm to 11pm on Wednesday and Saturday – check the calendar for details.

Summa Summarum LIVE MUSIC

(Map p376; Klappergasse 3; 🕐8pm-1am Tue-Sun; 🚋14/18 Lokalbahnhof) This *Musikkeller* (music cellar), an intimate basement venue with vaulted stone ceilings and just a half-dozen tables, features traditional New Orleans jazz on Wednesday and Friday and singer-songwriters (blues, rock etc) on Thursday and Saturday; Tuesday is open mic night. The music lasts from about 9pm to midnight.

Theatre, Classical & Dance

Frankfurt has over 30 different theatre, classical music and dance venues around town.

Städtische Bühnen PERFORMING ARTS

(Map p376; ☎069-2124 9494; www.buehnen-frankfurt.de; Untermainanlage 11; [S]Willy-Brandt-Platz) The city's huge cultural complex includes **Oper Frankfurt** (Map p376; www.oper-frankfurt.de), Frankfurt's main opera company, and **Schauspiel Frankfurt** (Map p376; www.schauspielfrankfurt.de), its largest theatre company. Tickets can be booked by phone or online.

Alte Oper CLASSICAL MUSIC

(Map p376; www.alteoper.de; Opernplatz 1; 🕐closed mid-Jul–late Aug; [U]Alte Oper) The 'old opera house', Alte Oper, hosts frequent concerts of symphonic and chamber music in its two halls, which seat 2450 and 720 respectively.

English Theatre THEATRE
(Map p376; ☎069-2423 1620; www.english-theatre.de; Gallusanlage 7; ⏲season late Aug-Jun, box office noon-6pm Mon, 11am-6.30pm Tue-Fri, 3-6.30pm Sat, 3-5pm Sun; [S]Willy-Brandt-Platz) Continental Europe's largest English-language theatre company stages first-rate plays and musicals, with top actors hired after casting calls in London and New York.

Bockenheimer Depot DANCE
(Map p388; ☎069-2124 9494; www.bockenheimer-depot.de; Carlo-Schmid-Platz 1; [S]Bockenheimer Warte) This century-old former tram depot hosts innovative dance productions by the Forsythe Company (www.theforsythecompany.com) as well as Städtische Bühnen theatre and opera productions.

Shopping

The eminently strollable Zeil (p375) is the main shopping precinct, but for serious splurging, head to nearby **Goethestrasse** and its surrounding streets, where you'll find the city's chicest fashion boutiques and most glamorous jewellery stores. Fressgass, the pedestrian zone between Opernplatz and Börsenstrasse, is filled with tantalising gourmet shops.

GAY & LESBIAN FRANKFURT

The beating heart of gay and lesbian Frankfurt is north of the Zeil around Schäfergasse and, a block further north, Alte Gasse, with a bevy of clubs and cafes. For the low-down on the scene, check out www.inqueery.de or www.travelgayeurope.com/frankfurt.

Gay pride peaks during mid-July's **Christopher Street Day** (p382).

Bar Central (Map p376; Elefantengasse 11-13; ⏲8pm-2am Sun-Thu, to 3am Fri & Sat; [S]Konstablerwache) Frankfurt's most popular gay bar, stylish Bar Central has regular themed nights including jazz on Sundays. Cash only.

La Gata (Map p376; www.club-la-gata.de; Seehofstrasse 3; ⏲8pm-1am Mon, Wed & Thu, 9pm-3am Fri & Sat, 6pm-1am Sun; 🚋14/18 Frankensteiner Platz) Opened in 1971, this is Frankfurt's sole women-only lesbian bar.

Young clothing designers have shops in Sachsenhausen around the intersection of Brückenstrasse and Wallstrasse.

★**Handwerkskunst am Römer** GIFTS
(Map p376; www.cuckoo-clocks.biz; Braubachstrasse 39; ⏲10am-6.30pm Mon-Fri, to 6pm Sat; [S]Dom/Römer) Exquisite handcrafted souvenirs at this timeless shop include traditional toy-soldier nutcrackers, adorable 'smokers' (incense burners) depicting peddlers, miners, organ-grinders and so on, cuckoo clocks, music boxes, tiny wooden figurines and Christmas decorations.

Frankfurter Fass FOOD & DRINK
(Map p376; www.frankfurter-fass.de; Töngesgasse 38; ⏲10am-6.30pm Mon-Fri, to 5pm Sat; [S]Hauptwache) Pick up *Apfelwein* as well as apple brandy, regional wines, vinegars, oils, spirits, salts, mustard and other local delicacies like Frankfurt bonbons filled with cider liqueur at this emporium.

Töpferei Maurer CERAMICS
(Map p376; www.keramik-maurer.de; Wallstrasse 5; ⏲9am-6pm Mon-Fri, to 1pm Sat; [R]Lokalbahnhof) At this traditional Sachsenhausen ceramics manufacturer, you can buy an authentic *Bembel* made either here on the premises or at Töpferei Maurer's larger factory nearby. The iconic blue-painted, grey-coloured jugs here range from thimble-sized to barrel-like (mounted on cast-iron stands to facilitate pouring the apple wine).

Wohnen und Spielen TOYS
(Map p376; www.wohnenundspielen.de; Grosse Friedberger Strasse 32; ⏲10am-7pm Mon-Fri, to 5pm Sat; [R]Konstablerwache) A Frankfurt institution, this toy shop has been delighting kids for decades with handcrafted dolls, pull-along wooden toys, teddy bears and jigsaws as well as musical instruments.

Kleidoskop FASHION
(Map p376; www.kleidoskop.de; Töngesgasse 38; ⏲11am-7pm Mon-Fri, to 6pm Sat; [S]Hauptwache) Women's clothes, shoes, handbags and belts by Frankfurt's young, up-and-coming designers are stocked at this stark, stylish boutique, along with French, Belgian and Italian labels.

Skyline Plaza MALL
(Map p388; www.skylineplaza.de; Europa Allee 6; ⏲10am-8pm Mon-Wed, to 9pm Thu-Sat; [S]Messe) Near the Messe, this spiffing new mall has 130 shops and a range of restaurants. It's a great place to unwind, thanks to its enor-

ⓘ TICKETS FOR CULTURAL EVENTS

Last-minute tickets can generally be purchased an hour or so before performance time at each venue's *Abendkasse* (evening ticket window).

Tickets for rock, pop and classical concerts, operas, musicals, plays and sports events (except football/soccer) are available from Frankfurt Ticket. Tickets ordered through its website (€5 surcharge) can be printed out.

Frankfurt Ticket Main Office (Map p376; ☑ 069-134 0400; www.frankfurtticket.de; ☺ 10am-7pm Mon-Fri, to 4pm Sat; Ⓢ Hauptwache) Underground in the Hauptwache U-Bahn/S-Bahn station, on the B Level facing KFC. Posters and brochures announcing upcoming events line the walls, making this a good place to assess your options for going out.

Frankfurt Ticket Office (Map p376; Opernplatz 1, Alte Oper; ☺ 10am-6.30pm Mon-Fri, 10am-2pm Sat; Ⓢ Alte Oper) Alte Oper branch.

Frankfurt Ticket Office (Map p388; Ludwig Erhard Anlage 1 in the Festhalle, Messe; ☺ 1-6pm Mon-Fri during trade fairs only; Ⓡ Messe) Messe branch.

mous, grassy rooftop **Skyline Garden**, with ping-pong tables, a putting green and an urban vineyard, plus a double-storey **spa** (Map p388; www.meridianspa.de; ☺ 7am-11pm Mon-Fri, 9am-10pm Sat & Sun; Ⓢ Messe) with saunas, a gym and 20m, circular swimming pool topped by a glass dome.

Schaumainkai   MARKET
(Map p376; ☺ 8am-2pm Sat) Hundreds of tables and blankets spread out on the pavement are piled high with an incredible array of second-hand goods at this flea market; come early for finds. It takes place on alternate weeks in Sachsenhausen, along the riverfront Schaumainkai between the Eisener Steg and Hobeinsteg pedestrian bridges (tram 16 Schweizerstrasse-Gartenstrasse); and at the Osthafen, along Lindleystrasse, about 1km southeast of the zoo (U-Bahn Osthahnhof).

ⓘ Information

DANGERS & ANNOYANCES

The area east of the Hauptbahnhof is a base for Frankfurt's trade in sex and illegal drugs, and has *Druckräume*, centres where needles are distributed and the drug-dependent can shoot up.

You might want to avoid Elbestrasse and Taunusstrasse, which have the city's largest concentration of sex shows, go-go bars, short-time hotels, sleazy casinos and shifty characters.

Frequent police and private security patrols of the train station and the surrounding streets keep things under control, but it's always advisable to use big-city common sense.

DISCOUNT CARDS

Benefits of the **Frankfurt Card** (one/two days €9.90/14.50, for up to five people €20/29.50) include free public transport (including to/from

the airport); 50% discount at 28 museums, the PalmenGarten and the zoo; and 15% off opera tickets. It's available at the airport's Hotels & Tours desk (so you can use it for the train ride into the city), the tourist office, the Verkehrsinsel and some hotels.

MEDICAL SERVICES

To find a *Notdienstapotheke* (duty pharmacy) open after-hours, check the window of any pharmacy or check www.aponet.de (in German). Pharmacies at the Hauptbahnhof and the airport are open until late at night.

Unfallklinik (Centre for Trauma Surgery; ☑ 069-4750; www.bgu-frankfurt.de; Friedberger Landstrasse 430; ☺ 24hr; ☐ 18 Walter-Kolb-Siedlung) Accident and emergency treatment, 5km northeast of the centre.

Vertragsärztlicher Bereitschaftsdienst (VBF; ☑ 116 117; www.bereitschaftsdienst-frankfurt. de; ☺ 24hr) Doctors make house (or hotel) calls.

TOURIST INFORMATION

Tourist Office (☑ 069-2123 8800; www. frankfurt-tourismus.de) Frankfurt's tourist office has two branches: one at the Hauptbahnhof (Main Train Station; Map p376; ☑ 069-2123 8800; www.frankfurt-tourismus. de; Main Hall, Hauptbahnhof; ☺ 8am-9pm Mon-Fri, 9am-6pm Sat & Sun; Ⓡ Hauptbahnhof) and a smaller office at Römer (Map p376; ☑ 069-2123 8800; www.frankfurt-tourismus. de; Römerberg 27; ☺ 9.30am-5.30pm Mon-Fri, to 4pm Sat & Sun; Ⓢ Dom/Römer), in the central square.

Verkehrsinsel (☑ 01801-069 960; www.rmv. de; Zeil 129; ☺ 9am-8pm Mon-Fri, 9.30am-6pm Sat; Ⓢ Hauptwache) In a round, glass pavilion, Verkehrsinsel provides public transport information, including timetables, and sells local and DB tickets.

WHEELCHAIR ACCESSIBILITY

For details on access to sights, activities, the Messe and public transport, download the outstanding 89-page, English-language booklet *Barrier-free Frankfurt* from www.frankfurt-tourismus.de/barrier-free.html. The same site has information and links for information on using the public transport system. While buses have ramps, not all U-Bahn and S-Bahn stations have lifts/elevators yet.

The website www.frankfurt-handicap.de also has useful information in English.

ⓘ Getting There & Away

AIR

Frankfurt Airport (FRA; www.frankfurt-airport.com; ☎; 🚈 Flughafen Regionalbahnhof) Located 12km southwest of the centre, Frankfurt Airport is Germany's busiest, with the highest cargo turnover and the third-highest passenger numbers in Europe (after London's Heathrow and Paris' Charles de Gaulle). Its two terminals are linked by the free SkyLine elevated railway (every two to three minutes), and free buses (every 10 minutes). Left-luggage lockers per two/24 hours cost €4.50/7.

Frankfurt-Hahn Airport (HHN; www.hahn-airport.de) Frankfurt-Hahn Airport – a US Air Force base during the Cold War – is 110km west of Frankfurt (near the Moselle Valley). It's served by budget carriers, primarily Ryanair.

BUS

Eurolines (www.eurolines.de) can take you inexpensively to cities all around Europe (but not within Germany). It uses the main **bus station** (Map p376; Mannheimer Strasse 15; 🚈 Frankfurt Hauptbahnhof).

CAR & MOTORCYCLE

Major car rental companies have desks at both Frankfurt Airport and Frankfurt-Hahn Airport.

At the Hauptbahnhof, Avis, Europcar, Hertz and Sixt have offices next to the tourist office.

RIDE SERVICE

The **Mitfahrzentrale** (📞 069-194 40; www.mitfahrzentrale.de; Baselerplatz; ⏰ 9.30am-6.30pm Mon-Fri, 10am-2pm Sat; 🚈 Hauptbahnhof) matches travellers with drivers going to the same destination. Typical all-up fares, including fees, are Berlin (€30), Cologne (€11), Heidelberg (€10), Munich (€22), Nuremberg (€10) and Stuttgart (€13). It's best to make reservations two or three days ahead, but last-minute bookings are often possible. Drivers meet passengers at the office.

TRAIN

Hauptbahnhof The main train station, about 1km west of the Altstadt and 1km southeast of the Messe, is Germany's most frequented, with convenient trains to pretty much everywhere. Lockers for left luggage are available (per 72 hours small/large €3/5).

Major services include:
- **Berlin** (€89, 4¼ hours, two per hour)
- **Cologne** (€39, 1¼ hours, up to four per hour Monday to Saturday, up to three per hour Sunday)
- **Heidelberg** (€19, one hour, every 20 minutes)
- **Mainz** (€11, 35 minutes, hourly)
- **Munich** (€59, 3¾ hours, up to three per hour Monday to Saturday, hourly Sunday)
- **Nuremberg** (€35, 2½ hours, up to two per hour)
- **Stuttgart** (€35, 1½ hours, up to two per hour)

Frankfurt Airport Fernbahnhof From Frankfurt Airport's long-distance train station (Terminal 1), you can travel directly to destinations across Germany, often by superfast IC and ICE trains.

Major services include:
- **Cologne** (€45, 1¼ hours, up to four per hour Monday to Saturday, up to three per hour Sunday)
- **Hamburg** (€79, four hours, hourly)
- **Hanover** (€57, 2½ hours, up to two per hour)
- **Munich** (€79, 3½ hours, hourly Monday to Friday, up two Saturday, up to three Sunday)
- **Nuremberg** (€41, 2¾ hours, up to two per hour)
- **Stuttgart** (€45, 1¼ hours, up to two per hour Monday to Saturday, hourly Sunday)

ⓘ Getting Around

TO/FROM THE AIRPORT
Frankfurt Airport

Train The Flughafen Regionalbahnhof (Airport Regional Train Station; Terminal 1) handles regional train and S-Bahn connections; services begin at about 4.30am and end at 12.30am. S-Bahn commuter rail lines S8 and S9 shuttle between the airport and city centre (one-way €4.55, 15 minutes), stopping at Hauptbahnhof, Hauptwache and Konstablerwache, as well as (in the other direction) Wiesbaden and Mainz. To get to Darmstadt, change to the S3.

Intercity trains use the airport's modern, glass-roofed Fernbahnhof (Long-Distance Train Station).

Bus Bus 61 links the Südbahnhof in Sachsenhausen with Terminals 1 and 2 every 15 minutes (€2.75, 10 minutes, every 30 minutes on Saturday and Sunday).

Lufthansa Buses (www.lufthansa.com) link Terminal 1 with Heidelberg (€24, one hour, every 1½ hours) and Saarbrücken (€27, two hours, four per day). Buses run from 7.30am to 10.30pm.

> **ⓘ TRAIN DISCOUNTS**
>
> Day passes often work out costing *much* less than standard one-way fares, especially for groups:
>
> **Baden-Württemberg-Ticket** (1 day for 1 person €23, additional person €5) For travel in the Heidelberg area. Same conditions as the Rheinland-Pfalz-Ticket.
>
> **Hessenticket** (1 day €32) Allows a group of up to five people travelling together to take regional trains (those designated RB, RE and IRE, ie any trains except D, IC, EC or ICE) anywhere within the German federal state of Hesse plus Mainz and Worms any time after 9am (all day on Saturday, Sunday and public holidays) – an incredible deal.
>
> **Rheinland-Pfalz-Ticket** (1 day for 1 person €24, additional person €4) Valid from 9am to 3am the following day (all day on weekends and holidays) for up to five people travelling together in both Rhineland-Palatinate and Saarland, plus adjacent parts of Hesse (including Wiesbaden) and Baden-Württemberg (including Mannheim). Parents and grandparents can bring along their own children or grandchildren under age 15 for free.

Taxi A taxi from the airport to the city centre costs about €25 to €35.

Frankfurt-Hahn Airport

Buses (www.bohr.de; passenger €15, luggage €8) link Frankfurt-Hahn Airport with the real Frankfurt airport (Terminal 2 only) and Frankfurt's Hauptbahnhof (Mannheimer Strasse; 1¾ hours); book ahead to ensure a place.

BICYCLE

Cycling is a great way to get around Frankfurt, which is criss-crossed with designated bike lanes.

Call-a-Bike (☑ 069-4272 7722; www.callabike-interaktiv.de) To use Deutsche Bahn's share bicycle scheme, register by phone with your credit card number then go to one of Frankfurt's 72 Call-a-Bike Stations and phone to get the lock code to pick up a bicycle. Costs are €0.08 a minute and up to €15 for 24 hours.

Next Bike (☑ 030-6920 5046; www.nextbike.de; per hr/24hr €1/9) After registering with a credit card, go to one of Frankfurt's dozens of pick-up points throughout the city and use the app to get the lock code.

CAR & MOTORCYCLE

Traffic flows smoothly in central Frankfurt, but the many one-way streets mean a good sat nav/GPS can save a lot of time and frustration.

Throughout the centre you'll see signs indicating the way to the nearest *Parkhaus* (parking garage) and the number of spaces left. City centre street parking is generally limited to one hour.

In many areas, parking on one side of the street is reserved for *Bewohner* (local residents) whose cars have a special sticker. Signs list the hours during which restrictions apply.

PUBLIC TRANSPORT

Frankfurt's excellent transport system, part of the **RMV** (Rhein-Main-Verkehrsverbund; www.rmv.de) network, integrates all bus, *Strassenbahn* (tram), S-Bahn (commuter rail) and U-Bahn (metro/subway) lines.

➤ Tickets can be purchased at transit stops from *Fahrkartenautomaten* (ticket machines). Zone 50 encompasses most of Frankfurt, excluding the airport. Machines accept euro coins and bills (up to €10 or €20) and chip-and-pin credit cards, which excludes many US-issued cards (and even some international chip-and-pin cards).

➤ An *Einzelfahrt* (single-ride) ticket costs €2.75 (for children aged six to 14 years €1.60); it's time-stamped when you buy it and so is valid only for travel you begin immediately. For trips of less than 2km, buy a *Kurzstrecke* (short-distance journey) ticket (€1.75).

➤ A *Tageskarte* (all-day ticket), valid from the start of service until 3.30am the next day, costs €6.80 (€8.85 including the airport); a *Gruppentageskarte* (all-day collective ticket), for up to five people, is just €10.50 (€15.80 including the airport) – a superb deal.

➤ A *Wochenkarte* (weekly pass, valid for any seven consecutive days), sold at the airport's DB ticket office and available from some ticket machines, costs €24.70 (including the airport) and is also great value.

➤ **Nachtbus** (night bus; Map p376; www.nachtbus-frankfurt.de) lines, whose numbers begin with 'n', leave from Konstablerwache half-hourly (hourly for some suburban destinations) from 1.30am to 4am daily. For destinations outside of the city, the Nachtbus service runs only on Friday and Saturday nights and holiday eves. Tickets cost the same as for daytime transport, or you can use an all-day ticket or weekly pass.

➤ Inspectors frequently check to make sure passengers have valid tickets. The fine for travelling *schwarz* ('black', ie without a ticket) is €40.

TAXI

Taxis have a €2.75 flagfall (€3.25 at night); travel costs €1.65 per kilometre (€1.75 at night), with a waiting charge of €26 per hour (€32 at night). A fifth passenger costs €7 extra. (Don't look for a cab at the Thurn-und-Taxis-Palais, named after a German princely family.)

There are taxi ranks throughout the city.

Taxi Frankfurt (☑069-230 001; www.taxi-frankfurt.de)

Time Car (☑069-203 04; www.timecar.de)

AROUND FRANKFURT

Wiesbaden

☑0611 / POP 273,871

Lined with magnificent neoclassical buildings that were rebuilt after WWII, the state capital of Hesse, 40km west of Frankfurt across the Rhine from Mainz, is one of Europe's oldest spa towns, with 14 hot springs still flowing today.

Wiesbaden's name translates as 'meadow baths', reflecting both its thermal baths and its beautiful expanses of parkland. The city lies at the eastern edge of the Rheingau wine-growing region, which stretches along the right (northern) bank of the Rhine west to the Rüdesheim area of the Romantic Rhine.

Renowned Russian novelist Fyodor Dostoevsky (1821–81) amassed huge debts at the city's gambling tables in the 1860s, which inspired his masterpiece, *The Gambler.*

Home to the European headquarters of the US Army, Wiesbaden has a strong US military presence, with around 19,000 US citizens based here.

◉ Sights & Activities

◉ City Centre

Wiesbaden's walkable city centre is 1km north (along Bahnhofstrasse) from the Hauptbahnhof. The main shopping precinct is around the pedestrianised **Langgasse**, lined with stately 19th-century buildings, and its southern continuation, Kirchgasse.

A good place to start exploring Wiesbaden is the **Schlossplatz**, where you'll find the **Marktbrunnen** (Löwenbrunnen; Market Fountain; 1537), the **Altes Rathaus** (Old Town Hall; 1610) and, across the square, the **Neues Rathaus** (New Town Hall; 1884–87). On the north side is the neoclassical Stadtschloss (1840), built for Duke Wilhelm von Nassau and now home of the Hessischer Landtag (Hessian state parliament).

⭐**Marktkirche** CHURCH
(www.marktkirche-wiesbaden.de; ☺2-6pm Tue, Thu & Fri, 10-11.30am & 2-6pm Wed, 10-11am & noon-2pm Sat, 2-5pm Sun Mar-Dec, shorter hours Jan & Feb) The Protestant neo-Gothic Marktkirche, built of bright red bricks from 1852 to 1862, has a **Glockenspiel** (carillon; ☺rings 9am, noon, 3pm & 5pm daily, concerts noon-12.30pm Sat) – the 45 bronze bells weigh between 13kg and 2200kg. Schedules for regular organ concerts are posted on the website.

⭐**Kurhaus Wiesbaden** HISTORIC BUILDING
(www.wiesbaden.de; Kurhausplatz 1; ☺24hr, closed during events) Built in 1907, the neoclassical Kurhaus is now the city's convention centre. Ornate interior spaces include the **main hall**, with its marble floor, granite columns, Greco-Roman–style statuary and sparkling dome mosaics, and the **casino** (Wiesbaden Casino; www.casino-wiesbaden.de; admission €2.50; ☺2.45pm-3am Sun-Thu, to 4am Fri & Sat). ID required; men will need a jacket, button-down shirt and nonsports shoes.

Out front, the aptly named **Bowling Green** is flanked by an elegant, 129m-long **colonnade** and, opposite, the Hessisches Staatstheater (p401), whose arcade shelters stylish boutiques.

Museum Wiesbaden MUSEUM
(www.museum-wiesbaden.de; Friedrich-Ebert-Allee 2; adult/child €10/free; ☺10am-5pm Wed & Fri-Sun, to 8pm Tue & Thu) Paintings from the 12th to 19th centuries and some 100 works by the Russian expressionist Alexei Jawlensky (1864–1941), who lived in Wiesbaden for the last 20 years of his life, are highlights of Wiesbaden's art museum, along with late-20th-century installations, objects, sculptures and paintings, and a natural sciences section featuring geological, mineral and botanical exhibits. Don't miss the dazzling gilded hall mosaic dating from just before WWI.

Michelsberg Synagogue Memorial MEMORIAL
(www.am-spiegelgasse.de; Michelsberg 24) The site of Wiesbaden's largest pre-war synagogue, built in 1869 and destroyed in 1938, is marked by a memorial that includes an outline of the structure (in dark paving stones on the footpaths and street) and historic photos and biographical information on 1507 Wiesbaden Jews who perished in the Holocaust.

★ **Kaiser-Friedrich-Therme**   THERMAL BATHS
(www.wiesbaden.de; Langgasse 38-40; per hr May-Aug €4.50, Sep-Apr €6; ◎10am-10pm, to midnight Fri & Sat Sep-Apr, women only Tue) Built in 1913 on the site of a Roman steam bath, the gorgeous Kaiser-Friedrich-Therme, still run by the city, lets you experience 'Irish-Roman' spa culture with saunas and pools fed by water naturally heated to 66.4°C. Bathrobes and towels can be rented; swimsuits are banned in the sauna (you can wear a towel) and optional elsewhere. Shower before entering the pools. The minimum age for the sauna is 16, but kids can access the bathing area.

Kochbrunnen   HOT SPRINGS
(Kranzplatz; ◎24hr) If you're game to taste-test the hot spa waters for which the city is known (and named), which are said to have wonderful pharmacological powers, head to the Kochbrunnen. Inside the stone pavilion are four free-flowing spouts. A sign recommends drinking no more than 1L a day, though if you can down more than a mouthful you deserve a beer.

There's another hot springs tap at the **Bäckerbrunnen** (Grabenstrasse; ◎24hr), a little brick building a block south of Goldgasse.

◉ **Neroberg**

About 2km northwest of the centre, the Neroberg is a 245m-high hill that's home to one of the oldest vineyards in the area.

Russian Orthodox Church   CHURCH
(www.roc-wiesbaden.de; Christian-Spielmann-Weg 2; admission by donation; ◎10am-6pm Mon-Fri, 10am-4.45pm Sat, 12.30-6pm Sun May-Oct, 10am-5pm Apr, 10am-4pm Nov-Mar) The five glinting gold onion domes of this Russian Orthodox Church, built between 1847 and 1855, rise above a canopy of trees 600m southeast of the Neroberg hill.

Nerobergbahn   FUNICULAR
(www.nerobergbahn.de; one-way/return adult €2.70/3.50, child €1.35/1.75; ◎9am-8pm May-Aug, 10am-7pm Apr, Sep & Oct) The easiest way to get up the Neroberg is aboard this 1888, water ballast–powered funicular railway. The top car is filled with up to 7000L of water, making it heavier than the bottom car, to which it's attached by a 452m-long cable. When the heavier car reaches the bottom, the water is pumped out and back up the hill.

Opelbad   SWIMMING POOL
(adult/child €8.20/3; ◎7am-8pm May-Sep) Attractions on the Neroberg include this

---

ⓘ CYCLING PARADISE

Delightful long-distance bike trails (www.radwanderland.de and www.radroutenplaner.hessen.de) – many following decommissioned rail lines, with gentle gradients – run along the Rhine, the Moselle, the German Wine Route and in the Saarland. Almost all cities and towns have bike rental options.

Tourist offices can supply cycling maps that include elevation charts, and outline your public transport options (so, for example , you can catch a ride up the hill and cycle back down).

Bicycles can be taken aboard all regional trains for no charge except between 6am and 9am from Monday to Friday, when you need a special ticket (from €1.80). You can also take bikes aboard ferries for a small charge (€1 to €2.50).

Bauhaus-style outdoor swimming pool complex, built in 1934.

⟲ Tours

City Walking Tour   WALKING TOUR
(www.wiesbaden.de; Marktplatz 1; adult/child €6.50/1.80; ◎10.30am & 2.30pm Sat May-Oct, 10.30am Sat Feb-Apr & Nov) Wiesbaden's tourist office runs 90-minute walking tours of the city in English and German; it also has an English-only tour at 2pm Saturday from June to September.

🛏 Sleeping

Room rates rise only moderately during Frankfurt's trade fairs, making Wiesbaden a reasonably priced base.

DJH Hostel   HOSTEL $
(☑0611-486 57; www.jugendherberge.de; Blücherstrasse 66; dm/s/d/q €28/35.50/69/134; ☎) Behind its functional exterior, this recently modernised 238-bed hostel 1.2km west of the city centre has squeaky-clean rooms and helpful staff. Amenities include table football, billiards, air hockey, and a barbecue area. From the Hauptbahnhof or the centre, take bus 14 to Gneisenaustrasse.

Citta Trüffel Hotel   BOUTIQUE HOTEL $$
(☑0611-990 5510; www.citta-hotel.de; Webergasse 6-8; s/d weekdays from €115/145, weekends €95/125; ✳☎) Just 300m from the Altstadt, this ultrastylish business hotel's 27 sleek, spacious rooms have natural materials, cool

Wiesbaden

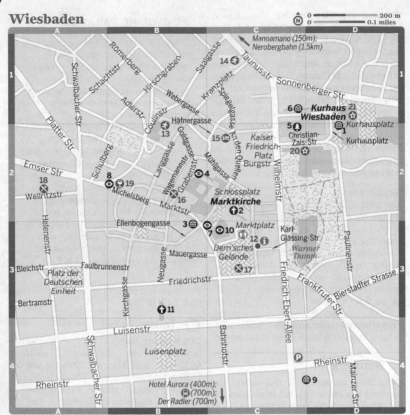

neutral colour schemes, designer lighting and parquet floors, as well as huge, state-of-the-art bathrooms. Some rooms open onto balconies.

Hotel Aurora
HOTEL **$$**

(☑ 0611-373 728; www.aurora-wiesbaden.de; Untere Albrechtstrasse 9; s/d from €69/89; P@🖀) Friendly and bright, this 31-room gem, in a late-19th-century building with high ceilings (but no lift/elevator), is just three blocks north along Bahnhofstrasse from the Hauptbahnhof, but peaceful and quiet. The pretty courtyard garden has umbrella-shaded tables, where breakfast is served in fine weather.

✕ Eating

Restaurant-lined Goldgasse, a block north of the Stadtschloss, is the heart of Wiesbaden's dining district.

Trüffel Feinkost
DELI **$**

(www.trueffel.net; Webergasse 6-8; ⊙9am-7pm Mon-Fri, 8am-4pm Sat) Gourmet goods at this tantalising deli range from cheeses, salamis, antipasti and artisan breads to ready-to-eat dishes like spaghetti bolognese with parmesan, bratwurst and potato salad, and schnitzel with rosemary potatoes.

Food Market
MARKET **$**

(Dern'sches Gelände; ⊙7am-2pm Wed & Sat) Food stalls set up twice weekly next to the tourist office on the Schlossplatz.

★ das!Burger
BURGERS **$$**

(☑ 0611-5808 9030; www.das-burger.com; Grabenstrasse 16; burgers €8-12; ⊙11am-11pm Tue-Sat, noon-10pm Sun) 🖉 Towering burgers made with locally sourced produce include the Alamo (cheddar, beef, onion rings, pickles and BBQ sauce), Farmhouse (bacon, beef, tomato, fried egg and goats cheese), and the brilliantly named Lousy Hunter (seared haloumi cheese, pickled red onions, grilled peppers and zucchini, and olive and mush-

Wiesbaden

room tapenade, cooked on its own grill). There's a fantastic range of craft beers.

Harput Restaurant　TURKISH $$
(📞 0611-406 196; www.harputrestaurant.de; Wellritzstrasse 9; mains €7.50-12; ☺ 7am-1am Sun-Thu, to 2am Fri & Sat) In the heart of Wiesbaden's Turkish quarter, you can feast on Anatolian breads and mains such as skewers of grilled meat at this hugely popular sit-down Turkish restaurant.

🍸 Drinking

Manoamano　COCKTAIL BAR
(www.manoamano-bar.de; Taunusstrasse 31; ☺ 6.30pm-2am Mon-Sat) Wiesbaden's coolest cocktail bar has a 9m-long LED light wall, custom-made luminescent panels on its walls and ceiling, and amazing cocktails: elderflower Collins, made with Wiesbaden-distilled Amato gin, chocolate martinis and raspberry mojitos, as well as seasonal specials and infused vodkas.

Irish Pub　PUB
(http://theirish.pub/wiesbaden; Michelsberg 15; ☺ 5pm-1am Mon-Thu, 5pm-2am Fri, 1pm-2am Sat, 3pm-1am Sun; 🛜) Expats congregate at this sprawling, Irish-run basement establishment for live music (from 9.30pm on Thursday, Friday and Saturday), karaoke (from 9.30pm on Tuesday and Sunday), open mic night (Wednesday) and, of course, Guinness.

☆ Entertainment

Tickets for events can be puchased at the tourist office.

Hessisches Staatstheater　PERFORMING ARTS
(📞 0611-132 340; www.staatstheater-wiesbaden.de; Christian Zais Strasse 3) The Hessian State Theatre puts on operas, operettas, ballet, classical music, musicals, plays and events for children.

Kulturzentrum Schlachthof　LIVE MUSIC
(📞 0611-974 450; www.schlachthof-wiesbaden.de; Murnaustrasse 1) Live music and top-name DJs 500m south of the Hauptbahnhof make this venue a huge draw for music lovers, with events most nights.

Murnau Filmtheater　CINEMA
(www.murnau-stiftung.de; Murnaustrasse 6; adult/child €6/5) Art-house films screen at this cinema 500m south of the Hauptbahnhof.

❶ Information

Tourist Office (📞 061-172 9930; www.wiesbaden.de; Marktplatz 1; ☺ 10am-6pm Mon-Fri, 10am-3pm Sat, 11am-3pm Sun Apr-Sep, 10am-3pm Sat Oct-Mar) If you're travelling with kids, pick up a *Leisure Guide for Families*.

❶ Getting There & Away

Train Frequent S-Bahn trains link Wiesbaden with Frankfurt's Hauptbahnhof (€8.10). S1 (42 minutes) goes direct; S8 and S9 serve Frankfurt Airport (€4.55, 30 minutes) before continuing to Frankfurt's Hauptbahnhof. S8 also serves Mainz (€7, 13 minutes), a major rail hub.

DB trains run by Vias also serve Frankfurt (€8, 40 minutes). An all-day ticket for travel between Wiesbaden and Frankfurt, including the use of local trams and buses, costs €15.80.

Bus Buses (www.eswe-verkehr.de) linking the Hauptbahnhof with the city centre include 1,

4, 8, 14, 27 and 47. A single ticket costs €2.70; a day pass for one/up to five people costs €6.50/9.70. The **Eswe Verkehr bus Information office** (Platforms A & B, Hauptbahnhof; ◷ 6am-7pm Mon-Fri, 10am-5pm Sat) has transport maps.

ℹ Getting Around

Der Radler (◰ 0611-953 050; www.bau-hauswerkstaetten.de; Hauptbahnhof; per hr/day €2/10, electric bikes per day €20; ◷ 8am-6pm Mon-Fri, 9am-1pm Sat May-Sep, 8am-6pm Mon-Fri Oct-Apr) Rents bikes; helmets and child seats cost €3 each. From the train station, take the exit next to Track 11 and turn left.

Taxi Wiesbaden (◰ 0611-999 99; www. taxi-wiesbaden.de)

Mainz

◰ 06131 / POP 201,961

Strategically situated at the confluence of the Rhine and Main Rivers, Mainz has a sizable university, pretty pedestrian precincts and a *savoir vivre* dating from Napoleon's occupation (1797–1814). Strolling along the Rhine and sampling local wines in a half-timbered Altstadt tavern are as much a part of any Mainz visit as viewing the fabulous Dom, Chagall's ethereal windows in St-Stephan-Kirche, or the first printed Bible in the bibliophile paradise of the Gutenberg Museum. The city has been the capital of the German federal state of Rhineland-Palatinate since 1946.

◉ Sights

The broad **Marktplatz**, Mainz' central market square, and the adjacent **Liebfrauenplatz** are the focal point of the Altstadt. South of the squares, pedestrian-only **Augustinerstrasse** is lined with handsome five-storey houses (some half-timbered) and shops.

★ Mainzer Dom   CHURCH

(◰ 06131-253 412; www.mainz-dom.de; Markt 10; ◷ 9am-6.30pm Mon-Fri, to 4pm Sat, 12.45-3pm, 4-6.30pm Sun, shorter hours Nov-Feb) Topped by an octagonal tower, Mainz' famous cathedral, built from deep red sandstone in the 12th century, is quintessentially Romanesque. Its predecessor went through a literal baptism by fire when it burned down in 1009 on the day of its consecration. Over the centuries seven coronations were held here.

★ Gutenberg-Museum Mainz   MUSEUM

(www.gutenberg-museum.de; Liebfrauenplatz 5; adult/child €5/2; ◷ 9am-5pm Tue-Sat, 11am-5pm Sun) A heady experience for book lovers, the Gutenberg Museum commemorates native son Johannes Gutenberg who in the 15th century ushered in the information age here by perfecting moveable type. Highlights include very early printed masterpieces – kept in a walk-in vault – such as three extremely rare (and valuable) examples of Gutenberg's original 42-line Bible. Many of the signs are in English, as is a 15-minute film. An audioguide costs €3.50.

In the museum's **Druckladen** (Print Shop; www.gutenberg-druckladen.de; ◷ 9am-5pm Mon-Fri, 10am-3pm Sat) FREE across tiny Seilergasse, you can try out Gutenberg's technology yourself, with instruction on the art of hand-setting type – backwards, of course. Nearby, master craftsmen produce elegant posters, certificates and cards using the labour-intensive technologies of another age.

★ Landesmuseum Mainz   MUSEUM

(www.landesmuseum-mainz.de; Grosse Bleiche 49-51; adult/child €6/3; ◷ 10am-8pm Tue, 10am-5pm Wed-Sun) Highlights of this well-laid-out state museum include an ensemble of exquisite *Jugendstil* pieces, outstanding collections of Renaissance and 20th-century German paintings, and baroque porcelain and furniture. Rare artefacts from the Merovingian and Carolingian periods include 4th- to 7th-century tombstones in Latin. Mainz' illustrious medieval Jewish community is represented by gravestones from the 11th to 13th centuries. Audioguides cost €1.

★**Heiligtum der Isis
und Mater Magna** ARCHAEOLOGICAL SITE
(www.isis-mainz.de; Römer Passage 1; admission by
donation; ⊙10am-6pm Mon-Sat) In a darkened,
dungeon-like space, a glass walkway leads you
around this extraordinary Roman archaeological site, which was discovered in 1999 during
the construction of the Römer Passage shopping mall. Brilliantly illuminated artefacts
discovered during excavations include ceremonial bowls, Roman tablets, statues, coins,
and dried fruits like figs from other climates.
Signs are in German but an English brochure
is available. The easy-to-miss, office-like entrance is on the mall's ground floor, just inside
the western entrance.

St-Peterskirche CHURCH
(www.sankt-peter-mainz.de; Petersstrasse 3;
⊙9am-6pm Apr-Oct, to 5pm Nov-Mar) Completed in 1762, the Church of St Peter is a worthy
showcase for the exuberant glory of the rococo style, with a richly adorned and gilded
pulpit and altars, putti-decorated columns
and white-and-pink colour scheme.

Augustinerkirche CHURCH
(Augustinerstrasse 34; ⊙8am-5pm Mon-Fri, hours
vary Sat & Sun) Part of the local Catholic semi-
nary, the classically baroque Augustinerkirche,
built from 1768 to 1772, was unscathed by
WWII so all its rich decor is original, including
its elaborate organ loft and a delicate ceiling
fresco by Johann Baptist Enderle.

St-Ignazkirche CHURCH
(Kapuzinerstrasse 36; ⊙9.30am-7pm) Dating
from 1773, this church marks the transition
from rococo to neoclassicism – the baroque
baldachin (over the altar) and organ sit in a
space defined by Corinthian columns and a
neoclassical dome.

St-Stephan-Kirche CHURCH
(www.st-stephan-mainz.de; Kleine Weissgasse 12;
⊙10am-5pm Mon-Sat, noon-5pm Sun Mar-Oct,
10am-4.30pm Mon-Sat, noon-4.30pm Sun Nov-Feb)
This would be just another Gothic church
rebuilt after WWII were it not for the nine
brilliant-blue, stained-glass windows created by the Russian-Jewish artist Marc
Chagall (1887–1985) in the final years of
his life, which serve as a symbol of Jewish–
Christian reconciliation.

Museum für Antike Schiffahrt MUSEUM
(www.rgzm.de; Neutorstrasse 2b; ⊙10am-6pm
Tue-Sun) FREE The extraordinary remains

**MEDIEVAL MONASTERY:
KLOSTER EBERBACH**

Kloster Eberbach (http://kloster-eber-
bach.de; Eltville; adult/child incl audioguide
€8/5; ⊙10am-6pm) Dating from the
12th century, this one-time Cistercian
monastery, in an idyllic little valley 17km
west of Wiesbaden, went through periods as a lunatic asylum, jail, sheep pen
and accommodation for WWII refugees.
Today you can explore the 13th- and
14th-century **Kreuzgang** (cloister), the
monks' baroque **refectory** and their
vaulted Gothic **Mönchsdormitorium**
(dormitory), as well as the austere Romanesque **Klosterkirche** (basilica).

At the **Vinothek** (http://kloster-eber-
bach.de; ⊙10am-7pm Apr-Oct, 10am-4pm
Sat & Sun Nov-Mar) you can taste and
buy the superb wines produced by the
government-owned Hessische Staats-
weingüter (Hessian State Winery).

of five wooden ships of the Romans' Rhine
flotilla, used around AD 300 to thwart the
Germanic tribes then threatening Roman
settlements, are the centrepiece of the Museum of Ancient Seafaring. Also on display are
two full-size replicas of Roman ships and a
collection of scale-model ships kids will love.
Signs are in English.

Riverfront Promenade PARK
(Adenauer-Ufer & Stresemann-Ufer) A parade
of barges along the Rhine pass by Mainz'
grassy riverfront promenade – a great spot
for a cycle, stroll or picnic.

☞ Tours

Tourist Office Walking Tours WALKING TOUR
(tour €10; ⊙11am & 2pm Sat May-Oct, 2pm Sat
Nov-Apr) Informative guides take you on
45-minute walking tours of the city, departing from the tourist office.

🛏 Sleeping

During Frankfurt's trade fairs, room prices
in Mainz rise only moderately.

The tourist office has a **room reservations hotline** (☎06131-242 828; ⊙9am-5pm
Mon-Fri, 10am-4pm Sat); bookings can be made
in person, by phone or via www.touristik-
mainz.de.

Mainz

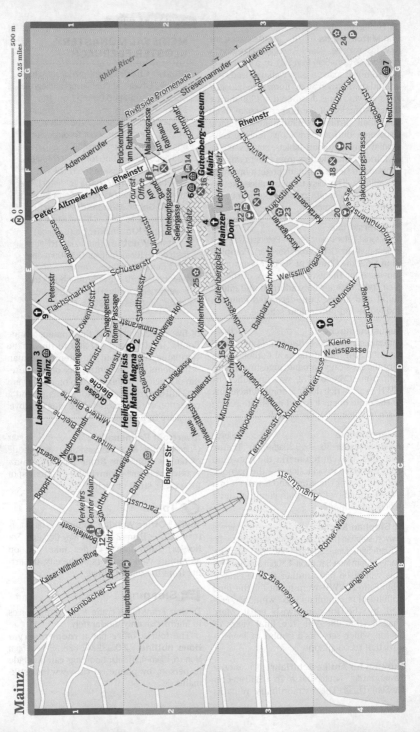

N

0

500 m

0.25 miles

Rhine River

Riverside Promenade

Adenauerufer

Peter-Altmeier-Allee

Rheinstr

Stresemannufer

Lauterenstr

Holzstr

Rheinstr

Weintorstr

Kapuzinerstr

Dagobertstr

Neutorstr

Jakobsbergstrasse

Windmühlenstr

Karlstr

Augustinerstr

Kirschgarten

Grebenstr

Liebfrauenplatz

Gutenberg-Museum Mainz

Fischtorplatz

Am Fischtor

Mailandsgasse

Am Rathaus

Brückenturm am Rathaus

Tourist Office

Am Brand

Rotekopfgasse

Seilergasse

Quintinsstr

Marktplatz

Mainzer Dom

Gutenbergplatz

Schusterstr

Bauerngasse

Flachsmarktstr

Peterstr

Löwenhofstr

Stadthausstr

Emmeranstr

Synagogenstr

Römer Passage

Am Kronberger Hof

Kötherhofstr

Ludwigsstr

Gutenbergplatz

Schillerplatz

Gaust

Ballplatz

Bischofsplatz

Weisslliliengasse

Stefansstr

Eisgrubweg

Kleine Weissgasse

Landesmuseum Mainz 3

Grosse Bleiche

Mittlere Bleiche

Margaretengasse

Klarastr

Lothartstr

Hintere Bleiche

Neubrunnenstr

Kaiserstr

Bopstr

Heiligtum der Isis und Mater Magna 2

Steingasse

Grosse Langgasse

Neue Schillerstr

Universitätsstr

Münsterstr

Schillerstr

Schillerplatz

Emmerich-Joseph-Str

Walpodenstr

Terrassenstr

Kupferbergterrasse

Gaust

Augustusstr

Römer-Wall

Langenbstr

Antonsuberg-Str

Binger Str

Bahnhofstr

Gärtnergasse

Parcusstr

Schottstr

Bonifatiusstr

Verkehrs Center Mainz

Kaiser-Wilhelm-Ring

Bahnhofplatz

Hauptbahnhof

Mombacher Str

Mainz

DJH Hostel　　　　　　　　　　　　　HOSTEL **$**
(☑ 06131-853 32; www.jugendherberge.
de; Otto-Brunfels-Schneise 4; dm/s/d from
€22.50/28/56; P �) On the grounds of the
leafy urban oasis Mainzer Volkspark, footsteps from the riverfront, this modernised
173-bed hostel has one-, two- and four-bed
rooms, all with private bathroom. Great
amenities include a barbecue area, kids'
playground, and a bar, bistro and cafe. It's
3.3km southeast of the Hauptbahnhof; take
bus 62 or 63 to the Am Viktorstift stop.

Hotel Hof Ehrenfels　　　　　　　　HOTEL **$$**
(☑ 06131-971 2340; www.hof-ehrenfels.de; Greben-
strasse 5-7; s/d/tr weekdays €80/100/120, weekends
€70/90/110; ☎) Housed in a 15th-century, one-
time Carmelite convent, this 22-room place
has spectacular views of the Dom. Rooms are
spacious and modern; there's a walled court-
yard garden with umbrella-shaded tables, and
a *Weinhaus* with a lengthy local wine list.

Guesthouse Mainz　　　　　　　APARTMENT **$$**
(☑ 06131-2702 7110; www.guesthouse-mz.de;
Kaiserstrasse 20; s/d/tr studios weekdays from
€99/119/139, weekends from €85/99/119; ☺ reception 7am-8pm Mon-Fri, to 11pm Sat & Sun; ☎)
Contemporary, light-filled studio apartments
here come with well-equipped kitchenettes
with hotplates, fridges, microwaves and cof-
feemakers, making them a perfect base for
exploring the city and region. Call ahead if
you'll be arriving outside reception hours.

Hotel Schwan　　　　　　　　　　HOTEL **$$**
(☑ 06131-144 920; www.mainz-hotel-schwan.de;
Liebfrauenplatz 7; s/d €87/114; ☎) You can't
get more central than this family-run place,
that's been around since 1463. The 22 well-lit
rooms have baroque-style furnishings. Kai-
ser Joseph II stayed here in 1777.

Hotel Hammer　　　　　　　　　　HOTEL **$$**
(☑ 06131-965 280; www.hotel-hammer.com; Bahn-
hofplatz 6; s/d weekday from €92/102, weekend
from €79/98; ✳ @ ☎) Handy for the train
station, the 37-room, business-oriented
Hammer has 37 sound proof rooms with
plum-toned fabrics, natural timbers and
bright bathrooms. The free sauna is a welcome bonus.

✖ Eating

Food Market　　　　　　　　　　　MARKET **$**
(Marktplatz & Liebfrauenplatz; ☺ 7am-2pm Tue, Fri
& Sat) Along the north and east sides of the
Dom, this big, open-air market's colourful
stalls spill over with fruit, vegetables, chees-
es, sausages, breads and ready-to-eat dishes.

Heiliggeist　　　　　　　　　　INTERNATIONAL **$$**
(☑ 06131-225 757; www.heiliggeist-mainz.de; Mai-
landsgasse 11; mains €12-23.50; ☺ kitchen 4-11pm
Mon-Fri, 9am-11pm Sat & Sun) Soaring Gothic
vaults make this 15th-century former hos-
pital a fabulously atmospheric spot to try
inventive twists on German cuisine: veal
sausages with crisped onions and wasabi
hash browns, grilled salmon with thyme
butter and stuffed tomatoes, wild herb ri-
sotto with artichokes and grilled feta, and
carrot cake with lime sorbet and passion-
fruit sauce. Weekend breakfast is served
until 4pm.

FRANKFURT & SOUTHERN RHINELAND MAINZ

⭐ Zur Kanzel
GERMAN, FRENCH **$$**

(☑ 06131-237 137; www.zurkanzel.de; Grebenstrasse 4; mains €8-23.50; ⊙ kitchen 5-11pm Mon-Fri, noon-4pm & 6-11pm Sat) Germany meets France at this dark-timber-panelled *Weinstube* in dishes like grilled tuna with riesling and sage sauce, garlic-crusted rack of lamb with wilted spinach, schnitzel with Frankfurt-style *Grüne Sosse* and rump steak with herb butter, as well as garlic snails. All ingredients are fresh, so the menu evolves with the seasons; there's a lovely summer courtyard. Cash only.

Weinstube Lösch
GERMAN **$$**

(☑ 06131-220 383; www.weinstube-loesch.de; Jakobsbergstrasse 9; mains €8.80-24.50; ⊙ kitchen 3-10pm Tue-Fri, 2-10pm Sat, noon-10pm Sun) Traditional, timber-lined Lösch is a wonderful spot for local Mainz specialities, such as sausage casserole with bacon and cabbage and medallions of pork with liver-stuffed potato dumplings, as well as succulent steaks. It serves its own wines from its Bingen estate, as well as local producers in the Mainz region. Tables are set up on the cobblestones in summer.

El Chico
STEAK **$$$**

(☑ 06131-238 440; Kötherhofstrasse 1; mains €15.50-28.50; ⊙ 6-11pm; 🕸) Widely believed to serve Mainz' finest steaks (from Argentina) and lamb chops (from New Zealand), as well as desserts like crispy, flaky apple strudel, El Chico has the ambience of an intimate bistro, with fresh flowers and candles on the tables. Its popularity means reservations are crucial all week, year round.

🍺 Drinking

Eisgrub-Bräu
MICROBREWERY

(www.eisgrub.de; Weissliliengasse 1a; ⊙ 11.30am-midnight Sun-Thu, to 1am Fri & Sat) Take a seat in this down-to-earth microbrewery's warren of vaulted chambers or on the heated pavement terrace and order a mug of *Dunkel*

(dark) or *Hell* (light) – or, if you're planning to settle in for a while – a 3L/5L *Bierturm* (beer tower).

Weingut Michel
WINE BAR

(www.michel-wein.de; Jakobsbergstrasse 8; ⊙ 4pm-midnight) Mainz' only *Weingut* winery to exclusively serve its own wines occupies a vine-draped stone building that's housed a wine bar since 1756. Along with superb whites including riesling and Blanc de Noir, there are feisty reds (Dornfelder, Merlot) and sparkling wines.

Weinstube Hottum
WINE BAR

(Grebenstrasse 3; ⊙ 4pm-midnight) Behind a plain, olive-green-painted facade is one of the Altstadt's cosiest wine taverns. Dating from 1791, it serves wines purely from the Rheingau and Rheinhessen regions.

⭐ Entertainment

Mainz is large and lively enough to have a diverse range of cultural offerings.

The tourist office has event guides and sells tickets. Gigs are listed at *Der Mainzer* (www.dermainzer.net).

KuZ
LIVE MUSIC

(☑ 06131-286 860; www.kuz.de; Dagobertsstrasse 20b) Concerts by German and international bands, dance parties, theatre for kids...the happening *KulturZentrum* (cultural centre) has it and more. It's housed in a red-brick building that began life in the 19th century as a military laundry.

Frankfurter Hof
LIVE MUSIC

(☑ 06131-220 438; www.frankfurter-hof-mainz. de; Augustinerstrasse 55) Performances by up-and-coming artists and big-name international acts are organised and hosted by this cultural venue. Some events take place at other venues around the city, such as open-air summer concerts.

Staatstheater
PERFORMING ARTS

(☑ 06131-285 1222; www.staatstheater-mainz. com; Gutenbergplatz 7) The state theatre stages plays, opera and ballet. Students get significant discounts.

ℹ Information

Tourist Office (☑ 06131-242 888; www. mainz-tourismus.com; Rheinstrasse 66; ⊙ 9am-5pm Mon-Fri, 10am-4pm Sat, 11am-3pm Sun Apr-Oct, 9am-5pm Mon-Fri Nov-Mar)

❶ Getting There & Away

Train From the Hauptbahnhof, S-Bahn line S8 goes via Frankfurt airport (€4.10, 20 minutes, frequent) to Frankfurt's Hauptbahnhof (€8.10, 40 minutes). A day ticket that takes in both Mainz and Frankfurt, including S-Bahn commuter trains, local trams and buses, costs €15.80.

A major rail hub, Mainz' Hauptbahnhof has at least hourly regional services to Bingen (€8.40, 15 to 40 minutes) and other Romantic Rhine towns, Koblenz (€20 to €22, one hour, every 30 minutes), Saarbrücken (€32.30, 2¼ hours, up to three per hour) and Worms (€12.50, 25 to 40 minutes, every 15 minutes).

Bus Buses to **Hahn Airport** (www.hahn-airportshuttle.de; one way €13.50, 70 minutes, up to 12 per day) depart from in front of the Hauptbahnhof.

❶ Getting Around

Bicycle Zweirad Boxx (www.zweiradboxx.de; Nackshrasse 14; bikes per day €8-15, tandem or electric bikes €25; ⊙10am-6pm Mon, Wed & Fri, 2-7pm Tue & Thu, 10am-2pm Sat Mar-Oct, 10am-6pm Mon, Wed & Fri, 10am 2pm Sat Nov-Feb) rents bikes.

Public Transport Mainz operates its bus and tram system jointly with Wiesbaden. Single tickets cost €2.70; day passes for individuals/groups of up to five are €6.50/9.70. Details on public transport in the region are available at the **Verkehrs Center Mainz** (☑06131-127 777; www.mvg-mainz.de; Bahnhofplatz 6a; ⊙7am-7pm Mon-Fri, 9am-2pm Sat).

Darmstadt

☑ 06151 / POP 149,052

Beautiful *Jugendstil* architecture and excellent museums are the biggest draws of this strollable city 35km south of Frankfurt, easily reached by frequent S-Bahn trains.

Famed for its technical university, Darmstadt is a designated *Wissenschaftsstadt* (City of Science). The super-heavy element Darmstadtium (Ds; atomic number: 110) was first created at Darmstadt's GSI Helmholtzzentrum für Schwerionenforschung (GSI Helmholtz Centre for Heavy Ion Research) in 1994. The city's glass-and-stone conference centre is also called the Darmstadtium.

The surrounding area has some fascinating sights, including the Unesco-listed archaeological site Grube Messel, and fabled castle Burg Frankenstein.

◉ Sights & Activities

Mathildenhöhe AREA
(www.mathildenhoehe.eu) Established in 1899 at the behest of Grand Duke Ernst Ludwig, the former *Künstlerkolonie* (artists colony) at Mathildenhöhe is famous for its Darmstädter *Jugendstil* architecture.

FORTY-TWO LINES THAT CHANGED THE WORLD

Johannes Gutenberg, the inventor of printing with moveable type, is one of those rare epochal figures whose achievements truly changed the course of human history.

Little is known about Gutenberg the man, who was born in Mainz in the late 1300s, trained as a goldsmith and then, in the late 1420s, left for Strasbourg (now in France), where he first experimented with printing technology. By 1448 he was back in Mainz, still working on his top-secret project and in debt to some rather impatient 'venture capitalists'. But eventually his perseverance paid off and he perfected a number of interdependent technologies:

➡ Metal type that could be arranged into pages.

➡ Precision moulds to produce such type in large quantities.

➡ A metal alloy from which type could be cast.

➡ A type of oil-based ink suitable for printing with metal type.

➡ Press technology derived from existing wine, paper and bookbinding presses.

Despite several lawsuits, by 1455 Gutenberg had produced his masterpiece, the now-legendary Forty-Two-Line Bible, so-named because each page has 42 lines. Thus began a new era in human history, one in which the printed word – everything from Martin Luther's *Ninety-Five Theses* to the *Declaration of the Rights of Man* to Nazi propaganda – was to become almost universally accessible. In all of human history, arguably only two other inventions have come close to having the same impact on the availability of information: the alphabet and the internet.

The area is surrounded by a lovely hilltop park with fountains. From the centre, take bus F.

➡ **Museum Künstlerkolonie**

(Olbrichweg 13; adult/child €5/3; ⊘ 11am-6pm Tue-Sun Apr-Sep, 11am-5pm Tue-Sun Oct-Mar) Displays supremely elegant *Jugendstil* furniture, tableware, textiles, ceramics and jewellery.

➡ **Ausstellungsgebäude Mathildenhöhe**

(adult €5-8, student €3-6; ⊘ 11am-6pm Tue, Wed & Fri-Sun, to 9pm Thu Apr-Sep, 11am-5pm Tue, Wed & Fri-Sun, to 9pm Thu Oct-Mar) Puts on temporary art exhibitions.

➡ **Russian Orthodox Chapel**

(☑ 06151-424 235; Nikolaiweg 18; ⊘ 10am-1pm & 2-4pm Tue-Sat, 2-4pm Sun) Mathildenhöhe's western slope is graced by the three golden onion domes of a mosaic-adorned Russian Orthodox chapel. It was built from 1897 to 1899 for the last Russian Tsar, Nicholas II, who married a local gal, Princess Alix von Hessen (Grand Duke Ernst Ludwig's younger sister), in 1894.

Luisenplatz   SQUARE

Darmstadt's focal point is 18th-century Luisenplatz, a veritable hive of activity thanks to the adjacent shopping precinct, which stretches south from the LuisenCenter shopping mall for several pedestrianised blocks.

In the centre of Luisenplatz, a 39m-high column, erected in 1844, holds aloft a statue of Grand Duke Ludwig I of Hesse and the Rhine (1753–1830). The square itself is named after his wife, Grand Duchesse Louise (1761–1829).

Luisenplatz is 1.5km east of the Hauptbahnhof, linked by trams 2, 3 and 5.

Hessisches Landesmuseum   MUSEUM

(www.hlmd.de; Friedensplatz 1; adult/child €6/free; ⊘ 10am-6pm Tue, Thu & Fri, 10am-8pm Wed, 11am-5pm Sat & Sun) An exceptional selection of works by Joseph Beuys is the highlight of the wide-ranging art collection at the Hesse State Museum. It's located two blocks northeast of Luisenplatz.

Schlossmuseum   MUSEUM

(☑ 06151-240 35; www.schlossmuseum-darmstadt. de; Marktplatz 15; adult/child €4/2; ⊘ tours 10am, 11.30am, 1pm, 2.30pm & 4pm Fri-Sun) Ornate furnishings, carriages and paintings pack the Schlossmuseum, one block east of Luisenplatz. It occupies the southeast corner of the Schloss complex, one-time resi-

dence of the landgraves and grand dukes of Hessen-Darmstadt. Rebuilt after WWII damage, it is now part of the **university** (TU Darmstadt; www.tu-darmstadt.de; Karolinenplatz 5). The only way to visit is by compulsory tours (in German; some guides speak English).

Jugendstilbad   SWIMMING POOL

(www.jugendstilbad.de; Mercksplatz 1; swimming pools 2hr/4hr/all day €6/8.20/10.40, incl spa €9.30/12.10/14.30, incl spa & saunas €13.60/16.40/19.70; ⊘ 10am-10pm, to midnight 2nd Fri of month, to 2am last Sat of month) This historic swimming and spa complex looks just as gorgeous as it did when it opened in 1909. It has a year-round outdoor pool, superb *Jugendstil* indoor pool, children's pools and 10 dry and wet saunas. Some areas are *textilfrei* (clothing-free). You can rent a towel (€5) and bathrobe (€5). It's one block east of the Schloss along Landgraf-Georg-Strasse.

Grosser Woog   LAKE

For open-air swimming in warm weather, head to this natural lake four blocks south of Mathildenhöhe. It's served by bus L from the city centre.

☞ Tours

Tourist Office Tours   TOUR

(tours from €5) The tourist office runs tours of the city and Matildenhöhe (some in English); schedules are posted online.

🛏 Sleeping

If you'll be visiting the Frankfurt area during a big trade fair, staying in Darmstadt is a good way to avoid spending a fortune on a room. Local prices rise only moderately during fairs, and train travel to Frankfurt's Hauptbahnhof can take as little as 20 minutes. Book early, though, as rooms fill up fast.

DJH Hostel   HOSTEL $

(☑ 06151-452 93; www.darmstadt.jugendherberge. de; Landgraf-Georg-Strasse 119; dm/s €26/36; 🛜) This basic, 130-bed hostel has a superb setting on the shores of the Grosser Woog lake. From the city centre take bus L to the 'Woog' stop.

★**Hotel Jagdschloss Kranichstein**   HISTORIC HOTEL $$

(☑ 06151-130 670; www.hotel-jagdschloss-kranichstein.de; Kranichstein Strasse 261; d from €95; 🅿@🛜) Set on 4.2 hectares of forest and parkland 5km northeast of Darmstadt, this 1580-built hunting lodge is now a magnificent hotel, with contemporary countrified rooms throughout the estate's buildings. Breakfast starts from €17; epicurean options include a game-specialist restaurant, bar/bistro, and *Bierstube* (tavern) in the armoury, opening to a beer garden, plus gourmet hampers for summer picnicking in the grounds.

Hotel Prinz Heinrich HOTEL **$$**
(☑06151-813 70; www.hotel-prinz-heinrich.de; Bleichstrasse 48; s/d weekdays from €65/85, weekends from €55/65; ☎) A traditional atmosphere, friendly service and fresh renovations with new bathrooms, comfy beds and outsized photos on the walls make this 60-room hotel a great-value choice. Singles are small but serviceable. It's midway between the Hauptbahnhof and Luisenplatz.

Best Western Hotel BUSINESS HOTEL **$$$**
(☑06151-281 00; www.bestwestern.de; Grafenstrasse 31, 3rd fl; s/d weekday €135/155, weekend €89/104; P✿@☎) The entrance, through a parking garage, is unpromising, but inside, the Best Western's lobby is pristine and its 77 quiet, neutral-toned rooms are spacious, modern and comfortable; higher-priced rooms have air-conditioning. Best of all is the central location, just two blocks south-west of Luisenplatz.

✗ Eating & Drinking

In the warm season you'll find outdoor cafes two blocks southeast of Luisenplatz on the Marktplatz.

★Elisabeth CAFE **$**
(www.suppkult.de; Schulstrasse 14; dishes €3.80-5.80; ⊙11am-4.30pm Mon-Fri, to 4pm Sat; ✔♿) Hidden down a passageway in a picnic-table-filled courtyard, this wonderful spot specialises in homemade soups (which change daily): pork meatballs and split green peas; curried apple and potato; lentil, carrot and leek; and roast tomato with sheep's cheese, all served with home-baked sourdough or rye bread. Salads are also available as meals. Finish off with fabulous cakes.

City Braustübl GERMAN **$$**
(☑06151-255 11; www.city-braustuebl.de; Wilhelminenstrasse 31; mains lunch €6-7, dinner €7-18; ⊙11am-midnight; ☎) At this classic brewery-affiliated restaurant, with wood-plank floors, hops hanging from the rafters and a beer garden out back, you can wash down hearty Bavarian and Hessian dishes with a Darmstädter beer brewed over near the Hauptbahnhof. It's three blocks south of Luisenplatz.

ⓘ DARMSTADT CARD

The **Darmstadt Card** (one/two days €6/9) buys you unlimited use of public transport and reduced-price entry to museums. It's sold at the tourist office.

An Sibín Irish Pub IRISH PUB
(www.ansibin.com; Landgraf-Georg-Strasse 25; ⊙6pm-1am Sun-Wed, to 3am Thu-Sat) There's always something happening at this Irish pub and live concert venue: Tuesday is quiz night, Wednesday is open mic night and on Thursday there's karaoke, all from 9pm. For live music, come by on Monday, Friday or Saturday after 9.30pm. Filling pub grub includes full Irish breakfasts, baked potatoes, and fish and chips.

☆ Entertainment

Darmstadt has plenty of student-oriented nightspots and concert venues.

Centralstation LIVE MUSIC
(www.centralstation-darmstadt.de; Im Carree; ⊙11am-2am Mon-Thu, to 4am Fri & Sat) In the courtyard across Luisenstrasse from the tourist office, the city's first electric power plant, built in 1888, is now a multipurpose cultural centre hosting concerts (especially jazz but also pop and classical) and housing an upstairs cocktail lounge. On Friday and Saturday nights from 10pm to 4am it transforms into a disco.

Goldene Krone LIVE MUSIC
(www.goldene-krone.de; Schustergasse 18; ⊙7pm-late Mon-Sat) An old student favourite, this sociable bar is known for its concerts as well as dance parties, many held on Friday and Saturday nights starting at 9pm. The entrance is on Holzstrasse, a block east of the Marktplatz.

ⓘ Information

Tourist Office (☑06151-134 513; www.darmstadt-tourismus.de; Luisenplatz 5; ⊙10am-6pm Mon-Fri, to 4pm Sat, to 2pm Sun Apr-Sep, 10am-6pm Mon-Fri, to 4pm Sat Oct-Mar) Darmstadt's tourist office is in the northeastern corner of the LuisenCenter shopping mall, with direct access from Luisenplatz; look for a sign reading 'Darmstadt Shop'. It sells cultural events tickets and an informative booklet on Mathildenhöhe (€3).

WORTH A TRIP

FRANKENSTEIN'S CASTLE

Burg Frankenstein (www.franken-stein-restaurant.de; Mühltal; admission by donation; ⊙ castle 9am-sunset except during events) Built by Lord Konrad II Reiz von Breuberg around 1250, this hulking, partly ruined hilltop castle was visited by Mary Shelley on her German travels in 1814, inspiring the title of her famous novel and its protagonist. Tours are in German but you're free to walk around the castle and grounds. It's home to a restaurant and events including one of Europe's largest Halloween parties. From Darmstadt, it's 13km south, high up in the forest, via the B426.

Other events here include medieval banquets, costumed adventure castle days, live music including jazz, and theatre nights – schedules are posted online.

❶ Getting There & Around

Frequent S-Bahn (S3) trains link Darmstadt with Frankfurt's Hauptbahnhof (€9, 30 minutes), but it's faster to take one of DB's RB, IC or ICE trains (€9, 16 minutes). A day ticket that takes in both cities, including local trams and buses, costs €14.40.

In Darmstadt, the DB Service counter inside the Hauptbahnhof can supply you with a free map of the city. Trams 2, 3 and 5 link the Hauptbahnhof with Luisenplatz. A single ticket costs €1.30.

HEIDELBERG & AROUND

Heidelberg

📞 06221 / POP 152,435

Surrounded by forest 93km south of Frankfurt, Germany's oldest and most famous university town is renowned for its baroque Altstadt, spirited student atmosphere, beautiful riverside setting and evocative half-ruined hilltop castle, which draw 11.8 million visitors a year. They follow in the footsteps of the late-18th- and early-19th-century romantics, most notably the poet Goethe. Britain's William Turner also loved Heidelberg, which inspired him to paint some of his greatest landscapes.

In 1878, Mark Twain began his European travels with a three-month stay in Heidelberg, recounting his observations in *A Tramp Abroad* (1880). Heidelberg's rich literary history, along with its thriving contemporary scene involving authors, translators, publishing houses, bookshops, libraries, festivals and events, saw it named a Unesco City of Literature in 2014.

Heidelberg's Altstadt has a red-roofed townscape of remarkable architectural unity. After having been all but destroyed by French troops under Louis XIV (1690s), it was built pretty much from scratch during the 18th century. Unlike the vast majority of German cities, it emerged from WWII almost unscathed. Today, Heidelberg is one of Germany's most enchanting cities. The longer you stay, the more heart-stopping panoramas and hidden treasures you'll discover.

⊙ Sights

Heidelberg's Altstadt runs along the left (south) bank of the Neckar River from Bismarckplatz east to the hillside Schloss. One of Europe's longest pedestrian zones, the 1600m-long Hauptstrasse, runs east–west through the Altstadt, about 200m south of the Neckar.

⊙ Schloss

★**Schloss Heidelberg** CASTLE
(📞 06221-658 880; www.schloss-heidelberg.de; adult/child incl Bergbahn €6/4, tours €4/2, audioguide €4; ⊙ grounds 24hr, castle 8am-6pm, English tours hourly 11.15am-4.15pm Mon-Fri, 10.15am-4.15pm Sat & Sun Apr-Oct, reduced tours Nov-Mar) Towering over the Altstadt, Heidelberg's ruined Renaissance castle cuts a romantic figure, especially across the Neckar River when illuminated at night. Attractions include the world's largest wine cask and fabulous views. It's reached either via a steep, cobbled trail in about 10 minutes or by taking the **Bergbahn** (cogwheel train) from Kornmarkt station. The only way to see the less-than-scintillating interior is by tour, which can be safely skipped. After 6pm you can stroll the grounds for free.

Once you arrive up top, you'll be struck by the far-reaching views over the Neckar River and the Altstadt rooftops. Show your ticket to enter the **Schlosshof**, the castle's central courtyard, which is framed by reconstructed Gothic and Renaissance buildings with elaborate facades. The most eye-catching belongs to the **Friedrichsbau**, which is festooned with lifesize sculptures of kings and emperors.

You can't miss the **Grosses Fass**, the world's largest wine cask, with a capacity of about 228,000L. Also worthwhile is a spin around the surprisingly interesting Deutsches Apotheken-Museum.

Deutsches Apotheken-Museum MUSEUM
(German Pharmacy Museum; www.schloss-heidelberg.de; incl in Schloss Heidelberg admission; ☉10am-6pm Apr-Oct, to 5.30pm Nov-Mar) The German Pharmacy Museum, off the Schlosshof at Schloss Heidelberg, illustrates the history of Western pharmacology, in which Germany played a central role. Exhibits include pharmacies from the early 1700s and the Napoleonic era. Kids can use a mortar and a pestle to blend their own herbal tea. Most signs are in English.

⊙ Altstadt

The Hauptstrasse passes by a series of attractive public squares, many with historic or modern fountains.

Marktplatz SQUARE
The Marktplatz is the focal point of Altstadt street life. The trickling **Hercules fountain** (Marktplatz) – that's him up on top of the pillar – in the middle is where petty criminals were chained and left to face the mob in the Middle Ages.

Heiliggeistkirche CHURCH
(☑06221-980 30; www.ekihd.de; Marktplatz; tower adult/child €2/1; ☉church 11am-5pm daily, tower 11am-5pm Mon-Sat, 12.30-5pm Sun Apr-Oct, 11am-3pm Fri & Sat, 12.30-3pm Sun Nov-Mar) For bird's-eye views, climb 208 stairs to the top of the tower of Heidelberg's famous church, constructed between 1344 and 1441, which was shared by Catholics and Protestants from 1706 until 1936 (it's now Protestant).

The church is often used for concerts (adult/child from €10/6), including half-hour organ recitals (€4/2) held at 5.15pm Sunday to Friday from June to September; see www.studentenkantorei.de for a full calendar of events.

Ruprecht-Karls-Universität UNIVERSITY
(Heidelberg University; www.uni-heidelberg.de) Established in 1386 by Count Palatinate Ruprecht I, Germany's oldest and most prestigious university comprises 12 faculties with 30,000 German and international students, and has an esteemed alumni that includes a roll-call of Nobel Laureates.

The most historic facilities are around **Universitätsplatz**, dominated by the **Alte Universität** (1712–28; on the south side) and the **Neue Universität** (1931; on the north side), the 'old' and 'new' university buildings respectively. Nearby stands the **Löwenbrunnen** (Lions Fountain).

Studentenkarzer HISTORIC SITE
(Student Jail; ☑06221-543 554; www.uni-heidelberg.de; Augustinergasse 2; adult/child incl Universitätsmuseum €3/2.50; ☉10am-6pm Tue-Sun Apr-Sep, 10am-4pm Tue-Sat Oct-Mar) From 1823 to 1914, students convicted of misdeeds such as public inebriation, loud nocturnal singing, freeing the local pigs or duelling were sent to this student jail for at least 24 hours. Judging by the inventive wall graffiti, some found their stay highly amusing. Delinquents were let out to attend lectures or take exams. In certain circles, a stint in the Karzer was considered a rite of passage.

Universitätsmuseum MUSEUM
(www.uni-heidelberg.de; Grabengasse 1; adult/child incl Studentenkarzer €3/2.50; ☉10am-6pm Tue-Sun Apr-Sep, 10am-4pm Tue-Sat Oct-Mar) The three-room University Museum, inside the Alte Universität building, has paintings, portraits, documents and photos documenting the university's mostly illustrious history. Only the signs on the Third Reich period are in English but the admission fee includes an English audioguide.

You can visit the adjacent **Alte Aula** (Old Assembly Hall; ☉closed during academic events), a neo-Renaissance hall whose rich decoration dates from 1886.

Jesuitenkirche CHURCH
(☉9.30am-6pm May-Sep, to 5pm Oct-Apr) Rising above an attractive square just east of Universitätsplatz, the red-sandstone Jesuits' church is a fine example of 18th-century baroque. This part of town was once the focal point of Heidelberg's Jewish quarter.

Heidelberg Altstadt

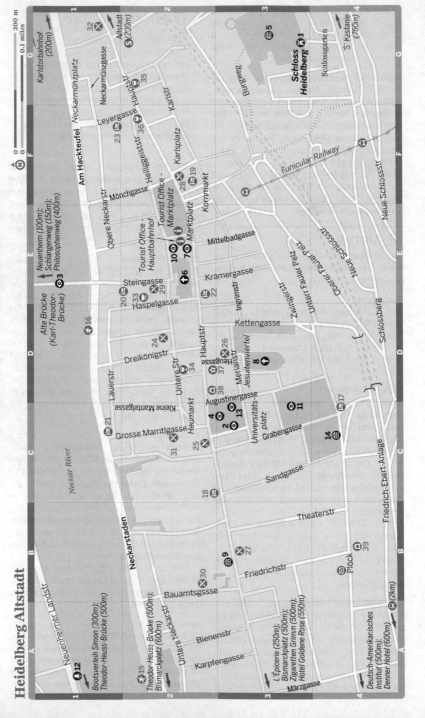

Heidelberg Altstadt

The **Schatzkammer** (Treasury; admission €3; ☉10am-5pm Tue-Sat, 1-5pm Sun Jun-Oct, 1-5pm Sat & Sun Nov-May) displays precious religious artefacts.

Alte Brücke   BRIDGE
(Karl-Theodor-Brücke) Heidelberg's 200m-long 'old bridge', built in 1786, connects the Altstadt with the river's right bank and the **Schlangenweg** (Snake Path), whose switchbacks lead to the Philosophenweg (Philosophers' Walk).

Next to the tower gate on the Altstadt side of the bridge, look for the brass sculpture of a monkey holding a mirror. It's the 1979 replacement of the 17th-century original sculpture.

Kurpfälzisches Museum   MUSEUM
(www.museum-heidelberg.de; Hauptstrasse 97; adult/child €3/free; ☉10am-6pm Tue-Sun) The city-run Palatinate Museum has well-presented exhibits on Heidelberg's eventful history and is especially strong on the Roman period – exhibits include original wood beams from a 3rd-century bridge. To learn about really ancient local life, check out the replica of the 600,000-year-old jawbone of *Homo heidelbergensis* (Heidelberg Man),

unearthed about 18km southeast of here in 1907 (the original is stored across the river at the university's palaeontology institute).

Universitätsbibliothek   MUSEUM
(Plöck 107-109; ☉exhibition 10am-6pm) **FREE**
The University Library was built in massive Wilhelmian style from 1901 to 1905. Upstairs you can see rare books and prints from its superb collections in the corner **Ausstellungsraum** (exhibition room).

◎ Neuenheim

Superb views of the town extend from the north (right) bank of the Neckar.

★**Philosophenweg**   TRAIL
(Philosophers' Walk; south bank of the Neckar River) Winding past monuments, towers, ruins, a beer garden and an enormous **Thingstätte** (amphitheatre; built by the Nazis in 1935), the 2.5km-long Philosophers' Walk has captivating views of Heidelberg's Schloss, especially at sunset when the city is bathed in a reddish glow. Access is easiest via the steep Schlangenweg from Alte Brücke. Don't attempt to drive up as the road is narrow and there's nowhere to turn around up the top.

WORTH A TRIP

EVOLUTIONARY DISCOVERIES

Grube Messel (Messel Pit; ☑ 0615-971 7590; www.grube-messel.de; Rossdörfer Strasse 108; visitor centre adult/child €10/8, guided pit tour €7; ⊙ 10am-5pm, tour by reservation) A Unesco World Heritage Site, this one-time coal and oil shale quarry 10km northeast of Darmstadt is renowned for its superbly preserved animal and plant remains from the Eocene era (around 49 million years ago). Early horses found here illustrate the evolutionary path towards the modern beast. A pretty half-timbered house 3km south of the visitor centre houses a fossil-filled **museum** (www.messelmuseum.de; Langgasse 2; ⊙ 11am-5pm Apr-Oct, 11am-5pm Sat & Sun Nov-Mar) **FREE**. You can visit the pit with a German-speaking guide or pre-arrange an English-speaking tour (extra €20 per group).

Other interesting finds from the site are showcased at the **Hessisches Landesmuseum** (p408) in Darmstadt and the **Senckenberg Museum** (p381) in Frankfurt.

Neuenheim River Bank PARK
(Uferstrasse) The Neckar's grassy northern bank between Theodor-Heuss-Brücke and Ernst-Walz-Brücke is a favourite student hang-out when the weather is warm. Small cafes sell snacks and drinks including beer.

Botanischer Garten der Universität PARK
(University Botanical Garden; http://botgart.hip.uni-heidelberg.de; Im Neuenheimer Feld 340; ⊙ outdoor areas dawn-dusk, hothouses 9am-4pm Mon-Thu, 9am-2.30pm Sat, 10am-5pm Sun, closed Fri Apr-Oct, shorter hours Nov-Mar) **FREE** Orchids, ferns and Madagascan succulents thrive in the verdant University Botanical Garden, part of the university's right-bank Neuenheimer Feld campus. The garden is 2.5km northwest of Bismarckplatz, served by trams 4 and 5.

🏃 Activities

Solarschiff RIVER CRUISE
(www.hdsolarschiff.com; Alte Brücke; adult/child €8/3.50; ⊙ every 90min 10am-6pm Tue-Sun Mar-Oct) 🚤 One of the most peaceful ways to appreciate Heidelberg's charms is to get out on the river. Solarschiff's solar-panelled boat engine is silent – all you hear during a 50-minute cruise, apart from onboard commentary in English and German, is the water and the distant sounds of the city.

Bootsverleih Simon BOAT RENTAL
(☑ 06221-411 925; 3-/4-person pedalos per 30min €10/12; ⊙ 2pm-dusk Mon-Sat, 11am-dusk Sun Apr-early Oct) To take to the river under your own steam, hire a pedalo (pedal boat) on the north shore of the Neckar, just east of Theodor-Heuss-Brücke.

**Rhein-Neckar
Fahrgastschifffahrt** RIVER CRUISE
(Weisse Flotte; ☑ 06221-201 81; www.weisse-flotte-heidelberg.de; adult/child to Neckarsteinach return €16.50/9; ⊙ mid-Apr–late Nov) Day trips run up and down the Neckar; it takes 90 minutes one-way to reach Neckarsteinach.

From April to October, between 10am and 5pm daily, the company also operates a six-stop ferry along the Neckar, from the Ernst-Walz-Brücke to the Alte Brücke (per stop adult/child €2/0.50, entire length €3/1, hop-on, hop-off €10/5).

👉 Tours

Tourist Office Walking Tours WALKING TOUR
(www.heidelberg-marketing.de; adult/child €7/5; ⊙ English tours 10.30am Thu-Sat Apr-Oct) One-and-a-half-hour English-language tours taking in the Altstadt's highlights depart from the Marktplatz (Rathaus) tourist office.

🎊 Festivals & Events

Heidelberg has a packed year-round calendar of events; check with the tourist office to find out what's on while you're in town.

Schlossbeleuchtungen FIREWORKS
(Castle Illumination; ⊙ 10.15pm on 1st Sat Jun, 2nd Sat Jul & 1st Sat Sep) The Schloss, the Alte Brücke and the Altstadt are lit up by fantastic fireworks that commemorate the French assault on the Schloss in 1693. The best views are from both banks of the Neckar, west of the Alte Brücke.

Heidelberger Herbst STREET CARNIVAL
(⊙ 10am-11pm last Sat in Sep) Heidelberg's huge street party has music, arts and crafts, buskers, food and general merrymaking throughout the Altstadt, kicking off from the Marktplatz.

Weihnachtsmarkt CHRISTMAS MARKET
(⊙ 11am-10pm 23 Nov-22 Dec) Around 140 stalls take over the Altstadt's public squares, including the Marktplatz, Universitätsplatz

and the Kornmarkt, during Heidelberg's magical Christmas market.

🛏 Sleeping

Bargains are thin on the ground in Heidelberg and its popularity with tourists means finding a bed can be tricky, so booking ahead is advisable any time of year but especially in summer and during the Christmas season. Many places to stay don't include breakfast in the rate but can provide it for an extra charge.

Steffis Hostel
HOSTEL $

(☑ 06221-778 2772; www.hostelheidelberg.de; Alte Eppelheimer Strasse 50; dm from €18, s/d/f without bathroom from €45/56/100; ☉ reception 8am-10pm; 🅿 @ ⊛ 🛜) In a 19th-century tobacco factory a block north of the Hauptbahnhof, accessed via an industrial-size lift/elevator, Steffis offers bright, well-lit dorms and rooms (all with shared bathrooms), a colourful lounge that's great for meeting fellow travellers, a spacious kitchen and an old-school hostel vibe. Breakfast costs €3. Perks include tea, coffee and free bike rental.

DJH Hostel
HOSTEL $

(☑ 06221-651 190; www.jugendherberge-heidelberg.de; Tiergartenstrasse 5; dm €33.40, 26yr & under €27.40; 🛜) Although it's a long haul 5km northwest of the Altstadt, on the north bank of the river, and often filled with big groups of noisy schoolkids, this modern 447-bed hostel is very comfortable, with impeccable dorms. Rates include a big buffet breakfast. From the Hauptbahnhof, take bus 32.

★Hotel Villa Marstall
HISTORIC HOTEL $$

(☑ 06221-655 570; www.villamarstall.de; Lauerstrasse 1; s €95-165, d €115-185; ☉ reception 7am-10pm Mon-Sat, 8am-6pm Sun; ⊛ 🛜) A 19th-century neoclassical mansion directly overlooking the Neckar River, Villa Marstall is a jewel with cherrywood floors, solid-timber furniture and amenities including a lift/elevator. Exquisite rooms are decorated in whites, creams and bronzes, and come with in-room fridges (perfect for chilling a bottle of regional wine). A sumptuous breakfast buffet (€10) is served in the red-sandstone vaulted cellar.

★Arthotel Heidelberg
BOUTIQUE HOTEL $$

(☑ 06221-650 060; www.arthotel.de; Grabengasse 7; s €109-172, d €125-198; 🅿 ⊛ 🛜) This charmer is a winning blend of historic setting and sleek contemporary design. Equipped with huge bathrooms (tubs!), the 24 rooms are spacious and purist – except for three that sport painted ceilings from 1790. There's a courtyard as well as a roof garden (but avoid rooms below it in summer, when you can hear people walking above). Breakfast costs €12.90.

Hotel Goldener Hecht
HOTEL $$

(☑ 06221-166 025; www.hotel-goldener-hecht.de; Steingasse 2; s €60-76, d €76-97; 🛜) Footsteps from the Alte Brücke, this atmospheric hotel has just 13 rooms, six with bridge views; the three corner rooms are bright and gorgeous. One drawback to being so central: it can be noisy at night, especially on summer weekends. Goethe was once turned away for lack of space, so book ahead. Breakfast costs €11.

Hotel zum Ritter St Georg
HISTORIC HOTEL $$

(☑ 06221-1350; www.ritter-heidelberg.de; Hauptstrasse 178; s/d from €109/129; 🛜) Set in an ornate, late-Renaissance mansion built by a Huguenot cloth merchant in 1592, Hotel zum Ritter St Georg's cheaper rooms are an anticlimax after the opulent facade, but the spacious Superior (28 sq metres) and De Luxe (35 sq metres) rooms, some with church views, are bright and really lovely. Breakfast costs €15.

Hotel am Kornmarkt
HOTEL $$

(☑ 06221-905 830; www.hotelamkornmarkt.de; Kornmarkt 7; d/tr/f from €90/125/135, s/d without bathroom €68/75; 🛜) In a fantastic location just a block from the Marktplatz, this hotel is low on frills but great value. The 20 rooms are comfortable and spotless; some have Kornmarkt views. Breakfast costs €9.

Hotel Regina
HOTEL $$

(☑ 06221-536 40; www.hotel-regina.de; Luisenstrasse 6; s €75-90, d €88-135; 🛜) Central but quiet, just west of the Altstadt and 200m west of Bismarckplatz, the welcoming Regina occupies a brick-and-stone building built a century ago. The 15 attractive rooms, decked out in tones of orange, green and white, are all outfitted with bright, all-tile bathrooms.

Hotel Goldene Rose
HOTEL $$

(☑ 06221-905 490; www.hotel-goldene-rose.de; St-Anna-Gasse 7; s/d from €100/115; 🛜) At the western end of the Hauptstrasse, the rose-toned, gold-trimmed Hotel Goldene Rose has 37 surprisingly modern rooms that are compact but quiet, comfortable and well-kept.

Denner Hotel
HOTEL $$

(☑ 06221-604 510; www.denner-hotel.de; Bergheimer Strasse 8; s/d from €91/119; 🛜) An almost-boutique hotel a block west of the Altstadt's western edge, Denner has 18 uniquely decorated rooms, with details such as designer furniture, hardwood floors and stencilled walls; some have four-poster beds. Rooms 14 and 26 have neoclassical balconies overlooking Bismarckplatz.

Kulturbrauerei Hotel
HOTEL $$

(☑ 06221-502 980; www.heidelberger-kultur-brauerei.de; Leyergasse 6; d €120-180; ☎) This stylish Altstadt hotel above the eponymous microbrewery has romantic cream-coloured rooms with polished parquet floors, classical furniture and large windows. Breakfast is €12 for hotel guests (€15 for nonguests).

★ Hip Hotel
BOUTIQUE HOTEL $$$

(☑ 06221-208 79; www.hip-hotel.de; Hauptstrasse 115; s €95-180, d €150-210, tr €190-240; @☎) Snooze in a Fijian beach shack complete with sandy bay, a woodsy Canadian hunter's cottage, or a topsy-turvy Down Under room where everything (paintings, doors, bed) is upside down. In an age in which cities are awash in 'theme hotels', this 27-room place is both genuinely creative and heaps of fun. The Amsterdam room is wheelchair-accessible. Breakfast costs breakfast €12.

Eating

The Altstadt, especially around Steingasse and Untere Strasse, is chock-full of restaurants, cafes, pubs and beer gardens. Cosy restaurants frequented by students and locals are tucked away on the side streets south of the Hauptstrasse and west of the Kornmarkt.

Many of Heidelberg's traditional pubs are also atmospheric places to dine on hearty German cuisine.

Joe Molese
DINER $

(www.joemolese.com; Steingasse 16a; dishes €5-12; ⊙11am-11pm Sun-Thu, to midnight Fri & Sat) Amazing sandwiches like pastrami, tomato and honey-mustard vinaigrette; brie, rocket and truffle oil; or wild smoked salmon with lemon juice and olive oil are the standout at Joe's, but it also has fantastic salads, chicken drumsticks, burgers and buffalo wings. Black-and-white chequerboard tiling and fire-engine-red walls give it a souped-up New York deli vibe.

Smoothies range from strawberry and basil to pineapple and lime, or you can order beer, wine and cocktails.

Gundel
CAFE, BAKERY $

(www.gundel-heidelberg.de; Hauptstrasse 212; dishes €2-8; ⊙cafe 8am-6pm Tue-Sun, bakery 6am-7pm Tue-Fri, 6am-6pm Sat, 7am-6pm Sun) Gundel's bakery section has 30 kinds of bread

and rolls, as well as delectable pastries. It's a great stop to stock up for a river or forest picnic; alternatively, you can dine on-site at the wicker-chair-filled cafe, which serves light bites like salads, soups, quiches, sausages, pickled herring fillets and jacket potatoes.

Die Kuh Die Lacht
BURGERS $

(www.diekuhdielacht.com; Hauptstrasse 133; mains €6.50-10; ⊙11am-11pm Mon-Sat, noon-10pm Sun; 🖝) Since it opened in 2015, this sleek burger joint has been packed to the rafters. Its 18 different, all-natural burgers are handmade on the premises, with choices like chicken caesar, barbecued beef, a Mexican burger with beans and corn, as well as vegie options including a tofu burger and a falafel burger. Sides include onion rings or fried bacon.

Falafel
FALAFEL $

(Merianstrasse 3; dishes €3.50-8.50; ⊙11.30am-11pm; ✍) This aromatic spot serves some of the tastiest Syrian-style falafel in Germany, along with kebabs, hummus, baba ganoush and Middle Eastern salads. Enter via Heugasse.

Gelato To Go
GELATERIA $

(Hauptstrasse 100; ice cream from €1; ⊙11am-7pm Mon-Sat, noon-7pm Sun; 🖝) The Hauptstrasse is sprinkled with ice-cream shops but Gelato To Go trumps them all (hence the constant queue out the door, even in winter). In addition to the classics, flavours span sea salt caramel, lime mint, cinnamon, chocolate chilli, crème brûlée, lemon vodka, chestnut, tiramisu, watermelon and shredded-chocolate straciatella. Some of its ice creams are organic and/or gluten-free.

★ 'S' Kastanie
GERMAN $$

(☑ 06221-728 0343; www.restaurant-s-kastanie.de; Elisabethenweg 1; 2-course lunch menu €9, mains €12-28; ⊙11.30am-2.30pm & 6-10pm Wed-Fri, 5-10pm Sat, 11.30am-8pm Sun) A panoramic terrace provides sweeping views of the river at this gorgeous 1904-built former hunting lodge, with stained glass and timber panelling, set in the forest near the castle. Chef Sven Schönig's stunning creations include a sweet potato and goats' cheese tower with papaya, and goose-stuffed ravioli.

Café Weinstube Burkardt
CAFE $$

(www.burkardt-heidelberg.de; Untere Strasse 27; mains €7.50-22; ⊙9am-11pm Tue-Sat, to 6pm Sun) Charming Burkardt's latest incarnation sees it hitting its stride. A superb selection of wines from villages around Heidelberg are available by the glass, and the food is first-rate: paella, risotto with mushroom and asparagus, roast gnocchi with ham and rocket, and spinach frittata. The courtyard abuts the house where Friedrich Ebert, German President during the Weimar Republic, was born.

Schnitzelbank
GERMAN $$

(🖉 06221-211 89; www.schnitzelbank-heidelberg.de; Baumamtsgasse 7; mains €15-22; ☺5pm-1am Mon-Thu, 11.30am-1am Fri & Sun) Small and often jam-packed, this cosy wine tavern has you sampling the local tipples (all wines are regional) and cuisine while crouched on wooden workbenches from the time when this was still a cooperage. It's these benches that give the place its name, incidentally, not the veal and pork schnitzel on the menu. Other specialities include *Schäufele* (stuffed pig's stomach).

★ Zur Herrenmühle Heidelberg
GERMAN $$$

(🖉 06221-602 909; www.herrenmuehle-heidelberg.de; Hauptstrasse 239; mains €23-31, 3-/4-/5-/6-course menus from €46/72/82/92; ☺6-10pm Tue-Sat) A flour mill from 1690 has been turned into an elegant and highly cultured place to enjoy refined 'country-style' cuisine, such as saffron-crusted dorade royale with baby spinach and creamed potato, beneath weighty, 300-year-old wooden beams with candles flickering on the tables. Book ahead.

Weisser Bock
INTERNATIONAL $$$

(🖉 06221-900 00; www.weisserbock.de; Grosse Mantelgasse 24; mains €20-35; ☺kitchen 5-10pm Mon-Thu, noon-10pm Fri & Sat) Dark-wood panelling, linen-bedecked tables and low lighting make an elegant backdrop for newly interpreted classical dishes. Each is prepared with fresh ingredients that play off each other: scallop tartare with wasabi or wild garlic and chilli prawns for starters, followed by lamb loin with basil risotto or grilled tuna with rosemary potatoes, and dark chocolate cake with elderflower sorbet.

The bar serves cocktails until late.

🍸 Drinking

Heidelberg's student population fuels the party, especially at the weekend. For a pub crawl, you can't beat pedestrianised Untere Strasse, which student revellers keep lively until very late on weekends.

KulturBrauerei
MICROBREWERY

(www.heidelberger-kulturbrauerei.de; Leyergasse 6; ☺7am-midnight) With its wood-plank floor, chairs from a Spanish monastery and black iron chandeliers, this brewpub is an atmospheric spot to quaff the house brews (including many seasonal specialities) in the enchanting beer garden. Soak them up with time-tested local dishes such as homemade sausages with cream cheese, radish and dark bread. It also has some lovely hotel rooms.

Zum Roten Ochsen
PUB

(Red Ox Inn; www.roterochsen.de; Hauptstrasse 217; mains €11.90-24.50; ☺5pm-12.30am Tue-Sat) Fronted by a red-painted, blue-grey-shuttered facade, Heidelberg's most historic student pub has black-and-white frat photos on the dark wooden walls and names carved into the tables. Traditional dishes focus on regional fare, such as deer ragout with cranberries, croquettes and red cabbage. Along with German luminaries, visitors who've raised a glass here include Mark Twain, John Wayne and Marilyn Monroe.

Chocolaterie Yilliy
CAFE

(www.chocolaterie-heidelberg.de; Haspelgasse 7; ☺10am-8pm Sat-Thu, to 10pm Fri) Especially when the weather's chilly, this is a wonderful spot to warm up with a wickedly thick house-speciality hot chocolate in flavours like hazelnut, cointreau, chilli or praline. The airy space has a laid-back lounge-room vibe, with a book swap, piano and regular acoustic gigs.

Destille
BAR

(www.destilleonline.de; Untere Strasse 16; ☺noon-2am Sun-Thu, to 3am Fri & Sat) An enormous tree frames the bar of this mellow pub, which is famed for its *Warmer Erpel* ('warm duck'; spicy schnapps). It also serves various other schnapps, such as green melon, as well as *Apfelwein*.

Frollein Bent
BAR

(www.frolleinbent.de; Neckarmünzgasse 1; ☺2pm-midnight Tue-Sun Apr-Sep, 5pm-midnight Fri-Sun Oct-Mar) With just 13 seats, the interior of this retro-style bar can be cramped but its big draw is its sundrenched terrace on a riverfront square – a fabulously scenic spot to enjoy a Brazilian-invented, German-adopted caipirinha, other cocktails like mojitos and G&Ts, or Italian Sequella coffee.

Nachtschicht
CLUB

(www.nachtschicht.com; Bergheimerstrasse 147; ☺10pm-5am Thu, 8pm-5am Fri, 11pm-5am Sat) In an old tobacco factory just north of Hauptbahnhof, Nachtschicht is one of Heidelberg's more popular party venues; events are listed on its online calendar. Cheap cover (around €3 to €6), cheap drinks and an easy door.

☆ Entertainment

The city's effervescent cultural scene includes concerts, films and dance and theatre performances. **Zigaretten Grimm** (☑06221-209 09; Sophienstrasse 11; ☺9am-7pm Mon-Fri, 10am-5pm Sat), a tobacco shop at Bismarckplatz (east of the Alstadt), sells tickets for concerts and other cultural events.

Karlstorbahnhof   CULTURAL VENUE
(☑06221-978 911; www.karlstorbahnhof.de; Am Karlstor 1; ☺closed Aug) Within an old train station, this beloved cultural centre has an art-house cinema screening non-dubbed films; theatre, cabaret and comedy performances (some in English); a hugely popular disco, Klub K (11pm to 5am Friday and Saturday); and a diverse range of concerts. It's 100m east of the Karlstor, the towering stone gate at the eastern end of the Altstadt.

Gloria und Gloriette   CINEMA
(☑06221-253 19; www.gloria-kamera-kinos.de; Hauptstrasse 146; tickets €6-8) Right on the Hauptstrasse, this cute little cinema with just 131 seats shows art-house films, some in English.

Deutsch-Amerikanisches Institut   CULTURAL CENTRE
(German-American Institute; ☑06221-607 30; www.dai-heidelberg.de; Sofienstrasse 12; ☺ticket office 1-6pm Mon-Fri) The German-American Institute hosts concerts, lectures and films several times a week.

🛍 Shopping

Amble along traffic-free Hauptstrasse for souvenirs, brand-name shops and fine window displays, or find one-off galleries and speciality shops in Altstadt backstreets such as Plöck.

★**Heidelberger Zuckerladen**   FOOD & DRINK
(www.heidelbergerzuckerladen.de; Plöck 52; ☺noon-7pm Tue-Fri, 11am-5pm Sat) The dentures and dentist's chair in the window of this old-time sweet shop hint at what will happen to your gnashers if you overindulge on the Zuckerladen's bonbons, liquorice laces and fizzy sherbet.

L'Épicerie   FOOD & DRINK
(www.lepicerie.de; Hauptstrasse 35; ☺1-7pm Mon, 11am-7pm Tue-Fri, 10am-6pm Sat) In a courtyard off Hauptstrasse, foodie haven L'Épicerie is filled with luscious pralines, spices, oils and preserves.

Bären Treff   FOOD & DRINK
(www.baeren-treff.de; Hauptstrasse 144; ☺10am-7pm Mon-Sat) This entire shop is dedicated to chewy gummi bear sweets (with free samples). A poster on the wall shows how they're made.

ℹ Information

Tourist Office (☑06221-584 4444; www.heidelberg-marketing.de) There are branches at Hauptbahnhof (☑06221-584 4444; www.heidelberg-marketing.de; Willy-Brandt-Platz 1; ☺9am-7pm Mon-Sat, 10am-6pm Sun Apr-Oct, 9am-6pm Mon-Sat Nov-Mar), right outside the main train station, and on Marktplatz (www.heidelberg-marketing.de; Marktplatz 10; ☺8am-5pm Mon-Fri, 10am-5pm Sat), in the old town.

ℹ Getting There & Away

Train From the **Hauptbahnhof** (Willy-Brandt-Platz), 3km west of the Schloss, there are at least hourly train services to/from Frankfurt (€18 to €29, one hour to 1½ hours) and Stuttgart (€19 to €39, 40 minutes to 1½ hours), as well as frequent S-Bahn services to Mannheim (€7, 15 minutes) and Speyer (€12, 50 minutes). From Mannheim you can connect to German Wine Route towns.

Bus The fastest way to reach **Frankfurt airport** (www.lufthansa.com; Frankfurt Airport) is the eight-seat **Lufthansa's Airport Shuttle** (www.lufthansa.com; Kurfürsten-Anlage 1-3, Crowne Plaza Hotel; one-way €25). It runs every 1½ hours; journey time is one hour.

To get to Frankfurt-Hahn airport (2¼ hours, four daily), you can take the **Hahn Express** (Bus 140; ☑06221-782 525; www.hahn-express.de; one-way adult/child €20/10), which stops at the Hauptbahnhof.

ℹ Getting Around

BICYCLE

Fahrradverleih (☑06221-654 4460; www.fahrradverleih-heidelberg.de; Neckarstaden 52; per day €18; ☺10am-1pm & 2-6pm Tue-Fri, 10am-6pm Sat, 2-6pm Sun) Convenient bike rental in the Altstadt with cycling maps.

VBI (☑06221-656 6377; www.vbi-heidelberg.de; Hauptbahnhof; per day €10; ☺7am-6pm Mon & Fri, 10am-6pm Tue-Thu) Bike rental, repair and secondhand sales at the Hauptbahnhof, next to Track 1, at Platform 1b.

CAR

Street parking in the city centre is almost completely reserved for residents, so there's really no way to avoid the fees at the city's 19 **parking garages** (http://parken.heidelberg.de; per hr €0.50-1.50, per day €12-15). The website has live updates of parking space availability in each garage. Some hotels offer discount vouchers.

PUBLIC TRANSPORT

Tram 5 and buses 10, 33, 34, 41 and 42 link the Hauptbahnhof with Bismarckplatz – the main hub for Heidelberg's public transport (www.vrn. de) – and parts of the Altstadt. The quickest way from the Hauptbahnhof to the eastern part of the Altstadt is to take an S-Bahn train one stop to the Altstadt station. The tourist office can supply you with a pocket-sized *Linienplan* transport map.

Standard single tickets cost €2.40. For travel within the city centre (ie within the area between the Hauptbahnhof, the Schloss and the start of the Philosphenweg), a ticket costs just €1.60. A Ticket 24 for one/five people, valid for 24 hours in up to three zones, costs €6.40/16.40; a 3-Tages-Karte, valid for three days, costs €15.20 per person. Tickets are sold at tram-stop ticket machines and by bus drivers.

TAXI

Taxis (☑ 06221-302 030; www.taxizentrale-heidelberg.de) line up outside the Hauptbahnhof. Count on paying about €10 from the Hauptbahnhof to the Alte Brücke.

Speyer

☑ 06232 / POP 49,764

Scarcely damaged during WWII, the handsome town of Speyer is crowned by a magnificent Romanesque cathedral. Easily explored on foot, its centre is home to some outstanding museums and the remains of a medieval synagogue.

First a Celtic settlement, then a Roman market town, Speyer gained prominence in the Middle Ages under the Salian emperors, hosting 50 imperial parliament sessions (1294–1570).

In 1076, the king and later Holy Roman Emperor Heinrich IV, having been excommunicated by Pope Gregory VII, launched his penitence walk to Canossa in Italy from Speyer. He crossed the Alps in the middle of winter, an action that warmed the heart of the pope, who revoked his excommunication. He lies buried in the Kaiserdom.

In 1529, pro-Luther princes 'protested' a harsh anti-Luther edict issued by the Diet of Speyer, thereby starting the use of the term 'Protestant'.

⊙ Sights

Roman troops and medieval emperors once paraded down 'Via Triumphalis'. Now known as **Maximilianstrasse**, Speyer's pedestrian-only shopping precinct is 800m long, linking the Kaiserdom with the Altpörtel. Striking baroque buildings along Maximilianstrasse include the **Rathaus** (at No 13), with its red-orange facade and lavish rococo 1st floor (open for concerts and events), and the **Alte Münze** (Old Mint; at No 90).

Street numbers along Maximilianstrasse begin at the Kaiserdom, run sequentially along the south side to the Altpörtel, and then continue along the north side back to the Kaiserdom – be prepared for confusion!

★ **Kaiserdom**   CATHEDRAL

(http://bistum-speyer.de; Domplatz; crypt adult/child €3.50/1, tower €6/3; ⊙ cathedral & crypt 9am-7pm Apr-Oct, to 5pm Nov-Mar, tower 10am-5pm Mon-Sat & noon-5pm Sun Apr-Oct) **FREE** Begun in 1030 by Emperor Konrad II of the Salian dynasty, this extraordinary Romanesque cathedral has been a Unesco World Heritage Site since 1981. Its square red towers and green copper dome float majestically above Speyer's rooftops; you can climb the 304 steps of the **southwest tower** to reach the 60m-high viewing platform for a spectacular panorama. Other highlights include the fascinating crypt and 19th-century paintings in the **Kaisersaal**.

Atmospheric **organ concerts** (www.dommusik-speyer.de; adult/child €10/5) often take place here.

The cathedral's interior is startling for its awesome dimensions (it's an astonishing 134m long); walk up the side aisles to the elevated altar area to get a true sense of its size.

To the right of the altar, steps lead down to the darkly festive **crypt**, whose candy-striped Romanesque arches – like those on the west front – recall Moorish architecture (ask for an English-language brochure). Stuffed into a side room, up some stairs, are the sandstone **sarcophagi** of eight emperors and kings, along with some of their queens. **Tours** (adult/child including crypt entry €7.50/4) of the cathedral and crypt take place in English at 11am Saturday from April to October. You can rent a 45-minute audioguide (adult/child including crypt entry €7/4) at the crypt entrance.

Behind the Dom, the large **Domgarten** (cathedral park) stretches towards the Rhine.

★ **Altpörtel**   GATE

(adult/child €1/0.50; ⊙ 10am-noon & 2-4pm Mon-Fri, 10am-5pm Sat & Sun Apr-Oct) The 55m-high,

13th-century Altpörtel, the city's western gate, is the only remaining part of the town wall. The clock (1761) has separate dials for minutes and hours. On the 2nd floor, a permanent exhibition covers the history of Speyer. Breathtaking views unfold from the top of the Altpörtel on a clear day.

★ Judenhof
SYNAGOGUE

(Jews' Courtyard; Kleine Pfaffengasse 21; admission €3; ⊙10am-5pm Apr-Oct, 10am-4pm Tue-Sun Nov-Mar) A block south of the Rathaus, the 'Jews' Courtyard' is one of the most important medieval Jewish sites in Germany: the remains of a Romanesque-style synagogue that was consecrated in 1104 and used until 1450. Highlights include the 13th-century women's section, a **Mikwe** (ritual bath) from the early 1100s – the oldest, largest and best preserved north of the Alps – and a small **museum** covering the city's storied medieval Jewish community. Signs are in English and German.

A curious fact: everyone with the surname of Shapira (or Shapiro) is descended from Jews who lived in Speyer during the Middle Ages.

Dreifaltigkeitskirche
CHURCH

(Trinity Church; http://dreifaltigkeit-speyer.de; Grosse Himmelsgasse 3a; ⊙9am-5pm Mon-Fri, 10am-3pm Sat, 10am-2pm Sun Apr-Oct, 9am-5pm Mon-Fri, 10am-noon Sat Nov-Mar) Consecrated in 1717, 200 years to the day after Luther posted his 95 Theses, this harmonious church, half a block north of Maximilianstrasse, is a superb example of Protestant baroque. Almost all the rich interior decor is original. Double-sided front pews, installed in 1890, allowed worshippers to face both the altar then shift sides to see the pulpit during the sermon. There's 30 minutes of organ music every Saturday at 11.30am year-round, plus every Sunday at 11.30am from April to October.

Historisches Museum der Pfalz
MUSEUM

(Historical Museum of the Palatinate; www.museum.speyer.de; Domplatz 4; adult/student incl audioguide €7/5; ⊙10am-6pm Tue-Sun) Mind-boggling exhibits at this treasure-packed museum across from the Kaiserdom include the **Goldener Zeremonialhut von Schifferstadt**, an ornate gilded hat shaped like a giant thimble, which dates from the Bronze Age (around 1300 BC), and Celtic artefacts such as **two bronze wheels** (circa 800 BC). In the **Wine Museum**, an amphora from about AD 325 contains what may be the world's oldest wine. Emperor Konrad II's surprisingly simple 11th-century bronze crown is the prized exhibit of the **Domschatz** (cathedral treasury).

Technik Museum
MUSEUM

(www.technik-museum.de; Am Technik Museum 1; adult/child €14/12; ⊙9am-6pm Mon-Fri, to 7pm Sat & Sun) At this technology extravaganza 1km south of the Kaiserdom across the A61 highway, you can climb aboard a Boeing 747-230 (and wonder how on earth they got the aircraft here, much less mounted it 28m off the ground), a 1960s U-boat that's claustrophobic even on dry land, and a mammoth Antonov An-22 cargo plane with an all-analogue cockpit and a nose cone you can peer out of. Other highlights include the Soviet space shuttle *Buran*.

There are also military jets and helicopters from both sides of the former Iron Curtain, and a superb collection of vintage automobiles and fire engines.

The **Wilhelmsbau** showcases some extraordinary automated musical instruments – all in working order – including a Hupfeld Phonoliszt-Violina, a player-piano that also bows and fingers two violins, and a Roland orchestrion (1928), which simulates the sound of a soprano accompanying an orchestra.

🛏 Sleeping

DJH Hostel
HOSTEL $

(☑06232-615 97; www.jugendherberge.de; Geibstrasse 5; dm/d €28/75) A bright, cheery hostel on the banks of the Rhine, 300m east of the Technik Museum and right next door to the Bademaxx swimming complex, this DJH has 176 beds spread across 51 rooms, all with private bathroom. It's linked to the Hauptbahnhof and city centre by the City-Shuttle bus.

★ Hotel Domhof
HOTEL $$

(☑06232-132 90; www.domhof.de; Bauhof 3; s/d from €101/125; P❋@🛜) A hotel has stood on this epicentral spot next to the Kaiserdom since the Middle Ages, hosting emperors, kings and councillors over the centuries. The current incarnation opened in 1990 – Speyer's 2000th anniversary. Wrapped around an ivy-covered, cobbled courtyard, its 49 autumnal-hued rooms have parquet floors, bright bathrooms and leafy views. Wi-fi and parking cost €5 each for 24 hours.

Hotel Zum Augarten
HOTEL $$

(☑06232-754 58; www.augarten.de; Rheinhäuser Strasse 52; s/d from €65/85; P🛜) A 20-minute, 1.7km walk south of the centre, and just 500m from the Technik Museum in a suburban setting, this pale-orange-painted, family-run hotel offers a warm welcome. Its 16 rooms are modern and some have soothing plum-toned colour schemes. The separate guesthouse has longer-term, apartment-style accommodation – contact the hotel for availability and rates.

Hotel Speyer HOTEL $$
(☑ 06232-671 00; www.hotel-speyer.de; Am Technik Museum 1; caravan site €22, s/d from €65/95; P 🎇) Part of the Technik Museum complex, this motel-like establishment has 108 practical rooms (some of which face the museum's Boeing 747) as well as a 90-space **caravan park** (no tents). The City-Shuttle bus links it with the Hauptbahnhof and city centre. Guests at both the hotel and the caravan park get discounted Technik Museum entry.

🍴 Eating & Drinking

When the weather's warm, outdoor cafe terraces set up along Maximilianstrasse and nearby streets such as Kleine Pfaffengasse.

Domhof-Hausbrauerei GERMAN $$
(www.domhof.de; Grosse Himmelsgasse 6; mains €7-23; ⊙ kitchen 11.30am-11pm; 🎇👶) Footsteps from the Kaiserdom, this historic brewery has a courtyard beer garden shaded by chestnut trees. The menu includes regional favourites, some prepared using the three beers brewed on the premises (light, dark and wheat), such as fried local sausages with sauerkraut cooked in light beer, and liver dumplings in dark-beer-and-beef broth.

Rabennest GERMAN $$
(☑ 06232-623 857; www.weinstube-rabennest.de; Korngasse 5; mains €8-18; ⊙ kitchen 11am-11pm Mon-Sat) A half-timbered, green-shuttered building houses this timber-panelled, two-storey *Weinstube*, which serves Palatinate specialities such as *Handkäse mit Musik* with riesling bread, *Leberknödel* (liver meatballs in beef broth), *Pfälzer Bauernsteak* (pork steak with mushrooms, onions and bacon) and *Saumagen* (stuffed pig's stomach) with herb bread. In summer tables are set up on the cobblestones out front. Reservations are recommended.

Maximilian INTERNATIONAL $$
(www.cafe-maximilian.de; Korngasse 15; mains €11-18; ⊙ kitchen 8am-11pm Mon-Fri, 9am-11pm Sat & Sun; 🚲) Always buzzing, this local favourite by the Altpörtel serves 11 different breakfasts, from traditional German spreads to eggs Benedict and French toast, as well as weekday lunch specials (€5.90) of a soup or salad with a hot dish, and an à la carte menu spanning sausage platters, steaks, burgers and pastas. It also has **guest rooms and apartments** (☑ 06232-100 2500; www.mein-maximilian.de; Korngasse 15; s/d/apt from €90/100/130; 🎇).

Alter Hammer WINE BAR
(www.alter-hammer.de; Leinpfad 1c; ⊙ 11.30am-11pm Mon-Sat, 11am-11pm Sun) On the grassy banks of the Rhine, this half-timbered manor house has a sprawling, 360-seat beer garden, open March to October, canopied by linden trees. Its lengthy local wine list includes house-made *Glühwein* in winter. Traditional German fare, vegetarian options and a kid's menu make it a perfect place to while away a few hours. Cash only.

ℹ Information

Tourist Office (☑ 06232-142 392; www.speyer.de; Maximilianstrasse 13; ⊙ 9am-5pm Mon-Fri, 10am-3pm Sat, 10am-2pm Sun) Situated 200m west of the Kaiserdom, next to the historic Rathaus.

ℹ Getting There & Around

S-Bahn (S3 and S4) trains link the Hauptbahnhof with Mannheim (€5.40, 40 minutes, every 30 minutes) and Heidelberg (€9.70, 50 minutes, every 30 minutes). Change at Mannheim to reach the German Wine Route towns.

The convenient City-Shuttle minibus (bus 565; day pass €1.10) links the Hauptbahnhof, Maximilianstrasse, the Dom, Festplatz, the Technik Museum and the youth hostel at 10- to 15-minute intervals from 6am (9am on Sunday) to 8pm.

ℹ CYCLING AROUND SPEYER

Several excellent cycling paths fan out around Speyer.

The **Kaiser-Konrad-Radweg** links Speyer's Kaiserdom with Bad Dürkheim's Rathaus (32.5km each way), on the German Wine Route; the 120km **Salier-Radweg** circuit also takes in Worms. Starting from Basel, Switzerland, the 420km-long **Veloroute Rhein** follows the Rhine north to Worms.

The tourist office has cycling information; alternatively, visit **Outdoor Active** (www.outdooractive.com) with downloadable links, maps and more.

WORTH A TRIP

FAST CARS: HOCKENHEIMRING GRAND PRIX TRACK

HockenheimRing (☑ 06205-950 222, track reservations 06205-950 6005; www.hockenheimring.de; Hockenheim) The hallowed HockenheimRing, 22km southwest of Heidelberg just east of the A6, has three circuits and stands accommodating up to 120,000 fans. It hosts some of Germany's most famous car races, including the Formula One German Grand Prix (in even-numbered years), with the opportunity to test out the track yourself.

Motorsports fans can get a look behind the scenes on an **Insider Tour** (adult/child incl museum €12/6.50; ⊙ 11am except during races, advance bookings required Dec-Mar), in English and German. Tickets are sold at the **Motor Sport Museum** (adult/child €6/3; ⊙ 10am-5pm Apr-Oct, 10am-5pm Fri-Sun Nov-Mar, longer hours on race days).

The museum has a fantastic collection of historic motorcycles, some a century old, and a fine ensemble of historic race cars. Upstairs, check out the reconstruction of the world's first motorcycle, built of wood by Maybach and Daimler in 1885.

If roaring along on a speed-limitless Autobahn doesn't get the adrenalin pumping any more, you can take to the Hockenheim track when it isn't being used for a race:

➡ **Action Track Days** (per person €399) Three laps on the Grand Prix course with a professional driver in a superfast racing car, eg a Porsche GT3, a Mercedes SLK 350 or an Audi R8 V10.

➡ **Drifttaxi** (€229) Lets you experience high-speed skids with a professional driver.

➡ **Race'n'roll** (€399) Drive a superfast race car yourself.

➡ **Touristenfahrten** (per 15 minutes €15) Drive your own car around the track.

You can rent a bicycle, borrow cycling maps and get touring advice at **Radsport Stiller** (☑ 06232-759 66; www.stiller-radsport.de; Gilgenstrasse 24; bike/tandem per day €10/20; ⊙ 9.30am-12.30pm & 2-6.30pm Mon-Fri, 9am-2pm Sat, 1-5pm Sun), a first-rate bike shop a block southwest of the Altpörtel.

Schloss Schwetzingen

Schloss Schwetzingen PALACE (Schwetzingen Palace; www.schloss-schwetzingen. de; off Carl Theodor Strasse, Schwetzingen; adult/child gardens €5/2.50, incl Schloss tour €9/4.50, cheaper in winter; ⊙ gardens 9am-7.30pm late Mar-late Oct, 9am-4pm late Oct-late Mar, English palace tours 2pm Sat & Sun Apr-Oct) The enchanting **gardens** of Schloss Schwetzingen, the grand baroque-style summer residence of Prince-Elector Carl Theodor (1724–99), are wonderful for a family outing or a romantic stroll, especially on a sunny day.

The only way to see the furnished Schloss **interior** is on a tour. Download the free map-brochure *Schwetzingen Castle Garden* or buy it at the ticket desk (€1.50). Schloss Schwetzingen is 10km west of Heidelberg and 8km south of Mannheim (served by buses), just east of the A6.

Of Versaillian proportions and inspiration, Schloss Schwetzingen's gardens are a beguiling mix of exquisite French formality and meandering, English-style landscaping. Scattered around the gardens are burbling fountains and 'follies', architectural flights of fancy. Among them is an ersatz *Moschee* (mosque), an extraordinary complex in pink, decorated with Turkish crescents, that mixes 18th-century German baroque with 'exotic' styling inspired by Constantinople. As you wander, keep an eye out for strutting peacocks.

There is a couple of cafes on-site.

Mannheim

☑ 0621 / POP 314.931

Surrounded by factories and heavy-industry plants, Mannheim, situated between the Rhine and Neckar Rivers, near their confluence, isn't Germany at its prettiest. Industrial giants based here include Daimler (automotive), John Deere (agricultural machinery), Caterpillar (construction machinery), ABB (electrical equipment), Fuchs Petrolub (chemicals), IBM (computers), Roche (pharmaceuticals), Unilever (consumer goods) and Siemens (engineering). However, Mannheim compensates with an energetic cultural scene and decent shopping in its busy city centre.

Two important transportation firsts took place in Mannheim: Karl Drais created the world's first bicycle in 1817, and Karl Benz built the world's first automobile to combine an internal combustion engine and integrated chassis in 1885; the three-wheeled vehicle was patented in 1886.

◎ Sights

★ Barockschloss Mannheim PALACE

(www.schloss-mannheim.de; cnr Bismarckstrasse & Breite Strasse) Mannheim's most famous sight is the mustard-yellow-and-red sandstone Schloss, Germany's largest baroque palace. Now occupied by the University of Mannheim, the 450m-long structure was built over the course of 40 years in the mid-1700s but was almost completely destroyed during WWII.

Off the main courtyard are the **Schloss Museum** (Ehrenhof; adult/child incl audioguide €6/3, incl guided tour in English €8/4; ⊙10am-5pm Tue-Sun) and baroque **Schlosskirche** (⊙10am-5pm).

In the Schloss Museum, you can see the impressively rococo **Kabinettsbibliothek**, saved from wartime destruction thanks to having been stored off-site, and several go-for-baroque halls – each a feast of stucco, marble, porcelain and chandeliers – rebuilt after the war.

The Schlosskirche was constructed between 1720 and 1731, and was rebuilt after the war. Mozart performed here in 1777. It belongs to the Alt-Katholiken (Old Catholics), a movement that split with Rome over papal infallibility in the 1870s and is now part of the Anglican Communion.

Kunsthalle Museum MUSEUM

(www.kunsthalle-mannheim.de; Friedrichsplatz 4; adult/child €9/6; ⊙11am-6pm Tue & Thu-Sun, to 8pm Wed) Mannheim's premier gallery is a vast repository of modern and contemporary art by masters such as Cézanne, Degas, Manet, Kandinsky and Rodin. The permanent collection has often been stored away to make space for blockbuster exhibitions, but that will change with the opening of a €70 million metal-encased, glass-roofed new 16,000-sq-metre exhibition space in 2017.

Jesuitenkirche CHURCH

(Jesuit Church; www.jesuitenkirche.de; A4, 2; ⊙10am-7pm) A sumptuously ornate baroque vision, glowing with gold leaf, the Jesuitenkirche was built between 1733 and 1760. When Mozart spent time in Mannheim in the late 1700s, he praised its acoustics and atmosphere. Like the rest of the city, the church suffered damage during WWII, but it has since been fully restored.

Friedrichsplatz PARK

Five blocks northeast of the Hauptbahnhof, Friedrichsplatz is an oasis of manicured lawns, lovely flower beds and art-nouveau fountains. Its centrepiece is the 60m-high **Wasserturm** (Water Tower), a bit of 19th-century civil architecture that has become one of the city's symbols. An elegant ensemble of red sandstone edifices, many with arcades, lines the perimeter.

🛌 Sleeping

Arabella Pension HOTEL $

(☑0621-230 50; www.pension-arabella-mannheim.de; M2, 12; s/d/tr from €28/46/63; 🛜) Super-centrally situated just two blocks north of the Schloss, the Arabella has 18 bright, spacious, ultra-budget rooms with shared bathrooms (and no breakfast). Reception is closed Sunday afternoon – call ahead if you'll be arriving then.

Central Hotel HOTEL $$

(☑0621-123 00; www.centralhotelmannheim.de; Kaiserring 26-28; s €68-145, d €78-165; 🅿🛜) The aptly named Central Hotel, just two blocks north of the Hauptbahnhof, offers snazzy design at reasonable prices. Its 34 rooms are bright and modern, though singles can be small. For a cityscape panorama, ask for one of the three corner rooms. Breakfast costs €10; on-site parking is available for €10.

Maritim Parkhotel LUXURY HOTEL $$

(☑0621-158 80; www.maritim.de; Friedrichsplatz 2; d from €118; 🅿🌸@🛜♨) Built in 1901 in the sumptuous style of the Renaissance, this supremely elegant 173-room hotel overlooks Friedrichsplatz. Amenities include a swimming pool, sauna and steam bath, two top-notch restaurants and, often, live lobby music in the evenings. Many rooms have balconies or terraces. Breakfast costs €20.

🍴 Eating

Mannheim's attractive Marktplatz is flanked by cafes with alfresco seating in summer.

★ Café Prag CAFE $

(E4, 17; dishes €1.50-3.50; ⊙10am-7pm Mon-Sat, 1-6pm Sun) A former tailor's shop and cigar store, built in 1902, is now an arty cafe with *Jugendstil* woodwork, cranberry-red walls and a pre-war Central European feel. Smooth jazz on the stereo makes a perfect backdrop for enjoying an espresso and light refreshments like croissants or rhubarb cake.

ℹ NAVIGATING MANNHEIM

Mannheim is famous for its quirky – indeed, unique – chessboard street layout. The city centre, which measures 1.5km by 1.5km, is divided into four quadrants by two perpendicular, largely pedestrianised shopping streets, the north–south Breite Strasse and the east–west Planken. At their intersection is the grassy Paradeplatz, with a fountain in the middle.

The streets don't have names. Instead, each rectilinear city block has an alphanumeric designation. Starting at the Schloss, as you move north the letters go from A up to K for blocks west of Breite Strasse and from L to U for blocks east of it. The numbers rise from 1 to 7 as you move away – either east or west – from Breite Strasse. The result is addresses such as 'Q3, 16' or 'L14, 5' (the latter numeral specifies the building) that sound a bit like galactic sectors.

Südlandhaus

DELI $

(www.suedlandhaus.de; P3, 8-9; ⏱9.30am-7pm Mon-Fri, to 5.30pm Sat) Filled with German and international wines, cheeses, breads, sausages, hams, antipasti items like olives, liqueurs and chocolates, this aromatic food emporium is the ultimate place to pick up picnic fare.

Kochstation

ITALIAN $

(www.kochstation.de; O4, 3; mains €6.50-9.50; ⏱11am-8pm Mon-Sat) Not an Italian restaurant in the traditional sense, Kochstation cooks up contemporary dishes at its central open kitchen, with the option to mix and match seven types of fresh pasta and 15 different sauces. At the back there's an airy glass-roofed atrium dining space, as well as an alfresco courtyard with umbrella-shaded communal tables.

Self-caterers can buy take-away ingredient packs; it also runs cookery courses.

Wochenmarkt

MARKET $

(Marktplatz; ⏱8am-2pm Tue, Thu & Sat) Lively farmers markets set up on the Marktplatz three times weekly, selling fresh fruit, vegetables, fish, spices, wine, flowers and snacks to eat on the go as you browse the stalls.

Gasthaus Zentrale

GERMAN $$

(N4, 15; mains €6.30-19.50; ⏱kitchen 9.30am-midnight) Dark and rustic, and opening to a terrace in warm weather, this welcoming place three blocks east of Paradeplatz rustles up salads, steaks, schnitzel and other pub favourites. Great-value daily specials (not available Sunday) cost €6 to €9.

Café Journal

CAFE $$

(www.cafejournal-mannheim.de; H1, 15; mains €8-14; ⏱8.30am-11.30pm Mon-Sat, 9.30am-11.30pm Sun; 🎵) In a prime people-watching location on Mannheim's Marktplatz, French-styled Café Journal serves pan-European creations like Mediterranean vegetable strudel, salmon and spinach lasagne with Prosecco sauce, homemade sausages with spring onion and radish, and lamb with rosemary sauce and asparagus. Mid-week lunch specials cost just €6; breakfast is available until 3pm daily. Live jazz plays every Wednesday evening and Sunday afternoon.

ℹ Information

Tourist Office (☎0621-293 8700; www.tourist-mannheim.de; Willy-Brandt-Platz 3; ⏱9am-7pm Mon-Fri, 10am-1pm Sat) Just across the square from the Hauptbahnhof. An audioguide tour of the city per three hours/day costs €7.50/10.

ℹ Getting There & Around

Mannheim is a major rail hub on the Hamburg–Basel line serving Frankfurt (€19, 45 minutes, up to four per hour). Frequent S-Bahn trains link the Hauptbahnhof with Heidelberg (€4.90, 20 minutes).

Worms

☎06241 / POP 79,727

Worms (starts with a 'V' and rhymes with 'forms') has played a key role at pivotal moments in European history. In AD 413 it became capital of the legendary, if short-lived, Burgundian kingdom whose rise and fall was chronicled in the 12th-century *Nibelungenlied*. Later hijacked by Wagner and the Nazis, the epic poem is featured in a local museum and the annual theatre festival, Nibelungen-Festspiele.

After the Burgundians, just about every other tribe in the area had a go at ruling Worms, including the Huns, the Alemans and finally the Franks, and it was under the Frankish leader, Charlemagne, that the city flourished in the 9th century. The most impressive reminder of the city's medieval heyday is its majestic, late-Romanesque Dom.

A Jewish community, renowned for the erudition of its rabbis, thrived here from the 10th century until the 1930s, earning Worms the moniker 'Little Jerusalem'.

◉ Sights

Pedestrianised Wilhelm-Leuschner-Strasse leads from the Hauptbahnhof for 500m southeast to Lutherplatz, on the northwest edge of the half-oval-shaped Altstadt, where the impressive **Luther Memorial** honours the Protestant reformer. From here, it's 150m southeast to pedestrianised **Kämmererstrasse**, the old city's main commercial thoroughfare, and 300m south to the Dom.

Kaiserdom   CHURCH
(www.wormser-dom.de; Domplatz; ⊗9am-6pm Apr-Oct, 10am-5pm Nov-Mar, closed during Sun morning Mass) FREE Worms' skyline, such as it is, is dominated by the four towers and two domes of the magnificent Kaiserdom (Dom St Peter und St Paul), built in the 11th and 12th centuries in the late-Romanesque style. Inside, the lofty dimensions impress as much as the lavish, canopied high altar (1742) in the east choir, designed by the baroque master Balthasar Neumann. Details of concerts are listed on the website.

In the cathedral's south transept, a scale model shows the enormity of the original complex. Nearby stairs lead down to the stuffy crypt, which holds the stone sarcophagi of several members of the Salian dynasty of Holy Roman emperors.

Alte Synagoge   SYNAGOGUE
(Rashi Shul; Synagogenplatz, Judengasse; ⊗10am-12.30pm & 1.30-5pm Apr-Oct, 10am-noon & 2-4pm Nov-Mar, closed to visitors Sat morning) FREE Worms' famous Old Synagogue, founded in 1034, was destroyed by the Nazis, but in 1961 it was reconstructed using, as much as possible, stones from the original. Men are asked to cover their heads inside.

In the garden, stone steps lead down to an extraordinary, Romanesque-style **Mikwe** (ritual bath) built in the 1100s.

Jüdisches Museum   MUSEUM
(Raschi-Haus; Hintere Judengasse 6; adult/child €1.50/0.80; ⊗10am-12.30pm & 1.30-5pm Apr-Oct, to 4.30pm Nov-Mar) Behind Worms' Alte Synagoge, the Jewish Museum introduces the city's storied Jewish community through exhibits such as parchment manuscripts, documents and plans, and a menorah (seven-armed candlestick), as well as a model of the synagogue

depicting its location around the year 1600. The museum also sells several informative English booklets on Jewish Worms.

Alter Jüdenfriedhof   CEMETERY
(Willy-Brandt-Ring 21; ⊗8am-dusk Sep-Jun, to 8pm Jul & Aug, closed Jewish holidays) FREE Inaugurated in 1076, the Old Jewish Cemetery, also known as the Heiliger Sand ('holy sand'), is one of the oldest Jewish burial grounds in Europe. It is situated 250m west of the Dom; turn left at the fountain roundabout on Andreasstrasse.

The most revered gravestone is that of Rabbi Meir of Rothenburg (1215–93), a Talmudic commentator still read today. Rabbi Meir died in captivity after being imprisoned by King Rudolf of Habsburg for attempting to lead a group of persecuted Jews to Palestine (emigration would have cut the king's income from a tax only Jews had to pay). It's on the left just after you enter, the left-hand gravestone of the two that are topped with large piles of pebbles (left by visitors as tokens of respect) and Western Wall–style prayer notes.

Nibelungen Museum   MUSEUM
(www.nibelungen-museum.de; Fischerpförtchen 10; adult/child €5.50/3.50; ⊗10am-5pm Tue-Fri, to 6pm Sat & Sun) The *Nibelungenlied* is the ultimate tale of love and hate, treasure and treachery, revenge and death, with a cast including dwarves, dragons and bloodthirsty *Überfrauen* (superwomen). Richard Wagner set the poem to music, Fritz Lang turned it into a silent movie in 1924 and the Nazis abused its mythology, seeing in dragon-slayer Siegfried the quintessential German hero. The Nibelungen Museum's multimedia exhibit seeks to rescue the epic from the Nazis' manipulations. Audioguides (included in admission) are available in English.

Museum der Stadt Worms   MUSEUM
(City Museum; Weckerlingplatz 7; adult/child €2/1, special exhibitions €3/1.50; ⊗10am-5pm Tue-Sun) Exhibits at Worms' city museum bring its fascinating history to life. Highlights include Bronze Age women's jewellery, a superb collection of delicate Roman glass excavated from local graves, and a section on the Middle Ages. It's two blocks south of the Dom, behind the youth hostel.

✸ Festivals & Events

Nibelungen-Festspiele   CULTURAL
(www.nibelungenfestspiele.de; ⊗late Jul–mid-Aug) The saga of the Burgundian kingdom is

celebrated at the two-week Nibelungen-Festspiele, featuring theatre productions on an open-air stage in front of Worms' cathedral.

🛏 Sleeping

Kriemhilde
HOTEL $

(☏ 06241-911 50; www.hotelkriemhilde.de; Hofgasse 2-4; s/d €55/78; 🛜) Wake up to the peal of the Dom bells at this friendly, family-run inn. It faces the north side of the mighty cathedral, which can be glimpsed from some of the 18 streamlined, sparingly furnished rooms and from the terrace. There's a wine cellar and restaurant serving hearty German cuisine.

DJH Hostel
HOSTEL $

(☏ 06241-257 80; www.jugendherberge.de; Dechaneigasse 1; dm/s/d €21.50/33.50/54; 🅿) In a superb location facing the south side of the Dom, this 121-bed hostel has spick-and-span rooms with two to six beds and private bathrooms. There are four lounge areas, a beer garden and a bistro, as well as free parking out the front.

Parkhotel Prinz Carl
HOTEL $$

(☏ 06241-3080; www.parkhotel-prinzcarl.de; Prinz-Carl-Anlage 10-14; s/d from €88/131; 🅿🛜) Housed in handsome barracks built during the reign of the last Kaiser, the Prinz Carl has 90 spacious, comfortable rooms including rooms especially designed for business travellers, with good-sized desks. There's a classy restaurant and bar; staff are exceptionally helpful. It's peacefully situated on the northern edge of town, 500m north of the Hauptbahnhof through a chestnut-shaded park.

🍴 Eating

Italian restaurants cluster a block southeast of the Dom at the corner of Gerberstrasse and Wollstrasse. Cheap eats are available up towards the Hauptbahnhof, along pedestrianised Wilhelm-Leuschner-Strasse.

Schnitzelhütt
GERMAN $$

(☏ 06241-594 343; www.schnitzelhuett.de; Rathenaustrasse 31; mains €8.40-19; ⊙11am-10.30pm Sun-Thu, to 11.30pm Fri & Sat) No fewer than 22 varieties of pork or chicken schnitzel are served at this exposed brick-and-timber city-centre restaurant with barrel tables: gorgonzola-topped, Dijon mustard-doused, slathered in sherry-cream sauce, Swiss-style with cheese and ham, Hawaiian-style with pineapple, plus a fiery *Teufelsschnitzel* (devil schnitzel) with corn, kidney beans, pepperoni, olives and fresh chilli. Other dishes include rump steaks, burgers and meal-sized salads.

Trattoria-Pizzeria Pepe e Sale
ITALIAN $$

(☏ 06241-258 36; www.pepe-e-sale.de; Wollstrasse 12; pizzas & pasta €5.50-8, mains €9.50-21.50; ⊙11am-11.30pm; 🍴) Warm and welcoming, this time-honoured, Italian-run trattoria/pizzeria serves scores of varieties of pizzas and pastas along with classic Italian mains such as veal in Marsala or Sambuca-cream sauce, chicken with pesto, grilled calamari, and perch with rich homemade tomato sauce. There's an atmospheric dining room with chunky wooden tables and open wine racks and an alfresco summer terrace.

Café TE
INTERNATIONAL $$

(Bahnhofstrasse 5; mains €6.30-18; ⊙kitchen 4pm-midnight Mon-Sat, to 10pm Sun; 🛜) Just south of the Hauptbahnhof, sociable TE ('Trans Europa') has communal tables within a huge building. It's a student favourite for its different special each night (Monday is burger night, Tuesday is pizza night and so on). Cash only.

🍷 Drinking

★ Hagenbräu
MICROBREWERY

(www.hagenbraeu.de; Am Rhein 3; ⊙10am-11pm Mon-Fri, 9am-11pm Sat & Sun Mar-Oct, 11am-11pm Wed-Fri, 10am-11pm Sat, 10am-9pm Sun Nov-Feb) Producing four varieties of beer each month (light, dark, wheat beer, and a seasonal brew such as potato beer), this half-timbered microbrewery is one of several hugely popular beer gardens along the Rhine, just north of the bridges, with chestnut-shaded tables stretching down to the water's edge. Filling Rheinhessisch-style fare is served from 11.30am to 10pm.

Nearby is a **statue of Hagen** tossing the Nibelung treasure into the Rhine.

Strand Bar 443
BEER GARDEN

(http://strandbar443-worms.de; Am Rhein 9; ⊙3pm-midnight Mon-Thu, 2pm-1am Fri, noon-1am Sat, 10am-midnight Sun Apr-Sep) Tiki huts and sandy beaches lined with sun lounges are the last thing you'd expect to find along the Rhine, but this beach bar sees this stretch of riverbank transformed into a tropical paradise come summer. There's a big barbecue area, DJs most nights and lush cocktails (plus soft drinks for the kids). Hours can vary depending on the weather.

ℹ Information

Tourist Office (☏ 06241-853 7306; www.worms.de; Neumarkt 14; ⊙9am-6pm Mon-Fri, 10am-2pm Sat & Sun Apr-Oct, 9am-5pm Mon-

Fri Nov-Mar) Friendly, helpful office; also sells local events tickets.

ℹ Getting There & Around

Worms is 75km southwest of Frankfurt.

Frequent trains serve Worms; destinations include:

➡ **Darmstadt** (from €12.50, one hour)

➡ **Deidesheim** (€15.50, 1¼ hours)

➡ **Frankfurt** (from €13.30, 1¼ hours)

➡ **Mainz** (€12.50, 26 to 44 minutes)

➡ **Mannheim** (€8.50, 15 minutes)

➡ **Speyer** (€13.50, 45 minutes; change in Mannheim)

Bicycles can be rented at **Radhaus-Mihm** (☑ 06241-242 08; Von Steuben-Strasse 8; per day/weekend €5/7.50; ⊙ 9.30am-12.30pm & 1.30-6pm Mon-Fri, 10am-1pm Sat, shorter hours in winter), under the tracks from the Hauptbahnhof. The tourist office sells cycling maps.

Lorsch Abbey

Lorsch Abbey CHURCH
(Kloster Lorsch; www.kloster-lorsch.de; Nibelungenstrasse 35, Lorsch; adult/child €5/3; ⊙ 10am-5pm Tue-Sun, English tours 11am & 4pm Mar-Oct, 11am & 4pm Sat & Sun Nov-Feb) Founded around AD 760 and Unesco listed in 1991, Lorsch Abbey, in the charming village of Lorsch, was an important religious site in its Carolingian heyday (8th to 10th centuries). Preserved medieval buildings include the rare, Carolingian-era Königshalle and the Altenmünster; museum exhibits cover the history of the abbey, life in Hesse, and tobacco, which was cultivated in Lorsch in the late 17th century.

Lorsch is 30km south of Darmstadt via the A5 or picturesque Bergstrasse (B3); there's no public transport.

GERMAN WINE ROUTE

One of Germany's oldest touring routes, the Deutsche Weinstrasse (www.deutsche-weinstrasse.de), inaugurated in 1935, traverses the heart of the Palatinate (Pfalz) – a region of vine-covered hillsides, rambling forests, ruined castles, picturesque hamlets and, of course, exceptional wine estates. Starting in Schweigen-Rechtenbach, on the French border (5km from the delightful Alsatian town of Wissembourg), it winds north – through Germany's largest contiguous wine-growing area – for 85km to Bockenheim an der Wein-

strasse (not to be confused with the Frankfurt district of Bockenheim), 15km west of Worms.

Blessed with a moderate climate that allows almonds, figs, kiwi fruit and even lemons to thrive, the German Wine Route is especially pretty during the spring bloom (March to mid-May). Weinfeste (wine festivals) run from March to mid-November (especially on weekends); check with tourist offices for dates. The grape harvest (September and October) is also a lively time to visit.

In part because of its proximity to France, the Palatinate is a renowned culinary destination. Tourist offices can supply lists of visitable wineries.

The Pfälzerwald (www.pfaelzerwald.de), the hilly forest that runs along the western edge of the German Wine Route, was declared (along with France's adjacent Vosges du Nord area) a Unesco Biosphere Reserve in 1993. Hiking and cycling options abound here.

ℹ Getting There & Away

The **Rhein-Haardtbahn** (www.rnv-online.de) light rail line links Bad Dürkheim with Mannheim (€5.40, 55 minutes, at least hourly). Change at Mannheim for Frankfurt (€19 to €24, 1¾ hours).

The RNV-Express goes to Heidelberg's Hauptbahnhof and Bismarckplatz (€9.70, 1¼ hours, every 30 minutes). The trip from Speyer requires a change at Schifferstadt (€8.30, one hour, every 30 minutes).

ℹ Getting Around

The German Wine Route is most easily explored by car. Cycling here is also a pleasure, thanks to

---

JEWISH WORMS

Starting in the 900s, Jewish life in Worms – known as Varmaiza in medieval Jewish texts – was centred on **Judengasse**, in the northeast corner of the Altstadt, 1km northeast of the Dom (on foot, take Kämmererstrasse). Today, it's where you'll find a medieval synagogue, a 12th-century ritual bath and Worms' Jewish museum.

Before 1933, 1100 Jews lived in the city. A Jewish community was re-established in the late 1990s and now numbers 140 souls, almost all of them from the former USSR.

For more information, visit www.worms.de, which has a dedicated Jewish Worms section in English.

FRANKFURT & SOUTHERN RHINELAND LORSCH ABBEY

a multitude of *Radwanderwege* (bike paths and cyclable back roads; www.radwanderland.de) such as the Radweg Deutsche Weinstrasse. Area tourist offices sell various excellent cycling maps and have details on bike rentals.

Germany's superb transport network, however, means it's possible to get almost everywhere – including to trail heads and from hike destinations – by public transport. Local trains that take bicycles (p399) link Deidesheim and Bad Dürkheim (€2.40, seven minutes, every 30 minutes) and head south to Neustadt an der Weinstrasse and beyond.

Neustadt an der Weinstrasse

☑ 06321 / POP 52,164

Vineyards fan out around Neustadt, a busy wine-producing town at the heart of the German Wine Route. A half-timbered Altstadt, historic hilltop castle and some outstanding places to eat and drink make it an unmissable stop.

⊙ Sights & Activities

Neustadt has a largely pedestrianised Altstadt teeming with half-timbered houses, especially along Mittelgasse, Hintergasse, Metzgergasse and Kunigundenstrasse. It's anchored by the Marktplatz, a cobbled square flanked by the baroque Rathaus and the Gothic Stiftskirche.

★ Hambacher Schloss   CASTLE
(Hambacher Castle; ☑ 06321-926 290; www.hambacher-schloss.de; Wolfsburg; adult/child €4.50/1.50, incl tour €8/5; ⊙ castle 10am-6pm Apr-Oct, 11am-5pm Nov-Mar, tours hourly 11am-4pm Apr-Oct, 11am, noon and 2pm Sat & Sun Nov-Mar) Atop a forested Pfälzerwald hill 6km southwest of the centre, this 'cradle of German democracy' is where idealistic locals, Polish refugees and French citizens held massive protests for a free, democratic, united Germany on 27 May 1832, hoisting the black, red and gold German flag for the first time. An exhibition commemorates the event, known as the Hambacher Fest. Audioguides (€3) and tours are available in English. Bus 502 (17 minutes, hourly) runs from the Hauptbahnhof.

The castle's restaurant is excellent.

Stiftskirche   CHURCH
(☑ 06321-841 79; http://stiftskirchengemeinde-nw.de; Marktplatz; adult/child church tour €3/1, tower tour €3/1; ⊙ 8am-4pm Mon-Thu, 8am-noon Fri, 9am-2pm Sat) Built from red sandstone, the

14th- and 15th-century Gothic Stiftskirche has been shared by Protestant and Catholic congregations since 1708. Recent renovations revealed frescos from 1410 that depict a snapshot of life at the time, with bakers, crafts people and market traders. Guided tours of the church take place at 4pm on Friday. Every Saturday at noon guided tours take you into the tower, reached by 184 steps. Many tours are in English – phone ahead to confirm your spot.

Weingut Kriegshaeuser   WINERY
(☑ 06321-836 09; www.kriegshaeuser-wein.de; Kreuzstrasse 4, Diedesfeld; ⊙ 10am-6pm Mon-Fri, to 5pm Sat, to noon Sun Apr-Oct, shorter hours Nov-Mar) A beautiful half-timbered building houses this charming *Weingut*, which offers tastings of its riesling, Pinot blanc, Spät, Cabernet Dorsa and sparkling wines from its vineyards dating from 1594. It's just off the Weinstrasse (L512) 5km south of the centre.

🛏 Sleeping & Eating

★ Gästehaus-Weingut
Helbighof   GUESTHOUSE $$
(☑ 06321-327 81; www.helbighof.de; Andergasse 40; d €81; P 🛜) Beneath the Hambacher Schloss amid sprawling vineyards, this charming family-run winery has just five guest rooms, so book well ahead. The pick is room 3, with balconies on two sides. Its superb wines are sold at its honour bar; a sun terrace overlooks the vines. Turn right after Andergasse 36, then immediately left to reach the driveway. Cash only.

Herve's Crêperie   CRÊPERIE $
(www.hervescreperie.de; Hauptstrasse 121; savoury galettes €3.70-6.30, sweet crêpes €2.50-6; ⊙ 11.30am-9pm Wed-Fri, to 4pm Sat) Newly relocated to a contemporary, airy space in the town centre, this wonderfully authentic Breton crêperie serves savoury buckwheat-flour *galettes* like *forestière* (with mushrooms and cream sauce) and tri-colour (Rustique, St-Agur blue and Raclette cheese with cranberry jam), and sweet crêpes such as caramelised apples with Calvados, or salted caramel, washed down with bowls of traditional cider.

★ Restaurant 1832   MODERN GERMAN $$
(☑ 06321-959 7860; www.hambacherschloss.eu; Hambacher Schloss, Wolfsburg; mains €13-21.50; ⊙ 10am-8pm Apr-Oct, to 6pm Nov-Mar) Inside the Hambacher Schloss, opening to a courtyard, Restaurant 1832 is reason enough to make the trip up the hill, with inspired modern

German cuisine: liver dumpling soup; tagliatelle with roasted asparagus in fig sauce; fried calf's liver with glazed grapes and potato and celery cake; red mullet, shrimp and clams baked in parchment with cuttlefish risotto.

Urgestein
MODERN GERMAN $$$

(☑ 06321-489 060; www.restaurant-urgestein.de; Rathausstrasse 6; 4-course vegetarian menu €85, 5-/6-course menus €100/120, paired wines extra €30-50; ⊙ 6-10pm Tue-Sat; ✔) For a gastronomic extravaganza, book a table at Benjamin Peifer's Michelin-starred, vaulted brick cellar restaurant within a half-timbered town-centre house. Exquisite dishes might include pickled trout with sauerkraut and horseradish, followed by steamed liver dumplings with riesling foam, hay-roasted pigeon with foie gras mousse, and nougat ganache with hazelnut yoghurt. Live jazz plays in the summer courtyard.

❶ Information

Tourist Office (☑ 06321-926 870; www.neustadt.eu; Hetzelplatz 1; ⊙ 9.30am-6pm Mon-Fri, 10am-2pm Sat Apr-Oct, 9.30am-5pm Mon-Fri Nov-Mar) Diagonally across Bahnhofplatz from the Hauptbahnhof, with information on local sights, hiking, cycling and wine festivals.

Deidesheim

☑ 06326 / POP 3704

Awash with pale purple-flowering wisteria in the springtime, diminutive Deidesheim is one of the German Wine Route's most picturesque – and upmarket – villages. Perfect for a romantic getaway, it offers plenty of opportunities for wine tasting, relaxed strolling and sublime dining.

Deidesheim is a 'Cittaslow' town, an extension of the Slow Food movement that aims to rebalance modern life's hectic pace not only through 'ecogastronomy' but also local arts, crafts, nature, cultural traditions and heritage.

◎ Sights

Museum für Weinkultur
MUSEUM

(Museum of Wine Culture; Marktplatz 8; ⊙ 4-6pm Wed-Sun Mar-Dec) FREE A Marktplatz landmark with a canopied outdoor staircase, the **Altes Rathaus** (old town hall) dates from the 16th century. Inside is the three-storey Museum of Wine Culture, featuring displays on winemakers' traditional lifestyle and naive-art portrayals of the German Wine Route. An English brochure is available.

Pfarrkirche St Ulrich
CHURCH

(Marktplatz; ⊙ 8am-5pm) Right on the Marktplatz, this late-Gothic, three-nave columned church was built between 1440 and 1480 and is the only remaining large mid-15th-century church in the Palatinate.

Deutsches Film-und Fototechnik Museum
MUSEUM

(www.dftm.de; Weinstrasse 33; admission €2.50; ⊙ 2-6pm Wed-Sat, 11am-6pm Sun) Down an alleyway across from the Rathaus, the German Film & Photography Museum has an impressive collection of historic photographic and movie-making equipment. Check out the vintage film-dispensing vending machine by the entrance.

Geissbockbrunnen
FOUNTAIN

(Bahnhofstrasse) Near the tourist office, the whimsical 'Goat Fountain' (1985) celebrates a quirky local tradition. For seven centuries, the nearby town of Lambrecht has had to pay an annual tribute of one goat for using pastureland belonging to Deidesheim. The presentation of this goat, which is auctioned off to raise funds for local cultural activities, culminates in the raucous Geissbockfest.

⚡ Activities

Deidesheim is home to 10 **winemakers** (some closed Sunday) that welcome visitors – look for signs reading *Weingut* (winery), *Verkauf* (sale) and *Weinprobe* (wine tasting) and ring the bell. Many can be found along the small streets west of Pfarrkirche St Ulrich.

The tourist office has maps for several signposted **walking routes** and **cycling routes** through vineyards and the Pfälzerwald.

Gepäckservice Pfalz
CYCLING

(☑ 06326-982 284; www.gepaeckservice-pfalz.de; Kirschgartenstrasse 49; bikes per day €10; ⊙ 9am-5pm Apr-Oct) Owned by Olympic cycling champion Stefan Steinweg, Gepäckservice Pfalz rents bikes and arranges luggage and bike transport. It's 500m southwest of the tourist office.

✦ Festivals & Events

Geissbockfest
CULTURAL

(Goat Festival; ⊙ May or Jun) This lively festival celebrates Deidesheim's time-honoured goat presentation. Check dates with the tourist office.

Weihnachtsmarkt   CHRISTMAS MARKET

(◷late Nov-late Dec) Deidesheim is famed for its Christmas market, the region's largest, held on the four weekends (Friday evening, Saturday and Sunday) before Christmas.

🛏 Sleeping & Eating

The town's speciality, *Saumagen* (stuffed pig's stomach), appears on menus everywhere.

Gästehaus Ritter von Böhl   GUESTHOUSE $

(✉06326-972 201; www.gaestehaus-ritter-von-boehl.de; Weinstrasse 35; s/d/tr from €55/80/117; ◷reception 8am-6pm; Ⓟ) Set around a wisteria-wrapped courtyard, this guesthouse belongs to and occupies part of the grounds of a charity hospital (now an old-age home) founded in 1494. It has 22 apricot-toned rooms and a bright breakfast atrium.

★Deidesheimer Hof   BOUTIQUE HOTEL $$

(✉06326-968 70; www.deidesheimerhof.de; Am Marktplatz; s/d from €85/125; Ⓟ❄@ⓦ) In a story-book gabled building, this renowned hostelry has 28 individually decorated, ultra-spacious rooms (the smallest are 25 sq metres), and two fine restaurants: **St Urban** (mains €17.50-28; ◷11am-10pm), whose regional offerings include *Saumagen*, made with chestnuts in autumn; and, in the vaulted basement, the gourmet **Schwarzer Hahn** (mains €44-59, 4-course menu €95; ◷6-10pm Tue-Sat), which specialises in creative French- and Palatinate-style *haute cuisine*.

Ketschauer Hof   BOUTIQUE HOTEL $$$

(✉06326-700 00; www.ketschauerhof.com; Ketschauerhofstrasse 1; s/d from €195/230; ❄ⓦ) A one-time winemaker's mansion has been turned into a romantic hotel that blends traditional luxury with contemporary styling. Its 17 rooms are light-filled and airy. Also here are two gourmet restaurants, **LA Jordan** (5-/7-course menus from €105/135; ◷6.30-10pm Tue-Sat) and **Bistro 1718** (mains €15-33; ◷noon-10pm), which specialises in steaks; from 3pm to 6pm it serves light refreshments like cakes. Reserve well ahead for weekend stays.

Turmstüb'l   GERMAN $$

(✉06326-981 081; www.turmstuebel.de; Turmstrasse 3; mains €10-17; ◷6pm-midnight Tue-Sat, noon-11pm Sun) Tucked down an alley opposite the church, this artsy wine cafe serves seasonal dishes like white asparagus with poached eggs and parsley, and regional specialities such as *Saumagen*, as well as over a dozen wines by the glass.

Gasthaus zur Kanne   GERMAN $$$

(✉06326-966 00; www.gasthauszurkanne.de; Weinstrasse 31; mains €19-23, 4-/5-/6-course menus €49/59/65; ◷noon-2pm & 6-10pm Wed-Sun) The Palatinate's oldest inn, dating from 1160, serves refined, contemporary regional cuisine in an elegant space with parquet floors. Its menu changes daily but might include porcini-stuffed *Saumagen,* venison with riesling jus, or smoked trout with cream and horseradish. Reservations are recommended.

🛍 Shopping

Wine shopping aside, galleries and artisans' studios (such as jewellery makers and potters) can be visited along the **Kunst und Kultur** (Art and Culture) Circuit; look for dark-blue-on-yellow 'K' signs.

ℹ Information

Tourist Office (✉06326-967 70; www.deidesheim.de; Bahnhofstrasse 5; ◷9am-12.30pm & 1.30-5pm Mon-Thu, to 6pm Fri, 9am-12.30pm Sat Apr-Oct, 9am-noon & 2-5pm Mon-Fri Nov-Mar) Situated 150m across the car park from the Bahnhof.

Bad Dürkheim

✉06322 / POP 18.222

Adorned with plenty of splashy fountains, the attractive spa town of Bad Dürkheim is famous for its salty thermal springs and lovely parks – and what's claimed to be the world's largest wine festival, as well as the world's largest wine barrel.

◉ Sights & Activities

Bad Dürkheim's number-one photo opp is the enormous **Dürkheimer Riesenfass** ('giant barrel') with a diameter of 13.5m and volume of 1,700,000L, which contains the Restaurant Dürkheimer Fass.

Glorious walking options include **Weinwanderwege** (vineyard trails) from St Michaelskapelle, a chapel atop a little vine-clad hill northeast of the tourist office, to Honigsäckel and the Hochmess vineyards (a 6km circuit); and forest trails to two historic ruins, Limburg and Hardenburg (4km west of town). The tourist office has maps.

The 130km-long **Kaiser-Konrad-Radweg** bike path to Speyer starts here.

Kurgarten   PARK

(◷24hr) Between the Hauptbahnhof and the tourist office lies the grassy Kurpark, an azalea- and wisteria-filled public garden where you'll find the tiny **Isenach River**, with landscaped banks and a **children's playground**.

Kurzentrum SPA
(☑ 06322-9640; www.kurzentrum-bad-duerkheim. de; Kurbrunnenstrasse 14; treatments from €15; ⊘ 9am-8pm Mon-Fri, 9am-5pm Sat, 9am-2.30pm Sun) The modern Kurzentrum has a spa and wellness facilities. In the lobby, warm, salty spring water flows from a fountain; for a free taste – it's said to be good for your digestion – ask at reception for a conical cup.

Salinarium SWIMMING POOL
(www.salinarium.de; Kurbrunnenstrasse 28; pools adult/child €6.30/3.50, saunas €12.90/10; ⊘ 9am-6pm Mon, 9am-10pm Tue & Thu, 6.45am-10pm Wed, 9am-11pm Fri, 9am-9pm Sat & Sun) Water babies of all ages will love the city-run Salinarium, a year-round complex of outdoor (April to September) and indoor swimming pools. There's a 100m-long spiral water slide, whirlpools, a children's pool and seven saunas. Lockers require a €1 deposit.

⚝ Festivals & Events

Dürkheimer Wurstmarkt WINE
(www.duerkheimer-wurstmarkt.de; ⊘ 2nd & 3rd weekends in Sep) The Dürkheimer Wurstmarkt ('sausage market', named for the area where it's held, which once hosted the town's eponymous *Wurst* market) bills itself as the world's largest wine festival. Much of the action takes place around the enormous Dürkheimer Riesenfass wine barrel, home to Restaurant Dürkheimer Fass.

🛏 Sleeping

Bad Dürkheim makes an ideal overnight stop, with a good selection of reasonably priced hotels.

Marktschänke HOTEL $$
(☑ 06322-952 60; www.marktschaenke-bad-duerkheim.de; Marktgasse 1; s/d/studio from €80/88/130; ⚹) Freshly renovated in 2015, this central spot 250m southwest of the train station, off the Obermarkt, has seven streamlined rooms (six doubles, plus a studio suite with two balconies). Its family-friendly restaurant, serving Palatinate-meets-Mediterranean cuisine, has a local following.

Hotel Weingarten PENSION $$
(☑ 06322-940 10; www.hotelweingarten.de; Triftweg 11a-13; s/d from €73/100; ⊘ reception 7am-6pm Mon-Sat, 7am-2pm Sun; Ᵽ ⚹) Next door to a winery owned by the same family, the aptly named 'wine garden' has 18 lovingly cared-for rooms, some with balconies. Breakfast includes homemade jam and locally sourced produce. Call ahead if you'll be arriving outside reception hours. It's 1km northeast of the train station along Manheimerstrasse.

Kurparkhotel CASINO HOTEL $$$
(☑ 06322-7970; www.kurpark-hotel.de; Schlossplatz 1-4; s/d from €140/182; Ᵽ @ ⚹ ⚹) Occupying a yellow, neoclassical building on the edge of the Kurpark, this landmark hotel has 113 unexpectedly contemporary, spacious rooms, all with minibars and most with balconies overlooking the Kurpark's manicured gardens. Rates include spa use and casino entry, and drop for stays of longer than one night.

✗ Eating & Drinking

Restaurants with warm-season terraces can be found on Römerplatz and along nearby Kurgartenstrasse.

Restaurant Dürkheimer Fass GERMAN $$
(☑ 06322-2143; www.duerkheimer-fass.de; St Michaels-Allee 1; mains €13-23; ⊘ 11am-10.30pm Apr-Oct, shorter hours Nov-Mar; ☖) This convivial spot occupies the Dürkheimer Riesenfass, the gargantuan wine barrel that's had a restaurant inside since a master cooper built it out of 200 pine trees in 1934. Dishes range from suckling pig and liver dumplings to perch fillet with *Grüne Sosse*. There's a summer beer garden.

Petersilie Bier & Weinstube WINE BAR
(www.weinstube-petersilie.de; Römerplatz 12; ⊘ 11.30am-11pm) On the town's liveliest square, Petersilie is a great spot to try local wines (including organic wines) by the glass or to knock back a frothy beer. Umbrella-shaded tables spill onto the square in warm weather. Bar snacks include its own gold-medal-winning *Pfälzer Saumagen* (chestnut-stuffed pig's stomach pâté), *Flammkuchen* (regional-style pizza) and potato soup.

ℹ Information

Tourist Office (☑ 06322-935 140; www. bad-duerkheim.com; Kurbrunnenstrasse; ⊘ 9am-5pm Mon-Fri, 10am-2.30pm Sat & Sun Mar-Oct, 9am-5pm Mon-Fri Nov-Feb) Inside the Kurzentrum spa complex. It has a useful walking-tour map in English.

THE ROMANTIC RHINE VALLEY

Between Rüdesheim and Koblenz, the Rhine cuts deeply through the Rhenish slate mountains, meandering between hillside castles and steep fields of wine-producing grapes to create a magical spell of beauty and legend. This is Germany's landscape at its most dramatic – forested hillsides alternate with craggy cliffs and near-vertical terraced vineyards. Idyllic villages appear around each bend, their half-timbered houses and Gothic church steeples seemingly plucked from the world of fairy tales.

High above the river, busy with barge traffic, and the rail lines that run along each bank, are the famous medieval castles. Most were built by a mafia of local robber barons – knights, princes and even bishops – who extorted tolls from merchant ships by blocking their passage with iron chains. Time and French troops under Louis XIV laid waste to many of the castles but several were restored in the 19th century, when Prussian kings, German poets and British painters discovered the gorge's timeless beauty. Today, some have been reincarnated as hotels and, in the case of Burg Stahleck, as a hostel.

In 2002, Unesco designated these 65 kilometres of riverscape, more prosaically known as the Oberes Mittelrheintal (www.welterbe-mittelrheintal.de), as a World Heritage Site.

A popular summer and early autumn tourist destination, the area all but shuts down in winter. Hotel prices are highest on weekends from May to mid-October, but are still remarkably reasonable.

🏃 Activities

Cycling
The **Rhein-Radweg** (www.rheinradweg.eu) stretches for 1230km from Andermatt, Switzerland to the Hoek van Holland, near Rotterdam. Between Bingen and Koblenz it runs along the left (more-or-less west) bank, as well as on a growing number of sections of the right bank. It links up with two other long-distance bike paths: the 207km **Nahe-Hunsrück-Mosel-Radweg** (www.naheland-radtouren.de), which follows the Nahe River from Bingen southwest to Trier, and the 311km **Mosel-Radweg** (www.mosel-radweg.de), which runs along the Moselle River from Koblenz to Traben-Trarbach, Bernkastel-Kues, Trier and on to Thonville, France.

Bicycles can be taken on regional trains, car ferries and river ferries, making it possible to ride one way (such as down the valley) and take public transport the other.

Walking
The Rhine Valley is superb territory for hikers. Almost every village has hiking options – tourist offices can supply suggestions and maps. A one-way hike can be turned into a circuit by combining walking with ferries, trains and buses.

Two challenging but achingly beautiful long-distance hiking trails run along the Romantic Rhine, with variants continuing downriver to Bonn and upriver to Mainz and beyond, including the 199km **Rhein-BurgenWeg** (www.rheinburgenweg.com), linking Rolandsbogen, near Bonn, with Bingen, passing some 40 castles; and the 320km **Rheinsteig** (www.rheinsteig.de), linking Wiesbaden with Bonn – the prettiest section of this tough, hilly trail is between Rüdesheim and Loreley.

ℹ Getting Around

BOAT
River travel is a relaxing and very romantic way to see the castles, vineyards and villages of the Romantic Rhine.

➜ From about Easter to October (winter services are very limited), passenger ships run by **Köln-Düsseldorfer** (Köln-Düsseldorfer; ☑ 0221-208 8318; www.k-d.com) link Rhine villages on a set timetable.

➜ You can travel to the next village or all the way from Mainz to Koblenz (one-way/return €50/55, downstream/upstream 5½/eight hours).

➜ Within the segment you've paid for (eg Boppard–Rüdesheim, which costs €25.40/26.80 one-way/return), you can get on and off as many times as you like, but make sure to ask for a free stopover ticket each time you disembark.

➜ Many rail passes (such as Eurail) get you a free ride or discount on normal KD services, although you still need to register at the ticket counter.

➜ Children up to the age of four travel for free, while those up to age 13 are charged a flat fee of €6 regardless of distance.

➜ Return tickets usually cost only slightly more than one-way.

➜ To bring along a bicycle, there's a supplement of €2.80.

Several smaller companies also send passenger boats up and down the river:

Bingen-Rüdesheimer (www.bingen-ruedesheimer.com)

Hebel Linie (www.hebel-linie.de)

Loreley Linie (www.loreley-linie.com)

Rössler Linie (www.roesslerlinie.de)

BUS & TRAIN

Bus and train travel, perhaps combined with mini-cruises by boat and car ferry, are a convenient way to go village-hopping, get to a trailhead or return to your lodgings at the end of a hike or bike ride.

Villages on the Rhine's left bank (eg Bingen, Bacharach, Oberwesel and Boppard) are served regularly by local trains on the Koblenz–Mainz run. Right-bank villages such as Rüdesheim, Assmannshausen, Kaub, St Goarshausen and Braubach are linked hourly to Koblenz' Hauptbahnhof and Wiesbaden by the RheingauLinie.

It takes about 1½ hours to travel by train from Koblenz, along either riverbank, to Mainz or Wiesbaden.

CAR FERRY

No bridges span the Rhine between Koblenz and Mainz; the only way to cross the river along this stretch is by *Autofähre* (car ferry).

Prices vary slightly but you can figure on paying about €4.20 per car, including the driver; €1.20 per car passenger; €1.30 per pedestrian (€0.80 for a child); and €2.50 for a bicycle, including the rider.

Ferry services generally operate every 15 or 20 minutes during the day and every 30 minutes early in the morning and late at night:

Bingen-Rüdesheim (www.bingen-ruedesheimer.com; ⊙5.30am-9.45pm Sun-Thu, 5.30am-12.50am Fri & Sat May-Oct, 5.30am-9.45pm Nov-Apr)

Boppard-Filsen (www.faehre-boppard.de; ⊙6.30am-10pm Jun-Aug, 6.30am-9pm Apr, May & Sep, 6.30am-8pm Oct-Mar)

Niederheimbach-Lorch (www.mittel-rhein-faehre.de; ⊙6am-7.50pm Apr-Oct, 6am-6.50pm Nov-Mar)

Oberwesel-Kaub (www.faehre-kaub.de; ⊙6am-8pm Mon-Sat, 8am-8pm Sun Apr-Sep, 6am-7pm Mon-Sat, 8am-7pm Sun Oct-Mar)

St Goar-St Goarshausen (www.faehre-loreley.de; ⊙5.30am-midnight Mon-Sat, 6.30am-midnight Sun)

Rüdesheim & Around

☑06722 / POP 9733

Some three million day-tripping coach tourists descend on Rüdesheim each year. Depending on how you look at it, the town centre – and especially its most famous feature, a medieval alley know as Drosselgasse – is either a touristy nightmare or a lot of kitschy, colourful fun. If you're looking for a souvenir thimble, this is definitely the place to come. But there's also wonderful walking in the greater area, which is part of the Rheingau wine region, famed for its superior rieslings.

Rüdesheim and Bingen across the river are the only Romantic Rhine towns to have a passenger-only ferry in addition to car ferries.

◉ Sights & Activities

The tunnel-like **Drosselgasse** alley is the Rhine at its most colourfully touristic – music blares from the pubs, which heave with rollicking crowds. At the top of Drosselgasse, **Oberstrasse** is similarly overloaded. To get away from the throngs all you have to do is wander a few blocks in any direction.

You can also find serenity on delightful **vineyard walks** (p437) in the surrounding area.

Siegfried's Mechanisches Musikkabinett   MUSEUM
(www.smmk.de; Oberstrasse 29; tour adult/child €6.50/3; ⊙10am-6pm Mar-Dec) Situated 50m to the left from the top of Drosselgasse, this fun museum has an often-surprising collection of 18th- and 19th-century mechanical musical instruments that play themselves as you're shown around on the compulsory 45-minute tour.

Weinmuseum   MUSEUM
(www.rheingauer-weinmuseum.de; Rheinstrasse 2; adult/child incl audioguide €5/3; ⊙10am-6pm mid-Mar–Oct) The 1000-year-old Brömserburg castle near the Bingen car-ferry dock now houses the Wine Museum, filled with winemaking and wine-drinking paraphernalia from Roman times onwards. The tower offers great river views.

✦ Festivals & Events

Weihnachtsmarkt   CHRISTMAS MARKET
(⊙23 Nov-23 Dec) Rüdesheim is famous for its *Weihnachtsmarkt* (Christmas market), with 120 stalls crowding Drosselgasse and Oberstrasse.

▭ Sleeping & Eating

★**Rüdesheimer Schloss**   BOUTIQUE HOTEL **$$**
(☑06722-905 00; www.ruedesheimer-schloss.com; Steingasse 10; s €95-115, d €125-155, ste €155-165; P◈) Truly good places to sleep and eat are thin on the ground in Rüdesheim, but this 18th-century building has 26 stunning

Romantic Rhine Valley

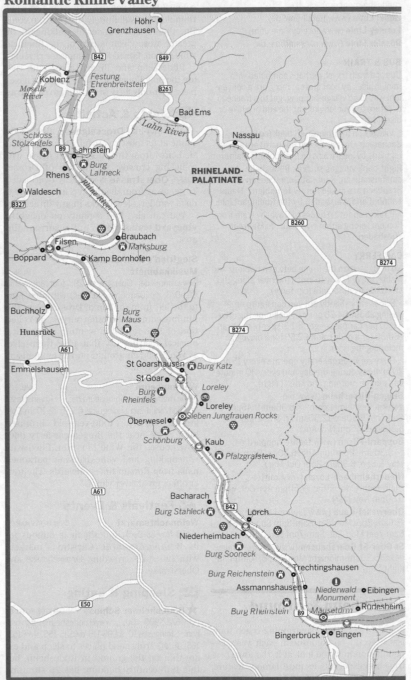

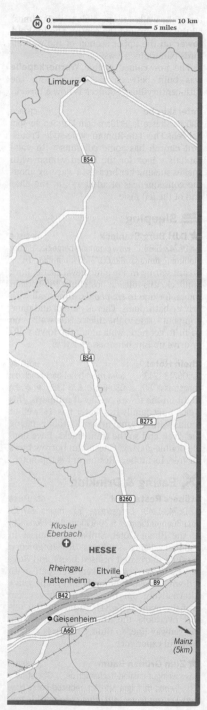

contemporary rooms designed by local and regional artists. Its restaurant is excellent, serving dishes like cheese and riesling soup, veal liver with truffled mash, and roast duck stuffed with dates and figs, with a live pianist and after-dinner dancing.

ℹ Information

Tourist Office (☑ 06722-906 150; www. ruedesheim.de; Rheinstrasse 29a; ☺8.30am-6.30pm Mon-Fri, 10am-4pm Sat & Sun Apr-Oct, 10am-4.30pm Mon-Fri Nov-Mar) At the eastern edge of the town centre.

Bingen

☑ 06721 / POP 24,077

Thanks to its strategic location at the confluence of the Nahe and Rhine Rivers, Bingen has been coveted by warriors and merchants since its founding by the Romans in 11 BC. These days it's a busy working town that's less touristy – and less cute – than its smaller neighbours.

Bingen has two train stations: the Hauptbahnhof, just west of the Nahe in Bingerbrück; and the more central Bahnhof Bingen Stadt, just east of the town centre. Passenger ferries to Rüdesheim leave from the town centre's riverfront promenade; car ferries dock about 1km upriver (east) from the centre.

◉ Sights

Museum am Strom   MUSEUM
(Museumsstrasse 3; adult/child €3/2; ☺10am-5pm Tue-Sun) On Bingen's riverside promenade, this one-time power station now displays exhibits on Rhine romanticism, both engraved and painted. Other highlights include a set of surgical instruments – from scalpels and cupping glasses to saws – left behind by a Roman doctor in the 2nd century AD.

Mäuseturm   CASTLE
(☺closed to the public) The Mouse Tower, on an island near the confluence of the Nahe and Rhine, is where – according to legend – Hatto II, the 10th-century archbishop of Mainz, was devoured alive by mice as punishment for his oppressive rule. In fact, the name is probably a mutation of *Mautturm* (toll tower), which reflects the building's medieval function.

ℹ Information

Tourist Office (☑ 06721-184 205; www.bingen. de; Rheinkai 21; ☺9am-6pm Mon-Fri, 9am-5pm Sat, 10am-1pm Sun May-Oct, 9am-6pm

Mon-Fri, 9am-1pm Sat Apr, 9am-6pm Mon, 9am-4pm Tue-Thu, 9am-1pm Fri Nov-Mar)

Burg Rheinstein

Burg Rheinstein CASTLE
(www.burg-rheinstein.de; adult/child €5/3; ⊙9.30am-6pm mid-Mar–Oct, 10am-5pm Sat & Sun mid-Nov–mid-Mar) In the 1820s, privately owned Rheinstein, 6km downriver from Bingen, became the first Rhine castle to be converted – by Prussian royalty (a branch of the Hohenzollerns) – into a romantic summer residence complete with turrets and battlements. Today, the neo-Gothic interior is furnished more-or-less as it was over a century ago. Highlights include a tiny chapel, the **Rittersaal** (Knights' hall) and 14th- to 19th-century stained-glass windows brought from Cologne and Düsseldorf churches. A path leads from parking places along the B9.

Also here are two apartments for rent (€125 and €175; minimum stay two nights), and a castle tavern.

Burg Reichenstein

Burg Reichenstein CASTLE
(✏06721-6117; www.burg-reichenstein.de; adult/child €5/3.50; ⊙10am-6pm Tue-Sun Mar–mid-Nov, 10am-5pm Tue-Sun mid-Nov–Feb) Looming above the village of Trechtingshausen, 8km downriver from Bingen, mighty Burg Reichenstein harbours a lavish collection of furnishings, armour, hunting trophies – even cast-iron oven slabs. To get a taster of what living here would be like, book into one of its 21 individually designed rooms (doubles from €94). Its fine-dining restaurant has seasonal regional menus and monumental views.

Bacharach

✏06743 / POP 1877
One of the prettiest of the Rhine villages, tiny Bacharach – 24km downriver from Bingen – conceals its considerable charms behind a 14th-century wall. From the B9, go through one of the thick arched gateways under the train tracks and you'll find yourself in a medieval old town filled with half-timbered mansions.

◉ Sights & Activities

The best way to get a sense of the village and its hillside surrounds is to take a stroll on top of the walls – it's possible to walk almost all the way around the centre. The **lookout tower** on the upper section of the wall affords panoramic views.

The now-ruined Gothic **Wernerkapelle** was built between 1289 and 1430; the 12th-century Burg Stahleck is now a hostel.

Peterskirche CHURCH
(Blücherstrasse 1; ⊙10am-6pm Mar-Sep, to 4pm Nov-Feb) This late-Romanesque-style Protestant church has some columns with vivid capitals – look for the naked woman with snakes sucking her breasts (a warning about the consequences of adultery), at the altar end of the left aisle.

⊨ Sleeping

★**DJH Burg Stahleck** HOSTEL $
(✏06743-1266; www.jugendherberge.de; Burg Stahleck; dm/s/d €21.50/27/54; ⓟ@) In a dream setting inside a medieval castle, Burg Stahleck, this hillside hostel has 168 beds in rooms for one to six people, almost all with private bathrooms. There's pinball and ping-pong but – due to the thick castle walls – no wi-fi. To get here, walk along the town walls or drive up Blücherstrasse for 1km.

Rhein Hotel HOTEL $$
(✏06743-1243; www.rhein-hotel-bacharach.de; Langstrasse 50; s €39-68, d €78-136; ⓟ❄ⓢ) Right on the town's medieval ramparts, this welcoming family-run hotel has 14 well-lit rooms with original artwork. Rooms facing the river, and so the train tracks, have double double-glazing. Guests can borrow bikes for free. Its Stübers Restaurant is top-notch.

✕ Eating & Drinking

Stübers Restaurant GERMAN $$
(✏06743-1243; Langstrasse 50; mains €17-23; ⊙11.30am-2.15pm & 5.30-9.15pm Wed-Mon; ✿) At the Rhein Hotel, Stübers specialises in regional dishes such as *Rieslingbraten* (riesling-marinated braised beef) and *Steeger Hinkelsdreck* (chicken-liver pâté with red wine, toasted almonds and grape jelly). Alternatively, opt for a four-course vegan or fish menu (€32/34). Although the terrace overlooks the Rhine, it's metres from the railway line, so dining inside is a more peaceful experience.

★**Zum Grünen Baum** WINE BAR
(www.weingut-bastian-bacharach.de; Oberstrasse 63; ⊙noon-midnight Apr-Oct, reduced hours Nov-Mar) Dating from 1421, this olde-worlde tav-

ern serves some of Bacharach's best whites; the *Weinkarussel* (€22.50) lets you sample 15 of them. Its nearby **Vinothèque** (www.weingut-bastian-bacharach.de/vinothek; Koblenzer Strasse 1; ☺3-5pm Mon-Fri, 11am-6pm Sat & Sun Apr-Oct, 3-5pm Mon-Fri Nov-Mar), by contrast, is state of the art. Owner Friedrich Bastian is a renowned opera singer, so music (and culinary) events take place year-round, including on Bastian's private river island with its own vineyard.

❶ Information

Tourist Office (☎ 06743-919 303; www.rhein-nahe-touristik.de; Oberstrasse 10; ☺9am-5pm Mon-Fri, 10am-3pm Sat & Sun Apr-Oct, 9am-1pm Mon-Fri Nov-Mar) Information about the entire area includes details of day hikes through the vineyards.

Pfalzgrafstein

Pfalzgrafstein CASTLE
(www.burg-pfalzgrafenstein.de; adult/child €3/2; ☺10am-6pm Tue-Sun Apr-Oct, 10am 5pm Mar, 10am-5pm Sat & Sun Nov, Jan & Feb, closed Dec) Across the river from the village of Kaub, the boat-shaped toll castle Pfalzgrafstein, built in 1326, perches on an island in the middle of the Rhine. A once-dangerous rapid here (since modified) forced boats to use the right-hand side of the river, where a chain

forced ships to stop and pay a toll. Pick up an audioguide (€2) to learn more about its history. To get here, hop on a **Fährboot** (adult/child €2.50/1; ☺every 30min 10am-6pm Tue-Sun Apr-Oct, 10am-5pm Mar, 10am-5pm Sat & Sun Nov, Jan & Feb, closed Dec) next to Kaub's car ferry dock.

Oberwesel

📋 06744 / POP 2838

Oberwesel is known for its 3km-long medieval town wall, sporting the remains of 16 guard towers, that wraps around much of the picturesque Altstadt; a path lets you walk along the top of most of it. The old town is separated from the river by the rail line, laid in 1857.

◎ Sights

Oberwesel Kulturhaus MUSEUM
(www.kulturhaus-oberwesel.de; Rathausstrasse 23; adult/child €3/1; ☺10am-5pm Tue-Fri, 2-5pm Sat & Sun Apr-Oct) Every April, Oberwesel crowns not a *Weinkönigin* (wine queen), as in most Rhine towns, but a *Weinhexe* (wine witch) – a good witch, of course – who is said to protect the vineyards. Photos of all the *Weinhexen* crowned since 1946 are on display in the cellar of Oberwesel's Kulturhaus, whose local history exhibits feature 19th-century engravings of the Romantic Rhine and models of

---

VINEYARD WALKS

For a stunning Rhine panorama, head up the wine slopes west of Rüdesheim to the **Niederwald Monument**. Erected between 1877 and 1883, this bombastic monument celebrates the Prussian victory in the Franco-Prussian War and the creation of the German Reich, both in 1871. You can walk up via the Rüdesheimer Berg vineyards – signposted trails include one that begins at the P2 car park (one block above Oberstrasse) – but to save climbing 203 vertical metres, it's faster to glide above the vineyards aboard the 1400m-long **Seilbahn** (Kabinenbahn; www.seilbahn-ruedesheim.de; Oberstrasse 37; adult/child one-way €5/2.50, return €7/3.50, with Sesselbahn €8/4; ☺10am-5.30pm Mon-Fri, to 6pm Sat & Sun May-Sep, 10am-5pm Mon-Fri, to 5.30pm Sat & Sun Apr & Oct) cable car.

From the monument, a network of trails leads to destinations such as the **Jagd-schloss** (2km), a one-time hunting lodge that's now a hotel and restaurant; and, down the hill, the romantic ruin of **Burg Ehrenfels** (Ruine Ehrenfels).

North of the Jagdschloss, you can follow part of the Rheinsteig long-distance path down to **Assmannshausen**, a sedate castle 5km downriver from Rüdesheim that's known for its *Spätburgunder* (Pinot noir) red wines. Or you can head down to Assmannshausen on the **Sesselbahn** (Sessellift; www.seilbahn-assmannshausen.de; Niederwaldstrasse 34; adult/child one-way €5/2.50, return €7/3.50, with Seilbahn €8/4; ☺10am-5.30pm Mon-Fri, to 6pm Sat & Sun May-Sep, 10am-5pm Mon-Fri, to 5.30pm Sat & Sun Apr & Oct) and return to Rüdesheim on foot (via hillside vineyards and Burg Ehrenfels), by train or by passenger ferry.

A round-trip **Ring-Ticket** (adult/child €14/7) includes the Seilbahn, the Sesselbahn and the ferry.

Rhine riverboats. An excellent English visitors' brochure is available at reception.

Liebfrauenkirche
CHURCH

(Kirchstrasse; ⊙10am-noon & 2-5pm Apr-Oct, 2-4pm Nov-Mar) In the southern Altstadt, the High Gothic Liebfrauenkirche, known as the 'red church' for the colour of its facade, dates from the 15th century and has an impressive gilded altar.

St-Martins-Kirche
CHURCH

(Martinsberg; ⊙10am-6pm) Easily spotted on a hillside at the northern end of town is the 14th-century St-Martins-Kirche, popularly known as the 'white church', which has painted ceilings, a richly sculpted main altar and a tower that once formed part of the town's defences.

🛏 Sleeping & Eating

DJH Hostel
HOSTEL $

(☏06744-933 30; www.jugendherberge.de; Am dem Schönberg; dm/d from €22.50/56; P 🛜 🏊) Commanding views stretch from the terrace and some of the rooms of this modern, 264-bed place perched up near the Schönburg, a steep 800m walk from the town. Amenities include an indoor swimming pool.

Hotel Römerkrug
HOTEL $$

(☏06744-7091; www.hotel-roemerkrug.rhinecastles.com; Marktplatz 1; s/d from €50/80; 🛜) Facing the Rathaus in the prettiest part of town, the half-timbered Römerkrug is run by three generations of a friendly local family. Three of its 10 rooms have ancient roof beams. Regional specialities at its excellent restaurant include trout.

Schönburg
HISTORIC HOTEL $$$

(☏06744-939 30; www.hotel-schoenburg.com; Auf Schönburg; d incl 4-course dinner menu €250-350; P 🛜) Sumptuous Schönburg castle's 24 palatial rooms are richly furnished with antiques and chandeliers; some have four-poster beds and open fireplaces. Rates include a lavish breakfast as well as a gastronomic four-course dinner menu of delicacies like white tomato soup, trout tartare, quail breast with truffled cabbage and lime curd with orange foam and wild raspberry ice cream. The restaurant is also open to nonguests (noon to 2pm and 6.30pm to 9pm Tuesday to Sunday; three-/four-course menus from €35/58).

The castle was saved from ruin when a New York real-estate millionaire purchased it in 1885. Legend has it this was once the home of seven beautiful but haughty sisters who rejected all potential suitors until all seven were turned into stone and submerged in the Rhine. Try to spot them from the **Siebenjungfraublick** (Seven Virgins Viewpoint), reached by a lovely vineyard trail beginning at the town's downriver edge.

Hotel Weinhaus Weiler
GERMAN $$

(☏06744-930 50; Marktplatz 4; mains €13-27.50, 3-course dinner menu €39.50; ⊙kitchen 11am-10pm Apr-Oct, shorter hours Nov-Mar) Above all, this half-timbered treasure by the town walls is a superb place to dine on dishes like riesling-marinated steak with raisins, almonds and apple compote or pork medallions with wild forest mushrooms. Its 10 rooms, including a two-storey tower suite with rooftop terrace, are absolute gems (doubles from €78) but, like many Mittelrhein properties, noisy due to passing trains.

🍷 Drinking

★ Günderode Haus
BEER GARDEN

(www.guenderodefilmhaus.de; Siebenjungfrauenblick; ⊙11am-6pm Sat-Thu, to 8pm Fri Apr-Oct, reduced hours Nov-Mar) Hidden sky-high up a steep vineyard-striped hillside, Günderode Haus' flagstone terrace is an incredible spot for a glass of wine, beer or brandy, with sweeping views over the Rhine. Traditional food includes wild boar sausages with rosemary potatoes. From Oberwesel, take the K93 east for 600m, turn right (north) onto the K95; after 1km, the car park's on your right.

The adjacent 200-year-old half-timbered house was used as a film set for *Heimat 3* (2004) and now has a cinema room and hosts live music and literary events, as well as wine tastings.

Historische Weinwirtschaft
WINE BAR

(www.historische-weinwirtschaft.de; Liebfrauenstrasse 17; ⊙4-10pm Mon & Wed-Sat, noon-10pm Sun) A half-timbered, slate-walled house with exposed timber ceiling beams and creaky timber floors is a fantastically atmospheric setting for sampling local wines. Picnic tables are set up in the ivy-clad summer courtyard shaded by magnolias.

ⓘ Information

Tourist Office (☏06744-710 624; www.oberwesel.de; Rathausstrasse 3; ⊙9am-1pm & 2-5pm Mon-Thu, 9am-1pm & 2-6pm Fri, 9am-1pm Sat Jun-Oct, 9am-1pm & 2-5pm Mon-Thu, 9am-1pm & 2-6pm Fri Apr & May, 9am-1pm & 2-5pm Mon-Thu, 9am-1pm Fri Nov-Mar) Across the street from the Rathaus.

Loreley & St Goarshausen

📞 06771 / POP 1292

The most fabled spot along the Romantic Rhine, Loreley is an enormous, almost vertical slab of slate that owes its fame to a mythical maiden whose siren songs are said to have lured sailors to their death in the river's treacherous currents. Heinrich Heine told the tale in his 1824 poem *Die Lorelei*.

👁 Sights & Activities

Lorelei Sculpture   SCULPTURE

At the tip of a narrow breakwater jutting into the Rhine, a bronze sculpture of Loreley's famous maiden perches lasciviously atop a rocky platform. Access to the breakwater car park is 2.5km south of St Goarshausen. From the car park, you can walk the 600m out to the sculpture, from where there are fantastic views of both riverbanks, but be aware that the rough path is made from jagged slate and the gentler sandy lower path is often underwater.

Burg Maus   CASTLE

(Burg Peterseck; ⊘ closed to the public) Two rival castles stand either side of the village of St Goarshausen. Burg Peterseck was built by the archbishop of Trier to counter the toll practices of the powerful Katzenelnbogen family. The latter responded by building a much bigger castle high on the other side of town, Burg Neukatzenelnbogen (dubbed Burg Katz, meaning 'Cat Castle'). Highlighting the obvious imbalance of power between the Katzenelnbogens and the archbishop, Burg Peterseck was soon nicknamed Burg Maus ('Mouse Castle').

Loreley Besucherzentrum   MUSEUM

(📞 06771-599 093; www.loreley-besucherzentrum. de; Loreleyring 7; adult/child €2.50/1.50, parking €2; ⊘ 10am-6pm Apr-Oct, 10am-5pm Mar, 11am-4pm Sat & Sun Nov-Feb) On the edge of the plateau above the Loreley outcrop, 4km southeast of St Goarshausen, this visitors centre covers the Loreley myth and local flora, fauna, shipping and winemaking traditions through an English-signed multimedia exhibit and German-language 3D film.

A 300m gravel path leads to a **viewpoint** at the tip of the Loreley outcrop, 190m above the river.

From April to October, bus 595 runs from St Goarshausen's Marktplatz. Alternatively, the 400-step Treppenweg begins at the base of the breakwater.

St Goar

📞 06741

A car ferry connects St Goarshausen with its twin across the river, St Goar. It's lorded over by the sprawling ruins of **Burg Rheinfels** (www.st-goar.de; adult/child €5/2.50; ⊘ 9am-6pm mid-Mar–late Oct, 11am-5pm late Oct–mid-Nov), once the mightiest fortress on the Rhine. Built in 1245 by Count Dieter V of Katzenelnbogen as a base for his toll-collecting operations, its size and labyrinthine layout are astonishing. Kids (and adults) will love exploring the subterranean tunnels and galleries (bring a torch). It's a 20-minute uphill walk, or you can take the Burg Express Shuttle from St Goar's Marktplatz, or drive (parking €2). The complex incorporates a romantic, antique-furnished **hotel** (📞 06741-8020, www.schloss-rheinfels.de; s/d weekday from €95/130, weekend €110/140; 🅿 @ 🔄 🐾) with three restaurants (rustic, semi-formal and gourmet).

About 1.5km north of St Goar, the dining room and terrace at **Weinhotel Landsknecht** (📞 06741-2001; www.hotel-landsknecht. de; Aussiedlung Landsknecht 4; mains €14-27.50, 4-course dinner menu €42; ⊘ noon-2.30pm & 6-9pm Apr-Oct, noon-2.30pm & 6-9pm Wed-Sun Nov, Dec & Mar, closed Jan & Feb) make you feel like you're on board a cruise boat, with close-up, uninterrupted river views. Sensational home cooking covers a broad range, from pickled salmon with quince mousse to schnitzel with mushroom and riesling sauce, and red-wine-marinated plums with rosemary-and-vanilla ice cream. Many of its **rooms** (doubles from €90) also have Rhine views.

Boppard

📞 06742 / POP 15,240

Scenically located on a horseshoe bend in the river, Boppard (pronounced bo-*part*) is one of the Romantic Rhine's prettiest towns, not least because its riverfront and historic centre aren't split by the rail line but are both on the same side of the tracks. Many of its charming half-timbered buildings house cosy wine taverns serving excellent riesling from grapes grown near here in some of the Rhine's steepest vineyards.

From Boppard, fantastic hiking trails fan out into the countryside.

⊙ Sights & Activities

Just off Boppard's main commercial street, the pedestrianised, east–west oriented Oberstrasse, is the ancient **Marktplatz**, whose modern fountain is a favourite local hang-out.

Outdoor enthusiasts can tackle some superb hillside **hiking trails** (p441).

Ask at the tourist office about seasonal wine-tasting sessions.

Severuskirche CHURCH
(⊙8am-6pm Apr-Oct, to 5pm Nov-Mar) The late-Romanesque 13th-century Severuskirche is built on the site of Roman military baths. Inside are polychrome wall paintings, a hanging cross from 1225 in the choir, and spiderweb-like vaulted ceilings.

Rheinallee PROMENADE
Lined with boat docks, hotels, cafes, restaurants and wine taverns, Boppard's beautiful pedestrian promenade runs along the riverfront. There are grassy areas for picnicking and a **children's playground** upriver from the car-ferry dock.

Römer-Kastell ARCHAEOLOGICAL SITE
(Roman Fort; cnr Angertstrasse & Kirchgasse; ⊙24hr) **FREE** A block south of the Marktplatz, the Roman Fort (also known as the Römerpark) has 55m of the original 4th-century Roman wall and graves from the Frankish era (7th century). A wall panel shows what the Roman town of Bodobrica looked like 1700 years ago.

⊨ Sleeping & Eating

Hotel Günther HOTEL $$
(☑06742-890 90; www.hotelguenther.de; Rheinallee 40; s/d from €78/88; ⊙closed most of Dec; @🛜) Watch boats and barges glide along the mighty Rhine from this bright, welcoming waterfront hotel: of its 19 plain but perfectly comfortable rooms, 15 have river-facing balconies. There's a lift, and bike rental is from €6.50 per day.

Hotel Bellevue HOTEL $$
(☑06742-1020; www.bellevue-boppard.de; Rheinallee 41; s/d from €85/120; P🛜≋) Built in beautiful art nouveau style in 1910, this classy, Best Western–affiliated hotel has 93 brightly carpeted rooms, many with views of the Rhine. The relaxing indoor swimming pool, along with a steam bath, sauna and gym, are all free for guests; breakfast costs €11. Its gourmet restaurant, Le Chopin, is a stunner straight out of *la belle époque*.

Chocobar CAFE $
(Kronengasse 20; dishes €4-7.50; ⊙9am-7pm Mon-Sat, to 6pm Sun Apr-Oct, shorter hours Nov-Mar) Facing the Marktplatz, with a large outdoor terrace spilling onto the square, this is a fabulous bet for breakfast, including a 'chocolate breakfast' of a croissant, chocolate spread, three chocolate truffles, and to drink, one of its wonderfully thick, rich hot chocolates (traditional, orange, chilli or caramel). It also serves panini, *Flammkuchen* and cakes, and sells handmade imported chocolates.

Severus Stube GERMAN $$
(☑06742-3218; www.severus-stube.de; Untere Marktstrasse 7; mains €8.50-18.50; ⊙11.30am-2pm & 5-10pm Fri-Tue, 5-10pm Wed) Smoked trout roasted in herb butter, pheasant with roast potatoes and bacon, braised beef in horseradish sauce and warm apple strudel with vanilla custard are among the reasonably priced dishes served up at high-backed wooden booths in Severus Stube's cosy, timber-panelled dining room, and on the cobbled alleyway in summer. Reservations are recommended.

☕ Drinking

Teehäusje CAFE
(www.boppard-teehaeusje.de; Untere Marktstrasse 10; ⊙10am-6pm Mon-Wed, 10am-1pm Fri & Sat, closed Thu & Sun) The oldest and cutest of Boppard's half-timbered buildings, built in 1519, now houses a delightful tea shop selling over 100 varieties of tea, and serving them at its tiny on-site tearoom.

Weinhaus Heilig Grab WINE BAR
(www.heiliggrab.de; Zelkesgasse 12; ⊙3pm-midnight Wed-Mon) Across the street from the Hauptbahnhof, Boppard's oldest wine tavern, dating back over 200 years, offers a cosy setting for sipping 'Holy Sepulchre' rieslings. In summer you can sit outside under the chestnut trees, where live music plays on weekends. It also has five guest rooms (doubles €63 to €79).

Weingut Felsenkeller WINE BAR
(www.felsenkeller-boppard.de; Mühltal 21; ⊙3-11pm Mon, Wed, Thu & Sun, to midnight Fri & Sat Apr-Oct, shorter hours Nov-Mar) Across the street from the Sesselbahn station, next to a little stream, this homey place serves its own and other local growers' wines along with hearty German fare like schnitzels.

ⓘ Information

Tourist Office (☑06742-3888; www.boppard-tourismus.de; Marktplatz; ⊙9am-6.30pm

Mon-Fri, 10am-2pm Sat May-Sep, 9am-5pm
Mon-Fri Oct-Apr)

Braubach

📞 02627 / POP 3036

Framed by forested hillsides, vineyards and rose gardens, the 1300-year-old town of Braubach, 8km south of Koblenz on the Rhine's right bank, centres on its small, half-timbered Marktplatz.

High above Braubach are the dramatic towers, turrets and crenellations of the 700-year-old **Marksburg** (www.marksburg. de; adult/child €64; ⏰ 10am-5pm mid-Mar–Oct, 11am-4pm Nov–mid-Mar), which is unique among the Rhine fastnesses as it was never destroyed. The compulsory tour takes in the citadel, the Gothic hall and the large kitchen, plus a grisly torture chamber, with its hair-raising assortment of pain-inflicting nasties. English tours are offered at 1pm and 4pm from late March to October.

Koblenz

📞 0261 / POP 106,000

At the confluence of the Rhine and Moselle Rivers and the convergence of three low mountain ranges – the Hunsrück, the Eifel and the Westerwald – Koblenz' roots go all the way back to the Romans, who founded a military stronghold here (calling it Confluentes) because of the site's supreme strategic value.

Today, this park- and flower-filled city is the northern gateway to the Romantic Rhine and the bottom of the Moselle Valley, making it an ideal gateway for exploring the region.

◉ Sights

Koblenz' core is shaped like the bow of a ship seen in profile, with the Rhine to the east, the Moselle to the north and the Deutsches Eck at the tip of the bow.

Koblenz' Altstadt, most of it rebuilt after WWII, surrounds the northern end of **Löhrstrasse**, the city's main pedestrian-only shopping street. Its intersection with Altengraben is known as **Vier Türme** (Four Towers) because each of the 17th-century corner buildings sports an ornately carved and painted oriel.

★ **Deutsches Eck**   SQUARE

At the point of confluence of the Moselle and the Rhine, the 'German Corner' is dominated by a soaring **statue of Kaiser Wilhelm I** on horseback, in the bombastic style of the late 19th century. After the original was destroyed in WWII, the stone pedestal

---

HILLSIDE HIKES

Boppard is a jumping-off point for some superb hiking.

→ **Vierseenblick** The peculiar geography of the Four-Lakes-View panoramic outlook creates the illusion that you're looking at four separate lakes rather than a single river. The nearby Gedeonseck affords views of the Rhine's hairpin curve. To get up here you can either hike for 1.4km or – to save 240 vertical metres – take the 20-minute **Sesselbahn** (chair lift; http://sesselbahn-boppard.de; adult/child return €7.50/4.50, one-way €4.80/3; ⏰ 10am-5pm Apr-Oct) chairlift over the vines from the upriver edge of town.

→ **Klettersteig** This 2½- to three-hour cliffside adventure hike (a 6.2km round trip) begins at the upriver edge of town right next to the Sesselbahn. Decent walking or climbing shoes are a must; optional climbing equipment can be rented at the Aral petrol station for €5 (plus €20 deposit). Some vertical sections involve ladders; less vertiginous alternatives are available – except at the Kletterwand, a hairy section with steel stakes underfoot. It's possible to walk back to town via the Vierseenblick.

→ **Hunsrück Trails** Germany's steepest scheduled railway route, the **Hunsrückbahn** (adult/child one-way €2.90/1.75; ⏰ hourly 10am-6pm Apr-Oct, to 4pm Nov-Mar), travels through five rail tunnels and across two viaducts on its 8km journey from Boppard's Bahnhof to Buchholz (a new section continues for 7km from Buchholz to Emmelshausen, though there's little to see here). From Buchholz, many people hike back via the Mörderbachtal to Boppard, but Buchholz is also the starting point for an excellent 17km hike via the romantic Ehrbachklamm (Ehrbach gorge) to Brodenbach (on the Moselle), from where you can take a bus to Koblenz, with connections to Boppard.

remained empty – as a testament to lost German unity – until, post-reunification, a copy was re-erected in 1993. Flowcry **parks** stretch southwest, linking up with a grassy **riverfront promenade** running southward along the Rhine.

★**Mittelrhein-Museum**   MUSEUM
(www.mittelrhein-museum.de; Zentralplatz 1; adult/child €10/7; ☉10am-6pm Tue-Sun) Spread over 1700 sq metres of the striking new glass Forum Confluentes building, Koblenz' Mittelrhein-Museum's displays span 2000 years of the region's history, including artworks, coins, ceramics, porcelain, furniture, miniature art, textiles, militaria and more. Don't miss the collection of 19th-century landscape paintings of the Romantic Rhine by German and British artists.

Ludwig Museum   MUSEUM
(www.ludwigmuseum.org; Danziger Freiheit 1; adult/child €5/3; ☉10.30am-5pm Tue-Sat, 11am-6pm Sun) Once the property of the Order of the Teutonic Knights, the Deutschherrenhaus is now home to the Ludwig Museum, which showcases post-1945 and contemporary art from France and Germany.

Basilika St Kastor   CHURCH
(www.sankt-kastor-koblenz.de;   Kastorhof 4; ☉9am-6pm) Adjoining a lovely formal garden is Koblenz' oldest church, Basilika St Kastor. Established in the 9th century, it was rebuilt in the 12th century. The entrance is on the west side.

Liebfrauenkirche   CHURCH
(www.liebfrauen-koblenz.de; ☉8am-6pm Mon-Sat, 8.30am-6pm Sun) In the Altstadt, the arched walkway at Am Plan's northeastern corner leads to the Catholic Liebfrauenkirche, built in a harmonious hotchpotch of styles. Of Romanesque origin, it has a Gothic choir (check out the stained glass), painted vaulting above the central nave, and baroque onion-domed turrets. It was destroyed in 1944 and rebuilt in 1955.

Historiensäule   SCULPTURE
(Josef-Görres-Platz) The History Column portrays 2000 years of Koblenz history in 10 scenes perched one atop the other – the WWII period, for instance, is represented by a flaming ruin. An English-language panel provides context.

Festung Ehrenbreitstein   FORTRESS
(www.diefestungehrenbreitstein.de; adult/child €6/3, incl cable car €11.80/5.60; ☉10am-6pm Apr-Oct, to 5pm Nov-Mar) On the right bank of the Rhine, 118m above the river, this mighty fortress proved indestructible to all but Napoleonic troops, who levelled it in 1801. A few years later the Prussians, to prove a point, rebuilt it as one of Europe's mightiest fortifications. Today there are fabulous views from its ramparts and a regional museum and restaurants inside; an audioguide costs €2. It's accessible by car, on foot or by cable car.

Schloss Stolzenfels   CASTLE
(www.schloss-stolzenfels.de; adult/child €4/2.50; ☉9am-6pm Apr-Sep, to 5pm Oct, Nov & Mar, 10am-5pm Sat & Sun Jan-Feb, closed Dec) A vision of crenellated towers, ornate gables and medieval-style fortifications, Schloss Stolzenfels rises above the Rhine's left bank 5km south of the city centre. In 1823, the future Prussian king Friedrich Wilhelm IV had the castle – ruined by the French – rebuilt as his summer residence; guests included Queen Victoria. Today, the rooms remain largely as the king left them, with paintings, weapons, armour and furnishings from the mid-19th century.

Take bus 650 from the Hauptbahnhof.

☞ **Tours**

Romantic Old Town
Walking Tour   WALKING TOUR
(www.koblenz-touristik.de; adult/child €7/3.50; ☉English tours 3pm Sat Apr-late Oct) Departing from the tourist office, this 90-minute tour takes you through the Aldstadt, stopping at sights such as the Basilika St Kastor, and Liebfrauenkirche, as well as Deutsches Eck. Tours in German run more frequently.

KD Cruises   BOAT TOUR
(☎0261-310 30; www.k-d.com; Konrad-Adenauer-Ufer; ☉Apr-Oct) KD operates popular cruises from Koblenz along the Rhine as far north as Bonn (one-way/return €19.40/22.60) and as far south as Mainz (one-way/return €25.80/28.60). It also runs trips southwest along the Moselle to Cochem (one-way/return €32/37.60).

🛌 **Sleeping**

Hotel Jan van Werth   HOTEL **$**
(☎0261-365 00; www.hoteljanvanwerth.de; Von-Werth-Strasse 9; s/d from €47/70, without bathroom from €42/57; @🛜) This long-time budget favourite, with a lobby that feels like someone's living room, offers exceptional value. No surprise, then, that its cute, colourful 17 rooms are often booked out (especially

given that Koblenz has no hostels); definitely reserve ahead. It's conveniently situated four blocks north of the Hauptbahnhof.

★ **Hotel Stein** BOUTIQUE HOTEL **$$**
(☏0261-963 530; www.hotel-stein.de; Mayener Strasse 126; s/d from €85/110; P 🛜) Decorated in zesty colours like tangerine contrasted with dark timbers, Stein's 30 contemporary rooms are all soundproofed for a peaceful night's sleep. The hotel is situated across the Moselle River 2km north of Koblenz' city centre but you won't need to leave to dine: its superb gourmet restaurant Schiller's utilises premium ingredients like white asparagus, scampi, foie gras and truffles.

Hotel Morjan HOTEL **$$**
(☏0261-304 290; www.hotel-haus-morjan.de; Konrad Adenauer Ufer; s/d/f from €65/90/140; P @ 🛜) In an unbeatable location facing the Rhine about 300m south of the Deutsches Eck, this late-20th-century hotel has 42 dated but bright rooms with minibars, half with river views and some with balconies. Wi-fi can be patchy; parking is (very) limited but free.

✗ Eating & Drinking

Many of Koblenz' restaurants and pubs are in the Altstadt, especially along the streets south of Florinsmarkt, and by the Rhine.

Cafe Miljöö CAFE **$**
(www.cafe-miljoeoe.de; Gemüsegasse 8; mains €8-15; 🕑 kitchen 9am-10pm Apr-Oct, shorter hours Nov-Mar; 🛜🍴) Cosy cafe-restaurant 'Milieu' (pronounced like the French) has fresh flowers, changing art exhibits, and a fantastic selection of coffees (40 kinds!), teas and homemade cakes. Ten different breakfasts (including Mediterranean, with feta, olives, salami, espresso and a glass of wine; Dutch, with chocolate sprinkles; Swiss, with hot chocolate and sliced apple and honey; 'hangover', with multivitamin juice) are available until 5pm.

Einstein CAFE **$$**
(www.einstein-koblenz.de; Firmungstrasse 30; mains €9-22; 🕑 kitchen 9am-10pm Mon-Sat, 10am-10pm Sun) Grilled calf's liver with masala jus; gilthead, tiger prawn and lime risotto; ribbon noodles with feta, spinach and tomatoes; and chocolate cannelloni with almond mascarpone and orange sorbet are among the choices at this elegant crimson-toned cafe/bar. It also has lighter bites like soups and salads. Live music often plays on weekends.

Da Vinci INTERNATIONAL **$$$**
(☏0261-921 5444; www.davinci-koblenz.de; Firmungstrasse 32b; 3-course lunch menu €30, 4-/5-/6-course dinner menus €72/83/95, with wine €92/108/125; 🕑 noon-2.30pm & 6-9.30pm Tue-Sat) Prints of Da Vinci's works hang on the marine-blue walls beneath the chandeliers of this refined Michelin Bib Gourmand–rated restaurant. Inspired multicourse menus served at white-clothed tables might include smoked cockles with green asparagus and fennel, or ox tail with truffled local potatoes. The mostly local wine list is extensive; bookings are recommended.

Alte Weinstube Zum Hubertus WINE BAR
(www.weinhaus-hubertus.de; Florinsmarkt 6; 🕑 3.30pm-midnight Mon-Fri, noon-midnight Sat & Sun) Specialising in Rhine and Moselle wines by the glass and/or bottle, rustic Alte Weinstube Zum Hubertus occupies a half-timbered house dating from 1689, with an open fireplace, antique furniture and dark-wood panelling. In summer, seating spills onto the square.

Absintheria BAR
(http://absintheria-koblenz.de; Florinsmarkt; 🕑 8pm-1am Sun-Thu, to 3am Fri & Sat) The concealed location in a vaulted former wine cellar beneath Florinsmarkt, flickering with candlelight and centered on a green neon backlit bar, adds to the clandestine feel of this absinthe bar. Over 100 different types of the 'green fairy' are available; it also serves absinthe-laced cocktails. Live blues and jazz often play.

ℹ Information

Tourist Office (☏0261-194 33; www.koblenz-touristik.de; Zentralplatz 1; 🕑 10am-6pm) In the Forum Confluentes.

ℹ Getting There & Away

Train Koblenz has two train stations, the main Hauptbahnhof on the Rhine's left bank about 1km south of the city centre, and Koblenz-Ehrenbreitstein on the right bank (right below Festung Ehrenbreitstein).

Regional trains serve villages on both banks of the Romantic Rhine, including Bingen (€13.30 to €17, 30 to 50 minutes, every 30 minutes).

Frequent Hauptbahnhof services:

➡ **Bonn** (€12 to €15, 30 minutes to one hour)
➡ **Cologne** (€20 to €24, 25 minutes to 1½ hours)
➡ **Frankfurt** (€20 to €25, 50 minutes to one hour)

→ **Mainz** (€26 to €32, 1½ to 2½ hours)

→ **Traben-Trarbach** (€14.40, 1¼ hours)

→ **Trier** (€22.70, 1½ to two hours)

Bus Some Romantic Rhine villages are also served by buses (www.rmv-bus.de) that stop outside the Hauptbahnhof. Bus 650 goes to Boppard via Schloss Stolzenfels, while bus 570 goes to Braubach/Marksburg.

The Fahrplan Rhein-Mosel-Bus services link Koblenz with Frankfurt-Hahn Airport (€11.30, 1¼ hours, six per day).

Boat Several boat companies have docks on Konrad-Adenauer-Ufer, which runs along the Rhine south of the Deutsches Eck.

ⓘ Getting Around

Bus 1 (€1.80, twice an hour, hourly after 8pm) links the Hauptbahnhof with the Deutsches Eck.

Fahrrad Zangmeister (☏ 0261-323 63; www.fahrrad-zangmeister.de; Stegemannstrasse 33; bike/electric bike per day €10/25; ⏱10am-6.30pm Mon, Tue, Thu & Fri, 10am-2pm Wed, 10am-4pm Sat) One of Germany's oldest bike shops, Fahrrad Zangmeister was founded, unbelievably, way back in 1898.

THE MOSELLE VALLEY

Wending between vertiginous vine-covered slopes, the Moselle (in German, Mosel) is narrower than its neighbour, the Rhine, and has a more intimate charm. The German section of the river, which rises in France then traverses Luxembourg, flows for 195km from Trier to Koblenz on a slow, winding course, with entrancing scenery around every hairpin bend: brightly coloured, half-timbered medieval villages, crumbling hilltop castles, elegant *Jugendstil* villas, and ancient wine warehouses.

Exploring the wineries of the Moselle Valley is an ideal way to get to know German culture, interact with locals and, of course, sample some truly exceptional wines. Look for signs reading *Weingut, Weinprobe, Wein Probieren, Weinverkauf* and *Wein zu Verkaufen*. In spring pale-purple wisteria flowers, trailing from stone houses, anticipate the bunches of grapes that will ripen in autumn. From around April to mid-November, numerous wine festivals take place in the towns and villages; for a complete list visit www.mosel-weinfeste.de.

Wonderful walking trails allow you to explore the Moselle's banks and hillsides, where you'll find Europe's (and reputedly the world's) steepest vineyard, the Brem-

mer Calmont (www.calmont-region.de) just north of Bremm, with a 65-degree gradient.

The summer (July to August) and autumn (September to October) months are peak season in the Moselle. Almost all Moselle towns have a summertime camping ground, most right on the breeze-cooled riverbanks. From November to about Easter, the majority of towns in the valley are very quiet, and some hotels shut down. You can book accommodation at www.mosellandtouristik.de.

🏃 Activities

Cycling
Superb cycling paths traverse the countryside along and near the Moselle, including the 275km-long **Mosel-Radweg**, which runs from Thionvielle, France, skirting the Luxembourg border, to Koblenz. Tourist offices have maps.

Walking
The Moselle Valley is especially scenic walking country. Variants of the **Mosel Erlebnis Route** (www.mosel-erlebnis-route.com) follow the entire Moselle Valley along both banks of the river.

Expect some steep climbs if you venture away from the river, such as on the long-distance **Moselhöhenweg**, which sticks to high ground, but offers spectacular vistas.

Bookshops and tourist offices carry good maps, including *Mosel Erlebnis Route* (€9.50).

ⓘ Getting There & Around

Driving is the easiest way to see the Moselle, which, unlike the Romantic Rhine, is spanned by plenty of bridges.

Currently under construction, the *Hochmoselbrücke* (High Moselle Bridge) will link Ürzig and Zeltingen-Rachtig, with a carriageway stretching 158m above the river. It's part of a new highway connection, the 'Hochmoselübergang' (B50), providing a fast link to the Frankfurt area and beyond. Environmental concerns have seen it beset by delays, but it's expected to open in 2018. Check its progress via webcam at www.b50hochmoselbruecke.de.

The valley is also well served by public transport.

→ Frankfurt-Hahn Airport is just 21km east of Traben-Trarbach. A **shuttle bus** (Rhein-Mosel-Bus; www.hahn-airport.de) links the airport with the railhead of Bullay (€7.90, 30 minutes, nine daily); two shuttle-bus services continue on to Cochem (€9.50, 40 minutes).

➡ The rail line linking Koblenz with Trier (€22.70, 1½ to two hours, at least hourly) follows the Moselle (and stops at its villages) only as far upriver as Bullay. (Koblenz–Bullay €15.60, 45 minutes, hourly; Trier–Bullay €12.10, 45 minutes, two per hour).

➡ From Bullay, small shuttle trains run along a spur line that terminates in Traben-Trarbach (€3.90, 20 minutes, up to four per hour).

➡ The villages between Traben-Trarbach and Trier, including Bernkastel-Kues, are served year-round by bus 333 (www.moselbahn.de, day ticket €5.80, six daily Monday to Friday, three daily Saturday and Sunday). From April to October its popular RegioRadler service has bicycle trailers (bicycle per trip €2.80; online reservations recommended).

➡ **Kolb** (www.moselrundfahrten.de) is the Moselle's main boat operator, offering sightseeing cruises as well as one-way transport. Most services run from April to October.

Alken

☑ 02605 / POP 655

Dominated by a majestic castle, Alken is one of the Moselle's oldest villages, tracing its roots to Celtic and Roman times. It's also one of the valley's prettiest, with geranium-filled window boxes emblazoning its half-timbered houses, and vestiges of its medieval walls.

◉ Sights & Activities

Burg Thurant   CASTLE
(www.thurant.de; adult/child €3.50/2.50; ☉10am-6pm May–mid-Nov, to 5pm Mar-Apr, closed mid-Nov–Feb) Built on Roman foundations from 1197, this mighty castle on the hilltop above Alken has an intriguing history. From 1246 to 1248 it was fought over by the archbishops of Cologne and Trier, and divided in two parts (separated by a wall). The peace agreement dated 17 September 1248 is one of the oldest surviving documents in the German language. Fascinating displays include medieval torture devices; the watchtower is accessible by ladder. Leaflets are available in English.

⌂ Sleeping & Eating

Hotel-Gasthaus Burg Thurant   HOTEL $
(www.turmgasthaus.de; Moselstrasse 15; s/d €48/70) Next to the old bell tower (once part of the medieval walls), this charmer has stylish rooms with iron beds, pewter- and sky-blue fabrics, and bright, white modern bathrooms. Two of its four rooms overlook the river; the other two have castle views. Its restaurant, with a fireplace

and exposed stone walls, serves excellent local food and wine.

Winzerstube Brachtendorf   GERMAN $$
(www.winzerhofbrachtendorf.de; Moselstrasse 13; mains €6-11.50; ☉4pm-midnight Mon & Wed-Fri, 2pm-midnight Sat & Sun) The summer terrace facing the river at Winzerstube Brachtendorf makes an ideal spot to sample the Brachtendorf family's wines, peach liqueur and apple-and-pear brandy – along with dishes like homemade *Griebenschmalz* (lard spread, served in a clay pot with bread), *Tresterfleisch* (wine-marinated pork) and *Winzersülze* (pork jelly, accompanied by warm potato salad). Double rooms start from €64.

Burg Eltz

★ **Burg Eltz**   CASTLE
(www.burg-eltz.de; Burg-Eltz-Strasse 1, Wierschem; tour adult/child €9/6.50; ☉9.30am-5.30pm Apr-Oct) At the head of the beautiful Eltz Valley, a side valley of the Moselle, Burg Eltz is one of the most romantic medieval castles in Germany. Never destroyed, this fairy-tale vision of turrets, towers, oriels, gables and half-timber has jutted forth from a rock framed by thick forest for nearly 900 years and is still owned by the original family. The decorations, furnishings, tapestries, fireplaces, paintings and armour you will see during the 45-minute English-language tour are also centuries old.

From the Eltz car park it's a shuttle bus ride (€2) or 1.3km walk to the castle. From Koblenz, boats and trains also go to Moselkern village, from where it's a lovely 5km walk to the castle.

Cochem

☑ 02671 / POP 5215

Inundated with visitors most of the year, Cochem is the Moselle at its most touristy, with a bank of pastel-coloured, terrace-fronted restaurants lining the waterfront. Its tangle of narrow alleyways and dramatic castle precipitously perched on a rock, however, are well worth a stop.

The town is a key transport hub, with a train station and regular bus and boat services in season.

◉ Sights

Reichsburg   CASTLE
(☑02671-255;   www.burg-cochem.de; Schlossstrasse 36; tours adult/child €6/3; ☉tours

9am-5pm mid-Mar–Oct, 10am-3pm Nov & Dec, 11am, noon & 1pm Wed, Sat & Sun Jan–mid-Mar) Like many others in the area, Cochem's original 11th-century castle fell victim to French troops in 1689, then stood ruined for centuries until wealthy Berliner Louis Ravene snapped it up for a pittance in 1868 and had it restored to its current – if not always architecturally faithful – glory. The 40-minute tours (in German but English leaflet/audioguide available) take in the decorative rooms that reflect 1000 years' worth of tastes and styles.

Its restaurant hosts four-hour banquets (€49) on Friday and Saturday evenings in summer, attended by costumed staff, with wine served in a clay tumbler that you get to keep and culminating in a knighting ceremony.

🛏 Sleeping & Eating

Pension Gundert　　　　HOTEL **$**
(☑ 02671-910 224; www.pension-gundert.de; Ravenestrasse 34; s/d €45/78; P @ 🛜) A lavish stone building houses this river-facing hotel. Its 12 rooms, by contrast, are simple but comfortable, with cane and pine furniture. Cyclists can take advantage of lock-up parking; if you're not travelling by bike, you can rent one here for €5 per day.

Alt Thorschenke　　　　GERMAN **$$**
(☑ 02671-7059; www.thorschenke.de; Brückenstrasse 3; mains €10.50-19; ⊗ kitchen 11am-10pm Apr-Oct, reduced hours Nov-Mar) Wedged into the old medieval walls, away from the busy riverfront restaurants, Alt Thorschenke is a diamond find for regional specialities, such as herring with apple and onions, pork neck with mustard-cream sauce, and several different types of schnitzel, washed down with wines from local producers. Upstairs are 27 small but charming rooms (doubles from €99), some with four-poster beds.

🛈 Information

Tourist Office (☑ 02671-600 40; www. cochem.de; Endertplatz 1; ⊗ 9am-5pm Mon-Sat, 10am-3pm Sun May-Oct, 9am-5pm Mon-Fri Apr, 9am-1pm & 2-5pm Mon-Fri Nov-Mar)

Beilstein

☑ 02673 / POP 137
On the right bank of the Moselle about 50km upriver from Koblenz, Beilstein is a pint-sized village straight out of a story book. Centred on the Marktplatz, dating from 1322, its cluster of half-timbered houses are surrounded by steep vineyards.

◉ Sights & Activities

Burg Metternich　　　　CASTLE
(admission €2.50; ⊗ 9am-6pm Apr-Nov) Above the village looms Burg Metternich, a ruined hilltop castle reached via a footpath off Im Mühlental (at the top of cobbled Bachstrasse). Built in 1129, it was destroyed by French troops in the Nine Years' War (1688–97) in 1689. Today you can visit the ruins and have a glass of local wine at the courtyard cafe.

Karmeliterkirche St Josef　　　CHURCH
(www.st-josef-beilstein.de; ⊗ 8am-6pm) Up a steep staircase from Fürst-Metternich Strasse, this baroque 17th-century Carmelite monastery church has a spectacular interior with a vaulted ceiling supported by soaring apricot-coloured columns. The Kloster Restauant Café has a sheltered inner courtyard as well as a panoramic terrace.

🛏 Sleeping & Eating

Hotel Altes Zollhaus　　　HOTEL **$$**
(☑ 02673-1850; www.hotel-lipmann.de; Moselstrasse 26; s/d from €90/100; ⊗ Apr-Oct; P 🛜) Right by the river, this historic half-timbered former toll house contains snug rooms with floral fabrics, a beautiful slate bar, a vine-draped river-view terrace, and a restaurant serving hearty German and international fare. The Lipmann family, whose record of hosting visitors in Beilstein stretches back to 1795, runs another flowery hotel on the hillside, Hotel Am Klosterberg (doubles from €120).

🍷 Drinking

Zehnthauskeller　　　　WINE BAR
(www.zehnthauskeller.de; Marktplatz; ⊗ 11am-10pm Tue-Sat, noon-10pm Sun) Starting in 1574, the Zehnthauskeller was used to store wine delivered as a tithe; it now houses a romantically dark, vaulted wine cellar where you can try six wines for €8.90, served by dirndl-wearing staff. Live music plays on summer evenings.

🛈 Information

Tourist information is available on the village website www.beilstein-mosel.de.

Note that Beilstein has no ATMs.

Moselle Valley

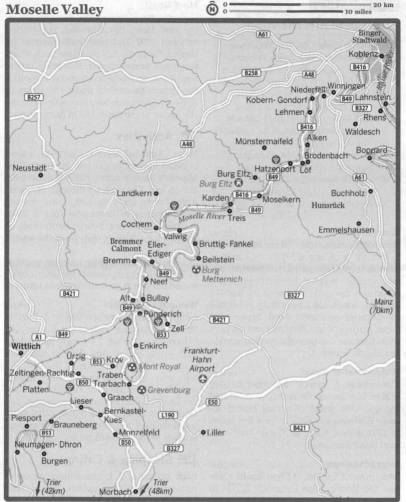

Traben-Trarbach

☎ 06541 / POP 5740

Elegant Traben-Trarbach makes an excellent base for exploring the valley by bike or car. A major centre of the wine trade a century ago, the town's winemakers still welcome visitors for tastings and sales.

Traben, on the Moselle's left bank, lost its medieval appearance to three major fires but was well compensated with beautiful *Jugendstil* villas, many of them designed by Berlin architect Bruno Möhring, whose works also include the ornate 1898 bridge gate, the medieval-style Brückentor, across the river in Trarbach. The two towns united in 1904.

◎ Sights

Traben is where you'll find amenities including the tourist office, the end-of-the-line train station (linked by small shuttle trains to the railhead of Bullay), the adjacent bus station, and the commercial centre.

Both banks of the Moselle have grassy riverfront promenades that are perfect for strolling.

WINE BENEATH THE VINES

Weinhaus Ibald (☑02605-2043; www.weinhaus-ibald.de; Moselstrasse 34, Hatzenport; ☺10am-11pm Easter-Oct, shorter hours Nov-Mar) Occupying a 1547 half-timbered building, wonderfully local Weinhaus Ibald specialises in rieslings, sparkling Spätlese, Dornfelder reds and Fruchsaft (fruit wine); the ultimate spot for a glass is on the vine-shaded terrace. Food ranges from homemade onion soup to sausage platters and gorgeous cakes including rhubarb topped with meringue.

You can also stay in its simple but comfortable rooms (doubles from €60).

Buddha Museum   MUSEUM
(www.buddha-museum.de; Bruno-Möhring-Platz 1, Trarbach; adult/child €15/7.50; ☺10am-6pm Tue-Sun) A magnificent 1906 *Jugendstil* former winery designed by architect Bruno Möhring is the unlikely home of the Buddha Museum, which has a beautifully presented collection of over 2000 wood, bronze and paper statues of the Buddha from all over Asia. Upstairs the peaceful rooftop garden has Moselle views.

Mittelmosel-Museum   MUSEUM
(Casinostrasse 2, Trarbach; adult/child €2.50/1; ☺10am-5pm Tue-Sun Easter-Oct) A furnished baroque villa proud of having hosted Johann Wolfgang von Goethe for a few hours in 1792 is now home to Traben-Trarbach's local history museum.

Fahrradmuseum   MUSEUM
(Moselstrasse 2, Trarbach; ☺2-6pm Mon-Fri, 10am-6pm Sat, 10am-1pm Sun Easter-Oct) FREE To check out a collection of historic bicycles as well as high-tech carbon fibre bikes from the 2000 Olympics, head up the stairs from the Wein-Kontor wine shop.

Grevenburg   RUIN
(Trarbach) The Grevenburg castle, built in the mid-1300s, sits high in the craggy hills above Trarbach, with incredible valley views. Because of its strategic importance, it changed hands 13 times, was besieged six times and was destroyed seven times – no wonder that two walls are all that remain. It's reached via a steep 500m-long footpath, the **Sponheimer Weg**, that begins a block north of the bridge (there's no access by car). Its cafe serves wine, beer and *Flammkuchen*.

Mont Royal   RUIN
(Traben) Above Traben are the remains of the vast Mont Royal fortress, constructed between 1687 and 1698 and designed by Vauban for Louis XIV as a base from which to project French power. Ruinously expensive, it was dismantled before completion by the French themselves under the Treaty of Ryswick. The 1.5km-long footpath up to the site begins at the upper end of Römerstrasse.

🏃 Activities

From Traben-Trarbach, Bernkastel-Kues is 24km upriver by car but, because of the Moselle's hairpin curve, just 6.5km over the hill on foot. The walk up through the forest from Traben-Trarbach and down through the vineyards to Bernkastel-Kues is wonderfully scenic but poorly signposted, so be sure to pick up a map from the tourist office.

Wine tastings and cellar tours are available in Traben-Trarbach; contact the tourist office to find out what's on while you're in town.

Weingut Louis Klein   WINERY
(☑06541-6246; www.klein-wein.de; Enkircher Strasse 20, Trarbach; tastings per 6 wines €10; ☺10am-6pm Mon-Sat, 10am-noon Sun) Along with whites like riesling, Rivaner and Pinot blanc, Louis Klein is one of the few Moselle wine producers to specialise in reds, including Pinot Meunier, Pinot noir, Cabernet Dorio, Cabernet Sauvignon, Merlot, and Dornfelder. It occupies a monumental stone warehouse on the river; you can also arrange tastings in the vineyard among the vines.

🛏 Sleeping & Eating

Both Traben and Trarbach have plenty of restaurants and wine taverns. A local (non-alcoholic) speciality is the local bottled spring water, Trarbacher.

For an impossibly romantic meal (and/or accommodation), head southeast of Traben-Trarbach to Liller's Historische Schlossmühle (p452).

DJH Hostel   HOSTEL $
(☑06541-9278; www.jugendherberge.de; Hirtenpfad 6, Traben; dm/d €21.50/54; P@🕏) All rooms at this modern, 172-bed hostel have private bathrooms. It's a 1.2km walk up the hillside from the train station, past the fire station.

Central Hotel   HOTEL $$
(☑06541-6238; www.central-hotel-traben.de; Bahnstrasse 43, Traben; s €41-52, d €72-84, apt

per week €370-600; P 🛜) In the same family for three generations, this welcoming hotel 50m east of the tourist office and bang in the centre of Traben has a handy elevator and 32 modest but spotless rooms, as well as three apartments for weekly rental.

★Hotel Bellevue HISTORIC HOTEL $$$
(🗗 06541-7030; www.bellevue-hotel.de; An der Mosel 11, Traben; s/d from €95/145; 🛜 ❄) Topped by a Champagne-bottle-shaped slate turret, this exquisite *Jugendstil* river-facing hotel was built in 1903 by Bruno Möhring, with an oak staircase in the lobby and beautiful stained-glass windows in its gourmet restaurants Belle Epoque and Michelin-starred Clauss Feist. Individually designed rooms are overwhelmingly romantic; amenities include bike and canoe hire, a pool and a sauna.

★Alte Zunftscheune GERMAN $$
(🗗 06541-9737; www.zunftscheune.de; Neue Rathausstrasse 15, Traben; mains €11.50-20; ☻kitchen 5-11pm Tue-Fri, 11.30am-3pm & 5-11pm Sat & Sun Easter-Oct, reduced hours Nov-Easter; 🎵) Dine on delicious Moselle-style dishes like homemade black pudding and liver sausage, pork medallions with riesling cream sauce, or grilled rump steak with asparagus and fried potatoes in a series of wonderfully atmospheric rooms chock-full of rustic bric-a-brac, with beautiful timber staircases. Its cellar still has its original 1890s lighting. Reservations are recommended. Cash only.

Die Graifen MEDITERRANEAN $$$
(🗗 06541-811 075; www.graifen.de; Wolfer Weg 11; mains €17-27; ☻kitchen 3-11pm Wed-Fri, 12.30-11.45pm Sat & Sun) In a prime riverside setting, Die Graifen has a shaded summer garden and glass-roofed, gas-heated winter garden. The menu is inspired: wild boar mousse with beetroot carpaccio, braised veal with truffled potato cakes, homemade avocado and spinach tortellini with buffalo mozzarella and tomato foam, and dark praline ice cream with hazelnut and nougat brûlée.

ℹ Information

Tourist Office (🗗 06541-839 80; www.traben-trarbach.de; Am Bahnhof 5, Traben; ☻10am-5pm Mon-Fri, 11am-3pm Sat May-Aug, 10am-6pm Mon-Fri, 11am-3pm Sat Sep & Oct, 10am-4pm Mon-Fri Nov-Apr; 🛜)

Bernkastel-Kues

🗗 06531 / POP 6840
These charming twin towns are the hub of the *Mittelmosel* ('Middle Moselle', ie Central Moselle) region. Bernkastel, on the right (eastern) bank, is a symphony in half-timber, stone and slate and teems with wine taverns. Kues, the birthplace of theologian Nicolaus Cusanus (1401–64), is less quaint but is home to some key historical sights.

⊙ Sights & Activities

The Kues shoreline has a lovely riverfront promenade.

Marktplatz SQUARE
(Bernkastel) Bernkastel's pretty Marktplatz, a block inland from the bridge, is enclosed by a romantic ensemble of half-timbered houses with beautifully decorated gables. Look for the medieval iron handcuffs, to which criminals were attached, on the facade of the old **Rathaus**.

Pfarrkirche St Michael CHURCH
(Bernkastel; ☻9am-6pm) Facing the bridge, this partly 14th-century-Gothic church has an ornate interior and some colourful stained glass. The tower was originally part of the town's fortifications.

Burg Landshut RUIN
(Bernkastel; ☻beer garden 10am-6pm Fri-Wed Easter-Nov) A rewarding way to get your heart pumping is hoofing it from the Marktplatz up to Burg Landshut, a ruined 13th-century castle – framed by vineyards and forests – on a bluff above town. It's a very steep 750m from town; allow 30 minutes. You'll be rewarded with glorious river valley views and a refreshing drink in the **beer garden**. An hourly shuttle bus from the riverfront costs €5 uphill, €3.50 downhill or €7 return.

St-Nikolaus-Hospital HISTORIC BUILDING
(www.cusanus.de; Cusanusstrasse 2, Kues; guided tour €5; ☻9am-6pm Sun-Fri, 9am-3pm Sat, guided tour 10.30am Tue & 3pm Fri Apr-Oct) **FREE** Most of Kues' sights, including the Mosel Vinothek (p450), are conveniently grouped near the bridge in the late-Gothic St-Nikolaus-Hospital, an old-age home founded by Cusanus in 1458 for 33 men (one for every year of Jesus' life). You're free to explore the cloister and Gothic *Kapelle* (chapel) at leisure, but the treasure-filled library can only be seen on a guided tour.

Mosel Vinothek
WINE TASTING

(www.moselvinothek.de; ⏰10am-6pm Apr-Oct, 11am-5pm Nov, Dec, Feb & Mar) In the cellar of the Vinothek, you can indulge in an 'all you can drink' wine tasting (€18) with about 150 vintages to choose from. In winter the selection is more limited but costs just €12.

It's adjacent to a small **wine museum** (☑06531-4141; www.moselweinmuseum.de; Cusanusstrasse 2, Kues; adult/child €5/3; ⏰10am-6pm Apr-Oct, 11am-5pm Nov, Dec, Feb & Mar), with interactive screens (best appreciated by German speakers).

👉 Tours

The tourist office rents out **audioguides** (three hours/all day €6/8).

For a gentle bike ride, the **Mosel-Maare-Radweg** (www.maare-moselradweg.de), linking Bernkastel-Kues with Daun (in the Eifel Mountains), follows an old train line so the gradients are reasonable. From April to October, you can take RegioRadler bus 300 up (adult/bicycle transport €12.35/3, 1½ hours, every two hours) and ride the 57km back down to Bernkastel-Kues. **Fun Bike Team** (☑06531-940 24; www.funbiketeam.de; Schanzstrasse 22, Bernkastel; 7-speed/tandem per day €11/19; ⏰9am-6.30pm Mon-Fri, 9am-2pm Sat Mar-Oct, 9am-1pm & 2-6.30pm Mon, Tue, Thu & Fri, 1-6.30pm Thu & 9am-2pm Sat Nov-Mar) rents bikes.

MTB Trailscout
BICYCLE TOUR

(☑017 620 730 681; www.mtbtour-mosel.de; tours €17-26; ⏰Easter-Oct) Guided mountain bike tours offer a local perspective of the valley (English tours are possible by arrangement). Two- to three-hour beginner tours cover 25km; experienced (and fit!) mountain bikers can take a challenging 50km tour. Rates don't include bikes; rent them from Fun Bike Team (p450), or **Fahrräder Wildmann** (☑06532-954 367; www.fahrraeder-wildmann.de; Uferallee 55, Zeltingen-Rachtig; bikes per day from €90; ⏰9.30am-1pm & 2.30-6pm Mon-Fri, 9.30am-1pm & 4-6pm Sat, 9.30am-noon & 4-6pm Sun Apr-Oct, reduced hrs Nov-Mar), which has pick-up, drop-off and luggage-transport services.

🛏 Sleeping & Eating

Bernkastel has restaurants along the waterfront and in the Altstadt's squares and narrow, pedestrian-only streets. In Kues there are several restaurants near the bridge.

Doctor Weinstube
HISTORIC HOTEL $$

(☑06531-966 50; www.doctor-weinstube-bernkastel.de; Hebegasse 5, Bernkastel; s/d from €55/93;

🅿) A partly half-timbered building in the heart of the Altstadt houses this recently renovated hotel. Spacious rooms have light-toned fabrics and contemporary bathrooms; some have exposed wooden beams. German classics such as schnitzels and sausages are served at its restaurant; the vaulted cellar contains a bar hosting live music on summer weekends (its thick stone walls provide effective soundproofing).

Christiana's Wein & Art Hotel
BOUTIQUE HOTEL $$

(☑06531-6627; www.wein-arthotel.de; Lindenweg 18, Kues; s/d from €60/89; 🅿🛜) Each of the 17 rooms at this sleek new hotel is named after a Moselle vineyard and some have dramatic outsized photos of wine glasses or barrels. Bathrooms are state of the art; higher-priced rooms have spas. Its steakhouse restaurant overlooks the vineyards. Lock-up bike storage is available.

Rotisserie Royale
MODERN EUROPEAN $$

(☑06531-6572; www.rotisserie-royale.de; Burgstrasse 19, Bernkastel; mains €13.50-19.50; ⏰noon-2pm & 5-9pm Thu-Tue) Seriously good cooking inside this half-timbered house spans starters like pan-fried foie gras on a potato and apple rösti or salmon carpaccio with lime and olive marinade, followed by mains such as pike perch with potato soufflé and riesling foam, or braised rabbit with snow peas, and decadent desserts like chocolate mousse on eggnog foam with walnut sorbet.

🍷 Drinking

For a change from wine, don't miss the monastery-housed Kloster Machern (p453).

★Weinstube Spitzhäuschen
WINE BAR

(☑06531-7476; www.spitzhaeuschen.de; Karlstrasse 13, Bernkastel; ⏰from 4pm Mon-Fri, from 3pm Sat & Sun Easter-Oct, from 3pm Sat Nov-Dec, other times by appointment) Wine bars don't come cuter than this crooked half-timbered building (the Moselle's oldest, dating from 1416), which resembles a giant bird's house: its narrow base is topped by a much larger, precariously leaning upper floor which allowed carriages to pass through the narrow alley to the marketplace. Taste over 50 of the Schmitz family's local wines; small snacks are also available.

ℹ Information

Tourist Office (☑06531-500 190; www.bernkastel.de; Gestade 6, Bernkastel; ⏰9am-5pm Mon-Fri, 10am-5pm Sat, 10am-1pm Sun May-

Oct, 9.30am-4pm Mon-Fri Nov-Apr) Reserves hotel rooms, sells hiking and cycling maps and has an ATM.

Trier

📞 0651 / POP 106,544

A Unesco World Heritage Site since 1986, Germany's oldest city is home to its finest ensemble of Roman monuments, among them a mighty gate, amphitheatre, elaborate thermal baths, imperial throne room, and the country's oldest bishop's church, which retains Roman sections. Architectural treasures from later ages include Germany's oldest Gothic church, and Karl Marx' baroque birthplace.

Trier's mostly pedestrianised city centre is filled with cafes and restaurants, many inside gorgeous Gothic or baroque buildings. Wineries are scattered throughout the surrounding vineyards.

The city's proximity to both Luxembourg and France is apparent in its cuisine and the local esprit, enlivened by some 15,000 students from its renowned university.

⦿ Sights & Activities

⭐ Porta Nigra
GATE

(adult/child €3/2; ⊗ 9am-6pm Apr-Sep, to 5pm Mar & Oct, to 4pm Nov-Feb) This brooding 2nd-century Roman city gate – blackened by time (hence the name, Latin for 'black gate') – is a marvel of engineering since it's held together by nothing but gravity and iron clamps.

In the 11th century, the structure was turned into a church to honour Simeon, a Greek hermit who spent six years walled up in its east tower. After his death in 1134, he was buried inside the gate and later became a saint.

Stadtmuseum Simeonstift
MUSEUM

(adult/child €5.50/4; ⊗ 10am-5pm Tue-Sun) Adjoining the Porta Nigra, in the 11th-century priests' residence Simeon's College (retaining an original 1060-laid oak beam floor in the double-storey cloister), Trier's city museum brings alive two millennia of local history through paintings, sculptures, porcelain, textiles and more. Highlights include the **Trier Kino** (Trier Cinema), where you can see 80 short films of Trier, some made as far back as 1904. Admission includes a free audioguide.

Hauptmarkt
SQUARE

Anchored by a 1595 **fountain** dedicated to St Peter and the Four Virtues, Trier's central market square is surrounded by medieval and Renaissance architectural treasures such as the **Rotes Haus** (Red House), and the **Steipe**, which now houses a cafe and the Spielzeugmuseum, as well as the Gothic St-Gangolf-Kirche.

Small market stalls (flowers, sausages etc) set up most days, except Sunday.

Spielzeugmuseum
MUSEUM

(Toy Museum; www.spielzeugmuseum-trier.de; Dietrichstrasse 50/51; adult/child €4.50/2.50; ⊗ 11am-5pm Tue-Sun) Upstairs from the cafe Zur Steipe on the Hauptmarkt, the Spielzeugmuseum is chock-full of miniature trains, dolls, wooden soldiers and other childhood delights. It's also accessible from Hauptmarkt 14; an entrance for visitors with limited mobility is located at Jakobstrasse 4-5.

St-Gangolf-Kirche
CHURCH

(⊗ 7am-6.30pm) Topped by a 62m-high tower, the Gothic St-Gangolf-Kirche was built in the early 15th century on the site of a 14th-century tower. It's reached via a flowery portal on the Hauptmarkt.

⭐ Trierer Dom
CATHEDRAL

(📞 0651-979 0790; www.dominformation.de; Liebfrauenstrasse 12, cnr of Domfreihof; ⊗ 6.30am-6pm Apr-Oct, to 5.30pm Nov-Mar) **FREE** Looming above the Roman palace of Helena (Emperor Constantine's mother), this is Germany's oldest bishop's church and still retains Roman sections. Today's edifice is a study in nearly 1700 years of church architecture with Romanesque, Gothic and baroque elements. Intriguingly, its floorplan is of a 12-petalled flower, symbolising the Virgin Mary.

To see some dazzling ecclesiastical equipment and peer into early Christian history, head upstairs to the **Domschatz** (Cathedral

---

ℹ️ **BOAT & BIKE COMBO**

From May to October, boats run by **Kolb** (📞 02673-1515; www.moselrundfahrten.de; ⊗ May-Oct) link Bernkastel with Traben-Trarbach (one-way/return €13/19, two hours, five daily). You can take along a bicycle for €2, making it easy to sail one way and ride the 24km back.

In Traben-Trarbach, **Zweirad Wagner** (📞 06541-1649; www.zweirad-wagner.de; Brückenstrasse 42, Trarbach; per day €8.50; ⊗ 9am-12.30pm & 2-6pm Mon-Fri, 9am-1pm Sat) rents bikes; in Bernkastel-Kues try **Fun Bike Team** (p450).

WORTH A TRIP

FAIRY-TALE HIDEAWAY

Liller's Historische Schlossmühle
(☑ 06543-4041; www.hostorische-schloss-muehle.de; An der Landstrasse 190; mains €18.50-32, 5-/7-course menu €59/79; ⊗ kitchen noon-9pm Thu-Tue) A wonderland of waterwheels, wooden furniture and fairylights, this ancient mill was moved stone by stone in 1804 to its magical spot in the forest 21km southeast of Traben-Trarbach. Venison carpaccio marinated in plum brandy, trout terrine with dandelion salad and wild garlic-crusted veal with chanterelle ragout encapsulate the flavours of the countryside. Upstairs are enchanting **rooms** (☑ 06543-4041; www.historische-schlossmuehle.de; An der Landstrasse 190; s/d/ste from €91/134/197; ℗ 🐾).

All rooms are exquisitely decorated with antiques; some have woodland themes (Fox, Owl, Dormouse, et al) and one has a clawfoot bath. Breakfast is served in the ochre-toned, wood-beamed Napoleon room; there's a library with a crackling open fire, as well as a lakeside summer terrace.

Treasury; adult/child €1.50/0.50; ⊗ 10am-5pm Mon-Sat, 12.30-5pm Sun Mar-Oct & Dec, 11am-4pm Tue-Sat, 12.30-4pm Sun & Mon Nov & Jan-Mar) or around the corner to the **Bischöfliches Dom-und Diözesanmuseum** (☑ 0651-710 5255; www.bistum-trier.de/museum; Windstrasse 6-8; adult/child €3.50/2; ⊗ 9am-5pm Tue-Sat, 1-5pm Sun).

★ **Liebfrauenbasilika**   CHURCH
(Church of Our Lady; www.trierer-dom.de; Liebfrauenstrasse; ⊗ 10am-7pm Mon-Fri, 11am-4.30pm Sat, 12.30-6pm Sun Apr-Oct, 10am-5pm Mon-Fri, 11am-4.30pm Sat, 12.30-5pm Sun Nov-Mar) Germany's oldest Gothic church was built in the 13th century. It has a cruciform structure supported by a dozen pillars symbolising the 12 Apostles (look for the black stone from where all 12 articles of the Apostle's Creed painted on the columns are visible) and some colourful postwar stained glass.

★ **Konstantin Basilika**   CHURCH
(☑ 0651-425 70; www.konstantin-basilika.de; Konstantinplatz 10; ⊗ 10am-6pm Mon-Sat, 1-4pm Sun Apr-Oct, 10am-noon & 2-4pm Mon-Sat, 1-4pm Sun Nov-Mar) Constructed around AD 310 as Con-

stantine's throne room, the brick-built basilica is now an austere Protestant church. With built-to-impress dimensions (some 67m long, 27m wide and 33m high), it's the largest single-room Roman structure still in existence. A new organ, with 87 registers and 6500 pipes, generates a seven-fold echo.

Palastgarten   PARK
Stretching south from Konstantinplatz, the lawns, daffodil beds, statues and fountains of the formal Palace Garden are perfect for a stroll, especially on warm summer days. The pink and gold rococo confection at the northern end is the **Kurfürstliches Palais** (Prince Electors' Palace; interior closed to the public).

★ **Rheinisches Landesmuseum**   MUSEUM
(Roman Archaeological Museum; www.landesmuseum-trier.de; Weimarer Allee 1; adult/child €6/3; ⊗ 10am-5pm Tue-Sun) A scale model of 4th-century Trier and rooms filled with tombstones, mosaics, rare gold coins (including the 1993-discovered Trier Gold Hoard, the largest preserved Roman gold hoard in the world, with over 2600 gold coins) and some fantastic glass are highlights of this museum, which affords an extraordinary look at local Roman life. Admission includes an audioguide.

★ **Kaiserthermen**   ROMAN SITE
(Imperial Baths; Weberbachstrasse 41; adult/child €3/2; ⊗ 9am-6pm Apr-Sep, to 5pm Mar & Oct, to 4pm Nov-Feb) Get a sense of the layout of this vast Roman thermal bathing complex with its striped brick-and-stone arches from the corner lookout tower, then descend into an underground labyrinth consisting of cavernous hot and cold water baths, boiler rooms and heating channels.

★ **Amphitheater**   ROMAN SITE
(Olewiger Strasse; adult/child €3/2; ⊗ 9am-6pm Apr-Sep, to 5pm Mar & Oct, to 4pm Nov-Feb) Trier's Roman amphitheatre could accommodate 20,000 spectators for gladiator tournaments and animal fights. Beneath the arena are dungeons where prisoners sentenced to death waited next to starving beasts for the final showdown.

Thermen am Viehmarkt   ROMAN SITE
(Forum Baths; Viehmarktplatz; adult/child €3/2; ⊗ 9am-5pm Tue-Sun) Found by accident in 1987 during the construction of a parking garage, buried beneath WWII air-raid shelters, the remains of a 17th-century Capucinian monastery, one-time vineyards and ceme-

teries, these thermal baths are sheltered by a dramatic glass cube. The site is closed on Tuesday when Monday is a public holiday.

Karl Marx Haus
HISTORIC SITE
(www.fes.de/Karl-Marx-Haus; Brückenstrasse 10; adult/child €4/2.50; ⊙10am-6pm Apr-Oct, 2-5pm Mon, 11am-5pm Tue-Sun Nov-Mar) The early-18th-century baroque town house in which the author of *The Communist Manifesto* and *Das Kapital* was born in 1818 now houses exhibits that cover Marx' life, work, allies and enemies, social democracy, his decades of exile in London, where he died in 1883, and his intellectual and political legacy. Admission includes an audioguide that opens with the stirring cadences of *L'Internationale*.

Römerbrücke
ROMAN SITE
(Roman Bridge; western end of Karl Marx Strasse) Spanning the Moselle, Germany's oldest bridge uses 2nd-century stone pilings (AD 144–52), built from black basalt from the Eifel mountains, which have been holding it up since legionnaires crossed on chariots.

Weinkulturpfad
HIKING
(Wine Culture Path) Panoramic views unfold from **Petrisberg**, the vine-covered hill just east of the Amphitheatre. Halfway up, the Weinkulturpfad leads through the grapes to Olewig (1.6km). Next to the Petrisberg/Aussicht stop for buses 4 and 85, a **multilingual panel** (Sickingenstrasse) traces local history from the first known human habitation (30,000 years ago) through the last ice age to the Romans.

Tours

City Walking Tour
WALKING TOUR
(adult/child €6.50/3; ⊙1pm May-Oct) Guided 75-minute walking tours in English begin at the tourist office.

Kolb
BOAT TOUR
(☑0651-263 37; www.moselrundfahrten.de; Georg-Schmitt-Platz 2; ⊙Apr-Oct) Cruise along the Moselle for 45 minutes across the border into Luxembourg (one-way/return €9/13), or choose from a range of river tours within Germany such as a 4¼-hour trip to Bernkastel (one-way/return €24/30).

Sleeping

Trier is a popular weekend getaway and hotel prices rise on Friday and Saturday.

Hille's Hostel
HOSTEL $
(☑0651-6998 7026, outside office hours 0157 8856 9594; www.hilles-hostel-trier.de; Gartenfeldstrasse 7; dm from €15, s/d from €40/50, without bathroom from €36/46; ⊙reception 8-11am & 2-7pm May-Oct, 9-11am & 3-6pm Nov-Apr; @🛜) Freshly renovated and operated by new management since late 2014, this laid-back indie hostel has a piano in the common kitchen and 12 attractive, spacious rooms, most with private bathrooms. Breakfast costs €6. Outside office hours, call ahead to arrange your arrival.

DJH Hostel
HOSTEL $
(☑0651-146 620; www.jugendherberge.de; An der Jugendherberge 4; dm/d €22.50/56; P@🛜) Right on the Moselle, 1km northeast of the tourist office, this 228-bed hostel has spick-and-span rooms with bathrooms and a maximum of just four beds. There's a piano and a sprawling summer beer garden.

★Becker's Hotel
DESIGN HOTEL $$
(☑0651-938 080; www.beckers-trier.de; Olewiger Strasse 206; s €60-75, d €110-170, tr €150-225; P✿@🛜) In the peaceful wine district of Olewig, across the creek from the old monastery church, 3km southeast of the centre, classy Becker's pairs supremely tasteful rooms – some ultramodern, others rustically traditional – with stellar dining (p456).

WORTH A TRIP

DIVINE BREWS

Kloster Machern (www.klostermachern.de; An der Zeltinger Brücke, Zeltingen-Rachtig; ⊙bar 11am-2am Easter-Oct, reduced hours Nov-Easter) The Moselle might be better known for its wine but a former Cistercian monastery, founded in the 13th century, now houses this extraordinary brewery, with a bar made from a copper vat and strung with dry hops, a wicker-chair-filled terrace, and excellent local cuisine. Brews, including a *Dunkel* (dark), *Hell* (light) and *Hefe-Weizen* (wheat beer), are also sold at its **shop** (noon to 5pm). Also here is a **museum** (10am to 6pm Easter to October, reduced hours at other times; adult/child €3/1.50) exhibiting religious iconography, plus puppets, toys and model railways. It's 7km northwest of Bernkastel-Kues.

Trier

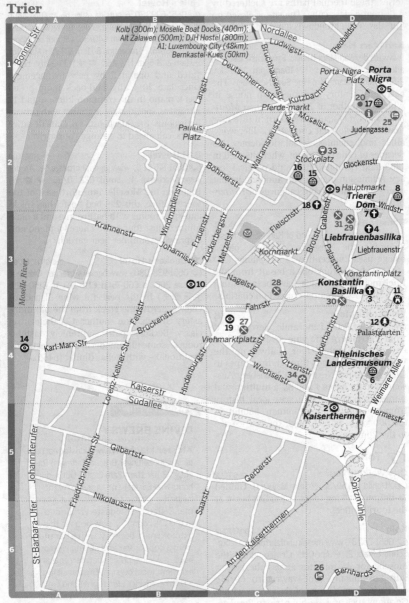

Hotel Petrisberg   HOTEL **$$**

(☎ 0651-4640; www.hotel-petrisberg.de; Sickingen-strasse 11; s €68-75, d €97-105; P @ ☎) Incredible views of the city and Roman Ampitheater extend from this traditional, hillside-perched hotel; try for a front room, which comes with a balcony that's idyllic for enjoying a glass of Moselle (the in-house honour bar has wine and beer). It's a great option for cyclists, with lock-up bike storage. A zigzag path leads down the hill into Trier.

pool and Finnish sauna. The 36 rooms are decorated with honey-toned woods.

Hotel Römischer Kaiser
HOTEL **$$**

(✆ 0651-977 0100; www.friedrich-hotels.de; Porta-Nigra-Platz 6; s/d from €86/116; [P][☎]) Convenient to the train station and the old city, this 1894-built hotel offers 43 bright, comfortable rooms with solid wood furnishings, parquet floors and spacious bathrooms.

✗ Eating & Drinking

In the warmer months, cafes fill the Altstadt's public squares, including the Hauptmarkt and Kornmarkt.

Traditional *Weinstuben* are scattered throughout the Olewig district, 3km southeast of the centre.

Kartoffel Kiste
GERMAN **$**

(www.kiste-trier.de; Fahrstrasse 13-14; mains €6-17; ⊙ kitchen 11.30am-10pm; [☑][📶]) Fronted by a bronze fountain, local favourite Kartoffel Kiste specialises, as its name suggests, in baked, breaded, gratinéed, soupified and sauce-doused potatoes. If you're after something heartier (albeit pricier), it also does great schnitzel and steaks.

Zuppa
CAFE **$**

(www.zuppa-trier.de; Sichelstrasse 18; dishes €3-5.50; ⊙ 11am-5pm Mon-Fri, noon-4pm Sat; [☑]) Five different soups served with sourdough bread are the mainstay of this bright little hole in the wall: two vegetarian, one vegan and two meat-based. Soups change daily but might include lentil and spinach, potato with pork sausage, curried pumpkin, and asparagus and cabbage. Finish off with semolina or almond cake.

Food Market
MARKET **$**

(Viehmarktplatz; ⊙ 7am-2pm Tue & Fri Apr-Sep, from 8am Tue & Fri Oct-Mar) The city centre's largest outdoor market is a perfect place to pick up fresh local produce for a riverside picnic.

★ Weinwirtschaft Friedrich-Wilhelm
MODERN GERMAN **$$**

(✆ 0651-9947 4800; www.weinwirtschaft-fw.de; Weberbach 75; mains €11-26; ⊙ kitchen noon-2pm & 6-10pm Mon-Sat, wine shop 9am-6pm Mon-Sat) A historic former wine warehouse with exposed brick and hoists now houses this superb restaurant. Creative dishes incorporate local wines, such as trout poached in sparkling white wine with mustard sauce and white asparagus; local sausage with riesling sauerkraut and fried potatoes.

Hotel Villa Hügel
BOUTIQUE HOTEL **$$**

(✆ 0651-937 100; www.hotel-villa-huegel.de; Bernhardstrasse 14; s/d from €108/148; [P][@][☎][🏊]) Begin the day with sparkling wine at a lavish breakfast buffet at this stylish hillside villa, and end it luxuriating in the 12m indoor

Trier

◎ Top Sights

◎ Sights

● Activities, Courses & Tours

● Sleeping

● Eating

● Drinking & Nightlife

● Entertainment

Vines trail over the trellis-covered garden; the attached wine shop is a great place to stock up.

Zum Domstein   ROMAN $$
(☑0651-744 90; www.domstein.de; Hauptmarkt 5; mains €9-18.50, Roman menu €17-31; ☺kitchen 8.30am-11pm, Roman menu 6-9.30pm) Feast like a Roman on dishes based on the recipes of 1st-century local chef Marcus Gavius Apicius: mulled Moselle white wine followed by barley soup, pine nut–stuffed sausage, artichokes with boiled eggs, ham with figs and almonds, and wine-sautéed pears with custard, honey and green peppercorns. The Roman menu is available of an evening; during the day it serves more conventional German and international fare.

Weinstube Kesselstadt   GERMAN $$
(☑0651-411 78; www.weinstube-kesselstatt.de; Liebfrauenstrasse 10; mains €7-24; ☺kitchen 11.30am-2.30pm & 6-10pm, bar 10am-midnight) Dining on quality regional produce – and sampling the local whites – is a serious pleasure at this charming *Weinstube*, either in the barrel-filled, dark-timber interior housing a huge wooden wine press, or in the tree-shaded, flower-filled summer garden facing the cathedral. Seasonal specialities utilise ingredients like mushrooms, game or asparagus. Order at the bar.

Alt Zalawen   GERMAN $$
(☑0651-286 45; www.altzalawen.de; Zurlaubener Ufer 79; mains €7-18; ☺kitchen 11am-10pm, closed Sun Nov-Mar; ☜) The pick of the cluster of bar/restaurants right on the riverfront with terraces extending to the footpath/cycleway running along the grassy bank, timber-panelled Alt Zalawen is a picturesque spot for traditional German specialities (schnitzels, sausages, *Spätzle*). If you're here in December, it's fêted for serving the best roast goose in town.

★**Weinhaus Becker**   INTERNATIONAL $$$
(☑0651-938 080; www.beckers-trier.de; Olewiger Strasse 206; 1-course lunch menu incl wine & coffee €18, 3-course lunch menu €28, mains €21-34; ☺noon-2pm & 6-10pm) Within the Becker's Hotel complex, 3km southeast of the centre, this supremely elegant winehouse serves sublime internationally influenced dishes like ribeye with green beans, bacon and baked potato with sour cream, accompanied by (very) local wines made from grapes grown on the hillside opposite. Also here is the ultragourmet, twin-Michelin-starred **Becker's Restaurant** (5-/8-course dinner menu €125/149; ☺7-9pm Tue-Sat).

Safari Haus   CLUB
(www.trierwirdwild.de; Stockplatz 2a; ☺10pm-4am Thu, to 5am Fri & Sat) Set over two storeys in a baroque stone building, Safari is Trier's best

club, with international DJs spinning hip-hop, dance, house and electronica.

☆ Entertainment

The tourist office has details on concerts and other cultural activities and sells tickets.

TuFa PERFORMING ARTS
(📞 0651-718 2410; www.tufa-trier.de; Wechsel-strasse 4-6) This vibrant cultural events venue, housed in a former *Tuchfabrik* (towel factory), hosts cabaret, live music of all sorts, theatre and dance performances.

❶ Information

Tourist Office (📞 0651-978 080; www.trier-info.de; ⊙ 9am-6pm Mon-Sat, 10am-5pm Sun May-Oct, shorter hours Nov-Apr)

❶ Getting There & Away

Trier has frequent train connections to Saar-brücken (€17.90, one to 1½ hours, two per hour) and Koblenz (€22.70, 1½ to two hours, two per hour).

There are also regular trains to Luxembourg City (same-day return €17.90, one hour, at least hourly), with onward connections to Paris (€59 to €93, 3½ hours, at least hourly).

❶ Getting Around

The city centre is easily explored on foot. A bus ride (see www.swt.de) costs €2, a public transport day pass costs €5.80. The Olewig wine district is served by buses 7 and 84.

Bikes in tip-top condition can be rented at the Hauptbahnhof's **Radstation** (Fahrradser-vicestation; 📞 148 856; adult/child/electric bike per day from €12/6/30; ⊙ 9am-6pm mid-Apr–Oct, 10am-6pm Mon-Fri Nov–mid-Apr), next to track 11, and from the tourist office. Staff are enthusiastic about cycling and can provide tips on routes.

SAARLAND

The French influence on this border region is apparent in all sorts of subtle ways. While the tiny federal state of Saarland is now solidly within German boundaries, many locals are bilingual and the standard greeting is not 'hallo' but 'salü', from the French 'salut'. Their French heritage, although somewhat imposed, means Saarlanders have an appreciation of good cuisine (with numerous Michelin-starred restaurants), fine wine and a laid-back lifestyle – 'Saarvoir vivre', it's called.

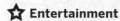
❶ TRIER DISCOUNT CARDS

The **Antiquities Card** (2/4 Roman sites & Rheinisches Landesmuseum €10/15) is a great deal for Trier's most interesting antiquities. Sold at the tourist office and each site.

Using the **TrierCard** (adult/family €9.90/21) for three consecutive days you get 10% to 25% off museum and monument admissions, unlimited use of public transport, and other discounts. Sold only at the tourist office.

Over the centuries, France and Germany have played ping pong with Saarland, coveting it for its valuable natural resources. In the 20th century, the region came under French control twice – after each of the world wars – but in both cases (in referendums held in 1935 and 1955) its people voted in favour of rejoining Germany.

Long a land of coal and heavy industry, Saarland has in recent decades cleaned up its air and streams and reoriented its struggling economy towards high-technology and ecotourism. The capital, Saarbrücken, is a vibrant city with excellent museums and a fine, French-accented culinary scene. Rolling hills and forest cover much of the countryside, which can be explored not only by car or public transport but also on foot or by bicycle. Cycling paths include the 356km, circular **Saarland-Radweg** and the 98km **Saar-Radweg** (VeloRoute SaarLorLux), along the (mostly) beautiful Saar River. The region's industrial heritage is celebrated in places such as the historic Völklinger Hütte ironworks.

Saarbrücken

📞 0681 / POP 176,996
The Saarland capital has considerable historical charm. Vestiges of its 18th-century heyday as a royal residence under Prince Wilhelm Heinrich (1718–68) survive in the baroque town houses and churches designed by his prolific court architect, Friedrich Joachim Stengel. The historic centre around St Johanner Markt brims with excellent restaurants and cafes.

Saarbrücken is home to the main Universität des Saarlandes (Saarland University) campus, whose students add to the city's dynamic energy.

◉ Sights

◉ Right Bank

From the Hauptbahnhof, at the northwestern end of the city centre, pedestrian-only Reichsstrasse and its continuation Bahnhofstrasse – the attractive main shopping street – lead 1km southeast to St Johanner Markt.

St Johanner Markt   SQUARE
The heart of Saarbrücken (and its nightlife hub), historic St Johanner Markt is a long, narrow public square anchored by an ornate **fountain** designed by Friedrich Joachim Stengel and flanked by some of the town's oldest buildings.

Basilika St Johann   CHURCH
(www.basilika-sb.de; Katholisch-Kirch-Strasse 26; ⊙9.30am-7.15pm Mon, Fri & Sat, 8.30am-7.15pm Tue, Thu & Sun, 8.30am-5pm Wed) This dazzlingly baroque Catholic church, designed by Stengel, will wow you with its gleaming gold altars, pulpit, organ case and overhead rayburst design. As you face the facade, the entrance is to the left around the side.

Moderne Galerie   MUSEUM
(www.kulturbesitz.de; Bismarckstrasse 11-15; adult/child €5/free; ⊙10am-6pm Tue & Thu-Sun, to 10pm

Wed) One of Saarland's cultural highlights, the Saarland Museum's Moderne Galerie covers European art from the late 1800s to the present and is especially noteworthy for its works of German Impressionism (eg Slevogt, Corinth and Liebermann), French Impressionism (eg Monet, Sisley and Renoir) and Expressionism (eg Kirchner, Marc and Jawlensky). The Galerie der Gegenwart focuses on contemporary art.

◉ Left Bank

Schlossplatz   SQUARE
Crossing the Saar River via the pedestrians-only Alte Brücke takes you over the autobahn and up to the Stengel-designed baroque Schlossplatz, around which you'll find the city's museums showcasing history and pre-19th-century art. The dominant building here is the **Saarbrücker Schloss,** which mixes several architectural styles from Renaissance to baroque to neoclassical. The northern wing was once used by the Gestapo as offices and detention cells.

Historisches Museum Saar   MUSEUM
(www.historisches-museum.org; Schlossplatz 15; adult/student €5/3; ⊙10am-6pm Tue, Wed & Fri-Sun, to 8pm Thu) The Saarbrücker Schloss'

CYCLE TOURING: FIVE RIVERS IN FIVE DAYS

Trier makes an ideal base for day trips by bike, with five different riverside bike paths (www.radwanderland.de) to choose from. Trains and RegioRadler buses (www.moselbahn.de), which have bike trailers make it possible to ride one way (ie downhill) and take public transport the other.

Esterbauer (www.esterbauer.com) publishes Bikeline cycling guides (€13.90), which include 1:60,000-scale maps.

➡ **Kylltal-Radweg** Paralleling the rail line to Cologne, this route leads 122km north along the Kyll (pronounced *kool*) River. Take the train between Erdorf and Kyllburg (five to seven minutes) to avoid a killer hill.

➡ **Mosel-Radweg** (www.mosel-radweg.de) Begining in Thionville, France, the 275km Mosel-Radweg passes through Trier before continuing downriver to Koblenz. Parts are served by RegioRadler bus 333.

➡ **Ruwer-Hochwald-Radweg** (www.ruwer-hochwald-radweg.de) This 50km bike path runs along a one-time rail line south along the Ruwer River and then west, crossing seven bridges. It's served by RegioRadler bus 290, operating Monday, Wednesday and Friday to Sunday.

➡ **Saar-Radweg** Travels south from Trier for 130km along the mostly gorgeous, partly industrial Saar River to Saarbrücken and on to Sarreguemines, France.

➡ **Sauertal-Radweg** From Wasserbillig, 13km west of Trier via the Mosel-Radweg, this 53km path follows a decommissioned rail line north along the Sauer River into Luxembourg. Northern variants follow the Prüm and Nims Rivers. Parts are served by RegioRadler bus 441.

basement and a modern annex house the well-designed Museum of Regional History. The section covering Saarland from 1870 to the 1950s includes a 1904 film of Saarbrücken street life. From here you can descend to the castle's massive bastions and **Kasematten** (casemates; English brochure available). Other exhibits look at Saarland under French rule (1920–35) and during the Nazi era.

Alte Sammlung — MUSEUM
(www.kulturbesitz.de; adult/child €5/free, after 3pm Tue free; ☺ 10am-6pm Tue & Thu-Sun, to 10pm Wed) The Saarland Museum's Alte Sammlung ('old collection') displays a millennium's worth of paintings, porcelain, tapestries and sculptures from southwest Germany and the Alsace and Lorraine regions of France.

Museum für Vor- und Frühgeschichte — MUSEUM
(Museum of Early History & Prehistory; www.kulturbesitz.de; adult/child €5/free, after 3pm Tue free; ☺ 10am-6pm Tue & Thu-Sun, to 10pm Wed) Fans of the Romans, the Celts and their predecessors won't want to miss the Museum für Vor-und Frühgeschichte. The star exhibit here is resplendent gold jewellery from around 400 BC, discovered in the tomb of a Celtic princess at Bliesbruck-Reinheim.

Museum in Der Schlosskirche — MUSEUM
(www.kulturbesitz.de; ☺ 10am-6pm Tue & Thu-Sun, to 10pm Wed) **FREE** The Museum in der Schlosskirche, inside a desanctified late-Gothic church, features religious art from the 13th to 19th centuries. Highlights include the elaborate tombs of three 17th and 18th-century princes.

Ludwigskirche — CHURCH
(www.ludwigskirche.de; Ludwigsplatz; ☺ 10am-6pm Tue-Sun Apr-Dec, noon-5pm Tue, 10am-5pm Wed-Sat Jan-Mar) The star at Stengel's handsome Ludwigsplatz, flanked by stately baroque town houses, is his masterpiece, Ludwigskirche. A Protestant church built in 1775 and rebuilt after WWII, it sports a facade festooned with biblical figures and a brilliant white interior with stylish stucco decoration.

☞ Tours

★ Saarbrücker Personenschiffahrt — BOAT TOUR
(www.xn–personenschifffahrt-saarbrcken-ufd. de; city river cruise adult/child €10/7; ☺ city river cruise 12.30pm, 4.15pm & 5.15pm Apr-Oct, reduced schedule Nov-Mar) From its dock in front of the Staatstheater, Saarbrücker Personenschiffahrt runs one-hour city cruises.

For a cross-country trip, you can take a day cruise (adult/child return €19.50/11) to Sarreguemines, France, on Tuesday, the town's colourful market day. It departs from Saarbrücken at 8am, returning at 3.15pm year-round.

Other options include cruises along the Saar River to Saarschleife (€14/7).

One-way tickets and bicycle transport are available by request.

⏻ Sleeping

DJH Hostel — HOSTEL $
(☎ 0681-330 40; www.jugendherberge.de; Meerwiesertalweg 31; dm/d €22.50/56; P ☎) This modern, 192-bed hostel, 1.5km northeast of the city centre, is a 20-minute walk from the Hauptbahnhof and 100m from a supermarket, with en suite rooms and dorms, a barbecue area and a lockable bike storage room. It's served by buses 101, 102 and 150 from the Rathaus and, Monday to Friday, by buses 112 and 124 from the Hauptbahnhof.

Hotel Stadt Hamburg — HOTEL $$
(☎ 0681-379 9890; www.hotel-stadt-hamburg-saarbruecken.de; Bahnhofstrasse 71-73, 3rd fl; s/d from €63/87; P ☎) An unpromisingly small street door leads to this striking establishment. Its 24 rooms are decorated with colourful original watercolours, oils and collages (the owner is an artist), and have contemporary, immaculate bathrooms. It can be noisy at night due to the cafes downstairs but the trade-off is the central location and on-site parking (per day €10; book ahead).

Hotel Madeleine — HOTEL $$
(☎ 0681-857 780; www.hotel-madeleine.de; Cecilienstrasse 5; s/d from €85/91; @☎) 🖉 Impressively eco-conscious, this central, friendly family-run hotel has 28 bright rooms with bold wallpapering, fabrics and furniture like clear-plastic chairs that are comfortable if compact (doubles are 12 to 14 sq metres). Several rooms have church views. Breakfasts are mostly organic, with vegetarian and vegan options. Free bikes are available (subject to availability) for a spin around town.

★ Hotel am Triller — DESIGN HOTEL $$
(☎ 0681-580 000; www.hotel-am-triller.de; Trillerweg 57; s/d/ste from €82/98/165; P @☎⯎) Uphill from Schlossplatz, this 110-room hotel has art-filled public areas and creative rooms, some with themes such as Musée de

SAARLAND SPECIALITIES

Many local *saarländische* dishes revolve around potatoes – look for *Dibbelabbes* (potato casserole with dried meat and leeks), *Hoorische* (half-cooked, half-raw potato dumplings, literally 'hairy ones', in reference to the coarse surface), and *Gefillde* (*Hoorische* filled with minced meat and liver sausage).

In the French tradition, meals are often served with a basket of crunchy baguette-style bread.

Paris, the seductive, red-clad Moulin Rouge, Planet Ocean with porthole-shaped paintings of reefs and fish, and La Mer, with a tropical island sailing theme, complete with a waterbed. Its all-organic Mediterranean restaurant, Panorama, has 270-degree views over the city.

✗ Eating & Drinking

Saarbrücken's restaurant, cafe and bar scene centres on St Johanner Markt and nearby Saarstrasse, Am Stiefel and Kappenstrasse, with cheaper eats along Kaltenbachstrasse.

The city's lively student nightlife district is four long blocks northeast of St Johanner Markt, around the intersection of Nauwieserstrasse and Cicilienstrasse.

★ Kalinski   CAFE $
(www.kalinskibrueder.de; Kaltenbachstrasse 4; dishes €2-6; ⊙11am-11pm Mon-Thu, to 3am Fri & Sat, to 10pm Sun) ✐ Saarbrücken's hippest eatery is this *Wurstwirtschaft* and gin bar, which sizzles up street-food-style *Currywurst* (including a fabulous tofu and wheatgerm vegetarian sausage with spicy tomato sauce), pulled pork burgers, *Spätzle*, and meatballs, accompanied by potato or sweet-potato fries. Everything, down to the condiments, is preservative-free and made daily on the premises from local produce. Seats spill onto the front pavement.

Zum Stiefel   GERMAN $$
(☎0681-936 450; www.stiefelgastronomie.de; Am Stiefel 2; mains €9-21; ⊙restaurant 11.45am-2pm & 5.30-10.30pm Mon-Sat, brewery 11.30am-1am Mon-Sat, 5.30-11pm Sun) One kitchen covers two dining options at this brewery and German restaurant. **Zum Stiefel** features good-value classic German and *saarländische* dishes, including *Gefillde* (meat-filled potato dump-

lings). Next door (the entrance is around the corner), **Stiefel-Bräu**, Saarbrücken's oldest microbrewery, also serves meals (from Monday to Saturday) and three beers brewed according to an old Broch family recipe (including on Sunday evening).

Jens Jakob das
Restaurant   MODERN FRENCH $$$
(☎0681-968 1988; www.jjdasrestaurant.jensjakob-gourmetworld.com; Mainzer Strasse 10; 3-course lunch menu €24, 4-/5-/6-course dinner menus €84/94/104; ⊙noon-2.30pm & 6.30-11pm Tue-Thu, noon-2.30pm & 7-11.45pm Fri & Sat) Until recently, Jens Jakob had his two-Michelin-star restaurant here. But his new approach sees him creating simplified, casual dishes inside a glass-box kitchen. Menus might include foie gras and passionfruit, buttermilk-marinated Faroe Islands salmon and asparagus, sweetbread ravioli with spinach and parmesan foam, quail and mushroom mousse, and strawberry and rhubarb with cheese dumplings and quark ice cream.

★ Baker Street   BAR
(www.bakerstreetsb.de; Mainzer Strasse 8; ⊙2pm-midnight Mon-Thu, 2pm-2am Fri, 10am-2am Sat, 10am-midnight Sun) Named after Sherlock Holmes' fictional home, this fabulous Victorian-era-themed bar with crackling open fireplaces bills itself as a 'criminal tea room and pub'. Vintage furniture including studded leather couches and book-lined shelves fill Watson's Club; homemade scones with clotted cream are served in the Tea Room; and you can sip British beers like Newcastle Brown Ale in the colonial-style Adventure Salon.

Sunday brunch (€14.50; 10am to 1pm), has a cult following. Other events range from bingo to murder mystery nights and magic shows.

☆ Entertainment

Garage   LIVE MUSIC
(www.garage-sb.de; Bleichstrasse 11-15) Industrial 1920s brick surrounds provide great acoustics at this live music venue, where punk, alternative, metal and rock bands take to the stage. Concerts generally start around 7pm; on Friday and Saturday from 11pm to 5am, it also hosts a small nightclub, **Kleiner Klub** (www.kleinerklub.de) with dance, techno and reggae nights.

Staatstheater   THEATRE
(☎box office 0681-3092 486; www.theater-saarbruecken.de; Schillerplatz) The grandiose,

golden-hued Staatstheater was built on Hitler's orders to thank the Saarlanders for their 1935 vote to rejoin Germany. It opened in 1938 with Richard Wagner's *The Flying Dutchman* and today presents opera, ballet, classical music concerts, drama and musicals.

❶ Information

Tourist Office (📞0681-9590 9200; www.saarbruecken.de; Rathausplatz 1; ⊙9am-6pm Mon-Fri, 10am-4.30pm Sat) Inside the Rathaus St-Johann, a red-brick neo-Gothic structure built from 1897 to 1900, this helpful office has region-wide info and sells cycling guides as well as tickets for cultural events.

❶ Getting There & Away

Saarbrücken's Hauptbahnhof has rail connections to Mainz (€32.30, two hours, at least hourly) and, via Völklingen, to Trier (€17.90, 1¼ hours, every 30 minutes).

Trains run south to the lovely French city of Metz (€17.90, one hour, every two hours) – ideal for a cross-border day trip.

❶ Getting Around

Saarbrücken has an extensive, integrated bus and rail network (www.saarbahn.de) that includes one tram line, called S1. Tickets within the city (Zone 111) cost €2.50 (€1.90 for up to five stops); a day pass for one/five people costs €5.50/10.60.

By Schulz (📞0681-925 5252; www.bikes-ebikes.de; Vorstadtstrasse 53; bike rental half-day/day/week €12/20/110; ⊙10am-6pm Mon-Fri, to 4pm Sat) Great-value weekend rentals, from 1pm Friday to 1pm Monday, cost €35.

Taxi Saarbrücken (📞0681-330 33; http://taxi-sb.de)

Around Saarbrücken

Völklinger Hütte   HISTORIC SITE
(www.voelklinger-huette.org; adult/child €15/13, after 3pm Tue free; ⊙10am-7pm Apr-Oct, 10am-6pm Nov-Mar) The hulking former ironworks of Völklinger Hütte, about 14km northwest of Saarbrücken, are one of Europe's great heavy-industrial relics. Opened in 1873, 17,000 people worked here by 1965 – the height of Germany's post-WWII boom. The plant blasted its last pig iron in 1986 and was declared a Unesco World Heritage Site in 1994.

Trains link Saarbrücken with Völklingen (10 minutes), from where it's a three-minute walk.

By car, take the A620 to Völklingen and follow the signs to the *'Weltkulturerbe'*.

Both Dickensian and futuristic, dystopian and a symbol of renewal, the plant's massive scale dwarfs humans, who nevertheless managed to master the forces of fire, wind and earth in order to smelt iron, without which civilisation as it is today could not exist. Fine views of the whole rusty ensemble can be had from atop a 45m blast furnace (helmet required). Parts of the vast complex are being reclaimed by trees, shrubs and mosses. Brochures and all signs are in German, English and French.

Colourful works of modern art make a particularly cheerful impression amid the ageing concrete and rusted pipes, beams, conveyors and car-sized ladles. Check out the website for details on exhibitions and events (like summertime jazz concerts). At night, the compound is luridly lit up like a vast science-fiction set.

Saarschleife   AREA
The most scenic spot along the Saar River is the Saarschleife, where the river makes a spectacular, almost unbelievable hairpin turn, flowing 10km to return to a point just 2km from where it started. In a large nature park about 5km northwest of Mettlach (towards Nennig), the best viewing point is Cloef, a 1.7km walk east through the forest from the village of Orscholz.

The Saarschleife is 60km northwest of Saarbrücken along the A620 and A8.

Cologne & Northern Rhineland

POP 17.8 MILLION (NORTH RHINE–WESTPHALIA)

Best Places to Eat

➡ Salon Schmitz (p474)

➡ Altes Gasthaus Leve (p517)

➡ Bistrot B (p474)

➡ Münstermann Kontor (p499)

➡ Holstein's Bistro (p517)

Best Museums

➡ Römisch-Germanisches Museum (p471)

➡ Beethoven-Haus Bonn (p479)

➡ Kunstsammlung Nordrhein-Westfalen (p493)

➡ Museum Folkwang (p507)

➡ Felix-Nussbaum-Haus (p519)

Why Go?

Cologne's iconic Dom has twin towers that might as well be twin exclamation points after the word 'welcome'. Flowing behind the cathedral, the Rhine River provides a vital link for some of the region's highlights: Düsseldorf, with its great nightlife and fabulous shopping, and Bonn, which hums to Beethoven. Away from the river, Aachen still echoes to the beat of the Holy Roman Empire and Charlemagne.

Much of Germany's 20th-century economic might stemmed from the Northern Rhineland industrial region known as the Ruhrgebiet. Now cities such as Essen are transforming old steelworks and coal mines into cultural centres and more, Dortmund is embracing its amazing football record and literally scoring with it, while ancient Münster is a hive of students on bikes day and night, making it endlessly interesting and vibrant.

When to Go

Sure it's cold in December but Cologne's Christmas market will warm you up. Just a couple of months later, the city's Carnival is one of Europe's best. Although the region has plenty of beer gardens and restaurants that delight with warm-weather tables, much of what's best happens indoors so you really can visit at any time. The best reason to come in summer might be for walks along the Rhine, hikes in the Eifel National Park or partying in Münster's parks.

COLOGNE

☏ 0221 / POP 1 MILLION

Cologne (Köln) offers seemingly endless attractions, led by its famous cathedral whose filigree twin spires dominate the skyline. It's regularly voted the country's single most popular tourist attraction. The city's museum landscape is especially strong when it comes to art, but also has something in store for fans of chocolate, sports and even Roman history. Its people are well known for their liberalism and joie de vivre, and it's easy to have a good time right along with them year-round in the beer halls of the Altstadt (old town) or during the springtime Carnival.

Cologne is like a 3D textbook on history and architecture. Drifting about town you'll stumble upon an ancient Roman wall, medieval churches galore, nondescript postwar buildings, avant-garde structures and even a new postmodern quarter right on the Rhine. Germany's fourth-largest city was founded by the Romans in 38 BC and given the lofty name Colonia Claudia Ara Aggripinensium. It grew into a major trading centre, a tradition it solidified in the Middle Ages and continues to uphold today.

◎ Sights

Plan on at least a couple days to explore Cologne's wealth of sights. The city maintains an excellent website (www.museenkoeln.de) with info on most of Cologne's museums. The **MuseumsCard** (per person/family €18/30) includes most of the museums and is good for two consecutive days.

◎ Altstadt

The Altstadt hugs the river bank between two bridges, Hohenzollernbrücke and Deutzer Brücke. You can spend half a day or more just strolling and soaking in it. Cologne's medieval heyday is reflected in its wealth of Romanesque churches, which were constructed between 1150 and 1250, and survived largely intact until WWII. About a dozen have been rebuilt since and offer many unique architectural and artistic features. Even if you're pushed for time, try seeing at least a couple of the ones mentioned here.

See www.romanische-kirchen-koeln.de for good info on all the churches.

★ **Kölner Dom**　　　　　CATHEDRAL
(Cologne Cathedral; ☏ 0211-1794 0200; www.koelner-dom.de; tower adult/concession €4/2; ☺ 6am-9pm May-Oct, to 7.30pm Nov-Apr, tower 9am-6pm May-Sep, to 5pm Mar-Apr & Oct, to 4pm Nov-Feb) Cologne's geographical and spiritual heart – and its single-biggest tourist draw – is the magnificent Kölner Dom. With its soaring twin spires, this is the Mt Everest of cathedrals, jam-packed with art and treasures. For an exercise fix, climb the 533 steps up the Dom's south tower to the base of the steeple that dwarfed all buildings in Europe until Gustave Eiffel built a certain tower in Paris. The underground Domforum visitor centre is a good source of info and tickets.

The Dom is Germany's largest cathedral and must be circled to truly appreciate its dimensions. Note how its lacy spires and flying buttresses create a sensation of lightness and fragility despite its mass and height.

This sensation continues inside, where a phalanx of pillars and arches supports the lofty nave. Soft light filters through the medieval stained-glass windows as well as a much-lauded recent window by contemporary artist Gerhard Richter in the transept. A kaleidoscope of 11,500 squares in 72 colours, Richter's abstract design has been called a 'symphony of light'. In the afternoon especially, when the sun hits it just so, it's easy to understand why.

The *pièce de résistance* among the cathedral's bevy of treasures is the Shrine of the Three Kings behind the main altar, a richly bejewelled and gilded sarcophagus said to hold the remains of the kings who followed the star to the stable in Bethlehem where Jesus was born. The bones were spirited out of Milan in 1164 as spoils of war by Emperor Barbarossa's chancellor and instantly turned Cologne into a major pilgrimage site.

Other highlights include the Gero Crucifix (970), notable for its monumental size and an emotional intensity rarely achieved in those early medieval days; the choir stalls from 1310, richly carved from oak; and the altar painting (c 1450) by Cologne artist Stephan Lochner.

During your climb up to the 95m-high viewing platform, take a breather and admire the 24-tonne Peter Bell (1923), the largest free-swinging working bell in the world.

To get more out of your visit, invest €1 in the information pamphlet or join a **guided tour** (adult/concession €8/6; ☺ tours in English 10.30am & 2.30pm Mon-Sat, 2.30pm Sun Apr-Oct, less often other times).

Construction began in 1248 in the French Gothic style but proceeded slowly and was

Cologne & Northern Rhineland Highlights

1 Feeling your spirits soar as you climb the majestic loftiness of Cologne's **Dom** (cathedral; p463)

2 Losing count of the little glasses of *Kölsch* beer you've drunk at Cologne's **beer halls** (p475)

3 Deciding if Düsseldorf's iconic **Altbier** (p499) is better than Cologne's *Kölsch*

4 Experiencing a 21st-century spin on the industrial age at the **Zollverein coal mine** (p507) in Essen

5 Stepping back to the Middle Ages in **Aachen** (p486), with memories of Charlemagne round every corner

6 Enjoying the vibrant life of **Münster** (p512), where great history combines with youthful pleasures

7 Roaming the beautiful Ahr Valley via the **Rotweinwanderweg** (p484), which links wineries and villages

8 Basking in the ethereal green glow of the native limestone churches in medieval **Soest** (p521)

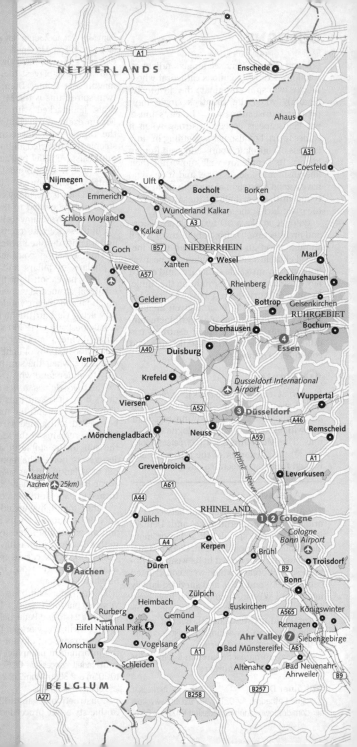

eventually halted in 1560 when funds ran out. The half-built church lingered for nearly 300 years and even suffered a stint as a horse stable and prison when Napoleon occupied the town. A few decades later, a generous cash infusion from Prussian King Friedrich Wilhelm IV finally led to its completion in 1880, 632 years after it started. Luckily, it escaped WWII bombing raids with nary a shrapnel wound and has been a Unesco World Heritage Site since 1996.

➡ **Domschatz-kammer**

(Cathedral Treasury; ☑ 0221-1794 0300; Dom; adult/concession €5/2.50; ⊙ 10am-6pm) Reliquaries, robes, sculptures and liturgical objects are handsomely presented in medieval vaulted rooms below the main floor of the Dom. Standouts include a Gothic bishop's staff from 1322 and a 15th-century sword.

★ **Museum Schnütgen** MUSEUM

(☑ 0221-2212 2310; www.museenkoeln.de; Cäcilienstrasse 29; adult/concession €6/3.50; ⊙ 10am-6pm Tue-Sun, to 8pm Thu) East of the Neumarkt, the Cultural Quarter encompasses the Museum Schnütgen, a repository of medieval religious art and sculpture. Part of the exhibit shows the beautiful setting of the Romanesque Cäcilienkirche (Cecily Church). Also part of the atrium complex is the Rautenstrauch-Joest-Museum.

Schokoladenmuseum MUSEUM

(Chocolate Museum; ☑ 0221-931 8880; www.schokoladenmuseum.de; Am Schokoladenmuseum 1a; adult/concession €9/6.50; ⊙ 10am-6pm Tue-Fri, 11am-7pm Sat & Sun, last entry 1hr before closing; ⚑) At this high-tech temple to the art of chocolate-making, exhibits on the origin of the 'elixir of the gods', as the Aztecs called it, and the cocoa-growing process are followed by a live-production factory tour and a stop at a chocolate fountain for a sample.

Upstairs are departments on the cultural history of chocolate, advertising, and porcelain and other accessories. Stock up on your favourite flavours at the downstairs shop.

Deutsches Sport & Olympia Museum MUSEUM

(German Sport & Olympic Games Museum; ☑ 0221-336 090; Im Zollhafen 1; adult/concession €6/3; ⊙ 10am-6pm Tue-Fri, 11am-7pm Sat & Sun) In a 19th-century customs building, the Deutsches Sport & Olympia Museum is an imaginative Germany-focused tribute to the sporting life from antiquity to today. There are exhibits on the 1936 Berlin and 1972 Munich Olympic Games and on such modern-day heroes as Steffi Graf and Michael Schumacher. Interactive displays allow you to experience a bobsled run or a bike race, and on the miniature football field on the rooftop you can kick with a view of the cathedral.

NS Dokumentationszentrum MUSEUM

(☑ 0221-2212 6332; www.museenkoeln.de; Appellhofplatz 23-25; adult/concession €4.50/2; ⊙ 10am-6pm Tue-Fri, 11am-6pm Sat & Sun) Cologne's Third Reich history is poignantly documented in the NS Documentation Centre. In the basement of this otherwise mundane-looking building was the local Gestapo prison where scores of people were interrogated, tortured and killed. Inscriptions on the basement cell walls offer a gut-wrenching record of the emotional and physical pain endured by inmates. Executions often occurred in the courtyard.

Kölnisches Stadtmuseum MUSEUM

(Cologne City Museum; ☑ 0221-2212 2398; www.museenkoeln.de; Zeughausstrasse 1-3; adult/concession €5/3; ⊙ 10am-8pm Tue, to 5pm Wed-Sun) The Kölnisches Stadtmuseum, in the former medieval armoury, explores all facets of Cologne history. There are exhibits on Carnival, *Kölsch*, eau de cologne and other things that make the city unique. A huge and amazing model re-creates the city in 1571 and is minutely detailed.

Kolumba MUSEUM

(☑ 0221-933 1930; www.kolumba.de; Kolumbastrasse 4; adult/child €5/free; ⊙ noon-5pm Wed-Mon) Art, history, architecture and spirituality form a harmonious tapestry in this spectacular collection of religious treasures of the Archdiocese of Cologne. Called Kolumba, the building encases the ruins of the late-Gothic church of St Kolumba, its layers of foundations going back to Roman times and the Madonna in the Ruins chapel, built on the site in 1950. Exhibits span the arc of religious artistry from the early days of Christianity to the present. Don't miss the 12th-century carved ivory crucifix.

Other exhibits include Coptic textiles, Gothic reliquaries and medieval painting juxtaposed with works by Bauhaus legend Andor Weininger in edgy room installations.

The museum is yet another magnificent design by Swiss architect Peter Zumthor, 2009 winner of the Pritzker Prize, the 'architectural Oscar'.

Museum Ludwig
MUSEUM

(☑0221-2212 6165; www.museum-ludwig.de; Heinrich-Böll-Platz; adult/concession €11/7.50, more during special exhibits; ⊘10am-6pm Tue-Sun) A mecca of contemporary art, Museum Ludwig presents a tantalising mix of works from all major phases. Fans of German expressionism (Beckmann, Dix, Kirchner) will get their fill here as much as those with a penchant for Picasso, American pop art (Warhol, Lichtenstein) and Russian avant-garde painter Alexander Rodchenko. Rothko and Pollock are highlights of the abstract collection, while Gursky and Tillmanns are among the reasons the photography section is a must stop.

Wallraf-Richartz-Museum & Fondation Corboud
MUSEUM

(☑0221-2212 1119; www.wallraf.museum; Obenmarspforten; adult/concession €8/4.50; ⊘10am-6pm Tue-Sun, to 9pm Thu) A famous collection of European paintings from the 13th to the 19th centuries, the Wallraf-Richartz-Museum occupies a postmodern cube designed by the late OM Ungers. Works are presented chronologically, with the oldest on the 1st floor where standouts include brilliant examples from the Cologne School, known for its distinctive use of colour. The most famous painting is Stefan Lochner's *Madonna of the Rose Bower*.

Upstairs are Dutch and Flemish artists, including Rembrandt and Rubens, Italians such as Canaletto and Spaniards such as Murillo. The top floor shines the spotlight on the 19th century with Germany's largest collection of impressionist paintings, including masterpieces by Monet, Van Gogh, Cezanne, Gauguin and all the other heavy hitters of the genre.

Rautenstrauch-Joest-Museum
MUSEUM

(Cultures of the World Museum; ☑0221-2213 1356; www.museenkoeln.de; Cacilienstrasse 29-33; adult/concession €6/3.50; ⊘10am-6pm Tue-Sun, to 8pm Thu) This museum boldly makes a statement with a huge rice boat from Sulawesi that fills the lobby. Over three floors there are exhibits on the cultures of the world; fear not about getting your knuckles rapped – these are interactive and you're encouraged to touch.

Gross St Martin
CHURCH

(☑0221-1642 5650; An Gross-St-Martin 9; ⊘8.30am-7.30pm Tue-Sat, 1-7pm Sun) Winning top honours for Cologne's most handsome exterior is Gross St Martin, whose ensemble of four slender turrets grouped around a central spire towers above Fischmarkt in

COLOGNE'S LOVE LOCKS

A blight to some, an ode to eternal romance to others, Cologne was one of the first European cities to be festooned with love locks, each engraved with some romantic slogan, proclamation of love or simply the names of people meant to be locked together for the ages. What at first looks like modern art on Cologne's iconic **Hohenzollernbrücke** railway bridge over the Rhine are in reality tens of thousands of locks in myriad shapes and colours. (Unlike Paris, Cologne has made no effort to halt the practice.)

On sunny weekends, you'll see people engaging in rituals grand and humble as they affix new locks to the railings and – inevitably – you might catch a delocking ceremony, whereby evidence of someone's now unpermanent love is removed and usually tossed in the drink, followed by much of the same.

the Altstadt. Dating from the 12th century, its location was once an island in the Rhine.

St Maria im Kapitol
CHURCH

(☑0221-214 615; Marienplatz 19; ⊘10am-6pm Mon-Sat, noon-6pm Sun) The striking clover-leaf choir is an architectural feature pioneered at this 11th-century Romanesque church, where major treasures include a carved door and a spectacularly ornate Renaissance rood screen.

Museum für Angewandte Kunst
MUSEUM

(Museum of Applied Arts; ☑0221-2212 3860; www.makk.de; An der Rechtschule; adult/concession €6/3.50; ⊘11am-5pm Tue-Sun) The Museum für Angewandte Kunst consists of a series of period rooms tracing European design from the Middle Ages to today. Keep an eye out for a 15th-century Venetian wedding goblet, a silver service by Henry van de Velde and life-sized animals made of Meissen porcelain.

Käthe Kollwitz Museum
MUSEUM

(☑0221-227 2899; www.kollwitz.de; Neumarkt 18-24; adult/concession €4/2; ⊘10am-6pm Tue-Fri, 11am-6pm Sat & Sun) The Käthe Kollwitz Museum has graphics and sculptures by the acclaimed socialist artist. A highlight is the haunting cycle called *Ein Weberaufstand* (A Weavers' Revolt, 1897). Enter through an arcade, then take the glass-walled lift to the 4th floor.

Cologne

A **B** **C** **D**

1

Brüsseler Str

Christophstr/Mediapark ⓤ

Schmaliestr

ⓤ **Hans-Böckler-Platz/Bf West**

Probstgasse

19 ✚

2

Hildebold-platz

Gereonshof

Gereonsdriesch

Steinfelder Gasse

Mohrenstr

🍴 **59** Bismarckstr

Venloer Str

Au dem Berlich

Friesenplatz 🍴 **55**

17 ❗

Am Römerturn

Underground (1.8km)

Brüsseler Str

Antwerpener Str

Friesen-platz

ⓤ **Friesenstr**

43 ✕ **45** ✕

Helenenstr

St-Apern Str

3

46 ✕

BELGISCHES VIERTEL

Hohenzollernring

Friesenwall

Brüsseler Platz

Maastrichter Str

Ehrenstr

Gertrudenstr

Richmodstr

Wolfstr

Lütticher Str

Flandrische Str

51 🍴

4

Mittelstr

Mittelstr

65 🛏 **9** 🏛

Aachener Str

44 ✕ Hahnenstr

Pfeilstr

Neumarkt

Moltkestr

58 🍴

ⓤ **Rudolfplatz**

Rudolf-platz

Cäcilienstr

33 🍴

Richard-Wagner-Str

Handelstr

5

29 🍴

Engelbertstr

Schaafenstr

54 🍴

Mauritiussteinweg

Clemensstr

Jülicher Str

30 🍴

ZÜLPICHER VIERTEL

Rubenstr

Bayardsgasse

32 🍴

Mozartstr

Mauritiuswall

Thieboldsgasse

Lindenstr

Roonstr

6

Kleiner Griechenmarkt

Rathenau-platz

47 🍴

39 ✕

Görresstr

Zülpicher Platz

Friedrichstr

Rothgerberbach

40 ✕

Hohenstaufenring

7

Dasselstr

Zülpicher Str

Hochstadenstr

36 ✕

Barbarossa-platz

41 ✕

A **B** **C** **D**

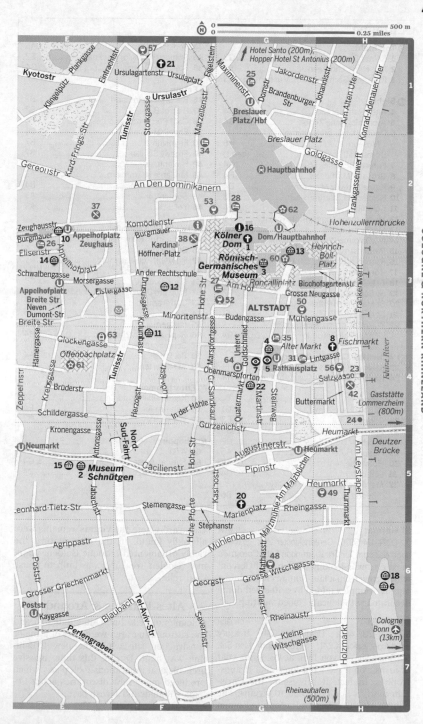

Cologne

St Gereon CHURCH
(☑ 0221-474 5070; Gereonskloster 2-4; ◷ 10am-noon & 3-5pm Tue-Fri, 10am-noon Sat) Cologne's most eccentric-looking church is St Gereon, which grew from a late-Roman chapel into a massive complex lidded by a 10-sided dome decorated with delicate ribbed vaulting.

St Ursula CHURCH
(☑ 0221-133 400; Ursulaplatz 24; treasury adult/concession €2/1; ◷ 10am-6pm Mon-Sat, 3-4.30pm Sun) If you look at Cologne's coat of arms, you'll see what looks like 11 apostrophes. In fact, it represents the Christian martyrs St Ursula and 10 virgins. The church of St Ursula stands atop the Roman graveyard where the virgins' remains were allegedly found. In the 17th century, the richly ornamented baroque Goldene Kammer (Golden Treasury) was built to house their relics.

◎ Altes Rathaus & Around

Cologne's old city hall (Altes Rathaus) and the surrounding area were part of a major construction site while the new U-Bahn line was built. During this time, massive archeological excavations took place, which produced many new discoveries about Cologne's Roman and Jewish past.

★ **Römisch-Germanisches Museum** MUSEUM
(Roman Germanic Museum; ☑ 0221-2212 4438; www.museenkoeln.de; Roncalliplatz 4; adult/concession €9/5; ⊙ 10am-5pm Tue-Sun) Sculptures and ruins displayed outside the entrance are merely the overture to a full symphony of Roman artefacts found along the Rhine. Highlights include the giant Poblicius tomb (AD 30–40), the magnificent 3rd-century Dionysus mosaic, and astonishingly well-preserved glass items. Insight into daily Roman life is gained from toys, tweezers, lamps and jewellery, the designs of which have changed surprisingly little since Roman times.

Plenty of remnants of the Roman city survive around the museum, including a street leading to the harbour and two wells. Other vestiges from the ancient settlement include a **Roman arch** from the former town wall outside the Dom and the **Römerturm**, a tower standing among buildings at the corner of St-Apern-Strasse and Zeughausstrasse.

Altes Rathaus HISTORIC BUILDING
(Rathausplatz; ⊙ 8am-4pm Mon & Wed-Thu, to 6pm Tue) **FREE** Dating from the 15th century and much restored, the old city hall has fine bells that ring daily at noon and 5pm. The Gothic tower is festooned with statues of old city notables, and the plaza out front is popular with wedding parties.

Future Jüdisches Museum HISTORIC SITE
(Jewish Museum; www.museenkoeln.de; Rathausplatz) Cologne had a large Jewish population in the 12th and 13th centuries, and the foundations of a large neighbourhood have been uncovered as part of the new U-Bahn line construction, which included improvements to the Roman Praetorium site and exhibit in the same area. A new Jewish museum based on these discoveries is set to rise behind the Rathaus, with work begun in 2012 but unlikely to be completed until at least 2017. In the meantime, at times the subterranean parts of a medieval synagogue here are open to the public. Visit the work site for more details.

Archäologische Zone HISTORIC SITE
(Archeology Zone; ☑ 0221-2213 3422; Kleine Budengasse 2; adult/concession €3.50/3; ⊙ 10am-5pm Tue-Sun) Cologne used the construction of the U-Bahn line to also build this grand new museum, which is located under the Rathausplatz and fully encompasses two ma-

jor parts of the city history. At the deepest level is the Praetorium, which has relics of a Roman governor's palace. One level up you'll find relics from the Jewish community that was here in the Middle Ages, including a *mikveh* (community bath). Although work is ongoing, there is usually some access to the site.

◉ **Brüsseler Platz**
The heart of the ever-so-lively-and-trendy Belgisches Viertel neighbourhood, Brüsseler Platz is a lush square surrounding **St Michael's Church**. Locals play chess, make out, sip a beer or catch up on the gossip. It's a good place for a picnic from one of the many ethnic markets on the surrounding streets.

🏌 **Activities**
Cologne's dense network of bike routes along the Rhine and throughout the city make it a fine place to cycle. Pick up a bike map at the tourist office.

★ **Radstation** BICYCLE RENTAL, TOURS
(☑ 0221-139 7190; www.radstationkoeln.de; Breslauerplatz, Hauptbahnhof; per 3hr/day €5/10; ⊙ 5.30am-10.30pm Mon-Fri, 6.30am-8pm Sat, 8am-8pm Sun) Bike rental place under the train station. It also offers excellent three-hour **tours** (Marksmann-gasse; tours €17.50; ⊙ 1.30pm Apr-Oct) in English that start from a small stand in the Altstadt on the Rhine near the Deutzer Brücke.

👉 **Tours**
For an excellent DIY 2km walking tour, start at the Dom and walk down to the river, turn south and head to the bridge over the Rhine River, the Deutzer Brücke. Cross east, watching the boat traffic below. On the east bank, follow the river promenade north, soaking up the sweeping view of the Cologne skyline across the water. Take the pedestrian path along the busy side of the Hohenzollernbrücke, the busy railway bridge, back west across the Rhine. All manner of trains will pound past you, just a few metres away, before the return walk to the Dom.

KD River Cruises BOAT TOUR
(☑ 0221-258 3011; www.k-d.com; Frankenwerft 35; adult/concession €10/6; ⊙ 10.30am-5pm Apr-Oct) One of several companies offering one-hour spins taking in the splendid Altstadt

panorama; other options include brunch and sunset cruises.

✨ Festivals & Events

★ Karneval
PARADE

(Carnival; www.koelnerkarneval.de; ⊙ usually Feb) Cologne's Carnival is one of Europe's most raucous. There are myriad events, parades and parties before everything comes to a halt on Ash Wednesday.

Christopher Street Day
GAY & LESBIAN

(www.colognepride.de; ⊙ early Jul) More than a million people descend on Cologne for one of the top LGBT pride events in Europe.

🛏 Sleeping

Cologne often hosts trade shows, which can cause hotel rates to double and triple. Otherwise, you'll find good-value options across the walkable central area.

Meininger Hotel Cologne City Center
HOSTEL, HOTEL €

(☑ 0221-9976 0965; www.meininger-hotels.com; Engelbertstrasse 33-35; dm/s/d from €20/50/80; @ 🛜) In a former hotel, this flashpacker hostel and hotel in the cool Zülpicher Viertel is loaded with retro appeal. The 52 modern rooms feature lockers, reading lamps, a small TV and

---

HARBOUR REDUX:
....

London has its Docklands, Düsseldorf its Medienhafen, Hamburg is building HafenCity and now Cologne has joined the revitalised-harbour trend with the Rheinauhafen. South of the Altstadt, this urban quarter has sprung up along a 2km stretch between the Severinsbrücke and Südbrücke bridges. Dozens of 19th-century brick buildings have second lives as office, living and entertainment spaces, juxtaposed with contemporary designs ranging from bland to avant-garde. The most dramatic change to Cologne's skyline comes courtesy of a trio of Kranhäuser (Crane Houses), huge inverted L-shaped structures that are an abstract interpretation of historic harbour cranes. There are some shops, restaurants and cafes as well as a riverside promenade but, as with all projects of this type, it'll be a while before the quarter's true character and personality make it a compelling place to visit.

---

private bathrooms. Freebies include linen and towels in the dorms. It's got six floors served by one lift and you can rent a bike.

Pension Otto
PENSION €

(☑ 0157-8595 2825; www.pensionotto.de; Pension Otto Richard-Wagner-Strasse 18; s/d from €50/70) This pension occupies the 1st floor of a beautiful 100-year-old apartment building in the heart of the Belgisches Viertel. The five rooms have terrazzo floors and shared bathrooms. There's no TV but you might just enjoy pondering the elaborate wall tiles. This is excellent-value, basic accommodation.

Station Hostel for Backpackers
HOSTEL €

(☑ 0221-912 5301; www.hostel-cologne.de; Marzellenstrasse 44-56; dm €17-20, s/d from €32/50; @ 🛜) Near the Hauptbahnhof, this is a hostel as hostels should be: central, convivial and economical. A lounge gives way to clean, colourful rooms sleeping one to six people. There's lots of free stuff, including linen, internet access, lockers, city maps and guest kitchen. Some private rooms have their own bathrooms.

★ Hopper Hotel et cetera
HOTEL €€

(☑ 0221-924 400; www.hopper.de; Brüsseler Strasse 26; s/d from €80/110; 🅿 @ 🛜) A waxen monk welcomes you to this former monastery whose 49 rooms sport eucalyptus floors, cherry furniture and marble baths along with lots of useful features like fridges. The sauna and bar, both in the vaulted cellars, are great places for reliving the day's exploits. The cheapest singles are dubbed 'monastic cells'.

Cerano Hotel
HOTEL €€

(☑ 0221 925 7300; www.cerano-hotels.de; Elisenstrasse 16; s/d from €70/80; 🛜) This unassuming five-storey hotel is a short walk from the train station and is peppered with extra touches: mineral water, juices and more apples than you'd find in an orchard. Many of the rooms have large work desks and windows that provide natural light. The staff are helpful, there's a lift and the breakfast is very good.

Appartel am Dom
HOTEL €€

(☑ 0221 160 780; www.appartelamdom.de; Allerheiligenstrasse 2; s/d from €70/80; 🛜) A real find about two minutes' walk from the train station, this welcoming hotel offers large and very comfortable rooms. There's a lift and some rooms have balconies and Dom

FOOLS, FLOATS & REVELRY

Carnival in Cologne is one of the best parties in Europe and a thumb in the eye of the German work ethic. Every year at the onset of Lent (late February/early March), a year of painstaking preparation culminates in the 'three crazy days' – actually more like six.

It all starts with *Weiberfastnacht,* the Thursday before Ash Wednesday, when women rule the day (and do things like chop off the ties of their male colleagues/bosses). The party continues through the weekend, with more than 50 parades of ingenious floats and wildly dressed lunatics dancing in the streets. By the time it all comes to a head with the big parade on *Rosenmontag* (Rose Monday), the entire city has come unglued. Those still capable of swaying and singing will live it up one last time on Shrove Tuesday before the curtain comes down on Ash Wednesday.

'If you were at the parade and saw the parade, you weren't at the parade,' say the people of Cologne in their inimitable way. Translated, this means that you should be far too busy singing, drinking, roaring the Carnival greeting '*Alaaf!*' and planting a quick *Bützchen* (kiss) on the cheek of whoever strikes your fancy, to notice anything happening around you. Swaying and drinking while crammed like sardines in a pub, or following other costumed fools behind a huge bass drum leading to God-only-knows-where, you'll be swept up in one of the greatest parties the world knows.

views. All rooms have fridges, and some have small cooking areas with sinks and microwaves.

Hotel Chelsea HOTEL €€
(☑0221-207 150; www.hotel-chelsea.de; Jülicher Strasse 1; s/d from €65/80; P❄@☎) Those fancying an artsy vibe will be well sheltered in this self-proclaimed 'hotel different'. Originals created by international artists in exchange for lodging grace the public areas and 38 rooms and suites. The eye-catching deconstructivist rooftop extension houses a penthouse. The cafe is excellent.

Hopper Hotel St Antonius HOTEL €€
(☑0221-166 00; www.hopper.de; Dagobertstrasse 32; s/d from €90/125; P❄@☎; U-BahnEbertplatz) History and high-tech mix nicely at this 54-room posh retreat with plenty of eye candy for the style-conscious. The romantic courtyard garden and small spa in the brick-vaulted cellar are great bliss-out spots. It's handy to the Hauptbahnhof.

Lint Hotel HOTEL €€
(☑0221-920 550; www.lint-hotel.de; Lintgasse 7; s/d from €90/100; ☎) This cute, contemporary and intimate hotel in the heart of the Altstadt has 18 rooms with hardwood floors, warm colours and lots of wood. The generous breakfast buffet should tide you through the afternoon.

Stern am Rathaus HOTEL €€
(☑0221-2225 1750; www.stern-am-rathaus.de; Bürgerstrasse 6; s/d from €80/100; ☎) This small, contemporary hotel has eight nice-

ly spruced up, luxuriously panelled rooms spread over three floors. It's in a quiet side street smack dab in the Altstadt yet close to sights and plenty of restaurants. Kudos for the extra-comfortable beds, the personalised service and the high-quality breakfast buffet.

Excelsior Hotel Ernst HOTEL €€€
(☑0221-2701; www.excelsiorhotelernst.com; Trankgasse 1-5; s/d from €180/200; ❄@☎) Luxury is taken very seriously at this traditional hotel with a pedigree going back to 1863. Some of the plushly furnished rooms overlook the majestic Cologne cathedral. If that doesn't wow you enough, perhaps a meal at the Michelin-starred restaurant will.

Dom Hotel LUXURY HOTEL €€€
(☑0221-202 4250; www.domhotel.com; Domkloster 2a; r from €250; ❄@☎) This temple to overnight stays is right on the plaza with Cologne's iconic cathedral. Built in 1857, it has had numerous renovations through the years. However, the most recent will transform the hotel into the epitome of modern luxury when it reopens in 2017. New rooftop venues will have magnificent views.

✗ Eating

Cologne's multiculturalism lets you take a culinary journey around the world. The Belgisches Viertel and streets in and around Zülpicher Platz and Ehrenstrasse are ideal areas for making a tasty discovery.

Cologne's unmissable beer halls (p475) offer not only the local brew but also excellent meals at good prices. And be sure to sample some of Cologne's *Schwarzbrot* (black bread), which many claim is Germany's best.

Engelbät
EUROPEAN €

(☑ 0221-246 914; www.engelbaet.de; Engelbertstrasse 7; crepes €5-8.50; ⊗11am-1am) 🖋 This cosy restaurant-pub is famous for its habit-forming crepes, which come in 40 varieties – sweet, meat or vegetarian. Also popular for weekend breakfast (served until 3pm). Outside of summer, there's often live jazz at night. The sidewalk tables are popular.

Madame Miammmiam
BAKERY €

(☑ 0221-271 9242; madamemiammmiam.de; Antwerpener Strasse 39; treats from €3; ⊗11am-6.30pm Tue-Thu, to 7pm Fri & Sat, 1-5pm Sun) A luscious and spunky bakery that captures the Belgisches Viertal vibe, come here for amazing cupcakes, tarts, cookies and more. Then repair to Brüsseler Platz to enjoy.

Freddy Schilling
BURGERS €

(☑ 0221-1695 5515; www.freddyschilling.de; Kyffhäuserstrasse 34; burgers €6-10; ⊗noon-11pm Sun-Tue, to 11pm Fri & Sat) A wholewheat bun provides a solid framework for the moist patties made with beef from happy cows and drizzled with Freddy's homemade 'special' sauce. Pair it with a side of Rosi's: small butter-and-rosemary tossed potatoes.

★ Salon Schmitz
MODERN EUROPEAN €€

(☑ 0221-9229 9594; www.salonschmitz.com; Aachener Strasse 28; mains from €10; ⊗9am-late, hours vary by venue) Spread over three historic row houses, the Schmitz empire is your one-stop for excellent food and drink. From the casual bistro to excellent seasonal meals in the restaurant to the takeaway deli, you'll find something you like at Schmitz almost any time of day. Wash it all down with the house-brand *Kölsch*.

No matter whether you prefer sidling up to the long bar or grabbing a comfy sofa in the retro lounge, Schmitz is a perfect pitstop for relaxed chats over coffee, cocktails or creative bar meals. There are plenty of tables outside.

★ Bei Oma Kleinmann
GERMAN €€

(☑ 0221-232 346; www.beiomakleinmann.de; Zülpicher Strasse 9; mains €13-21; ⊗5pm-midnight Tue-Thu & Sun, to 1am Fri & Sat) Named for its long-time owner, who was still cooking almost to her last day at age 95 in 2009, this perennially booked, grafitti-covered restaurant serves oodles of schnitzel, made either with pork or veal and paired with homemade sauces and sides. Pull up a seat at the

small wooden tables for a classic Cologne night out.

Gaststätte Lommerzheim
GERMAN €€

(☑ 0221-814 392; Siegesstrasse 18; mains €11-20; ⊗11am-2.30pm & 4.30pm-late) The best reason to wander east across the Hohenzollernbrücke railway bridge over the Rhine is this delightfully old-school pub serving some of the finest pork chops around. Just tell the waiter what sides you want (fries, potato salad etc), then quaff some beer while you wait for your thick, juicy chop.

Feynsinn
INTERNATIONAL €€

(☑ 0221-240 9210; www.cafe-feynsinn.de; Rathenauplatz 7; mains €7-20; ⊗9am-late) 🖋 This well-respected Zülpicher Viertel restaurant weaves organic seasonal ingredients into sharp-flavoured dishes. The owners raise their own meat. Get a table overlooking the park for a meal or just a drink.

Café Reichard
CAFE €€

(☑ 0221-257 8542; www.cafe-reichard.de; Unter Fettenhennen 11; mains €6-16; ⊗8.30am-8pm) There are plenty of cafes around the Dom, but this slightly hidden one is a true luxe gem. Cologne grannies have been bringing there granddaughters here for luscious cakes and treats for generations. Great people-watching from the terrace tables.

Yo!
INTERNATIONAL €€

(☑ 0221-1706 5617; Neue Maastrichter Strasse 2; mains €8-16; ⊗9am-1am) Mismatched chairs set the vibe at this Belgisches Viertel 1960s throwback. Huge candles add to the atmosphere while the views from the sidewalk tables add interest. The food has global inspirations and there are lots of specials. Think lots of whole grains and fresh veggies.

Haxenhaus
GERMAN €€

(☑ 0221-947 2400; www.haxenhaus.de; Frankenwerft 19; mains €10-20; ⊗11am-midnight) While the Altstadt has no shortage of mediocre restaurants aimed at beer-swilling tourists, this old place stands out for serving up classic German fare (eight kinds of *haxe* – meat knuckles). Patio tables have river views.

★ Bistrot B
EUROPEAN €€€

(☑ 0221-1398 6777; www.lapoeledor.de; Komödienstrasse 50; menus from €31; ⊗noon-2pm & 5-10pm Tue-Sat) Classic French cooking by chef Jean-Claude Bado stars at this prim little bistro that's one of Cologne's most popular restaurants. The dishes are inventive, seasonal and remarkably good value given the talents at

DON'T MISS

KÖLSCH BEER & BEER HALLS

Cologne has a its own style of beer, *Kölsch*, which is unlike any other in Germany. It's light, hoppy and slightly sweet, always crisp, and served cool. Unlike the vast steins used elsewhere for suds serving, in Cologne your *Kölsch* comes in *stangen*: skinny, straight glasses that only hold 0.2L.

In traditional Cologne beer halls and pubs you don't order beer so much as subscribe. The constantly prowling waiters will keep dropping off the little glasses of beer until you indicate you've had enough by placing a beer mat on top of your glass.

A ceaseless flow of *stangen* filled with *Kölsch*, coupled with earthy humour and platters of meaty local foods, are the hallmarks of Cologne's iconic beer halls. Look for the days when each place serves glorious potato pancakes (*Kartoffelpuffer* or *Reibekuchen* in local dialect).

Päffgen (0221-135 461; www.paeffgen-koelsch.de; Friesenstrasse 64-66; mains €6-20; ⊘10am-midnight Sun-Thu, to 12.30am Fri & Sat) Busy, loud and boisterous, Päffgen has been pouring *Kölsch* since 1883 and hasn't lost a step since. In summer you can enjoy the refreshing brew and local specialities (€1.10 to €10.70) beneath starry skies in the beer garden.

Potato pancakes are served on Tuesdays from September to April.

Brauhaus Peters (0221-257 3950; www.peters-brauhaus.de; Mühlengasse 1; mains €6-18; ⊘11am-12.30am) This beautifully restored 19th-century pub draws a crowd knocking back their *Kölsch* in a web of highly individualistic nooks, including a room lidded by a kaleidoscopic stained-glass ceiling. On Tuesday, insiders invade for the freshly made potato pancakes. The wood carving over the main entrance translates as: 'Hops and malt, God preserves'. Outside tables abound.

Früh am Dom (0221-261 3215; www.frueh-am-dom.de; Am Hof 12-18; mains €4-20; ⊘8am-midnight) This warren of a beer hall near the Dom epitomises Cologne earthiness. Tuck into hearty meals amid loads of knick-knacks or out on the flower-filled terrace next to a fountain. It's also known for plate-covering breakfasts. Imbibe on the terrace or in the echoey basement.

Schreckenskammer (0221-132 581; www.schreckenskammer.com; Ursula-gartenstrasse 11; mains €7-17; ⊘11am-1.45pm & 4.30-10.30pm Mon-Sat) Empty chairs are a rare sight at this locals' favourite. There's a fine beer garden, excellent food, and should you need divine inspiration for just one more *stangen*, Romanesque St Ursula is just across the square.

Brauerei Zur Malzmühle (0221-210 117; www.muehlenkoelsch.de; Heumarkt 6; mains €6-16; ⊘10am-midnight) Expect plenty of local colour at this convivial beer hall off the beaten tourist track. It brews *Kölsch* with organic ingredients and is also known for its lighter *Malzbier* (malt beer, 2% alcohol).

Gaffel am Dom (0221-913 9260; www.gaffelamdom.de; Bahnhofsvorplatz 1; mains €5-15; ⊘11.30am-late) Right in the shadow of the Dom, this otherwise standard-issue Cologne beer hall is notable for one reason: they serve the city's best potato pancakes every day of the week.

work in the kitchen. Bentwood chairs add curvaceous charm to the simple dining room.

Sorgenfrei MODERN EUROPEAN €€€
(0221-355 7327; www.sorgenfrei-koeln.com; Antwerpener Strasse 15; mains €17-35, 2-course lunch €17, 3-/4-course dinner €35/43; ⊘noon-3pm Mon-Fri, 6pm-midnight Mon-Sat) A huge wine-by-the-glass menu is but one draw of this Belgische Viertel fine-dining treasure. Dishes are prepared with the same attention to detail yet

lack of pretension found throughout this small restaurant. Hardwood floors encourage a casual vibe that goes well with salads and simple mains at lunch and more complex creations for dinner.

 Drinking & Nightlife

Cologne's thirst parlours range from grungy to grand. Centres of action include the Altstadt, the student flavoured Zülpicher

Viertel and the more grown-up Belgisches Viertel, zinging bar and pub quarters.

★ **Biergarten Rathenauplatz**   BEER GARDEN
(☎0221-801 7349; www.rathenauplatz.de; Rathenauplatz; ⊙noon-11pm Apr-Oct) A large, leafy park has one of Cologne's best places for a drink: a community-run beer garden. Tables sprawl under huge, old trees, while simple snacks such as salads and very good *frikadelle* (spiced hamburger) issue forth from a cute little hut. Prices are cheap; beers come from nearby Hellers Brewery – try the organic lager. Proceeds help maintain the park.

★ **Stadtgarten**   CLUB
(☎0221-952 9940; www.stadtgarten.de; Venloer Strasse 40; ⊙hours vary) Surrounded by a small park, this Belgisches Viertel favourite hosts vibrant dance parties and live jazz, soul and world music concerts in its cellar hall, but is also a great spot for a drink (in the summer beer garden).

Gebäude 9   CLUB
(☎0221-814 637; www.gebaeude9.de; Deutz-Mülheimer Strasse 127-129) This ex-factory is an essential indie-rock concert venue in town. DJs take over at other times, and there's also an eclectic program of nonmainstream plays and films. Take tram 3 or 4 to KölnMesse/Osthallen.

Papa Joe's Jazzlokal   LOUNGE
(☎0221-257 7931; www.papajoes.de; Buttermarkt 37; ⊙8pm-3am) Jazz riffs nightly in this museumlike place where the smoky brown walls are strewn with yesteryear's photographs. There really is a Joe and he is a true jazz lover. There's a second, less intimate location, Papa Joe's Klimperkasten, on Alter Markt.

GAY & LESBIAN COLOGNE

Next to Berlin, Cologne is Germany's most gay-and-lesbian-friendly city. The rainbow flag flies especially proudly in the so-called 'Bermuda Triangle' around Rudolfplatz, which explodes into a non-stop party zone at weekends. Another major romping ground is the Heumarkt area (especially Pipinstrasse), which draws more sedate folks and leather and fetish lovers. **Cologne Pride** in June basically serves as a warm-up for the Christopher Street Day (p472), which brings more than a million people to Cologne.

Six Pack   BAR
(☎0221 254 587; Aachener Strasse 33; ⊙8pm-5am) This is a must-stop on any Belgisches Viertel pub crawl. Pass through the battered door, belly up to the super-long bar and pick from several dozen varieties of beer, all served by the bottle from a giant fridge. It gets seriously jammed after midnight.

Capri Lounge   COCKTAIL BAR
(☎0221-820 3360; www.capri-lounge.com; Benesisstrasse 61; ⊙8pm 3am Tue-Sat) High style mixes well here – as do the cocktails. The tiled bar is a work of art but you may want to stay outside enjoying some of Cologne's best people-watching. There are several all-day cafes with terraces nearby.

Blue Lounge   CLUB
(☎0221-271 7117; http://blue-lounge.com; Mathiasstrasse 4-6; ⊙from 9pm Wed-Sun) A smooth dance and cocktail bar with a crowd as mixed as the music: house, Latin, pop, current hits, blues, disco and more.

Ixbar   CLUB
(☎0221-6777 0578; www.i-like-x.de; Mauritiuswall 84) Hard driving music bar with top DJs.

Underground   CLUB
(☎0221-542 326; www.underground-cologne.de; Vogelsanger Strasse 200; ⊙7pm-late Mon & Wed-Sat) This complex combines a pub and two concert halls where indie and alternative rock bands hold forth several times a week. Otherwise, it's party time with different music nightly (no cover and cheap drinks keep the crowd young). There's a beer garden in summer. To get here, take U3 or U4 to Venloer Strasse/Gürtel.

Club Bahnhof Ehrenfeld   CLUB
(http://cbe-cologne.de; Bartholomäus-Schink-Strasse 65/67) As legendary as it is sweaty, this vast club packs in hundreds of partiers into a space under train tracks. Hip hop, jazz and house are just some of the eclectic line-up. Locals love to slum it here long after they claim to have outgrown it. Take U3 or U4 to Venloer Strasse/Gürtel.

☆ **Entertainment**

Major listings are in *Kölner Illustrierte* (mainstream, www.koelner.de) and *StadtRevue* (alternative, www.stadtrevue.de). Buy tickets at www.koelnticket.de.

Kölner Philharmonie   CLASSICAL MUSIC
(☎0221-280 280; www.koelner-philharmonie.de; Bischofsgartenstrasse 1) The famous Kölner

Philharmoniker is the 'house band' in this grand, modern concert hall below the Museum Ludwig.

Schauspiel THEATRE
(☑ 0221-2212 8400; www.buehnenkoeln.de; Offenbachplatz) Repertory theatre based at the Schauspiel, in the same massively remodeled complex as the Opernhaus (opera). The box office for both is in the Opernhaus foyer.

🛍 Shopping

Cologne is a good place to shop, with eccentric boutiques, designer and vintage stores, plus the usual selection of chain and department stores. And of course there are classic outlets for its namesake smelly stuff.

Hohe Strasse is one of Germany's oldest pedestrianised shopping strips, and along with its side street In der Höhle, it's where you'll find all the mainstream chains and department stores. Smaller fashion and shoe shops culminate in Schildergasse in the Neumarkt, where the Neumarkt-Galerie mall is easily recognised by the upturned ice-cream cone on the roof, designed by Claes Oldenburg and Coosje van Brugge.

Mittelstrasse and Pfeilstrasse are lined with exclusive fashion, jewellery and home-accessory shops, while Ehrenstrasse is easily Cologne's most creative strip, with designer boutiques mixing with more offbeat fare. Funky music shops, vintage clothing dealers and the-next-hot-desginer-shops are scattered about the streets near Belgisches Viertel and Brüsseler Platz.

4711 PERFUME
(☑ 0221-2709 9910; www.4711.com; cnr Glockengasse & Schwertnergasse; ⊗ 9.30am-6.30pm Mon-Fri, to 6pm Sat) A classic gift for Mum is a bottle of eau de cologne, the not terribly sophisticated but refreshing perfume created – and still being produced – in, yes, Cologne. The most famous brand is 4711, named after the number of the house where it was invented, which now houses this glossy shop. Note the cutesy carillon on the facade with characters from Prussian lore parading hourly from 9am to 9pm.

Farina-House PERFUME
(☑ 0221-399 8994; Obenmarspforten 21; tour adult/child €5/free; ⊗ 10am-7pm Mon-Sat, to 4pm Sun) Learn all about stories behind the scent at this longtime Cologne producer, which offers hourly guided tours (some in English) as well as a huge shop.

Mayersche Buchhandlung BOOKS
(☑ 0221-203 070; www.mayersche.de; Neumarkt 2; ⊗ 9am-8pm Mon-Sat) Large bookstore with a good English-language selection.

ℹ Information

The **KölnCard** (24hr €9) offers free public transport and discounted admission, tours, meals and entertainment. It's available at the tourist office and participating venues.

There is free public wi-fi in the area around the Dom.

Post Office (☑ info 0221-925 9290; Breite Strasse 6-26, WDR Arkaden shopping mall; ⊗ 9am-7pm Mon-Fri, to 2pm Sat)

ReiseBank (☑ 0221-134 403; Hauptbahnhof; ⊗ 7am-10pm) Exchange services and money transfers.

Tourist Office (☑ 0221-346 430; www.cologne-tourism.com; Kardinal-Höffner-Platz 1; ⊗ 9am-8pm Mon-Sat, 10am-5pm Sun) Excellent; near the cathedral. The app is well done.

ℹ Getting There & Away

AIR

About 18km southeast of the city centre, **Cologne-Bonn Airport** (CGN; www.airport-cgn.de) has direct flights to 130 cities and is served by numerous airlines, with destinations across Europe.

BUS

Eurolines runs buses in all directions, including Paris (7½ hours) and Amsterdam (5¼ hours). The central bus station is on Breslauer Platz, behind the Hauptbahnhof.

TRAIN

Cologne's beautiful Hauptbahnhof sits just an incense waft away from the landmark Dom. Services are fast and frequent in all directions. A sampling: Berlin (€117, 4¼ hours), Frankfurt (€71, 1¼ hours) and Munich (€142, 4½ hours). In addition there are fast Thalys and ICE trains to Brussels (where you can connect to the Eurostar for London) and Paris.

ℹ Getting Around

TO/FROM THE AIRPORT

The S13 train connects the airport and the Hauptbahnhof every 20 minutes (€2.80, 15 minutes). Taxis charge about €30.

CAR & MOTORCYCLE

Central Cologne is now a low-emission zone, meaning that your car needs to display an *Umweltplakette* (emission sticker). Rental cars automatically have the sticker, but if you're driving your own vehicle, you'll need to obtain one. Your

ⓘ REGIONAL TRAIN PASSES

There are several deals available for getting around Cologne and the surrounding state of North Rhine–Westphalia by public transport. The **SchönerTag-Ticket** buys one day of unlimited travel within the state from 9am to 3am the following day (midnight to 3am the next day on weekends). You can only use RE, RB and S-Bahn trains, as well as buses, U-Bahn and trams. The ticket costs €28.50 for single travellers and €41 for groups of up to five people.

best option is to stash the car in one of the many large parking buildings and forget it.

PUBLIC TRANSPORT

Cologne's comprehensive mix of buses, trams, and U-Bahn and S-Bahn trains is operated by **VRS** (☑ 01803-504 030; www.vrsinfo.de) in cooperation with Bonn's system. Short trips (up to four stops) cost €1.90, longer ones €2.40. Day passes are €6.80 for one person and €9.60 for up to five people travelling together. Buy your tickets from the machines at stations and aboard trams; be sure to validate them.

TAXI

Call ☑ 0221-2882 or ☑ 0221-194 10.

THE RHINELAND

Linked by the iconic river, a host of cities and villages in the Rhineland are worth your time.

Brühl

☑ 02232 / POP 44,400

Brühl wraps an astonishing number of riches into a pint-size package. The town, halfway between Cologne and Bonn, languished in relative obscurity until the 18th century, when archbishop-elector Clemens August (1723–61) – a friend of Casanova and himself a lover of women, parties and palaces – made it his residence. His two made-to-impress rococo palaces, at opposite ends of the elegant Schlosspark, landed on Unesco's list of World Heritage Sites in 1984.

⊙ Sights & Activities

Brühl's two palaces are a wonderful 30-minute stroll apart on a wide 2.5km

promenade through the Schlosspark. Schloss Augustusburg is close to the train station and presents a dramatic vision as you arrive. A combined ticket for all the sites costs adult/concession €12/7.

★ **Schloss Augustusburg**   PALACE
(☑ 02232-440 00; www.schlossbruehl.de; Max-Ernst-Allee; adult/concession €8/5; ☺ 9am-1pm & 1.30-4pm Tue-Fri, 10am-5pm Sat & Sun, site closed Dec-Jan) The larger and flashier of Brühl's palaces, Schloss Augustusburg is a little jewel-box inside a moat. It was designed by François Cuvilliés. On guided tours you'll learn fascinating titbits about hygiene, dating and other aspects of daily life at court. The architectural highlight is a ceremonial staircase by Balthasar Neumann, a dizzying symphony in stucco, sculpture and faux marble. At most times, visits are only by guided tour.

Jagdschloss Falkenlust   HISTORIC BUILDING
(☑ 02232-440 00; www.schlossbruehl.de; Otto-Weis-Strasse; adult/concession €6/4; ☺ 9am-1pm & 1.30-4pm Tue-Fri, 10am-5pm Sat & Sun, site closed Dec-Jan) Besides Schloss Augustusburg, François Cuvilliés also dreamed up Jagdschloss Falkenlust, a hunting lodge where Clemens August liked to indulge his fancy for falconry. Though small, it's almost as opulent as the main palace. A particular gem is the adjacent chapel, which is awash with shells, minerals and crystals.

Max Ernst Museum   MUSEUM
(☑ 02232-579 3110; www.maxernstmuseum.com; Comesstrasse 42; adult/child €8/free; ☺ 11am-6pm Tue-Sun) A short stroll from the palaces is the Max Ernst Museum, where nine rooms trace all creative phases of the Brühl-born Dadaist and surrealist (1891–1976). We especially enjoyed examples of his artistic innovations such as frottage (floorboard rubbings) and the spooky collage novels, which are graphic works exploring the darkest crevices of the subconscious.

Phantasialand   THEME PARK
(☑ 02232-362 00; www.phantasialand.de; Berggeiststrasse 31-41; day pass adult/child €45/24; ☺ 9am-6pm Apr-Jun & Sep-Oct, to 8pm Jul-Aug, special winter hours) Fantasy replaces the reality of Brühl's palaces at Phantasialand, one of Europe's earliest (since 1967), most popular and best Disneyland-style amusement parks. The park has six themed areas – Chinatown, Berlin, Mexico, Fantasy, Mystery and Deep in Africa – each with its own roller coasters, gondolas, flight simulators, water

rides and other thrills, plus song and dance shows. Children under four enter free.

ℹ Getting There & Away

Brühl is regularly served by regional trains from Cologne (€3.80, 15 minutes) and Bonn (€5, 10 minutes). The Hauptbahnhof is opposite Schloss Augustusburg, with the compact town centre behind the palace. Shuttle buses to Phantasialand leave from outside the station. You can rent bikes at the station.

Bonn

📞 0228 / POP 310,000

When this relaxed city on the Rhine became West Germany's 'temporary' capital in 1949 it surprised many, including its own residents. When in 1991 a reunited German government decided to move to Berlin, it shocked many, especially its own residents.

A generation later, Bonn is doing just fine, thank you. It has a healthy economy and lively urban vibe. For visitors, the birthplace of Ludwig van Beethoven has plenty of note, not least the great composer's birth house, a string of top-rated museums, a lovely riverside setting and the nostalgic flair of the old government quarter.

◉ Sights

Bonn can be seen on an easy day trip from Cologne or as a stop on the busy Rhine railway line. There is a concentration of sights in the Altstadt but others are rather removed from the centre.

◉ Altstadt

You can easily explore all of Bonn's old town on foot.

★ Münster Basilica CATHEDRAL

(📞 0228-985 880; www.bonner-muenster.de; Münsterplatz; ⊗ 7am-7pm) A good place to start exploring Bonn's historic centre is on Münsterplatz, where the landmark Münster Basilica was built on the graves of the two martyred Roman soldiers who later got promoted to be the city's patron saints. It got its Gothic look in the 13th century but the Romanesque origins survive beautifully in the ageing cloister (open till 5pm). It's interior is redolent with centuries of burnt incense.

On the square outside the church, a buttercup-yellow baroque Palais (palace; now the post office) forms a photogenic backdrop for the Beethoven Monument (1845).

★ Beethoven-Haus Bonn MUSEUM

(📞 0228-981 7525; www.beethoven-haus-bonn. de; Bonngasse 24-26; adult/concession €6/4.50; ⊗ 10am-6pm Apr-Oct, 10am-5pm Mon-Sat, 11am-5pm Sun Nov-Mar) One of the world's most famous composers, Beethoven was born in 1770 in this rather humble town house. Today it displays a predictable array of scores, letters, paintings and instruments, including his last grand piano. Of note are the huge ear trumpets he used to combat his growing deafness. Tickets are also good for the adjacent **Digitales Beethoven-Haus**, where you can experience the composer's genius during a spacey, interactive 3D multimedia show.

Contemplate his life in a near-hidden garden out back, and stroke your inner Schroeder (of *Peanuts* fame) in the Beethoven-bust-filled gift shop.

Altes Rathaus HISTORIC BUILDING

(Markt) In the Altstadt's other main square, the triangular Markt, the baroque Altes Rathaus (old town hall) absolutely glistens with silver and gold trim. Politicians from Charles de Gaulle to John F Kennedy have waved to the crowds from its double-sided staircase.

Kurfürstliche Residenz HISTORIC BUILDING

(Electoral Residence; Regina-Pacis-Weg) To the south is the palatial 1705 Kurfürstliche Residenz, once the immodest home of the archbishop-electors of Cologne and part of Bonn's university since 1818. Its south side

---

A RHINE DAY OUT

You can experience the sweeping beauty of the Rhine River fully on this circular day trip from Cologne, which includes a short ferry ride and a good walk.

Catch a train south (hourly, one hour) on the right bank of the Rhine to the small riverside village of **Erpel**. Walk about 200m down to the waterfront and catch a small ferry (€1, every 30 minutes) across the river to **Remagen**. Check out the remains of the famous bridge, then begin your walk north along the Rhine path. The views of passing boats are endlessly engaging and there is a sharp bend in the river to add interest. After about 5km you'll reach another small riverside village, **Oberwinter**, which has frequent trains back to Cologne (40 minutes).

opens up to the expansive Hofgarten (Palace Garden), a popular gathering place for students.

Arithmeum
MUSEUM

(☑ 0228-738 790; www.arithmeum.uni-bonn.de; Lennéstrasse 2; adult/child €3/2; ☺ 11am-6pm Tue-Sun) The Arithmeum explores the symbiosis of science, technology and art. On view are hundreds of mechanical calculators and historic mathematics books but also an out-there exhibit on the aesthetics of microchips. Design your own or study their beauty through a polarisation microscope. Work your way down from the top floor of this large but minimalist glass-and-steel cube. It's on the southeast corner of the Altstadt by the Hofgarten.

LandesMuseum Bonn
MUSEUM

(Rhineland Regional Museum; ☑ 0228-207 00; www.landesmuseum-bonn.lvr.de; Colmantstrasse 14; adult/child €8/free; ☺ 11am-6pm Tue-Fri & Sun, from 1pm Sat) South of the Hauptbahnhof, the LandesMuseum presents its rich collections in such themed exhibits as Epochs, Gods and Power. Highlights include a 40,000-year-old Neanderthal skull and a rare blue Roman glass vessel from the 1st century AD. The museum cafe is good.

◉ Bundesviertel

From 1949 to 1999, the nerve centre of West German political power lay about 1.5km southeast of the Altstadt along Adenauerallee. These days the former government quarter has reinvented itself as the home of the United Nations and other international and federal institutions. The airy and modern **Plenary Hall**, where the Bundestag (German parliament) used to convene, now hosts international conferences. Nearby, the high-rise nicknamed **Langer Eugen** (Tall Eugen), where members of parliament kept their offices, is now a UN campus. Officially retaining their former purposes are the stately **Villa Hammerschmidt**, still a secondary official residence of the federal president, and the neoclassical **Palais Schaumburg**, now serving as the chancellor's Bonn office.

★ Haus der Geschichte
MUSEUM

(Museum of History; ☑ 0228-916 50; www.hdg.de; Willy-Brandt-Allee 14; ☺ 9am-7pm Tue-Fri, 10am-6pm Sat & Sun) **FREE** The Haus der Geschichte der Bundesrepublik Deutschland presents a smart and fun romp through recent German history, starting from the end of WWII. Walk

through the fuselage of a Berlin Airlift '*Rosinenbomber*', watch classic clips in a 1950s cinema, imagine free love in a VW microbus, examine Erich Honecker's arrest warrant, stand in front of a piece of the Berlin Wall or see John F Kennedy's famous '*Ich bin ein Berliner*' speech. U-Bahns 16, 63 and 66 stop here.

◉ Museumsmeile

Bonn's Museum Mile sits opposite the government quarter, on the western side of the B9. U-Bahns 16, 63 and 66 stop here.

Museum Koenig
MUSEUM

(☑ 0228-912 20; www.zfmk.de; Adenauerallee 160; adult/concession €5/2.50; ☺ 10am-6pm Tue & Thu-Sun, to 9pm Wed; ⊞) Across from the Villa Hammerschmidt, the Museum Koenig is a natural history museum but it's hardly your usual dead-animal zoo. The 'Savannah' exhibit re-creates an entire habitat with theatrical flourishes: elephants drinking at a watering hole, a jaguar holed up with its kill and vultures surveying the scene from above. Other highlights include a talking baobab tree in the 'Rainforest', a colossal sea elephant in the 'Arctic' and a condor with a 3m wingspan in the 'World of Birds'.

Kunstmuseum Bonn
MUSEUM

(Bonn Art Museum; ☑ 0228-776 260; www.kunstmuseum-bonn.de; Friedrich-Ebert-Allee 2; adult/concession €7/3.50; ☺ 11am-6pm Tue & Thu-Sun, to 9pm Wed) Beyond its dramatic foyer, the Kunstmuseum Bonn presents 20th-century works, especially by August Macke and other Rhenish expressionists, as well as such avant-gardists as Beuys, Baselitz and Kiefer. It has a vigorous schedule of special exhibitions.

Bundeskunsthalle
EXHIBITION SPACE

(Kunst-und Ausstellungshalle der Bundesrepublik Deutschland; ☑ 0228-917 1200; www.bundeskunsthalle.de; Friedrich-Ebert-Allee 2; adult/concession €10/6.50; ☺ 10am-9pm Tue & Wed, to 7pm Thu-Sun) Adjoining the Kunstmuseum Bonn, the Kunst-und Ausstellungshalle der Bundesrepublik Deutschland is another striking space with a name that's a mouthful. It has special exhibitions of everything from serious art to images from space probes.

Deutsches Museum Bonn
MUSEUM

(☑ 0228-302 255; www.deutsches-museum-bonn.de; Ahrstrasse 45; adult/concession €6/4; ☺ 10am-6pm Tue-Sun; ⊞) Did you know that the airbag and MP3 technology were invented in Germany? You will, after visiting the Deutsches Museum Bonn. This pint-size subsidiary of the blockbuster Munich mothership highlights German technology since WWII with plenty of buttons to push and knobs to pull. It's around 2km south of the centre; take U-Bahn 16 or 63.

◉ Nordstadt

Also referred to as Northern Altstadt, Nordstadt is a former working-class quarter whose web of narrow streets has grown pockets of hipness. Cafes, restaurants, boutiques and galleries have sprouted along Breite Strasse, Heerstrasse and the connecting side streets. The quarter is prettiest in spring when the cherry trees are in bloom.

August-Macke-Haus   MUSEUM
(☑ 0228-655 531; www.august-macke-haus.de; Bornheimer Strasse 96; adult/concession €5/4; ⊙ 2.30-6pm Tue-Fri, 11am-5pm Sat & Sun) The Expressionist painter August Macke (1887–1914) lived in this neighbourhood in the three years before he died on the battlefields in WWI. At his neoclassical home, you can soak up the master's aura in his recreated studio and see some originals; the finest works, though, are not far away at the Kunstmuseum Bonn (p480). The house is about 1km from the train station. Take tram 16, 18 or 63.

◉ Poppelsdorf & Around

About 2km south of the Altstadt, elegant and leafy Poppelsdorf is anchored by Schloss Poppelsdorf, an electoral palace now used by the university. Students and locals populate the bars and eateries along Clemens-August-Strasse, which runs south of the palace to the hillside Kreuzbergkirche.

Doppelkirche Schwarzrheindorf   CHURCH
(☑ 0228-461 609; Dixstrasse 41; ⊙ 9am-6.30pm Tue-Sat, 11.30am-6.30pm Sun, upper church Sat & Sun only) The 12th-century Doppelkirche Schwarzrheindorf is a magnificent 'double church' where the nobility sat on the upper level and the parishioners on the lower. The beautiful Romanesque architecture is impressive, as is the restored Old Testament fresco cycle in the lower church. It's across the river from Poppelsdorf in the suburb of Schwarzrheindorf; take bus 550 or 640 from the Hauptbahnhof to Schwarzrheindorf-Kirche.

Kreuzbergkirche   CHURCH
(www.kreuzberg-bonn.de; Stationsweg 21; ⊙ 9am-6pm Apr Oct, to 5pm Nov-Mar) This rococo

gem is lavishly decorated with gilded faux marble, frescos and a Balthasar Neumann–designed version of the Holy Steps.

☞ Tours

Beethoven fans can follow in his footsteps, either via a free Beethoven Walk pamphlet or an iTour audio guide (rental €7.50), both available at the tourist office.

Given the diffuse nature of cycling routes in Bonn and the riverside, touring by bike is an ideal way to see the city.

★ Bonn Walking Tour   WALKING TOUR
(☑ 0228-775 000; Tourist Office, Windeckstrasse 1; adult/concession €9/5; ⊙ 11am Sat May-Oct) Follow the life of Beethoven and explore the Altstadt on these 90-minute English-language walking tours that leave from the tourist office.

★ Weg der Demokratie   WALKING TOUR
(Path of Democracy; www.wegderdemokratie.de) A good way to explore the Bundesviertel is by following the Weg der Demokratie, a self-guided walking tour taking in 18 key historic sites. It starts at the Haus der Geschichte der Bundesrepublik Deutschland. There are interesting signs explaining things in English; the brochure from the tourist office is useful.

Radstation   BICYCLE RENTAL
(☑ 0228-981 4636; www.radstationbonn.de; Quantiusstrasse 4-6; per day from €8; ⊙ 6am-10.30pm Mon-Fri, 7am-10.30pm Sat, 8am-10.30pm Sun) Bike rental and cycling maps; on the southeast side of the Hauptbahnhof via the subterranean passageway.

Big City Tour   TOUR
(Windeckstrasse 1, Tourist Office; adult/concession €16/8; ⊙ 2pm daily Apr-Oct, Sat Nov-Mar) A combination bus and walking tour run by the tourist office, this 2½-hour tour takes in almost everything.

Weisse Flotte Rhein   BOAT TOUR
(☑ 0228-636 363; www.weisse-flotte-rhein.info; Alter Zoll docks; one way/return to Königswinter €9/11.50; ⊙ Apr-Oct) Offers popular boat trips several times daily up the Rhine to destinations that include Königswinter (45 minutes).

🛏 Sleeping

Accommodation – like Bonn – is spread out. There are some decent places in the Altstadt and some more atmospheric hotels along the Rhine.

Max Hostel   HOSTEL €
(☑0228-8234 5780; max-hostel.de; Maxstrasse 7; dm €20-24, s/d from €33/52; ☺check-in 4-8pm; ☎) Choose from brightly decorated rooms with one to eight beds at this modern hostel close to the centre. There are 48 beds total and it's in a quiet location. The breakfast buffet is €6.50; bed linen is €2.50. It's near the Stadthaus tram stop.

★**Villa Esplanade**   HOTEL €€
(☑0228-983 800; www.hotel-villa-esplanade.de; Colmantstrasse 47; s/d from €80/105; ℙ☺☎) Inside a stately late-19th-century building, this charming hotel has 17 bright rooms with very high ceilings, wooden floors and fridges. Days start with a heaping breakfast buffet served in a lovely room with ornate stucco ceilings. It's close to the train station.

Hotel Löhndorf   HOTEL €€
(☑0228-634 726; www.hotel-loehndorf-bonn.de; Stockenstrasse 6; s €55-80, d €100-150; ☺@☎) This 13-room property is wonderfully quiet and is atmospherically close to the Hofgarten and the Rhine. There's a cheery breakfast room and a bamboo-lined patio. Bonus: a handy honour bar in the lounge and free access to the adjacent gym and sauna. Economy singles with share bathrooms are great value.

Altes Treppchen   GUESTHOUSE €€
(☑0228-625 004; www.treppchen.de; Endenicher Strasse 308; s/d from €75/105; ℙ) ✿ In the suburb of Endenich, this rustic inn is a true gem that's been in the same family for 500 years. The nine rooms are simple but squeaky clean and most of them are decent sized. The restaurant is loaded with olde-world ambience and fresh, seasonal fare. The owners have a strong green ethos.

Ameron Hotel Königshof   HOTEL €€€
(☑0228-260 10; www.hotel-koenigshof-bonn. de; Adenauerallee 9; r €110-250; ℙ✳@☎) Sit back on the leafy terrace and enjoy sweeping views of the Rhine from this luxurious understated hotel that dates from the 1950s. Rooms have a relaxed elegance. There are good walks along the river and strolls in the neighbouring Stadtgarten. The stylish restaurant, Oliveto, is known for its Med-influenced fare.

🍴 Eating & Drinking

The largely pedestrianised historic Altstadt brims with options, including all of those listed below. For offbeat choices head to Heerstrasse and Wolfsstrasse just northwest of the Altstadt.

Eislabor   ICE CREAM €
(☑0228-9268 7172; http://eislabor.info; Maxstrasse 16; snacks from €2; ☺11am-9pm) What better on hot Bonn day (yes, they have them) than the über-fresh ice cream from this cone-sized artisanal shop?

Cafe Blüte   CAFE €
(☑0228-9629 9944; Heerstrasse 61; snacks from €3; ☺8am-8pm; ☎) Walls lined with colourful containers of the owner's favorite teas are matched by mismatched but comfy chairs and tables at this neighbourhood favourite. The delicious cakes change daily; light meals and breakfasts are served throughout the day.

★**Pastis**   FRENCH €€
(☑0228-969 4270; pastisbonn.com; Rheingasse 5; mains €7-19; ☺noon-8pm Tue-Sat, kitchen till 7pm) This little bistro-deli is so fantastically French you'll feel like donning a beret and affecting a silly accent. Dine on unfussy gourmet cuisine – paired with great wines, *bien sûr* – or get a superlative picnic from the deli. Enjoy the outdoor tables.

Bottler Cafe & Brasserie   BRASSERIE €€
(☑0228-9090 2999; www.bottler-bonn.de/; Vivatsgasse 8; mains €5-17; ☺9am-10pm) Right across from Bonn's landmark Sterntor, the old city gate, is this all-around good restaurant. Whether it's a quick breakfast, coffee and a cake (great pastries!) or a more elaborate seafood or pasta meal, Bottler is always busy *and* good.

Brauhaus Bönnsch   BREWERY €€
(☑0228-650 610; www.boennsch.de; Sterntorbrücke 4; mains €7-15; ☺11am-1am; ♿) The unfiltered ale is a must at this congenial brew-pub adorned with photographs of famous politicians great and failed: from Willy Brandt to, yes, Arnold Schwarzenegger. Schnitzel, various pork cuts and sausage dominate the menu, but the *Flammkuchen* is always a crowd-pleaser.

Cafe Spitz   CAFE €€
(☑0228-97 430; www.spitz-bonn.de; Sterntorbrücke 10; mains €5-16; ☺9am-1am Mon-Thu, to 2am Fri & Sat, 10am-midnight Sun) This spare and stylish place is often mobbed, especially during the after-work cocktail happy hour. The menu revolves around salad, pizza and pasta supplemented by changing black-

board specials. The corner location affords great people-watching from the outdoor tables.

Pawlow

BAR

(☑ 0228-653 603; Heerstrasse 64; ☺ 11am-1am Sun-Thu, 11am-to late Fri & Sat) Generations of *bon vivants* have followed the Pavlovian bell to this northern Altstadt institution. A cafe in the daytime with a fine terrace, it morphs into a DJ bar at night with electro, punk and '60s sounds heating up a chatty, boozy crowd.

Biergarten Alter Zoll

BEER GARDEN

(☑ 0228-241 243; http://alterzoll.de; Brassertufer 1, Stadtgarten; snacks from €3; ☺ 11am-midnight Apr-Oct) Here's a Bonn drinking game: every time a barge passes below this beer garden with gorgeous views of the Rhine, have a drink. You won't last an hour. Bonn's Stadtgarten is a little leafy gem next to the Altstadt with an old bastion overlooking the river. The beer and sausages here are standard but the surroundings are anything but.

☆ Entertainment

It won't surprise you to learn that Bonn's entertainment scene is strong in the field of classical music. A cultural highlight is the **Beethovenfest** (www.beethovenfest.de) in early September with several dozen concerts held in venues around town. Book event tickets at **Bonn Ticket** (www.bonnticket.de).

Kammermusiksaal

VENUE

(☑ 0228-981 7515; www.beethoven-haus-bonn.de; Bonngasse 24-26) This chamber music hall is part of the Beethoven House complex.

Beethovenhalle

CONCERT HALL

(☑ 70228-22 20; www.beethovenhalle.de; Wachsbleiche 17) The Beethovenhalle is Bonn's premier concert hall.

❶ Information

Bonn Regio WelcomeCard (per person/family 24hr €9/19) This is better value than most of these schemes: besides unlimited public transport, it gives free (rather than reduced) admission to over 20 museums, plus discounts on tours, thermal baths and more. It's sold at the tourist office and some hotels.

Tourist Office (☑ 0228-775 000; www.bonn-region.de; Windeckstrasse 1; ☺ 10am-6pm Mon-Fri, to 4pm Sat, to 2pm Sun) Has excellent free information and tours in English. It's 200m north of the train station.

❶ Getting There & Away

Cologne Bonn Airport (CGN; www.airport-cgn.de) has flights across Europe.

Bonn's daggy train station looks like improvement stopped in 1989 when the wall fell. It's linked by train to Cologne many times hourly by U-Bahn lines U16 and U18, regional trains (€8, 30 minutes) and ICs. There are frequent trains across the region including the scenic ride upriver to Koblenz (€13, 45 minutes).

You can also travel the Rhine by boat, to/from Cologne and south to/from Koblenz and beyond on **KD** (www.k-d.com; to Cologne €17, to Koblenz €37).

❶ Getting Around

Cologne Bonn Airport is about 25km northeast of the city centre. Express bus SB60 makes the trip between the airport and Hauptbahnhof every 20 or 30 minutes between 5.30am and midnight (€8, 32 minutes). For a taxi to/from the airport budget about €40.

Buses, trams and the U-Bahn make up the public transport system, which is operated by the **VRS** (☑ 01803-504 030; www.vrsinfo.de). It extends as far as Cologne and is divided into zones. All you need to travel within Bonn is a City Ticket for €2.80 per trip or €8.30 for a 24-hour pass. All tickets must be validated when boarding.

For a taxi, call ☑ 0228-555 555.

Siebengebirge

Steeped in legend, the densely forested hills of the Siebengebirge (Seven Mountains) rise above the right bank of the Rhine, just a few kilometres south of Bonn. Closer inspection actually reveals about 40 peaks, but only the seven most prominent give the region its name.

At 461m, the **Ölberg** may be the highest, but the 321m **Drachenfels** is the most heavily visited of these 'mountains'. Since 1883, some 32 million day-trippers have reached the top aboard the **Drachenfelsbahn** (☑ 02223-920 90; www.drachenfelsbahn-koenigswinter.de; Drachenfelsstrasse 53, Königswinter; one way/return adult €7.50/9, child €5/5.50; ☺ 9am-7pm May-Sep, shorter hours Oct-Apr), a nostalgic cogwheel train that rattles along for 1.5km. Prices are a bit steep, but so is the paved path should you prefer to walk.

The walking route leads past restaurants and various attractions, including the 1913 **Nibelungenhalle** (☑ 02223-241 50; www.nibelungenhalle.de; adult/concession €5/3; ☺ 10am-6pm mid-Mar–Nov, Sat & Sun only other times), a templelike shrine to the composer Richard Wagner decorated with scenes from his opera cycle *Ring of the Nibelungen*. Tickets include access to the Drachenhöhle, a cave inhabited by a 13m-long stone dragon and, strangely enough, a small reptile zoo.

Further uphill loom the fairy-tale turrets of the neo-Gothic Schloss Drachenburg (✆ 02223-901 970; www.schloss-drachenburg.de; adult/concession €6/5; ☻ 11am-6pm Apr-Oct, shorter hours other times), which looks medieval but was actually built in the 1880s. It houses exhibits on the building's rather short history. More interesting are the lovely grounds with their terraces, fountains and tower, which can be climbed for expansive views.

Views are at least as nice (and free) from the medieval Burg Drachenfels at the top of the mountain, which has remained a ruin since the Thirty Years' War (1618–48).

The Drachenfels rises above the town of Königswinter, which is served by the U66 from Bonn Hauptbahnhof. A more atmospheric approach is by one of the Weisse Flotte Rhein (p481) boats that leave from Bonn.

Remagen

✆ 02642 / POP 16,100

Remagen, 20km south of Bonn, was founded by the Romans in AD 16 as Rigomagus, but the town would hardly figure in the history books were it not for one fateful day in early March 1945. As the Allies raced across France and Belgium to rid Germany of Nazism, the Wehrmacht tried frantically to stave off defeat by destroying all bridges across the Rhine.

But the Brücke von Remagen (the steel rail bridge at Remagen) lasted long enough for Allied troops to cross the river, contributing significantly to the collapse of Hitler's western front. One of the bridge's surviving basalt towers now houses the Friedensmuseum (Peace Museum; ✆ 02642-218 63; www.bruecke-remagen.de; adult/child €3.50/1; ☻ 10am-5pm early Mar–mid-Nov, to 6pm May-Oct), with a well-presented exhibit on Remagen's pivotal role in WWII. Note the many memorial plaques to the battle placed by a generation of soldiers now all but passed.

The bridge and museum are a 15-minute walk along the Rhine promenade south from the train station, which has frequent services towards both Cologne and Koblenz.

The Ahr Valley & the Eifel

The Eifel, a rural area of gentle hills, tranquil villages and volcanic lakes, makes for a good respite from the mass tourism of the Moselle and Rhine Valleys. Its subtle charms are best sampled on a bike ride or a hike, though it also has a few headline attractions, including a world-class car-racing track, a stunning Romanesque abbey and a lovely wine region, the Ahr Valley.

The Ahr River has carved a scenic 90km valley stretching from Blankenheim, in the High Eifel, to its confluence with the Rhine near Remagen. This is one of Germany's few red-wine regions – growing *Spätburgunder* (pinot noir), in particular – with vineyards clinging to steeply terraced slopes along both banks. The quality is high but the yield small, so very few wine labels ever make it beyond the area – all the more reason to visit and try them for yourself.

Bad Neuenahr-Ahrweiler

✆ 02641 / POP 27,500

Bad Neuenahr and Ahrweiler are a bit of an odd couple: two small towns joined together by government edict. The spouse listed second, Ahrweiler, should come first in terms of appeal. It's an attractive medieval town encircled by a wall and criss-crossed by pedestrianised lanes lined with half-timbered houses.

Bad Neuenahr, by contrast, is a spa town. Although its healing waters have been sought out by the moneyed and the famous (including Karl Marx and Johannes Brahms) for a century and a half, it's rather on the bland side.

◉ Sights & Activities

The two towns are about 3km apart; you can walk between them along the narrow Ahr River. There are many more hikes through the hillside vineyards. The tourist office has information.

★ **Rotweinwanderweg** WALKING
(Red Wine Trail; www.ahr-rotweinwanderweg.de/) Well-signed paths abound throughout the vineyards of the Ahr Valley, but this is easily the most alluring. Wander amid the grapes and soak up the hills from Bad Bodendorf in the east to Altenahr in the west. The full length is almost 36km, but it's broken up by cute villages with train stops and wine tasting rooms. The segment from Bad Neuenahr

to Ahrweiler (7.4km), for instance, loops up beautifully into the hills. Tourist offices have the route brochure.

◉ AHRWEILER

Ahrweiler preserves an atmospheric, pedestrianised Altstadt, almost entirely encircled by a medieval town wall with four gates. The focal point is the Marktplatz and its yellow Gothic church, Pfarrkirche St Laurentius, beautifully decorated with floral frescoes from the 14th century, old wood carvings and luminous stained-glass windows, some of which show farmers working their vineyards.

Museum Roemervilla   MUSEUM
(☑ 02641-5311; www.museum-roemervilla.de; Am Silberberg 1; adult/concession €5/2.50; ☺ 10am-5pm Tue-Sun Apr–mid-Nov, closed mid-Nov–Mar) Ahrweiler's Roman roots spring to life at the Museum Roemervilla on the northwest edge of town. Protected by a lofty glass and wood structure are the surprisingly extensive 1st- to 3rd-century ruins – a veritable Rhenish Pompeii – which reveal the posh standard of living enjoyed by wealthy Romans.

Dokumentationsstätte Regierungsbunker   HISTORIC SITE
(Government Bunker Documentation Site; ☑ 02641-917 10; www.regbu.de; Am Silberberg 0; adult/child €8/free; ☺ 10am-5pm Wed, Sat, Sun & holidays early Mar–mid-Nov, closed mid-Nov–early Mar) During the Cold War, there was no vast, top-secret bunker complex bored into the hillside 500m up the slope from the Museum Roemervilla – at least not officially. Now, however, you can see the truth at a 200m section of the nuclear-proof former 'Emergency Seat of the Constitutional Organs of the Federal Republic of Germany'. There's a real Dr Strangelove quality to what comforts the bureaucrats thought would be good to have at hand as the world ended.

◉ BAD NEUENAHR

The focal point of Bad Neuenahr, bisected by the Ahr, is the stately Kurhaus, an art nouveau structure built in 1903; next door is the casino. The nearby riverbanks are great for strolling.

Ahr Thermen   SPA
(☑ 02641-911 760; www.ahr-thermen.de; Felix-Rütten-Strasse 3; day pass €16; ☺ 9am-11pm or midnight) Neuenahr owes its 'Bad' reputation' (ie its spa status) to its mineral springs, whose soothing qualities are accessible at this spa. Besides swimming pools, options include a surge channel, a 37°C whirlpool and various saunas. Discounts are available.

🛏 Sleeping & Eating

Ahrweiler (eg around Marktplatz) teems with traditional restaurants and Weinstuben, all serving the tasty local reds. The Meyer-Näkel label is especially prized.

Kleine Herberge   GUESTHOUSE €
(☑ 02641-378 1024; www.kleineherberge.de; Adenbachhutstrasse 8, Ahrweiler; s €55-58, d €58-69) Just inside the Adenbachtor, the gate closest to the train stop, this 1898 house has been turned into a stylish two-room guesthouse. There's a garden out back where you can chill out after hillside wanderings. Rates include breakfast.

★Prümer Gang   HOTEL €€
(☑ 02641-4757; www.pruemergang.de; Niederhutstrasse 58, Ahrweiler; s/d from €76/130, restaurant menu €40-50; ☺ restaurant noon-2pm Wed-Sun, 6-10pm Tue-Sun; ☻ 🎅) Behind the vintage facade is this modern and stylish 12-room hotel. The decor is all wood and light colours, which might put you in the mood for a ramble. The restaurant serves creative, seasonal fare in elegantly relaxed surrounds.

Hotel Garni Schützenhof   GUESTHOUSE €€
(☑ 02641-902 83; www.schuetzenhof-ahrweiler. de; Schützenstrasse 1, Ahrweiler; s/d incl breakfast from €52/85; P ☻ 🎅) Facing the Ahrtor, one of Ahrweiler's landmark town gates, this unpretentious, welcoming family-run hotel has 14 spacious rooms.

Hotel & Restaurant Hohenzollern   HOTEL €€
(☑ 02641-9730; www.hotelhohenzollern.com; Am Silberberg 50; s/d from €80/125; P ☻ 🎅) This elegant hillside hotel, right on the Rotweinwanderweg, has unbeatable valley views and a top-end restaurant (menus from €60) with local, French and Italian dishes. From Ahrweiler's Museum Roemervilla, head up the narrow road 700m through the forest.

Das Kleine Caféhaus   CAFE €
(☑ 02641-5061; daskleinecafehaus.de; Niederhutstrasse 65, Ahrweiler; mains from €5; ☺ 8am-5pm) Before your wine adventure begins – or when you need a break – stop by this top-class cafe for delicious, cakes, breakfasts and more. The baked goods are artful. The sidewalk tables refreshing.

ℹ Information

Ahrweiler Tourist Office (☑ 02641-917 10; www.ahrtaltourismus.de; Blankartshof 1; ⏱ 9am-5.30pm Mon-Fri, 10am-3pm Sat & Sun) On the south side of town, sells walking and cycling maps of the area.

ℹ Getting There & Away

By train, skip the 'Ahrweiler' stop and use 'Ahrweiler Markt', which is just north of the old town. From the main Bahnhof in Bad Neuenahr it's a five-minute walk to the centre, which is around car-free Poststrasse.

Hourly trains serve the towns from Bonn (€5, 40 minutes) and Remagen, where you change for travel south to Koblenz.

Altenahr

☑ 02643 / POP 1700

Surrounded on all sides by craggy peaks, steep vineyards and rolling hills, Altenahr may just be the most romantic spot in the Ahr Valley. The landscape is best appreciated by taking a 20-minute uphill walk from the Bahnhof to the 11th-century **Burgruine Are**, a ruined hilltop castle, whose weather-beaten stone tower stands guard over the valley.

Altenahr is the western terminus of the Rotweinwanderweg. A dozen more trails can be picked up in the village centre (eg the 7km **Geologischer Wanderweg**) or at the top of the **Ditschardhöhe**, whose 'peak', at 354m, is most easily reached by the **Seilbahn** (chairlift; ☑ 02643-8383; Seilbahnstrasse 34; ascent/return adult €5/7, child €4/5; ⏱ 10am-5pm or later Easter-Oct). In the town centre, parts of the Romanesque **Pfarrkirche Maria Verkündigung** (Church of the Annunciation) date from the late 1100s.

🛏 Sleeping & Eating

DJH Hostel HOSTEL €
(☑ 02643-1880; www.jugendherberge.de; Langfigtal 8; dm/d €23/56) Altenahr's 92-bed hostel is beautifully located in the Langfigtal nature park, overlooking the Ahr.

Hotel Zum Schwarzen Kreuz HOTEL €€
(☑ 02643-1534; www.zumschwarzenkreuz.de; Brückenstrasse 5-7; s/d from €50/70) In the heart of town, this half-timbered fantasy place offers retro flair, a quiet library with overstuffed chairs and 30 rooms (some with balconies); rates include breakfast. The restaurant does Eifel specialities (mains €9 to €20) and *Flammkuchen*.

ℹ Getting There & Away

Trains run on the line through Ahrweiler (€4, 20 minutes).

Nürburgring

The Nürburgring (www.nuerburgring.de), a historic Formula One race car track, has hosted many spectacular races with legendary drivers since its completion in 1927. The 20.8km, 73-curve **Nordschleife** (North Loop) was not only the longest circuit ever built but also one of the most difficult, earning the respectful moniker 'Green Hell' from racing legend Jackie Stewart.

After Niki Lauda's near-fatal crash in 1976, the German Grand Prix moved to the Hockenheimring near Mannheim, but in 1995 Formula One returned (in odd-numbered years) to the 5148m **Grand-Prix-Strecke** (South Loop), built in 1984. The complex hosts dozens of races a year.

⦿ Sights & Activities

If you have your own car or motorcycle, you can discover your inner Michael Schumacher by taking a spin around the Nordschleife for €27 per 15-minute circuit. Check the website for Open Nordschleife times and dates.

There are all sorts of options for joining a driver in a high-performance machine like a BMW M5 for a 'co-pilot ride' starting at €225; nonrace periods only.

Backstage Tour TOUR
(Info center Nürburgring; tour €7.50; ⏱ 10am, noon, 2pm & 4pm) Glimpse behind the scenes at Nürburgring with a 90-minute tour, usually in German with printed material in English.

ℹ Information

Info center (☑ 02691-302 630; www.nuerburgring.de; Ring Boulevard; ⏱ 9am-6pm) The hub for all things Nuerburgring: learn about the circuit, find out all the ways you can go fast, pick up pre-booked tickets and more.

ℹ Getting There & Away

The Nürburgring is off the B258, reached via the B257 from Altenahr. It is 60km west of Koblenz.

Aachen

☑ 0241 / POP 240,100

Aachen has been around for millennia. The Romans nursed their war wounds and stiff joints in the steaming waters of Aachen's mineral springs, but it was Charlemagne who put the city firmly on the European map. The emperor, too, enjoyed a dip now and then, but it was more for strategic reasons that he made Aachen the geographical and political capital of his vast Frankish Empire in 974 – arguably the first empire with European dimensions.

Today, Aachen should be on any visitor's itinerary. It is still a quintessentially international city, and has a unique appeal thanks to its location in the border triangle with the Netherlands and Belgium. And Charlemagne's legacy lives on in the stunning Dom, which in 1978 became Germany's first Unesco World Heritage Site as well as the new Centre Charlemagne.

◉ Sights

Appreciating the Dom and wandering Aachen's medieval streets can easily fill a day. Everything is reachable on foot.

★**Aachener Dom**   CATHEDRAL
(🅙0241-447 090; www.aachendom.de; Münsterplatz; ⊙7am-7pm Apr-Dec, to 6pm Jan-Mar) It's impossible to overestimate the significance of Aachen's magnificent cathedral. The burial place of Charlemagne, it's where more than 30 German kings were crowned and where pilgrims have flocked since the 12th century. Before entering the church, stop by **Dom Information** (🅙0241-4770 9145; www.aachendom.de; Johannes-Paul-II-Strasse; ⊙10am-5pm Jan-Mar, to 6pm Apr-Dec) for info and tickets for tours and the cathedral treasury.

The oldest and most impressive section is Charlemagne's palace chapel, the Pfalzkapelle, an outstanding example of Carolingian architecture. Completed in 800, the year of the emperor's coronation, it's an octagonal dome encircled by a 16-sided ambulatory supported by antique Italian pillars. The colossal brass chandelier was a gift from Emperor Friedrich Barbarossa, during whose reign Charlemagne was canonised in 1165.

Pilgrims have poured into town ever since that time, drawn as much by the cult surrounding Charlemagne as by his prized relics: Christ's loincloth from when he was crucified, Mary's cloak, the clothes used for John the Baptist when he was beheaded and swaddling clothes from when Jesus was an infant. These are displayed once every seven years (next in 2021) and draw 100,000 or more of the faithful.

To accommodate these regular floods of the visitors, a Gothic choir was docked to the chapel in 1414 and filled with such priceless treasures as the pala d'oro, a gold-plated altar-front depicting Christ's Passion, and the jewel-encrusted gilded copper pulpit, both fashioned in the 11th century. At the far end is the gilded shrine of Charlemagne that has held the emperor's remains since 1215. In front, the equally fanciful shrine of St Mary shelters the cathedral's four prized relics.

Unless you join a **guided tour** (adult/concession €4/3; ⊙tours 11am-5.30pm Mon-Fri, 1-5pm Sat & Sun, 2pm tour in English daily), you'll barely get a glimpse of the white marble of Charlemagne's imperial throne in the upstairs gallery. Reached via six steps – just like King Solomon's throne – it served as the coronation throne of those 30 German kings between 936 and 1531.

High mass at 10am Sundays is a full-on religious experience.

➜ ★**Domschatzkammer**
(Cathedral Treasury; 🅙0241-4770 9127; www.aachendom.de; Johannes-Paul-II-Strasse; adult/concession €5/4; ⊙10am-1pm Mon, to 5pm Tue-Sun Jan-Mar, 10am-1pm Mon, to 6pm Tue-Sun Apr-Dec) The cathedral treasury is a veritable mother lode of gold, silver and jewels. Items

---

REDECORATING THE DOM

Like the stereotypical suburban housewives who never know when to leave well enough alone, the caretakers of the Dom have been on a centuries-long remodelling binge. The result is that very little of what you see dates to Charlemagne's time. For instance, the interior of the main part of the church was redone for the umpteenth time in the 19th century, when vast amounts of Byzantine gilt and stained glass were introduced. At that time, churches across Europe thought to be as old as the Dom were scoured for design ideas, which explains why you can see echoes of Hagia Sophia in İstanbul.

The inside of the dome overhead dates from the 17th century ...and on it goes. Other than possibly the hidden relics and Charlemagne's bones, the oldest authenticated item in the Dom is the 12th-century chandelier, which was a gift from Emperor Friedrich Barbarossa.

DON'T MISS

MARIA LAACH ABBEY CHURCH

Abteikirche Maria Laach (Maria Laach Abbey Church; ☑02652-590; www.maria-laach.de; Maria Laach; parking €2; ⊙visitor centre 1-5pm Sun-Mon, 10am-5pm Tue-Sat Easter-Oct, shorter hours other times) Serenely nestled in beautiful countryside, Abteikirche Maria Laach is one of the finest examples of a Romanesque church in Germany. Part of a nine-century-old Benedictine abbey, it is next to a volcanic lake, the Laacher See, surrounded by a 21-sq-km nature reserve.

You enter the church via a large Vorhalle (portico; restored in 2009), a feature not usually found north of the Alps. Note the quirky carvings on and above the capitals and the Löwenbrunnen (Lion Fountain), reminiscent of Moorish architecture. The interior is surprisingly modest, in part because the original furnishings were lost during the 1800s. In the west apse lies the late-13th-century, recumbent, statue-adorned tomb of abbey founder Heinrich II of Palatine (laminated information sheets in six languages are available). The east apse shelters the high altar with its wooden canopy; overhead is an early-20th-century Byzantine-style mosaic of Christ donated by Kaiser Wilhelm II. The entrance to the 11th-century crypt is to the left of the choir.

Across the path from the Klostergaststätte (restaurant), a 20-minute film looks at the life of the 46 monks, who take the motto *Ora et labora* (pray and work) very seriously indeed. They earn a living from economic activities such as growing organic apples and raising house plants, available for purchase in the Klostergärtnerei (nursery); and they pray five times a day. Attending Gottesdienst (prayer services; hours posted at the church entrance) is worthwhile if only to listen to the ethereal chanting in Latin and German.

Various trails take walkers up the forested hill behind the abbey; options for circum-ambulating the Laacher See include the lakefront **Ufer-Rundweg** (8km) and two hillier trails (15km and 21km).

Next to the car park, a small shop sells fruits and vegetables grown by the monks, as well as other organic edibles.

Maria Laach is about 25km northwest of Koblenz and 18km southeast of Ahrweiler. It is served hourly by bus 312 from Mendig, the nearest town with a train station.

of particular importance include a silver and golden bust of Charlemagne, a 10th-century bejewelled processional cross known as the Lotharkreuz, a 1000-year-old relief-decorated ivory situla (a pail for holy water) and the marble sarcophagus that held Charlemagne's bones until his canonisation; the relief shows the rape of Persephone. Get tickets at Dom Information.

Rathaus HISTORIC BUILDING
(Town Hall; ☑0241-432 7310; Markt; adult/concession incl audioguide €5/3; ⊙10am-6pm) Fifty life-size statues of German rulers, including 30 kings crowned in town between 936 and 1531 AD, adorn the facade of Aachen's splendid Gothic town hall. It was built in the 14th century atop the foundations of Charlemagne's palace, of which only the eastern tower, the Granusturm, survives. Inside, the undisputed highlight is the Krönungssaal (coronation hall) with its epic 19th-century frescoes and replicas of the imperial insig-

nia: a crown, orb and sword (the originals are in Vienna). The Rathaus faces the Markt.

Katschhof SQUARE
It's worth finding a comfy spot to sit and contemplate this deeply historic square. At the north end is the backside of the Rathaus; across from it is the Dom and its complex of buildings. To the west is a mishmash of old buildings that have parts dating back to when this was part of Charlemagne's palace.

Centre Charlemagne MUSEUM
(☑0241-432 4919; www.route-charlemagne.eu; Katschhof 1; adult/concession €5/3; ⊙10am-6pm Tue-Sat) Overlooking the Katschof and right in the midst of where the great man walked, this museum looks at not only the life and times of Charlemagne but also Aachen's dramatic history. Multimedia exhibits bring the Roman era to life, and significant moments ever since. Begin your Route Charlemagne walk here; there is a huge amount of info in English.

Couven Museum MUSEUM
(www.couven-museum.de; Hühnermarkt 17; adult/
concession €5/3; ⊙10am-6pm Tue-Sun) This
small applied arts museum re-creates the
living spaces and lives of 17th- and 18th-
century patricians.

Suermondt Ludwig Museum MUSEUM
(☑0241-479 800; www.suermondt-ludwig-
museum.de; Wilhelmstrasse 18; adult/concession
€5/3; ⊙noon-6pm Tue, Thu & Fri, noon-8pm Wed,
11am-6pm Sat & Sun) Of Aachen's two art museums, the Suermondt Ludwig Museum is
especially proud of its medieval sculpture
but also has fine works by Cranach, Dürer,
Macke, Dix and other masters.

Puppenbrunnen FOUNTAIN
(Puppet Fountain; Krämerstrasse) A modern
fountain that's a crowd-pleasing work of
mechanical art; look for the cock on top
(a symbol of Napoleon's love for Aachen).
Other details (all with meaning), include a
horse, professor, canon and more. The *Charlemagne Guides You Through Aachen* brochure explains all.

**Ludwig Forum
für Internationale Kunst** MUSEUM
(Ludwig Forum for International Art; ☑0241-180
7104; www.ludwigforum.de; Jülicherstrasse 97-109,
adult/concession €5/3; ⊙noon-6pm Tue, Wed &
Fri, noon-8pm Thu, 11am-6pm Sat & Sun) In a former umbrella factory, the Ludwig Forum für
Internationale Kunst trains the spotlight on
contemporary art (Warhol, Immendorf, Holzer, Penck, Haring) and also stages progressive changing exhibits.

Activities

In fine weather, get off the asphalt and onto
the trails of the densely forested spa garden
north of the Altstadt. A brisk 20-minute
walk takes you up the 264m-high **Lousberg**
hill, where the entire city panorama unfolds
before you. Get there by cutting north on
Kupferstrasse from Ludwigsallee, then left
on Belvedereallee.

You can cycle the 100km **Vennbahn**
(www.vennbahn.eu), a disused railway line
that goes to Luxembourg.

Carolus Thermal Baths SPA
(☑0241-182 740; www.carolus-thermen.de; Stadt-
garten/Passstrasse 79; admission with/without
sauna from €24/12; ⊙9am-11pm) Oriental
pools, honey rubs, deep-tissue massages and
soothing saunas are among the relaxation
options at the Carolus-Thermen, a snazzy

bathing complex on the edge of the Stadt-
park (city park).

Radstation BICYCLE RENTAL
(☑0241-4501 9502; Hauptbahnhof; per day from
€5; ⊙5.30am-10.30pm Mon-Fri, 10am-6pm Sat &
Sun) Rent all manner of bikes at this full-
service shop right in the train station.

Tours

Old Town Guided Tour WALKING TOUR
(adult/concession €9/4.50; ⊙11am Sat Apr-
Dec) The tourist office runs 90-minute
English-language walking tours.

Sleeping

There are good choices around the Dom and
the historic quarters. Chain hotels dot the
ring roads.

Hotel Stadtnah HOTEL €
(☑0241-474 580; www.hotelstadtnah.de; Leydel-
strasse 2; s/d from €58/71; ❀🛜) The rate reflects the basic decor and amenities, but this
16-room budget special near the Hauptbahnhof should do in a snap. It shares ownership
with the Hotel Am Bahnhof around the corner, which has similar prices and amenities.

A&O Aachen HOSTEL, HOTEL
(☑0241-463 073 300; www.aohostels.com; Hack-
länderstrasse 5; dm/s/d from €20/50/70; 🛜)
Vast and utilitarian, you can't beat this flashpacker haven's location next to the train station and close to the centre. All rooms have
private bathrooms and there is a lift. At busy
times rates can soar past those of plusher
digs in town.

★**Hotel Drei Könige** HOTEL €€
(☑0241-483 93; www.h3k-aachen.de; Büchel 5;
s €90-130, d €120-160, apt €130-240; 🛜) The

ROUTE CHARLEMAGNE

The Route Charlemagne is designed to
showcase Aachen's 1200-year tradition
as a European city of culture and science. The city's sites are linked together
and many have special exhibits related
to the theme.

The excellent brochure, *Charlemagne
Guides You Through Aachen*, takes you
past all the sites. Pick up a copy at the
logical starting place for the tour, the
Centre Charlemagne, or at the tourist
office.

Aachen

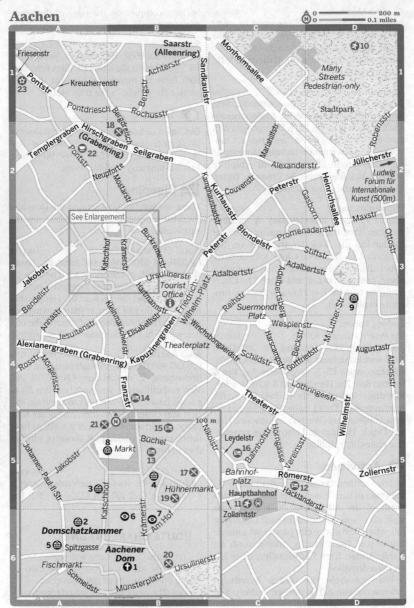

radiant Mediterranean decor is an instant mood-warmer at this family-run favourite with its doesn't-get-more-central location. Some of the nine rooms are a tad twee; the four two-room apartments sleep up to four. Breakfast, on the 4th floor, comes with dreamy views over the rooftops and the cathedral.

Aquis Grana City Hotel   HOTEL **€€**
(📞 0241-4430; www.hotel-aquis-grana.de; Büchel 32; s/d from €80/100; 🅿 🛜) The best quarters

Aachen

at this gracious hotel have terrace and balcony views of the town hall. But even in the most modest of the 98 rooms, you couldn't be any closer to the heart of town. The hotel offers a full range of services, including a bar and a restaurant.

Hotel Benelux   HOTEL €€
(☏ 0241-400 030; www.hotel-benelux.de; Franzstrasse 21-23; s/d from €100/130; 🛜) Though on a busy street, this well-run place has 33 quiet, uncluttered rooms reached via art-filled floors. Fuel up with a generous breakfast served tableside and wrap things up with a sunset drink in the rooftop garden. There's a small gym to work out the kinks.

🍴 Eating & Drinking

Aachen is the birthplace of the famous (and tasty) *Printen*, crunchy spiced cookies spiked with herbs or nuts and drenched in chocolate or frosting. You'll find them sold in bakeries across town.

Ponstrasse (locals say 'Ponte') is good for restaurant browsing and bar-hopping.

★ Café zum Mohren   CAFE €
(☏ 0241-352 00; www.cafezummohren.de; Am Hof 4; mains €4-8; ⊙ 10am-6pm) There's nary a lick of *Printen* anywhere to be seen at this cute little cafe just off the tourist trail. Have waffles for breakfast or sumptuous cakes and tortes throughout the day. Outside tables overlook the Hof, a small colonnaded portico that dates from Roman times.

Nobis   BAKERY, CAFE €
(☏ 0241-968 000; www.nobis-printen.de; Münsterplatz; snacks from €3; ⊙ 7am-7pm Mon-Fri, 7.30am-6pm Sat, 9am-6pm Sun) This gorgeous bakery, where you can watch the bakers at work, is right across from the Dom. It has a stunning array of sandwiches and other goods ready to eat at tables on the square or as a picnic in the nearby parks. Get your *Printen* in the elegant adjoining shop.

Alt-Aachener Café-Stuben   CAFE €
(Van den Daele; ☏ 0241-357 24; www.kockartz.be; Büchel 18; treats from €3; ⊙ 9am-6.30pm Mon-Fri, 10am-6pm Sat & Sun) Leather-covered walls, tiled stoves and antiques forge the yesteryear flair of this rambling cafe institution that dates from 1890 (the building goes back to 1655). Come for all-day breakfast, a light lunch, divine cakes or just to pick up the housemade *Printen*.

★ Am Knipp   GERMAN €€
(☏ 0241-331 68; www.amknipp.de; Bergdriesch 3; mains €9-20; ⊙ 5-11pm Wed-Mon) Hungry grazers have stopped by this traditional inn since 1698, and you too will have a fine time enjoying hearty German cuisine served amid a flea market's worth of knick-knacks or, if weather permits, in the big beer garden.

Zum goldenen Einhorn   GERMAN €€
(☏ 0241-326 93; Markt 33; mains €9-20; ⊙ 11am-11.30pm) You won't feel the sharp end of the namesake golden unicorn at this main square restaurant that goes one better than most of its neighbours. The schnitzels are crispier, the pork juicier, potatoes mashier...

COLOGNE & NORTHERN RHINELAND AACHEN

well, you get the point. And if you're at one of the thicket of tables outside, just look up for that view of the Rathaus.

Magellan CAFE
(☑0241-401 6440; www.magellan-ac.de; Pontstrasse 78; mains €8-12; ☉10am-1am Sun-Thu, to 2am Fri & Sat) This cocktail bar and cafe has a surprising garden setting right near the centre of town. There's even a little stream running past garden tables where you can enjoy refreshments under the stars and food with Mediterranean flair.

☆ Entertainment

For listings, pick up the free *Klenkes* (www.klenkes.de) in cafes and the tourist office.

Apollo Kino & Bar BAR, CLUB
(☑0241-900 8484; www.apollo-aachen.de; Pontstrasse 141-149; ☉vary) This cavernous basement joint does double duty as an art-house cinema and a sweaty dance club. Top DJs rule on Saturdays, salsa on Wednesdays, and on other nights it could be anything from dancehall to disco, house to punk.

ⓘ Information

There's free wi-fi in the centre around the Dom. Look for businesses with the 'Aachen WiFi' logo and ask for a free password.

Tourist Office (☑0241-180 2960; www.aachen-tourist.de; Friedrich-Wilhelm-Platz; ☉9am-6pm Mon-Fri, to 4pm Sat & Sun Apr-Dec, 9am-6pm Mon-Fri, to 2pm Sat Jan-Mar, 10am-2pm Sun Easter-Dec) Local tourist information.

ⓘ Getting There & Away

Regional trains to Cologne (€17, one hour) run twice hourly, with some proceeding beyond. Aachen is a stop for high-speed trains to/from Brussels and Paris.

ⓘ Getting Around

The Hauptbahnhof is a 10- to 15-minute signed walk to the tourist office and the Altstadt.

Bus tickets for travel within central Aachen cost €2.65; drivers sell tickets.

Eifel National Park

It's hard to imagine that until 2005 Belgian troops used much of this beautiful national park for military exercises. Now it's a natural playground amid beautiful mountains and valleys.

◉ Sights & Activities

Nationalpark Eifel PARK
(Eifel National Park; ☑02444-951 00; www.nationalpark-eifel.de) Wild cats, beavers, kingfishers, bats and owls are just some of the critters you might spot in Eifel National Park, North Rhine–Westphalia's only national park. It protects about 110 sq km of beech forest, rivers and lakes, and is filled with interesting plants and wildlife. In spring, a sea of wild narcissus floods the valleys.

The park's developed centre, Forum Vogelsang, is a good starting point for hikes. Staff at the visitor centre hand out advice and maps. Information and informative exhibits can also be found at all the park entrances, including Simmerath-Rurberg, Schleiden-Gemünd, Heimbach and Nideggen.

Forum Vogelsang MUSEUM
(☑02444-915 790; www.vogelsang-ip.de; off Neukirchen Strasse, Neukirchen; guided tour adult/child €5/free, parking €3; ☉8am-8pm Apr-Oct, 8am-5.30pm Nov-Mar, guided tour in German 2pm) A focal point of Eifel National Park is Forum Vogelsang, a vast complex built by the Nazis as a party leadership training centre and later used as military barracks by the Belgians. It has exhibits on the national park and the Eifel region, as well as a documentation centre about the indoctrination and educational system in the Nazi state.

ⓘ Getting There & Away

The park is some 50km southeast of Aachen and 70km southwest of Cologne near the border with Belgium.

From Cologne, regional trains make the trip to Kall several times hourly, where you can switch to the weekends-only Nationalpark shuttle bus SB8 to Vogelsang. The park website has details of additional options.

Düsseldorf
☑0211 / POP 594,000

Düsseldorf impresses with boundary-pushing architecture, zinging nightlife and an art scene to rival many higher-profile cities. It's a posh and modern city that seems all buttoned-up business at first glance: banking, advertising, fashion and telecommunications are among the fields that have made North Rhine–Westphalia's capital one of Germany's wealthiest cities. Yet all it takes is a few hours of bar-hopping around the Altstadt, the historical quarter along the

Rhine, to realise that locals have no problem letting their hair down once they shed those Armani jackets.

The Altstadt may claim to be the 'longest bar in the world' but some attention has strayed to Medienhafen, a redeveloped harbour area and a festival of international avant-garde architecture. Older neighbourhoods are also evolving. Case in point: Flingern, which has gone from drab to fab in recent years and has a multifaceted arty boho scene.

◉ Sights

Düsseldorf has long had a love affair with art, dating back to Jan Wellem's generous patronage, and the city has several high-calibre museums to prove it. Those museums and a stroll through the reconstructed Altstadt can easily fill a day – and that's before you allow time for some *Altbier*.

◉ Altstadt & Around

Düsseldorf's Altstadt, a mostly pedestrianised web of lanes cuddling up to the Rhine, is rightly (in)famous for its lively nightlife. But it has some interesting sights that recall its ages-old wealth.

Marktplatz   SQUARE
(Marktplatz) The historic Marktplatz is framed by the Renaissance Rathaus (town hall; 1573) and accented by a bronze equestrian statue of Jan Wellem. The art-loving 17th-century ruler lies buried nearby in the Andreaskirche.

Andreaskirche   CHURCH
(☑0211-363 40; www.dominikaner-duesseldorf.de; Andreasstrasse 27; ☺7.30am-6.30pm Mon-Sat, 8.30am-7pm Sun) This early baroque church (it was built from 1622 to 1629) is drenched in fanciful white stucco. Six baroque saint sculptures from the original altar are integrated into the sanctuary. More religious art awaits in the treasury in the upstairs gallery. A great time to visit is for the free organ concert at 4.30pm on Sundays.

St Lambertuskirche   CHURCH
(Church of St Lambert; ☑0211-132 326; lambertuspfarre.de; Stiftsplatz; ☺8am-5pm) The twisted tower of the 14th-century St Lambertuskirche shadows treasures that span several centuries. Look for the Gothic tabernacle, the Renaissance marble tombs, baroque altars and modern windows.

★Kunstsammlung Nordrhein-Westfalen   MUSEUM
(Art Collection of North Rhine Westphalia; www.kunstsammlung.de; combined ticket adult/concession €18/4) The regional art museum is spread over two separate buildings. Its diversity and richness reflect the high importance art has in local life. During opening hours, a shuttle bus runs every 20 minutes between K20 and K21.

➡ K20 Grabbeplatz
(☑0211-838 1130; Grabbeplatz 5; adult/child €12/2.50; ☺10am-6pm Tue-Fri, 11am-6pm Sat & Sun) A collection that spans the arc of 20th-century artistic vision gives the K20 an enviable edge in the art world. It encompasses major works by Picasso, Matisse and Mondrian and more than 100 paintings and drawings by Paul Klee. Americans represented include Jackson Pollock, Andy Warhol and Jasper Johns. Düsseldorf's own Joseph Beuys has a major presence as well.

➡ K21 Ständehaus
(☑0211-838 1630; Ständehausstrasse 1; adult/child €12/2.50; ☺10am-6pm Tue-Fri, 11am-6pm Sat & Sun) A stately 19th-century parliament building forms a fabulous dichotomy to the cutting-edge edge art of the K21 – a collection showcasing only works created after the 1980s. Large-scale film and video installations and groups of works share space with site-specific rooms by an international cast of artists including Andreas Gursky, Candida Höfer, Bill Viola and Nam June Paik.

Kunsthalle   MUSEUM
(Art Hall; ☑0211-899 6243; www.kunsthalle-duesseldorf.de; Grabbeplatz 4; adult/child €6/free; ☺11am-6pm Tue-Sun) Across the square from K20, a brutalist '60s cube houses the Kunsthalle, which hosts contemporary art shows. The bookstore is superb.

Rheinuferpromenade   PROMENADE
(Rhine River Walk) Burgplatz marks the beginning of the Rheinuferpromenade, whose cafes and benches fill with people in fine weather, creating an almost Mediterranean flair.

Schlossturm   HISTORIC BUILDING
(Palace Tower; Burgplatz 30) Looking a bit forlorn by the river, the Schlossturm is all that's left of the electors' palace, which burned down in 1872.

Rheinturm   TOWER
(Stromstrasse 20; adult/child €5/2.50; ☺10am-11.30pm) Spearing the sky at the southern

Düsseldorf

COLOGNE & NORTHERN RHINELAND DÜSSELDORF

Düsseldorf International (8km)

13

Joseph-Beuys-Ufer

14
Ehrenhof
Oederallee

Schelbenstr
Inselstr
Arnoldstr
Fischerstr
Nordstr
Kaiserstr
Duisburger Str
Sternstr
Feldstr
Rücenstr
Taunstr

23
Gartenstr

Oberkasseler Brücke

47
Tonhalle Hofgartenrampe
Fritz-Roeber-Str
Maxim-Weyhe-Allee

5

Hofgarten
Jan-Wellem-Platz

Reuterkaserne
Ritterstr
31
41 Ratinger Str
Altestadt
Stiftsplatz
Grabbeplatz 6
Mühlenstr
1
18
Burgplatz
17
Marktplatz
40
Kurze Str Andreasstr
42
39
16 12
Zollstr Altstadt
20
Tourist Office - Altstadt
Rheinartstr
43

10
44
Heinrich-Heine-Allee
Hofgartenstr
Schadow-platz
8 Cornelius-platz
Heinrich-Heine-Allee
19
Blumenstr

Rhine River

Rheinuferpromenade
Rheinufertunnel

Schossufer
Jalengasse
Mertensgasse
Bolker Str
Berger Str
Flingerstr
Wallstr

2 34
Schulstr
4
Citadellstr
30
25
Backerstr
Bäckerstr

Grabenstr Königstr
ALTSTADT
Carlsplatz
32
Benratherstr
Steinstr
Steinstrasse/Königsallee

Königsallee
Königsallee
Grünstr
Stresemanestr
Alexanderstr

Mediciplatz
45 3 35
Bastionstr
Bilker Str
29
38
Südstr
Hohe Str
Kasernenstr
Breite Str

Rheinkniebrücke
Mannesmannufer
Rathausufer
Berger Allee
Postsr

9
46
Thomasstr
Horion-platz
Apolloplatz
15

Haroldstr
Graf-Adolf-Platz
Graf-Adolf-Str
Bahnstr
Berliner Allee

28
Ernst-Reuter-Platz

Kavalleriestr
Reichsstr
Elisabethstr
Adersstr
Luisenstr

Neusserstr
Medienhafen (1.5km)
Fürstenwall

Standehausstr
7
Friedrichstr
Herzogstr
48
Talstr
Jahnstr

22

end of the Rhine promenade, the Rheinturm (which is brilliantly lit at night) has an observation deck at the 168m level of its overall height of 240m. The views are as sweeping, although the phrase 'on a clear day you can see Essen' may not inspire. There are various cafes, bars and a revolving restaurant should the mere thought of Essen get you hungry. Near the base is the Landtag, the state parliament.

Hetjens Museum
MUSEUM

(☑ 0211-899 4210; www.duesseldorf.de; Schulstrasse 4; adult/concession €4/2; ☺ 11am-5pm Tue-Sun, from 1pm Sat) A short detour off the Rheinuferpromenade takes you to the Hetjens Museum, known for its survey of 8000 years of ceramic art from around the world.

Filmmuseum
MUSEUM

(☑ 0211-899 2232; www.duesseldorf.de/filmmuseum; Schulstrasse 4; adult/concession €5/2.50; ☺ 11am-5pm Tue & Thu-Sun, to 9pm Wed) This small musuem trains the spotlight on the technology, history and mystery of movie-making. Its Black Box art-house cinema presents retrospectives, rare flicks and silent movies with live organ accompaniment.

Mahn-und Gedenkstätte Düsseldorf
MEMORIAL

(Memorial Düsseldorf; ☑ 0211-899 6144; www.gedenk-dus.de; Mühlenstrasse 6; ☺ 11am-5pm Sun-Fri, 1-5pm Sat) FREE A few steps west of Marktplatz is this memorial with exhibits on local persecution and resistance during the Third Reich. It reopened in 2015 after a complete reconstruction. Among the new permanent exhibits is 'Düsseldorf children and youth in the Third Reich'.

NRW-Forum Düsseldorf
GALLERY

(☑ 0211-892 6690; www.nrw-forum.de; Ehrenhof 2; adult/concession €6/3.50; ☺ 11am-8pm Tue-Sun, to 10pm Fri) For Zeitgeist-capturing exhibits, swing by the NRW-Forum Düsseldorf. It targets the lifestyle-savvy crowd with changing exhibits on fashion, media, design, photography and architecture.

Museum Kunstpalast
MUSEUM

(☑ 0211-899 0200; www.smkp.de; Ehrenhof 5; adult/child €12/1; ☺ 11am-6pm Tue-Sun, to 9pm Thu) Stuffy no more, the Kunstpalast presents its well-respected collection in paradigm-shifting ways. Old masters are juxtaposed with contemporary young dogs and non-Western works to reveal unexpected connections between the ages and artistic

Düsseldorf

trends. Temporary exhibitions further reinforce the theme.

Heinrich Heine Institut MUSEUM
(☎0211-899 2902; www.duesseldorf.de; Bilker Strasse 12-14; adult/child €4/free; ☺11am-5pm Tue-Fri & Sun, 1-5pm Sat) For a literary kick, swing by the Heinrich Heine Institut, where letters, portraits, first editions and manuscripts document this famed Düsseldorfer's career. Heine's birth house at Bolkerstrasse 53 now contains a literary bookshop and reading room.

KIT – Kunst im Tunnel GALLERY
(☎0211-892 0769; www.kunst-im-tunnel.de; Mannesmannufer 1b; adult/concession €4/3; ☺11am-6pm Tue-Sun) Young artists – many from the local art academy – get the nod in this underground exhibition space housed in a spectacularly adapted tunnel below the Rhine promenade. The entrance is via a glass pavilion.

◎ Medienhafen

South of the Altstadt, the Medienhafen (Media Harbour) is an office quarter that's been wrought from the remains of the old city harbour. It's Düsseldorf's largest and most progressive urban construction project, but despite a few trendy restaurants and shops, there's a paucity of life on the streets as yet.

Modern architecture fans, however, will want to head right down. The most eye-catching structure is clearly the warped **Neuer Zollhof**, a typically sculptural design by Frank Gehry. Moored nearby is Claude Vasconi's **Grand Bateau**, built to resemble an ocean liner. A pedestrian bridge links to another quay dominated by William Alsop's **Colorium**, easily recognised by its kaleidoscopic glass facade. Recent additions include **Hafen** by Helmut Jahn.

◎ Königsallee & Hofgarten

Banks and boutiques are the ammo of the Königsallee (Kö for short), one of Germany's most expensive shopping strips. Otherwise, there's little of actual merit here, although the art nouveau facade of the **Kaufhof** (Königsallee 1-9) department store and the landmark **Triton fountain** (Konigsallee) deserve a look.

Hofgarten

PARK

When you've had your shopping fill, head on over to the pleasant Hofgarten, dotted with statues of Heinrich Heine, Robert Schumann and other German greats.

◉ Schloss Benrath

Schloss Benrath

MUSEUM

(☑ 0211-899 3832; www.schloss-benrath.de; Benrather Schlossallee 100-106; combined ticket adult/concession €12/4; ⊙ 11am-5pm Tue-Sun; ⊛) Elector Carl Theodor was a man of deep pockets and good taste, as reflected in his vast and exquisite pleasure palace and gardens, where he came to relax and frolic. Designed by Frenchman Nicolas de Pigage, the three-winged palace centres on the **Corps de Logis** (adult/child €9/3), the former residential tract, where tours (in German) offer a glimpse of the elector's lifestyle. The complex is about 10km south of the city centre and reached by tram 701 and U74 in about 30 minutes.

The other wings contain an old-school **natural history museum** (adult/child €6/3) and a **museum of European garden history** (adult/child €6/3) that will probably grow on you.

✯ Activities

Radstation

BICYCLE RENTAL

(☑ 0211-514 4711; Willi-Becker-Allee 8a; rental per day from €8; ⊙ 7am-9pm Mon-Fri, 10am-8pm Sat & Sun) In the southeast corner of the train station, Radstation rents out a range of bikes. A natural first place to ride is the Rheinuferpromenade.

⌗ Tours

Old Town Walk

WALKING TOUR

(☑ 0211-1720 2854; www.duesseldorf-tourismus. de; Old Town Tourist Office, Marktsrasse; tours €11; ⊙ 3pm Sun-Thu, 3pm & 4pm Fri, 2pm Sat Apr-Oct, 3pm Fri & Sat, 11am Sun Nov-Mar) Explore the Altstadt on these bilingual (German and English) walking tours.

Hop On Hop Off City Tour

BUS TOUR

(☑ 0211-1720 2854; www.visitduesseldorf.de; Tourist Office, Immermannstrasse 65; adult/child €15/free; ⊙ 10.30am-4.30pm) This bus tour of the city, operated by the tourist office, is a good way to get a handle on the sprawl that is Düsseldorf in 90 minutes. There are a few caveats: the 'Hop On Hop Off' aspect is slightly dubious as you can wait a long time

between buses and the roof may stay closed even on nice days.

🛌 Sleeping

Düsseldorf's hotels cater primarily to business travellers, which explains why prices can triple during big trade shows held not only here but as far away as Cologne and Essen. Fortunately, bargains abound on weekends and in summer. Prices quoted here are outside trade-show spikes.

Hotel Berial

HOTEL €

(☑ 0211-490 0490; www.hotelberial.de; Gartenstrasse 30; s/d incl breakfast from €60/70; @ ☎) This well-kept property is a fine choice for wallet-watching nomads. The 40 rooms boast decor that's nothing to tweet about, but all the expected comforts and amenities are here. The Hofgarten is a couple of minutes away – perfect for jogging off your jet lag.

Backpackers-Düsseldorf

HOSTEL €

(☑ 0211-302 0848; www.backpackers-duesseldorf.de; Fürstenwall 180; dm €19-25; ⊙ reception 8am-10pm; ℙ@☎) Düsseldorf's adorable indie hostel sleeps 60 in clean four- to 10-bed dorms outfitted with individual backpack-sized lockers. It's a low-key place with a kitchen and a relaxed lounge where cultural and language barriers melt quickly. The vending machine is filled with beer. Rates include a small breakfast; linen costs €3.

★ Hotel Windsor

HOTEL €€

(☑ 0211-914 680; www.sir-astor.de; Grafenberger Allee 36; s/d from €100/110; ℙ 🖰@☎) With the same owner as the Sir & Lady Astor, the Windsor commits itself to the British country tradition. Behind the sandstone facade of this 100-year-old mansion await 18 rooms where you can unwind beneath stucco-ornamented ceilings surrounded by antiques and sedate prints.

Sir & Lady Astor

GUESTHOUSE €€

(☑ 0211-173 370; http://hotel.sir-astor.de; Kurfürstenstrasse 18 & 23; s/d from €70/80; 🖸@☎) Never mind the ho-hum setting on a residential street near the Hauptbahnhof: this unique twin boutique hotel brims with class, originality and charm. Check-in is at Sir Astor, furnished in 'Scotland-meets-Africa' style, while Lady Astor across the street goes more for French floral sumptuousness. With a huge fan base, great value and only 36 rooms in total, book early.

Stage 47 BOUTIQUE HOTEL €€

(📞0211-388 030; www.stage47.de; Graf-Adolf-Strasse 47; r €130-180; P❄@🅿) Behind the drab exterior, movie glamour meets design chic at this boutique hotel. Rooms are named for famous people, who appear in enormous black-and-white prints peering onto your bed, so let's hope you like who you sleep with...nice touches include a Nespresso coffeemaker.

Hotel Orangerie HOTEL €€

(📞0211-866 800; www.hotel-orangerie-mcs.de; Bäckergasse 1; r €110-200; ⊖🅿) Ensconced in a neoclassical mansion in a quiet corner of the Altstadt, this place puts you within staggering distance of pubs, the river and museums, yet offers a quiet and stylish refuge to retire to. Some of the 27 sparsely decorated rooms skimp somewhat on size but all are as bright, modern and uncluttered as the lobby and breakfast room (rates include breakfast).

Max Hotel Garni PENSION €€

(📞0211-386 800; www.max-hotelgarni.de; Adersstrasse 65; s/d €65/80; @🅿) Upbeat, contemporary and run with personal flair, this charmer is a favourite Düsseldorf bargain. The 11 rooms are good-sized and decked out in bright hues and warm woods. Rates include coffee, tea, soft drinks and a regional public transport pass; breakfast costs €7.50. The reception isn't always staffed, so call ahead to arrange an arrival time.

Hotel Mondial HOTEL €€

(📞0211-173 9920; www.nk-hotels.de; Graf-Adolf-Strasse 82; s €57-77, d €77-90; 🅿) In a veritable ghetto of mid-priced hotels near the Hauptbahnhof, the Mondial stands out for having small but sparkling rooms and service that borders on the jolly. Try for a room facing the street on the 5th floor and you'll get a small terrace.

✕ Eating

The heart of the Altstadt is a mass of places to eat of widely variable quality. Head over to Ratinger Strasse and Hohe Strasse for choices that are less visitor-swamped.

★ Café Hüftgold CAFE

(www.cafehueftgold.de; Ackerstrasse 113; snacks from €3; ⊗8am-7pm Mon-Wed, to 10pm Thu-Sat, 10am-10pm Sun) A Flingern Boho classic, Café Hüftgold is renowned for its amazing cakes, tortes and more baked goodness. The coffee and sandwiches are good as well.

★ Libanon Express MIDDLE EASTERN €

(📞0211-134 917; www.libanon-restaurant.de; Berger Strasse 19-21; mains €3-12; ⊗noon-11pm; 🖋) Crammed with mirrors and tiles, this cafe serves great kebabs, felafel and other Middle Eastern specialities. Its takeaway is a standout among competitors counting on customers to be too drunk to notice their poor fare. The adjoining sit-down restaurant has outdoor tables with a front seat on Berger Strasse frivolity; inside it's all *Arabian Nights* fantasy.

Kaffeerösterei Röstzeit CAFE €

(📞0211-8774 4590; www.roestzeit.de; Oststrasse 115; snacks €3-7; ⊗9am-6pm Mon-Fri, 10am-5pm Sat) 🖋 The smell of freshly roasted coffee may just snatch you up and pull you right inside this cool and casual cafe that takes its java *very* seriously. The beans are organic and the small plates of perfect little sandwiches or tasty tortes are ideal snacks.

Bäckerei Hinkel BAKERY €

(📞0211-8620 3421; www.baeckerei-hinkel.de; Hohe Strasse 31; snacks from €2; ⊗6am-6.30pm Mon-Fri, to 4pm Sat) This traditional bakery is an institution that has people queuing patiently for its excellent breads and cakes. Buy the fixings for a perfect picnic – it blows away anything you've had from a train station chain bakery.

★ Brauerei im Füchschen GERMAN €€

(📞0211-137 470; www.fuechschen.de; Ratinger Strasse 28; mains €6-16; ⊗9am-1am Mon-Thu, to 2am Fri & Sat, to midnight Sun) Boisterous, packed and drenched with local colour – the 'Little Fox' in the Altstadt is all you expect a Rhenish beer hall to be. The kitchen makes a mean *Schweinshaxe* (roast pork leg). The high-ceilinged interior echoes with the mirthful roar of people enjoying their meals. This is one of the best *Altbier* breweries in town.

Bistro Zicke BISTRO €€

(📞0211-327 800; www.bistro-zicke.de; Bäckerstrasse 5a; dishes €6-15; ⊗9am-1am) Arty types jam this staple in a quiet corner tucked away from the Altstadt bustle. Linger over breakfast (served until 3pm, on weekends till 4pm) or come for fresh and tasty soups, salads and various hot plates that change daily. Marble tables add class.

Restaurant Takumi JAPANESE €€

(📞0211-179 3308; Immermannstrasse 28; mains €8-16; ⊗noon-10pm) All you need to know about this seeming hole-in-the-wall is that you'll find a good portion of Düsseldorf's expat Japanese community here lined up for some of Germany's best noodle soups. The ramen noodles are made to perfection and slurp-worthy broth is both hearty and complex.

Carlsplatz   MARKET €€
(www.carlsplatz.net; cnr Hohe Strasse & Benrather Strasse; mains €5-20; ⊗ Mon-Sat) A former fruit and vegetable market has been transformed into a foodies playground. Scores of cafes, luxe food vendors, stand-up takeaways and others dish up a huge range of food that's always fresh and seasonal. Prices and hours vary widely, but prepare for some happy grazing: a wurst here, a glass of wine there, fresh berries over there...

★**Münstermann Kontor**   MODERN EUROPEAN €€€
(☑ 0211-130 0416; www.muenstermann-delikatessen.de; Hohe Strasse 11; menus €20-50; ⊗ 11am-10pm Mon-Fri, to 6pm Sat) This legendary long-running delicatessen has morphed into a legendary bistro serving Düsseldorf's best seasonal and locally sourced fare. Book early to enjoy the creative dishes that issue forth from the busy open kitchen. The vibe is energetic; try for a sidewalk table to enjoy the stylish Hohe Strasse scene.

Sila Thai   THAI €€€
(☑ 0211-860 4427; www.sila-thai.com; Bahnstrasse 76; mains €17-25; ⊗ noon-3pm & 6pm-1am) Even simple curries become culinary poetry at this Thai gourmet temple with its fairy-tale setting of carved wood, rich fabrics and imported sculpture. Like a trip to Thailand without the long flight. Book ahead.

🍷 Drinking & Nightlife

Düsseldorf's beverage of choice is *Altbier*, a dark, hoppy beer that's just slightly heavy. Think of it as the pepper to rival Cologne's salt (*Kölsch*).

★**Zum Uerige**   BEER HALL
(☑ 0211-866 990; www.uerige.de; Berger Strasse 1; ⊗ 10am-midnight) This cavernous brew pub is the quintessential Düsseldorf haunt to try the city's typical *Altbier*. The suds flow so quickly from giant copper vats that the waiters – called *Köbes* – simply carry huge trays of brew and plonk down a glass whenever they spy an empty. Even on a cold day, the outside tables are alive with merriment.

FLINGERN FLING

Once all working-class, Flingern, a neighbourhood east of the Hauptbahnhof, is now the centre of Düsseldorf's stylish hipness. The main strip is a 1km-stretch of leafy Ackerstrasse, where retail therapy gets a unique twist in indie boutiques stocked with vintage frocks, edgy jewellery, whimsical tees, handmade accessories and gourmet foods.

There are cafes by the dozen; try arty, punky Café Hüftgold or join the mixed and merry mobs on the terrace at Beethoven (p502).

Getting there is easy: from the Hauptbahnhof it's either a 15-minute walk via Worringer Strasse or a short ride on tram 709 or 719 to Wetterstrasse (head north for a couple of minutes to get to Ackerstrasse).

★**Stone Im Ratinger Hof**   CLUB
(☑ 0211-210 7828; www.stone-club.de; Ratinger Strasse 10; cover varies; ⊗ Wed, Fri & Sat) The venerable Ratinger Hof is the place for indie and alt sounds. Depending on the night, tousled boho types, skinny-jean emos and sneaker-wearing students thrash it out to everything from noise pop to indietronic to punk and roll.

★**Destille**   BAR
(☑ 0211-327 181; www.destille-duesseldorf.de; Bilker Strasse 46; mains from €8; ⊗ 4pm-midnight, from 10am Sat) The kind of neighbourhood bar that makes you want to move to the neighbourhood. Saturday mornings are 'breakfasts with authors' – when local authors give talks – on other days there is live jazz, while you can expect art exhibitions any time. The small menu has numerous vegetarian choices.

Melody Bar   COCKTAIL BAR
(☑ 0211-329 057; Kurze Strasse 12; ⊗ 9pm-3am Wed-Sat) After 10pm you may have to shoehorn your way into this jewel of a cocktail bar that's an island of sophistication amid the boisterous Altstadt thirst parlours. The drinks are excellent, the owner couple gracious and the crowd mixed.

Salon des Amateurs   LOUNGE
(☑ 0211-899 6243; www.salondesamateurs.de; Grabbeplatz 4; ⊗ noon-1am Tue-Sun, to 5am Fri & Sat) Tucked into the Kunsthalle, this

Historic Marvels

Germany's history has been shaped by many players. Hear the whispers of the past as you nose around medieval castles, crane your neck to take in lofty cathedrals and explore the cobbled tangle of towns founded centuries before Columbus set sail. If only stones could talk...

Beauteous Bamberg

1 Germany teems with towns drenched in history, but Bamberg (p276) is a particularly delightful web of medieval lanes, with a lordly cathedral, well-kept historic buildings and some of Germany's best beer. The Altes Rathaus is a shutterbug favourite.

Europe's Roots

2 Few people have shaped Europe as much as Charlemagne. And few German cathedrals have as illustrious a history as Aachen's (p486), where the Frankish king-turned-emperor is buried and which witnessed the coronations of over 30 kings between AD 936 and 1531.

Joyful Sanctuaries

3 Lift your spirits at the heavenly rococo Wieskirche pilgrimage church (p233), rising like a vision from an emerald Bavarian meadow. With angels flitting across frescoed ceilings and an altar that is a symphony of colour, its beauty will resonate even with nonbelievers.

Fairy-tale Fantasy

4 Before touring Schloss Neuschwanstein in Füssen, glimpse an insight into 'Mad' King Ludwig II's mind on a spin around his childhood home, Schloss Hohenschwangau (p231. A romantic neo-gothic extravaganza, it is festooned with mythological murals and still furnished in the original 19th-century style.

1 Altes Rathaus (p277), Bamberg 2 Aachener Dom (p487) 3 Wieskirche, Bavaria 4 Schloss Hohenschwangau, Füssen

tunnel-shaped cafe-lounge pulls off an artsy vibe without a single canvas. Museum-goers arrive in the afternoon for tea and a chat, while scenesters keep the bar and little dance floor hopping after dark.

Beethoven BAR
(📇 0211-2339 8687; Ackerstrasse 106; ⏲ 10am-1am) Stop off for coffee and a snack or go with the majority and plunge into the drink menu. This Flingern classic caters to a mixed crowd who whoop it up on the terrace.

Sub CLUB
(📇 0211-865 890; www.sub-duesseldorf.de; Bolker Strasse 14; ⏲ from 10pm Wed, Fri & Sat) Getting past the door can be tough, but if you succeed you'll have a fine time inside this glitzy basement haunt designed to look like a subway station. Tip: dress nicely, smile and don't arrive drunk.

Em Pöötzke BAR
(📇 0211-326 973; www.jazz-em-poetzke.de; Mertensgasse 6; ⏲ 8pm-1am Mon-Fri, to 2am Sat) Jazz blares live and recorded every night

---

WHERE TO DRINK IN THE ALTSTADT

With the 'world's longest bar' hype, the Altstadt may seem like one big festive drunk, but there are distinct personalities to various streets. Here's a guide as you go on the prowl.

➤ **Andreasstrasse** A good place to find a classy cafe or restaurant with a free table outside.

➤ **Berger Strasse** Excellent casual restaurants and what seems like a hectare of outdoor tables.

➤ **Bolker Strasse** A nightmare of fake ethnic restaurants geared towards the undiscerning; bad bars and a mural of a man pooping.

➤ **Hunsrückenstrasse** Fake Irish bars – need we say more?

➤ **Rheinartstrasse** The merry crowds spilling out of Zum Uerige set the tone.

➤ **Kurze Strasse** Slightly mellow, restaurants with tables outside, not a mob scene.

➤ **Mertensgasse** Quieter than others, few outside tables, several late-night clubs.

---

that this narrow little Altstadt joint is open. Duck off the narrow street and choose from an array of whiskies and *Altbiers*.

☆ Entertainment

Check listings site Coolibri (www.coolibri.de) for current goings-on in 'D-Town'.

★ **Marionetten-Theater** THEATRE
(📇 0211-328 432; www.marionettentheater-duesseldorf.de; Bilker Strasse 7; tickets €15-24; 📷) Generations of kids and adults have been enthralled by the adorable marionettes that sing, dance and act their way through beautifully orchestrated operas and fairy tales at this venerable venue. Pure magic.

Roncalli's Apollo Varieté THEATRE
(📇 0211-828 9090; www.apollo-variete.de; Apolloplatz 1; tickets €14-39) No German skills are needed to enjoy the line-up of acrobats, comedians, magicians, artistes and other variety acts performing under the starry-sky ceiling of a nostalgic theatre hall.

Tonhalle CLASSICAL MUSIC
(📇 0211-899 6123; www.tonhalle-duesseldorf.de; Ehrenhof 1) The imposing domed Tonhalle, in a converted 1920s planetarium, is the home base of the Düsseldorfer Symphoniker (Düsseldorf Symphony Orchestra).

Deutsche Oper Am Rhein OPERA
(📇 0211-892 5211; operamrhein.de; Heinrich-Heine-Allee 16a; tickets €15-100) Düsseldorf's renowned opera house.

🛍 Shopping

The big noise is all about the big names with the big prices in the Königsalle. Think of it as duty-free luxury goods without the savings. Closer to the Altstadt, check out streets like Benratherstrasse and Hohe Strasse for interesting and creative boutiques. Finally, there is Flingern, with everything for sale you can imagine along Ackerstrasse.

Buchhaus Stern-Verlag BOOKS
(📇 0211-388 10; www.buchhaus-sternverlag.de; Friedrichstrasse 24-26; ⏲ 9.30am-8pm Mon-Sat; ☎) Great bookshop with huge international selection and a cafe.

ℹ Information

The **Düsseldorf Card** (24/48/72hr €9/14/19) offers free public transport and discounted museum admission. Available from the tourist office.

ReiseBank (✆ 0211-364 878; Konrad-Adenauer-Platz 14, Hauptbahnhof; ⊙7am-10pm Mon-Sat, 8am-9pm Sun) Exchange and money transfer services.

Tourist Office – Altstadt (✆ 0211-1720 2840; www.duesseldorf-tourismus.de; cnr Marktstrasse & Rheinstrasse; ⊙10am-6pm) Right in the heart of the old centre.

Tourist Office – Hauptbahnhof (✆ 0211-1720 2844; www.visitduesseldorf.de; Immermannstrasse 65b; ⊙9.30am-7pm Mon-Fri, to 5pm Sat) The main tourist office, across from the train station; has an exchange window.

❶ Getting There & Away

AIR

Düsseldorf International Airport (DUS; www.dus-int.de) has three terminals and is served by a wide range of airlines.

BUS

Düsseldorf's central bus station is on Worringer Strasse, about 250m north of the Hauptbahnhof main exit. From here, Eurolines services include daily buses to Paris (7½ hours), Warsaw (20 hours) and London (13½ hours).

TRAIN

Düsseldorf is part of a dense S-Bahn and regional train network in the Rhine-Ruhr region, with services to Cologne (€12, 30 minutes). ICE/IC train links include Berlin (€111, 4¼ hours), Hamburg (€82, 3¾ hours) and Frankfurt (€82, 1½ hours).

❶ Getting Around

The Hauptbahnhof (main train station) is on the southeastern edge of the city centre. From here it's about a 20-minute walk along Bismarckstrasse and Blumenstrasse to the Königsallee, with the Altstadt just beyond. Alternatively, any U-Bahn from the Hauptbahnhof to Heinrich-Heine-Allee will put you right in the thick of things.

TO/FROM THE AIRPORT

The airport is about 7km north of the Altstadt.

S-Bahns, regional RE and long-distance trains connect the airport with Düsseldorf Hauptbahnhof, and cities beyond, every few minutes. The free SkyTrain links the airport terminals with the Flughaven Bahnhof station, although the S11 goes direct to the terminals. A taxi into town costs about €20.

CAR & MOTORCYCLE

Central Düsseldorf is now a low-emission zone, meaning that your car needs to display an *Umweltplakette* (emission sticker). Rental cars automatically have the sticker, but if you're driving your own vehicle you'll need to obtain one.

PUBLIC TRANSPORT

Rheinbahn (www.rheinbahn.de; single-ride/daypass €2.60/6.60) Operates an extensive network of U-Bahn trains, trams and buses throughout Düsseldorf. Tickets are available from bus drivers and orange vending machines at U-Bahn and tram stops, and must be validated upon boarding.

TAXI

Taxi (✆ 0211-212 121)

Lower Rhine

North of Düsseldorf, the Rhine widens and embarks on its final headlong rush towards the North Sea, traversing the sparsely populated Lower Rhine (Niederrhein). It's a flat, windswept plain that feels like Holland without the windmills and yields a few offbeat surprises.

The region has its own airport, the tiny **Airport Weeze** (www.airport-weeze.de), which is a hub for RyanAir (which, in its own inimitable fashion, calls the airport 'Düsseldorf-Weeze' even though D-town is over 80km away).

Xanten

☎ 02801 / POP 21,700

Some of the region's most interesting museums capture Xanten's role as the hub of the Lower Rhine, going all the way back to when it was founded as a Roman military camp in 12 BC. Within a century it grew into a respectable settlement called Colonia Ulpia Traiana. At its peak, some 15,000 people milled about town, enjoying a surprisingly high standard of living.

Xanten's next heyday – in medieval times – is best symbolised by the majestic Dom that dominates the tangled old town with its stately gates, cheerful mills and historic fountains. The town is also the mythological birthplace of Siegfried, the dragon-slaying hero of the 12th-century Nibelungen epic, which became the subject of Richard Wagner's Ring opera cycle 700 years later.

Xanten enjoys an annual highlight during its huge Christmas market in December.

◉ Sights & Activities

You can still find traces of the Middle Ages in Xanten's surviving fragments of walls and entry towers. Bikes are an ideal way to visit the extended sights.

★ **RömerMuseum** MUSEUM

(⌖ 02801-988 9213; www.apx.lvr.de; Siegfriedstrasse 39; adult/child incl Archäologischer Park €9/free; ⊙ 9am-6pm Mar-Oct, 10am-4pm Nov-Feb; 🚼) The grand building west of the Archäologischer Park houses the RömerMuseum, which takes you on a journey through 400 years of Roman presence in the Lower Rhine region. Modern and interactive, the exhibit kicks off with the arrival of the Roman legions and ends with the colony's 4th-century demise at the hands of marauding Germanic tribes. The complex is about 1km northwest of the train station and town centre.

The museum was built on the foundations of the Grosse Thermen thermal baths, which have been partly excavated and can be admired in an adjacent hall.

Make your way along the floating ramps to learn how the Roman folk earned their money, worshipped, educated their kids, played and buried their dead. A highlight among the locally excavated treasures is a Roman ship.

Archäologischer Park MUSEUM

(Archaeological Park; ⌖ 02801-988 9213; www.apx.lvr.de; Wardter Strasse 2; adult/child incl Römer-Museum €9/free; ⊙ 9am-6pm Mar-Oct, 10am-4pm Nov-Feb; 🚼) The old Roman colony has been reborn as an archaeological park, an open-air museum that features faithfully reconstructed buildings to help amateurs visualise what the Roman town looked like. The originals were torn down and used in building the medieval town. Kids will enjoy the two imaginative playgrounds: one a Roman fort, the other water-themed (bring a towel). The Archaeological Park adjoins the RömerMuseum.

The self-guided tour takes you past such sites as the Amphitheatre, which seats 12,000 people during Xanten's summer music festival; the Spielehaus, where you can play early versions of backgammon and Nine Men's Morris; a Roman hostel complete with hot baths and restaurant; and the majestic Hafentempel (harbour temple).

Dom St Viktor CHURCH

(⌖ 02801-713 10; www.stviktor-xanten.de; Kapitel 8; ⊙ 10am-6pm Mon-Sat, 12.30-6pm Sun Apr-Oct, to 5pm Nov-Mar) The crown jewel of Xanten's Altstadt is the Dom St Viktor, which has Romanesque roots but is now largely Gothic. It is framed by a walled close, called an 'Immunity', which can only be entered from the Markt.

The soaring five-nave interior brims with treasures, reflecting the wealth Xanten enjoyed in the Middle Ages. Foremost is the Marienaltar, halfway down the right aisle, whose base features an intricately carved version of the *Tree of Jesse* by Heinrich Douvermann (1535).

The candelabrum in the central nave, with its *Doppelmadonna* (Double Madonna, 1500), is another masterpiece. A stone sarcophagus in the crypt holds the remains of St Viktor, the Roman martyr who became Xanten's patron saint. Look for the preserved original statues behind glass outside.

Siegfried Museum Xanten MUSEUM

(⌖ 02801-772 200; www.siegfriedmuseum-xanten.de; Kurfürstenstrasse 9; adult/child €4/free; ⊙ 10am-5pm Mon-Sat, 11am-4pm Sun; 🚼) Wagner's *Der Ring des Nibelungen* (The Ring of the Nibelung), which is legendary for its length (15 hours over four epic operas), has Siegfried the dragonslayer as its main character. An obsession for many, this museum in the Altstadt lays out the stories and myths using family-friendly displays – kids can dress up as knights.

With reality lost in the mists of time, Wagner's tales of the House of Burgundy, and Norse settlers who settled in northern German from around the 6th century, include kings, rivalries, invasions and dragons.

Stiftsmuseum MUSEUM

(Monastic Museum; www.stiftsmuseum-xanten.de; Kapitel 21; adult/child €4/free; ⊙ 10am-5pm Tue-Sat, to 6pm Sun) This museum in the 1000-year-old abbey near the Dom contains treasures, including reliquaries, sculptures and graphics. The illuminated manuscripts always amaze with their detailed, hand-drawn beauty.

EBike 4 All BICYCLE RENTAL

(⌖ 02838-778 074; http://ebike4all-xanten.de; off Bahnhofstrasse, Bahnhof; rental per day from €9; ⊙ 10am-8pm Mon-Sat, to 4pm Sun Apr-Sep) In the train station, there's a large selection for rent, including electric bikes.

🛏 Sleeping & Eating

★ **Neumaier** HOTEL €€

(⌖ 02801 715 70; www.hotel-neumaier.de; Orkstrasse 19-21; s/d from €70/100; 🅿 🛜) The 16 rooms are sprightly at this family-run hotel close to the Markt in the Altstadt. Cute touches abound, including house plants and rubber ducks for rooms with bathtubs. There's a beautiful beer garden in a courtyard that makes a perfect pause between the town's museums.

Hotel van Bebber   HOTEL €€
(☑02801-6623; www.hotelvanbebber.de; Klever Strasse 12; s/d from €80/110; P🐾🖥🛜) Queen Victoria and Churchill have slept in this old-school 35-room hotel, where waiters wear tuxedos and the reception is past a gallery of mounted animal heads. Rooms reflect the history, with open beams and antiques.

★ Emilie's Le Petit Joli   CAFE €
(☑02801-985 0961; www.lepetitjoli.de; Klever Strasse 6; mains €4-8; ☺9am-6pm Thu-Sun) Emilie has a reason to smile – as do her many happy customers: the food here, from breakfasts to afternoon cakes, is sensational. The menu changes daily, but whatever you order, whether in the artfully chaotic dining room or in the lovely garden, will be a delight.

Zur Börse   GERMAN €€
(☑02801-1441; zurboersexanten.de; Markt 12; mains €8-18; ☺11am-10pm Wed-Mon) Waiters in chequered aprons bustle between tables inside and out at this smart restaurant in the very heart of town. There are good beers on tap and the menu is thick with classic dishes. Look for the yellow bunnies perched in the upstairs windows.

ⓘ Information

Tourist Office (☑02801-983 00; www.xanten. de; Kurfürstenstrasse 9; ☺10am-5pm Mon-Sat, 11am-4pm Sun) The tourist office is right in the Altstadt.

ⓘ Getting There & Around

Trains run on a branch line from Duisberg (€13, 45 minutes, hourly), which has good connections.

Xanten's compact Altstadt is about a 10-minute walk northeast of the train station via Hagenbuschstrasse or Bahnhofstrasse.

Kalkar & Around

☑02824 / POP 13,800

About 15km north of Xanten, Kalkar boasts a pretty medieval core centred on a proud **Rathaus**. It's renowned for its woodcarving traditions.

◉ Sights

★ St Nikolaikirche   CHURCH
(☑02824-976 510; www.stnicolai.de; Jan-Joest-Strasse 6; ☺10am-noon & 2-5.30pm Apr-Oct,

2-3.30pm Nov-Mar) Dating from the 13th century, St Nikolaikirche is famous for its nine masterful altars chiselled by members of the Kalkar woodcarving school. Top billing goes to the High Altar, which depicts the Passion of Christ in heart-wrenching detail. Another eye-catcher is the Seven Sorrows Altar, by Henrik Douvermann, at the end of the right aisle. Note the oak-carved *Jesse's Root,* which wraps around the entire altar.

For a little comic relief, lift the first seat on the left in the back row of the choir chairs (with you facing the altar) to reveal a monkey on a chamber pot.

Schloss Moyland   CASTLE
(☑02824-951 060; www.moyland.de; Am Schloss 4; adult/concession €7/3; ☺11am-6pm Mon-Fri, 10am-6pm Sat & Sun Apr-Sep, 11am-5pm Oct-Mar) With its Rapunzel towers and Romeo-and-Juliet balcony, Schloss Moyland is an unexpected sight amid the dull expanses of the Lower Rhine flatlands. The 'medieval' fairy-tale looks are deceiving: they're a 19th-century creation. Today, the castle houses a private modern-art collection that includes a huge assortment of works by Joseph Beuys. The labyrinthine interior is smothered in drawings, paintings and etchings. For a breather, take a spin around the lovely park with its old trees and wacky sculptures.

ⓘ Getting There & Away

Bus 44 makes regular trips from Xanten's Bahnhof to the Markt in Kalkar, but the service is infrequent on weekends.

Schloss Moyland is about 4km northwest of Kalkar off the B57 and is well signposted.

THE RUHRGEBIET

Once known for its belching steelworks and filthy coal mines, the Ruhrgebiet – a sprawling post-industrial region of 53 cities and 5.3 million people – has worked hard in recent years to reinvent itself for the future.

In the meantime, rather than eschew the Ruhrgebiet's heritage, the people have embraced it. Many of the dormant furnaces, steel works, coking plants and other vestiges of the industrial age have been rebooted in creative ways. You can see cutting-edge art in a huge converted gas tank or free-climb around a blast furnace. Tours and parks embrace the muscular legacy of this vast and defunct industrial complex.

INDUSTRIAL HERITAGE TRAIL

Most of the smokestacks and mines are eerily silent today, but many of the Ruhr region's 'cathedrals of industry' have taken on a new life as museums, concert halls, cinemas, restaurants, lookouts, playgrounds and other such venues. Dozens of them are linked along the 400km **Industrial Heritage Trail** (www.route-industriekultur.de) that takes in such cities as Dortmund, Essen, Duisburg and Bochum. Most sites are also served by public transport.

The route has several dedicated visitors centres, including one at Zollverein (p507) in Essen. Virtually any tourist office in the Ruhrgebiet will also have plenty of details, including lots of info in English.

For travellers, the Ruhrgebiet delivers a trainload of surprises and unique sights, locations and experiences. You'll find old masters, great architecture from Gothic to Bauhaus to postmodern, cutting edge culture and much more.

ℹ Information

The **Ruhr.TopCard** (adult/child €50/35, www. ruhrtopcard.de) gives free public transport and free and discounted admission to 90 attractions, including theme parks, museums and tours, during the course of a calendar year. It's available from local tourist offices.

The region's tourist authority, **Ruhr Tourismus** (www.ruhr-tourismus.de), has an excellent range of information in English.

ℹ Getting Around

The Ruhrgebiet has a complex web of public transport systems made up of U-Bahns, buses and trams in cities and linked together by frequent S-Bahns and trains.

The region is divided into zones by the transport authority **VRR** (www.vrr.de). Check the displays on ticket machines to determine how much you'll pay for your ticket.

All cities covered in the Ruhrgebiet section have introduced low-emission zones in their city centres, so your car needs to display an *Umweltplakette* (emission sticker). Rental cars automatically have the sticker, but if you're driving your own vehicle you'll need to obtain one.

Essen

🖉 0201 / POP 566,900

It's taken a few decades, but Germany's seventh-largest city has mastered the transition from industrial powerhouse to city of commerce and culture. A visit with Van Gogh? Go to the Museum Folkwang. Emperor Otto III's gem-studded childhood crown? Head for the cathedral treasury. A Unesco-listed Bauhaus-style coal mine with a fabulous museum? Look no further than Zollverein.

◉ Sights

Essen's sights are scattered about. If you only have time for one, make it Zollverein, with its myriad attractions. With more time, give the city centre a wander. All this can be done on an easy day trip from Cologne or Münster.

◉ Zollverein

The former Zollverein coal mine was recognised as a Unesco World Heritage Site in 2001. In operation until 1986, the sprawling site has since been rebooted as a cultural hub with museums, performance spaces, artists' studios, cafes and some unusual playgrounds. The centrepiece is the old coal-washing plant, a beautiful Bauhaus-style behemoth that houses the main museum and the visitors centre. Start your visit with a ride on the giant exterior escalator that points the way like a huge orange arrow.

Be sure to walk the grounds, which encompass dozens of large industrial buildings spread out over a wooded expanse with some parklike areas. The site is also an excellent place for cycling; you can rent bikes near the visitors centre. Attractions are grouped into three main areas. In the vast coking plant there is a Ferris wheel (Sonnenrad) and an ice-skating rink on the old barge canal that operates seasonally. Cafes and restaurants are scattered about.

Tram 107 travels to Zollverein from the Hauptbahnhof.

★ **Ruhr Museum** MUSEUM
(🖉 0201-2468 1444; www.ruhrmuseum.de; Fritz-Schupp-Allee 15; adult/child €8/free; ⊙ 10am-6pm) The former coal-washing plant provides an edgy setting for the Ruhr Museum. Exhibits span the history of the Ruhr Region in an easily accessible and engaging

fashion. Just as the coal was transported on conveyor belts, a long escalator whisks you up to the foyer from where you descend into the dark bowels of the building. With its raw stone walls, steep steel stairs, shiny aluminium ducts and industrial machinery, the space itself has all the drama and mystique of a movie set (*Blade Runner* comes to mind).

Don't miss the section showing the poor conditions of the workers and how an effort to strike for better conditions in the 1920s was brutally crushed. It still has echoes today.

Panorama VIEWPOINT
(Ruhr Museum; admission incl with Zollverein Museum; ☺10am-6pm) Feel like a coal miner as you climb dozens of steps up from the Ruhr Museum to the summit of the coal-washing building, where a large viewing platform lets you ponder the vast scope of Zollverein, with the Ruhrgebiet as a backdrop. There's also a multimedia presentation on industrial culture.

Red Dot Design Museum MUSEUM
(☎0201-301 0425; www.red-dot.org; Gelsenkirchener Strasse 181; adult/child €6/free; ☺11am-6pm Tue-Sun) The Red Dot Design Museum is in the stoker's hall, creatively adapted by British architect Norman Foster. In a perfect marriage of space and function, this four-storey maze showcases the best in contemporary design amid the original fixtures: bathtubs balancing on grated walkways, bike helmets dangling from snakelike heating ducts, and beds perching atop a large oven. All objects are winners of the Red Dot award, the 'Oscar' of the design world.

Zollverein Visitors Centre TOURIST INFORMATION
(☎0201-246 810; www.zollverein.de; Gelsenkirchener Strasse 181; ☺10am-6pm) The best place to get a handle on Zollverein's vast site and myriad attractions. It's near the tram stop and also has information on the entire Ruhrgebiet.

⊙ City Centre

★Museum Folkwang MUSEUM
(☎0201-884 5314; www.museum-folkwang.de; Goethestrasse 41; ☺10am-6pm Tue-Sun, to 8pm Thu & Fri) FREE A grand dame among Germany's art repositories, the Museum Folkwang has sparkling digs designed by British star architect David Chipperfield. Galleries radiate out from inner courtyards and gardens of the glass-fronted building, providing a progressive setting for such 19th- and 20th-century masters as Gauguin, Van Gogh and Mark Rothko.

Dom CATHEDRAL
(☎0201-220 4206; www.domschatz-essen.de; Burgplatz 2; treasury adult/concession €4/2; ☺6.30am-6.30pm Mon-Fri, 9am-7.30pm Sat, 9am-8pm Sun, treasury 10am-5pm Tue-Sat, 11.30am-5pm Sun) Essen's medieval Dom is an island of quiet engulfed by the commercialism of pedestrianised Kettwiger Strasse, the main shopping strip. It has a priceless collection of Ottonian works, all about 1000 years old. Not to be missed is a hauntingly beautiful Golden Madonna, set in her own midnight-blue chapel matching the colour of her eyes. The treasury presents more fancy baubles, including a crown worn by Holy Roman Emperor Otto III, in a modern, intimate fashion.

Alte Synagoge SYNAGOGUE
(☎0201-884 5218; www.alte-synagoge.essen.de; Steeler Strasse 29; ☺10am-6pm Tue-Sun) East of the cathedral, the grand Alte Synagoge miraculously survived WWII largely intact. A memorial site since 1980, it is a Jewish cultural centre.

⊙ Werden

Lining a pastoral stretch of Ruhr, the half-timbered houses and cobbled lanes of the suburb of Werden intimate at what a preindustrial Ruhrgebiet must have looked like. The village today mixes low-key modernity with a sprinkling of medieval structures. Take a breather in the lovely park on an island in the river.

The S6 follows a leafy route to Werden from the Hauptbahnhof.

Basilika St Ludgerus CHURCH
(☎0201-491 801; www.schatzkammer-werden.de; Brückstrasse 54; treasury adult/concession €3/2; ☺treasury 10am-noon & 3-5pm Tue-Sun) Werden's main sight is solid-stone St Ludgerus (1175), a beautiful late-Romanesque church named for the Frisian missionary buried here. It has an impressive exterior as well as a commendable treasury housed in the old abbey. The interior has sumptuous carvings.

🛏 Sleeping

Hotels in the centre cater for business visitors and are mostly nondescript and overpriced. The more charming places are in the suburbs.

★ **Hotel Résidence** BOUTIQUE HOTEL **€€**
(☑ 02054-955 90; www.hotel-residence.de; Auf der Forst 1; s/d from €95/125; P ⊜ ⊗) Posh and petite, this 17-room hotel in an art nouveau villa in the historic suburb of Kettwig appeals to refined tastes. Dinner in the vaunted namesake **restaurant** (www.hotel-residence.de; Auf der Forst 1; menus from €120; ⊙5-10pm Tue-Sat), which boasts two Michelin stars for chef Berthold Buehler, is a special delight during summer when you can dine in the garden.

Mintrops City Hotel
Margarethenhöhe HOTEL **€€**
(☑ 0201-438 60; www.mmhotels.de; Steile Strasse 46; r €70-150; P ⊜ ⊗) A former Krupp guesthouse has been reborn as a cheerful 30-room hotel, filled with light, art and designer touches. It's about 5km south of the centre in the Margarethenhöhe, a garden-like art nouveau workers' colony. Take the U17 to Laubenweg.

✗ Eating

There's a dearth of interesting restaurants in the city centre, which is also dead after dark. Head south to Rüttenscheider Strasse (known as 'Rü' locally), where you have your pick from dozens of eateries. Take the U11 or tram 107 to Martinstrasse or Rüttenscheider Stern.

Orkide Döner Kebab TURKISH **€**
(☑ 0201-797 408; cnr Klarastrasse & Rüttenscheider Strasse; mains €4-10; ⊙11.30am-10pm Mon-Sat) People come from all over, passing a lot of other Döner places on the way, to enjoy the piquant goodness. Germany's favourite fast food is given great treatment in an appropriately casual setting. The sauces and fillings are just that much better than the rest. The Rüttenscheider Stern U-Bahn stop is right out front.

★ **Miamamia** CAFE **€€**
(☑ 0201-874 2562; www.miamamia.de; Rüttenscheider Strasse 183; mains €6-16; ⊙9am-10pm Mon-Sat) An Italian treasure! This cafe is beautifully situated in an old house and offers easily the best coffee in the region. Also enjoy paninis and other simple Med classics. Retreat to tables in the garden or soak up the Rü scene out front.

♀ Drinking & Nightlife

Zeche Carl CLUB
(☑ 0201-834 4410; www.zechecarl.de; Wilhelm-Nieswandt-Allee 100; ⊙cafe & beer garden 5-11pm Tue-Fri, 11am-11pm Sat) The machine hall and washrooms of a former coal mine have been restyled as an alternative cultural centre with live concerts, parties, cabaret, theatre and art exhibits. The cafe has a beer garden plus a wide range of small and large plates. Take U11 or U17 to Karlsplatz.

❶ Information

Tourist Office (☑ 0201-887 2048, 0201-194 33; www.essen.de; Am Hauptbahnhof 2; ⊙9am-6pm Mon-Fri, 10am-4pm Sun)

❶ Getting There & Around

There are frequent ICE and IC trains in all directions and RE and S-Bahn trains to other Ruhrgebiet cities departing every few minutes and other cities in the region such as Düsseldorf (€11, 30 minutes).

The Hauptbahnhof's Nord (north) exit drops you right onto the centre's main drag, the pedestrianised Kettwiger Strasse.

Essen's major sights are spread out, but all are accessible by U-Bahn, S-Bahn or trams. The handiest line is tram 107, which shuttles between the Zollverein coal mine, the Museum Folkwang and the Rüttenscheid Strasse dining and nightlife.

For a taxi, call ☑ 866 55.

Dortmund

☑ 0231 / POP 572,000

Football (soccer) is a major Dortmund passion. Borussia Dortmund, the city's Bundesliga (Germany's first league) team, has been national champion an impressive eight times, including the 2011–12 season and runners-up 2013–14. So it's appropriate that the city is home to the new German Football Museum.

As the largest city in the Ruhrgebiet, Dortmund built its prosperity on coal, steel and beer. These days, the mines are closed, the steel mills quiet and more Zeitgeist-compatible high-tech industries have taken their place. Only the breweries are going as strong as ever, churning out oceans of beer and ale, much of it for export.

◉ Sights

Besides the German Football Museum, Dortmund continues the Ruhrgebiet theme of industrial resuse with a brewery-turned-art-centre right by the station and a string of beautiful churches in its centre. You can easily experience it in a few hours.

Commerce coexists with religious treasures in Dortmund's city centre, just south of the Hauptbahnhof. The trio of churches conveniently line up along the pedestrianised Westenhellweg.

★**DFB-Museum** MUSEUM
(German Football Museum; ☑0231-476 4660; www.fussballmuseum.de; Königswall; adult/concession €17/14; ⊙9am-5pm Tue-Sun) Classic scenes of German football triumphs play across the facade of this vast shrine to the nation's passion. Right outside the Hauptbahnhof, the museum has 6900 sq metres of exhibits dedicated to the nation's football passions and triumphs. Storylines familiar to every fan are explored, such as the battle in the heat between Germany and Italy at the World Cup semifinals in Mexico City in 1970.

★**Zollern Colliery** MUSEUM
(☑0231-696 1111; www.lwl-industriemuseum.de; Grubenweg 5; adult/child €5/2; ⊙10am-6pm Tue-Sun; ☐462, 378, ☐Bövinghausen) The Zollern II/IV Coal Mine was considered a 'model mine' when operation began in 1902. It boasted state-of-the-art technology and fantastic architecture, including an art nouveau machine hall and a castlelike administration building adorned with gables and onion-domed towers. An innovative exhibit documents the harsh realities of life as a miner, with plenty of interactive and children-oriented programs. It's one of eight industrial museums across the region linked under the banner LWL Industrial Museum.

Dortmunder U GALLERY
(☑0231-502 4723; www.dortmunder-u.de; Leonie-Reygers-Terrasse; ⊙Tue-Wed & Sat-Sun 11am-6pm, to 8pm Thu-Fri) FREE You can see it from afar – the golden 'U' atop the tower of the defunct Union Brauerei. Once one of Dortmund's largest and most famous breweries, the protected landmark has been reborn as a cultural centre and home to the Museum am Ostwall. Many exhibitions outside the museum are free and there are great views from the top-floor cafe. It's a five-minute walk east of the train station.

Museum Am Ostwall MUSEUM
(☑0231-502 3248; www.museumamostwall.dortmund.de; Dortmunder U, Leonie-Reygers-Terrasse; adult/concession €5/2.50; ⊙Tue-Wed & Sat-Sun 11am-6pm, to 8pm Thu-Fri) The top three floors of Dortmunder U are home to an art-world star thanks to the Ostwall's far-reaching collection of all major 20th- and 21st-century

genres – expressionism to art informel, fluxus and op-art to concrete art. This translates into works by Macke, Nolde, Beuys and Paik, and living artists including Jochen Gerz, and Anna and Bernhard Blume.

Mahn- und Gedenkstätte Steinwache MEMORIAL
(☑0231-502 5002; www.ns-gedenkstaetten.de; Steinstrasse 50; ⊙10am-5pm Tue-Sun) FREE This municipal memorial uses the original rooms and cells of a Nazi prison as a backdrop for a grim exhibit about Dortmund during the Third Reich. Over 66,000 people were imprisoned here, with many tortured and killed. It's north of the Hauptbahnhof, just beyond the multiplex cinema.

Petrikirche CHURCH
(www.stpetrido.de; Westenhellweg; ⊙10am-5pm) The 14th-century Petrikirche's show-stopper is the massive Antwerp altar (1520), featuring 633 individually carved and gilded figurines in scenes depicting the Easter story. Note that the altar is closed in summer, exposing only the panels' painted outer side.

Reinoldikirche CHURCH
(www.sanktreinoldi.de; Ostenhellweg 2; tower admission €1.50; ⊙10am-6pm Mon-Sat, from 1pm Sun) Dating from 1280, this church is named after the city's patron saint. As the story goes, after the monk Reinold was martyred in Cologne, the carriage containing his coffin rolled all the way to Dortmund, stopping on the site of the church. There's a statue of him, opposite Charlemagne, at the entrance to the choir. Of outstanding artistic merit is the late-Gothic high altar. There are good views from the bell tower.

Marienkirche CHURCH
(www.st-marien-dortmund.de; Ostenhellweg; 0231-526 548; ⊙10am-noon & 2-4pm Tue-Fri, to 1pm Sat) Marienkirche is the oldest of Dortmund's churches, and its Romanesque origins are still visible in the round-arched nave. The star exhibit here is the Marienaltar (1420), with a delicate triptych by local son Conrad von Soest. In the northern nave is the equally impressive Berswordt Altar (1385). Both were saved from wartime destruction; the churches all needed massive reconstruction.

🍴 Sleeping & Eating

Non-chain hotel choices are few. The best local beer is *Dortmunder Kronen,* a fine, hoppy pilsener consumed in vast quantities on match days.

Cityhotel Dortmund HOTEL €€
(☑0231-477 9660; www.cityhoteldortmund.de; Silberstrasse 37-43; s/d incl breakfast from €75/90; P🖭🕭@🛜) A mousy grey facade hides this jewel, where a palette evoking the ocean, sun and sand gives rooms and public areas a cheerful and fresh look. The 50 rooms are quiet. It's 200m southwest of the train station.

Brauhaus Wenkers GERMAN €€
(☑0231-527 548; www.wenkers.de; Betenstrasse 1; mains €7-20; ☺11am-midnight) A legendary place for quaffing before and after football matches, long-running Wenkers has a sea of tables outside on a centrally located square. It brews its own beer (try the dark one) and the German classics spill over the plates.

Zum Alten Markt GERMAN €€
(☑0231-572 217; www.altermarkt-dortmund.de; Markt 3; mains €8-15) Traditional Westphalian fare is served to hordes of appreciative locals in the very centre of the city. Pray to the gods of digestion at one of the nearby churches.

☆ Entertainment

★**Borussia Dortmund** FOOTBALL
(☑01805-309 000; www.bvb.de; Strobelallee 50; tickets €17-60) Dortmund's famous and massively popular *and* successful Bundesliga soccer team plays its home games at the legendary Westfalenstadion, now branded **Signal Iduna Park** (www.signal-iduna-park.de;

tours adult/concession €12/8; ☺tours times vary depending on matches). Guided tours of the 80,000-seat stadium, Germany's largest, are popular. Take U-Bahn 45.

ℹ Information

Tourist Office (☑0231-189 990; www.dortmund-tourismus.de; Königswall 18a; ☺10am-6pm Mon-Fri, to 1pm Sat) Opposite the Hauptbahnhof's south exit.

ℹ Getting There & Around

There are frequent ICE and IC trains in all directions and RE and S-Bahn trains to other Ruhrgebiet cities departing every few minutes.

Elsewhere in the Ruhrgebiet

The Ruhrgebiet has plenty of other places of interest, many of them on the Industrial Heritage Trail. All of the cities listed below have frequent train service from across the region.

Bochum

☑0234 / POP 362,000

Though indeed no beauty, as one of Grönemeyer's lyrics says, Bochum is a Ruhrgebiet party hub, with most of the action concentrated in the so-called **Bermuda Dreieck** (Bermuda Triangle). Formed by Kortumstrasse, Vikto-

---

THE KRUPP DYNASTY – MEN OF STEEL

Steel and Krupp are virtual synonyms. So are Krupp and Essen. For it's this bustling Ruhrgebiet city that is the ancestral seat of the Krupp family and the headquarters of one of the most powerful corporations in Europe.

It all began rather modestly in 1811 when Friedrich Krupp and two partners founded a company to process 'English cast steel' but, despite minor successes, he left a company mired in debt upon his death in 1826. Enter his son Alfred, then the tender age of 14, who would go on to become one of the seminal figures of the industrial age.

It was through the production of the world's finest steel that the 'Cannon King' galvanised a company that – by 1887 – employed more than 20,000 workers. In an unbroken pattern of dazzling innovation, coupled with ruthless business practices, Krupp produced steel and machinery that was essential to the world economy.

But Krupp also provided womb-to-tomb benefits to its workers at a time when the term 'social welfare' had not yet entered the world's vocabulary.

Krupp will forever be associated, however, with the Third Reich. Not only did the corporation supply the hardware for the German war machine, but it also provided much of the financial backing that Hitler needed to build up his political power base. Krupp plants were prime targets for Allied bombers. After the war, the firm slowly lost its way and in 1999 merged with once arch-rival Thyssen.

An excellent source for an understanding of what the Krupp family has meant to Germany is William Manchester's brilliant chronicle *The Arms of Krupp* (1964).

riastrasse and Brüderstrasse, it's just a five-minute walk from the Hauptbahnhof.

◎ Sights

★ **Eisenbahnmuseum** MUSEUM
(Train Museum; ☑ 0234-492 516; www.eisenbahn museum-bochum.de; Dr-C-Otto-Strasse 191; adult/concession €7.50/4; ☺ 10am-5pm Tue-Fri & Sun Mar–mid-Nov; ⚑) It's a bit away from the centre, but fans of historic trains have plenty to admire at this vast museum. It displays around 180 steam locomotives (many puffing away), and coaches and wagons dating back as far as 1853. From Bochum Hauptbahnhof take tram 318 (or from Essen, the S3) to Bochum-Dahlhausen, then walk for 1200m or take the historic shuttle (Sundays only).

Deutsches Bergbau-Museum MUSEUM
(German Mining Museum; ☑ 0234-587 70; www. bergbaumuseum.de; Am Bergbaumuseum 28; adult/concession €6.50/3; ☺ 8.30am-5pm Tue-Fri, 10am-5pm Sat & Sun) Bochum is worth a quick stop if only to get 'down and dirty' in the German mining museum, one of the nation's most-visited museums. Besides learning about all aspects of life *unter Tage* (below ground), you can descend into the earth's belly for a spin around a demonstration pit followed by a ride up the landmark winding tower for commanding views. U-Bahn 35 goes to the museum from the Hauptbahnhof.

Oberhausen
☑ 0208 / POP 213,000
A former blast furnace is now one of Germany's most innovative exhibition spaces – not just a metaphor for once proudly industrial Oberhausen but for the entire Ruhrgebiet.

◎ Sights

Gasometer Oberhausen GALLERY
(☑ 0208-850 3730; www.gasometer.de; Arenastrasse 11; prices vary by exhibition; ☺ 10am-6pm Tue-Sun) This barrel-shaped tower – spectacularly lit at night – once stored gas to power blast furnaces. One of Germany's most exciting and popular art and exhibit spaces, the Gasometer Oberhausen is draws crowds with its site-specific installations by top artists, Bill Viola and Christo and Jeanne-Claude included. Top off your visit – literally – by riding a pair of lifts to a 117m-high platform for sweeping views over the entire western Ruhrgebiet. From Oberhausen's train station, take any bus or tram from Terminal 1 to Neue Mitte.

Duisburg
☑ 0203 / POP 486,000
Duisburg, about 25km west of Essen, is home to Europe's largest inland port, the immensity of which is best appreciated on a boat tour (p512). Embarkation is at the Schwanentor, which is also the gateway to the **Innenhafen Duisburg** (inner harbour), an urban quarter with a mix of modern and restored buildings infused with restaurants, bars, clubs and attractions set up in the old storage silos.

◎ Sights & Activities

★ **Landschaftspark Duisburg-Nord** PARK
(Landscape Park Duisburg-Nord; ☑ 0203-429 1942; www.landschaftspark.de; Emscherstrasse 71; admission free, activities vary; ☺ park 24hr, visitor centre 9am-6pm Mon-Fri, 11am-6pm Sat & Sun; ⚑) Molten iron used to flow 24/7 from the fiery furnaces of this decommissioned iron works that is now a unique performance space and an all-ages adventure playground. You can free-climb its ore bunkers, take a diving course in the former gas tank, climb to the top of the blast furnace or picnic in a flower garden. From Duisburg train station take tram 903 to the stop Landschaftspark-Nord, then walk along Emscherstrasse (around seven minutes).

Lehmbruck Museum MUSEUM
(☑ 0203-283 3294; www.lehmbruckmuseum.de; Friedrich-Wilhelm-Strasse 40; adult/child €8/free; ☺ noon-6pm Wed, Fri & Sat, noon-9pm Thu, 11am-6pm Sun) Great art awaits at this renowned modern art museum, which presents a survey of 20th-century international sculpture – think Giacometti, Calder, Ernst and Chillida. About 40 sculptures are planted throughout the lovely surrounding park. It's a five-minute walk from the Hauptbahnhof.

Museum Küppersmühle MUSEUM
(☑ 0203-3019 4811; www.museum-kueppers-muehle.de; Philosophenweg 55, Duisburg; adult/concession €9/6; ☺ 2-6pm Wed, 11am-6pm Thu-Sun) A half-century of German art is on display at the Museum Küppersmühle in a mill storage building converted by Swiss Pritzker Prize–winning architects Herzog & de Meuron. From Baselitz to Kiefer to Richter, all the big names are showcased beneath the lofty ceilings, as are up to six international art exhibits annually. From the train station, take bus 934 to Hansegracht.

Weisse Flotte Duisburg BOAT TOUR
(☑0203-713 9667; www.wf-duisburg.de; Schwanentor; adult/concession €14/7; ☺Apr-Nov) Explore the labyrinthine workings of Europe's busiest inland port on a cruise. The dock at Schwanentor is a 1.3km walk through the centre from the train station, or it's well served by public transport.

Bottrop
☑02041 / POP 116.000

About 13km north of Essen, post-industrial Bottrop is the birthplace of Josef Albers (1888–1976), the Bauhaus artist famous for his explorations of colour and spatial relationships, squares in particular.

◉ Sights

Josef Albers Museum MUSEUM
(☑02041-297 16; www.bottrop.de/mq; Im Stadtgarten 20; ☺11am-5pm Tue-Sat, 10am-5pm Sun) FREE In this musem the city honours its famous son, who fled the Nazis for the US in 1933. His abstract works combine bold use of colour with geometric forms. Presented in a starkly minimalist space are examples from Albers' key series 'Homage to the Square', as well as early lithographs from the Bottrop period. From Bottrop Hauptbahnhof take bus SB16 to Im Stadtgarten.

Tetraeder SCULPTURE
(Tetrahedron; Beckstrasse; ☺24hr) FREE Deceptively wire-like from afar, the Tetraeder is one of the most striking stops on the Industrial Heritage Trail. The airy 60m-high installation is made from steel pipes, gracing the top of a former slag heap turned landscape park. You can climb the Tetraeder via 'floating' staircases suspended from steel cables, which lead to viewing platforms. Views of the surprisingly green, yet undeniably industrial, surrounds are impressive rather than conventionally beautiful. At night, the illuminated Tetraeder glows from afar.

MÜNSTER & OSNABRÜCK

Catholic Münster and protestant Osnabrück are forever linked – at least in the minds of suffering high-school history students – as the dual sites chosen to sign the Peace of Westphalia, the series of treaties that ended the Thirty Years' War (one of the longest and comparatively most destructive wars in his-

tory). Today you can find echoes of the event in both towns, which have plenty to please visitors beyond memories of the treaty.

Münster
☑0251 / POP 296.600

There are some 500,000 bicycles in Münster – and that's just an example of the exuberance found in this captivating city, one of the most appealing between Cologne and Hamburg.

It's beautiful centre was rebuilt after the war and features many architectural gems. Yet Münster is not mired in nostalgia. Its 50,000 students keep the cobwebs out and civic pride is great – the town's main cultural treasures have enjoyed ambitious renovations and enhancements. Plan on at least a couple nights here – sampling the many great pubs and restaurants alone will necessitate it.

◉ Sights

Münster's Altstadt is encircled by the 4.8km **Promenade**, a car-free ring trail built through parkland on top of the former city fortifications; it's hugely popular with cyclists, joggers, lovers and walkers.

On any warm days, especially the first ones of spring, you'll find thousands of locals sunbathing, partying, barbecueing and much more on the grassy parkland along the Aasee near Adenauerallee.

The architect who left his mark on Münster more than any other was Johann Conrad Schlaun (1695–1773). He was a master of the Westphalian baroque, a more subdued, less exuberant expression of the style than in southern Germany. A most exquisite example of Schlaun's vision is the 1757 **Erbdrostenhof** (Salzstrasse 38), a lavish private mansion. Nearby, the equally stunning 1753 **Clemenskirche** (Klemensstrasse) boasts a domed ceiling-fresco supported by turquoise faux-marble pillars. Less pristinely preserved is the 1773 **Schloss** (Schlossplatz), the former residence of the prince-bishops and now the main university building.

Dom St Paul CATHEDRAL
(☑0251-495 6700; www.paulusdom.de; Domplatz 28; ☺6.30am-7pm Mon-Sat, to 7.30pm Sun) The two massive towers of Münster's cathedral, Dom St Paul, match the proportions of this 110m-long structure and the vast square it overlooks. It's a three-nave construction

built in the 13th century, a time when Gothic architecture began overtaking the Romanesque style in popularity. Enter from Domplatz via the porch (called the 'Paradise'), richly festooned with sculptures of the apostles. Inside, pay your respects to the statue of St Christopher, the patron saint of travellers.

Make your way to the southern ambulatory with its astronomical clock. This marvel of 16th-century ingenuity indicates the time, the position of the sun, the movement of the planets, and the calendar. Crowds gather daily at noon (12.30pm Sunday) when the carillon starts up.

The Dom reopened in 2013 after a massive reconstruction that included a new roof among other improvements (work was delayed after the first new roof's copper was found to have the wrong shade of green). Archaeological excavations at the same time found parts of previous cathedrals on the site, predating the current structure. Note how the aggressively restored golden-hued stones on the west facade glow at sunset.

Domkammer HISTORIC BUILDING
(Cathedral Treasury; ☑0251-495 333; www.domkammer-muenster.de; Münster Dom; adult/child €3/free; ⊙11am-4pm Tue-Sun) The Domkammer, which is reached via the Dom's hidden cloisters, counts an 11th-century, gemstudded golden head reliquary of St Paul among its finest pieces.

◉ Around Domplatz

Northwest of the Dom, the Aa is a burbling little stream whose tree-lined promenade makes for relaxed strolling.

★**LWL-Museum für Kunst und Kultur** MUSEUM
(Museum for Art and Culture; ☑0251-590 701; www.lwl-museum-kunst-kultur.de; Domplatz 10; adult/concession €8/4; ⊙10am-6pm Tue-Sat) A vast new wing and a new name are among the sweeping changes to this state museum that opened in 1908 as the Westfälisches Landesmuseum. In its 51 rooms, you'll find many of the sculptures purged from the churches by the Anabaptists (p516). The collection spans from the Middle Ages to the latest avant-garde creations. Works are displayed by theme as opposed to merely chronologically. Contemporary painters Conrad von Soest, August Macke, Simon Hantaï and others also get their due.

Kunstmuseum Picasso MUSEUM
(☑0251-414 4710; www.kunstmuseum-picasso-muenster.de; Königsstrasse 5; adult/concession €10/8; ⊙10am-6pm Tue-Sun) One of the 20th century's most famous artists gets the spotlight in this 18th-century nobleman's house. Changing exhibits are drawn from the collection of some 800 graphic works, including a near complete series of Picasso's lithographs.

Überwasserkirche CHURCH
(Near Water Church; Überwasserkircheplatz) The Überwasserkirche (officially known as Liebfrauenkirche) is a 14th-century Gothic hall church with handsome stained-glass windows. The nickname was inspired by its location right by the Aa.

◉ Prinzipalmarkt

The most interesting street in Münster's Altstadt is the Prinzipalmarkt, lined by restored Patrician town houses with arcades sheltering elegant boutiques and cafes and other medieval landmarks.

Historisches Rathaus HISTORIC BUILDING
(Historic City Hall; ☑0251-492 2724; Prinzipalmarkt 8-9; Friedenssaal adult/child €2/1.50; ⊙Friedenssaal 10am-5pm Tue-Fri, to 4pm Sat & Sun) The key building on the Prinzipalmarkt is this Gothic gem, with its elegant filigree gable. In 1648 an important subtreaty of the Peace of Westphalia was signed here, marking the first step in ending the calamitous Thirty Years' War. You can visit the spot of the signing, the splendidly wood-carved Friedenssaal.

Stadtweinhaus HISTORIC BUILDING
(City Wine House; Prinzipalmarkt 10) Immediately to the left of the Historisches Rathaus is this beautifully porticoed Renaissance building.

St Lambertikirche CHURCH
(☑0251-448 93; www.st-lamberti.de; Lambertikirchplatz; ⊙9am-6pm Mon-Sat, from 10am Sun) One of Münster's finest churches, the late-Gothic St Lambertikirche was built in 1450. See those three wrought-iron cages dangling from the openwork spire? They once displayed the corpses of the Anabaptist leader Jan van Leyden and his cohorts after they were defeated in 1535 by troops of the prince-bishop. Before their execution, the trio was publicly tortured with red-hot tongs.

Münster

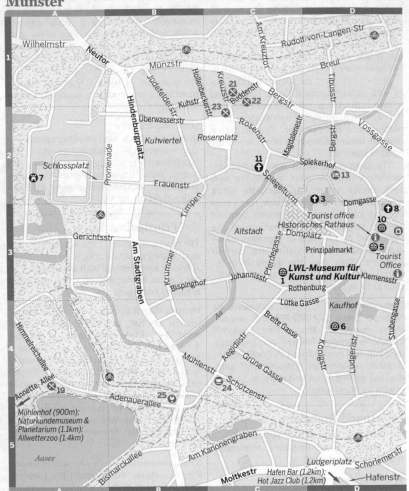

Stadtmuseum MUSEUM
(City Museum; ☎ 0251-492 4503; www.stadt-muen ster.de; Salzstrasse 28; ⊙ 10am-6pm Tue-Fri, 11am-6pm Sat & Sun) FREE The city's museum has a fascinating collection of town models showing how Münster grew and changed from the 16th century onwards. Also included are the once-red-hot tongs used on Jan van Leyden and his unlucky colleagues.

◎ Aasee

Southwest of the Altstadt, the Aasee is another recreational getaway. Come for a picnic by the lake, a stroll along its promenade or go for a spin on the water itself. Family-friendly attractions abound.

Mühlenhof-Freilichtmuseum MUSEUM
(Mühlenhof Open Air Museum; ☎ 0251-981 200; www. muehlenhof-muenster.org; Theo-Breider-Weg 1; adult/concession €5/3; ⊙ 10am-6pm Mar-Oct, 11am-4pm Sun-Fri Nov-Feb; 🚼) A fun open-air museum where you can stroll among historical Westphalian buildings, including a mill and bakery.

LWL-Museum für Naturkunde MUSEUM
(Natural History Museum; ☎ 0251-591 05; Sentruper Strasse 285; museum adult/child €5.50/3,

Münster

◎ Top Sights
1 LWL-Museum für Kunst und Kultur...C3

◎ Sights
2 Clemenskirche E3
3 Dom St Paul...D2
  Domkammer .... (see 3)
4 Erbdrostenhof...E3
5 Historisches Rathaus............................D3
6 Kunstmuseum Picasso D4
7 Schloss..A2
8 St Lambertikirche.................................D3
9 Stadtmuseum E3
10 Stadtweinhaus.......................................D3
11 Überwasserkirche..................................C2

⊕ Activities, Courses & Tours
12 Radstation F5

◎ Sleeping
13 Hotel Busche am Dom D2
14 Hotel Foldmann......................................E3
15 Hotel Horstmann...................................E5
16 Hotel Marco Polo F5
17 Hotel Mauritzhof...................................F4
18 Sleep Station F4

◎ Eating
19 A2 am See...A4
20 Altes Gasthaus Leve.............................E3
21 Cavete C1
22 Drübbelken...C1
  Holstein's Bistro........................ (see 13)
23 Pinkus Müller...C2

◎ Drinking & Nightlife
24 Cafe Gasolin C4
25 Kruse-Baimken B5
26 Pension Schmidt....................................E3

◎ Entertainment
27 Black Box E5

◎ Shopping
28 Poertgen Herder D3

planetarium €5.50/3, both €9.50/5; ⊙9am-6pm Tue-Sun) Dinosaurs and the universe are the stars at this large state-run nature museum that also has a popular planetarium.

◉ Hafen

A 10-minute walk southeast of the Hauptbahnhof takes you to the Hafen, Münster's partly revitalised old harbour. What were once derelict halls and brick warehouses have been updated with avant-garde architectural elements and now house artists' studios and creative offices in a string of buildings called the **Kreativkai**. There are a few cafes and nightspots; you can promenade along the waterfront and watch cargo barges cutting along the Dortmund–Ems canal.

To get to the Hafen, exit the Hauptbahnhof to the east via Bremer Platz, follow Bremer Strasse south, cross Hansaring and it will be on your left. It's about a 500m walk.

🕴 Activities

Join the scores of other cyclists and discover why Münster is such a popular place to ride a bike. From bounding over the

THE ANABAPTISTS

They did like to argue. The Anabaptists were a religious movement that swept through Europe in the early 16th century. Starting in Zurich, Anabaptists spread through much of Germany and beyond. But like many cultish groups, their true believers had sharp disagreements among themselves. The name alone was cause for strife as it referred to the core tenet that adults should be 'rebaptised' into the faith. However, many claimed that any original baptism as an infant hadn't counted because non-Anabaptist religions were not valid, thus your Anabaptist baptism was the first. And so it went.

Other beliefs included polygamy and community ownership of goods. The movement reached its apex at Münster in 1534, when a Dutchman named Jan van Leyden and a crew of followers managed to take over the town. Soon they had baptised over 1000 new followers.

Some rather extreme personalities also emerged: Jan Matthys marched out to confront a vast army of besiegers from the Catholic church who planned to retake the city. He was promptly beheaded and his genitals nailed to a town gate. Meanwhile, van Leyden proclaimed himself king and took 16 wives, which worked out to be about one for each month he was in power; besiegers overran the Münster in 1535 and had van Leyden and many Anabaptists tortured and killed. Three of the bodies ended up in the cages you can still see today in St Lambertikirche.

After the defeat at Münster, the movement was never the same. It had managed to bring both Catholics and Protestants together as both mercilessly tortured and killed Anabaptists. Splinters of the old faith eventually formed what later became Amish and Mennonites, among others.

cobblestones of Domplatz to staging your own F1 on the park promenade, you'll have a ball. The tourist office has cycling maps for routes around the region. Many use Münster as a base for exploring the castles of Münsterland (p518).

Radstation BICYCLE RENTAL
(☑ 0251-484 0170; www.radstation.de; Berliner Platz 27a; 1/3 days from €8/20; ☉5.30am-11pm Mon-Fri, 7am-11pm Sat & Sun) At the Hauptbahnhof, Radstation has a range of bikes.

🛏 Sleeping

Sleep Station HOSTEL €
(☑ 0251-482 8155; www.sleep-station.de; Wolbecker Strasse 1; dm €16-26, s/d €40/56; ☉reception 8am-12.30pm & 5-9pm; ☺@) Münster's hostel is 200m from the Hauptbahnhof. Dorms are clean but basic and sleep three to eight; some singles and doubles have private bathrooms. Perks include free coffee and tea, a small breakfast and kitchen use.

Hotel Horstmann HOTEL €
(☑ 0251-417 040; www.hotel-horstmann.de; Windthorststrasse 12; s/d from €62/82; ☎) Good basic accommodation is the motto at this five-storey hotel on the busy main pedestrian street. Rooms are large, clean and the staff is especially helpful. Good breakfasts.

★**Hotel Busche am Dom** HOTEL €€
(www.hotel-busche.de; Bogenstrasse 10; s/d from €70/105) A family-run hotel with a fantastic central location. This central hotel has 13 comfortable rooms in muted pastels. You'll hear the bells ringing on the hour. Enjoy a buffet breakfast at an outside table.

★**Hotel Feldmann** BOUTIQUE HOTEL €€
(☑ 0251-414 490; www.hotel-feldmann.de; An der Clemenskirche 14; s/d from €76/106; ☎) Four generations of the same family have run this refined hotel. The 20 rooms have an understated elegance; some have huge, glassy walk-in showers. The restaurant is good and you can relax with a drink after a hard day enjoying yourself at one of the outdoor tables on the quiet pedestrian lane overlooking the Clemenskirche.

Hotel Mauritzhof HOTEL €€
(☑ 0251-417 20; www.mauritzhof.de; Eisenbahnstrasse 17; r €95-160; ☺✳☎) Bold hues, a harmonious interplay of glass and wood and extravagant designer furniture (Vitra, Driade, Kartell) give this 39-room property a mod edge. Rooms facing the promenade have a balcony; XXL-sized beds are available upon request. Wind down the day in the reading room.

Hotel Marco Polo HOTEL €€
(☑ 0251-9609 2000; www.hotel-marcopolo.de; Bremer Platz 36; s/d from €80/100; ☎) On the far side of the train tracks from the Altstadt but not on the wrong side of the tracks, the Marco Polo honours its name by naming each room after a world city. For instance, Madrid comes with a toy bull and matador. The decor is basic and the breakfast good.

Factory Hotel HOTEL €€
(☑ 0251-418 80; www.factoryhotel-muenster.de; An der Germania Brauerei 5; s/d from €100/110; P ⊜ ❀ ☎) This sleek hotel marries the historical with the contemporary in the defunct Germania Brewery. The 144 large and modern rooms have an industrial vibe with white linens, metal and concrete; some come with a balcony overlooking an artificial lake. Entertainment includes restaurants and a stylish bar. It's about 2km north of the city centre.

✖ Eating

Most places in Munster are good just for a meal or drink or vice-versa. Besides its namesake pub, look for the local brew Pinkus Müller on better taps around town.

★ Altes Gasthaus Leve GERMAN €€
(☑ 0251-455 95; www.gasthaus-leve.de; Alter Steinweg 37; mains €7-18; ☺ 11.30am-11pm) Münster's oldest inn (since 1607) has painted tiles, oil paintings and copper etchings that form a suitably rustic backdrop to the hearty Westphalian fare. Besides seasonal specials, stalwart dishes such as lima-bean stew and sweet-and-sour beef are delicious. Despite being ever busy, the staff are cheery. In spring try a surprising *Altbierbowle* (dark Pinkus Müller beer with strawberries) – it's almost addictive.

★ Holstein's Bistro MODERN EUROPEAN €€
(☑ 0251-449 44; www.butterhandlung-holstein.de; Bogenstrasse 9; mains €8-16; ☺ 11.30am-7pm Tue-Fri, 11am-5pm Sat; ☑) ✔ Münster's slow food outpost has been raising the bar of inventive seasonal fare for almost 20 years. The ever-changing menu reflects what's fresh, but there's usually a variety of soups, salads, pastas and more on offer. Snare one of the tables in the shadow of the Dom along the alley. An excellent deli adjoins.

★ Pinkus Müller BREWERY €€
(☑ 0251-451 51; www.pinkus.de; Kreuzstrasse 4; mains €8-26; ☺ noon-midnight Mon-Sat) One of Germany's best small brewers, Pinkus

Müller has a namesake pub and restaurant in the heart of the nightlife-filled Kuhviertel. It has a swath of tables out front under a big tree and tables scattered in a warren of timeless carved wood rooms. Enjoy German standards along with great beers such as the very hoppy Extra.

A2 am See CAFE €€
(☑ 0251-284 6840; www.a2amsee.de; Annette-Allee 3; mains €8-20; ☺ 11am-midnight Sun-Thu, 9.30am-late Fri & Sat) Location, location, location. A2, right on the Aasee, certainly has got it. The glass walls and designer furniture scream trendy, but this bar-bistro-restaurant actually appeals to a diverse range of imbibers and munchers who come for the views. The vast waterside terrace is a must at sunset.

Drübbelken GERMAN
(☑ 0251-421 15; www.druebbelken.de; Buddenstrasse 14; mains €9-25; ☺ 11.30am-midnight) A Westphalian version of a half-timbered house (the stucco is coloured rather than, say, a Bavarian beige) houses this ancient restaurant that has been churning out topnotch earthy German fare forever. Of course, the beer is Pinkus; watch for their many seasonal specials.

Cavete GERMAN €€
(☑ 0251-457 00; www.muenster-cavete.de; Kreuzstrasse 38; mains €8-12; ☺ 6pm-2am) For a relaxed pint, steer to the Kuhviertel, the traditional student quarter north of the Dom. Cavete has been a late-night classic for generations. Find a seat at one of the battered old wooden tables and enjoy housemade noodles with schnitzel.

☕ Drinking & Nightlife

★ Kruse-Baimken BEER GARDEN
(☑ 0251-463 87; www.kruse-baimken.de; Am Stadtgraben 52; ☺ noon-1am) Huge trees soar over the passel of tables at this oh-so-lovely beer garden right off the promenade and near the Aasee. Unsurprisingly it gets very crowded, especially as the food is just that much better than beer garden average – the sausages smokier, the salads fresher. In cold months, the action moves inside, where there's an ambitious modern German menu.

Hafen Bar COCKTAIL BAR
(☑ 0251-289 7810; Hafenweg 26; ☺ 6pm-late) For a glamour vibe without the velvet rope, beat a trail to this stylish glass cube in the Hafen's

Kreativkai. Soft lighting gives even pasty-faced hipsters a healthy glow. Good playlists.

Pension Schmidt CAFE
(☑0251-9795 7050; www.pensionschmidt.se; Alter Steinweg 37; ☺noon-5am) Given the quality of the coffee at this hipster cafe, it's unlikely you'll wish it was a real pension, even if the sofas for lounging on are very comfortable. Events include poetry readings, live bands and jazz 'breakfasts' that start at noon.

Cafe Gasolin CAFE
(☑0251-510 5897; www.cafe-gasolin.de; Aegidiistrasse 45; snacks from €3; ☺11am-3am) This cleverly converted 1950s petrol station has cakes, snacks and coffee. It's a good place for that final drink when everything else is closed. Prices are low, quality is not; huge patio.

☆ Entertainment

Münster's party-happy students fuel an eclectic pub and club scene. The Haven's Kreativkai quarter is breeding a few interesting places.

★Hot Jazz Club JAZZ
(☑0251-6866 7909; www.hotjazzclub.de; Hafenweg 26b; ☺hrs vary) The best reason to head out to the Hafen, this subterranean bar keeps it real with live music of all stripes, as long as it's jazz. Check the schedule in case it's an off night. There's usually live jazz Sunday afternoons.

Black Box CULTURAL CENTRE
(☑0251-548 95; www.blackbox-muenster.de; Achtermannstrasse 12) This performance venue and culture centre sees a huge range of acts in any given week. Classical mixes with jazz which mixes with house; well-known DJs often appear to try out something experimental.

🛍 Shopping

The least appealing part of Münster is the chain-filled shopping drag Königstrasse. You'll find much more appealing retail action amid the colonnades on Prinzipalmarkt.

Poertgen Herder BOOKS
(☑0251-490 140; Salzstrasse 56; ☺10am-6pm Mon-Sat) Fine selection of English books, as befits a university town.

ℹ Information

You can find more info on many of Münster's sites at www.muenster.de.

Tourist Office (☑0251-492 2710; www.tourismus.muenster.de; Heinrich-Brüning-Strasse 9; ☺10am-6pm Mon-Fri, to 1pm Sat) The main office has plenty of info (much in English).

Tourist Office Historisches Rathaus (☑0251-492 2724; Prinzipalmarkt 10; ☺10am-5pm Tue-Fri, to 4pm Sat & Sun) A good source of information.

ℹ Getting There & Away

The **Münster Osnabrück International Airport** (FMO; www.fmo.de) has mostly internal German flights and a few charters to holiday spots.

Münster is on a main train line with regular links to points north including Hamburg (€58, 2¼ hours) and south to Cologne (€35, 1¾ hours).

ℹ Getting Around

Buses connect the airport and the Hauptbahnhof every half-hour (40 minutes). Bus drivers sell single tickets for €2.80 (from machines €2.50), as well as day passes for €4.70 (valid after 9am).

Münsterland

Münster is surrounded by Münsterland, a flat and rural region that's home to about 100 castles and palaces, some of which are still owned and inhabited by the landed gentry. Many are protected by water-filled moats, which today offer little protection from tax assessors.

The region is a dream for cyclists, with over 4500km of well-signposted trails (called *Pättkes* in local dialect), including the scenic 100 Schlösser Route (www.100-schloesser-route.de), which links 100 palaces. Bicycles can be hired in Münster and at practically all local train stations. Public transport for the castles can be convoluted, especially at weekends. The route website has downloadable maps and much more info for cyclists.

◉ Sights

The following trio of castles offer the greatest tourist appeal and are relatively accessible from Münster.

Burg Hülshoff CASTLE
(☑02534-1052; www.burg-huelshoff.de; Schonebeck 6; adult/concession €5/3.50, park & castle free, combo ticket incl Haus Rüschhaus €8/6; ☺11am-6.30pm Apr-Oct, limited hours Mar & Nov) In Havixbeck, about 10km west of Münster, Burg Hülshoff is the birthplace of one of Germany's pre-eminent women of letters,

Annette von Droste-Hülshoff (1797–1848). The red-brick Renaissance chateau is embedded in a lovely – partly groomed, partly romantic – park. The interior, which consists of period rooms furnished in the style of the poet's day, can be explored with an English-language audioguide.

Haus Rüschhaus　　　　HISTORIC BUILDING
(☑ 02533-1317; http://haus-rueschhaus.de; Am Rüschhaus 81; adult/concession €5/3.50, park & castle free, combo ticket incl Burg Hülshoff €8/6; ☺ tours hourly 11am-noon & 2-4pm Tue-Sun May-Sep, limited hours Apr & Oct, garden 24hr) Annette von Droste-Hülshoff did some of her finest writing at the smallish Haus Rüschhaus, where she lived for 20 years from 1826. The building was once the private home of star architect Johann Conrad Schlaun, who magically morphed a farmhouse into a baroque mini-mansion backed by a formal garden. It's in the suburb of Nienberge, about 3km north of Burg Hülshoff, and served by bus 5 from Münster's Hauptbahnhof (€2.80, 20 minutes).

★**Burg Vischering**　　　　CASTLE
(☑ 02591-799 00; www.burg-vischering.de; Berenbrok 1, Lüdinghausen; adult/child €2.50/1; ☺ 10am-1pm & 1.30-5.30pm Tue-Sun Apr-Oct, to 4.30pm Nov-Mar) The quintessential medieval moated castle, Burg Vischering is Westphalia's oldest (1271), and the kind that conjures romantic images of knights and damsels. Surrounded by a system of ramparts and ditches, the complex consists of an outer castle and the main castle, now a museum. Burg Vischering is 30km southwest of Münster. Ask at the Hauptbahnhof about regional train connections to Lüdinghausen.

Osnabrück

☑ 0541 / POP 155,600

'Zum Glück komm' ich aus Osnabrück', or 'Thankfully I come from Osnabrück': locals like to boast. That's something you might understand when you discover your own quietly evocative corner of the old town. Osnabrück is easily visited on a daytrip from Münster or when passing by on a train.

◉ Sights

You'll need a little fortitude to penetrate past gaudy and charmless shopping streets to find Osnabrück's charming, albeit small, old quarter, which eddies around Dom St Peter and Marienkirche.

★**Felix-Nussbaum-Haus**　　　　MUSEUM
(☑ 0541-323 2237; www.osnabrueck.de/fnh; Lotter Strasse 2; adult/concession €5/3; ☺ 11am-6pm Tue-Fri, 10am-6pm Sat & Sun) Osnabrück-born Jewish painter Felix Nussbaum (1904–44) is renowned for his works, which have shades of Van Gogh and Henri Rousseau. In 1944, after several years in exile, arrest in Belgium and successful escape in France, Nussbaum was denounced and finally deported from Belgium to Auschwitz, where he died. Shaped like an interconnected series of concrete shards, with slit windows and sloping floors, the Felix-Nussbaum-Haus captures the artist's brilliance and is an early masterpiece by Daniel Libeskind.

The building uses space magnificently to illustrate the absence of orientation in the artist's eventful and tragic life. Libeskind designed it in 1998, before his much-lauded and famous Jewish museum in Berlin. One of Nussbaum's most famous paintings is *Self-portrait with Jewish Pass*, from around 1943. It hauntingly captures what he felt living a life on the run. The museum shares an entrance with the **Kulturgeschichtliches Museum** (entry included in price), which has cabinets designed by Libeskind holding works by Albrecht Dürer. The local Museum of Cultural History adjoins.

Rathaus　　　　HISTORIC BUILDING
(Markt; ☺ 8am-6pm Mon-Fri, 9am-4pm Sat, 10am-4pm Sun) It was on the Rathaus steps that the Peace of Westphalia was proclaimed on 25 October 1648, ending the Thirty Years' War. The preceding peace negotiations were conducted partly in Münster, about 60km south, and partly in the Rathaus' Friedenssaal (Peace Hall). On the left as you enter the Rathaus are portraits of the negotiators. Also look around the Schatzkammer (Treasure Chamber) opposite,

especially for the 13th-century *Kaiserpokal* (Kaiser goblet).

Dom St Peter
CATHEDRAL

(☑0541-184 90; Domplatz; treasury adult/concession €5/3.50; ⊗Dom 8am-6pm, treasury 10am-6pm Tue-Sun) The unbalanced towers are just one of the idiosyncratic architectural features that makes Osnabrück's cathedral an intriguing place. Parts date from 1100, and given that the holy complex got rough treatment in WWII, it's fascinating to explore the surviving labyrinth, finding the cloister and discovering golden relics in the *Domschatz-kammer* (treasury).

Marienkirche
CHURCH

(Markt; ⊗10am-noon, 3-5pm Apr-Sep, 10.30am-noon & 2.30-4pm Oct-Mar) The four richly ornamented cross gables of the Marienkirche loom above the square, painstakingly rebuilt after burning down during WWII.

Erich Maria Remarque Friedenszentrum
MUSEUM

(Erich Maria Remarque Peace Centre; ☑0541-323 2109; www.remarque.uos.de; Markt 6; ⊗10am-1pm & 3-5pm Tue-Fri, 11am-5pm Sat & Sun) FREE This small museum uses photos and documents to chronicle the writer Erich Maria Remarque's life (1898–1970) and work (*All Quiet on the Western Front* et al).

Half-Timbered Houses
HISTORIC BUILDINGS

Several half-timbered houses survived WWII. At Bierstrasse 24 is the baroque **Romantik Hotel Walhalla**, with a portal flanked by cheeky cherubs. There's a good row of shops at **Hackenstrasse 3**. At **Krahnstrasse 4** you'll find a beautiful house (1533), with a cafe taking up the ground floor. At **Krahnstrassehe 7** is the best of the bunch, the Renaissance Haus Willmann (1586), with its carved circular motifs and small relief of Adam and Eve.

🍴 Sleeping & Eating

Intour Hotel
HOTEL €€

(☑0541-963 860; www.intourhotel.de; Maschstrasse 10; s €57-72, d €69-79; P⊕🐾🛜) Situated just outside the old quarter and handy to Felix-Nussbaum-Haus, this hotel looks unprepossessing from the outside but is modern, with unfussy decor. Take buses 31, 32 or 33 to Weissenburgstrasse from the train station or Neuer Markt.

★ Barösta Kaffeebar
CAFE €

(☑0541-7706 6946; www.baroesta.de; Redlingerstrasse 1; mains €4-9; ⊗8am-7pm) A fine choice for a superb coffee or a meal, you can literally follow your nose to the source of the fresh-roasted aromas. The menu changes daily but is simple and seasonal – think good baked goods, sandwiches, salads, soups, housemade chocolate and more.

Konditorei Ulrich Läer
CAFE €

(☑0541-222 44; Krahnstrasse 4; treats from €3; ⊗8am-6pm Mon-Sat) In one of Osnabrück's prettiest authentic half-timbered houses, this bakery and cafe near the Rathaus is suitably luxe. Pastries and cakes might take your fancy. Watch the passing parade of locals from a pair of tables out front.

Hausbrauerei Rampendahl
GERMAN €€

(☑0541-245 35; www.rampendahl.de; Hasestrasse 35; meals €7-24; ⊗11am-11pm Mon-Sat, to 9.30pm Sun) This restaurant and microbrewery near the Dom is about as hearty as they come, serving substantial dishes to accompany the house beers. It has various cheaper and ever-changing lunch or dinner deals. The unfiltered lager is excellent.

ℹ Information

Tourist Information (☑0541-323 2202; www.osnabrueck.de; Bierstrasse 22/23; ⊗9.30am-6pm Mon-Fri, 10am-4pm Sat) Close to the Rathaus; more gifts than info.

ℹ Getting There & Away

Trains to Hanover (€27, 1¼ hours) and Münster (€13, 30 minutes) leave twice an hour.

ℹ Getting Around

Single bus tickets cost €2.60 and day tickets €5.10.

The Hauptbahnhof is on the town's eastern edge. The Altstad is a bland 15-minute walk. Shorten your exposure to Osnabrück's less salubrious side by taking bus 81 or 82 to the Theatre stop.

OSTWESTFALEN

The rolling hills and forests make for pleasant and scenic driving in Ostwestfalen. Both terrain and elevations get more dramatic in the Sauerland, where there are winter sports. Nestled within it all are some interesting towns such as church-filled Soest.

Soest

☑ 02921 / POP 48,700

One of northwest Germany's most appealing towns, Soest is a tranquil place of half-timbered houses and a clutch of treasure-filled churches that reflect the wealth it enjoyed during its Hanseatic League days. Although bombed in WWII, this maze of idyllic, crooked lanes has been beautifully rebuilt and preserves much of its medieval character. Little channels of running water are utterly charming.

But Soest's one remarkable feature is it's stone: a shimmering greenish local sandstone used in building the town wall, churches and other public structures.

Only 45km southeast of Münster, Soest is compact enough to be explored on a day trip or as a side trip en route to somewhere else.

◉ Sights & Activities

Much of Soest's historic centre lies within a moated defensive wall, which today has a park-like appearance and is great for strolling and picnicking. The town is home to some of Westphalia's most important churches. Several are near the Markt, which features the **Rathaus**, a baroque confection with an arched portico on the western side.

The **Grosser Teich** is a placid duck pond and park where the tourist office occupies an old water mill.

★**St Maria zur Wiese** CHURCH
(Wiesenkirche; Wiesenstrasse; ⊗11am-6pm Mon-Sat, noon-6pm Sun Apr-Sep, to 4pm Oct-Mar) Close to the train station, this exquisite late-Gothic church is easily recognised by its neo-Gothic twin spires, which are undergoing restoration. One is complete and is aglow with green, while the other is under wraps until at least 2020. The interior is bathed in colours from stained-glass windows, including one from 1520 showing Jesus and his disciples enjoying a Westphalian Last Supper of ham, beer and pumpernickel bread (native to Soest).

★**St Patrokli** CHURCH
(www.sankt-patrokli.de; Propst-Nübel-Strasse 2; ⊗10am-5.30pm) Ponder the balance and beauty of the soaring yet dignified tower of St Patrokli, a three-nave 10th-century Romanesque structure partly adorned with delicate frescoes. The west side is especially elaborate.

Nikolai-Kapelle CHURCH
(Thomästrasse; ⊗11am-noon Tue-Thu & Sun Apr-Nov) The tiny Nikolaikapelle is a few steps southeast of St Patrokli. Its almost mystical simplicity is enlivened by a masterful altar painting attributed to 15th-century master Conrad von Soest (who was born in Dortmund).

St Maria zur Höhe CHURCH
(Hohnekirche; www.hohnegemeinde.de; Hohe Gasse; ⊗10am-5.30pm Apr-Sep, to 4pm Oct-Mar) St Maria zur Höhe is a squat and architecturally less refined 13th-century hall church. Its sombreness is brightened by beautiful ceiling frescoes, an altar ascribed to the Westphalian painter known as the Master of Liesborn, and the *Scheibenkreuz*, a huge wooden cross on a circular board more typically found in Scandinavian churches; in fact, it's the only such cross in Germany. Look for the light switch on your left as you enter to shed some light on the matter.

Petrikirche CHURCH
(Petrikirchhof 10; ⊗9.30am-5.30pm Tue-Sat, 2-5.30pm Sun) Petrikirche has Romanesque origins in the 8th century and a choir from Gothic times, all topped by a baroque onion dome. It's adorned with wall murals and features an unusual modern altar made from the local green sandstone, glass and brushed stainless steel.

Grünsandstein-Museum MUSEUM
(Green Sandstone Museum; ☑02921-150 11; www.gruensandsteinmuseum.de; Walburgerstrasse 56; ⊗10am-5pm Mon-Sat, 2-5pm Sun) **FREE** The church of St Maria zur Wiese's restoration workshop operates this museum, where you can learn about the origin of Soest's ethereal green stone.

🛏 Sleeping & Eating

Local specialities include the Soester pumpernickel, a rough-textured rye bread made entirely without salt, and the *Bullenauge* (bull's eye), a creamy mocha liqueur.

Hotel Im Wilden Mann HOTEL €€
(☑02921-150 71; www.im-wilden-mann.de; Am Markt 11; s/d from €55/90; P🜚) This central landmark in a portly half-timbered town house offers the opportunity to connect to the magic of yesteryear in a dozen comfortable rooms furnished in white minimalist style. The casual, timbered **restaurant** (mains €8-22; ⊗noon-10pm Mon-Sat, to 9pm Sun) is all about traditional local food.

WORTH A TRIP

KALKRIESE

Varusschlacht Museum & Park Kalkriese (☑ 05468-920 4200; www.kalkriese-varuss chlacht.de; off N218, Bramsche-Kalkriese; adult/child €7/4.50; ☉ 10am-6pm Apr-Oct, 10am-5pm Tue-Sun Nov-Mar; ⊕) You don't need to be a history buff (or even a fan of Russell Crowe in *Gladiator*) to come to this museum and park, although by the time you leave you'll have a fine idea about how rebellious Germanic tribes won a major victory over their Roman masters somewhere in the Osnabrück region in AD 9 – defeating three of military commander Publius Quinctilius Varus' legions. The site is about 16km north of Osnabrück.

Only in 1987 was this likely candidate for the site of the so-called Battle of Teutoberg Forest uncovered. In 2000, the battlefield was opened as an archaeological park to display the Germans' dirt ramparts and explain how they did it. Since then, facilities have expanded steadily and you'll find exhibits on the artefacts dug up so far, as well as high-tech displays and re-enactments that show how the Germanic tribes had such good luck against the Romans.

Hotel Stadt Soest
HOTEL **€€**

(☑ 02921-362 20; www.hotel-stadt-soest.de; Brüderstrasse 50; s/d from €55/80; ☞) Close to the train station, this modest family-run hotel has 20 decent-sized rooms accented by bright basic colours – some orange here, some green there. It's at the start of the pedestrian zone.

★ Brauhaus Zwiebel
GERMAN

(☑ 02921-2921 4424; http://brauhaus-zwiebel.de; Ulricherstrasse 24; ☉ 11am-midnight) A one-stop shop for myriad forms of pleasure in Soest, this long-running brewery produces a bevy of excellent seasonal beers through the year, which can all be enjoyed in the beer garden. The food is predictably hearty and tasty (yes, many dishes come with *zwiebel* – onion), while various games keep the mood boisterous and jolly.

Brauerei Christ
BREWERY **€€**

(☑ 02921-155 15; www.brauerei-christ.com; Walburger Strasse 36; mains €10-20; ☉ noon-late) Dating from 1584, history oozes from every nook and cranny of this warren of living-room-style rooms stuffed with musical instruments, oil paintings and unique knick-knacks. Hunker down at polished tables for Westphalian specialities or any of its four schnitzel variations. Nice beer garden.

ⓘ Information

Tourist Office (☑ 02921-6635 0050; www.soest.de; Teichsmühlengasse 3; ☉ 9.30am-4.30pm Mon-Fri, 10am-3pm Sat year-round, 11am-1pm Sun Apr-Oct; ☞) The tourist office has its own little waterwheel.

ⓘ Getting There & Around

Soest's regular train connections include Dortmund (€13, 45 minutes), Paderborn (€13, 40 minutes) and Münster (€16, 50 minutes).

The train station is on the north side of the ring road enclosing Soest's historic centre. Follow the pedestrianised Brüderstrasse south.

Paderborn
☑ 05251 / POP 143,600

About 50km east of Soest, Paderborn is the largest city in eastern Westphalia. It derives its name from the Pader which, at 4km, is Germany's shortest river.

Charlemagne used Paderborn as a power base to defeat the Saxons and convert them to Christianity, giving him the momentum needed to rise to greater things. A visit by Pope Leo III in 799 led to the establishment of the Western Roman Empire, a precursor to the Holy Roman Empire, and Charlemagne's coronation as its emperor in Rome the following year.

Paderborn remains a pious place to this day – churches abound, and religious sculpture and motifs adorn facades, fountains and parks. Many of the city's 14,000 students are involved in theological studies. It's a good stop if you're passing by on the train.

⊙ Sights & Activities

Most sights cluster in the largely pedestrianised **Altstadt**, which is easily explored on foot. To get there from the Hauptbahnhof, exit right onto Bahnhofstrasse and continue for 10 minutes straight via the rather schlocky **Westernstrasse**, the main shopping street. The scent of cheap perfume samples will tell you've arrived, but press on because once you reach the Dom, it's like you've entered another village entirely – a small but charming and very evocative village.

Should you weary of walking, however, at the foot of the Abdinghofkirche lies the **Paderquellgebiet**, a small park perfect for relaxing by the astonishing 200 springs that feed the Pader.

Dom
CATHEDRAL

(✆ 05251-125 1287; Markt 17, Paderborn; ⊙ 7am-6.30pm) Paderborn's massive (104m long!) Dom, a three-nave Gothic hall church, is a good place to start your explorations. Enter through the southern portal (called 'Paradise'), adorned with delicate carved figures, then turn your attention to the high altar and the pompous memorial tomb of Dietrich von Fürstenberg, a 17th-century bishop.

Signs point the way to the Dom's most endearing feature, the so-called Dreihasenfenster, a unique trompe l'oeil window in the cloister. Its tracery depicts three hares, ingeniously arranged so that each has two ears, even though there are only three ears in all.

The hall-like crypt, one of the largest in Germany, contains the grave and relics of St Liborius, the city's patron saint. A 4th-century priest in today's France, his remains were sent to Paderborn in the 8th century as a gift.

Erzbischöfliches Diözesanmuseum
MUSEUM

(Archbishop's Diocesan Museum; ✆ 05251-125 1400; www.dioezesanmuseum-paderborn.de; Markt 17; adult/child €3.50/1.50; ⊙ 10am-6pm Tue-Sun) The famous 1627 Liborius shrine is housed in an attractive modernist structure outside the Dom. It brims with church treasures, the most precious of which are kept in the basement, including the gilded shrine and prized portable altars. Upstairs, the one piece not to be missed is the Imad Madonna, an exquisite 11th-century linden-wood statue.

Rathaus
HISTORIC BUILDING

(Rathausplatz) Paderborn's proud Rathaus (1616) with ornate gables, oriels and other decorative touches, is typical of the Weser Renaissance architectural style.

Marktkirche
CHURCH

(Market Church; Rathausplatz; ⊙ 9am-6pm) South of the Rathaus is the Marktkirche, aka Jesuitenkirche, a galleried basilica where pride of place goes to the dizzyingly detailed baroque high altar. A soaring symphony of wood and gold, it's an exact replica of the 17th-century original destroyed in WWII.

Marienplatz
SQUARE

Rathausplatz blends into Marienplatz with its delicate **Mariensäule** (St Mary's Column) and **Heising'sche Haus**, an elaborate 17th-century patrician mansion that shares a wall with the tourist office. The **Abdinghofkirche** (Am Abdinghof; ⊙ 11am-6pm) is easily recognised by its twin Romanesque towers. Once a Benedictine monastery, it's been a Protestant church since 1867 and is rather austere with its whitewashed and unadorned walls and flat wooden ceiling.

Carolingian Kaiserpfalz
HISTORIC SITE

East along Am Abdinghof to the north of the Dom are the remnants of the Carolingian **Kaiserpfalz**, Charlemagne's palace where that historic meeting with Pope Leo took place. It was destroyed by fire and replaced in the 11th century by the Ottonian-Salian **Kaiserpfalz**, which has been reconstructed as faithfully as possible atop the original foundations. The only original palace building is the twee **Bartholomäuskapelle** next door. Consecrated in 1017, it's considered the oldest hall church north of the Alps and enjoys otherworldly acoustics.

Museum in Der Kaiserpfalz
MUSEUM

(✆ 05251-105 110; www.kaiserpfalz-paderborn. de; Am Ikenberg 2, Carolingian Kaiserpfalz; adult/child €3.50/1.50; ⊙ 10am-6pm Tue-Sun) The museum inside the Kaiserpfalz presents excavated items from the days of Charlemagne, including drinking vessels and fresco remnants.

Schloss Neuhaus
PALACE

(✆ 05251-801 92; www.schlosspark-paderborn. de; Schlossstrasse 10; ⊙ park 24hr, event hours vary) Schloss Neuhaus, a moated palace, is reached by a lovely riverside walk about 5km northwest of the Paderquellgebiet. It hosts frequent cultural events in summer.

Heinz Nixdorf Museumsforum
MUSEUM

(HNF; ✆ 05251-306 600; www.hnf.de; Fürstenallee 7; adult/concession €7/4; ⊙ 9am-6pm Tue-Fri, 10am-6pm Sat & Sun) You don't have to be a techie to enjoy this museum, a high-tech romp through 5000 years of information technology, from cuneiform to cyberspace. Established by the local founder of Nixdorf computers (since swallowed by bigger

SIEGEN

Wedged into a valley hemmed by dense forest, Siegen (pop 103,000) is the commercial hub of the Siegerland and birthplace of the painter Peter Paul Rubens (1577–1640).

For centuries it was ruled by the counts of Nassau-Oranien, the family that ascended to the Dutch throne in 1813. One of two palaces from those glory days that survived the bombing squadrons of WWII is well worth a stop if you're in the area. Otherwise Siegen is short on charm.

Direct trains depart hourly for Cologne (€22, 1½ hours).

Oberes Schloss (☑ 0271-230 410; Burgstrasse 10; museum adult/concession €3.50/1.50; ⊙ museum 9am-5pm Mon-Sat, 11am-3pm Sun) From Markt, Burgstrasse slopes up to the Oberes Schloss, a classic medieval fortress and the ancestral home of the rulers of Nassau-Oranien. Its labyrinth of rooms now houses the Siegerlandmuseum, which would be a mediocre collection of old paintings were it not for its nine Rubens originals, including a self-portrait and a large-scale work viscerally depicting a lion hunt. Other rooms cover aspects of local history.

Nikolaikirche (Markt; ⊙ 10am-6pm Mon-Fri, to noon Sat Apr-Oct) Halfway up the hill looms Siegen's signature landmark, the late Romanesque Nikolaikirche. It's easily recognised by the golden crown atop the steeple, placed there by a local ruler in 1652 to commemorate his promotion from count to prince.

corporations), it displays all manner of once-high-tech gadgets from the predigital age, but most memorable is the replica of Eniac, a room-sized vacuum-tube computer developed for the US Army in the 1940s. Catch bus 11 from the Hauptbahnhof to Museumsforum.

Radstation BICYCLE RENTAL
(☑ 05251-870 740; www.paderborner-radstation. de; Bahnhofstrasse 29; per day from €9; ⊙ 5.30am-10.30pm) At the train station, it rents bicycles. Head off to Schloss Neuhaus.

🛏 Sleeping & Eating

Near the Rathaus, the Rathauspassage has delis and markets where you can assemble a fine picnic to enjoy in the Paderquellgebiet.

★ Galerie-Hotel Abdinghof HOTEL €€
(☑ 05251-122 40; www.galerie-hotel.de; Bachstrasse 1; s/d incl breakfast from €80/100; ℗ ⊛ ⊜) Paderborn's most evocative sleeping option is this hotel in a 1563 stone building overlooking the Paderquellgebiet. Famous artists – Michelangelo to Picasso – inspired the decor of the 11 rooms, furnished in styles ranging from country-rustic to elegant-feminine. Original art graces the downstairs cafe-restaurant.

Eiscafe Artusa ICE CREAM €
(☑ 05251-288 7625; artusa.state-art.de; Westernstrasse 2; treats from €2; ⊙ 9am-8pm) Enjoy Pa-

derborn's best ice cream and gelato at this always-crowded cafe overlooking Marienplatz.

Le Maison BISTRO €€
(☑ 05251-878 6280; www.lamaison-paderborn. de; Rathauspassage, Rosenstrasse 13-15; mains €7-20; ⊙ 9am-midnight Sun-Thu, to 2am Fri & Sat) A thoroughly French bistro hidden away in the modern warren of the Rathauspassage. Tables spill outside and you can linger over one of many coffee varietes. Plates include excellent salads, pasta and various meaty mains. Enjoy drinks while debating the rise of Charlemagne late into the night.

ℹ Information

Tourist Office (☑ 05251-882 980; www.paderborn.de; Marienplatz 2a; ⊙ 10am-6pm Mon-Fri, to 4pm Sat Apr-Oct, to 5pm Mon-Fri, to 2pm Sat Nov-Mar) Local information.

ℹ Getting There & Away

Paderborn has direct trains every two hours to Kassel-Wilhelmshöhe (€26, 1¼ hours) and regional connections to Dortmund (€24, 1¼ hours) and other Ruhrgebiet cities. Trains to Soest (€13, 40 minutes) leave twice hourly.

SAUERLAND

This hilly forested region is popular as an easy getaway for nature-craving Ruhrgebiet residents and hill-craving Dutch tourists.

There are a few museums and castles sprinkled about, but the Sauerland's primary appeal lies in the outdoors. Some 20,000km of marked hiking trails, mostly through beech and fir forest, spread across five nature parks. Cyclists and mountain bikers can pick their favourites from dozens of routes. In winter some of the steeper slopes around **Winterberg** come alive with downhill skiiers. Under it all, is Attendorn's famous cave, the **Atta-Höhle**.

The Sauerland is best explored with your own wheels; you can get loads of info from the regional tourist office (www.sauerland. com).

Altena

☑ 02352 / POP 18.500

In a steep, narrow valley carved by the Lenne River, Altena has built its fortune on producing industrial wire since making mail-shirts for medieval knights. Its famous fortress is the reason to stop off. It's a 15-minute walk from the train station. Altena is served by regional trains running between Hagen and Siegen.

◉ Sights

Burg Altena CASTLE
(☑ 02352-966 7033; www.burg-altena.de; Fritz-Thomee-Strasse 80; adult/concession €5/2.50; ⊙ 9.30am-5pm Tue-Fri, 11am-6pm Sat & Sun) This fairy-tale medieval castle started out as the home of the local counts, then served military purposes under the Prussians before becoming, in 1912, the birthplace of the youth hostel movement. The world's first hostel, with dark dorms sporting wooden triple bunks, can be seen in the museum. You'll also see some fancy historic weapons and armour and an exhibit on the Sauerland under the Nazis.

Admission is also good at the nonelectrifying **Deutsches Drahtmuseum**, about 300m downhill, which covers wire and all its uses.

Central Germany

Best Places to Eat

➡ Anna Amalia (p553)

➡ Weinrestaurant Turmschänke (p557)

➡ Zum Wenigemarkt 13 (p546)

➡ Immergrün (p592)

➡ Pho Vang (p536)

Best Places to Stay

➡ Hardenberg Burghotel (p542)

➡ Romantik Hotel auf der Wartburg (p557)

➡ Hotel am Hoken (p575)

➡ Design Apartments Weimar (p551)

Why Go?

Central Germany's captivating landscapes await. From Thuringian Forest hikes, steam-train journeys deep into the Harz Mountains and riverside rambles past Saale-Unstrut vineyards to medieval castle ruins and restored Renaissance palaces, this region is the stuff of both fairy tale and history.

If you fancy yourself a philosopher, head to Weimar, Erfurt, Lutherstadt Eisleben and Lutherstadt Wittenberg, former stamping grounds of cultural titans such as Goethe, Schiller, Luther (harbinger of the Reformation) and Bach. Design-heads will delight in Dessau-Rosslau, birthplace of Bauhaus, while anyone with a camera will appreciate the time-capsule villages of Goslar, Wernigerode and Quedlinburg, all strikingly well preserved.

With outdoor options galore, sparkling and red wines to discover, a fairy-tale road to follow and health spas to soak away the days travels, the bucolic heartland of Germany is sure to delight.

When to Go

The warmer months from April to October are the best time to visit, when museums and sights have longer opening hours, leafless landscapes burst back to life, and the region's hiking and cycling is at its finest.

As the days grow shorter, the Saale-Unstrut wine region, the Harz and the Thuringian Forest are all picturesque autumn destinations, though weather can be fickle.

In winter, cross-country ski-hikes are popular in the Harz. For anyone who's dressed for the conditions, hiking here under blue skies and upon frozen ground can also be invigorating.

History

Life has been present in the hilly Thuringian forests and on the fertile plains of Saxony-Anhalt for thousands of years. Historical artefacts from as far back as the late stone age have been uncovered here, and the cities of Halle and Magdeburg are among Germany's oldest, dating well beyond 1200 years. Hildesheim celebrated is 1000th birthday in 2015.

In more recent times, many of the larger cities across the region suffered heavy allied bombing in WWII. Kassel was one of the most targeted, where over 10,000 civilians were killed and the city was razed. Magdeburg, Dessau and Weimar also all suffered heavy losses. From 1949 to 1990 much of what is now known as Central Germany belonged to the former German Democratic Republic (GDR; East Germany). Although it's difficult (but not impossible) to find signs of the former border today, there's still a discernible difference between what was 'West' and what was 'East', particularly in terms of architecture.

FAIRY-TALE ROAD

The 600km **Märchenstrasse** (Fairy-Tale Road; www.deutsche-maerchenstrasse.com) is one of Germany's most popular tourist routes. It's made up of cities, towns and hamlets in four states (Hesse, Lower Saxony, North Rhine–Westphalia and Bremen), which can often be reached by using a choice of roads rather than one single route. The towns are associated in one way or another with the works of Wilhelm and Jakob Grimm. Although most towns can be easily visited using public transport, a car is useful for getting a feel for the route.

The Grimm brothers travelled extensively through central Germany in the early 19th century documenting folklore. Their collection of tales, *Kinder- und Hausmärchen,* was first published in 1812 and quickly gained international recognition. It includes such fairy-tale staples as 'Hansel and Gretel', 'Cinderella', 'The Pied Piper', 'Rapunzel' and scores of others.

There are over 60 stops on the Fairy-Tale Road. Major ones include (from south to north): Hanau, about 15km east of Frankfurt, the birthplace of Jakob (1785–1863) and Wilhelm (1786–1859); Steinau, where the Brothers Grimm spent their youth; Marburg, in the university of which the brothers studied for a short time; Kassel, with a museum dedicated to the Grimms; Göttingen, where the brothers served as professors in the university before being expelled in 1837 for their liberal views; Bad Karlshafen, a meticulously planned white baroque village; Bodenwerder, where the rambling Münchhausen Museum is dedicated to the legendary Baron von Münchhausen, (in) famous for telling outrageous tales; and Hamelin (Hameln), forever associated with the legend of the Pied Piper.

ℹ️ Getting There & Around

BICYCLE

Visit www.weser-radweg.de for details of the much-loved riverside Weser Radweg (Weser Cycle Path), which also connects with some Fairy-Tale Road villages.

BOAT

From April to October, boats operated by **Flotte Weser** (📞 05151-939 999; www.flotte-weser.de) travel from Hamelin to Bodenwerder on Wednesday, Saturday and Sunday (€13.50, 3½ hours). A range of cruises and packages are available.

CAR

Hanau and Steinau are each a short drive from Frankfurt am Main. The road route is marked with signs along the way. From Hanau, take the A66 to Steinau, north of which the route leaves the autobahn and travels along minor roads. Following the B83 along the Weser River is a highlight. The Märchenstrasse website has a downloadable map that provides an overview of the routes and towns; a good German road map is also useful, as it will illustrate minor roads through the countryside. Factor in time to stop, walk around and explore the countryside along the way.

TRAIN & BUS

The Fairy-Tale Road is more of a road trip than a route to be followed by public transport, but catching trains and buses is easy if you want to take in the highlights. Take day trips from Frankfurt am Main to Hanau and Steinau, or take a train further afield to Marburg, Kassel or Göttingen.

From the Hauptbahnhof at Hamelin, bus 520 follows the Weser to/from Holzminden (€17, 1½ hours) via Bodenwerder (€13) hourly on weekdays and every couple of hours on weekends. From Holzminden at least five trains leave daily for Bad Karlshafen (€12, 50 minutes), with a change at Ottbergen. Direct trains run every two hours from Bad Karlshafen to Göttingen (€17, one hour).

Central Germany Highlights

1 Delighting in Kassel's cascading **Herkules** (p534) or invoking your inner child at **Grimmwelt** (p535)

2 Touring Dessau's **Bauhaus** (p583) gems to study the origins of modernist architecture and design

3 Wandering cobblestoned streets past half-timbered houses in medieval **Quedlinburg** (p574)

4 Hiking (p574) or catching a GDR-era **stream train** (p573) to the top of the Brocken, the Harz' highest peak

5 Exploring the fascinating history of Goslar at the **Rammelsberg** (p568) mines and **Kaiserpfalz** (p567) residence

6 Walking in Luther's footsteps in **Eisleben** (p594) and **Wittenberg** (p579)

7 Marvelling at Germany's long archaeological history at the **Landesmuseum für Vorgeschichte** (p591) in Halle

8 Sampling three palaces and three eras in one swoop at the magnificent **Dornburger Schlösser** (p562)

9 Remembering those lost in war at the haunting **Gedenkstätte Buchenwald** (p553)

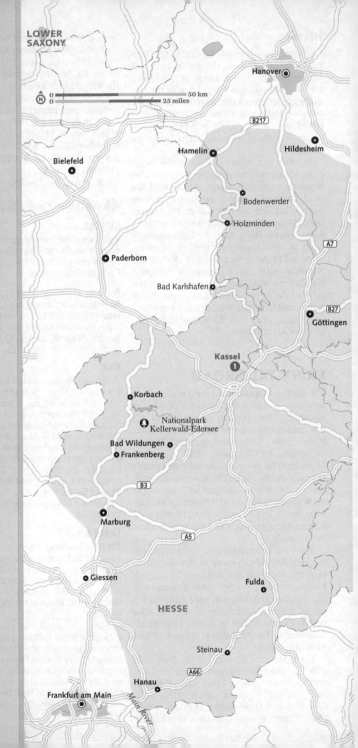

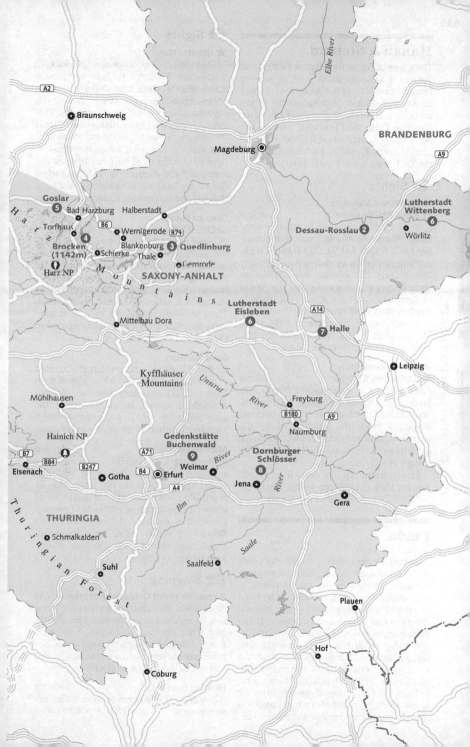

Hanau & Steinau

The towns of Hanau (population 88,200) and Steinau (population 10,900) are so close to Frankfurt am Main that it is easy to visit them on day trips. Hanau, birthplace of the Brothers Grimm, is within 30 minutes of Frankfurt. Closer to Fulda than Frankfurt, Steinau (an der Strasse) is situated on the historic trade road between Frankfurt am Main and Leipzig. Each town has one main attraction.

◉ Sights

**Historisches Museum
Schloss Philippsruhe** MUSEUM
(🎫 06181-295 564; www.hanau.de/kultur/museen/hanau; Philippsruher Allee 45, Hanau; adult/concession €4/3; ⊙ 11am-6pm Tue-Sun) Located within Philippsruhe Palace, dating from the early 18th century, this museum has displays on town history and arts and crafts. The parks and gardens (free) are a beautiful place to stroll in snow or in summer.

Hourly regional trains from Frankfurt am Main stop at Hanau West (€7.50, 30 minutes), a short walk from the palace.

**Brüder Grimm-Haus
and Museum Steinau** MUSEUM
(🎫 06663-7605; www.brueder-grimm-haus.de; Brüder Grimm-Strasse 80, Steinau; adult/concession €6/3.50; ⊙ 10am-5pm) These twinned musuems inside the building where the Grimm family lived from 1791 to 1796 house exhibits on the brothers, their work and the history of Steinau.

Hourly trains run to Steinau from Frankfurt am Main (€13.50, one hour). The house is a 20-minute walk from the train station.

Fulda

🎫 0661 / POP 65,000
Although it's not officially on the Fairy-Tale Road, photogenic Fulda, about 30 minutes northeast of Steinau (by car or train), is well worth a side trip for those interested in sumptuous baroque architecture, historic churches and religious reliquaries. A Benedictine monastery was founded here in 744, and today Fulda has its own bishop. The Hauptbahnhof is about 600m east of the main sights, at the northeastern end of Bahnhofstrasse. In the Altstadt (old town), shutterbugs will find plenty of opportunities for happy snapping and there's a handful of top spots to pause for a meal or a glass of wine.

◉ Sights

★ Stadtschloss CASTLE
(🎫 0661-1020; adult/concession €3.50/2.30; ⊙ 10am-5pm Tue-Sun) Fulda's spectacular Stadtschloss was built from 1706 to 1721 as the prince-abbots' residence. It now houses the city administration and function rooms. Visitors can enter the ornate **Historiche Räume** (historic rooms) including the grandiose banquet hall, the octagonal Schlossturm (tower; April to October only) for great views of the town, and the magnificent **Schlossgarten** (palace gardens) where locals play *pétanque* (boules) and sunbathe in summer.

Dom zu Fulda CATHEDRAL
(🎫 0661-874 57; www.bistum-fulda.de; Domplatz 1; ⊙ 10am-6pm Mon-Fri, to 3pm Sat, 1-6pm Sun) Inside the baroque Dom (cathedral), built from 1704 to 1712, you'll find gilded furnishings, plenty of *putti* (figures of infant boys), some dramatic statues (such as to the left of the altar) and the tomb of St Boniface, who died a martyr in 754. There are organ recitals (€3.50) here at noon every Saturday during May, June, September, October and December.

Dommuseum MUSEUM
(🎫 0661-872 07; www.bistum-fulda.de; Domplatz 2; adult/concession €2.10/1.30; ⊙ 10am-5.30pm Tue-Sat, 12.30-5.30pm Sun) Reached through a delightful garden, reliquaries include the spectacular Silver Altar and a spooky object reported to be part of the skull of St Boniface.

Michaelskirche CHURCH
(Michaelsberg 1; ⊙ 10am-5pm) Fulda's history started here. A still-standing reminder of the abbey that made this town, this remarkable church was the monastic burial chapel. Beneath classic witch's-hat towers, a Carolingian rotunda and crypt recall Fulda's flourishing Middle Ages, when the abbey scriptorium churned out top-flight illuminated manuscripts.

🛏 Sleeping

Romantik Hotel Goldener Karpfen HOTEL $$
(🎫 0661-868 00; www.hotel-goldener-karpfen.de; Simpliziusbrunnen 1; s/d/ste from €95/135/285; 🅿✳@🖥) An elegant, historic hotel with traditional and designer rooms (only the latter have air-con), and a restaurant (mains €16 to €32, open 11am to 11pm).

Holiday Inn Fulda HOTEL $$
(🎫 0661-833 00; www.holiday-inn-fulda.de; Lindenstrasse 45; s/d from €93; 🅿✳@🖥) This

well-maintained, early '90s hotel has friendly, helpful, English-speaking staff. Spotless rooms feature comfortable bedding, large-screen TVs and excellent showers. There's an impressive breakfast buffet.

Arte Altstadt Hotel
HOTEL **$$**

(☑0661-2502 9880; www.altstadthotel-arte.de; Doll 2; s/d from €69/99; P❄@🖤) In a great spot on the fringe of the Altstadt, this modern hotel has fresh, bright rooms in a variety of sizes and configurations. Parking is available (at additional cost).

Eating & Drinking

Wirtshaus Schwarzer Hahn
GERMAN **$$**

(☑0661-240 312; www.schwarzerhahn-fulda.de; Friedrichstrasse 18; mains €6-18; ⊙11.30am-10.30pm; 🖤) The walls of this atmospheric little restaurant are plastered with photographs of local and family history; it's a great spot to dine if you're seeking that authentic small-town German experience. It features a hearty menu of fish soups, salmon, steak and schnitzels (the Schwaben-Glück, with creamy mushroom sauce, triumphs). Vegetarian options available.

Vini & Panini
ITALIAN **$$**

(☑0661-774 93; www.vini-panini.de; Steinweg 2-4; mains €8-18; ⊙9am-9pm Mon-Sat; 🖤) Stop by this popular Italian eatery in the heart of the Altstadt for delicious pizza, pasta and crostini. Dine inside or alfresco in the square and pair off your meal with a thoughtfully selected, well-priced wine.

Dachsbau
MODERN EUROPEAN **$$$**

(☑0661-741 12; www.dachsbau-fulda.de; Pfandhausstrabe 8; mains €20-30; ⊙noon-2pm & 6-10pm Wed-Sun) Upmarket, romantic and a treat for the tastebuds, historic Dachsbau is a food-lover's delight. It serves traditional German and European cuisine, using fresh local ingredients, in an elegantly rustic dining room.

Viva Havanna
BAR

(☑0661-227 11; www.vivahavanna-fulda.de; Bonifatiusplatz 2; ⊙11am-midnight) Come for a *Cuba libre*, a beer or a wine, if only to sit on the wonderful terrace with its unbeatable views of the palace.

ⓘ Information

Tourist Office (☑0661-102 1814; www.tourismus-fulda.de; Bonifatiusplatz 1; ⊙8.30am-6pm Mon-Fri, 9.30am-4pm Sat & Sun) Has English-language maps and brochures on Fulda and the Fairy-Tale Road.

ⓘ Getting There & Around

Frequent InterCity Express (ICE) trains connect Fulda with Frankfurt am Main (€31, one hour), Kassel (€32, 30 minutes) and Erfurt (€39, 1¼ hours).

Regional trains connect Fulda with Steinau (€8.10, 30 minutes).

Hahner Zweiradtechnik (☑933 9944; www.hahner-zweirad.de; Beethovenstrasse 3; bikes per day from €13; ⊙9am-6pm Mon-Fri, 9am-1pm Sat) rents out bicycles. Bike path options are signposted down by the river.

Marburg

☑06421 / POP 81,150

Hilly and historic Marburg is 90km north of Frankfurt. It's a delight to wander around the narrow lanes of the town's vibrant Altstadt, sandwiched between a palace (above) and a spectacular Gothic church (below). On the south side of the focal Marktplatz, is the historic **Rathaus** (1512). From there it's a steep climb to the Lutheran **St-Marien-Kirche**, an imposing red-brick church with great views over the lower town. At the base of the Altstadt's Reitgasse are the **Universitätskirche** (early 1300s), a former Dominican monastery, and the neo-Gothic **Alte Universität** (1891), still a well-used part of Philipps-Universität, the world's oldest Protestant university. Founded in 1527, it once counted the Brothers Grimm among its students, who now number almost 26,000.

Visit on a day trip from Frankfurt, or consider spending the night here if you're heading deeper into Central Germany.

⊙ Sights & Activities

Landgrafenschloss
CASTLE

(☑06421-991 20; www.uni-marburg.de/uni-museum; Schloss 1; adult/concession €4/3; ⊙10am-6pm Tue-Sun) Perched at the highest point in town, a steep walk up from St-Marien-Kirche or the Marktplatz, is the massive Landgrave Castle, built between 1248 and 1300. It offers panoramic views of bucolic hills, jumbled Marburg rooftops and the **Schlosspark**, which hosts concerts and open-air films. The castle museum has exhibits on cultural history from prehistoric to modern times.

Elisabethkirche
CHURCH

(☑06421-654 97; www.elisabethkirche.de; Elisabethstrasse; adult/concession €2/1.50; ⊙9am-5pm Apr-Oct, 10am-4pm Nov-Mar) Built between 1235 and 1283, with two high spires added later, the Protestant Elisabethkirche is considered to be Germany's earliest pure-Gothic church. The highlight inside is the **Hohe Chor** (high choir), where you can see beautiful Gothic stained glass behind an astounding stone *Hochaltar* (high altar). The cathedral also houses the elegant **Elisabeth-Schrein** (Elisabeth Shrine), dedicated to St Elisabeth, whose burial here made the church a site of pilgrimage in the Middle Ages. The church is located about 100m south of Bahnhofstrasse.

Marburger Kunstverein GALLERY
(☑ 06421-258 82; www.marburger-kunstverein.de; Gerhard-Jahn-Platz 5; ⊘ 11am-5pm Tue & Thu-Sun, to 8pm Wed) FREE Experimental music meets contemporary art in this compact gallery.

Mittelalterliche Synagoge RUIN
(Willy-Sage-Platz) Beneath this giant glass cube lie the excavated remains of a 13th- and 14th-century synagogue.

Bootsverleih Marburg BOATING, BICYCLE RENTAL
(☑ 06421-804 8467; www.boats-and-bikes.de; Auf dem Wehr 1a; electro-bikes/pedal-boats per hour €4.50/10; ⊘ 9am-9pm) Electro-bikes, row-boats and pedal-boats for hire on the east bank of the Lahn, just south of Weidenhäuser Brücke.

Velociped CYCLING
(☑ 06421-886 890; www.velociped.de; Alte Kasseler Strasse 43; ⊘ 9am-5.30pm Mon-Fri) Everything to know about cycling around Germany and more, 400m north of the station. A huge range of tours and hire options are available. Check the website for prices.

🛏 Sleeping & Eating

DJH Hostel HOSTEL $
(☑ 06421-234 61; www.djh-hessen.de/jugendherbergen/marburg; Jahnstrasse 1; dm/s/d incl breakfast €22/33/56; @ ☎) This clean, well-run youth hostel is located 500m south of the centre on the river and the Lahntal Radweg (Lahntal Bike Route). Staff can help plan outings, rent canoes and arrange bike hire. Take bus 3 to the Auf der Weide bus stop. Linen is included and there's no surcharge if you're over 27.

Vila Vita Rosenpark HOTEL $$
(☑ 06421-600 50; www.rosenpark.com; Anneliese Pohl Allee 7-17; s/d from €116/126; P ❋ @ ☎ ☲) Marburg's swankiest and priciest digs are in a lovely spot by the river, a short stroll from the station. If you're going to splurge, superior or double rooms and suites offer better value at almost twice the size of classic single rooms. An expansive wellness centre, day spa and two restaurants come with the package.

Welcome Hotel Marburg HOTEL $$
(☑ 06421-9180; www.welcome-hotel-marburg.de; Pilgrimstein 29; s/d from €93/122; ❋ @ ☎) Just below the Altstadt, this central hotel has 147 bright, spacious rooms with large windows. Ask for a quieter room at the rear of the building.

Hostaria Del Castello HOTEL $$
(☑ 06421-243 02; www.del-castello.de; Marktplatz 19; s €55-84, d €78-108; @) In the thick of things, 50m up the hill from the Markt, this Italian-run establishment has seven rooms and a downstairs restaurant.

★ Café Barfuss CAFE $
(☑ 06421-253 49; www.cafebarfuss.de; Barfüsserstrasse 33; meals €4-15; ⊘ 10am-1am; ☑) A local institution, Barfuss is a no-fuss, offbeat place with a steady stream of student diners who favour its menu of hearty, healthy plates, including great breakfasts and vegetarian options.

Bückingsgarten GERMAN $$
(☑ 06421-165 7771; www.bueckingsgarten-marburg.de; Landgraf-Philipp-Strasse 6; mains €8-24; ⊘ noon-10pm) Choose from two separate menus at this historical restaurant with a spectacular hilltop position adjacent to the castle. Dine inside for more upmarket ambience and fare, or enjoy a beer and casual meal in the brer garden: both have excellent views.

Zur Sonne GERMAN $$
(☑ 06421-171 90; www.zur-sonne-marburg.de; Markt 14; mains €12-28; ⊘ 8am-2pm & 6-10pm; ☑) In the heart of the Markt, this delightful restaurant feels as though it's been serving meals to scholars and students since time immemorial. Enjoy traditional German fare in the rustic dining rooms or alfresco in the square.

KostBar MODERN EUROPEAN $$
(☑ 06421-161 170; www.kostbar-marburg.de; Barfüsserstrasse 7; mains €8-18; ⊘ noon-11pm; ☑) This modern bar-restaurant offers well-prepared soups, salads and vegetarian meals as well as healthy approaches to the standard chicken, fish and meat offerings, all concocted from a creative blend of ingredients.

🍷 Drinking & Entertainment

For listings, look no further than the free *Marburger Magazin Express* (www.marbuch-verlag.de).

Delirium mit Frazzkeller PUB
(☑ 06421-649 19; Steinweg 3; ⊘ 8pm-3am) Delirium is upstairs, Frazzkeller is downstairs,

and both of these student hang-outs scream 1970s and have great views over the Unterstadt (yes, even from the cellar). The house drink is Roter Korn, a redcurrant liqueur.

Trauma im G-Werk   CLUB
(✆06421-889 772; www.cafetrauma.de; Afföllerwiesen 3a; ☺event hours vary) This versatile, über-cool space hosts semi-regular parties, DJs, art shows, installations, live music, cinema and cultural events. Check the website.

Café Vetter   CAFE
(✆06421-258 88; www.cafe-vetter-marburg.de; Reitgasse 4; ☺9am-6pm) The same family has been tending this tearoom for five generations, amid wicker-back chairs and classic 1970s lamps. The house-speciality chocolate-cream cake is best enjoyed with the fine panoramas.

Jazzclub Cavete   JAZZ
(www.jazzini.de; Steinweg 12; ☺8pm-1am) A prime port of call for jazz lovers, with open-stage nights (no cover charge) on Monday and frequent concerts.

ℹ Information

Post Office (Bahnhofstrasse 6; ☺9am-6pm Mon-Fri, to 12.30pm Sat)

Tourist Office (✆06421 991 20; www.marburg.de; Pilgrimstein 26; ☺9am-6pm Mon-Fri, 10am-2pm Sat) Books inexpensive private rooms and has free maps of town. In summer an information point is also open on Markt.

ℹ Getting There & Away

BICYCLE
The 245km Lahntal Radweg runs along the Lahn all the way to the Rhine.

CAR
From Marburg the next major stop on the Fairy-Tale Road is Kassel. Follow the B3/B62 north out of town toward Neustadt and Bad Wildungen for the Nationalpark Kellerwald-Edersee or Fritzlar (direct route) to Kassel.

TRAIN
There are frequent connections with Frankfurt am Main (from €15, one hour) and Kassel (from €21, one hour).

ℹ Getting Around

BUS
The Hauptbahnhof is linked to Rudolphsplatz (where Pilgrimstein meets Universitätsstrasse) by buses 2 and 6.

LIFT
About 100m north of the tourist office, free **public lifts** (inside Parkhaus Oberstadt, Pilgrimstein; ☺6am-2am) whisk you up to Wettergasse in the Altstadt. A thigh-toughening alternative is nearby Enge Gasse, a monstrously steep stone staircase that was once a sewage sluice.

Nationalpark Kellerwald-Edersee

Nationalpark Kellerwald-Edersee   NATIONAL PARK
(www.nationalpark-kellerwald-edersee.de) Hesse's first national park, established in 2004, encompasses the **Kellerwald**, one of the largest extant red-beech forests in Central Europe, and the **Edersee**, a serpentine artificial reservoir 55km northeast of Marburg and about the same distance southwest of Kassel. Animals such as red deer roam the park, while honey buzzards, eagles and various species of bat might be seen overhead. Keep an eye out for vibrantly mottled fire salamanders in the park's many spring-fed creeks.

For information and insights into the area's ecosystems, head to the striking **visitors centre** (✆05635-992 781; www.national parkzentrum-kellerwald.de; B252, Vöhl-Herzhausen; e-bikes per day €20; ☺10am-6pm Apr-Oct, to 5pm Nov-Mar) at the western end of the Edersee, on the northern edge of Kirchlotheim. Here and at other points you can rent e-bikes and ride around the lake on a comfortable day tour, changing the battery at points along the way. Bike trails also run through the forest itself, and the park's lush landscapes offer excellent hiking. Walking trails include the **Kellerwaldsteig** (marked 'K') and the **Urwaldsteig-Edersee** (marked 'UE'). Shorter hiking circuits are marked with animal or plant icons. The lake has swimming, canoeing and sailing.

Buses lead into the park from the train stations in Bad Wildungen and Frankenberg, and from Korbach, which is linked to Kassel by the RE04 train. Bus 555 links the NationalparkZentrum with both Frankenberg and Korbach. A one-way ticket with the train and bus from Kassel to Korbach and on to the national park office costs €16; the trip takes 2¾ hours. Bus 521 goes from Bad Wildungen to the Edersee.

Nordhessische Verkehrsbund (✆0180 234 0180; www.nvv.de; one way from €5.40) operates public transport into the park.

Kassel

✔ 0561 / POP 192,880

Although wartime bombing and postwar reconstruction left Kassel looking undeniably utilitarian, you'd hardly know it today. Visitors to this culture-rich, sprawling hub on the Fulda River will discover a pleasant, modern city with several interesting and unusual museums and a one-of-a-kind baroque park – Bergpark Wilhelmshöhe – which boasts a handsome palace and the gargantuan Herkules Wasserspiel (water feature).

Most museums, hotels and dining options are located downtown, whereas the castle, gardens and Herkules are in Bad Wilhelmshöhe, at the western end of the stately 4.5km-long Wilhelmshöher Allee, which runs west to east through town. Allow a full day to explore the Bad Wilhelmshöhe attractions.

◉ Sights

Bergpark Wilhelmshöhe   PARK
(www.museum-kassel.de; ⊙ 9am-sunset) FREE
Situated 6.5km west of Kassel HBF station, and 3km west of Kassel Wilhelmshöhe station, in the enchanting **Habichtswald** nature park, this spectacular baroque parkland takes its name from Schloss Wilhelmshöhe, the late 18th-century palace situated inside the expanse. You can spend an entire day here walking through the forest, enjoying a romantic picnic and exploring the castles, fountains, grottoes, statues and water features; the Herkules statue and water feature and Löwenburg castle are also here.

There are a number of transport options to get to the park. Tram 1 to the Wilhelmshöhe terminus drops you close by if you want to visit Schloss Wilhelmshöhe (a short walk or take bus 23 for one stop) or just want to stroll around. To get to the Herkules

---

100 DAYS OF ART

Every five years Kassel hosts **dOCU-MENTA** (www.documenta.de), one of Europe's most important contemporary art exhibitions, lasting 100 days. Popping up next in 2017 and then 2022, the event draws around one million visitors – expect more indoor and outdoor festivities, installations and exhibitions within exhibitions than even the most seasoned art aficionado could digest in, well...one hundred days.

---

statue, take tram 3 to the Druseltal terminus and then bus 22 (once or twice an hour from 8am to 7pm or 8pm) to the Herkules stop. From the statue you can also walk down the hill to reach the palace.

★ **Herkules**   STATUE
(www.museum-kassel.de; Schlosspark Wilhelmshöhe 26 (Herkules-Terrassen); adult/concession €3/2; ⊙ 10am-5pm mid-Mar–mid-Nov) Declared a Unesco World Heritage site in 2013, the 8.25m-high copper Herkules statue stands atop a towering stone pyramid atop an octagonal amphitheatre atop an imposing hill at the western end of Bergpark Wilhelmshöhe, some 600m above sea level. It was erected between 1707 and 1717. Even more phenomenal than the statue itself is the engineering genius at the heart of its 1¼-hour **Wasserspiele** cascade, which takes place every Wednesday, Sunday and public holiday from 1 May to 3 October.

The water begins its tumble at 2.30pm from up top, near Herkules. From there, you can walk down with the crowds via the **Teufelsbrücke** (Devil's Bridge) and the **Aquädukt** to the **Grosse Fontäne** (Large Fountain) to watch the water emerge in a 50m-high jet. Once a month during the summer months, there's a spectacular nighttime illumination; check with Kassel's tourist offices for dates.

Unfortunately, scaffolding from ongoing restoration works is visible around the statue itself, and likely to remain for some time.

Schloss Wilhelmshöhe   PALACE
(☎ 0561-316 800; www.museum-kassel.de; Schlosspark 1; adult/concession €6/4, Weissenstein wing incl tour €4/3; ⊙ 10am-5pm Tue & Thu-Sun, to 8pm Wed) Home to Elector Wilhelm and later to Kaiser Wilhelm II, Wilhelmshöhe Palace (1786–98) at the foot of Bergpark Wilhelmshöhe today houses one of Germany's best art collections (especially of Flemish and Dutch baroque painting), featuring works by Rembrandt, Rubens, Jordaens, Lucas Cranach the Elder, Dürer and many others in the **Gemäldegalerie** (painting gallery). The 23 rooms of the **Weissenstein** wing comprise the oldest part of the palace, dating from 1790, and are filled with original furnishings and paintings.

The **Antikensammlung** is an excellent collection of Egyptian, Etruscan, Greek and Roman statuary and vases.

Löwenburg   CASTLE
(☎ 0561-316 800; www.museum-kassel.de; Bergpark Wilhelmshöhe; adult/student €4/2; ⊙ tours

hourly 10am-4pm Tue-Sun Mar-Oct, to 3pm Nov-Feb) Situated within Bergpark Wilhelmshöhe, the 'Lion's Castle' was built between 1793 and 1801 in a medieval style. Tours take in the **Rüstkammer** (Museum of Armaments) and **Ritterzeitsmuseum** (Museum of Chivalry). Bus 23 will get you here.

★ Grimmwelt   MUSEUM

(☑0561-598 610; www.grimmwelt.de; Weinbergstrasse; adult/concession €8/6; ⊙10am-6pm Tue-Sun) Occupying a prime position atop the Weinberg bunker in the scenic Weinbergpark, Kassel's newest musuem, opened in September 2015, could be described as an architect-designed walk-in sculpture housing the most significant collection of Brother's Grimm memorabilia on the planet. Visitors are guided around original exhibits, state-of-the-art installations, and fun, hands-on activities, aided by entries from the Grimm's German dictionary: there were more to these famous brothers than just fairy tales, didn't you know?

Museum für Sepulkralkultur   MUSEUM

(Museum of Sepulchral Culture; ☑0561-918 930; www.sepulkralmuseum.de; Weinbergstrasse 25-27; adult/concession €6/4; ⊙10am-5pm Tue & Thu-Sun, to 8pm Wed) Billed as 'a meditative space for funerary art', this museum aims at burying the taboo of discussing death. The permanent collection includes headstones, hearses, dancing skeleton bookends and sculptures depicting death. Take trams 1 or 3 to Weigelstrasse.

Fridericianum   MUSEUM

(☑0561-707 2720; www.fridericianum.org; Friedrichsplatz 18; adult/concession €5/3, Wed free; ⊙11am-6pm Tue-Sun) This excellent contemporary art museum hosts changing exhibitions exploring relevant, topical themes. The historical context of the gallery itself nicely contrasts the works being displayed.

Neue Galerie   GALLERY

(☑0561-3168 0400; www.museum-kassel. de; Schöne Aussicht 1; adult/concession €4/2; ⊙10am-5pm Tue, Wed & Fri-Sun, to 8pm Thu) The recently restored Neue Galerie showcases paintings and sculptures by German artists from 1750 to the present, as well as exhibits from past dOCUMENTA exhibitions.

Documenta Halle   GALLERY

(☑0561-707 270; www.documentahalle.de; Du-Ry-Strasse 1; ⊙10am-6pm Tue-Sun) Changing exhibitions on modern art.

ⓘ WHERE TO WATCH THE WASSERSPIELE?

If you're coming to see the Herkules' Wasserspiele, the burning question is: where's the best vantage point? To make the most of your visit, it's a good idea to head to the top nice and early, so you can take a look around the Herkules statue itself and admire the views. Around 2pm, walk down to the base of the statue and get a good spot for the release of the water at 2.30pm; you can watch it cascade down the hill, then follow the other pilgrims through the park to see the full show. Patience is a virtue. Bring a tripod if you plan to shoot some video.

🛏 Sleeping

The tourist office books private rooms from around €25 per person.

Pentahotel Kassel   BOUTIQUE HOTEL $

(☑0561-933 9887; www.pentahotels.com, Bertha-von-Suttner Strasse 15; d from €55; P✳🐾) This modern, central hotel has compact, stylish rooms with ambient lighting, arty design elements and free high-speed wi-fi. There's a bar and restaurant and free late checkout of 3pm on Sundays (subject to availability).

DJH Hostel   HOSTEL $

(☑0561-776 455; www.djh-hessen.de/jugendherbergen/kassel; Schenkendorfstrasse 18; dm/s/d incl breakfast €24/34/55; P☺@🐾) Opposite a small park, the hostel's proximity to the railway lines might bother light sleepers. Linen is included and there's no surcharge if you're over 27. Situated about 1km west of Kassel Hauptbahnhof, or take tram 4 or 7 from Königsplatz to Querallee.

Kurpark Hotel Bad Wilhelmshöhe   BOUTIQUE HOTEL $$

(☑0561-318 90; www.kurparkhotel-kassel.de; Wilhelmshöher Allee 336; s/d from €105/137; P✳🐾🏊) In an excellent location near the castle and train station, this stylish hotel offers well-appointed rooms and common areas, a restaurant and an indoor pool.

Schlosshotel Bad Wilhelmshöhe   HOTEL $$

(☑0561-308 80; www.schlosshotel-kassel.de; Schlosspark 8; s/d from €119/149; P🐾) In an idyllic garden setting on the fringe of Bergpark Wilhelmshöhe, this luxe hotel is built in the Bauhaus style. Rooms are stylish and comfortable with large windows and garden views. Drop some cash in the day spa if you fancy: you will be rejuvenated.

Tryp by Wyndham   HOTEL **$$**
(☑0561-703 330; www.trypkassel.com; Erzbergerstrasse 1-5; s/d from €65/75; [P][@][🛜]) A quality hotel with bright, modern rooms situated 500m northeast of Kassel Hauptbahnhof or 600m north of Scheidemannplatz. Take bus 52 or tram 7 from Kassel-Wilhelmshöhe train station to Scheidemannplatz.

🍴 Eating & Drinking

The free monthly *Frizz* (www.frizz-kassel. de) has nightlife and entertainment listings.

★Pho Vang   VIETNAMESE **$**
(☑0561-937 5136; Garde-du-Corps Strasse 1; mains €6-16; ⊘11.30am-3pm & 5-10pm Mon-Sat; 🍴) There are many mediocre Southeast Asian restaurants in Germany. Spotless Pho Vang is an exception, delivering authentic Vietnamese *pho* noodle soups and other traditional dishes that aren't altered too drastically to suit the European palate. It's cheap and delicious, with plenty of options for vegetarians.

Lohmann   GERMAN **$$**
(☑0561-701 6875; www.lohmann-kassel.de; Königstor 8; mains €8-18; ⊘noon-11pm Sun-Fri, 5-11pm Sat) With roots that go back to 1888, this popular, family-run *Kneipe* (pub) has an old-style birch-and-maple-shaded beer garden with an outdoor grill. Schnitzel (always pork) features heavily on the menu.

Matterhorn Stübli   SWISS **$$**
(☑0561-399 33; www.matterhornstuebli.de; Wilhelmshöher Allee 326; mains €14-22; ⊘5.30-11pm Tue-Sat, noon-2pm & 5.30-11pm Sun; 🍴) If you love cheese, fondue, schnitzel, or all three, you're well advised to hotfoot it to this quaint Swiss restaurant. If you like mushrooms as well, try the *Original Züri Geschnätzläts:* veal escalopes served with mushrooms and crispy rösti.

Gaststube
Kleines Schweinchen   GERMAN **$$**
(☑0561-940 480; www.steinernes-schweinchen. de; Konrad-Adenauer-Strasse 117; mains €9-22; ⊘5-10pm; 🍴) One of a trio of dining options under the tutelage of acclaimed chef Jürgen Richter, this 'little piggy' – the most casual of the three – offers hearty, homestyle German fare in the style of a woodsy, country inn.
    The restaurant is 5km southwest of Kassel-Wilhelmshöhe station (take bus 51 or 52 to the stop Brasselsberg) within the Zum Steinernes Schweinchen hotel.

El Erni   SPANISH **$$$**
(☑0561-710 018; www.el-erni.de; Parkstrasse 42, Ecke Querallee; mains €16-31; ⊘6-10pm Mon-Sat) For quality modern-Spanish cuisine in an upmarket setting, head to this refined restaurant and choose between delicious tapas to share, or from a menu of fish, chicken or meat-based mains. Better still, try both.

Bolero   BAR
(☑0561-4501 0632; www.bolerobar.de; Schöne Aussicht 1a; ⊘10am-midnight Mon-Fri, 9am-1am Sat & Sun) The best reason to visit this sleek, modern chain-restaurant is to sip a cocktail and enjoy the wonderful views from the terrace. Oh, and the daily happy hour (5pm to 7pm) followed by the jumbo hour (7pm to 9pm).

Shamrock   IRISH PUB
(☑0561-202 8630; www.irishpubkassel.com; Bürgermeister Brunner Strasse 19; ⊘4.30pm-2am) Popular with locals and travelers alike, this jovial haunt brings together lovers of Guinness, Irish music and football.

❶ Information

Sold at tourist offices and some hotels, the great-value **Kassel Card** (1 or 2 persons per 24/72hr €9/12) gets you discounts on a bunch of attractions and free use of public transport.
Tourist Office Innenstadt (☑0561-707 707; www.kassel-marketing.de; Wilhelmsstrasse 23; ⊘9am-6pm Mon-Sat)
Tourist Office Kassel-Wilhelmshöhe (☑0561-340 54; www.kassel-tourist.de; Kassel-Wilhelmshöhe Train Station; ⊘9am-6pm Mon-Sat)

❶ Getting There & Away

Kassel has two main train stations. Kassel Hauptbahnhof, in the centre of town, is served by regional (RE) trains, but it's more likely that you'll be arriving into Kassel-Wilhelmshöhe (Fernbahnhof) station, 3.5km to the west, which handles both regional and IC/ICE trains. ICE or IC connections from Kassel-Wilhelmshöhe include Fulda (€32, 30 minutes), Marburg (€20.70, one hour), Göttingen (€18, 18 minutes) and Frankfurt am Main (from €43, two hours).

❶ Getting Around

BICYCLE
Fahrradhof (☑313 083; www.fahrradhof.de; Wilhelmshöher Allee 253; bikes per 24hr/week €10/50; ⊘9am-1pm & 2-6.30pm Mon-Fri, 9am-3pm Sat) Rent city and trekking bikes and

buy cycling maps from this outfitter on the east side of Kassel-Wilhelmshöhe train station, just past track 11.

TRAM

Tram 1 runs the length of Wilhelmshöher Allee, linking the city centre with Wilhelmshöhe. Trams 1, 3 and 4 go from Kassel-Wilhelmshöhe train station to the centre. Almost all the city's tram lines stop at Königsplatz.

Göttingen

0551 / POP 116,650

With over 30,000 students, this historic town nestled in a corner of Lower Saxony near the Hesse border offers a good taste of university-town life in Germany's north. Since 1734, the Georg-August Universität has sent more than 40 Nobel Prize winners into the world. As well as all those award-winning doctors and scientists, alumni include the fairy-tale-writing Brothers Grimm (as German linguistic teachers) and Prussian chancellor Otto von Bismarck (as a student).

Be sure to stroll around the pleasant Markt and nearby Barfüsser-strasse to admire the *Fachwerk* (half-timbered) houses.

Sights & Activities

Gänseliesel MONUMENT

(Markt) The city's symbol, the *Gänseliesel* (little goose girl) statue is hailed locally as the most kissed woman in the world – not a flattering moniker, you might think, but enough to make her iconic. After graduating, doctoral students climb up to peck her on the cheek.

Altes Rathaus HISTORIC BUILDING

(Markt 9; 9.30am-6pm Mon-Sat, 10am-4pm Sun) FREE The Old Town Hall was built in 1270 and once housed the merchants' guild. Inside, later decorations added to its Great Hall include frescos of the coats of arms of the Hanseatic cities and local bigwigs, grafted onto historic scenes. It's particularly lovely at dusk.

Göttinger Wald FOREST

Göttinger Wald (Göttingen Forest) is one of the best mixed forest stands of predominantly beech and oak in the region. It's easily reached by following Herzberger Landstrasse east from the centre of town to the point near where it forms a hairpin bend, and turning into Borheckstrasse. From there, a bitumen track open to hikers and cyclists winds toward Am Kehr, 45 minutes away, where there's a small Bavarian-style beer garden.

Bismarckturm TOWER

(adult/concession €2/1; 11am-6pm Sat, Sun & holidays Apr-Sep) Göttingen's stone Bismarck Tower, completed in 1898, has a viewing platform 31m above the ground from where you can see as far as the Göttingen Forest to the east, the Werra mountains to the south and the Weser mountains to the west.

City Wall WALKING

Taking a stroll along the 18th-century former city wall, now an attractive tree-lined path, is one of the best ways to introduce yourself to this historic, pedestrian-friendly town.

Festivals & Events

Händel Festival MUSIC

(www.haendel-festspiele.de) Lovers of classical music flock to town for this extravaganza held in late May and early June. Enquire about tickets at the tourist office.

Sleeping

Hostel 37 HOSTEL $

(0551-6344 5177; www.hostel37.de; Groner Landstrasse 7; dm from €18; office 3-9pm;) This modern hostel has four- and six-bed dorm rooms and a brilliant downtown location.

WORTH A TRIP

SOME ROCOCO WITH YOUR BAROQUE?

Schloss Wilhelmsthal (05674-6898; www.museum-kassel.de; Calden; adult/concession €4/3; 10am-4pm Tue-Sun) About 12km northwest of Kassel you'll find one of Germany's best-preserved and most beautiful rococo palaces, built by Landgrave Wilhelm VIII as a leisure palace between 1747 and 1761. The magnificent baroque park-like grounds are free to explore, while the sumptuous interior can be visited on a (highly recommended) hourly guided tour. Among the many delightful rooms, visitors love the master kitchen, where the *Bratenwendemaschine* (roast turning machine) still functions.

To get here from Kassel, take the B7 north to Calden and follow the signs, or from Wilhelmshöhe, take the L3217 north and follow the signs.

Park Inn by Radisson
HOTEL $$
(☑0551-270 7070; www.parkinn.com; Kasseler Landstrasse 25c; r from €89; ⓟ✳@🛜) This ultra-modern chain hotel approximately 2.5km from downtown has 114 air-conditioned rooms with large flat-screen TVs, comfortable bedding, great showers and free wi-fi. It's a good choice for self-drivers, although parking attracts an additional fee (€6).

Hotel Stadt Hannover
HOTEL $$
(☑0551-547 960; www.hotelstadthannover.de; Goetheallee 21; s/d from €84/118; ⓟ@🛜) Beyond the art-nouveau etched-glass door and quaint entrance hall, you'll find modern, comfortable rooms with free wi-fi. There's a choice of bathtub or shower, and the prices vary according to the size of the room and the standard of furnishings.

Gebhards Hotel
HOTEL $$$
(☑0551-49 680; www.gebhards-hotel.de; Goetheallee 22-23; s/d from €104/158; ⓟ@🛜) With a robust sandstone facade, and art-deco details within, this charming hotel boasts a large spa, a compact sauna and an excellent restaurant. Service is straight out of the good ol' days.

Freizeit In
HOTEL $$$
(☑0551-900 10; www.freizeit-in.de; Dransfelder Strasse 3; s/d incl breakfast from €120/160; ⓟ✳@🛜🏊) More than 200 comfortable and stylish rooms in a variety of configurations, 24-hour reception, numerous dining options, and an enormous day-spa and wellness centre make this resort-style hotel a top choice if you decide to linger a little longer. It's located on the outskirts of town.

✖ Eating

Nudelhaus
GERMAN, EUROPEAN $
(☑0551-442 63; Rote Strasse 13; mains €5-9; ⊙11.30am-11pm) You're spoiled for choice at this always-busy, central eatery, which specialises in the humble German noodle (try the green-ribbon variety) and a range of European dishes (such as delicious garlic mushrooms), as well as traditional Italian pastas, pizza and seafood. The smoky central beer garden is often packed.

Cron & Lanz
CAFE $
(☑0551-560 22; Weender Strasse 25; cakes from €4; ⊙8.30am-7pm Mon-Sat, 1-6.30pm Sun) This ornate Viennese-style cafe is Göttingen's dignified haunt for connoisseurs of chocolate and other calorie bombs.

Zum Szultenburger
GERMAN $$
(☑0551-431 33; Prinzenstrasse 7; mains €8-20; ⊙noon-2.30pm & 5.30-11pm Tue-Sat) This traditional German pub does things to the humble schnitzel that will make your mouth water. It's cosy and cheap, the varied menu is all kinds of delicious, and the staff seem happy to be here, which makes all the difference. Cash only.

Myer's
INTERNATIONAL $$
(☑0551-499 7888; www.das-myers.de; Lange-Geismar-Strasse 47; mains €6-18; ⊙9am-midnight Mon-Sat, 10am-11pm Sun, closed Sun Jul & Aug; ✍) This rambling cafe-bar-restaurant is great if you can handle the noise. Every now and again the skilled chefs whip up a delicious surprise or two to complement the pastas, salads, pancakes, pizzas and vegetarian or meat dishes on its large year-round or smaller seasonal menus. Smokers can sit upstairs.

★Gauss
GERMAN $$$
(☑0551-566 16; www.restaurant-gauss.de; Obere Karspüle 22, enter on Theaterstrasse; 3-/4-/5-course menu from €45/55/68; ⊙6pm-midnight Tue-Sat; ✍) Arguably Göttingen's finest gourmet experience features exquisite haute cuisine that constantly evolves with the availability of fresh, seasonal ingredients. Course menus are complimented by à-la-carte options, and vegetarians are well catered for.

🍷 Drinking & Entertainment

Monster Café
CAFE
(☑0551-4997 7779; Goetheallee 13a; ⊙11am-midnight Mon-Thu, to 1.30am Fri & Sat, noon-midnight Sun) Lively student cafe-bar with an art edge.

Savoy
CLUB
(☑0551-531 4145; www.club-savoy.de; Berliner Strasse 5; admission €4-8; ⊙Wed, Fri & Sat from 11pm) Göttingen's leading club plays mainstream and house music; it's spread over a couple of levels.

Apex
LIVE PERFORMANCE
(☑0551-468 86; www.apex-goe.de; Burgstrasse 46; ⊙5.30pm-midnight Mon-Sat) Apex offers the perfect trio of art gallery, performance venue, and restaurant serving quality light dishes.

Junges Theater
THEATRE
(☑0551-495 015; www.junges-theater.de; Hospitalstrasse 6) Göttingen's Junges Theater has been on the scene since the late 1950s and enjoys a high reputation throughout Germany.

ⓘ Information

Pickup up a **GöCard** (per 1/3 days €5/12) from the tourist office for a variety of local discounts and free travel on all municipal buses.

Post Office (Groner Strasse 15-17; ⊙9am-6pm Mon-Fri, 10am-1pm Sat)

Tourist Office (☑ 0551-499 800; www.goet tingen-tourismus.de; Markt 9, Altes Rathaus; ⊙9.30am-6pm Mon-Sat, 10am-4pm Sun) Free bilingual English-German brochures and walking maps are available, as well as a variety of interesting themed tours – including those delving into Göttingen's underworld.

ⓘ Getting There & Away

CAR

Göttingen is on the A7 running north–south. The closest entrance is 3km southwest along Kasseler Landstrasse, an extension of Groner Landstrasse. Pick up the B27 southwest to the Weser River and northeast to the Harz Mountains for Fairy-Tale Road towns.

TRAIN

Frequent direct ICE services to Hanover (€28, 35 minutes), Kassel (€18, 18 minutes), Hamburg (€63, two hours), Frankfurt (€64, 1¾ hours), Munich (€112, 3¾ hours) and Berlin-Hauptbahnhof (€80, 2¼ hours). Direct regional services go to Kassel (€15, one hour), Weimar (€18, two hours) and Goslar (€17.30, 1¼ hours).

ⓘ Getting Around

Single bus tickets cost €2, 24-hour tickets €4.60. For a taxi, call ☑ 340 34.

Bad Karlshafen

☑ 05672 / POP 3530

Bad Karlshafen's orderly streets and white-washed baroque buildings were built in the 18th century for landgrave Karl von Hessen-Kassel by French Huguenot refugees. The town was planned with an impressive harbour and a canal connecting the Weser with the Rhine to attract trade, but the Landgrave died before his designs were completed. The only reminder of his grand plans is a tiny *Hafenbecken* (harbour basin) trafficked by white swans.

Although it's lost a little of its grandeur, Bad Karlshafen remains a popular summer destination, with motorhomes and tents lining up along the northern banks of the Weser. Take a stroll around the compact town centre on the river's southern bank, with the *Hafenbecken* and its surrounding square, Hafenplatz, at its western end.

◉ Sights

Deutsches Huguenotten Museum MUSEUM (German Huguenot Museum; ☑ 05672-1410; www.huguenot-museum-germany.com; Hafenplatz 9a; adult/concession €4/2; ⊙10am-5pm Tue-Fri, 11am-6pm Sat & Sun mid-Mar–Oct, 10am-noon Mon-Fri Nov–mid-Mar) This interesting museum traces the history of the French Huguenot refugees in Germany.

🛏 Sleeping

There's no shortage of accommodation in this sweet, sleepy spa town.

Hotel-Pension Haus Fuhrhop HOTEL $ (☑ 05672-404; www.pension-fuhrhop.de; Friedrichstrasse 15; s/d/tr €39/80/90) This charming *pension* in the centre of town has spacious and comfortable rooms with a modern, stylish character.

Helmarshausen DJH Hostel HOSTEL $ (☑ 05672-1027; www.djh-hessen.de/jh/helmarshausen; Gottsbürener Strasse 15; dm/s/d incl breakfast €21/28/45; [P🛜]) Situated at the start of forest trails in a lovely half-timbered building 3km from Hafenplatz in the town of Helmarshausen. Linen is included and there's no surcharge if you're over 27. Take bus 180 to Helmarshausen Mitte.

Hotel zum Schwan HOTEL $$ (☑ 05672-104 445; www.hotel-zum-schwan-bad-karlshafen.com; Conradistrasse 3-4; s/d €48/86; [P🛜]) Landgrave Karl's former hunting lodge is now one of the better hotels in town, with views of the harbour and a lovely rococo dining room.

ⓘ Information

Tourist Office (☑ 05672-999 922; www.bad-karlshafen.de; Hafenplatz 8; ⊙10am-noon & 2-4pm Mon-Thu, 10am-noon Fri & Sat) Has local maps and guides to the area.

Hamelin

☑ 05151 / POP 57,350

If you have a phobia about rats, you might give this picturesque town on the Weser River a wide berth. According to the tale of *The Pied Piper of Hamelin*, in the 13th century the Pied Piper *(Der Rattenfänger)* was employed by Hamelin's townsfolk to lure its nibbling rodents into the river. When they refused to pay him for his services, he picked up his flute and lured their children away. Today the rats rule once again – cute, fluffy stuffed rats, wooden rats, and tiny rats adorning the sights around town.

Rats aside, Hamelin (Hameln, in German) is a pleasant town with half-timbered houses and opportunities for cycling along the Weser River, on the eastern bank of which lies Hamelin's circular **Altstadt**. The main streets are Osterstrasse, which runs east–west, and Bäckerstrasse, running north–south. Hamelin's heart is its **Markt**, the northern continuation of which, **Pferdemarkt**, is home to an interesting sculpture by artist Wolfgang Dreysse, dealing with the collapse of the East German border.

Sights

Museum Hamelin
MUSEUM

(✆ 05151-202 1215; www.museum-hameln.de; Osterstrasse 8-9; adult/concession €5/4; ⊙ 11am-6pm Tue-Sun) Many of Hamelin's finest buildings were constructed in the Weser Renaissance style, which has strong Italian influences. Today two of the best provide the location for the town's revamped museum, which has an excellent permanent exhibition on regional history from the earliest times to the present. The **Leisthaus** at number 9 was built for a patrician grain trader during 1585–89. The **Stiftsherrenhaus**, dating from 1558, is Hamelin's only surviving building decorated with human figures.

Hochzeitshaus
HISTORIC BUILDING

(Osterstrasse 2) Situated on the corner of Markt and Osterstrasse is the Hochzeitshaus (1610–17), partly used today as city council offices and as a police station. The **Rattenfänger Glockenspiel** at the far end of the building chimes daily at 9.35am and 11.35am, while a carousel of Pied Piper figures twirls at 1.05pm, 3.35pm and 5.35pm.

Schloss Hämelschenburg
CASTLE

(✆ 05151-951 690; www.schloss-haemelschenburg.de; Schlossstrasse 1, Emmerthal; tours adult/concession €7/4.50; ⊙ tours 11am, noon, 2pm, 3pm & 4pm Tue-Sun Apr-Sep) Some 15km southwest of Hamelin in pretty parkland near a tributary of the Weser River lies this Renaissance palace dating from 1588 to 1613. The castle is among the best of its kind in Germany, and was built on a former pilgrimage road that eventually led to Santiago de Compostella in Spain. Tours take you through rooms decked with original Renaissance furnishings and paintings.

Getting here can be half the fun if you cycle along the Weser River bicycle path (heading south). Otherwise, take bus 40 (€2.70, 30 minutes) to the residence from Hamelin station.

Sleeping & Eating

Ask at the tourist office about staying at the local camping ground, a 15-minute walk north of town.

Mercure Hamelin
HOTEL $$

(✆ 05151-7920; www.mercure.com; 164er Ring 3; s/d from €69/79; P ﹫ ﹡) Just outside the city walls, this freshly and tastefully refurbished tourist hotel benefits from airy rooms, some with balconies and lovely views. Bonuses include the swimming pool and a fantastic buffet-breakfast spread.

Hotel La Principessa
HOTEL $$

(✆ 05151-956 920; www.laprincipessa.de; Kupferschmiedestrasse 2; s/d €78/99; P ﹫) Cast-iron balustrades, tiled floors throughout, gentle Tuscan pastels and ochre shades make this Italian-themed hotel an unusual and distinguished option. There's a junior suite, and out back some giant rats for the kids to mess with.

Komfort-Hotel Garni Christinenhof
BOUTIQUE HOTEL $$

(✆ 05151-950 80; www.christinenhof-hameln.de; Alte Marktstrasse 18; s/d incl breakfast €90/115; P ﹫ ﹡) Historic outside, modern within, this quaint hotel has some neat touches, such as a tiny swimming pool in the vaulted cellar, a sauna, compact but pleasant and uncluttered rooms, and a generous buffet breakfast.

★ Rattenfängerhaus
GERMAN $$

(✆ 05151-3888; www.rattenfaengerhaus.de; Osterstrasse 28; mains €10-23; ⊙ 11am-10pm) One of Hamelin's finest ornamental Weser Renaissance–style buildings, the Rattenfängerhaus (from 1602) is also home to a favourite, unashamedly tourist-centric restaurant, which has been serving 'rats' tails' flambéed at your table since 1966; don't fret – it's all a pork-based ruse. Aside from the novelty dishes, standard schnitzels, herrings, vegie dishes and 'rat killer' herb liquor are also offered.

Klütturm
MODERN EUROPEAN $$

(✆ 05151-962 620; www.kluetturm-restaurant.de; Klütturm 1; mains €12-22) If you fancy a splurge, take a drive into the hills above Hamelin to this classy hotel-restaurant serving well-executed modern-European dishes. The setting is wonderful, with an expansive terrace and magnificent views. If you find yourself in the mood, you can also stay the night.

BODENWERDER-POLLE

If Bodenwerder's most famous son were to have described his little home town, he'd probably have painted it as a huge, thriving metropolis on the Weser River. But then Baron Hieronymous von Münchhausen (1720–97) was one of history's most shameless liars. He gave his name to a psychological condition – Münchhausen's syndrome, or compulsive exaggeration of physical illness – and inspired the cult film of British director Terry Gilliam, *The Adventures of Baron Munchausen*. Drive in or get bus 520 from Hameln (€4, 40 minutes); no trains run to Bodenwerder.

South of Bodenwerder, the village of Polle occupies a lovely spot on the Weser River. The 520 bus continues here from Bodenwerder (€2, 25 minutes).

Münchhausen Museum (☑ 05533-409 147; Münchhausenplatz 1; adult/child €2.50/1.50; ☉ 10am-5pm Apr-Oct) Bodenwerder's principal attraction struggles a little with the difficult task of conveying the chaos and fun associated with the 'liar baron' – a man who liked to regale dinner guests with his Crimean adventures, claiming he had, for example, tied his horse to a church steeple during a snow drift and ridden around a dining table without breaking one teacup. Among other artefacts, it also has paintings and displays of Munchhausen books in many languages.

Burgruine Polle (☑ 05535-411; www.weserbergland-tourismus.de/poi/detail/burg-polle; Amtsstrasse 4a, Polle; adult/concession €2/1; ☉ 10am-7pm May-Oct) About 15km south of Bodenwerder, in the tiny village of Polle, you'll find this wonderfully accessible hilltop castle ruin (dating to around 1285) affording beautiful views over the Weser River valley below. You can climb to the top of the tower or just admire the views from the quirky sculpture garden within the garden walls. This is an offbeat, special spot.

Tourist Office (☑ 05533-405 41; www.muenchhausenland.de; Münchhausenplatz 3; ☉ 9am-noon & 2-5pm Mon-Fri, 10am-12.30pm Sat) The tourist office has information on canoe and bicycle hire in town, arranges accommodation, and can answer other queries.

ⓘ Information

Tourist Office (☑ 05151-957 823; www.hameln.com; Diesterallee 1; ☉ 9am-6pm Mon-Fri, 9.30am-3pm Sat, to 1pm Sun; ⌨ Bürgergarten) Look for the rat symbols throughout the streets, along with information posts offering a glimpse into Hameln's history and its restored 16th- to 18th-century architecture.

ⓘ Getting There & Around

BICYCLE

Jugendwerkstatt Hameln (☑ 05151-609 770; Ruthenstrasse 10; bikes per day €5; ☉ 7am-5pm Mon-Fri, 9am-1pm Sat)

BUS

Buses 1 to 7 are just some of the bus lines that will take you into town from Hauptbahnhof.

CAR

Take the B217 to/from Hanover.

TRAIN

Frequent S-Bahn trains (S5) head to Hameln from Hanover's Hauptbahnhof (€12, 45 minutes). Regular direct trains connect Hanover's airport with Hameln (€15.10, one hour).

THURINGIA

Taking in the historical heavyweights of Weimar and Erfurt, smaller, scenic towns such as Mühlhausen and Eisenach, and the fascinating Kyffhäuser Mountains, Thuringia, Germany's sixth-smallest state, packs a punch with its wonderful blend of rich culture and bucolic nature, earning itself the moniker, 'the green heart of Germany'.

Weimar, where cultural trailblazers Goethe and Schiller did their thing, and nearby Erfurt, Thuringia's lively, historic and attractive capital, are must-sees on any comprehensive Germany itinerary. Nearby Jena is an important centre for optics and a fun, university town. Mühlhausen has a charming medieval atmosphere and access to the nearby Hainich National Park. The sprawling Thuringian Forest (Thüringer Wald in German) and the city of Eisenach are famed for the spectacular castle, Wartburg, where Luther sought protection after being excommunicated.

Throughout the region, dense forests, pristine rivers and scenic landscapes await. The area is well serviced by rail, but hiring a car

SLEEP LIKE A ROYAL

Ever wanted to sleep in a castle? Or play prince and princess in a palace? There are numerous castle hotels throughout Germany, but Central Germany has two of particular note. If you have the time, inclination and some breathing space in the budget, consider spending a night somewhere truly special – one might even say, straight from a fairy tale...

Hardenberg Burghotel (☑ 05503-9810; www.burghotel-hardenberg.de; Hinterhaus 11a, Nörten-Hardenberg; d incl breakfast from €192; P ✳ ☎) This gem of a hotel, under the luxury Relais & Chateaux banner, lies some 15km due north of Göttingen, in Count von Hardenberg's estate, at the foot of historic castle ruins. Spacious rooms are elegantly furnished, service is top-notch, and the delightful manicured grounds, golf course and sumptuous dining offerings await your pleasure.

Schlosshotel Münchhausen (☑ 05154-706 00; www.schlosshotel-muenchhausen.com; Schwöbber 9, Aerzen bei Hameln; s/d tithe barn from €110/140, castle from €135/180, ste €345-445; P ☮ ✳ ☎) Palatial Schlosshotel Münchhausen, 15km outside Hameln, is a popular spot for weddings and high-end functions. Stylish, contemporary rooms in the main wing have historic touches, while the suites have tasteful period furnishings. Rooms in the adjacent Tithe barn are entirely modern. Two restaurants, lavish spa facilities and two golf courses set in 8 hectares of parkland round off this luxurious option.

will afford you the freedom to explore the secret miles of mountain and country roads and the innumerable quaint villages they serve.

ℹ Getting There & Around

The **Thuringia Card** (1-day adult/concession €17/12, 3-day adult/concession €37/24), available at tourist offices across Thuringia, offers considerable savings, especially if you plan to explore the region for a few days. Benefits include free admission to over 200 attractions and free or discounted public transport. See www.thuringia-tourism.com for the low-down.

Erfurt has direct high-speed train connections to Hanover, Kassel and Frankfurt, while nearby Weimar is similarly connected to Berlin and Leipzig.

The A4 autobahn leads into the region here between Fulda and Kassel and comes within close proximity of Eisenach, Gotha, Erfurt, Weimar and Jena, making it particularly convenient for self-drivers. Wthout your own wheels you'll be dependent on buses to get to Hainich National Park or the Kyffhäuser Mountains.

Erfurt

☑ 0361 / POP 204,880

Thuringia's capital is a scene-stealing mix of sweeping squares, cobblestone alleyways, perky church towers, idyllic riverside backdrops and architecture spanning the ages. On the little Gera River, Erfurt was founded by the indefatigable missionary St Boniface as a bishopric in 742, and was catapulted to prominence and prosperity in the Middle Ages when it began producing a precious blue pigment from a woad plant. In 1392 rich merchants founded the university, allowing students to study common law, rather than religious law. Its most famous graduate was Martin Luther, who studied philosophy here before becoming a monk at the local Augustinian monastery in 1505.

Today Erfurt is proof that with forethought and planning, technology and history can coexist gracefully: Erfurt's appearance honours its medieval roots, while adding often classy, sometimes quirky, contemporary flourishes.

◉ Sights

Erfurt has a number of lovely squares to stroll between. Be sure to visit Domplatz, the largest; Anger, a transport and shopping hub where old meets new; Wenigemarkt, the perfect place for a casual meal; and Fischmarkt, Erfurt's central square, where you'll find the neo-Gothic Rathaus and a collection of spectacular historical buildings, including the Renaissance Haus zum Breiten Herd and the Gildehaus with its facade depicting the four virtues.

Erfurter Dom   CATHEDRAL
(Mariendom; ☑ 0361-646 1265; www.dom-erfurt.de; Domplatz; ⊙ 9.30am-6pm Mon-Sat, 1-6pm Sun May-Oct, to 5pm Nov-Apr) Erfurt's cathedral, where Martin Luther was ordained a priest, has origins as a simple 8th-century chapel that grew into the stately Gothic pile

you see today. Standouts in its treasure-filled interior include the stained-glass windows; the *Wolfram,* an 850-year-old bronze candelabrum in the shape of a man; the Gloriosa bell (1497); a Romanesque stucco Madonna; and the intricately carved choir stalls.

The steps buttressing the cathedral make for a dramatic backdrop for the popular **Domstufen-Festspiele**, a classical-music festival held in July or August.

Krämerbrücke
BRIDGE

(Merchants' Bridge) Flanked by cute half-timbered houses on both sides, this charming 1325 stone bridge is the only one north of the Alps that's still inhabited. People live above little shops with attractive displays of chocolate and pottery, jewellery and basic souvenirs. See the bridge from above by climbing the tower of the **Ägidienkirche** (usually open 11am to 5pm) punctuating its eastern end.

Severikirche
CHURCH

(Domplatz; ⊙9am-6pm Mon-Sat, 1-6pm Sun) The Severikirche, together with Erfurt's Dom forming the ensemble on Domplatz, is a five-aisled hall church (1280) with prized treasures that include a stone Madonna (1345), a 15m-high baptismal font (1467) and the sarcophagus of St Severus.

★ Zitadelle Petersberg
FORTRESS

(⊉0361-664 00; tour adult/concession €8/4; ⊙7pm Fri & Sat May-Oct) Situated on the Petersberg hill northwest of Domplatz, this citadel ranks among Europe's largest and best-preserved baroque fortresses. It sits above a honeycomb of tunnels, which can be explored on two-hour guided tours run by the tourist office. Otherwise, it's free to roam the external grounds and to enjoy fabulous views over Erfurt.

Augustinerkloster
CHURCH

(⊉0361-576 600; www.augustinerkloster.de; Augustinerstrasse 10; tour adult/concession €6/4; ⊙tours 9.30am-5pm Mon-Sat, 11am & noon Sun Apr-Oct, 9.30am-3.30pm Mon-Fri, to 2pm Sat & 11am Sun Nov-Mar) It's Luther lore galore at the very monastery where the reformer lived from 1505 to 1511, and where he was ordained as a monk and read his first Mass. You're free to roam the grounds, visit the church with its ethereal Gothic stained-glass windows and attend the prayer services. Guided tours of the monastery itself take in the cloister, a re-created Luther cell and an exhibit on Luther's life in Erfurt. You can sleep here, too. Enter from Comthurgasse.

Alte Synagoge
SYNAGOGUE

(⊉0361-655 1520; www.juedisches-leben.cr-furt.de; Waagegasse 8; adult/concession €8/5; ⊙10am-6pm Tue-Sun) This is one of Europe's oldest Jewish houses of worship, with roots in the 12th century. Exhibits document the history of the building and showcase a cache of treasures unearthed during excavations nearby, including rings, brooches, cutlery and, most famously, a very rare golden Jewish marriage ring from the early 14th-century.

Angermuseum
MUSEUM

(⊉0361-655 1651; www.angermuseum.de; Anger 18; adult/concession €6/4; ⊙1-7pm Tue-Fri, 11am-7pm Sat & Sun) Housed inside a fully restored baroque building dating from the early 18th century, the Angermuseum has a strong collection of medieval art, paintings ranging from the 17th century to contemporary times, and Thuringian faience (glazed earthenware). A highlight is the *Heckelraum* on the ground floor, which has expressionist frescos by the artist Erich Heckel.

Stadtmuseum
MUSEUM

(⊉0361-655 5659; www.stadtmuseum-erfurt. de; Johannesstrasse 169; adult/concession €5/3; ⊙10am-5pm Tue-Sun) Inside the magnificent portal of the **Haus am Stockfisch**, the Stadtmuseum has exhibits ranging from a medieval bone-carver's workshop to displays on Erfurt in GDR times.

Museum für Thüringer Volkskunde
MUSEUM

(⊉0361-655 5612; www.volkskundemuseum-erfurt. de; Juri-Gagarin-Ring 140a; adult/concession €6/4; ⊙10am-6pm Tue-Sun) This folklore museum is one of the largest of its kind in Germany, with an interesting collection that focuses on the applied arts, with household objects, furnishings and tools of all sorts. Its centrepiece is an exhibit on 19th-century village life.

Egapark Erfurt
GARDENS

(Erfurter Gartenausstellung; ⊉0361-564 37 37; www.egapark-erfurt.de; Gothaer Strasse 38; adult/concession €8/6.50; ⊙9am-6pm) It's easy to spend hours amid the kaleidoscopic flower beds, romantic rose garden, Japanese rock garden and greenhouses of the rambling Egapark, about 4km west of the city centre (take tram 2 from Anger). It's so huge that there's even a little trolley to whisk around the foot-weary. Part of the park is the medieval **Cyriaksburg** citadel, now home to a horticultural museum; climb to the top for fantastic views.

Erfurt

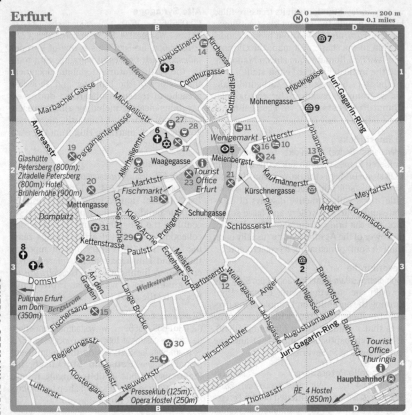

Michaeliskirche
CHURCH

(cnr Michaelisstrasse & Allerheiligenstrasse; ⊙11am-4pm Mon-Sat) The old university church boasts a magnificent organ (1652), made by local master Ludwig Compenius, and was a key gathering place of leading local dissidents during the final days of the GDR.

🛏 Sleeping

The Erfurt tourist office has access to a large array of private rooms and apartments starting at €20 per person. Visitors pay a 5% tax on accommodation to fund cultural upkeep.

Opera Hostel
HOSTEL $

(☎0361-6013 1360; www.opera-hostel.de; Walkmühlstrasse 13; dm €15-22, s/d/tr €49/60/81, linen €2.50; @🛜) This upmarket hostel in a historic building scores big with wallet-watching global nomads. Rooms are bright and spacious, many with an extra sofa. Make friends in the communal kitchen and on-site lounge-bar.

From the train station, take bus 51 (direction: Hochheim) to 'Alte Oper'.

Re_4 Hostel
HOSTEL $

(☎0361-600 0110; www.re4hostel.de; Puschkinstrasse 21; dm/s/d/apt from €14/28/56/120, linen €2; P @) If you've ever spent a night in a police lock-up, staying in this former police station might give you flashbacks. It's run by an energetic, clued-in crew, happy to help you make the most out of your stay in Erfurt. Self contained apartments are available. It's a 1.5km walk southwest of the station.

Rad-Hof
PENSION $

(☎0361-602 7761; www.rad-hof.de; Kirchgasse 1b; s/d incl breakfast from €33/66; @🛜) The owners of this cyclist-friendly guesthouse, next to the Augustinian monastery and near the pub quarter, have gone the extra mile in renovating the building with natural materials, such as wood and mud. No two rooms are alike. Take tram 1 or 5 to Augustinerstrasse.

Erfurt

★ **Hotel Brühlerhöhe** BOUTIQUE HOTEL $$
(☑0361-241 4990; www.hotel-bruehlerhoe he-erfurt.de; Rudolfstrasse 48; s/d from €80/95; P☏) This Prussian officers' casino turned chic city hotel gets high marks for its opulent breakfast spread (€12.50) and smiling, quick-on-their-feet staff. Rooms are cosy and modern with chocolate-brown furniture, thick carpets and sparkling baths. It's a short tram ride into the town centre.

Evangelisches Augustinerkloster zu Erfurt GUESTHOUSE $$
(☑0361-664 0110; www.augustinerkloster.de; Augustinerstrasse 10; s/tw €52/84; P) This venerable monastery offers an unusual retreat from the rat race of everyday life – a bible, but no television, telephones or internet, in rooms barely larger than a monk's cell. It's undeniably a special and tranquil place, where you can allow your social networking accounts to digitally rust.

Take tram 1 or 5 to Augustinerstrasse.

Mercure Erfurt Altstadt HOTEL $$
(☑0361-594 90; www.accorhotels.com; Meienbergstrasse 26-27; s/d from €89/109; P✱☏) The best thing about this above-average tourist hotel is its prime location a few blocks from lovely Wenigemarkt and the Anger transit hub. Rooms tend to be a little pricey for their styling, but are bright and comfortable. Wi-fi is free. Online bargains can be found.

Hotel Krämerbrücke BOUTIQUE HOTEL $$
(☑0361-674 00; www.ibbhotelerfurt.com; Gotthardtstrasse 27; d from €94; P✱@☏) This bright hotel, in a brilliant spot near a willow-fringed arm of the Gera River, gets a thumbs-up from design-minded travellers. Rooms of varying sizes are spread over two buildings, one an annexe on the historic Krämerbrücke. Limited parking is available.

Ibis Erfurt Altstadt HOTEL $$
(☑0361-664 10; www.ibis.com/Erfurt; Barfüsserstrasse 9; s/d from €65/80; P@☏) You'll be pleasantly surprised by the larger-than-usual rooms and decent bathrooms at this non-standard Ibis in a quiet, central setting opposite the Barfüsserkirche. Take tram 1, 2, 3, 4, 5 or 6 to Anger.

Hotel am Kaisersaal HOTEL $$
(☑0361-658 560; www.hotel-am-kaisersaal.de; Futterstrasse 8; s/d from €89/104; P☏) Ultra modern and uber stylish after a recent makeover, rooms in this highly rated hotel might easily entice you to stay in bed. Request a room facing the yard if street noise disturbs you easily. Take tram 1 or 5 to Futterstrasse.

Pullman Erfurt am Dom LUXURY HOTEL $$$
(☑0361-644 50; www.pullmanhotels.com/Erfurt; Theaterplatz 2; s/d from €102/129; P✱☏) Situated about 300m west of Domplatz (off Lauentor), Erfurt's only all-out luxury address has 160 rooms that exude effortless sophistication thanks to classy decor and a

soothing natural-hued colour scheme. Sightseeing fatigue quickly fades in the impeccable Zen-inspired wellness area. Take tram 4 from Hauptbahnhof to Theater.

🍴 Eating

Altstadt Cafe
CAFE $

(☑0361-562 6473; www.erfurt-altstadtcafe.de; Fischersand 1; mains €5-9; ⊙11.30am-11pm Mon-Fri, noon-10pm Sat, 2-7pm Sun) Chatty mothers, foot-weary sightseers and people catching up on their reading gather at this historic cafe in a 14th-century building. The terrace overlooking the Gera is enchanting in fine weather.

Faustfood
BARBECUE $

(☑0361-786 9969; www.faustfood.de; Waagegasse 1; items from €3.50; ⊙11am-11pm Tue-Sat, to 7pm Sun) It's a clever name and a clever concept: traditional Thuringian grills (*Rostbrätel* and bratwurst) alongside more international meaty treats such as spare ribs, steak and cheeseburgers. Dine in or takeaway, but you might want to head elsewhere if you're vegetarian.

KEKOA
BUFFET $

(www.kekoa-food.de; Marktstrasse 38b; salads from €3.50; ⊙11.30am-8pm Mon-Sat; ☑) 🌿 The focus of this fresh, funky soup, salad and sandwich bar, which uses local ingredients and special sauces, is good health (well, with the exception of the amazing fries) and sustainability. Cheap and cheery.

Drogerie Bistro
BISTRO $

(☑0361-642 2850; Wenigemarkt 8; items €6-12; ⊙noon-11pm Tue-Sat) If atmosphere and ambience are high on your list of priorities, you'll love this cosy little bistro in the Wenigemarkt. Homestyle cooking with a French bent includes the likes of seasonal soups, salads, quiches and pasta, but you're also more than welcome to pop in for a glass of wine or coffee and cake. Cash only.

⭐ Zum Wenigemarkt 13
GERMAN $$

(☑0361-642 2379; www.wenigemarkt-13.de; Wenigemarkt 13; mains €10-18; ⊙11.30am-11pm) This upbeat restaurant in a delightful spot serves traditional and updated takes on Thuringian cuisine, starring regionally hunted and gathered ingredients where possible. Tender salt-encrusted pork roast and trout drizzled with tangy caper-and-white-wine sauce are both menu stars.

Fellini
ITALIAN $$

(☑0361-642 1375; www.fellini-erfurt.de; Fischmarkt 3; mains €12-22; ⊙10am-11pm) You can't beat the Fischmarkt location of this smart Italian affair where local suits and casual tourists dine side by side. Expect well-prepared traditional Italian staples, good old-fashioned service and tourist prices.

Glashütte Petersberg
EUROPEAN $$

(☑0361-601 5094; www.glashuette-petersberg. de; Petersberg 11; mains €9-19; ⊙10am-11pm) The main reason you'll want to come to this glass cube perched high atop Erfurt's only significant hill is for the fabulous views of the cathedral and city below. The menu offers a varied selection of modern German and European fare.

Gingko
JAPANESE $$

(☑0361-601 5415; www.ginkgo-menu.de; Pergamentergasse 6; mains €12-26; ⊙5-11pm Tue, 11am-2pm & 5-10pm Wed-Sat, 2-11pm Sun) Behind an unassuming storefront tucked away in a side street off Domplatz, you'll find this purveyor of authentic Japanese sushi, run by the engaging Mr and Mrs Saburi. Their story is a fascinating one: be sure to enquire if you have the chance. You won't find real-deal sushi and sashimi like this for miles. Priced accordingly.

Zum Goldenen Schwan
GERMAN $$

(☑0361-262 3742; www.zum-goldenen-schwan. de; Michaelisstrasse 9; mains €9-20; ⊙11am-1am) This authentic inn serves all the usual Thuringian classics, but if you're up to mounting your own *Survivor* challenge, try something called *Puffbohnenpfanne* (fried broad beans with roast bacon), an Erfurt speciality. Excellent house brews wash everything down well.

Schnitzler
GERMAN $$

(☑0361-644 7557; www.schnitzler-restaurant.de; Domplatz 32; mains €7.50-19; ⊙11am-11pm) While these aren't necessarily the best schnitzels to be found in Germany, it simply shouldn't be possible for any self-proclaimed schnitzel lover to pass by a restaurant that pays homage to the crumbed cutlet: there's an enormous variety to choose from, the prices are reasonable, and service comes with a smile.

La Gondola
ITALIAN $$

(☑0361-660 3920; Kürschnergasse 1/2; mains €7-16; ⊙11am-11pm) What's so great about this uber-casual Italian joint where nary a word of English is spoken and the meals are tasty and reasonably priced, but nothing to write home about? Well, you couldn't find a lovelier spot to sip a beer or dine with a friend overlooking a little tributary of the Gera, as if in Venice. Keep it a secret.

Si Ju INTERNATIONAL **$$**
(☑ 0361-655 2295; www.si-ju-erfurt.de; Fischmarkt 1; mains €7.50-15; ☺ 11am-midnight Mon-Sat; ☎) This restaurant-lounge combo is a fashionable stop any time for diners and drinkers of all ages. The daily breakfast buffet (from 11.30am) is usually a winner.

Drinking & Nightlife

Erfurt's former university quarter to the north and east of Fischmarkt is a hub of nightspots, pubs and bars. Much of the action can be found along Michaelisstrasse and Futterstrasse.

Engelsburg CLUB
(☑ 0361-244 770; www.eburg.de; Allerheiligenstrasse 20-21; ☺ noon-2am) Good times are pretty much guaranteed at this venerable venue, no matter whether you hunker down for beer and chat in the Steinhaus pub (also an eating option), report to the dance floor of the medieval cellar labyrinth, or go highbrow at the upstairs Café DuckDich cultural forum.

Hemingway BAR
(☑ 0361-551 9944; www.hemingway-erfurt.de; Michaelisstrasse 26; ☺ 6pm-midnight) Everything the macho scribe loved is here in abundance, from cigar humidors with personal drawers to 148 types of rum and 30 different daiquiris. The Africa Lounge has a local Bambi, though, not an elephant bagged beneath Kilimanjaro.

Modern Masters COCKTAIL BAR
(☑ 0361-550 7255; www.modern-masters.de; Michaelisstrasse 48; ☺ 6pm-2am Tue-Sat) Urbane and sophisticated, this cocktail bar offers an impressive range of more than 220 cocktail concoctions.

Weinstein LeBar WINE BAR
(Kleine Arche 1; ☺ 7pm-late Sun-Fri, 8pm-late Sat) This unassuming wine bar has soft music, candlelight, and as many as 50 wines by the glass, including some hard-to-get bottles from the nearby Saale-Unstrut Valley. A basic snack menu is available.

Presseklub CLUB
(☑ 0361-789 4565; www.presseklub.net; Dalbergsweg 1; ☺ 8pm-late Tue-Sun) A former gathering spot for media types, this club is now a delightful dance party location with a chic interior. Every second Friday is gay night, under the 'Test It Party' banner.

Dubliner PUB
(☑ 0361-789 2595; www.dublinererfurt.de; Neuwerkstrasse 47a; ☺ 4pm-1am) On weekends it seems as though everybody's popping by to knock back pints of Kilkenny or Guinness at this boisterous Irish thirst parlour. Smokers can sit downstairs.

☆ Entertainment

Consult the free zines *Dates, Takt* (www.takt-magazin.de) and *Blitz* (www.blitz-world.de) for event listings. Throughout summer, from the end of May, Friday classical concerts take place beneath the linden trees in the romantic courtyard of Michaeliskirche. Organ concerts are held year-round in the Predigerkirche and Michaeliskirche (Wednesday at noon), and in the Dom (Saturday).

DasDie Brettl PERFORMING ARTS
(☑ 0361-551 166; www.dasdielive.de; Lange Brücke 29) Cabaret, musicals and concerts take centre stage in this cultural centre.

Theater Waidspeicher THEATRE
(☑ 0361-598 2924; www.waidspeicher.de; Domplatz 18) Not only children will be enchanted by the adorable marionettes and puppets that perform at this cute theatre in a historic wood storehouse (reached via Mettengasse).

ℹ Information

Post Office (Anger 66; ☺ 9am-7pm Mon-Fri, to 1pm Sat)

Tourist Office Erfurt (☑ 0361-664 00; www.erfurt-tourismus.de; Benediktsplatz 1; ☺ 10am-6pm Mon-Fri, to 2pm Sat & Sun) Sells the ErfurtCard (€14.90 per 48 hours), which includes a city tour, public transport, and free or discounted admissions.

Tourist Office Thuringia (☑ 0361-374 20; www.thuringia-tourism.com; Willy-Brandt-Platz 1; ☺ 9am-7pm Mon-Fri, 10am-4pm Sat & Sun) Opposite the Hauptbahnhof.

ℹ Getting There & Away

AIR

Flughafen Erfurt (☑ 0361-656 2200; www.flughafen-erfurt.de; Binderlebener Landstrasse 100) The tiny Erfurt airport is about 6km west of the city centre and is served by Air Berlin and a few charter airlines.

CAR

Erfurt is just north of the A4 and is crossed by the B4 (Hamburg to Bamberg) and the B7 (Kassel to Gera). The A71 autobahn runs south to Schweinfurt via Ilmenau, Oberhof and Meiningen.

TRAIN

Direct IC/ICE trains connect Erfurt with Berlin (€61, 2½ hours), Dresden (€53, 2½ hours) and

Frankfurt am Main (€55, 2¼ hours). Direct trains also go to Meiningen (€19.80, 1½ hours) and Mühlhausen (€12.20, 45 minutes). Regional trains to Weimar (€5, 15 minutes) and Eisenach (€12.10, 45 minutes) run at least hourly.

ℹ Getting Around

BICYCLE

Fahrradstation (☏ 0361-644 1506; www.fahr radstation-erfurt.de; Bahnhofstrasse 22; bikes per 24hr €15; ⊙10am-7pm Mon-Fri, to 2pm Sat)

Radhaus Am Dom (☏ 0361-602 0640; www. radhaus-erfurt.de; Andreasstrasse 28; bikes per 24hr from €12; ⊙10am-6pm Mon-Fri, to 2pm Sat)

BUS & TRAM

Tram 4 directly links the airport with Anger in the city centre (€1.90, 25 minutes). Trams 3, 4 and 6 run from Hauptbahnhof via Anger and Fischmarkt to Domplatz. Tickets for trams and buses in the central (yellow) zone cost €1.90, or €4.90 for a day pass.

TAXI

Call ☏ 511 11 or ☏ 555 55 or check out www. bettertaxi.de.

Weimar

☏ 03643 / POP 63,320

Historical epicentre of the German Enlightenment, Weimar is an essential stop for anyone with a passion for German history and culture. A pantheon of intellectual and creative giants lived and worked here: Goethe, Schiller, Bach, Cranach, Liszt, Nietzsche, Gropius, Herder, Feininger, Kandinsky...the list goes on. You'll see them memorialised on the streets and in museums across town. In summer, Weimar's many parks and gardens lend themselves to quiet contemplation of the town's intellectual and cultural onslaught.

Weimar is also the place where, post WWI, the constitution of the German Reich, known as the Weimar Republic (1919–1933), was drafted, though there are few reminders of this historical moment. Nearby, the ghostly ruins of the Buchenwald concentration camp provide reminders of the terrors of the Nazi regime.

It's a 20-minute walk south of Weimar station to the start of the historic centre at Goetheplatz.

◉ Sights & Activities

★**Goethe-Nationalmuseum**   MUSEUM
(☏03643-545 400; www.klassik-stiftung.de; Frauenplan 1; adult/concession €12/8.50; ⊙9.30am-

6pm Tue-Sun Apr-Oct, to 4pm Nov-Mar) This museum has the most comprehensive and insightful exhibit about Johann Wolfgang von Goethe, Germany's literary icon. It incorporates his home of 50 years, left pretty much as it was upon his death in 1832. This is where Goethe worked, studied, researched, and penned *Faust* and other immortal works. In a modern annexe, documents and objects shed light on the man and his achievements, not only in literature, but also in art, science and politics.

If you're a Goethe fan, you'll get the chills when seeing his study, and the bedroom where he died, both preserved in their original state. To gain the most from your visit, use the free audioguide.

Schillers Wohnhaus   MUSEUM
(☏03643-545 400; www.klassik-stiftung.de; Schillerstrasse 12; adult/concession €7.50/6; ⊙9.30am-6pm Tue-Sun Apr-Oct, to 4pm Nov-Mar) The dramatist Friedrich von Schiller (a close friend of Goethe) lived in Weimar from 1799 until his early death in 1805. Study up on the man, his family and his life in Thuringia in a recently revamped exhibit before plunging on to his private quarters, including the study with his deathbed and the desk where he wrote *Wilhelm Tell* and other famous works.

Fürstengruft   TOMB
(☏03643-545 400; www.klassik-stiftung.de; Am Poseckschen Garten; adult/concession €4/3; ⊙10am-6pm) Goethe and, to a lesser extent, Schiller (more about that soon) are interred at the **Historischer Friedhof** (Historical Cemetery) in this neoclassical mausoleum, along with Duke Carl August. The mausoleum dates from 1828 and houses almost 50 sarcophagi. Schiller's, however, is empty today, after tests showed that his remains originated from several different people!

Park an der Ilm   PARK
This sprawling park provides a bucolic backdrop to the town, and is also home to a trio of historic houses, including the **Goethes Gartenhaus** (adult/concession €4.50/3.50; ⊙10am-6pm Wed-Mon), where Goethe lived from 1776 to 1782; the **Römisches Haus** (adult/concession €3.50/3; ⊙10am-6pm Wed-Mon), the local duke's summer retreat, with period rooms and an exhibit on the park; and the **Liszt-Haus** (Liszt House; Marienstrasse 17; adult/concession €4/3; ⊙10am-6pm Tue-Sun Apr-Sep, to 4pm Sat & Sun Oct-Mar), where the composer resided from 1869 to 1886.

★ **Herzogin Anna Amalia Bibliothek**   LIBRARY

(📞03643-545 400; www.anna-amalia-bibliothek. de; Platz der Demokratie 1; adult/concession incl audioguide €7.50/6; ⊘9.30am-2.30pm Tue-Sun) Assembled by literature-loving local duchess Anna Amalia (1739–1807), this Unesco World Heritage library has been beautifully reconstructed after a monumental fire in 2004 destroyed much of the building and its priceless contents. Some of the most precious tomes are housed in the magnificent Rokokosaal (Rococo Hall), and were once used by Goethe, Schiller and other Weimar hot shots, who are depicted in busts and paintings.

Entry by timed ticket is capped at fewer than 300 people per day; book in advance or start queuing before the ticket office opens.

Schloss Belvedere   PALACE

(📞03643-545 400; www.klassik-stiftung.de; Belvedere Park; adult/concession €6/4.50; ⊘10am-6pm Apr-Dec) Set in the lovely Belvedere Park, this palace has displays of glass, porcelain, faience and weapons from the late 17th and 18th centuries. The easiest way to reach it is by bus 1 from Goetheplatz.

Schloss Tiefurt   PALACE

(📞03643-545 400; www.klassik-stiftung.de; Hauptstrasse 14; adult/concession €6/4.50; ⊘10am-6pm Tue-Sun Apr-Sep) Originally this (relatively) small house from 1800 was leased to the tenant who ran the estate of the duchess Anna Amalia, but Anna took it over and turned it into her 'temple of the muses'. The period rooms give you an impression of the age and of Anna's intellectual gatherings where Goethe, Schiller and Herder were regulars.

Take Bus 3 from Goetheplatz.

Weimar Haus   MUSEUM

(📞03643-901 890; www.weimarhaus.de; Schillerstrasse 16; adult/concession €7/5.50; ⊘9.30am-6.30pm) The Weimar Haus is a history museum for people who hate history museums. Sets, sound and light effects, wax figures and even an animatronic Goethe accompany you on your 30-minute journey into Thuringia's past, from prehistory to the Enlightenment. The production values can be comical, but the entertainment factor is inarguably high.

Haus Hohe Pappeln   HISTORIC BUILDING

(📞03643-545 400; www.klassik-stiftung.de; Belvederer Allee 58; adult/concession €3/2; ⊘11am-4pm Tue-Sun Apr-Oct) Belgian art-nouveau architect, designer and painter, Henry van de Velde is considered a pioneer of modernity. In 1902

WHY THE WEIMAR REPUBLIC?

Despite its name, the Weimar Republic (1919–33), Germany's first dalliance with democracy, was never actually governed from Weimar. The town on the Ilm River was merely the place where, in 1919, the National Assembly drafted and passed the country's first constitution.

Assembly delegates felt that the volatile and explosive political climate rocking post-WWI Berlin would threaten the democratic process if it took place there, and looked for an alternative location. Weimar had several factors in its favour: a central location, a suitable venue (the Deutsches Nationaltheater) and a humanist tradition entirely antithetical to the militaristic Prussian spirit that had led to war.

Weimar's spot in the democratic limelight, however, lasted only briefly. With the situation in Berlin calming down, the delegates returned to the capital just one week after passing the constitution on 31 July.

---

he founded the arts and crafts seminar in Weimar that Walter Gropius later developed into the Bauhaus. For nine years, starting in 1908, van de Velde and his family lived in this house, which looks a bit like a ship on its side and features natural stone, stylised chimneys, loggias and oversized windows.

Take bus 1 or 12 to Papiergraben.

Nietzsche Archiv   HISTORIC BUILDING

(📞03643-545 400; www.klassik-stiftung.de; Humboldtstrasse 36; adult/concession €3/2; ⊘11am-4pm Tue-Sun Apr-Oct) Belgian architect, designer and painter Henry van de Velde added some art-nouveau touches to this house, where the philosopher Friedrich Nietzsche spent his final years in illness.

Bauhaus Museum   MUSEUM

(📞03643-545 400; www.klassik-stiftung.de; Theaterplatz 1; adult/concession €4/3; ⊘10am-6pm Apr-Oct, to 4pm Nov-Mar) Considering that Weimar is the 1919 birthplace of the influential Bauhaus movement, this museum is a rather modest affair. A new, representative museum is expected to open in 2018.

Haus am Horn   HISTORIC BUILDING

(📞03643-583 000; www.hausamhorn.de; Am Horn 61; ⊘11am-5pm Wed, Sat & Sun Apr-Oct)

CENTRAL GERMANY WEIMAR

Weimar

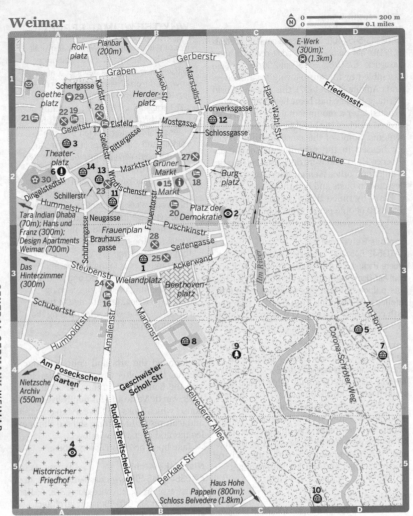

Weimar's only truly Bauhaus building. Today, it's used for exhibitions and events.

Stadtschloss Weimar
MUSEUM

(Schlossmuseum; ☎03643-545 400; www.klassik-stiftung.de; Burgplatz 4; adult/concession €7.50/6; ☉10am-6pm Tue-Sun) Situated in the former residential palace, which was rebuilt in 1789–1803 after a fire, the Schlossmuseum houses works of art dating from the Middle Ages to the turn of the 20th century. Not to be missed is the gallery containing the works of Lukas Cranach the Elder and

of other European masters such as Rodin, Tischbein and Caspar David Friedrich.

Wittumspalais
MUSEUM

(☎03643-545 400; www.klassik-stiftung.de; Theaterplatz; adult/concession €6/4.50; ☉10am-6pm) This is the palace in which the duchess Anna Amalia lived from 1774, after the residiential palace (today the Schlossmuseum) burned. Rooms contain period furniture and paintings, culminating in the Green Salon, the living room of the duchess.

Weimar

Belvedere Express   BUS TOUR
(☑ 905 882; www.belvedere-express.de; Markt 2; adult/concession €18/16) Aimed at the German market, Weimar's classy city tour might be a little pricey, but it does provide a good low-down on all the sights with a video commentary, as long as you ask for the English headphones.

⎍ Sleeping

Visitors to Weimar pay a supplement of €1 to €2 per person per night for the upkeep of cultural sites.

Labyrinth Hostel   HOSTEL $
(☑ 03643-811 822; www.weimar-hostel.com; Goetheplatz 6; dm/s/d from €16/32/44, linen €2.50; @ 🛜) Loads of imagination has gone into this professionally run hostel with artist-designed rooms. In one double, for example, the bed perches on stacks of books, while another comes with a wooden platform bed. Bathrooms are shared, as is the kitchen and lovely rooftop terrace. Breakfast costs €3.

Die Kleine Residenz   PENSION $
(☑ 03643-743 270; www.residenz-pension.de; Grüner Markt 4; d from €70; @) With an enviable location in the heart of Weimar's Altstadt, this little inn offers comfortable, light-filled rooms with high-speed internet and en-suite bathrooms in a variety of configurations, and a lovely little terrace restaurant downstairs.

★ Design Apartments Weimar   APARTMENT $$
(☑ 03643-217 149; www.hier-war-goethe.nie. de; Fuldaer Strasse 85; apt per person from €59; 🛜) Get in quick to snap up one of these enormous, self-contained, fully renovated heritage apartments that could have been plucked from the pages of a Taschen design book. You'd be hard-pressed to find friendlier, kinder hosts anywhere. This is surely the perfect home-base for exploring the delights of Weimar and Thuringia. Exceptional value.

Hotel Elephant   LUXURY HOTEL $$
(☑ 03643-8020; www.luxurycollection.com/elephant; Markt 19; s/d from €115/130, ste €220-599; P ❄ @ 🛜) From the elegant art-deco lobby of this charmer, it's luxury all the way from here to the top. For over 300 years, this classic has wooed statesmen, artists, scholars and the merely rich with first-class service and amenities. Prices vary by demand and day; check the website.

Romantik Hotel Dorotheenhof   HOTEL $$
(☑ 03643-4590; www.dorotheenhof.com; Dorotheenhof 1; s/d from €69/105; P 🛜) Located 3km north of Weimar in the suburb of Schöndorf, this excellent conference and tourist hotel is set in its own large park and gardens; rooms are modern and tastefully decorated. It's best if you have your own transport (take Friedrich-Ebert-Strasse north), but bus 7 from Hauptbahnhof runs out here daily.

Casa dei Colori PENSION $$

(☎03643-489 640; www.casa-colori.de; Eisfeld 1a; d incl breakfast from €100; P 🐕) Possibly Weimar's most charming boutique pension, the Casa convincingly imports cheerfully exuberant Mediterranean flair to central Europe. The mostly good-sized rooms are dressed in bold colours and come with a small desk, a couple of comfy armchairs and a stylish bathroom.

Amalienhof HOTEL $$

(☎03643-5490; www.amalienhof-weimar.de; Amalienstrasse 2; s/d incl breakfast from €60/80; P 🐕) The charms of this hotel are manifold: classy antique furnishings, richly styled rooms that point to history without burying you in it, and a late breakfast buffet for those who take their holidays seriously. It's a splendid choice. Parking is included.

Hotel Anna Amalia HOTEL $$

(☎03643-495 60; www.hotel-anna-amalia.de; Geleitstrasse 8-12; s/d/apt from €60/87/125; P 🐕) With a Mediterranean air and a fresh colour scheme, this family-run hotel near Goetheplatz exudes good cheer. For more panache and elbow room, book one of the apartments.

✖ Eating

Tara Indian Dhaba VEGETARIAN $

(☎03643-900 0744; www.tara-weimar.de; Erfurter Strasse 4; mains €7-12; ☉11am-9pm; 🐕) Vegetarians rejoice! In the heart of meat-loving Germany, vegie nirvana can be pinpointed right here in Weimar. Spic and spartan, Tara offers a wonderful selection of wholly vegetarian and vegan cuisine, from fresh salads and creamy soups to rich curries and aromatic tandoori dishes, all spiced to your liking. Fill your belly for under a tenner.

Crêperie du Palais CREPERIE $

(☎03643-401 581; www.creperie-weimar.de; Am Palais 1; mains €4-11; ☉11am-11pm; 🐕) For a little taste of France, pop into this delightful, petite cafe, which serves not only crêpes but also fondue and a range of vegetarian options.

Gasthof Luise GERMAN $$

(☎03643-905 819; www.gasthof-luise-weimar.de; Wielandplatz 3; €7-14; ☉5pm-midnight) There's nothing fancy about this traditional Thuringian diner, which exudes a dark woodsy atmosphere. Despite sometimes surly staff, it's cosy, comfortable and frequented by local students and workers alike: great for people-watching. Hearty eats include to-die-for fries, bratwurst and local speciality *Thüringer Rostbrätel:* char-grilled marinated pork neck. Wednesday is beer night.

Gretchen's Cafe & Restaurant MODERN EUROPEAN $$

(☎03643-457 9877; http://gretchens-weimar.de; Seifengasse 8; mains €12-23; ☉9am-11pm) 🍴 This passionately locavore cafe serves all manner of decadent cakes, tortes and coffee by day, then transforms into an intimate house of just eight tables in the evening, serving mod-Med cuisine; reservations essential. Be sure to sip a beverage on the wonderful rooftop terrace.

Hans und Franz GERMAN $$

(☎03643-457 3987; www.hanzundfranz.com; Erfurter Strasse 23; mains €8-14; ☉6-11pm Mon-Sat, noon-2pm & 6-11pm Sun; 🐕) There's something of a mid-century vibe at this happy haunt

---

GOETHE – THE LITERARY LION

Johann Wolfgang von Goethe (1749–1832) is the grandaddy of German literature and philosophy. He lived to be 82, having written novels, essays, treatises, scientific articles, travelogues, plays and poetry. A consummate politician, Goethe was a classic 'Renaissance' man, capable in many disciplines: during his life he served as town planner, architect, social reformer and scientist.

Born in Frankfurt am Main and trained as a lawyer, Goethe overcame the disadvantages of a wealthy background and a happy childhood to become the driving force of the 1770's *Sturm und Drang* (Storm and Stress) literary movement. Though he worked and experimented in various styles throughout his life, his work with Friedrich Schiller fostered the theatrical style known as Weimar classicism. Goethe himself once described his work as 'fragments of a great confession'.

His defining play in two parts, *Faust,* is a lyrical but highly charged retelling of the classic legend of a man selling his soul for knowledge. It's still regularly performed throughout Germany today. The beloved **Goethe-Schiller Denkmal** (Goethe-Schiller Monument; Theaterplatz 2), directly in front of Weimar's Deutsches Nationaltheater (p554), still pulls a crowd.

FORMER BUCHENWALD CONCENTRATION CAMP

Gedenkstätte Buchenwald (☑430 200; www.buchenwald.de; Gedenkstätte Buchenwald; ⊙9am-6pm Apr-Oct, to 4pm Nov-Mar), the sombre former concentration camp 10km northwest of Weimar, has been preserved as a memorial site. Between 1937 and 1945, hidden from the awareness of Weimarers and surrounding villagers, some 56,500 of the 250,000 men, women and children who were incarcerated here were murdered. Visitors are encouraged to wander quietly and freely around the numerous intact structures. Tours are available.

Before you enter the main compound, you'll notice an enormous monument to your left, which you can walk right up to. The monument is perched atop a small mountain with remarkable views; publications from the museum store explain the symbolic significance of its many elements.

The camp's prisoners included Jews and homosexuals from 18 nations, German anti-fascists, prominent German thinkers and social democrats, and Soviet and Polish prisoners of war. Many were exploited in the production of weapons, subject to torture and medical experimentation or sent on death marches. On 11 April 1945, as US troops approached and the SS guards fled, the emaciated prisoners rebelled, overwhelming the remaining guards and liberating themselves.

After the war, Soviet victors re-utilised the site as Special Camp No 2 and worked 7000 so-called anti-communists and ex-Nazis to death. Their bodies were found in mass graves north of the camp and near the Hauptbahnhof.

To get here, take bus 6 (direction Buchenwald) from Goetheplatz in Weimar. By car, head north on Ettersburger Strasse from Weimar station and turn left onto Blutstrasse.

serving up local specialities such as *Thuringian Klösse* (dumplings) with red cabbage, and meaty German favourites, intelligently balanced with a few nice options for vegetarians and vegans. And, yes, the schnitzel is good.

JoHanns Hof
GERMAN $$
(☑03643-493 617; www.restaurant-weimar.com; Scherfgasse 1; lunch special €6.50, mains €12-25; ⊙11.30am-2.30pm & 5-11pm Mon-Sat) JoHanns is a breezy and elegant port of call for inspired modern German cuisine and perfectly prepared choice cuts of steak, paired with a carefully curated selection of wines from the nearby Saale-Unstrut region. For a break from sightseeing, tuck into the value-priced weekday lunch specials in the cosy courtyard.

Residenz-Café
INTERNATIONAL $$
(☑03643-594 08; www.residenz-cafe.de; Grüner Markt 4; breakfast €2.90-6.40, mains €5-13; ⊙8am-1am; ☑) Locally adored 'Resi' is a Viennese-style coffeehouse and a jack of all trades – everyone should find something to their taste here, no matter where the hands are on the clock. The 'Lovers' Breakfast' comes with sparkling wine, the cakes are delicious and the salads crisp, but perhaps the most creativity goes into the weekly specials.

Zum Weissen Schwan
GERMAN $$
(☑03643-908 751; Frauentorstrasse 23; mains €11-22; ⊙noon-10pm Tue-Sat) At this venerable inn, you can fill your tummy with Goethe's favourite dish, which actually hails from his home town of Frankfurt (boiled beef with herb sauce, red beet salad and potatoes). The rest of the menu, though, is midrange Thuringian.

★Anna Amalia
INTERNATIONAL $$$
(☑03643-8020; www.restaurant-anna-amalia.com; Markt 19; 3-/5-/7-course menu from €65/85/110; ⊙6.30-10pm Tue-Sat Mar-Dec) Inside the Hotel Elephant Weimar, this highly acclaimed gourmet act is one for those who appreciate a true fine-dining experience. Dress to impress, expect the chef to wow your palate, wait for the staff to make you feel more important than you know you are, and leave plenty of room on the credit card.

Anno 1900
INTERNATIONAL $$$
(☑03643-903 571; www.anno1900-weimar.de; Geleitstrasse 12a; mains €21-27; ⊙11am-midnight Mon-Fri, 9am-midnight Sat & Sun) Send your taste buds on a wild ride in this elegant art-nouveau pavilion. How about ostrich fillet with carrot-rocket fettucine followed by chocolate-orange crème brûlée? It's adventurous, but most of the time it works.

☕ Drinking & Entertainment

Planbar   BAR
(☎ 03643-502 785; www.planbar-we.de; Jakob-
splan 6; ⊙ 6pm-1am) This is a good-looking
bar with an unpretentious, all-ages crowd
that likes to knock back the mojitos, flirt
with the bartenders and wave to the DJs.

Das Hinterzimmer   BAR
(☎ 03643-457 3852; www.dashinterzimmer.de;
Trierer Strasse 33; ⊙ 9pm-2am) 'The Backroom', a
classy, chilled neighbourhood bar, warms up
later in the evening.

Kasseturm   CLUB
(☎ 03643-851 670; www.kasseturm.de; Goetheplatz 10; ⊙ 6pm-1am Tue-Sun) The well-loved
Kasseturm has been a student club in Weimar since 1962, hosting parties, concerts
and drum workshops, among other things.
Three floors of action for young and old.

Deutsches Nationaltheater   THEATRE
(German National Theatre; ☎ 03643-755 334;
www.nationaltheater-weimar.de; Theaterplatz 2;
tickets from €10; ⊙ Sep-Jun) Expect a grab bag
of classic and contemporary theatre, opera
and concerts at this esteemed space.

E-Werk   PERFORMING ARTS
(☎ 03643-748 868; www.ewerkweimar.info; Am
Kirschberg 4) The Deutsches Nationaltheater
troupe and others perform in this former
tram depot, which also has a cinema, live
music, cultural events and an excellent exhibit of works by contemporary avant-garde
artist Rebecca Horn.

ℹ Information

Post Office (Goetheplatz 7-8; ⊙ 9am-6.30pm
Mon-Fri, to noon Sat)

Roxanne Internet Café (☎ 03643-800 194;
Markt 21; per 30min €1.50; ⊙ 10.30am-late
Mon-Fri, 2pm-late Sat & Sun) Internet termi-
nals, wi-fi and good coffee.

Tourist Office (☎ 03643-7450; www.weimar.
de; Markt 10; ⊙ 9.30am-7pm Mon-Sat, to 3pm
Sun Apr-Oct, 9.30am-6pm Mon-Fri, to 2.30pm
Sat & Sun Nov-Mar) Pick up a great-value
WeimarCard (€27.50 for two days) for free
admission to most museums, free iGuides, free
travel on city buses and discounted tours.

ℹ Getting There & Away

CAR
Weimar is situated on the A4 autobahn, which
connects Eisenach and Erfurt in the west with
Dresden in the east.

TRAIN
Direct IC/ICE trains run to Frankfurt am Main
(€58, 2¾ hours), Leipzig (€24, 1¼ hours),
Dresden (€47, 2¾ hours) and Berlin (€58, 2¼
hours). Frequent regional trains go to Erfurt
(€5, 15 minutes), Eisenach (€15, one hour),
Gotha (€13, 35 minutes) and Jena (€5, 15
minutes).

ℹ Getting Around

BICYCLE
Grüne Liga (☎ 03643-492 796; www.
grueneliga-thueringen.de; Goetheplatz 9b; city
bikes per 24hr from €8; ⊙ 9am-3pm Mon-Fri,
to noon Sat) Enter from Rollplatz. Call ahead
for rentals from November to March.

BUS
A single ride/day pass costs €1.90/4.90. Bus
1 connects Goetheplatz in the centre with
Hauptbahnhof.

CAR
Note that driving in the Altstadt is severely
restricted; it's best to park outside the centre.
There's a free lot at Hermann-Brill-Platz, about a
10-minute walk northwest from the Altstadt.

TAXI
Call ☎ 03643-903 600 or try www.bettertaxi.de.

Schmalkalden
☎ 03683 / POP 20.700
Schmalkalden's old town groans and creaks
under the sheer weight of its half-timbered
houses and is crowned by a handsome hilltop castle, Schloss Wilhelmsburg. About
40km south of Eisenach, the little town
played a big role during the Reformation. It
was here in 1531 that the Protestant princes established the Schmalkaldic League
to counter the central powers of Catholic
emperor Charles V. Although they suffered
a daunting military defeat in 1546, they
managed to regroup and eventually got the
emperor to sign the Peace of Augsburg in
1555, which allowed each of the German
states to choose between Lutheranism and
Catholicism.

It's about a 10-minute walk from the
train and bus stations to the Altmarkt,
with its handsome **Rathaus** (1419), which
once functioned as the meeting place of the
Schmalkaldic League. The incongruous towers of the late-Gothic **Stadtkirche St Georg**
(1437–1509) overlook the square.

⊙ Sights & Activities

Schloss Wilhelmsburg · PALACE
(☑03683-403 186; www.museumwilhelmsburg.
de; Schlossberg 9; adult/concession €3.50/2;
☉10am-6pm Apr-Oct) Overlooking the town,
the late-Renaissance Schloss Wilhelmsburg
was conceived by Landgrave Wilhelm IV
of Hessen as a hunting lodge and summer
residence in the 1580s. Since then, it has
largely kept its original design, with lavish
murals and stucco decorating most rooms,
of which the **Riesensaal**, with its coffered
and painted ceiling, is the most impressive.
The playfully decorated **Schlosskirche** has
a rare wooden organ, thought to be the oldest working organ of its type in Europe.

Viba Nougat Welt · MUSEUM
(☑03683-692 1600; www.viba-sweets.de/
worlds-of-experience; Nougat-Allee 1; ☉10am-8pm)
FREE This company has been seducing sweet-
tooths with its range of soft nougats and chocolate treats for over a century. Here at their
flagship factory and visitor centre, you can observe the production process, gorge yourself
on high-sucrose delights or take a course to
earn your Viba nougat diploma.

Mart-Luther-Weg · HIKING
Schmalkalden is the western terminus of this
17km easy-to-moderate hiking trail that ends
at Tambach-Dietharz, from where there are
bus services back to town (weekdays only;
check with the tourist office for times).

Mommelstein-Radweg · CYCLING
A recommended cycling route is the 28km
Mommelstein Bike Trail, which follows a
former railway line and some forest trails
through a tunnel and viaduct (the tourist
office has maps and directions).

⊨ Sleeping & Eating

Teichhotel · HOTEL $$
(☑03683-402 661; www.teichhotel.de; Teichstrasse
21; s/d €55/86; 🅿) Expect plain but comfortable rooms in this hotel located just outside
the Altstadt. There's a restaurant on-site.

Stadthotel Patrizier · HOTEL $$
(☑03683-604 514; www.stadthotel-patrizier.de;
Weidebrunner Gasse 9; s/d incl breakfast €79/109)
A historic hotel in the heart of town with 14
spotless, well-appointed rooms.

Maykel's · GERMAN $$
(☑03683-608 970; www.maykels.eu; Lutherplatz
1; mains €10-22; ☉10am-11pm Mon-Sat) A relaxed pub-restaurant with good salads, pasta,
Flammkuchen (Alsatian pizzas) and meat-
based mains. There's a terrace out front if you
just feel like a beer or some delicious gelati.

ⓘ Information

Tourist Office (☑03683-403 182; www.
schmalkalden.com; Auer Gasse 6-8; ☉10am-
5pm Mon-Fri, to 1pm Sat) This helpful, modern
office has brochures and maps, and can assist
with event bookings.

ⓘ Getting There & Around

BICYCLE
Fahrrad Anschütz (☑03683-403 909; www.
fahrrad-anschuetz.de; Stiller Gasse 17; bikes
per day from €10; ☉9am-6pm Mon-Fri, to noon
Sat) Rents out city, touring and mountain bikes.

CAR
Schmalkalden is about 6km east of the B19,
which connects Eisenach and Meiningen.

TRAIN
Schmalkalden is served by the private Süd-
Thüringen-Bahn (www.sued-thueringen-bahn.
de). Going to Erfurt (€17.90, two hours) requires
a change in Zella-Mehlis; for Eisenach (€10, one
hour), change in Wernshausen.

Eisenach

☑03691 / POP 37,600
The modest appearance of hilly Eisenach, a
small town on the edge of the Thuringian
Forest, belies its association with two German heavyweights: Johann Sebastian Bach
and Martin Luther. Luther went to school
here and later returned to protective custody in the Wartburg, now one of Germany's
most famous castles and a Unesco World
Heritage site. A century later, Bach, the
grandest of all baroque musicians, was born
in a wattle-and-daub home and attended the
same school as Luther had. Eisenach also
has a century-old automotive tradition – the
world's first BMW rolled off the local assembly line in 1929. And when it's time to shake
off culture and civilisation, remember that
the famous Rennsteig hiking trail is only a
hop, skip and jump away.

⊙ Sights

★ Wartburg · CASTLE
(☑03691-2500; www.wartburg-eisenach.de; Auf
der Wartburg 1; tour adult/concession €9/5, museum & Luther study only €5/3; ☉tours 8.30am-5pm
Apr-Oct, 9am-3.30pm Nov-Mar, English tour 1.30pm)

When it comes to medieval castles and their importance in German history, Eisenach's Wartburg is the mother lode. This huge medieval castle is where Martin Luther went into hiding in 1521 after being excommunicated and placed under papal ban. During his 10-month stay, he translated the New Testament from Greek into German, contributing enormously to the development of the written German language. Allow at least two hours: one for the guided tour, the remainder for the museum and the views.

According to legend, the first buildings were put up in 1067 by the hilariously named local ruler Ludwig the Springer in an effort to protect his territory. In 1206 Europe's best minstrels met for the medieval version of *Pop Idol*, a song contest later immortalised in Richard Wagner's opera *Tannhäuser*. Shortly thereafter, Elisabeth, the most famous Wartburg woman, arrived. A Hungarian princess, she was married off to the local landgrave at age four and later chose to abandon court life for charitable work, earning canonisation quickly after her death in 1235.

To walk to Wartburg from the Markt, head one block west to Wydenbrugkstrasse, then turn southwest along Schlossberg through the forest via Eselstation (takes about 40 minutes, and some parts are rather steep). A more scenic route is via the Haintal (50 minutes).

From April to October, bus 10 runs hourly 9am to 5pm from the Hauptbahnhof (with stops at Karlsplatz and Mariental) to the Eselstation, from where it's a steep 10-minute walk up to the castle. In winter buses are available on demand; call ☑ 228 822 for a pick-up.

Bachhaus
MUSEUM

(☑ 03691-793 40; www.bachhaus.de; Frauenplan 21; adult/concession €8.50/4.50; ☉ 10am-6pm) Johann Sebastian Bach, who was born in Eisenach in 1685, takes the spotlight in one of Germany's best biographical museums. Exhibits trace his professional and private life through bilingual panelling, and culminate in a modern annexe, where you can sit in suspended bubble chairs and listen to the wide range of musical contributions made by this versatile genius. Admission includes a 20-minute concert played on antique instruments.

Automobile Welt Eisenach
MUSEUM

(☑ 03691-772 12; www.ame.eisenachonline.de; Friedrich-Naumann-Strasse 10; adult/concession €5/3.50; ☉ 11am-5pm Tue-Sun) Cars, cars, cars! Production revved up in Eisenach in 1896 with the Wartburg, a model based on the French Decauville. This museum celebrates this history by displaying pretty much the entire product range, including an 1899 Wartburg Dixi, a 1936 BMW 328 sports car and other rare vintage vehicles and assorted memorabilia, many from the GDR era.

Reuter-Wagner Museum
MUSEUM

(☑ 03691-743 294; Reuterweg 2; adult/concession €4/2; ☉ 11am-5pm Tue-Sun) This museum, housed in a villa once owned by writer Fritz Reuter, hosts exhibits on Richard Wagner's life and times. Located at the foot of the Wartburg, the inspiration for Wagner's *Tannhäuser*, it's like stepping back in time.

Lutherhaus
HISTORIC BUILDING

(☑ 03691-298 30; www.lutherhaus-eisenach.com; Lutherplatz 8; adult/concession €6/4; ☉ 10am-5pm, closed Mon Nov-Mar) Displays in the house where Martin Luther lived as a schoolboy.

Georgenkirche
CHURCH

(Marktgasse; ☉ 10am-noon & 2-4pm) The baptismal church of St Elizabeth and Johann Sebastian Bach. The reformer Martin Luther preached here while under papal ban. From June to September, free 30-minute organ concerts take place at 11am Monday to Saturday.

Predigerkirche
MUSEUM

(☑ 03691-784 678; www.predigerkirche.eisenachonline.de; Predigerplatz 2; adult/concession €4/2; ☉ 11am-5pm Tue-Sun) Exquisite collection of medieval sculpture, paintings and liturgical objects.

🛏 Sleeping

Pentahotel Eisenach
HOTEL $

(☑ 03691-815 7900; www.pentahotels.com; Weinbergstrasse 5; d from €63; ▣✳🛜) Good for self-drivers, this quirky chain hotel on the outskirts of town has lovely forest views, comfortable, modern rooms, free wi-fi and a friendly bar-restaurant. A good breakfast buffet and excellent rates seal the deal.

Residenzhaus
PENSION $

(☑ 03691-214 133; www.residenzhaus-eisenach.de; Markt 9b; s/d without bathroom €25/50, d with bathroom €60) If you want basic, modern comforts in a historic, central setting without shelling out big money, lug your luggage up the spiral stone staircase of this nice, no frills inn. Breakfast is €6.

Hotel Villa Anna
BOUTIQUE HOTEL $$

(☑ 239 50; www.hotel-villa-anna.de; Fritz-Koch-Strasse 12; s €80, d €100-120; ▣😊🛜) This fantastic boutique hotel at the foot of the Wartburg has classy, spacious rooms. The beds are ultra comfy and most feature a decent desk. Take bus 3, 10 or 11 to Prinzenteich.

Hotel Haus Hainstein   HOTEL $$
(☑ 03691-2420; www.haushainstein.de; Am Hainstein 16; s/d incl breakfast from €60/86; [P]) A stately art-nouveau villa in the leafy, hilly area south of town provides the charismatic setting of this small hotel, which has bright, stylish rooms, its own chapel (for weddings), a restaurant and views of the Wartburg. Buses 3, 10 and 11 to Wandelhalle stop within 500m.

★Romantik Hotel
auf der Wartburg   HOTEL $$$
(☑ 03691-7970; www.wartburghotel.de; Auf der Wartburg 2; s/d incl breakfast from €145/240; [P]🛈) Built in 1914, this hotel has subdued colours and furnishings to match the location on the historic Wartburg. The gorgeous singles with alcove beds are called 'Luther' rooms, but, for space and luxury, book in the 'Romantik' category. While you're not staying in the castle, you can't get any closer: the location is amazing.

✗ Eating

Zucker + Zimt   CAFE $$
(☑ 03691-741 141; www.zucker-zimt-eisenach.de; Markt 2; mains €6-15; ⊙10am-8pm) A whiff of urbanity in ye-olde Eisenach, this upbeat cafe, dressed in mod apple green, fully embraces the 'bio' trend. Organic and fair-trade ingredients find their destination in light creative mains, bagel sandwiches, stuffed crêpes and homemade cakes.

Villa Antik   MODERN EUROPEAN $$
(☑ 03691-658 0286; www.villaantik-eisenach.com; Wartburgallee 55; mains €12-20; ⊙2-11pm Wed-Sat, 11am-11pm Sun) Having undergone a complete transformation in 2015, this classy upmarket Modern European restaurant is now even more refined. One to dress up for.

Brunnenkeller   GERMAN $$
(☑ 03691-212 358; www.brunnenkeller-eisenach.de; Markt 10; mains €10-18; ⊙11am-10pm Apr-Oct, 5.30-10pm Mon-Sat & 11am-3pm Sun Nov-Mar) Linen-draped tables beneath an ancient vaulted brick ceiling set the tone of this traditional chow house in a former monastery cellar. Predictably, meals are honest-to-goodness German and regional classics.

Trattoria La Grappa   ITALIAN $$
(☑ 03691-733 860; www.lagrappa-eisenach.de; Frauenberg 8 10; mains €7-21; ⊙11.30am-2.30pm & 5.30-11.30pm Tue-Sun) The sunny terracotta terrace of this local favourite takes you straight back to the homeland. Pizza, pasta, fish, soup, salad and meat dishes are tasty and generously portioned. Cash only.

★Weinrestaurant
Turmschänke   GERMAN $$$
(☑ 03691-213 533; www.turmschaenke-eisenach.de; Karlsplatz 28; mains from €15-26, 3-course menu from €35; ⊙6-11pm Mon-Sat) This hushed hideaway in Eisenach's only surviving medieval city gate scores a perfect 10 on the 'romance meter'. Walls panelled in polished oak, beautiful table settings and immaculate service complement Ulrich Rösch's flavour-packed concoctions.

🛈 Information

Post Office (Markt 16; ⊙9am-6pm Mon-Fri, to noon Sat)

Tourist Office (☑ 03691-792 30; www.eisenach.info; Markt 24; ⊙10am-6pm Mon-Fri, to 5pm Sat & Sun) The Eisenach tourist office has Rennsteig cycling and hiking brochures and maps, and sells the great-value Thuringia Card (€17/12 for a one-day adult/concession pass or €37/24 for a three-day pass).

🛈 Getting There & Around

BICYCLE
Zweirad Henning (☑ 03691-784 738; www.fahrrad-eisenach.de; Schmelzerstrasse 4-6; bikes per day €10; ⊙9am-6pm Mon-Fri, to 1pm Sat) Rents out bikes, but you may need to book in advance.

BUS
Buses 1, 2, 5 and 12 run from the bus station opposite Hauptbahnhof to Markt.

CAR
Eisenach is on the A4 autobahn and is crossed by the B7, B19 and B84.

TRAIN
Direct regional trains run frequently to Erfurt (€12.10, 45 minutes), Gotha (€9, 25 minutes) and Weimar (€15, one hour). Eisenach is connected by direct ICE trains with Frankfurt am Main (€49, 1¾ hours).

Mühlhausen
☑ 03601 / POP 33,470

Mühlhausen flaunts medieval charisma. Encircled by nearly intact fortifications, its historic centre is a warren of cobbled alleyways linking proud churches and half-timbered houses. In the early 16th century, the town became a focal point of the Reformation and a launch pad for the Peasants' War of 1525, led by local preacher Thomas Müntzer. The decisive battle took place on the Schlacht-berg in nearby Bad Frankenhausen, where the rebellion was quickly crushed. Müntzer was decapitated outside the Mühlhausen town gates.

The GDR regime hailed the reformer as a great hero and an early social revolution-ary. Numerous sites remain around town that uphold his memory. With reunifica-tion, Mühlhausen became united Germa-ny's most central town, located a mere 5km north of the country's precise geographical centre in Niederdorla.

The town's main shopping street is Stein-weg (near Obermarkt).

◉ Sights

Town Fortification
TOWER

(Am Frauentor; adult/concession €3/2; ◷10am-5pm mid-Apr–Sep) One of the best places to admire the beauty of Mühlhausen's Altstadt is from the 330m section of the town forti-fication accessible through **Inneres Frauen-tor**. Originally the 12th-century fortification ran for 2.8km around the town, from which a remarkable 2km remain today. Chart the rest of your explorations from the viewing platform in the **Rabenturm** (Raven's Tower).

Divi-Blasii-Kirche
CHURCH

(◷03601-446 516; Untermarkt; ◷10am-5pm Mon-Thu & Sat, 1-5pm Sun) This Gothic church was built by the Teutonic Knights in the 13th and 14th centuries, based on the style of French Gothic cathedrals. It was here that in 1707–08 Johann Sebastian Bach worked as an organist.

Kornmarktkirche
MUSEUM

(◷5660; Ratsstrasse; adult/concession €3/2; ◷10am-5pm Tue-Sun) This former church is today a museum about the German Peas-ants' War and the Reformation. It can be easily reached from the nearby Divi-Blasii-Kirche via the pedestrianised Linsenstrasse.

Rathaus
HISTORIC BUILDING

(Ratsstrasse 19; ◷10am-4pm Tue-Sun) Mühl-hausen's Rathaus is an architecturally in-triguing hotchpotch of Gothic, Renaissance and baroque styles. Inside, pay special atten-tion to the Great Hall and the Councillors' Chamber.

Marienkirche
CHURCH

(St Mary's Church; ◷03601-870 023; adult/concession €3/2; ◷10am-5pm Tue-Sun) Thurin-gia's second-largest church, after the Dom in Erfurt, Marienkirche is now used as a memorial museum to Thomas Müntzer who preached here to his rebel followers in 1525 before the disastrous Schlachtberg battle.

🛏 Sleeping & Eating

An Der Stadtmauer
HOTEL $

(◷03601-465 00; www.muehlhausen-hotel.de; Breitenstrasse 15; s/d from €39/58; P ◷) The tasteful fittings, comfort and old-town lo-cation make this an excellent choice. Some rooms open onto a courtyard and there's a small bar and beer garden.

RENNSTEIG RAMBLE

Germany's oldest and most popular long-distance trail, the 169km Rennsteig, is a back-woodsy hike along forested mountain ridges from Hörschel (near Eisenach) to Blanken-stein on the Saale River. It's one place you can pack away the guidebook and just explore the villages you ramble by. If you press ahead as far as the Bavarian border region, the local dialect becomes incomprehensible even to many Germans.

The trail is marked by signposts reading 'R', and is best hiked in May/June and Sep-tember/October. You should be moderately fit, with good shoes and a set of strong thighs to carry you for six or seven days. Day hikes offer a taste of the trail with lodging options aplenty in the villages below. The Rennsteig bike trail also begins in Hörschel and travels over asphalt, soft forest soil and gravel, mostly paralleling the hiking trail.

A time-honoured tradition for Rennsteig ramblers is to pick up a pebble from the Wer-ra River at the beginning of your hike, carry it with you and throw it back into the Saale River upon completing the trail.

The tourist office in Eisenach has hiking and cycling brochures and maps. From the office, bus 11 or regional bus 31 will drop you at the **Hohe Sonne** trail head, right on the Rennsteig hiking trail, although you could also hike there (or back) via the craggily ro-mantic **Drachenschlucht** gorge.

DJH Hostel HOSTEL **$**
(☑ 03601-813 318; www.muehlhausen.jugendherberge.de; Auf dem Tonberg 1; dm incl breakfast from €21.50; **P**@☎) This small hostel is about 2.5km west of the Hauptbahnhof. Take bus 5 to Blobach, then walk 500m.

Brauhaus zum Löwen HOTEL **$$**
(☑ 03601-4710; www.brauhaus-zum-loewen.de; Felchtaer Strasse 2-4; s/d €60/89; **P**☎) Conversation flows as freely as the beer at this classic brewpub, where you can get fed and fuelled among the copper vats before retiring to boldly pigmented, country-style rooms. Adjacent you'll find the Leo disco (Wednesday to Saturday), which is the focal point for Mühlhausen nightlife.

Landhaus Frank Zum Nachbarn GERMAN **$$**
(☑ 03601-812 513; www.landhaus-frank.de; Eisenacher Landstrasse 34; mains €12-20; ☉11.30am-10pm) Book ahead for one of the best local restaurants for regional cuisine. Take bus 151, 152 or 153 to the *Friedhof* (cemetery) nearby if you haven't got your own wheels.

ℹ Information

Tourist Office (☑ 03601-404 770; www.muehlhausen.de; Ratsstrasse 20; ☉9am-5pm Mon-Fri, 10am-4pm Sat & Sun) You'll find this quiet little office between Obermarkt and Untermarkt, near the Rathaus.

ℹ Getting There & Away

Mühlhausen is at the crossroads of the B249 from Sondershausen and the B247 from Gotha. Regional trains link Mühlhausen with Erfurt (€12.20, 45 minutes), Kassel (€15, 1½ hours) and Gotha (€8.10, 25 minutes).

Kyffhäuser Mountains

Though not particularly mighty or tall, there's an undeniable mystique to the densely forested Kyffhäuser low-mountain range, historically known as the site of a bloody battle in the Peasants' War of 1525 that left at least 6000 dead.

There is little public transport in this sparsely populated area, but bike trails and roads are well signposted. The main town is Bad Frankenhausen.

◉ Sights

Kyffhäuser Denkmal MONUMENT
(☑ 034651-2780; www.kyffhaeuser-denkmal.de; Kyffhäuser Denkmal, Steinthaleben; adult/concession €5/2.50; ☉9.30am-6pm) The Kyffhäuser were once home to one of Germany's largest medieval castles, the Reichsburg, built in the 12th century during the reign of Emperor Friedrich Barbarossa. According to legend, Barbarossa lies in eternal sleep in the belly of the mountain. In the 19th century, Emperor Wilhelm I was seen as Barbarossa's spiritual successor and in 1896, this statue, showing the emperor on horseback beneath a 60m high tower on which Barbarossa sits on a stone throne, was erected atop the Reichsburg ruins.

To get to the monument, follow the B85 north from Bad Frankenhausen for about 10km, then turn right at the sign and continue for another 2km.

Barbarossahöhle CAVE
(☑ 034671-545 13; www.hoehle.de; Mühlen 6, Rottleben; adult/child €7.50/4; ☉10am-5pm) One of the largest of its type in Europe, this gypsum cave is on a grand scale. Hourly tours last about 50 minutes and take you past shimmering underground lakes and bizarre gypsum sheets that hang from the ceiling, as well as slabs described by legend as Barbarossa's table and chair.

The caves are 7km west of Bad Frankenhausen, north of Rottleben.

Panorama Museum MUSEUM
(☑ 034671-6190; panorama-museum.de; Am Schlachtberg 9, Bad Frankenhausen; adult/concession €5/4; ☉10am-6pm Tue-Sun) This museum looms on the very site where thousands of peasants were slaughtered in 1525 during the Peasants' War. There's one very special painting inside the giant cylindrical structure: called *Frühbürgerliche Revolution in Deutschland* (Early Civil Revolution in Germany), it measures an astonishing 14m by 123m and was inaugurated in 1989.

The museum is on the Schlachtberg, about 3km north of Bad Frankenhausen.

ℹ Information

Tourist Office (☑ 034671-717 16; www.kyffhaeuser-tourismus.de; Anger 14, Bad Frankenhausen; ☉9.30am-6pm Mon-Fri, to 12.30pm Sat, 10-11.30am Sun) Can help with maps, directions and general information.

ℹ Getting There & Around

Bad Frankenhausen is 60km north of Erfurt off the B4. As the town is no longer served by train, it's a hassle to get here without two or four wheels. If you're determined, get yourself to nearby Sondershausen from where you can catch bus 530 to Bad Frankenhausen (€3.20, 35 minutes).

WALKING ABOVE THE TREETOPS

The Unesco World Heritage **Hainich National Park** (www.nationalpark-hainich.de), located 15km southwest of Mühlhausen, protects Germany's largest coherent deciduous forest. There's hiking and cycling, of course, but the park's key draw is the **Baumkronenpfad** (Tree Top Trail; www.baumkronen-pfad.de; Thiemsburg 1, Schönstedt; adult/concession/family €8.50/3/20; ⊙ 10am-7pm Apr-Oct, reduced hours Nov-Mar) elevated trail, meandering through the treetops an impressive 44m above the forest floor. Enjoy magnificent views over the park and observe its flora and fauna from this unique perspective.

On weekends from April to October, the Wunderbare Wanderbus runs between Wartburg (Eisenach) and Bad Langensalza, which is accessible by train from Mühlhausen (15 minutes) and Erfurt (45 minutes), stopping at the Baumkronenpfad.

Gotha

☎ 03621 / POP 44,330

Once described as Thuringia's wealthiest and most beautiful city, Gotha has seen better days. Although it now lacks the tourist draw of neighbouring towns, it remains a pleasant stop, dominated by the grand Schloss Friedenstein. This gracious edifice was built by Duke Ernst I (1601–75), the founder of the House of Saxe-Coburg-Gotha, whose descendants reinvented themselves as the House of Windsor after WWI and now occupy the British royal throne.

◉ Sights & Activities

Schloss Friedenstein   MUSEUM
(☎ 03621-823 40; www.stiftungfriedenstein.de; Schloss Friedenstein; adult/concession €10/5, audioguide €2.50; ⊙ 10am-5pm Tue-Sun) This horseshoe-shaped palace is the largest surviving early baroque palace in Germany. Much of the compound is now the **Schlossmuseum** (Palace Museum), a glorious assembly of art collections displayed in lavish baroque and neoclassical apartments. The picture gallery features priceless works by Rubens, Tischbein, Cranach and other old masters, as well as the radiant *Gothaer Liebespaar*

(Pair of Lovers) painted around 1480 by an anonymous artist known only as Master of the Housebook.

Upstairs is the exuberantly stucco-ornamented **Festsaal** (Festival Hall), as well as the neoclassical wing, the sculpture collection of which includes a famous Renaissance work by Conrad Meit called *Adam und Eva*. Other highlights include the **Kunstkammer**, a curio cabinet jammed with exotica, and the **Schlosskirche** (Palace Church) in the northeastern corner. The southwest tower contains the stunning **Ekhof-Theater**, one of the oldest baroque theatres in Europe, dating from the late 1700s. This hosts performances during the popular **Ekhof Festival** in July and August.

Tickets double as the Friedenstein-Karte, which provides admission to several other sights in Gotha.

Rathaus   HISTORIC BUILDING
(Hauptmarkt; tower €1; ⊙ 11am-6pm) Hauptmarkt is dominated by the picturesque Rathaus, with its colourful Renaissance facade and 35m-tall tower. It started out as a storage house in 1567, later served as ducal pad of Ernst I while Schloss Friedenstein was under construction, and only became a town hall in 1665. The 14th-century **Wasserkunst** (cascading fountain) originally supplied the city with water, but is now purely decorative.

Thüringerwaldbahn   TRAM
(www.waldbahn-gotha.de; per zone €1.50, day ticket €9.10) Gotha's city tram 4 curves around the ring road, crawls through some unlovely suburbs and then just keeps on going – like a local version of the Hogwarts Express – straight into the fairy-tale world of the Thuringian Forest, winding for about 45 minutes to Friedrichroda (three zones), a town of some 7400 people located 20km south of Gotha, and then on to Tabarz (four zones).

The tram departs Gotha every 30 to 60 minutes and takes one hour; take the tram in reverse to return to Gotha.

ⓘ Information

Tourist Office (☎ 03621-5078 5712; www.gotha.de; Hauptmarkt 33; ⊙ 9am-6pm Mon-Fri, 10am-3pm Sat, to 2pm Sun)

ⓘ Getting There & Around

It's a brisk 15-minute walk from the Hauptbahnhof via Schloss Friedenstein to the Neumarkt and Hauptmarkt central squares.

CAR
Gotha is just north of the A4 and is crossed by the B247 and B7.

TRAIN
Direct trains connect Gotha to Eisenach (€9, 25 minutes), Erfurt (€8.50, 16 minutes), Weimar (€13, 35 minutes) and Mühlhausen (€8.10, 25 minutes).

Jena
☑ 03641 / POP 107,700

Although signs of WWII and GDR aesthetics remain, Jena is a pleasant town with a lovely setting on the Saale River, flanked by rugged limestone hills and blessed with a climate mild enough for orchids and grape vines. Although it's also an old university town (since 1558), and Goethe was here, too, Jena has an entirely different feel from Weimar, some 20km to the west. The birthplace of precision optics – pioneered here by Carl Zeiss, Ernst Abbe and Otto Schott – it is Jena's pedigree as a city of science that sets it apart from other Thuringian towns. Today several museums and the world's oldest public planetarium attest to this legacy.

Around 19,000 students inject a dose of youth and vigour; close investigation will unearth fun, fringe, Berlin-esque hang-outs and tasty cheap eats. Less touristy than nearby Weimar and Erfurt, you'll find lovely art-nouveau neighbourhoods and challenging trails leading to glorious viewpoints outside the city centre.

⊙ Sights

Optisches Museum MUSEUM
(Optical Museum; ☑ 03641-443 165; www.optischesmuseum.de; Carl-Zeiss-Platz 12; adult/concession €5/4, combination ticket with Zeiss Planetarium €11/9; ☺ 10am-4.30pm Tue-Fri, 11am-5pm Sat) Carl Zeiss began building rudimentary microscopes in 1846 and, with Ernst Abbe's help, developed the first scientific microscope in 1857. Together with Otto Schott, the founder of Jenaer Glasswerke (glass works), they pioneered the production of optical precision instruments, which eventually propelled Jena to global prominence in the early 20th century. Their life stories and the evolution of optical technology are the themes of this interactive museum featuring 3-D holograms.

Rathaus HISTORIC BUILDING
(Markt 1) Situated at the southern end of the town square, Jena's town hall (1380) is graced with an astronomical clock in its baroque tower. Every hour, on the hour, a little door opens and a devil/fool called Schnapphans appears, trying to catch a golden ball (representing the human soul) that dangles in front of him. The square itself is anchored by a **statue of Prince-Elector Johann Friedrich I**, founder of Jena's university and popularly known as 'Hanfried'.

Stadtmuseum & Kunstsammlung Jena MUSEUM, GALLERY
(City Museum & Art Collection; ☑ 03641-498 261; www.stadtmuseum.jena.de; Markt 7; Stadtmuseum adult/concession €4/2.40, Kunstsammlung €8/5; ☺ 10am-5pm Tue, Wed & Fri, 3-10pm Thu, 11am-6pm Sat & Sun) This handsome building with a half-timbered upper section, at the northern end of the town square, houses the Stadtmuseum, where you can learn how the city evolved into a centre of philosophy and science, and the Kunstsammlung, with changing exhibitions and a permanent collection of mostly 20th-century works.

Botanischer Garten GARDENS
(☑ 03641-949 274; www.spezbot.uni-jena.de/botanischer-garten; Fürstengraben 26; adult/concession €4/2; ☺ 10am-6pm) Goethe himself planted the ginkgo tree in these wonderful botanic gardens boasting more than 12,000 plants from every climatic zone on earth.

Schillers Gartenhaus HISTORIC BUILDING
(Schiller's Garden House; ☑ 03641-931 188; Schillergässchen 2; adult/concession €2.50/1.30; ☺ 11am-5pm Tue-Sun) Goethe is credited with recruiting Schiller to Jena University in 1789. The playwright enjoyed Jena so much that he stayed for 10 years, longer than anywhere else, in what is now known as Schillers Gartenhaus. He wrote *Wallenstein* in the little wooden shack in the garden, where he and Goethe liked to wax philosophical.

JenTower TOWER
(☑ 03641-208 000; www.jentower.de; Leutragraben 1; viewing platform €3; ☺ viewing platforms 10am-11pm) Built in 1972, but deceptively modern in appearance, the 128m-tall cylindrical JenTower was intended to be a Zeiss research facility, but proved unsuitable. There's a shopping mall at ground level and two open-air observation decks at the top.

Universität

Jena – Collegium Jenense UNIVERSITY

(Kollegiengasse) Jena's university faculties are spread throughout town, but this was where the university was founded as Collegium Jenense in 1558, in a former monastery. Enter the courtyard to admire the coat of arms of Johann Friedrich I and to check out the free exhibit (in German) on the university's illustrious history.

Zeiss Planetarium PLANETARIUM

(☑ 03641-885 488; www.planetarium-jena.de; Am Planetarium 5; adult/concession €8.50/7) The world's oldest public planetarium (1926) has a state-of-the-art dome projection system, making it a heavenly setting for cosmic laser shows paying tribute to music legends such as Pink Floyd and Queen, or sending the kids deep into outer space. Show times and pricing varies by program; check the website for details.

Stadtkirche St Michael CHURCH

(Parish Church; Kirchplatz; ⊙10am-5pm Tue-Sun May-Sep) This Gothic church one block north of the town square is famous for having Martin Luther's original engraved tombstone (there's another in the Schlosskirche in the town of Wittenberg that is actually a 19th-century replica).

Schott Glasmuseum MUSEUM

(☑ 03641-681 5304; www.schott.com/jena; Otto-Schott-Strasse 13; ⊙1-5pm Tue-Fri) FREE An interactive multimedia exhibition with audioguides in English on the history, production and technology of glass.

★ Dornburger Schlösser PALACE

(☑ 036497-222 91; www.dornburg-schloesser. de; Max-Krehan-Strasse 2, Dornburg; combination ticket (Renaissance & Rococo) €4; ⊙10am-5pm Thu-Tue Apr-Oct) About 15km north of Jena, you'll find this hillside trilogy of magnificently restored palaces in medieval, Renaissance and rococo styles, with stunning views and immaculate gardens. The **Altes Schloss**, the oldest, blends Romanesque, late-Gothic and baroque elements, but can only be viewed from the outside. You can enter both the 1539 **Renaissance Palace** (where Goethe sought solitude after the death of his patron, Duke Carl August) and the youngest, most beautiful **Rococo Palace**, used for temporary exhibitions, concerts and weddings.

It won't cost you a cent to stroll around the beautiful gardens, enjoying the wonderful views and admiring the palaces from the outside.

Trains travel frequently from Jena-Paradies to Dornburg (€3.80, 12 minutes), from where it's a steep 20- to 30-minute climb.

★✰ Festivals & Events

Kulturarena Jena MUSIC

(☑ 03641-498 060; www.kulturarena.com) This international music festival – with blues, rock, classical and jazz – gets the town rocking through July and August.

🛏 Sleeping

Hotel Rasenmühle BOUTIQUE HOTEL $

(☑ 03641-534 2130; www.hotel-rasenmuehle. de; Burgauer Weg 1a; s/d incl breakfast €48/55; P �) The best thing about this modern, well-priced, sparsely decorated 11-room private hotel is its green, leafy location in the midst of Jena's Paradies park. Most rooms have views over the Saale River or parklands. Free wi-fi and parking are a nice bonus, and a communal kitchen is available to guests.

Alpha One Hostel Jena HOSTEL $

(☑ 03641-597 897; www.hostel-jena.de; Lassallestrasse 8; dm/s from €15/25, linen €2.50; @) Jena's indie hostel is in a quiet street within staggering distance of the Wagnergasse pubs. The decent-sized rooms are splashed in bright colour; those on the 3rd floor have great views and room 16 even has a balcony. Breakfast is €4.50. The closest tram stop is Ernst-Abbe-Platz (tram 5, 25 or 35).

Ibis Jena City HOTEL $

(☑ 03641-8130; www.ibis.com/Jena; Teichgraben 1; r from €69; P) This chain contender has all the prerequisites to give you a good night's sleep and puts you smack dab in the thick of things. Wi-fi is free in the lobby. Bus 15 from Jena-West runs to Holzmarkt. From Jena-Paradies it's a short walk north.

★ Scala Turm Hotel BOUTIQUE HOTEL $$

(☑ 03641-311 3888; www.scala-jena.de; Leutragraben 1, JenTower; s/d from €99/135; P) This boutique hotel (Germany's second-highest at 120m), atop the JenTower, boasts 17 over-sized rooms that afford amazing views of the town and countryside. Slick, super-stylish, modern and minimalist, Scala Turm has all the right ingredients to make your night something special. The hotel's eponymous restaurant is equally impressive, so you'll not have to wander far to dine.

Steigenberger
Esplanade Jena
LUXURY HOTEL $$

(☑03641-8000; www.steigenberger.com/Jena/Steigenberger-Esplanade; Carl-Zeiss-Platz 4; r from €94; P✴@☎) Jena's premier abode is a hulking, professional outfit with 140 good-sized rooms and suites of varying configurations in a great downtown location. Furnishings are well made and reasonably stylish, having seen some recent updates. There's free low-bandwidth wi-fi, but you'll have to pay more for decent speed and for parking.

Hotel Vielharmonie
HOTEL $$

(☑03641-796 2171; www.hotel-vielharmonie.de; Bachstrasse 14; s/d from €53/80) This central, well-priced hotel still feels new. It's rooms are compact, simple and stylish, but the generous use of the red colour palette may not be to everyone's liking. The hotel's best feature are some cute attic rooms with small terraces and/or kitchenettes.

Eating

Café Immergrün
BISTRO $

(☑03641-447 313; www.cafe-immergruen.com; Jener Gasse 6; items €3.50-6; ☺11am-1am Mon-Sat, 10am-1am Sun) Sink deep into a plump sofa for intense tête-à-têtes or gather your posse in the leafy garden at this self-service bistro-pub, tucked off a quiet side street just north of the JenTower. The cheap meals (mostly pasta, rice and baguettes) make it popular with students.

Landgrafen Jena
MODERN EUROPEAN $$

(☑03641-507 071; www.landgrafen.com; Landgrafenstieg 25; mains €10-21; ☺3-11pm Tue-Thu, 11.30am-11pm Fri & Sat, 11.30am-8pm Sun) High in the hills, with stunning views over Jena, this smart, multipurpose restaurant is fresh from extensive renovations. There's a summer beer garden with bratwursts, beverages and playthings for the kids, but the real appeal lies within the stylish terrace (for casual eats) or the dressy, upmarket dining room.

Restauration Stilbruch
INTERNATIONAL $$

(☑03641-827 171; www.stilbruch-jena.de; Wagnergasse 2; mains €7-24; ☺8.30am-1am Mon-Thu, 9am-3am Fri & Sat, to 2am Sun; ✑) The competition is great on Wagnergasse, Jena's pub mile, but this multilevel contender is a fascinating stop for drinks and a bite from the something-for-everybody menu, and even better for weekend brunch (though you might have to fight for a seat). For privacy, snag the table atop the spiral staircase; for people-watching, sit outside.

Gasthaus Zur Noll
GERMAN $$

(☑03641-597 710; www.zur-noll.de; Oberlauengasse 19; mains €9-18; ☺10.30am-11pm; P☎) You'll find classic Thuringian hospitality galore in this woody, historic charmer. Perfect for sampling hearty rustic fare, the menu is updated constantly, but always features German and traditional Thuringian cooking prepared from fresh, local ingredients.

Schnitzelparadies
GERMAN $$

(☑03641-628 724; www.schnitzelparadies-jena.de; Grietgasse 2; schnitzel €9-16; ☺11am-10pm Tue-Sun) The name says it all: get ready for schnitzels galore. This popular downtown joint serves up more variations of the humble cutlet than you can begin to imagine, has an extensive beer menu for you to pair them with, and presents them to you with a smile. Fun and tasty.

Fuchsturm Berggäststatte
GERMAN $$

(☑03641-360 606; www.fuchsturmgaststaette.de; Turmgasse 26; mains €9-18; ☺11.30am-9pm Tue-Fri, 11am-11pm Sat, 10am-8pm Sun) Beneath the ancient Fuchsturm castle tower, this atmospheric dining hall serves hearty traditional fare alongside pastas, salads and fish dishes.

🍷 Drinking & Entertainment

Der Strand 22
BAR

(☑03641-423 7665; www.derstrand22.de; Vor dem Neutor 5, Paradiespark; ☺10am-midnight May-Sep) Open only in the summer months, this riverside beer garden, bar and club-in-the-park is *the* place to hang out. It's lovely, plays great music, makes killer drinks, serves cold beer, has tasty snacks and is a hub for culture and the arts. What are you waiting for?

Grünowksi
CAFE

(☑03641-446 620; www.gruenowski.de; Schillergässchen 5; ☺noon-midnight) Hippies, hipsters and the simply hip flock here for the chilled vibe and the soul-warming food from Grünowksi's kitchen. Inside it's full of casual nooks and crannies to command, or there's a rambling beer garden outside. Eat, drink and be merry.

Rosenkeller
CLUB

(☑03641-931 190; rosenkeller.org; Johannisstrasse 13; ☺8pm-2am Fri-Sun) This historic club in a network of cellars has plied generations of students with booze and music and is still among the best places in town to meet some friendly locals.

Volksbad Jena
LIVE PERFORMANCE

(☑03641-498 300; www.volksbad-jena.de; Knebelstrasse 10) You can't swim in water in this century-old public pool any longer, instead you'll be showered with cultural events ranging from the mainstream to the offbeat. Opposite Jena-Paradies station.

Kassablanca Gleis 1
LIVE PERFORMANCE

(☑03641-282 60; www.kassablanca.de; Felsenkellerstrasse 13a) Near Jena-West train station, this joint feeds the cultural cravings of the indie crowd with a potpourri of live concerts, dance parties, readings, experimental theatre, movies and other distractions. Cheap drinks fuel the fun.

ⓘ Information

Bagels & Beans (☑03641-219 291; Leutragraben 2-4; internet per min €0.05, wi-fi per 30min €1.50; ☺8am-8.30pm Mon-Fri, 9am-7pm Sat, 10am-6pm Sun; ☏) Internet and cheap bagels in a pleasant atmosphere.

Tourist Office (☑03641-498 050; www.jena. de; Markt 16; ☺10am-7pm Mon-Fri, to 4pm Sat & Sun) Purchase the JenaCard (€11.90) here for 48 hours of discounted tours and admissions and free public transport. A variety of guided and self-guided walking and cycling tours are also available.

ⓘ Getting There & Away

CAR
Jena is just north of the A4 from Dresden to Frankfurt, and west of the A9 from Berlin to Munich. The B7 links it with Weimar, while the B88 goes south to Rudolstadt and Saalfeld.

TRAIN
Direct trains depart from Jena-West to Weimar (€5, 15 minutes) and Erfurt (€8.50, 30 minutes); for Eisenach (€15, 1½ hours) change in Weimar. Two-hourly ICE trains to Berlin (€63, 2¼ hours) depart from Jena-Paradies, as do at least hourly services to Saalfeld (€10, 30 minutes).

ⓘ Getting Around

Jena has two train stations. Long-distance trains arrive at Jena-Paradies, a 10-minute walk south of Markt. Regional trains from Erfurt or Weimar stop at the tiny Jena-West station, a 20-minute walk from Markt. To get to Markt from Jena-West, turn left onto Westbahnhofstrasse and turn right into Kollegienstrasse. Bus 15 runs twice-hourly from Jena-West to Holzmarkt, 150m south of Markt along Löbderstrasse.

BICYCLE
Fahrrad Kirscht (☑03641-441 539; Löbdergraben 8; bikes per 1st 24hr €15, extra days €10; ☺9am-7pm Mon-Fri, to 4pm Sat)

BUS
Single/daily bus or tram tickets cost €1.90/4.90.

TAXI
Call ☑03641-458 888 or try www.bettertaxi.de.

Saale-Unstrut Region

The wine-growing region along the rivers Saale and Unstrut provides a wonderfully rural summer retreat. Europe's most northerly wine district produces crisp whites and fairly sharp reds, which you can enjoy at wine tastings, sometimes right at the estates. The 60km bicycle-friendly Weinstrasse (Wine Road) meanders through the region, past steeply terraced vineyards, castle-topped hills and small family-owned farms. Local tourist offices can help with information and maps.

Naumburg
☑03445 / POP 23,900

At the confluence of the Saale and Unstrut Rivers, Naumburg has a handsome Altstadt with a striking Renaissance Rathaus and the Marientor double gateway.

◎ Sights

Dom
CHURCH

(☑03445-230 1133; www.naumburger-dom.de; Domplatz 16-17; adult/concession €6.50/4.50; ☺9am-6pm Mon-Sat, noon-6pm Sun) The enormous Cathedral of Sts Peter and Paul is a masterpiece of medieval architecture. While the crypt and the east choir feature elements of the Romanesque, the famous west choir is a prime example of early Gothic design. Here you'll find a dozen monumental statues of the cathedral founders, the work of the so-called Master of Naumburg. Medieval stained-glass windows are augmented by ruby-red modern panes by Neo Rauch, one of the premier artists of the New Leipzig School.

Nietzsche Haus
MUSEUM

(☑03445-201 638; www.mv-naumburg.de/ nietzsche haus; Weingarten 18; adult/concession €3/2; ☺2-5pm Tue-Fri, 10am-5pm Sat & Sun) Friedrich Nietzsche (1844–1900) spent most of his childhood in this modest home, acquired by his mother after the death of her husband. In 1890 she brought her son back here to nurse him as he was going slowly mad, allegedly as a result of syphilis. The exhibit consists mostly of photos, documents and reams of biographical text about one of Germany's greatest philosophers.

✸ Festivals & Events

Kirschfest   FOOD
(Cherry Festival; www.kirschfest.de) In late June, the normally sedate town of Naumburg goes wild during the Kirschfest, a celebration of food, drink, music, a parade and fireworks.

🛏 Sleeping & Eating

DJH Hostel   HOSTEL $
(✆ 03445-703 422; www.jugendherberge.de/jh/naumburg; Am Tennisplatz 9; dm incl breakfast under/over 27yr €21/24, linen €3.50; 🅿 🛜) Naumburg's large and well-equipped hostel is 1.5km south of the town centre.

Hotel Stadt Aachen   HOTEL $$
(✆ 03445-2470; www.hotel-stadt-aachen.de; Markt 11; s €62-69, d €83-95, tr €105) Comfortable traditional hotel on the bustling main square.

Bocks   INTERNATIONAL $$
(✆ 03445-261 5110; Steinweg 6; €10.50-24; ⏰ 10am-9pm; ✒) Naumberg's top eatery boasts charming decor, two rooms, a cafe area, and excellent meat dishes, pasta and other fare.

ℹ Information

Tourist Office (✆ 03445-273 125; www.naumburg-tourismus.de; Markt 12; ⏰ 9am-6pm Mon-Fri, to 4pm Sat, 10am-1pm Sun) Maps and audio tours available.

ℹ Getting There & Around

BICYCLE
Radhaus Steinmeyer (✆ 03445-203 119; www.radhaus-naumburg.de; Bahnhofstrasse 46; bikes per day from €10) Rents bikes in the summer.

BOAT
MS Fröhliche Dörte (✆ 03445-202 830; www.froehliche-doerte.de) The MS *Fröhliche Dörte* runs to Freyburg between April and October, taking 70 minutes (adult/child one way €9/5, return €15/8). It departs Naumburg at 11am, 1.30pm and 4pm.

CAR
From Halle or Leipzig, take the A9 to either the B87 or the B180 and head west; the B87 is less direct and more scenic, though it's the first exit from the A9.

TRAIN
Regional trains chug to Naumburg from Halle (€8.10, 45 minutes), Jena (€8.10, 45 minutes) and Weimar (€9.70, 35 minutes). A local line runs to Freyburg (€2.80, eight minutes). Direct ICE services run to Leipzig (€19, 40 minutes).

TRAM
Departing from in front of the station, the Naumburger Strassenbahn, a GDR-era tram (€1.90) will drop you at Theaterplatz, near Markt. By foot, walk along Rossbacher Strasse (keep bearing left and uphill) past the cathedral.

Freyburg

🌐 034464 / POP 3630

With its cobblestone streets and medieval castle clinging to vine-covered slopes, the little village of Freyburg has a rustic, vaguely French atmosphere. Sparkling wine production has been the main source of income here since the middle of the 19th century, and to this day Freyburg is home to Germany's most famous bubbly brand, Rotkäppchen Sekt (named for the Little Red Riding Hood from the Grimm fairy tale). The town seriously comes alive for its wine festival in the second week of September.

👁 Sights

⭐ Schloss Neuenburg   CASTLE
(✆ 355 30; www.schloss-neuenburg.de; Schloss 25; adult/concession €6/3.50, with tour €8/6.50, tower €1.50/1; ⏰ 10am-6pm daily, tower Tue-Sun) This large medieval castle on the hill above town is one of Freyburg's highlights. It houses an excellent museum that illuminates various aspects of medieval life. The complex includes a rare Romanesque two-storey (or 'double') chapel and a free-standing tower, the Dicker Wilhelm, which has further historical exhibitions and splendid views.

Rotkäppchen Sektkellerei   WINERY
(✆ 340; www.rotkaeppchen.de; Sektkellereistrasse 5; 45min tours €5; ⏰ tours 11am & 2pm daily, also 12.30pm & 3.30pm Sat & Sun) Established in 1856, and the biggest sparkling-wine producer in Germany, the Rotkäppchen Sektkellerei is one of the few companies that survived the GDR and, since reunification, has acquired enough muscle to buy other brands, including Mumm. Tours include the historic cellars and the production facilities. Between 10am and 5pm, you can also taste and buy a whole range of Sekt at the shop out front.

SAALFELD: FAIRIES IN THE GROTTOES?

Gables, turrets and gates provide a cheerful welcome to Saalfeld, which has been sitting prim and pretty along the Saale River for 1100 years. Aside from the handsome medieval town centre, it lures visitors with one of Thuringia's more interesting natural attractions, the Feengrotten (Fairy Grottoes), now heavily targeted toward children.

Saalfeld is linked to Weimar via the B85 and to Jena by the B88. Regional trains run frequently to Jena (€9.70, 45 minutes).

Feengrotten (Fairy Grottoes; ☎ 03671-550 40; www.feengrotten.de; Feengrottenweg 2; adult/child €11/6.50, with Grottoneum & Fairy World adult/child €15/8.50; ⏰ 9.30am-5pm) These former alum slate mines (from 1530 to 1850) were opened for tours in 1914 and rank among the world's most colourful grottoes, imbued with shades of brown, ochre, sienna, green and blue. Small stalactites and stalagmites add to the surreal appearance, the highlight of which is the Fairytale Cathedral and its Holy Grail Castle. The **Feenweltchen** (open May to October) is an outdoor trail, weaving its way through a fun obstacle course of elves, fairies and spirits. Year-round, the **Grottoneum** museum has interactive exhibits on mining, the caves and how they came about.

Buses make the 3km trip from Saalfeld Bahnhof and Markt to the grottoes every half-hour. For a taxi, call ☎ 511 115.

ℹ Information

Tourist Office (☎ 03445-272 60; www.freyburg-info.de; Markt 2; ⏰ 9am-5pm Mon-Thu, to 6pm Fri, 8am-2pm Sat)

ℹ Getting There & Around

BICYCLE
The well-marked bicycle route between Naumburg and Freyburg makes for a wonderful ride.

BOAT
MS Fröhliche Dörte (☎ 03445-202 830; www.froehliche-doerte.de) The 19th-century MS Fröhliche Dörte tootles its way along the Unstrut between April and October. The 40-minute one-way journey from Freyburg to Naumburg costs €9/5 per adult/concession, and €15/8 return. It departs Freyburg at 12.15pm, 2.45pm and 5.15pm.

CAR
The B180 to Naumburg follows the river.

TRAIN & BUS
Freyburg is about 9km north of Naumburg and served by trains (€2.80, eight minutes) and buses (€2.50, 23 minutes).

HARZ MOUNTAINS

What the Harz Mountains – Northern Germany's only serious uplands – lack in alpine dramatics, they make up for in atmosphere and accessibility. The long-time subject of legend and lore, the mountains are easily and inexpensively reached from Berlin and other towns. There's excellent hiking and good mountain-biking in the warmer months and equally impressive cross-country skiing in the winter, though serious downhill skiers will head further south.

Straddling parts of the three German states of Lower Saxony, Saxony-Anhalt and Thuringia, the mountains ward a number of delightful historical villages. These include historic Goslar and charming Quedlinburg, as well as Wernigerode, from where you can catch an old-world steam train to the summit of the Harz' highest peak, the Brocken, at 1142m – that is, if you don't have the energy to make the hike. Many do, especially on Walpurgisnacht (30 April) when all and sundry hit the trails to celebrate a pagan festival.

The main information centre for the Harz Mountains is the Harzer Verkehrsverband (p569) in Goslar, but information on the Eastern Harz is best picked up in towns there, particularly in Wernigerode.

A local Kurtaxe (resort tax; ranging from €0.75 to €3 per night) is charged in most towns.

ℹ Getting There & Away

BUS
BerlinLinienBus (www.berlinlinienbus.de) and **Meinfernbus** (www.meinfernbus.de) operate low-cost services from Berlin's Hauptbahnhof to Quedlinburg, Wernigerode and Goslar. Most services also stop at Magdeburg. Fares fluctuate; check the websites for details.

CAR

If you're driving, the area's main arteries are the east–west B6 and the north–south B4, which are accessed via the A7 (skirting the western edge of the Harz on its way south from Hanover) and the A2 (running north of the Harz between Hanover and Berlin).

TRAIN

The area's main towns of Goslar, Wernigerode and Quedlinburg are serviced by frequent trains; visit the website of **Deutsche Bahn** (www.bahn. de) for details.

ℹ️ Getting Around

The Harz is one part of Germany where you'll rely on buses as much as trains, and the various local networks are fast and reliable. Narrow-gauge steam trains run to the Brocken and link major towns in the Eastern Harz.

Having your own wheels makes exploring this pretty area that much more enjoyable.

Goslar

📱 05321 / POP 41,750

Gorgeous Goslar is a tourist hub. Its beautiful medieval Altstadt and Unesco World Heritage–listed Rammelsberg mine attract visitors by the busload, especially in the summer, when it's best to book ahead.

Founded by Heinrich I in 922, the town's early importance centred on mining silver. Its Kaiserpfalz (Imperial Palace) was the seat of the Saxon kings from 1005 to 1219. Goslar fell into decline after a second period of prosperity in the 14th and 15th centuries, relinquishing its mine to Braunschweig in 1552 and then its soul to Prussia in 1802.

Post WWII, it was the most important town west of the former border between the Western and Eastern Harz.

👁 Sights

One of the nicest things to do in Goslar is to wander through the historic streets around the Markt. Hotel Kaiserworth (p568) on Markt was erected in 1494 to house the textile guild, and sports almost life-size figures on its orange facade. The **market fountain**, celebrating Goslar's status as a free imperial city, dates from the 13th century. Opposite the Rathaus is the **Glockenspiel,** a chiming clock depicting four scenes of mining in the area. It plays at 9am, noon, 3pm and 6pm.

Kaiserpfalz CASTLE
(📞05321-311 9693; Kaiserbleck 6; adult/concession €7.50/4.50; ⏰10am-4pm) Goslar's pride and joy is its reconstructed 11th-century Romanesque palace. After centuries of decay, the building was resurrected in the 19th century and adorned with interior frescos of idealised historical scenes. On the southern side is St Ulrich Chapel, housing a sarcophagus containing the heart of Heinrich III. Behind the palace, in pleasant gardens, is an excellent sculpture by Henry Moore called the *Goslarer Krieger* (Goslar Warrior).

Domvorhalle HISTORIC BUILDING
(Kaiserbleek; ⏰9am-5pm) FREE Below the Kaiserpfalz, the Domvorhalle is all that remains of the once magnificent St Simon and St Jude Cathedral. Within it you can see the 11th-century Kaiserstuhl, the throne used by Salian and Hohenstaufen emperors.

CENTRAL GERMANY GOSLAR

CLIMBING THE BROCKEN: THE GOETHEWEG TRAIL

From 1945 to 1989 the Harz region was a front line in the Cold War, and the Brocken was used by the Soviets as a military base. For 28 years the top was off limits, but today you can hike alongside the trainline above soggy moorland to reach the open, windy summit. There are prettier landscapes and hikes in the Harz, but the Brocken summit (1142m) draws up to 50,000 avid hikers on a summer's day. There are several approaches, including one from Schierke, but the 8km Goetheweg trail, beginning in Torfhaus, is the easiest and most popular approach from the Western Harz.

The hike begins through bog then follows a historic aqueduct before crossing the Kaiserweg, a sweaty 11km trail from Bad Harzburg. Things get steep as you walk the former border between East and West Germany. Once at the top, you'll find the **Brockenhaus** (www.nationalpark-brockenhaus.de; adult/concession €4/3; ⏰9.30am-5pm), with its interactive displays, a cafe where you can refuel, and a viewing platform. In summer, weather permitting, rangers conduct one-hour tours of the plateau.

Bus 820 stops at Torfhaus (€3.90, 20 minutes) on the well served Bad Harzburg–Braunlage route.

Rathaus   HISTORIC BUILDING

(Markt; Huldigungssaal adult/child €3.50/1.50; ☺11am-3pm Mon-Fri, 10am-4pm Sat & Sun Apr-Oct & Dec) The impressive late-Gothic Rathaus is most beautiful at night, when light shining through stained-glass windows illuminates the stone-patterned town square. The highlight inside is a beautiful cycle of 16th-century religious paintings in the **Huldigungssaal** (Hall of Homage).

Goslarer Museum   MUSEUM

(☑05321-433 94; Königstrasse 1; adult/concession €4/2; ☺10am-5pm Tue-Sun) This museum offers a good overview of the natural and cultural history of Goslar and the Harz. One room contains the treasures from the former Goslar Dom, and there's also a cabinet with coins dating from the 10th century.

Mönchehaus Museum   GALLERY

(☑05321-295 70; www.moenchehaus.de; Mönchestrasse 3; admission €5; ☺10am-5pm Tue-Sat) Set in a 16th-century half-timbered house, this museum has changing exhibits of modern art, including works by the most recent winner of the prestigious Kaiserring art prize; past winners include Henry Moore, Joseph Beuys and Rebecca Horn. Look for the interesting sculptures in the peaceful garden.

Museum im Zwinger   MUSEUM

(☑05321-431 40; www.zwinger.de; Thomasstrasse 2; adult/concession €5/2.50; ☺11am-4pm Tue-Sat mid-Mar–Oct) A 16th-century tower with a collection of such late-medieval delights as torture implements, coats of armour and weapons used during the Peasant Wars.

Zinnfiguren-Museum   MUSEUM

(☑05321-258 89; www.zinnfigurenmuseum-goslar.de; Klapperhagen 1; adult/concession €4/2; ☺10am-4pm Tue-Sun) This museum boasts a colourful collection of painted pewter figures.

Musikinstrumenten- und
Puppenmuseum   MUSEUM

(☑05321-269 45; Hoher Weg 5; adult/child €3/1.50; ☺11am-5pm) A private museum sprawling over five floors, with musical instruments, dolls, and a porcelain collection housed in the cellar.

★Rammelsberg
Museum & Besucherbergwerk   MUSEUM

(Rammelsberg Museum & Visitors' Mine; ☑05321-7500; www.rammelsberg.de; Bergtal 19; adult/concession €13/8; ☺9am-6pm, last admission 4.30pm) About 2km south of the town centre, the shafts and buildings of this 1000-year-old mine are now a museum and Unesco World Heritage site. Admission includes a German-language tour and a pamphlet with English explanations of the 18th- and 19th-century Roeder Shafts, the mine railway and the ore-processing section. Bus 803 stops here.

🛏 Sleeping

DJH Hostel   HOSTEL $

(☑05321-222 40; www.djh-niedersachsen.de/jh/goslar; Rammelsberger Strasse 25; dm incl breakfast from €22.50; P@☎) Take bus 803 to Theresienhof to reach this pretty hostel out near the mining museum. Facilities are excellent, with single and twin rooms and six- to eight-bed dorms, as well as barbecue and sports areas.

★Hotel Alte Münze   BOUTIQUE HOTEL $$

(☑05321-225 46; www.hotel-muenze.de; Münzstrasse 10-11; s/d from €69/99; P☎) There's very little not to like about this boutique hotel in the heart of the Altstadt, with a history of over 500 years on the site. Operating as a mint in a previous incarnation, the hotel's hotchpotch of rooms have been beautifully brought up to date with spotless new bathrooms, flat-screen TVs and wi-fi to complement the antique-y, creaky, medieval vibe.

Schiefer   BOUTIQUE HOTEL $$

(☑05321-382 270; www.schiefer-erleben.de; Markt 6; d incl breakfast from €109; P✳☎) In a prime Markt location, Schiefer brings a touch of the modern to ancient Goslar. Rooms and maisonette apartments are tastefully furnished and spotlessly clean. There's on-site parking at the rear of the hotel (a blessing in largely pedestrian-only Goslar) and breakfast is served in your room. Highly recommended.

Hotel Kaiserworth   HOTEL $$

(☑05321-7090; www.kaiserworth.de; Markt 3; s/d from €79/129; P⊜☎) This magnificent 500-year-old former merchant-guild building has tasteful rooms and a good restaurant open daily from 6am to 11pm. Insomniacs should head for the hotel's Café Nouvelle, which is open until 2am or the last customer.

Niedersächsischer Hof   HOTEL $$

(☑05321-3160; www.niedersaechsischerhof-goslar.de; Klubgartenstrasse 1; s/d from €79/109; P☎) Opposite the train station, the 'Hof' toys with the idea of being an art hotel (the kids will love the piece near the foyer with the cindered toy cars), and has bright rooms well insulated against the bustle outside. Prices fluctuate according to the date, so call ahead.

ⓘ WATCH YOUR SPEED

If you've decided to rent a car to experience the thrill of autobahn driving or to get off the beaten track, you're well advised to pay attention to your speed. Although you're free to (safely) burn rubber on designated stretches of major autobahns, speed limits apply everywhere else. On regional highways and roads in the Harz, it's common for the speed limit to drop from 100km/h to 70km/h, then to 50km/h, and 30km/h when approaching villages. Coming off an autobahn at 150km/h onto a sparsely trafficked rural highway, there's a natural tendency to keep driving a little faster than you should. Don't.

Mobile police patrols and fixed position speed cameras (Radarkontrole) are commonplace and pop up without warning. While you won't lose points on your home licence, you will be fined: the faster you're driving over the limit, the higher the fine, so driving 45km/h in a 30km/h zone is considered the same as doing 115km/h in a 100km/h zone. Rental-car companies process speed camera fines and automatically deduct the amount from your credit card.

Das Brusttuch   HOTEL $$
(☑ 05321-346 00; www.brusttuch.de; Hoher Weg 1; s/d from €89/119; P 🤖 🛁) The soft colours and smart rooms in this historic hotel, dating from 1521, make it a comfortable snooze zone. It's very central and some rooms have double doors to the hallway.

✖ Eating

Soup & Soul Kitchen   VEGETARIAN $
(☑ 05321-756 3341; www.soulkitchen.house; Petersilienstrasse 5-7; mains €6-14; ⊙ noon-8pm Tue-Sun; ☑) ✿ Locally sourced organic and bio-dynamic fruit and vegetables are used to create the hearty and delicious vegan and vegetarian soups, salads and pastas at Goslar's hippest healthy hang-out.

Barock-Café Anders   BAKERY $
(☑ 05321-238 14; Hoher Weg 4; cakes from €3; ⊙ 8.30am-6pm) Breathe in the smell of fresh baking as soon as you walk through the door; it's unlikely you'll be able to leave without a pastry for the road.

Das Schwarze Schaf   INTERNATIONAL $$
(☑ 05321-319 5111; www.dasschwarzeschaf-goslar. de; Jakobikirchhof 7; mains €8-13; ⊙ 11am-8.30pm; ☑) This sleek eatery has a large menu of salads, pasta, Flammkuchen, stir-fries and grills, all served at wooden tables in a bright Asian-European-crossover atmosphere. Dishes can also be ordered takeaway.

Die Butterhanne   GERMAN $$
(☑ 05321-228 86; www.butterhanne.de; Marktkirchhof 3; mains €9-16; ⊙ 8.30am-midnight) The fare is traditional, the outdoor seating is nice and on the first Saturday of the month the tables are cleared and the place morphs into a throbbing nightspot from 10pm. The

name refers to a famous local frieze showing a milkmaid churning butter while clutching her buttock to insult her employer – don't try it on disco night.

Restaurant Aubergine   MEDITERRANEAN $$
(☑ 05321-421 36; www.aubergine-goslar.de; Marktstrasse 4; mains €9-20; ⊙ noon-2.30pm & 6-11.30pm) Good-quality cuisine, crisp tablecloths and service, and a classy atmosphere.

Brauhaus   GERMAN $$
(☑ 05321-685 804; www.brauhaus-goslar.de; Marktkirchhof 2; mains €7-19; ⊙ 11am-11pm) Goslar's newcomer to the gastronomic and drinking scene is a gastro pub that brews four types of beer in its copper vats beyond the bar and serves meals focusing mostly on steaks and other meats, some of them organic and locally produced.

ⓘ Information

Harzer Verkehrsverband (☑ 05321-340 40; www.harzinfo.de; Marktstrasse 45, Bäckergildehaus; ⊙ 8am-5pm Mon-Thu, to 2pm Fri) Come here for all things Harz.

Post Office (Klubgartenstrasse 10; ⊙ 9am-6pm Mon-Fri, to 12.30pm Sat)

Tourist Office (☑ 05321-780 60; www.goslar. de; Markt 7; ⊙ 9.15am-6pm Mon-Fri, to 4pm Sat, to 2pm Sun) Unmissable in the Markt, this office can help with bookings and maps in English.

ⓘ Getting There & Away

BUS

BerlinLinienBus (www.berlinlinienbus.de) and **Meinfernbus** (www.meinfernbus.de) run daily services to Berlin via Magdeburg. Prices fluctuate and schedules change; check the websites for details.

Goslar

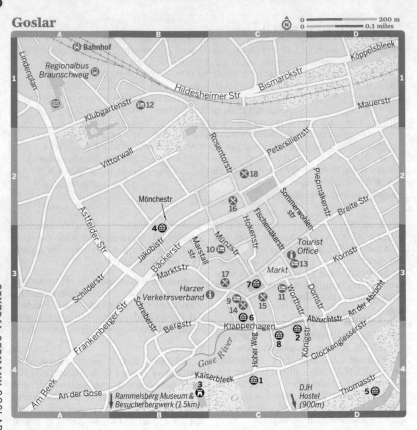

Goslar

◉ Sights
1 Domvorhalle	C4
2 Goslarer Museum	C4
3 Kaiserpfalz	B4
4 Mönchehaus Museum	B3
5 Museum im Zwinger	D4
6 Musikinstrumenten- und Puppenmuseum	C3
7 Rathaus	C3
8 Zinnfiguren-Museum	C4

🛏 Sleeping
9 Das Brusttuch	C3
10 Hotel Alte Münze	C3
11 Hotel Kaiserworth	C3
12 Niedersächsischer Hof	B1
13 Schiefer	C3

🍴 Eating
14 Barock-Café Anders	C3
15 Brauhaus	C3
16 Das Schwarze Schaf	C2
Die Butterhanne	(see 15)
17 Restaurant Aubergine	C3
18 Soup & Soul Kitchen	C2

Regionalbus Braunschweig (RBB; ☏ 05321-194 49; www.rbb-bus.de; Hildesheimer Strasse 6) The office of Regionalbus Braunschweig, from where buses depart, has free timetables for services throughout the Harz region. Bus 831 runs between Goslar and Altenau in the south via Clausthal-Zellerfeld; 830 runs to Clausthal-Zellerfeld via Hahnenklee. Change to the 840 at Clausthal-Zellerfeld for St Andreasberg.

CAR & MOTORCYCLE
The B6 runs north to Hildesheim and east to Bad Harzburg, Wernigerode and Quedlinburg. The north–south A7 is reached via the B82. For Hahnenklee, take the B241.

TRAIN

Bad Harzburg–Hanover trains stop here often, as do trains on the Braunschweig–Göttingen line. There are direct trains to Wernigerode (€10, 40 minutes, every two hours) and other services requiring a change at Vienenburg.

ⓘ Getting Around

Local bus tickets cost €2.40. To book a taxi, ring ☑1313 or try www.bettertaxi.de.

Bad Harzburg

☑ 05322 / POP 17,300

Parts of this quiet mountain spa town, just 9km from Goslar, could use a little TLC, but it remains in favour with visitors seeking the healing properties of its curative spas. Otherwise, the main attraction is the nearby Harz National Park and its trails, which offer excellent access to some typically picturesque Harz landscapes.

⊙ Sights & Activities

Marked hiking trails lead into the national park from Berliner Platz. Popular trails include those to Sennhütte (1.3km), Molkenhaus (3km) and scenic Rabenklippe (7km), overlooking the Ecker Valley. Molkenhaus and Rabenklippe have restaurants.

★ **Baumwipfelpad** FOREST
(☑05322-877 7920; Nordhäuser Strasse 2d; adult/concession €8/7.50; ⊙10am-4pm) The Harz' newest attraction, opened in May 2015, this 1km-long elevated walking trail traverses 18 platforms and bridges to reach an observation platform 26m up among the ancient treetops of the Kalten Valley.

Grosser Burgberg RUIN
(cable car adult/child return €3/2; ⊙9am-5pm) Take the pleasant 3km walk (or hop the cable car) from town to the summit of this hill, which boasts the ruins of an 11th-century fortress built by Heinrich IV. From there you can stroll around the fortress ruins or set out on longer hikes or mountain-bike rides.

From here, the Kaiserweg trail leads to Torfhaus and connects to the Brocken. If snow conditions are good, it's possible to ski cross-country to/from Torfhaus, which has equipment-hire facilities.

Sole Therme SPA
(☑05322-753 30; www.sole-therme-bad-harzburg. de; Nordhäuser Strasse 3; sauna & therme €13; ⊙8am-9pm Mon-Sat, to 7pm Sun) This local mega-spa has mildly heated indoor and outdoor saltwater pools and six types of sauna, including a salt grotto: rub a handful of white gold onto your skin, let it do the trick, then wash it off in the water cascade. Remember: wear bathers in the pool, but not in the sauna.

🛏 Sleeping & Eating

Plumbohms HOTEL $$
(☑05322-3277; www.plumbohms.de; Herzog-Wilhelm-Strasse 97; s/d from €95/120; P❄🛜🏊) These pleasant suites, featuring natural fittings and fibres, enjoy a central location.

Hotel Tannenhof-Solehotel HOTEL $$
(☑05322-968 80; www.solehotels.de; Nordhäuser Strasse 6; s/d from €74/124; P🛜) If you're coming to town to soak in the waters or bake in the sauna, this is the only hotel with direct access to the town's famed pools. Rooms vary in size and decor. Suites on the top level have been recently refurbished.

Albert's Corner GERMAN $$
(☑05322-516 98; www.alberts-corner.de; Herzog-Wilhelm-Strasse 118; mains €7-19) There's something about humble Albert's that just beckons you to enter: you'll be greeted warmly and can relax and sip on a hot drink or cold beer, soaking up the woodsy mountain atmosphere. When it's time to eat, tuck into fish, schnitzel or a steak that won't break the bank.

Braunschweiger Hof MODERN EUROPEAN $$$
(☑05322-7880; www.hotel-braunschweiger-hof. de; Herzog-Wilhelm-Strasse 54; mains €10-24; ⊙noon-2.30pm & 5-10pm; P🛜) Possibly Bad Harzburg's finest dining can be found here in the Braunschweiger Hof hotel. Select from a diverse menu of modern German and European cuisine that caters to even the most discerning palate.

ⓘ Information

Haus der Natur (☑05322-784 337; www. haus-der-natur-harz.de; Berliner Platz; adult/concession €3/1; ⊙10am-5pm Tue-Sun) Harz National Park information centre, with a small interactive exhibition that kids will enjoy.

Tourist Office (☑05322-753 30; www.bad-harzburg.de; Nordhäuser Strasse 4; ⊙9am-6pm Mon-Fri, 10am-4pm Sat & Sun)

ⓘ Getting There & Around

BICYCLE

Bike House Harz (☑05322-987 0623; www. bike-house-harz.de; Ilsenburger Strasse 112; bikes per day from €25)

BUS

Bus 810 leaves Bad Harzburg regularly for Goslar (€3.90, 20 minutes) and travels via the cable-car station; bus 260/874 heads for Wernigerode (€4.60, one hour). Bus 820 shuttles almost hourly to Torfhaus (€4, 25 minutes).

CAR

Bad Harzburg is on the A395 to Braunschweig; the B4 and B6 lead to Torfhaus and Wernigerode, respectively.

TRAIN

Frequent train services link Bad Harzburg with Goslar (€3.90, 12 minutes), Hanover (€21, 1¼ hours), Braunschweig (€13.10, 45 minutes) and Wernigerode (€8.10, 30 minutes).

Wernigerode

☑03943 / POP 35,050

The Central Harz area is mostly within former East Germany and the major hub here is Wernigerode. A bustling, attractive town on the northern edge of the Harz, Wernigerode is a good starting point for exploring the eastern regions of the Harz National Park. The winding streets of the Altstadt are flanked by pretty half-timbered houses, and high above the Altstadt hovers a romantic ducal castle from the 12th century. This is the northern terminus of the steam-powered narrow-gauge *Harzquerbahn,* which has chugged along the breadth of the Harz for almost a century; the line to the summit of the Brocken (1142m), the highest peak in northern Germany, also starts here.

◉ Sights

Marktplatz   SQUARE

Dominating Wernigerode's town square, the spectacular towered **Rathaus** began life as a theatre around 1277, only to be given its mostly late-Gothic features in the 16th century. The artisan who carved its 33 wooden figures is said to have fallen foul of the authorities; if you look closely you can see a few of his mocking touches. The neo-Gothic **fountain** (1848) was dedicated to charitable nobles, whose names and coats of arms are immortalised on it.

★ Schloss Wernigerode   CASTLE

(☑03943-553 040; www.schloss-wernigerode.de; adult/concession €6/5, tower €1; ☉10am-5pm, closed Mon Nov-Apr) Originally built in the 12th century to protect German Kaisers on hunting expeditions, Schloss Wernigerode was enlarged over the years to reflect late-Gothic

and Renaissance tastes. Its fairy-tale facade came courtesy of Count Otto of Stolberg-Wernigerode in the 19th century. The museum inside includes portraits of Kaisers, beautiful panelled rooms with original furnishings, the opulent **Festsaal** (Banquet Hall) and stunning **Schlosskirche** (1880), with its altar and pulpit made of French marble.

You can walk (1.5km) or take a Bimmelbahn wagon ride (adult/child return €5/2) from Marktstrasse. In summer, horse-drawn carts make the trek from Marktplatz.

Oberpfarrkirchhof   NEIGHBOURHOOD

Follow the small Klint south from Marktplatz (the street on the right-hand side if you face the town hall) past some historic buildings to eventually reach Oberpfarrkirchhof, which surrounds the Gothic- and later, neo-Gothic-styled **Sylvestrikirche**. Here you'll also find the **Gadenstedtsches Haus** (1582) with its Renaissance oriel on the south side of the neighbourhood.

Breite Strasse   NEIGHBOURHOOD

Essentially the main street of Wernigerode, Breite Strasse accommodates the pretty **Café Wien** building (1583) at number 4, today a dignified cafe and worthwhile stopover for both architectural and gastronomic reasons. It's almost impossible to miss the carved facade of the **Krummelsches Haus** at number 72, as it depicts various countries symbolically; America is portrayed, strangely enough, as a naked woman riding an armadillo.

🛏 Sleeping

Schlossidyll   PENSION $

(☑0162-925 7515; www.schlossidyll.net; Freilandstieg 14; d/apt from €49/79; [P][❄][🛜]) With views to the castle, this six-room boutique *Pension* in the hills above Wernigerode, a short walk from the Altstadt, could be one of the town's best-kept secrets. Spacious rooms and apartments boast stylish, quality furnishings and clever design. Breakfast is available and there's a jacuzzi and sauna on-site. Excellent value.

DJH Hostel   HOSTEL $

(☑03943-606 176; www.jugendherberge.de/jh/wernigerode; Am Eichberg 5; dm under/over 27yr €21/24, linen €3.50; [🛜]) On the edge of the forest about 2.5km west of town in Hasserode, this hostel has two-, three- and four-bed dorms with bathrooms. There's also a sauna and solarium here, and nearby is the large Brockenbad swimming complex. Take bus 1 or 4 to Hochschule Harz and follow the signs for 500m.

NARROW-GAUGE RAILWAYS

Fans of old-time trains will be in their element on any of the three narrow-gauge railways crossing the Harz. This 140km integrated network – the largest in Europe – is served by 25 steam and 10 diesel locomotives, which tackle gradients of up to 1:25 (40%) and curves as tight as 60m in radius. Most locomotives date from the 1950s, but eight historic models, some from as early as 1897, are proudly rolled out for special occasions.

The network, a legacy of the GDR, consists of three lines.

The **Harzquerbahn** runs 60km on a north–south route between Wernigerode and Nordhausen. The serpentine 14km between Wernigerode and Drei Annen Hohne includes 72 bends; you'll get dropped off on the edge of Harz National Park.

From the junction at Drei Annen Hohne, the **Brockenbahn** begins the steep climb to Schierke and the Brocken. Trains to the Brocken (via Drei Annen Hohne) can be picked up from Wernigerode and Nordhausen; single/return tickets cost €24/12 from all stations. Many visitors take the train to Schierke and then follow a trail on foot to the Brocken summit (1142m).

The third service is the **Selketalbahn**, which begins in Quedlinburg and runs to Eisfelder Talmühle or Hasselfelde. At Eisfelder Tal, you can change trains for other lines. The picturesque Selketalbahn crosses the plain to Gernrode and follows Wellbach, a creek with a couple of good swimming holes, through deciduous forest to Mägdesprung, before joining the Selke Valley and climbing past Alexisbad to high plains around Friedrichshöhe, Stiege and beyond.

Passes for three/five days on all three lines cost €74/111 per adult (children half-price). Check in with the folks at **Harzer Schmalspurbahnen** (☏ 5580; www.hsb-wr.de; Hauptbahnhof, Wernigerode) for timetables.

★ **Hotel Gothisches Haus** LUXURY HOTEL **$$**
(☏ 03943-6750; www.travelcharme.com; Am Markt 1; s/d from €99/129, ste from €275; P ❄ 🛜) The warm Tuscan colours and thoughtful design of this luxury hotel make it a very attractive option, and the wellness area is hard to beat, with three saunas and a 'beach' with real sand.

HKK Hotel Wernigerode HOTEL **$$**
(☏ 03943-9410; www.hkk-wr.de; Pfarrstrasse 41; s/d incl breakfast €82/112; P ❄ 🛜) This modern 258-room conference hotel is popular with bus and tour groups. It has spacious rooms, fast free wi-fi, and a convenient location a few minutes' walk from the Altstadt and station.

✖ Eating & Drinking

Orchidea Huong VIETNAMESE, JAPANESE **$$**
(☏ 03943-625 162; www.orchidea-huong.de; Klintgasse 1; mains €9-24; ⊙ 5-10pm Mon & Wed-Fri, noon-3pm & 5-10pm Sat & Sun) If you need a break from heavy German food, this interesting establishment incorporates Restaurants Lan (Vietnamese) and Hanazono (Japanese). For authenticity, err on the Vietnamese side, though the Japanese menu is also well executed.

Casa Vita MEDITERRANEAN **$$**
(www.casa-vita-wr.de; Marktstrasse 35; mains €8-18; ⊙ 5-10pm; 🖋) This bistro and bar has an attractive, spacious interior, a courtyard and a beer garden – all rounded off with a homely Mediterranean ambience. There's a diverse menu including a number of pizzas, many under €10, and a range of vegetarian options.

Weisser Hirsch GERMAN **$$**
(☏ 03943-602 020; www.hotel-weisser-hirsch.de; Marktplatz 5; mains €11-24; ⊙ 11am-10pm) Crisp white tablecloths, glistening cutlery and wild hare on the menu underscore a traditional but enticing culinary approach at the 'White Stag'. Four- and five-course menus are available (from €24.50 to €50). It's popular with travel groups, so it can be hit and miss with timing, and you may have to wait. Reservations advised.

Bodega SPANISH **$$**
(☏ 03943-9492 6330; www.bodega-wernigerode. de; Marktstrasse 12; tapas from €3.90, mains €9-19; ⊙ 5-10pm Tue-Fri & Sun, noon-10pm Sat) For authentic Spanish flavours and ambience, look no further than this popular, atmospheric hang-out, with tapas to share, vegetarian options, and plenty of seafood and meat on the menu.

Brauhaus PUB
(☏ 695 727; www.brauhaus-wernigerode.de; Breite Strasse 24; ⊙ 11.30am-midnight) This sprawling, multilevel pub has a dance floor upstairs on

Saturday nights. The Sky sportsbar on the 2nd floor is a popular haunt for watching local and international matches. Meals are available.

❶ Information

Post Office (Burgstrasse 19; ⏱ 9am-6pm Mon-Fri, to 12.30pm Sat)

Tourist Office (☎ 03943-553 7835; www.wernigerode-tourismus.com; Marktplatz 10; ⏱ 9am-7pm Mon-Fri, 10am-4pm Sat, to 3pm Sun) Tourist information, free map and free room-booking service.

❶ Getting There & Around

BICYCLE

Bad-Bikes (☎ 03943-626 868; www.badbikes-online.de; Breite Strasse 48a; bikes per day from €20)

BUS

Bus 253 runs to Blankenburg and Thale, while bus 257 serves Drei Annen Hohne and Schierke.

In town, buses 1 and 2 run from the bus station to the Rendezvous bus stop just north of the Markt, connecting with bus 3. Tickets cost €1.20 or are free with the Kurkarte, which your hotel will provide upon check-in.

TAXI

Call ☎ 03943-633 053 or try www.bettertaxi.de.

TRAIN

There are frequent trains to Goslar (€10, 40 minutes) and Halle (€23.20, 1¼ hours). Change at Halberstadt for Quedlinburg (€10, 45 minutes) and Thale (€12.10, one hour).

Schierke

☎ 039455 / POP 600

Just 16km southwest of Wernigerode, in the foothills of the Brocken at an altitude of 650m, Schierke is a popular starting point for hiking explorations within the Harz National Park and up the mountain. A rambling, mostly modern village, it's the last stop for the Brockenbahn before it climbs to the summit. Schierke has an upper town on the main road to the Brocken and a lower town in the valley of the Kalte Bode River.

🏃 Activities

Hiking   HIKING

You can hike to the Brocken via the bitumen Brockenstrasse (12km), closed to private cars and motorcycles. More interesting is the 7km hike via Eckerloch. Marked trails also lead to the rugged rock formations of Feuer-steinklippen (30 minutes from the Kurverwaltung) and Schnarcherklippen (1½ hours).

On the night of 30 April, **Walpurgisnacht**, Schierke attracts a veritable throng of visitors, most of whom set off on walking tracks to the Brocken.

Cross-Country Ski Hire   SKIING
(☎ 039455-409; Brockenstrasse 14a; per day from €15; ⏱ 9am-5pm Mon-Fri) Winter cross-country ski hire is available from an outlet alongside the Stöber Eck store.

❶ Information

Nationalparkhaus Schierke (☎ 039455-477; Brockenstrasse; ⏱ 8.30am-4.30pm) The mother lode of hiking brochures and information on the national park; 1km north of the tourist office toward the Brocken.

Tourist Office (☎ 039455-8680; www.schierke-am-brocken.de; Brockenstrasse 10; ⏱ 9am-noon & 1-4pm Mon-Fri, 10am-noon & 2-4pm Sat, 10am-noon Sun) Find trail maps and brochures and book accommodation here.

❶ Getting There & Around

The frequent bus 257 connects Schierke with Wernigerode (€2.90, 30 to 45 minutes). Narrow-gauge railway services run between Wernigerode and Schierke (single/return €10/15, one hour).

Driving from the west, take the B27 from Braunlage and turn off at Elend. From Wernigerode, take Friedrichstrasse.

Quedlinburg

☎ 03946 / POP 25,920

Little Quedlinburg, situated on a fertile plain at the northern cusp of the Harz Mountains, is the most spectacular of the historic towns in the Harz region. Since becoming a Unesco World Heritage site in 1994, restoration of the 1400 or so centuries-old half-timbered houses lining the town's cobblestone streets is largely complete, and the spectacular, intact Altstadt now has a wonderful mix of original, innovative options for wining, dining and resting your head.

In the 10th century the Reich was briefly ruled from here by two women, Theophano and Adelheid, successive guardians of the child-king Otto III. Quedlinburg itself is closely associated with the *Frauenstift,* a medieval foundation for widows and daughters of the nobility that enjoyed the direct protection of the Kaiser.

QUEDLINBURG'S HISTORIC BUILDINGS

With so many historic buildings, Quedlinburg is one town in which it's nice just to stroll the streets and soak up the atmosphere. The **Rathaus** (1320) dominates Markt, and in front of this is a **Roland statue** from 1426. Just behind the Rathaus is the **Marktkirche St Benedikti** (1233), and nearby is the **Gildehaus zur Rose** (1612) at Breite Strasse 39. Running off Markt is the tiny **Schuhhof**, a shoemakers' courtyard, with shutters and stablelike 'gossip doors'. **Alter Klopstock** (1580), which is found at Stieg 28, has scrolled beams typical of Quedlinburg's 16th-century half-timbered houses.

From Stieg 28 (just north of Schuhhof), it's a short walk north along Pölle to **Zwischen den Städten**, a historic bridge connecting the old town and Neustadt, which developed alongside the town wall around 1200 when peasants fled a feudal power struggle on the land. Behind the Renaissance facade, tower and stone gables of the **Hagensches Freihaus** (1558) is now the Hotel Quedlinburger Stadtschloss. Many houses in this part of town have high archways and courtyards dotted with pigeon towers. A couple of other places of special note are the **Hotel zur Goldenen Sonne** building (1671) at Steinweg 11 and **Zur Börse** (1683) at number 23.

Although the Altstadt gets crowded in summer and on weekends, Quedlinburg is always worth a visit. On quieter weekdays and in spring or autumn, it's the perfect spot to stop for a night or two.

⊙ Sights

Stiftskirche St Servatius CHURCH
(☑ 03946-2730; Schlossberg 1; adult/concession €4.50/3; ⊙ 10am-6pm Tue-Sat) This 12th-century church is one of Germany's most significant from the Romanesque period. Its treasury contains valuable reliquaries and early bibles. The crypt has some early religious frescos and contains the graves of Heinrich and his widow, Mathilde, along with those of the abbesses.

Schlossmuseum MUSEUM
(☑ 03946-905 681; Schlossberg 1; adult/concession €4.50/3; ⊙ 10am-5pm) The Schlossberg, on a 25m-high plateau above Quedlinburg, was first graced with a church and residence under Henry the Fowler. The present-day Renaissance Schloss contains the Schlossmuseum, with some fascinating Ottonian-period exhibits dating from 919. A multimedia display explains how the Nazis used the site for propaganda by staging a series of events to celebrate Heinrich, whose life they skewed to justify their own ideology and crimes.

Fachwerkmuseum im Ständerbau MUSEUM
(☑ 03946-3828; Wordgasse 3; adult/concession €3/2; ⊙ 10am-5pm Fri-Wed) Germany's earliest half-timbered houses were built using high perpendicular struts. The building from 1310 that now houses the Fachwerkmuseum im Ständebau is a perfect illustration of this,

and inside there are exhibits on the style and construction technique.

Lyonel-Feininger-Galerie GALLERY
(☑ 03946-689 5930; www.feininger-galerie.de; Finkenherd 5a; adult/concession €6/3; ⊙ 10am-5pm Wed-Mon) This purpose-built gallery exhibits the work of influential Bauhaus artist Lyonel Feininger (1871–1956). Feininger was born in New York and came to Germany at the age of 16, later fleeing the Nazis and returning to the US in 1937. The original graphics, drawings, watercolours and sketches on display are from the period 1906 to 1936.

Klopstockhaus MUSEUM
(☑ 03946-905 691; Schlossberg 12; adult/concession €3.50/2.60; ⊙ 10am-5pm Wed-Sun) The early classicist poet Friedrich Gottlieb Klopstock (1724–1803) is one of Quedlinburg's most celebrated sons. He was born in this 16th-century house, which is now a museum containing some interesting exhibits on Klopstock himself and Dorothea Erxleben (1715–62), Germany's first female doctor.

✪ Festivals & Events

A program of classical music is held in the Stiftskirche every year from June to September. For tickets and information, contact the tourist office.

🛏 Sleeping

★**Hotel am Hoken** HOTEL $
(☑ 03946-525 40; www.hotel-am-hoken.de; Hoken 3; s/d from €49/69; 🅿 ❀ 🛜) This wonderfully romantic hotel off Markt exemplifies traditional style and elegance, and has warm,

accommodating staff, but it's not for everyone: floors and furnishings are in attractive timber, which means everything creaks a little, and due to the building's age, there's only a narrow winding staircase to reach the rooms.

Hotel zur Goldenen Sonne   HOTEL $

(☏ 03946-962 50; www.hotelzurgoldenensonne.de; Steinweg 11; s/d from €49/69; ℗) Both the old and new buildings of this hotel have decent rooms, but those in the old building are better.

DJH Hostel   HOSTEL $

(☏ 03946-811 703; www.jugendherberge-quedlinburg.de; Neuendorf 28; dm under/over 27yr €19.50/22.50, linen €3.50) This excellent DJH hostel offers four- and 10-bed dorms in a quiet and very central location. It's relatively small and fills quickly in summer.

Romantik Hotel am Brühl   BOUTIQUE HOTEL $$

(☏ 03946-961 80; www.hotelambruehl.de; Billungstrasse 11; s/d/apt from €86/113/176; ℗✳🛜) Well-appointed, spacious rooms and suites are individually styled in this impressive boutique hotel on the outskirts of the Altstadt. The apartments are an excellent option for those traveling with children or in a small group. A plentiful breakfast buffet is included.

Hotel Zum Bär   HOTEL $$

(☏ 03946-7770; www.hotelzumbaer.de; Markt 8-9; s/d from €58/70; ℗🛜) Expect spacious, well-styled rooms and a good mid-priced restaurant downstairs in this traditional hotel in the heart of the old town.

Ringhotel Theophano   HOTEL $$

(☏ 03946-963 00; www.hoteltheophano.de; Markt 13-14; s/d from €69/99; ℗@🛜) Each room is decorated in individual style at this rambling, rustic hotel. Most are spacious and very comfortable, but the many staircases (no lift) and low thresholds might be a problem for some. Doubles are reduced Sunday to Thursday.

Wyndam Garden Quedlinburger Stadtschloss   HOTEL $$

(☏ 03946-526 00; www.wyndham.com; Bockstrasse 6/Klink 11; d from €64; ℗🛜) Tasteful features and the wellness area (including Finnish sauna, steam bath and whirlpool) of this hotel in a restored Renaissance residence make it worth considering.

✖ Eating

Heilemann's FachwerQ   ITALIAN $

(☏ 03946-519 8051; www.fachwerq-quedlinburg.de; Markstrasse 10; bruschetta €6-12; ⊙10am-8pm Wed-Mon; 🖉) This awesome little bruschetta-ria overlooking the Marktkirche St Benedikti doles out a clever selection of delicious bruschetta on freshly baked bread, with local tomatoes and other goodies. Pasta, wine, coffee and beer are also served.

Mom's Burgers   BURGERS $

(☏ 03946-528 2415; www.momsburger.de; Marktstrasse 15; burgers €4.50-11; ⊙noon-7pm) The name says it all: if you're craving a burger without the fast-food feel, this cute little hole-in-the-wall will likely satisfy. It's sweet and squeaky clean, and the burgers are pretty darn good, made from fresh, locally sourced ingredients.

Kartoffelhaus No 1   GERMAN $

(☏ 03946-708 334; www.kartoffelhausno1.de; Breite Strasse 37; dishes €4-12; ⊙11am-midnight) Tasty potato and grill dishes – nothing more, nothing less – are served here in large quantities. Enter from Klink.

Münzenberger Klause   GERMAN $$

(www.muenzenberger-klause.de; Pölle 22; mains €9-18; ⊙11am-11pm Tue-Sat) Serving traditional German fare, this atmospheric restaurant is loved by locals and visitors alike. If you're seeking hearty comfort food, look no further.

Brauhaus Lüdde   GERMAN $$

(☏ 03946-705 206; www.hotel-brauhaus-luedde.de; Blasiistrasse 14; mains €9-18; ⊙11am-midnight Mon-Sat, to 10pm Sun) After the arrival of a coach group, the average age can soar to 70 years, decreasing slowly as the night grinds on in this lively microbrewery. Decent food and good boutique beer (despite some rather flatulent names for the local drop) are the order of the day in Lüdde.

Hössler   SEAFOOD $$

(☏ 03946-915 255; Steinbrücke 21; mains €7-15; ⊙8am-7.30pm Mon-Fri, 9am-8pm Sat, 2-7pm Sun) This is an excellent fish cafeteria, with a restaurant through the passage. The same meals are cheaper in the front section. It doesn't look much from the outside, but the fish is delish and the portions are generous.

Zum Roland   CAFE $$

(☏ 03946-4532; www.cafe-roland.de; Breite Strasse 2-6; cakes from €4, mains €8-15; ⊙10am-10pm; 🖐) Sprawling through seven houses, this cafe does decent if unspectacular international nosh and a delicious apple strudel. There's a kid's table and small play area.

Zum Goldenen Drachen   CHINESE $$
(✆03946-700 386; Schmale Strasse 1a; dishes €6.50 15; ⊙noon-9pm; ✐) There's nothing mind-blowing about this Chinese restaurant, but it's not disappointing either. There's lots of vegetarian options if you're needing a break from all the meat and cheese. Convenient and inexpensive.

ℹ Information

Post Office (Bahnhofstrasse; ⊙9am-6pm Mon-Fri, to noon Sat)

Tourist Office (✆03946-905 625; www. quedlinburg.de; Markt 2; ⊙9.30am-6pm Mon-Fri, to 3pm Sat, to 2pm Sun) Tourist information, maps and guided tours to sights.

ℹ Getting There & Away

BUS

The bus office inside the train station hall has timetables and information. Buses to Thale leave from the bridge in front of the train station (stops 8 and 9).

CAR

The Strasse der Romanik (Romanesque Road; not to be confused with the Romantic Road in Bavaria) theme road follows the L239 south to Gernrode and connects towns that have significant Romanesque architecture. The B6 runs west to Wernigerode, Goslar, the A395 (for Braunschweig) and the A7 between Kassel and Hanover. For Halle take the B6 east, and for Halberstadt the B79 north.

TRAIN

From Quedlinburg there are frequent services to Thale (€2.50, 12 minutes). For trains to Wernigerode (€10, 40 minutes), change at Halberstadt. The narrow-gauge *Selketalbahn* (p573) runs to Gernrode (€5, 15 minutes) and beyond. There are no left-luggage lockers, and the station hall isn't always open.

ℹ Getting Around

It's easy to wander around the Aldstadt, indeed, there are many sections where vehicles are not permitted. **2Rad Pavillon** (✆03946-709 507; www.zweiradpavillon.de; Bahnhofstrasse 1b; bikes per day from €10; ⊙9am-6pm Mon-Fri, 9.30am-noon Sat) hires out bicycles.

Gernrode

✆039485 / POP 5600

With a magnificent Romanesque church and, inexplicably, the world's largest wooden thermometer and largest Skat (a card game) table, Gernrode makes an ideal day trip only a short 8km hop south of Quedlinburg. Hikers and picnickers will enjoy this pretty town and, for steam-train enthusiasts, it is a lovely place to pick up the narrow-gauge railway if you're planning to travel deeper into the mountains.

◉ Sights

Stiftskirche St Cyriakus   CHURCH
(Burgstrasse 3; guided tour €3; ⊙9am-5pm Mon-Sat, noon-5pm Sun Apr-Oct, tours 3pm daily year-round) This church is one of the purest examples of Romanesque architecture from the Ottonian period. Construction of the basilica, which is based on the form of a cross, was begun in 959. Especially noteworthy is the early use of alternating columns and pillars, later a common Romanesque feature. The octagonal **Taufstein** (Christening stone), whose religious motifs culminate in the Ascension, dates from 1150. You can also see enclosed in glass **Das Heilige Grab**, an 11th-century replica of Christ's tomb in Jerusalem.

ℹ Information

Tourist Office (✆039485-354; www.gernrode. de; Suderode Strasse 8; ⊙9am-4pm Mon-Fri) The tourist office is a 10-minute walk from the Hauptbahnhof and another 10 minutes from the town centre.

ℹ Getting There & Away

Regular bus services for Thale and Quedlinburg stop at the Hauptbahnhof and in the town centre. The *Selketalbahn* (p573) passes through Gernrode from Quedlinburg; buy tickets at the Hauptbahnhof.

Thale

✆03947 / POP 10,300

Situated below the northern slopes of the Harz Mountains, once-industrial Thale has turned to tourism for its future. Its main attraction is the sensational landscape of rugged cliffs flanking the Bode River, and a lush valley ideal for hiking.

The two cliffs at the head of the valley are known as Hexentanzplatz and Rosstrappe. These once boasted Celtic fortresses and were used by Germanic tribes for occult rituals and sacrifices.

Postmodern pagans gather in grand style and numbers each year on 30 April to celebrate **Walpurgisnacht** here.

⊙ Sights & Activities

Hexentanzplatz — LOOKOUT
(cable car return €5.50; ⊘ 9.30am-6pm) Of the two rocky bluffs flanking the Bode Valley, Hexentanzplatz is the most developed and popular. Take the cable car to the top for spectacular views and crisp, fresh air.

Rosstrappe — LOOKOUT
(chairlift return €3.80; ⊘ 9.30am-6pm Easter-Sep, 10am-4.30pm Oct-Easter) Rosstrappe takes its name from what is supposedly a horse's hoof print, visible in stone on the cliff, left by the mythical Brunhilde when she sprang over the gorge on horseback to avoid marrying the giant Bodo. Considering that Bodo, who leapt after her, landed in a watery grave, horse and all, you're probably better off taking the chairlift or one of the trails up here. Go early or late in the day to avoid crowds.

Signs direct you to the chairlift from the Thale Hauptbahnhof, near where the **Presidentenweg** hiking trail also begins.

Hexensteig — WALKING
The Bode Valley Hexensteig walking trail (blue triangle, 10km) between Thale and Treseburg is highly recommended. If you take the bus from Thale to Treseburg, you can walk downstream and enjoy the most spectacular scenery at the end. WVB bus 264 does the trip from April to early November, and QBus 18 runs via Hexentanzplatz from April to October.

Another 10km trail (red dot) goes from Hexentanzplatz to Treseburg; combine with the valley walk to make a round trip.

ℹ Information

Tourist Office (☑ 03947-776 8000; www.bodetal.de; Bahnhofstrasse 1; ⊘ 8am-6pm Mon-Fri, 9am-3pm Sat & Sun) Pick up the English-language brochure *LegendaryThale*, or book a themed tour with a witch.

ℹ Getting There & Around

BUS
The bus station is located alongside the train station. For Wernigerode, take bus WVB 253.

CAR
Karl-Marx-Strasse leads to the main junction for roads to Quedlinburg and Wernigerode.

TAXI
Call ☑ 2505 or 2435 or try www.bettertaxi.de.

TRAIN
Frequent trains travel to Quedlinburg (€2.70, 12 minutes) and Wernigerode (change in Halberstadt; €12.10, one hour).

SAXONY-ANHALT

This otherwise unassuming region in the former GDR is best known today for Lutherstadt Eisleben and Lutherstadt Wit-

---

WALPURGISNACHT

The Bode Valley was first inhabited by Celts, whose fortresses were conquered by Germanic tribes and used for pagan rituals before Charlemagne embarked upon campaigns to subjugate and Christianise the local population during the 8th-century Saxon Wars. Today Harz mythology blends these pagan and Christian elements.

One popular – but misleading – explanation for the Walpurgisnacht festival (a pagan festival held on the night of 30 April, when everyone dresses up as witches and warlocks) is that it was an invention of the tribes who, pursued by Christian missionaries, held secret gatherings to carry out their rituals. They are said to have darkened their faces one night and, armed with broomsticks and pitchforks, scared off Charlemagne's guards, who mistook them for witches and devils. In fact the name 'Walpurgisnacht' probably derives from St Walpurga, an 8th-century abbess, but the festival tradition may also refer to the wedding of the gods Wodan and Freya.

According to local mythology, witches and warlocks gather on Walpurgisnacht at locations throughout the Harz before flying off to the Brocken on broomsticks or goats. There they recount the year's evil deeds and top off the stories with a bacchanalian frenzy, said to represent copulation with the devil. Frightened peasants used to hang crosses and herbs on stable doors to protect their livestock; ringing church bells or cracking whips were other ways to prevent stray witches from dropping by!

Head to the Harz on 30 April today and you'll be swept up in a sea of strange faces, dark-cloaked goths, squealing teens and spooky families: think Halloween on a mountaintop.

KZ-GEDENKSTÄTTE MITTELBAU DORA

During the final stages of WWII, when Hitler's grand plan turned to conducting war from underground bunkers, **KZ-Gedenkstätte Mittelbau Dora** (☏03631-495 820; www. dora.de/29; Kohnsteinweg 20, Nordhausen; ⊙10am-6pm Tue-Sun Apr-Sep, to 4pm Oct-Mar) was established as a satellite of the Buchenwald concentration camp (p553), after British bombers destroyed missile plants in Peenemünde. At least 20,000 prisoners were worked to their deaths here. After years of decay under the GDR, the memorial today gives an insight into the horrors that unfolded here, and includes a modern museum that explains the background of the camp and the experiences of the prisoners.

From late 1943, thousands of mostly Russian, French and Polish POWs (many who had survived Auschwitz) toiled under horrific conditions digging a 20km labyrinth of tunnels in the chalk hills north of Nordhausen, within which were built the V1 and V2 rockets that rained destruction on London, Antwerp and other cities during the final stages of the war. The US army reached the gates in April 1945, cared for survivors and removed all missile equipment before turning the area over to Russia.

Visitors are free to roam the grounds, crematorium and museum. The tunnels (which are the diameter of an aircraft hangar) are only accessible on free 90-minute guided tours, which run at 11am and 2pm Tuesday to Friday and at 11am, 1pm and 3pm on weekends. Within the dank walls you can see partially assembled rockets that have lain untouched for over 50 years.

There is limited public transport to the site, which is best reached by private vehicle. The nearest station (tram 10 and Harzquerbahn from Nordhausen) is Nordhausen-Krimderode, from where it's a 20-minute walk.

tenberg, two towns inextricably linked with religious reformer Martin Luther. The 500th anniversary of the Reformation in 2017 stimulated much restoration work in both of the Lutherstadts in preparation for an influx of Protestants from around the globe (see www.luther2017.de for more information).

History buffs could head also to Magdeburg, the state capital, and Halle, birthplace of heavyweight baroque composer Georg Händel. Both cities celebrated their 1200th birthdays in recent years and have invested much in improving their visual appeal and tourist infrastructure as a whole.

Students of architecture and lovers of design should beeline for Dessau-Rosslau, birthplace of Bauhaus and an easy day trip from Berlin.

Lutherstadt Wittenberg

☏ 03491 / POP 50,400

As its full name suggests, Wittenberg is first and foremost about Martin Luther (1483–1546), the monk who triggered the German Reformation by publishing his 95 theses against church corruption in 1517. A university town since 1502, Wittenberg back then was a hotbed of progressive thinking that also saw priests get married and educators

such as Luther's friend Philipp Melanchthon argue for schools to accept female pupils.

Today, Wittenberg retains its significance for the world's 340 million Protestants, including 66 million Lutherans, as well as for those who simply admire Luther for his principled stand against authority. Sometimes called the 'Rome of the Protestants', its many Reformation-related sites garnered the city World Heritage status in 1996.

◉ Sights & Activities

★ **Lutherhaus** MUSEUM
(☏03491-420 3118; www.martinluther.de; Collegienstrasse 54; adult/concession €6/4; ⊙9am-6pm) Even those with no previous interest in the Reformation will likely be fascinated by the state-of-the-art exhibits in the Lutherhaus, the former monastery turned Luther family home, operated as a museum since 1883. Through an engaging mix of accessible narrative, artefacts, famous oil paintings and interactive multimedia stations, you'll learn about the man, his times and his impact on world history. Highlights include Cranach's *Ten Commandments* in the refectory and an original room furnished by Luther in 1535.

Melanchthon Haus
MUSEUM

([☎]03491-420 3110; www.martinluther.de; Collegienstrasse 60; adult/concession €4/2.50; [⏱]10am-6pm) An expert in ancient languages, Philipp Melanchthon helped Luther translate the bible into German from Greek and Hebrew, becoming the preacher's friend and most eloquent advocate. This museum, expanded in 2013, occupies his former quarters. The historic wing authentically recreates the atmosphere in which Melanchthon lived. The modern annexe houses an exhibition on Melanchthon's life, work and influence.

Schlosskirche
CHURCH

(Castle Church; [☎]03491-402 585; www.schloss kirche-wittenberg.de; Schlossplatz; [⏱]10am-6pm Mon-Sat, 11.30am-6pm Sun) Did he or didn't he nail those 95 theses to the door of the Schlosskirche? We'll never know for sure, for the original portal was destroyed by fire in 1760 and replaced in 1858 with a massive bronze version inscribed with the theses in Latin. Luther himself is buried inside below the pulpit, opposite his friend and fellow reformer Philipp Melanchthon.

Under extensive restoration at the time of writing and with restricted visiting hours, the Schlosskirche is due to reopen before the 2017 celebrations commemorating the 500th anniversary of the Reformation; check the website for updates.

Stadtkirche Wittenberg
CHURCH

([☎]03491-628 30; www.stadtkirchengemein de-wittenberg.de; Jüdenstrasse 35; [⏱]10am-6pm Mon-Sat, 11.30am-6pm Sun) The Stadt- und Pfarrkirche St Marien (Stadtkirche Wittenberg) was where Martin Luther's ecumenical revolution began, with the world's first Protestant worship services in 1521. It was also here that Luther preached his famous Lectern sermons in 1522, and where he married ex-nun Katharina von Bora three years later. Ongoing renovations continue.

The church's centrepiece is the large altar, designed by Lucas Cranach the Elder and his son. The side facing the nave shows Luther, Melanchthon and other Reformation figures, as well as Cranach himself, in biblical contexts. The altar is also painted on its reverse side. On the lower rung, you'll see a seemingly defaced painting of heaven and hell; medieval students etched their initials into the painting's divine half if they passed their final exams, and into purgatory if they failed.

Haus der Geschichte
MUSEUM

(House of History; [☎]03491-409 004; www.pflug cv.de; Schlossstrasse 6; adult/concession €6/4.50; [⏱]10am-6pm Tue-Sun) If you want to catch a glimpse of daily life in the region, especially life beyond the former Iron Curtain, pop by the Haus der Geschichte. The ground floor has a long-running special exhibition on German–Russian relations (many Russian soldiers were stationed in Lutherstadt Wittenberg during the GDR era), and other sections have living rooms, kids' rooms and kitchens from the GDR era and before. The top floor is dedicated to children's toys from this same 60-year period.

Luthereiche
LANDMARK

(Luther Oak; cnr Lutherstrasse & Am Bahnhof) This oak tree marks the spot where, on 10 December 1520, Luther burned the papal bull (a treatise issued by then Pope Leo X ordering his excommunication) and a number of other books on church law; the tree itself was only planted around 1830.

Cranach-Höfe
GALLERY

(Markt 4; admission €4/3; [⏱]10am-5pm Mon-Sat, 1-5pm Sun) Lucas Cranach's old residential and work digs have been rebooted as a beautifully restored cultural complex built around two courtyards that often echo with music and readings. There's a permanent exhibit on the man, his life and his contemporaries.

Historische Druckerstube
GALLERY

(Historical Print Shop; Schlossstrasse 1; tour €2.50; [⏱]9am-noon & 1-5pm Mon-Fri, 10am-1.30pm Sat) This gallery is part of the Cranachhöfe complex of courtyards (accessed separately from the main courtyards). It sells ancient-looking black-and-white sketches of Martin Luther, both typeset and printed by hand. Take a tour to hear the owner explain the sketches and early printing techniques.

Hundertwasserschule
ARCHITECTURE

(Hundertwasser School; [☎]03491-877 780; www. hundertwasserschule.de; Strasse der Völkerfreundschaft 130; tours adult/concession €2/1; [⏱]1.30-4pm Tue-Fri, 10am-4pm Sat & Sun) How would you like to study grammar and algebra in a building where trees sprout from the windows and gilded onion domes balance above a rooftop garden? This fantastical environment is everyday reality for the lucky pupils of Wittenberg's Hundertwasserschule. It's the penultimate work of eccentric Viennese artist, architect and eco-visionary Friedensreich Hundertwasser, who was famous for

Lutherstadt Wittenberg

Lutherstadt Wittenberg

quite literally thinking 'outside the box'. In Wittenberg, he transformed a boxy GDR-era concrete monstrosity into this colourful and curvy dreamscape.

The school is a 20-minute walk northeast of the centre. From the Markt, head east on Jüdenstrasse, turn left into Neustrasse and continue into Geschwister-Scholl-Strasse. Turn left into Sternstrasse, right into Schillerstrasse, and the school is at the next intersection on the left. You can view the exterior any time, but tours of the interior wait for at least four participants before they start. Ring ahead for tours in English.

Trabant Tours DRIVING TOUR
(☑498 610; www.trabant-mieten.de; Schlossplatz 2; tours per 4hr from €55) *Good Bye, Lenin!* fans might get a kick out of negotiating Wittenberg's streets squeezed behind the wheel of a tinny East German Trabant car. Note that this is a self-drive option.

✨ Festivals & Events

Luthers Hochzeit RELIGIOUS
(www.lutherhochzeit.de) Wittenberg is busiest during Luther's Wedding Festival in early or mid-June.

Wittenberger Reformationsfest RELIGIOUS
(www.wittenberger-reformationsfest.de) Beginning on 31 October and running into November, this annual festival celebrates and commemorates the start of the Reformation.

🛏 Sleeping

The tourist office operates a free room reservation service. Private rooms start at €19 per person.

Am Schwanenteich
PENSION $

(☑ 03491 402 807; www.wittenberg-schwanenteich. de; Töpferstrasse 1; s/d from €43/84; P ❋ 🐾) If it's friendly, familiar ambience and pleasant, comfortable, spotlessly clean rooms you seek, this humble *Pension* fits the bill. Great value.

DJH Hostel
HOSTEL $

(☑ 03491-505 205; www.jugendherberge-wittenberg.de; Schlossstrasse 14/15; dm under/over 27yr €22/25; P @ 🐾) Wittenberg's excellent youth hostel has 40 bright rooms sleeping up to six people that come with bathrooms, reading lamps and private cabinets. Linen is included.

Stadthotel Wittenberg Schwarzer Baer
HOTEL $$

(☑ 03491-420 4344; www.stadthotel-wittenberg. de; Schlossstrasse 2; s/d €65/80; P 🐾) The modern rooms in this 500-year-old heritage-listed building (no lift) are light and airy, with wooden floors and cork headboards.

Alte Canzley
HOTEL $$

(☑ 03491-429 190; www.alte-canzley.de; Schlossplatz 3-5; s/d from €79/90; P @ 🐾) This lovely boutique hotel is located in a 14th-century building opposite the Schlosskirche. Each of the eight spacious units are furnished in dark woods and natural hues, named for a major historical figure and equipped with a kitchenette.

Luther Hotel
HOTEL $$

(☑ 03491-4580; www.luther-hotel-wittenberg.de; Neustrasse 7-10; s/d/ste from €89/109/155; P 🐾) You'll sleep like an angel in this sparkling, modern place affiliated with a Christian charity organisation. Expect good-sized and cheerfully coloured rooms, most of them with unimpeded Stadtkirche views. Some rooms have several beds, and there are also double junior suites. A sauna invites post-sightseeing unwinding. Internet performance, however, could do with some improvement.

WITTENBERG WORSHIP

Wittenberg English Ministry
(☑ 03491-498 610; www.wittenberg-english-ministry.com; Schlossplatz 2) From May to October, a changing roster of Lutheran guest preachers, usually from the US, hold free English-language services in Wittenberg's Schlosskirche or Stadtkirche.

🍴 Eating & Drinking

Bittersüss
CAFE $

(☑ 03491-876 4030; www.meinbittersuess.de; Schlossstrasse 22; items from €4; ⊙ noon-6pm Mon & Sun, to 10pm Tue-Sat; 🐾) There's not a lot of bitter but a whole lot of sweet to this handsome, family-run cafe-by-day (serving delicious cakes, waffles, coffee and ice-cream) and bar-by-night (with some easy libations for the grown-ups). There's free wi-fi, too.

Vino
MEDITERRANEAN $$

(☑ 03491-769 0565; www.restaurant-vino.de; Mittelstrasse 3; mains €8-19; ⊙ 5-11pm Mon-Sat) Antipasti, tapas, salads or pasta dishes form the perfect accompaniment to the global wine menu at this modern, upmarket bistro.

Brauhaus Wittenberg
GERMAN $$

(☑ 03491-433 130; www.brauhaus-wittenberg.de; Markt 6, Im Beyerhof; mains €8-18; ⊙ 11am-11pm) Wittenberg's brewhouse, with its cobbled courtyard, indoor brewery and shiny copper vats, thrums with the noise of people having a good time. The menu is hearty, but also features smaller dishes for waist-watchers. Oh, and there's beer also. Lots of fun.

Tante Emmas Bier- & Caféhaus
GERMAN $$

(☑ 03491-419 757; www.tante-emma-wittenberg. de; Markt 9; mains €9-17; ⊙ 9am-5pm Mon, to midnight Tue-Sun) Take a step back to the 'good old times' in this German country kitchen, where servers wear frilly white aprons and the room is chock-full of bric-a-brac – from dolls and books to irons and a gramophone.

Flower Power
BAR

(☑ 03491-660 666; www.flowerpower.eu; Bügermeisterstrasse 21; ⊙ 8pm-3am) Catch live bands, croon karaoke or hit the floor for a party in the town's grooviest venue.

Independent
BAR

(Collegienstrasse 44; ⊙ 11am-2am Mon-Sat, 5pm-2am Sun) Alt-flavoured pub among several interesting venues along Collegienstrasse.

ℹ️ Information

Post Office (Wilhelm-Weber-Strasse 1; ⊙ 9am-6pm Mon-Fri, to 12.30pm Sat)

Tourist Office (☑ 03491-498 610; www.wittenberg.de; Schlossplatz 2; ⊙ 9am-6pm Mon-Fri, 10am-4pm Sat & Sun)

ℹ️ Getting There & Around

Wittenberg is on the main train line to Halle and Leipzig (both €13.30, one hour). ICE (€31, 45

LUTHER LORE

It's been so often repeated that Luther nailed a copy of his revolutionary theses to the door of Wittenberg's Schlosskirche on 31 October 1517 that only serious scholars continue to argue to the contrary. Certainly, Luther did write 95 theses challenging some of the Catholic practices of the time, especially the selling of 'indulgences' to forgive sins and reduce the buyer's time in purgatory. However, it's another question entirely as to whether he publicised them in the way popular legend suggests.

Believers point to the fact that the Schlosskirche's door was used as a bulletin board of sorts by the university, that the alleged posting took place the day before the affluent congregation poured into the church on All Saints' Day (1 November), and the fact that at Luther's funeral, his influential friend Philipp Melanchthon said he witnessed Luther's deed. But Melanchthon didn't arrive in town until 1518 – the year *after* the supposed event. It's also odd that Luther's writings never once mentioned such a highly radical act.

While it is known that he sent his theses to the local archbishop to provoke discussion, some locals think it would have been out of character for a devout monk, interested mainly in an honest debate, to challenge the system so flagrantly without first exhausting all options. In any event, nailed to the church door or not, the net effect of Luther's theses was the same. They triggered the Reformation and Protestantism, altering the way that large sections of the world's Christian population worship to this day.

minutes) and RE trains (€23.50, 1¼ hours) travel to Berlin. Coming from Berlin, be sure to board for 'Lutherstadt Wittenberg', as there's also a Wittenberge west of the capital.

The town itself is tiny and best explored on foot or by bike. Parking enforcement is quite stringent, so use the car parks on the fringes of the Altstadt (such as near Elbtor and along Fleischerstrasse).

Fahrradhaus Kralisch (☑ 403 703; www.fahrradhaus-kralisch.de; Jüdenstrasse 11; bikes per 24hr €7; ☉ 9am-6pm Mon-Fri, to noon Sat)

Dessau-Rosslau

☑ 0340 / POP 86,030

Officially known as Dessau-Rosslau since the 2007 merger with its neighbour across the Elbe, this little town was the birthplace of the most influential design school of the 20th century – Bauhaus. A mecca for architecture and design students, there's nowhere else you'll find a greater concentration of structures from Bauhaus' most creative period: 1925 to 1932.

Dessau-Rosslau is an easy day trip from Berlin, but spending a night in the area will allow more time to contemplate the beauty of the stark, utilitarian Bauhaus sites in contrast to the opulent splendour of the numerous palaces of the surrounding Garden Realm.

The Bauhaus mainstay is an easy walk west of the Hauptbahnhof. The town centre is southeast, about 15-minutes away. Pedestrianised Zerbster Strasse is the main drag, leading to the Markt, town hall and the Rathaus-Center shopping mall.

⦿ Sights

There are three main Bauhaus locations in Dessau-Rosslau: the Bauhausgebäude, where it all started, the Meisterhäuser (Master's Houses) and the Törten Estate.

Exemplifying the Bauhaus credo of 'design for living', four of the original seven Meisterhäuser, where the Bauhaus' leading lights lived as neighbours, have been reconstructed after years of decay: Gropiushaus, Haus Feininger, Haus Muche/Schlemmer and Haus Kandinsky/Klee. They can be found on leafy Ebertallee, a 15-minute walk west of the Hauptbahnhof.

★ **Bauhausgebäude**   ARCHITECTURE
(Bauhaus Building; ☑ 0340 650 8250; www.bauhaus-dessau.de; Gropiusallee 38; exhibition adult/concession €7.50/4.50, tour €5; ☉ 10am-6pm, tours 11am & 2pm, also noon & 4pm Sat & Sun) It's almost impossible to overstate the significance of this building, erected in 1925–26, as a school of Bauhaus art, design and architecture. Today a smattering of lucky students from an urban studies program use some of the building, but much of it is open to the public. An audioguide is included with the admission fee, so you can tour the building and exhibition by yourself, although certain rooms are only revealed on a guided tour.

Two key pioneers of modern architecture, Walter Gropius and Ludwig Mies van der

CENTRAL GERMANY DESSAU-ROSSLAU

Rohe, served as the school's directors. Gropius claimed that the ultimate of all artistic endeavours was architecture, and this building was the first real-life example of his vision. It was revolutionary, bringing industrial construction techniques, such as curtain walling and wide spans, into the public domain and presaging untold buildings worldwide. The school also disseminated the movement's ideals of functionality and minimalism.

Gropiushaus   ARCHITECTURE
(☑0340-3406 5080; www.meisterhaeuser.de; Ebertallee 59; ☺11am-5pm) Walter Gropius' house is the most recently reconstructed of the Master's Houses, opening to the public in 2014. The building houses the ticket office for the remaining three Meisterhäuser, and is also used for special events. You're free to wander the perimeter of the building.

Kurt Weill Zentrum
in Haus Feininger   ARCHITECTURE
(☑0340-619 595; www.meisterhaeuser.de; Ebertallee 63; 3-house ticket adult/concession €7/5.50; ☺11am-5pm) Haus Feininger, former home of Lyonel Feininger, now pays homage to Dessau-born Kurt Weill, who later became playwright Bertolt Brecht's musical collaborator in Berlin, and composed *The Threepenny Opera* and its hit 'Mack the Knife' (immortalised by a rasping Louis Armstrong).

Haus Muche/Schlemmer   ARCHITECTURE
(☑0340-882 2138; www.meisterhaeuser.de; Ebertallee 65/67; 3-house ticket adult/concession €7/5.50; ☺11am-5pm) The Haus Muche/Schlemmer makes it apparent that the room proportions used, and some of the design experiments, such as low balcony rails, don't really cut it in the modern world. At the same time, other features are startlingly innovative. The partially black bedroom here is intriguing; look out for the leaflet explaining the amusing story behind it – Marcel Breuer apparently burst in to paint it when reluctant owner Georg Muche was away on business.

Haus Kandinsky/Klee   ARCHITECTURE
(☑0340-661 0934; www.meisterhaeuser.de; Ebertallee 69/71; 3-house ticket adult/concession €7/5.50; ☺11am-5pm) The Haus Kandinsky/Klee is most notable for the varying pastel shades in which Wassily Kandinsky and Paul Klee painted their walls (re-created today). There's also biographical information about the two artists and special exhibitions about their work.

Törten Estate   ARCHITECTURE
(Am Dreieck 1; tours €4; ☺tours 3pm Tue-Sun) The leafy Törten Estate, in Dessau's south, built in the 1920s, is a prototype of the modern working-class estate. Although many of the 300-plus homes have been altered in ways that would have outraged their purist creator Walter Gropius (patios and rustic German doors added to a minimalist facade?), others retain their initial symmetry. To reach Törten, take tram 1 toward Dessau Süd, get off at Damaschkestrasse and follow the signs saying 'Bauhaus Architektur'.

You're free to roam the streets, but be aware that this is a residential area. To peek inside, head to Konsumgebäude and Moses-Mendelssohn-Zentrum.

Konsumgebäude   HISTORIC BUILDING
(Co-Op Building; ☑0340-650 8251; www.bauhaus-dessau.de; Am Dreieck 1; admission €2; ☺11am-3.30pm Tue-Sun) The former Konsumgebäude today houses an information centre with a permanent exhibition on the history of the Törten housing estate.

Moses-Mendelssohn-Zentrum   MUSEUM
(☑0340-850 1199; www.mendelssohn-dessau.de; Mittelring 38; admission €2; ☺noon-4pm Tue-Sun) Located within the Törten Estate, this exhibition tracks the life and accomplishments of the Dessau-born humanist philosopher Moses Mendelssohn, the godfather of the Jewish Enlightenment.

Technikmuseum Hugo Junkers   MUSEUM
(☑0340-661 1982; www.technikmuseum-dessau.de; Kühnauer Strasse 161a; adult/concession €5/2; ☺10am-4pm Tue-Sun) Aviation fans will be wowed by the vintage aircraft at the Technikmuseum Hugo Junkers. Tram 1 goes straight to the museum (get off at Junkerspark) from the Hauptbahnhof.

🏃 Activities

Elberadweg   CYCLING
(Elbe River Bike Trail; www.elberadweg.de) Dessau is an ideal hub for cycling part of this bike trail, one of Germany's top three cycling routes. The trail wends its way some 860km west alongside the Elbe River, from the Czech border to Cuxhaven. The scenic 360km stretch in Saxony-Anhalt is particularly popular.

The tourist office in Dessau can give you information on the Fürst Franz Garden Realm Tour (68km), which travels between all the palaces around Dessau and Wörlitz, and passes the biosphere reserve information office.

✸ Festivals & Events

Kurt Weill Festival MUSIC
(www.kurt-weill.de) Although more closely associated with Berlin, and later New York, the composer Kurt Weill was born in Dessau. Every March the city hosts a Kurt Weill Festival, reprising and updating his collaborations with Bertolt Brecht, such as *The Threepenny Opera*. Performances take place in Dessau and surrounds.

🛏 Sleeping

★ Bauhaus 'Prellerhaus' HOSTEL $
(📞 0340-650 8318; www.bauhaus-dessau.de; Gropiusallee 38; s/d from €35/55; 🅿) This is one for architecture and design purists who'll first need to come to terms with the fact that all rooms share showers and toilets. If you can swallow that, you'll be able to channel your modernist dream into something highly functional by staying in these minimally super-cool former students' rooms.

Hotel-Pension An den 7 Säulen HOTEL $
(📞 0340-619 620; www.hotel-7-saeulen.de; Ebertallee 66; s/d incl breakfast from €55/75; 🅿) Rooms at this small pension are clean and nicely renovated; the owners are friendly, the garden is pleasant and the breakfast room overlooks the Meisterhäuser across the leafy street. Take bus 11 to Kornerhaus from Hauptbahnhof and walk back to Ebertallee.

DJH Hostel HOSTEL $
(📞 0340-619 803; www.jugendherberge.de/en/youth-hostels/dessau-rosslau701; Ebertallee 151; dm under/over 27yr €22/25, linen €3.50; 🅿@🛜) Cheerful dorms sleeping from two to seven people, each with their own bathroom. Close to the main Bauhaus sights. Take bus 11 to Ebertallee from the train station.

Radisson Blu Hotel Fürst Leopold HOTEL $$
(📞 0340-251 50; www.hotel-dessau-city.de; Friedensplatz; r from €70; 🅿✳🛜) Dessau's grandest hotel offers excellent facilities and value, with a bar, restaurant, fitness area and beauty spa. Prices vary by demand, mostly between €75 and €110. Take tram 1, 2 or 3 one stop from the train station to Theater or follow Fritz-Hesse-Strasse.

NH Dessau HOTEL $$
(📞 0340-251 40; www.nh-hotels.com/NH-Dessau; Zerbster Strasse 29; r from €69; 🅿✳@🛜) This

modern hotel in white-grey tones is set in the pedestrianised strip leading to the Rathaus and tourist office. Wrap up a day on the tourist track with a session in the rooftop sauna with attached terrace. Prices vary according to demand. Take bus 12 from the train station to Zerberstrasse.

🍴 Eating

Cafe-Bistro im Bauhaus Dessau CAFE $
(📞 0340-650 8444; www.klubimbauhaus.de; Gropiusallee 38; items from €4; ⊗ 8am-midnight Mon-Sat, to 6pm Sun; 🛜) Breakfasts, salads, snacks and *Flammkuchen* are served in the congenial cafe and snack bar in the basement of the Bauhaus Building.

★ Kornhaus CAFE $$
(📞 0340-6501 9963; www.kornhaus-dessau.de; Kornhausstrasse 146; mains €10-21) This striking Bauhaus riverside beer-and-dance hall was designed by Carl Fieger, a Gropius assistant. Apart from being a piece of modern architectural history, it offers the perfect spot to sit and enjoy a beer and some refreshingly light, modern German fare in the sun.

Brauhaus Zum alten Dessauer PUB FOOD $$
(📞 0340-220 5909; www.alter-dessauer.de; Lange Gasse 16; mains €9-20; ⊗ 11am-midnight) This fun, friendly, lively brewhouse serves excellent modern and traditional German food, including all the staples and, of course, a wide range of house-brewed beer. What more could you ask for at the end of a long day of sightseeing?

Ratskeller GERMAN $$
(📞 221 5283; www.ratskeller-dessau.de; Zerbsterstrasse 4a; mains €8-22; ⊗ 11am-10pm) There's one in almost every town; this Ratskeller is open and airy with tables outside to enjoy

BAUHAUS: DESIGN FOR LIFE

'Less is more' said the third and final Bauhaus director, Ludwig Mies van der Rohe. Given that this school survived fewer than 15 years, yet exerted more influence on modern design than any other, van der Rohe was probably right. As Frank Whitford put it in *Bauhaus: World of Art* (1984): 'Everyone sitting on a chair with a tubular steel frame, using an adjustable reading lamp or living in a house partly or entirely constructed from prefabricated elements is benefiting from a revolution...largely brought about by the Bauhaus'.

Founded in Weimar in 1919 by Berlin architect Walter Gropius, this multidisciplinary school aimed to abolish the distinction between 'fine' and 'applied' arts, and to unite the artistic with daily life. Gropius reiterated that form follows function and exhorted his students to craft items with an eye toward mass production. Consequently, Bauhaus products stripped away decoration and ornamentation and returned to the fundamentals of design, with strong, clean lines.

From the very beginning, the movement attracted a roll call of the era's greatest talents, including Lyonel Feininger, Wassily Kandinsky, Paul Klee, László Moholy-Nagy and Oskar Schlemmer, plus now legendary product designers Marianne Brandt, Marcel Breuer and Wilhelm Wagenfeld. After conservative politicians closed the Weimar school in 1925, the Bauhaus crew found a more welcoming reception in industrial Dessau.

Even here, though, right-wing political pressure continued against what was seen as the Bauhaus' undermining of traditional values, and Gropius resigned as director in 1928. He was succeeded by Swiss-born Hannes Meyer, whose Marxist sympathies meant that he, in turn, was soon replaced by Ludwig Mies van der Rohe. The latter was at the helm when the school moved to Berlin in 1932 to escape Nazi oppression, but to no avail. Just one year later, the Nazis dissolved the school and its leading lights fled the country.

But the movement never quite died. After WWII, Gropius took over as director of Harvard's architecture school, while Mies van der Rohe (the architect of New York's Seagram Building) held the same post at the Illinois Institute of Technology in Chicago. Both men found long-lasting global fame as purveyors of Bauhaus' successor, the so-called International Style.

the view of the square. Standard German fare, including a wide range of schnitzels, and plenty of good beer, is on offer.

★ **Pächterhaus** GERMAN $$$
(☑0340-650 1447; www.paechterhaus-dessau.de; Kirchstrasse 1; mains €18-25; ☉noon-3pm & 6-10pm Tue-Sun) 🍴 Foodies won't mind making the small detour to this gorgeously restored half-timbered farmhouse where seasonal and locally sourced ingredients get the gourmet treatment. In fine weather do anything to bag a table on the idyllic terrace beneath a canopy of vines. Take bus 11 to Kirchstrasse.

ℹ Information

Bauhaus Stiftung (Bauhaus Foundation; ☑0340-650 8250; www.bauhaus-dessau.de; Gropiusallee 38; ☉10am-6pm) For info on, and tours of, Bauhaus buildings (also in English).
Post Office (Kavalierstrasse 30-32; ☉8.30am-6.30pm Mon-Fri, 9am-12.30pm Sat)

Tourist Office (☑0340-204 1442; www. dessau-rosslau-tourismus.de; Zerbster Strasse 2c; ☉10am-6pm Mon-Fri, to 1pm Sat)

ℹ Getting There & Around

BICYCLE

Beckers Radhaus (☑0340-216 8989; www.beckers-radhaus.de; Kavalierstrasse 82; bikes per day from €15; ☉9am-6pm Mon-Fri, 10am-3pm Sat)
Mobilitätszentrale (☑0340-213 366; Hauptbahnhof; bikes per 2hr from €5; ☉7am-5pm Mon-Fri, 9am-1pm Sat) Look for the little booth opposite the station for nicely priced bike hire.

BUS

Bus and tram tickets for a single/day pass cost €1.80/4.90.

CAR

The Berlin–Munich autobahn (A9) runs east of town.

TRAIN

Direct regional services connect to Berlin (€24.50, 1½ hours), Lutherstadt Wittenberg

(€8.10, 30 minutes), Leipzig (€12.10, 45 minutes), Halle (€14.50, 55 minutes) and Magdeburg (€12.10, 50 minutes).

Gartenreich Dessau-Wörlitz

Aside from being a mecca of modern architecture, Dessau-Rosslau and its surrounds are home to the Gartenreich Dessau-Wörlitz (Garden Realm), one of the finest garden ensembles in Germany. The parks reflect the vision of Prince Leopold III Friedrich Franz von Anhalt-Dessau (1740–1817). A highly educated man, he travelled to Holland, Italy, France and Switzerland for inspiration on how to apply the philosophy of the Enlightenment to the design of a landscape that would create a harmony of nature, architecture and art. Each of the six English-style gardens comes with its own palace and other buildings, in styles ranging from neoclassical to baroque to neo-Gothic. They were added to Unesco's World Heritage list in 2000 and are also protected under the Biosphärenreservat Mittelelbe (www.mittelelbe.com).

The six parks are scattered over 142 sq km. The most central is Georgium, just five minutes' walk from Dessau Hauptbahnhof. The most impressive, Wörlitz, is situated about 18km east of Dessau, making it also the most distant.

All parks are free and can be roamed during daylight hours (most aren't fenced off), but the palaces charge admission and have their own opening hours.

⊙ Sights

Schloss & Park Georgium   PALACE, GARDENS
(☑ 039404-613 874; www.gartenreich.com; Puschkinallee 100; palace adult/concession €3/2; ⊙ 10am-5pm Tue-Sun) Just a five-minute walk from Dessau Hauptbahnhof, the sprawling 18th-century Park Georgium is anchored by the neoclassical palace, now a picture gallery showcasing German and Dutch old masters, including Rubens and Cranach the Elder. The leafy grounds are also dotted with ponds and fake Roman ruins, including a triumphal arch and a round temple. Restoration of the palace was still well underway at the time of writing.

Schloss & Park Grosskühnau   GARDENS
(www.gartenreich.com; Ebenhanstrasse 8; ⊙ 11am-6pm Tue-Sun) Completed in 1780, neo-classical Schloss Grosskühnau is situated at the edge of Lake Grosskühnau, about 4km west of Dessau-Rosslau. Visitors are free to roam the delightful gardens, which include vineyards and partially restored fruit plantations. The palace currently houses the administrative offices of Kulturstiftung DessauWörlitz and is not open to the public.

Schloss & Park Luisium   PALACE, GARDENS
(☑ 039404-218   3711; www.gartenreich.com; Schloss Luisium, Dessau-Rosslau; palace admission €7.50; ⊙ 11am-5pm Sat & Sun Apr-Nov) East of central Dessau, about 4km toward Wörlitz, Schloss Luisium is an intimate neoclassical refuge framed by an idyllic English garden scattered with neo-Gothic and classical follies. It is reached via bus 13 to Vogelherd.

Schloss & Park Mosigkau   PALACE, GARDENS
(☑ 039404-521 139; www.gartenreich.com; Knobelsdorffallee 3, Dessau-Rosslau; palace admission €7.50; ⊙ 11am-6pm Wed-Sun May-Sep, 11am-7pm Sat & Sun Apr & Oct) About 7km southwest of central Dessau, Schloss Mosigkau is a petite rococo palace that's been called a 'miniature Sanssouci'. Many of the 17 rooms retain their original furnishings, although the highlight is the **Galleriesaal**, with paintings by Rubens and van Dyck. In summer, play hide-and-seek in the leafy labyrinth. To get here, take bus 16 to Schloss.

Schloss & Park Oranienbaum   PALACE, GARDENS
(☑ 039404-202 59; www.gartenreich.com; Oranienbaum-Wörlitz; palace admission €7.50; ⊙ 10am-5pm Tue-Sun May-Sep) Ongoing restoration continues at this delightful Dutch-inspired baroque ensemble, south of Wörlitz, but visitors can access most of the rooms and in some cases, take part in the restoration process. Oranienbaum is 14km southeast of Dessau or 6km south of Wörlitz. To get here, take bus 331.

★ Wörlitz Park & Schloss Wörlitz   GARDENS, PALACE
(☑ 039404-310 09; www.woerlitz-information.de; Förstergasse 26, Wörlitz; palace tours €5; ⊙ 10am-6pm Apr-Oct, 10am-4pm Mon-Fri Nov-Mar) With peacocks feeding on the lawn before a neo-Gothic house, a tree-lined stream flowing toward a Grecian-style temple and a gap in a hedge framing a distant villa, the 112-hectare English-style Wörlitz Park is the pinnacle of Prince Leopold's garden region. Take your sweet time to saunter amid this mosaic of paths, hedges and follies, but don't even think about having a picnic on the sprawling lawns:

even walking on them is very much *verboten*, as is bicycling within park grounds.

On the edge of the park nearest the town lies Prince Leopold's former country house, the neoclassical Schloss Wörlitz, which is still filled with original late-18th-century furniture and decorations.

Bus 334 does the 30-minute trip from Dessau to Wörlitz roughly every two hours between 6am and 5.30pm. From late March to early October, there's also a 35-minute train service on Wednesday, Saturday and Sunday. Check the timetable carefully before heading out or check with the information kiosk Mobilitätszentrale (p586) outside the train station. By road from Dessau, take the B185 east to the B107 north, which brings you right into town.

ℹ Information

Information Centre (☑ 034904-4060; www. mittelelbe.com; Am Kapenschlösschen 3, Oranienbaum) On the way to Schloss Oranienbaum, this nature-focused information centre for the Biosphärenreservat Mittelelbe can point you to the nearby **beaver compound**, where you can watch the animals through a screen.

Wörlitz-Information (☑ 034905-310 09; www. woerlitz.de; Förstergasse 26; ☺ 9am-6pm) Come here to the outskirts of Wörlitz park for comprehensive information on all the Garden Realm parks and palaces. There's also a booking service.

Magdeburg

☑ 0391 / POP 230,000

Few people could deny that Magdeburg is aesthetically challenged, thanks to WWII bombs and socialist city planners. Yet this is one of the country's oldest cities, founded some 1200 years ago and home to Germany's first Gothic cathedral. Magdeburg's newest architectural attraction is the whimsical Grüne Zitadelle (Green Citadel), the last building of eccentric artist-architect Friedensreich Hundertwasser.

The Elbe River, too – demoted to industrial waterway in GDR times – is again a vital part of Magdeburg's green side, lined with beer gardens, beach bars, a promenade and a paved bikeway. The most historic parts of town are Hegelstrasse and nearby Hasselbachplatz.

⊙ Sights

Dom　　　　　　　　　　　　　CHURCH
(www.magdeburgerdom.de; Am Dom 1; tour adult/ concession €3/1.50; ☺ 10am-5pm) Magdeburg's main historical landmark traces its roots to 937 when Otto I founded a Benedictine monastery and built it into a fully fledged cathedral within two decades. After a fire destroyed the original a couple of centuries later, it was rebuilt as a Gothic three-aisled basilica with transept, choir and pointed windows. Today it's the burial place of Otto I and his English wife Editha, packed with artistic highlights ranging from the delicate 13th-century **Magdeburg Virgins sculptures** to a haunting **antiwar memorial** by Ernst Barlach.

Grüne Zitadelle　　　　　ARCHITECTURE
(Green Citadel; ☑ 0391-620 8655; www.gruene-zitadelle.de; Breiter Weg 9; tour adult/concession €6/5; ☺ information office 9am-2pm) Completed in 2005, this piglet-pink building with trees growing from its facade and meadows sprouting on its rooftops was the final design of Viennese artist Friedensreich Hundertwasser. It reflects his philosophy of creating unique spaces in harmony with nature, an 'oasis for humanity'. Inside are offices, flats and shops, as well as a small hotel and a cafe. If you understand German, join the one-hour guided tours to learn more about the man and his intriguing vision.

**Elbauenpark
& Jahrtausendturm**　　　　PARK, TOWER
(www.elbauenpark.de; adult/concession incl Jahrtausendturm & butterfly house €3/2; ☺ park 9am-8pm, butterfly house 10am-6pm, Jahrtausenturm 10am-6pm Tue-Sun Apr-Oct) The Elbauenpark was carved out of the landscape for a 1999 garden exhibition, and has rose, sculpture and other gardens and a butterfly house. Its most unusual attraction, though, is the conical, 60m-high Jahrtausendturm (Millennial Tower), which bills itself as the world's tallest wooden tower. Inside is a display on history from ancient times to the present, including a Foucault pendulum. Take tram 5 to Herrenkrug or tram 6 to Messegelände.

**Kunstmuseum Kloster
Unser Lieben Frauen**　　　　GALLERY
(☑ 0391-565 020; www.kunstmuseum-magdeburg. de; Regierungsstrasse 4-6; adult/concession €4/2; ☺ 10am-5pm Tue-Sun, to 6pm Sat & Sun) Magdeburg's oldest building, a decommissioned medieval monastery, is now a museum presenting regional sculptures and contemporary art from Saxony-Anhalt. The front door, designed by popular local artist Heinrich Apel (b 1935), is fun: knock with the woman's necklace and push down on the man's hat to enter. Admission to the cloister is free.

Kulturhistorisches Mueum
MUSEUM

(☎ 0391-540 3501; www.khm-magdeburg.de; Otto-von-Guericke-Strasse 68-73; adult/concession €5/3; ⏱ 10am-5pm Tue-Fri, to 6pm Sat & Sun) This recently restored and enlarged museum boasts the original **Magdeburger Reiter statue** from 1240. A gilded copy is on Alter Markt.

Rathaus
HISTORIC BUILDING

(Alter Markt) After the original bronze door of the Rathaus on Alter Markt was destroyed by WWII bombing, local artist Heinrich Apel designed the current bronze relief door, based on the original's 17th-century design.

🛏 Sleeping & Eating

DJH Hostel
HOSTEL $

(☎ 0391-532 1010; www.jugendherberge.de/jh/magdeburg; Leiterstrasse 10; dm under/over 27yr €22.50/25.50; ℗ @ 🛜) Rooms in this large, modern hostel have shower and toilet attached and there's a family floor with a kiddie romper room. Linen is included.

★ Grüne Zitadelle
BOUTIQUE HOTEL $$

(☎ 0391-620 780; www.arthotel-magdeburg.de; Breiter Weg 9; s/d from €97/109; ℗ ❄ 🛜) Housed in the Green Citadel, a design by the Austrian architect Friedenreich Hundertwasser, this hotel has bold colours, organic shapes and all-natural materials. The nicest rooms face the inner courtyard and provide access to a grassy terrace. Those facing the street are air-conditioned.

Herrenkrug Parkhotel an der Elbe
HERITAGE HOTEL $$

(☎ 0391-850 80; www.herrenkrug.de; Herrenkrug 3; s/d from €86/122; ℗ @ 🛜 🏊) Rise to chirping birds at this riverside mansion, then take a wake-up stroll through the surrounding park. Rooms are spacious and stylish, with access to the sauna and steam bath included in the rate. The hotel's best feature is its bold, handsome art-deco facade: one for lovers of the period. Take tram 6 to Herrenkrug.

Residenz Joop
BOUTIQUE HOTEL $$

(☎ 0391-626 20; www.residenzjoop.de; Jean-Burger-Strasse 16; s/d from €88/112; ℗ ❄ @ 🛜) Nothing is too much trouble for your hosts in this place with tastefully appointed rooms. Take tram 3 or 9 to Am Fuchsberg.

★ Qilin
ASIAN $$

(☎ 0391-243 9944; www.qilin-md.de; Leiterstrasse 1; lunch specials from €6, mains €9-18; ⏱ 11.30am-2.30pm & 5-11pm Mon-Sat, noon-9pm Sun) Magde-

burg's culinary scene won't blow you out of the Elbe, but this small, sleek pan-Asian eatery is excellent – it serves soups, sushi variations, fried seafoods, salads, noodles and superb stir-fries (all without MSG), complemented by a strong wine and cocktail list.

Bralo House
STEAK $$

(☎ 0391-535 7708; www.bralo-house.de; Domplatz 12; mains €12-36; ⏱ 11am-11pm Mon-Sat) An extensive wine list accompanies a wide range of steaks, salads and burgers, cooked to your liking at this popular, central haunt. There's not a lot for either vegetarians or pescetarians.

Liebig Lounge
INTERNATIONAL $$

(☎ 0391-555 6754; www.liebig-lounge.de; Liebigstrasse 1-3; snacks from €5, mains €9-18; ⏱ 10am-midnight) Diners range from tattooed hipsters to helmet-headed grannies in this trendy cafe-bar-restaurant with large outdoor terrace.

Die Saison
INTERNATIONAL $$$

(☎ 0391-850 80; www.herrenkrug.de; Herrenkrug Parkhotel an der Elbe, Herrenkrug 3; mains €22-36; ⏱ noon-3pm & 5-11pm) Classic German cuisine gets a modern international twist within the ornately detailed dark-green walls of this robust hotel's stylish art-deco dining room.

🍷 Drinking & Nightlife

The nightlife action revolves around the Hasselbachplatz. For listings, pick up a copy of *DATEs, Urbanite* (www.urbanite.de/magdeburg) or *Kulturfalter* (all free, all in German).

Café Central
CAFE, BAR

(☎ 0391-239 5671; www.cafecentral.cc; Leibnitzstrasse 34; ⏱ 7.30pm-2am) This hip bar-cum-

Magdeburg

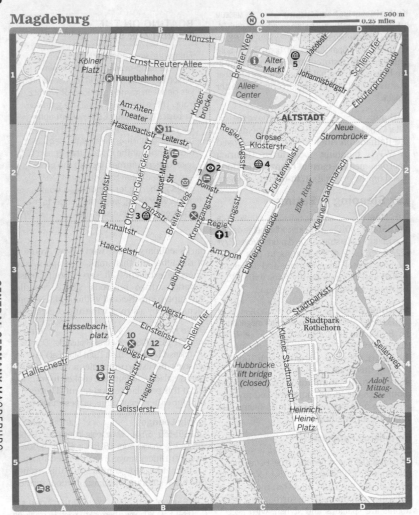

Magdeburg

literary-salon re-creates the early 1900s with antique velvet sofas, flocked wallpaper and Persian carpets. There are comedy shows, public readings, films or lectures many evenings. It's worth visiting just for the cosy decor.

Stern
CLUB

(☑0391-580 2219; http://stern.klamsi.biz; Sternstrasse 9; ⊗7pm-late Mon-Sat, 8pm-late Sun) Magdeburg's 'it' venue features two floors of lounges and a compact dance floor. Dress to impress and show your best moves.

Factory
CLUB

(☑0391-5907 9530; www.factory-magdeburg.de; Karl-Schmidt-Strasse 26-29) Live music and parties here in all musical directions. Check the homepage for what's on when.

ℹ Information

Post Office (Breiter Weg 203-206; ⊗9am-7pm Mon-Fri, to noon Sat)

Tourist Office (☑0391-194 33; www.magdeburg-tourist.de; Ernst-Reuter-Allee 12; ⊗10am-6.30pm Mon-Fri, to 4pm Sat) Throughout town, bilingual information panels provide background about key sights, but grab your brochures here.

ℹ Getting There & Away

Magdeburg is directly connected to Berlin-Hauptbahnhof (€29, two hours), Leipzig (€29, 1¼ hours) and Dessau (€12.10, 50 minutes). For Lutherstadt Wittenberg (€17.90, 70 minutes), change in Rosslau.

Magdeburg is just south of the A2 to Berlin or Hanover and also served by the A14 to Leipzig.

ℹ Getting Around

BICYCLE

Little John Bikes (☑0391-733 0334; www.littlejohnbikes.de; Alter Markt 13-14; bikes per day from €12; ⊗10am-7pm Mon-Fri, to 4pm Sat) This full-service bike shop also rents two-wheelers.

BUS & TRAM

Single/daily tickets cost €1.80/4.90. Buy from vending machines at a stop and punch on-board.

TAXI

Call ☑0391-737 373 or try www.betterdaxi.de.

Halle

☑0345 / POP 231,450

Once a hotbed for the GDR's chemical industry, Halle is most famous for being the birthplace of Georg Friedrich Händel. When the

---

> ### CANAL IN THE SKY
>
> You'll rub your eyes in disbelief when you first see **Wasserstrassenkreuz** (www.wasserstrassenkreuz-magdeburg.de): a massive water-filled bridge straddling the Elbe River. About 15km northeast of central Magdeburg, the Wasserstrassenkreuz is Europe's longest canal bridge and a miracle of modern engineering. The 918m-long 'bathtub' links two major shipping canals and has made life a lot easier for barge captains navigating between Berlin and western Germany.
>
> You can drive yourself here (take Magdeburg-Rothensee exit off the A2) or rent a bicycle and pedal along the scenic Elberadweg (p584).

GDR collapsed, the chemical factories gradually disappeared and the smoke began to clear. Change was slow, but some intelligent planning and major projects leading up to Halle's 1200th birthday in 2006, combined with the presence of some 25,000 students attending the Martin Luther University, has injected a strong dose of vibrancy into this very old town.

Halle has a handful of impressive museums spanning themes as diverse as art, archaeology and the Beatles.

◉ Sights

★ Landesmuseum für Vorgeschichte
MUSEUM

(State Museum of Pre-History; ☑0345-524 7363; www.lda-lsa.de/en/state_museum_of_prehistory; Richard Wagner Strasse 9; adult/concession €5/3; ⊗9am-5pm Tue-Fri, 10am-6pm Sat & Sun) The entrance fee is a small price to pay for a glimpse at this phenomenal collection of major archaeological finds, one of the most significant in Europe. Priceless permanent exhibits shed light on the early to late stone age and early bronze age. Highlights include the famous bronze Nebra Sky Disk (the oldest known concrete depiction of astronomical phenomena), the oldest known recorded fingerprint, and the graves of Eulau. There's usually a special visiting exhibition, and audioguides are available.

Kunstmuseum Moritzburg
GALLERY

(Moritzburg Art Gallery; ☑0345-212 5911; www.kunstmuseum-moritzburg.de; Friedemann-Bach-Platz 5; adult/concession €8/6; ⊗10am-6pm

Thu-Tue) The late-Gothic Moritzburg castle forms a fantastic setting for this superb permanent art collection. The addition of a glass and aluminium roof over the north and west wings, which had been ruined since the Thirty Years' War (1618–48), nearly doubled the exhibition area. Airy and sky-lit, the new space is entirely dedicated to modern art. Older parts of the castle showcase works from medieval times to the 19th century.

Händel-Haus   MUSEUM
([☎] 0345-500 900; www.handel-house.com; Grosse Nikolaistrasse 5; adult/concession €4/2.50; ⊙ 10am-6pm Tue-Sun) The house in which (1685–1759) was born is now the Händel-Haus. An exhibit charts the composer's life, achievements and impact on the evolution of classical music, with an emphasis on his wider European career. Descriptions are in German and English, and the free audioguide is also useful.

Marktkirche Unser Lieben Frauen   CHURCH
(Marktplatz 12; Luther exhibit €2; ⊙ 10am-5pm Mon-Sat, 3-5pm Sun, organ music noon Tue & Thu, also noon Sat May-Sep) Halle's central square has no fewer than five towers. One of these is the freestanding belltower known as Roter Turm, but the other four rise up from the bulky late-Gothic Marktkirche. Inside is its prized possession, Luther's original death mask of wax (ask the attendant to take you into the separate room). It also has a Renaissance pulpit from which he preached.

Beatles Museum   MUSEUM
([☎] 0345-290 3900; www.beatlesmuseum.net; Alter Markt 12; adult/child €6/3; ⊙ 10am-6pm Tue-Sun) Take a 'magical mystery tour' through the life and music of the Fab Four at the Continent's only full-time, but heavily commercial, Beatles Museum. Überfan Rainer Moers has amassed enough knick-knacks to cram three floors with baby photos, birth certificates, album covers, film posters, wigs, jigsaws and even talcum powder – nothing is too trivial to be displayed.

★☆ Festivals & Events

Händel Festival   MUSIC
(www.handel-festival.com) Concerts galore each year in May/June in celebration of Halle's favourite son.

🛏 Sleeping & Eating

Dormero Rotes Ross   HOTEL $
([☎] 0345-233 430; www.dormero-hotel-rotes-ross.de; Leipziger Strasse 76; d from €59; [P][⊕][❄][🖥]) This four-star hotel boasts lots of marble, dark woods, heavy curtains and old-world-style furnishings. It has excellent amenities, including a sauna and wellness area with whirlpools, and benefits from a central location. Online specials are available.

Dorint Charlottenhof Halle   HOTEL $$
([☎] 0345-292 30; www.dorint.com/halle; Dorotheenstrasse 12; r from €89; [P][❄][🖥]) For large, comfortable rooms of an international standard, free wi-fi, impeccable service and stylish hotel amenities, such as whirlpool, gym and sauna, check in to the Dorint Charlottenhof. Early bird specials are available online. Walk from Hauptbahnhof or take any tram one stop to Riebeckplatz.

Ankerhotel Halle   HOTEL $$
([☎] 0345-232 3200; www.ankerhof.de; Ankerstrasse 2a; s/d/ste from €75/105/150; [P][❄][@]) Walls clad in local stone and ceilings supported by heavy wooden beams hark back to the 19th century, when this was the Royal Customs Office. Completely modernised, it's now one of Halle's most charming hotels, with stylish and good-sized rooms; the nicest have river views. There's even a gym and sauna for sweating it out. Take tram 2, 5, 10 or 11 to Ankerstrasse.

Ökoase   VEGETARIAN $
([☎] 0345-290 1604; www.oekoase-halle.de; Kleine Ulrichstrasse 2; mains €6-12; ⊙ 8.30am-4.30pm Mon-Sat; [✓]) Vegetarian eatery with soup, salads and main dishes with curry and other infusions changing on a weekly basis.

★ Immergrün   INTERNATIONAL $$
([☎] 0345-521 6056; www.restaurant-immergruen.de; Kleine Klausstrasse 2; mains €13-19; ⊙ 5pm-midnight Tue-Sat) You're strongly advised to make advance reservations for a table at this highly lauded establishment. Clever, creatively prepared seasonal fish, poultry and meat dishes are served from a small menu that changes monthly and usually features a 'green' theme. Multicourse menus are available.

Osteria da Salvatore   ITALIAN $$
([☎] 0345-681 9610; www.osteria-salvatore.de; Bergstrasse 7; mains €8-22; ⊙ 11am-midnight) There are several Italian places along the main restaurant strip, Kleine Ulrichstrasse, but this *osteria* on the corner of Bergstrasse is the local favourite for its delicious home-

made pastas and cross-regional selection of mains. Students, office workers and anyone else with an appetite for good Italian food come here. Lone diners will also feel very comfortable.

Hallesches Brauhaus GERMAN $$
(☑ 0345-212 570; www.halleschesbrauhaus.de; Grosse Nikolaistrasse 2; mains €9-15; ☺ 4pm-midnight Mon-Fri, 11am-midnight Sat, noon-9pm Sun) This brewhouse is a local institution, known for its crisp light and heavy dark beers, lively atmosphere and hearty pub fare, including *Flammkuchen*.

 Drinking & Entertainment

Finding a party pen to match your mood is easy in Halle's trifecta of fun strips: Kleine Ulrichstrasse, Sternstrasse and the Bermudadreieck (around Seebener Strasse and Burgstrasse near Burg Giebichstein). Also consult the free magazines *Blitz* or *Frizz*.

Potemkin CAFE
(☑ 0345-959 8138; Kleine Ulrichstrasse 27; ☺ 9am-midnight) Potemkin is a sleek and fashionable drinking spot with an extraordinary selection of teas, breakfasts and the occasional snack. It can, however, get a little smoky in the main room.

Turm CLUB
(☑ 0345-548 4686; www.turm-halle.de; Friedemann-Bach-Platz 5; ☺ Wed, Fri & Sat) In the Moritzburg, this old student club has DJs pressing out the latest sounds and various events, including poetry slams some Sundays; check the website for event times.

Objekt 5 LIVE MUSIC
(☑ 0345-4782 3360; www.objekt5.de; Seebener Strasse 5) This classic venue has folk, rock, occasional avant-garde concerts and regular DJs. Check the program. Take tram 8 to Burg Giebichenstein, the castle ruin nearby.

ⓘ Information

Bahnhofslounge Bastian (☑ 0345-685 8790; 1st fl, Hauptbahnhof; ☺ 24hr; 🛜) A 24/7 lounge with free wi-fi, as well as internet access.
Post Office (Marktplatz 20; ☺ 9.30am-8pm Mon-Sat)
Tourist Office (☑ 0345-122 9984; www.stadtmarketing-halle.de; Marktplatz 13; ☺ 9am-7pm Mon-Fri, 10am-4pm Sat) Sells the Halle Welcome Card (€7.50/15 for one/three days), good for free public transport and discounted tours and museum admissions.

ⓘ Getting There & Around

AIR
Leipzig-Halle Airport (www.leipzig-halle-airport.de) lies midway between both cities, and is served by domestic and international flights. The airport is linked with Halle Hauptbahnhof by RE (€4.80, 11 minutes) and hourly IC (€6, 10 minutes) trains.

CAR
From Leipzig, take the A14 west to the B100. The A14 connects Halle and Magdeburg in about one hour. The B91 runs south from Halle and links up with the A9 autobahn, which connects Munich and Berlin.

TRAIN
Leipzig and Halle are linked by frequent IC (€10, 25 minutes) and cheaper regional trains. IC and ICE trains also service Magdeburg (€21, 50 minutes) and Berlin (€47, 1¼ hours), respectively. Local trains connect Halle with Lutherstadt Eisleben (€8.10, 40 minutes) and Lutherstadt Wittenberg (€13.30, one hour).

TRAM
Trams 2, 5, 7 and 9 run from the train station to the Marktplatz. Rides cost €1.80 (€1.30 for up to four stops) or €4 for day cards. Buy tickets from machines at many stops.

Lutherstadt Eisleben

☑ 03475 / POP 26,190
It seems odd for a well-travelled man whose ideas revolutionised Europe to have died in the town where he was born. However, as native son Martin Luther (1483–1546) himself put it before spinning off his mortal coil here, '*Mein Vaterland war Eisleben*' ('Eisleben was my fatherland'). This former mining town focuses almost exclusively on the devout follower. Everywhere you turn, it's Luther, Luther, Luther.

ⓞ Sights

Luther's Sterbehaus MUSEUM
(Luther's Death House; ☑ 03475-714 7840; www.martinluther.de; Andreaskirchplatz 7; adult/concession €4/2.50; ☺ 10am-5pm, closed Mon Nov-Apr) Luther returned to Eisleben in January 1546 to help settle a legal dispute for the Count of Mansfeld, but he was already ill and died on 18 February, a day after finalising an agreement. This museum, expanded and updated in 2013, focuses on three themes: how the culture of death has evolved over the centuries; Luther's thoughts about death; and the last 24 hours of his life. The museum's prize

literary exhibit is a bible from 1541 – the last Luther worked on.

Luther's Geburtshaus
MUSEUM

(Luther's Birthplace Museum; ☑03475-714 7814; www.martinluther.de; Lutherstrasse 15; adult/concession €4/2.50; ☉10am-5pm, closed Mon Nov-Apr) This house where the famous reformer was born has been a memorial site since 1693, though it has been updated since then! The original house is furnished in period style, while annexe-wing exhibits focus on Luther's family and aspects of the society in which he grew up.

St Annenkirche
CHURCH

(☉10am-4pm Mon-Sat, noon-4pm Sun May-Oct) While district vicar, Martin Luther stayed in the apartments of the St Annenkirche, 10 minutes west of the Markt in the hills above Eisleben. This church also features a stunning Steinbilder-Bibel (stone-picture bible; 1585), the only one of its kind in Europe, and a wittily decorated pulpit.

St Andreaskirche
CHURCH

(Andreaskirchplatz; admission €1; ☉10am-4pm Mon-Sat, 11am-4pm Sun May-Oct) Luther delivered his last sermons in the St Andreaskirche, a late-Gothic hall church on the hill behind the central Markt.

St Petri Pauli Kirche
CHURCH

(Andreaskirchplatz; admission €1; ☉10am-4pm Mon-Sat, 11am-4pm Sun May-Oct) Remarkable for being the church where Luther was baptised.

🛏 Sleeping & Eating

Mansfelder Hof
HOTEL $

(☑03475-612 620; www.mansfelderhof.de; Hallesche Strasse 33; s/d incl breakfast €49/69; P🏠) Behind its vine-covered, faded green stucco facade, this hotel turns out to have modern if rather generic rooms; the quietest are those facing the rear of the hotel. The restaurant serves Greek food.

★ Hotel Graf von Mansfeld
HOTEL $$

(☑03475-663 00; www.hotel-eisleben.de; Markt 56; s/d/ste from €65/95/125; P@🏠) Eisleben's premier in-town hotel is a classic

outpost of charm and tradition. Although over 500 years old, it has seriously slicked-up rooms with four-poster beds, and bright and airy flair. No two rooms are alike. The partner-run wellness area has three saunas for an extra fee.

Deckert's Hotel am Katherinsift
HOTEL $$

(☑03475-632 670; www.deckerts-hotel.de; Sängerhauser Strasse 12/13; s/d incl breakfast €65/85; P🏠) This small hotel in a historic building offers a great location a few minutes' walk from the Markt and spotless, light-filled rooms with neutral furnishings and modern conveniences. Recommended.

Plan B
CAFE $

(☑03475-711 788; Markt 33; items from €4; ☉10am-6pm Mon-Fri, noon-6pm Sat) This sleek modern cafe-bar offers a contrast to the historic aspects of Eisleben. As well as serving wine and cocktails (in broad daylight), it does *Flammkuchen,* antipasti and salads.

Fellini
ITALIAN $$

(☑03475-748 015; Sangerhäuser Strasse 10; mains €8-24; ☉11am-2.30pm & 5.30-11pm) Friendly, efficient table service, a busy atmosphere, tasty authentic pizza and pasta (the carbonara is just right – not too creamy), reasonable prices and a nice ambience both indoors and alfresco, earn Fellini's our warm recommendation.

ⓘ Information

Tourist Office (☑03475-602 124; www.eisleben-tourist.de; Hallesche Strasse 4; ☉10am-5pm Mon & Wed-Fri, to 6pm Tue, to 1pm Sat)

ⓘ Getting There & Around

There are frequent trains to Halle (€8.10, 40 minutes), where you can change for Lutherstadt Wittenberg (€21.30, 1¾ hours), Leipzig (€15.70, 70 minutes), Magdeburg (€27, 1½ hours) and Weimar (€25.10, 2¼ hours). Eisleben is a half-hour drive west of Halle on the B80.

Most sights are knotted together around the Markt, just north of Hallesche Strasse, the main thoroughfare. To get there from the station, it's a 15-minute walk via Bahnhofsring (turn left on leaving the station) and Bahnhofstrasse. Buses going past Markt usually meet the trains.

Lower Saxony & Bremen

AREA 47,960 SQ KM

Best Places to Eat

➡ Pier 51 (p605)

➡ Bremer Ratskeller (p626)

➡ Natusch (p632)

➡ Zum Schwejk (p611)

➡ Kleiner Olymp (p627)

Best Places to Stay

➡ Ritz Carlton Wolfsburg (p619)

➡ Althoff Hotel Fürstenhof (p611)

➡ Van der Valk Hotel Hildesheim (p613)

➡ Atlantic Grand (p626)

➡ Central Hotel Kaiserhof (p603)

Why Go?

Lower Saxony (Niedersachsen) is the largest German state after Bavaria. West to east, it stretches from the World Heritage Wattenmeer tidal flats and the intriguing East Frisian Islands, to Wolfsburg, global HQ of das auto, Volkswagen. Green and liveable, its capital, Hanover, was named Unesco City of Music in 2014, but is better known for its annual CeBit and Messe tech tradeshows, where geeks and suits unite en masse. The state's patchwork of vibrant towns and villages, none with more than a few hundred thousand inhabitants, should pique your interest. Between them is a diverse landscape of forests, farmlands, river plains, heath and moors that will beckon your return to nature.

Bremen, the smallest of the German states, packs a punch for its size. In Bremem City a wealth of fine architecture and cobblestone streets, engaging, educational museums, a vibrant riverfront and happening, modern, multicultural vibe keep things interesting.

At the mouth of the Weser, Bremen's 'daughter' port, Bremerhaven, upholds a rich seafaring tradition and is itself home to two of Germany's most original, instructive and entertaining museums.

When to Go

There are few outdoor advantages to travelling in this area in winter: expect grey, windy weather and double-digit subzero temperatures in a harsh year. Fortunately, there's a healthy quota of museums, galleries, concert halls and theatres to provide plenty of indoor pursuits over those colder months.

From April to September, life moves outdoors. Spring heralds a welcome explosion of colour in endless fields of golden yellow canola and manicured floral gardens. It's warm enough to dine al fresco, picnic, cycle and hike comfortably, walk the Wattenmeer tidal flats and sojourn on the white sands of the East Frisian Islands. Summer sees long days, social beer gardens and breathtaking late-hour sunsets on the North Sea coast.

Lower Saxony & Bremen Highlights

① Contemplating the atrocities of war at **Bergen-Belsen** (p611) concentration camp

② Journeying the world at Bremerhaven's **Deutsches Auswanderer Haus** (p631) and **Klimahaus 8° Ost** (p631) museums

③ Admiring the golden archangel of **Böttcherstrasse** (p620) in Bremen

④ Hiking across tidal flats to an **East Frisian Island** (p637)

⑤ Admiring the art in Hanover's world-class **Sprengel Museum** (p599)

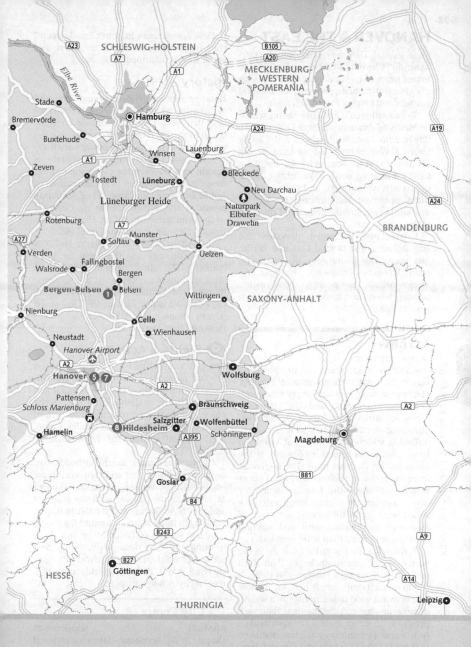

HANOVER & THE EAST

State capital Hanover (Hannover, in German: don't leave out that second 'n'!) is the urban heart of Lower Saxony with a wealth of cultural attractions, picturesque parks and gardens and plenty of top-notch nosh.

To its south, you'll find Hildesheim, whose residents celebrated their city's 1200th birthday in 2015. East of Hildesheim is the lovely town of Wolfenbüttel and its intimate big brother, medieval Braunschweig, the 'Lion City'. Continuing north is Wolfsburg, headquarters of Volkswagen; and Celle, with its many preserved half-timbered houses. All are within easy striking distance of the capital by road or rail.

Further east, the region dissolves into Brandenburg, and beyond that into Berlin, just under two hours away by high-speed train. The states of Hessen, Thuringia and Saxony-Anhalt, along with their castles, palaces, forests and gardens, lie south, from west to east.

Hanover

📞 0511 / POP 522,700

Lacking the high profile of neighbouring Hanse city states Hamburg and Bremen, Hanover is today known for its mammoth CeBit computer expo and the Hannover Messe industrial technology trade fair, each attracting over 200,000 visitors a year.

Buried within its identity, but visible to those with patience and a keen eye, is the lesser known fact that from 1714, monarchs from the house of Hanover also ruled Great Britain, and the entire British Empire, for over a century. In a cruel irony, extensive Allied bombing in 1943 wiped out much of Hanover's rich architectural and cultural heritage, with more than 6000 lives lost.

Perhaps it's this paradox of once being part of something much larger than itself that makes Hanover's character so difficult to pin down. Local's love it here for the low cost of living, good public transport, a wealth of museums and cultural sites and Hanover's proximity to green spaces: the spectacularly baroque Herrenhäuser Gärten, southern manmade Lake Maschsee and Europe's largest urban forest, the Eilenriede. That said, most Germans groan at the first mention of Hanover, whose dialect is regarded as the closest tongue to High German. Perhaps it's a complex socio-linguistic thing; perhaps they're just jealous.

First appearances mightn't knock you off your feet, but spend a little time here and you'll soon be charmed.

History

Hanover was established around 1100 and became the residence of Heinrich der Löwe later that century. An early Hanseatic city, by the Reformation it had developed into a prosperous seat of royalty and a power unto itself.

A link was created with the monarchy of Britain in 1714, when the eldest son of Electress Sophie of Hanover (a granddaughter of James I of England; James VI of Scotland), ascended the British throne as George I while simultaneously ruling Hanover. This British–German union lasted until 1837.

In 1943 up to 80% of the centre and 50% of the entire city was destroyed by Allied bombing. The rebuilding plan included creating sections of reconstructed half-timbered houses and painstakingly rebuilding the city's prewar gems, such as the Opernhaus (Opera House), Marktkirche and Neues Rathaus (New Town Hall).

⊙ Sights & Activities

The city has painted a *Roter Faden* (red line) on pavements around the centre. Follow it with the help of the multilingual *Red Thread Guide,* available from the tourist office, online at www.roterfaden-hannover.de, or download the app, for a quick 4.2km, do-it-yourself loop of the city's 36 highlights.

Of Hanover's many neighbourhoods, two of the most interesting and visit-worthy are once-working-class Linden-Limmer (known as Linden), now popular with the students and the tragically hip, and the Oststadt, particularly in the side streets around the pedestrianised section of Lister Meile and those fronting the Eilenriede where you'll find some beautiful heritage architecture that survived WWII. Both are quickly and easily reached by public transport.

⊙ City Centre

Altstadt NEIGHBOURHOOD

Despite WWII bombing, Hanover's restored old town remains appealingly quaint. The red-brick, Gothic **Marktkirche** (Market Square) in the market square has original elements, as do both the **Altes Rathaus** (Altstadt) (begun 1455), across the market, and the nearby **Ballhof** (Altstadt) (1649–

64), a hall originally built for 17th-century badminton-type games. An entire row of half-timbered houses has been re-created along Kramerstrasse and Burgstrasse near the Marktkirche, and here you also find **Leibnizhaus**, once the home of mathematician and philosopher Gottfried Wilhelm Leibniz (1646–1716), with its reconstructed Renaissance facade. In front of the Leibnizhaus is the **Oskar-Winter-Brunnen** (Oskar Winter Fountain; Kramerstr). If you make a wish and turn the small brass ring embedded in the ironwork three times, local lore has it that your wish will come true.

★ **Neues Rathaus**　　HISTORIC BUILDING
(Trammplatz 2; lift adult/concession €3/2; ⊙9.30am-6.30pm Mon-Fri, 10am-6.30pm Sat & Sun, lift closed mid-Nov–Mar; Ⓤ Hannover Kröpcke, Hannover Aegidientorplatz) An excellent way to get your bearings in Hanover is to visit the Neues Rathaus (built 1901–13) and travel 98m to the top in the curved lift (the only one of its kind) inside its green dome. There are four observation platforms offering panoramic views as far as the Deister hills. The cabin can take only five people at a time so expect queues. In the downstairs lobby, city models show Hanover from the Middle Ages to today.

★ **Sprengel Museum**　　MUSEUM
(☎0511-438 75; www.sprengel-museum.com; Kurt-Schwitters-Platz; adult/concession €7/4, Fri free; ⊙10am-6pm Wed-Sun, to 8pm Tue) The Sprengel Museum is held in extremely high esteem, both for the design of the building as well as for the art housed inside. Its huge interior spaces are perfectly suited to displaying its modern figurative, abstract and conceptual art, including a few works by Nolde, Chagall and Picasso. At the core of the collection are 300 works by Niki de Saint Phalle, a selection of which is usually on show. Check the website for visiting exhibitions.

Take bus 100 from Kröpcke station to the Maschsee/Sprengel Museum stop.

Aegidienkirche　　MEMORIAL
(Aegidius Church; ☎0511-3018 6611; cnr Breite Strasse & Osterstrasse; ⊙carillon 9.05am, 12.05pm, 3.05pm & 6.05pm; Ⓤ Hannover Kröpcke) In 1943 this former Gothic church dating from 1347 was bombed. It was never repaired or reconstructed and today stands as a reminder to the horrors of war. Inside the ruin is the Peace Bell donated by sister city Hiroshima. Every 6 August at 8.15am, the date and time

---

ⓘ **'EXPERIENCE' BUSES 100 & 200**

You can easily take in the main sights by foot in Hanover by following the red line on the pavement, but buses 100 (clockwise) and 200 (anticlockwise) are also handy for getting around. They run every 10 to 15 minutes. The most convenient section is bus 100 south from Hauptbahnhof to the Maschsee. Good places to pick up the 100/200 are Lister Meile, Kröpke and Maschsee/Sprengel Museum near the football stadium.

of the atomic detonation at Hiroshima, a delegation from both cities meets here to ring the bell.

Maschsee　　LAKE
(Rudolf-von-Bennigsen-Ufer) This artificial lake, built by the unemployed in one of the earliest Nazi-led public-works projects, is now a favourite spot for boating and swimming. It's certainly the most central, at just 30 minutes' walk from the Hauptbahnhof and directly alongside the AWD-Arena, Hanover's football stadium. Ferries – some solar-powered – ply the lake from Easter to October in good weather, and there are sailing, pedal and rowing boats for hire.

Take bus 100 from Kröpcke station to the Maschsee/Sprengel Museum stop.

Strandbad　　BEACH
(www.das-strandbad.de; Beach; adult/child €2.30/1.40; ⊙10am-8pm May-Aug) This popular swimming beach is situated on the southeast bank of the Maschsee, Hanover's large lake, where you'll also find inline skaters gliding by in the shade of neighbouring trees. The closest stop is Döhrener Turm on the tram/U-Bahn lines 1, 2 and 8. Walk west for 15 minutes to Maschsee. You can also walk 15 minutes along the lake from Maschsee/Sprengel Museum stop (bus 100).

Kestner Gesellschaft　　GALLERY
(Kestner Society; http://kestnergesellschaft.de; Goseriede 11; adult/concession €7/5; ⊙11am-6pm Tue, Wed & Fri-Sun, to 8pm Thu; Ⓤ Hannover Steintor) It's always worth checking listings for the Kestner Gesellschaft. Having exhibited works by Otto Dix, Georg Grosz, Wassily Kandinsky and Paul Klee before they became famous, the society is still originating shows that later tour Europe. Its wonderfully light, high-ceilinged premises were once a bathhouse.

Hanover

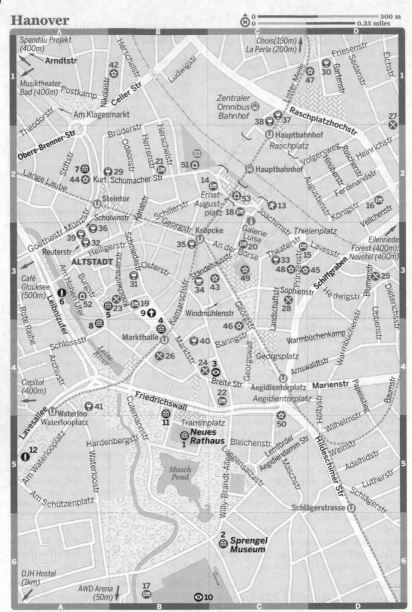

LOWER SAXONY & BREMEN HANOVER

Museum August Kestner MUSEUM
(📞0511-427 30; www.museum-august-kestner.
de; Trammplatz 3; adult/concession €5/3, Fri
free; ⏰11am-6pm Tue & Thu-Sun, to 8pm Wed;
Ⓤ Aegidientorplatz, Markthalle) Decorative
arts through the ages are the focal point
of the Kestner Museum, where you'll see
everything from Bauhaus-style cutlery to
a very impressive collection of Greek and
Egyptian antiquities.

Hanover

Die Nanas   SCULPTURE

(Leibnizufer) Hanover's city fathers and mothers were inundated with nearly 20,000 letters of complaint when these three earth-mama sculptures were first installed beside the Leine River in 1974. Now, the voluptuous and fluorescent-coloured 'Sophie', 'Charlotte' and 'Caroline', by French artist Niki de Saint Phalle, are among the city's most recognisable, and most loved, landmarks. Indeed, *Die Nanas* helped make de Saint Phalle famous.

Waterloo Memorial   MONUMENT

(Waterlooplatz; Ⓤ Hannover Waterloo) This 46.3m column commemorates the victory of German, British and Prussian forces over Napoleon in the Battle of Waterloo in June 1815.

◉ Around the Centre

★**Herrenhäuser Gärten**   GARDENS

(☏ 0511-1683 4000; www.hannover.de/Herrenhausen; Herrenhäuser Strasse 4; general admission free; ☺ 9am-6pm (grotto to 5.30pm) Apr-Oct, to 4.30pm (grotto to 4pm) Nov-Mar; Ⓤ Hannover Herrenhäuser Gärten) Proof that Hanover is not all buttoned-down business are the grandiose baroque Royal Gardens of Herrenhausen, about 5km north of the city centre, which are considered one of the most important historic garden landscapes in Europe. Inspired by the gardens at Versailles, they're a great place to slow down and smell the roses for a couple of hours, especially on a blue-sky day.

Four gardens make up the ensemble. The oldest, the baroque **Grosser Garten and Berggarten**, is pay-for-admission; **Georgeangarten** (George Garden) and **Welfengarten** (Welf Garden) are free and open to the public day and night. East of the Grosser Garten, beyond a small canal, the lake-dotted Georgengarten counts the Wilhelm-Busch-Museum (p602) among its treasures.

→ **Grosser Garten**

(☑ 0511-1683 4000; www.herrenhaeuser-gaerten. de; Herrenhäuser Strasse 4; combination ticket adult/concession €8/4; ⊘ 9am-6pm (later in summer); ⓢ Hannover Herrenhäuser Gärten) The jewel in the crown of the Herrenhäuser Gärten is grand both in format and history, having been laid out as a baroque garden in 1714 under the tutelage of the French landscape gardener Martin Charbonnier. The garden contains statues, fountains, a maze and the coloured tile walls of the Niki de Saint Phalle Grotto (creator of the city's much-loved *Die Nanas* sculptures). The Grosse Fontäne is Europe's tallest, jetting water up to 80m.

In summer the synchronised **Wasserspiele** (Fountain Display; ⊘ 11am-noon & 3-5pm Mon-Fri, 11am-noon & 2-5pm Sat & Sun Apr-Oct) water fountains always pull a crowd, as do nightly garden Illuminations, summer concerts and fireworks competitions. Dates and times vary: check the 'Events' section of the website for details.

Combination ticket entry includes admission to Berggarten and Museum Schloss Herrenhäusen.

→ **Berggarten**

(☑ 0511-1683 4000; www.herrenhaeuser-gaerten. de; Herrenhäuser Strasse 4; combination ticket adult/concession €8/4; ⊘ 9am-6pm (later in summer); ⓢ Hannover Herrenhäuser Gärten) The oldest botanical garden in Germany is redolent with a mind-boggling assortment of global flora and features 300-year-old lime trees lining an avenue leading to a mausoleum holding the remains of George I of England.

Combination ticket entry includes admission to Grosser Garten and Museum Schloss Herrenhäusen.

Museum Schloss Herrenhäusen   MUSEUM
(☑ 0511-1684 4543; www.herrenhaeuser-gaerten. de; Herrenhäuser Strasse 3; combination ticket adult/concession €8/4; ⊘ 11am-6pm; ⓤ Hannover Herrenhäuser Gärten) Opened in 2013, this spectacular reconstruction was built to the original plans for the early-19th-century palace that was destroyed by bombing in 1943. It features an authentic facade and a state-of-the-art modern interior, primarily used for high-end conferences and events. This small museum is the only part of the complex open to visitors. It features displays on the baroque era and the fascinating period in Hanover's history when the British Empire was ruled from here.

Combination ticket entry includes admission to Grosser Garten and Berggarten.

Eilenriede Forest   FOREST
(Fritz-Behrens-Allee) At over 640 hectares, Europe's largest city forest, beginning about 1km northeast of the Hauptbahnhof, is also known as Hanover's *grüne Lunge* (green lung). It is well frequented and loved by locals who picnic, play and cycle through the enchanting woods, luminous green in the summertime, where it's easy to imagine you're not in the middle of a city of half a million people.

Bus 100 going north to Emmichplatz stops at the entrance arch.

Wilhelm-Busch-Museum   MUSEUM
(☑ 0511-1699 9911; www.karikatur-museum.de; Georgengarten; adult/concession €6/4; ⊘ 11am-

---

GLOBAL GIANTS: CEBIT & MESSE

Trade fairs in Hanover are a time-honoured tradition. The first export fair was held in August 1947 in the midst of all the rubble from WWII. As most hotels had been destroyed, the mayor made an appeal to citizens to provide beds for foreign guests. The people did, the money came and it's become a tradition; about a third more beds are available in private flats at fair time (the only time they're offered) than in hotels, which book out months in advance at elevated rates.

There are two 'world's biggest' trade fairs held in Hanover each year. The pre-eminent fair today is CeBIT, a business IT and computer expo, held every March. During it's glory days of the late 90s, the fair recorded as many as 800,000 attendees. The other is Hannover Messe, an industrial technology trade show in late April.

The Messegelände fairgrounds are in the city's southeast, served by tram/U-Bahn 8 (and 18 during fair times) to Entrance Nord as well as the S4 S-Bahn, IC and ICE trains. Tram/U-Bahn 6 and 16 serve the eastern part of the fairgrounds.

During major fairs there's a full-service tourist office at the airport and an information pavilion at the fairgrounds, in addition to the main tourist office.

6pm Tue-Sun) Contains a wealth of caricature, including works by caricature greats Busch, Honoré Daumier and William Hogarth.

🎭 Festivals & Events

CeBIT TRADE FAIR
(www.cebit.de; ⊘ Mar) In early March Hanover is overtaken by tech-heads for the world's largest computer expo.

Hannover Messe TRADE FAIR
(www.hannovermesse.de; ⊘ Apr) At the end of April, the world's largest industrial technology fair attracts more than 6000 exhibitors and 200,000 visitors.

Enercity Swinging Hannover JAZZ FESTIVAL
(www.swinginghannover.de) Visitors come from afar for this international jazz festival, held over two days around Ascension Day in May/June.

International Fireworks Competition FIREWORKS
Held over five evenings from May to September in the skies above the Herrenhäuser Garten, this prestigious spectacle of light and sound attracts the world's most accomplished pyrotechnicians.

Maschseefest CULTURAL
(www.maschseefest.de; ⊘ late Jul-early Aug) This annual festival by the lake features a packed calendar of events in, on and around the Maschsee, including a range of performances and fun activities for all ages.

🛏 Sleeping

The tourist office books accommodation, including an inventory of private rooms rooms, for a €2.50 fee. During trade shows, the rates listed below can increase dramatically. Check the city website (www.hannover.de) to ensure your dates don't unintentionally coincide with a trade show.

Campingplatz Arnumer See CAMPGROUND $
(☑ 05101-3534; http://camping-hannover.de; Osterbruchweg 5, Arnum-Hemmingen; adult €6, car €2-4, tent €5; @ 🛜) In a leafy lakeside location south of the city, this extremely well-equipped camping ground with wi-fi everywhere has a playground and separate areas for tents and caravans. Take bus 300 to Arnum Mitte, from where it's a five-minute walk. By road, take A7 south to Laatzen, or B3 from Arnum, and follow the signs. Cottages and apartments are available.

★ Courtyard Hannover Maschsee HOTEL $
(☑ 0511-366 000; www.marriott.com; Arthur-Menge-Ufer 3; d from €79; P ⊖ ❄) The boxy 70s exterior of this hotel belies its ultra-modern, stylish interior; all common areas and guestrooms have been fully renovated. Standard rooms are comfortable, good-looking and functional. Perhaps its best feature is the lakefront location boasting a wonderful outlook from the shores of the shimmering Maschsee. Bus 100 runs to the door.

GästeResidenz PelikanViertel APARTMENT $
(☑ 0511-399 90; www.gaesteresidenz-pelikanviertel.de; Pelikanstrasse 11; s/d from €49/69; P 🛜 ; Ⓤ 3, 7 or 9 to Pelikanstrasse) Upmarket student residence meets budget hotel at this well-managed complex with a wide range of minimalist rooms, some split over two levels. Stays of seven days or longer are excellent value.

DJH Hostel HOSTEL $
(☑ 0511-131 7674; www.jugendherberge.de/jh/hannover; Ferdinand-Wilhelm-Fricke-Weg 1; dm under/over 27yr from €23.30/27.30; P @ 🛜 ; Ⓤ 3 or 7 to Bahnhof Linden/Fischerhof) This huge, spacelab-like structure houses a modern hostel with breakfast room and terrace-bar overlooking the river. It's only a short walk from here to the Maschsee. Linen is included.

City Hotel Königstrasse HOTEL $
(☑ 0511-410 2800; www.smartcityhotel.com; Königstrasse 12; s/d/tr €60/69/99; P @ 🛜) This convenient business hotel is a few minutes by foot from Hauptbahnhof. Prices rise according to the day of week and demand. Breakfast costs €9.50.

★ Central Hotel Kaiserhof HOTEL $$
(☑ 0511-368 3114; www.centralhotel.de; Ernst Aug Platz 4; d/ste from €79/180) Directly opposite Hanover's handsome, historic Hauptbahnhof. With a lovely terrace bar-restaurant overlooking Ernst August Platz, this well-maintained, small but elegant private hotel has neutrally decorated rooms of varying sizes, comfortable bedding, an excellent breakfast buffet and friendly, helpful staff.

City Hotel am Thielenplatz HOTEL $$
(☑ 0511-327 691; www.smartcityhotel.com/thielenplatz; Thielenplatz 2; s/d from €75/80; P 🛜) This very central 'budget boutique' beauty has a reception and bar (open until 5am) restyled with leather seating, black-and-white leaf-patterned wallpaper and lots of wood laminate. All rooms have been renovated, mostly in a minimalist style.

Novotel
HOTEL **$$**

(☑ 0511-390 40; www.novotel.com; Podbielskistrasse 21/23; d from €110; P ⊜ ❄ 🐾 🛜; Ⓤ 3 to Hannover List Platz) In one of Hanover's most beautiful neighbourhoods, one street back from the Eilenriede forest and a hop, skip and a jump from the Lister Meilie shopping street, is this top-choice chain hotel. The boxy-but-stylish designer rooms feature great beds, showers and fast wi-fi. Service and amenities are outstanding, with two good restaurants, a gym and plenty of parking.

Arabella Sheraton Pelikan
HOTEL **$$**

(☑ 0511-909 30; www.sheratonhannoverpelikan.com/en; Podbielskistrasse 145; r from €89; ❄ @ 🛜; Ⓤ 3, 7 or 9 to Pelikanstrasse) Fat beds with thick mattresses and plump cushions dominate the rooms of this luxury hotel, where high ceilings alleviate any feeling of being cramped. Set on a redeveloped factory site in the suburbs, it feels like a hideaway village, with the renowned restaurant 5th Ave and Harry's New York bar. There's a fitness centre (free use) next door.

Loccumer Hof
HOTEL **$$**

(☑ 0511-126 40; www.loccumerhof.de; Kurt-Schumacher-Strasse 14-16; s/d from €99/139; P @ 🛜) 🖋 Some of the stylish and well-decorated rooms here are themed by nations ('Australia'), elements ('Air') and feng shui. Others are low-allergy. Rates are often lower for advance or internet bookings (from €59 for singles).

Lühmanns Hotel am Rathaus
HOTEL **$$**

(☑ 0511-326 268; www.hotelamrathaus.de; Friedrichswall 21; s/d from €89/120; @ 🛜) Posters from the nearby Kestner Museum and artworks adorn the halls here, and the rooms themselves are tastefully decorated. Although the hotel is on a busy street, good double-glazing keeps the rooms very quiet.

Hotel Wiehberg
HOTEL **$$**

(☑ 0511-879 990; www.hotel-wiehberg.de; Wiehbergstrasse 55a; s/d incl breakfast from €78/95; P 🛜; Ⓤ 1 to Wiehbergstrasse) Modernistic and evoking a 'Zen' feel, this hotel makes excellent use of natural lighting and shadow, and features low Japanese-style beds set on rails. These are designed for trade-fair guests who want to share rooms without getting too snug. If guests do want to get snug, they can push the beds together. The hotel is in a leafy residential neighbourhood.

Hanns-Lilje-Haus
HOTEL **$$**

(☑ 0511-124 1698; www.hanns-lilje-haus.de; Knochenhauerstrasse 33; s/d from €69/89; 🛜) Though church-owned, this hotel has no qualms about welcoming unmarried or gay couples. Large, spartan rooms make interesting use of space to create a bright, pleasant atmosphere and feature some good design elements and a splash of colour.

Kastens Hotel Luisenhof
HOTEL **$$**

(☑ 0511-304 40; www.kastens-luisenhof.de; Luisenstrasse 1-3; s/d/ste from €99/109/199; P ❄ @ 🛜) This grand dame still looks pretty good in spite of being over 150 years old. Myriad wellness offerings include massages and an upper-level spa and fitness centre. The Piano Suite literally comes with a piano. Early and internet booking can bring good deals.

Grand Hotel Mussmann
HOTEL **$$$**

(☑ 0511-365 60; www.grandhotel.de; Ernst-Aug-Platz 7; s/d from €124/154; ❄ @ 🛜) The central, four-star Mussmann is one of Hanover's old dames that has been revamped into a stylish, modern hotel with rooms named after famous Hanover landmarks. Rooms and suites are spacious and well appointed, though the rates seem a little steep.

🍴 Eating

Spandau Projekt
INTERNATIONAL **$**

(☑ 0511-1235 7095; www.spandauprojekt.de; Engelbosteler Damm 30; mains €6-12; ⊙ noon-10pm Mon-Fri, from 10am Sat & Sun; 🛜 🍴) Retro-'70s Spandau in Hanover's Nordstadt is more like a place in Berlin's Kreuzberg – where students from the nearby university and the local Turkish community rub shoulders. The varied menu features curries, salads, soups and pastas. It's great for breakfast on weekends and people-watching anytime.

Markthalle
MARKET **$**

(www.hannover-markthalle.de; Kamarschstrasse 49; dishes €3.50-10; ⊙ 7am-8pm Mon-Wed, to 10pm Thu & Fri, to 4pm Sat; 🍴) This huge covered market of food stalls and gourmet delicatessens is fantastic for a quick bite, both carnivorous and vegetarian.

Fischers
MEXICAN **$**

(☑ 0511-441 404; www.estrella-gastro.de; Limmerstrasse 49; menu items €3.50-15.50; ⊙ 6pm-midnight) In the hip, arty suburb of Linden you'll find this spicy little number that will awaken your senses to the flavours of Mexico. There's a broad menu of small plates, plenty of vegetarian options and all the favourites – tacos, fajitas, margaritas – served up in a smart and stylish setting. The Leinaustrasse tram/subway stop is just outside.

Denn's Biomarkt   SUPERMARKET $
(denns-biomarkt.de; Marktstrasse 45; ⊘8am-8pm Mon-Sat; 🖉) A large organic supermarket, Denn's has everything from fruit and veggies to wines, aquaculture fish and meats – perfect for a wholesome picnic in one of Hanover's parks. There are also locations in Linden and Oststadt: check the website for details.

Café Mezzo   CAFE $
(🖉 0511-314 966; www.cafe-mezzo.de; Lister Meile 4; dishes from €3.50; ⊘9am-2am Tue-Thu, to 3am Fri & Sat, to midnight Sun & Mon; 🛜) This classic bar and cafe used to be a student hang-out, but today attracts a balance of ages. It's popular any time of day (including for breakfast), but doubles as a place to warm up in the evening before moving on to a club or performance.

★Pier 51   INTERNATIONAL $$
(🖉0511-807 1800; www.pier51.de; Rudolf von Bennigsen Ufer 51; mains €10-22; ⊘noon-midnight) Romantic at sundown, Pier 51 is walled with glass and juts out over the Maschsee. Expect light pasta dishes and a small selection of fish, poultry and red meats on a changing menu. All dishes can be ordered in half-servings for little over half the price. Book at least a few days ahead if you want a window seat at dinner.

Take tram/U-Bahn 1, 2 or 8 to Altenbeken Damm and walk 10 minutes to the Maschsee.

★Basil   FUSION $$
(🖉0511-622 636; www.basil.de; Dragonerstrasse 30; menus €14.50-26.50; ⊘6-10pm Mon-Sat) These former stables to the north of town now house a hip fusion restaurant, with a high arched ceiling, pressed tablecloths and memorable creative cuisine. Dress to be seen. Course menus offer the best value. Take tram/U-Bahn 1 or 2 to Dragonerstrasse.

Weinstube Ristorante Leonardo   ITALIAN $$
(🖉0511-321 033; www.weinstube-leonardo.de; Sophienstrasse 6; mains €14-28; ⊘noon-2.30pm & 6-10pm Mon-Fri, from 6pm Sat) Tucked away in a side street behind the Hauptbahnhof is this delightfully old-fashioned restaurant serving primarily Italian fare of the masterfully crafted variety. The restaurant itself is quite small and has been something of a local secret; book ahead if you can.

Hiller   VEGETARIAN $$
(🖉0511-321 288; www.hannover-vegetarisch.de; Blumenstrasse 3; mains €8-12; ⊘noon-11pm Mon-Sat; 🖉) Germany's oldest vegetarian restau-

rant is a tad hushed and old fashioned, but the interior, with colourful draped cloth on the walls, is cheery. Food is well prepared and excellent value.

La Perla   ITALIAN $$
(🖉0511-661 186; www.ristorante-laperla.de; Bürgerstrasse 1; mains €8-20; ⊘noon-10pm) This tidy, no-fuss Italian on the corner of Lister Meile, replete with candles in silver holders and old-fashioned service from jovial Italian staff, also has a great patio out front. You'll find tasty, well-priced authentic pasta, pizza and all the usual takes on meat, fish and poultry. It's one of those places that's either full or you'll have the place to yourself.

Choi's   KOREAN $$
(🖉0511-313 132; www.restaurant-chois.de; mains €9-16; ⊘noon-3pm & 6-10pm Mon-Sat) You can smell the traditional Korean cooking as you climb the stairs to this spotless family affair on the Lister Meile. Traditional Korean meals and some hybrid German-Chinese dishes are served. The lunch time buffet is great value (adult/concession €8/6) and the Korean dumplings (fried or steamed) are hard to resist.

Tomo Sushi   JAPANESE $$
(🖉0511-343 443; Volgersweg 18; mains €8-24; ⊘noon-3pm & 6-10pm Mon-Fri, 6-10pm Sat & Sun) Run by a friendly Japanese and Korean husband and wife team, this tidy little restaurant feels like something you'd find in a rural Japanese town. There's a wide range of sushi and *donburi* (dishes served on rice) and bento boxes are available.

🍸 Drinking & Nightlife

Hanover has two main clusters of clubs and bars. One place to head is the red-light district of Steintor (cheekily nicknamed Stöhntor by locals, meaning 'Moaning Gate'), in a former strip- and sex-club stronghold. The other is around the revamped Raschplatz, behind the Hauptbahnhof. Many of the clubs around Steintor have free admission, so you can look inside and pick and choose if you like. Hanover's cultural centres, clubs and music venues are also good places for a drink.

Auszeit   BAR
(🖉0511-336 5588; www.auszeit-hannover.de; Friesenstrasse 15; ⊘5pm-1am Mon-Sat) This colourful, ambient Oststadt lounge-bar is a bit of this and a bit of that, with something for everyone. There's an inviting loft seating

area upstairs and a generous happy 'hour': all cocktails are €4.30 until 8pm.

Schöne Aussichten 360° BAR
(☑0511-982 6833; http://beach.sceneevents. de; Röselerstrasse 7, Parkdeck level 6) Putting a beach club atop a carpark (with deckchairs and sand) is a very Berlin thing to do and it works, bringing out that sense of fun in people. It's open in the warmer months; check the website for the current event details.

Jack the Ripper's London Tavern PUB
(☑0511-169 5395; www.jacktherippers.de; Georgstrasse 26; ☺noon-1am) In the heart of Kröpcke, this popular British basement pub is famous for its beef pies, fish and chips, and vaulted ceiling. It's a good spot to watch football.

Brauhaus Ernst August PUB
(www.brauhaus.net; Schmiedestrasse 13; ☺8am-3am Mon-Thu, to 5am Fri & Sat, 9am-3pm Sun) A Hanover institution, this sprawling brewpub makes a refreshing unfiltered pilsner called *Hannöversch*. A party atmosphere reigns nightly, helped along by a varied roster of live bands and DJs.

Bronco's BAR
(Schwarzer Bär 7; ☺from 5pm Mon-Sat) Bronco's brings together the features of a bar, club and lounge in decor that snaps up the best of the 1960s and '70s. You'll find a good selection of cocktails, as well as DJs and a small dance floor. Take tram 9 or 17 to Schwarzer Bär.

HeimW BAR
(☑0511-235 2303; www.heim-w.de; Theaterstrasse 6; ☺10am-1am Mon-Thu & Sun, to 2am Fri & Sat) This long, narrow bar has lights shaped like huge droplets of water about to land on your head, an atrium ceiling, potted palms beside cream leather banquettes, and intriguing artwork on the walls. Salads, pasta, tapas, breakfast, burgers and classic German meat dishes are also served here (€5 to €17.90).

Waterloo BEER GARDEN
(☑0511-156 43; www.waterloo-biergarten.de; Waterloostrasse 1; ☺11am-1am) Hanover's most popular beer garden has a lovely stand of trees, low prices and a large screen that shows German League football matches, and always the Hannover 96 game.

Holländische Kakao-Stube CAFE
(☑0511-304 100; www.hollaendische-kakao-stube. de; Ständehausstrasse 2-3; ☺9am-7.30pm Mon-Fri, to 6.30pm Sat) With the blue-and-white square-patterned floor matching the Delft pottery, and a curved ship's staircase and maritime paintings creating a subtle nautical feel, this historic Dutch coffeehouse has many fans, young and old.

Eve Klub CLUB
(☑0511-262 5151; www.eve-klub.de; Reuterstrasse 3-4; ☺mostly Fri & Sat) This former striptease bar has kept the red lamps over the tables and red corduroy sofas.

200 Ponies CLUB
(☑0511-160 4124; www.200ponies.com; Goseriede 4, Tiedthof; ☺Wed, Fri & Sat) If you're young and frisky, head to the Tiedhof courtyard and this den of hormones.

Kiez Klub CLUB
(☑0511-268 5286; www.kiez-klub.de; Scholvinstrasse 5; ☺midnight-6am Mon-Thu, 11pm-9am Fri & Sat) Minimal house, techno house, electro house, hip hop you don't stop...

Osho Diskothek CLUB
(☑0511-642 2785; www.osho-disco.de; Raschplatz 7l; ☺10pm-4am Wed-Sun) Fondly called 'Baggi' by the Hanoverians, Osho offers classic disco hits for the over-25s.

Palo Palo CLUB
(☑0511-7902 0210; www.palopalo.de; Raschplatz 8a; ☺11pm-6am Fri, Sat & Mon) On Hanover's nightlife calendars for over two decades, this club spins dance classics, soul, R&B and hip hop, with a high see-and-be-seen factor.

Rocker CLUB
(☑0511-514 5492; www.rocker-hannover.de; Reuterstrasse 5; ☺9pm-7am Thu-Sun) The only club in Hanover committed to rock draws a crowd committed to rocking out.

☆ Entertainment

For listings, check out the local edition of *Prinz*, in German (www.prinz.de/hannover).

Cinemas

Astor Grand CINEMA
(☑01805-333 966; www.astor-grandcinema.de; Nikolaistrasse 8) Hanover's newest premium cinema complex is one of Germany's largest, with 10 screens, luxury seating and state-of-the-art, well... everything.

Hochhaus-Lichtspiele CINEMA
(☑0511-144 54; www.filmkunstkinos-hannover.de; Goseriede 9) This spacious art-house cinema is on the top floor of a magnificent expressionist building designed by Fritz Höger, the

architect of Hamburg's Chilehaus. Check listing times, as the box office only opens just before screenings.

Theatre & Classical Music

Staatsoper Hannover   PERFORMING ARTS
(☑ 0511-9999 1111; www.staatsoperhannover.de; Opernplatz 1) Housed in the 19th-century Opera House that was lovingly restored after suffering WWII damage. Classical music as well as ballet and opera are performed.

Schauspielhaus   THEATRE
(☑ tickets 0511-9999 1111; www.schauspielhannover. de; Prinzenstrasse 9) Home to the Staatstheater Hannover and sometimes used to host international performances.

GOP Varieté Theatre   THEATRE
(☑ 0511-301 8670; www.variete.de/hannover; Georgstrasse 36) An old-school type of variety theatre with dancing, acrobatics, circus-style acts, magic, music and more, housed in the Georgspalast. It also boasts a much-lauded restaurant.

Marlene Bar & Bühne   PERFORMING ARTS
(☑ 0511-368 1687; www.marlene-hannover.de; cnr Alexanderstrasse & Prinzenstrasse; free-€15) Hanover's popular cabaret venue.

Neues Theater   THEATRE
(☑ 0511-363 001; www.neuestheater-hannover.de; Georgstrasse 54) Excellent performances of contemporary theatre.

Theater am Aegi   THEATRE
(☑ 0511-989 3333; www.theater-am-aegi.de; Aegidientorplatz) Comedies and theatre with musical accompaniment.

Live Music
Check the websites of the following venues (usually under 'Programm'), or listings, for dates and prices of events.

Café Glocksee   CLUB
(☑ 0511-161 4712; www.cafe-glocksee.de; Glockseestrasse 35; ☺ 9pm-5am Tue, 11pm-6am Fri & Sat) Part live-music venue, part club, the Glocksee has everything from techno and trance DJs to grungy gigs. Take tram 10 or 17 to Goetheplatz.

Capitol   LIVE MUSIC
(☑ 0511-444 066; www.capitol-hannover.de; Schwarzer Bär 2; ☺ box office 9.30am-6.30pm Mon-Fri) This former movie theatre has rock, pop, house, soul and more on weekends and frequently during the week. Take tram 9 or 17 to Schwarzer Bär.

Kulturzentrum Faust   PERFORMING ARTS
(☑ 0511-455 001; www.kulturzentrum-faust.de; Zur Bettfedernfabrik 1-3, Linden; ☺ box-office 10am-noon & 2-5pm Mon-Fri) Ska from Uruguay, Chinese new year festivals, disco, reggae, heavy-metal gigs, hip hop, multimedia installations, quiz evenings, book readings and film evenings – all this happens, and more, in this former factory complex. The 1960s concert hall is complemented by a pub-bar, Mephisto, beer garden and cafe. Take tram 10 to Leinaustrasse.

Musiktheater Bad   PERFORMING ARTS
(☑ 0511-169 4138; www.musiktheater-hannover.de; Am Grossen Garten 60; ☺ box-office 10am-3pm Mon-Fri) In this large old building and its surrounding grounds, you'll find a mixed bag of live music, music theatre and dance offerings. It's great in summer when there's an outdoor stage. Take tram 5 to Herrenhäuser Markt and walk for 20 minutes.

Jazz Club Hannover   JAZZ
(☑ 0511-454 455; www.jazz-club.de; Am Lindener Berg 38) Hanover's premier jazz club, with top acts from Germany and abroad. Take tram 9 to Nieschlagstrasse.

Pavillon   PERFORMING ARTS
(☑ 0511-235 5550; www.pavillon hannover.de; Lister Meile 4, office 9am-6pm) This huge circular

***

GAY & LESBIAN HANOVER

With Berlin so close at hand, Hanover's gay scene has seen better days but there's a handful of friendly establishments here. The most up-to-date source for listings is http://gay-szene.net.

Café Konrad (☑ 0511-323 666; www.cafe-konrad.de; Knochenhauerstrasse 34; meals from €7; ☺ 10am-midnight Sun-Thu, to 1am Fri & Sat, breakfast to 4pm) This convivial LGBT cafe has a changing menu of weekly specials and is the epicentre of Hanover's gay grapevine.

Schwule Sau (www.schwulesauhannover. de; Schaufelder Strasse 30a) This alternative gay and lesbian centre, refitted in 2015, regularly hosts concerts, theatre and club nights. Take the U6 or 11 to Kopernikusstrasse from Kröpcke.

Martinos (☑ 0511-388 3301; martinos-hannover.de; Gretschenstrasse 16; ☺ 5pm-3am Sun-Thu, to 5am Fri & Sat) A cafe and bar with lots of events. Take the tram 3, 7 or 9 to Sedanstrasse/Listermeile.

venue has a cafe-bar, theatre and rooms used as venues where you can catch a wide program of jazz, off-beat rock, world music and whatever else anyone decides to put on there.

Sport

AWD Arena
STADIUM

(www.hannover96.de; U Waterloo) This football stadium with a capacity of 49,000 is home turf for Hannover 96 football club. You can pick up available tickets at the ground on the same day for league matches or anytime from the DB service point inside the Hauptbahnhof. Those with extra tickets (scalpers if it's a big match) sell them on the tree-lined alley leading to the ground.

Follow the stream of fans or take tram 3, 7 or 9 from Hauptbahnhof to Waterloo and follow the signs for about 500m, or bus 100 from Kröpke to Maschsee/Sprengel Museum.

🛍 Shopping

Hanover's compact city centre makes it ideal for shopping, although most of what you will find is modern, international fashion. A pedestrianised zone full of shops extends south from the Hauptbahnhof, along Bahnhofstrasse, Georgstrasse and Karmarschstrasse. Lister Meile has some great shops.

Leine Flea Market
MARKET

(Am Hohen Ufer; ⊙8am-4pm Sat) Germany's first flea market , established in 1967, is still going strong in a lovely spot along the Leine River Canal.

Ernst-August-Galerie
SHOPPING CENTRE

(Ernst-Aug-Platz 2) A large, modern complex alongside the train station.

Niki de Sainte Phalle Promenade
MALL

(Bahnhofstrasse) A subterranean shopping strip running below the street.

ℹ Information

DISCOUNT CARDS

Available from the tourist office and DB service point inside the main train station, **Hannover-Card** (1/2/3 days €9.50/15/18) offers unlimited public transport and discounted admission to museums.

EMERGENCY

Call ☏ 0511-314 044 for the Medical Emergency Service.

Diakoniekrankenhaus Friederikenstift
(☏ 0511-304 31; www.diakoniekrankenhaus-friederikenstift.de; Marienstrasse 37)

Police (☏110; Raschplatz)

MONEY

Reisebank (Hauptbahnhof; ⊙8am-10pm Mon-Sat, 9am-10pm Sun) Reisebank has ATMs plus currency exchange services, inside the station.

POST

Post Office (Ernst-Aug-Platz 2; ⊙9.30am-7.30pm Mon-Fri, to 3pm Sat) The post office is inside the Ernst-August-Galerie.

TOURIST INFORMATION

Hannover Tourist Information (☏information 0511-1234 5111, room reservations 0511-1234 5555; www.hannover-tourismus.de; Ernst-Aug-Platz 8; ⊙9am-6pm Mon-Fri, 10am-3pm Sat & Sun) One of Germany's most multilingual tourist bureaus provides a plethora of pro-Hanover materials and is especially useful during trade fairs, when they're able to book a secret treasure trove of private rooms.

ℹ Getting There & Away

AIR

Hanover Airport (www.hannover-airport.de) has many connections, including **Lufthansa** (www.lufthansa.com) and **Air Berlin** (www.airberlin.com) to/from London-Stansted, **Germanwings** (www.germanwings.com) to/from the UK, Moscow and many other destinations, and **TuiFly** (www.tuifly.com) to/from Moscow, as well as many holiday destinations. The S-Bahn (S5) takes 18 minutes from the airport to the Hauptbahnhof (€3).

BUS

Long-distance and international services leave from the full-service **Zentraler Ombnibus Bahnhof** (ZOB; Central Bus Station; Rundestrsse 12) bus station, making coach travel to/from Hanover more convenient than ever before.

Eurolines Germany (☏ 0511-940 42 69; www.eurolines.de/en/home; Rundestrasse 12; ⊙9am-8.30pm Mon-Fri, till 2pm Sat & Sun) Serves long-distance routes in Europe including daily services from Hanover to Warsaw (return €126) and Moscow (return €215) with a change in Minsk, among other destinations. Ensure you have the correct visas!

MeinFernbus (☏0180-515 9915; www.mein fernbus.de) This long-distance coach operator travels to some 200 destinations in Germany, Denmark, the Netherlands, France, Italy, Austria, Croatia and the Czech Republic.

Berlinlinienbus (☏030-338 4480; www.berlin-linienbus.de) Long-distance coach company connecting Berlin, Hamburg and many other German cities with around 250 destinations in Germany and Europe.

CAR & MOTORCYCLE

Nearby autobahns run to Hamburg, Munich, Frankfurt and Berlin, with good connections to

NEUSCHWANSTEIN OF THE NORTH

Nobles the world over will tell you that ancestral homes can be such a huge financial burden to maintain, especially when they're turreted castles; this one has been tenuously compared to Germany's famous Neuschwanstein.

In late 2005, the family of Prince Ernst August of Hanover (Princess Caroline of Monaco's husband) auctioned off some 25,000 household objects to raise money for the upkeep of their 130-room neo-Gothic fancy. Now a small part of the palace, **Schloss Marienburg** (05069-348 000; www.schloss-marienburg.de; Schloss Marienburg, Pattensen; tour adult/concession 16yr €8/6; 10am-6pm early Mar-Oct), is open to the public.

Admission is by a one-hour tour, either with a tour guide or using an audioguide (English, French, Polish, Russian and Spanish available). Tours include the Knight's Hall, Queen's Library and more.

From Hanover, you can take the B3 28km south or the A7 south and exit 62 to Hildesheim. Take the B1 out of Hildesheim and continue 7km until you come to Mahlehrten. Turn right for Nordstemmen and you should see the castle. By public transport, the best way is to take bus 300 to the stop 'Pattensen', then change to bus 310 to stop 'Marienburg Abzweig Nord'. From there it's 1.5km to the castle.

Bremen, Cologne, Amsterdam and Brussels. Major car rental firms have prominent desks in the Hauptbahnhof.

Sixt (01805-252 525; www.sixt.com; 6am-9pm Mon-Fri, 9am-6pm Sat, 9am-9pm Sun)

Europcar (0511-363 2993; www.europcar.de; 7.30am-9pm Mon-Fri, 9am-4.30 Sat, 11am-8pm Sun)

TRAIN

Hanover is a major rail hub for European and national services, with frequent ICE trains to/from Hamburg Hauptbahnhof (€46, 1¼ hours), Bremen (€33, one hour), Munich (€132, 4¼ hours), Cologne (€72, 2¾ hours) and Berlin (€68, 1¾ hours), among others. Left-luggage lockers are accessible 24 hours.

❶ Getting Around

BIKE

Fahrradstation am Bahnhof (0511-353 9640; www.step-hannover.de/startseite/angebote/radstation; Fernoroder Strasse 2; bicycle per day €7.50; 6am-11pm Mon-Fri, 8am-11pm Sat & Sun) Rents bikes.

PUBLIC TRANSPORT

The transit system of buses and tram/U-Bahn lines (so-called *Stadtbahn* or 'city rail' because some are trams on lines underground) is run by **Üstra** (166 80; www.uestra.de; 6am-11pm Mon-Fri, to 8pm Sat, 7am-8pm Sun). Board most U-Bahn lines, including U-Bahn 8 to the Messe (fairgrounds; €2.60, 19 minutes) from within the north of the Hauptbahnhof (follow signs towards Raschplatz).

Lines U10 and U17 are different. These are overground trams leaving south of the station near the tourist office. Note that the late-night service of the U10 also begins on the north side.

Most visitors only travel in the central 'Hannover' zone, where single tickets are €2.60 and good-value day passes cost €5. If you wish to travel in two/three zones, singles cost €3.30/4.20, while day passes cost €6.40/8.

TAXIS

Call 8484, 2143 or 3811, or try www.better-taxi.de/en. From the centre to the fairgrounds, a taxi costs about €35; to the airport it's about €20.

Celle

05141 / POP 70,745

With 400 half-timbered houses and its Ducal Palace dating back to the 13th century, Celle is graced with a picture-book town centre that is among the most attractive in the region. The white-and-pink Ducal Palace, Celle's centrepiece set in small gardens, contrasts with the ultramodern Kunstmuseum, which is illuminated at night into a '24-hour' museum and successfully creates an interesting contrast of old and new.

To reach the centre from the train station, follow Bahnhofstrasse and turn left at the end of the street.

◉ Sights

Celler Schloss   PALACE, MUSEUM
(Ducal Palace; 05141-909 0851; residenzmuseum.celle.de; Schlossplatz 1; with tour adult/concession €7/5, entrance only €5; 10am-5pm Tue-Sun) Celle's wedding-cake Schloss was built in 1292 by Otto Der Strenge (Otto the Strict)

> ### ❶ EXPLORING THE ALTSTADT
>
> A good way to experience Celle is to take a stroll around the Altstadt. First, pop into the tourist office in the Weser Renaissance-style **Altes Rathaus** (from 1561–79) for an ex(Celle)nt (sic) English walking map. One block south, on the corner of Poststrasse and Runde Strasse, is the ornate **Hoppener Haus** (1532). If you backtrack north past the tourist office and turn right into Neue Strasse, highlights include the **Green House** (1478) with the crooked beam at No 32 and the ornately (and humorously) decorated **Fairy-Tale House** at No 11.

as a town fortification and in 1378 was expanded and turned into a residence. The last duke to live here was Georg Wilhelm (1624–1705), and the last royal was Queen Caroline-Mathilde of Denmark, who died here in 1775. Today it houses administrative offices and the Palace Museum.

One-hour guided tours depart at 11am, 1pm and 3pm from Tuesday to Friday and Sunday, and hourly from 11am to 3pm on Saturday. These take you into sections of the palace you can't otherwise visit, such as the Renaissance Schlosskapelle (Palace Chapel), the 19th-century Schlossküche (Palace Kitchen) and – rehearsals permitting – the baroque Schlosstheater (Palace Theatre).

Kunstmuseum   GALLERY
(☑ 05141-125 44; www.kunst.celle.de; Schlossplatz 7; adult/concession incl Bomann-Museum €5/3, Fri free; ⏰ 10am-5pm Tue-Sun) Billed as the world's first 24-hour art gallery, Celle's sexy cubed Kunstmuseum, housing the Robert Simon Collection, isn't actually open around the clock. Rather, during regular opening hours, you can admire the indoor collection of modern art, including the focal point 'Light Room' by Otto Piene. As night descends, the 'nocturnal museum' glows and oozes different colours as the actual building morphs into an artwork to be observed, with light and a few sounds.

Bomann-Museum Celle   MUSEUM
(☑ 05141-125 44; www.bomann-museum.de; Schlossplatz 7; adult/concession incl Kunstmuseum €5/3; ⏰ 10am-5pm Tue-Sun, last entry 4.15pm) This museum for cultural history was com-

pletely updated in 2013 and houses a broad historic collection alongside a new collection on the work, lives and times of ordinary people in the region.

Stadtkirche   CHURCH
(www.stadtkirche-celle.de; An der Stadtkirche 8; tower adult/concession €2/1; ⏰ church 10am-6pm Tue-Sat year-round, tower 10-11.45am & 2-4.45pm Tue-Sat Apr-Oct) The highlight of the 13th-century Stadtkirche is the 235 steps you can climb to the top of the church steeple for an amazing view of the city: not for those who suffer vertigo. The city trumpeter climbs 220 steps to the white tower below the steeple for a trumpet fanfare in all four directions at 9.30am and 5.30pm daily.

Synagogue   SYNAGOGUE
(Im Kreise 24; ⏰ 3-5pm Tue-Thu, 9-11am Fri, 11am-noon Sun) **FREE** Dating back to 1740, Celle's synagogue is the oldest in northern Germany. It was partially destroyed during Kristallnacht and looks just like any other half-timbered house from the outside. Once a new Jewish congregation formed in 1997, services began to be held here regularly. Changing exhibitions on Jewish history take place next door. The synagogue is at the southeastern end of the Altstadt, in the town's former ghetto.

🛏 Sleeping & Eating

The tourist office can help with camping, 4km from the centre.

You can find numerous eating and drinking options along Schuhstrasse and Neue Strasse, as well as on Am Heiligen Kreuz.

Hotel am Hehlentor   INN $
(☑ 05141-885 600; www.hotel-am-hehlentor.de/en; Nordwall 62/63; s/d from €59/79; P🛈) This quaint, well-maintained inn benefits from a great position on the fringe of the Altstadt, with comfortable homely rooms and a hearty breakfast spread equating to good value.

DJH Hostel   HOSTEL $
(☑ 05141-532 08; www.jugendherberge.de/jh/celle; Weghausstrasse 2; dm under/over 27yr €20.70/24.70; P🛈) This rambling youth hostel inside a former school building caters mostly to school groups in its four- to six-bed dorms. It's a 25-minute walk from the train station, or take bus 2 to Jugendherberge from the top of Bahnhofstrasse, opposite the station. Linen is included.

Hotel Celler Hof HOTEL $$

(☑05141-911 960; www.cellerhof.de; Stechbahn 11; s/d €85/120; P@⊛) The friendly staff, Finnish sauna, tasteful furnishings and central location make this a good all-round option. All rooms have a writing desk, and there's a small lobby bar for relaxing.

★ Althoff Hotel Fürstenhof HOTEL $$$

(☑05141-2010; www.fuerstenhof.de; Hannoversche Strasse 55/56; d from €180; P⊛⊛) In a converted baroque palace, much of this luxury hotel has been extensively refurbished to the highest modern standard. Executive double rooms exude style, sophistication and comfort. The hotel's two restaurants offer a gourmet fine-dining experience: dress to impress. Of course, there's a pool and day-spa for guests.

Taj Mahal Tandoori INDIAN $

(☑05141-978 5060; tajmahal-celle.de; Mauernstrasse 34/Ecke Kleiner Plan; dishes from €7.50; ⊙noon-3pm & 6-11pm) If you're needing a break from heavy German food and fancy something spicy and aromatic, you'll delight in the well-presented range of curries (including a good selection of vegetarian dishes), tandoor dishes and biryani. The lunch specials are great value.

★ Zum Schwejk CZECH $$

(☑05141-233 53; www.zum-schwejk-celle.de; Kanzleistasse 7; mains €12-28) Primarily hearty Czech meals with some German twists are served up in this wonderful historic haus with an excellent balcony dining area. Come for comfort food, old-school Euromantic ambience and cold beer...you'll leave very slowly and need a nap. Highly recommended.

Restaurant Bier Akademie GERMAN $$

(☑05141-234 50; www.bier-akademie-celle.de; Weisser Wall 6; mains €9-28; ⊙noon-2pm & 5-10pm Mon-Thu, 6-10pm Fri & Sat) This family-run restaurant serves an excellent range of beef, poultry and lamb as well as pork, but its speciality is a local roulade, which you can order as a starter or main course. It's just northeast of Schlossplatz.

❶ Information

Tourist Office (☑05141-1212; www.region-celle.com; Markt 14-16; ⊙9am-6pm Mon-Fri, 10am-4pm Sat, 11am-2pm Sun) There's a wealth of English language information available here, as well as some interesting guided tours (from €3.50; in German).

❶ Getting There & Away

CAR

The B3 from Hanover goes straight into the centre of town.

TRAIN

Several trains each hour to Hanover take from 20 minutes (IC; €12) to 45 minutes (S-Bahn; €9.50). There are also IC services to Hamburg (€31, 1¼ hours).

❶ Getting Around

BIKE

Fahrradhaus Jacoby (☑05141-254 89; www.jacoby-bikes.de; Bahnhofstrasse 27; bicycle hire per day €8.50; ⊙9am 1pm & 3-6pm Mon-Fri, 9am-1pm Sat) Try Fahrradhaus Jacoby for bike hire.

BUS

City buses 2 and 4 run between the Hauptbahnhof and Schlossplatz, the two main stations. Single tickets are €2.10 and day passes €5.70.

HORSE

Horse-drawn carriage rides (from €5 per person) depart between April and October from the corner of Bergstrasse and Poststrasse.

TAXI

Call ☑444 44 or ☑280 01 or try www.better-taxi.de/en. Expect to pay €40 each way between Celle and Bergen-Belsen.

Bergen-Belsen

★ Gedenkstätte Bergen-Belsen MEMORIAL

(Bergen-Belsen Memorial Site; ☑05051-475 90; www.bergen-belsen.de; Anne-Frank-Platz, Lohheide; ⊙documentation centre 10am-6pm Apr-Sep, 10am-5pm Oct-Mar, grounds until dusk) **FREE** The Nazi-built camp at Bergen-Belsen began its existence in 1940 as a POW camp, but became a concentration camp after being taken over by the SS in 1943, initially to imprison Jews as hostages in exchange for German POWs held abroad. In all, 70,000 prisoners perished here, most famously Anne Frank. The modern Documentation Centre poignantly chronicles the fates of the people who passed through here.

Unlike Auschwitz in Poland, none of the original buildings remain from the most infamous concentration camp on German soil. Yet the large, initially peaceful-looking lumps of grassy earth – covered in beautiful purple heather in summer – soon reveal their true identity as mass graves. Signs indicate approximately how many people lie in each – 1000, 2000, 5000, an unknown number...

Tens of thousands of prisoners from other camps near the front line were brought to Belsen in the last months of WWII, causing overcrowding, an outbreak of disease and even more deaths. Despite attempts of the SS to hide evidence of their inhumane practices, by destroying documents and forcing prisoners to bury or incinerate their deceased fellow inmates, thousands of corpses still littered the compound when British troops liberated the camp on 15 April 1945.

After WWII, Allied forces used the troop barracks here as a displaced persons' (DP) camp, for those waiting to emigrate to a third country (including many Jews who went to Israel after its establishment in 1948). The DP camp was closed in September 1950.

The Documentation Centre today is one of the best of its kind and deals sensitively with the lives of the camp prisoners – before, during and after incarceration. The exhibition is designed to be viewed chronologically, and part of it focuses on the role of Bergen-Belsen in the early years as a POW camp for mostly Soviet prisoners of war. About 40,000 POWs died here from 1939 to 1942, largely due to atrocious conditions. As you move through the exhibition you can listen to original-language descriptions through headphones (also subtitled on the screens), read documents and explanations, and watch a 25-minute documentary about the camp. This film includes a moving testimony from one of the British cameramen who filmed the liberation. Subtitled screenings rotate between different languages.

In the several hectares of cemetery within the gates is a large stone obelisk and memorial, with inscriptions to all victims, a cross on the spot of a memorial initially raised by Polish prisoners, and the Haus der Stille, where you can retreat for quiet contemplation.

A gravestone for Anne Frank and her sister, Margot, has also been erected (not too far from the cemetery gates, on the way to the obelisk). The entire family was initially sent to Auschwitz when their hiding place in Amsterdam was betrayed to police, but the sisters were later transferred to Belsen. Although no one knows exactly where Anne lies, many pay tribute to their 15-year-old heroine at this gravestone.

Other monuments to various victim groups, including a Soviet memorial, are dotted across the complex.

ⓘ Getting There & Away

BUS

Getting to the memorial by bus is possible but difficult, and it's best to either have your own transport or find people to share a taxi. On Saturdays, a direct bus departs Schlossplatz in Celle at 9am but you need to take a taxi back. The tourist office in Celle has a timetable sheet with a sketch map.

CAR

Driving from Celle, take Hehlentorstrasse north over the Aller River and follow Harburger Strasse north out of the city. This is the B3; continue northwest to the town of Bergen and follow the signs to Belsen.

TAXI

Call ☒ 05051-5555. Expect to pay €18 one way from the village of Bergen to the camp or €40 one way from Celle.

Hildesheim
☒ 05121 / POP 102,800

Hildesheim certainly put on its fancy pants in preparation for its 1200th birthday in 2015. It's hard to believe that Hildesheim was razed by bombing on 22 March 1945 and that its pretty, medieval-looking 'Altstadt' is a post-WWII reconstruction. There are three Unesco World Heritage sites in the Hildesheim area and history buffs will find it worth considering an overnight stop here. If you're visiting Hanover for a trade fair and find no rooms in the capital, Hildesheim makes an excellent alternative base with some decent modern hotels.

◎ Sights & Activities

One of the tragedies of Hitler's excursion into megalomania was the horrendous damage inflicted upon once-magnificent architectural gems such as Hildesheim. After WWII, key parts of the old town such as the Markt were lovingly reconstructed in their former style. Here you'll find, (clockwise from north) the Rokokohaus, Wollenweberhaus, Wedekindhaus, Knochenhauerhaus and Bäckeramtshaus.

The Marktbrunnen fountain in front of the Rathaus has bells that play folk songs at noon, 1pm and 5pm daily.

Bus 1 from Hauptbahnhof to Rathausstrasse drops you near Markt.

★ Dommuseum
MUSEUM

(📞 05121-307 760; www.dommuseum-hildesheim.de/en; Domhof; adult/concession €6/4; ⊙10am-5pm Tue-Sun) Reopened in 2015 after a five-year renovation and expansion process, this engaging museum showcases 1000 years of church history in the cloisters of World Heritage-listed Mariendom Cathedral. Its permanent exhibition explores church-life and religious history 'From the Middle Ages to the Modern', including a priceless, rare collection of treasures, reliquaries and artifacts.

Take bus 1 from Hauptbahnhof to Bohlweg.

Mariendom
CHURCH

(St Mary's Cathedral; 📞 05121-179 1646; www.dom-hildesheim.de/en; Domhof 17; adult/concession €4/3; ⊙10am-6pm) Reopened in 2014 after a painstaking renovation and restoration process, Hildesheim's Unesco World Heritage–listed cathedral took its present form in 1061 and was virtually rebuilt after WWII bombing. It's famous for the almost 5m-high Bernwardsturen, bronze doors with bas-reliefs dating from 1015. These depict scenes from the Bible's Old and New Testaments. The church's wheel-shaped chandelier and the Christussäule (Column of Christ) are also from the original cathedral.

Be sure to look out for the Tausend-Jähriger Rosenstock (1000-year-old rose-bush) located in the cathedral cloister.

To reach the Dom from Hauptbahnhof, take bus 1 to Bohlweg.

St Michaeliskirche
CHURCH

(📞 05121-344 10; www.michaelis-gemeinde.de; Michaelisplatz 2; ⊙10am-4pm) **FREE** The Unesco-protected Church of St Michael was built in the Romanesque style in 1022 and reconstructed after war damage. Unusual features inside are the alternation of round columns and square pillars as supports, its painted wooden ceiling, a late-12th-century chancel barrier decorated with angels, the cloisters and a crypt containing Bernward, the bishop of Hildesheim from 993 to 1022, who commissioned many artists and strove to make Hildesheim a cultural centre in his day.

Bus 1 to Museum drops you within a few minutes' walk of the church.

Stadtmuseum
MUSEUM

(📞 05121-299 3685; www.stadtmuseum-hildesheim.de; Markt 7-8; adult/concession €2.50/2; ⊙10am-6pm Tue-Sun) This town museum is located in

the reconstructed Knochenhauerhaus, one of Germany's most intricate half-timbered houses. Exhibits are spread over five floors, starting with changing exhibitions on the ground floor, leading into the town's history, and finally a silverware collection on the top floor.

Roemer-und Pelizaeus-Museum
MUSEUM

(📞 05121-936 90; www.rpmuseum.de; Am Steine 1-2; adult/concession €10/8; ⊙10am-6pm Tue-Sun) This museum houses one of Europe's best collections of Egyptian and Peruvian art and artefacts. There are dozens of mummies, scrolls, statues and wall hangings, but the life-size re-creation of an Egyptian tomb (of Sennefer) is a particular highlight. Take bus 1 from Hauptbahnhof to Museum.

JoBeach
SWIMMING

(📞 05121-281 5112; www.jowiese.de; Lucienvörder Allee 1; adult/child €3.90/2.50; ⊙6am-8pm) This attractive swimming complex in landscaped parklands features outdoor splash, swimming and diving pools and its own 'beach' on a private lake (June to October). It's a great spot to cool down on a hot summer's day.

🛏 Sleeping

Its proximity to Hanover means Hildesheim often takes overflow guests during trade fairs, when accommodation prices rise phenomenally.

Ibis Styles Hildesheim
HOTEL $

(📞 05121-912 8700; www.ibis.com; Zingel 26; d/tw incl breakfast from €59; 🅿 ❄ 🛜) This shiny low-cost hotel in the centre of town is Hildesheim's newest and best-value option, with bright, fresh everything, splashes of colour and a fantastic location. Standard rooms have a full double bed: no pesky singles.

DJH Hostel
HOSTEL $

(📞 05121-427 17; www.djh-niedersachsen.de/jh/hildesheim; Schirrmannweg 4; dm under/over 27yr from €22.30/26.30; 🅿 @) This hostel is inconveniently located on the edge of town and close to forest, but it's well run and modern. From Hauptbahnhof, take bus 1 to Schuhstrasse and change to 4 in the direction of Im Koken-Hof. Get off at the Triftstrasse stop and walk the remaining 750m uphill. Linen is included.

★ Van der Valk Hotel Hildesheim
HOTEL $$

(📞 05121-3000; www.vandervalk.de; Markt 4; s/d from €74/84; @ 🛜 🌊) Behind its historic frontage on the central market place, this luxury

WORTH A TRIP

BAUHAUS: FAGUS FACTORY
....
Fagus Werk (Fagus Factory; ☑ 05181-7914; www.fagus-werk.com/en; Hannover-sche Strasse 58, Alfeld; adult/concession €8/6; ☺ 10am-4pm) Designed and built by Bauhaus founder, Walter Gropius in 1911, this factory, which has been producing shoe lasts for over 100 years, is regarded as the first building in the world conforming to the modern architectural style. Given Unesco World Heritage status in 2011, sections of the building have been turned into a gallery that focuses on Gropius' life, the Bauhaus movement, the history of the Fagus company and footwear in general. Guided factory tours are recommended.

It's just over a five-minute walk to the factory from Alfeld station, serviced by regional trains from Hanover (€10.60, 30 minutes) and a 30-minute drive from Hildesheim.

hotel reveals a surprisingly large interior, with a flagstone-floored atrium entrance giving way to tasteful rooms in subtle tones. The pool and Finnish sauna are a bonus.

Novotel HOTEL $$
(☑ 05121-171 70; www.accorhotels.com; Bahnhof-sallee 38; r from €89; ⓟ@�?) Hildesheim's classy Novotel features exposed stone walls, gentle tones and cosy designer-chic style. It's set back from the street in quiet grounds and has excellent dining and bar facilities.

✖ Eating & Drinking
There are quite a few eating and drinking options along the popular Friesenstrasse (just behind Schuhstrasse), where the pubs and bars usually sell cheap meals.

Café Desseo MEDITERRANEAN $
(☑ 05121-399 27; www.cafedeseo.de; Hinden-burgplatz 3; items from €3; ☺ from 8am Mon-Sat, from 9am Sun; ☎) Generally billed as a tapas bar, this excellent venue is actually more of an all-rounder, with sandwiches, delicious wraps, pasta, pizza and other dishes right up to the top-of-the-range steak. In summer there's outdoor seating. Breakfasts are a hit.

Nil im Museum INTERNATIONAL $$
(☑ 05121-408 595; www.nil-restaurant.de; Am Steine 1; mains €8-19; ☺ 11am-6pm Tue-Sun) This relaxed restaurant in the Roemer- und Pelizaeus-Museum serves delicious antipasti, pasta and salads, along with poultry and red-meat main courses. There's music on Monday ('anything but mainstream').

Schlegels Weinstuben INTERNATIONAL $$$
(☑ 05121-331 33; schlegels-weinstuben.de; Am Steine 4-6; mains €11.50-22.50; ☺ 6-11pm Mon-Sat) The lopsided walls of this rose-covered, 500-year-old house add to its charm. Inside are historic rooms and a round, glass-topped table fashioned from a well, where you can dine overlooking the water. Select the changing seasonal and regional cuisine from the blackboard brought to your table; book ahead.

ⓘ Information
Il Giornale (☑ 05121-123 30; www.internet-ca-fe-hildesheim.de; Judenstrasse 3-4; per hr €2; ☺ 8am-8pm Mon-Sat) Internet access in an Italian cafe atmosphere.

Post Office (Bahnhofsplatz 3-4; ☺ 8.30am-6pm Mon-Fri, to 1pm Sat)

Tourist Office Hildesheim (☑ 05121-179 80; www.hildesheim.de; Rathausstrasse 20; ☺ 10.30am-6pm Mon-Fri, 9am-3pm Sat, 11am-3pm Sun) Helpful staff can provide a range of bilingual information and maps, in addition to making accommodation reservations.

ⓘ Getting There & Around

BUS
Most sights in Hildesheim are within walking distance of the centre, but from Hauptbahnhof bus 1 is useful as it passes Schuhstrasse (for Markt and the tourist office), Bohlweg (for the ca-thedral sights) and Museum (for the Roemer- und Pelizaeus-Museum). Single tickets cost €2.35 (60 minutes); day tickets cost €5.10.

CAR
The A7 runs right by town from Hanover, while the B1 goes to Hamelin.

TRAIN
Frequent regional and suburban train services operate between Hildesheim and Hanover (€8.20, 30 minutes), while ICE trains to/from Braunschweig (€15, 25 minutes) and Göttingen (€26, 30 minutes) stop here on the way to/from Berlin (€63, 1¾ hours).

Braunschweig
☑ 0531 / POP 248,900
Still famous as the city of Heinrich der Löwe (Henry the Lion), nine centuries after this powerful medieval duke made it his capital,

Braunschweig (Brunswick) reveals its past with a reconstructed town centre: 90% of the city's buildings were destroyed in WWII. Its handful of museums and impressive buildings make it an interesting place to while away a day or two.

◉ Sights

Braunschweig's **Altstadtmarkt** is an appealing square with the step-gabled Renaissance **Gewandhaus** (built 1303; facade redesigned 1590) and the Gothic **Altstadt Rathaus**.

Head to the oldest part of town, the area known as the **Magniviertel**, for handsome, half-timbered houses, cafes and bars.

Braunschweiger Löwe   MONUMENT

(Burgplatz) Braunschweig's identity is intricately tied up with Heinrich der Löwe, a duke who was responsible for colonising the eastern regions of Germany beyond the Elbe and Saale. The Brunswick lion statue is based on the original lion Heinrich ordered to be made in 1166 as a symbol of his power and jurisdiction, and today it's the symbol of the city; you can see the original at Burg Dankwarderode.

Dom St Blasii   CHURCH

(St Blasius Cathedral; ☑ 0531-243 350; www.braunschweigerdom.de; Domplatz 5; crypt admission €1; ⊙ 10am-5pm) The tomb of Heinrich der Löwe, the powerful duke who made Braunschweig his capital in the 12th century, can be found lying alongside his wife Mathilde in the crypt of Dom St Blasii. The Nazis decided to co-opt his image and in 1935 exhumed his tomb to conduct an 'archaeological investigation'. The corpse found inside had one short leg and dark hair, which threw the master-race propagandists into a spin and raised doubt as to whether it's really Heinrich inside.

Burg Dankwarderode   MUSEUM

(☑ 0531-1215 2618; www.museum-braunschweig. de; Burgplatz 4; adult/concession €5/2.50; ⊙ 10am-5pm Tue & Thu-Sun, 1-8pm Wed) This former castle of Heinrich der Löwe is now a museum housing a glittering medieval collection, including golden sculptures of arms, medieval capes and Braunschweig's symbol, the original bronze lion statue cast in 1166. Upstairs is a huge, spectacularly adorned Knights' Hall, which contains the pick of the crop from the Herzog Anton Ulrich Museum until it reopens after restoration in late 2016.

Landesmuseum   MUSEUM

(State Museum; ☑ 0531-121 50; www.landesmuseum-bs.de; Burgplatz; adult/concession €4/2; ⊙ 10am-5pm Tue-Sun) This chronologically ordered museum features engaging exhibits, starting with a large Foucault pendulum illustrating the principle of the Earth's rotation, leading to artefacts narrating Germany's past, including eclectic objects like the strands of hair allegedly belonging to Heinrich der Löwe and his wife Mathilde. They are in cases of silver, gold and marble, specially constructed in 1935 as part of Hitler's propaganda offensive to present Heinrich posthumously as one of his own.

Schlossmuseum   MUSEUM

(☑ 0531-470 4876; www.schlossmuseum-braunschweig.de; Schlossplatz 1; admission incl audioguide €3/1.50; ⊙ 10am-5pm Tue-Sun) Braunschweig's Ducal Palace was badly damaged in WWII and demolished in 1960. The present building is an impressive reconstruction completed in 2007, using original elements. Its palace museum uses multilingual, interactive technology to explain the region's rulers and history, and features rooms with original furnishings from the 19th century.

🛏 Sleeping & Eating

DJH Hostel   HOSTEL $

(☑ 0531-866 8850; http://braunschweig.jugendherberge.de/en; Wendenstrasse 30; dm under/over 27yr from €26.90/30.90) This sparkling jewel in the crown of the DJH Hostel Network was opened in 2015 and offers the newest, cheapest digs in town.

★ Steigenberger Parkhotel   HOTEL $$

(☑ 0531-482 220; http://en.steigenberger.com/ Braunschweig; Nimes-Strasse 2; r from €78) The best thing about this popular 163-room business/conference hotel is its wonderful location in the middle of Burgerpark. Rooms are spacious, stylish and well appointed. There's free wi-fi, three restaurants, an excellent day spa and an outdoor pool in the summer months.

Frühlings-Hotel   HOTEL $$

(☑ 0531-243 210; www.fruehlingshotel.de; Bankplatz 7; s/d from €79/99; P @ 🛜) Friendly good-humoured staff, a stylish ground floor with reception and guest lounge, plus varying categories of comfortable rooms make this an excellent choice. Tram M5 from Hauptbahnhof to Friedrich-Wilhelm-Strasse stops nearby.

★ Mutter Habenicht GERMAN $

(☑ 0531-459 56; www.mutter-habenicht.de; Papenstieg 3; mains €6-19; ☺ noon-2:30pm & 6-10pm) This 'Mother Hubbard' dishes up filling portions of schnitzels, potatoes, steaks, spare ribs and the occasional Balkan dish in the dimly lit, bric-a-brac-filled front room, or in the small beer garden out the back.

Kegel Bahnhof GERMAN $$

(☑ 0171-4000 0444; www.kegel-bahnhof.de; Kurt-Schumacher-Strasse 11; mains €8-18; ☺ 3-11pm Mon-Sat) A few minutes walk from the station, this rustic and railroad-y, train-themed restaurant (and bowling alley!) oozes ambience and is fun for adults and kids alike. Tasty German meals are made from fresh local ingredients and the menu features seasonal specials and a great selection of German beer.

Ox STEAK $$$

(☑ 0531-243 900; www.oxsteakhouse.com; Güldenstrasse 7; mains €18-48; ☺ noon-2.30pm & 6-11pm) Ox bills itself as the best steakhouse in town, and there can be little doubt about this for its prime and choice American beef and lamb. Connoisseurs of schnapps will soon be hailing the waiter for the trolley, which is filled with excellent, often lesser-known local and international varieties.

🍷 Drinking & Entertainment

The Magniviertel has a smattering of traditional pubs, while Kalenwall has a string of clubs that are mostly open on Friday and Saturday. Useful listings can be found in the tourist office's *Braunschweig Bietet* or the quarterly *Hin & Weg*.

Strupait CAFE

(☑ 0531-2392 9494; www.strupait.de; Magnitorwall 8; cakes from €4; ☺ 9am-10pm Tue-Thu, 10am-10pm Fri & Sat, 10am-6pm Sun) Nestled on a corner in the Magniviertel, this cafe and bar also serves a few light dishes such as quiche to accompany the wine in an elegant interior. It has outside seating in summer.

Lindbergh Palace CLUB

(www.disko-kolchose.de; Kalenwall 3; ☺ 10pm-5am Thu-Sat, 9pm-late Fri & Sat) One of Braunschweig's premier clubs for those into soul, funk and electro.

Staatstheater Braunschweig
'Grosses Haus' PERFORMING ARTS

(☑ ticket office 0531-123 4567; www.staatstheater-braunschweig.de; Am Theater/Steinweg) This historic venue is used for classical music, theatre, dance and opera. The tourist office sells tickets, or turn up an hour before the event for rush tickets.

ℹ Information

Main Post Office (Berliner Platz 12-16; ☺ 9am-7pm Mon-Fri, 10am-1pm Sat) Alongside the Hauptbahnhof.

Tourist Service Braunschweig (☑ 0531-470 2040; www.braunschweig.de; Kleine Burg 14; ☺ 10am-7pm Mon-Fri, to 4pm Sat) Helpful staff hawk an array of English-language literature and maps.

ℹ Getting There & Away

CAR

The A2 runs east–west between Hanover and Magdeburg across the northern end of the city. This connects with the A39 about 25km east of the city, which heads north to Wolfsburg. The A39 also heads south from the city.

TRAIN

There are regular RE services to Hanover (€12.90, 45 minutes) and IC trains to Leipzig (€45, two hours). ICE trains go to Berlin (€58, one hour 20 minutes) and Frankfurt (€91, 2¾ hours).

ℹ Getting Around

Braunschweig is at the heart of an integrated transport network that extends throughout the region and as far south as the Harz Mountains. Ninety-minute bus and tram tickets cost €2.20; 24-hour tickets €5.50. Any bus or tram going to 'Rathaus' from the Hauptbahnhof will get you to the centre in 10 minutes; these leave from the same side as the public transport information booth just outside the train station. Trams 1 or 2 and bus 420 are among these. The M5 tram is useful, connecting the train station with Friedrich-Wilhelm-Platz via Am Magnitor and passing the Herzog Anton Ulrich Museum.

If driving, be aware that there are one-way systems all around the Altstadt. Alternatively, there's parking by the train station.

Wolfenbüttel

☑ 05331 / POP 53,400

'Alles mit Bedacht' (Everything with prudence) was the expression favoured by Duke August II (1579–1666), who founded Wolfenbüttel's famous library and turned the town into a cultural centre in the mid-17th century. This friendly, charming little town is a true delight, about 10 minutes by train from Braunschweig – practically a

suburb, though worlds away in terms of its feel and architecture.

First mentioned in 1118, Wolfenbüttel was virtually untouched by WWII, and it's almost a time capsule of half-timbered houses – there are over 600 of them, almost all beautifully restored.

Stadtmarkt, the town centre, is a five-minute walk northeast of Hauptbahnhof.

In the late 16th century, Dutch workers came to Wolfenbüttel and built an extensive canal system, remnants of which today survive in a quarter of town known as **Klein Venedig** (Little Venice). To reach it from Schlossplatz, walk east along Löwenstrasse to Krambuden and north up Kleiner Zimmerhof.

◎ Sights

Schloss Museum
MUSEUM

(☑ 05331-924 60; www.schlosswolfenbuettel.de; Schlossplatz 13; adult/child €5.50/free; ⊙ 10am-5pm Tue-Sun) Wolfenbüttel's pretty Palace Museum showcases the living quarters of the Braunschweig-Lüneburg dukes, and have been preserved in all their glory of intricate inlaid wood, ivory walls, brocade curtains and chairs. A highlight is the large collection of porcelain. Visiting exhibitions frequently grace its rooms.

Herzog August Bibliothek
MUSEUM, LIBRARY

(Herzog August Library; ☑ 05331-8080; www. hab.de; Lessingplatz 1; adult/concession €5/2; ⊙ 10am-5pm Tue-Sun) This hushed building one of the world's best reference libraries for 17th-century books (if you're a member, that is). Its collection of 800,000 volumes also includes what's billed as the 'world's most expensive book' (€17.5 million at the time of purchase in the 1980s): the *Welfen Evangelial*, a gospel book once owned by Heinrich der Löwe. The original is only on show sporadically, but an impressive facsimile is permanently displayed in the vault on the first floor.

ⓘ Information

Tourist Office (☑ 05331-862 80; www.wolfen-buettel.com; Stadtmarkt 7; ⊙ 10am-6pm Mon-Fri, to 2pm Sat & Sun) Take Bahnhofstrasse north to Kommisstrasse. This joins Kornmarkt, the main bus transfer point.

ⓘ Getting There & Away

Trains connect Wolfenbüttel with Braunschweig's Hauptbahnhof.

Wolfsburg

☑ 05361 / POP 121,750

Arriving in Wolfsburg by train, the first thing you see is an enormous, almost surreal, VW emblem on the side of a factory. It's an image that could have been ripped straight from Fritz Lang's classic film *Metropolis*. Volkswagen is the world's second-largest vehicle manufacturer, and its global headquarters is right here, employing about 40% of Wolfsburg's residents. Company town though it might be, most visitors won't experience so much of that side of things: Wolfsburg is set up quite brilliantly as a modern daytripper's destination, quickly and easily reached by rail between Hanover and Berlin.

Five shiny state-of-the-art museums, covering automobiles, technology, science and modern art, make Wolfsburg a worthwhile visit for travelling families and enquiring minds. Some excellent accommodation options across all price categories make it smart to spend a night here, if you're planning on covering more than one museum.

◎ Sights

★ Autostadt
THEME PARK, MUSEUM

(Car City; ☑ 05361-400; www.autostadt.de/en; Stadtbrücke; adult/concession €15/12, car tower discovery adult/concession €8/6; ⊙ 9am-6pm) A hit with boys of all ages, Autostadt is a celebration of all things automobile, spread across 25 hectares. A visit to this theme park-museum kicks off with a broad view of automotive design and engineering in the Konzernforum, then breaks off into exhibits relating to a bunch of European automobile makers, from Volkswagen to Audi, Bentley, Lamborghini, Seat and Skoda.

Many exhibits are interactive and most have signage in German and English.

Included in the tour is a 45-minute return Maritime Panorama Tour along the Aller River to the outlying district of Fallersleben. Unfortunately, you can't get off the boat.

For a pure, competitive adrenaline rush, ring ahead to organise an English-speaking instructor for the park's obstacle courses and safety training (costing between €28 and €35 each). You'll need a valid licence, of course, and to be comfortable with a left-hand-drive car. The park even has a minicourse, with toy models that can be driven by kids.

★**Phaeno** MUSEUM
(☑05361-890 100; www.phaeno.de; Willy Brandt-Platz 1; adult/concession €12.50/8; ⊙9am-5pm Tue-Fri, from 10am Sat & Sun) The glass-and-concrete building that houses this brilliant and engaging science centre was designed by British-based Iraqi architect Zaha Hadid. Inside are over 300 hands-on physics exhibits and experiments (with instructions and explanations in both German and English), great for inquisitive minds, young and old. It's a couple of minutes by foot from the train station.

AutoMuseum MUSEUM
(http://automuseum.volkswagen.de/en; Dieselstrasse 35; adult/concession/family €6/3/15; ⊙10am-6pm Tue-Sun) Wolfsburg's original Volkswagen Museum has a collection that includes a vehicle used in the *The Love Bug* movie, a Beetle built from wood, the original 1938 Cabriolet presented to Adolf Hitler on his 50th birthday, and the bizarre 'See-Golf', a Golf Cabriolet from 1983 with hydraulic pontoons that extend outwards to make it amphibious. Take bus 208 to Automuseum.

Kunstmuseum GALLERY
(Art Museum; ☑05361-266 90; www.kunstmuseum-wolfsburg.de; Porschestrasse 53; adult/concession €8/4; ⊙11am-8pm Tue, to 6pm Wed-Sun) Wolfsburg's excellent art gallery stages temporary exhibitions of modern art. Buses 201 and 202 from the bus station run there.

Planetarium Wolfsburg PLANETARIUM
(☑05361-8902 5510; www.planetarium-wolfsburg.de; Uhlandweg 2; adult/concession/family €7/5/15) Built in 1982 after VW bartered Golfs for Zeiss projectors with the GDR, this planetarium stages laser and rock shows, star shows and spoken-word performances set to the stars. Show times vary; see the website.

🛏 Sleeping

DJH Hostel HOSTEL $
(☑05361-133 37; www.djh-niedersachsen.de/jh/wolfsburg; Kleiststrasse 18-20; dm under/over 27yr €26.90/30.90; 🅿@🛜) This hostel inside a former fire department building has bright dorms furnished in light-coloured woods. Each dorm has its own bathroom as well as a table with seating. Buses 201, 202, 203 and 204 stop close by. Linen is included.

Innside by Melia HOTEL $$
(☑015 5294; www.melia.com; Heinrich-Nordhoff-Strasse 2; s/d from €94/111) Opened in 2014, this spotless, stylish property is in a great spot a hop, skip and a jump from the station. Its slick black and sleek steel guestrooms

afford every comfort and convenience, including ports in all the right places, wi-fi and a killer LED smart TV.

★**Ritz-Carlton**   HOTEL **$$$**
(☑05361-607 000; www.ritzcarlton.com; Stadtbrücke; r/ste from €305/405; P❈🤖🛋) This hotel is a hard act to beat. The hotel swimming pool is integrated into the harbour basin of the canal, giving it a lakeside feel, while the building forms a stunning arc on one side of Autostadt. The decor is elegant and breathes natural tones. Expect full five-star facilities, complemented by a Michelin-starred restaurant and numerous bars. You can take high tea overlooking the harbour.

✖ Eating & Drinking

Wolfsburg's Autostadt complex has a wide range of restaurants, including a couple in the foyer that you can eat in without having to pay admission.

Wolfsburgers do much of their drinking in Kaufhof – not the department store but a small strip of bars, pubs and a few eateries west of Porschestrasse. The best thing is to wander along and see what appeals.

Vini D'Italia   ITALIAN **$$**
(☑05361-154 46; http://viniditalia-wolfsburg.de; Schillerstrasse 25; dishes €9.50-21.50; ⊙10am-8pm Mon-Sat) This Italian *bottega* acts as a wine store and a small eatery with antipasti and salads for €5 to €8. You can choose from the main menu or the daily lunch menu (€9.50), or simply treat yourself to the daily specialities.

An Nam   VIETNAMESE **$$**
(☑05361-275 7651; www.an-nam.net; Willi-Brandt-Platz 8; mains €8-25; ⊙8.30am-11pm) This clean and bright, centrally located Vietnamese eatery has fresh and flavourful dishes (including *pho*) that haven't been vastly altered from their original styles back home.

Trattoria Incontri   ITALIAN **$$**
(☑05361-437 254; Goethestrasse 53-55; blackboard mains €20-24, pasta €10-15; ⊙lunch & dinner Mon-Sat, 4pm-midnight Sun) On a patch of Goethestrasse with several restaurants and bars, this Italian trattoria is one of the most popular and offers mains from a changing blackboard menu.

🛍 Shopping

Designer Outlets   SHOPPING CENTRE
(☑05361-893 500; www.designeroutlets-wolfsburg. de/en; An der Vorburg 1; ⊙10am-7pm Mon-Sat)

Folks from Hanover come to Wolfsburg just to shop at this massive outlet centre with over 70 stores selling discounted big-name collections. There's a tax-free shopping service too. How much more can you fit in your luggage?

ℹ Information

Main Post Office (Porschestrasse 22-24; ⊙8.30am-6.30pm Mon-Fri, 9am-1pm Sat)

Tourist Office (☑05361-899 930; www. wolfsburg.de; Willy Brandt-Platz 3; ⊙9am-6pm Mon-Sat, 10am-3pm Sun) In the train station. Friendly, helpful staff will load you up with brochures and maps and can help with hotel bookings. You can also rent bikes here from €7.50 per day (book ahead).

ℹ Getting There & Away

CAR

From Braunschweig, take the A2 east to the A39 north, which brings you right into town. Alternatively take the B248 north to the A39.

TRAIN

Frequent IC train services go to Berlin (from €41, 1½ hours) and Hanover (€18, 30 minutes). ICE trains are slightly faster and more expensive. Regional and IC trains go to Braunschweig (€12, 16 minutes).

ℹ Getting Around

BIKE

Zweirad Schael (☑05361-140 64; www. zweirad-schael.de; Kleiststrasse 5) Rents out bicycles from €10 per day.

BUS

Single bus tickets, valid for 90 minutes, cost €2.20 and a day pass costs €5.50. The major bus transfer point (ZOB) is at the northern end of Porschestrasse, near the train station. Buses 203, 204, 206 and 214 go regularly to Fallersleben from here.

TAXI

There are taxi ranks at the Hauptbahnhof and at the northern end of Porschestrasse. Alternatively, call ☑230 23 or try www.bettertaxi.de/en.

BREMEN & THE EAST FRISIAN COAST

They tell us there's an old German saying that 'people from Lübeck drink beyond their means, people from Hamburg eat beyond their means and people from Bremen live beyond their means'. It might never have been true, but it's certainly evident that Bremeners like to enjoy the finer things in life. Bremen, an outward-looking, cultural and industrial capital of its own city state, is a clear urban triumph and a highlight of any visit to the region, along with its 'daughter' city Bremerhaven, at the mouth of the River Weser and Worpswede, the century old artists' colony on the moors.

If you like peat bogs, tidal flats, birdlife and blustery bike rides by the sea, you'll especially enjoy visiting the East Frisian coast and islands, ideally suited to slowing down the pace and immersing yourself in nature.

While rail connections to and around Bremen are excellent, you'll find a combination of buses, boats and trains necessary for exploring outlying regions and the islands. Renting a vehicle can help to keep things simple and off-schedule, so as not to interrupt your unwinding.

Bremen City

📞 0421 / POP 546,450

Bremen, one of Gemany's three city states (along with Berlin and Hamburg), has a justified reputation for being among the country's most outward-looking and hospitable places, with a population that strikes a good balance between style, earthiness and good living.

Nature is never far away here, but Bremen is better known for its fairy-tale character, unique expressionist quarter and one of Germany's most exciting football teams. That nature would get its chance to win back a few urban patches did seem likely from the late 1960s, when the population, having peaked at over 600,000, began to decline. Something else happened, however, to clinch it: in 1979 Bremen was the first to elect Green Party candidates to its state parliament, unwittingly becoming the cradle of a Green movement worldwide. Today, it's also one of Europe's leaders in science and technology, home to Airbus' Defence and Space headquarters and a major Mercedes Benz plant.

More populous than Hanover, Bremen scrapes in as Germany's 10th largest city, but feels quite the contrary, offering a relaxed, unhurried lifestyle. Closer inspection reveals some vibrant districts with fine restaurants and fun bars, a selection of excellent museums, a beautiful Altstadt and some tall tales to complement its legitimate history – likely proof that the people of Bremen are also among Germany's most gregarious.

History

Bremen's origins go back to a string of settlements that developed near today's centre from about AD 100, and one settlement in particular that in 787 was given its own bishop's seat by Charlemagne. In its earliest days, it was known as the 'Rome of the North' and developed as a base for Christianising Scandinavia. Despite this, it gradually shed its religious character, enjoying the greater freedom of being an imperial city from 1186, joining the Hanseatic League in 1260, and in 1646 coming directly under the wing of the Kaiser as a free imperial city; today it is a 'Free Hanseatic City'.

⊙ Sights

Most of Bremen's major sights are in the centre, but its many neighbourhoods each have a different feel.

Böttcherstrasse (www.boettcherstrasse. de) was transformed into a prime example of mostly Expressionist architecture in the 1920s at the instigation of coffee merchant Ludwig Roselius. Many of its ornate red-brick facades house artesanal shops and art museums. Its most striking feature is Bernhard Hoetger's golden Lichtbringer (Bringer of Light) relief that keeps an eye on the north entrance.

Hugging the Weser River, Schlachte is a waterfront ramble with lots of bars and restaurants. Sights on the Weser outside the centre can be easily reached by public transport. The Kulturmeile and Das Viertel neighbourhood is a walk or short tram ride east of the centre and is one of Bremen's liveliest and most interesting areas, packed with restaurants and lots of bars. Areas north and east of the centre have a sprinkling of sights that are usually best reached by tram or bus.

⊙ Markt & Böttcherstrasse

Markt　　　　　　　　　　　　SQUARE

Bremen's Unesco World Heritage–protected Markt is striking, especially for its ornate, gabled and sculpture-festooned Rathaus (town hall; 1410). In front stands a 5.5m-high medieval statue of the knight Roland (1404), the symbolic protector of Bremen's civic rights and freedoms.

THE FANTASTIC FOUR

In the Brothers Grimm fairy tale, the 'Bremer Stadtmusikanten' (Town Musicians of Bremen) never actually make it to Bremen, but when you arrive in the city you might enjoy a quick reminder of what the fuss was about. Starting with a donkey, four overworked and ageing animals, fearing the knacker's yard or the Sunday roasting pan, run away from their owners. They head for Bremen intending, like many young dreamers, to make their fortune as musicians.

On their first night on the road, they decide to shelter in a house. It turns out to be occupied by robbers, as our heroes discover when they climb on the donkey to peer through the window. The sight of a rooster atop a cat, perched on a dog, which is sitting on a donkey – and the 'musical' accompaniment of braying, barking, meowing and crowing – startles the robbers so much, they flee. The animals remain and make their home 'where you'll probably still find them today'.

On Sunday from May to September, this story is charmingly re-enacted (at noon) in Bremen's Markt.

On the town hall's western side is a sculpture of the Town Musicians of Bremen (1951). Local artist Gerhard Marcks cast them in their most famous pose, scaring the robbers who invaded their house, with the rooster atop the cat, perched on the dog, on the shoulders of the donkey.

Dom St Petri   CHURCH

(St Petri Cathedral; ☑ 0421-334 71 42; www.stpetridom.de; Sandstrasse 10-12; tower adult/concession €1/0.70, museum €3/2; ⊙10am-5pm Mon-Fri, till 2pm Sat, 2-5pm Sun) Bremen's Protestant main church has origins in the 8th century and got its ribbed vaulting, chapels and two high towers in the 13th century. Aside from the imposing architecture, the intricately carved pulpit and the baptismal font in the western crypt deserve a closer look. For panoramic views, climb the 265 steps to the top of the south tower (April to October). The Dom-museum displays religious artefacts and treasures found here in a 1970s archaeological dig.

Bleikeller   CRYPT

(Lead Cellar; www.stpetridom.de; Sandstrasse 10-12; adult/child €1.40/1; ⊙10am-5pm Wed-Fri, to 1.45pm Sat, noon-4.45pm Sun Apr-Oct) Located inside Dom St Petri but accessed via a separate entrance south of the main door, the Lead Cellar was formerly the cathedral's cellar and today is a crypt in which bodies have mummified in the incredibly dry air. You can see eight preserved bodies in open coffins here, including a Swedish countess, a soldier with his mouth opened in a silent scream and a student who died in a duel in 1705. It's more than a little creepy.

Roselius-Haus Museum   MUSEUM

(☑ 0421-336 5077; www.museen-boettcherstrasse.de; Böttcherstrasse 6-10; combined ticket adult/concession €6/4; ⊙11am-6pm Tue-Sun; ☒ stop Domsheide) A combined museum with its neighbour, the Paula Modersohn-Becker Museum, this 16th-century house contains a private collection of art from medieval times to the baroque era, which belonged to none other than Ludwig Roselius, the man who gave the world decaffeinated coffee and used the money from his beans and other ventures to bankroll the expressionist Böttcherstrasse in the 1930s.

Paula Modersohn-Becker
Haus Museum   MUSEUM

(☑ 0421-336 5077; www.museen-boettcherstrasse.de; Böttcherstrasse 6-10; combined ticket adult/concession €6/4; ⊙11am-6pm Tue-Sun) Twinned with the Roselius-Haus Museum, this building is the work of Bernhard Hoetger, the creative mind behind much of Böttcherstrasse. It's now home to the Paula Modersohn-Becker Haus Museum and showcases the art of the eponymous painter, Paula Modersohn-Becker (1876–1907), an early expressionist and member of the Worpswede colony.

👁 Schnoor

This maze of narrow, winding alleys was once the fishermen's quarter and later a red-light district. Today its teeny cottages house boutiques, restaurants, cafes and galleries. Though geared to tourists, Schnoor is a pretty place for a stroll and a fun word to say out

Bremen City

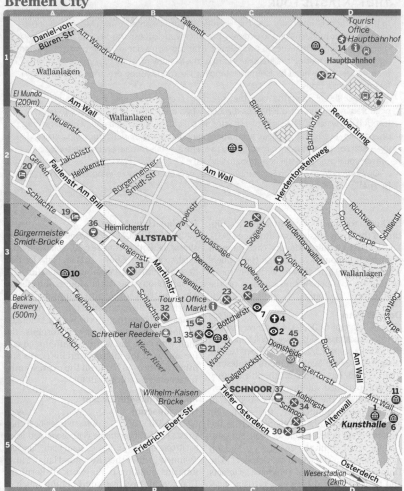

LOWER SAXONY & BREMEN BREMEN CITY

loud. Its restaurants are popular with locals in the evenings.

👁 Schlachte & the Weser

★ Beck's Brewery
BREWERY

(📞0421-5094 5555; www.becks.de/besucherzentrum; Am Deich 18/19; tours €10.90; ⏰10am, 11.30am, 1pm, 3pm, 4.30pm & 6pm Thu-Sat) Two-hour tours of one of Germany's most internationally famous breweries must be booked online. The 3pm tour is also in English. Minimum age 16. Meet at the brewery's visitor centre, reached by taking tram 1, 2 or 3 to Am Brill.

Weserburg Museum
für Moderne Kunst
GALLERY

(Weserburg Museum of Modern Art; 📞0421-598 390; www.weserburg.de; Teerhof 20; adult/concession €8/5; ⏰10am-6pm Tue-Sun) Situated on an island in the Weser River, across from the Schlachte promenade, this museum showcases German and international artists in changing, hot-off-the-press exhibitions.

Hafenmuseum
Speicher XI
MUSEUM

(Harbour Museum Warehouse 11; ☑ 0421-716 8518; www.hafenmuseum-speicherelf.de; Am Speicher XI; adult/concession €5/3.50; ⊙ 11am-6pm Tue-Sun) This former harbour warehouse has a strong permanent exhibition focusing on Bremen's waterside history and the workers who have played a part in making it happen, including a section on forced labourers during WWII. Special exhibitions elaborate on the waterside theme. Take bus 26 to Speicher XI.

◉ Kulturmeile & Das Viertel

★ Kunsthalle
GALLERY

(☑ 0421-329 080; www.kunsthalle-bremen.de; Am Wall 207; adult/concession €8/5; ⊙ 10am-6pm Wed-Tue, to 9pm Tue) For art lovers, the highlight of Bremen's *Kulturmeile* (Cultural Mile) is the Kunsthalle, which presents a large permanent collection of paintings, sculpture and copperplate engraving from the Middle Ages to modern times, as well as changing exhibitions. Some of the masterpieces in the collection are over 600 years old.

Gerhard Marcks Haus
GALLERY

(☑ 0421-989 7520; www.marcks.de; Am Wall 208; adult/concession €5/3.50; ⊙ 10am-6pm Tue-Wed & Fri-Sun, to 9pm Thu) Gerhard Marcks (1889–1981), the man responsible for Bremen's famous Stadtmusikanten sculpture on Markt, is among Germany's greatest sculptors. He was born in Berlin and was one of the artists condemned as 'degenerate' by the Nazis in the 1930s and forbidden from exhibiting his work until after WWII. In 1966 he transferred much of his work into a foundation in Bremen, culminating in this excellent museum with exhibits of his own works as well as those of modern and contemporary sculptors.

Wilhelm Wagenfeld Haus
MUSEUM

(☑ 0421-339 9933; www.wwh-bremen.de; Am Wall 209; adult/concession €3.50/1.50; ⊙ 3-9pm Tue, 10am-6pm Wed-Sun) Wilhelm Wagenfeld (1900–90) was a Bauhaus luminary whose foundation today promotes contemporary design in its many facets and forms in special exhibitions, including, for instance, photography.

◉ North & East of the Centre

★ Universum Science Center
MUSEUM

(☑ 0421-334 60; www.universum-bremen.de; Wiener Strasse 1a; adult/child €16/11; ⊙ 9am-6pm Mon-Fri, 10am-6pm Sat & Sun; ⬚ Universität/NW1) Bremen has a strong aerospace industry, and space buffs will enjoy the eye-catching, oyster-shaped Universum Science Center, where you can make virtual trips to the stars, as well as to the ocean floor or the centre of the earth. Great for kids.

Übersee Museum
MUSEUM

(Overseas Museum; ☑ 0421-160 380; www.ueber-see-museum.de; Bahnhofplatz 13; adult/concession €6.50/4.50; ⊙ 9am-6pm Tue-Fri, from 10am Sat &

Bremen City

Sun) Right by the station, the Übersee Museum takes you to all continents of the world and offers an insight into natural evolution with its dazzling collection of exotic artefacts. It can call on about 1.1 million objects, including African art, tropical plants and gold from South America.

Dutch Windmill HISTORIC BUILDING
(Am Wall) The city's typical Dutch windmill today houses a restaurant and adds a rural flavour to the parkland tracing the part of town where Bremen's city fortifications once were.

Botanika GARDENS
(📞 0421-427 066; www.botanika.net; Deliusweg, Rhododendron-Park; adult/concession €10.50/9.50; ⊙ 9am-6pm Mon-Fri, 10am-6pm Sat & Sun; 🚃 Horner Kirche) If you're a plant lover, don't miss a trip to Botanika and its replicated Asian landscapes from the Himalayas to New Guinea. Admission to the rhododendron park, where you'll find 2000 rhododendrons and azaleas, is free.

⌲ Tours

City Tour BUS TOUR
(www.bremen-tourism.de; €17.90; ⊙ Tue-Sun) Departing from platform L outside the Hauptbahnhof at 11am and from Domsheide in front of the concert hall at 12.30pm, guided tours in German and English give you the best overview of Bremen's neighbourhoods and sights. Take the tour first, then explore for yourself later. Look for the distinctive 'Der Bremen Bus'.

Hal Över Schreiber Reederei BOAT TOUR
(📞 0421-338 989; www.hal-oever.de; Schlachte 2 & Martinianleger; ⊙ office 9am-5pm Mon-Fri) Operates a 75-minute Weser and harbour tour three to five times daily from January to November as well as infrequent scheduled ferry services along the Weser between April and September, as far as Bremerhaven, with numerous stops per route. There are also sailings from Bremen-Vegesack to Worpswede.

Check the English language website for the latest schedules and pricing.

Mercedes Benz Factory Tour TOUR

(www.bremen-tourism.de/mercedes-benz-factory-tour-bremen; adult/concession €15/10; ⊘ 2.30pm Fri May-Oct) Bookable only through the tourist office, English-language tours of Mercedes Benz' Bremen plant, which produces the SL, SLK, C-Class, E-Class Coupé and the GLK luxury models, run on Fridays only from May to October.

Airbus Defence
& Space Tour SCIENCE & TECHNOLOGY

(www.bremen-tourism.de/airbus; adult/concession €16.50/13.50; ⊘ 2pm & 4pm Sat) Truly unique, these fascinating two-hour tours of Airbus Defence & Space facility, which built major sections of the International Space Station, must be booked in advance online, or through the tourist office. For security, you must carry your passport with you at all times.

🛏 Sleeping

Bremen charges a city tax of €1 to €3 per guest per night, added when you pay your bill.

★ Courtyard by Marriott HOTEL $

(☏ 0421-696 400; www.marriott.com; Theodor-Heuss Allee 2; d & tw from €79) This station-side chain hotel in the restored heritage Lloyd Building is recommended for a bunch of reasons: convenience and value; airy, oversized, light-filled rooms; comfy beds; and friendly helpful staff. Modern bathrooms are delights of German design: think super-soaker tubs and floating toilets. It's worth paying the few extra euros for a larger room in the Lloyd building.

Prizeotel Bremen City HOTEL $

(☏ 0421-222 2100; www.prizeotel.com/bremen[]; Theodor-Heuss-Allee 12; s/d from €59/64; ⓟ ❋ 🛜) This funky, fresh and fluoro design hotel won't be everyone's cup of tea, but if you like it, you'll love it. Ultra-modern, compact rooms are quiet despite their proximity to the rail lines: the hotel is a five-minute walk from the station. All rooms feature 32-inch TV's, 'mega beds' and 'maxi showers'.

Townside Hostel Bremen HOSTEL $

(☏ 0421-780 15; www.townside.de; Am Dobben 62; dm from €15, s/d with bathroom from €46/64; 🛜) This bright, professionally run hostel is right in the middle of Bremen's nightlife quarter and handy to Werder Bremen's stadium. Breakfast costs €5.50. Take tram 10 from Hauptbahnhof to Humboldtstrasse or tram 2 or 3 to Sielwall.

Jugendherberge Bremen HOSTEL $

(☏ 0421-163 820; http://bremen.jugendherbergen-nordwesten.de; Kalkstrasse 6; dm under/over 27yr €27/31, s/d from €37/64; @ 🛜) Looking like a work of art from the exterior, with a yellow-and-orange Plexiglas facade and slit windows, this hostel has comfortable rooms, a rooftop terrace and a bar-breakfast room with huge glass windows overlooking the Weser River. Linen is included. Take tram 1 to Am Brill from Hauptbahnhof.

Camping Stadtwaldsee CAMPGROUND $

(☏ 0421-841 0748; www.camping-stadtwaldsee.de; Hochschulring 1; per adult/tent/car €12/4/3.50) This camping ground features modern amenities, a supermarket and Oliver's restaurant close by. Take the A27 to the university exit in Bremen Nord. Tram 6 to Universität/NW1 is close, or change here to bus 28 to Campingplatz.

SAMBA ON THE WESER

As weird as it sounds, every year in January or February, Bremen celebrates a popular **Karneval** (www.bremer-karnival.de; ⊘ Jan/Feb) that has become the largest samba festival in Europe. Okay, so the competition for samba carnivals in Europe isn't exactly enormous, but you can expect about 10,000 people to take to the streets in Bremen. It all began when the 1st Bremer Samba Group swung into action in 1986, and today this merrymaking continues.

As the www.bremer-karnival.de (in German) website puts it, the festival celebrates 'the road from the dark, cold time to brightness and warmth', when 'the foreign, the bizarre, the grotesque and the exotic invade the streets'. Each year the carnival takes a different theme. To get into the swing of things, follow the parade from Markt along Ostertorsteinweg and into Das Viertel. Open-air stages are set up, mostly on Ostertorsteinweg. Dress up warm, weird and inappropriately, and get down to the beat!

Hotel Bremer Haus
HOTEL $

(☑ 0421-329 40; www.hotel-bremer-haus.de; Löningstrasse 16/20; s/d from €42/57; P@🖥) The yellow exterior of this place is somewhat unappealing and its rooms could be considered a tad drab, but they're spotlessly clean and very well maintained. There's a small foyer lounge for mulling over the newspapers and 24-hour reception. Room rates are hard to beat, making the hotel extremely popular with business travellers. Even cheaper advance rates are available.

★ Atlantic Grand
HOTEL $$

(☑ 0421-620 620; www.atlantic-hotels.de; Bredenstrasse 2; r from €109) Pitched around a central courtyard, moments from Bremen's quirky Böttcherstrasse, the simple, effortlessly stylish, dark-wooded rooms with chocolate leather armchairs and top-notch service from attentive staff make this classy hotel an excellent choice.

Radisson Blu
HOTEL $$

(☑ 0421-369 60; www.radissonblu.com/hotel-bremen; Böttcherstrasse 2; r from €94; P🖥✳🖥✳) The 235 guestrooms and suites of this sprawling, full-service international hotel in a premium location by the Markt have been renovated to a high standard. The hotel has annexed what was formerly the Haus Atlantis building, whose striking Himmelssaal room is now an event space. Ask at reception: if its not in use, you can take a look.

Hotel Residence
HOTEL $$

(☑ 0421-348 710; www.hotelresidence.de; Hohenlohestrasse 42; s/d/apt from €70/80/105; P@🖥) This century-old terrace, now a charming hotel, also boasts some funky apartments. The main building has rooms facing the street, while the newer extension backs onto the railway line but is still reasonably quiet. A sauna, solarium, bar and dining room complete the package. Rooms and apartments are furnished in differing styles.

Hotel Überfluss
DESIGN HOTEL $$$

(☑ 0421-322 860; www.hotel-ueberfluss.de; Langenstrasse 72; s/d from €132/169; ✳🖥✳) Just metres above river level, this cutting-edge cool hotel is a good choice for design-minded urban nomads. Black, white and chrome create a sleek, postmodern vibe that extends to the rooms, which feature open bathrooms and Yves Rocher products. Suites have river views and a private sauna and whirlpool – perfect for a honeymoon. Breakfast costs €12.50.

Park Hotel Bremen
HOTEL $$$

(☑ 0421-340 80; www.park-hotel-bremen.de; Im Bürgerpark; s/d from €129/149, ste from €635; P🖥@🖥✳) Although its exterior is certainly dated, this domed lakeside mansion, surrounded by parkland, impresses through its sheer extravagance and could be considered Bremen's only true five-star, grand hotel. It offers access to excellent spa, fitness and beauty facilities, a heated outdoor pool and views over the lake in a 'spa resort' ambience.

Eating

Town Centre

Beck's Bistro
BISTRO $$

(☑ 0421-326 553; www.becks-bistro-bremen.de; Am Markt 9; mains €7-14; ⊙ 9am-11pm) It's worth dining here once if only for the incredible Markt location and outlook: when you're sitting in the terrace on a sunny day sipping a cold Beck's and overlooking the phenomenal architecture of the Markt, you won't be too concerned about what you're eating. Fortunately, the menu of casual European bistro fare is full of cheap and cheerful treats.

★ Bremer Ratskeller
GERMAN $$

(☑ 0421-321 676; www.ratskeller-bremen.de; Am Markt 11; mains €10-20; ⊙ 11am-11pm) Ratskellers were traditionally built underneath the Rathaus in every German town to keep the citizens and civil servants fed. Bremen's is quite the experience, with high vaulted ceilings, an atmosphere that's the real deal on the historical Richter scale (in business since 1405!) and good, heavy, no-fuss German food and beer. What's not to like?

Edel Weiss
AUSTRIAN $$

(☑ 0421-2427 8094; www.edelweiss-bremen.de; Bahnhofsplatz 8; mains €9-20; ⊙ noon-11pm Mon-Fri, from 10am Sat & Sun) Opposite the station, this friendly haunt is famed for its hearty fare and friendly staff: schnitzel and, in season, *spargel* (white asparagus) galore. It's a good first foray into Bremen's tasty restaurant scene.

Chu Ba
VIETNAMESE $$

(☑ 0421-6659 7731; http://chu-ba.de; Knochenhauerstrasse 3-4; mains €13-18; ⊙ noon-3pm & 6-10pm) A compact menu with weekly specials keeps things simple for the uninitiated who might be delighting in the flavours and aromas of Saigon for the first time. This is not your average Vietnamese takeaway joint by any means. Sit back, relax and let your palate enjoy the subtle awakenings that fine Vietnamese cuisine brings.

Ständige Vertretung
GERMAN $$

(☎0421-320 995; www.staev.de; Böttcherstrasse 3-5; mains €9-20; ⊗11.30am-11pm) An offshoot of Berlin's best-known restaurant for home-sick Rhineland public servants, this large, bustling place thrives on its political theme and solid cuisine, washed down with Rhineland wines and beer.

✖ Schlachte & Around

Luv
INTERNATIONAL $$

(☎0421-165 5599; www.restaurant-luv.de; Schlachte 15-18; mains €9-37; ⊗11am-late Mon-Fri, 10am-late Sun) This upbeat bistro has a lounge-bar feel and a menu strong on salads and pasta complemented by mostly meaty mains, including a respectable lava-grill burger, a giant Wiener schnitzel and locally caught fish. In good weather, sit beneath the twinkling lights at the outdoor tables over-looking the Weser River.

El Mundo
INTERNATIONAL $$

(☎0421-384 010; www.elmundo-bremen.de; Konsul-Smidt-Strasse 10a; mains €9-54) This huge restaurant, with enormous chandeliers and portion sizes almost as big, often gets long queues for a table (which some feel are not justified). However, if you're lucky with your timing or have made a reservation, you might be impressed by the diverse international menu and top-notch service. Many mains are under €15.

Le Gril by Loui and Jules
STEAK $$

(☎0421-3017 4443; www.loui-jules.com; Schlachte 36; mains €12-36; ⊗noon-3pm & 6-11pm Mon-Fri, 6-11pm Sat) Located inside Hotel Überfluss, this surf 'n' turf place does excellent wood-coal grills, with steaks starting from €20, but also has many cheaper dishes, including an inexpensive burger and midrange seafood.

Osteria
ITALIAN $$

(☎0421-339 8207; www.osteria-bremen.de; Schlachte 1; mains €8-24; ⊗noon-1am Mon-Fri, 6pm-1am Sat; ✔) Crisp tablecloths and good service are hallmarks of this formal but relaxed Italian restaurant serving a range of grilled meats and seafood. For vegetarians ithere is a fine selection of meat-free pasta dishes.

✖ Schnoor

★Kleiner Olymp
GERMAN $$

(☎0421-326 667; www.kleiner-olymp.de; Hinter der Holzpforte 20; mains €7-19; ⊗11am-11pm) This homely kitchen in Schnoor has a wonderful atmosphere, delicious (and not too heavy) North German cuisine and very reasonable prices. With a selection of mouthwatering soups and starters, seafood (not pork, for a change) features predominantly and appropriately on the menu. Enjoy!

Schröter's
MEDITERRANEAN $$

(☎0421-326 677; www.schroeters-schnoor.de; Schnoor 13; mains €8-29; ⊗noon-11pm) A modern bistro with artful decoration, Schröter's is known for its antipasti and abundant Mediterranean mains, from risotto to fish. It is a veritable warren of rooms, including a Toulouse-Lautrec room upstairs, decorated with plenty of copies of the painter's pictures. Course menus are available.

Katzen Café
INTERNATIONAL $$

(☎0421-326 621; www.katzen-cafe.de; Schnoor 38; mains €12-26; ⊗noon-11pm) This popular Moulin Rouge–style restaurant opens out into a rear sunken terrace bedecked with flowers. The menu runs the gamut from Alsatian to Norwegian, with seafood a strong theme.

✖ Das Viertel

This arty, student neighbourhood is where to head for cheaper meals or simply a glass of wine or beer over something tasty.

Engel Weincafe
CAFE $

(☎0421-6964 2390; www.engelweincafe-bremen.de; Ostertorsteinweg 31; dishes €4-13; ⊗8am-1am Mon-Fri, 10am-1am Sat & Sun; 🔊✔) Exuding the nostalgic vibe of a former pharmacy, this popular hang-out gets a good crowd no matter where the hands on the clock. Come for breakfast, a hot lunch special, crispy *Flammekuche* (French pizza), carpaccio or pasta, or just some cheese and a glass of wine.

Piano
INTERNATIONAL $

(☎0421-785 46; www.cafepiano-bremen.de; Fehrfeld 64; mains €7-13; ⊗9am-1am; ✔) An enduringly popular cafe, this bustling place serves pizza, pasta, a few heartier dishes and veggie casseroles to a broad neighbourhood mix, from media types checking proofs to young mums. Breakfast can also be ordered until 4pm Saturday and 5pm Sunday

LOCAL KNOWLEDGE

HITTING THE BEACH: CAFE SAND

On an island in the Weser River, **Café Sand** (☑ 0421-556 011; www.cafe-sand.de; Strandweg 106; ☺ from noon Mon-Sat, from 10am Sun, closing hours vary) makes you feel light years away from the city. It's favoured by everyone from swimmers and tanners to families and fans of Werder Bremen football club. Get here on foot via the Wilhelm-Kaisen-Brücke (bridge) or by ferry from the Osterdeich (return €2.60, from 3pm Friday, noon Saturday and 10am to 6pm Sunday).

Casa
MEDITERRANEAN $$

(☑ 0421-326 430; www.casa-bremen.com; Ostertorsteinweg 59; mains €10-27; ☺ 11.30am-11pm Mon-Fri, from 10am Sat & Sun) This long-standing local favourite evokes a slight Mediterranean vibe, both in its looks and through its menu, which includes salads, pastas and an inspired selection of tapas. Top marks, though, go to the lava-grill fish and meat dishes (including a signature burger), made with quality organic meats. Breakfast is till noon weekdays and till 3pm weekends.

Rotkäppchen
CAFE $$

(☑ 0421-754 46; Am Dobben 97; breakfast from €3, mains €6-13; ☺ 9am-11pm Mon-Fri, from 10am Sat & Sun; ☎☑) Art posters, drawings and even one or two vinyl records adorn the walls and shelves in this student cafe with an art edge; there's a winter garden and outdoor summer seating. Breakfast on weekends is until 3.30pm.

🍷 Drinking & Nightlife

The waterfront Schlachte promenade has a respectably long line of bars catering to all tastes. For either a slightly older, alternative feel or for a student vibe, head to Das Viertel and just walk along Ostertorsteinweg ('O-Weg'). Auf den Höfen, north of O-Weg and also part of Das Viertel, has a good selection of bars. Check listings mags, such as *Prinz* or *Bremen4U*, for more details.

Clubbing in Bremen is relatively cheap; expect to pay €4 to €8 at the door for regular nights, although special events may cost more.

Bremen is generally a safe town to walk around day or night, but the teenage club mile of Rembertiring, near the main train station, has been a problem zone in recent years. Video cameras and a strong police presence point to its potential for sudden violence. Use big-city sense here.

★ Wohnzimmer
BAR

(www.wohnzimmer-bremen.de; Ostertorsteinweg 99; ☺ from 4pm May-Aug, from 10am Sep-Apr) This bar and lounge mostly gets a relaxed 20s and early 30s crowd, who hang out on the sofas – which explains the name 'Living Room' – or lounge around on the mezzanine levels.

Studio
COCKTAIL BAR, LOUNGE

(☑ 0421-745 77; www.stu-dio.de; Auf den Häfen 12; ☺ from 7pm Tue-Sat) This venue, situated in the small lane known as Auf den Höfen, has changed names over the years but the design and concept remain much the same: a favourite bar, lounge and cocktail place among students, with occasional events.

Lagerhaus
BAR

(☑ 0421-701 0000; www.kulturzentrum-lagerhaus.de; Schildstrasse 12/19; ☺ from 6pm) This once-dilapidated warehouse off Ostertorsteinweg was squatted by young revolutionaries in the 1970s and later became a cultural centre. Today it houses a pub with an alternative flavour downstairs a disco for a 20- to 30-something crowd upstairs. Concerts and performance art are held here, too.

Bodega Del Puerto
BAR

(☑ 0421-178 3797; www.bodega-bremen.de; Schlachte 31; ☺ noon-11pm) Essentially, the point of the Schlachte is exploration – to walk along it and see which bar you most like the look of. This one is the prime choice for a Spanish-style place with decent tapas from €2.80 (mixed tapas €12.80 to €13.80).

Feldmann's Bierhaus
PUB

(☑ 0421-168 9212; www.feldmanns-bierhaus.de; Schlachte 19; dishes ; ☺ 11am-11pm) A slightly older crowd can be found chatting and lingering over the wide range of Haake-Beck beers in this modern *Bierhaus* on the Schlachte bar and restaurant drag; it also sells food (dishes €5 to €14).

Cafe Tölke
CAFE

(☑ 0421-324 330; Schnoor 23a; ☺ 10am-7.30pm) This taste of a Viennese coffeehouse in Bremen will please even the most discerning tipplers of the regally roasted bean. Furnishings are original sofas, mirrors and chairs from the Austrian capital, but offering a less stuffy, more Hanseatic interpretation.

★ **Lila Eule** LIVE MUSIC
(www.lilaeule.de; Bernhardstrasse 10; ⊙ from 8pm)
A decade or more is a long time to be a hot
tip, but this gem off Sielwall has pulled it
off. A student crowd gathers here for parties
and events, but it's also a very alternative
place to watch the Werder Bremen football
team; most Werder matches are shown here.
Thursday night is the legendary student
bash.

Modernes CLUB
(www.modernes.de; Neustadtwall 28; ⊙ Thu-Sat)
South of the river in Neustadt, this club converted from an old movie theatre also hosts
live music and remains Bremen's best club,
bar none. The centrepiece is the domed roof
that can be opened to let in some much-needed air towards the end of the evening. Take
tram 4, 5 or 6 to Leibnizplatz.

NFF Club CLUB
(www.nffclub.de; Katharinenstrasse 12-14; ⊙ Fri
& Sat) With a futuristic-looking bar, a chic
dance floor and lots of cocktails, Nur Für
Freunde (Just for Friends) is the place for
house, dance and electro. It's also where famous German and international DJs come to
spin tunes.

☆ **Entertainment**

Theatre & Music

Theater Bremen PERFORMING ARTS
(✏ tickets 0421-365 3333; www.theatrebremen.
com; Goetheplatz 1-3; ⊙ 11am-6pm Mon-Fri, to
2pm Sat) Bremen's main company has several theatres in the one complex: Theater am
Goetheplatz, where well-known 1970s film
director Rainer Werner Fassbinder honed
his craft with the company; the attached
Neues Schauspielhaus with new interpretations of classics and avant-garde drama;
and the small and versatile Brauhauskeller
(Brewery Cellar) with anything from Elvis
musicals to Edward Albee.

Die Glocke CONCERT VENUE
(✏ 0421-336 699; www.glocke.de; Domsheide) Bremen's concert hall stages classical concerts,
opera and a large variety of special events,
many by visiting performers, in a venue
whose acoustics are considered to be among
Europe's very best.

Schlachthof LIVE MUSIC
(✏ 0421-377 750; www.schlachthof-bremen.de;
Findorffstrasse 51; ⊙ bar from 4pm Mon-Sat, from
10am Sun; 🚊 25, Theodor-Heus-Allee stop) Ethnic
and world-music concerts, theatre, cabaret
and variety are all complemented here by
parties, art exhibitions and a bar.

Theater am Leibnizplatz THEATRE
(✏ 0421-500 333; www.shakespeare-company.
com; Am Leibnizplatz; 🚇 Leibnizplatz) The highly acclaimed Bremer Shakespeare Company
mixes the Bard (in German) with fairy tales
and contemporary works.

Sport

Weserstadion STADIUM
(✏ ticket hotline 01805-937 337; www.weserstadion.
de; Franz-Böhmert-Strasse 1a) The local Bundesliga team Werder Bremen is less a football
team than a sporting religion. Worship takes
place at the Weserstadion, where a seat costs
€20 to €40. Call the ticket hotline or go down
on your knees outside the stadium and beg.
Take tram 3 to Weserstadion, or tram 2 or 10
to St Jürgen-Strasse, then follow the crowds.

🛍 **Shopping**

Reacquaint yourself with the Brothers
Grimm fairy tale 'The Town Musicians of
Bremen' via one of the many English-language editions. Otherwise, the most obvious buy in Bremen is sweets. Both Böttcherstrasse and the Schnoor Viertel are full of
interesting jewellery, from antique silver and

GAY & LESBIAN BREMEN

Bremen's gay and lesbian scene is, like
the city itself, small and friendly. A handful of bars and clubs in An der Weide and
its extension Ausser der Schleifmühle
make up the main quarter for guys.

Cafe Kweer (✏ 0421-700 008;
www.ratundtat-bremen.de; Theo-
dor-Körner-Strasse 1, Rat & Tat Zentrum;
⊙ 8pm-midnight Fri, 3-6pm Sun) Part of
the information centre for gay men and
lesbians, this place turns into a dance
club on Fridays with everything from
1920s sounds to urban lounge. On
Sundays it's a place for coffee, cake and
a chat, and whenever Werder Bremen
plays it shows match. There are also
special events, so check the website.

Queens (✏ 0421-325 912; www.
queens-bremen.de; Ausser der Schleifmühle
10; ⊙ 8pm-midnight Sun-Thu, to 7am Fri &
Sat) One of Bremen's longest-running
gay bars has a cool '70s atmosphere
and appeals to a mainstream crowd.

LOWER SAXONY & BREMEN BREMEN CITY

oodles of amber to modern designer pieces. Ostertorsteinweg, in Das Viertel, is the place to look for funky streetwear.

Flea Market MARKET
(www.breminale.de; Burgerweide; ⏲7am-3pm Sun) A renowned flea market is held in spring and summer on Bürgerweide (a short walk north of Hauptbahnhof) and at the Hansa Carré at Pfalzburger Strasse 41 at other times of year.

Hachez CHOCOLATE
(☎0421-509 000; www.hachez.de; Am Markt 1) The local purveyor of chocolate and specialities such as *Kluten* (peppermint sticks covered in dark chocolate).

Information

Get the excellent-value **ErlebnisCARD** (adult and up to 2 children for 1/2 days €8.90/11.50, up to 5 adults for 1/2 days €18.50/22.90) for free public transport and discounts on sights. It's available from tourist offices.

Police (☎3621; Am Wall 201)

Post Office (Domsheide 15; ⏲9am-7pm Mon-Fri, 9am-1pm Sat)

Tourist Office Hauptbahnhof (☎0421-308 0010; www.bremen-tourism.de; Hauptbahnhof; ⏲10am-4pm, extended hours in summer) Handily located at the main train station.

Tourist Office Markt (☎0421-308 0010; www.bremen-tourism.de; Langenstrasse 2-4; ⏲10am-4pm, extended hours in summer) Bremen's full-service tourist office has friendly staff who can help you navigate through the multitude of excellent English language maps, pamphlets and programs. A wide range of tours are available.

Getting There & Away

AIR

Bremen airport (www.airport-bremen.de) is about 3.5km south of the city centre and well connected to the city by the line 6 tram. Fly from here to destinations in Germany and Europe. Airline offices here include Air Berlin (p608) and Lufthansa Airlines (p608). Low-cost carrier **RyanAir** (www.ryanair.com) flies to Dublin, Edinburgh and London Stansted.

BOAT

You can reach Bremen by boat with **Hal Över Schreiber Reederei** (☎0421-338 989; www.hal-oever.de; Schlachte 2, Martinianleger; ⏲office 9am-3pm Mon & Fri, to 5pm Wed).

BUS

Check pricing and schedules buses online. Long-distance services depart from and arrive into the ZOB (Bust station) on Breitenweg in front of the Hauptbahnhof.

Agentur Grajan (☎0421-157 00; Breitenweg 13, ZOB bay 10) Find this agent for Eurolines tickets at bus bay 10.

Eurolines (☎069 790 3501; www.eurolines.com) Regular services run from Bremen to Amsterdam (€41, six hours), London (€92, 12¾ hours), Moscow (€115, 44 hours; Belarus visa required) and other European destinations. Sale fares to Amsterdam can be as low as €9!

CAR & MOTORCYCLE

The A1 (from Hamburg to Osnabrück) and the A27/A7 (Bremerhaven to Hanover) intersect in Bremen. The city is also on the B6 and B75. All major car-rental agencies have branches at the airport.

Avis (☎0421-558 055; www.avis.com; Hauptbahnhof, Bahnhofsplatz) This office is found inside the main train station.

Sixt (☎0421-258 3953; www.sixt.de; Theodor-Heuss-Allee 6) Conveniently located adjacent the train station.

Europcar (☎0421-557 440; www.europcar.com; Breitenweg 32) This office is a few blocks from Hauptbahnhof.

TRAIN

Frequent IC trains go to Hamburg (€28, one hour), Hanover (€33, one hour) and Cologne (€67, three hours). Less frequent IC trains go to Berlin (€79, four hours).

Getting Around

AIRPORT

Tram 6 travels between the Hauptbahnhof and the airport (€2.60, 15 minutes).

BIKE

Radstation (☎0421-169 01 00; www.1-2-3rad.de; per day from €9.50; ⏲8am-10pm Mon-Fri, 9am-8pm Sat & Sun) For bike rental, contact the Radstation just outside the Hauptbahnhof (bring your passport).

BUS & TRAM

The city's public transport is operated by **Verkehrsverbund Bremen/Niedersachsen** (☎01805-826 826; www.bsag.de). Main hubs are in front of the Hauptbahnhof and at Domsheide near the Rathaus. A €2.60 single fare covers most of the Bremen city area, while a day pass (Tageskarte) costs €7.50.

TAXI

A taxi from the airport costs about €15. Call ☎0421-144 33 or ☎0421-140 14 or try www.bettertaxi.de/en.

Bremerhaven

📞 0471 / POP 108,500

Anyone who has dreamt of running away to sea will love Bremerhaven's waterfront Havenwelten area, with its old ships, rusty docks and glistening modern buildings pointing to a recent re-imagining of its harbour as a place to play and learn.

Bremerhaven has long been a conduit that gathered the 'huddled masses' from the verdant but poor countryside and poured them into the world outside. Of the millions who landed at New York's Ellis Island, a large proportion sailed from here, and an enticing exhibition at the German Emigration Centre allows you to share their history. Continuing on this global theme, the neighbouring Klimahaus museum takes you on a fascinating journey around the world and its changing climes. If you have an inquisitive mind, both museums are reason enough to come to town.

The city runs north–south along the eastern bank of the Weser River. For the museums and zoo, get on any bus leaving from in front of the Sparkasse building outside Hauptbahnhof and disembark at the 'Havenwelten' stop, about 1.7km northwest. The Schaufenster Fischereihafen (fishing harbour) is 2km southwest of the station.

◎ Sights

★**Deutsches Auswandererhaus** MUSEUM
(German Emigration Centre; 📞 0471-902 200; www.dah-bremerhaven.de; Columbusstrasse 65; adult/concession €12.60/10.60; ⊙ 10am-6pm Mar-Oct, 10am-5pm Nov-Feb) Standing on the spot where more than 7.2 million emigrants set sail for the US, South America and Australia between 1830 and 1942, this spectacular museum does a superb job commemorating some of their stories. The visitor relives stages of their journey, which begins at the wharf where passengers huddle together before boarding 'the ship', clutching the biographical details of one particular traveller and heading toward your new life. Everything is available in both German and English.

A second exhibit, opened in 2012, reverses the theme and tells of immigration *to* Germany since the 17th century. Contributions these new arrivals have made to German society are explained in the setting of a 1970s shopping mall. The museum also provides free access to two international online databases where you can try tracing your German forebears and there's a retro cinema screening related short films.

★**Klimahaus Bremerhaven 8° Ost** MUSEUM
(Climate House; 📞 0471-902 0300; www.klimahaus-bremerhaven.de; Am Längengrad 8; adult/concession/family €15/11/45; ⊙ 10am-6pm, longer hours in summer) Shiny, space-age Klimahaus Bremerhaven 8° Ost offers a journey around the world along the longitudinal meridian 8° east, through climate zones in Switzerland, Italy, Niger, Cameroon, Antarctica, Samoa, Alaska and Germany. The educational displays are aimed at kids but are adult-friendly. Temperatures soar and plummet considerably and accordingly, so along with sensible shoes to scale Swiss mountains and cross African rope bridges, wear two layers of clothing: seriously! Allow at least three hours to get the most from the experience.

Zoo am Meer ZOO
(📞 0471-308 4141; www.zoo-am-meer-bremerhaven.de; H-H-Meier-Strasse 6; adult/child €8.50/5; ⊙ 9am-7pm) The Zoo am Meer isn't spectacular on the face of things, but it enthrals kids, partly because the enclosures are cleverly built into one big artificial 'rock' formation. They'll see a polar bear (or if he's sleeping, a fluffy pile of fur on a rock), polar foxes, seals, penguins, pumas and chimpanzees. Check the website or ask at the tourist office for feeding times.

Schaufenster Fischereihafen HARBOUR
(🚌 505, 506 to Schaufenster Fischereihafen) Situated a few kilometres south of Bremerhaven's train station, this 'window to the fishing harbour' is, true to its name, a fishing harbour. Today, one of the fish-packaging halls has been converted into fish restaurants, bars and small shops.

Deutsches Schiffahrtsmuseum MUSEUM
(German Maritime Museum; 📞 0471-482 070; www.dsm.museum; Hans-Scharoun-Platz 1; adult/concession €6/4; ⊙ 10am-6pm) A highlight here is the reconstructed *Bremer Hansekogge*, a merchant boat from 1380, reassembled (in part) from pieces rescued from the deep. Some of the boats bobbing on the harbour have additional entrance fees.

Kunstmuseum & Kunsthalle Bremerhaven GALLERY
(Art Museum & Art Hall; 📞 0471-468 38; www.kunstverein-bremerhaven.de; Karlsburg 1 & 4; combined ticket adult/concession €5/3; ⊙ 11am-6pm Tue-Fri,

to 5pm Sat & Sun) The permanent exhibition of paintings focuses on Weser artists; changing exhibitions are staged in the adjacent Kunsthalle. It's just north of the bridge, near the main sights.

Historisches Museum Bremerhaven
MUSEUM

(Bremerhaven Museum of History; ☑ 0471-308 160; www.historisches-museum-bremerhaven.de; An der Geeste 1; adult/concession €5/3.80; ☺10am-5pm Tue-Sun) Exhibits on the history and development of the region, as well as temporary exhibitions. An online emigration database (www.dad-recherche.de) based on passenger lists can be used for searching for ancestors. Located just south of the bridge.

🍴 Sleeping & Eating

Bremerhaven is easy to do on a short trip – not being a nightlife capital of Germany, most people take in the city while based in Bremen.

Havenhostel Bremerhaven
HOSTEL $

(☑0471-309 6690; www.havenhostel.de; Bürgermeister-Smidt-Strasse 209; dm/s from €25/65; P☺🐾🛜) This smart hostel with 24-hour reception has fantastic dorms and private rooms with high ceilings and large windows. It's some away from the sights but buses 505 and 506 go to the door (Rotersand stop). You'll find supermarkets nearby and some bars and restaurants south on Bürgermeister-Smidt-Strasse. Breakfast is available.

Atlantic Hotel SAIL City
HOTEL $$

(☑0471-309 900; www.atlantic-hotels.de/sailcity/en; Am Strom 1; d from €109; @🛜) Looking like a slightly smaller version of Dubai's Burj Al Arab hotel, this striking sail shaped hotel is unmissable in Bremen. Interiors are tasteful without being ostentatious, and there's a sauna and wellness area with excellent views. Service and facilities are top-notch.

Räucherei Herbert Franke
SEAFOOD $$

(☑0471-742 06; www.fisch-franke.de; Am Pumpwerk 2; small/large baskets €6/16; ☺8am-4.30pm Mon-Fri, to 1pm Sat) Connoisseurs of delicious smoked fish will find an absolute highlight at this family-run place with a long tradition of hand-smoking. Cats will be following you around for days afterwards. Take bus 505 or 506 to Schaufenster Fischereihafen.

Olympisches Feuer
GREEK $$

(☑0471-544 14; www.olympisches-feuer.com; Hafenstrasse 119; mains €8-15; ☺6-10pm) You've come as far as Bremerhaven, so why not be surprised by the quality and authenticity of this excellent Greek taverna, about as far on the other side of the continent from the homeland as you can be. It's all here: gyros, saganaki, calamari, dolmades, moussaka, steak, seafood, salad! Big helpings, low prices. Yum.

★ Natusch
SEAFOOD $$$

(☑0471-710 21; www.natusch.de; Am Fischbahnhof 1; mains €14-36; ☺noon-3pm & 5.30-10pm Tue-Sun) Located between Fischereihafen I and Fischereihafen II at the fishing harbour, you'll find this wonderful seafood restaurant, with a woody, sea-shanty atmosphere and expertly prepared, mouthwatering seafood fresh from the boat. Priced accordingly. Take bus 505 or 506 to Schaufenster Fischereihafen.

ⓘ Information

Tourist Office (☑0471-414 141; www.bremerhaven.de/tourism; H-H-Meier-Strasse 6; ☺10am-5pm) Cross from the bridge behind the Auswandererhaus – it's located inside the building ahead.

Tourist Office Schaufenster Fischereihafen (☑0471-414 141; www.bremerhaven.de/tourism; Am Schaufenster 6; ☺10am-5pm) Located at the Fischkai, near the FMS *Gera* ship. Also rents bicycles (till 5pm on day of rental, €7.50 to €10) as well as e-bikes (per day €25) and Segways (per hour €25).

ⓘ Getting There & Around

BUS

The **bus ticket office** (Friedrich-Ebert-Strasse 73 d-f; ☺7am-6pm Mon-Fri, 8am-1pm Sat) outside Bremerhaven's train station has free maps of town. Within Bremerhaven, single tickets/day passes cost €2.60/7.50. From the train station, buses 502, 506 and 509 stop at Havenwelten, near the Alter Hafen (Old Harbour) and Neuer Hafen (New Harbour). Buses 505 and 506 go to Schaufenster Fischereihafen, in the other direction.

CAR

Bremerhaven is quickly reached via the A27 from Bremen; get off at the Bremerhaven-Mitte exit.

TRAIN

Frequent trains connect Bremen and Bremerhaven (€12.10, 40 minutes).

Worpswede

☑04792 / POP 9500

Worpswede was originally a settlement of turf diggers, but from 1894 an artists' colony was established here by the architects and painters who became associated with

Bremen's Böttcherstrasse. Today it is a cute artisans' town that lends itself to mooching around in sunny weather. Outside Germany, the community's most famous member was the poet Rainer Maria Rilke, who dedicated several books to this pretty Niedersachsen village. Other major names involved include the painter Paula Modersohn-Becker and Otto Modersohn, plus the future designer of Böttcherstrasse, Bernhard Hoetger, architect and painter Heinrich Vogeler and, the first to move here, painter Fritz Mackensen.

Today, not only can you visit their buildings and view their art in some seven museums, but you can also shop for porcelain, jewellery, posters, soap made from moor products and other trinkets. Throw in plenty of opportunities to stop for coffee and cakes, enjoy a spa, or go hiking, cycling or canoeing, and Worpswede makes a pleasant outing for anyone.

◎ Sights

Grosse Kunstschau GALLERY
(☑04792-4792 1302; www.worpswede-museen.de; Lindenallee 5; adult/concession €8/5; ◎11am-5pm Tue-Sun) Designed by Bernhard Hoetger in 1927, this exhibition space is part art deco and part tepee, with a round skylight that complements the wooden floors. Its permanent exhibition is a who's who of the artists' colony, but there is also a regularly changing exhibition included in the admission.

Niedersachsenstein MONUMENT
A highlight of Worpswede is the stroll to the 55m-tall Weyerberg dune, less than a kilometre from the centre, where you find the Niedersachsenstein, a contentious sculpture looming like a giant eagle. This is the work of Bernhard Hoetger, the man responsible for much of Bremen's Böttcherstrasse. Follow Lindenallee from the tourist office and then follow the trails off to the right.

Barkenhoff GALLERY
(☑04792-49 72 39 68; www.worpswede-museen.de/barkenhoff; Ostendorfer Strasse 10; adult/concession €4/2; ◎10am-6pm) The creative heart of the Worpswede artists' colony was this half-timbered structure remodelled in the art nouveau style by its owner Heinrich Vogeler. Today it houses the Heinrich-Vogeler-Museum, with paintings and applied arts.

Worpsweder Bahnhof HISTORIC BUILDING
(Bahnhofstrasse) This Art Nouveau former railway station designed by Heinrich Vogeler is pretty as a picture. Today, only the infrequent *Moor Express* from Bremen (www.evb-elbe-weser.de) stops here.

❶ Information

Tourist Office (☑04792-935 820; www.worpswede.de; Bergstrasse 13; ◎10am-5pm) Sells the new Museum Card (adult/concession €15/10) providing admission to Worpswede's four museums. Can assist with accommodation bookings.

❶ Getting There & Around

BICYCLE
Fahrradladen Eckhard Eyl (☑04792-2323; Finddorfstrasse 28) Hires out bikes. From the tourist office, you can walk there in less than 10 minutes by taking the path between the bank and the Village Hotel am Weyerberg to Finddorfstrasse and going right.

BUS
From Bremen's central bus station, bus 670 (€5.80 one way) makes the 50-minute trip about 20 times a day during the week and every two hours on weekends. See www.fahrplaner.de or check the timetable at the departure point (platform G) in Bremen; ask the driver to drop you near the tourist office ('Insel').

TRAIN
The vintage **Moor Express** (☑04/61-993 116; www.evb-elbe-weser.de; one way adult/child/family €6.50/3.50/15) runs between Worpswede and Bremen (and on to Stade) four times each way every Saturday and Sunday from May to October. First and last services from Worpswede to Bremen are 8.04am and 6.04pm. First and last services to Worpswede from Bremen are 9.08am and 7.08pm. The train station is about 1km north of the tourist office on Bahnhofstrasse (follow Strassentor or Bauernreihe north).

Oldenburg
☑0441 / POP 162,200
Being shuffled between Danish and German rule has left the relaxed capital of the Weser-Ems region with a somewhat difficult-to-pin-down identity. Most of its medieval buildings were destroyed in a huge fire in 1676, while others were later refashioned at various stages according to the prevailing architectural style of the time. Today it's principally a business destination, but it makes a good day trip from Bremen or stopover on the way to the East Frisian Islands.

Exit the Hauptbahnhof (Bahnhof Sud) from the 'Stadtmitte' side to reach the centre of town.

◉ Sights

Landesmuseum für Kunst und Kulturgeschichte MUSEUM
(Museum of Art & Cultural History; ☑0441-220 7300; www.landesmuseum-oldenburg.niedersachsen.de; Schlossplatz 1; adult/concession incl Augeum & Prinzenpalais €6/4; ☺10am-6pm Tue-Sun) Housed inside the pale yellow Renaissance-baroque Schloss (1607) at the southern end of the Altstadt shopping district (on Schlossplatz, just south of Markt), this museum chronicles the area's history from the Middle Ages. On the 1st floor you'll find the Idyllenzimmer, with 44 paintings by court artist Heinrich Wilhelm Tischbein, a friend of Goethe, which explains why he was often known by his double-banger moniker 'Goethe-Tischbein'.

Augusteum MUSEUM
(☑0441-220 7300; www.landesmuseum-oldenburg.niedersachsen.de; Elisabethstrasse 1; incl in Landesmuseum ticket adult/concession €6/4; ☺10am-6pm Tue-Sun) Part of Oldenburg's Museum of Art & Cultural History, the Augusteum showcases European paintings – with a strong focus on Italian and Dutch masters – from the 16th to the 18th century. The gallery also features changing exhibitions.

Prinzenpalais MUSEUM
(☑0441-220 7300; www.landesmuseum-oldenburg.niedersachsen.de; Damm 1; incl in Landesmuseum ticket adult/concession €6/4; ☺10am-6pm Tue-Sun) One of the three buildings comprising Oldenburg's Museum of Art & Cultural History, this branch focuses on German artists, beginning with Romanticism and neoclassicism of the mid-19th century and culminating in post-1945.

Landesmuseum Natur und Mensch MUSEUM
(Natural History Museum; ☑0441-924 4300; www.naturundmensch.de; Damm 38-44; adult/concession €4/2.50; ☺9am-5pm Tue-Fri, 10am-6pm Sat & Sun) This natural history museum showcases the ecology of Lower Saxony's landscapes and has a huge chunk (or wall) of peat bog, with niches containing bodies from the Roman period.

⊨ Sleeping & Eating

DJH Hostel HOSTEL $
(☑0441-871 35; http://oldenburg.jugendherbergen-nordwesten.de; Alexanderstrasse 65; dm under/over 27yr €22/26; Ⓟ☺) It is highly advisable to book ahead for this large and rambling hostel, which closes from 11.30pm till 7am.

It's about 20 minutes by foot north of the Hauptbahnhof, or take bus 302, 303 or 322 to Von-Finckh-Strasse. Linen is included.

Rosenbohm Designhotel DESIGN HOTEL $$
(☑0441-8006 3444; http://hotel-rosenbohm.de; Pferdemarkt 7; s/d from €110/135; Ⓟ☎) This plush design hotel has eight spacious rooms with lush bedding and plush furniture.

Der Schwan PUB FOOD $$
(☑0441-261 89; www.schwan-oldenburg.de; Stau 34; mains €6-20; ☺9am-midnight) A decent all-rounder, the Swan has a great riverside spot where you can drink and dine in the sunshine (weather permitting). Things get livelier of an evening.

Kleine Burg MODERN EUROPEAN $$$
(☑0441-158 55; www.kleineburg-ol.de; Burgstrasse 2; mains €14-29; ☺noon-3pm & 5-10pm Mon-Fri, noon-10pm Sat) Homemade pasta, truffles, avocado, goats cheese, lamb, fish, decadent deserts: all of these specialities can be found on the varied menu in this smart central eatery. Highly recommended.

ℹ Information

Post Office (Bahnhofsplatz 10; ☺8am-6pm Mon-Fri, 9am-1pm Sat)

Tourist Office (☑0441-3616 1366; www.oldenburg-tourist.de; Kleine Kirchenstrasse 14; ☺10am-6pm Mon-Fri, to 2pm Sat) Has maps and accommodation guides that are also available from the DB Service Point inside the train station.

ℹ Getting There & Around

BICYCLE

Fahrrad Station Oldenburg (☑0441-218 8250; Hauptbahnhof; ☺6.30am-8pm Mon-Sat) Rents out bikes from €7 per day and e-bikes from €19. Deposit is €50/100 respectively; bring your passport.

CAR

Oldenburg is at the crossroads of the A29 to/from Wilhelmshaven and the A28 (Bremen–Dutch border).

BUS

Many buses, including bus 315, run to the Landesmuseum on Schlossplatz from Hauptbahnhof. Bus 315 to Am Festungsgraben is the best one for Augusteum and Prinzenpalais; take bus 315, 270 or 280 to Staatsarchive for the Landesmuseum Natur und Mensch. Single bus tickets (valid for one hour) for the entire city cost €2.60 and day passes €7.50.

TRAIN

There are trains at least once an hour to Bremen (€8, 30 minutes), Emden (€25.60, one hour) and beyond.

Emden & Around

📞 04921 / POP 51,600

You're almost in Holland here, and it shows – from the flat landscape, dykes and windmills outside Emden to the lackadaisical manner in which locals pedal their bikes across the town's canal bridges. The Dutch, as well as Germans, have shaped Emden, and the local Plattdütsch dialect sounds like a combination of English, German and – guess what? – Dutch. While in most senses Emden stoically defies the adjective 'spectacular', the Kunsthalle and Ostfriesisches Landesmuseum (both closed on Monday) and the pretty coastal landscape of its environs do make it worthwhile.

◎ Sights & Activities

The tourist offices have information on canal tours and canoe hire, and can give tips on a favoured East Frisian pastime: cycling.

★ Kunsthalle   GALLERY

(📞 04921-975 050; www.kunsthalle-emden.de; Hinter dem Rahmen 13; adult/concession €8/6; ◷ 10am-5pm Tue-Fri, 11am-5pm Sat & Sun) Focusing on 20th-century art, the white-and-exposed-timber, light-flooded rooms of Emden's art gallery show off a range of big, bold canvases. There are some works by Max Beckmann, Erich Heckel, Alex Jawlensky, Oskar Kokoschka, Franz Marc, Emil Nolde and Max Pechstein, although most of the artists are more obscure. Several times a year, the museum closes its doors for a week while exhibitions are changed. Follow the signs from the tourist office.

Bunkermuseum   MUSEUM

(📞 04921-322 25; www.bunkermuseum.de; Holzsägerstrasse; adult/child €2/1; ◷ 10am-1pm & 3-5pm Tue-Fri, to 1pm Sat & Sun May-Oct) The labyrinth of WWII civilian air-raid shelters at the Bunkermuseum includes testimonies from those who sheltered here, offering a moving insight into part of history.

Ostfriesisches Landesmuseum   MUSEUM

(Regional History Museum; 📞 04921-872 058; www.landesmuseum-emden.de; Brückstrasse 1, Rathaus; adult/concession €6/free; ◷ 10am-6pm

Tue-Sun) The award-winning Ostfriesisches Landesmuseum has an interesting and varied collection illustrating themes of local history and life in the region. Not surprisingly, its picture gallery has a strong focus on Dutch artists. In the late 16th century a large number of Protestant Dutch fled to Emden to escape religious persecution in the Spanish-ruled low countries. Glass painting established itself here then. Later, the Emden-born painter Ludolf Backhuysen returned to work here. His work forms the backbone of the gallery.

Other sections of the museum cover the Frisian coast and cartography, prehistory and 20th-century landscape painting; a highlight is a stunning collection of armour.

EMS   BOAT TOUR

(📞 04921-890 70; www.ag-ems.de; adult/concession €7/5.50) Harbour cruises are run by EMS several times daily between early April and late October from the Delfttreppe steps in the harbour. The company also runs services to the East Frisian Island of Borkum and North Frisian Island of Helgoland.

⌷ Sleeping & Eating

The tourist office at the train station is a well-run outfit with a walk-in and advance room-booking service. Options are not abundant, so it pays to use it.

Emden is not really the place for outrageous nights, but if you explore Neuer Markt you'll find a few places to drink.

DJH Hostel   HOSTEL $

(📞 04921-237 97; www.jugendherberge.de/jh/emden; An der Kesselschleuse 5, off Thorner Strasse; dm under/over 27yr €26/30; ◷ closed Nov-Feb; 🅿️ @) Popular with schools and other groups, this hostel has a canal-side location and offers plenty of outdoor opportunities. Take bus 503 to Realschule/Am Herrentor. Linen is included.

Hotel am Boltentor   HOTEL $$

(📞 04921-972 70; www.hotel-am-boltentor.de; Hinter dem Rahmen 10; s/d/tr from €76/96/120; 🅿️) Hidden by trees from the main road nearby and close to the main sights, this homey red-brick hotel has the quietest location in town, plus comfy and well-equipped rooms.

Goldener Adler   HOTEL $$

(📞 04921-927 30; www.goldener-adler-emden.de; Neutorstrasse 5; s/d from €75/90) Rooms in this no-nonsense hotel are comfortable but tending to small; it is right in the centre of town and on the water.

Carlino Osteria Enoteca
ITALIAN $$

(Alter Markt 9; lunch special €6.50, pizza & pasta €6.50-9.50, meat & fish mains €14.50-20; ☺ lunch & dinner Tue-Sun; 🖉) This highly rated Italian restaurant near the tourist office pavilion offers a respite from traditional fare; the fettucine with a pork game ragout for €18 complements mainstays such as a rump steak (€17.50).

Ming Ming
CHINESE $$

(🖉 04921-4921 4848; Auricher Strasse 153; mains €9-24; ☺ noon-3pm & 6-11pm) This restaurant serves a diverse menu of regional Chinese cuisine and has an excellent, well-stocked buffet. Service is prompt, helpful and friendly.

Hafenhaus
SEAFOOD $$

(🖉 04921-689 5690; www.hafenhaus.com; Promenade Am Alten Binnenhafen 8; mains €12-35) On the Promenade, this fancy, modern seafood restaurant has a wonderful outdoor deck and pontoon in the warmer months.

ℹ Information

Tourist-Information Emden Pavillon am Stadtgarten (🖉 04921-974 00; www.emden-touristik. de; Alter Markt 2a; ☺10am-6pm Mon-Fri, to 2pm Sat) Just north of the central Ratsdelft harbour, near the car park and taxi stand.

Tourist Office (🖉 04921-974 00; www.emden-touristik.de; Bahnhofsplatz 11, Im Bahnhof; ☺8am-6pm Mon-Fri, 10am-4pm Sat, also 11am-3pm Sun Apr-Oct) Main tourist office, with an efficient hotel and private-room booking service.

ℹ Getting There & Around

Emden is connected by rail to Oldenburg (€17.20, 70 minutes) and Bremen (€25.60, 1¾ hours). Despite its relative remoteness, the town is easily and quickly reached via the A31, which connects with the A28 from Oldenburg and Bremen. The B70/B210 runs north from Emden to other towns in Friesland and to the coast.

Emden is small enough to be explored on foot but also has a bus system (€1.50 per trip). The best transport method is bicycle.

Jever

🖉 04461 / POP 13,900

Famous for its pilsner beer, the capital of the Friesland region is also known for 'Fräulein Maria', who peers out from at-tractions and shop windows in Jever. She was the last of the so-called *Häuptlinge* (chieftains) to rule the town in the Middle Ages, and although Russia's Catherine the Great got her hands on Jever for a time in the 18th century, locals always preferred their home-grown queen. Having died unmarried and a virgin, Maria is the German equivalent of England's (in truth more worldly) Elizabeth I.

With its Russian-looking castle, Jever is worth a brief visit, if only en route to the East Frisian Islands.

◉ Sights & Activities

Schloss
PALACE

(🖉 04461-969 350; www.schlossmuseum.de; adult/concession €6/3; ☺10am-6pm Tue-Sun) Looking like a prop from the film *Doctor Zhivago,* the onion-shaped dome is literally the crowning feature of Jever's 14th-century Schloss. The town's 18th-century Russian rulers added it to a building built by Fräulein Maria's grandfather, chieftain Edo Wiemken the Elder. Today the palace houses the Kulturhistorische Museum des Jeverlandes, with objects chronicling the daily life and craft of the Frieslanders. The *pièce de résistance* is the magnificent audience hall from 1560, with a carved, coffered oak ceiling of great intricacy.

From May to October you're able to climb the 67m-high tower, affording panoramic views of the East Frisian coastal landscape.

Stadtkirche
CHURCH

(www.kirche-jever.de; Am Kirchplatz 13; ☺8am-6pm) Many of Jever's sights are in some way connected to Fräulein Maria, the last of Jever's chieftains. The most spectacular is in the Stadtkirche, where you'll find the lavish memorial tomb of her father, Edo Wiemken (1468–1511). The tomb is another opus by Cornelis Floris and miraculously survived eight fires. The church itself succumbed to the flames and was rebuilt in a rather modern way; the main nave is opposite the tomb, which is now behind glass.

Friesisches Brauhaus zu Jever
BREWERY TOUR

(🖉 04461-137 11; www.jever.de; Elisabethufer 18; tours adult/concession €8/4; ☺10am-6pm Mon-Fri, to 2pm Sat) This Friesisches Brauhaus has been producing amber liquid since 1848 and allows visitors a peek behind the scenes. Two-hour weekday tours travel through the brewery's production and bottling facilities, as well as a small museum, whereas 1½-hour Saturday tours only include the museum. Reservations are essential. You must be over 16 to take a tour.

🛏 Sleeping & Eating

For a drink and other eating options, the area around Markt has a few decent places.

DJH Hostel HOSTEL $
(☑ 04461-909 202; www.jugendherberge.de/jh/jever; Dr-Fritz-Blume-Weg 4; dm under/over 27yr €29/33; ⊗ closed Dec–mid-Jan; ℗ @ 🛜) Jever's cute *Jugendherberge* (youth hostel) is like a little village, with a series of green and red-brick bungalows grouped around the reception. Dorms are clean, modern and comfortable.

★ Im Schützenhof HOTEL $$
(☑ 04461-9370; www.schuetzenhof-jever.de; Schützenhofstrasse 47; s/d from €64/94; ℗ 🛜) This hotel, a 10-minute walk south of the train station, has comfortable modern rooms and an annexed wellness area with Finnish sauna, pool and steam bath. Updated premier rooms are excellent: light-filled, comfortable, airy and well decorated. The on-site restaurant is also worthy of your patronage.

Am Elisabethufer HOTEL $$
(☑ 04461-949 640; www.jever-hotel-pension.de; Elisabethufer 9a; s/d from €52/84; ℗ @ 🛜) Frilly lampshades, floral duvet covers and an assortment of knick-knacks are par for the course in Jever's *Pensionen*, and exactly what you'll find in this attractive and comfortable place with free internet (using an adapter in the power socket) and wi-fi in all rooms and renovated bathrooms. From the tourist office, it's a short walk north along Von-Thünen-Ufer.

Haus der Getreuen GERMAN $$
(☑ 04461-748 5949; www.hausdergetreuen.de; Schlachtstrasse 1; mains €11-24; ⊗ noon-2pm & 5.30-9.30pm Tue-Fri) With an historic dining room and outside seating, Haus der Getreuen is well known for its tasty regional dishes, especially fish.

ℹ Information

Tourist Office (☑ 04461-710 10; www.stadt-jever.de; Alter Markt 18; ⊗ 9am-6pm Mon-Fri, to 1pm Sat)

ℹ Getting There & Around

The train trip to Jever from Bremen (€21.30, 1¾ hours) involves at least one change, in Sande, and sometimes one in Oldenburg too. By road, take the exit to the B210 from the A29 (direction: Wilhelmshaven).

Jever is small enough to explore on foot.

East Frisian Islands

Trying to remember the sequence of the seven East Frisian Islands, Germans – with a wink of the eye – recite the following mnemonic device: '*Welcher Seemann liegt bei Nanni im Bett?*' (which translates rather

---

WALKING TO THE ISLANDS

When the tide recedes on Germany's North Sea coast, it exposes the mudflats connecting the mainland to the East Frisian Islands, and that's when hikers and nature-lovers make their way barefoot to Baltrum and its sister 'isles'. This involves wallowing in mud or wading knee-deep in seawater, but it's one of the most popular outdoor activities in this flat, mountainless region. The Wadden Sea in the Netherlands and Germany became a World Heritage Site in 2009.

Wattwandern, as such trekking through the Wadden Sea National Park is called, can be dangerous as the tide follows channels that will cut you off from the mainland unless you have a guide who knows the tide times and routes. Tourist offices in Jever and Emden can provide details of state-approved ones, including **Martin Rieken** (☑ 04941-8260; www.wattfuehrung-rieken.de) and **Johann Behrends** (☑ 04944-913 875; www.wattwandern-johann.de).

Coastal tours cost from €7 to €15, but if a ferry is needed for one leg of the trip, count on paying about €25. Necessary gear includes shorts or short trousers and possibly socks or trainers that you don't mind getting seriously muddy (although many guides recommend going barefoot). In winter, wet-weather footwear and very warm gear is necessary.

ⓘ RESORT TAX

Each of the East Frisian Islands charges a *Kurtaxe* (resort tax), entitling you to entry onto the beach and offering small discounts for museums etc. It's typically €3.50 a day, and if you're staying overnight it's simply added to your hotel bill. Remind your hotel to give you your pass should they forget.

saucily as 'Which seaman is lying in bed with Nanni?').

Lined up in an archipelago off the coast of Lower Saxony like diamonds in a tiara, the islands are (east to west): Wangerooge, Spiekeroog, Langeoog, Baltrum, Norderney, Juist and Borkum. Their long sandy beaches, open spaces and sea air make them both a nature-lovers' paradise and a perfect retreat for those escaping the stresses of the world. Like their North Frisian cousins Sylt, Amrum and Föhr, the islands are part of the Wadden Sea (Wattenmeer) National Park. Along with coastal areas of the Netherlands, Germany's Wadden Sea is a Unesco World Heritage Site.

The main season runs from mid-May to September. Be aware, however, that the opening hours of tourist offices in coastal towns change frequently and without notice. Call ahead if possible but note that you might not always be able to reach an English speaker and not all relevant websites have English pages.

ⓘ Getting There & Away

Most ferries sail according to tide times, rather than on a regular schedule, so it's best to call the local ferry operator or visit the Deutsche Bahn website (www.bahn.de/nordseeinseln) for information on departure times on a certain day. Tickets are generally offered either as returns – sometimes valid for up to two months – or cheaper same-day returns.

In most cases (apart from Borkum, Norderney and Juist), you will need to change from the train to a bus at some point to reach the harbour from where the ferry leaves. Sometimes these are shuttle buses operated by the ferry company, or scheduled services from **Weser-Ems Bus** (☑ 04921-97 400; www.weser-ems-bus.de). For planning bus connections from Norden and Esens to ferry harbours, the tourist office in Emden has useful transport information.

Light aircraft also fly to every island except Spiekeroog. Contact **Luftverkehr Friesland Harle** (☑ 04464-948 10; www.inselflieger.de).

ⓘ Getting Around

Only Borkum and Norderney allow cars, so heading elsewhere means you'll need to leave your vehicle in a car park near the ferry pier (about €5 per 12 hours).

Wangerooge

The second-smallest of the East Frisian Islands (after Baltrum) is inhabited by just under 1000 people and is the easternmost of the group, lying about 7km off the coast in the region north of Jever. While crunching sand between your toes and watching huge tanker ships lumber past on their way to and from the ports at Bremerhaven, Hamburg and Wilhelmshaven, it's easy to feel like a willing castaway here.

⊙ Sights

Lighthouse   LIGHTHOUSE
(www.leuchtturm-wangerooge.de; adult/child €2/1; ⊙10am-1pm & 2-5pm Mon-Wed, 10am-1pm Thu, 10am-noon & 2-5pm Fri-Sun) If you're feeling active you can climb the 161 steps of Wangerooge's 39m-tall lighthouse dating from 1855.

Nationalparkhaus   INFORMATION
(www.nationalparkhaus-wangerooge.de; Friedrich-Aug-Strasse 18; ⊙9am-6pm Mon-Fri, 10am-noon & 2-5pm Sat & Sun) Head to this National Parks office to learn more about the plant, bird and sea life that call the Wattenmeer home.

ⓘ Information

Kurverwaltung (Spa Administration; ☑ 04469-990; www.wangerooge.de; Strandpromenade 3; ⊙9am-3pm Mon-Fri, to noon Sat & Sun) When you arrive on the island, hit this local information hot spot to get your bearings. They can also help find accommodation if you decide to stick around.

Verkehrsverein (☑ 04469-948 80; www.westturm.de; Hauptbahnhof; ⊙9am-5pm Mon-Fri, to noon Sat) You can book a room at one of the island's plentiful lodgings through this agency.

ⓘ Getting There & Away

The ferry to Wangerooge leaves from Harlesiel two to five times daily (1½ hours), depending on the tides. An open return ticket costs €30.90

(two-month time limit), and a one-way ticket is €21.90. This includes the tram shuttle to the village on the island (4km). Large pieces of luggage are an extra €3.40 each, and a bike is €12.10 each way. The ferry is operated by **DB** (☑ in Harlesiel 04464-949 411, on Wangerooge 04469-947 411; www.siw-wangerooge.de).

To reach Harlesiel, take bus 211 from Jever train/bus station (€3.80, 40 minutes).

Spiekeroog

Rolling dunes dominate the landscape of minuscule Spiekeroog; about two-thirds of its 17.4 sq km is taken up by these sandy hills. It's the tranquillity of this rustic island that draws people. There are also plenty of baths for swimming, but if you're looking to just hit the beach, another island might be a better bet: all that sand and all those dunes mean it can be a fair hike before you reach the water's edge.

Spiekeroog is not only car-free but discourages bicycles too.

◉ Sights & Activities

Mussel Museum   MUSEUM
(admission €1; ⊘ 9am-12.30pm & 2-5pm Mon-Fri, 9am-12.30pm Sat & Sun) Shellers of the world will take delight in this little museum, with over 3000 shells of all varieties.

Pferdebahn   TRAIN TOUR
(adult/child return €3/2; ⊘ departs 10am, 10.45am, 3pm & 3.45pm Mon-Fri, 2pm or 2.30pm Sun Apr-Sep) The must-do activity on the island is to ride this horse-drawn train that runs on rails and dates back to 1885.

ⓘ Information

Tourist Office (☑ 04976-919 3101; www.spiekeroog.de; ⊘ 9am-12.30pm & 2-5pm Mon-Fri, 9am-12.30pm Sat & Sun) In 'Haus Kogge', these friendly folk will let you know what's open in terms of food, lodging and activities.

ⓘ Getting There & Away

From the ferry departure point in Neuharlingersiel, it takes 40 to 55 minutes to reach Spiekeroog. Ferry times depend on the tides, so same-day returns aren't always possible. Go to www.spiekeroog.de for the latest schedules.

From Jever, catch a train to Esens and change to a bus to Neuharlingersiel (€10, 50 minutes). From Emden, take a train to Norden and change there for a bus to Neuharlingersiel (€17.80, 1¾ hours). Check connections on www.bahn.de before setting out.

Spikeroog Ferry (☑ in Neuharlingersiel 04974-214, in Spiekeroog 04976-919 3133; www.spiekeroog.de) Prices are €17.90/9 (adult/concession) for one-way or same-day return tickets. If you plan on returning at a later date, the fare is €26.80/13.40. Three pieces of luggage per person are carried free of charge.

Spiekeroog Express (☑ 0171-892 3992; express@spiekeroog.de; one-way €25) The *Spiekeroog Express* water taxi does the trip from Neuharlingersiel to Spikeroog in 15 minutes.

Langeoog

Floods and pirates make up the story of Langeoog, whose population was reduced to a grand total of two following a horrendous storm in 1721. By 1830 it had recovered sufficiently to become a resort town.

The island boasts the highest elevation in East Frisia – the 20m-high Melkhörndüne – and the grave of Lale Anderson, famous for being the first singer to record the WWII song 'Lili Marleen'. On a sunny day, however, the most popular thing to do is to stroll

LOWER SAXONY & BREMEN EAST FRISIAN ISLANDS

SLOW TRAVEL IN EAST FRISIA

One of the pleasures of travelling around East Frisia is that – intentionally or not – you can really slow down and enjoy the ride. A good way of taking advantage of the bike paths and waterways is by using the so-called **Paddel und Pedal stations** (www.paddel-und-pedal.de). These allow you to combine kayaking or Canadian canoe paddling with cycling, using some of the 21 stations scattered around the countryside. You can paddle to one, hire another kayak there, or switch to bicycle, then choose your next destination/station and set off again.

To give just one of many options, from **Emden** (☑ 04921-890 7219, 0160-369 2739; Marienwehrster Zwinger 13) you can hire a single kayak (€18), paddle about 11km (three hours) to the quarry lake **Grosses Meer** (☑ 04942-576 838; Langer Weg 25, in Südbrookmerland), which is in parts a nature reserve, then change to a bicycle (€10 per day) and ride back, or head deeper into East Frisia. Local tourist offices can help with planning.

along the 14km-long beach. The nearest mainland port is Bensersiel. Langeoog is your best bet if you're looking for a quiet, day-return beach trip.

Sights

Schiffahrtsmuseum   MUSEUM
(Haus der Insel; adult/concession €2.50/1.50; ⊙10am-noon & 3-5pm Mon-Thu, 10am-noon Fri Easter-Oct) Nautical tradition is showcased in this maritime museum, where you can also view a sea rescue ship.

Water Tower   TOWER
(adult €1; ⊙10am-noon Mon-Fri Easter-Oct) Visit Langeoog's symbol, the water tower, which has an exhibition on drinking water on the ground floor.

Information

Room Reservations (☑04972-693 201; zimmernachweis@langeoog.de; ⊙9am-noon & 2-5pm Mon-Thu, 9am-noon Fri) If you get here and decide you just can't leave, head upstairs to the first floor of the island's 'train station' where these friendly folk will help you find a bed.

Tourist Office (☑04972-6930; www.langeoog. de; Hauptstrasse 28; ⊙9am-noon & 2-5pm Mon-Thu, 9am-noon Fri) Inside the Rathaus you'll find the friendly staff of this welcoming tourist office.

Getting There & Away

From Jever, take the train to Esens and change to a bus for Bensersiel (€9.50, 40 minutes). From Emden, take the train to Norden and change to a bus for Bensersiel (€15, 1½ hours). Check connections on www.bahn.de before setting out.

Langeoog Ferry (☑04971-928 90; www.schiffahrt-langeoog.de) The ferry shuttles between Bensersiel and Langeoog around five times daily. The trip takes about one hour and costs €24 return. Luggage is €3 per piece; bikes are not carried.

Baltrum

The smallest inhabited East Frisian Island, delightful Baltrum is just 1km wide and 5km long, and peppered with dunes and salty marshland. It's so tiny that villagers don't bother with street names but make do with house numbers instead. Numbers have been allocated on a chronological basis; houses No 1 to 4 no longer exist so the oldest is now No 5.

As the island closest to the mainland, Baltrum is the most popular destination for Wattwanderungen guided tours. The closest mainland port is Nessmersiel.

Sights

Nationalpark Haus-Gezeitenhaus   MUSEUM
(National Park House-Tide House; house No 177; ⊙10am-noon & 3-7pm Tue-Fri, 3-7pm Sat & Sun) FREE If you just can't stand lying on the pristine white sand a moment longer, head here to this little exhibition on 'Wildlife and the Wattenmeer'.

Information

Kurverwaltung (☑04939-800; www.baltrum. de; house No 130; ⊙9am-noon & 3-5pm Mon-Fri, 10am-noon Sat) Your onestop shop for island information.

Room Reservation Service (☑04931-938 3400; www.zimmervermittlung-baltrum.de; Norden; ⊙8am-8pm Mon-Fri, 10am-6pm Sat & Sun) This room reservation service based in Nordern can help with accommodation.

Getting There & Away

From Emden, take a train to Norden and change to a bus to Nessmersiel (€6.50, 45 minutes).

Baltrum Linie (☑in Baltrum 04939-913 00, in Nessmersiel 04933-991 606; www.baltrum-linie.de; one way €15) Ferries leave from Nessmersiel and take 30 minutes. Departures depend on the tides, which means day trips aren't always possible. Tickets are €15 one way or €21/28 for a same-day/open return. Concessions are half-price. Bikes cost €8 each way.

Norderney

'Queen of the East Frisian Islands', Norderney was Germany's first North Sea resort. Founded in 1797 by Friedrich Wilhelm II of Prussia, it became one of the most famous bathing destinations in Europe, after Crown Prince Georg V of Hanover made it his summer residence, and personalities such as Chancellor Otto von Bismarck and composer Robert Schumann visited in the 19th century.

Now 'Lüttje Welt' ('Little World', as the 5800 islanders call Norderney, for the way fog makes it seem like it's the only place on earth) is complementing its image of tradition and history with some decidedly modern touches. Its wonderful art-deco **Kurtheater** was built as a private theatre in 1893, but with the advent of film it morphed gradually from 1923 into a cinema, which is what it is mainly used for today. Another gem is the neoclassical **Conversationshaus** (1840), which today houses the tourist office.

Norddeich is the mainland town servicing both Nordeney and Juist islands, and it's worth considering spending a night here before heading over. Of all the islands, Nordeney has the best amenities for tourism, including plenty of restaurants.

◉ Sights & Activities

Nationalpark-Haus   INFORMATION
(☑ 04932-2001; www.nationalparkhaus-norderney. de; Am Hafen 1; ⊗ 9am-6pm Tue-Sun) FREE On the harbourfront, you'll find this small exhibition and the opportunity to take a walk into the Wattenmeer: dates and times are published on the website during the summer season.

★ Bade:haus   SPA
(www.badehaus-norderney.de; Am Kurplatz 3; pool/ sauna per 4hr €18/25; ⊗ 9.30am-9.30pm, women only from 2pm Wed) You'll love the Bade:haus, in the former art-nouveau sea-water baths. This sleek stone-and-glass complex is now an enormous thalassotherapy centre, with warm and cold swimming pools, a rooftop sauna with views over the island, relaxation areas where you can lie back on lounges and drink Frisian tea, and much more – all split between the 'Wasserebene' (Water Level), where you can bathe in the pools or bob around in the wave pool, and the 'Feuerebene' (Fire Level) zone for saunas.

🛏 Sleeping

★ Hotel Fährhaus   HOTEL $$
(☑ 04931-988 77; www.hotel-faehrhaus.de; Hafenstrasse 1, Norddeich; d from €105; ﹡) This delightful hotel by the ferry terminal in Norddeich is a great place to spend the night before or after your visit to the island. Rooms have been brightly refurbished, there's an excellent restaurant – great for dinner and with one of the best breakfast spreads we've seen – and even a rooftop infinity pool and sauna! Late night summer sunsets are breathtaking.

Haus am Meer   HOTEL $$
(☑ 04932-8930; www.hotel-haus-am-meer.de; Damenpfad 35, Nordeney; r from €79) Rates on Nordeney fluctuate wildly as demand and occupancy ebbs and flows. This is a great option if you can get a good rate, with wonderful, tastefully furnished ocean-facing rooms and day-spa facilities.

ℹ Information

Harbour Service Centre (Ferry Harbour; ⊗ 6am-6pm) Tourist information by the harbour.

Tourist Office (☑ 04932-891 900, room reservations 04932-891 300; www.norderney.de; Conversationshaus; Am Kurplatz 1; ⊗ 9am-6pm Mon-Fri, 10am-1pm Sat, 11am-1pm Sun) Nordeney's tourist office can provide information or book rooms.

ℹ Getting There & Away

There are trains (€10.30, 35 minutes) from Emden to Norddeich Mole, the ferry landing stage. **Reederei Frisia** (☑ 04931-9870; www. reederei-frisia.de; adult return €19.50, bikes €9.50) *Reederei Frisia* leaves Norddeich every one to two hours, roughly from 6am to 6pm daily (later some days in summer). The journey takes 50 minutes and any DB office can provide details.

Juist

Juist, shaped like a snake, is 17km long and only 500m wide. The only ways to travel are by bike, horse-drawn carriage or on your own two feet. Here, you're often alone with the screeching seagulls, the wild sea and the howling winds. Forest, brambles and elderberry bushes blanket large sections of the island.

One peculiarity of Juist is the idyllic **Hammersee** – a bird sanctuary and the only freshwater lake on all the islands (no swimming). In 1651 Juist was torn in two by a storm tide, but in the early 20th century it was decided to close off the channel with dunes, eventually creating a freshwater lake.

◉ Sights

Juister Küstenmuseum   MUSEUM
(Coastal Museum; www.kuestenmuseum-juist.de; Loogster Pad 29; adult/child €2.50/1.50; ⊗ 9.30am-1pm & 2.30-5pm Tue-Fri, 9.30am-1pm Sat, 2.30-5pm Sun) This little museum has exhibits on coastal and island life.

ℹ Information

Tourist Office (☑ information 04935-809 107, room reservations 04935-809 222; www.juist. de; Strandstrasse 5; ⊗ 9am-12.30pm & 2.30-6pm Mon-Fri, 9am-12.30pm Sat, 10am-12.30pm Sun) Friendly staff are found here, in the

Rathaus. Someone also meets all ferry arrivals, regardless of time.

⊙ Getting There & Away

Trains from Emden (€9.70, 35 minutes) travel straight to the landing dock in Norddeich Mole. **Reederei Frisia** (⊘ 04931-9870; www. reederei-frisia.de) Reederei Frisia operates the ferries from Norddeich to Juist (adult day/normal return €22/32.50, 1½ hours); children are half-price and bikes cost €13 return. You can also ask any DB office for details.

Borkum

The largest of the East Frisian Islands – once even larger before it was ripped apart by a flood in the 12th century – has a tough seafaring and whaling history. Reminders of those frontier times are the whalebones that you'll occasionally see, stacked up side by side or as unusual garden fences. In 1830, however, locals realised that reinventing itself as a 'seaside' resort was a safer way to earn a living, and today many of the island's 5500 inhabitants are involved in the tourism industry in one way or another.

Borkum is popular with German and Dutch families who rent houses and come for their summer holidays.

⊙ Sights

Heimatmuseum MUSEUM
(Local History Museum; ⊘ 04922-4860; museum: adult/child €3/1.50, lighthouse €1.50; ⊙ 10am-5pm Tue-Sun Apr-Oct, 3 5pm Tue & Sat Nov-Mar) To learn about the whaling era and other stages in the life of Borkum, visit this museum at the foot of the old lighthouse.

Borkumriff MUSEUM
(www.feuerschiff-borkumriff.de; Am Nordufer; adult/child €3/2, incl tour €4/2; ⊙ 9.45am-5.45pm Tue-Sun, tours 10.45am, 11.45am, 1.45pm & 2.45pm) This fire ship turned museum has an exhibition on the Wadden Sea National Park.

ⓘ Information

Tourist Office (⊘ 04922-9330; www.borkum. de; Am Georg-Schütte-Platz 5; ⊙ 9am-5pm Mon-Fri, 10am-1pm Sat & Sun) Also handles room reservations.

ⓘ Getting There & Away

AG-Ems (⊘ 01805-180 182; www.ag-ems.de) All-year boats depart twice to six times daily to/from Emden for Borkum. AG-Ems runs car ferries (adult same-day/open return €19/36, two to three hours). Bike transport costs €13 return. AG-Ems also has faster catamarans (€29.80/58, one hour); bikes aren't permitted. Transporting a car on the ferry costs around €77, depending on size.

Hamburg & the North

POP 6.3 MILLION / AREA 30,728 SQ KM

Best Places to Eat

➡ Anna Sgroi (p662)

➡ Söl'ring Hof (p691)

➡ Restaurant (p665)

➡ Freustil (p710)

➡ Speicher 8 (p708)

Best Beaches

➡ Sylt (p688)

➡ Darss-Zingst Peninsula (p705)

➡ Warnemünde (p701)

➡ Göhren (p711)

➡ Usedom Island (p714)

Why Go?

Head to Germany's north because you love the water: from the posh pleasures of Sylt in the west, to the fabled Baltic heritage of historic towns like Lübeck, Wismar, Stralsund and Greifswald. Here, you can sense the legacy of the Hanseatic League in beautiful old quarters created with iconic black and red bricks.

Even inland there is water. Mecklenburg's lakes are a maze of places to paddle. But really, most visitors will be happiest right at the edge of the sea. There are beaches everywhere, and while the temperatures aren't tropical, the drama of the crisp sea crashing onto the white sand is irresistible.

Finally, there is Hamburg, a city with a love of life that ignites its fabled clubs, and where proximity to the water has brought the city both wealth and vigour through the centuries.

When to Go

Summer seems the obvious time to hit northern Germany but let's be honest, just because it's August it doesn't mean you won't be wrapped up in a blanket on a Baltic beach. So free yourself from bikini-clad fantasies and go to the coast anytime to enjoy its often breathtaking beauty.

The best reason to go in summer is for the days that go on and on and on. Sitting outside a Hamburg cafe and enjoying the passing pedestrian parade in daylight at 10pm is a delight.

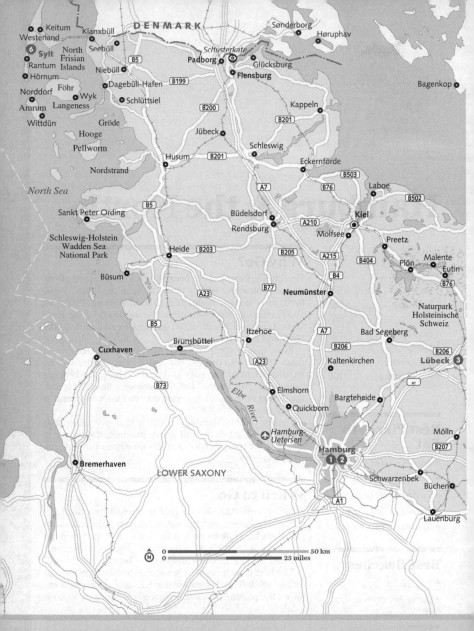

Hamburg & the North Highlights

1 Having a hard day's night – like the Beatles – in **Hamburg's innumerable places of pleasure** (p665), no matter what your taste

2 Discovering a world of enormous ships on a **Hamburg harbour tour** (p658)

3 Enjoying Hanseatic drama at Lübeck's **Europäisches Hansemuseum** (p674)

4 Cycling past Schwerin's **palace** (p692) and the beautiful surrounding lakes

5 Revelling in the soaring heights of Stralsund's **Nikolaikirche** (p705), which proclaims this proud city's heritage

6 Finding your own perfect beach far from the chattering masses on **Sylt** (p688)

7 Letting your feet decide which way to go amid the highlight-speckled streets of **Wismar** (p703)

HAMBURG

📍 040 / POP 1.8 MILLION

Hamburg's historic label, 'The gateway to the world', might be a bold claim, but Germany's second-largest city and biggest port has never been shy. Hamburg has engaged in business with the world ever since it joined the Hanseatic League back in the Middle Ages. Its role as a centre of international trade in the late 19th and early 20th centuries brought it great wealth (and Unesco World Heritage recognition in 2015), a legacy that continues today: it's one of Germany's wealthiest cities.

Hamburg's maritime spirit infuses the entire city; from architecture to menus to the cry of gulls, you always know you're near the water. The city has given rise to vibrant neighbourhoods awash with multicultural eateries, as well as the gloriously seedy Reeperbahn red-light district. Hamburg nurtured the early promise of the Beatles, and today its distinctive live- and electronic-music scene thrives in unique harbourside venues.

The city's attractions are only matched by its inherent tempting spirit. Come, Hamburg says, have a ball.

History

Hamburg's commercial character was forged in 1189, when local noble Count Adolf III persuaded Emperor Friedrich I (Barbarossa) to grant the city free trading rights and an exemption from customs duties. This transformed the former missionary settlement and 9th-century moated fortress of Hammaburg into an important port and member of the Hanseatic League.

The city prospered until 1842, when the Great Fire destroyed a third of its buildings. It joined the German Reich in 1871, but the city was then involved in two devastating world wars. After WWI, most of Hamburg's merchant fleet (almost 1500 ships) was forfeited to the Allies. WWII saw more than half of Hamburg's housing, 80% of its port and 40% of its industry reduced to rubble; tens of thousands of civilians were killed.

In the postwar years, Hamburg harnessed its resilience to participate in Germany's economic miracle (*Wirtschaftswunder*). Its harbour and media industries are now the backbone of its wealth. The majority of Germany's largest publications are produced here, including news magazines *Stern* and *Der Spiegel*.

◉ Sights & Activities

To really see and explore Hamburg, count on spending at least three days prowling its neighbourhoods, waterfront, museums, shops and more.

◉ Altstadt

The centre of old Hamburg is also the hub of the modern city. Largely reconstructed after WWII, the city's ages-old wealth is apparent as you stroll among its most important civic and commercial institutions. In Hanseatic times, this was where you found the rich merchants and their businesses along the canals.

★ Chilehaus   HISTORIC BUILDING

(Map p654; 📍 040-349 194 247; www.chilehaus. de; Fischertwiete 2; Ⓢ Messberg) One of Hamburg's most beautiful buildings is the crowning gem of the new Unesco-anointed Kontorhaus District. The brown-brick 1924 Chilehaus is shaped like an ocean liner, with remarkable curved walls meeting in the shape of a ship's bow and staggered balconies that look like decks.

Designed by architect Fritz Höger for a merchant who derived his wealth from trading with Chile, the building is a leading example of German Expressionist architecture. It's situated alongside other so-called 'Backsteingotik' buildings (*Backstein* refers to a specially glazed brick; *gotik* means 'Gothic') in the Kontorhaus District, which was one of Europe's first purpose-built office building developments. Note the stylistically similar 1927 Spinkenhof building across the street.

Rathaus   HISTORIC BUILDING

(Map p648; 📍 040-428 312 064; Rathausmarkt 1; tours adult/under 14yr €4/free; ⊙ tours half-hourly 10am-3pm Mon-Fri, to 5pm Sat, to 4pm Sun, English tours depend on demand; Ⓢ Rathausmarkt, Jungfernstieg) With its spectacular coffered ceiling, Hamburg's baroque Rathaus is one of Europe's most opulent, and is renowned for its Emperor's Hall and Great Hall. The 40-minute tours take in only a fraction of this beehive of 647 rooms. A good secret to know about is the inner courtyard, where you can take a break from exploring the Rathaus to rest on comfy chairs with tables.

North of here, you can wander through the Alsterarkaden, the Renaissance-style arcades sheltering shops and cafes alongside a canal or 'fleet'.

Deichstrasse   STREET

(Map p648; U Rödingsmarkt) Hamburg's Great Fire of 1842 broke out in Deichstrasse, which features a few restored 18th-century homes, most now housing restaurants. You can get a feel for the old canal and merchants quarter here, thanks to their mostly historic appearance.

★**Hamburger Kunsthalle**   MUSEUM

(Map p654; ☑040-428 131 200; www.hamburger-kunsthalle.de; Glockengiesserwall; adult/child €12/free; ☉10am-6pm Tue, Wed & Fri-Sun, to 9pm Thu; ⓢHauptbahnhof) A treasure trove of art from the Renaissance to the present day, the Kunsthalle spans two buildings linked by an underground passage. The main building houses works ranging from medieval portraiture to 20th-century classics, such as Klee and Kokoschka. There's also a memorable room of 19th-century landscapes by Caspar David Friedrich. Its stark white modern cube, the Galerie der Gegenwart, showcases contemporary German artists.

Look for Rebecca Horn, Georg Baselitz and Gerhard Richter, alongside international stars, including David Hockney, Jeff Koons and Barbara Kruger. The view out of the gallery's huge picture windows is also worthy of framing.

Museum für Kunst und Gewerbe   MUSEUM

(Museum for Art & Trade; Map p654; ☑040-428 542 732; www.mkg-hamburg.de; Steintorplatz 1; adult/child €10/free; ☉10am-6pm Tue-Sun, to 9pm Thu; ⓢHauptbahnhof) The Museum für Kunst und Gewerbe is lots of fun. Its vast collection of sculpture, furniture, fashion, jewellery, posters, porcelain, musical instruments and household objects runs the gamut from Italian to Islamic, Japanese to Viennese and medieval to pop art, and includes an art nouveau salon from the 1900 Paris World Fair. The museum cafe is part of the exhibition space.

Deichtorhallen   GALLERY

(Hall of Contemporary Art/House of Photography; Map p654; ☑040-321 030; www.deichtorhallen.de; Deichtorstrasse 1-2; adult/child €10/free; ☉11am-6pm Tue-Sun; ⓢSteinstrasse) Two grandly restored brick market halls built in 1911 and 1913 respectively, are home to high-profile special exhibitions of modern art and photography.

★**Zweiradperle**   BICYCLE RENTAL

(Map p654; ☑040-3037 3474; Altstädter Strasse 3-7; rental per day from €14, tour incl rental from €25; ☉9am-7pm Mon-Fri, 10am-6pm Sat & Sun, tour 10am daily; U Steinstrasse) Offers a range

---

ⓘ SAVING ON ADMISSIONS

Besides the widely promoted **Hamburg Card** (p669), there are other ways to save on admission to Hamburg's sights. Many museums now give free admission to anyone under 18.

The **Kunstmeile Hamburg** (Museum Mile; ☑040-428 134 110; www.kunstmeile-hamburg.de; adult/child €29/free) is a joint admission ticket for five of Hamburg's art museums, including the Hamburger Kunsthalle, Museum für Kunst und Gewerbe and Deichtorhallen. Buy it at the museums.

---

of rental bikes (including helmets and locks), as well as tours. The three-hour tour is a great introduction to the city. Has a cool cafe and plenty of cycling info.

◉ **Neustadt**

The Neustadt blends seamlessly with the Altstadt in the posh surrounds of the Binnenalster. The mood is set by the elegant Renaissance-style arcades of the **Alsterarkaden** (Map p648; off Poststrasse; ⓢHamburg Jungfernstieg), which shelter upscale shops and cafes alongside the Alsterfleet canal.

Further south, the district blends into the heart of the port area.

St Michaelis Kirche   CHURCH

(Church of St Michael; Map p648; ☑040-376 780; www.st-michaelis.de; Englische Planke 1; tower adult/child €5/3.50, crypt €4/2.50, combo ticket €7/4; ☉9am-7.30pm May-Oct, 10am-5.30pm Nov-Apr, last admission 30min before closing; ⓡStadthausbrücke) 'Der Michel', as it is affectionately called, is one of Hamburg's most recognisable landmarks and northern Germany's largest Protestant baroque church. Ascending the tower (by steps or lift) rewards visitors with great panoramas across the city and canals. The crypt has an engaging multimedia exhibit on the city's history.

Krameramtswohnungen   HISTORIC BUILDINGS

(Map p648; Krayenkamp 10; ⓡStadthausbrücke) In an alley off Krayenkamp 10 are the Krameramtswohnungen, a row of tiny half-timbered houses from the 17th century that, for nearly 200 years, were almshouses for the widows of members of the Guild of Small Shopkeepers. Today they house shops and restaurants, plus a

Hamburg Central City

A **B** **C** **D**

Langenfelder Str

Altonaer Str

Sternschanze

Sternschanzenpark

Sternschanze

Rentzelstr

1

37

45

Sternschanze

32

40

61

54

Max-Brauer-Allee

Susannenstr

Bartelsstr

Kampstr

Lagerstr

47

Karolinenstr

20

SCHANZENVIERTEL

Stresemannstr

Schulterblatt

Lippmannstr

38

Schanzenstr

Sternstr

Grabenstr

Glashüttenstr

Wohlers Allee

Bernstorffstr

Neuer
Pferdemarkt

Beckstr

Vorwerkstr

SCHANZENVIERTEL

Marktstr

Marktstr

Messehallen

2

77

71

Intervention

Feldstrasse

Feldstr

Thadenstr

Neuer Kamp

69

Otzenstr

53

3

HEILIGENGEISTFELD

73

Gilbertstr

36

Grosse
Wallanlagen

Paul-Roosen-Str

64

Annenstr

49 41

Budapester Str

Glacischaussee

16

Holstenwall

Petersstr

4

60

Clemens-Schultz-Str

Rendsburgerstr

50

30

Talstr

Grosse Freiheit

Simon-von-Utrecht-Str

Millerntorplatz

St Pauli

24

70

Millerntorplatz

Helgoländer Allee

Hütten

58

65

Seilerstr

Holstenstr

Reeperbahn

Reeperbahn

Reeperbahn

ST PAULI

5

6

Hans-
Albers-
Platz

59

8

74 66

Kastanienallee

Gerhardstr

13

Balduinstr

Davidstr

Hopfenstr

Zirkusweg

Böhmkenstr

Venusberg

Hein
Köllisch
Platz

Erichstr

62

31

Seewartenstr

34 68

Elbpark

Friedrichstr

56

Bernhard-Nocht-Str

St-Pauli-Hafenstr

Landungsbrücken

43

6

17

57

67

48

28

Port
Area

Tourist
Information
am Hafen

25

19

Rambachstr

51

1

Fischmarkt

Elbe
River

St Pauli
Harbour

St Pauli Elbtunnel

Johannisbollwerk
Vorsetzen

Ditmar-Koel-Str

7

Norderelbstr

A **B** **C** **D**

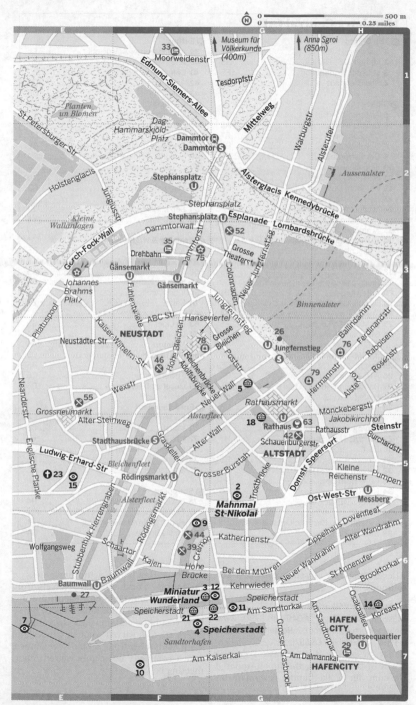

0   500 m
0.25 miles

Museum für
Völkerkunde
(400m)

Anna Sgroi
(850m)

33 Moorweidenstr

Edmund-Siemers-Allee

Tesdorpfstr

Planten
un Blomen

St Petersburger Str

Dag-
Hammarskjöld-
Platz

Dammtor

Dammtor S

Mittelweg

Warburgstr

Alsterufer

Aussenalster

Holstenglacis

Junglusst

Stephansplatz U

Stephansplatz

Alsterglacis Kennedybrücke

Kleine
Wallanlagen

Gorch-Fock-Wall

Stephansplatz U

Esplanade Lombardsbrücke

Dammtorwall

⊗ 52

Drehbahn

35 ☆
75

Grosse
Theaterstr

Binnenalster

Gänsemarkt

Dammtorstr

Colonnaden

Neuer Jungfernstieg

Johannes
Brahms
Platz

Gänsemarkt U

Fuhlentwiete

Kaiser-Wilhelm-Str

Jungfernstieg

ABC Str

Hansaviertel

Grosse
Bleichen

26

NEUSTADT

Neustädter Str

78 🏛

Reichenbrücke

Hohe Bleichen

Adolfsbrücke

Poststr

Jungfernstieg U
S

Ballindamm

Ferdinandstr

Raboisen

76 🔒

Rosenstr

46

Neuer Wall

Wexstr

5 🏛

79 🔒

Hermannstr

Joy

Alste

55

Grossneumarkt

Alter Steinweg

Alsterfleet

Rathausmarkt

18 🏛 Rathaus

42 ⊗

Schauenburgerstr

Rathausstr

63

Mönckebergstr

Jakobikirchhof

Steinstr

Stadthausbrücke S

Gaskeller

Alter Wall

ALTSTADT

Domstr Speersort

Burchardstr

Ludwig-Erhard-Str

Bleichenfleet

Rödingsmarkt U

Grosser Burstah

Trostbrücke

Kleine
Reichenstr

Pumpen

Englische Planke

🛈 23

15

Alsterfleet

Rödingsmarkt

Neanderstr

2

Mahnmal
St-Nikolai

Ost-West-Str U
Messberg

Stubbenhuk

Herrengraben

Schaartor

Rödingsmarkt

9

⊗ 44
Cremon

39 ⊗

Katherinenstr

Zippelhaus Dovenfleet

Alter Wandrahm

St Annenufer

Brooktorkai

Wolfgangsweg

Baumwall

Kajen

Hohe
Brücke

Bei den Mühren

Neuer Wandrahm

Baumwall U

Kehrwieder

3 12

Miniatur
Wunderland

Speicherstadt

Am Sandtorkai

14 🏛

27

Speicherstadt

21 🏛

22

11

HAFEN
CITY

Osakallee

Koreastr

7

4 Speicherstadt

Sandtorhafen

Am Sandtorkai

Grosser Grasbrook

Am Sandtorpark

29

Überseequartier U

10

Am Kaiserkai

Am Dalmannkai

HAFENCITY

Hamburg Central City

◉ Top Sights
1	Fischmarkt	A6
2	Mahnmal St-Nikolai	G5
3	Miniatur Wunderland	F6
4	Speicherstadt	F7

◉ Sights
5	Alsterarkaden	G4
6	Beatles-Platz	A5
7	Cap San Diego	E7
8	Davidwache	B5
9	Deichstrasse	F6
10	Elbphilharmonie	F7
11	HafenCity InfoCenter	G6
12	Hamburg Dungeon	G6
13	Herbertstrasse	B5
14	Internationales Maritimes Museum	H6
15	Krameramtswohnungen	E5
16	Museum für Hamburgische Geschichte	D4
17	Park Fiction	A6
18	Rathaus	G5
19	Rickmer Rickmers	D6
20	Rote Flora	B1
21	Speicherstadt Museum	F7
22	Spicy's Gewürzmuseum	G7
23	St Michaelis Kirche	E5
24	Star Club Memorial	A4

⊕ Activities, Courses & Tours
25	Abicht	D6
26	ATG Alster-Touristik	G4
27	Barkassen-Centrale Ehlers	E6
	Hadag	(see 25)
28	Maritime Circle Line	B6

⊜ Sleeping
29	25hours Hotel HafenCity	H7
30	East	C4
31	Empire Riverside	B5
32	Fritz im Pyjama Hotel	C1
33	Hotel Bellmoor	F1
34	Hotel Hafen	C6
35	Hotel SIDE	F3
36	Hotel St Annen	B4
37	Instant Sleep Backpacker Hostel	B1
38	Superbude St Pauli	B2

⊗ Eating
39	Alt Hamburger Aalspeicher	F6
40	Altes Mädchen	C1
41	Café Mimosa	B4
42	Café Paris	G5
43	Cafe Sul	D6
44	Deichgraf	F6
45	Die Herren Simpel	B1
46	Edelcurry	F4
47	Erikas Eck	C2
48	Fischbrötchenbude Brücke 10	B6
49	Konditorei Holger Rönnfeld	B4
50	Le Kaschemme	C4
51	Lusitano	D6
52	Matsumi	G3
53	Nil	B3
54	Super Mercato Italiano	B1
55	Thämer's	E4

⊙ Drinking & Nightlife
56	Amphore	B6
57	Golden Pudel Club	A6
58	Gretel & Alfons	A5
59	Hasenschaukel	B5
60	Indra Club	B4
61	Katze	B1
62	Komet Musik Bar	B5
63	Le Lion	G5
64	Luba Luft	B4
65	Molotow	A5
66	Prinzenbar	C5
67	StrandPauli	B6
68	Tower Bar	C6
69	Uebel und Gefährlich	C3

⊕ Entertainment
70	Kaiserkeller	B4
71	Knust	C3
72	Laeiszhalle	E3
73	Millerntor-Stadion	C3
74	Schmidt Tivoli	B5
75	Staatsoper	F3

ⓐ Shopping
76	Dr Götze Land & Karte	H4
77	Flohschanze	C2
78	Hanse CD Im Hanse Viertel	F4
79	Thalia Bücher	G4

little summer-only museum relating to the buildings.

Museum für Völkerkunde   MUSEUM
(Museum of Ethnology; ☑ 040-428 8790; www.voelkerkundemuseum.com; Rothenbaumchaussee 64; adult/child €8.50/free; ⊙10am-6pm Tue-Sun, to 9pm Thu; ⓈHallerstrasse, Dammtor) North of the Altstadt, the much-updated Museum für Völkerkunde demonstrates seafaring Hamburg's acute awareness of the outside world. Modern artefacts from Africa, Asia and the South Pacific are displayed alongside traditional masks, jewelcry, costumes and musical instruments. There are also carved wooden canoes and giant sculptures from Papua New Guinea, and a complete, intricately carved Maori meeting hall.

☉ St Georg

This neighbourhood of large 19th-century apartment blocks for Hamburg's upper middle class hit a nadir in the 1970s when thoughtless postwar reconstruction combined with a massive influx of drug dealing and prostitution to give it a very sleazy reputation.

Things are much gentrified now (look for great shops and cafes), as shown in St Georg's central square, the **Hansaplatz**. Completely renovated in 2011 and fully pedestrianised, the square's centrepiece is its **fountain** (Map p654; Hansaplatz; U Hauptbahnhof, S Hauptbahnhof). Completed in 1878, it shows important figures in Hamburg's past, including Emperor Constantine the Great and Charlemagne, and is surmounted by a figure showing the might of the Hanseatic League.

Segelschule Pieper BOATING
(Map p654; ☑040-247 578, www.segelschule-pie per.de; An der Alster; row boat per hr from €18; ☉10am-9pm Apr–mid-Oct; S Hauptbahnhof) Hire your own boat for rowing or paddling (sailing requires a certificate). The calm on the water amid the city and the views are a delight.

☉ Speicherstadt & HafenCity

The seven-storey red-brick warehouses lining the **Speicherstadt** archipelago are a well-recognised Hamburg symbol, stretching to Baumwall in the world's largest continuous warehouse complex. Their neo-Gothic gables and (mostly) green copper roofs are reflected in the narrow canals of this free-port zone. Historic boats line the waterways.

A separate free port became necessary when Hamburg joined the German Customs Federation on signing up to the German Reich in 1871. An older neighbourhood was demolished – and 24,000 people displaced – to make room for the construction of the Speicherstadt from 1885 to 1927. This area was spared wartime destruction; in 2015 it made Unesco's World Heritage list in recognition of its historic role in rapidly expanding world trade.

The Speicherstadt merges into Europe's biggest inner-city urban development, **HafenCity**. Here, a long-derelict port area of 155 hectares is being redeveloped with restaurants, shops, apartments, schools and offices. In the next 20 years, it's anticipated that some 40,000 people will work and 12,000 will live here. For the moment, however, it can seem a bit bleak as only some projects are complete and large swathes of land are vacant.

A new underground line, the U4, links HafenCity from the Überseequartier stop to the rest of the city. The website, www. hafencity-map.de, has details on the area.

★**Miniatur Wunderland** MUSEUM
(Map p648; ☑040-300 6800; www.miniatur-wunderland.de; Kehrwieder 2; adult/child €13/6.50; ☉9.30am-6pm Mon, Wed & Thu, to 7pm Fri, to 9pm Tue, 8am-9pm Sat, 8.30am-8pm Sun; S Messberg) Even the worst cynics are quickly transformed into fans of this vast miniature world that goes on and on. The model trains wending their way through the Alps are impressive – but slightly predictable. But when you see a model A380 swoop out of the sky and land at the fully functional model of Hamburg's airport, you can't help but gasp and say OMG! On weekends and in summer holidays, prepurchase your ticket online to skip the queues.

DON'T MISS

HAMBURG'S SOARING WAR SURVIVOR

Mahnmal St-Nikolai (Memorial St Nicholas; Map p648; ☑040-371 125; www.mahnmal-st-nikolai.de; Willy-Brandt-Strasse 60; adult/child €5/3; ☉10am-6pm May-Sep, to 5pm Oct-Apr; S Rödingsmarkt) St Nikolai church was the world's tallest building from 1874 to 1876, and it remains Hamburg's second-tallest structure (after the TV tower). Mostly destroyed in WWII, it is now called Mahnmal St-Nikolai. You can take a glass lift up to a 76.3m-high viewing platform inside the surviving spire for views of Hamburg's centre, put into context of the wartime destruction.

The crypt houses an unflinching underground exhibit on the horrors of war, focusing on three events in World War II: the German bombing of Coventry in 1940; the German destruction of Warsaw and Operation Gomorrha; and the combined British and American bombing of Hamburg over three days and nights in 1943 that killed 35,000 and incinerated much of the centre. Note that St-Nikolai remains open despite any scaffolding for reconstruction.

The current display is an extraordinary 1300 sq metres; tiny details abound as days change to night. The next addition will include Italy, which you can watch being built.

Internationales Maritimes Museum MUSEUM
(International Maritime Museum; Map p648; ☎040-3009 3300; www.internationales-maritimes-museum.de; Koreastrasse 1; adult/concession €12.50/9; ⏲10am-6pm Tue, Wed & Fri-Sun, to 8pm Thu; [S] Messberg) Hamburg's maritime past – and future – is fully explored in this excellent private museum that sprawls over 10 floors of a revamped brick shipping warehouse. Considered the world's largest private collection of maritime treasures, it includes a mind-numbing 26,000 model ships, 50,000 construction plans, 5000 illustrations, 2000 films, 1.5 million photographs and much more.

The collection is well presented so you can easily dip in and out of what interests you most about 3000 years of maritime history.

Speicherstadt Museum MUSEUM
(Map p648; www.speicherstadtmuseum.de; Am Sandtorkai 36; adult/child €3.50/2; ⏲10am-5pm Mon-Fri, to 6pm Sat & Sun Apr-Oct, 10am-5pm Tue-Sun Nov-Mar; [S] Messberg, Baumwall) A century-old warehouse is the atmospheric backdrop for exhibitions on Hamburg's trading role, especially within its namesake district.

Spicy's Gewürzmuseum MUSEUM
(Map p648; ☎040-367 989; www.spicys.de; Am Sandtorkai 34; adult/child €5/2; ⏲10am-5pm Tue-Sun, also Mon Jul-Oct; [S] Messberg) This spice and herb museum invites you to exercise your olfaction to the fullest.

HafenCity InfoCenter EXHIBITION
(Map p648; ☎040-3690 1799; www.hafencity.com; Am Sandtorkai 30; ⏲10am-6pm Tue-Sun; [S] Messberg) You can pick up brochures and check out detailed architectural models and installations that give a sense of the immensity of the project. The centre offers a program of **free guided tours** through the evolving district.

Elbphilharmonie ARTS CENTRE
(Elbe Philharmonic Hall; Map p648; ☎040-3576 6666; www.elbphilharmonie.de; 6 Marco-Polo-Terrassen; [S] Baumwall) A squat brown-brick former warehouse at the far west of HafenC-

HAMBURG'S NEIGHBOURHOODS

Hamburg is as watery as Venice and Amsterdam. Set around two lakes, the Binnenalster and Aussenalster (Inner and Outer Alster Lakes), in the city centre, it's also traversed by three rivers – the Elbe, the Alster and the Bille – and a grid of narrow canals called *Fleete*.

The half-moon-shaped city centre arches north of the Elbe and is bisected diagonally by the Alsterfleet, the canal that once separated the now almost seamless Altstadt (old town) and Neustadt (new town).

Within the sprawling city are distinct neighbourhoods, which include:

- **Altstadt** The biggest churches, museums and department stores.
- **Neustadt** Leafier and less corporate-office-filled than the Altstadt, although still very much part of the centre.
- **St Georg** East of the Hauptbahnhof; gentrified in parts and also accented with Balkan, Middle Eastern and African flavours, it's the hub of Hamburg's gay scene.
- **Speicherstadt & HafenCity** The former is an atmospheric restored warehouse district with interesting attractions; the latter is a new city being built from scratch.
- **Port Area** Just what the name implies, the city's front porch, with views of passing ships and myriad attractions.
- **St Pauli** Includes the notorious Reeperbahn strip of sin and frolic, plus leafier quarters and port area views.
- **Schanzenviertel & Karolinenviertel** North of St Pauli and home to old hippies, young Goths and Hamburg's most creative and alternative scene.
- **Altona & Elbmeile** The former is gentrified and merges with the waterfront of the latter. The family-filled neighbourhood of Ottensen abuts on the west.
- **Blankenese** Some 8km west of Altona, it's a wealthy enclave with narrow historic streets and sweeping views of the Elbe.

Western Hamburg

Western Hamburg

ity is the base for the architecturally bold new Elbphilharmonie, which will become a major concert hall. Pritzker Prize–winning Swiss architects Herzog & de Meuron are responsible for the design, which captivates with its details like the 1096 individually curved glass panes. Also captivating for lo-cals is the building's huge cost overruns and planned completion date, which was once 2010 but is now 2017.

Hamburg Dungeon   AMUSEMENT PARK
(Map p648; ☎040-3005 1519; www.thedungeons. com; Kehrwieder 2; adult/child €24/19; ⊗10am-

East Central Hamburg

N 0 ————————————— 500 m
0 ————————————— 0.25 miles

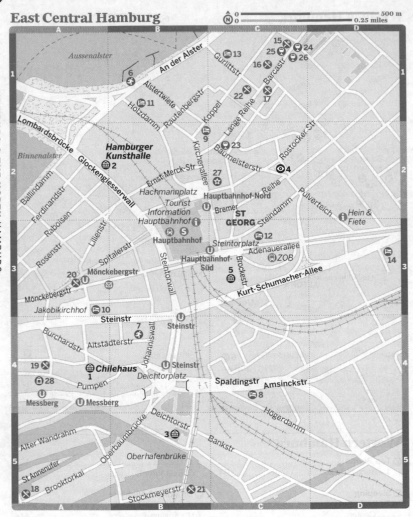

6pm Jul & Aug, 10am-5pm Mar-Jun & Sep-Dec, 11am-5pm Jan & Feb; S Messberg) This camped-up chamber of horrors is brought to life by actors, incorporating various thrill rides, and is housed in an old warehouse. It's pricey and not recommended for kids under 10, which limits its appeal to a rather narrow range.

◉ Port Area

Sprawling over 75 sq km (12% of Hamburg's entire surface area), Hamburg's huge port receives some 12,000 ships each year, which deliver and take on some 70 million tonnes of goods.

Climbing the steps above the Landungs-brücken U-/S-Bahn station to the **Stint-fang stone balcony** offers a sweeping panorama, while dozens of port and Elbe River cruises, starting at the St Pauli Harbour Landungsbrücken, put you right in the middle of the action. On a sunny day, the **Landungsbrücken promenade** here is hugely popular with locals and tourists alike.

East Central Hamburg

Rickmer Rickmers MUSEUM
(Map p648; ☑040-319 5959; www.rickmer-rick-mers.de; Ponton 1a; adult/child €5/3; ☺10am-6pm, longer hours Jun-Aug) The 1886 three-masted steel windjammer *Rickmer Rickmers* is now a museum ship; from the restaurant on deck you have fine harbour views.

Cap San Diego HISTORIC SITE
(Map p648; ☑040-364 209; www.capsandiego.de; 3 Baumwall; adult/child €7/3; ☺10am-6pm; Ⓢ Baumwall) The beautiful 1961 freighter, the 10,000-tonne *Cap San Diego,* is open to tours that give a good feel for when sea voyages were a relaxing and low-key way to tour the world. There are also special exhibitions.

◎ St Pauli

Even those not interested in lurid late nights usually pay a quick trip to the St Pauli's **Reeperbahn** to see what the fuss is all about. Sure, it's tamer than the Amsterdam scene (which is itself becoming tamer), but it's still Europe's biggest in terms of the number of businesses. Long established as a party place, the Reeperbahn is flooded by crowds of thousands from around 4pm on weekends, cruising the sleazy collection of bars, sex clubs, variety acts, pubs and cafes collectively known as the 'Kiez'.

While the sex industry is still in full swing, some of the harsher edges are gone, although prostitutes dressed as schoolgirls are still much in evidence. The once 'daring' sex shops are now marked by tired displays of sun-faded dildos in the windows. Still, many can't resist some safe titillation and on summer evenings, walking tour groups of bug-eyed tourists jostle each other along the streets.

Herbertstrasse STREET
(Map p648; Herbertstrasse; Ⓡ Reeperbahn) Along Davidstrasse, a painted tin wall bars views into Herbertstrasse, a block-long bordello that's off-limits to men under 18 and to women of all ages. It's the notorious sinful centre of the district.

Davidwache BUILDING
(Map p648; Spielbudenplatz 31, cnr Davidstrasse; Ⓡ Reeperbahn) South of the Reeperbahn stands the star of many a German crime film and TV show, the Davidwache. This brick police station, festooned with ornate ceramic tiles, is the base for 150 officers, who keep the surrounds reasonably tame.

---

❶ THE PRICE OF SEX

Especially at the sex clubs on and near St Pauli's **Grosse Freiheit**, doorstaff try to lure in the passing crowd with bargain shows, leaving customers to discover the mandatory drink minimum (usually at least €25) once inside. Ask at the bar how much drinks cost; you can easily spend €100 for a couple of watery cocktails.

Museum für Hamburgische Geschichte MUSEUM (Museum of Hamburg History; Map p648; ☑040-428 412 380; www.hamburgmuseum.de; Holstenwall 24; adult/child €9/free; ☺10am-5pm Tue-Sat, to 6pm Sun; ⊞; ⓢSt Pauli) Hamburg's history museum has lots of kid-friendly features: it's chock-full of intricate ship models, has a large model train set (which runs on the hour), and even the actual bridge of the steamship *Werner*, which you can clamber over. As it chronicles the city's evolution, it reveals titbits such as the fact that the Reeperbahn was once the home of rope makers (*Reep* means 'rope'). There is a good exhibit on the history of the city's Jewish population.

Park Fiction PARK (Map p648; www.park-fiction.net; Antonistrasse) Hamburg's maritime tableau spreads out before this park created by local residents and overlooking the Elbe. Pick up some beer and have your own sunset happy hour lounging on the grass under the fake palm trees.

⊙ Schanzenviertel & Karolinenviertel

North of St Pauli lie the lively Schanzenviertel and Karolinenviertel districts, bordered by the U-Bahn Feldstrasse, S-/U-Bahn Sternschanze and Stresemannstrasse, which retain a strong sense of Hamburg's

---

THE BEATLES IN HAMBURG – FOREVER

I was born in Liverpool, but I grew up in Hamburg.
John Lennon

It was the summer of 1960 and a fledgling band from Liverpool had been assured a paying gig in Hamburg, if only it could come up with a drummer. After a frantic search, Pete Best joined John Lennon, Paul McCartney, George Harrison and Stuart Sutcliffe in August that year.

The Beatles opened on the notorious Grosse Freiheit to seedy crowds of drunks and whores. After 48 consecutive nights of six-hour sessions, the Beatles' innate musical genius had been honed. The magnetism of the group that would rock the world began drawing loyal crowds. But complications ensued when an underage George was deported in November, and Paul and Pete were arrested for attempted arson. All escaped the German authorities and returned to England. There, as 'The Beatles: Direct from Hamburg', they had their Merseyside breakthrough.

In 1961 the Beatles returned to Hamburg. During a 92-night stint, they made their first professional recording. Soon manager extraordinaire Brian Epstein and the recording genius (now Sir) George Martin arrived on the scene. The Beatles began their career with EMI; Pete Best was replaced by Ringo Starr, a more professional drummer; Stuart Sutcliffe quit the band; and they went on to fame and fortune.

You can still find traces of their time in Hamburg:

➡ **Indra Club** (p666) The group's small first venue is open again and has live acts many nights. The interior is vastly different.

➡ **Kaiserkeller** (Map p648; Grosse Freiheit 36; ⓢHamburg Reeperbahn) One of the more respectable clubs today on the Grosse Freiheit, this second venue for the Beatles survives in a much-altered form.

➡ **Gretel & Alfons** (Map p648; Grosse Freiheit 29; ⓢHamburg Reeperbahn) A late-night cafe and bar that is little changed from when the boys would unwind here after shows.

➡ **Star Club** (Map p648; Grosse Freiheit 39; ⓢHamburg Reeperbahn) The seminal venue for the Beatles opened in 1962. It has since burnt down and there is a sad historical marker. Thai karaoke now echoes off the walls.

➡ **Beatles-Platz** (Map p648; ⓢHamburg Reeperbahn) Designed like a vinyl record, it has abstract steel sculptures resembling cookie cutters of the fab four (including a hybrid of Ringo Starr and Pete Best).

Beatles Tour (☑040-3003 3790; www.hempels-musictour.com; tour €34; ☺6pm Sat; ⓢFeldstrasse) For an entertaining look at the Beatles in Hamburg, try this Beatles tour offered by the fun-filled and engaging Stephanie Hempel.

countercultural scene. Creative media types mix with students amid a landscape of multicultural cafes and restaurants, as well as offbeat shops, particularly along **Marktstrasse**.

Rote Flora CULTURAL CENTRE
(Map p648; ☎040-439 5413; www.nadir.org; Schulterblatt 71; 🕐hours vary) One of the most outstanding remnants of the area's rougher days, the graffiti-covered Rote Flora looks one step away from demolition. Once the famous Flora Theatre, it's now an alternative cultural centre with a calendar of new music, protests and events. The city protected it from gentrification in 2014.

Altona & Elbmeile

To the west of the Schanzenviertel, Altona is gentrified and a good place to take a neighbourhood stroll. It also has its share of offbeat shops and buzzing restaurants.

Altona stretches from the village-like centre around its S-Bahn and train stations to the waterfront, where a string of restaurants stretch along the Elbmeile, along with waterfront bars and cafes.

★ **Altonaer Balkon** VIEWPOINT
(Altona Balcony; Map p653; off Klopstockstrasse; [S] Hamburg Königstrasse) Thrill to some of Hamburg's best harbour views from this accurately named and quite pretty park.

Blankenese

Once a former fishing village and haven for cut-throat pirates, Blankenese, 8km west of Altona, now boasts some of the finest and most expensive houses in Germany. For visitors, the area's attractiveness lies in its hillside labyrinth of narrow, cobbled streets, with a network of 58 stairways (4864 steps in total) connecting them.

Süllberg Hill VIEWPOINT
(Süllbergweg) The best views of the Elbe (nearly 3km wide here) and its container ships are from the 75m-high Süllberg hill. To get to Süllberg, take the S-Bahn to Blankenese, then bus 48 to Waseberg – having passed the beachfront restaurants and cafes – where you'll see a sign pointing to the nearby Süllberg. If you alight at the Krögers Treppe (Fischerhaus) bus stop, head up the Bornholdt Treppe and Süllbergweg. Or get off once the road starts winding and explore.

Further Afield

★ **Auswanderermuseum BallinStadt** MUSEUM
(Emigration Museum; ☎040-3197 9160; www.ballinstadt.de; Veddeler Bogen 2; adult/child €12.50/7; 🕐10am-6pm Apr-Oct, 10am-4.30pm Nov-Mar; 🚉Veddel) Sort of a bookend for New York's Ellis Island, Hamburg's excellent emigration museum in the original halls looks at the conditions that drove about 5 million people to leave Germany for the US and South America in search of better lives from 1850 until the 1930s. Multilingual displays address the hardships endured before and during the voyage and upon arrival in the New World. About 4km southeast of the city centre, BallinStadt is easily reached by S-Bahn.

Bullenhuser Damm Schule HISTORIC SITE
(Bullenhuser Damm School; ☎040 428 1310; www.kz-gedenkstaette-neuengamme.de; Bullenhuser Damm 92-94; 🕐10am-5pm Sun; 🚉Rothenburgsort) [FREE] During WWII, 20 Jewish children were chosen by Dr Josef Mengele at Auschwitz and sent to Neuengamme concentration camp (see p671) near Hamburg for medical experiments. In 1945, with the German war effort collapsing, the children and their adult minders (other prisoners) were brought to this otherwise unremarkable school in a grimy industrial area of southeast Hamburg and murdered. In a war filled with horror, this story stands out. Today there are exhibits about the children in a basement display area.

A nearby **memorial garden** along Grossmanstrasse is planted with roses. Read about this atrocity and the children at www.kinder-vom-bullenhuser-damm.de.

Tierpark Hagenbeck ZOO
(☎040-530 0330; www.hagenbeck-tierpark.de; Lokstedter Grenzstrasse 2; adult/child from €20/15; 🕐9am-7pm Jul & Aug, 9am-6pm Sep-Oct & Mar-Jun, 9am-4.30pm Nov-Feb; 👪; [S] Hagenbecks Tierpark) The 2500 animals that live in Hamburg's zoo have open enclosures over 27 hectares. In addition to elephants, tigers, orang-utans, toucans and other creatures, you'll find a replica Nepalese temple, a Japanese garden, an art deco gate and a huge aquarium. A petting zoo, pony rides, a miniature railway and playground mean you'll have to drag the kids away at the end of the day. It is 5km northwest of the centre.

Tours

Boat Tours

For port tours, it's easiest to just go to Landungsbrücken and pick a boat that's leaving when you want.

You can also float past elegant buildings aboard an Alster Lakes cruise.

★Maritime Circle Line BOAT TOUR
(Map p648; ☎040-2849 3963; www.maritime-circle-line.de; Landungsbrücken 10, Jetty 10; adult/child €16/8; ⏲3 times daily; [S] Landungsbrücken) Harbour shuttle service connecting Hamburg's maritime cultural attractions, including the Auswanderermuseum BallinStadt and Miniatur Wunderland. The entire loop takes around 95 minutes; you can hop on or off at any of its stops.

★Barkassen-Centrale Ehlers BOAT TOUR
(Map p648; ☎040-319 916 170; www.barkassen-centrale.de; Vorsetzen-Angleger; tours from adult/child €18/8; ⏲daily) Offers the usual one-hour harbour tour, but also runs a fascinating two-hour tour of the harbour, as well as canal and specialised trips in historic boats.

Abicht BOAT TOUR
(Map p648; ☎040-317 8220; www.abicht.de; Brücke 1; 1hr tour adult/child €18/9; ⏲noon Apr-Oct; [U] Hamburg Landungsbrücken) This company's harbour tours are rightly popular; it also offers Saturday-evening tours taking you past the illuminated warehouses (departure times vary according to tides).

Hadag BOAT TOUR
(Map p648; ☎040-311 7070; www.hadag.de; Brücke 2; 1hr harbour trip adult/child from €18/9; ⏲several times daily Apr-Sep, Sat & Sun Oct-Mar; [U] Hamburg Landungsbrücken) Harbour tours plus more adventuresome trips to the Lower Elbe (April to September). Also offers a hop-on, hop-off service along the Elbe.

ATG Alster-Touristik BOAT TOUR
(Map p648; ☎040-3574 2419; www.alstertouristik.de; Jungfernstieg pier; tours adult/child from €15/7.50; ⏲daily Apr-Oct; [S] Jungfernstieg) Runs a hop-on, hop-off service between nine landing stages around the lakes. There are a lot of other tours on offer – especially interesting are the canal tours.

> **SIGHTSEEING LIKE A REAL HAMBURGER**
>
> This maritime city offers a bewildering array of boat trips, but locals will tell you that you don't have to book a cruise to see the port – the city's **harbour ferries** will take you up the river on a regular public transport ticket, and you can avoid hokey narration!
>
> One oft-recommended route is to catch **ferry 62** from Landungsbrücken to Finkenwerder, then change for the 64 to Teufelsbrücke. From Teufelsbrücke, you can wander along the Elbe eastwards to Neumühlen, from where you can catch bus 112 back to the Altona S-Bahn station or ferry 62 back to Landungsbrücken.
>
> On land, the **U3 U-Bahn line** is particularly scenic, especially the elevated track between the St Pauli and Rathaus U-Bahn stations.

Bus Tours

Hamburg's numerous bus tour companies compete in name only. In reality, they are one big cartel with fixed prices and at times mediocre service.

There are four tour routes:

➡ **Route A** The most popular, it gives a good overview of Hamburg. You can hop on and hop off the buses of the various companies using the same ticket.

➡ **Route B** Visits far-flung maritime sights, but uses motorways for part of the route and interesting vistas can fly past.

➡ **Routes C & D** Variations on Route A.

On the tours:

➡ On sunny days, look for buses with open tops. Some drivers refuse to open the tops, creating rolling saunas.

➡ English narration *may* be provided, despite promises otherwise. Check before you board.

➡ Don't expect route maps.

➡ Complete route loops take about 90 minutes.

➡ Most tours stop at both Landungsbrücken and the Hauptbahnhof (Kirchenallee exit).

➡ Buy tickets on board.

Walking Tours

Dozens of walking tours operate throughout the city, many with specific themes, such as red-light tours, 'historic hooker' tours, Beatles tours (see p656), culinary tours and more. Tourist offices have full details.

✺ Festivals & Events

Hafengeburtstag FESTIVAL
(Harbour Birthday; www.hafengeburtstag.de;
☉ early May) The city's biggest annual event
is this three-day gala. It commemorates
Emperor Barbarossa granting Hamburg
customs exemption and is energetically celebrated with harbourside concerts, funfairs
and gallons of beer.

Hamburger Dom CARNIVAL
(www.hamburger-dom.de; Heiligengeistfeld; attraction costs vary; ☉ late Mar, late Jul, late Nov; Ⓢ Feldstrasse) Established in 1329, the month-long
Hamburger Dom is held three times a year
and is one of Europe's largest and oldest
funfairs. This colourful carnival takes place
on Heiligengeistfeld, between St Pauli and
Schanzenviertel.

🛏 Sleeping

Hamburg is big, so you might consider
where you'll be spending your time before
you decide where to stay. Booking ahead is
a good idea any time of year and is essential
on weekends, during festivals and throughout summer.

🛏 Altstadt & Neustadt

You'll find every chain hotel imaginable in
the centre of the city.

**A&O Hamburg
Hauptbahnhof** HOSTEL, HOTEL €
(Map p654; ☎ 030-809 475 110; www.aohostels.
com; Amsinckstrasse 10; dm from €20, s/d from
€50/60; Ⓟ ☺ @ ☎; ⓇHauptbahnhof) A 300m
suitcase-drag from the Hauptbahnhof, this
central branch of the institutional-style A&O
chain has some 900 beds in rooms with private bathrooms. Those deep inside the labyrinthine building can feel claustrophobic;
try for one overlooking the street. Prices can
skyrocket depending on demand. There are
three other Hamburg branches.

★Henri Hotel HOTEL €€
(Map p654; ☎ 040-554 357 557; www.henri-ho-
tel.com; Bugenhagenstrasse 21; r €110-180; ☎;
Ⓢ Mönckebergstrasse) Kidney-shaped tables,
plush armchairs, vintage typewriters – the
Henri channels the 1950s so successfully that
you half expect to run into Don Draper. Its
65 rooms and studios are a good fit for urban lifestyle junkies who like the alchemy of
modern comforts and retro design. For more

elbow room get an L-sized room with a king-
size bed.

Hotel SIDE HOTEL €€€
(Map p648; ☎ 040-309 990; www.side-hamburg.de;
Drehbahn 49; r €145-300; Ⓟ ☺ ✳ @ ☎ ☎; Ⓢ Gänsemarkt) A stylish alternative to the city centre's chain business hotels, this Matteo Thun-
designed stunner is built around a soaring
prism-shaped central atrium. Suites feature
vividly coloured free-standing bath-tubs
and soothing shades. The 8th-floor chill-out
lounge opens to a panoramic sun deck.

🛏 St Georg

Convenient to the Hauptbahnhof, St Georg
is ripe with midrange hotels, some much
better than others. Without a booking, be
ready to leave your bag in a locker and compare a few. Note that the area around the
Steindamm and Hansaplatz can be seedy.

Alpha Hotel-Pension PENSION €
(Map p654; ☎ 040-245 365; www.alphahotel.biz;
Koppel 4-6; r €45-100; ☺ ☎; ⓇHauptbahnhof)
An excellent choice only 300m from the
Hauptbahnhof. The 21 rooms here are basic
but comfortable. The reception staff are especially warm and helpful. If it's your first
visit to Hamburg, your every question will
be answered with aplomb. Some rooms
share baths, others have access to a tiny
rooftop playground.

★Hotel Wedina HOTEL €€
(Map p654; ☎ 040-280 8900; www.hotelwedi-
na.de; Gurlittstrasse 23; r €125-245; Ⓟ @ ☎;
Ⓢ Hauptbahnhof) Margaret Atwood, Jonathan
Franzen and Martin Walser are among the
literary greats who've stayed at this loveable
lair. Rooms are spread over five brightly
pigmented buildings that in different ways
express the owners' love for literature, architecture and art. It's close to the train station and the Alster lakes. The breakfasts are
especially good.

Hotel Village HOTEL €€
(Map p654; ☎ 040-480 6490; www.hotel-village.de;
Steindamm 4; r €50-150; @ ☎; Ⓢ Hauptbahnhof)
You can tell this edgy gem was once a bordello: the 20 boudoirs feature various kitsch
mixes of red velvet, gold flock wallpaper and
leopard prints, and several have huge mirrors above the bed. It attracts a mix of gay
and straight guests. Economy rooms have
bathrooms outside the room.

Junges Hotel　　　　　　　HOTEL €€
(Map p654; ☑040-419 230; www.jungeshotel.de;
Kurt-Schumacher-Allee 14; r €100-175; P@ ☎;
Ⓢ Berliner Tor, Ⓡ Berliner Tor) A corrugated metal
exterior fronts lots of blond wood in this airy,
modern 128-room hotel less than five minutes' walk from the Berliner Tor U-Bahn/S-
Bahn station. Extra guests can be accommodated in some double rooms, with beds that
drop down from the wall (like in a train sleeper compartment). Some rooms have fridges.

★**Hotel Atlantic**　　　LUXURY HOTEL €€€
(Map p654; ☑040-288 80; www.kempinski.
com; An der Alster 72-79; s/d from €160/190;
❋ ☎ ⛵; Ⓢ Hauptbahnhof Nord) Imagine yourself aboard a luxury ocean liner in this
grand 252-room hotel, which opens onto
Holzdamm. Built in 1909 for luxury-liner
passengers departing for America, it has
ornate stairwells, wide hallways and subtle
maritime touches. It has all the services of a
five-star hotel; many rooms have lake views.

🛏 Speicherstadt & HafenCity

25hours Hotel HafenCity　　HOTEL €€
(Map p648; ☑040-855 870; www.25hours-hotel.
de; Überseeallee 5; r €100-200; P ☎; Ⓢ Überseequartier) Offbeat decor, an infectious
irreverence and postmodern vintage flair
make this pad a top choice among global
nomads. Sporting maritime flourishes, the
decor channels an old-timey seaman's club
in the lobby, an excellent restaurant and the
170 cabin-style rooms. Enjoy views of the
emerging HafenCity neighbourhood from
the rooftop sauna.

🛏 St Pauli

St Pauli offers greatly divergent accommodation: wild near the Reeperbahn, leafy in
its genteel neighbourhoods and flashy on its
knoll overlooking the bright lights of the city
and harbour.

★**Superbude St Pauli**　　HOTEL, HOSTEL €
(Map p648; ☑040-807 915 820; www.superbude.
de; Juliusstrasse 1-7; dm/r from €20/60; @ ☎;
Ⓢ Sternschanze, Ⓡ Sternschanze, Holstenstrasse)
The young and forever-young mix and mingle without a shred of prejudice at this rocking design hotel-hostel combo that's all about
living, laughing, partying and, yes, even
sleeping well. All rooms have comfy beds and
sleek private baths, breakfast is served until
noon and there's even a 'rock star suite' with
an Astra beer as a pillow treat.

East　　　　　　　　　　　HOTEL €€
(Map p648; ☑040-309 933; www.east-hamburg.
de; Simon-von-Utrecht-Strasse 31; r €100-210;
❋ ☎; Ⓢ St Pauli) In an old iron foundry, East's
bold and dramatic design never fails to impress. The walls, lamps and huge pillars of
this hotel's public areas emulate organic
forms – droplets, flowers, trees – giving it
a warm, rich and enveloping feel. Rooms
come with handmade furniture and are accented with tactile fabrics and leather. It's
on a cool St Pauli street.

Hotel St Annen　　　　　　HOTEL €€
(Map p648; ☑040-317 7130; www.hotelstannen.
de; Annenstrasse 5; r €80-140; P ➡@ ☎; Ⓢ St
Pauli) Tucked away in one of the few quiet
streets between the Reeperbahn and Schanzenviertel, this 36-room hotel is a favourite
with business people for its whitewashed,
restful-hued modern rooms and shaded
back garden and terrace.

Hotel Hafen　　　　　　　HOTEL €€
(Map p648; ☑040-311 1370; www.hotel-hafen-ham-
burg.de; Seewartenstrasse 9; r €110-180; @ ☎;
Ⓢ Landungsbrücken) Location, location, location. This privately owned behemoth of
a hotel (353 rooms) looms over the heart
of Hamburg's harbour from a small hill. If
you're lucky enough to score a harbour-
facing room, the views are extraordinary. In
addition to the refurbished, historic main
building, a former seafarer's home, there are
modern wings. Decor verges on frumpy.

Empire Riverside　　　　　HOTEL €€€
(Map p648; ☑040-311 190; www.empire-riverside.
de; Bernhard-Nocht-Strasse 97; r €130-190; P ❋ ☎;
Ⓢ St Pauli) Sparing splashes of colour bright-
en its restaurant, bars and 327 streamlined
rooms with floor-to-ceiling windows, most
with harbour views. Those on the higher of
the 20 floors may not leave as they'll be captivated by the goings on of all Hamburg around
them. There's a good spa and exercise room.

🛏 Schanzenviertel & Karolinenviertel

Edgy neighbourhoods deserve edgy – yet
restful – rooms, which you'll find here.

Instant Sleep Backpacker Hostel　HOSTEL €
(Map p648; ☑040-4318 2310; www.instantsleep.
de; Max-Brauer-Allee 277; dm/s/d from €19/50/60;
@ ☎; Ⓡ Sternschanze) Artistic murals – from
green stripes to golden Buddhas – adorn
this chilled-out pad in the happening

Schanzenviertel. Airy dorms (three to 12 beds) and private rooms house 50 proper beds (no bunks), though all share bathrooms. Some of Hamburg's most ideal cafes for hanging out are just around the corner.

★ **Hotel Bellmoor** HOTEL €€
(Map p648; ☎040-413 3110; www.hotel-bellmoor.de; Dammtorpalais, Moorweidenstrasse 34, 4th fl; s/d from €80/120; 📶; 🚉Dammtor) White embossed wallpaper and vintage advertising posters line the halls of this traditional hotel in a grand old apartment block that has been converted into several hotels. Rooms 14 (single) and 34 (twin) feature art-nouveau bathrooms with stained-glass windows and tiled tubs. Economy singles are like old sailing-ship cabins. Views over Hamburg's rooftops unfurl from the sunlit breakfast room.

★ **Fritz im Pyjama Hotel** BOUTIQUE HOTEL €€
(Map p648; ☎040-314 838; www.fritz-im-pyjama.de; Schanzenstrasse 101-103; s/d from €75/90; 📶; [S]Sternschanze) This stylish town-house hotel sits smack dab in the heart of the Schanzenviertel party zone. Rooms are smallish, with wooden floors, angular furniture and large windows; seven of the 17 have a balcony. Those without are quieter as they face the courtyard.

🛏 Altona & Elbmeile

Of all the areas to stay in Hamburg, this option feels the most residential; the charms of the city are a short S-Bahn ride away.

Schanzenstern Altona PENSION €
(Map p653; ☎040-3991 9191; schanzenstern.com; Kleine Rainstrasse 24-26; dm/s/d from €20/50/75, apt from €85; 🚭@📶; 🚉Altona) A mix of families and slightly more grown-up backpackers inhabit these sparkling rooms (with private bathrooms), and self-catering apartments. Staff are wired into what's happening around Hamburg. Dorms have two to seven beds. There is another property in St Pauli.

Meininger Hotel Hamburg City Center HOSTEL, HOTEL €
(Map p653; ☎040-2846 4388; www.meininger-hotels.com; Goetheallee 11; dm €20-30, s/d from €70/75; [P]@📶; 🚉Altona) The Hamburg branch of this upscale chain of hostel-hotels is conveneint to Altona train station and the many enticements of the neighbourhood. The 116 rooms are in a modern six-storey building with a lift. There's a laundry, storage lockers, games room, bar and more.

🍴 Eating

Virtually every part of Hamburg has good dining options ranging from humble to fine. Unsurprisingly, seafood is a favourite in this port city, with everything from traditional regional specialities to sushi on offer. You'll also find a truly global variety of foods reflecting this city's international links and traditions.

🍴 Altstadt

Many of the restaurants in the Altstadt cater to bankers and other office workers, but there are alternatives, including touristy Deichstrasse, which is lined with atmospheric old buildings – a rarity in this area.

★ **Mö Grill** GERMAN €
(Map p654; ☎040-335 529; Mönckebergstrasse 11; mains from €4; ⏲10am-7pm; [S]Mönckebergstrasse) You can smell the curry and see the crowds from two streets away at this very popular venue for that beloved German fast food, the *Currywurst*. Locals agree that the versions here (and at a second stand across the street) are about the best anywhere.

Goot GERMAN €
(Map p654; ☎040-6730 6171; www.goot-hamburg.de; Depenau 10; mains €5-9; ⏲11.30am-4pm; [S]Messberg) Top regional ingredients are used in fresh lunches served in a casual setting. There are vegetarian soups and salads plus sandwiches featuring roasted meats. Nab a table outside.

Café Paris FRENCH €€€
(Map p648; ☎040-3252 7778; www.cafeparis.net; Rathausstrasse 4; mains €15-26; ⏲9am-11.30pm; [S]Rathaus) Within a spectacularly tiled 1882 butchers' hall and adjoining art-deco salon, this elegant yet relaxed brasserie serves classical French fare like *croque-monsieur* (toasted ham-and-cheese sandwich), *croque-madame* (the same, but with a fried egg) and *steak tartare* (minced meat, but pan-fried, not raw). Its breakfast for two is a splendid feast.

Deichgraf GERMAN €€€
(Map p648; ☎040-364 208; www.deichgraf-hamburg.de; Deichstrasse 23; mains €18-30; ⏲noon-3pm Mon-Fri, 5.30-10pm Mon-Sat; [S]Rödingsmarkt) In a prime setting, with the water on one side and long street-side tables on the

other, Deichgraf excels in Hamburg specialities cooked to a high standard. The menu changes seasonally and much of the food is sourced from the region.

🍴 Neustadt

Look for luxe cafes under the beautiful columned arcades of the Alsterarkaden and the appropriately named Colonnaden.

Edelcurry GERMAN €
(Map p648; ☎040-3571 8350; www.edelcurry.de; Grosse Bleichen 68; mains from €4; 🕐11am-10pm Mon-Sat, noon-8pm Sun; [S] Rödingsmarkt) The humble *Currywurst* gets the royal treatment here. Choose from three flavours of sausage (classic, fruity or spicy) and add on a side of fresh-cut fries that are the best you'll find this side of Belgium.

Thämer's GERMAN €€
(Map p648; ☎040-345 077; Grossneumarkt 10; mains €8-18; 🕐noon-midnight; [R] Stadthausbrücke) The leafy Grossneumarkt is a relaxed change from the more chi chi parts of the Neustadt, and for decades Thämer's has anchored a prime spot with dozens of covered tables on the square. There's more inside the vaguely divey bar. Hearty German meals plus burgers are the speciality, the beer list is tops.

★**Anna Sgroi** ITALIAN €€€
(☎040-2800 3930; www.annasgroi.de; Milchstrasse 7; lunch menus from €32, dinner mains €38-42; 🕐noon-2.30pm Wed-Fri, 7-10.30pm Wed-Sat; [S] Hallerstrasse) Lauded chef Anna Sgroi has taken the foods of her southern Italian childhood and elevated them to culinary heights. A seemingly mundane dish like stuffed artichokes is sublime and that's just to start. While never the same, expect dishes with bold flavours, the finest ingredients and flawless execution. Service is smooth and unfussy.

Matsumi JAPANESE €€€
(Map p648; ☎040-343 125; www.matsumi.de; Colonnaden 96; meals from €18; 🕐noon-2.30pm & 6.30-10pm Tue-Sat; [S] Stephansplatz) Celebrated sushi chef Hideaki Morita creates excellent Japanese fare at this 2nd-floor restaurant where virtually everything is unassuming, except for the food. Besides sushi, there are various teriyaki grills, a bevy of tempura dishes and *washinabe* (a stew of fish and vegetables that boils at your table). Explore the sake menu.

🍴 St Georg

You'll be spoiled for choice strolling Lange Reihe, with dozens of options ranging from fancy to simple, German to Asian, breakfast to post-midnight.

★**Café Gnosa** CAFE €
(Map p654; ☎040-243 034; www.gnosa.de; Lange Reihe 93; mains €7-14; 🕐10am-1am) With its abstract art and in-house bakery, Café Gnosa draws an affable gay and straight crowd in

HISTORY OF THE HAMBURGER

A classic *Calvin and Hobbes* comic strip once asked if hamburgers were made out of people from Hamburg. And while Hamburg's citizens are, of course, known as Hamburgers, it was the city's role as an international port that gave rise to its most famous namesake.

The origins of the ubiquitous fast food date back to the 12th century. The Tartars (Mongolian and Turkish warriors) wedged pieces of beef between their saddles and the horses' backs, softening the meat as they rode until it was tender enough to be eaten raw, and the practice soon spread to Russia. By the 17th century, Hamburg ships brought 'steak tartare' (named after the Tartars) back to Germany, which visiting seafarers then referred to as 'steak in the Hamburg style'. These patties of salted minced beef – usually slightly smoked and mixed with breadcrumbs and onions – were highly durable, making them ideal for long sea voyages.

Hamburg emigrants to America continued making the patties, which they served in bread. (As for who in America officially launched the burger remains a fanatical culinary debate.)

American chains have invaded Hamburg, as they have everywhere. Although known here, too, as hamburgers or burgers, the original style of patty is rarely called Hamburg-anything in Germany, but rather *Frikadelle, Frikandelle* or *Bulette*, all staples of train station sausage stands.

St Georg. The curved glass windows give it an art deco vibe. There are outside tables.

Peaberries
CAFE €

(Map p654; ☑ 040-2419 2862; Gurlittstrasse 46; mains from €3; ⊙ 7am-6pm Mon-Fri, 9am-4pm Sat; ⊠ Hauptbahnhof) Perfect for that much-needed pause, this cute little cafe has excellent coffee drinks as well as tasty baked goods, including the best bagels in town.

Café Koppel
VEGETARIAN €

(Map p654; ☑ 040-249 235; www.cafe-koppel.de; Lange Reihe 66; mains €5-10; ⊙ 10am-11pm; ☑; ⓢ Hauptbahnhof) Set back from busy Lange Reihe in the gallery Koppel 66, this vegie cafe is a refined oasis (with a summer garden). The menu could be an ad for the fertile fields of northern Germany, as there are baked goods, salads, soups and much more made with fresh seasonal ingredients.

Cox
MODERN EUROPEAN €€€

(Map p654; ☑ 040-249 422; www.restaurant-cox. de; Lange Reihe 68; mains lunch €10-18, dinner €17-25; ⊙ noon-2.30pm Mon-Fri, 6.30-10.30pm daily; ⊠ Hauptbahnhof) Behind its opaque glass doors, this upmarket bistro was part of the original vanguard of St Georg's gentrification. Its changing menu of dishes reflects the foods of the season and influences from across the continent.

Speicherstadt & HafenCity

Speicherstadt has a couple of excellent traditional restaurants amid its old restored warehouses. HafenCity has a few newish eateries but until it gets more built up, they have a slightly soulless feel among the never-ending construction.

Oberhafen Kantine
GERMAN €€

(Map p654; ☑ 040-3280 9984; www.oberhafen-kantine-hamburg.de; Stockmeyerstrasse 39; mains €7-16; ⊙ noon-10pm; ⊠ Steinstrasse) Since 1925, this slightly tilted brick restaurant has served up the most traditional Hamburg fare. Here you can order a 'Hamburger' and you get the real thing: a patty made with various seasonings and onions. Roast beef and fish round out a trip back to the days when the surrounding piers echoed to the shouts of seafarers.

Fleetschlösschen
BISTRO €€

(Map p654; ☑ 040-3039 3210; www.fleetschloesschen.de; Brooktorkai 17; mains €7-12; ⊙ 8am-10pm; ⓢ Messberg) Timelessly cute, this former customs post overlooks a Speicherstadt canal

and has a narrow steel spiral staircase to the toilets. There's barely room for 20 inside, but its outdoor seating areas are brilliant in sunny weather. Choose from sandwiches, soups, salads and various small plates of tasty treats.

Port Area

Right on the water you'll find a plethora of ice-cream stands, fried-fish stalls and other vittles-pushers for the strolling masses. But step slightly inland and there are good places for a coffee or a meal in the old ethnic neighbourhoods. Fancy seafood places around Landungsbrücken are skippable.

★ Fischbrötchenbude Brücke 10
FISH €

(Map p648; ☑ 040-3339 9339; www.bruecke-10. de; Landungsbrücken, Pier 10; sandwiches €2.50-7.50; ⊙ 10am-10pm Apr-Oct, to 8pm Nov-Mar; ⓢ Landungsbrücken, ⊠ Landungsbrücken) There are a gazillion fish sandwich vendors in Hamburg, but we're going to stick our neck out and say that this vibrant, clean and contemporary outpost makes the best. Try a classic *Bismarck* (pickled herring) or *Matjes* (brined), or treat yourself to a bulging shrimp sandwich. Lovely tables outside.

Cafe Sul
CAFE €

(Map p648; ☑ 040-3179 7486; www.cafe-sul.de; Ditmar-Koel-Strasse 10; mains €5-9; ⊙ 8am-midnight; ⓢ Baumwall) A perfect place of refuge from the fried-fish-clutching mobs of the port area, this cafe lives up to its name with a cheery disposition, even on a cloudy day. The front opens to the street and there is an excellent breakfast and tapas menu.

Lusitano
PORTUGUESE €€

(Map p648; ☑ 040-315 841; Rambachstrasse 5; mains €8-20; ⊙ noon-11pm; ⓢ Baumwall) As unadorned as a piece of salt cod, this little restaurant in Hamburg's old Portuguese neighbourhood captures the bright flavours of the Mediterranean. Dishes like spicy sausages and pasta will warm your heart, but the seafood is the real star. Order the Gambas James Brown and be prepared for feel-good garlicky prawns as volatile as the namesake singer. Book ahead.

St Pauli

Note that it's easy to escape the clamour of St Pauli's manufactured sleaze by getting just a few streets off the Reeperbahn, where you can find quiet squares and cool cafes.

In fact, the further you get from the Reeperbahn, the better your odds of having something tasty to eat (unless it's 4am, in which case the gaggle of fast-fooderies along this notorious street will do just fine).

★ **Konditorei Holger Rönnfeld** BAKERY €
(Map p648; ☎040-313 536; www.hochzeitstorten-hamburg.de; Hein-Hoyer-Strasse 52; snacks from €2; ⏲6.30am-6pm Mon-Fri, to 4pm Sat; 🚆Reeperbahn) Sweet offerings abound at this aromatic and traditional bakery. Try a *nussecken,* a crunchy, nutty, triangular-shaped pastry.

Café Mimosa CAFE €
(Map p648; ☎040-3202 7989; www.cafemimosa.de; Clemens-Schultz-Strasse 87; mains €4-12; ⏲10am-7pm Tue-Sun; [S]St Pauli) This gem of a neighbourhood cafe is the go-to place for warm brioches, some of the yummiest cakes in town, plus daily changing lunch specials. Camp out inside among theatrical flourishes or grab a table outside.

Le Kaschemme EUROPEAN €€
(Map p648; ☎040-5190 6370; www.le-kaschemme.de; Rendsburger Strasse 14; mains €8-16; ⏲6pm-midnight Mon-Sat, 5-10.30pm Sun; [S]St Pauli) The perfect place for a beverage while you plan your night out in St Pauli, this clean-lined pub has a good menu of dishes that range from Italian to German. There are sidewalk tables and when you're ready to move on, you will go far in this cafe-filled area until you find another good spot.

Nil INTERNATIONAL €€€
(Map p648; ☎040-439 7823; www.restaurant-nil.de; Neuer Pferdemarkt 5; mains €17-24; ⏲6-10.30pm Wed-Mon; [S]Feldstrasse) There's a lot more than nothing here at this hip tri-level restaurant. The varied and inspired slow-food menu is steered by the seasons and whatever regional suppliers have in store. Flavour pairings can be adventurous. The summer garden tables are dreamy.

🍴 Schanzenviertel & Karolinenviertel

Ethnic and offbeat dining options abound in these edgy areas while cafes hum to animated conversations about the topics of the day. Head to Susannenstrasse for an array of Turkish and Asian choices.

Die Herren Simpel CAFE €
(Map p648; ☎040-3868 4600; www.dieherrensimpel.de; Schulterblatt 75; dishes €4-8; ⏲5pm-late Mon-Fri, noon-late Sat, 2-8pm Sun; 📶; 🚆Sternschanze) The sky-blue mural with huge white flowers behind the bar has become this cafe's signature. Its tiny entrance opens to a spacious series of retro rooms, with garden tables out back. There's a fantastic range of breakfasts, plus sandwiches and warm snacks like *Flammkuchen* (Alsatian-style pizza). The long drinks menu includes various coffees, teas, beer and wine.

Super Mercato Italiano CAFE €
(Map p648; ☎040-434 114; www.super-mercato-italiano.net; Schulterblatt 82; snacks from €3; ⏲8am-6pm Mon-Sat; 🚆Sternschanze) The alt-vibe is perfectly contrasted by this very traditional Italian cafe and grocery, facing the inspirational near-ruin of the Rote Flora cultural centre. Any of three generations of owners will make you a perfect coffee, which you can enjoy on the wide pavement out front amid a plethora of adjoining ethnic cafes.

HAMBURG'S FISH MARKET

Fischmarkt (Map p648; Grosse Elbstrasse 9; ⏲5-9.30am Sun Apr-Oct, 7-9.30am Sun Nov-Mar; 🚌112 to Fischmarkt, 🚆Reeperbahn) Here's the perfect excuse to stay up all Saturday night. Every Sunday in the wee hours, some 70,000 locals and visitors descend upon the famous Fischmarkt in St Pauli. The market has been running since 1703, and its undisputed stars are the boisterous *Marktschreier* (market criers) who hawk their wares at full volume. Live bands also entertainingly crank out cover versions of ancient German pop songs in the adjoining **Fischauktionshalle** (Fish Auction Hall).

Vendors artfully arrange their bananas, cherries, kumquats and whatever else they've picked up that week (some comes direct from farms but a lot comes from wholesalers). Others pile up eels, shellfish, cacti and all manner of goods. It's not yet 5am as the first customers begin to trundle in. 'Don't be shy, little girl,' a vendor might shout with a lascivious wink to a 60-year-old, waggling a piece of eel in front of her face. Almost always, the 'girl' blushes before taking a hearty bite as the crowd cheers.

★Altes Mädchen MODERN EUROPEAN €€
(Map p648; ☎040-800 077 750; www.altes-maedchen.com; Lagerstrasse 28b; mains €9-22; 🕑noon-late Mon-Sat, from 10am Sun; [S] Sternschanze) The lofty red-brick halls of a 19th-century animal market have been upcycled into a hip culinary destination that includes a coffee roastery, a celebrity chef restaurant, and this beguiling brewpub with a central bar, in-house bakery and garden.

Erikas Eck GERMAN €€
(Map p648; ☎040-433 545; www.erikas-eck.de; Sternstrasse 98; mains €6-18; 🕑5pm-2pm; 🚆Sternschanze) This pit-stop institution originally fed hungry workers from the nearby abattoir (today the central meat market) and now serves wallet-friendly but waist-expanding portions of schnitzel and other trad German fare to a motley crowd of clubbers, cabbies and cops 21 hours a day.

🍴 Altona & Elbmeile

In the village-like area around Altona train station, you'll find dozens of casual and ethnic eateries, especially in the gentrified climes of Ottensen to the west.

Hamburg's western riverfront, from Altona to Övelgönne, known as the Elbmeile (Elbe Mile), has a dense concentration of popular and trendy restaurants – many drawing menu inspiration from the waterfront location.

★Eiscafe Eisliebe ICE CREAM €
(Map p653; ☎040-3980 8482; Bei der Reitbahn 2; ice cream from €1.50; 🕑noon-9pm; 🚆Altona) Some of the yummiest ice cream you'll ever taste is scooped from this little hole-in-the-wall (look for the queues). On any given day, you'll find around a dozen of its handmade, all-natural flavours. Fresh berry creations are the stuff of fantasy.

★Mikkels CAFE €
(Map p653; ☎040-7699 5072; www.mikkels.de; Kleine Rainstrasse 10; mains from €4; 🕑9am-6pm Tue-Sat, 10am-6pm Sun; 🚆Altona) Even if you miss the morning at this cheery spot, which mixes affability with pastel style, you can still sit outside and catch the afternoon sun. Baked goods are fabulous and egg dishes are all-organic. The coffee? Good, as you'd expect.

Mercado DELI €
(Map p653; ☎040-398 6840; www.mercado-hh.de; Ottenser Hauptstrasse 10; meals €4-9; 🕑9am-8pm; 🚆Altona) Forage for prime picnic fare (or eat here) at this market hall by Altona station. Stalls have everything from fresh Med fare to fine wines by the glass.

Atlantik Fisch SEAFOOD €€
(Map p653; ☎040-391 123; www.atlantik-fisch.de; Grosse Elbstrasse 139; mains €8-16; 🕑6am-4pm Mon-Fri, from 7am Sat; 🚌112, 🚆Altona) It doesn't get fresher than this Elbmeile gem. One of Hamburg's top seafood vendors has a simple cafe where top-notch dishes are served to thankful diners sitting inside and out on wooden benches.

★Restaurant MODERN EUROPEAN €€€
(Map p653; ☎040-3990 7772; kleine-brunnenstrasse.de; Kleinen Brunnenstrasse 1; lunch mains €12-16, dinner mains €20-23; 🕑noon-3pm Mon-Sat, 6-10pm daily; 🚆Altona) The heart of Northern Germany's slow food movement beats in this exquisite bistro. Menus change daily and *always* reflect what's in season and fresh. Preparations are simple, allowing flavours to shine. There's summer seating outside; book in advance.

Fischereihafen SEAFOOD €€€
(Map p653; ☎040-381 816; www.fischereihafenrestaurant.de; Grosse Elbstrasse 143; lunch mains €10-13, dinner mains €19-55; 🕑11.30am-10pm; 🚆Altona) Near the Elbmeile waterfront, Fischereihafen serves some of Hamburg's finest fish, including regional specialities, to a well-heeled clientele. No-frills outside, its 1st-floor, elegant maritime-themed dining room overlooks the Elbe. Lobster here comes in many forms. The Oyster Bar is a gentrified treat.

🍷 Drinking & Nightlife

Hamburg's nightlife choices deserve every bit of their legendary status. Live music alone is reason enough to come to Hamburg. And the city continues to breed and support new bands, acts, DJs, sounds, grooves and more. It is renowned for its electro-punk sound, which started in the 1980s and has evolved and morphed endlessly.

Clubkombinat (www.neu.clubkombinat.de) has club listings.

Many of the cafes listed under eating are excellent venues for enjoying just a drink.

🍷 Altstadt

Le Lion COCKTAIL BAR
(Map p648; ☎040-334 753 780; www.lelion.net; Rathausstrasse 3; 🕑8pm-3am or later; [S] Rathaus) Easily the classiest, most exclusive bar (by

virtue of size) you'll find in Hamburg – if you find it. Look for the buzzer in a lion's head and if there's space, they'll let you into this little lair of serious cocktails. Better yet, book a table in advance.

 St Georg

Bar M & V
BAR

(Map p654; ☑040-2800 6973; www.mvbar.de; Lange Reihe 22; ⊗5pm-2am; ⓡHauptbahnhof) The drinks menu is like a designer catalogue at this grand old St Georg bar that's had a beautiful restoration. Settle into one of the wooden booths, smell the freesias and enjoy the merry mixed crowd.

Kyti Voo
BAR

(Map p654; ☑040-2805 5565; www.kytivoo.de; Lange Reihe 8; ⊗10am-midnight; ⓡHauptbahnhof) A mixed crowd mixes it up with mixed drinks until very late. At sunnier (or less dark) times, the coffees are much coveted.

Frau Möller
BAR

(Map p654; ☑040-2532 8817; fraumoeller.com; Lange Reihe 96; ⊗11am-4am Sun-Thu, to 6am Fri & Sat, kitchen closes 3 hours before bar; ⓡHauptbahnhof) It's 3am Saturday and you can't live without a pork steak? Head to this St Georg institution where outside tables wrap around the corner location and the kitchen stays open late. Besides good German standards, the wine and beer lists are the best you'll find at 5am.

Generation Bar
GAY

(Map p654; ☑040-2880 4690; www.generation-bar.de; Lange Reihe 81; ⊗4pm-2am Sun-Thu, to 4am Fri & Sat; ⓡHauptbahnhof) A popular gay bar right in the middle of the St Georg gay strip. The red light adds to the hazy mood – this is a smokers joint.

 St Pauli

These days the Reeperbahn and surrounding streets feature mainstream musicals, and while stylish nightclubs entertain a hip, moneyed clientele until dawn, edgy bars happily serve a beer to anyone with €3. You can still hear up-and-coming music acts.

★Golden Pudel Club
LIVE MUSIC

(Map p648; ☑040-3197 9930; www.pudel.com; St-Pauli-Fischmarkt 27; ⊗11pm-6am; ⓡReeperbahn) In a 19th-century bootleggers' jail, this tiny bar-club is run by members of the legendary ex-punk band Die Goldenen Zitro-

nen and is an essential stop on the St Pauli party circuit. Night after night it gets packed to the rafters for its countercultural vibe, quality bands and DJs, and relaxed crowd.

★Amphore
CAFE

(Map p648; ☑040-3179 3880; www.cafe-amphore.de; Hafenstrasse 140; ⊗11am-late Tue-Sun; ⓡReeperbahn) Amphore has views out to the Elbe from a grassy verge with tables on sand as well as pavement tables for neighbourhood gawking. Inside it's woodsy in a nonfussy way. Blankets keep you cosy outside and it has good mini-pizzas.

★Indra Club
CLUB

(Map p648; www.indramusikclub.com; 64 Grosse Freiheit; ⊗9pm-late Wed-Sun; ⓡReeperbahn) The Beatles' small first venue is open again and has live acts many nights. The interior is vastly different from the 1960s and there is a fine beer garden.

★Hafenklang
MUSIC BAR

(Map p653; ☑040-388 744; www.hafenklang.org; Grosse Elbstrasse 84; ⓡKönigstrasse) A collective of Hamburg industry insiders present established and emerging DJs and bands, as well as clubbing events and parties. Look for the spray-painted name on the graffiti-covered dark-brick harbour store above a blank metal door.

Prinzenbar
BAR, CLUB

(Map p648; ☑040-3178 8310; www.docks-prinzenbar.de; Kastanienallee 20; ⊗10pm-4am or later; ⓢSt Pauli, ⓡReeperbahn) With its cheeky cherubs, stucco flourishes and sparkling chandeliers, this intimate club has luxe looks but is in fact a former cinema that now hosts stylish electro parties, concerts, queer bashes and indie nights in the heart of St Pauli.

Hasenschaukel
LIVE MUSIC

(Map p648; ☑040-1801 2721; www.hasenschaukel.de; Silbersackstrasse 17; ⊗9pm-1am Tue-Thu & Sun, 9pm-4am Fri & Sat; ⓡReeperbahn) The booking policy at this unhurried pocket-size club with plush decor skews towards lo-fi indie-folk-rock and usually features pre-stardom international artists along with DJ sets. Grab a vegan midnight snack if the vintage doll lamps get too trippy after a few beers.

Luba Luft
COCKTAIL BAR

(Map p648; ☑040-4819 4332; www.lubaluft.de; Am Brunnenhof 2-4; ⊗8pm-late Tue-Sat; ⓡReeperbahn) A loungey bar with dark-corner sofas and mod touches like chairs out of a '60s fantasy. Gets a relaxed mix of locals.

Komet Musik Bar   BAR
(Map p648; ☑040-2786 8686; www.komet-st-pauli.de; Erichstrasse 11; ☺9pm-late; ⑤St Pauli) Vinyl and only vinyl spins at this treasure of a music bar. Nightly themes range from ska and rocksteady to '60s garage punk and hip hop. Order a Helga, a sweetish house drink that will have everything sounding dreamy in no time.

Molotow   CLUB
(Map p648; ☑040-310 845; www.molotowclub.com; Nobistor 14; ⑧Reeperbahn) This legendary indie club still rocks on as hot 'n heavy as ever after moving to new digs after its Reeperbahn location was torn down.

Tower Bar   LOUNGE
(Map p648; ☑040-311 13; www.hotel-hafen-hamburg.de; Seewartenstrasse 9; ☺6pm-2am; ⑤Landungsbrücken) For a low-key evening with harbour views that will keep you entranced, drop by this 14th-floor lounge at the Hotel Hafen.

☺ Schanzenviertel & Karolinenviertel

★Katze   BAR
(Map p648; ☑040-5577 5910; Schulterblatt 88; ☺3pm-midnight Mon-Thu, 6pm-3am Fri, 1pm-3am Sat, 3pm-midnight Sun; ⑤Sternschanze) Small and sleek, this 'kitty' (Katze = cat) gets the crowd purring for well-priced cocktails (best caipirinhas in town) and great music (there's dancing on weekends). It's one of the most popular among the watering holes on this main Schanzenviertel booze strip.

Uebel und Gefährlich   CLUB
(Map p648; www.uebelundgefaehrlich.com; Feldstrasse 66; ⑤Feldstrasse) DJ sets, live music and parties rock this soundproof WWII bunker.

☺ Altona & Elbmeile

Café Knuth   CAFE
(Map p653; ☑040-4600 8708; www.cafeknuth.com; Grosse Rainstrasse 21; ☺9am-late; ⑧; ⑧Altona) Students, creative types and work colleagues come to chat in its split-level lounge areas. Or grab a picnic table outside and enjoy your drinks in the open air. Get here early and you can have breakfast.

Familien-Eck   PUB
(Map p653; ☑040-9823 7896; www.familieneck.de; Friedensallee 2-4; ☺3pm-5am; ⑧Altona) It's just a hole-in-the-wall, but this place is everything a good Hamburg neighbourhood joint should be: friendly, unassuming, yet always ready to take the piss. Locals pop in, down a quick drink, joke, gossip and hurry on out.

☆ Entertainment

Live Music
Many clubs and bars are renowned for their live music by bands new, old and mega.

Fabrik   LIVE PERFORMANCE
(Map p653; ☑040-391 070; www.fabrik.de; Barnerstrasse 36; ⑧Altona) They're making beautiful music in this former factory that's an iconic Altona venue, where the music ranges from classical to club and the program spans theatre to film.

Knust   LIVE PERFORMANCE
(Map p648; ☑040-8797 6230; www.knusthamburg.de; Neuer Kamp 30; ⑤Feldstrasse) In

---

HAMBURG'S UNLIKELY BEACH BARS
When it comes to city beaches, you have to salute Hamburgers for their can-do spirit. Undeterred either by the working harbour or by their renowned Schmuddelwetter (drizzly weather), they've built their own little sandy enclaves on the banks of the Elbe, where they can enjoy a beer on the sand, no matter what the weather.

Strandperle (☑040-880 1112; www.strandperle-hamburg.de; Oevelgönne 60; ☺10am-11pm Mon-Fri, 9am-11pm Sat & Sun May-Sep, shorter hours Oct-Apr; ☐112) Hamburg's original beach bar is a must for primo beer, burgers and people-watching. All ages and classes gather, mingle and wriggle their toes in the sand, especially at sunset, right on the Elbe as huge freighters glide past. Get here by taking ferry 62 from Landungsbrücken or bus 112 from Altona station to Neumühlen/Oevelgönne.

StrandPauli (Map p648; ☑040-2261 3105; www.strandpauli.de; St-Pauli-Hafenstrasse 89; ☺11am-11pm; ☐112) Tuesday is tango night at StrandPauli, a Gilligan's Island stretch of sand built over the water overlooking the busy docks.

addition to excellent live music gigs and experimental DJ sets, this former slaughterhouse hosts anything from acoustic raves to spoken word.

Theatre

Deutsches Schauspielhaus Theatre THEATRE

(Map p654; ☎040-248 713; www.schauspielhaus.de; Kirchenallee 39; 🚆Hauptbahnhof) Germany's largest and most important theatre presents imaginative interpretations of the classics (Shakespeare, Goethe, Chekhov et al) alongside new works.

Schmidt Tivoli THEATRE

(Map p648; ☎040-3177 8899; www.tivoli.de; Spielbudenplatz 27-28; [S]St Pauli) This plush theatre stages a cornucopia of saucy musical reviews, comedies, soap operas and variety shows. Midnight shows follow the main performance. The newly opened adjoining **Schmidtchen** showcases young talent in a smaller venue.

Opera & Classical Music

Laeiszhalle CLASSICAL MUSIC

(Map p648; ☎040-346 920; www.elbphilharmonie.de; Johannes-Brahms-Platz; [S]Messehallen) Hamburg's longtime premier address for classical concerts and opera is this splendid neo-baroque edifice, home to the State Philharmonic Orchestra, among others. When/if the Elbphilharmonie (p652) finally opens, many performances will move there.

> **GAY & LESBIAN HAMBURG**
>
> Hamburg has a thriving gay and lesbian scene. Much of the action is centred on the St Georg area but mixed venues are found across the city and, in essence, the 'gay and lesbian friendly' label could be applied to most night spots in the city.
>
> ➡ Look for venues in *hinnerk* (www.hinnerk.de).
>
> ➡ Men can find information at the gay centre **Hein & Fiete** (Map p654; ☎040-240 440; www.heinfiete.de; Pulverteich 21; 🕑4-9pm Mon-Fri, to 7pm Sat; [S]Hauptbahnhof).
>
> ➡ Women can contact the lesbian centre **Intervention** (Map p648; ☎040-245 002; www.intervention-hamburg.de; Glashüttenstrasse 2; 🕑hours vary; [U]Feldstrasse).

Staatsoper OPERA

(Map p648; ☎040-356 868; www.hamburgische-staatsoper.de; Grosse Theaterstrasse 25; [S]Stephansplatz) Among the world's most respected opera houses, the Staatsoper has been directed by the likes of Gustav Mahler and Karl Böhm during its 325-year-plus history.

Sport

Barclaycard Arena STADIUM

(www.barclaycard-arena.de; Sylvesterallee 7) Hamburg's huge Barclaycard Arena (previously sponsored by O2) was extensively refurbished for the 2006 football World Cup, and is home to Bundesliga club **Hamburger SV** (www.hsv.de). Take S-Bahn 21 or 3 to 'Stellingen', which is linked by free shuttle buses to the stadium.

Millerntor-Stadion STADIUM

(Map p648; ☎tickets 040-3178 7451; Heiligengeistfeld; [S]Feldstrasse) Favourite local football team **FC St Pauli** (www.fcstpauli.com) plays at home in the multi-use Millerntor stadium.

Shopping

Hamburg's shopping may not come close to its nightlife in profile, but there are numerous neighbourhoods where you will find many interesting finds– from mainstream to offbeat – as you explore the city.

Altstadt

West of the Hauptbahnhof, along Spitalerstrasse and Mönckebergstrasse (known as the 'Mö'), you'll find the large department stores and mainstream boutiques.

★**Dr Götze Land & Karte** BOOKS

(Map p648; ☎040-357 4630; www.landundkarte.de; Alstertor 14-18; 🕑10am-7pm Mon-Fri, 10am-6pm Sat; [S]Mönckebergstrasse) Enormous range of guidebooks and maps. Browse the world.

Robert Morat Gallerie ARTS

(Map p654; ☎040-3287 0890; www.robertmorat.de; Kleine Reichenstrasse 1; 🕑noon-6pm Tue-Fri, noon-4pm Sat; [S]Messberg) Artful photos, exhibitions and rare books vie for your attention at this elegant shop.

Thalia Bücher BOOKS

(Map p648; ☎040-3095 4980; www.thalia.de; Ballindamm 40; 🕑10am-8pm Mon-Sat) Has a large selection of English-language books.

Neustadt

Upmarket shops are located within the triangle created by Jungfernstieg, Fuhlentwiete and Neuer Wall. Most of them are in a network of elegant shopping arcades.

Hanse CD Im Hanse Viertel MUSIC
(Map p648; ☎040-340 561; www.hanse-cd.de; Grosse Bleichen 36; ⌚10am-7pm Mon-Fri, to 4pm Sat; [S] Jungfernstieg) Not for music streamers: this exquisite little shop huddled amid some very posh brethren sells CDs and DVDs with rare and hard-to-find music and film.

Schanzenviertel & Karolinenviertel

Hamburg's countercultural scene has retro and vintage clothing and music shops, particularly along Marktstrasse, where you'll find everything from '70s sportswear to Bollywood fashions. Bartelsstrasse is another good bet for unusual wares.

Flohschanze MARKET
(Map p648; Neuer Kamp 30; ⌚8am-4pm Sat; [S] Feldstrasse) Hamburg's best flea market is nirvana for thrifty trinket hunters and vintage junkies, with hundreds of vendors holding forth outdoors in the hip Karolinenviertel.

Altona & Elbmeile

Gentrified with designer boutiques yet still retaining some offbeat shops, especially along Hauptstrasse and the western stretch of Ottenser Hauptstrasse.

Krupka SHOES
(Map p653; ☎040-3990 3847; krupka-schuhe.de; Ottenser Hauptstrasse 55; ⌚10am-7pm Mon-Fri, to 4pm Sat; [R] Altona) Stylish shoe heaven: rare brands of women's shoes plus Krupka's own designs are sold in this leather-scented shop. It's one of many alluring boutiques in the immediate area.

Information

DANGERS & ANNOYANCES

Although mostly safe and wealthy, Hamburg is also undeniably sleazy in parts, with red-light districts around the Hauptbahnhof and Reeperbahn. Steindamm and Hansaplatz in St Georg are also dicey, both day and night. However, there's a strong police presence in these areas, too.

DISCOUNT CARDS

In addition to free public transport in the region, the Hamburg Card (one to five days €9.50 to €40.50) provides discounts on museums, tours and more. If you plan on buying Day Passes for transport, then the card can be a good deal, otherwise the discounts are not that large. It's sold at tourist offices and some hostels and hotels.

EMERGENCY

Police (Kirchenallee exit, Hauptbahnhof) Cop shop.

INTERNET ACCESS

You can find free wi-fi around the city. For services like printing, ask at your accommodation.

POST

Post Office (Map p654; ☎01802-3333; Mönckebergstrasse 7; ⌚9am-7pm Mon-Fri, 9am-3pm Sat) Among many choices, the post office near the Hauptbahnhof is the most convenient.

TOURIST INFORMATION

Useful websites:

➡ **www.hamburg-tourism.de** Run by the tourist office.

➡ **www.hamburg.de** Run by the city.

Tourist Information Airport (Terminals 1 & 2; ⌚6am-11pm) On the arrival level, between the terminals.

Tourist Information Hauptbahnhof (Map p654; Hauptbahnhof, near Kirchenallee exit; ⌚9am-7pm Mon-Sat, 10am-6pm Sun; [S] Hauptbahnhof, [R] Hauptbahnhof) Busy all the time.

Tourist Information am Hafen (Map p648; btwn piers 4 & 5, St Pauli Landungsbrücken; ⌚9am-6pm Sun-Wed, to 7pm Thu-Sat; [S] Landungsbrücken) No hotel bookings.

Getting There & Away

AIR

Despite their marketing hype, the 'Hamburg' services by Ryanair and Wizzair use Lübeck's airport (p680).

Hamburg Airport (HAM; www.airport.de; [R] Hamburg Airport) Hamburg Airport has frequent flights to domestic and European cities, including on Lufthansa and most other major European carriers. Low-cost carriers include Air Berlin, EasyJet and Germanwings.

BOAT

Hamburg is a popular port of call for cruise ships. There are two main places they dock.

Hamburg Cruise Center Altona (Map p653; www.hamburgcruisecenter.eu; Van-der-

Smissen-Strasse 5; 112) A popular dock for large cruise ships.

Hamburg Cruise Center HafenCity (www. hamburgcruisecenter.eu; Grosser Grasbrook; S Überseequartier) Many large cruise ships dock here, close to HafenCity.

BUS
ZOB (Zentraler Omnibusbahnhof, Central Bus Station; Map p654; 040-247 576; www. zob-hamburg.de; Adenauerallee 78; Hauptbahnhof) Long-distance destinations include Sweden, the Netherlands, Eastern Europe, the Balkans and more.

TRAIN
Frequent trains serve regional and long-distance destinations from Hamburg. There are two main-line stations worth noting:

Hamburg Hauptbahnhof (Main Train Station; Hauptbahnhof) The most important station and an attraction in itself, the views to the busy tracks from the concourses are legendary.

There are direct ICE/IC services to Berlin-Hauptbahnhof (€45, 1¾ hours), Cologne (€51, four hours), Frankfurt (€49, 3½ hours) and Munich (€81, 5¾ hours). A direct service to Copenhagen (€69, five hours) runs several times a day.

Hamburg Altona (Altona) Many Hamburg trains, including long-distance services, begin or end their journeys at this medium-sized station in the heart of its namesake west Hamburg neighbourhood.

⊙ Getting Around

TO/FROM THE AIRPORT
The S1 S-Bahn connects the airport directly with the city centre, including the Hauptbahnhof. The journey takes 25 minutes and costs €3.10.

BICYCLE
Many hostels and some hotels arrange bike rental for guests. Zweiradperle (p647) is also a good source.

StadtRad Hamburg (www.stadtradhamburg. de; 1st 30min free, then per min €0.08) Run by Deutsche Bahn, operates from U-Bahn and S-Bahn stations and other key points across the city. Rentals are bright-red, seven-gear bikes. You can register online or at the rental sites.

CAR & MOTORCYCLE
Driving around town is easy: thoroughfares are well signposted, and parking stations plentiful.

PUBLIC TRANSPORT
HVV (040-194 49; www.hvv.de) operates buses, ferries, U-Bahn and S-Bahn and has several info centres, including at the Jungfernstieg S-/U-Bahn station, and the Hauptbahnhof.

The city is divided into zones. Ring A covers the city centre, inner suburbs and airport. Kids under six travel free. Day Passes cover travel for one adult and up to three children aged six to 14.

S-/U-Bahn tickets must be purchased from machines at stations; bus tickets are available from the driver. Ticket types include the following:

TICKET GROSSBEREICH/ RING A & B REGION	PRICE
Short Journey/Kurzstrecke (only two to three stops)	€1.50
Single/Einzelkarte	€3.10
9-Hour Day Pass/9-Uhr-Tageskarte (after 9am)	€6
Day Pass/Ganztageskarte (good 6am to 6am the next day)	€7.50
Group Day Pass/Gruppen-karte (after 9am, up to 5 people of any age)	€11.20

If you catch an express bus (Schnellbus), it costs an extra €2.10.

Services run around the clock on weekends and the night before a public holiday; between approximately 12.30am and 4am Sunday to Thursday the night bus network takes over, converging on Rathausmarkt.

Bikes are allowed free of charge aboard S-/U-Bahn trains and buses outside peak hours (6am to 9am and 4pm to 6pm) and on ferries any time.

TAXI
Taxi Hamburg (040-666 666; www.taxiham burg.de)

AROUND HAMBURG

Although dominated by its namesake city, Hamburg State does encompass part of the Altes Land, a fertile area reclaimed from marshy ground by Dutch experts in the time of the Middle Ages. Flatness as a terrain feature takes on its own certain stark beauty.

With Germany's good train system and great-value day passes, destinations in surrounding states make easy day trips, such as the picturesque town of Lüneburg. Lübeck is a very popular day trip, as is Bremen.

HAMBURG'S CONCENTRATION CAMP

KZ-Gedenkstätte Neuengamme (Neuengamme Concentration Camp; ☎ 040-428 131 500; www.kz-gedenkstaette-neuengamme.de; Jean-Dolidier-Weg 75; ⊕ 9.30am-4pm Mon-Fri year-round, noon-7pm Apr-Sep, noon-5pm Oct-Mar) In 1938, the Nazis converted an old brick factory 25km southeast of Hamburg into a concentration camp. Over the next seven years, countless numbers of people were imprisoned here. At least 42,900 were killed, either directly murdered or due to the horrible living conditions.

Exhibits recount the Holocaust, both locally and nationally. Only a few historic buildings remain, but the general layout of the huge camp is shown. Take the S-Bahn to Bergedorf, then bus 227 or 327 (about one hour, €8.10).

Much less known than other camps such as Sachsenhausen near Berlin, Neuengamme was only fully opened as a memorial in 2005, after prisons on the site had been closed. Its setting amid vast expanses of flat farmland adds a mundane horror.

You can spend a couple of hours wandering the site, reading the plaques that explain what happened where and going inside surviving buildings for the many exhibits. Combine your time here with a visit to **Bullenhuser Damm Schule** (p657) in Hamburg for a gruelling window into the horrors of 75 years ago.

Stade

☑ 04141 / POP 46,000

You half expect some Pied Piper-type character to come tooting around a corner as you wander the ancient lanes of Stade, a stand-in for everybody's idea of a perfectly clichéd old German village.

Easily reached in an hour by public transit from Hamburg, Stade makes an ideal escape from the urban hustle and is a great day trip. First mentioned in the 10th century, Stade has half-timbered buildings, a series of little canals and some moody old churches.

◎ Sights

Stade's compact Altstadt is surrounded by defensive canals. The most interesting part is the north end, about a 10-minute walk from the train station.

The **Alter Haven** was once the town's trading hub and the narrow canal here is fronted on both sides by rows of restored 17th-century merhcant's houses along Wasser West and Wasser Ost. It's an authentic brick and half-timbered spectacle. Good streets for exploring include Hökerstrasse and Bäckerstrasse.

Holzkran   HISTORIC BUILDING
(Fischmarkt; ⊕ hours vary, generally 10am-4pm Apr-Oct) This old crane was used for unloading canal boats. It has local information provided by volunteers and displays about the town's history inside.

St Wilhadi Kirche   CHURCH
(off Flutstrasse; ⊕ 11am-4pm Mon-Sat Apr-Oct, 11.30am-1.30pm Mon-Sat Nov-Mar) Stade's oldest building is this hulking church, which has parts dating to the 14th century. Keeping the building standing to the present day is the stuff of drama, what with wars, lightning and waterlogged ground. Note the heavy buttresses on the exterior and the bands of iron around the pillars in the detail-packed interior. The small history brochure is a good read.

✖ Eating

The usual assortment of cafes around the Alter Haven allow you to sip refreshments while soaking up the scene.

Ratskeller Stade   GERMAN €€
(☑ 04141-787 228; www.ratskeller-stade.de; Hökerstrasse 10; mains €9-15; ⊕ noon-10pm) A cut above your average Ratskeller, Stade's is on a shady back lane near St Wilhadi. It has its own brewery, fine hearty, meaty fare and plenty of outdoor tables.

❶ Getting There & Away

From Hamburg, the S3 line and hourly express trains from the Hauptbahnhof reach Stade in one hour. Tickets cost €8.40 one way, so buy the day pass '9-Uhr Tageskarte Ring ABCDE' for €15.90.

Lüneburg

☑ 04131 / POP 73,600

An off-kilter church steeple, buildings leaning on each other and houses with swollen 'beer-belly' facades: in parts it looks like the charming town of Lüneburg has drunk too much of the Pilsner lager it used to brew. Of course, the city's wobbly angles and uneven pavements have a more prosaic cause. For centuries until 1980, Lüneburg was a salt-mining town, and as this 'white gold' was extracted from the earth, shifting ground and subsidence caused buildings to tilt sideways.

Its wobbly comic-book streets aside, Lüneburg is a lovely town with attractive stepped-gable facades and Hanseatic architecture. It has a lively student population.

The Ilmenau River sits between the Hauptbahnhof and the city centre that begins 500m to its west.

◉ Sights & Activities

You can fully explore the old town on foot in half a day. Many tourists enjoy touring the surrounding region, the Lüneburger Heide, by bike; Lüneburg's tourist office can outline dozens of routes; one is windmill-themed.

Markt   SQUARE
(Markt) The name Lüneburg hails from the Saxon word *hliuni* (refuge), which was granted at the Ducal Palace to those fleeing other territories. However, many sources mistakenly assume Lüneburg's name has something to do with Luna, the Roman goddess of the moon. This is reflected on the large Markt, where authorities at one time seem to have liked this idea, erecting a **fountain** with a statue of the Roman goddess.

Besides the Rathaus, notable buildings around the Markt include the **Court of Justice**, the little gated-in, grotto-like area with paintings depicting scenes of justice being carried out throughout the centuries; and the former Ducal Palace, now a courthouse.

★ Rathaus   HISTORIC BUILDING
(☑04131-207 6620; Markt; tours adult/child €5/3; ⊙tours 11am & 2pm Tue-Sun Jan-Mar, noon & 3pm Tue-Sat, 11am & 2pm Sun Apr-Dec) The medieval Rathaus has a spectacular baroque facade, added in 1720 and decorated with coats of arms and three tiers of statues. The top row represents (from left to right): Strength, Trade, Peace (the one with the staff), Justice and Moderation. The steeple, topped with 41 Meissen china bells, was installed on the city's 1000th birthday in 1956. Tours cover the lavishly restored interior.

★ Am Sande   STREET
The cobbled, slightly wobbly street and square Am Sande is full of red-brick buildings with typically Hanseatic stepped gables. Even among these striking buildings, the black-and-white **Industrie und Handelskammer** (Trade and Industry Chamber; 1548) at the far western end stands out.

St Johanniskirche   CHURCH
(☑04131-445 42; www.st-johanniskirche.de; Am Sande; ⊙10am-5pm Mon-Sat, 11am-4pm Mar-Oct, shorter hours Nov-Feb) At the eastern edge of the Am Sande stands the 14th-century St Johanniskirche, whose 108m-high spire leans 2.2m off centre. Local legend has it that the architect was so upset by this crooked steeple that he tried to do himself in by jumping off it. He fell into a hay cart and was saved, but, celebrating his escape later in the pub, drank himself into a stupor, fell over, hit his head and died after all.

The inside of the church is, well, a lot more believable than the legend; there's an impressive organ dating to 1551, carvings and stained-glass windows, both ancient and modern. Overall it has a rich interior, unlike the stark spaces of so many postwar-reconstructed churches.

Auf dem Meere   STREET
If you continue west along Waagestrasse from the Markt and veer left, you'll come to Auf dem Meere, a particularly striking Lüneburg street. Here the wavy pavements have pushed facades sideways or made buildings buckle in the middle. All the way to St Michaeliskirche the street feels wonky. Look at the steps leading to the church!

Deutsches Salzmuseum   MUSEUM
(☑04131-450 65; www.salzmuseum.de; Sülfmeisterstrasse 1; adult/child €6/4; ⊙9am-5pm Mon-Fri Apr-Sep, from 10am Oct-Mar, 10am-5pm Sat & Sun year-round) The Deutsches Salzmuseum explains (in German only) how Lüneburg's precious food preservative made the town such an important player in the Hanseatic League. Displays are peppered with old salt implements.

SaLü Salztherme   SPA
(Spa Baths; ☑04131-723 110; www.kurzentrum.de; Uelzener Strasse 1-5; adult/child from €8/5; ⊙10am-11pm Mon-Sat, 8am-9pm Sun) With Lüneburg having made its fortune from salt, where better to try the mineral's therapeutic properties than at the town's salt baths. You can bathe in saltwater at 36°C and try out the single-sex or mixed sauna area, water fountains and whirlpool.

🛏 Sleeping

DJH Hostel
HOSTEL €

(🖉04131-418 64; lueneburg.jugendherberge.de; Soltauer Strasse 133; dm under/over 27yr €25/29; P🖘@🛜) After sundown, the lights glow a warm welcome from the glass-walled stairwell of this spacious and relatively luxurious 148-bed hostel. It's 4km southwest of the Markt, right near the university. Bus services – 5011 or 5012 from the train station to Scharnhorstrasse/DJH – don't run late.

★ Hotel Scheffler
HOTEL €€

(🖉04131-200 80; www.hotel-scheffler.de; Bardowicker Strasse 7; s/d from €73/100; P🖘🛜) The hotel most in keeping with Lüneburg's quirky character, this 16-room place just off the Markt greets you with brickwork, stained glass, carved wooden stair-rails, animal trophies and indoor plants. The bright rooms are less idiosyncratic; there's a restaurant on-site.

Hotel Bremer Hof
HOTEL €€

(🖉04131-2240; www.bremer-hof.de; Lüner Strasse 12-13; s/d from €70/100; P🖘🛜) This ivy-covered 54-room hotel offers rooms for most budgets, from plain and inexpensive in a modern annex to historic rooms with beamed ceilings in the main building. It has been in the same family since 1889 and is just northeast of the Markt.

🍴 Eating & Drinking

The restaurant-lined Schröderstrasse leads from the Markt; it's alive at night with students enjoying beer specials. Also popular is Am Stintmarkt down by the river, where many places have outdoor tables that let you hear the water sluicing through the locks.

Annàs Café
CAFE €

(🖉04131-884 3181; www.annas-cafe.de; Am Stintmarkt 12a; mains €3-9; ⏱8am-9pm; 📶) Frilly and cute, Anna's has fabulous baked goods, including some alluring cakes. Breakfasts are served with verve while lunch is a mix of fresh salads, sandwiches and specials. Bric-a-brac on the tables jostles for space with kids' books.

★ News Cafe
CAFE €€

(🖉04131-401 144; www.news-lueneburg.de; Schröderstrasse 5; mains €5-16; ⏱8.30am-1am) There's a reason why you see a cross-section of all Lüneburg at this ever-busy cafe: it does everything just right. Menu specials change with the seasons and even a simple sandwich is a work of art. The healthy breakfasts

make you want to explore, while the long drinks menu rewards a long day touring.

Gasthausbrauerei und Brennerei Nolte
BREWERY

(🖉04131-522 32; www.gasthausbrauereinolte.de; Dahlenburger Landstrasse 102; mains €12-18; ⏱4-11pm Wed-Sat, 11am-10pm Sun) They've been brewing here since 1906; the dark beer is especially good out in the garden. Unlike many beer-centric places, food is taken seriously at this local legend; fish is house-smoked, the menu lists the provenance of the dishes and you can enjoy regional specialities like sour pork in aspic. It's about 500m east of the train station.

Pons
BAR

(🖉04131-224 935; pons-lueneburg.de; Salzstrasse am Wasser 1; ⏱from 1pm) If Pons looks this cracked, crooked and uneven when you walk in of an evening, just imagine how it will seem when you stagger out after a few drinks. This ex-1970s hippie joint still hews to an off-kilter vibe. The beer's cheap as are the simple plates of food. Settle in at a waterside table under the trees.

ℹ Information

Lüneburg Tourist-Information Office
(🖉04131-207 6620; www.lueneburg.de; Am Markt; ⏱9.30am-4pm daily May-Oct, closed Sun Nov-Apr) Offers city tours and has info on trips to the surrounding Lüneburger Heide.

ℹ Getting There & Away

There are frequent IC train services to Hamburg (€13, 30 minutes) and Hanover (€28, one hour). A web of cheaper regional trains provide these and more links from the station, which is 300m east of the centre.

ℹ Getting Around

You'll have no problem walking any place you'd like to reach in the old town from the train station. The **Rad am Hauptbahnhof** (🖉04131-266 350; radspeicher.de; Bahnhofstrasse 4; per 3hr/day €5/10; ⏱9am-6pm) rents bikes.

SCHLESWIG-HOLSTEIN

Sandy beaches, jaunty red-and-white striped lighthouses, deep fjords carved by glaciers, sandpipers and seals have made this sweeping peninsula between the North and Baltic Seas Germany's most elite summer retreat.

> ### ⓘ SCHLESWIG-HOLSTEIN TOURIST INFO
> ·······················
> Schleswig-Holstein's tourism website (www.sh-tourismus.de) is an excellent resource, especially for activities.

Much of the peninsula's interior is comprised of seemingly never-ending expanses of flat, green farmland interrupted only by wind farms and grazing black-and-white-splotched cows. But its coastline – and especially the North Frisian Islands off Schleswig-Holstein's western coast – remain the country's answer to the Côte d'Azur.

Of course, the fickle northern European climate makes it a funny sort of answer, as cold winds and dark clouds periodically drive the hardiest holidaymakers from their *Strandkörbe* (sheltered straw 'beach basket' seats).

Even if it's only as a day trip from Hamburg, don't miss Lübeck, the magnificently preserved medieval headquarters of the Hanseatic League.

Schleswig-Holstein belonged to neighbouring Denmark until 1864 and you'll find Scandinavian overtones throughout the region, particularly in Flensburg and Schleswig.

Lübeck

🏛 0451 / POP 211,700

A 12th-century gem boasting more than 1000 historical buildings, Lübeck's picture-book appearance is an enduring reminder of its role as one of the founding cities of the mighty Hanseatic League and its moniker, 'Queen of the Hanse'. Behind its landmark Holstentor (gate), you'll find streets lined with medieval merchants' homes and spired churches forming Lübeck's 'crown'.

Recognised by Unesco as a World Heritage Site in 1987, today this thriving provincial city retains many enchanting corners to explore, including a fab musuem that tells the Lübeck story.

⊙ Sights

You can easily spend two days wandering amid Lübeck's steeple-punctuated sights.

There must be something in the water in Lübeck, or maybe it's the famous marzipan. The city has connections to two Nobel Prize-winning authors (Günter Grass and Thomas

Mann), as well as the Nobel Peace Prize-winning former chancellor Willy Brandt.

★ Holstentor   LANDMARK

(Holsten Gate) Built in 1464 and looking so settled-in that it appears to sag, Lübeck's charming red-brick city gate is a national icon. Its twin pointed cylindrical towers, leaning together across the stepped gable that joins them, captivated Andy Warhol (his print is in the St Annen Museum), and have graced postcards, paintings, posters and marzipan souvenirs. Discover this and more inside the **Museum Holstentor** (🏛 0451-122 4129; Holstentor; adult/child €6/2; ⊙ 10am-6pm Apr-Dec, 11am-5pm Tue-Sun Jan-Mar), which sheds light on the history of the gate and on Lübeck's medieval mercantile glory days.

The latin inscription on the west face *'concordia domi foris pax'* means 'harmony at home and peace abroad'.

★ Europäisches Hansemuseum   MUSEUM

(European Hanseatic Museum; 🏛 0451-809 0990; www.hansemuseum.eu; An der Untertrave 1; combined ticket adult/child €14.50/8.50; ⊙ 10am-6pm Mar-Oct, to 5pm Nov-Mar) Opened in 2015, this brilliant museum tells the remarkable story of the Hanseatic League, Lübeck and the region. For 600 years, city states in Northern Europe and along the Baltic discovered that shared interests in trade made everybody's life better than war. Transfixing exhibits use every modern technology to tell a story as dramatic as anything on *Game of Thrones*. The complex includes the beautifully restored medieval **Castle Friary**.

★ Museumsquartier St Annen   MUSEUM

(Museum Quarter St Annen; 🏛 0451-122 4137; museumsquartier-st-annen.de; St-Annen-Strasse; adult/child €10/4; ⊙ 10am-5pm Tue-Sun Apr-Dec, 11am-5pm Tue-Sun Jan-Mar) This newly designated museum quarter includes an old synagogue, church and medieval buildings along its uneven streets. The namesake **St Annen Museum** details the diverse history of the neighbourhood as it traces 700 years of art and culture. The adjoining **St Annen Kunsthalle** has ecclesiastical art (including Hans Memling's 1491 Passion Altar) and contemporary art including Andy Warhol's print of Lübeck's Holstentor. There's a chic little **cafe** in the courtyard.

Renovations of the many historic buildings in and around St-Annen-Strasse are ongoing.

Marienkirche CHURCH
(St Mary's Church; ☎0451-397 700; www.st-marien-luebeck.com; Marienkirchhof 1; adult/child €2/1.50; ⏲10am-6pm Apr-Sep, to 5pm Oct, to 4pm Tue-Sun Nov-Mar) This fine Gothic church boasts the world's highest brick-vaulted roof and was the model for dozens of churches in northern Germany. Crane your neck to take in the painted cross-vaulted ceilings supported by slender, ribbed pillars. A WWII bombing raid brought down the church's bells, which have been left where they fell in 1942 and have become a famous symbol of the city.

Also note the astronomical clock in the north aisle next to modern glass windows inspired by a medieval Dance of Death mural destroyed by the war. Outside there's a little devil sculpture with an amusing folk tale (in German and English).

Rathaus HISTORIC BUILDING
(Town Hall; ☎0451-122 1005; Breite Strasse 62; adult/concession €4/2; ⏲tours 11am, noon & 3pm Mon-Fri, 1.30pm Sat & Sun) Sometimes described as a 'fairy tale in stone', Lübeck's 13th- to 15th-century Rathaus is widely regarded as one of the most beautiful in Germany. Inside, a highlight is the *Audienzsaal* (audience hall), a light-flooded hall decked out in festive rococo.

Petrikirche CHURCH
(Church of St Peter; ☎0451-397 730; www.st-petri-luebeck.de; Petrikirchhof 1; tower adult/child €3/2; ⏲9am-8pm Apr-Sep, 10am-7pm Oct-Mar) Thanks to a lift, even the fitness-phobic get to enjoy panoramic views from the 50m-high platform in the tower of the 13th-century Petrikirche. No longer an active parish, the starkly whitewashed interior hosts exhibits and events.

Theater Figuren Museum MUSEUM
(Museum of Theatre Puppets; ☎0451-786 26; www.theaterfigurenmuseum.de; Am Kolk 14; adult/child €6/2; ⏲10am-6pm Apr-Oct, 11am-5pm Tue-Sun Nov-Mar; 👪) Even if you think you eschew puppets, don't miss this wondrous collection of some 1200 puppets, props, posters and more from Europe, Asia and Africa. The artistry is amazing, as is the ancient alley where it's located; try to catch a performance at its theatre (p680).

Salzspeicher HISTORIC BUILDINGS
(off Holstenbrücke) Just behind the Holstentor (to the east) stand the Salzspeicher: six gabled brick shop-filled buildings once used to store salt transported from Lüneburg. It was then bartered for furs from Scandinavia and used to preserve the herrings that formed a substantial chunk of Lübeck's Hanseatic trade.

Dom CATHEDRAL
(☎0451-747 04; www.domzuluebeck.de; Domkirchhof; ⏲10am-6pm Apr-Oct, 10am-4pm Nov-Mar) The Dom was founded in 1173 by Heinrich der Löwe when he took over Lübeck. Locals like to joke that if you approach the Dom from the northeast, you have to go through *Hölle* (hell) and *Fegefeuer* (purgatory) – the actual names of streets – to see **Paradies** (paradise), the lavish vestibule to the Dom. Although spartan, the interior has good displays showing reconstruction after the 1942 bombing raid.

SMOKIN' FISH

The smooth, oily fillets of northern fish are smoked for hours until they have a tangy, buttery softness that melts in your mouth. No wonder people love it. Here are some good places:

➡ **Hamburg** There's smoked fish by the tonne at Hamburg's Sunday **Fischmarkt** (p664) or order some house-smoked eel at **Alt Hamburger Aalspeicher** (Map p648; ☎040-362 990; www.aalspeicher.de; Deichstrasse 43; mains €12-28; [S] Rödingsmarkt).

➡ **Sylt** Just saying '**Gosch** (p690)' brings knowing nods of satisfaction from those who've had this seafood legend's smoked fish in its many varieties.

➡ **Wismar** Ancient techniques dating to Hanseatic times make the young smoked eel here especially succulent (p704).

➡ **Binz** Just follow your nose to the glorified beach hut, **Fischräucherei Kuse** (p710).

➡ **Stralsund** The harbour is ringed with stands selling smoked fish.

➡ **Wieck** Right at the sea, this tiny town has some excellent smoked fish stands, while **Fischer-Hütte** (p713) specialises in smoked herring.

Lübeck

Könemann Schiffahrt dock
(boats to Travemünde) (200m)

Schwartauer Allee

Holstenhafen

An der Untertrave

Fischergrube

23

32

Beckergrube

Breite Str

Fackenburger Allee

39

Willy-Brandt-Allee

Wallhafen

20 27

Mengstr

19

Fünfhausen

3

Alfstr

Fischstr

10

Schüsselbuden

Königstr

Hauptbahnhof

Braunstr

12

Markt

An der Untertrave

Holstenbrücke
Holstenorplatz

Holstenstr

41

28

Lindenplatz

Holstentor 1

Kohlmarkt

Sandstr

Hansestr

18 24

21

13

17

14

11

Am Kolk

Königstr

Lindenstr

Nebenhofstr

38

Gr Petersgrube

Mühlenstr

40

Depenau

Moislinger Allee

Possehlstr

Thrave River

Marlesgrube

Pferdemarkt Parade

Dankwartsgrube

MALERWINKEL

Hartengrube

Domkirchhof

36

Lachswehrallee

Stadtgraben

An der Obertrave

Wallstr

4

Musterbahn

Mühlendamm

Mühlenteich

Gänge & Höfe
HISTORIC BUILDING

(Histo) In the Middle Ages, Lübeck was home to numerous craftspeople and artisans. Their presence caused demand for housing to outgrow the available space, so tiny single-storey homes were built in courtyards behind existing rows of houses. These were then made accessible via little walkways from the street.

Almost 90 such *Gänge* (walkways) and *Höfe* (courtyards) still exist. The most famous include the **Füchtingshof** (Glockengiesserstrasse 25), with its beautiful carvings, and the 1612 **Glandorps Gang** (Glockengiesserstrasse 41-51), which you can peer into.

Buddenbrookhaus
MUSEUM

(☎0451-122 4190; www.buddenbrookhaus.de; Mengstrasse 4; adult/child €6/2.50; ☯10am-6pm Apr-Dec, 11am-5pm Jan-Mar) The winner of the 1929 Nobel Prize for Literature, Thomas Mann, was born in Lübeck in 1875 and his family's former home is now the Buddenbrookhaus. Named after Mann's novel of a wealthy Lübeck family in decline, *The Buddenbrooks* (1901), this museum is a monument to the author of such classics as *Der Tod in Venedig* (Death in Venice) and *Der Zauberberg* (The Magic Mountain).

It also covers his brother Heinrich, who wrote the story that became the Marlene

is filled with the author's *leitmotifs* – flounders, rats, snails and eels – brought to life in bronze and charcoal, as well as in prose. The small bookshop is excellent.

You can view a copy of the first typewritten page of *Die Blechtrommel* (The Tin Drum; 1959). Grass died in Lübeck in 2015.

Willy Brandt House   MUSEUM
(📞 0451-122 4250; www.willy-brandt.de; Königstrasse 21; ⏱ 11am-5pm Tue Sun Jan-Mar, 11am-6pm daily Apr-Dec) [FREE] Besides Günter Grass, Lübeck's other big Nobel Prize winner, Willy Brandt, was chancellor of West Germany (1969–74) and was honoured for his efforts to reconcile with East Germany. Exhibits capture the tense times of the Cold War and Brandt's role at this pivotal time. He was born in this house in 1913.

Heiligen-Geist-Hospital   HISTORIC BUILDING
(Holy Spirit Hospital; Königstrasse; ⏱ 10am-5pm Tue-Sun, 10am-4pm Dec-Feb) The former Heiligen-Geist-Hospital has an elegant old entryway and a few resonances of Germany's first hospital (dating back to 1227). Through an early-Gothic hall church, you'll find a warren of small living cubicles dating from 1820, which gave refuge to aged seafarers. Part of the complex is used for December's Christmas market.

Katharinenkirche   CHURCH
(www.museumskirche.de; cnr Glockengiesserstrasse & Königstrasse) Art lovers will enjoy the Katharinenkirche for its sculptures by Ernst Barlach and Gerhard Marcks, plus *The Resurrection of Lazarus* by Tintoretto. It has no tower owing to the rules of the Cistercian order that built it in the 14th century. At time of research it was closed for ongoing restoration; meanwhile, ponder the animated statues on the facade.

🏃 Activities

You can enjoy plenty of walking in Lübeck. For respite from crowds and summer heat, consider two areas refreshing for their beauty and serenity.

Head south along An der Obertrave southwest of the Altstadt; you'll pass one of Lübeck's loveliest corners, the **Malerwinkel** (Painters' Quarter), where you can take a break on garden benches among blooming flowers, gazing out at the houses and white-picket fences across the water.

Another lovely area lies along the canals southeast of the centre. Parks and small

Dietrich film *Der Blaue Engel* (The Blue Angel). There's a rundown of the rather tragic family history, too.

Günter Grass-Haus   MUSEUM
(📞 0451-122 4230; www.grass-haus.de; Glockengiesserstrasse 21; adult/child €7/2.50; ⏱ 10am-5pm Apr-Dec, 11am-5pm Jan-Mar) Born in Danzig (now Gdańsk), Poland, Günter Grass had been living just outside Lübeck for 13 years when he collected his Nobel Prize in 1999. But this postwar literary colossus initially trained as an artist, and he always continued to draw and sculpt. The Günter Grass-Haus

Lübeck

lakes like **Krähenteich** offer relaxed bucolic idyls amid passing swans and under the shade of trees.

Mietrad Mielke　　　　　BICYCLE RENTAL
(☑0176 2728 0353; Hüxterdamm 2; rental per day from €9; ☉10am-6pm Mon-Sat) This cheery English-speaking shop rents a huge range of bikes, including electric models.

👉 Tours

The Trave River forms a moat around the Altstadt, and cruising it aboard a boat is a fine way to get a feel for the city.

Quandt-Linie　　　　　　　BOAT TOUR
(☑0451-777 99; www.quandt-linie.de; Holstentorterrassen; adult/child from €14/7; ☉half-hourly 10am-6pm May-Oct) One-hour city tours leave from next to the Holstentor. Also offers tours to the seaside resort of Travemünde. Tours are less frequent November to April.

Open-Air City Tour　　　　　BUS TOUR
(www.sv-luebeck.de; An der Untertrave; adult/child €9/5; ☉hourly 10am-4pm May-Oct) Open-top buses make 50-minute circuits of the historic city.

🛌 Sleeping

Rucksackhotel　　　　　　　HOSTEL €
(☑0451-706 892; www.rucksackhotel-luebeck. com; Kanalstrasse 70; dm/s/d from €18/30/45; P@☎) This 30-bed family-run hostel has a relaxed atmosphere and good facilities, including a well-equipped kitchen and round-the-clock access. The decor is colourful, with the odd tropical touch.

Campingplatz Schönböcken　CAMPGROUND €
(☑0451-893 090; www.camping-luebeck.de; Steinrader Damm 12; per tent €4-5, adult/child €6/2) This modern campground is a good bet for its grassy sites, kiosk, restaurant, entertainment room and children's playground. It's a 10-minute bus ride west of the city centre (take bus 2).

★ Klassik Altstadt Hotel　BOUTIQUE HOTEL €€
(☑0451-702 980; www.klassik-altstadt-hotel.de; Fischergrube 52; s/d from €50/120; ☎) Each of the 29 rooms at this elegantly furnished boutique hotel is dedicated to a different, mostly German, writer or artist, such as Thomas Mann and Johann Sebastian Bach. Single rooms (some share baths and are great value) feature travelogues by famous authors.

★ **Hotel zur Alten Stadtmauer** HOTEL €€
(☑ 0451-737 02; www.hotelstadtmauer.de; An der Mauer 57; s/d from €65/95; P 🛜) With pine furniture and splashes of red and yellow, this simple 24-room hotel is a great place to wake up. Back rooms overlook the lakes and three are in a historic guesthouse. The real star of your stay, however, is the bounteous breakfast buffet, with many homemade preserves and other touches. Parking is 200m distant.

Hotel Lindenhof HOTEL €€
(☑ 0451-872 100; www.lindenhof-luebeck.de; Lindenstrasse 1a; s/d from €90/120; P @ 🛜) Most of the 66 rooms at this family-run hotel in a quiet side street are compact, but the opulent breakfast buffet, friendly service and little extras (such as free biscuits and newspapers) propel the Lindenhof into a superior league.

Hotel an der Marienkirche HOTEL €€
(☑ 0451-799 410; www.hotel-an-der-marienkirche.de; Schüsselbuden 4; s/d from €60/100; 🛜) This small, good-value hotel exudes cheery, contemporary Scandinavian flair and is equipped with top-quality hypo-allergenic mattresses and crispy linen. One of the 18 rooms even has a view of the namesake church.

Baltic Hotel HOTEL €
(☑ 0451-855 75; www.baltic-hotel.de; Hansestrasse 11; s/d from €70/100; ⊘ reception 6.30am-10pm; 🛜) This rambling older hotel is one of many close to the bus and train stations. It's clean and run by helpful staff. Rooms vary greatly in size, although none seem as large as the excellent breakfast buffet. Decor is simple, parking is limited and a few rooms lack internet access.

Park Hotel am Lindenplatz HOTEL €€
(☑ 0451-871 970; www.parkhotel-luebeck.de; Lindenplatz 2; s/d from €60/80; P @ 🛜) Inside a well-preserved art nouveau building, this small, intimate hotel has 24 low-lit, neutral-toned rooms that offer respite after a day tackling the sights. A lift helps you take a load off.

★ **Hotel Anno 1216** DESIGN HOTEL €€€
(☑ 0451-400 8210; www.hotelanno1216.com; Alfstrasse 38; s/d from €115/160) The name at this excellent hotel isn't fanciful, as parts of this beautifully gabled brick building date back 800 years. The rooms have high ceilings and are large (the singles are bigger than most other hotel doubles) and have simply elegant furnishings like large, enveloping leather easy chairs. Breakfasts (extra) are organic.

✗ Eating & Drinking

★ **Amaro** CAFE €
(☑ 0451-2963 0801; www.amaro-luebeck.de; Glockengiesserstrasse 67; snacks from €3; ⊘ 10am-6pm Mon-Fri, 10am-4pm Sat) This prim little corner cafe makes its own fabulous range of chocolates using top ingredients from around the world. There is a variety of coffees and liquors that you can enjoy amid the luscious smells inside or at tables out front.

Café Niederegger CAFE €
(☑ 0451-530 1126; www.niederegger.de; Breite Strasse 89; mains €4-15; ⊘ 9am-7pm Mon-Fri, to 6pm Sat & Sun) Milky marzipan coffee, marzipan ice cream and a host of other sweet and savoury snacks and light meals are served at the cafe inside Lübeck's iconic marzipan shop (p680).

Krützfeld DELI €
(☑ 0451-728 32; Hüxstrasse 23; snacks from €2; ⊘ 8am-6pm Tue-Fri, 8am-2pm Sat) This classic deli has been serving all manner of fresh and smoked seafood for decades. There's no better place in town to assemble a picnic.

★ **Grenadine** BISTRO €€
(☑ 0451-307 2950; www.grenadine-hl.de; Wahmstrasse 40; mains €7-15; ⊘ 9am-late; 🛜) This narrow, elongated bar leads through to a garden out back. Enjoy bistro fare amid chic, retro-minimalist style. The long drinks menu goes well with tapas choices. Sandwiches, salads and pasta plus a gorgeous breakfast buffet are served.

Schiffergesellschaft GERMAN €€
(☑ 0451-767 76; www.schiffergesellschaft.com; Breite Strasse 2; mains €10-25; ⊘ kitchen 11.30am-11pm, bar 10am-1am) In the historic seafarers' guild hall (1535), Lübeck's most atmospheric – if not best – restaurant is a veritable museum. Ships' lanterns, old model ships and revolving Chinese-style silhouette lamps dangle from the beamed ceiling of this wood-lined dining room. White-aproned waitstaff deliver regional specialities to tables here or in the hidden garden out back. Book ahead for dinner.

Brauberger GERMAN €€
(☑ 0451-714 44; www.brauberger.de; Alfstrasse 36; mains €10-18; ⊘ 5pm-midnight Mon-Thu, 5pm-late Fri & Sat) The air is redolent of hops at this traditional German brewery. Get a stein of the one house brew, the superbly sweet, cloudy *Zwickelbier,* and tuck into a sizeable schnitzel or other traditional fare. There are

outside tables in back and student specials for pitchers.

Vai
MODERN EUROPEAN €€€

(☑ 0451-400 8083; www.restaurant-vai.de; Hüxstrasse 42; lunch mains €9, dinner mains €17-30; ⊙ 11am-10pm Mon-Sat) Glossy, richly grained timber lines the walls, tables and even the alfresco courtyard of this sleek, stylish restaurant. The good-value top-end lunches are popular and feature pasta, seafood and salads. The menu is more complex at night with steaks and lobster appearing. Great wine list; book ahead.

Die Zimberei
MODERN EUROPEAN €€€

(☑ 0451-738 12; www.zimberei.de; Königstrasse 5-7; mains €15-28, menus from €38; ⊙ 5-9.30pm Tue-Sat) Take one historic Hanseatic merchant's house, mix in three beautifully restored ballrooms and season with restored elegant gardens. The result is this excellent restaurant which serves modern takes on local meats and seafood.

★ Im Alten Zolln
PUB

(☑ 0451-723 95; www.alter-zolln.de; Mühlenstrasse 93-95; ⊙ 11am-late; 🛜) This classic pub inhabits a 16th-century customs post. There's an excellent beer selection. Patrons people-watch from terrace and sidewalk tables in summer and watch bands (rock and jazz) inside in winter. Fortify yourself with schnitzel and Lübeck's best roast potatoes.

Jazz-Café
BAR

(☑ 0451-707 3734; Mühlenstrasse 62; ⊙ 4pm-late Sun-Fri, noon-late Sat) Live jazz only plays once a month but the sound system can always be counted on for good tunes at this sleek, glass-fronted bar, which has moodily lit tables out front.

CafeBar
BAR

(☑ 0451-4893 8679; www.cafebar-luebeck.de; Hüxstrasse 94; ⊙ 11am-late) Cafe by day, bar by... you get it. During daylight hours savour coffee drinks while grazing fresh and tasty casual fare. But the real appeal here are the night-time hippin' hot DJs who mix techno, R&B and groovy sounds.

Tibia Tick
BAR

(☑ 0451-758 58; Dr-Julius-Leber-Strasse 76) Tiny and divey in the best possible ways, this little bar is welcoming and utterly pretension-free. Candles flicker on tables. It's at the cool (east) end of the Dr-Julius-Leber-Strasse bar strip.

☆ Entertainment

Local listings include *Piste* (www.piste.de) and *Ultimo* (www.ultimo-luebeck.de). Check organ recital schedules for the churches at the tourist office.

Figurentheater
THEATRE

(☑ 0451-700 60; www.figurentheater-luebeck.de; Am Kolk 20-22; tickets €6-18; ⊙ Tue-Sun; 🖰) This adorable puppet theatre, which is part of the museum here (p675), puts on a children's show at 3pm, and another for adults on some evenings at 7.30pm, as well as occasional performances in English.

Musikhochschule Lübeck
LIVE MUSIC

(☑ 0451-150 50; www.mh-luebeck.de; Grosse Petersgrube 17-29) High-calibre concerts take place throughout the summer and winter semesters at this music academy.

🔒 Shopping

Hüxstraase is one of Germany's best shopping streets. It's lined with an array of creative and interesting boutiques, clothing stores, bookshops, cafes and much more. Nearby Schlumacherstrasse is also good.

★ Niederegger
FOOD

(☑ 0451-530 1126; www.niederegger.de; Breite Strasse 89; ⊙ 9am-7pm Mon-Fri, 9am-6pm Sat, 10am-6pm Sun) Lübeck's mecca for marzipan lovers, the almond confectionery from Arabia, which has been made locally for centuries. Even if you're not buying, the shop's elaborate seasonal displays are a feast for the eyes. In its small museum, **Marzipan-Salon**, you'll learn that in medieval Europe marzipan was considered medicine, not a treat. At the back there's an elegant cafe (p679).

🛈 Information

Get free wi-fi all over Lübeck by logging into luebeck.freifunk.net.

Tourist Office (☑ 0451-889 9700; www.luebeck-tourismus.de; Holstentorplatz 1; ⊙ 9am-7pm Mon-Fri, 10am-4pm Sat, 10am-3pm Sun May-Aug, reduced hours Sep-Apr) Sells the HappyDay Card (per 24/48/72hr €12/14/17) with discounts and free public transport. Also has a cafe and internet terminals.

🛈 Getting There & Away

AIR

Lübeck Airport (LBC; www.flughafen-luebeck.de; Blankenseer Strasse 101) Lübeck's airport is 10km south of the centre via the A207. Low-cost carriers Ryanair and Wizzair serve the airport, which they euphemistically call Hamburg-Lübeck. Buses take passengers straight to Hamburg (one-way €11.50, one hour), while bus 6 (€3) serves Lübeck's Hauptbahnhof and central bus station.

BOAT

Ferries sail from nearby Travemünde to Baltic destinations.

BUS

Regional and local buses use the Central Bus Station near the Hauptbahnhof. Berlinlinienbus. de serves Kiel and Berlin.

TRAIN

Lübeck has connections every hour to Hamburg (€14, 45 minutes) and Kiel (€18, 1¼ hours).

❶ Getting Around

Lübeck's Altstadt (old town) is on an island encircled by the canalised Trave River. The Hauptbahnhof and central bus station are 500m west of the Holstentor.

Lübeck's centre is easily walked. Many streets are pedestrianised and off limits to all but hotel guest vehicles.

Bus tickets cost €1.80; day cards cost €5.20. Higher-priced tickets are valid for Travemünde.

Travemünde

☑ 04502 / POP 13,900

Writer Thomas Mann declared that he spent his happiest days in Travemünde, just outside Lübeck (which bought it in 1329 to control the shipping coming into its harbour). Its 4.5km of sandy beaches at the point where the Trave River flows into the Baltic Sea make it easy to see why. Water sports are the main draw, along with a colourful **sailing regatta** (www.travemuender-woche.com) in the last week of July.

The town is all wide streets and has a certain 1960s feel. Vorderreihe on the waterfront is lined with pricey shops and cafes.

◉ Sights

Passat   MUSEUM
(☑ 04502-122 5202; www.ss-passat.com; Am Priwallhafen 16a; adult/child €4/2; ⊗ 10am-5pm Apr-Oct) The town takes great pride in its historic four-masted sailing ship-turned-museum, Passat, which used to do the run around South America's Cape Horn in the early to mid-20th century. A regular passenger ferry (€1) crosses the river to the ship.

❶ Getting There & Away

Travemünde is a gateway to Scandinavia, with major ferry lines sailing from its Skandinavienkai.

Hourly trains connect Lübeck to Travemünde (€3.20, 22 minutes), which has several train stations, including Skandinavienkai (for international ferries) and Strandbahnhof (for the beach and tourist office).

Könemann Schiffahrt (☑ 0451-280 1635; www.koenemannschiffahrt.de; adult one-way/return €14/20.50, child €6.50/11; ⊗ twice daily Apr–mid-Oct) Runs scenic ferries to/from Lübeck (1¾ hours). You can sail one-way and take the train the other.

Kiel

☑ 0431 / POP 240,000

Some locals admit Kiel, the capital of Schleswig-Holstein, has a city centre that's *grottenhässlich* (ugly as sin). And unfortunately it is true; it was obliterated during WWII by bombing raids on its U-boat pens and then rapidly rebuilt. Today, it is a series of charmless indoor malls linked by pedestrian bridges.

However, Kiel's grand harbour continues on as it has for centuries and this should be the focus of your visit. Huge ferries transport millions of passengers to and from Scandinavia, while summer sees locals strolling the long waterfront promenade.

◉ Sights & Activities

Follow Kiel's main thoroughfare, the pedestrianised Holstenstrasse, for about 1.5km northeast to the Schlossgarten to reach the waterfront (the port closer in is inaccesible due to ferry terminals). Amid the sparkling waters, you'll see new warships being built for nations worldwide and all manner of ships big and small.

The tourist office has maps for scores of bike rides along the waterfronts.

★ **Kiellinie**   PROMENADE
The magnificent waterfront promenade known as the Kiellinie begins northeast of the Schlossgarten. Sailing clubs, a tiny **aquarium** (☑ 0431-600 1637; Düsternbrooker Weg 20) **FREE**, cafes and restaurants line the way and there are an ever-changing series of vistas of the harbour and huge ships. Eventually the 3.5km-promenade becomes the Hindenburgufer. About 2km from the start at Reventloubrücke you can get hourly ferries back to near the train station or on to Laboe.

WORTH A TRIP

LÜBECK'S NATURAL PLAYGROUND

Naturpark Holsteinische Schweiz (www.naturpark-holsteinische-schweiz.de) Sprawling over 753 sq km between Lübeck to the south and Kiel to the north, the Naturpark Holsteinische Schweiz is the region's largest outdoor playground. Germany's propensity to label its most scenic areas 'Swiss' (the name translates as 'Holstein Switzerland') reflects the park's undulating green hills, golden fields and wildflower-strewn meadows. This verdant landscape is interspersed with a string of some 200 lakes, of which 70 are over one hectare in size.

The park's three main towns, each in idyllic lakeside settings, are **Eutin**, famed for its baroque castle amid English-style gardens; the spa resort of **Malente**; and **Plön**, on the shores of the park's largest lake, the Grosser Plöner See.

Plön's comprehensive **Tourist Info Grosser Plöner See** (☑ 04522-509 50; www.holsteinischeschweiz.de/ploen; Bahnhofstrasse 5, Plön; ⊗ 9am-6pm Mon-Fri, 10am-4pm Sat, 10am-2pm Sun Jun-Aug) can help with accommodation and a wealth of water-based activities from boat trips to fishing, swimming, windsurfing, kayaking and scuba diving.

Hiking and cycling trails criss-cross the park, as does a well-signed road network. Lübeck–Kiel trains stop in Eutin, Malente (Bad Malente-Gremsmühlen) and Plön.

Schiffahrtsmuseum MUSEUM
(Maritime Museum; ☑ 0431-901 3428; Am Wall 65; adult/child €3/1; ⊗ 10am-6pm May-Sep, to 5pm Oct-Apr) Atmospherically located in an imposing former fish market, Kiel's maritime museum tells the story of the city's maritime heritage. Newly redone, it's a great primer on the city and has paintings, models and engaging displays. The cafe overlooks the harbour.

Nord-Ostsee-Kanal CANAL
(viewing platform adult/child €2/1) The 99km-long Nord-Ostsee-Kanal reaches the Baltic Sea from the North Sea at Kiel, with some 60,000 ships passing through every year. It's easy to view the *Schleusen* (locks) at **Holtenau**, 7km north of Kiel. The viewing platform here is open from sunrise to sunset. There's a museum on the southern side of the canal. To get to the locks, take bus 11 to Wik, Kanal. A free ferry shuttles back and forth between the southern and northern banks.

Inaugurated in 1895, the canal is now the third-most trafficked in the world, after the Suez and Panama Canals.

Adler-Schiffe BOAT TOUR
(☑ 01805-123 344; www.adler-schiffe.de; Bahnhofskai; adult/child from €49/24.50; ⊗ Jun-Sep) Experience the full engineering glory of the Nord-Ostsee-Kanal and take in the passing ship traffic on an eight-hour journey with the *Raddampfer Freya*. The best way to appreciate the canal, this historic steamship sails to Rendsburg and back from Bahnhofskai in Kiel (some services are aboard regular boats).

Brücke Schleswig-Holstein BICYCLE RENTAL
(☑ 0431-237 7790; Hauptbahnhof; per day from €9; ⊗ 6am-7pm Mon-Fri, 8am-2pm Sat) Bikes can be rented at the south end of the train station.

☆ Festivals & Events

★ **Kieler Woche** REGATTA
(Kiel Week; www.kieler-woche.de; ⊗ late Jun) Kiel's biggest annual event is the giant weeklong Kieler Woche. Revolving around a series of yachting regattas, it's attended by more than 4000 of the world's sailing elite and half a million spectators. Even if you're not into boats, it's one nonstop party.

🛏 Sleeping & Eating

Kiel is best visited on your way to someplace else. Follow the waterfront and choose a seafood cafe for lunch.

Hotel Am Schwedenkai HOTEL €€
(☑ 0431-986 4220; www.hotel-am-schwedenkai.de; Holstenbrücke 28; s/d from €60/80; P ☻ 🖨 ☂) About midway between the train station and the Kiellinie, this 28-room hotel has great views of the nearby ferry docks. The building is modern and rooms have a Scandi sensibility and maritime blues and whites.

Kieler Brauerei BREWERY €
(☑ 0431-906 290; www.kieler-brauerei.de; Alter Markt 9; mains €7-13; ⊗ 10am-11pm) This city centre microbrewery produces a very fine unfiltered beer that's redolent with herbs and hops. The menu is casual and has German standards (yes, schnitzel) and locally caught seafood.

ℹ️ Information

Tourist Information Kiel (☎0431-679 100; www.kiel-sailing-city.de; Andreas-Gayk-Strasse 31; ☺9.30am-6pm Mon-Fri, 10am-2pm Sat) Tourist Information Kiel is about 300m north of the train station, next to the library.

ℹ️ Getting There & Away

Ferry services run between Kiel and Gothenburg, Oslo and Lithuania.

Numerous trains run between Kiel's shop-filled station and Hamburg (€27, 1¼ hours). Trains to Lübeck leave hourly (€23, 1¼ hours). There are regular local connections to Schleswig, Husum, Schwerin and Flensburg.

ℹ️ Getting Around

Local **bus** (www.vrk-sh.de) trips that include Laboe cost €2.50 one-way or €8 for a day card.

A ferry service along the firth runs daily until around 6pm (to 5pm on weekends) from the Bahnhofsbrücke pier behind the Hauptbahnhof. The trip to Laboe is €9.

Bikes can be rented from Brücke Schleswig-Holstein in the train station.

Laboe
☎04343

At the mouth of the Kiel firth, on its eastern bank, the village of Laboe is home to some surprising reminders of WWII as well as decent beaches, cheap and somewhat cheerful waterfront cafes, and thrilling views of the ceaseless water traffic of ships great and small.

◎ Sights

U-Boat 995   HISTORIC SITE
(☎04343-427 062; www.deutscher-marinebund.de; Strandstrasse 92; combined admission with Marine Ehrenmal adult/child €9.50/6.50; ☺9.30am-6pm Apr-Oct, 9.30am-4pm Nov-Mar) Hundreds of subs like this one that's literally beached once called Kiel home; Wolfgang Petersen's seminal film *Das Boot* (1981) was set on a similar U-boat. You can climb through its claustrophobic interior.

Marine Ehrenmal   MEMORIAL
(Naval Memorial; ☎04343-4948 4962; Strandstrasse 92; adult/child €6/4, combined admission with U-Boat 995 adult/child €9.50/6.50; ☺9.30am-6pm) Nearly 100m tall, this memorial was opened in 1936 to commemorate German seamen killed in WWI. After WWII it became a memorial for sailors killed in

both wars. In one room you can see every ship lost during the conflicts. It's often striking and you'll see that efforts to literally whitewash its Nazi past have been only partially successful.

ℹ️ Getting There & Away

From Kiel, take the ferry (the best way) or bus 100 or 102. It's about 18km by bike.

Schleswig
☎04621 / POP 24,100

Neat red-brick houses and manicured lawns don't begin to hint at the Viking past of this tidy town on the Baltic Sea's longest fjord. Although Schleswig is sleepy today, the tall cathedral spire rising proudly above the water hints at a more active past.

Founded in 804, after a major Viking community put down roots across the Schlei fjord, the town was the continent's economic hub for some 200 years. Later the Dukes of Gottorf made Schleswig their power base from the 16th to 18th centuries. And countless generations of fisherfolk and their families have left their marks.

You can enjoy the long local heritage at excellent museums and along the pretty waterfront.

◎ Sights & Activities

The local highlights are spread out (Schloss Gottorf is 1.5km from the train station; the old town and cathedral are another 2km east of there). With your own transport you can see everything in half a day, otherwise, plan on spending the day exploring.

Spend some time wandering the cobblestoned streets around the **Rathausmarkt**. The traditional fishing village of **Holm** is 500m southeast along the waterfront.

★ Schloss Gottorf   MUSEUM
(☎04621-8130; www.schloss-gottorf.de; Schlossinsel 1) The Dukes of Gottorf's castle in Schleswig is far more 18th-century palace than medieval fortress and today it is home to three remarkable museums.

The Schloss is 2km west of the Schleswig's old town (1.5km north of the Bahnhof).

➡ Schleswig-Holstein
Landesmuseum

(Schleswig-Holstein State Museum; Schloss Gottorf; adult/child €9/5.50; ☺10am-5pm Mon-Fri, 10am-6pm Sat & Sun Apr-Oct, 10am-4pm Tue-Fri, 10am-5pm Sat & Sun Nov-Mar) The

SCHLESWIG-HOLSTEIN'S OPEN-AIR MUSEUM

Schleswig-Holsteinisches Freilichtmuseum (Schleswig-Holstein Open-Air Museum; ☑ 0431-659 660; www.freilichtmuseum-sh.de; Alte Hamburger Landstrasse 97; adult/child Apr-Oct €8/2, Nov-Mar €3/1.50; ☺ 9am-6pm Apr-Oct, 11am-5pm Sun & holidays Nov-Mar) Beekeepers, bakers, potters and many more traditional craftspeople ply their trade 6km south of Kiel, in Molfsee. This excellent museum features some 70 traditional houses typical of the region, relocated from around the state. Take bus 501 from Kiel's central bus station.

Schleswig-Holstein Landesmuseum is filled with art treasures. A roomful of paintings by Lucas Cranach the Elder and a wood-panelled 17th-century wine tavern from Lübeck create a memorable first impression. There's also the rococo Plöner Saal, with faïence from the Baltic region; the artistic beauty and lavish detail of the stunning Schlosskapelle; and the elegant Hirschsaal, the former banquet hall named for the bas-reliefs of deer on the walls.

The more contemporary collection is equally noteworthy, including an entire *Jugendstil Abteilung* (art nouveau department), and 20th-century paintings, sketches, lithographs and woodcuts from German artists such as Emil Nolde and Ernst Barlach.

➡ **Archäologische Landesmuseum**

(Archaeological Museum; Schloss Gottorf; admission incl with Schleswig-Holstein Landesmuseum; ☺ same as Schleswig-Holstein Landesmuseum) The second museum, the Archäologische Landesmuseum, boasts the Nydam-Boot, a reconstructed and preserved 28-oar rowing boat from 350 BC, which is housed in its own hall.

➡ **Gottorfer Globus**

(Gottorf Globe; Schloss Gottorf; adult/child €7/5; ☺ 10am-5pm Mon-Fri, 10am-6pm Sat & Sun Apr-Oct) View a reconstruction of the famous Gottorfer Globus, which has been placed in its own house, a five-minute walk through the castle's lovely **formal gardens**. The exterior of the 3m-diameter globe shows how the continents and seas were thought to look in the 17th century. The real magic is inside, however. Several people can fit on a bench inside the globe and watch the Renaissance night sky change as the globe spins around them; eight minutes equals one day.

The original 17th-century globe was lauded as one of the wonders of the world – its first planetarium – but through war ended up being taken from Schleswig to St Petersburg. It's still there (albeit fire-damaged) in the Lomonosov Museum.

★ **Dom St Petri** CATHEDRAL

(☑ 04621-989 585; Süderholmstrasse 2; ☺ 9am-5pm Mon-Sat, 1.30-5pm Sun May-Sep, 10am-4pm Mon-Sat, 1.30-4pm Sun Oct-Apr) With its steeple towering above the Altstadt (old town), the Dom St Petri provides an excellent point of orientation. It's also home to the intricate **Bordesholmer Altar** (1521), a carving by Hans Brüggemann. The 12.6m by 7.14m altar, on the wall furthest from the entrance, shows more than 400 figures in 24 scenes relating the story of the Passion of Christ – the result of extraordinary artistry and patience.

Owing to its flock of seafarer worshippers, the church has many elaborate ship models scattered about its interior, which was untouched by the war.

Stadtmuseum Schleswig MUSEUM

(☑ 04621-936 820; www.stadtmuseum-schleswig.de; Friedrichstrasse 9-11; adult/child €5/2.50; ☺ 10am-5pm Tue-Sun; 🚼) Schleswig's city museum incorporates a treacly (and kid-friendly) **Teddy Bear Haus** in a half-timbered building off the courtyard. More sober displays outline the city's history. It's a signposted five-minute walk north of the Bahnhof.

Wikinger Museum MUSEUM

(Viking Museum; ☑ 04621-813 222; www.haithabu.de; Haddebyer Noor 5, Haddeby; adult/child €7/5; ☺ 9am-5pm Apr-Oct, 10am-4pm Tue-Sun Nov-Mar; 🚼) Vikings ruled from their base here at Haithabu, across the Schlei from Schleswig, some 1000 to 1200 years ago.

Located just outside the historic settlement (now an archaeological site), this kid-friendly museum features replica huts and actors showing how Viking families lived their daily lives (but without the smells etc), and has halls filled with displays.

The museum lies east of the B76 that runs between Schleswig and Kiel, about 3km from Schleswig's Bahnhof. Otherwise, take bus 4810; alight at Haddeby.

Kappeln VILLAGE

(B199) This tiny fishing village is near the mouth of the Schlei. It makes for a good stroll with some historic buildings and old boats. You can cycle here (about 32km), but the best way to arrive is on a tour boat.

Fahrradverleih Röhling BICYCLE RENTAL

(☑ 04621-993 030; www.fahrradverleih-schleswig. de; Knud-Laward-Strasse 30, Holm; per day from €7.50; ⊙ 9am-6pm Mon-Fri, 9am-12.30pm Sat) Choose from a range of bikes in old Holm, 500m east of the Altstadt.

☞ Tours

Several companies offer a vast array of boat trips 40km up the Schlei between April and October, departing from various landing docks.

Schleischifffahrt A Bischoff BOAT TOUR

(☑ 04621-233 19; www.schleischifffahrt.de; Gottorfer Damm 1; tours from €12, ⊙ Apr–mid-Sep) Located near the Schloss, offers journeys to destinations that include Kappeln.

🛏 Sleeping & Eating

Schleswig is a quiet place at night. You might consider a moonlit stroll along the small harbour. There are several cafe choices in the Altstadt and along the waterfront.

★ Hotel Alter Kreisbahnhof HOTEL €€

(☑ 04621-302 00; www.hotel-alter-kreisbahnhof. de; Königstrasse 9; s/d €60/95, mains €9-20; ⊙ restaurant 7am-9.30pm; ⓟ♿🛜) Some of the spacious rooms at this hotel-restaurant, based in a turreted former railway station, have water views. All have a modern decor that's literally peachy. The **restaurant** serves creative regional cuisine. It's nicely located in the Altstadt, 100m from the Dom.

Zollhaus HOTEL €€

(☑ 04621-290 340; zollhaus-zu-gottorf.de; Lollfuss 110; s/d from €85/115; ⓟ♿🛜) After a day sightseeing, you will enjoy the refined yet relaxed atmosphere and comfortable rooms at this 200-year-old customs house. The 10 rooms have a pastel-accented decor, and many look out to the terrace overlooking the grassy grounds. A cafe provides tasty refreshments. The waterfront and Schloss are both close by.

Esch am Hafen SEAFOOD €€

(☑ 04621-290 207; Hafengang 2; mains €5-20; ⊙ 10am-9pm Apr-Oct, shorter hours Nov-Mar) Like a cod in a school, this one-storey

GERMANY'S GREAT WALL?

Danevirke Museum (☑ 04621-378 14; www.dannewerk.com; Ochsenweg 5, Dannewerk; adult/child €3/1; ⊙ 10am-4pm Tue-Sun Mar-Nov) Northern Germany has its own version of the Great Wall of China: the Dannewerk, a 30km-long earth-and-stone wall that stretched across today's Schleswig-Holstein and protected the southern border of the Danish kingdom. A surviving section of the wall, which was maintained roughly from AD 650 to 1200, is located 3km southwest of Schleswig's train station in the tiny hamlet of Dannewerk. This small museum gives the history of the wall and also offers a glimpse into Danish culture.

modern restaurant right on the waterfront looks, at best, unassuming. And the menu certainly doesn't stand out: there's fish and chips, prawns in many forms and even *Currywurst.* But the service is quick, the prices are good and all the fish dishes are excellent.

Olschewski's SEAFOOD €€

(☑ 04621-255 77; www.hotelolschewski.de vu; Hafenstrasse 40; mains €10-20; ⊙ 11am-9pm Wed-Sun Oct-Apr, Wed-Mon May-Sep) Right across from the harbour on the edge of the Altstadt, Olschewski's is a local icon. The large and sunny terrace fills up fast on weekends when you can hear the clanking masts of nearby boats. Seafood is a speciality, especially the *Holmer-pot,* a rich combo of whitefish and wine. Good, creative specials. An annex has basic rooms (single/double from €55/77).

❶ Information

Tourist Office (☑ 04621-850 056; www.schleswig.de; Plessenstrasse 7; ⊙ 10am-6pm Mon-Fri, 10am-2pm Sat & Sun Jun-Sep, 10am-4pm Mon-Fri Oct-May, also 10am-2pm Sat Apr-May & Oct) Very helpful; in the Altstadt near the Dom. City maps and hotel brochures are available outside after hours.

❶ Getting There & Away

Direct regional trains to Hamburg (€25, 1½ hours) run hourly; trains to Flensburg (€9, 30 minutes), Kiel (€12, 50 minutes) and Husum (€9, 35 minutes) leave every hour.

❶ Getting Around

It's a 3.5km walk mostly along the water-front from the surprisingly ramshackle and service-free train station northeast to the Altstadt.

Tickets for Schleswig's buses cost €2; two buses an hour link the station and the Altstadt. A taxi from the Bahnhof to the Altstadt costs around €10.

Between May and September, ferries cross the Schlei from Schleswig Hafen (just south of the Dom) between 10.30am and 5pm daily (adult one-way/return €3/5).

Flensburg

☑ 0461 / POP 88,700

Situated on a busy industrial firth just 7km south of the Danish border, Flensburg is sometimes still dubbed 'Rumstadt' for its prosperous 18th-century trade in liquor with the Caribbean. Reminders of its sea-faring, rum-trading days echo across the port area.

◉ Sights

Most attractions run north–south parallel to the western bank of the firth, although the harbour retains a gritty feel. However, there are always an interesting array of old and historic boats tied up.

★Schiffahrtsmuseum MUSEUM

(Maritime Museum; ☑0461-852 970; www. schiffahrtsmuseum.flensburg.de; Schiffbrücke 39; adult/child €6/3, combined ticket incl Museumsberg Flensburg €8/4; ☉10am-5pm Tue-Sun) An engrossing museum right on the old harbour. Displays here give the history of rum and the seafarers who both shipped and drank it. Cool models show how ships were built before power tools. On the water, workshops show how old ships are restored.

Kaufmannshöfe HISTORIC BUILDINGS

(Merchants' Courtyards) Flensburg's Kauf-mannshöfe date from the 18th century, when Danish-ruled Flensburg provided supplies to the Danish West Indies (St Thomas, St Jan and St Croix) in exchange for sugar and rum.

Free town maps from the tourist office mark nearly every *Hof* (courtyard).

Designed to make it easier to load goods into ships, they typically consisted of a tall warehouse on the harbourside, behind which was a series of low workshops, wrapped around a central courtyard and leading to the merchants' living quarters.

Museumsberg Flensburg MUSEUM

(Municipal Museum; ☑0461-852 956; www.mu-seumsberg.flensburg.de; Museumsberg 1; adult/child €6/3, combined ticket incl Schiffahrtsmuseum €8/4; ☉10am-5pm Tue-Sun) This hilltop museum features two wings: one contains a collection of rooms and furniture from Schleswig-Holstein history, including a remarkably painted cembalo (early piano covered in murals). The second has excellent art nouveau works by Flensburg-born painter Hans Christiansen, as well as an Emil Nolde room.

Braasch HISTORIC BUILDING

(☑0461-141 600; www.braasch-rum.de; Rote Strasse 26-28; ☉10am-6.30pm Mon-Fri, 10am-4pm Sat) Some of the prettiest Kaufmanns-höfe can be found off the very picturesque Rote Strasse, which is up from the harbour by the Rathaus. While here, you can buy rum in drinkable and edible forms at this lavish shop, which has a small musuem.

☞ Tours

★MS Viking BOAT TOUR

(☑0461-255 20; www.viking-schifffahrt.de; Augus-tastrasse 9; adult/child return €10/4; ☉Tue-Sun Apr-May & Sep, daily Jun-Aug) The MS *Viking* operates scenic cruises to Glücksburg (one hour each way; four or five times a day), departing from where Norderhofenden meets Schiffbrücke.

🛏 Sleeping & Eating

Flensburg isn't exactly a barrel of rum at night, so it's best visited on the way elsewhere. You can find seaside hotels in nearby Glücksburg.

Hotel Dittmer's Gasthof HOTEL €€

(☑0461-240 52; www.dittmersgasthof.de; Neu-markt 2; s/d from €80/120; ☉reception 5am-10pm; 🅿🛜) This flower-festooned historic inn spans two buildings and is between the train station and the harbour, close to the Rathaus. Run by the same family for more than 100 years, the rooms are basic and tidy.

★Weinstube im Krusehof GERMAN €€

(☑0461-128 76; weinstube-flensburg.de; Rote Strasse 24; mains €11-14; ☉11.30am-10.30pm Mon-Sat) Wander through the covered passage built from old ship timbers into a courtyard of goodness at this wine restaurant in the old town. Run by the irrepressable Steffi, loyal regulars enjoy a fine selection of German wines along with *Flammenkuchen*, the Alsatian 'pizzas' with their cracker-crisp thin crusts and a variety of toppings.

ℹ Information

Flensburg Tourist Office (☑ 0461-909 0920; www.flensburg-tourismus.de; Rote Strasse 15-17; ⊙ 9am-6pm Mon-Fri, 10am-2pm Sat) In the old town close to the Rathaus.

ℹ Getting There & Away

Flensburg has hourly trains to Schleswig (€9, 30 minutes), Kiel (€18, 1½ hours) and on to Hamburg.

ℹ Getting Around

It is almost 1km from the train station to the Rathaus and the start of the main pedestrian zone at Holm on the southern end of town. From here, the base of the harbour is another 800m. Follow the small blue signs reading 'Altstadt/Zentrum'. Buses 1 and 5 link the Bahnhof to the centre and the harbour (€2.10).

Glücksburg

☑ 04631 / POP 5950

Overlooking the water 10km northeast of Flensburg, this small spa town is a timeless, upscale retreat overlooking the often chilly Baltic waters. It's a pleasant stroll around the lake up to the beach.

◉ Sights

Schloss Glücksburg   PALACE
(☑ 04631-442 330; www.schloss-gluecksburg.de; off Schlossallee; adult/child €8/3; ⊙ 10am-6pm daily May-Oct, 11am-4pm Sat & Sun Nov-Apr) Glücksburg is renowned for this horseshoe-shaped, blindingly white Renaissance palace, which appears to float in the middle of a large lake.

⌂ Sleeping & Eating

Strandhotel
Glücksburg   HOTEL €€
(☑ 04631-614 10; www.strandhotel-gluecksburg.de; Kirstenstrasse 6; s/d from €100/130; P⊕@🖤) The fabled 'white castle by the sea' counts Thomas Mann among its former guests. Rooms at this resplendent and sprawling beachfront villa (which dates to 1872) are now decked out in cool, beach pastel style. Decadences include a spa and restaurant serving a seasonal menu utilising local produce.

ℹ Getting There & Away

Buses run hourly between Glücksburg and Flensburg's central bus station (€2.90) or you can take the scenic route aboard the MS *Viking*.

Husum

☑ 04841 / POP 22,200

Warmly toned buildings huddle around Husum's photogenic *Binnenhafen* (inner harbour), colourful gabled houses line its narrow, cobbled lanes, and in late March and early April millions of purple crocuses bloom in Husum's Schlosspark. You can easily while away a couple hours in Husum.

◉ Sights

Ask at the tourist office for a map highlighting Husum's Cultural Trail. Many focus on author-extraordinaire Theodor Storm, right down to the fountain in the Markt, which shows Tine, a young Frisian woman who figures in a Storm novella.

Theodor-Storm-Haus   MUSEUM
(Theodor Storm House; ☑ 04841-803 8630; www.storm-gesellschaft.de; Wasserreihe 31-35; adult/child €3.50/2.50; ⊙ 10am-5pm Tue-Fri, 11am-5pm Sat, 2-5pm Sun & Mon Apr-Oct, shorter hours Nov-Mar) Even if you're not familiar with the 19-century author, his tidy wooden house will whet your appetite. Well-placed biographical titbits fill in the life of this novelist, poet and proud Schleswig-Holstein citizen in the small, intimate rooms where he lived and wrote works such as his seminal

---

COFFEE WITH A CREAMY KICK

If the cold wind's biting, warm up with one of the region's specialities, rum-laced coffee topped with cream, known as a *Pharisäer*. So the stories go, chilly locals in the region infused their strong, sweetened coffee with a shot of rum. But, to hide the presence of alcohol from their priest, they smothered the top with cream. The priest, however, quickly caught on, decrying them as Pharisees (his point being that they were following the letter, not the spirit, of the law). The name stuck, as did the surreptitious drinking technique – don't stir it; instead, slurp the hot coffee through the cream.

HAMBURG & THE NORTH SYLT

North Frisian novella *Der Schimmelreiter* (The Rider on the White Horse).

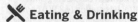 **Eating & Drinking**

Cafes and restaurants abound around the Marienkirche, the Markt and the *Binnenhafen*. Pick up fresh food at Husum's **market** (Thursday and Saturday), which has been held since 1465.

Husums Brauhaus   GERMAN €€
(☑ 04841-896 60; www.husums-brauhaus.de; Neustadt 60-68; mains €7-20; ☺ 5pm-late) The in-house microbrewery at Theodor Storm Hotel has a good range of brews, a beer garden and casual German fare.

ⓘ Information

Husum Tourist Office (☑ 04841-898 70; www.tourismus-husum.de; Grossstrasse 27; ☺ 9am-6pm Mon-Fri & 10am-4pm Sat Apr-Oct, to 5pm Mon-Fri Nov-Mar) Can book rooms and offers plenty of town info.

ⓘ Getting There & Around

There are regular direct train connections to Hamburg (€30, two hours) and Schleswig (€9, 30 minutes), plus several links daily to Westerland on Sylt (€18, 1¼ hours).

Husum is walkably compact and extremely well signposted. The Bahnhof lies 700m south of the city centre.

Sylt

☑ 04651 / POP 15,200

The star of Germany's North Frisian Islands, glamorous Sylt has designer boutiques housed in quintessential reed-thatched cottages, gleaming luxury automobiles jamming the car parks, luxurious accommodation and some of the country's most acclaimed restaurants.

This anchor-shaped island is attached to the mainland by a narrow causeway. On its west coast, the North Sea's fierce surf and strong winds gnaw at Sylt's shoreline. By contrast, the eastern Wadden Sea shore is tranquil and, yes, silty. At low tide, the retreating shallows expose vast mudflats called the Watt.

Outside of the pockets of excess (such as Kampden), Sylt's candy-striped lighthouses rise above wide expanses of shifting dunes, fields of gleaming yellow-gold rape flower and expanses of heath. Dotted along the beaches are saunas, where the idea is to heat up and then run naked into the chilly North Sea.

It's easy to lose the glamour and crowds on the beaches, in the dunes or on a hiking or bike trail, where the size of your wallet matters little.

Sylt is 38.5km long and measures only 700m at its narrowest point.

WORTH A TRIP

AT HOME WITH EMIL NOLDE

Bright flowers, stormy seas, red-lipped women with jaunty hats and impressionistic seaside watercolours: these are some of the recurring themes of great Schleswig-Holstein painter Emil Nolde. Born in 1867 in Nolde village near the Danish border (from whence he took his name), he first gained fame for producing postcards in which he gave mountains human features.

In 1927 Nolde and his wife Ada built a home and studio in Seebüll. Here, banned from working by the Nazis, he proceeded to produce 1300 'unpainted pictures' in secret.

Nowadays Nolde, who died in 1956, is considered one of the great 20th-century watercolourists, and his work is found across Schleswig-Holstein (and far beyond), including the **Schleswig-Holstein Landesmuseum** (p683) in Schleswig and the **Museumsberg Flensburg** (p686).

Emil Nolde Stiftung (☑ 04664-983 930; www.nolde-stiftung.de; Neukirchen bei Seebüll; adult/child €8/free; ☺ 10am-6pm Mar-Nov) By far the biggest and most impressive collection of Nolde's work is in his architecturally arresting former atelier at Seebüll. The exhibition is worth a half day's excursion, which is lucky because it's fairly remote – you'll need your own wheels to visit the location, which is almost on the Danish border. There's a suitably arty **cafe**.

⊙ Sights

⊙ Westerland

The island's largest town (with 9000 permanent residents) is an unattractive mess of concrete towers and tawdry commercial strips, such as the pedestrianised Friedrichstrasse. Once off the train from the mainland, don't linger.

⊙ Keitum

Historic reed-thatched houses strangled with ivy, lush gardens of colourful blooms, stone walls and the occasional garden gate made from two curving whalebones combine to create the island's prettiest village.

Keitum was once Sylt's most important harbour, which is recalled in its late-Romanesque sailors church, **St Severin**, with its Gothic altar and chancel, and heritage-listed gravestones in the cemetery.

Altfriesisches Haus HISTORIC BUILDING
(Old Frisian House; ☑ 04651-311 01; www.soelring-foriining.de; Am Kliff 13; adult/child €5/2.50; ⊙ 10am-5pm Mon-Fri, 11am-5pm Sat & Sun Apr-Oct, noon-4pm Wed-Sat Nov-Mar) The days before tourism are recalled in this 1739 house made from brick and thatch.

⊙ Wenningstedt

The best of Sylt's Stone Age graves are in the family-oriented resort town of Wenningstedt.

Denghoog ARCHAEOLOGICAL SITE
(☑ 04651-328 05; www.soelring-foriining.de; Am Denghoog; adult/child €4/2; ⊙ 10am-5pm Mon-Fri & 11am-5pm Sat & Sun Apr-Oct) Enter the 5000-year-old Denghoog, next to the town church, which measures 3m by 5m and is nearly 2m tall in parts. The outer walls consist of 12 stones weighing around 40 tonnes. How Stone Age builders moved these is a Stonehenge kind of mystery.

⊙ Kampen

Hermès, Cartier and Louis Vuitton boutiques ensconced in traditional reed-thatched houses signal that this little village is the island's ritziest. Each summer, aristocrats and German celebrities come to see and be seen along the main promenade, Stroenwai, which is called the Whisky Mile

WADDEN SEA

The vast tidal and mudflats that extend from Denmark around the German coast to the Netherlands have been named the **Wadden Sea World Heritage Site** (www.waddensea-worldheritage.org) by Unesco. Tidal flats, gullies, salt marshes and dunes form a diverse and lively natural area that includes the North Frisian Islands such as Sylt. It's an amazing ecosystem with many forms of life ranging from porpoises offshore to exotic molluscs that can breathe both air and water. See it all on a **Wattwandern Tour** (p690).

for all of its attitude-filled nightclubs. Watch for paparazzi hiding in the bushes.

People-watching aside, the principal reason to visit is the stunning **Uwe Dune**, at 52.5m Sylt's highest natural elevation. You can climb the wooden steps to the top for a 360-degree view over Sylt and, on a good day, to neighbouring Amrum and Föhr islands.

⊙ List

Everything in List is dubbed 'Germany's northernmost' – harbour, beach, restaurant etc... It's a windswept, tranquil land's end, but things usually liven up in the harbour when the ferry from Rømø (Denmark) deposits day-tripping Danes.

The privately owned Ellenbogen ('elbow') peninsula is at Sylt's far northern tip. The beaches here are off limits for swimming because of dangerous currents but are dramatically backed by 35m-high shifting dunes. There's sublime hiking here; ask at your accommodation or the tourist office.

Erlebniszentrum Naturgewalten MUSEUM
(Forces of Nature Centre; ☑ 04651-836 190; www.naturgewalten-sylt.de; Hafenstrasse 37; adult/child €14/8.50; ⊙ 10am-7pm Jul & Aug, 10am-6pm Sep-Jun) Dedicated to the North Sea, this state-of-the-art ecological museum has multimedia exhibits that keep both kids and adults entertained (especially on rainy days). It's housed in a vivid-blue 'wave'-like building powered by renewable energy. Everyone enjoys the *seehund* (seal) webcam.

◉ West Coast Beaches

To beat the crowds on the long west-coast strand, pick the parking area with the fewest cars – you'll find great variations. Conversely, some of the beach areas boast high-profile cafes and activities centres and have quite a scene. At many beach areas you can rent the classically German *Strandkorb*, a roofed wicker beach chair.

☞ Tours

Tourist offices have details on the oodles of island tours (foot, bus, bike etc). There's a head-spinning array of **boat cruises**, mostly operated by Adler-Schiffe (www.adler-schiffe.de). Many include visits to nearby islands such as Amrum and Föhr and leave from Hörnum on Sylt's southern tip.

★ Wattwandern Tour — BOAT, WALKING TOUR
(Tideland Tour; ☑ 01805-123 344; www.adler-schiffe.de; Hörnum; adult/child €32/21.50; ☺ 2-3 times per week late May-early Oct) See the Unesco-recognised Wadden Sea up close. Really up close. Take a boat from Hörnum to the nearby islands of either Amrum or Föhr (depending on tides) then walk across the mud for 8km to the other and take the boat back to Sylt. You will be amazed at how the seemingly desolate expanses come to life up close.

Seal Colonies Boat Tour — BOAT TOUR
(☑ 01805-123 344; www.adler-schiffe.de; Hörnum; adult/child from €18.50/14.50; ☺ daily Apr-Oct; ♠) See seals basking on the sandbanks on this 1½-hour boat tour from Hörnum, one of the most popular tours.

☱ Sleeping

Tourist websites have details of the island's plethora of accommodation options, including holiday apartments and private rooms. In season many require minimum stays of two nights or more.

DJH Hostel Dikjen Deel — HOSTEL €
(☑ 04651-835 7825; www.jugendherberge.de; Fischerweg 36-40, Westerland; dm under/over 26yr €25/30; ☺ closed late Dec; ☎) Set amid the dunes, Westerland's 114-bed hostel is a 45-minute walk from the Bahnhof. Alternatively, take bus 2 in the direction of Rantum/Hörnum to the Dikjen Deel stop. To get further away from it all, try the DJH hostels at List-Mövenberg and Hörnum.

Campingplatz Rantum — CAMPGROUND €
(☑ 04651-807 55; www.camping-rantum.de; Hörnumer Strasse 3, Rantum; per adult/child €5/3, tent €7.50-9.50, car €2.50; ☺ Apr-Oct; ℗☎) In a natural area of rolling dunes south of Westerland; great facilities including a bakery, restaurant and sauna.

Kamps — GUESTHOUSE €€
(☑ 04651-983 90; www.kamps-sylt.de; Gurtstich 41, Keitum; r from €170, apt from €160; ℗) Inside a traditional thatched-roof house in oh-so-quaint Keitum, this eight-room guesthouse plus apartments surprises with colours as bold as a Sylt sunrise on a clear day. And you'll probably catch the sunrise as you'll be waiting for the fab breakfasts that include the family's homemade jams, waffles, luscious breads and more.

★ Bundersand — RESORT €€€
(☑ 04651-460 70; www.budersand.de; Am Kai 3, Hörnum; s/d from €250/320; ℗◉☎✖) The 21st-century architecture is almost as stunning as the views at Sylt's most luxurious hotel. Many rooms have terraces with their own gardens where you can tickle your toes on grass while looking far out to the North Sea. The spa is legendary; use it to work out kinks generated on the beautiful private golf course.

Village — BOUTIQUE HOTEL €€€
(☑ 04651-469 70; www.village-kampen.de; Alte Dorfstrasse 7, Kampen; r from €310; ℗☎✖) A thatched fantasy of a boutique hotel with a mere 15 rooms but service standards worthy of a palace. Discretion is the rule here, whether it's at the indoor pool or out in the lovely gardens. Strolling the town starts outside the gate. Food, such as breakfast, is superb.

✖ Eating & Drinking

Sylt attracts some of Germany's top chefs. But the island's most quintessential dish is a simple and delicious fish sandwich from home-grown chain, Gosch. Also look for oysters from Germany's only oyster farm, in List. In high season, the clubs on the Kampen's Whisky Mile go till dawn – and beyond.

Gosch — SEAFOOD €€
(☑ 04651-870 383; www.gosch.de; Hafenstrasse 16, List; mains €4-20; ☺ 11.30am-9pm) The site of Gosch's original kiosk in List harbour is now this nationwide chain's maritime-themed flagship, Alte Bootshalle. But across the island you'll find branches offering its de-

SYLT ACTIVITIES

Sylt's **windsurfing** is known as the most radical on the World Cup windsurfing tour, which finishes here each September when winds and waves are wild. Yet beginners shouldn't be deterred.

Besides rental gear, there are **water sports** schools in every town where you can learn to master kitesurfing, regular surfing, catamaran sailing and much more.

For the less energetic, the German love of **spas** is sated in almost every town and resort hotel.

Horseback riding, whether on the beach or through the flatlands and along the marshes on the Wadden Sea side, is popular. As is **walking** – all those dunes beckon. Whether Nordi-style using poles (rentals widely available) or just serenely strolling, walking is hugely popular all over Sylt. You will find vehicle-free trails stretching in all directions.

And if you like a slightly quicker pace, **cycling** is almost as popular as walking here. Rental shops are everywhere (rates start at €7 per day), including ginormous ones near the Westerland train station.

licious fish sandwiches, seafood pasta, smoked fish and *Rösti* (potato cakes), lobster and caviar.

Coming to Sylt without visiting Gosch would be like coming to Germany without ordering a beer. Established by eel seller Jürgen Gosch some three decades ago, it's a Sylt institution. Its List location with its vast deli is a fantasyland for seafood lovers.

★ **Söl'ring Hof** MODERN EUROPEAN €€€
(☐ 04651-836 200; www.soelring-hof.de; Am Sandwall 1, Rantum; mains from €44; ☺ 6.30-9.30pm May-Oct, closed Wed & Sun, shorter hours other times) You'd come here just for the location set among dunes. From the terrace you can hear the crash of the surf, muted by blowing grasses. But Chef Johannes King's kitchen is the draw, with breathtaking takes on local, seasonal produce and seafood.

Sansibar LOUNGE
(☐ 04651-964 646; www.sansibar.de; Hörnumer Strasse 80, Rantum; ☺ 11am-late, shorter hours in winter) Drink among the dunes in this large grass-roof beach shack for the elite. Yes there's a fine restaurant, but the real reason to come is for that selfie which looks stolen from the pages of *Hello!* Sunset drinks on the terrace is the classic Sylt high-season extravagence.

❶ Information

All communities on Sylt charge hotel guests a *Kurabgabe* (guest tax) of about €3 to €5 per day, depending on the season. It entitles you to small discounts at museums and access to the beaches. Day trippers will need to buy a *Tageskarte* (day pass) from tourist offices or the kiosks at beach entrances.

Westerland has the main tourist offices, convenient for when you arrive on the island. (Other towns have offices but they are usually only open a few hours on weekdays.) A great source of info is www.sylt.de.

Tourist Information Desk (www.westerland. de; Bahnhofplatz, Westerland; ☺ 9am-6pm) Inside the train station. A good first stop.

❶ Getting There & Away

There is no direct land access to Sylt, although you can bring your car. You'll need to come by ferry or train.

A **car ferry** (☐ 0180-310 3030; www.sylt-faehre.de; one-way/return from €45/76) runs from Rømø in Denmark to List (one-way per foot passenger/car and passengers €7/43.50).

There are ferries to/from Amrun and Föhr.

AIR

Flughafen Sylt (GWT; Sylt Airport; www. flughafen-sylt.de; Westerland) Sylt's airport is served by Air Berlin and Lufthansa, which have flights to major German cities, although mostly around summer weekends.

TRAIN

Sylt is connected to the mainland by a causeway used exclusively by trains.
➡ IC trains serve Hamburg Hauptbahnhof (€50, 3¼ hours) a few times a day, while regional trains have hourly services to Hamburg Altona (€30, 3½ hours) via Husum. Important: make sure you're sitting in the correct part of the train, as they sometimes split en route.
➡ Vehicles use the **Sylt Shuttle** (www.syltshut tle.de; one-way/return Fri-Mon €51/90, return Tue-Thu €77) from Niebüll. There are hourly crossings in both directions; it doesn't take

reservations and foot and bicycle passengers aren't allowed. With loading and unloading, expect the journey to take about an hour and be prepared to queue at busy times.

Note that interest by another operator in the car train has sparked DB to announce that beginning in 2016 it may run the Sylt Shuttle every half hour and include passenger- and bike-carrying cars that start in Hamburg.

❶ Getting Around

Sylt is well covered by **buses** (www.svg-sylt. de; fares €2-7), which run at about 20-minute intervals on the main routes. Some buses have bike racks.

Regional trains to/from Westerland stop in Keitum.

Helgoland

Helgoland's former rulers, the British, really got the better deal in 1891 when they swapped it for then German-ruled Zanzibar. But Germans today are very fond of this lonesome North Sea outcrop of red sandstone rock and its fresh air and warm weather, courtesy of the Gulf Stream.

The 80m-tall **Lange Anna** (Long Anna) rock on the island's southwest edge is a compelling sight, standing alone in the ocean. There are also WWII bunkers and ruins to explore, and resurging numbers of Atlantic grey seals. Cycling is not permitted on the tiny 4.2-sq-km island.

By an old treaty, Helgoland is not part of the EU's VAT area, so many of the 1130 residents make their living selling duty-free cigarettes, booze and perfume to day trippers who prowl the main drag, Lung Wai (long way). To swim, many head to neighbouring **Düne**, a blip in the ocean that is popular with nudists.

Helgoland makes an easy day trip from several points, but if you want to stay, there are more than 1000 hotel beds. Get more information at www.helgoland.de.

❶ Getting There & Away

Ferries here take up to four hours. Return trips are timed to allow three to four hours on the island. Services include:

Reederei Rahder (☑ 04834 3612; www.rahder. de; Büsum; day trips from adult/child €39/22; ☺ Apr-Oct) Boats run from Büsum, which is on the rail network.

Helgoline (☑ 0180-522 1445; www.helgoline. de; from Hamburg adult/child from €70/35, from Cuxhaven €57/29; ☺ from Hamburg 9am,

Cuxhaven 11.30am Apr-Oct) Fast ferries run from Hamburg and Cuxhaven; there are also cheaper, slower boats.

SCHWERIN & THE MECKLENBURG LAKE PLAINS

At the doorstep of the appealing state capital, Schwerin, the wilderness area of the Mecklenburg Lake Plains spreads across the centre of the state, and shelters the pristine Müritz National Park. Meandering through charming little villages and hamlets, many roads in the area are canopied by trees that were planted by medieval fish merchants to shield wagons from the heat of the summer sun.

Schwerin

☑ 0385 / POP 103,000

Picturesquely sited around seven lakes (or possibly more depending on how you tally them), the centrepiece of this engaging city is its Schloss (castle), built in the 14th century during the city's six centuries as the former seat of the Grand Duchy of Mecklenburg.

Schwerin has an upbeat, vibrant energy on its restored streets that befits its role as the capital of Mecklenburg-Western Pomerania. Cafes, interesting shops and flashes of its regal past make wandering a delight.

◉ Sights & Activities

★ **Schloss & Gardens**   PALACE
(☑ 0385-525 2920; www.schloss-schwerin.de; Burg Island; adult/child €6/free; ☺ 10am-6pm Tue-Sun mid-Apr–mid-Oct, to 5pm mid-Oct–mid-Apr) Gothic and Renaissance turrets, Slavic onion domes, Ottoman features and terracotta Hanseatic step gables are among the mishmash of architectural styles that make up Schwerin's inimitable Schloss, which is crowned by a gleaming golden dome. Nowadays the Schloss earns its keep as the state's parliament building.

Crossing the causeway south from the palace-surrounding **Burggarten** brings you to the baroque **Schlossgarten** (Palace Garden), intersected by several canals.

Schwerin derives its name from a Slavic castle known as Zuarin (Animal Pasture) that was formerly on the site, and which was

OTHER NORTH FRISIAN ISLANDS

Sylt may be the star of the 14 North Frisian Islands, but the others also have many charms. With their grass-covered dunes, shifting sands, birds, seal colonies, lighthouses and rugged cliffs, these islands are the domain of nature lovers and those looking for restful retreats. Föhr and Amrum are both large and have myriad appeal.

Both islands have scores of places to stay, from hostels to apartments.

Föhr

Closer to the mainland, cloud-shaped Föhr is known as the green isle, although there's also a good sandy beach in the south. Its main village, **Wyk**, has plenty of windmills. In the north you'll find 16 tiny Frisian hamlets tucked behind dikes up to 7m tall. In the old days, Föhr's men went out to sea to hunt whales.

The church of **St Johannis** in Nieblum dates from the 12th century and is sometimes called the 'Frisian Cathedral' because it seats up to 1000 people.

For info, check www.foehr.de.

Amrum

Amrum is the smallest North Frisian Island; you can walk around it in a day. It's also the prettiest, with reed-thatched Frisian houses, a patchwork of dunes, woods, heath and marsh, and glorious Kniepsand – 12km of fine, white sand, sometimes up to 1km wide – that takes up half the island.

Crowning the central village of **Wittdün** is northern Germany's tallest lighthouse, which stands 63m tall. The island's largest village is **Nebel**.

Much of Amrum is under protection, so you must stick to the marked paths. There are some fine walks, including the 10km walk from the lighthouse to the village of **Norddorf** through the pine forest, or the 8km return hike from Norddorf along the safe swimming beach to the tranquil **Ood Nature Reserve**, an ideal place to observe bird life.

For info, www.amrum.de is a good source.

Getting There & Around

Ferries to Föhr and Amrum are operated by **WDR** (☑ 01805-080 140; www.faehre.de; return adult/child Föhr €9/4.50, Amrum €13/7, bikes €6, cars from €60) from Dagebüll Hafen (which has a train service that connects to the main line at Niebüll). Regular ferries link Föhr, Amrum and Sylt.

Buses take you around the islands; there are bike-rental places in every village.

---

first mentioned in AD 973. In a niche over the main gate, the **statue of Niklot** depicts a Slavic prince, who was defeated by Heinrich der Löwe in 1160.

Inside the palace's opulently furnished rooms, highlights include a huge collection of Meissen porcelain and richly coloured stained-glass windows in the **Schlosskirche**.

The Burggarten most notably features a wonderful **orangerie** overlooking the water, with a conservatory restaurant and terrace cafe (open May to October). A handful of statues, a grotto and lookout points are also here.

★**Pfaffenteich**   LAKE

Schwerin's central lake was created by a dam in the 12th century. Through the centuries it was surrounded by some of the city's most elegant buildings. At the southwest corner, the vividly orange **Arsenal** (Alexandrinenstrasse 1) dates from 1840. You can cross the waters on a small **ferry** (Pfaffentiech; adult/child €2/1; ☺10am-6pm Tue-Sun Apr-Sep) that makes four stops.

Galerie Alte & Neue Meister   MUSEUM
(Gallery of Old & New Masters; ☑0385-595 80; www.museum-schwerin.de; Alter Garten 3; adult/child €8/free; ☺10am-6pm Tue-Sun & noon-8pm Thu mid-Apr–mid-Oct, 10am-5pm Tue-Sun & 1-8pm Thu other times) Revel in the Flemish masterpieces collected by the Mecklenburg dukes in the 17th and 18th centuries at this impressive museum with wide-ranging collections. Works include oils by Lucas Cranach the Elder, as well as paintings by

Schwerin

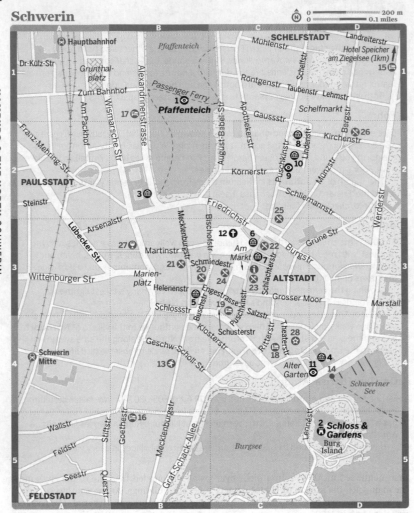

Brueghel, Rembrandt and Rubens. The 15 statues in the Ernst Barlach room provide a small taste of the sculptor's work. There's a typically amusing and irreverent Marcel Duchamp collection.

Schwerin Dom　　　　　　　CATHEDRAL
(📞 0385-565 014; www.dom-schwerin.de; Am Dom 4; tower adult/child €2/1; ⏱11am-5pm Mon-Sat, noon-5pm Sun) Above the Markt, the soaring Gothic Dom is a superb example of north German red-brick architecture. You can climb up to the viewing platform of its 19th-century cathedral tower (118m), which

is a mere 50cm taller than Rostock's Petri-kirche. Down on earth, check out the elaborately carved pews. Berlin's airport builders can take heart – construction lasted from 1270 to 1892.

Altstadt　　　　　　　HISTORIC SITE
The bustling **Markt** is home to the **Rathaus** and the colonnaded neoclassical **Neues Gebäude** (1780–83). The latter is fronted by a lion monument honouring the town's founder, Heinrich der Löwe. A walk southwest of the Rathaus to the appropriately named **Engestrasse** (Narrow Street) brings

Schwerin

you past a lovely example of the city's earliest **half-timbered houses** (Buschstrasse 15), which dates back to 1698.

Schelfstadt SQUARE
North of the Markt along Puschkinstrasse is Schelfstadt, a planned baroque village that was autonomous until Schwerin's mid-19th-century expansion. The restored 1737 **Schleswig-Holstein-Haus** (☑ 0385-555 524; www.schwerin.de; Puschkinstrasse 12; admission varies; ◎ 10am-6pm) contains a gallery that features changing contemporary art exhibitions. Just north of here is the early-18th-century baroque **Schelfkirche** (Nikolaikirche) and **Schelfmarkt**, the former town market, with its half-timbered surrounds.

Cycling Routes CYCLING
Schwerin is a great place to bike. There are routes short and long around the city and out into the countryside. The tourist office can offer advice. Ask for the **Stadt-Rund-Tour** (City Round Trip) map which covers the area's most important and beautiful sights in 18km.

Fahrrad Rachow BICYCLE RENTAL
(☑ 0385-565 795; www.fahrradrachow.de; Mecklenburgstrasse 59; per day from €7; ◎ 9am-6pm Mon-Fri, 10am-1pm Sat) Excellent long-running shop with a big selection of rental bikes. Usually has a summer location in the train station with longer hours.

◎ Tours

Weisse Flotte BOAT TOUR
(☑ 0385-557 770; www.weisseflotteschwerin.de; Werderstrasse; adult/child from €13.50/7; ◎ Apr-Oct) Choose from three different 90-minute tours of Schwerin's lakes and waterways.

◎ Festivals & Events

Schlossfestspiele THEATRE
(www.theater-schwerin.de; ◎ Jul) The highlight of Schwerin's cultural calendar is the Schlossfestspiele, when open-air opera concerts are performed on a stage near the Burggarten.

◎ Sleeping

Hostel Heintzes Töchter HOSTEL €
(☑ 0385-479 2968; www.hostel-schwerin.de; Werderstrasse 49; dm/d from €15/50, breakfast €4.50; ◎ reception 8am-10pm; @ ⑦) Rent a bike, do laundry or just enjoy the vibe at this well-located 35-bed indie hostel. There's a back terrace for chilling or grilling.

★ **Hotel Niederländischer Hof** HOTEL €€
(☑ 0385-591 100; www.niederlaendischer-hof. de; Karl-Marx-Strasse 12-13; s/d from €100/115; P ⑦) Overlooking the Pfaffenteich, this regal 1901-established hotel has 33 elegant rooms with black marble bathrooms, a library warmed by an open fire, and a lauded restaurant. The decor is plushly period with whimsical touches.

Zur guten Quelle
HOTEL €€

(☑ 0385-565 985; www.zur-guten-quelle.m-vp.de; Schusterstrasse 12; s/d from €60/90; 🅿 🛜) One of Schwerin's prettiest half-timbered houses, bang in the heart of the Altstadt. Zur guten Quelle is known for its cosy traditional restaurant and beer garden, but it also has six simple but comfortable rooms. Many have ancient timbers running right through the rooms.

Hotel Am Schloss
PENSION €€

(☑ 0385-593 230; www.hotel-am-schloss.m-vp.de; Heinrich-Mann-Strasse 3; s/d from €70/95; 🅿 🛜) There are 25 modern rooms spread across seven floors served by a lift in this basic but comfortable pension. It is located in an old commercial bakery and warehouse. Take tram 3, 5, 7 or 19 from the train station to Schlossblick.

Hotel Speicher am Ziegelsee
HOTEL €€

(☑ 500 30; www.speicher-hotel.de; Speicher-strasse 11; s/d from €85/105; 🅿 😊 @ 🛜) This tall heritage-listed former warehouse with a waterfront location and its own pier has been fitted out with streamlined rooms in comforting neutral hues. You can unwind in its spa, bar and fine-dining restaurant. It's 2km north of the Dom.

Pension am Theater
PENSION €€

(☑ 0385-593 680; www.pensionamtheater.m-vp. de; Theaterstrasse 1-2; s/d from €60/80; 🅿 😊) In the shadow of the huge theatre building and (just) within sight of the castle, this ideally located pension has 18 warm-hued, stylish and spacious rooms. It's a low-key place, although if you get one of the rooms with a terrace, you will have scored!

🍴 Eating & Drinking

★ Rösterei Fuchs
CAFE €

(☑ 0385-593 8444; www.roesterei-fuchs.de; Am Markt 4; mains €4-8; ⊘ 9am-8pm Mon-Fri, to 6pm Sat & Sun) The aroma of fresh coffee fills this chic cafe, which roasts its own coffee in-house and also sells beans as well as gourmet chocolates. Drop by for an espresso or other warming drink. Breakfasts are fresh and healthy while sandwiches and beautiful baked goods fill out the day. Outside tables peek at the Rathaus.

Die Suppenstube
CAFE €

(☑ 0172 382 5038; Puschkinstrasse 55; mains €4-6; ⊘ 11am-4pm Mon-Fri; 😊) Light fittings made from cutlery, stripped floorboards and bare tables provide a minimalist contrast with the historic half-timbered walls of this house on the edge of the Markt. The soups here are tops, as are the desserts. Hide out in the small beer garden out back.

Zum Freischütz
PUB FOOD €

(☑ 0385-561 431; www.zum-freischuetz.de; Ziegen-markt 11; mains €6-10; ⊘ 11am-late Mon-Fri, 6pm-late Sat & Sun) Overlooking Schwerin's old goat market (note the life-size bronze goat), this storied, characterful pub has an old interior that features wooden chairs dating back decades. When one collapses, there's free beer. Sandwiches, soups and various cheap specials are served long into the night.

Konditorei & Cafe Rothe
CAFE €

(☑ 0385-564 148; www.cafe-rothe.de; Am Markt 11; snacks from €3; ⊘ 9am-7pm Mon-Sat, to 6pm Sun) Much better than your usual city main square cafe, Rothe has superlative cakes, tarts and other delights. Ponder all the pleasure in the glass display cases, then settle back with a coffee drink outside while watching the passing parade.

Der Käseladen Mühlenberg
DELI €

(☑ 0385-568 328; Mecklenburgstrasse 37; snacks from €2; ⊘ 9am-6pm Mon-Fri, 9am-2.30pm Sat) A beautiful cheese store. The engaging owner will help you assemble a fabulous picnic to enjoy in the Schlossgarten.

Weinhaus Wöhler
GERMAN €€

(☑ 0385-555 830; www.weinhaus-woehler.de; Puschkinstrasse 26; mains €9-22; ⊘ 11.30am-2.30pm Tue-Sun, 5.30-10pm Tue-Sat; 🛜) In addition to wood-lined dining rooms dimly lit by stained glass, a large beer garden and a tapas/cocktail bar, this historic (1895) half-timbered inn also offers 12 upscale rooms (€80 to €150). The seasonal regional menu is best enjoyed amid the grape vines on the terrace.

★ Buschérie
MODERN EUROPEAN €€€

(☑ 0385-923 6066; www.buscherie.de; Buschstrasse 9; mains €16-25; ⊘ 11.30am-late) Although historic and half-timbered, Buschstrasse is very much the modern bistro. Enjoy seasonal foods of the region at an outdoor table with the Dom seeming to loom overhead. From mains to small plates, everything is well priced. Stop in for just a glass of wine from the long list and listen to live jazz some nights.

Zum Stadtkrug
BREWERY

(☑ 0385-593 6693; www.altstadtbrauhaus.de; Wismarsche Strasse 126; mains €10-20; ⊘ 11am-11pm)

The dark beer brewery at this 1936-established pub consistently rates among the best in Germany. It's full of antique brewing equipment, and it opens to an inviting beer garden. The menu features a familiar – albeit well-prepared – assortment of schnitzels and porky mains. Sandwiches are excellent.

☆ Entertainment

Staatstheater Schwerin THEATRE
(☎0385-530 00; www.theater-schwerin.de; Alter Garten) The state theatre offers a varied range of concerts and theatrical performances.

🛍 Shopping

Schwerin has huge malls like those around **Marienplatz**, but the real fun is found in the many interesting little shops. Stroll **Buschstrasse** for everything from handmade goods to model trains and **Münzstrasse** for a string of creative boutiques.

ℹ Information

Tourist Office (☎0385-592 5212; www.schwerin.com; Rathaus, Am Markt 14; ⊙9am-6pm Mon-Fri, 10am-6pm Sat & Sun)

ℹ Getting There & Around

Hourly train links include Hamburg (from €29, one hour), Rostock (from €18, one hour), Stralsund (from €32, two hours) and Wismar (€9, 30 minutes).

Buses and trams cost €1.80/5.50 for a single/day pass.

Güstrow

☎03843 / POP 30,500
Best known for its stately Renaissance Schloss, this charming 775-plus-year-old town is also the place where famed 20th-century sculptor Ernst Barlach spent most of his working life. You can view dozens of his deeply felt, humanist works at several locations.

◉ Sights

Güstrow has been beautifully restored and you can spend a couple of good hours just wandering its cobblestoned streets in the old town. Be sure to check out the **fountain** with an imposing statue of Prince Heinrich Borwin II, who founded the town in 1228. It is at the crux of the both ancient and modern commercial street, **Pferdemarkt** (horse market).

WORTH A TRIP

LUDWIGSLUST

Schloss Ludwigslust (☎03874-571 90; www.schloss-ludwigslust.de; Schloss Strasse, Ludwigslust; adult/child €3.50/free; ⊙10am-6pm Tue-Sun mid-Apr–mid-Oct, to 5pm mid-Oct–mid-Apr) Such was the allure of this palace, that when the ducal seat moved 36km north to Schwerin in 1837, some family members continued living here until 1945. Now part of the Schwerin State Museum, its high point is the stately, gilt-columned, high-ceilinged **Golden Hall**. After lavish renovations, the East Wing is set to reopen in 2016.

A planned baroque town, Ludwigslust showcases a neat, orderly layout that is an attraction in itself.

Trains run from Schwerin every two hours (€9, one hour).

A bike is a good way to explore the various Barlach sights.

Schloss Güstrow PALACE
(☎03843-7520; www.schloss-guestrow.de; Franz-Parr-Platz 1; adult/child €5/3.50; ⊙10am-6pm Tue-Sun mid-Apr–mid-Oct, to 5pm mid-Oct–mid-Apr) Güstrow's fabulous Renaissance 16th-century Schloss is home to an historical museum as well as a cultural centre, period art exhibitions and occasional concerts. You can tour rooms that recall the luxe excesses of its royal residents. The formal **gardens** are an exercise in orderly flora.

Güstrow Dom CATHEDRAL
(www.dom-guestrow.de; Philipp-Brandin-Strasse 5; ⊙10am-5pm daily mid-May–mid-Oct, reduced hours rest of year) Built between 1226 and 1335, the richly ornamented Gothic Dom contains a copy of Ernst Barlach's *Hovering Angel*, a memorial for the fallen soldiers of WWI; this copy was made secretly from the original mould after the Nazis destroyed the original sculpture.

Gertrudenkapelle GALLERY
(☎03843-844 000; Gertrudenplatz 1; adult/child €4/2.50; ⊙10am-5pm Tue-Sun Apr-Oct, 11am-4pm Tue-Sun Nov-Mar) The Ernst Barlach memorial in the Gertrudenkapelle displays many of his original works. It is about 300m west of the Pferdemarkt fountain in a large grassy park surrounded by housing.

Atelierhaus GALLERY
(☑ 03843-822 99; www.ernst-barlach-stiftung.de; Heidberg 15; adult/child €6/4; ☺ 10am-5pm Tue-Sun Apr-Oct, 11am-4pm Tue-Sun Nov-Mar) Based on sketches he made in Russia, Ernst Barlach's squarish sculptures began bearing the same expressive gestures and hunched-over, wind-blown postures of the impoverished people he encountered. Banned by the Nazis, he died in 1938; after the war his works gained full appreciation.

Many of his bronze and wood carvings are housed along with a biographical exhibition at his former studio, the Atelierhaus, 4km south of the city at Inselsee; take bus 204 or 205.

Fahrradhaus Karasch BICYCLE RENTAL
(☑ 03843-681 193; fahrradhaus-karasch.de; Speicherstrasse 1; per day from €9; ☺ 9am-6pm Mon-Fri, 9am-noon Sat) Directly across from the train station. Another good source is the Gästehaus Am Schlosspark.

🛌 Sleeping & Eating

Güstrow is a good day trip from across the region but by spending the night, you might just hear the echoes of the regal past on the cobblestones.

Gästehaus Am Schlosspark HOTEL €
(☑ 03843-245 990; www.gaestehaus-guestrow.de; Neuwieder Weg; s/d from €50/60; 🅿 @ 🛜) This great-value hotel overlooks the Schloss and its gardens. Most of the 100 modern rooms have views and some have small kitchen facilities. You can rent bikes (from €9 per day) to explore the area.

Cafe Küpper CAFE €
(☑ 03843-682 485; Domstrasse 15; cakes from €3; ☺ 9am-6pm) The perfect pause for your Güstrow visit. This cafe has been creating luscious cakes in the shadow of the Dom since 1852.

ℹ️ Information

Güstrow Information (☑ 03843-681 023; www.guestrow-tourismus.de; Franz-Parr-Platz 10; ☺ 9am-7pm Mon-Fri, 10am-5pm Sat, 11am-5pm Sun May-Sep, closes 1 hour earlier rest of year) A good info source; there is a small free musuem covering Güstrow's history. Tours are offered.

ℹ️ Getting There & Around

Trains leave for Güstrow once or twice an hour from Rostock's Hauptbahnhof (€9, 25 minutes).

Services to/from Schwerin require a change in Bad Kleinen. The station is 700m northwest of the Pferdemarkt fountain.

Neubrandenburg

☑ 0395 / POP 65,900
Neubrandenburg has few pretensions. It bills itself as 'the city of four gates on the Tollensesee Lake', and that's pretty well what it is. A largely intact medieval wall, with those gates, encircles the 13th-century Altstadt (bustling with shoppers, who ignore some harsh GDR architecture). It is an interesting stop.

⊙ Sights

City Wall HISTORIC SITE
Neubrandenburg was founded in 1248 by Herbord von Raven, a Mecklenburg knight granted the land by Brandenburg Margrave Johann I, and building progressed in the usual order: defence system, church, town hall, pub. The security system was the 2.3km-long, 7.5m-high stone wall that survives today, with four city gates and 56 sentry posts built into it.

To navigate the circular wall, consider it as the rim of a clock face. The train station is at 12 o'clock.

The **Friedländer Tor** (2 o'clock), begun in 1300 and completed in 1450, was the first gate. **Treptower Tor** (9 o'clock) is the largest and contains an archaeological collection.

At the southern end of the city is the gaudy **Stargarder Tor** (6 o'clock). The simple brick **Neues Tor** (3 o'clock) fronts the east side of the Altstadt.

Southwest of the train station (at about 11 o'clock) is the city's former dungeon, the **Fangelturm**. You'll recognise it by its pointy tower.

Wedged into the stone circumference are the 27 sweet **half-timbered houses** that remain of the original sentry posts. When firearms rendered such defences obsolete in the 16th century, the guardhouses were converted into *Wiekhäuser*, homes for the poor, disadvantaged and elderly. Most of the surviving homes are now craft shops, galleries and cafes.

🍴 Eating

Wiekhaus 45 GERMAN €€
(☑ 0395-566 7762; www.wiekhaus45.de; 4th Ringstrasse 44; mains €9-20; ☺ 11am-11.30pm) Easily the most-appealing place to eat in Neu-

brandenburg is this renovated guardhouse set into the wall. Waiters zip up and down the narrow stairwell carrying huge portions of Mecklenburg specialities (start with the tasty onion soup served with fresh bread; look for fresh herring in season). There are outside tables in summer.

ℹ Information

Stadt Info (☎ 0395-194 33; www.neubranden-burg-touristinfo.de; Marktplatz 1; ⏱10am-6pm Mon-Fri, 10am-4pm Sat) Located in the centre of the old town in the newly renovated Haus der Kultur und Bildung.

ℹ Getting There & Away

Train service runs on two-hour intervals to/from Berlin (€30, 1¾ hours) and Stralsund (€18, 1¼ hours).

COASTAL MECKLENBURG – WESTERN POMERANIA

This spectacular stretch of the Baltic coast is certainly one of Europe's better-kept secrets. But Germans know better and flock in summer to its dazzling clean, white sand and glittering seas.

Hotspots during the all-too-brief beach-going season include three leafy resort islands: sprawling, villa-lined Rügen; car-free Hiddensee; and Usedom (which Germany shares with Poland). Warnemünde, the seaside resort near Rostock, is another sandy hotspot – when it's hot.

Stralsund is the prize town of the region, combining seaside charms with beautiful, old architecture. Other highlights include the gracious university town of Greifswald, which retains some exquisite medieval architecture, as does Wismar.

Rostock

☎ 0381 / POP 202,900

Rostock was devastated in WWII and later pummelled by socialist architectural 'ideals'. Its best feature – Warnemünde, which has one of Germany's most appealing beaches – is 13km northwest, where the Warnow River flows into the Baltic Sea.

This large port city *does* have small but attractive historic enclaves – but you generally have to wade past a landscape of concrete

MÜRITZ NATIONAL PARK

Müritz is commonly known as the land of a thousand lakes. While that's an exaggeration, there are well over 100 lakes here, as well as countless ponds, streams and rivers in this beautiful land midway between Berlin and Rostock.

Müritz National Park (☎ 039824-2520; www.mueritz-nationalpark.de) This serene national park consists of bog and wetlands, and is home to a wide range of waterfowl, including ospreys, white-tailed eagles and cranes. Its two main sections sprawl over 300 sq km to the east and (mainly) west of Neustrelitz, where the park's waterway begins on the Zierker See. Boardwalks and other features let you get close to nature.

The country road between Neustrelitz and Waren to the west cuts through the heart of the park and offers plenty of places to stop and admire the **beech forests**, which have been recognised by Unesco.

eyesores to reach them. Perhaps its best feature is the vibrant energy provided by the 11,000 university students.

◉ Sights

It takes just a couple of hours to see the city sights, which are found in the pedestrianised zone between Neuer Markt and Universitätsplatz, as well as the Alter Markt.

★ **Marienkirche** CHURCH
(☎ 0381-453 325; www.marienkirche-rostock. de; Am Ziegenmarkt; €1.50 donation requested; ⏱10am-6pm Mon-Sat, 11am-5pm Sun May-Sep, 10am-4pm Mon-Sat, 11am-noon Sun Oct-Apr) Central Rostock's pride and joy is the 13th-century Marienkirche, the only main Rostock church to survive WWII unscathed (although restorations are ongoing). Behind the main altar, the church's 12m-high **astrological clock** was built in 1472 by Hans Düringer. At the very top of the clock is a series of doors. At noon and midnight the innermost right door opens and six of the 12 apostles march out to parade around Jesus (Judas is locked out).

Zodiac symbols and moon phases feature in the centre, while the lower section has a disc that tells the exact day on which Easter falls in any given year. The replaceable discs are accurate for 130 years – the current one expires in 2017, and a new one is ready. The clock is the only one of its kind in the world still with its original mechanisms.

Also note the unusually tall, organically shaped **baroque organ** (1770).

Alter Markt   SQUARE
Red-brick and pastel-coloured buildings on this large market square hark back to the 14th- and 15th-century Hanseatic era.

Petrikirche   CHURCH
(🕿 0381-211 01; www.petrikirche-rostock.de; Alter Markt; tower adult/child €3/2; ☉ tower 10am-6pm May-Sep, 10am-4pm Oct-Apr) The Gothic Petrikirche has a 117m-high steeple – a mariner's landmark for centuries – that was restored in 1994, having been missing since WWII. There's a lift up to the 45m-high viewing platform.

Neuer Markt   SQUARE
Rostock's large, somewhat bland central square is dominated by the splendid 13th-century **Rathaus**. The building's baroque facade was added in 1727 after the original brick Gothic structure collapsed.

Opposite the Rathaus is a series of restored **gabled houses** and a stylised, sea-themed fountain, the **Möwenbrunnen** (2001), by artist Waldemar Otto. The explanatory plaque says the four figures are Neptune and his sons, although many believe they represent the four elements.

Kröpeliner Strasse &
Universitätsplatz   STREET, SQUARE
Kröpeliner Strasse, a broad, shop-filled, cobblestone pedestrian mall lined with 15th- and 16th-century burghers' houses, runs from Neuer Markt west to Kröpeliner Tor.

At the centre of the mall is Universitätsplatz, and its centrepiece, the crazy rococo **Brunnen der Lebensfreude** (Fountain of Happiness; some of the people and animals shown seem to be engaging in acts deemed illegal in more religiously conservative places). True to its name, the square

---

STRANDKORB

Only a country with a love of engineering and nontropical coasts would invent the *Strandkorb*, the iconic German wicker beach chair complete with its own roof and awning to deflect seaside breezes.

---

is lined with university buildings, including the handsome terracotta **Hauptgebäude** (1866–70), which replaced the famous 'White College'. The university itself is the oldest on the Baltic (founded in 1419).

Kulturhistorisches
Museum Rostock   MUSEUM
(🕿 0381-203 590; www.kulturhistorisches-museum-rostock.de; Klosterhof 7; ☉ 10am-6pm Tue-Sun) **FREE** The city's cultural history museum has an interesting collection including Victorian furniture and a few sculptures by Ernst Barlach. It's housed in the Kloster Zum Heiligen Kreuz, a convent established in 1270 by Queen Margrethe of Denmark.

City Walls & Gates   HISTORIC SITE
Today only two of 32 gates, plus a small brick section, remain of the old city wall. The 55m-high **Kröpeliner Tor** stands at the western end of Kröpeliner Strasse. From here, you can follow the *Wallanlagen* (city walls) through the pleasant park to Wallstrasse and the other surviving gate, the **Steintor**.

🕝 Tours

Reederei Schütt   BOAT TOUR
(🕿 0381-690 953; www.hafenrundfahrten-in-rostock.de; Stadthafen; harbour cruise adult/child €15/7.50; ☉ daily May-Oct) Offers some round-harbour trips and services from Rostock's harbour to Warnemünde (one-way/return €10/14); the pier is at the base of Schnickmannstrasse.

🛏 Sleeping

Hanse Hostel   HOSTEL €
(🕿 0381-128 6006; www.hanse-hostel.de; Doberaner Strasse 136; dm €14-18, r €24-56, breakfast €5.50; ☻@🖰) On the edge of Rostock's trendy bar district, the KTV, is this family-run operation with great facilities. Some private rooms share bathrooms. From the Hauptbahnhof, take tram 4 or 5 to the Kabutzenhof stop.

Hotel Verdi   HOTEL €€
(🕿 0381-252 240; www.hotel-verdi.de; Wollenweberstrasse 28; s/d/apt €70/90/100; 🖰) Opening to an umbrella-shaded, timber-decked terrace is this sparkling little hotel near the Petrikirche and Alter Markt, with a handful of attractively decorated rooms (some with kitchenettes), and two apartments with views.

Eating

Café Central CAFÉ €€
(☑0381-490 4648; Leonhardstrasse 20; mains €6-15; ⊙9am-late) In the heart of the KTV bar scene, Café Central has cult status among Rostock locals. Students, artists, hipsters and suited-up professionals all loll around sipping long drinks on the banquettes or at tables out front. There are a lot of cheap ethnic restaurants nearby. It's 500m northwest of the Kröpeliner Tor.

Zur Kogge GERMAN €€
(☑0381-493 4493; www.zur-kogge.de; Wokrenterstrasse 27; mains €9-20; ⊙11am-9pm Mon-Sat; ☻) At this Rostock institution, cosy wooden booths are lined with stained-glass Hanseatic coats of armour and monster fish threatening sailing ships, while life preservers hang from the walls, and ships lanterns are suspended from the ceiling. Local fish dishes dominate the menu.

Ursprung GERMAN €€
(☑0381-459 1983; www.ursprung-rostock.de; Alter Markt 16; mains €7-20; ⊙5pm-late Mon-Sat, from 10am Sun) You can let the hours slip past from one of the terrace tables here overlooking the historic square. The German food is typically hearty and well-priced. On many nights, the interior rocks to live bands.

🍷 Drinking & Nightlife

West of the Altstadt lies the student and nightlife district Kröpeliner Torvorstadt, commonly known as KTV.

Live gigs, DJs, concerts and a host of other events are listed at www.szenerostock.de.

★Studentenkeller Rostock BAR
(☑0381-455 928; www.studentenkeller.de; Universitätsplatz 5; ⊙5pm-late Tue-Sat) This cellar and garden joint has been rocking Rostock's learned youth for years. Check the website for parties, DJ sets and other events.

Mau Club CLUB
(☑0381-202 3576; www.mauclub.de; Warnowufer 56; ⊙varies by event) Everything from indie to punk to house infuses this former storage hall. It's well known for up-and-coming acts.

ℹ Information

Tourist-Information Rostock (☑0381-381 2222; www.rostock.de; Universitätsplatz 6; Rostock Card 24-/48-hours €12/16; ⊙10am-6pm Mon-Fri, 10am-3pm Sat & Sun May-Oct, 10am-5pm Mon-Fri, 10am-3pm Sat Nov-Apr)

Sells the Rostock Card, which is good for public transport and discounts to some attractions.

ℹ Getting There & Away

BOAT
Ferries sail to/from Denmark, Sweden, Latvia and Finland. Boats depart from the Überseehafen (overseas seaport), which is on the east side of the Warnow. Take tram 3 or 4 from the Hauptbahnhof, then change for bus 49 to Seehafen. There's an S-Bahn stop at Seehafen, but it's a 20-minute walk from the station to the piers.

TRAIN
There are frequent direct trains to Berlin (from €42, 2½ hours) and Hamburg (from €37, 2¼ hours), and hourly services to Stralsund (€16, one hour) and Schwerin (€18, one hour).

ℹ Getting Around

Journeys within Rostock cost €2/4.90 for a single/day pass. The Hauptbahnhof is about 1.5km south of the Altstadt.

Trams 5 and 6 travel from the Hauptbahnhof up Steinstrasse, around the very central Marienkirche and down Lange Strasse to the university.

Warnemünde

☑0381
Warnemünde is all about promenading, eating fish, sipping cocktails, and lazing in a *Strandkörbe* (sheltered straw 'beach basket' seat) on its long, wide and startlingly white **beach**.

Walking from Warnemünde's train station along **Alter Strom**, the boat-lined main canal, you'll pass a row of quaint cottages housing restaurants. Then you turn the corner into Am Leuchtturm and Seestrasse and see the sand.

For a fabulous view from above, climb the spiralling 135-step wrought-iron and granite staircase of the 1898-built **lighthouse**.

🛏 Sleeping

There are scads of places to stay. The tourist office website (www.warnemuende.de) is useful for ferreting out a bed.

Residenz Strandhotel HOTEL €€
(☑0381-548 060; www.residenz-strandhotel.de; Seestrasse 6; s/d from €90/155; P☻❄@☎) The balcony-clad exterior of this hotel manages to be somewhat attractive (an accomplishment locally). Inside, you'll find stylish rooms; go on, splurge for one with a seaview balcony.

HAMBURG & THE NORTH WARNEMÜNDE

Hotel-Pension Zum Kater GUESTHOUSE €€

(☑0381-548 210; www.pension-zum-kater.de; Alexandrinenstrasse 115; s/d from €75/110; ℙ) The beach is less than 10 minutes' stroll from this 19-room guesthouse. There's a supplement if you stay less than three nights on high-season weekends. Get a room with a roof terrace.

✖ Eating & Drinking

Fish – fresh, fried, baked, smoked, you name it – is the order of the day here. Both banks of the harbour are lined with kiosks and caravans selling inexpensive fish sandwiches – perfect if you're heading to the beach or a nearby bench along the harbourfront.

Fischerklause SEAFOOD €€

(☑0381-525 16; www.fischer-klause.de; Am Strom 123; mains €9-15; ⊙11.30am-10pm, closed Mon Nov-Mar; ☎) Fischerklause is one of the atmospheric salty seadog joints lining the western bank of Alter Strom, and attracts plenty of tourists (as does all of Warnemünde). Still, its ship's cabin decor (think topless mermaid statues) and its tasty seafood make it worth seeking out.

Brasserie MODERN EUROPEAN €€€

(☑0381-504 00; www.hohe-duene.de; Am Yachthafen 1, Hohe Dune; mains from €20; ⊙noon-10pm; ℙ) The views from the terrace are worth it alone, but the food at this creative restaurant is excellent. Seasonal produce goes into menus that feature locally caught seafood. Long lunches with wine are a good time to survey the yacht harbour. It's on the east side of the channel in the Hohe Dune resort. Book in season.

STRAWBERRY SURPRISE

Karls (☑0382-024 050; www.karls.de; Purkshof 2, off B105; ⊙8am-8pm May-Sep, to 7pm Oct-Apr; ♿) Gloriously hokey, Karls is a roadside attraction in the cheesiest tradition. The schtick here is fruit, strawberries to be exact. In this sprawling hodge-podge of a petting zoo, shops, playgrounds, shops, cafes and, yes, strawberry fields, you will find something for *anyone* in the family. The fresh strawberry ice cream (€1) is really good. Watch them make preserves, then listen to the mechanical bears sing Elvis. Karls is about 12km northeast of Rostock.

Schusters BAR

(☑0381-700 7835; www.schusters-strandbar.de; Seepromenade 1; ⊙10am-late Apr-Oct) Head here for sunset cocktails. It has a hip summer pavilion on the beach, not far from the iconic lighthouse.

❶ Getting There & Around

There are frequent S-Bahn trains between Rostock and Warnemünde (single/day pass €2/4.90, 22 minutes). You can also get a tour boat (p700).

Baltic Coastal Resorts

☑038203

Heiligendamm and Kühlungsborn are among the atmospheric beach resorts along the starkly beautiful coast west of Rostock.

Molli is a popular tourist train that travels along the coast from Bad Doberan. Alternate between taking the train and walking between stops for a gorgeous day out along the often wild Baltic shore.

◎ Sights & Activities

Heiligendamm BEACH

The 'white town on the sea' is Germany's oldest seaside resort, founded in 1793 by Mecklenburg duke Friedrich Franz I, and was fashionable throughout the 19th century as a playground of the nobility. You won't be able to miss the five gleaming white, heritage-listed buildings of the **Grand Hotel Heiligendamm** (www.grandhotel-heiligendamm.de) perched nearly on the beach.

Kühlungsborn BEACH

Kühlungsborn, the biggest Baltic Sea resort, with some 7500 inhabitants, has some lovely art deco buildings backing the beach and adjoining a dense 130-hectare forest. The east and west ends of the sand are linked by the Ostseeallee promenade, lined with hotels and restaurants.

★ Molli STEAM TRAIN

(Mecklenburger Bäderbahn Molli; ☑038293-431 331; www.molli-bahn.de; Bad Doberan Bahnhof; return adult/child €13.50/9.50; ⊙year-round; ♿) This historic steam train departs Bad Doberan's train station (where it links to the rail network) on average 11 times a day.

With a maximum speed of 45km/h, the train takes 15 minutes to reach the coast at Heiligendamm and 45 minutes in total to Kühlungsborn/West, with interim stops in Steilküste, Kühlungsborn/East and Kühlungsborn/Mitte.

Children love the dinky engine and carriages. There's a salon car on many journeys and the scenery is the best on the coast.

In 1886, the steam train 'Molli', as she's affectionately known, began huffing and puffing her way to Heiligendamm, carrying Germany's elite. In 1910, the line was extended west along the coast to Kühlungsborn.

For a particularly easy and enjoyable **walk**, you can get off at Heiligendamm and walk to the Steilküste station before picking up the train again.

Wismar

📞 03841 / POP 44,800

With its gabled facades and cobbled streets, this small, photogenic city looks essentially Hanseatic. But although it joined the Hanseatic trading league in the 13th century, it spent most of the 16th and 17th centuries as part of Sweden. There are numerous reminders of this era all over town. The entire Altstadt was Unesco-listed in 2002.

Wismar has been long popular with film-makers and its picturesque *Alter Hafen* (old harbour) starred in the 1922 Dracula movie *Nosferatu*.

◉ Sights & Activities

Wismar's Altstadt centres on the Markt, said to be the largest medieval town square in northern Germany. Wandering the sights can easily occupy a half day.

★ St-Nikolai-Kirche   CHURCH
(St-Nikolai-Kirchhof; www.kirchen-in-wismar.de; St-Nikolai-Kirkhof; admission €2; ⊙8am-8pm May-Sep, 10am-6pm Apr & Oct, 11am-4pm Nov-Mar) Of the three great red-brick churches that once rose above the rooftops before WWII, only the sober St-Nikolai-Kirche, the largest of its kind in Europe, was left intact. It has elaborate carvings and a font from its older sister church, the St-Marien-Kirche. The linden-tree-shaded **churchyard** is next to a small canal and is Wismar's loveliest spot.

Markt   SQUARE
Dominating the middle of the Markt is the 1602-built **Wasserkunst** (waterworks), an ornate, 12-sided well that supplied Wismar's drinking water until 1897 and is the town's landmark.

WORTH A TRIP

THE CHURCH OF 1.2 MILLION BRICKS

Münster Bad Doberan (📞038203-627 16; www.muenster-doberan.de; Klosterstrasse 2; adult/child €3/1; ⊙9am-6pm Mon-Sat, 11am-6pm Sun May-Sep, shorter hours rest of the year) The former summer ducal residence of Bad Doberan, about 15km west of Rostock, was once the site of a powerful Cistercian monastery. Construction of this magnificent Gothic church started in 1280 but the scale of the building meant it wasn't consecrated until 1368. Its treasures include an intricate **high altar** and an ornate **pulpit**.

Trains connect Bad Doberan with Rostock Hauptbahnhof (€9, 25 minutes) and Wismar (€9, 45 minutes) roughly hourly. The train station is 1km south of the Münster.

A massive restoration has made every one of the cathedral's 1.2 million bricks look like new – almost too new.

Organ recitals, as well as choir and band performances, are held from May to September, usually on Friday evenings at 7.30pm.

Behind it stands the red-brick **Alter Schwede**, which dates from 1380 and features a striking step buttress gable facade. It houses a restaurant and guesthouse, as well as a copy of one of the so-called Swedish Heads (see p704).

Rathaus   MUSEUM
(Markt; exhibition adult/child €3/2; ⊙exhibition 9am-5pm Apr-Sep, 10am-4pm Oct-Mar) The large Rathaus at the Markt's northern end was built between 1817 and 1819 and houses the excellent **Rathaus Historical Exhibition** in its basement. Displays include an original 15th-century *Wandmalerei* (mural) uncovered by archaeologists in 1985, a glass-covered medieval well, and the Wrangel tomb – the coffin of influential Swedish General Helmut V Wrangel and his wife, with outsized wooden figures carved on top.

Fürstenhof   HISTORIC BUILDING
(Vor dem Fürstenhof) Between the St-Marien and St-Georgen churches lies the restored Italian Renaissance Fürstenhof, now the city courthouse. The facades are slathered

in terracotta reliefs depicting episodes from folklore and Wismar's history.

St-Georgen-Kirche
CHURCH

(St-Georgen-Kirchhof; tower adult/child €3/2; ⏱9am-5pm Apr-Oct, 10am-4pm Nov-Mar) The massive red shell of the St-Georgen-Kirche has been extensively reconstructed and while work continues, the intention is to use it for cultural (Abba cover bands!) and religious purposes. In 1945 a freezing populace was driven to burn what was left of the church's beautiful wooden statue of St George and the dragon. It was bombed only three weeks before the war ended. The tower can be climbed.

St-Marien-Kirche Steeple
TOWER

(St-Marien-Kichhof; tower adult/child €3/2; ⏱9am-5pm Apr-Oct, 10am-4pm Nov-Mar, tower 11am-3pm) All that remains of 13th-century St-Marien-Kirche is its great brick steeple (1339), which rises above the city. A multimedia exhibit on medieval church-building techniques is housed in the tower's base. The tower can be climbed.

Schabbellhaus
MUSEUM

(www.schabbellhaus.de; Schweinsbrücke 8) The town's historical museum is in the Renais-

sance Schabbellhaus in a former brewery (1571), just south of St-Nikolai-Kirche across the canal. It is undergoing massive reconstruction at least until 2017.

Buddha Bikes
BICYCLE RENTAL

(☑03841-473 6202; www.buddha-bikes.de; Dankwartstrasse 49; per day from €7; ⏱9.30am-12.30pm & 3-6.30pm Mon-Fri, 10am-2pm Sat) Rents a variety of bikes and has route info; one street south of the Markt.

👉 Tours

Adler-Schiffe
BOAT TOUR

(☑01805-123 344; www.adler-schiffe.de; Hafen 7; adult/child €12/6.50; ⏱daily Apr-Oct) The ubiquitous tour company operates hour-long harbour cruises.

🎊 Festivals & Events

Annual events include Wismar's **Hafenfest** (Harbour Festival) in mid-June, featuring old and new sailing ships and steamers, music and food, and a free **street theatre** festival in July/August. Wismar also holds a **Schwedenfest** on the third weekend of August, commemorating the end of Swedish rule in 1903.

🛌 Sleeping

The Altstadt is dotted with places to stay.

Pension Chez Fasan
PENSION €

(☑03841-213 425; www.unterkunft-pension-wismar.de; Bademutterstrasse 20a; s/d from €27/50; ⏱reception 2-8pm) The 25 simple but perfectly comfortable rooms in these three linked houses, just one block north of the Markt, are fantastic value. Call ahead to make sure someone's around to let you in.

⭐ Hotel Reingard
HOTEL €€

(☑03841-284 972; www.hotel-reingard.de; Weberstrasse 18; s/d from €72/90; 🅿🛜) 🌿 Wismar's most charming hotel has a dozen artistic rooms, a little garden and wonderfully idiosyncratic touches such as a lightshow to classical music that plays across the facade daily at 8.30pm. The breakfast includes apples from the owners' trees and eggs from their chickens.

🍴 Eating & Drinking

If you're feeling adventurous, try *Wismarer Spickaal* (young eel smoked in a way that's unique to the region).

Along the Alter Hafen, seafood (including delicious fish sandwiches and smoked fish)

A SWEDISH HEADS-UP

A 'Swedish head' isn't (in this case, at least) something you need to successfully assemble a flat-pack IKEA bookcase. In Wismar, Swedish Heads refers to two baroque busts of Hercules, which once stood on mooring posts at the harbour entrance.

Semicomical, with great curling moustaches, wearing lions as hats and painted in bright colours (one red-and-white, the other yellow-and-blue), the statues are believed to have marked either the beginning of the harbour or the navigable channels within it. It's thought that before this they were ships' figureheads.

The original heads were damaged when a Finnish barge rammed them in 1902, at which time replicas were made. One original is now in the **Schabbellhaus**, the town museum that's closed for renovation until at least 2017. Two replicas guard the Baumhaus in Wismar's *Alter Hafen* (old harbour). They're also a boon for Wismar's souvenir sellers.

is sold directly from a handful of bobbing boats. Most are open 9am to 6pm daily, and from 6am on Saturday during Wismar's weekly **fish market**.

★**Café Glücklich** CAFE €

(☑03841-796 9377; Schweinsbrücke 7; mains €3-8; ⊙9am-6pm Sun-Thu, to 8pm Fri & Sat) Amid a few galleries, this artful cafe serves Wismar's finest coffee drinks. Breakfasts are as beautiful as they are delicious, while the meat and cheese platters are a treat. Cakes, crumbles and more require you to save room for dessert.

Börners Nikolaiblick GERMAN €€

(☑03841-224 066; www.börners-nikolaiblick.de; Frische Grube 8; mains €6-13; ⊙11am-2pm & 5pm late Wed-Mon; 🐾) Just across the canal from the lovely St-Nikolai-Kirche churchyard, this friendly pub cooks up fine schnitzels and fish dishes. It has a good beer list and you can take a load off at a table outside. Kids get their own menu.

Brauhaus am Lohberg BREWERY

(☑03841-250 238; www.brauhaus-wismar.de; Kleine Hohe Strasse 15; mains €7-15; ⊙11am-late) This imposing brick half-timbered building was once home to the town's first brewery, which opened in 1452. After a long pause, beer is brewing again in enormous copper vats. Enjoy local classics like *Sauerfleisch* (sour-spiced pork) and seafood; live music cranks up throughout summer.

❶ Information

Tourist Information (☑03841-251 3025; www.wismar.de; Lübsche Strasse 23a, Welt Erbe Haus; ⊙9am-5pm Apr-Sep, 9am-5pm Nov-Mar) Has regional info as well as details on Wismar's Unesco-recognised heritage.

❶ Getting There & Around

Trains travel every hour to/from Rostock (€13, 70 minutes) and Schwerin (€9, 35 minutes). The train station is 400m north of the Markt near the Alter Hafen.

Stralsund

☑03831 / POP 57,900

Stralsund was once the second-most important member of the Hanseatic League, after Lübeck, and its square gables interspersed with Gothic turrets, ornate portals and vaulted arches make it one of the leading examples of *Backsteingotik* (classic red-brick

DARSS-ZINGST PENINSULA

Nature lovers and artists will be captivated by the Darss-Zingst Peninsula. This far-flung splinter of land is home to 60,000 **migratory cranes** every spring and autumn.

The area is, well, picturesque, so not surprisingly it's home to an artists colony in **Ahrenshoop** (www.ostseebad-ahrenshoop.de), which has an especially wild and windblown **beach**. The tiny town of **Prerow** is renowned for its model-ship-filled **seafarer's church** and lighthouse.

Gothic gabled architecture) in northern Germany.

This vibrant city's historic cobbled streets and many attractions make it an unmissable stop in the region. Since 1990, the Stralsund's elected representative in parliament has been prime minister Angela Merkel.

◉ Sights

Stralsund's Unesco-recognised Altstadt is effectively on its own island, surrounded by lakes and the sea. You can easily spend a day wandering here. Among all the careful restorations, you'll discover oddly leaning, unreconstructed 17th-century buildings.

Alter Markt SQUARE

(Old Market) Stralsund's main square is a hub of its architectural treasures.

★**Nikolaikirche** CHURCH

(☑03831-299 799; www.nikolai-stralsund.de; Alter Markt; adult/child €2/free; ⊙9am-7pm Mon-Sat, noon-5pm Sun May-Sep, 10am-6pm Mon-Sat, noon-4pm Sun Oct-Apr) The main portal of the soaring Nikolaikirche is reached via an entrance off the Alter Markt. This masterpiece of medieval architecture dates to 1270 and is modelled on Lübeck's Marienkirche. Its interior is redolent with colour and is filled with art treasures. The **main altar** (1708), designed by the baroque master Andreas Schlüter, shows the eye of God flanked by cherubs and capped by a depiction of the Last Supper.

Also worth a closer look are the **high altar** (1470), 6.7m wide and 4.2m tall, showing Jesus' entire life, and, behind the altar, a 1394-built (but no longer operational) **astronomical clock**.

Stralsund

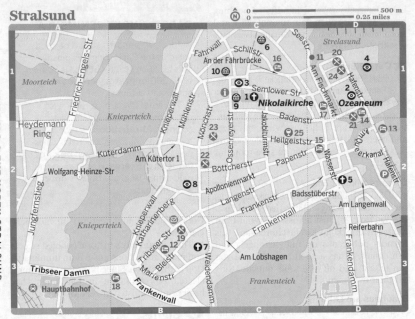

Rathaus
HISTORIC BUILDING

(Alter Markt) Seven copper turrets and six triangular gables grace the red-brick Gothic facade of the splendid 1370 Rathaus. The upper portion of the northern facade, or *Schauwand* (show wall), has openings to prevent strong winds from knocking it over. Inside, the sky-lit colonnade boasts shiny black pillars on carved and painted bases; on the western side of the building is an ornate portal.

Wulflamhaus
HISTORIC BUILDING

(Alter Markt 5) A beautiful 15th-century town house named after an old mayor, the turreted step gable imitates the Rathaus facade across the square.

Johanniskloster
HISTORIC BUILDING

(Schillstrasse 27) The Johanniskloster, a partially ruined former Franciscan monastery, is undergoing long-term restoration. It's famous for its 'smoking attic' (there was no chimney), chapter hall and cloister. Immediately west is a courtyard surrounded by small **medieval houses**.

Marienkirche
CHURCH

(☑03831-298 965; www.st-mariengemeinde-stralsund.de; Marienstrasse 16, off Neuer Markt; ☺9am-6pm) You'll need divine inspiration to guess the number of bricks used to build the massive 14th-century Marienkirche, a superb example of north German red-brick construction. You can climb the steep wooden steps up the tower for a sweeping view of the town, with its lovely red-tiled roofs, and Rügen Island. The ornate 17th-century **organ** is a stunner.

Meeresmuseum
AQUARIUM

(Maritime Museum; ☑03831-265 010; www.meeresmuseum.de; Katharinenberg 14-20; adult/child €9/4, combined ticket incl Ozeaneum €21/10; ☺10am-5pm daily Jul-Sep, 10am-5pm Tue-Sun Oct-Jun) The Meeresmuseum aquarium is in a 13th-century convent building. Exhibits include a very popular sea turtle tank and polychromatic tropical fish.

Heilgeistkirche
CHURCH

(Wasserstrasse) Don't miss the lovely ivy-covered face of this baroque 14th-century church.

Harbour Area

Stralsund has a deep relationship with the sea going back beyond Hanseatic times.

★Ozeaneum
AQUARIUM

(☑03831-265 0610; www.ozeaneum.de; Hafenstrasse 11; adult/child €16/7, combined ticket incl Meeresmuseum €21/10; ☺9.30am-8pm Jun-Sep, 9.30am-6pm Oct-May) In an arctic-white

Stralsund

◉ **Top Sights**
1 Nikolaikirche...C1
2 Ozeaneum..D1

◉ **Sights**
3 Alter Markt...C1
4 Gorch Fock 1...D1
5 Heilgeistkirche D2
6 Johanniskloster..C1
7 Marienkirche..B3
8 Meeresmuseum..B2
9 Rathaus...C1
10 Wulflamhaus..C1

◉ **Activities, Courses & Tours**
11 Weisse Flotte...D1

◉ **Sleeping**
12 Altstadt Hotel Peiss..................................B3

13 Hafenspeicher D2
14 Hiddenseer D1
15 Hotel Amber...D2
16 Hotel Scheelehof.......................................C1
17 Pension am Ozeaneum............................D1
18 Younior Hotel...B3

⊗ **Eating**
19 Brasserie Grand Café B3
20 Fischermann's..D1
21 Fischhalle..D1
22 Kaffeehaus Strahl.......................................B2
23 Nur Fisch...C2
24 Speicher 8..D1

◉ **Drinking & Nightlife**
25 T1...C2

wavelike building that leaps out from the surrounding red-brick warehouses, the state-of-the-art Ozeaneum takes you into an underwater world of creatures from the Baltic and North Seas and the Atlantic Ocean up to the polar latitudes. In a huge tank you can see what thousands of herring do before they end up dropping down northerner gullets.

Gorch Fock 1   SHIP
(☑03831-666 520; www.gorchfock1.de; Hafen; adult/child €4.50/2.50; ⊙10am-6pm Apr-Sep, to 4pm Oct-Mar) Built as a training ship by the German navy in 1933, the *Gorch Fock 1* is an 82m-long, steel three-masted barque with a history. The Russians took her as war booty and from there she went to Ukraine and the UK before ending up back in Stralsund, her original home port. As restoration continues, plans call for the ship to again sail the Baltic.

☞ Tours

The tourist office rents out English-language audioguide tours (€7).

Weisse Flotte   BOAT TOUR
(☑0180-321 2120; www.weisse-flotte.com; Hafen; adult/child €9.50/4.50; ⊙mid-May–Oct) Weisse Flotte offers one-hour harbour cruises, circling the island of Dänholm, between Stralsund and Rügen.

🎆 Festivals & Events

Wallensteintage   CARNIVAL
(www.wallensteintage.de; ⊙3rd week of Jul) Stralsund celebrates repelling an ene-

my invasion in 1628 with merriment and fireworks.

🛌 Sleeping

If everything is booked in the harbour area and old town, there are several midrange hotels by the train station you can try.

Hotel Amber   PENSION €
(☑03831-282 580; www.hotelamber.de; Heilgeist-strasse 50; s/d from €60/90; Ⓟ🖙) Perfectly located between the old town and the harbour, the Hotel Amber is also great value. The 12 rooms are simple with bright colour accents. Views from rooms on the 3rd floor include the harbour and city.

Younior Hotel   HOSTEL €
(☑0800-233 388 234; www.younior-hotel.de; Trib-seer Damm 78; dm €20-25, d €50-60; Ⓟ🖙) Situated in an expanse of parkland near the train station, this grand old 1897 building once housed Stralsund's railway offices. It's now a 300-bed hostel. Dorms have capsule-like triple-decker bunks in nine-bed rooms. Facilities include a guest-only bar, a barbecue area and a beach volleyball court.

Pension am Ozeaneum   PENSION €
(☑03831-666 831; www.pension-ozeaneum.com; Am Fischmarkt 2; s/d from €65/75; 🖙) There's nothing fancy about this basic 10-room place, however the location is unbeatable. Rooms have maroon and beige details plus small fridges.

★**Hotel Scheelehof**   BOUTIQUE HOTEL €€
(☎03831-283 300; www.hotel-stralsund-scheele-hof.de; Fährstrasse 23-25; r €105-145; 🕏) One of Stralsund's most appealing places to stay, the Scheelehof's 94 rooms are all individually decorated and scattered about several adjoining historic buildings. Furnishings have a luxurious period feel and there is a small spa. The hotel is noted for its bars and restaurants.

★**Altstadt Hotel Peiss**   HOTEL €€
(☎03831-303 580; www.altstadt-pension-peiss.de; Tribseer Strasse 15; s/d from €65/85; P🕏🕏) Fifteen spacious rooms with Paul Gauguin prints and sparkling bathrooms combine with cheery service at this bright and appealing guesthouse. The breakfast buffet is healthy and the host-family are very helpful. With a terrace, small garden and bike rack, it's especially popular with cyclists.

Hafenspeicher   APARTMENT €€
(☎03831-703 676, 0176 2210 9004; www.hafen-speicher-stralsund.de; Am Querkanal 3a; r €80-160; 🕏) One of Stralsund's oldest brick waterfront warehouses has been converted into a relaxed apartment-hotel. The design takes full advantage of the exisiting materials in the building. Rooms range from spacious doubles to rather large apartments; most have views over the water towards Rügen. All five floors are served by an elevator.

Hiddenseer   HOTEL €€
(☎03831-289 2390; www.hotel-hiddenseer.de; Hafenstrasse 12; s/d from €75/120; P🕏🕏) A prime harbourside location and 25 comfortable rooms make the Hiddenseer one of Stralsund's best options. The hotel is spread over three vintage buildings and although they lack lifts, the energetic staff will carry your bags up to your room. Some rooms have balconies and sweeping views to Rügen.

✗ Eating & Drinking

Smoked-fish stands dot the harbour area; many have quite elaborate menus although nothing costs more than €5.

Don't miss the more than a dozen beers brewed locally by Störtebeker Brewing.

★ **Fischhalle**   SEAFOOD €
(☎03831-278 366; Neue Badenstrasse 2; mains €4-10; 🕒9am-8pm May-Oct, to 6pm Nov-Apr) Choose your pleasure from the glass-fronted counters, order up, get a beer and wait for your meal's arrival at a picnic table inside or out. This über-casual fish bar has the best of the Baltic and beyond. People love the salmon and mussels. The local fish sandwiches are excellent.

Kaffeehaus Strahl   CAFE €
(☎03831-278 566; Mönchstrasse 46; mains €5-10; 🕒9am-6pm; 🕏) Displays of huge home-made cakes tempt you into this charming, old-fashioned cafe, which has many tables out front; also serves sandwiches.

★**Speicher 8**   MODERN GERMAN €€
(☎03831-288 2898; www.speicher8.de; Hafenstrasse 8; mains €10-20; 🕒10am-10pm) Simply roasted fish is one of the stars of this excellent casual restaurant in an old turreted building right on the waterfront. There are great tables out front; inside it's all glass and exposed wood. Celebrate your love by ordering a meat or fish platter for two. Both are beautfully presented. Sushi and vegie fare are also on offer.

Nur Fisch   SEAFOOD €€
(☎03831-306 609; Heilgeiststrasse 92; mains €5-15; 🕒10am-4pm Mon-Fri, 11am-3pm Sat) Simple canteen-style bistro dedicated to marine delights – from fish sandwiches to sumptuous platters of local seafood. Dishes include pasta, salads, smoked fish and seasonal specials.

Brasserie Grand Café   EUROPEAN €€
(☎03831-703 514; www.brasseriegrandcafe-hst.de; Neuer Markt 2; mains €8-18; 🕒9am-1am, kitchen to 11pm) Always crowded with locals, this fine bistro has tables scattered on the square, throughout several rooms and levels inside, and right on back to a beer garden. Food includes a great breakfast buffet, pasta and German staples. The *Fischpfanne Brasserie* is a delicious meal of three kinds of roasted fish fillets.

Fischermann's   SEAFOOD €€
(☎03831-292 322; www.fischermanns-restaurant.de; An der Fährbrücke 3; mains €9-16.50; 🕒11am-11pm; 🕏) Don't be dissuaded by Fischermann's touristy location in a tall red-brick warehouse on the waterfront. Diners pack its terrace like sardines on sunny days, enjoying its small but stellar selection of fish dishes –the views across to Rügen are just the bonus. Has the full range of Störtebeker beers.

T1 COCKTAIL BAR

(☎03831-282 8111; www.t1-stralsund.de; Heilgeist-strasse 64; ☺6pm-late) This hip yet refined cocktail lounge caters to an upscale crowd inside a central, step-gabled town house.

❶ Information

Tourist Office (☎03831-246 90; www.stralsundtourismus.de; Alter Markt 9; ☺10am-6pm Mon-Fri, to 4pm Sat & Sun May-Oct, 10am-5pm Mon-Fri, to 2pm Sat Nov-Apr) Tourist information and room bookings.

❶ Getting There & Away

BOAT
Services run to Rügen Island and Hiddensee Island.

TRAIN
Regional trains travel to/from Rostock (€16, one hour), Berlin Hauptbahnhof (from €44, 3¼ hours) and most major towns in the region at least every two hours.

❶ Getting Around

Your feet will do just fine in the Altstadt; the Rathaus is about 1km from the train station.

Rügen Island

With its white-sand beaches, canopies of chestnut, oak, elm and poplar trees, charming architecture and even its own national park, Rügen offers myriad ways to enjoy nature.

Frequented in the late 19th and early 20th centuries by luminaries including Bismarck, Thomas Mann and Albert Einstein, its chalk coastline was also immortalised by Romantic artist Caspar David Friedrich in 1818.

Although summer draws thousands to its shores, Rügen's lush 1000-sq-km surface area fringed by 574km of coastline means there are plenty of quiet corners to escape the crowds. You can appreciate Rügen on a day trip from Stralsund.

❶ Information

Every town has at least one tourist office dispensing local information. **Tourismuszentrale Rügen** (www.ruegen.de) provides island-wide information. Don't expect to find many spontaneous accommodation choices on summer weekends or anytime in August.

❶ Getting There & Away

BOAT
Adler-Schiffe (☎01805-123 344; www.adler-schiffe.de; adult/child €14.50/8; ☺Apr-Oct) connects Peenemünde on Usedom Island with Göhren, Sellin and Binz once daily.

International ferries to Trelleborg, Sweden, and Rønne, Denmark, sail from Sassnitz Mukran, about 7km south of Sassnitz' Bahnhof (linked by buses 18 and 20).

CAR & MOTORCYCLE
The toll-free Rügenbrücke and neighbouring Rügendamm (1936) bridges cross the Strelasund channel from Stralsund.

TRAIN
Direct IC trains connect Binz with Hamburg (€63, four hours) and beyond. There is an hourly Stralsund service (€13, 50 minutes). To get to Putbus, change RE trains in Bergen.

❶ Getting Around

Rügen is covered with trails that are perfect for bikes and hikers. Tourist offices sell oodles of maps and route guides.

BUS
RPNV Buses (☎03838-822 90; www.rpnv.de) link practically all communities, though service can be sporadic.

Fares are according to distance: Binz–Göhren, for example, costs €4.85. A day pass for the whole network is often a good deal (adult/child €12.10/8.70).

TRAIN
More than just a tourist attraction, the **Rügensche Bäderbahn** (RBB; www.ruegensche-baederbahn.de; day pass adult/child €22/11) steam train serves as a handy mode of transport as it chuffs between Putbus and Göhren. En route, it stops in Binz, Jagdschloss Granitz, Sellin and Baabe. Much of the narrow track passes through sun-dappled forest. Its nickname is the ironic 'Rasender Roland' (Rushing Roland).

The main interchange with the regular rail network is at Putbus. In Binz, the DB and RBB stations are 2km apart.

The route is divided into five zones, each costing €2. Bikes cost €3. There are family discounts.

Binz

☎038393 / POP 5500

Rügen's largest and most celebrated seaside resort, *'Ostseebad'* (Baltic Sea spa) Binz is an alluring confection of ornate, white Victorian-era villas, white sand and blue water. Its roads are signed in Gothic script and lined with coastal pines and chestnut trees. Even if all the signs of 21st-century capitalism abound, especially along jam-packed Hauptstrasse, you can still feel the pull of history amid the modern-day crowds.

⊙ Sights & Activities

Strandpromenade   STREET
(Binz) A highlight of Binz is simply strolling its 4km-long north–south beach promenade lined with elegant villas. At the southern end of the built-up area, you'll find the palatial **Kurhaus**, a lovely-looking 1908 building housing a luxury hotel. In front of it is the long pier. Strandpromenade continues further south from here, and becomes markedly less busy.

Prora   HISTORIC SITE
The beach just north of Binz still bears testament to Nazi plans to create the world's largest resort: six hideous six-storey buildings, each 500m long lining the sand. Begun in 1936, Prora was intended as a *Kraft-durch-Freude* (strength through joy) escape for 20,000 workers. The outbreak of WWII stopped its completion; no one has known what to do with it since. Much of it is a moody partial-ruin, with the echos of jackboots not far off.

★Dokumentationszentrum Prora   MUSEUM
(Prora Documentation Centre; ☑038393-139 91; www.proradok.de; Prora; adult/child €6/free; ☉10am-6pm Mar-Oct, 10am-4pm Nov-Feb; 🚌20, 23, 🚆Prora Nord) *'Macht Urlaub'* (power vacation) is a well-done exhibition on the Nazis and the role the workers resort Prora played in their 'strength through joy' schemes. You can easily spend an hour or more fully engrossed in the exhibits. Use the Prora Nord stop on local trains or bus line 20 or 23.

ⓘ WATER SPORTS

Sail & Surf Rügen (☑038306-232 53; www.segelschule-ruegen.de) Sail & Surf Rügen rents SUP (per day €35) as well as catamarans and windsurfing gear. It offers lessons for a variety of water sports and has locations across the island.

Zweiradhandel
Deutschmann   BICYCLE RENTAL
(☑038393-324 20; www.zweirad-deutschmann. de; Dollahnerstrasse 17, Ostseebad Binz Bahnhof; per day from €9; ☉9am-6pm Mon-Fri, 9am-noon & 5-6pm Sat & Sun) Has a huge selection of bikes right in the main train station.

🛏 Sleeping

Binz' abundant accommodation includes private rooms (many in historic properties) starting from €25 per person. In high season, minimum stays of three or more nights are common.

★Pension Haus Colmsee   PENSION €€
(☑038393-325 56; www.hauscolmsee.de; Strandpromenade 8; r €80-105; 🅿🐾) Relax in the leafy, quieter and altogether more pleasant eastern edge of town at this historic 1902 villa. Still family-run after all these years, the comfy but unadorned rooms include ones with sea views.

Hotel Imperial   HISTORIC HOTEL €€
(☑038393-1380; www.karin-loew-hotellerie.de; Strandpromenade 20; r €65-140) A classic survivor from the glory days of Binz, this 1903 hotel has a romantic turret and several rooms with balconies. It's as unadorned as the beach out front and offers a care-free escape in the centre of the action.

🍴 Eating

The beachfront Strandpromenade is lined with restaurants serving everything from pizzas and ice cream to creative seasonal cuisine.

★Fischräucherei Kuse   SEAFOOD €
(☑038393-322 49; Strandpromenade 3; dishes from €2; ☉9am-8pm) For some of the most delicious and certainly the cheapest fish on Rügen, follow your nose – literally – to the far southeast end of the Strandpromenade, where fish has been freshly smoked since 1900. Choose from fish sandwiches and meals; dine at its indoor tables, on the terrace or make a picnic.

★Freustil   MODERN GERMAN €€€
(☑038393-504 44; www.freustil.de; Zeppelinstrasse 8; menus €48-60; ☉noon-3pm & 6pm-midnight Tue-Sun May-Oct, shorter hours Nov-Apr) One of the region's top restaurants has value to match its relaxed vibe. Exquisitely prepared seasonal dishes, sourced locally, are combined in menus (one vegie) that delight with

their creativity. Why moan about autumn, when your mushrooms will star here? Tables outside let you revel in the long summer nights.

ℹ Information

Tourist Office (www.ostseebad-binz.de; Kurverwaltung, Heinrich-Heine-Strasse 7; ☺9am-6pm Mon-Fri, 10am-6pm Sat & Sun Feb-Oct, 9am-4pm Mon-Fri, 10am-4pm Sat & Sun Nov-Jan) Lots of maps, island guides and booking services.

ℹ Getting There & Around

Binz has two train stations: the main Ostseebad Binz Bahnhof, serving DB, RE and IC trains, and Binz LB, 2km southeast, serving the RBB steam train.

A daytime shuttle bus circles the Binz environs (adult/child €2.60/free).

Sellin

🕿 038303 / POP 2500

The symbol of 'Ostseebad' Sellin is its **Seebrüucke** (pier), an ornate, turreted pavilion sitting out over the water at the end of a long wooden causeway. The original pier was built in 1906. It's had a checkered history since: the not-terribly attractive modern pier you see now is somewhat modelled on a 1927 version.

The pier lies at the end of gently sloping **Wilhelmstrasse**, Rügen's most attractive main drag. It is lined with elegant villas, hotels and cafes and unlike so many local towns, didn't get a cheesy early-1990s makeover in the heady postreunification days. The pier is at the northwest end of Sellin's lovely white-sand **beach** and is 1.3km from the RBB train stop, Sellin Ost.

Göhren

🕿 038308 / POP 1300

On the Nordperd spit, Göhren's stunning 7km-long beach – divided into the sleepier Südstrand and the more developed Nordstrand – lives up to its hype as Rügen's best resort beach..

◎ Sights

Mönchgüter Museen   MUSEUM
(🕿 038308-2175; www.moenchguter-museen-ruegen.de; single museum adult/child €3/2.50, combined ticket €10/8; ☺10am-5pm Tue-Sun May-Oct, Sat & Sun Nov-Apr) Göhren has a collection of four historic sites, which to-

DON'T MISS

RÜGEN'S GRAND PALACE

Jagdschloss Granitz (🕿 038393-667 10; www.jagdschloss-granitz.de; Binz; adult/child €6/1; ☺9am-6pm daily May-Sep, to 4pm Apr & Oct, 10am-4pm Tue-Sun Nov-Mar) A grandiose hunting palace built in 1723 on top of the 107m-high Tempelberg, Jagdschloss Granitz was significantly enlarged and altered by Wilhelm Malte I in 1837. The results will remind you of salt and pepper shakers or a phallic fantasy, depending on your outlook. Malte's flights of fancy also gave Rügen the grandiose Putbus.

The **RBB steam train** stops at Jagdschloss and Garftitz, which serve the palace. Get off at one, enjoy some lovely hiking and reboard at the other.

The Jagdschlossexpress (adult/child €8/4) is a fake 'train' that trundles from Binz to the palace. If driving, the parking areas (per hour €2) are a 2km walk to the palace.

gether make up the Monchgüter Museen, including the historical **Heimatsmuseum** and the **Museumshof** farm, the unusual chimney-less **Rookhus** and the museum ship **Luise**. Visit just one or get a ticket for all four.

ℹ Getting There & Away

Göhren is the eastern terminus of the RBB steam train; the stop is a mere 200m from the sand. In summer, parking is awful; take the train.

Putbus

🕿 038301 / POP 2700

Putbus appears like a mirage from the middle of modest farming villages. At its heart lies a gigantic circular 19th-century plaza, known as the **Circus**, which has a 21m **obelisk** at the centre. Sixteen large, white neoclassical buildings surround it. You can still get a whiff of the GDR here. Some buildings are in better shape than others.

Nearby, the 75-hectare **English park** is filled with exotic botanical species. After you've soaked up the atmosphere (15 minutes should do it), head for a beach.

This is the hub for the **RBB steam train**; interchange with Germany's main rail network here.

Jasmund National Park

The rugged beauty of Jasmund National Park (www.nationalpark-jasmund.de) first came to national attention thanks to the romanticised paintings of Caspar David Friedrich in the early 19th century. His favourite spot was the Stubbenkammer, an area at the northern edge of the park, where jagged white-chalk cliffs plunge into the jade-coloured sea.

◉ Sights & Activities

By far the most famous of the **Stubbenkammer** cliffs is the **Königsstuhl** – at 117m, it's Rügen's highest point, although the scenery is often marred by everyone else trying to see it too. Fewer people make the trek a few hundred metres east to the **Victoria-Sicht** (Victoria View), which provides the best view of the Königsstuhl itself.

Nationalpark-Zentrum Königsstuhl   PARK
(☑ 38392-661766; www.koenigsstuhl.com; Sassnitz; adult/child €8.50/4; ◷ 9am-7pm Easter-Oct, 10am-5pm Nov-Easter) Admission to Jasmund National Park is through the Nationalpark-Zentrum Königsstuhl, which has multimedia displays on environmental themes, a 'climbing forest' and a cafe.

★ Adler-Schiffe   BOAT TOUR
(☑ 038392-3150; www.adler-schiffe.de; adult/child from €14/7.50; ◷ Apr-Oct) Operates daily trips around the chalk cliffs from Sellin, Binz and Sassnitz.

Coastal Walk   WALKING
If you're feeling energetic, a spectacular way to approach the area is by making the 10km trek from Sassnitz along the coast through the ancient forest of Stubnitz. The trail also takes you past the gorgeous **Wissower Klinken chalk cliffs**, another vista famously painted by Friedrich.

❶ Getting There & Away

Bus 20 and 23 go right to the Nationalpark-Zentrum Königsstuhl from the coastal towns. A Königsstuhl Ticket (adult/family €18/36) includes bus travel and entry. Drivers must leave vehicles in the (paid) parking lot in Hagen, then either catch the shuttle bus or walk 2.5km past the Herthasee lake through the forest.

Sassnitz

While most people only pass through Sassnitz (population 10,400), at the south-ern end of the national park, the town has been redeveloping its **Altstadt** and **harbour**. The latter is reached from the town bluff by a dramatic pedestrian bridge and is home to cafes and maritime museums.

Kap Arkona

Rügen ends at the rugged cliffs of **Kap Arkona**, with its famous pair of lighthouses: the square, squat **Schinkel-Leuchtturm**, completed in 1827, and the cylindrical **Neuer Leuchtturm**, in business since 1902.

A few metres east of the lighthouses is the **Burgwall**, a complex that harbours the remains of the Tempelburg, a Slavic temple and fortress. The castle was taken over by the Danes in 1168, paving the way for the Christianisation of Rügen.

Most people sail around the cape (without landing) on boat tours run by Adler-Schiffe.

Cars must be parked in the gateway village of Putgarten. You can take the **Kap Arkona Bahn** (☑ 038391-132 13; www.kap-arkona-bahn.de; adult/child €2/0.50) fake train or make the 1.5km journey by foot.

Greifswald

☑ 03834 / POP 54,200

The old university town of Greifswald, south of Stralsund, was largely unscathed by WWII thanks to a courageous German colonel who surrendered to Soviet troops.

The skyline of this former Hanseatic city – as once perfectly captured by native son Caspar David Friedrich – is defined by three churches: the 'Langer Nikolas' ('Long Nicholas'), 'Dicke Marie' ('Fat Mary') and 'Kleine Jakob' ('Small Jacob').

Greifswald has a pretty harbour in the charming district of Wieck; the entire area is worth a stop.

◉ Sights

Dom St Nikolai   CATHEDRAL
(☑ 03834-2627; Domstrasse; tower adult/child €3/1.50; ◷ 10am-4pm Mon-Sat, 11am-3pm Sun) The 100m onion-domed tower of the 14th-century Dom St Nikolai rises above a row of historic facades, giving the cathedral the nickname 'Long Nicholas'. The austere, whitewashed 19th-century interior is a dud but some Gothic carvings remain. Climb the tower for great views amid the scaffolding.

WORTH A TRIP

HIDDENSEE ISLAND

'Dat söte Länneken' (the sweet little land) is much mythologised in the German national imagination. This tiny patch off Rügen's western coast measures 18km long and just 1.8km at its widest point. What makes Hiddensee (population 1100) so sweet is its breathtaking, remote landscape. The heath and meadows of the **Dornbush** area, with the island's landmark lighthouse and wind-buckled trees, extend north of the village of **Kloster**, while **dunes** wend their way south from the main village of Vitte to Neuendorf. In the 19th and early 20th centuries, Hiddensee bewitched artists and writers including Thomas Mann and Bertolt Brecht, as well as Gerhart Hauptmann, who is buried here.

Cars are banned on Hiddensee but bike hire places are everywhere. Alternatively, you can see the island at a gentle pace aboard clip-clopping horse-drawn carriages. Horses appear well looked after.

The **tourist office** (www.seebad-hiddensee.de) has a summer branch at Kloster harbour. Inexpensive private rooms and simple guesthouses are available in Hiddensee's villages.

Getting There & Away

Reederei Hiddensee (✆ 0180-321 2150; www.reederei-hiddensee.de; return day tickets from Schaprode adult/child from €15.50/9.10, from Stralsund €19.10/9.40) Ferries run by Reederei Hiddensee leave Schaprode, on Rügen's western shore, up to 12 times daily year-round and run to Neuendorf, Kloster and Vitte. Services from Stralsund run up to three times daily between April and October.

Markt SQUARE
The richly ornamented buildings ringing the Markt hint at Greifswald's stature in the Middle Ages. The **Rathaus**, at the western end, started life as 14th-century shops. Among the red-brick **gabled houses** on the eastern side, the **Coffee House** (No 11) is gorgeous and a good example of a combined living and storage house owned by Hanseatic merchants.

Pommersches Landesmuseum MUSEUM
(www.pommersches-landesmuseum.de; Rakower Strasse 9; adult/child €5/3; ⊙10am-6pm Tue-Sun May-Oct, to 5pm Nov-Apr) This outstanding museum links three Franciscan monastery buildings via a 73m-long, glassed-in hall. There's a major gallery of paintings, including half a dozen by Caspar David Friedrich, as well as history and natural history exhibits.

Marienkirche CHURCH
(✆ 03834-2263; www.marien-greifswald.de; Brüggstrasse; ⊙10am-4pm Mon-Sat, 10.15am-noon Sun) The 12th-century red-brick Marienkirche is a square three-nave tower trimmed with turrets. It's easy to see why it's called 'Fat Mary'. Look for the 16th-century elaborately carved pulpit and frescos.

Wieck VILLAGE
The photogenic centre of this fishing village is a Dutch-style wooden **drawbridge**. The small harbour is often alive with fishing

boats landing – and selling – their catch. There's a good hike through a large park to the ruins of the 12th-century **Eldena Abbey** and the **beach**. It's an easy 5km bike ride east of Greifswald's Markt.

🛏 Sleeping & Eating

Wieck has some excellent stands for fresh and smoked fish.

Hotel Galerie HOTEL **€€**
(✆ 03834-773 7830; www.hotelgalerie.de; Mühlenstrasse 10; s/d from €80/90; ▣⊜🛜) The 13 rooms in this sparkling modern property are filled with a changing collection of works by contemporary artists. Room design is a cut above the usual hotel standard.

★**Fischer-Hütte** SEAFOOD **€€**
(✆ 03834-839 654; www.fischer-huette.de; An der Mühle 12, Wieck; mains €10-22; ⊙11.30am-11pm; 🚼) An exquisitely presented meal at the 'fisher's house' might start with Wieck-style fish stew and move onto the house speciality – smoked herring. You know everything is fresh as you can see the boats pulling up to the dock right outside.

Fritz Braugasthaus BREWERY **€€**
(✆ 03834-578 30; www.fritz-braugasthaus.de; Am Markt 13a; mains €8-16; ⊙11am-11pm) One of the most striking step-gabled red-brick buildings on the Markt is also a brewery. Besides

German classics like schnitzels, there are good burgers on the menu. Ingredients are sourced locally; there's outdoor seating.

ⓘ Getting There & Away

There are regular train services to Stralsund (€19, 21 minutes) and Berlin Hauptbahnhof (from €39, 2½ hours).

ⓘ Getting Around

It's easy to get around Greifswald's centre on foot; the Altstadt is 500m northeast of the train station.

You can reach Wieck via a 5km foot/bike path, or by bus 2 (€1.90) from the train station.

Usedom Island

Nicknamed Badewanne Berlins (Berlin's Bathtub) in the prewar period, Usedom Island is a holiday spot sought-after for its 42km stretch of beautiful beach. Its average of 1906 annual hours of sunshine make it the sunniest place in Germany.

Usedom (Uznam in Polish) lies in the delta of the Oder River about 30km east of Greifswald. The island's eastern tip lies across the border in Poland. Although the German side accounts for 373 sq km of the island's total 445 sq km, the population of the Polish side is larger (45,000 compared with 31,500 on the German side).

Woodsy bike and hiking trails abound. Elegant 1920s villas with wrought-iron balconies grace many traditional resorts along its northern spine, including Zinnowitz, Ückeritz, Bansin, Heringsdorf and Ahlbeck. All have tourist offices. Usedom Tourismus (www.usedom.de) has accommodation info island-wide.

Peenemünde

It was here, on the island's western tip, that Wernher von Braun developed the V2 rocket, first launched in October 1942. It flew 90km high and a distance of 200km before plunging into the Baltic – the first time in history that a flying object exited the earth's atmosphere. The rocket complex was destroyed by the Allies in July 1944, but the Nazis continued research and production, using slaves in the caves at Nordhausen in the southern Harz.

◉ Sights

Historisch-Technisches Museum MUSEUM (Historical & Technological Museum; ☑ 038371-5050; www.peenemuende.de; Im Kraftwerk; adult/concession €8/5; ⊙ 10am-6pm Apr-Sep, 10am-4pm Oct-Mar, closed Mon Nov-Mar) Peenemünde is immodestly billed as 'the birthplace of space travel' here. Displays – some in surviving buildings – do a good job of showing how the rockets were developed and the destruction they caused.

ⓘ Getting There & Around

Direct **UBB** (www.ubb-online.com) trains from Stralsund (and Greifswald) stop at coastal resorts before terminating in Świnoujście (Swinemünde in German), just over the Polish border. Peenemünde is on a branch line; change in Züssow (total time from Stralsund two hours). A day ticket costs €14.

Ferries run between Peenemünde and Rügen Island.

Look for **Usedom Rad** (www.usedomrad.de) stations all over the island and Greifswald. You can rent bikes from machines for €9 per day.

Understand Germany

Germany Today

Germany has always been hard to ignore. Today, Europe's most populous nation is also its biggest economic power and consequently has – albeit reluctantly – taken on a more active role in global politics, especially in the crises in Ukraine and Greece. A founding member of the European Union, it is solidly committed to preserving the alliance and making sure it is poised to deal with the political, social and military challenges of this increasingly uncertain and complex world.

Best on Film

The Lives of Others (Florian Henckel von Donnersmarck; 2006) The East German secret police (Stasi) unmasked.

The Downfall (Oliver Hirschbiegel; 2004) The final days of Hitler, holed up in his Berlin bunker.

Das Boot (Wolfgang Petersen; 1981) WWII submarine drama.

Wings of Desire (Wim Wenders; 1987) An angel in love with a mortal.

Metropolis (Fritz Lang; 1927) Seminal sci-fi silent movie about a proletarian revolt.

Run Lola Run (Tom Tykwer; 1998) Energetic drama set in Berlin.

Best in Print

Grimms' Fairy Tales (Jacob & Wilhelm Grimm; 1812) The classic!

The Rise & Fall of the Third Reich (William L Shirer; 1960) One thousand pages of powerful reportage.

Berlin Alexanderplatz (Alfred Döblin; 1929) Berlin in the 1920s.

The Tin Drum (Günter Grass; 1959) WWII seen through the eyes of a boy who refuses to grow up.

The Reader (Bernhard Schlink; 1995) Boy meets girl in WWII; girl gets put on trial for war crimes.

Europe's Economic Engine

Germany weathered the recent global fiscal crisis better than most industrial nations, in large part because it now bears the fruits of decade-old key reforms, especially the liberalisation of its labour laws. It is the fourth-largest economy in the world (after the US, Japan and China) and the largest in the European Union. With its solid manufacturing base and an economic backbone of small and medium-sized businesses, it has drawn worldwide admiration, as well as criticism, for its relentless reliance on exports (one in four euros is earned from exports) and for using the euro to serve its own interests.

The European Commission reported 0.7% growth in the German economy for the fourth quarter of 2014, while the eurozone as a whole grew a mere 0.3%. GDP is expected to grow by 1.75% in 2015. Manufacturing orders and exports, especially to hungry markets in South America, Asia and Eastern Europe, are up, helped along by a weak euro. At the same time, the unemployment rate has dropped to around 6% (among the lowest in the EU), the property market is sizzling and consumer confidence is high.

Political Leadership

Aware of the burden of their country's 20th-century history, modern German leaders have traditionally avoided taking on a major political or military role in Europe. However, changing circumstances that pose a threat to European stability have led to a more assertive German foreign policy in recent years. Long accused of being reluctant to make tough decisions, Chancellor Angela Merkel has emerged as Europe's chief diplomat, demonstrating a commitment to a coherent European foreign policy and a willingness to take on a leadership role.

Together with French president François Hollande, she has worked hard towards a peaceful resolution to the Russia–Ukraine conflict, which began in February 2014 with Russia's annexation of the Crimean Peninsula. Meetings, phone calls and, finally, marathon talks in Minsk in February 2015 produced a ceasefire, albeit a volatile one. Since fighting never fully stopped, the agreement did not, as Russia had hoped, lead to a lifting of economic sanctions imposed by democracies around the world, which Germany supports. The sanctions were reconfirmed at the G7 summit in 2015 until Russia agrees to a deal to end the Ukraine conflict.

Germany again took a leadership role in the Greek financial crisis, which began around 2010, when it became clear that Greece had taken on a much higher debt than previously disclosed and thus, at least in part, kicked off the euro crisis. Merkel's and Finance Minister Wolfgang Schäuble's tough stance on Greek debt reduction and financial bailouts have engendered criticism on all sides, especially, of course, in Greece itself.

Land of Immigration

Some 15 million people living in Germany have an immigrant background (foreign-born or at least one immigrant parent), accounting for about 18% of the total population. The largest group are people of Turkish descent, a legacy of the post-WWII economic boom, when 'guest workers' were recruited to shore up the war-depleted workforce. Many stayed. Immediately after reunification, Germany welcomed large numbers of repatriates from the former USSR and refugees from war-ravaged Yugoslavia. In recent years, factors such as the economic stability and a high standard of living in Germany have attracted migrants from new EU member nations Romania and Bulgaria, as have people from economically weaker countries like Spain, Greece and Italy.

Along with other European nations, Germany is also accommodating an enormous influx of refugees, especially from war-torn Syria, Libya and Afghanistan, as well as from poor non-EU countries such as Kosovo and Albania. Among certain population groups, the arrival of these new migrants and the perceived drain they put on Germany's economy and society has given rise to new nationalist and anti-immigrant movements like Pegida ('Patriotic Europeans against the Islamisation of the West') and parties such as the AfD (*Alternative für Deutschland,* Alternative for Germany).

Opinions may differ as to whether immigration enriches or endangers German culture, but there's no denying the fact that an ageing population and the world's lowest birth rate mean Germany has the fastest population decline among developed nations.

AREA: **357,672 SQ KM**

POPULATION: **81.1 MILLION**

GDP: **€3.85 TRILLION**

INFLATION: **0.3%**

UNEMPLOYMENT: **6.1%**

LIFE EXPECTANCY: **WOMEN 82.8 YEARS, MEN 77.7 YEARS**

if Germany were 100 people

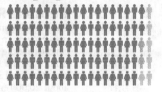

92 would be German
2 would be Turkish
6 would be other

belief systems
(% of population)

68   4   28

Christian   Muslim   Other

population per sq km

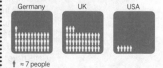

Germany   UK   USA

† ≈ 7 people

History

For most of its history, Germany was a patchwork of semi-independent principalities and city states, becoming a nation state only in 1871. Yet movements and events associated with its territory – from the Hanseatic League to the Reformation and the Holocaust – have shaped the history of Europe since the early Middle Ages. Charlemagne, Martin Luther, Otto von Bismarck and Adolf Hitler are just a few key figures whose impact resonates to present times when Germany is inextricably bound up within – and a leading proponent of – European unity.

Roots & Romans

The early inhabitants of present-day Germany were Celts and later nomadic German tribes. Under Emperor Augustus, the Romans began conquering the German lands from around 12 BC, pushing as far as the Rhine and the Danube. Attempts to expand their territory further east were thwarted in AD 9, when Roman general Varus lost three legions – about 20,000 men – in the bloody Battle of the Teutoburg Forest. The Germanic forces were led by Arminius, the son of a local chief who had been captured and brought to Rome as a hostage. Here he adopted Roman citizenship and received a military education, which proved invaluable in outwitting Varus.

For many years, Mount Grotenburg near Detmold in North Rhine–Westphalia was thought to have been the setting of the epic Teutoburg Forest battle, but no one can really say for sure where it happened. The most likely candidate is Kalkriese, north of Osnabrück, where in the 1990s archaeologists found face helmets, breast shields, bone deposits and other grisly battle remains. Today the site is a museum and park.

After Arminius' victory, the Romans never again attempted to conquer Germanic lands east of the Rhine, accepting the Rhine and the Danube as natural boundaries and consolidating their power by founding such colonies as Trier, Cologne, Mainz and Regensburg. They remained the dominant force in the region until 476.

Best Roman Sites

Trier

Xanten

Cologne

Aachen

Regensburg

Bingen

Mainz

TIMELINE

800–300 BC	100 BC–AD 9	4th Century
Germanic tribes and Celts inhabit large parts of northern and central Germany, but by around 300 BC the Celts have been driven back to regions south of the Main River.	The Romans clash with Germanic tribes until defeat at the Battle of the Teutoburg Forest halts Rome's expansion eastwards. The Romans consolidate territory south of the Limes.	The arrival of Hun horsemen triggers the Great Migration. Germanic tribes are displaced and flee to various parts of the Western Roman Empire. The Lombards settle in northern Italy.

Charlemagne & the Frankish Empire

Based on the Rhine's western bank, the Frankish Reich (Empire) existed from the 5th to the 9th centuries and was the successor state of the Western Roman Empire, which had crumbled in 476. Under the leadership of the Merovingian and later the Carolingian dynasties, it became Europe's most important political power in those early medieval times. In its heyday, the Reich included present-day France, Germany, the Low Countries (Netherlands, Belgium and Luxembourg) and half the Italian peninsula.

Its most powerful ruler was Charlemagne (r 768–814), a Carolingian. From his grandiose residence in Aachen, he conquered Lombardy, won territory in Bavaria, waged a 30-year war against the Saxons in the north and was crowned Kaiser by the pope in 800, an act that was regarded as a revival of the Roman empire. Charlemagne's burial in Aachen Dom (Aachen Cathedral) turned the court chapel into a major pilgrimage site.

After Charlemagne's death, fighting between his son and three grandsons ultimately led to the dissolution of the Frankish Reich in 843. The Treaty of Verdun split the territory into three kingdoms: the Westfrankenreich (West Francia), which evolved into today's France; the Ostfrankenreich (East Francia), the origin of today's Germany; and the Mittlere Frankenreich (Middle Francia), which encompassed the Low Countries and areas in present-day France and northern Italy.

The Middle Ages

Germany's strong regionalism has its roots in the early Middle Ages, when dynasties squabbled and intrigued over territorial spoils. The symbolic heart of power in the early Middle Ages was Charlemagne's burial place, the cathedral in Aachen. It hosted the coronation of 31 German kings from 936 until 1531, starting with Otto I (aka Otto the Great). Otto proved himself on the battlefield, first by defeating Hungarian troops and then by conquering the Kingdom of Italy. In 962 he renewed Charlemagne's pledge to protect the papacy, and the pope reciprocated by crowning him emperor, marking the birth of the Holy Roman Empire. For the next 800 years the Kaiser and the pope were strange, and often uneasy, bedfellows.

A power struggle between pope and Kaiser, who also had to contend with the local princes and prince-bishops, was behind many of the upheavals in the early Middle Ages. A milestone was the Investiture Conflict between Heinrich IV (r 1056–1106) and Pope Gregory VI over whether the pope or the monarch was entitled to appoint bishops, abbots and other high church officials. The pope responded by excommunicating Heinrich in 1076. Heinrich then embarked on a walk of penance to the castle of Canossa in Italy, where the pope was in residence. Contrite,

HISTORY CHARLEMAGNE & THE FRANKISH EMPIRE

For most of history, Germany was not a single country but a loose federation of fiefdoms known as the Holy Roman Empire of the German Nation. A proper nation state did not emerge until 1871.

For more on Germany's Roman ruins log on to www.historvius.com

The Holy Roman Empire was also known as the First Reich. The Second Reich refers to the German Empire (1871–1914) under Kaisers Wilhelm I and II, and the Third Reich, of course, to Adolf Hitler's rule from 1933 to 1945.

482–86	716–54	732	773–800
Clovis becomes king of the Franks and defeats the Romans in the Battle of Soissons in France. The last vestiges of the Western Roman Empire collapse and Romans seek protection with resettled Germanic tribes.	The English Benedictine monk St Boniface undertakes a journey to preach Christianity in Frisia, Hesse, Thuringia and Bavaria. His missionary activities end when he is killed in Frisia.	Charles Martel, king of the Franks, wins the decisive Battle of Tours and stops the progress of Muslims from the Iberian Peninsula into Western Europe, preserving Christianity in the Frankish Reich.	The Carolingian Charlemagne, grandson of Charles Martel, answers a call for help from the pope. In return, he is crowned emperor by the pope.

he reportedly stood barefoot in the snow for three days begging for the excommunication to be lifted. He was eventually absolved, but the investiture question held the Reich in the grip of civil war until a treaty signed in 1122 granted the emperor limited rights in selecting bishops.

Heinrich IV was a member of the Salians, one of several powerful dynasties that shaped the politics of the early Middle Ages. Others included the rival Hohenstaufen and Welf houses. One of the most powerful Welfs of the time was Heinrich der Löwe (Henry the Lion), who reigned over the duchies of Saxony and Bavaria, while also extending influence eastwards in campaigns to Germanise and convert the Slavs.

Heinrich, who was very well connected (his second, English wife Mathilde was Richard the Lionheart's sister), founded not only Braunschweig (where his grave is) but Munich, Lübeck and Lüneburg, too. At the height of his reign, his domain stretched from the north and Baltic coasts to the Alps, and from Westphalia to Pomerania (in Poland). Eventually, though, the Hohenstaufen under Friedrich I Barbarossa (r 1152–90) would regain the upper hand and take Saxony and Bavaria away from him.

In 1254, after the death of the last Hohenstaufen emperor, Friedrich II, the Reich plunged into an era called the Great Interregnum, when no potential successor could gain sufficient support, leaving the Reich rudderless until the election of Rudolf I in 1273. Rudolf was the first of 19 emper-

> The name Habsburg (Hapsburg) originates from *Habichts Burg* (literally 'Hawk Castle'), the spot on the Rhine (in present-day Switzerland, immediately across the border from Germany) from which the great Swabian family first hailed.

WHAT WAS THE HOLY ROMAN EMPIRE?

The Holy Roman Empire was a political union of feudal states that greatly influenced the history and evolution of Europe for over 800 years. Some historians peg its origins to Frankish king Charlemagne, who, in 800, was crowned emperor by Pope Leo III in Rome. It was the first time such a title had been bestowed in Western Europe since the collapse of the Roman Empire in the 5th century. However, not until the crowing of Otto I in 962 did the territory truly fall under German rule and would remain so almost exclusively until the abdication of Kaiser Franz II in 1806.

The empire sometimes included Italy, as far south as Rome. Sometimes it didn't – the pope usually had a say in that. It variously encompassed present-day Netherlands, Belgium, Switzerland, Lorraine and Burgundy (in France), Sicily, Austria and an eastern swath of land that today lies in the Czech Republic, Poland and Hungary. As such it was a decentralised, multi-ethnic mosaic with many languages. Unlike France, Spain or England, it was not a hereditary monarchy. Instead, emperors were selected by a small group of electors drawn from the ecclesiastical and political nobility, although the new king was usually – however distantly – related to the outgoing one. Since there was no capital city, rulers constantly moved from one city to the next.

Incidentally, the term 'Holy Roman Empire' was not used until the 13th century. In the 15th century, the words 'of the German nation' were added.

911	919–1125	1165	1241
Louis the Child dies without an heir at 18, and Frankish dukes in the eastern Reich bypass Charles the Simple in favour of their own monarch, electing the first truly German ruler.	Saxon and Salian emperors rule Germany, creating the Holy Roman Empire in 962, when Otto I is crowned Holy Roman Emperor by the pope, reaffirming the precedent established by Charlemagne.	Friedrich I Barbarossa is crowned in Aachen. He canonises Charlemagne and, while co-leading the Third Crusade, drowns while bathing in a river in present-day Turkey.	Hamburg and Lübeck sign an agreement to protect each other's ships and trading routes, creating the basis for the powerful Hanseatic League, which dominates politics and trade across much of Europe.

ors of the Habsburg dynasty that mastered the art of politically expedient marriage and dominated Continental affairs until the early 20th century.

In the 14th century, the basic structure of the Holy Roman Empire solidified. A key document was the Golden Bull of 1356 (so named for its golden seal), a decree issued by Emperor Charles IV that was essentially an early form of an imperial constitution. Most importantly, it set out precise rules for elections by specifying the seven *Kurfürsten* (prince-electors) entitled to choose the next king to be crowned Holy Roman Emperor by the pope. The privilege fell to the rulers of Bohemia, Brandenburg, Saxony and the Palatinate, as well as to the archbishops of Trier, Mainz and Cologne. A simple majority was sufficient in electing the next king.

As the importance of the minor nobility declined, the economic power of the towns increased, especially after many joined forces in a strategic trading alliance called the Hanseatic League. The most powerful towns, such as Cologne, Hamburg, Nuremberg and Frankfurt, were granted Free Imperial City status, which made them beholden directly to the emperor (as opposed to 'non-free' towns that were subordinate to a local ruler).

For ordinary Germans, times were difficult. They battled with panic lynching, pogroms against Jews and labour shortages – all sparked by the plague (1348–50) that wiped out 25% of Europe's population. While death gripped ordinary Germans, universities were being established all over the country around this time, with Heidelberg's the first, in 1386.

Reformation & the Thirty Years' War

In the 16th century, the Renaissance and humanist ideas generated criticism of rampant church abuses, most famously the practice of selling indulgences to exonerate sins. In the university town of Wittenberg in 1517, German monk and theology professor Martin Luther (1483–1546) made public his *Ninety-Five Theses,* which critiqued not only indulgences but also questioned papal infallibility, clerical celibacy and other elements of Catholic doctrine. This was the spark that lit the Reformation.

Threatened with excommunication, Luther refused to recant, broke from the Catholic Church and was banned by the Reich, only to be hidden in the Wartburg, a castle outside Eisenach in Thuringia, where he translated the New Testament into German.

It was not until 1555 that the Catholic and Lutheran churches were ranked as equals, thanks to Emperor Karl V (r 1520–58), who signed the Peace of Augsburg, allowing princes to decide the religion of their principality. The more secular northern principalities adopted Lutheran teachings, while the clerical lords in the south, southwest and Austria stuck with Catholicism.

But the religious issue refused to die. In 1618 it degenerated into the bloody Thirty Years' War, which Sweden and France had joined by 1635.

The German vernacular expression 'Gang nach Canossa' ('to go to Canossa') means to do penance and refers to Heinrich IV's 11th-century penitential walk from Speyer (Germany) to Canossa (Italy).

The use of the title Kaiser was a direct legacy of Roman times (the German word *Kaiser,* meaning 'emperor', is derived from 'Caesar').

Heinrich the Fowler: Father of the Ottonian Empire (2005), by Mirella Patzer, brings 10th-century Germany to life in a heady blend of history and fiction.

1245	1273	1338	1348–50
The chaotic period of the Great Interregnum begins when Pope Innocent IV deposes Friedrich II and a string of anti-kings are elected. Local bishops and dukes subsequently grab more power, weakening central rule.	The Great Interregnum ends when the House of Habsburg takes the reins of the Reich and begins its rise to become Europe's most powerful dynasty.	The Declaration of Rhense ends the need for the pope to confirm the Reich's elected Kaiser, abolishing the dependence whereby the pope crowned the Kaiser in exchange for loyalty and protection.	The plague wipes out 25% of Europe's population and pogroms are launched against Jews. The loss of workers leads to improved circumstances for able-bodied survivors.

What's in a name? Past German monarchs include Karl the Fat (r 881–87), Arnulf the Evil and Friedrich the Handsome (both medieval anti-kings), and the righteous Heinrich the Holy (r 1014–24).

Calm was restored with the Peace of Westphalia (1648), signed in Münster and Osnabrück, but it left the Reich – embracing more than 300 states and about 1000 smaller territories – a nominal, impotent state. Switzerland and the Netherlands gained formal independence, France won chunks of Alsace and Lorraine, and Sweden helped itself to the mouths of the Elbe, Oder and Weser Rivers.

Prussia on the Rise

As the power of the Holy Roman Empire waned, a new force to be reckoned with appeared on the horizon: Brandenburg-Prussia. Since 1411 the eastern duchy of Brandenburg had been under the rule of the Hohenzollern family, but remained pretty much on the fringes of power within the Reich. This changed in the 17th century under Friedrich Wilhelm (r 1640–88). Also known as the Great Elector, he took several steps that helped chart Brandenburg's rise to the status of a European powerhouse. He turned Berlin into a garrison town, levied a new sales tax, established the city as a trading hub by building a canal linking the Oder and Spree rivers, and encouraged the settlement of French refugees. Between 1680 and 1710, Berlin saw its population nearly triple to 56,000, making it one of the largest cities in the Holy Roman Empire. Seizing the opportuni-

THE HANSEATIC LEAGUE

The origins of the Hanseatic League go back to various guilds and associations established from about the mid-12th century by out-of-town merchants to protect their interests. After Hamburg and Lübeck signed an agreement in 1241 to protect their ships and trading routes, they were joined in their league by Lüneburg, Kiel and a string of Baltic Sea cities stretching east to Greifswald. By 1356 this had grown into the Hanseatic League, encompassing half a dozen other large alliances of cities, with Lübeck playing the lead role.

At its zenith, the league had about 200 member cities. It earned a say in the choice of Danish kings after fighting two wars against the Danes between 1361 and 1369. The resulting Treaty of Stralsund in 1370 turned it into northern Europe's most powerful economic and political entity. Some 70 inland and coastal cities – mostly German – formed the core of the Hanseatic League, but another 130 beyond the Reich maintained a loose association, making it truly international. During a period of endless feudal squabbles in Germany, it was a bastion of political and social stability.

By the 15th century, however, competition from Dutch and English shipping companies, internal disputes and a shift in the centre of world trade (from the North and Baltic Seas to the Atlantic) had caused a decline. The ruin and chaos of the Thirty Years' War in the 17th century delivered the final blow, although Hamburg, Bremen and Lübeck retained the 'Hanse City' title. The latter's new Europäisches Hansemuseum is a great place to learn more about this fascinating chapter in European history.

1414–18	1455	1517	1524–25
The Great Schism, which has plagued the Catholic Church since 1378, is resolved at the Council of Constance in southern Germany. In 1415 Bohemian reformer Jan Hus is burned at the stake.	Johannes Gutenberg of Mainz prints 180 copies of the Gutenberg Bible in Latin, using a moveable type system that revolutionises book printing and allows books to be published in large quantities.	Martin Luther makes public his Ninety-Five Theses in the town of Wittenburg. His ideas challenge the selling of indulgences, capturing a mood of disillusionment with the Church and among the clergy.	Inspired by the Reformation, peasants in southern and central Germany rise up against their masters, demanding the end of bonded labour. Luther at first supports the peasants, but later switches sides.

ty, his son, Friedrich III, promoted himself to King Friedrich I (elector 1688–1701, king 1701–13) of Prussia, making Berlin a royal residence and capital of Brandenburg-Prussia.

Friedrich's son, Friedrich Wilhelm I (r 1713–40) laid the groundwork for Prussian military might. Soldiers were this king's main obsession and he dedicated much of his life to building an army of 80,000, partly by instituting the draft (highly unpopular even then, and eventually repealed) and by persuading his fellow rulers to trade him men for treasure. History quite appropriately knows him as the *Soldatenkönig* (soldier king).

Ironically, these soldiers didn't see action until his son and successor Friedrich II (aka Frederick the Great; r 1740–86) came to power. Friedrich fought tooth and nail for two decades to wrest Silesia (in today's Poland) from Austria and Saxony. He also embraced the ideas of the Enlightenment, abolishing torture, guaranteeing religious freedom and introducing legal reforms. With some of the leading thinkers in town (Moses Mendelssohn, Voltaire and Gotthold Ephraim Lessing among them), Berlin blossomed into a great cultural capital and came to be known as 'Athens on the Spree'.

Napoleon & Revolutions

In the aftermath of the 1789 French Revolution, a diminutive Frenchman named Napoleon Bonaparte (Napoleon I) took control of Europe and significantly altered its fate through a series of wars. The defeat of Austrian and Russian troops in the Battle of Austerlitz in 1806 led to the collapse of the Holy Roman Empire, the abdication of Kaiser Franz II and a variety of administrative and judicial reforms.

Most German kingdoms, duchies and principalities aligned themselves with Napoleon in the Confederation of the Rhine. In his restructure of the map of the Europe, Bavaria fared especially well, nearly doubling its size and being elevated to kingdom in 1806. It was to be a short-lived confederation, though, for many of its members switched allegiance again after Napoleon got trounced by Prussian, Russian, Austrian and Swedish troops in the bloody 1813 Battle of Leipzig.

In 1815, at the Congress of Vienna, Germany was reorganised into the *Deutscher Bund,* a confederation of 39 states with a central legislative assembly, the *Reichstag,* established in Frankfurt. Austria and Prussia dominated this alliance, until a series of bourgeois democratic revolutions swept through German cities in 1848, resulting in Germany's first ever freely elected parliamentary delegation convening in Frankfurt's Paulskirche. Austria, meanwhile, broke away from Germany, came up with its own constitution and promptly relapsed into monarchism. As revolution fizzled in 1850, the confederation resumed, with Prussia and Austria again as dominant members.

One of the definitive histories on Prussia, Christopher Clark's *Iron Kingdom: The Rise and Downfall of Prussia* covers the period from 1600 to 1947, and shows the central role this powerhouse played in shaping modern Europe.

The first potato was planted in Germany in 1621, the Gregorian calendar was adopted in 1700 and Germany's first cuckoo clock started ticking in 1730.

1555	1618–48	1648	1740–86
The Peace of Augsburg allows princes to decide their principality's religion, putting Catholicism and Protestantism on an equal footing. Around 80% of Germany's population at this time is Protestant.	The Thirty Years' War sweeps through Germany, leaving its population depleted and vast regions reduced to wasteland. The Reich disintegrates into 300-plus states.	The Treaty of Westphalia ends the Thirty Years' War and formalises the independence of Switzerland, and of the Netherlands, which had been ruled by Spain since the early 16th century.	Brandenburg-Prussia becomes a mighty power under Friedrich the Great. Berlin becomes 'Athens on the Spree', as Absolutism in Europe gives way to the Enlightenment, heralding a cultural explosion.

In Bavaria, meanwhile, revolutionary rumblings brought out King Ludwig I's reactionary streak. An arch-Catholic, he restored the monasteries, introduced press censorship and authorised the arrest of students, journalists and university professors whom he judged to be subversive. Bavaria was becoming restrictive even as French and American democratic ideals flourished elsewhere in Germany.

On 22 March 1848 Ludwig I abdicated in favour of his son, Maximilian II (r 1848–64), who finally put into place many of the constitutional reforms his father had ignored, such as abolishing censorship and introducing the right to assemble. His son Ludwig II (r 1864–86) introduced further progressive measures early in his reign (welfare for the poor, liberalised marriage laws and free trade) but ultimately became caught up in a world inspired by mythology and focusing on building grand palaces such as Schloss Neuschwanstein, instead of running a kingdom. His death by drowning in shallow water in Lake Starnberg continues to spur conspiracy theories to this day.

Bismarck & the Birth of an Empire

The creation of a unified Germany with Prussia at the helm was the glorious ambition of Otto von Bismarck (1815–98), who had been appointed as Prussian prime minister by King Wilhelm I in 1862. An old-guard militarist, he used intricate diplomacy and a series of wars with neighbouring Denmark and France to achieve his aims. By 1871 Berlin stood as the proud capital of the Deutsches Reich (German Empire), a bicameral, constitutional monarchy. On 18 January the Prussian king was crowned Kaiser at Versailles, with Bismarck as his 'Iron Chancellor'.

Bismarck's power was based on the support of merchants and Junker, a noble class of nonknighted landowners. An ever-skilful diplomat and power broker, Bismarck achieved much through a dubious 'honest Otto' policy, whereby he brokered deals between European powers and encouraged colonial vanities in order to distract others from his own deeds. He belatedly graced the Reich with a few African jewels after 1880, acquiring colonies in central, southwest and east Africa, as well as numerous Pacific paradises, such as Tonga.

The early years of the German empire – a period called *Gründerzeit* (foundation years) – were marked by major economic growth, fuelled in part by a steady flow of French reparation payments. Hundreds of thousands of people poured into the cities in search of work in factories. New political parties gave a voice to the proletariat, especially the Socialist Workers' Party (SAP), the forerunner of the Sozialdemokratische Partei Deutschlands (Social Democratic Party of Germany; SPD).

Bismarck tried to make the party illegal but, when pressed, made concessions to the growing and increasingly antagonistic socialist move-

'Laws are like sausages. It's better not to see them being made.'

Otto von Bismarck

Bismarck to the Weimar Republic is the focus of Hans-Ulrich Wehler's *The German Empire 1871–1918*, a translation of an authoritative German work. For a revealing study of the Iron Chancellor himself, read *Bismarck, the Man and the Statesman* by AJP Taylor.

1789–1815	1806–13	1813 & 1815	1814–15
The French Revolution and, from 1803, the Napoleonic Wars sweep away the last remnants of the Middle Ages in Europe. Napoleon Bonaparte takes Berlin in 1806.	The Holy Roman Empire collapses and Napoleon creates the 16-member Confederation of the Rhine after defeating Austrian and Russian troops in the Battle of Austerlitz.	Napoleon suffers defeat near Leipzig in 1813. He subsequently abdicates and is exiled to Elba. He returns to power in 1815 but is defeated at Waterloo that same year.	The post-Napoleon Congress of Vienna redraws the map of Europe, creating in the former Reich the German Alliance, with 35 states.

ment, enacting Germany's first modern social reforms, though contrary to his true nature. When Wilhelm II (r 1888–1918) came to power, he wanted to extend social reform, while Bismarck envisioned stricter anti-socialist laws. By March 1890, the Kaiser had had enough and excised his renegade chancellor from the political scene. Bismarck's legacy as a brilliant diplomat unravelled as a wealthy, unified and industrially powerful Germany embarked upon a new century.

WWI & its Aftermath

The assassination on 28 June 1914 of Archduke Franz Ferdinand, heir to the Austrian throne, triggered a series of diplomatic decisions that led to WWI, the bloodiest European conflict since the Thirty Years' War. Initial euphoria and faith in a quick victory soon gave way to despair, as casualties piled up in the battlefield trenches and stomachs grumbled on the home front. When defeat came in 1918, it ushered in a period of turmoil and violence. On 9 November 1918 Kaiser Wilhelm II abdicated, bringing an inglorious end to the monarchy.

The seeds of acrimony and humiliation that later led to WWII were sown in the peace conditions of WWI. Germany, militarily broken, teetering on the verge of revolution and caught in a no-man's land between monarchy and modern democracy, signed the Treaty of Versailles (1919), which made it responsible for all losses inflicted upon its enemies. Its borders were trimmed and it was forced to pay high reparations.

The Weimar Republic

In July 1919 the federalist constitution of the fledgling republic was adopted in the town of Weimar, where the constituent assembly had sought refuge from the chaos of Berlin. Germany's first serious experiment with democracy gave women the vote and established basic human rights, but it also gave the chancellor the right to rule by decree – a concession that would later prove critical in Hitler's rise to power.

The Weimar Republic (1920–33) was governed by a coalition of left and centre parties, but pleased neither communists nor monarchists. In fact, the 1920s began as anything but 'golden', marked, as they were, by the humiliation of a lost war, hyperinflation, mass unemployment, hunger and disease.

Economic stability gradually returned after a new currency, the Rentenmark, was introduced in 1923 and with the Dawes Plan in 1924, which limited the crippling reparation payments imposed on Germany after WWI. But the tide turned again when the US stock market crashed in 1929, plunging the world into economic depression. Within weeks, millions of German were jobless, and riots and demonstrations again filled the streets.

Did you know that 9 November is Germany's 'date with destiny'? It was the end of the monarchy in 1918, the day of Hitler's Munich Putsch in 1923, the Night of Broken Glass in 1938, and the day the Wall fell in 1989.

After abdicating, Kaiser Wilhelm II was allowed to settle in Utrecht (the Netherlands) on the condition that he didn't engage in political activity. One of his final acts was to send a telegram to Hitler, congratulating him on the occupation of Paris.

1834	1848	1848	1866
The German Customs Union is formed under the leadership of Prussia, making much of Germany a free-trade area and edging it closer to unification; the Union reinforces the idea of a Germany without Austria.	*The Communist Manifesto* on class struggle and capitalism, by Trier-born Karl Marx and fellow countryman Friedrich Engels, is published in London by a group of Germans living in exile in Britain.	The March Revolution breaks out mainly in the Rhineland and southwest German provinces. Nationalists and reformers call for far-reaching changes; a first parliamentary delegation meets in Frankfurt.	Following a successful war against Denmark, Prussia defeats Austria in the Austro-Prussian War, and chancellor Otto von Bismarck creates a North German Confederation that excludes Austria.

Hitler's Rise to Power

In 1923 a postage stamp cost 50 billion marks, a loaf of bread 140 billion marks and US$1 was worth 4.2 trillion marks. In November, the new Rentenmark was traded in for one trillion old marks.

The volatile, increasingly polarised political climate led to clashes between communists and members of a party that had been patiently waiting in the wings – the Nationalsozialistische Deutsche Arbeiterpartei (National Socialist German Workers' Party, NSDAP, or Nazi Party), led by an Austrian failed artist and WWI corporal named Adolf Hitler. Soon jackboots, brown shirts, oppression and fear would dominate daily life in Germany.

Hitler's NSDAP gained 18% of the national vote in the 1930 elections. In the 1932 presidential election, Hitler challenged incumbent Reichspräsident (President of the Reich) Paul von Hindenburg, but only managed to win 37% of the second-round vote. However, a year later, on 30 January 1933, faced with failed economic reforms and persuasive right-wing advisors, Hindenburg appointed Hitler chancellor.

Hitler moved quickly to consolidate absolute power and to turn the nation's democracy into a one-party dictatorship. He used Berlin's Reichstag fire as a pretext to push through the Enabling Law, allowing him to decree laws and change the constitution without consulting parliament. When Hindenburg died a year later, Hitler merged the offices of president and chancellor to become Führer of the Third Reich.

The rise of the Nazis had instant, far-reaching consequences. Within three months of Hitler's power grab, all non-Nazi parties, organisations and labour unions ceased to exist. Political opponents, intellectuals and artists were rounded up and detained without trial; many went underground or into exile. There was a burgeoning culture of terror and denunciation, and the terrorisation of Jews began to escalate.

Hitler won much support among the middle and lower-middle classes by pumping large sums of money into employment programs, many involving rearmament and heavy industry. In Wolfsburg, Lower Saxony, affordable cars started rolling out of the first Volkswagen factory, founded in 1938.

During the hyperinflation of the early 1920s a man in Berlin was carting his pay home in a wheelbarrow when he was mugged. The thieves took the wheelbarrow...but left the money on the pavement.

That same year, Hitler's troops were welcomed into Austria. Foreign powers, in an attempt to avoid another bloody war, accepted this *Anschluss* (annexation) of Austria. Following this same policy of appeasement, the leaders of Italy, Great Britain and France ceded the largely ethnic-German Sudetenland of Czechoslovakia to Hitler in the Munich Agreement, signed in September 1938. By March 1939 he had also annexed Bohemia and Moravia.

Jewish Persecution

Jewish people were specifically targeted in what would become a long-term campaign of genocide. In April 1933 Joseph Goebbels, *Gauleiter* (district leader) of Berlin and head of the well-oiled Ministry of Propaganda, announced a boycott of Jewish businesses. Soon after, Jews were

1870–71	1890–91	1914–18	1915
Through brilliant diplomacy and the Franco-Prussian War, Bismarck creates a unified Germany, with Prussia at its helm and Berlin as its capital. Wilhelm I, king of Prussia, becomes Kaiser Wilhelm I.	Arising from mid-19th-century workers' parties, the Social Democratic Party of Germany (SPD) adopts its present name and a program strongly influenced by Marx's writings.	WWI: Germany, Austria-Hungary and Turkey go to war against Britain, France, Italy and Russia. Germany is defeated. Some 10 million soldiers and seven million civilians perish.	A German submarine sinks the RMS *Lusitania*, a British passenger ship carrying 1198 passengers, among them more than 120 Americans.

Germany's Changing Borders

HOLY ROMAN EMPIRE AT THE END OF THE THIRTY YEARS' WAR (PEACE OF WESTPHALIA, 1648)

GERMAN EMPIRE 1871–1918

GERMANY AFTER THE TREATY OF VERSAILLES (1919–38)

WEST GERMANY AND EAST GERMANY 1949–90

In 1923, Adolf Hitler tried to kick off a revolution from a beer hall in what became known as the Munich Putsch. He wound up in Landsberg Prison, where he penned *Mein Kampf*.

expelled from public service and banned from many professions, trades and industries. The Nuremberg Laws of 1935 deprived 'non-Aryans' of German citizenship and many other rights.

The international community, meanwhile, turned a blind eye to the situation in Germany, perhaps because many leaders were keen to see some order restored to the country after decades of political upheaval. Hitler's success at stabilising the shaky economy – largely by pumping public money into employment programs – was widely admired. The 1936 Olympic summer games in Berlin were a PR triumph, as Hitler launched a charm offensive. Terror and persecution resumed soon after the closing ceremony.

The targeting of Jews reached an early peak on 9 November 1938, with the Reichspogromnacht (often called Kristallnacht, or Night of Broken Glass). Using the assassination of a German consular official by a Polish

For a comprehensive overview of German history, visit the German Culture website www.german-culture.com.ua.

1918–19	1918–19	Mid-1920s	1933
Sailors' revolts spread across Germany, Kaiser Wilhelm II abdicates, and a democratic Weimar Republic is founded. Women receive suffrage and human rights are enshrined in law.	The 'war guilt' clause in the Treaty of Versailles, holding Germany and its allies financially responsible for loss and damage suffered by its enemies, puts the new republic on an unstable footing.	Amid the troubles of the Weimar Republic, Germans discover flamboyant pursuits. Cinemas attract two million visitors daily and cabaret and the arts flourish, but ideological differences increase.	Hitler becomes chancellor of Germany and creates a dictatorship through the Enabling Law. Only the 94 SPD Reichstag representatives present – those not in prison or exile – oppose the act.

Jew in Paris as a pretext, Nazi thugs desecrated, burned and demolished synagogues, Jewish cemeteries, property and businesses across the country. Jews had begun to emigrate after 1933, but this event set off a stampede.

The fate of those Jews who stayed behind deteriorated after the outbreak of WWII in 1939. In 1942, at Hitler's request, a conference in Berlin's Wannsee came up with the *Endlösung* (Final Solution): the systematic, bureaucratic and meticulously documented annihilation of European Jews. Sinti and Roma, political opponents, priests, gays and habitual criminals were targeted as well. Of the roughly seven million people who were sent to concentration camps, only 500,000 survived.

Resistance to Hitler was quashed early by the powerful Nazi terror machine, but it never vanished entirely. On 20 July 1944, Claus Schenk Graf von Stauffenberg and other high-ranking army officers tried to assassinate Hitler and were executed. Anti-Nazi leaflets were distributed in Munich and other cities by the Weisse Rose (White Rose), a group of Munich university students, whose resistance attempts cost most of them their lives.

> A comprehensive collection of fascinating Nazi propaganda material can be viewed at www.calvin.edu/academic/cas/gpa.

World War II

WWII began on 1 September 1939 with the Nazi attack on Poland. France and Britain declared war on Germany two days later, but even this could not prevent the quick defeat of Poland, Belgium, the Netherlands and France. Other countries, including Denmark and Norway, were also soon brought into the Nazi fold.

In June 1941 Germany broke its nonaggression pact with Stalin by attacking the USSR. Though successful at first, Operation Barbarossa quickly ran into problems, culminating in the defeat at Stalingrad (today Volgograd) the following winter, forcing the Germans to retreat.

With the Normandy invasion of June 1944, Allied troops arrived in formidable force on the European mainland, supported by unrelenting air raids that reduced Germany's cities to rubble and the country's population by 10%. The final Battle of Berlin began in mid-April 1945. More than 1.5 million Soviet soldiers barrelled towards the capital from the east, reaching Berlin on 21 April and encircling it on 25 April. Two days later they were in the city centre, fighting running street battles with the remaining troops, many of them boys and elderly men.

> Commenting on the Nazi party's torchlit procession through Berlin's Brandenburg Gate after taking power in January 1933, artist Max Liebermann famously commented: 'I couldn't possibly eat as much as I would like to puke.'

On 30 April the fighting reached the government quarter where Hitler was holed up in his bunker with his long-time mistress Eva Braun, whom he'd married just a day earlier. Finally accepting the inevitability of defeat, the couple killed themselves. As their bodies were burning in the chancellery courtyard, Red Army soldiers raised the Soviet flag above the Reichstag.

On 7 May 1945, Germany surrendered unconditionally. Peace was signed at the US military headquarters in Reims (France) and at the So-

1933–34	1935	1936	1937–45
The Nazi *Gleichschaltung* (enforced conformity) begins, signalling the death of tolerance and pluralism. The federal states become powerless, and opposition parties and free-trade unions are banned.	The Nuremberg Laws are enacted. A law for the 'protection of German blood and honour' forbids marriage between 'Aryans' and 'non-Aryans'. Another law deprives Jews and other 'non-Aryans' of German nationality.	Berlin hosts the Olympic Games. Embarrassingly for Hitler, who originally wanted to ban all black and Jewish athletes, African American Jesse Owens wins four gold medals in athletics.	Nazi Germany and Italy sign an agreement that allows several hundred thousand workers from Mussolini's Italy to boost labour for mostly war industries. Later, they become forced labourers.

viet military headquarters in Berlin. On 8 May 1945, WWII in Europe officially came to an end.

The Big Chill

At conferences in Yalta and Potsdam in February and July 1945, respectively, the Allies (the USA, the UK, the Soviet Union and France) redrew Germany's borders and carved up the country into four occupied zones.

Friction between the Western Allies and the Soviets quickly emerged. While the Western Allies focused on helping Germany get back on its feet by kick-starting the devastated economy, the Soviets insisted on massive reparations and began brutalising and exploiting their own zone of occupation. Tens of thousands of able-bodied men and POWs ended up in *gulags* (labour camps) deep in the Soviet Union. Inflation still strained local economies, food shortages affected the population, and the Communist Party of Germany (KPD) and Social Democratic Party of Germany (SPD) were forced to unite as the Sozialistische Einheitspartei Deutschlands (SED; Socialist Unity Party). In the Allied zones, meanwhile, democracy was beginning to take root, as Germany elected state parliaments (1946-47).

The showdown came in June 1948, when the Allies introduced the Deutschmark in their zones. The USSR regarded this as a breach of the Potsdam Agreement, under which the powers had agreed to treat Germany as one economic zone. The Soviets issued their own currency, the Ostmark, and announced a full-scale economic blockade of West Berlin. The Allies responded with the remarkable Berlin Airlift. For 11 months, American and British air crews flew in food, coal, machinery and other essential supplies to Tempelhof Airport in West Berlin. By the time the Soviets backed down, the Allies had made 278,000 flights, logged a distance equivalent to 250 round trips to the moon and delivered 2.5 million tonnes of cargo.

Two German States

In 1949 the division of Germany – and Berlin – was formalised. The western zones evolved into the Bundesrepublik Deutschland (BRD, Federal Republic of Germany or FRG) with Konrad Adenauer as its first chancellor and Bonn, on the Rhine River, as its capital. An economic aid package, dubbed the Marshall Plan, created the basis for West Germany's *Wirtschaftswunder* (economic miracle), which saw the economy grow at an average 8% per year between 1951 and 1961. The recovery was largely engineered by economics minister Ludwig Erhard, who dealt with an acute labour shortage by inviting about 2.3 million foreign workers, mainly from Turkey, Yugoslavia and Italy, to Germany, thereby laying the foundation for today's multicultural society.

The Soviet zone, meanwhile, grew into the Deutsche Demokratische Republik (DDR, German Democratic Republic or GDR) with East Berlin

One of a clutch of fabulous films by Germany's best-known female director, Margarethe von Trotta, *Rosenstrasse* (2003) is a portrayal of a 1943 protest by a group of non-Jewish women against the deportation of their Jewish husbands.

HISTORY THE BIG CHILL

1938	1939	1939–45	1940
The Munich Agreement allows Hitler to annex the Sudetenland, an ethnic-German region of Czechoslovakia. British Prime Minister Neville Chamberlain declares there will be 'peace in our time'.	WWII: Hitler invades Poland on 1 September. Two days later France and Britain declare war on Germany.	Millions of Jews are murdered during the Holocaust and 62 million civilians and soldiers die – 27 million in the Soviet Union alone.	The German Luftwaffe is defeated by the Spitfires of the RAF in the Battle of Britain, a major turning point in WWII. Hitler gives up on plans to invade Great Britain.

JEWS IN GERMANY

The first Jews arrived in present-day Germany with the conquering Romans, settling in important Roman cities on or near the Rhine, such as Cologne, Trier, Mainz, Speyer and Worms. As non-Christians, Jews had a separate political status. Highly valued for their trade connections, they were formally invited to settle in Speyer in 1084 and granted trading privileges and the right to build a wall around their quarter. A charter of rights granted to the Jews of Worms in 1090 by Henry IV allowed local Jews to be judged according to their own laws.

The First Crusade (1095–99) brought pogroms in 1096, usually against the will of local rulers and townspeople. Many Jews resisted, before committing suicide once their situation became hopeless. This, the *Kiddush ha-shem* (martyr's death), established a precedent of martyrdom that became a tenet of European Judaism in the Middle Ages.

In the 13th-century Jews were declared crown property by Frederick II, an act that afforded protection but exposed them to royal whim. Rabbi Meir of Rothenburg, who is buried in Europe's oldest Jewish cemetery in Worms, fell foul of King Rudolph I in 1293 for leading a group of would-be emigrants to Palestine; he died in prison. The Church also prescribed distinctive clothing for Jews at this time, which later meant that in some towns Jews had to wear badges.

Things deteriorated with the arrival of the plague in the mid-14th century, when Jews were persecuted and libellous notions circulated throughout the Christian population. The 'blood libel' accused Jews of using the blood of Christians in rituals.

Money lending was the main source of income for Jews in the 15th century. Expulsions remained commonplace, however, with large numbers emigrating to Poland, where the Yiddish language developed. The Reformation (including a hostile Martin Luther) and the Thirty Years' War brought difficult times for Jewish populations, but by the 17th century they were again valued for their economic contacts.

Napoleon granted Germany's Jews equal rights, but the reforms were repealed by the 1815 Congress of Vienna. Anti-Jewish feelings in the early 19th century coincided with German nationalism and a more vigorous Christianity, producing a large number of influential assimilated Jews.

By the late 19th century, Jews had equal status in most respects and Germany had become a world centre of Jewish cultural and historical studies. There was a shift to large cities, such as Leipzig, Cologne, Breslau (now Wrocław in Poland), Hamburg, Frankfurt am Main and the capital, Berlin, where a third of German Jews lived.

Germany became an important centre for Hebrew literature after Russian writers and academics fled the revolution of 1917. The Weimar Republic brought emancipation for the 500,000-strong Jewish community, but by 1943 Adolf Hitler had declared Germany *Judenrein* (literally 'clean of Jews'). This ignored the hundreds of thousands of Eastern European Jews incarcerated on 'German' soil. Around six million Jews died in Europe as a direct result of Nazism.

The number of Jews affiliated with the Jewish community in Germany is currently around 100,000 – the third largest in Europe – but there are many more who are not affiliated with a synagogue. Among them are many of the 250,000 Russian Jews who arrived in Germany between 1989 and 2005 to escape economic and political turmoil, as well as perceived widespread antisemitism.

1941–43	1945	1948–49	1949
Nazi Germany invades the USSR in June 1941, but the campaign falters almost from the outset and defeat in the Battle of Stalingrad in 1942–43 drains valuable resources.	Hitler commits suicide in a Berlin bunker while a defeated Germany surrenders. Germany is split into Allied- and Soviet-occupied zones; Berlin has its own British, French, US and Soviet zones.	The USSR blocks land routes to Allied sectors of Berlin when cooperation between the Allies and the Soviets breaks down. Over 278,000 US and British flights supply West Berlin during the Berlin airlift.	Allied-occupied West Germany becomes the FRG (Federal Republic of Germany), with Bonn as its capital. The GDR (German Democratic Republic;) is established in the Soviet-occupied zone, with Berlin as its capital.

as its capital and Wilhelm Pieck as its first president. A single party, the Sozialistische Einheitspartei Deutschlands (SED, Socialist Unity Party of Germany), led by party boss Walter Ulbricht, dominated economic, judicial and security policy. In order to suppress any opposition, the Ministry for State Security, or Stasi, was established in 1950.

Economically East Germany stagnated, in large part because of the Soviets' continued policy of asset stripping and reparation payments. Stalin's death in 1953 raised hopes for reform but only spurred the GDR government to raise production goals even higher. Smouldering discontent erupted in violence on 17 June 1953, when 10% of GDR workers took to the streets. Soviet troops quashed the uprising, with scores of deaths and the arrest of about 1200 people.

The Wall: What Goes Up...

Through the 1950s the economic gulf between the East and West Germany widened, prompting 3.6 million East Germans – mostly young and well educated – to seek a future in the West, thus putting the GDR on the brink of economic and political collapse. Eventually, this sustained brain and brawn drain prompted the East German government – with Soviet consent – to build a wall to keep its citizens in. Construction of the Berlin Wall, the Cold War's most potent symbol, began on the night of 13 August 1961.

This stealthy act left Berliners stunned. Formal protests from the Western Allies, as well as massive demonstrations in West Berlin, were ignored. Tense times followed. In October 1961, US and Soviet tanks faced off at the Berlin border crossing, Checkpoint Charlie, in a display of brinkmanship.

The appointment of Erich Honecker (1912–94) as leader of East Germany in 1971, combined with the *Ostpolitik* (East-friendly policy) of West German chancellor Willy Brandt (1913–92), allowed an easier political relationship between the East and the West. In September that year all four Allies signed a Four Power Accord that regulated access between West Berlin and West Germany, guaranteed West Berliners the right to visit East Berlin and the GDR, and even granted GDR citizens permission to travel to West Germany in cases of family emergency.

The accord also paved the way for the *Grundlagenvertrag* (Basic Treaty), signed a year later, in which the two countries recognised each other's sovereignty and borders and committed to setting up 'permanent missions' in Bonn and East Berlin.

In 1974 West Germany joined the G8 group of industrial nations. But the 1970s were also a time of terrorism, and several prominent business and political figures were assassinated by the anticapitalist Red Army Faction (RAF). In the same decade, antinuclear and green issues appeared onto the agenda, which ultimately lead to the founding of Die Grünen (the Green Party) in 1980.

Of the dozens of books covering Nazi concentration camps, *I Never Saw Another Butterfly: Children's Drawings and Poems from Terezín Concentration Camp 1942–1944*, edited by Hana Volavková, says it all. *This Way for the Gas, Ladies and Gentlemen*, by Tadeusz Borowski, is equally chilling.

HISTORY THE WALL: WHAT GOES UP...

1950	1951–61	1953	1954
The Christian Democratic Union (CDU) is founded at federal level in West Germany and Adenauer, known for his support for strong relationships with France and the US, is elected its first national chairman.	The economic vision of Ludwig Erhard unleashes West Germany's *Wirtschaftswunder* (economic miracle). The economy averages an annual growth rate of 8%.	Following the death of Stalin and unfulfilled hopes for better conditions in the GDR, workers and farmers rise up, strike or demonstrate in 560 towns and cities. Soviet troops quash the uprising.	West Germany wins the FIFA World Cup, a famous victory that becomes known as 'the miracle of Bern'.

...Must Come Down

Hearts and minds in Eastern Europe had long been restless for change, but German reunification caught even the most insightful political observers by surprise. The so-called *Wende* (turning point, ie the fall of communism) came about as a gradual development that ended in a big bang – the collapse of the Berlin Wall on 9 November 1989.

Prior to the Wall's collapse, East Germans were, once again, leaving their country in droves, this time via Hungary, which had opened its borders with Austria. The SED was helpless to stop the flow of people wanting to leave, some of whom sought refuge in the West German embassy in Prague. Meanwhile, mass demonstrations in Leipzig spread to other cities, including East Berlin.

As the situation escalated, Erich Honecker relinquished leadership to Egon Krenz (b 1937). And then the floodgates opened: on the fateful night of 9 November 1989, party functionary Günter Schabowski informed GDR citizens they could travel directly to the West, effective immediately. The announcement itself was correct but it was not supposed to be made until the following day, leaving border guards overwhelmed. Tens of thousands of East Germans jubilantly rushed through border points in Berlin and elsewhere in the country, bringing to an end the long, chilly phase of German division.

Reunification

The Germany of today, with 16 unified states, was hammered out after a volatile political debate and a series of treaties to end post-WWII occupation zones. The reunited city of Berlin became a city state. A common currency and economic union became realities in July 1990 and a mere month later the Unification Treaty was signed in Berlin. In September that year, representatives of East and West Germany, the USSR, France, the UK and the US met in Moscow to sign the Two-Plus-Four Treaty, ending postwar occupation zones and paving the way for formal German reunification. One month later, the East German state was dissolved; in December Germany held its first unified post-WWII elections.

In 1991 a small majority (338 to 320) of members in the Bundestag (German parliament) voted in favour of moving the government to Berlin and of making Berlin the German capital once again. On 8 September 1994 the last Allied troops stationed in Berlin left the city after a festive ceremony.

The single most dominant figure throughout reunification and the 1990s was Helmut Kohl, whose Christlich Demokratische Union Deutschlands (Christian Democratic Union; CDU)/Christlich-Soziale Union (Christian Social Union; CSU) and Freie Demokratische Partei

1955	1961	1963	1972
In a sign of increasing divisions between the two states, West Germany joins NATO while East Germany puts its name to the Warsaw Pact.	On the night of 12 August, the GDR government begins building the Berlin Wall, a 155km-long barrier surrounding West Berlin.	US President John F Kennedy professes his solidarity with the people of Berlin when giving his famous 'Ich bin ein Berliner' speech at the main town hall in West Berlin.	Social Democrat chancellor Willy Brandt's *Ostpolitik* thaws relations between the two Germanys. The Basic Treaty is signed in East Berlin, paving the way for both countries to join the UN.

(Free Democratic Party; FDP) coalition was re-elected to office in December 1990 in Germany's first postreunification election.

Under Kohl's leadership, East German assets were privatised; over-subsidised state industries were radically trimmed back, sold or wound up completely; and infrastructure was modernised (and in some cases over-invested in) to create a unification boom that saw the former East Germany grow by up to 10% each year until 1995.

Growth slowed dramatically from the mid-1990s, however, creating an eastern Germany that consisted of unification winners and losers. Those who had jobs did well, but unemployment was high and the lack of opportunities in a number of eastern regions was still causing many young people to try their luck in western Germany or in boom towns such as Leipzig. Berlin, although economically shaky, was the exception. Many public servants relocated there from Bonn to staff the ministries, and young people from all over Germany were attracted by its vibrant cultural scene.

Kohl's involvement in a party slush-fund scandal in the late 1990s financially burdened his own party and resulted in the CDU stripping him of his position as lifelong honorary chairman. In 1998 a coalition of the SPD and Bündnis 90/Die Grünen (Alliance 90/The Greens) parties defeated the CDU/CSU and FDP coalition.

The New Millennium

With the formation of a coalition government of SPD and Alliance 90/The Greens in 1998, Germany reached a new milestone. It marked the first time an environmentalist party had governed nationally – in Germany or elsewhere in the world. Two figures dominated the seven-year rule of the coalition: Chancellor Gerhard Schröder (b 1944) and the Green Party vice-chancellor and foreign minister Joschka Fischer (b 1948). Despite the latter's left-wing house-squatting roots in 1970s Frankfurt am Main, he enjoyed respect abroad and widespread popularity among Germans of all political stripes.

Under Schröder, Germany began to take a more independent approach to foreign policy, refusing military involvement in Iraq but supporting the USA, historically its closest ally, in Afghanistan and the war in Kosovo. Its stance on Iraq, which reflected the feelings of the majority of Germans, strained relations with the George W Bush administration.

The rise of the Greens and, more recently, the democratic socialist Die Linke (The Left), has changed the political landscape of Germany dramatically, making absolute majorities by the 'big two' (ie CDU/CSU and SPD) all the more difficult to achieve. The 2005 election brought a grand coalition of CDU/CSU and SPD with Angela Merkel (b 1954) as chancellor – the first woman, former East German, Russian speaker and

In early 2012 the tombstone on Hitler's parents' grave was removed from the Austrian village of Leonding, to prevent it becoming a shrine for neo-Nazis.

HISTORY THE NEW MILLENNIUM

After the Wall (1995), by Marc Fisher, is an account of German society, with emphasis on life after the Wende (fall of communism). Fisher was bureau chief for the Washington Post in Bonn and presents some perceptive social insights.

1972	1974	1977	1985
Munich hosts the Olympic Games, which end in tragedy when Palestinian terrorists murder two Israeli competitors and take nine hostage. A botched rescue operation kills all nine.	West Germany joins the G8 group of industrialised nations and hosts and wins the FIFA World Cup. The final is played at Munich's Olympic Stadium.	The Deutscher Herbst (German Autumn) envelops West Germany, when a second generation of the left-wing Red Army Faction (RAF) murders key business and state figures.	Teenage sensation Boris Becker wins Wimbledon tennis tournament. At the age of 17, he is the youngest player and first German to do so.

quantum chemist in the job. While many Germans hoped this would resolve a political stalemate that had existed between an opposition-led *Bundesrat* (upper house) and the government, political horse trading shifted away from the political limelight and was mostly carried out behind closed doors.

When the financial crisis struck in 2008, the German government pumped hundreds of billions of euros into the financial system to prop up the banks. Other measures allowed companies to put workers on shorter shifts without loss of pay and incentive schemes such as encouraging Germans to trade older cars for new ones.

The election of 2009 confirmed the trend towards smaller parties and a five-party political system in Germany. Both CDU/CSU and SPD lost a considerable number of votes to the FDP, Left and Green parties. Support for the Left had been consistently strong in eastern Germany, but success in 2009 allowed it to establish itself at the federal level. The 2013 election slightly reversed the trend, with the big parties gaining back some of the votes. The biggest loser that year was the FDP, which garnered a mere 4.8% (9.8% less than in 2009), thus falling below the 5% required for representation in the Bundestag.

ANGELA MERKEL – THE ENIGMATIC CHANCELLOR

Some say that she's enigmatic; others, that she likes to keep a low profile when political dissonance breaks out, especially within her own party. What is indisputable, however, is that Angela Merkel's rise to become German chancellor in 2005 brought about a number of firsts. She was Germany's first woman and first former East German in the job and, because of the latter, she also became the first Russian-speaking German chancellor.

Merkel was born in Hamburg in 1954 but grew up in the boondocks – in the Uckermark region (in Brandenburg, near the Polish border), where her father had a posting as a pastor in East Germany. She studied physics in Leipzig (and later earned a doctorate in quantum chemistry from the Academy of Sciences of the German Democratic Republic), entering politics as the GDR was falling apart. Soon she was honing her political skills in the ministries of a reunified Germany (Women and Youth was one ministry; Environment, Natural Protection and Reactor Safety was another) under Helmut Kohl, which is why she's sometimes called 'Kohl's foster child'. Her breakthrough came in the late 1990s when the reputations of several CDU high-flyers suffered as a result of a party slush fund.

While political commentators outside Germany have often compared her to the former UK prime minister Margaret Thatcher, Merkel's leadership style rarely has the bite of Britain's 'Iron Lady'. What Thatcher and Merkel do have in common, though, is that both have ranked among the *Forbes* 100 most powerful women in the world – Angela Merkel has topped the list since 2005.

1989	1989	1990	2005
Demonstrations are held in Leipzig and other East German cities. Hungary opens its border with Austria, and East Germans are able to travel to the West.	The Berlin Wall comes down, causing Communist regimes across Eastern Europe to fall like dominoes. East Germans flood into West Germany.	Berlin becomes the capital of reunified Germany. Helmut Kohl's conservative coalition promises East–West economic integration, creating unrealistic expectations of a blossoming economic landscape in the east.	Angela Merkel becomes Germany's first female chancellor, leading a grand coalition of major parties after the election results in neither the SPD nor the CDU/CSU being able to form its own government.

The 2013 election also saw the meteoric rise of a new conservative party, the Euro-sceptic Alternative für Deutschland (AfD, Alternative for Germany). Founded in April 2013, it scooped up 4.7% of the vote, with a platform advocating a return to the Deutschmark and other national currencies, a flat tax of 25% and tighter immigration laws. Voters were drawn from across the political spectrum but shared a general disillusionment with existing parties.

Although narrowly missing the 5% Bundestag threshold, the AfD has since gained representation in the European Parliament and in the state parliaments of Brandenburg, Saxony, Thuringia, Hamburg and Bremen. However, the election of the national conservative Frauke Petry as party leader at the AfD convention in July 2015 prompted thousands of more moderate members, including co-founder Bernd Lucke, to leave the party. A couple of weeks later, Lucke founded a new party, called Alfa.

In her convention speech, Petry garnered some of the biggest applause for her Islamophobic stance, which reflects her popularity among sympathisers of the anti-Islam, anti-immigrant Pegida ('Patriotic Europeans against the Islamisation of the West'), a populist movement founded in Dresden in October 2014. Although subject to strong criticism for its ties to the far right, Pegida quickly managed to attract thousands of followers and made headlines throughout the winter of 2014–15 with weekly demonstrations that peaked with 25,000 participants in January 2015. This sparked numerous, even bigger counter-rallies, as well as public condemnation by senior politicians, including Angela Merkel, and celebrities.

The issue fuelling support for both AfD and Pegida is the wave of economic and political refugees trying to enter Europe. In Germany, the level of immigration was expected to reach a 20-year high in 2015, with as many as 300,000 applications for asylum, a 50% increase from 2014. Xenophobia and frustration with existing immigration laws and policies have led to a number of arson attacks on shelters built for asylum seekers to live in while their applications grind through Germany's complex bureaucratic process.

Amid all these serious developments came a feel-good moment in 2014, when the German national soccer team won the FIFA World Cup for the fourth time. The title had previously been achieved in 1954, 1974 and 1990.

Daring Young Men: the Heroism and Triumph of the Berlin Airlift, by Richard Reeves, examines this 'first battle of the Cold War' by telling the stories of the American and British pilots who risked their lives to save their former enemies.

HISTORY THE NEW MILLENNIUM

2006	**2008**	**2009**	**2014**
Germans proudly fly their flag as the country hosts the FIFA World Cup for the first time as a unified nation.	The economic crisis bites deeply into German export industries. German banks are propped up by state funds as unemployment and state debt rise again.	The CDU/CSU and FDP achieve a majority in the federal election. Angela Merkel is re-elected as chancellor.	Germany's national football team wins the FIFA World Cup in Brazil.

The German People

When a 2013 BBC Worldwide poll found that Germany was considered the world's most popular country, it surprised many people, most of all the Germans themselves. Having been called arrogant, aggressive and humourless, they were hardly used to such positive feedback! But the poll shows that times are a-changing, proving that modern leadership, a belief in the power of diplomacy and, let's not forget, a pretty good national football team can ultimately make a difference.

The National Psyche

Some 15% of German beach tourists admit to having sunbathed in the nude, more than any other nation.

The German state of mind has long attracted speculation: two 20th-century wars and the memory of the Jewish Holocaust alone provide ample reason to consider the German psyche. Throw in Cold War division, a juggernaut-like economy that draws half of Europe in its wake and pumps enormous amounts of goods into the world economy, plus a crucial position at the crossroads of Europe, and this fascination is even more understandable.

Germans as a whole fall within the mental topography of northern Europe and are sometimes described as culturally 'low context'. That means, as opposed to the French or Italians, Germans like to pack what they mean into the words they use, rather than hint or suggest. Facing each other squarely in conversation, giving firm handshakes and hugs or kisses on the cheek among friends are also par for the course.

Many Germans are very much fans of their own folk culture. Even a young Bavarian from, say, the finance department of a large company, might don the dirndl (traditional Bavarian skirt and blouse) around Oktoberfest time and swill like a hearty, rollicking peasant. On Monday she'll be back at the desk, soberly crunching numbers.

Lifestyle

The German household fits into the general mould of households in other Western European countries. However, a closer look reveals some

---

OSTALGIE

Who would want to go back to East German times? Not many, but there was more to the GDR (German Democratic Republic; the former East Germany) than simply being a 'satellite of the Evil Empire', as Cold War warriors from the 1980s would portray it.

The opening lines of director Leander Haussmann's film *Sonnenallee* (1999) encapsulate this idea: 'Once upon a time, there was a land and I lived there and, if I am asked how it was, I say it was the best time of my life because I was young and in love'. Another film, the smash hit *Good Bye, Lenin!* (2003), looked at East Germany with humour and pathos. It also gave *Ostalgie* – from *Ost* (East) and *Nostalgie* (nostalgia) – the kick it needed to become a more-or-less permanent cultural fixture in Germany.

Whether it be in the form of grinning Erich Honecker doubles at parties, Spreewald cucumbers and GDR Club Cola, or the *Ampelmännchen* (the little green man that helped East German pedestrians cross the road), *Ostalgie* is here to stay. For a taste of what the East offered in daily life, check out the GDR museums in Berlin, Pirna and Radebeul.

distinctly German quirks, whether it be a compulsion for sorting and recycling rubbish, a taste for fizzy mineral water or a springtime obsession with asparagus.

Although tradition is valued and grandmother's heirlooms may still occupy pride of place in many a house, 3D smart TVs babble away in living rooms across the land and Germany boasts 71.7 million internet surfers (86% of the population), 23 million of whom also have a Facebook account. Eight in 10 Germans own a bike, but there's a car in almost every driveway, embodying the German belief that true freedom comes on four wheels and is best expressed by tearing along the autobahn at 200km/h or more. For many outsiders this high level of car use is incongruous with the Germans' green credentials.

One aspect of life many visitors can't help but notice is the high number of smokers, although levels are declining. Almost 29% of German men and 20% of women smoke, despite various smoking bans (which are different in each state). Alcohol consumption is also high and on the increase.

Smoking is the least of the problems continuing to plague the east of the country, where unemployment and a brain drain to the west dog the economy. Even when in employment, eastern Germans can expect to earn around 20% less than they would in the western states.

Birth rates are among the lowest in the world (8.2 babies per 1000 inhabitants) and have fallen steadily over the last decade, prompting fears that future labour market shortages will damage the economy. Although the traditional nuclear family is still the most common model, there is no social stigma attached to other family forms. Since one in three marriages end in divorce, many families today are so-called 'patchwork families', composed of divorced new partners and their children from a previous relationship.

Abortion is illegal (except when a medical or criminal indication exists), but it is unpunishable if carried out within 12 weeks of conception and after compulsory counselling. There is no 'gay marriage', although a law passed in 2001 made it possible for same-sex couples to register a civil partnership. Gays and lesbians walk with ease in most cities, especially Berlin, Hamburg, Cologne and Frankfurt am Main, although LGBT folk do encounter discrimination in certain eastern German areas.

German school hours, which are usually from 8am to 1pm (until 4pm for the less common 'all day' schools), and the underfunding of child care make combining career and children difficult for German women. On the plus side, parents enjoy equal rights for maternity and paternity leave.

On the whole, the number of women in employment is increasing. About 70% of working-age women are employed – high for an EU country – but lower than neighbours Switzerland, the Netherlands and the Scandinavian countries. Almost half of these women work part-time, and in eastern Germany women tend to have more of a presence at managerial level.

The official retirement age is 67, but changes may see this gradually increase to 69 in the coming decades.

Sport

Football

Football ignites the passion of Germans everywhere and has contributed to building Germany's self-confidence as a nation. Its national side has won the World Cup four times: in 1954, 1974, 1990 and 2014. West Germany's first victory against Hungary in Bern, Switzerland, was unexpected and quite miraculous for a country slumbering deeply in post-WWII depression. The miracle of Bern – as the victory was dubbed – sent national morale soaring.

Germany's first gay publication, *Der Eigene*, was published in 1896 and, with a few interruptions, continued until the early 1930s, when it was shut down by the Nazis.

Women's issues are lobbied by the Deutscher Frauenrat (German Women's Council; www.deutscher-frauenrat.de).

GREEN GERMANY

Germans are the original Greens. They cannot claim to have invented environmentalism, but they were there at the outset and it was they who coined the word to describe the movement. A few 'Values' and 'Ecology' parties were knocking around beforehand, but it was the group of politicians associated with Rudi Dutschke, Petra Kelly and artist Joseph Beuys who first hit on the name The Greens (Die Grünen) when contesting local and national elections in 1979 and 1980. They gained a strong foothold in Bremen, and other political groups across the world decided they quite liked the moniker.

The Greens' concern for the health of the planet and their strong opposition to nuclear power certainly struck a chord with the local populace. Contemporary Germans recycle vigilantly, often prefer to ride bicycles rather than catch buses, and carry their groceries in reusable cloth shopping bags; all this is simply second nature here.

Green ideology has also wielded an enormous influence on the political agenda. In the 1990s Greenpeace Germany made international news attempting to stop nuclear-waste transports in Lower Saxony and heavily populated North Rhine–Westphalia. German Greenpeace members also helped scuttle Shell's controversial plans to sink the *Brent Spar* oil platform in the North Sea.

Even more tellingly, the Greens were in government between 1998 and 2005, as the junior partner in Gerhard Schröder's coalition. Under the leadership of Joschka Fischer, the party had a major say in decisions to cut carbon emissions and to wind down the nuclear industry. In 2011 Germany announced the decision to phase out nuclear energy by 2022.

Germany has also hosted the World Cup twice, in 1974 and 2006. The first occasion was particularly special, as West Germany beat Holland 2-1 in the final, held at Munich's Olympic stadium.

Domestically, Germany's Bundesliga has fallen behind other European leagues, such as Spain's La Liga and England's Premier League, but still throws up some exciting duels. On the European stage, Germany's most successful domestic club is FC Bayern München, which has been Deutscher Meister (national champion) 25 times and has won the UEFA Champions League five times, the last time in 2012–13.

Women's football is growing in popularity, partly because of the success of the women's national team. Germany has won the FIFA Women's World Cup twice to date (in 2003 and 2007) and hosted the event in 2011.

Always a keen sporting nation, Germany has hosted the summer Olympics and football World Cup twice each. The Germans, it seems, are dastardly good at most sporting disciplines, and if your country has a national game, the Germans probably thrashed you at it a long time ago.

Tennis

Tennis was a minor sport until 1985, when the unseeded 17-year-old Boris Becker (b 1967), from Leinen near Heidelberg, became the youngest ever men's singles champion. Suddenly every German kid aspired to be the next Becker. The red-headed net-diver went on to win five more Grand Slam titles in his career. Even more successful was Steffi Graf (b 1969), who is among the few women to have won all four Grand Slam events in one year, and in 1988 – after also winning the gold in Seoul at the Olympics – the 'golden slam'.

Other Sports

Germany's most successful golfer, Bernhard Langer, is the son of a Russian prisoner of war who jumped off a Siberia-bound train and settled in Bavaria.

Though a relatively minor sport in Germany, basketball is gaining in popularity. Cycling boomed after Jan Ullrich (b 1973) became the first German to win the Tour de France in 1997. With seven world championships and more than 50 Grand Prix wins, Michael Schumacher (b 1969) was the most successful Formula One driver of all time, before suffering a major head injury in a skiing accident in 2013. After months in an induced coma, he returned to his home in September 2014, but remains paralysed and wheelchair-bound.

Multiculturalism

Germany has always attracted immigrants, be it French Huguenots escaping religious persecution (about 30% of Berlin's population in 1700 was Huguenot), 19th-century Polish miners who settled in the Ruhr region, post-WWII asylum seekers or foreign *Gastarbeiter* (guest workers) during the 1950s and 1960s to resolve labour shortages.

After reunification, the foreign population soared, as emigrants from the imploding USSR and the then war-ravaged Yugoslavia sought refuge. Between 1990 and 2011, Germany also accommodated around 1.4 million *Spätaussiedler* (people of German heritage), mainly from Russia, Poland and Kazakhstan. Germany has one of the highest percentage of international migrants in the world (19.5%). About 32.5% of these are from EU countries and almost 70% from Europe. Ethnic Turks form the largest single group (18.5%), followed by Poles (9.2%), Russians (7.7%), Kazakhs (5.8%) and Italians (4.9%).

There's no denying that this large immigrant population has contributed to the rise of extreme-right-wing movements, who oppose such a huge non-native presence in their country. Ironically, the problem is worst in the eastern states, where there are fewer immigrants. As across Europe, the debate as to whether Germany should promote a German *Leitkultur* (lead culture), as opposed to multiculturalism, polarises opinion.

In 2007 Würzburg-born Dirk Nowitzki (b 1978) won the NBA's Most Valuable Player Award, and was the first European player to be selected for the All-NBA First Team, made up of the best players in a season.

Religion

The constitution guarantees religious freedom; the main religions are Catholicism and Protestantism, with 24.2 million and 23.3 million members, respectively. Religion has a stronger footing in western Germany, especially Catholic Bavaria.

Unlike the Jewish community, which has grown since the early 1990s due to immigration from the former Soviet Union, the Catholic and Protestant churches are losing worshippers. This is attributed partly to the obligatory church tax (8% or 9% of total income tax paid) forked out by those registered with a recognised denomination. Most German Protestants are Lutheran, headed by the Evangelische Kirche (Protestant Church), an official grouping of a couple of dozen Lutheran churches, with headquarters in Hanover. In 2005, for the first time in almost five centuries, a German, Joseph Ratzinger (b 1927), became pope, taking the name Pope Benedict XVI. He resigned in 2013.

The largest Jewish communities are in Berlin, Frankfurt am Main and Munich. Countrywide 108 congregations are represented by the Zentralrat der Juden in Deutschland (Central Council of Jews in Germany). Around four million Muslims live in Germany, most of Turkish heritage.

The German Protestant Church is online at www.ekd.de; the Catholics are at www.catholic-hierarchy.org/country/de.html and the Central Council of Jews at www.zentral-ratdjuden.de.

THE GERMAN PEOPLE MULTICULTURALISM

Food & Drink

If we're honest, you probably didn't choose Germany for its food, right? But the culinary revolution that has been simmering for years under the sausage-cabbage-and-carbs layers is now finally bubbling to surface. Up and down the country you'll come across chefs playing up local, seasonal produce and making healthy and creative street food. There are exciting riffs on vegetarian and vegan food, and organic everything. Even some wines these days can rival the French and Italian old-timers. So dig in and drink up – you might just be surprised.

Local & Lighter

The German love of nature and eye for quality is reflected in what lands on the table. Long before 'seasonal' and 'local' were buzzwords, Germans made the most of locally grown produce. Menus burst with *Spargel* (asparagus) in spring and *Pfifferlinge* (chanterelles) in summer. In autumn the earthy delights of game, pumpkins and wild mushrooms enchant. Regional food at its best is about perfect timing, top-quality ingredients and dishes with natural, integral flavours.

Cheap frankfurters, frozen black forest gateau and Liebfraumilch (a sweet, white wine) may have tarnished Germany's culinary image in the past, but things are swiftly changing, with dishes getting lighter, healthier and more imaginative. Vegetarians, vegans and people with food allergies are well catered for – especially in big towns and cities. Germans like to shop at *Bauernmärkte* (farmers' markets) and *Biomärkte* (organic markets and supermarkets), where they can put a face and place to a product.

Germany is also raising the bar in the street-food stakes, where you can now find a world beyond the ubiquitous wurst (sausage) and kebab. The rest of the country, as always, is hot on the heels of Berlin, where food trucks and stands dish out everything from quirky takes on ceviche to *jiaozi* (Chinese dumplings), gourmet burgers made with 100% local beef and organic frozen yoghurt.

Sanddorn (sea buckthorn), nicknamed 'the Mecklenburg lemon', is a shrub berry with a subtle citrus flavour, used to great effect in teas, ice creams and other dishes.

German Classics

Metre-long bratwursts with litres of foamy wheat beer in Munich, snowball-sized dumplings with an avalanche of sauerkraut and roast pork in the Alps, salads swimming in dressing and cakes drowning in cream – every traveller has a tale of excess about German food.

On paper Germany's best-known specialities appear deceptively simple: wurst, *Brot, Kartoffeln* and sauerkraut (sausage, bread, potatoes and pickled cabbage). But, as any local will tell you, the devil is in the detail. Where else will you find so many kinds of sausage, such a cornucopia of bread and potatoes in so many guises? Elevated to near art forms, these staples both unite and divide the country: ingredients are often similar but regional recipes interpret them totally differently.

Sausage Country

In the Middle Ages, German peasants found a way to package and disguise animals' less appetising bits and the humble wurst was born. Today it's a noble and highly respected element of German cuisine, with strict rules determining varietal authenticity. In some cases, as with the finger-sized Nuremberg sausage, regulations even ensure offal no longer enters the equation.

There are more than 1500 sausage types, all commonly served with bread and a sweet *(süss)* or spicy *(scharf)* mustard *(Senf)*.

Bratwurst, served countrywide, is made from minced pork, veal and spices, and it is cooked in different ways: boiled in beer, baked with apples and cabbage, stewed in a casserole, grilled or barbecued.

The availability of other sausages differs regionally. A *Thüringer* is long, thin and spiced, while a wiener is what hot-dog fiends call a frankfurt. *Blutwurst* is blood sausage (not to be confused with black pudding, which is *Rotwurst*), *Leberwurst* is liver sausage and *Knackwurst* is lightly tickled with garlic.

Saxony has brain sausage *(Bregenwurst)* and Bavaria sells white rubbery *Weisswurst*, made from veal. Hamburg, Berlin and the Ruhrgebiet all claim to have invented the takeaway *Currywurst* (slices of sausage topped with curry powder and ketchup).

Daily Bread

In exile in California in 1941, German playwright Bertolt Brecht confessed that what he missed most about his homeland was the bread. Tasty and textured, often mixing wheat and rye flour, and available in 300 varieties, German bread is a world-beater. A visit to an old-fashioned *Bäckerei* (bakery), with yeasty smells wafting from ovens, bakers elbow-deep in dough and staff who remember customers by name, is a treat.

'Black' rye bread *(Schwarzbrot)* is actually brown, but a much darker shade than the slightly sour *Bauernbrot* – divine with a slab of butter. Pumpernickel bread is steamed instead of baked, making it extra moist, and actually *is* black. *Vollkorn* means wholemeal, while bread coated in sunflower seeds is *Sonnenblumenbrot*. If you insist on white bread *(Weissbrot)*, the Germans have that, too.

Fresh bread rolls (*Brötchen* in the north, *Semmel* in Bavaria and *Wecken* in southern Germany) can be covered in poppy seeds *(Mohnbrötchen)*, cooked with sweet raisins *(Rosinenbrötchen)* or sprinkled with salt *(Salzstangel)*.

King Kartoffel

Chipped, boiled, baked, mashed or fried: Germans are almost as keen as Russians about the potato. The *Kartoffel* is not only *Vegetable Nummer Eins* (first-choice vegetable) in any meat-and-three-veg dish, but it can also be incorporated into any course of a meal, from potato soup *(Kartoffelsuppe)* as a starter, to potato salad *(Kartoffelsalat)* with smoked fish, or potato pancakes *(Reibekuchen* or *Kartoffelpuffer)* as a sweet, sugar-sprinkled treat.

In between, you can try *Himmel und Erde* (Heaven and Earth), mashed potatoes and stewed apples served with black pudding, or potato-based *Klösse* dumplings. *Pellkartoffeln* or *Ofenkartoffeln* are jacket potatoes, usually capped with a dollop of *Quark* (a yoghurt-like curd cheese).

It's Pickled Cabbage

And finally we have the quintessential German side dish that many outside the country find impossible to fathom: sauerkraut. Before the 2006 FIFA World Cup, one football magazine bluntly suggested: 'It's pickled cabbage; don't try to make it sound interesting'. OK, we won't. It's shredded cabbage, doused in white-wine vinegar and slowly simmered. But if you haven't at least tried *Rotkohl* (the red-cabbage version of the white-cabbage sauerkraut), you don't know what you're missing. Braising

Quark, a yoghurt-like curd cheese, accounts for 50% of domestic cheese consumption in Germany. It is used in everything from potato dips and salad dressings to sauces to cheesecake.

The modern *Döner Kebab* (doner kebab) originates from Germany, not Turkey. In 1971 Turkish immigrants running the Berlin restaurant Hasir added salad to an age-old Turkish dish, and since then even outlets in Turkey have been making it this way.

SWEET TREATS

Unleash your sweet tooth on these German favourites:

→ **Black forest gateau** A multilayered chocolate sponge, cream and kirsch confection, topped with morello cherries and chocolate shavings.

→ **Nürnberg Lebkuchen** Totally moreish gingerbread made with nuts, fruit peel, honey and spices.

→ **Lübecker Leckerli** Honey-flavoured ginger biscuits. Also try the fabulous Lübeck marzipan.

→ **Dresden Stollen** Christmas wouldn't be the same without this spiced cake, loaded with sultanas and candied peel, sprinkled with icing sugar and spruced up with a ball of marzipan.

→ **Leipziger Lerche** As its name suggests, it was made with lark until songbird hunting was banned in 1876. Today it's shortcrust pastry filled with almonds, nuts and a cherry or spoon of jam.

→ **Aachener Printen** Aachen's riff on traditional *Lebkuchen* (gingerbread), these spicy, moreish biscuits are sweetened with beet syrup.

the cabbage with sliced apples and wine turns it into *Bayrischkraut* or *Weinkraut.*

Regional Flavours

Berlin

Alongside Hamburg, Berlin has one of the country's most dynamic and swiftly evolving restaurant scenes, but it can still lay claim to local delicacies. First up is *Eisbein* (pork knuckles with sauerkraut), then *Kohlsuppe* (cabbage soup) and *Erbsensuppe* (pea soup). Then there's the classic meaty treat on the hoof: the *Boulette,* a German-style hamburger, eaten with a dry bun and ketchup or mustard. Don't bypass the chance to give *Königsberger Klopse* (veal dumplings in caper sauce) a whirl, either.

Berlin is also where you'll find the country's highest concentration of Turkish *Döner Kebab* (doner kebab) spots, an essential end to any drink-fuelled night on the town. Germany's Turkish population invented the modern doner, adding salad and garlicky yoghurt sauce to spit-roasted lamb, veal or chicken in pita bread.

Bavaria

The Chinese say you can eat every part of the pig except the oink, and Bavarian chefs seem to be in full agreement. No part of the animal is spared their attention: they cook up its knuckles *(Schweinshax'n),* ribs *(Rippchen),* tongue *(Züngerl)* and belly *(Wammerl).* Pork also appears as *Schweinebraten* (a roast) and the misleadingly named *Leberkäse* (liver cheese), where it's combined with beef in a dish that contains no cheese – and in Bavaria at least – no liver. The Bavarians are also quite fond of veal *(Kalb).*

Dumplings are another staple, from potato-based *Klösse* and *Leberknödel* (liver dumplings) to sweet *Senfknödel,* made from *Quark,* flour and eggs, then dunked in milk. Dumplings also make a major appearance in the Franconian *Hochzeitsuppe* (wedding soup), a clear meat broth garnished with bread dumplings, liver dumplings and pancakes.

Music to the ears of Bavarian *biergarten* (beer garden) fans is that the *Brezel* (pretzel) and *Obazda* (Bavarian cheese) were given Protected Geographical Indication by the EU in 2014 and 2015, respectively.

Brezeln are traditional pretzels, covered in rock salt. Lore has it that they were born in Swabia in the 15th century when Tübingen University founder Count Eberhard im Bart, asked a baker from Bad Urach to create a pastry through which the sun could shine three times.

Stuttgart & the Black Forest

The food here, in the country's southwestern crook, is rich and earthy. Black Forest musts include *Bachforelle* (brook trout), fished from crystal-clear streams, *Schwarzwälderschinken* (dry-cured ham with a smoky aroma) and the world-famous, off-the-calorie-chart *Schwarzwälderkirschtorte* (black forest gateau). Seasonal additions to local menus include asparagus in spring/early summer and mushrooms and pumpkins in autumn. Another autumnal treat is *Zwiebelkuchen,* a deep-filled onion tart made with cream, egg, bacon and onions.

Swabian folk around Stuttgart are mad about *Spätzle,* egg-based noodles served as a main with cheese *(Käsespätzle),* or as a side dish with meat or fish. *Zwiebelrostbraten* (roast beef with onions and gravy) and *Maultaschen* (ravioli-like pockets stuffed with ground meat, onion and spinach) are other favourites.

Frankfurt & Southern Rhineland

Two former chancellors named dishes from Rhineland-Palatinate as their favourite: Helmut Kohl nominated *Saumagen,* a stuffed pork belly with pickled cabbage (vaguely resembling Scottish haggis), while post-WWII chancellor Konrad Adenauer preferred *Reibekuchen* (potato pancakes served with blueberry or apple sauce). Despite this, *Rheinischer Sauerbraten* (roast beef marinated in spiced vinegar and braised) is the region's signature dish.

Hesse produces outstanding cured and smoked hams, typically smoking them over juniper berries. Another regional favourite is pork in the form of *Sulperknochen,* a dish from trotters, ears and tails, served with mushy peas and pickled cabbage.

Saarland's neighbour is France and it shows. Fried goose liver and coq au vin are common, as is *Budeng mit Gellenewemutsch,* hot black pudding served with carrot and potato mash. When it comes to the crunch, though, Saarlanders revert to true German form, and *Schwenkbraten* (marinated pork grilled on a spit) is probably their most popular dish.

Central Germany

Saxony and Thuringia are slightly less meat-obsessed than some of their cousins. *Kartoffelsuppe* (potato soup) is a favourite, and *Leipziger Allerlei* (Leipzig hotpot) often comes in vegetarian versions. There are even lentils to be found in dishes such as *Linsensuppe mit Thüringer Rotwurst* (lentil soup with long, thin, spiced sausages).

Hamburg & the North

No two dishes better sum up northern Germany's warming, seafaring fodder than *Labskaus* and *Grünkohl mit Pinkel.* There are variations, but traditional *Labskaus* from Hamburg is a minced dish of salt herring, corned beef, pork lard, potato and beetroot, topped with gherkins and a fried egg. *Grünkohl mit Pinkel* combines steamed kale with pork belly, bacon and *Pinkelwurst* (a spicy pork, beef, oat and onion sausage from Bremen). *Aalsuppe* (eel soup) is sweet and sour – it's garnished with bacon and vegetables, and spiced with apricots, pears or prunes.

As you move towards Scandinavia, the German diet begins to encompass Nordic staples, such as rollmops and *Hering* (herring) in all its other guises (raw, smoked, pickled or rolled in sour cream).

Mecklenburg–Western Pomerania has a quite distinctive cuisine, with locals famed for liking things sweet and sour. Take *Mecklenburger Rippenbraten* (rolled pork stuffed with lemons, apples, plums and raisins), for example, *Mecklenburgische Buttermilchsuppe* (a sweet buttermilk soup flavoured with spices and jam) or the Russian-style *Soljanka* (sour soup with sausage or fish, garnished with lemon and sour cream). Other

Labskaus (a dish made of mashed potato, corned beef, onions and beets, often served with a fried egg) is a sailor's favourite and, some locals claim, brilliant hangover food – plenty of salt, plenty of fat and not too hard to chew.

When ordering food, a little knowledge of German can be a dangerous thing. Don't expect half a chicken when you order a *Halve Hahn* in Cologne – it's a rye roll with gouda cheese, gherkin and mustard. Similarly, *Kölscher Kaviar* is not caviar but black pudding. And *Nordseekrabben* in Hamburg and Lower Saxony? They're small prawns...of course.

typical mixes include raisins with cabbage, honey with pork, and plums with duck. Even the typical *Eintopf* (stew, often a potato version) is served with sugar and vinegar on the side.

Beer

Few things are as deeply ingrained in the German psyche as the love of beer. *Hopfen und Malz – Gott erhalt's!* (Hops and malt are in God's hands) goes the saying, which is fitting, given the almost religious intensity with which beer is brewed, consumed and celebrated – not least at the world's biggest festival, Oktoberfest. Brewing here goes back to Germanic tribes, and later monks, so it follows a hallowed tradition.

The 'secret' of the country's golden nectar dates back to the 1516 *Reinheitsgebot* (purity law) passed in Bavaria, demanding breweries use just four ingredients – malt, yeast, hops and water. Though it stopped being a legal requirement in 1987, when the EU struck it down as uncompetitive, many German brewers still conform to it anyway, seeing it as a good marketing tool against mass-market, chemical-happy competitors.

Kloster Weltenburg, near Kelheim (on the Danube), north of Munich, is the world's oldest monastery brewery, whose Weltenburg Barock Dunckel was presented with the World Beer Cup in 2004, 2008 and 2012. This light, smooth beer has a malty, toasty finish. Other connoisseurs believe the earthy Andechs Doppelbock Dunkel, produced by the Benedictines in Andechs near Munich, to be among the world's best.

The craft beer movement has also arrived in Germany, especially in the major cities. Berlin, as per usual, is leading the way, with places like Hops & Barley (p113), tapping unfiltered pilsner, dark and wheat beer in a former butcher's shop, and Hopfenreich (p111), the capital's first craft beer bar.

Beer Varieties

Despite often giving themselves only four ingredients to play with, Germans achieve distinctively different beers via subtle variations in the basic production process. At the simplest level, a brewer can choose a particular yeast for top or bottom fermenting.

The most popular form of brewing is bottom fermentation, which accounts for about 85% of German beers, notably the *Pils* (pilsner), popular throughout Germany, most *Bock* beers and the *Helles* (pale lager) type found in Bavaria.

Top fermentation is used for the *Weizenbier/Weissbier* (wheat/white beer) popular in Berlin and Bavaria, Cologne's *Kölsch* and the very few stouts brewed in the country.

Many beers are regional, meaning a Saxon Rechenberger cannot be found in Düsseldorf, where the locally brewed Altbier is the taste of choice.

Wine

'The Germans', wrote Mark Twain in *A Tramp Abroad* (1880), 'are exceedingly fond of Rhine wines; they are put up in tall, slender bottles, and are considered a pleasant beverage. One tells them from vinegar by the label'. He was not alone in his sentiments.

For decades the name of German wine was sullied by the cloyingly sweet Liebfraumilch and the naff image of Blue Nun. What a difference a decade makes. Thanks to rebranding campaigns, a new generation of wine growers and an overall rise in quality, German wine is staging a 21st-century comeback. In 2014 some 63 different medals were awarded to German wines, including to Horst Sauer, who received two Gold Outstandings at the International Wine and Spirit Competition in London for his Escherndorfer Lump Riesling Trockenbeerenauslese and Escherndorfer Lump Silvaner.

Thanks to the tradition of the *Reinheitsgebot* (purity law), German beer is supposed to be unique in not giving you a *Katzenjammer* or *Kater* (hangover).

Around 6.4 million litres of beer, give or take a stein, were downed by party-goers at Munich's Oktoberfest in 2014.

Some 1300 German breweries keep great beer-making traditions alive and turn out 5000 different beers. Eleven monasteries continue to produce beer today; these are known as *Klosterbrauerein*.

GERMANY'S BEER TOP 10

➡ **Pils** (pilsner) This bottom-fermented full beer, with pronounced hop flavour and creamy head, has an alcohol content around 4.8%.

➡ **Weizenbier/Weissbier** (wheat beer) Predominant in the south, especially in Bavaria, this contains 5.4% alcohol. A *Hefeweizen* has a stronger shot of yeast, whereas *Kristallweizen* is clearer, with more fizz. These beers are fruity and spicy, often recalling bananas and cloves. Decline offers of lemon as it ruins the head and – beer purists say – the flavour.

➡ **Dunkles** (dark lager) Brewed throughout Germany, but especially in Bavaria. With a light use of hops, it's full-bodied with strong malty aromas.

➡ **Helles** (pale lager) *Helles* (pale or light) refers to the colour, not the alcohol content, which is still 4.6% to 5%. Brewing strongholds are Bavaria, Baden-Württemberg and the Ruhr region. It has strong malt aromas and is slightly sweet.

➡ **Altbier** A dark, full beer with malted barley, from the Düsseldorf area.

➡ **Berliner Weisse** Berlin's top-fermented beer, which comes *rot* (red) or *grün* (green), with a *Schuss* (dash) of raspberry or woodruff syrup, respectively. A cool, fruity summer choice.

➡ **Bockbier** Strong beers with 7% alcohol. There's a '*Bock*' for every occasion, such as *Maibock* (for May/spring) and *Weihnachtsbock* (brewed for Christmas). *Eisbock* is dark and aromatic. *Bock* beers originate from Einbeck, near Hanover.

➡ **Kölsch** By law, this top-fermented beer can only be brewed in or around Cologne. It has about 4.8% alcohol, a solid hop flavour and a pale colour, and it is served in small glasses (0.2L) called *Stangen* (literally 'sticks').

➡ **Leipziger Gose** Flavoured with salt and coriander, this contrives to have a stingingly refreshing taste, with some plummy overtones. Tart like Berliner Weisse, it's often served with sweeteners, such as cherry *(Kirsch)* liqueur or the almond-flavoured *Allasch*.

➡ **Schwarzbier** (black beer) Slightly stronger, this dark, full beer has an alcohol content of 4.8% to 5%. It's fermented using roasted malt.

Even discerning wine critics have been pouring praise on German winemakers of late. According to Master of Wine Tim Atkin (www.timat kin.com), 'Germany makes the best rieslings of all', and, waxing lyrical on the country's Pinot noirs, he muses, 'if only the Germans didn't keep most of them to themselves'.

Grape Varieties

Having produced wines since Roman times, Germany now has more than 1000 sq km of vineyards, mostly on the Rhine and Moselle river-banks. Despite the common association with riesling grapes (particularly in its best wine regions), the less acidic Müller-Thurgau *(Rivaner)* grape is more widespread. Meanwhile, the Gewürztraminer grape produces spicy wines with an intense bouquet. What Germans call *Grauburgunder* is known to the rest of the world as Pinot gris.

German reds are light and lesser known. *Spätburgunder* (Pinot noir) is the best of the bunch and goes into some velvety, full-bodied reds with an occasional almond taste.

Wine Regions

There are 13 official wine-growing areas, the best being the Mosel-Saar-Ruwer region. It boasts some of the world's steepest vine-yards, where the predominantly riesling grapes are still hand-picked.

Top German Wine Producers

Dönnhoff
Award-winning rieslings.

Weingut Meyer-Näkel *Some of Germany's best Pinot noirs.*

Wittmann
Celebrated Rhein-hessen Silvaner and rieslings.

FOOD & DRINK WINE

For a comprehensive rundown of all German wine-growing regions, grape varieties, news of the hottest winemakers and information on tours or courses, visit www.winesofgermany.co.uk, www.germanwines.de and www.germanwineusa.org.

Slate soil on the hillsides gives the wines a flinty taste. Chalkier riverside soils are planted with the Elbling grape, an ancient Roman variety.

East of the Moselle, the Nahe region produces fragrant, fruity and full-bodied wines using Müller-Thurgau and Silvaner grapes, as well as riesling.

Riesling grapes are also the mainstay in Rheingau and Mittelrhein (Middle Rhine), two other highly respected wine-growing pockets. Rheinhessen, south of Rheingau, is responsible for Liebfraumilch, but also some top rieslings.

Other wine regions include Ahr, Pfalz (both in Rheinland-Palatinate), Hessische Bergstrasse (Hesse), Baden (Baden-Württemberg), Würzburg (Bavaria) and Elbtal (Saxony).

The Württemberg region, around Stuttgart, produces some of the country's best reds, while Saxony-Anhalt's Saale-Unstrut region is home to Rotkäppchen (Little Red Riding Hood) sparkling wine, a former GDR brand that's been a big hit in the new Germany.

Literature, Theatre & Film

Germany not only has a centuries-old literary tradition, but is also a nation of avid readers. Some 94,000 new books are released annually and Frankfurt's International Book Fair is the publishing world's most important gathering. Theatre, too, is a mainstay of the cultural scene, with hundreds of stages around the country and playwrights such as Lessing, Goethe and Brecht well known both inside and outside the country. In film Germany is not only a pioneer of the genre but, in the new millennium, has also gained international recognition with boundary-pushing movies.

Literature

Early Writing

Early forms of literary expression originated during the reign of Charlemagne (c 800); the most famous surviving work of this early period is the 11th century heroic epic poem *Hildebrandslied*. Medieval literature flourished in the 12th century, with *Minnesänger* (lyric poetry performed by bards, such as Walther von der Vogelweide) and more heroic poems, like the *Nibelungenlied*. A key figure in German writing was Protestant reformer Martin Luther, whose 1522 translation of the New Testament created a unified standard version of the German language.

A major work of the baroque period is Grimmelshausen's novel *Simplicissimus* (1668), which follows the adventures of a young ne'er do well in the Thirty Years' War. Another landmark is Christoph Martin Wieland's *Geschichte des Agathon* (Agathon; 1766–67), which is considered the first *Bildungsroman* (a novel showing the development of the hero) and an important piece of Enlightenment literature.

The rationality of the Enlightenment was followed by the *Sturm und Drang* (Storm and Stress) phase, which was characterised by emotional and subjective writing. The style was dominated by Germany's literary lion Johann Wolfgang von Goethe (eg *The Sorrows of Younger Werther*; 1774) and his friend Friedrich Schiller (eg *The Robbers*; 1781). Both of them later distanced themselves from the movement and ushered in what became known as Weimar Classicism, with its emphasis on humanist ideals.

Serious academics (they wrote *German Grammar* and *History of the German Language*), the Grimm brothers – Jacob and Wilhelm – are best known for their collection of fairy tales, myths and legends, published between 1812 and 1858. Heinrich Heine produced one of Germany's finest collections of poems, *Buch der Lieder* (Book of Songs) in 1827, but it was his more political writings that contributed to his work being banned under Prussian censorship laws in 1835.

Modernism & Modernity

In the 1920s Berlin became a literary hotbed, drawing writers like Alfred Döblin, whose *Berlin Alexanderplatz* (1929) is a stylised meander through the seamy 1920s, and Anglo-American import Christopher Isherwood, whose semi-autobiographical *Berlin Stories* formed the basis of the musical and film *Cabaret*. A key figure was Thomas Mann, recipient of

---

Berlin Cult Novels

Berlin Alexanderplatz (Alfred Döblin; 1929)

Goodbye to Berlin (Christopher Isherwood; 1939)

Alone in Berlin (Hans Fallada; 1947)

Wall Jumper (Peter Schneider; 1983)

Berlin Blues (Sven Regener; 2001)

Grimms' Fairy Tales by Jacob and Wilhelm Grimm is a beautiful collection of 210 yarns, passed orally between generations before being collected by German literature's most magical brothers.

Find reviews of the latest contemporary German books to be translated into English at www.new-books-in-german.com.

the 1929 Nobel Prize for Literature, whose greatest novels focus on social forms of the day. Mann's older brother, Heinrich, adopted a stronger political stance in his work; his *Professor Unrat* (1905) inspired the Marlene Dietrich film *Der Blaue Engel* (The Blue Angel). Erich Maria Remarque's antiwar novel *All Quiet on the Western Front* (1929) was banned (and burned) by the Nazis, but today remains a widely read German book.

The postwar literary revival was led by *The Tin Drum* (1959), by Nobel Prize–winner Günter Grass, tracing 20th-century German history through the eyes of a child who refuses to grow up. One of the first anti-Nazi novels published after WWII was Hans Fallada's *Alone in Berlin* (1947), based on a true story of a couple's entanglement in the German resistance. The book became a huge hit in the UK and the US after being translated into English in 2009.

Among East German writers, Christa Wolf is one of the best and most controversial, while Heiner Müller had the distinction of being unpalatable in both Germanys. His dense, difficult works include the *Germania* trilogy of plays.

Recent Trends

In the 1990s a slew of novels dealt with German reunification. Many of them are set in Berlin, including Thomas Brussig's tongue-in-cheek *Helden wie Wir* (Heroes like Us; 1998) and Jana Hensel's *Zonenkinder* (After the Wall; 2002), which reflects upon the loss of identity and the challenge of adapting to a new society. Günter Grass' *Ein weites Feld* (Too Far Afield; 1992) addresses 'unification without unity' after the fall of the Wall.

Berlin Alexanderplatz: The Story of Franz Biberkopf, by Alfred Döblin, is a masterful epic set in 1920s Berlin (film-maker Rainer Fassbinder made a 15-hour film adaptation).

The late novelist WG Sebald assured his place as one of Germany's best writers with his powerful portrayal of four exiles in *Die Ausgewanderten* (Emigrants; 1992). Russian-born author Wladimir Kaminer, whose Russendisko (Russian Disco; 2000) is made up of amusing, stranger-than-fiction vignettes has been wildly successful and widely translated. Foreign authors also continue to be inspired by Berlin. Ian McEwan's *The Innocent* (1990) is an old-fashioned spy story set in the 1950s, while the *Berlin Noir* trilogy (1989–91), by British author Philip Kerr, features a private detective solving crimes in Nazi Germany.

The Deutscher Buchpreis (German Book Award), the equivalent of Britain's Man Booker Prize and the US National Book Awards (in fiction), is a good guide to what's new each year. Search for short-listed and winning authors at www.deutscher-buchpreis.de.

Theatre

Germany has around 300 state, municipal, travelling and private theatres, most of them heavily government subsidised. In fact, box office takings account for only 10% to 15% of production costs on average.

Germany's theatre history begins in the Enlightenment; a key piece of this period is Gotthold Ephraim Lessing's *Nathan the Wise* (1779), which is a strong plea for religious tolerance. The Thuringian town of Weimar was a cultural hot spot in the 18th century, home to both Friedrich Schiller *(Don Carlos, Wallenstein, The Robbers)* and his even more famous friend Johann Wolfgang von Goethe, whose two-part *Faust* is a powerfully enduring drama about the human condition.

Woyzeck, by Georg Büchner, is another popular piece and, having anticipated Theatre of the Absurd, lends itself to innovative staging. In the early 20th century, Max Reinhardt became German theatre's most influential expressionist director, working briefly with dramatist Bertolt Brecht, whose *Threepenny Opera* (1928) enjoys international success to this day.

Read up-to-date reviews of the latest plays by German playwrights and other cultural offerings at www.goethe.de/enindex.htm.

Like many others, Brecht went into exile under the Nazis but returned in 1949 to establish the Berliner Ensemble, which remains one of Germany's seminal stages. Others include Berlin's Deutsches Theater and the Volksbühne Berlin, the Thalia Theater and the Deutsches Schauspielhaus in Hamburg, the Kammerspiele München, the Staatsschauspiel

Stuttgart and Schauspiel Hannover. Productions from these venue are regularly represented at the Deutsches Theatertreffen, a showcase of new plays held in Berlin every May. Contemporary playwrights to watch out for include Frank Castorf, Elfriede Jelinek, Rene Pollesch, Moritz Rinke, Botho Strauss, Rainald Goetz and Roland Schimmelpfennig.

Film

Before 1945

The legendary UFA (Universum Film AG), one of the first film studios in the world, began shooting in Potsdam, near Berlin, in 1912 and evolved into one of the world's most famous dream factories in the 1920s and early '30s, As early as 1919, Ernst Lubitsch produced historical films and comedies such as *Madame Dubarry,* starring Pola Negri and Emil Jannings; the latter went on to win the Best Actor Award at the very first Academy Awards ceremony in Hollywood in 1927. The same year saw the release of Walter Ruttmann's classic *Berlin: Symphony of a City,* a fascinating silent documentary that captures a day in the life of 1920s Berlin.

Other 1920s movies were heavily expressionistic, using stark contrast, sharp angles, heavy shadows and other distorting elements. Well-known flicks employing these techniques include *Nosferatu,* a 1922 Dracula adaptation by FW Murnau, and the ground-breaking *Metropolis* (1927), by Fritz Lang. One of the earliest seminal talkies was Josef von Sternberg's *The Blue Angel* (1930), starring Dietrich. After 1933, though, film-makers found their artistic freedom (not to mention funding) increasingly curtailed, and by 1939 practically the entire industry had fled to Hollywood.

Films made in Germany under the Nazis were mostly of the propaganda variety, with the brilliant, if controversial, director Leni Riefenstahl greatly pushing the genre's creative envelope. Her most famous film, *Triumph of the Will,* documents the 1934 Nuremberg Nazi party rally. *Olympia,* which chronicles the 1936 Berlin Olympic Games, was another influential work.

Some of the best films about the Nazi era include Wolfgang Staudte's *Die Mörder sind unter uns* (Murderers among Us; 1946); Fassbinder's *Die Ehe der Maria Braun* (The Marriage of Maria Braun; 1979); Margarethe von Trotta's *Rosenstrasse* (2003), and Oliver Hierschbiegel's Oscar-nominated *Der Untergang* (Downfall; 2004), depicting Hitler's final days, with the extraordinary Bruno Ganz in the role of the Führer.

After 1945

In the 1960s German film entered a new era with the Neuer Deutscher Film (New German Film), also known as Junger Deutscher Film (Young German Film), which brought directors Rainer Werner Fassbinder, Wim Wenders, Volker Schlöndorff, Werner Herzog and Margarethe von Trotta

Fritz Lang, the director of the famous film *Metropolis* (1927), fled to America after Goebbels offered him a position as head of the Nazi propaganda film unit.

LITERATURE, THEATRE & FILM FILM

Read what the critics say about 500-plus German films at www.german-cinema.de.

MARLENE DIETRICH

Marlene Dietrich (1901–92) was born Marie Magdalena von Losch into a good middle-class Berlin family. She first captivated audiences as a hard-living, libertine flapper in 1920s silent movies, but quickly carved a niche as the seductive femme fatale. The 1930 talkie *The Blue Angel* turned her into a Hollywood star and launched a five-year collaboration with director Josef von Sternberg. Dietrich built on her image of erotic opulence – dominant and severe but always with a touch of self-irony.

Dietrich stayed in Hollywood after the Nazi rise to power, though Hitler reportedly promised perks and the red-carpet treatment if she moved back to Germany. She responded with an empty offer to return if she could bring along Sternberg – a Jew and no Nazi favourite. She took US citizenship in 1937 and entertained Allied soldiers on the front.

After the war, Dietrich retreated slowly from the public eye, making occasional appearances in films but mostly cutting records and performing live cabaret. Her final years were spent in Paris, bedridden and accepting few visitors, immortal in spirit as mortality caught up with her.

TOP FIVE GDR RETRO FILMS

➡ *Good Bye, Lenin!* (2003), the cult box-office smash hit by Wolfgang Becker revolving around a son trying to re-create the GDR for his ailing, bedridden mother, whose health couldn't stand the shock of a fallen Wall.

➡ Leander Haussmann's nostalgia-inducing *Sonnenallee* (Sun Alley; 1999), set in a fantastical Wall-clad East Berlin in the 1970s.

➡ *Helden wie Wir* (Heroes like Us; 1999), directed by Sebastian Peterson and based on the novel by Thomas Brussig, sees the protagonist recount the story of his life, including how his penis allegedly leads to the collapse of the Berlin Wall.

➡ Leander Haussmann's humorous *Herr Lehmann* (Berlin Blues; 2003) relates the story of a bartending actor in West Berlin's bohemian Kreuzberg district just as the Wall comes down.

➡ Andreas Dresen's *Als wir träumten* (As We Were Dreaming; 2015) is a parable about friendship, betrayal, hope and illusion among a group of friends in Leipzig after the fall of the Wall.

to the fore. The impact of Fassbinder's *Die Sehnsucht der Veronika Voss* (Longing of Veronika Voss; 1981), Wenders' *Der Himmel über Berlin* (Wings of Desire; 1987), Herzog's *Aguirre, der Zorn Gottes* (Aguirre, the Wrath of God; 1972), Schlöndorff's film version of Grass' *Die Blechtrommel* (The Tin Drum; 1979) and the Schlöndorff-von Trotta co-production *Die Verlorene Ehre der Katharina Blum* (The Lost Honour of Katharina Blum; 1975) can still be felt on screens today.

The '70s also saw Wolfgang Petersen's first major release, the psychological thriller *Einer von uns beiden* (One or the Other of Us; 1974), starring Jürgen Prochnow. Prochnow returned as the lead character in Petersen's WWII submarine epic *Das Boot* (1981), which was nominated for six Oscars.

The first round of postreunification flicks were light-hearted comedy dramas, but towards the end of the 1990s filmic fare began to mature in terms of depth and quality, inspiring international critics to hail the birth of a new 'German Cinema'. A breakthrough film was *Lola Rennt* (Run Lola Run; 1998), which helped Tom Tykwer establish his reputation as one of Germany's best contemporary directors.

Another international runaway hit was *Good Bye, Lenin!*, Wolfgang Becker's witty and heart-warming tale of a son trying to re-create life in East Germany to save his sick mother. It was released in 2003, the same year Caroline Link won the Oscar for Best Foreign Language Film for *Nowhere in Africa*. In 2007 Florian von Donnersmarck was bestowed the same honour with *The Lives of Others* (2006), a ruthless portrayal of the stranglehold the East German secret police (Stasi) had on ordinary citizens. Also Oscar-nominated was Uli Edel's *Baader Meinhof Komplex* (Baader Meinhof Complex; 2008), which addresses a dark chapter in West German history: the terrorist group Red Army Faction in the late 1960s and early 1970s. Another important director with the finger on the pulse of contemporary Germany is Turkish-German Fatih Akin. His breakthrough movie *Gegen die Wand* (Head-On; 2004) is a story about love and the cultural conflicts encountered by two Turks brought up in Germany.

These days, 'Germany's Hollywood' is once again in Potsdam, where an average of 300 German and international productions are filmed on location and at the UFA successor Studio Babelsberg each year. Movies that were at least partially shot here include *The Reader, Valkyrie, Inglourious Basterds, The Ghost Writer, Anonymous, Cloud Atlas, The Monuments Men, The Grand Budapest Hotel, The Book Thief* and *Hunger Games* (parts 3 and 4).

Renamed DEFA (Deutsche Film-Aktienge-sellschaft), the illustrious UFA studios produced East German films until the fall of the Berlin Wall, most notably adaptations of German and Slavic fairy stories.

Music

Germany's reputation as a musical powerhouse is fuelled by such world-famous composers as Beethoven, Bach and Brahms. Today the country boasts 80 publicly financed concert halls, including internationally prestigious ones in Hamburg, Berlin, Dresden and Munich. But Germany has also punched well above its weight in the popular music arena and is one of the few countries outside the English-speaking world to have influenced rock, pop and electronic music in a significant way.

Classical Music

Medieval German music is closely associated with Walther von der Vogelweide (c 1170–1230), who achieved renown with love ballads. A more formalised troubadour tradition followed, but it was baroque composer and organist Johann Sebastian Bach (1685–1750) who most influenced early European music. His legacy can be explored in Bach museums in his birth town of Eisenach and in Leipzig, where he died.

Bach contemporary Georg Friedrich Händel (1685–1759) hailed from Halle in Saxony-Anhalt (his house is now a museum) but lived and worked almost exclusively in London from 1714, where he wrote operas and choral music. Händel's music found favour in the circle of Vienna's classical composers, which included Joseph Haydn (1732–1809), a teacher of Bonn-born Ludwig van Beethoven (1770–1827), who paved the way for Romanticism. Struck with deafness later in life, Beethoven's most famous works are his nine symphonies, which he composed along with piano sonatas, string quartets and choral works.

Among the Romantic composers, Felix Mendelssohn-Bartholdy (1809–47) is hailed as a genius. He penned his first overture at the age of 17 and later rediscovered works by JS Bach to give the latter the fame he enjoys today.

Born in Leipzig, Richard Wagner (1813–83) lords it over 19th-century German music. With his operas based on German mythology (most famously *The Ring of the Nibelungen*), he became Bavarian King Ludwig II's favourite composer. Hitler, who picked up on an anti-Semitic essay and some late-life ramblings on German virtues, famously turned Wagner into a postmortem Nazi icon. An annual summer music festival in Bayreuth celebrates Wagner's life and works.

Hamburg produced Johannes Brahms (1833–97) and his influential symphonies, plus chamber and piano works. Two figures whose legacies are tied to Bonn, Leipzig and Zwickau are composer Robert Schumann (1810–56) and his gifted pianist-spouse Clara Wieck (1819–96). Schumann (born in Zwickau) and Wieck (born in Leipzig) are buried in Bonn's Alter Friedhof.

The pulsating 1920s drew numerous classical musicians to Berlin, including Arnold Schönberg (1874–1951), whose atonal compositions turned music on its head, as did his experimentation with noise and sound effects. One of Schönberg's pupils, Hanns Eisler (1898–1962), went into exile in 1933, like Schönberg, but returned to East Berlin to teach in 1950. Among Eisler's works was the East German national anthem, *Auferstanden aus Ruinen* (Resurrected from Ruins), lyricless from 1961, when its proreunification words fell out of favour with party honchos.

Also working in Berlin, Paul Hindemith (1895–1963) explored the new medium of radio and taught a seminar on film music. He, too,

Singer Lena Meyer Landrut won the Eurovision Song Contest in 2010, becoming just the second German winner in the competition's history.

For more information, both practical and historical, on the Berlin Philharmonic Orchestra, visit www. berliner-philhar moniker.de.

GERMAN MUSIC IN 10 ALBUMS

→ *Brandenburg Concertos* (JS Bach)

→ *Water Music* (Händel)

→ *Nine Symphonies* (Beethoven)

→ *Violin Concerto* (Brahms)

→ *Autobahn* (Kraftwerk, 1974)

→ *Opium fuers Volk* (Die Toten Hosen, 1996)

→ *Mutter* (Rammstein, 2001)

→ *Nomad Songs* (Micatone, 2005)

→ *Sound So* (Wir sind Helden, 2007)

→ *Moderat II* (Moderat, 2013)

was banned by the Nazis and composed his most important orchestral compositions in exile. The Hindemith Institute (www.hindemith.org) in Frankfurt am Main promotes his music and safeguards his estate.

Perhaps better known is Dessau-born Kurt Weill (1900–50), another composer who fled the Nazi terror. He teamed up with Bertolt Brecht in the 1920s and wrote the music for the *The Threepenny Opera*, which premiered in 1928 with such famous songs as 'Mack the Knife'. Weill ended up writing successful Broadway musicals in New York.

The 1920s also gave birth to *Schlager* – light-hearted songs with titles like 'Mein Papagei frisst keine harten Eier' ('My Parrot Doesn't Eat Hard-Boiled Eggs'), which teetered on the silly and surreal. The most successful *Schlager* singing group was the a cappella Comedian Harmonists, who were famous for their perfect harmonies of voices that sounded like musical instruments.

After WWII, the southwestern towns of Darmstadt and Donaueschingen emerged as hubs of contemporary classical music based on constructivist compositional techniques and modal methods, with Karlheinz Stockhausen emerging as a key figure. The arrival of American experimental composer John Cage, a pioneer of chance composition, electroacoustic music and noise-as-music, at the International Music Institute Darmstadt is widely considered a turning point in the European post-WWII musical scene.

Contemporary Sounds

Since the 1960s, Berlin has spearheaded many of Germany's popular music innovations. Riding the New Age wave of the late '60s, Tangerine Dream helped to propagate the psychedelic sound, while a decade later Kreuzberg's subculture launched the punk movement at SO36 and other famous clubs. Regulars included David Bowie and Iggy Pop, who were Berlin flatmates in the 1970s. Bowie partly wrote and recorded his Berlin Trilogy (*Low, Heroes, Lodger*) at the city's famous Hansa Studios.

In East Germany, access to western rock and other popular music was restricted, while eastern musicians' own artistic freedom was greatly compromised, as all lyrics had to be approved and performances were monitored. Nevertheless, a slew of home-grown *Ostrock* (eastern rock) bands emerged. Some major ones like The Puhdys, Karat, Silly, City and Keimzeit managed to get around the censors by disguising criticism in seemingly innocuous metaphors or by deliberately inserting provocative lyrics they fully expected to be deleted. All built up huge followings in both Germanys.

Many nonconformists were placed under an occupational ban and prohibited from performing. Singer-songwriter Wolf Biermann became a cause célèbre when, in 1976, he was not allowed to return to the GDR from a concert series in the West, despite being an avid – albeit regime-critical – socialist. When other artists rallied to his support, they too were expatriated, including Biermann's stepdaughter Nina Hagen, an East Berlin pop singer who later became a West Berlin punk pioneer. The small but vital East German punk scene produced Sandow and Feeling B, members of whom went on to form the industrial metal band Rammstein in 1994. Known for provocative lyrics and intense sounds, the band is still Germany's top musical export today.

Once in West Berlin, Nina Hagen helped chart the course for Neue Deutsche Welle (NDW; German New Wave). This early '80s sound produced such bands as D.A.F., Trio, Neonbabies and Ideal, as well as Rockhaus in East Berlin. The same decade also saw the birth of Die Ärzte, Die Toten Hosen and the seminal Einstürzende Neubauten, who pioneered a proto-industrial sound. Düsseldorf-based Kraftwerk, meanwhile, created the musical foundations for techno, the club sound that would sweep across Germany after 1989, spawning Berlin's legendary Love Parade.

Members of the Neue Deutsche Welle always sang in German, an exception being the singer Nena, who successfully recorded her hit single '99 Red Balloons' in English, too. The NDW movement spawned the Hamburg School of musicians, with recognised acts such as Blumfeld, Die Sterne and the Tocotronic. The sensitive ballads and zeitgeist-capturing rock songs of 'Germany's Springsteen' Herbert Grönemeyer, who emerged in the 1980s, continue to resonate across generations.

Other fine German music originates from a jazz/breaks angle such as electrojazz and breakbeats that favour lush grooves, obscure samples and chilled rhythms. Remix masters Jazzanova are top dogs of the downtempo scene. Their Sonar Kollektiv label also champions similar artists, including Micatone. Reggae-dancehall made a splash with Seeed, whose frontman Peter Fox's solo album *Stadtaffe* (2008) was one of the best-selling albums in Germany of the same year. Also commercially successful is Culcha Candela, who have essentially pop-ified the Seeed sound. Home-grown rap and hip hop has a huge following, thanks to Sido, Fler, Bushido and Kool Savas. Also hugely successful are Berlin-based Casper and Marteria. K.I.Z., meanwhile, are more of a gangsta rap parody.

Dominated by disco in the 1970s and rap and hip hop in the 1980s, the club scene in the 1990s moved strongly towards electronic music, taking the impulses of Tangerine Dream and Kraftwerk to new heights.

The seed was sown in dark and dank cellar club UFO on Köpenicker Strasse in 1988. The 'godfathers' of the Berlin sound, Dr Motte, Westbam and Kid Paul, played their first gigs here, mostly sweat-driven acid house all-night raves. It was Motte who came up with the idea to take the party to the street with a truck, loud beats and a bunch of friends dancing behind it – and the Love Parade was born (it peaked in 1999 with 1.5 million people swarming Berlin's streets).

The Berlin Wall's demise, and the vacuum of artistic freedom it created, catapulted techno out of the underground. The associated euphoria, sudden access to derelict and abandoned spaces in eastern Berlin and lack of control by the authorities were all defining factors in making Berlin a techno mecca. In 1991 the techno-sonic gang followed UFO founder Dimitri Hegemann to Tresor, which launched camouflage-sporting DJ Tanith, along with trance pioneer Paul van Dyk. Today the Tresor label is still a seminal brand, representing Jeff Mills, Blake Baxter and Cristian Vogel, among many others.

Key label BPitch Control, founded by Ellen Allien in 1999, launched the careers of Modeselektor, Apparat (aka Sascha Ring), Sascha Funke and Paul Kalkbrenner. Another heavyweight is the collective Get Physical, which includes the dynamic duo M.A.N.D.Y., who fuse house and electro with minimal and funk to create a highly danceable sound. The charmingly named Shitkatapult, founded in 1997 by Marco Haas (aka T.Raumschmiere), is focused on minimalist styles and counts Apparat and Daniel Meteo among its artists.

'Once every generation, a German band achieves worldwide success... Yes, it's Nietzsche Rock!'

NME music magazine on popular metal band Rammstein.

Thomas Jerome's *Bowie in Berlin: A New Career in a New Town* (2008) offers cool insights into the heady years the 'Thin White Duke' spent in Berlin.

MUSIC CONTEMPORARY SOUNDS

Visual Arts

From 1200-year-old church frescoes to cutting-edge street art, you're never far from creative expression in Germany. While religious themes dominated the Middle Ages, the scope widened around the time of the Enlightenment and burst into a full spectrum of creativity in the 20th century, especially with seminal Weimar-era movements such as the Bauhaus and expressionism. With scores of museums, galleries, public art, art colonies and festivals, Germany's artistic world today continues to be vibrant, influential and reflective of the zeitgeist.

Middle Ages to the 19th Century

Peter Vischer the Elder, Veit Stoss and Tilman Riemenschneider are regarded as the greatest German sculptors of the late Gothic and early Renaissance period.

The origins of German medieval art can be traced to the Frankish Empire of Charlemagne (c 800). Frescoes from that period still grace the Stiftskirche St Georg on Reichenau Island, while those from Trier's St Maximin crypt are now on display at the city's Bischöfliches Dom- und Diözesanmuseum. Stained-glass enthusiasts will find colourful religious motifs lighting up Augsburg and Cologne cathedrals. By the 15th century, Cologne artists were putting landscapes on religious panels, some of which are on display in Hamburg's Kunsthalle.

The heavyweight of German Renaissance art, which flourished in the 15th century, is the Nuremberg-born Albrecht Dürer, the first artist to seriously compete with the Italian masters. Munich's Alte Pinakothek is one place showing several famous works, while his Nuremberg house is now a museum. In Wittenberg, Dürer influenced the court painter Lucas Cranach the Elder, whose *Apollo and Diana in a Forest Landscape* (1530) forms part of the collection at Berlin's Gemäldegalerie.

Two centuries later, during the baroque period, sculpture was integrated into Germany's buildings and gardens. A key work is Andreas Schlüter's *Great Elector on Horseback* in front of Berlin's Schloss Charlottenburg. Around the same time, it became fashionable to decorate palace walls and ceiling with trompe l'oeil frescoes to create the illusion of generous space. The one by Tiepolo gracing Balthasar Neumann's grand staircase in Würzburg's Residenz is a standout.

In the early 19th century, neoclassicism emerged as a dominant sculptural style. Leading the artistic pack was Johann Gottfried Schadow, whose *Quadriga* – the horse-drawn chariot atop Berlin's Brandenburg Gate – ranks among his finest works. In painting, neoclassicism ushered in a return to the human figure and an emphasis on Roman and Greek mythology. Johann Heinrich Tischbein's *Goethe in der Campagna* (1787), which depicts the famous writer in a classical landscape surrounded by antique objects, hangs in the Städel Museum in Frankfurt am Main.

Heart-on-your-sleeve romanticism, which drew heavily on emotion and a dreamy idealism, dominated the later 19th century, spurred by the awakening of a nationalist spirit after the Napoleonic Wars (1803–15). Caspar David Friedrich, best known for his moody, allegorical landscapes, was a key practitioner. Both Hamburg's Kunsthalle and Berlin's Alte Nationalgalerie have sizeable collections of his works, along with canvases by Philipp Otto Runge, intensely religious works by the Nazarenes and some later realistic paintings by Wilhelm Leibl.

Impressionism did not flourish nearly as much in Germany as it did in France. Key representatives include Max Liebermann, whose work was often slammed as 'ugly' and 'socialist', Fritz von Uhde, and Lovis Corinth, whose later work, *Childhood of Zeus* (1905) – a richly coloured frolic in nature with intoxicated, grotesque elements – can be admired in Bremen's Kunsthalle.

An art form popping up briefly in the final decade of the 19th century was *Jugendstil* (art nouveau), a florid, ornamental aesthetic inspired by printmaking that found expression less in visual art than in crafts and design. It was a reaction against the pompous eclecticism in vogue after the founding of the German Reich in 1871. In Munich the Neue Pinakothek is the place to head for some fine examples of this most elegant of styles, as is the Bröhan Museum in Berlin.

> *Jugendstil* – an alternative name in German for art nouveau – takes its name from the arts magazine *Jugend* (literally 'Youth'), first published in Munich in 1896.

Birth of Modernism

In the last decade of the 19th century, a number of artists banded together to reject the traditional teachings of the arts academics that stifled any new forms of expression. This led to the Munich Secession in 1892 and to the Berlin Secession in 1898. This new generation of artists preferred scenes from daily life to historical and religious themes, shunned studios in favour of natural outdoor light and inspired a proliferation of new styles. Famous secession members included Max Liebermann, Lovis Corinth, Max Slevogt, Max Beckmann, Käthe Kollwitz and Ernst Ludwig Kirchner.

Kirchner went on to found, along with Erich Heckel and Karl Schmidt-Rottluff, the artist group *Die Brücke* (The Bridge) in 1905 in Dresden. It turned the art world on its head with groundbreaking visions considered the dawn of German expressionism. As opposed to Impressionism, which focuses on passively depicting light and nature, expressionism is imbued with an emotional quality. Abstract forms, a flattened perspective and bright, emotional colours that the artists believed exuded a spiritual quality characterised this new aesthetic. Die Brücke moved to Berlin in 1911 and disbanded in 1913. The small Brücke Museum in Berlin has a fantastic collection of these influential artists.

In 1911 another seminal group of German expressionists banded together in Munich. Calling themselves *Der Blaue Reiter* (The Blue Rider), this loose association of painters centred on Vassily Kandinsky, Gabriele Münter, Paul Klee and Franz Marc, and remained active until 1914. Munich's Städtische Galerie im Lenbachhaus has a superb collection of Blaue Reiter paintings. Klee fans should also make a beeline to Düsseldorf's K20 Grabbeplatz and the Museum Berggruen in Berlin. A pilgrimage site for Marc aficionados is the Franz Marc Museum in Kochel am See in the Bavarian Alps, where the artist lived after 1908.

The most important woman painter of the period was Käthe Kollwitz, whose social and political awareness lent a tortured power to her lithographs, graphics, woodcuts, sculptures and drawings. Among her many famous works is *A Weavers' Revolt* (1897). There are museums dedicated to this extraordinary artist in Berlin and Cologne.

> Artist Joseph Beuys was a radio operator in a fighter plane shot down over the Crimea during WWII. He claims to have been nursed back to health by local Tartars, who covered him in tallow and wrapped him in felt. The two materials came to feature prominently in his later artworks.

Art in the Weimar Republic

The 1920s were one of the most prolific and creative periods in Germany's artistic history. Many different forms of expression flourished in this decade, a diversity fuelled by the monarchy's demise, political and economic instability and the memory of the horrors of WWI.

One artist especially haunted by his wartime experience was Otto Dix, who, in the early 1920s, produced a series of dark and sombre paintings depicting war scenes – disfigured and dying soldiers, and decomposing bodies – in graphic detail. Dix was greatly influenced by Dadaism, an avant-garde art movement formed in Zurich in 1916 as a reaction to the brutality of WWI.

Dada artists had an irrational, satirical and often absurdist outlook that was often imbued with a political undercurrent and a tendency to shock and provoke. Aside from Dix, artists associated with this movement included Kurt Schwitters, Hannah Höch and George Grosz. Along with Max Beckmann, Dix and Grosz went on to become key figures of the *Neue Sachlichkeit* (New Objectivity), an offshoot of expressionism that emerged later in the 1920s and was distinguished by an unsentimental, practical and objective look at reality.

After a creative surge in the 1920s, the big chill of Nazi conformity sent Germany into an artistic deep freeze in the 1930s and 1940s. Many artists were classified as degenerate and forced into exile, leading to a creative explosion among the Bauhaus movement protagonists who settled in the USA. Other artists were murdered, retreated from public life or put away their brushes and paints forever. In Quedlinburg a fine collection of works by Lyonel Feininger survived thanks to a local citizen, who hid them from the Nazis.

> The German Design Award is the country's most prestigious award for design (www.german-design-council.de). Another one is the Red Dot Design Award (http://en.red-dot.org).

Post-WWII

After WWII, Germany's art scene was as fragmented as the country itself. In the East, artists were forced to toe the socialist realism line, at least until the late 1960s, when artists of the so-called *Berliner Schule* (Berlin School), including Manfred Böttcher and Harald Metzkes, sought to embrace a more interpretative and emotional form of expression, inspired by the colours and aesthetic of Beckmann, Matisse, Picasso and other classical modernists. In the '70s, when conflicts of the individual in society became a prominent theme, underground galleries flourished in East Berlin and art became a collective endeavour. The Museum Junge Kunst in Frankfurt (Oder) presents a thorough survey of art created in the GDR.

In West Germany, the creative influence of expressionists such as Nolde, Schmidt-Rottluff and Kandinsky was revived, as a new abstract expressionism took root in the work of Stuttgart's Willi Baumeister and Ernst Wilhelm Nay in Berlin. Soon, however, artists eagerly embraced abstract art. Pioneers included Zone 5, which revolved around Hans Thiemann, and surrealists Heinz Trökes and Mac Zimmermann. In the 1950s and 1960s, Düsseldorf-based Gruppe Zero (Group Zero) plugged into Bauhaus, using light and space as a creative basis. The 'light ballets' of the late Otto Piene, relying on projection techniques, were among the best-known works. Celle's Kunstmuseum uses some of his light works for stunning effect.

In the 1960s social and political upheaval was a primary concern and a new style called 'critical realism' emerged, propagated by artists like Ulrich Baehr, Hans-Jürgen Diehl and Wolfgang Petrick. The 1973 movement, *Schule der Neuen Prächtigkeit* (School of New Magnificence), had a similar approach. In the late 1970s and early 1980s, expressionism found its way back onto the canvasses of Salomé, Helmut Middendorf and Rainer Fetting, a group known as the *Junge Wilde* (Young Wild Ones). One of the best-known German neo-expressionist painters is Georg Baselitz, who became internationally famous in the 1970s, thanks to his 'upside-down' works.

> For a comprehensive low-down of Germany's contemporary art scene and events, see www.art-in.de.

Another top contemporary German artist is Anselm Kiefer, some of whose works are in Berlin's Hamburger Bahnhof – Museum of Contemporary Art. A standout is his monumental *Census* (1967), which consists of massive lead folios arranged on shelves as a protest against a 1967 census in Germany.

The same museum also has a large permanent display of works by Düsseldorf's Joseph Beuys (1921–86), the enfant terrible of the post-WWII German art world and yet one of the most influential artists of the period.

DEGENERATE ART

Abstract expressionism, surrealism, Dadaism and other forms of modern art were considered 'Jewish subversion' and 'artistic Bolshevism' in the eyes of the Nazis and classified as *entartet* (degenerate). The art promoted instead looked back to a classical Greek and Roman aesthetic and favoured the depicting of racial purity and the use of epic styles.

In 1937, 650 paintings by 112 artists, including Klee, Beckmann, Dix, Kirchner, Marc and Grosz, were put on display in a major Degenerate Art Exhibition' in Munich. It was to serve as a counterpoint to the simultaneous Great German Art Exhibition at Munich's palatial Haus der Deutschen Kunst, which showcased Nazi-approved art by such artists as the sculptors Arno Breker and Georg Kolbe and painters Thomas Baumgartners and Ivo Salinger. With only 600,000 visitors, interest was low compared with the degenerate art show, which drew over two million people.

A year later, a law was passed allowing for the forced removal of degenerate works from private collections. While some art collectors saved their prized art from Nazi hands, many pieces were sold abroad for foreign currency. In 1939 about 4000 paintings were publicly burned in Berlin.

Beuys created a huge body of work that ranges from drawing, sculpture and installations to print-making and performance. His personal and provocative style created controversy wherever he lay his trademark hat and ultimately led to his dismissal from the Düsseldorf Art Academy, where he had been a professor. Other places with sizeable Beuys holdings include Darmstadt's Hessisches Landesmuseum (including his ground-breaking *Stuhl mit Fett;* Chair with Fat; 1963), the K20 Grabbeplatz in Düsseldorf and Schloss Moyland, near Kalkar, in North Rhine–Westphalia.

Other icons of contemporary German painting include Gerhard Richter and Sigmar Polke. Richter, who was born in Dresden and fled to West Germany in the early 1960s, made a huge splash in 2007 with a mesmerising stained-glass window in Cologne's cathedral. Polke, along with Richter and others, relied heavily on pop art and what they dubbed 'capitalist realism', which they used to describe a counterbalance in the West to socialist realism. Another heavy hitter, albeit from a younger generation, is Rosemarie Trockel, whose diverse and experimental works include drawings, sculpture, painting and video art. The Museum Ludwig in Cologne has works by her, as well as by Richter and Polke.

In the 1990s, the *Neue Leipziger Schule* (New Leipzig School) of artists emerged, achieving success at home and abroad with such superstar painters as Neo Rauch. Its return to representational painting may be regarded as a reaction to the dominance of conceptual art in previous decades.

These days abstraction has again become a focus, with a particular nod to its roots in modernism. There is no particular style but a diversity of expression and an idiosyncratic, personal approach to art. Underlying themes include the commercialisation of art and critical awareness of the impact of technology. Artists to keep an eye on include Andre Butzer, Isa Genzken, Thomas Zipp, Georg Herold, Alexandra Bircken, Jutta Köther, Max Frisinger and Corinne Wasmuth.

Photography is another area where Germany has long made a splash. In the 1920s and '30s, German photographers took two very different directions. Influenced by the Hungarian László Maholy-Nagy, some adopted a playful approach to light, figure, form and how they developed the resulting images in the darkroom. The other direction was a documentary-style New Objectivity, whose main protagonists were Albert Renger-Patzsch, August Sander and Werner Manz.

Bulgarian-American artist Christo and his wife Jeanne-Claude were responsible for possibly the best-known piece of public art of recent times in Germany. In 1995 they completely enveloped Berlin's Reichstag building in aluminium-coated fabric, attracting millions of visitors to the site.

Architecture

The bombs of WWII may have blasted away a considerable share of Germany's architectural heritage, but a painstaking postwar rebuilding program and a wealth of sites that survived with nary a shrapnel wound make Germany an architectural wonderland. Every building style from Roman amphitheatre to 21st-century skyscraper dot townscapes across the country. Of special interest are the many diverse Unesco-listed gems, including Bauhaus buildings in Dessau-Rosslau, the rococo Wieskirche pilgrimage church in southern Bavaria and the Zollverein coal mine in Essen.

Romanesque & Gothic

Among the grand buildings of the Carolingian period, Aachen's Charlemagne-built cathedral, remnants of one of his palaces in Paderborn, and Fulda's Michaelskirche are surviving masterpieces. A century on, Carolingian, Roman and Byzantine influences flowed together in a more proportional interior with round arches and integrated columns. Standouts among these Romanesque buildings are the elegant Stiftskirche St Cyriakus in Gernrode and the cathedrals in Worms, Speyer and Mainz.

Early Gothic architecture retained Romanesque elements, as seen in the cathedral in Magdeburg. The Unesco-listed Kloster Maulbronn, built in 1147 and considered among Europe's best-preserved medieval monastery complexes, combines Romanesque and Gothic elements.

Later churches sport purely Gothic traits, such as ribbed vaults, pointed arches and flying buttresses, to allow greater height and larger windows. There are many fine examples scattered across the country, including the churches and cathedrals in Cologne (Kölner Dom), Marburg (Elisabethkirche), Trier (Liebfrauenkirchc), Freiburg (Münster) and Lübeck (Marienkirche). After the 15th century, elaborately patterned vaults and hall churches emerged. Munich's Frauenkirche and Michaelskirche are typical of this late Gothic period.

Renaissance to Neoclassical

The Renaissance rumbled into Germany around the mid-16th century, bestowing Heidelberg and other southern cities with buildings bearing ornate leaf-work decoration and columns. In central Germany, the secular Weser Renaissance style resulted in such gems as Celle's ducal palace.

As the representational needs of feudal rulers grew in the 17th and 18th centuries, they invested heavily in grand residences. This was the age of baroque, a style that merged architecture, sculpture, ornamentation and painting. In northern Germany it retained a more formal and precise bent (as exemplified by the work of Johann Conrad Schlaun in Münster), never quite reaching the exuberance favoured in the south in such buildings as the Wieskirche or Munich's Schloss Nymphenburg. One of the finest baroque churches, Dresden's Frauenkirche, built in 1743, was destroyed in the 1945 firebombing of the city, but was reconstructed and reopened in 2005.

Berlin's Brandenburg Gate, based on a Greek design, is an exquisite example of neoclassicism. Turning away from baroque flourishes, this style drew upon columns, pediments, domes and other design elements that had been popular throughout antiquity. A leading architect of the era was Berlin-based Karl Friedrich Schinkel, whose colonnaded Altes Muse-

Dresden was delisted as a Unesco World Heritage Site in 2009, when local authorities insisted on building a modern bridge across the Elbe River.

um (Old Museum), Neue Wache (New Guardhouse) and the Konzerthaus (Concert Hall) still grace the capital. In Bavaria, Leo von Klenze chiselled his way through virtually every ancient civilisation, with eclectic creations such as the Glyptothek and Propyläen on Munich's Königsplatz.

The architecture in vogue after the creation of the German Empire in 1871 reflects the representational needs of the united Germany and tends towards the pompous. No new style as such emerged, as architects essentially recycled earlier ones (eg Romanesque, Renaissance, baroque, and sometimes all three woven together) in an approach dubbed *Historismus* (Historicism). As a result, many buildings look much older than they actually are. Berlin's Reichstag, Schloss Neuschwanstein in Füssen and the palace in Schwerin in northern Germany are all prominent examples.

Modern & Contemporary
20th Century

No architectural movement has had greater influence on modern design than the Bauhaus (p586), an architecture, art and design institute founded in 1919 Weimar by Walter Gropius. Based on practical anti-elitist principles bringing form and function together, it united architecture, painting, furniture design and sculpture. The school had its most fruitful period after moving to Dessau in 1925. Its school building, which is considered a landmark of modern, functionalist architecture, is open to visitors, as are the *Meisterhäuser* (private homes) of such Bauhaus teachers as Gropius, Vassily Kandinsky and Paul Klee. In Berlin the Bauhaus Archive, designed by Gropius in 1964, is a must-see.

The Bauhaus moved to Berlin in 1932, only to be shut down by the Nazis a year later. Hitler, who was a big fan of architectural monumentalism, put Albert Speer in charge of turning Berlin into the 'Welthauptstadt Germania', the future capital of the Reich. Today only a few buildings, including the Olympic Stadium and Tempelhof Airport, offer a hint of what Berlin might have looked like had history taken a different turn.

After WWII East Germany found inspiration in Stalin-era pomposity, impressively reflected in East Berlin's showcase boulevard Karl-Marx-Allee. The city's main square, Alexanderplatz, also got a socialist makeover in the 1960s, culminating in the construction of its 368m-high TV Tower (still Germany's tallest building) in 1969. Another (in)famous structure – the Berlin Wall – survives only in fragments.

Best Castles & Palaces

Schloss Neuschwanstein (p230)

Wartburg Castle (p555)

Schloss Sanssouci (p126)

Burg Eltz (p415)

Würzburg Residenz (p248)

Hohenzollern Castle (p321)

TOP UNESCO WORLD HERITAGE SITES IN GERMANY

➥ **Trier's Roman monuments** (p451) Germany's finest collection of Roman heritage.

➥ **Aachen Cathedral** (p487) Begun in the 8th century, this blockbuster building is the final resting place of Charlemagne.

➥ **Kaiserdom** (p419) Speyer's magnificent 11th-century cathedral holds the tombs of eight medieval German emperors.

➥ **Regensburg** (p289) An Altstadt (old town) crammed with Romanesque and Gothic edifices.

➥ **Kölner Dom** (p463) Cologne's 13th-century cathedral was completed over six centuries.

➥ **Potsdam's parks and palaces** (p126) Includes 500 hectares of parks and 150 buildings raised between 1730 and 1916.

➥ **Würzburg Residenz** (p248) This baroque 18th-century palace is perhaps Balthasar Neumann's finest creation.

➥ **Bauhaus sites** If you're interested in the early 20th-century Bauhaus movement, Weimar's Bauhaus Museum (p549) and Dessau's Bauhausgebäude (p583) are key.

By contrast, in West Germany, urban planners sought to eradicate any hint of monumentalism, instead embracing the reduced 'less is more' glass-and-steel aesthetic of the Bauhaus tradition. Ludwig Mies van der Rohe's Neue Nationalgalerie (New National Gallery) is a masterpiece, as is Hubert Petschnigg's slender Thyssenhaus (1960) in Düsseldorf. In 1972 Munich was graced with its splendid tent-roofed Olympiastadion.

Erich Mendelsohn and the Architecture of German Modernism, by Kathleen James, zooms in on Mendelsohn's expressionist buildings in Berlin and Frankfurt.

21st Century

After reunification, Berlin became the epicentre of contemporary building projects. On Potsdamer Platz, Italian architect Renzo Piano designed Daimler City (1998), while German-born (but Chicago-based) Helmut Jahn turned a playful hand to the glass-and-steel Sony Center (2000). Another notable Jahn creation in Berlin is the edgy Neues Kranzler Eck (2000).

Three spectacular successes in Germany by US star architect Daniel Libeskind are Osnabrück's Felix-Nussbaum-Haus (1998), Drseden's updated Militärhistorisches Museum (Military History Museum; 2011) and, most famously, the zinc-clad zigzag Jüdisches Museum (Jewish Museum; 2001) in Berlin. Also in Berlin, the haunting Holocaust Memorial (2005) is the work of New York–based Peter Eisenman, while the Hamburg-based architectural firm of Gerkan, Marg und Partner took glass-and-steel station architecture to new limits with the city's Hauptbahnhof (2006).

Frank Gehry has left his mark on German cities over the past two decades, first through the 1989 Vitra Design Museum in Weil am Rhein and later with his characteristically warped 1999 Neue Zollhof (New Customs House) in Düsseldorf's Medienhafen (Media Harbour), the Gehry-Tower (2001) in Hanover and the 1999 DZ Bank on Berlin's Pariser Platz.

The contrast of old and new in the extension of Cologne's Wallraf-Richartz-Museum (2001) by the late Oswald Mathias Ungers is a worthy addition to a city with one of the world's most beautiful cathedrals. In 2003 Axel Schultes and Charlotte Frank won the German Architecture Prize for their design of the Bundeskanzleramt (New Chancellery; 2001), which forms part of Berlin's new postreunification Government Quarter. Its historic anchor, the Reichstag, seat of Germany's parliament, got a modern landmark addition with its sparkling glass cupola (1999), part of Norman Foster's building makeover.

Munich architect Stephan Braunfels masterminded his city's modernist Pinakothek der Moderne (2002), while the Berlin firm of Sauerbruch Hutton designed the nearby Museum Brandhorst, whose facade consists of 36,000 colourful ceramic square tubes. In 2006 Munich's famous football team, FC Bayern München, moved into its sparkling Allianz Arena, a remarkable rubber-dinghy-like translucent object that pleases football and architecture fans alike. Not to be outdone, Stuttgart added the futuristic Porsche Museum to its cityscape in 2009.

In Hamburg, an old docklands area is being turned into the HafenCity, a new city quarter with futuristic architecture. There's a special focus on sustainable construction, with an award-winning standout being the Unilever building, which makes clever use of innovative LED lighting, a cooling double-layered outer shell and rooftop heat exchangers. Architecture and urban planning aficionados should also flock to the nearby island of Hamburg-Wilhelmburg, where a 2013 building exhibition produced a showcase of innovative, eco-sensitive buildings, including the striking new home of the State Ministry for Urban Development and the Environment.

Not all new construction has to be cutting-edge, as shown by the rebuilding of the Berlin City Palace, which began in 2013. Although planned to be a modern repository of museums and cultural institutions on the inside, its facade will be an exact replica of the baroque-style palace that was blown up by the East German government in 1951. Nearby Potsdam has also created a replica of its Prussian city palace, which opened in 2014 as the new home of the Brandenburg state parliament.

Landscapes & Wildlife

For centuries the epic beauty of Germany's landscapes has inspired artists and writers towards the lyrical and profound. The sprightly Rhine coursing through emerald vines, the wave-lashed Baltic coast, the glacier-licked summits of the Bavarian Alps – all have been immortalised by 19th-century Romantic painters and literary legends including Thomas Mann, Bertolt Brecht and Mark Twain. And, of course, the Brothers Grimm, who found in Germany's dark forests the perfect air of mystery for gingerbready tales of wicked witches and lost-in-the-woods children.

The Land

For all that has been publicised, much of Germany's loveliness remains unsung beyond its borders. Take Mecklenburg–Western Pomerania's beech forests, poppy-flecked meadows and lakes, or the East Frisian Islands' briny breezes and shifting sands, Saxon Switzerland's wonderland of sandstone pinnacles, or the Bavarian forest's primordial woodlands tinged with Bohemian melancholy. Who has heard of them? Bar the odd intrepid traveller, only the Germans.

The good news is that the national passion for outdoor pursuits and obsessive efficiency has made such landscapes brilliantly accessible. Every inch of the country has been mapped, cycling and hiking trails thread to its remotest corners, and farmhouses and mountain huts offer travellers shelter and sustenance. Life here is close to nature, and nature here is on a truly grand scale.

Across its 357,021 sq km, Europe's seventh-largest country embraces moors and heaths, mudflats, chalk cliffs, glacial lakes, river wetlands and dense forests. Hugged by Poland, the Czech Republic, Austria, Switzerland, France, Belgium, the Netherlands, Luxembourg and Denmark, the land is mountainous in the south but flat in the north. Many visitors are surprised to learn Germany even possesses low-lying islands and sandy beaches.

In the southeast are the Bavarian Alps, where the 2962m Zugspitze crowns the Northern Limestone Alps, and jewel-coloured lakes scatter the Berchtesgaden National Park. Rolling almost to the Swiss border in the southwest, the Black Forest presents a sylvan tableau of round-topped hills (the highest being 1493m Feldberg), thick fir forests and open countryside.

Starting its journey in Switzerland and travelling through Lake Constance (Germany's largest lake), the Rhine winds its 1320km-long way around the Black Forest, before draining into the North Sea. The Elbe, Oder and other German rivers likewise flow north, but the Danube flows east.

Moving towards the central belt, you'll find memorable vineyards and hiking areas in the warmer valleys around the Moselle River. The land just north was formed by volcanic activity. To the east is the holiday area of the Spreewald, a picturesque wetland with narrow, navigable waterways.

Where Germany meets Holland in the northwest and Denmark in the north, the land is flat; the westerly North Sea coast consists partly of drained land and dykes. To the east, the Baltic coast is riddled with bays and fjords in Schleswig-Holstein, but gives way to sandy inlets and beaches. At the northeastern tip is Germany's largest island, Rügen, renowned for its chalk cliffs.

Vital Statistics

Highest peak
Zugspitze (2962m) in the Bavarian Alps

Major rivers
Rhine, Danube, Elbe, Moselle, Main

Biggest lake
Lake Constance (536 sq km)

Tallest waterfall
Triberger Wasserfälle (163m)

Largest nature park Black Forest (12,000 sq km)

For the inside scoop on Germany's 104 nature parks and 16 national parks, visit www. natur parke.de; www.deutsche-nationalparks. com; www. germany.travel; and www.bfn.de

NATIONAL PARKS

Germany's vast and varied landscapes are protected to varying degrees by 104 nature parks, 15 biosphere reserves and 16 national parks. The Upper Middle Rhine Valley, the Wadden Sea and the beech forest of the Jasmund National Park are safeguarded as Unesco World Heritage Areas.

PARK & WEBSITE	FEATURES
Bavarian Forest (www.nationalpark-bayerischer-wald.de)	mountain forest & upland moors (243 sq km); deer, hazel grouse, foxes, otters, eagle owls, Eurasian pygmy owls; botany
Berchtesgaden (www.nationalpark-berchtesgaden.de)	lakes, subalpine spruce, salt mines & ice caves (210 sq km); eagles, golden eagles, marmots, blue hares
Black Forest National Park (www.schwarzwald-nationalpark.de)	meadows, mountains, spruce, pine & beech forests, valleys, moors and lakes (100 sq km)
Eifel (www.nationalpark-eifel.de)	beech forest (110 sq km); wild cats, beavers, kingfishers; wild yellow narcissus
Hainich (www.nationalpark-hainich.de)	mixed deciduous forest (76 sq km), beech trees; black storks, wild cats, rare bats
Hamburg Wadden Sea (www.national-park-wattenmeer.de)	mudflats, meadows & sand dunes (345 sq km); sea swallows, terns
Harz (www.nationalpark-harz.de)	rock formations, caves (247 sq km); black woodpeckers, wild cats, deer
Hunsrück-Hochwald (www.nationalpark-hunsrueck-hochwald.de)	Upland forests & fields (100 sq km); red deer, wild boar, black storks, wild cats
Jasmund (www.nationalpark-jasmund.de)	chalk cliffs, forest, creeks and moors (30 sq km); white-tailed eagles
Kellerwald Edersee (www.nationalpark-kellerwald-edersee.de)	beech & other deciduous trees, lake (57 sq km); black storks, wild cats, rare bats, stags
Lower Oder Valley (www.nationalpark-unteres-odertal.eu)	river plain (165 sq km); black storks, sea eagles, beavers, aquatic warblers, cranes
Lower Saxony Wadden Sea (www.nationalpark-wattenmeer.de)	salt-marsh & bog landscape (2780 sq km); seals, shell ducks
Müritz (www.nationalpark-mueritz.de)	beech, bogs & lakes (318 sq km); sea eagles, fish hawks, cranes, white-tailed eagles, Gotland sheep
Saxon Switzerland (www.nationalpark-saechsische-schweiz.de)	sandstone & basalt rock formations (93 sq km); eagle owls, otters, fat dormice
Schleswig-Holstein Wadden Sea (www.nationalpark-wattenmeer.de)	seascape of dunes, salt marshes & mudflats (4410 sq km); sea life, migratory birds
Vorpommersche Boddenlandschaft (www.nationalpark-vorpommersche-boddenlandschaft.de)	Baltic seascape (805 sq km); cranes, red deer, wild boar

The Wildlife

Animals

Snow hares, marmots and wild goats scamper around the Alps. The chamois is also fairly common here, as well as in pockets of the Black Forest, the Swabian Alps and Saxon Switzerland, south of Dresden.

A rare but wonderful Alpine treat for patient birdwatchers is a sighting of the golden eagle; Berchtesgaden National Park staff might be able to help you find one. The jay, with its darting flight patterns and calls imitating other species, is easy to spot in the Alpine foothills. Look for the flashes of blue on its wings.

Green information is posted on the website of the Federal Environment Agency (www.umweltbundesamt.de).

ACTIVITIES	BEST TIME TO VISIT	PAGE
walking, mountain biking, cross-country skiing	winter, spring	304
wildlife spotting, walking, skiing	winter, spring	246
walking, birdwatching, cycling, nature trails	spring through autumn	333
wildlife and flora spotting, hiking, hydrotherapy, spa treatments	spring, summer	492
walking	spring	560
birdwatching, mudflat walking	spring, autumn	689
climbing, walking	spring, summer, autumn; avoid weekends (busy)	566
ranger tours, hiking, cycling	spring through autumn	441
walking, cycling	avoid summer (paths like ant trails)	712
walking, wildlife spotting	spring, summer, autumn	533
walking, cycling, birdwatching	winter (birdwatching), spring (other activities)	Map p125
swimming, walking, birdwatching	late spring, early autumn	689
cycling, canoeing, birdwatching, hiking	spring, summer, autumn	699
walking, climbing, rock climbing	avoid summer (throngs with day trippers)	158
mudflat walking, tide watching, birdwatching, swimming	spring, autumn	689
birdwatching, water sports, walking	autumn (cranes), summer (water sports)	Map p8

Pesky but sociable racoons, a common non-native species, scoot about eastern Germany, and soon let hikers know if they have been disturbed with a shrill whistle. Beavers can be found in wetlands near the Elbe River. Seals are common on the North Sea and Baltic Sea coasts.

The north coast lures migratory birds. From March to May and August to October they stop over in Schleswig-Holstein's Wadden Sea National Park and the Vorpommersche Boddenlandschaft National Park while travelling to and from southerly regions. Forests everywhere provide a habitat for songbirds and woodpeckers.

Some animals are staging a comeback. Sea eagles, which had practically disappeared from western Germany, are becoming more plentiful in the east, as are falcons, white storks and cranes. The east also sees

Consisting mainly of firs and pines, the Black Forest derives its name from the dark appearance of these conifers when seen from the hillsides.

wolves, which regularly cross the Oder River from Poland, and Eurasian elk (moose), which occasionally appear on moors and in mixed forests.

The wild cat has returned to the Harz Mountains and other forested regions, but don't expect to see the related lynx. Having died out here in the 19th century, lynxes were reintroduced in the 1980s, only to be illegally hunted to the point of extinction again. Today, a few populate the Bavarian Forest National Park, although chances of seeing one in the wild are virtually zero.

Deer are still around, although with dwindling natural habitats and a shrinking gene pool, the Deutsche Wildtier Stiftung (www.deutschewild tierstiftung.de) has expressed concern for their future.

Plants

Despite environmental pressures, German forests remain beautiful places to wander away from crowds and get back to nature. At lower altitudes, they're usually a potpourri of beech, oak, birch, chestnut, lime, maple and ash that erupt into a kaleidoscope of colour in autumn. At higher elevations, fir, pine, spruce and other conifers are prevalent. Canopies often shade low-growing ferns, heather, clover and foxglove. Mixed deciduous forests carpet river valleys at lower altitudes.

In spring, Alpine regions burst with wildflowers – orchid, cyclamen, gentian, pulsatilla, Alpine roses, edelweiss and buttercups. Great care is taken not to cut pastures until plants have seeded and you can minimise your impact by sticking to paths, especially in Alpine areas and coastal dunes where ecosystems are fragile. In late August, heather blossom is the particular lure of Lüneburger Heide, northeast of Hanover.

Environmental Issues

Germans are the original Greens. They cannot claim to have invented environmentalism, but they were there at the outset and coined the word to describe the movement. Recycling, cycling, carrying groceries in reusable bags, shopping at *Biomärkte* (organic supermarkets) – it's all second nature here.

Nuclear power and its demise is still a hot topic. In the wake of the 2011 Fukushima disaster, Angela Merkel made the bold move to abandon nuclear power and shut down all of Germany's 17 nuclear plants by 2022 (eight have already closed).

In Frankfurt and Southern Rhineland, environmental concerns have delayed the construction of the Hochmoselbrücke (High Moselle Bridge) linking Ürzig and Zeltingen-Rachtig, though it is expected to open by 2018.

Travelling across Germany, you'll be struck by the number of wind turbines dotting the landscape, especially in the windswept north. In the EU, Germany blows away most of the competition, with some 23,000 wind turbines in action. In 2014 alone the country blazed ahead with a staggering 5.2GW of new wind power capacity. While other countries debate pros and cons, Germany has long embraced the technology to become Europe's leading producer of wind energy. These turbines provide roughly 8% of German electricity and there are plans – big plans – to build more offshore.

The country is setting a shining example when it comes to solar power, too. An article published by Bloomberg in April 2015 revealed that Germany was set for 'a season of solar power records' as it reached an 'all-time high of 27.7 gigawatts'. There are more than 1.4 million solar PV systems across Germany, which makes it the world leader in photovoltaics, with solar energy accounting for an estimated 6.9% of its electricity generation in 2014. If ecocities such as Freiburg, home to the 59-house PlusEnergy Solar Settlement, are anything to go by, Germany's future looks bright indeed.

But there have been a few gripes to rock the good ship green energy. Südlink, the new part of the national grid linked to green energy distribution, ran into stiff opposition in Bavaria. It seems the Bavarians want green energy but not the extra pylons.

Best Wildlife Spotting

North Sea
common seals, harbour porpoises

Black Forest
red deer, red squirrels

Bavarian Alps
chamois, marmots, ibex

Mecklenburg Lake Plains
otters

Lüneburger Heide *Heidschnucken (moorland sheep)*

Germany's 15 Unesco Biosphere Reserves include the Bavarian Forest, the Berchtesgaden Alps, the Spreewald and Rügen. For the low-down, visit www.unesco.org.

Brush up on your knowledge of German flora and fauna online at www.heimische-tiere.de, www.baumkunde.de and www.wald.de (all in German).

Survival Guide

Directory A–Z

Accommodation

Germany has all types of places to unpack your suitcase. Standards are generally high and even basic accommodation will likely be clean and comfortable. Reservations are a good idea between June and September, and around major public holidays, festivals, cultural events and trade shows. In this book, reviews are listed first by budget and then by author preference.

Costs

Accommodation costs vary wildly between regions, and between cities and rural areas. What gets you a romantic suite in a countryside inn in the Bavarian Forest may only be worth a two-star room in Munich. City hotels geared to the suit brigade often lure leisure travellers with lower rates on weekends. Seasonal variations are common in holiday regions, less so in the cities.

Reservations

Most tourist offices and properties now have an on-line booking function with a best-price guarantee. When making a room reservation directly with a smaller hotel or a B&B, tell your host what time they can expect you to arrive and stick to your plan or ring again. Many well-meaning visitors have lost rooms by showing up late.

If you've arrived in town and don't have reservations or online access, swing by the tourist office, where staff can assist you in finding last-minute lodgings. After hours, vacancies with contact details and addresses may be posted in the window or in a display case.

Categories

Budget stays will generally have you checking in at hostels, *Gasthof* (country inns), *Pensionen* (B&Bs or small hotels), simple family hotels or some Airbnb properties. Facilities may be shared. Midrange properties offer extra creature comforts, such as cable TV, wi-fi and private bathrooms. Overall, these constitute the best value for money. Top-end places come with luxurious amenities, perhaps scenic locations, special decor or historical ambience. Many also have pools, saunas and business centres.

AGRITOURISM

Family-friendly farm holidays offer a great opportunity to get close to nature in relative comfort. Kids get to interact with their favourite barnyard animals and maybe help with everyday chores. Accommodation ranges from bare-bones rooms with shared facilities to fully furnished holiday apartments. Minimum stays are common. Farm types include organic, dairy and equestrian farms, as well as wine estates. Note that places advertising *Landurlaub* (country holiday) no longer actively work their farms.

The German Agricultural Association inspects and controls the quality of hundreds of farms. Details are published on www.landreise.de, which also lets you contact individual properties directly. Another source is www.landsichten.de.

CAMPING

Camping grounds are well maintained but many get jam packed in summer. Book early or show up before noon to snap up any vacated spots. The core camping season runs from May to September, but quite a few sites are open year-round.

BOOK YOUR STAY ONLINE

For more accommodation reviews by Lonely Planet authors, check out http://lonelyplanet.com/hotels/germany. You'll find independent reviews, as well as recommendations on the best places to stay. Best of all, you can book online.

Many camping grounds are in remote locales that are not, or are only poorly, served by public transport, so having your own wheels is an asset. Camping on public land is not permitted and pitching a tent on private property requires the consent of the landowner.

Fees consist of charges per person (between €3 and €10), per tent (€6 to €16, depending on size) and per car or caravan (€3 to €20), plus additional fees for hot showers, resort tax, electricity and sewage disposal. A Camping Card International (www.campingcardinternational.com) may yield savings

The German National Tourist Office has an excellent searchable database with detailed information on 750 camping grounds, as well as a downloadable version of its *Camping in Germany* brochure at www.germany.travel/camping. A handy printed resource is the *BVCD Camping Guide* (www.bvcd.de), published by the Federal Association of the Camping Economy in Germany. It also sells the *Camping Europe Key* (€16), which provides liability insurance and some discounts.

DJH HOSTELS

Germany's 530 Hostelling International–affiliated *Jugendherbergen* (hostels) are run by the Deutsches **Jugendherbergswerk** (DJH; www.jugendherberge.de). Although they are open to people of all ages, they're especially popular with school and youth groups, families and sports clubs.

Aside from gender-segregated dorms, most hostels also have private rooms for families and couples, often with bathroom. If space is tight, hostels may give priority to people under 27, except for those travelling as a family. People over 27 are charged an extra €4 per night.

If you don't have an HI membership card from your home country, you need to buy either a Hostelling International Card for €18 (valid for one year) or collect six individual Welcome Stamps costing €3.50 per night. Both are available at any DJH hostel.

DJH hostels can be booked online at www.jugendherberge.de or www.hihostels.com.

INDEPENDENT HOSTELS

Independent hostels cater primarily for individual travellers and attract a more convivial, international crowd than DJH hostels. They're most prevalent in big cities like Berlin, Cologne and Hamburg, but there are now dozens in smaller towns throughout the country.

Hostels range from classic backpacker pads with large dorms and a communal spirit to modern 'flashpacker' properties that have a similar standard as budget hotels. Many also have private quarters with bathrooms and even apartments with kitchens. Dorms tend to be mixed, although some hostels also offer women-only units. Typical facilities include communal kitchens, bars, cafes, TV lounges, lockers, internet terminals and laundry facilities. Indie hostels have no curfew and staff tend to be savvy, multilingual and keen to help with tips and advice. Some charge a linen fee of around €3 per stay.

Some 60 indies in 34 cities have joined together in an alliance known as the Independent Hostels of Germany (www.german-hostels.de). The website has handy search filters (women-only dorms, credit cards accepted etc) and a best-price guarantee but, unfortunately, no booking function. Booking sites, with lots of information and reviews, include www.hostelworld.com, www.

hostels.com and www.hostelbookers.com.

HOTELS

Lonely Planet aims to feature well-situated, independent hotels that offer good value, a warm welcome, charm and character, as well as a palpable sense of place.

You'll find the gamut of options in Germany, from small family-run properties to international chains and luxurious designer abodes. Increasingly popular are budget designer chains (eg Motel One) geared towards lifestyle-savvy travellers.

In older, family-run hotels, rooms often vary dramatically in terms of size, decor and amenities. The cheapest may have shared facilities, while others come with a shower cubicle installed but no private toilet; only the pricier ones have their own bathrooms. Increasingly city hotels are not including breakfast in their room rate. Many hotels with a high romance factor belong to an association called Romantik Hotels & Restaurants (www.romantikhotels.com).

A growing number of properties are now entirely nonsmoking; others set aside rooms or entire floors for smokers.

WHICH FLOOR?

In Germany, as elsewhere in Europe, 'ground floor' refers to the floor at street level. The 1st floor (what would be called the 2nd floor in the US) is the floor above that. Lonely Planet follows German usage.

CHAIN HOTELS

Hotels chains stretch from nondescript establishments to central five-star properties with character and the gamut of amenities. Most conform to certain standards of decor, service and facilities (air-con, wi-fi, 24-hour check-in), and offer last-minute and/or weekend deals. International chains like Best Western, Holiday Inn, Hilton and Ramada are now ubiquitous on the German market, but there are also some home-grown contenders. Some properties belonging to the groups listed here are mentioned in the On the Road chapters of this guide. Check the websites for additional locations.

A&O (www.aohostels.com) Combines hostel and two-star hotel accommodation.

Dorint (www.dorint.com) Three-to five-star properties in cities and rural areas.

InterCity (www.intercityhotel.com) Good-value two-star chain usually located at train stations.

Kempinski (www.kempinski.com) Luxury hotel group with a pedigree going back to 1897.

Leonardo (www.leonardo-hotels.com) Three- to four-star city hotels.

Meininger Well-run hotel-hostel combo for city-breakers on a budget.

Motel One (www.motelone.com) Fast-growing chain of budget designer hotels.

Sorat (www.sorat-hotels.com) Four-star boutique hotels.

Steigenberger (www.steigenberger.com) Five-star luxury often in historic buildings.

PENSIONS, INNS & PRIVATE ROOMS

The German equivalent of a B&B, *Pensionen* are small and informal and an excellent low-cost alternative to hotels. *Gasthöfe/Gasthäuser* (inns) are similar, but usually have restaurants serving regional and German food to a local clientele. *Privatzimmer* are guest rooms in private homes, though privacy seekers may find these places a bit too intimate.

Amenities, room size and decor vary, often within a single establishment. The cheapest units may have shared facilities or perhaps a sink and a shower cubicle in the room but no private toilet. What rooms lack in amenities, though, they often make up for in charm and authenticity, often augmented by friendly hosts who take a personal interest in ensuring that you enjoy your stay.

Travellers in need of buckets of privacy, high comfort levels or the latest tech amenities may not feel as comfortable, although wi-fi, cable TV and other mod cons are becoming increasingly available in these places as well.

Some tourist offices keep lists of available rooms; you can also look around for *'Zimmer Frei'* (rooms available) signs in house or shop windows. They're usually quite cheap, with per-person rates starting at €15 and usually topping out at €30, including breakfast.

If a landlord is reluctant to rent for a single night, offer to pay a little extra. For reservations, try www.bed-and-breakfast.de, www.bedandbreakfast.de or www.bedandbreakfast.com.

FURNISHED FLATS

Renting a furnished flat is a hugely popular – and economical – lodging option. The benefit of space, privacy and independence makes them especially attractive to families, self-caterers and small groups. Peer-to-peer rental communities like Airbnb or its German competitors Wimdu and 9flats have also made enormous inroads.

Local tourist offices have lists of holiday flats (*Ferienwohnungen* or *Ferien-Appartements*) or holidays homes (*Ferienhäuser*). *Pensionen*, inns, hotels and even farmhouses also rent out apartments. International online agencies include

---

MY HOME IS MY CASTLE

If you're the romantic type, consider a fairy-tale getaway in a castle, palace or country manor dripping with character and history. They're typically in the countryside, strategically perched atop a crag, perhaps overlooking a river or rolling hills. And it doesn't take a king's ransom to stay in one. In fact, even wallet-watchers can fancy themselves knight or damsel when staying in a castle converted into a youth hostel (eg Burg Stahleck on the Rhine). More typically, though, properties are luxury affairs, blending the gamut of mod cons with baronial ambience and olde-worlde trappings, like four-poster beds, antique armoires and heavy curtains. Sometimes your hosts are even descendants of the original castle builders – often some local baron, count or prince. For details, see www.thecastles.de or www.germany-castles-hotels.com.

Climate

Berlin

Munich

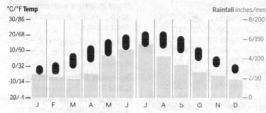

Frankfurt Am Main

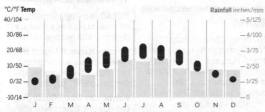

www.homeaway.com, www.forgetaway.com and www.interhomeusa.com.

Stays under a week usually incur a surcharge, and there's almost always a 'cleaning fee' of €20 or €30 added to the total.

You could alternatively consider a home exchange, where you swap homes and live like a local for free; see www.homeexchange.com for more on how it's done.

Customs Regulations

Goods brought in and out of countries within the EU incur no additional taxes, provided duty has been paid somewhere within the EU and the goods are for personal use. Duty-free shopping is only

available if you're leaving the EU.

Duty-free allowances (for anyone over 17) arriving from non-EU countries:

➡ 200 cigarettes or 100 cigarillos or 50 cigars or 250g of loose tobacco or a proportional combination of these goods

➡ 1L of strong liquor or 2L of less than 22% alcohol by volume, plus 4L of wine, plus 16L of beer

➡ other goods up to the value of €300 if arriving by land, or €430 if arriving by sea or air (€175 for under 15 years).

Discount Cards

Concession discounts are widely available for seniors, children and students. In some cases, you may be

asked to show ID or prove your age. Tourist offices in many cities sell Welcome Cards, which entitle visitors to discounts on museums, sights and tours, plus unlimited trips on local public transport. They can be good value if you plan on taking advantage of most of the benefits and don't qualify for any of the standard discounts.

If you qualify for one of the following discount cards, you can reap additional benefits on travel, shopping, attractions or entertainment:

Camping Card International (www.campingcardinternational.com) Up to 25% savings in camping fees and third-party liability insurance while on the camping ground.

International Student Identity Card (www.isic.org) The most popular discount card, but only for full-time students. Available at ISIC points (see website) and online. Cost vary by country and range from US$4 to US$25.

International Youth Travel Card (www.istc.org) Similar to ISIC but for nonstudents under 30 years of age. Available at ISIC points.

Electricity

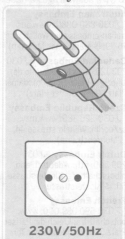

230V/50Hz

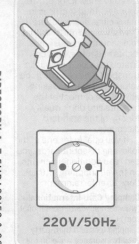

220V/50Hz

Embassies & Consulates

All foreign embassies are in Berlin, but many countries have consular offices in Frankfurt, Munich, Hamburg or Düsseldorf. Check online or call the embassy to find out which consulate is closest to your location. For German missions around the world and foreign missions in Germany not listed here, go to www.auswaertiges-amt.de.

Australian Embassy (☏030-880 0880; www.australian-embassy.de; Wallstrasse 76-79; ⓢMärkisches Museum)

Canadian Embassy (☏030-203 120; www.kanada-info.de; Leipziger Platz 17; ⓢPotsdamer Platz, ⓡPotsdamer Platz)

Czech Republic Embassy (☏030-226 380; www.mzv.cz/berlin; Wilhelmstrasse 44; ⓢMohrenstrasse)

Dutch Embassy (☏030-209 560; http://deutschland.nlbotschaft.org; Klosterstrasse 50; ⓢKlosterstrasse)

French Embassy (☏030-590 039 000; www.botschaft-frankreich.de; Pariser Platz 5; ⓢBrandenburger Tor, ⓡBrandenburger Tor)

Irish Embassy (☏030-220 720; www.dfa.ie; Jägerstrasse 51; ⓢHausvogteiplatz)

New Zealand Embassy (☏030-206 210; www.nzembassy.com; Friedrichstrasse 60; ⓢStadtmitte)

Polish Embassy (☏030-223 130; http://berlin.msz.gov.pl/de; Lassenstrasse 19-21; ⓡGrunewald)

Swiss Embassy (☏030-390 4000; www.eda.admin.ch/berlin; Otto-von-Bismarck-Allee 4a; ⌨100, ⓢBundestag)

UK Embassy (☏030-204 570; www.gov.uk/government/world/organisations/british-embassy-berlin; Wilhelmstrasse 70; ⓢBrandenburger Tor, ⓡBrandenburger Tor)

US Consulate (☏030-830 50; http://germany.usembassy.gov; Clayallee 170; ⓢOskar-Helene-Heim)

Food

German eating options (p740) match all tastes and travel budgets. The following price ranges refer to a standard main course. Unless otherwise stated 19% tax is included in the price.

€ less than €8
€€ €8 to €18
€€€ more than €18

Gay & Lesbian Travellers

Germany is a magnet for *schwule* (gay) and *lesbische* (lesbian) travellers, with the rainbow flag flying especially proudly in Berlin and Cologne. There are also sizeable communities in Hamburg, Frankfurt and Munich.

➟ Legal stuff: Homosexuality has been legal since the late 1960s. The age of consent is 14. There is no same-sex marriage, only registered partnerships.

➟ Attitudes are more conservative in the countryside, in older people and in the eastern states.

➟ As elsewhere, Germany's lesbian scene is less public than its male counterpart and is centred mainly on women's cafes and bars.

➟ Gay pride marches are held throughout Germany in springtime; the largest, in Cologne and Berlin, draw hundreds of thousands of rainbow revellers and friends.

Publications

Blu (www.blu.fm) Free print and online magazine with searchable, up-to-the-minute location and event listings.

L-Mag (www.l-mag.de) Bi-monthly magazine for lesbians. Available at newsagents.

Spartacus International Gay Guide Annual English-language travel guide for men. Available online, in bookstores and as an app.

Websites & Apps

BGLAD (www.bglad.com) International online resource and directory with hundreds of links.

German National Tourist Office (www.germany.travel/en/ms/lgbt/home/home.html?et_rp=1) Dedicated LGBT pages.

Patroc Gay Travel Guide (www.patroc.com) Travel information to 25 European destinations.

Spartacus World (www.spartacusworld.com) Hip hotel, style and event guide.

Health

Germany is a healthy place; your main risks are likely to be sunburn, foot blisters, insect bites, mild stomach problems and hangovers. Tap water is drinkable.

Before You Go

➟ A signed and dated letter from your doctor describing your medical conditions and medications, including generic names, is a good idea. It is illegal to import codeine-based medication without a doctor's certificate.

➟ No vaccinations are required for travel to

Germany, but the World Health Organization (WHO) recommends that all travellers be covered for diphtheria, tetanus, measles, mumps, rubella and polio.

Availability & Cost of Health Care

→ Excellent health care is widely available from *Rettungsstelle* (emergency rooms) at *Krankenhauser* (hospitals) and at *Arzt* (doctors' offices).

→ For minor illnesses or injuries (headache, bruises, diarrhoea), trained staff in pharmacies can provide advice, sell prescription-free medications and make doctors' referrals if further help is needed.

→ Condoms are widely available in drugstores, pharmacies and supermarkets. Birth control pills require a doctor's prescription.

Pharmacies

→ German *Drogerien* (chemists, drugstores) do not sell any kind of medication, not even aspirin. Even *rezeptfrei* (over-the-counter) medications for minor health concerns, such as a cold or upset stomach, are only available at an *Apotheke* (pharmacy).

→ For more serious conditions, you will need to produce a *Rezept* (prescription) from a licensed physician. If you take regular medication, be sure to bring a supply for your entire trip, as the same brand may not be available in Germany.

→ The names and addresses of pharmacies open after hours (these rotate) are posted in every pharmacy window, or call ☑01141.

Insurance

→ Comprehensive travel insurance to cover theft, loss

and medical problems is highly recommended.

→ Some policies specifically exclude dangerous activities, such as motorcycling, scuba diving and even trekking; read the fine print.

→ Check that the policy covers ambulance or an emergency flight home.

→ Before you leave, find out if your insurance plan makes payments directly to providers or reimburses you for health expenditures.

→ Paying for your airline ticket with a credit card sometimes provides limited travel accident insurance – ask your credit-card company what it is prepared to cover.

→ If you have to make a claim, be sure to keep all necessary documents and bills.

→ Worldwide travel insurance is available at www.lonelyplanet.com/travel-insurance. You can buy, extend and claim online anytime – even if you're already on the road.

→ Consider coverage for luggage theft or loss. If you already have a homeowner's or renter's policy, check what it will cover and only get supplemental insurance to protect against the rest.

→ If you have prepaid a large portion of your holiday, trip cancellation insurance is worthwhile.

Internet Access

→ Some cafes and bars have wi-fi hot spots that let laptop-toting customers hook up for free, although you usually need to ask for a password.

→ Many hotels have an internet corner for their guests, often at no charge. Note that in some properties wi-fi access may be limited to some rooms and/or public areas, so if you need in-room access be sure to specify at the time of booking.

→ Internet cafes seem to have the lifespan of a fruit fly, so listings are quickly outdated. Ask staff at your hotel for a recommendation.

→ Wi-fi is available for a fee on select ICE train routes, including Berlin to Cologne and Frankfurt to Munich and in DB Lounges (free in 1st class). Nearly 130 stations, including those in Berlin, Munich, Hamburg and Frankfurt, offer 30 minutes free wi-fi with registration via DeutscheTelekom.

→ Locate wi-fi hot spots at www.hotspot-locations.com.

EUROPEAN HEALTH INSURANCE CARD

Citizens of the EU, Switzerland, Iceland, Norway and Liechtenstein receive free or reduced-cost, state-provided (not private) health-care coverage with the European Health Insurance Card (EHIC) for medical treatment that becomes necessary while in Germany. It does not cover emergency repatriation home. Each family member needs a separate card. UK residents can find information on how to obtain the card at www.ehic.org.uk.

You will need to pay directly and fill in a treatment form; keep the form to claim any refunds. In general you can claim back around 70% of the standard treatment cost.

Citizens of other countries need to check whether there is a reciprocal arrangement for free medical care between their country and Germany.

Legal Matters

➨ The permissible blood-alcohol limit is 0.05%; drivers caught exceeding this are subject to stiff fines, a confiscated licence and even jail time. Drinking in public is not illegal, but be discreet.

➨ Cannabis *consumption* is not illegal, but the possession, acquisition, sale and cultivation of it is considered a criminal offence. There is usually no prosecution for possessing 'small quantities', although the definition of 'small' varies by state, ranging from 6g to 20g. Dealers face far stiffer penalties, as do people caught with any other recreational drugs.

➨ If arrested, you have the right to make a phone call and are presumed innocent until proven guilty, although you may be held in custody until trial. If you don't know a lawyer, contact your embassy.

Money

The unit of currency in Germany is the euro (€). Euros come in seven notes (€5, €10, €20, €50, €100, €200 and €500) and eight coins (€0.01, €0.02, €0.05, €0.10, €0.20, €0.50, €1 and €2).

ATMs & Debit Cards

➨ The easiest and quickest way to obtain cash is by using your debit (bank) card at a *Geldautomat* (ATM) linked to international networks such as Cirrus, Plus, Star and Maestro.

➨ ATMs are ubiquitous and usually accessible 24/7.

➨ ATM cards often double as debit cards, and many shops, hotels, restaurants and other businesses accept them for payment. Most cards use the 'chip and pin' system; instead of signing, you enter your PIN. If your card isn't chip-and-pin enabled, you may be able to sign the receipt, but ask first.

➨ Deutsche Bahn ticket vending machines in train stations and local public transport may not accept non-chip-and-pin cards.

Cash

Cash is king in Germany. Always carry some with you and plan to pay cash almost everywhere. It's also a good idea to set aside a small amount of euros as an emergency stash.

Credit Cards

➨ Credit cards are widely accepted, but it's best not to assume you'll be able to use one – ask first. Sometimes there's a minimum purchase amount. Even so, a piece of plastic is vital in emergencies and also useful for phone or internet bookings. Visa and MasterCard are more commonly accepted than American Express or Diner's Club.

➨ Cash advances on credit card via ATMs incur steep fees and you'll be charged interest immediately (ie, there's no grace period as with purchases).

➨ Report lost or stolen cards to the central number ☑116 116 or the following:

American Express ☑069-9797 1000

MasterCard ☑0800-819 1040

Visa ☑0800-814 9100

Moneychanging

➨ Commercial banks usually charge a stiff fee (€5 to €10) per foreign-currency transaction, no matter the amount, if they offer exchange services at all.

➨ *Wechselstuben* (currency exchange offices) at airports, train stations and in bigger towns usually charge lower fees. Traveller-geared Reisebank (www.reisebank. de) branches are ubiquitous in Germany and are usually found at train stations. They keep longer hours than banks and are usually open on weekends.

➨ Exchange facilities in rural areas are rare.

Tipping

Restaurant bills always include a *Bedienung* (service charge), but most people add 5% or 10%, unless the service was truly abhorrent. It's considered rude to leave the tip on the table. When paying, tell the server the total amount you want to pay (say, if the bill is €28, you say €30). If you don't want change back, say '*Stimmt so*' (that's fine). If you order food at a counter, don't tip.

SMOKING REGULATIONS

Germany was one of the last countries in Europe to legislate on smoking. However, there is no nationwide law, with regulations left to each of the 16 states, creating a rather confusing patchwork of antismoking laws. Generally, smoking is a no-no in schools, hospitals, airports, train stations and other public facilities. But when it comes to bars, pubs, cafes and restaurants, every state does it just a little differently. Since 2011, Bavaria has banned smoking practically everywhere, even in Oktoberfest tents. However, in most other states, lighting up is allowed in designated smoking rooms in restaurants and clubs. One-room establishments smaller than 75 sq metres may allow smoking, provided they serve no food and only admit patrons over 18. The venue must be clearly designated as a *Raucherbar* (smokers' bar).

WHERE & WHO	CUSTOMARY TIP
bar	€1, rounded to nearest euro
hotel porter	€1-1.50 per bag
restaurant	5-10%
room cleaners	€1-2 per day
taxi driver	10%, rounded to nearest euro
toilet attendant	€0.20-0.50
tour guide	€1-2 per person

Opening Hours

The following are typical opening hours in Germany, although these may vary seasonally and between cities and villages. For specifics, see individual listings. Where hours vary across the year, we've provided those applicable in high season.

Banks 9am to 4pm Monday to Friday, extended hours usually on Tuesday and Thursday, some open Saturday

Bars 6pm to 1am

Cafes 8am to 8pm

Clubs 11pm to early morning hours

Major stores and supermarkets 9.30am to 8pm Monday to Saturday (shorter hours outside city centres)

Post offices 9am to 6pm Monday to Friday, 9am to 1pm Saturday

Restaurants 11am to 11pm (food service often stops at 9pm in rural areas)

Photography

Germany is a photographer's dream. A good general reference guide is Lonely Planet's *Travel Photography*.

➡ Germans tend to be deferential around photographers and will make a point of not walking in front of your camera, even if you want them to.

➡ No one seems to mind being photographed in the context of an overall scene, but if you want a close-up shot, you should ask first.

➡ Many museums, palaces and some churches charge a separate 'photography fee' (usually €2 or €3) if you want to take (noncommercial) pictures.

Post

To send letters up to 20g to destinations within Germany costs €0.62 and €0.80 anywhere else in the world. For letters up to 50g, the rates are €0.85 and €1.50, respectively. For other rates, see www.deutschepost.de.

Mail within Germany takes one to two days for delivery; to the USA or other European countries it takes three to five days and to Australia five to seven days.

Public Holidays

Germany observes three secular and eight religious public holidays. Banks, shops, post offices and public services close on these days. States with predominantly Catholic populations, such as Bavaria and Baden-Württemberg, also celebrate Epiphany (6 January), Corpus Christi (10 days after Pentecost), Assumption Day (15 August) and All Saints' Day (1 November). Reformation Day (31 October) is only observed in eastern Germany (but not in Berlin).

The following are *gesetzliche Feiertage* (public holidays):

Neujahrstag (New Year's Day) 1 January

Ostern (Easter) March/April; Good Friday, Easter Sunday and Easter Monday

Christi Himmelfahrt (Ascension Day) Forty days after Easter

Maifeiertag/Tag der Arbeit (Labour Day) 1 May

Pfingsten (Whit/Pentecost Sunday and Monday) Fifty days after Easter

Tag der Deutschen Einheit (Day of German Unity) 3 October

Weihnachtstag (Christmas Day) 25 December

Zweiter Weihnachtstag (Boxing Day) 26 December

PRACTICALITIES

➡ **DVD** Germany is DVD region code 2.

➡ **Laundry** Virtually all towns and cities have a *Waschsalon* (launderette). Hostels often have washing machines for guest use, while hotels offer cleaning services.

➡ **Newspapers & Magazines** Dailies include the *Süddeutsche Zeitung, Die Welt* and *Der Tagesspiegel* (all quite centrist), and the more conservative *Frankfurter Allgemeine Zeitung. Die Zeit* is a weekly with in-depth reporting. *Der Spiegel* and *Focus* magazines are popular news weeklies.

➡ **Radio** Regional stations feature a mixed format of news, talk and music.

➡ **Weights & Measures** Metric system.

➡ **Women's Clothing** A German size 36 equals a US size 6 and a UK size 10, then increases in increments of two, making size 38 a US size 8 and UK size 12.

Telephone

German phone numbers consist of an area code, starting with 0, and the local number. Area codes are between three and six digits long; local numbers, between three and nine digits. If dialling from a landline within the same city, you don't need to dial the area code. You must dial it if using a mobile.

Calling Germany from abroad
Dial your country's international access code, then 49 (Germany's country code), then the area code (dropping the initial 0) and the local number.

Calling internationally from Germany Dial ⟋00 (the international access code), then the country code, the area code (without the zero if there is one) and the local number.

Calling on the Cheap

If you have access to a private phone, you can benefit from cheaper rates by using a 'Call-by-Call' access code (01016 or 01088). Rates change daily and are published in the newspapers, or online at www.billigertelefonieren.de (in German).

With a high-speed internet connection (preferably a free wi-fi hot spot) , you can make free Skype-to-Skype calls anywhere from a mobile or a computer. You can also buy Skype Credit and make inexpensive calls to a mobile

or landline number. Google Talk and FaceTime (for Apple devices only) work similarly.

Mobile Phones

➡ German mobile numbers begin with a four-digit prefix, such as 0151, 0157, 0170 or 0178.

➡ Mobile (cell) phones are called 'Handys' and work on GSM 900/1800. If your home country uses a different standard, you'll need a multiband GSM phone while in Germany. Check your contract for roaming charges.

➡ If you have an unlocked phone that works in Germany, you may be able to cut down on roaming charges by buying a prepaid, rechargeable local SIM card for €10, including calling time. The cheapest and least complicated of these are sold at discount supermarkets, such as Aldi, Netto and Lidl. Telecommunications stores (eg Telekom, O₂ and Vodaphone) also sell SIMs. Top-up cards are widely available in kiosks and supermarkets.

➡ If you want to purchase an inexpensive unlocked phone, try the electronics chains Media Markt and Saturn. Prices start at €20.

➡ Calls made to a mobile phone are more expensive than those to a landline, but incoming calls are free.

➡ The use of mobile phones while driving is *verboten* (forbidden), unless you're using a headset.

Phonecards

➡ Public pay phones are becoming increasingly rare and only work with Deutsche Telekom (DT) phonecards, available in denominations of €5, €10 and €20 at DT stores, post offices, newsagents and tourist offices. Calling internationally from pay phones is expensive.

➡ For long-distance or international calls, prepaid calling cards issued by other companies tend to offer better rates than DT's phone cards, although they may charge a per-call connection fee. Read the fine print on the card itself. These cards are widely available at newsagents and telephone call shops. They work from any phone.

Special Numbers

Customer service numbers in Germany often have prefixes that indicate the rate at which they're charged. The following table details the cost for calls made from landlines. Note that the per-minute charge can be as high as €0.42 for calls made from mobile phones.

NUMBER	COST
0800	free
01801	€0.04 per minute
01802	€0.06 per call
01803	€0.09 per minute
01804	€0.20 per call
01805	€0.14 per minute
01806	€0.20 per call
01807	first 30 seconds free, then €0.14 per minute
0900	up to €2 per minute

Time

Clocks in Germany are set to Central European time (GMT/UTC plus one hour). Daylight saving time kicks in at 2am on the last Sunday in March and ends on the last Sunday in October. The use of the 24-hour clock (eg 6.30pm is 18.30) is the norm. As daylight saving times vary across regions, the following time differences are indicative only.

CITY	NOON IN BERLIN
Auckland	11pm
Cape Town	1pm
London	11am
New York	6am
San Francisco	3am
Sydney	9pm
Tokyo	8pm

Toilets

➡ German toilets are sit-down affairs. Men are expected to sit down when peeing.

➡ Free-standing 24-hour self-cleaning toilet pods have become quite common. The cost is €0.50 and you have 15 minutes. Most are wheelchair-accessible.

➡ Toilets in malls, clubs, beer gardens etc, often have an attendant who expects a tip of between €0.20 and €0.50.

➡ Toilets in airports are usually free, but in main train stations they are often maintained by private companies like McClean, which charge as much as €1.50 for the privilege.

➡ Along autobahns, rest stops with facilities are spaced about 20km to 30km apart.

Tourist Information

➡ Just about every community in Germany has a walk-in tourist office where you can get advice and pick up maps and pamphlets, sometimes in English. Many also offer a room- and ticket-reservation service that's usually free. See the destination chapters for local offices.

➡ With few exceptions, at least one staff member will speak English and will be happy to make the effort to help you.

➡ A useful pre-trip planning source is the **German National Tourist Office** (www.germany.travel), where information is available in almost 30 languages.

Travellers with Disabilities

➡ Germany is fairly progressive when it comes to barrier-free travel. Access ramps and/or lifts are available in many public buildings, including train stations, museums, concert halls and cinemas. In historic towns, though, cobblestone streets make getting around difficult.

➡ Trains, trams, underground trains and buses are increasingly accessible. Some stations also have grooved platform borders to assist blind passengers in navigating. Seeing-eye dogs are allowed on all forms of public transport. For the hearing impaired, upcoming station names are often displayed electronically on public transport.

➡ Newer hotels have lifts and rooms with extra-wide doors and spacious bathrooms.

➡ Some car-rental agencies offer hand-controlled vehicles and vans with wheelchair lifts at no charge, but you must reserve them well in advance. In car parks and garages, look for designated spots marked with a wheelchair symbol.

➡ Many local and regional tourist offices have special brochures for people with disabilities, usually in German.

➡ Good general resources:

Deutsche Bahn Mobility Service Centre (☎01806-996 633, ext 9 for English; www.bahn. com) Train access information and route planning assistance. The website has useful information in English (search for 'barrier-free travel').

German National Tourist Office (www.germany.travel) Your first port of call, with inspirational information in English.

Visas

➡ EU nationals only need their passport or national identity card to enter, stay and work in Germany as a tourist. If you plan to stay longer, you must register with the authorities at the *Bürgeramt* (Citizens' Registration Office) within two weeks of your arrival.

➡ Citizens of Australia, Canada, Israel, Japan, New Zealand, Poland, Switzerland and the US only need a valid passport (no visa) if entering Germany as tourists for up to three months within a six-month period. Passports must be valid for another four months beyond the intended departure date. For stays exceeding 90 days, contact your nearest German embassy or consulate, and begin your visa application well in advance.

➡ Nationals from other countries need a Schengen Visa, named for the 1995 Schengen Agreement that abolished international border controls between most European countries. Applications for a Schengen

Visa must be filed with the embassy or consulate of the country that is your primary destination. It is valid for stays of up to 90 days. Legal residency in any Schengen country makes a visa unnecessary, regardless of your nationality.

➡ For full details, see www.auswaertiges-amt.de and check with a German consulate in your country.

Volunteering

Websites like www.goabroad.com and www.transitions-abroad.com throw up a wide spectrum of opportunities for volunteering in Germany: helping out on a family farm in the Alps, restoring a medieval castle in eastern Germany, helping kids or the elderly in Dresden, or teaching English to the long-term unemployed in Berlin are just some of the experiences awaiting those keen to volunteer their time and skills.

Here's a small selection of volunteer organisations:

Conversation Corps (www.geovisions.org) Volunteer 15 hours a week to teach a German family English in exchange for room and board.

Volunteers for Peace (www.vfp.org) US-based nonprofit offers a potpourri of opportunities, from construction to farm work or social work.

WWOOF (www.wwoof.de) Help out on a small organic farm harvesting, tending animals, bringing in the hay or gardening.

Transport

GETTING THERE & AWAY

Most travellers arrive in Germany by air, or by rail and road connections from neighbouring countries. Flights and tours can be booked online at lonelyplanet.com/bookings.

Entering the Country

Entering Germany is usually a very straightforward procedure. If you're arriving from any of the 25 other Schengen countries, such as the Netherlands, Poland, Austria or the Czech Republic, you no longer have to show your passport or go through customs in Germany, no matter which nationality you are. If you're coming in from non-Schengen countries, full border procedures apply.

Air

Frankfurt Airport is the main gateway for transcontinental flights, although Düsseldorf and Munich also receive their share of overseas air traffic. Until the opening of the new Berlin Brandenburg Airport, flights to Berlin will arrive at its two smaller international airports, Tegel and Schönefeld. There are also sizeable airports in Hamburg, Cologne/Bonn and Stuttgart, and smaller ones in such cities as Bremen, Dresden, Hanover, Leipzig-Halle, Münster-Osnabrück and Nuremberg.

Lufthansa, Germany's national flagship carrier and a Star Alliance member, operates a vast network of domestic and international flights and has one of the world's best safety records. Practically every other national carrier from around the world serves Germany, along with budget airlines

Air Berlin (www.airberlin.com), EasyJet (www.easyjet.com), Flybe (www.flybe.com), airBaltic (www.airbaltic.com), Ryanair (www.ryanair.com) and Germanwings (www.germanwings.com). Note that Ryanair usually flies to remote airports that are often little more than recycled military airstrips. Frankfurt-Hahn, for instance, is actually near the Moselle River, about 110km northwest of Frankfurt proper.

For details about individual airports, including information about getting to and from them, see the Getting There & Around sections in the On the Road chapters.

Land

Bicycle

Bringing a bicycle to Germany is much cheaper and less complicated than you might think.

CLIMATE CHANGE & TRAVEL

Every form of transport that relies on carbon-based fuel generates CO_2, the main cause of human-induced climate change. Modern travel is dependent on aeroplanes, which might use less fuel per kilometre per person than most cars but travel much greater distances. The altitude at which aircraft emit gases (including CO_2) and particles also contributes to their climate change impact. Many websites offer 'carbon calculators' that allow people to estimate the carbon emissions generated by their journey and, for those who wish to do so, to offset the impact of the greenhouse gases emitted with contributions to portfolios of climate-friendly initiatives throughout the world. Lonely Planet offsets the carbon footprint of all staff and author travel.

Eurotunnel bike shuttle service (☑in the UK 01303-282 201; www.eurotunnel.com) through the Channel Tunnel charges £18 (£22 in July and August) one way for a bicycle and its rider. You need to book at least 48 hours in advance.

A dismantled bike under 85cm tucked into a bike bag may be carried on board a **Eurostar train** (☑from outside the UK +44 1233 617 575, in the UK 03432 186 186; www.eurostar.com) as part of your luggage allowance. Larger bikes are charged £25 or £29 and require advance reservations. During peak travel periods, make sure there is sufficient space on the train before you complete your booking.

Deutsche Bahn charges €10 for transporting a bike internationally. You need to buy an *Internationale Fahrradkarte* and make reservations at least one day ahead.

On ferries, foot passengers can usually bring a bicycle, sometimes free of charge.

Bus

LONG-DISTANCE COACHES

Long-distance coach travel to Germany from such cities as Milan, Vienna, Amsterdam and Copenhagen has become a viable option thanks to a new crop of companies offering good-value connections aboard comfortable buses with snack bars and free wi-fi. Major operators include **MeinFernbus** (☑0180-515 9915; www.meinfernbus.de), **Flixbus** (☑01807 1239 9123; www.flixbus.com), **Megabus** (☑in the UK +44 900 1600 900; www.megabus.com), **Berlinlinienbus** (☑030-338 4480; www.berlinlinienbus.de) and **Eurolines** (www.eurolines.com). For routes, times and prices, check www.busliniensuche.de (also in English).

BUSABOUT

A backpacker-geared hop-on, hop-off service, **Busabout** (☑in the UK 8450 267 514; www.busabout.com) runs coaches along three interlocking European loops between May and October. Passes are sold online and through travel agents.

Germany is part of the north loop. Within Germany, the service stops in Berlin, Dresden, Munich and Stuttgart. Loops can be combined. In Munich, for instance, the north loop intersects with the south loop to Italy.

Trips on one loop start at €569, on two loops €979 and on three €1159. The Flexitrip Pass, which allows you to travel between cities across different loops, costs €489/537/569/599 for six/seven/eight/nine stops.

Car & Motorcycle

When bringing your own vehicle to Germany, you need a valid driving licence, car registration and proof of third-party insurance. Foreign cars must display a nationality sticker unless they have official European plates. You also need to carry a warning (hazard) triangle and a first-aid kit.

There are no special requirements for crossing the border into Germany by car. Under the Schengen Agreement there are no passport controls if entering the country from the Netherlands, Belgium, Luxembourg, Denmark, Austria, Switzerland, the Czech Republic and Poland.

For road rules and other driving-related information, see p784.

FROM THE EUROTUNNEL

Coming from the UK, the fastest way to the Continent is via the **Eurotunnel** (☑in Germany 01805-000 248, in the UK 08443 35 35 35; www.eurotunnel.com). These shuttle trains whisk cars, motorbikes, bicycles and coaches from Folkestone in England through the Channel Tunnel to Coquelles (near Calais, in France) in about 35 minutes. From there, you can be in Germany in about three hours. Loading and unloading takes about one hour.

Shuttles run daily round the clock, with up to four departures hourly during peak periods. Fares are calculated

BY SEA FROM THE UK

There are no direct ferry services between Germany and the UK, but you can go via the Netherlands, Belgium or France and drive or train it from there. For fare details and to book tickets, check the ferry websites or go to www.ferrybooker.com or www.ferrysavers.com.

Via France	P&O Ferries	Dover-Calais	www.poferries.com
	DFDS Seaways	Dover-Dunkirk	www.dfdsseaways.com
Via Belgium	P&O Ferries	Hull-Zeebrugge	www.poferries.com
Via the Netherlands	P&O Ferries	Hull-Rotterdam	www.poferries.com
	DFDS Seaways	Newcastle-Amsterdam	www.dfdsseaways.com
	Stena Line	Harwich-Hoek van Holland	www.stenaline.com

per vehicle, including up to nine passengers, and depend on such factors as time of day, season and length of stay. Standard one-way tickets start at £55. The website and travel agents have full details.

Train

Rail services link Germany with virtually every country in Europe. In Germany ticketing is handled by **Deutsche Bahn** (www.bahn.com). Long-distance trains connecting major German cities with those in other countries are called EuroCity (EC) trains. Seat reservations are essential during the peak summer season and around major holidays, and are recommended at other times.

Deutsche Bahn's overnight service is called **City Night Line** (⊘in Germany 0180-699 6633; www.nachtzugreise.de) and offers three levels of comfort:

➡ **Schlafwagen** (sleeping car, €46 to €176 supplement) Private, airconditioned compartment for up to three passengers; the deluxe version (1. Klasse) has a shower and toilet.

➡ **Liegewagen** (couchette; €21 to €70 supplement) Sleeps up to six people; when you book an individual berth, you must share the compartment with others; women may ask for a singlesex couchette at the time of booking but are advised to book early.

➡ **Sitzwagen** (seat carriage; €10 to €49 supplement) Roomy reclining seat. Useful websites:

➡ **www.raileurope.com** Detailed train information and ticket and train-pass sales from Rail Europe.

➡ **www.railteam.eu** Journey planner provided by an alliance of seven European railways, including Eurostar, Deutsche Bahn and France's SNCF. No booking function yet.

LOW-EMISSION STICKERS

To decrease air pollution caused by fine particles, most German cites now have low-emissions environmental zones that may only be entered by cars displaying an *Umweltplakette* (emissions sticker, sometimes also called *Feinstaubplakette*). And yes, this includes foreign vehicles. No stickers are needed for motorcycles.

The easiest way to obtain the sticker is by ordering it online from www.green-zones.eu, a handy website in many languages. The cost is €29.95. You can cut this amount in half if you order from the TÜV (Technical Inspection Authority) at www.tuev-sued.de or www.tuev-nord.de, both of which provide easy instructions in English. Once in Germany, stickers are also available from designated repair centres, car dealers and vehicle-licensing offices. Drivers caught without one will be fined €80.

➡ **www.seat61.com** Comprehensive trip-planning information, including ferry details from the UK.

EUROSTAR

Thanks to the Channel Tunnel, travelling by train between the UK and Germany is actually a fast and enjoyable option. High-speed **Eurostar** (⊘from outside the UK +44 1233 617 575, in the UK 03432 186 186; www.eurostar.com) passenger trains hurtle at least 10 times daily between London and Paris (the journey takes 2½ hours) or Brussels (two hours). In either city you can change to regular or other high-speed trains to destinations in Germany.

Eurostar fares depend on carriage class, time of day, season and destination. Children, rail-pass holders and those aged between 12 and 25 and over 60 qualify for discounts. For the latest fare information, including promotions and special packages, check the website.

RAIL PASSES

If you want to cover lots of territory in and around Germany within a specific time, a rail pass is a convenient and good-value option. Passes cover unlimited travel during their period of validity on

---

national railways as well as on some private lines, ferries and river-boat services.

There are two types: the Eurail Pass, for people living outside Europe, and the InterRail Pass, for residents of Europe, including residents of Russia and Turkey.

EURAIL

Eurail Passes (www.eurail.com) are valid for travel in up to 28 countries and need to be purchased – on the website, through a travel agent or at www.raileurope.com – before you leave your home country. Various passes are available:

➡ **Global Pass** Unlimited 1st-class travel for 15 or 21 consecutive days, or one, two or three months. There are also versions that give you five days of travel within a 10-day period or 10 or 15 days of travel within a two-month period. The 15-day continuous version costs €580.

➡ **Select Pass** Five, six, eight or 10 days of travel within two months in four bordering countries in 1st class; a five-day pass in three countries costs €413.

➡ **Regional Pass** Gets you around two neighbouring countries on four, five, six, eight or 10 days within two months. The Germany–Austria Pass for five days costs €263 in 2nd class or €328 in 1st class.

Groups of two to five people travelling together save 15% off the regular adult fares. If you're under 26, prices drop 35%, but you must travel in 2nd class. Children aged between four and 11 years get a 50% discount on the adult fare. Children under four years travel free.

The website has details, as well as a ticket-purchasing function allowing you to pay in several currencies.

INTERRAIL

InterRail Passes (www.interrail.eu) are valid for unlimited travel in 30 countries. As with the Eurail Pass, you can choose from several schemes.

➡ **Global Pass** Unlimited travel in 30 countries, available for 15 days (€414), 22 days (€484) or one month (€626) of continuous travel; for five travel days within a 10-day period (€264) or for 10 travel days within a 22-day period (€374).

➡ **Germany Pass** Buys three/four/six/eight days of travel within a one-month period for €205/226/288/319. This pass is not available if you are a resident of Germany.

Prices quoted are for one adult travelling in 2nd class. Different prices apply to 1st-class tickets and for travellers under 26 or over 60. Children under four travel for free and do not need a pass. Up to two children under 11 travel free with a child pass if accompanied by at least one person with an adult pass.

Boat
Lake Ferry

The Romanshorn–Friedrichshafen car ferry provides the quickest way across Lake Constance between Switzerland and Germany. It's operated year-round by **Schweizerische Bodensee Schifffahrt** (☑in Switzerland 071-466 7888; www.sbsag.ch), takes 40 minutes and costs €9.20/4.60 per adult/child. Bicycle fares are €6; car fares including driver start at €25.40.

Sea

Germany's main ferry ports are Kiel and Travemünde (near Lübeck) in Schleswig-Holstein, and Rostock and Sassnitz (on Rügen Island) in Mecklenburg–Western Pomerania. All have services to Scandinavia.

Timetables change from season to season.

Return tickets are often cheaper than two one-way tickets. Some ferry companies now set fares the way budget airlines do: the earlier you book, the less you pay. Seasonal demand is a crucial factor (school holidays and July and August are especially busy), as is the time of day (an early-evening ferry can cost much more than one at 4am). For overnight ferries, cabin size, location and amenities affect the price. Book well in advance if you're bringing a car.

People under 25 and over 60 may qualify for discounts. To get the best fares, check out the booking service offered by **Ferry Savers** (www.ferrysavers.com).

GETTING AROUND

Air

Most large and many smaller German cities have their own airports and numerous carriers operate domestic flights within Germany. Unless you're flying from one end of the country to the other, say Berlin to Munich or Hamburg to Munich, planes

INTERNATIONAL FERRY COMPANIES

COUNTRY	COMPANY	CONNECTION	WEBSITE
Denmark	Scandlines	Gedser-Rostock, Rødby-Puttgarden	www.scandlines.com
	Faergen	Rønne-Sassnitz	www.faergen.dk
Finland	Finnlines	Helsinki-Travemünde, Helsinki-Rostock	www.finnlines.com
Lithuania	DFDS Seaways	Klaipèda-Kiel	www.dfdsseaways.com
Norway	Color Line	Oslo-Kiel	www.colorline.com
Sweden	Stena Line	Trelleborg-Rostock	www.stenaline.com
	Finnlines	Malmö-Travemünde	www.finnlines.com
	Stena Line	Trelleborg-Rostock, Trelleborg-Sassnitz	www.stenaline.com
	TT-Line	Trelleborg-Rostock, Trelleborg-Travemünde	www.ttline.com

are only marginally quicker than trains once you factor in the time it takes to get to and from airports.

Lufthansa has the densest route network. The other main airlines offering domestic flights are:

➡ Air Berlin (www.airberlin. com) Flies to Berlin-Tegel, Cologne-Bonn, Dresden, Düsseldorf, Frankfurt, Friedrichshafen, Hanover, Karlsruhe-Baden-Baden, Leipzig-Halle, Memmingen, Münster-Osnabrück, Munich, Nuremberg, Paderborn, Saarbrücken, Stuttgart, Sylt.

➡ Germanwings (www. germanwings.com) Destination cities are Berlin-Schönefeld, Berlin-Tegel, Cologne-Bonn, Dortmund, Dresden, Düsseldorf, Hamburg, Hanover, Karlsruhe-Baden-Baden, Leipzig-Halle, Nuremberg, Rostock, Stuttgart, Usedom.

Bicycle

Cycling is allowed on all roads and highways but not on the autobahns (motorways). Cyclists must follow the same rules of the road as cars and motorcycles. Helmets are not compulsory (not even for children), but wearing one is common sense. Dedicated bike lanes are common in bigger cities.

On Public Transport

Bicycles may be taken on most trains but require a separate ticket (*Fahrradkarte*), costing €9 per trip on long-distance trains (IC and EC and City Night Line). You need to reserve a space at least one day ahead and leave your bike in the bike compartment, which is usually at the beginning or end of the train. Bicycles are not allowed on high-speed ICE trains.

The fee on local and regional trains (IRE, RB, RE, S-Bahn) is €6 per day. There is no charge at all on some local trains. For full details,

enquire at a local station or call ☑01805-99 66 33.

Many regional bus companies have vehicles with special bike racks. Bicycles are also allowed on practically all boat and ferry services.

Rental

Most towns and cities have some sort of bicycle-hire station, often at or near the train station. Hire costs range from €7 to €20 per day and from €35 to €85 per week, depending on the model of bicycle. A minimum deposit of €30 (more for fancier bikes) and/or ID are required. Some outfits also offer a repair service or bicycle storage facilities.

Hotels, especially in resort areas, sometimes keep a stable of bicycles for their guests, often at no charge.

Call a Bike (☑069-4272 7722; www.callabike.de) is an automated cycle-hire scheme operated by Deutsche Bahn (German Rail) in dozens of German towns and cities. In order to use it, you need a credit card to pre-register for free online or at one of the dozens of docking stations scattered around the central districts. The website has a map but is in German only, although there are English instructions at the docking stations. Once you're set up, select a bike and call the phone number marked on it in order to release the lock. When you're done, you must drop the bike at another docking station. The base fee for renting a bike is €0.08 per minute up to a maximum of €15 per 24 hours. Fees are charged to your credit card.

In around 30 German cities, competition for Call a Bike comes from **Nextbike** (☑030-6920 5046; www.next bike.de/en), which charges €1 per 30 minutes or €9 for 24 hours. Register for free via its website, via its smartphone app, by phone or at rental terminals. You'll need a credit or debit card.

Boat

Considering that Germany abuts two seas and has a lake- and river-filled interior, don't be surprised to find yourself in a boat at some point. For basic transport, ferry boats are primarily used when travelling to or between the East Frisian Islands in Lower Saxony; the North Frisian Islands in Schleswig-Holstein; Helgoland, which also belongs to Schleswig-Holstein; and the islands of Poel, Rügen and Hiddensee in Mecklenburg–Western Pomerania.

Scheduled boat services operate along sections of the Rhine, the Elbe and the Danube. There are also ferry services in river sections with no or only a few bridges, as well as on major lakes such as the Chiemsee and Lake Starnberg in Bavaria and Lake Constance in Baden-Württemberg.

From around April to October, local operators run scenic river or lake cruises lasting from one hour to a full day.

See the destination chapters for individual services.

Bus

Local & Regional

Buses are generally slower, less dependable and more polluting than trains, but in some rural areas they may be your only option for getting around without your own vehicle. This is especially true of the Harz Mountains, sections of the Bavarian Forest and the Alpine foothills. Separate bus companies, each with its own tariffs and schedules, operate in the different regions.

The frequency of services varies from 'rarely' to 'constantly'. Commuter-geared routes offer limited or no service in the evenings and at weekends, so keep this in mind or risk finding yourself stuck in a remote place on a Saturday night. Make it a habit to ask about special fare deals, such as daily or weekly passes or tourist tickets.

In cities, buses generally converge at the Busbahnhof or Zentraler Omnibus Bahnhof (ZOB; central bus station), which is often near the Hauptbahnhof (central train station).

Long-Distance Coaches

Thanks to the 2013 lifting of an anachronistic ban on long-distance domestic bus travel (passed in 1931 to protect the then state-owned railway system), the route network has grown enormously, making exploring Germany by coach easy, inexpensive and popular. Buses are modern, clean, comfortable and air-conditioned. Most companies offer snacks and beverages as well as free onboard wi-fi.

Fierce competition has kept prices extremely low. A trip from Berlin to Hamburg costs as little as €8, while the fare from Frankfurt to Munich averages €15.

MeinFernbus (www.mein fernbus.de), **Flixbus** (www. flixbus.com), **Postbus** (www. postbus.de), **Berlinlinienbus** (www.berlinlinienbus.de) and **Eurolines** (www.eurolines. com) are the biggest operators, but there are dozens of smaller, regional ones as well. A handy site for finding out which operator goes where, when and for how much is www.busliniensuche.de.

From April to October, special tourist-geared service the **Romantic Road Coach** (☎09851-551 387; www.romantic-road.com) runs one coach daily in each direction between Frankfurt and Füssen (for Schloss Neuschwanstein) via Munich; the entire trip takes around 12 hours. There's no charge for breaking the journey and continuing the next day. Note that buses get incredibly crowded in summer. Tickets

are available for the entire route or for short segments. Buy them online or from travel agents, **EurAide** (www.eu-raide.de; Desk 1, Reisezentrum, Hauptbahnhof; ◷10am-7pm Mon-Fri Mar-Apr & Aug-Dec, to 8pm May-Jul; ☒Hauptbahnhof, ☒Hauptbahnhof, ☒Hauptbahnhof) in Munich or *Reisezentrum* offices in larger train stations.

Car & Motorcycle

German roads are excellent and motoring around the country can be a lot of fun. The country's pride and joy is its 11,000km network of autobahns (motorways, freeways). Every 40km to 60km, you'll find elaborate service areas with petrol stations, toilet facilities and restaurants; many are open 24 hours. In between are rest stops (*Rastplatz*), which usually have picnic tables and toilet facilities. Orange emergency call boxes are spaced about 2km apart.

Autobahns are supplemented by an extensive network of *Bundesstrassen* (secondary 'B' roads, highways) and smaller *Landstrassen* (country roads). No tolls are charged on any public roads.

If your car is not equipped with a navigational system, having a good map or road atlas is essential, especially when negotiating the tangle of country roads. Navigating in Germany is not done by the points of the compass. That is to say that you'll find no signs saying 'north' or 'west'. Rather, you'll see signs pointing you in the direction of a city, so you'd best have that map right in your lap to stay oriented. Maps cost a few euros and are sold at bookstores, train stations, airports and petrol stations. The best are published by Freytag & Berndt, ADAC, Falk and Euromap.

Driving in the cities can be stressful thanks to congestion and the expense

and scarcity of parking. In city centres, parking is usually limited to car parks and garages charging between €0.50 and €2.50 per hour. Note that some car parks (*Parkplatz*) and garages (*Parkhaus*) close at night and charge an overnight fee. Many have special parking slots for women that are especially well lit and close to exits.

Many cities have electronic parking-guidance systems directing you to the nearest garage and indicating the number of available spaces. Street parking usually works on the pay-and-display system and tends to be short term (one or two hours) only. For low-cost or free long-term and overnight parking, consider leaving your car outside the centre in a Park & Ride (P+R) lot.

Automobile Associations

Germany's main motoring organisation, the **ADAC** (Allgemeiner Deutscher Automobil-Club; ☎for information 0800 510 1112, for roadside assistance 0180 222 2222; www.adac.de), has offices in all major cities and many smaller ones. Its roadside-assistance program is also available to members of its affiliates, including British (AA), American (AAA) and Canadian (CAA) associations.

Driving Licence

Drivers need a valid driving licence. International Driving Permits (IDP) are not compulsory, but having one may help German police make sense of your home licence (always carry that, too) and may simplify the car- or motorcycle-hire process.

Car Hire

As anywhere, rates for car hire vary considerably, but you should be able to get an economy-size vehicle from about €40 to €60 per day, plus insurance and taxes. Expect surcharges for rentals

German Autobahns

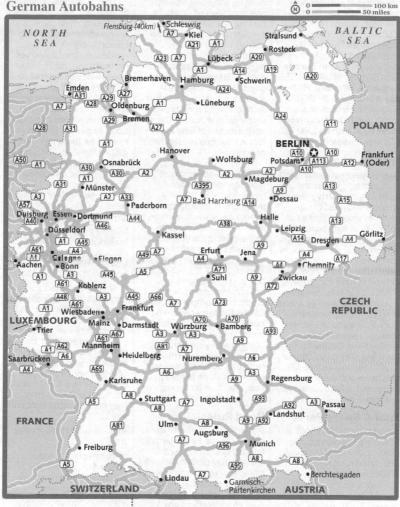

originating at airports and train stations, additional drivers and one-way hire. Child or infant safety seats may be hired for about €5 per day and should be reserved at the time of booking.

Rental cars with automatic transmission are rare in Germany and will usually need to be ordered well in advance.

To hire your own wheels, you'll need to be at least 25 years old and possess a valid driving licence and a major credit card. Some companies

lease to drivers between the ages of 21 and 24 for an additional charge (about €12 to €20 per day). Younger people or those without a credit card are usually out of luck. For insurance reasons, driving into an Eastern European country, such as the Czech Republic or Poland, is often a no-no.

All the main international companies maintain branches at airports, major train stations and towns. These include the following:

Alamo (☎0800 723 9253; www.alamo.com)

Avis (☎01806-217 702; www.avis.de)

Europcar (☎040-520 187 654; www.europcar.com)

Hertz (☎01806-333 535; www.hertz.com)

National (☎0800-723 8828; www.nationalcar.com)

Sixt (☎01806-25 25 25; www.sixt.de)

Pre-booked and prepaid packages arranged in your

home country usually work out much cheaper than on-the-spot rentals. The same is true of fly/drive packages. Deals can be found on the internet and through companies including **Auto Europe** (☑in Germany 0800-560 0333; www.autoeurope.com), **Holiday Autos** (☑in the UK 020 3740 9859; www.holidayautos.co.uk), and **DriveAway Holidays** (☑in Australia 1300 723 972; www.driveaway.com.au).

PEER-TO-PEER RENTALS

Peer-to-peer car rental is still in its infancy in Germany. The main service is **Drivy** (www.drivy.de). You need to sign up on its website, find a car you'd like to rent, contact the owner and sign the rental agreement at the time you're handed the keys. Renters need to be at least 21 years old and to have had a driving licence for at least two years. If your licence was not issued in an EU member country, Norway, Iceland or Liechtenstein, you need to have an International Driving Permit. Payment is by credit card or PayPal. Rentals include full insurance and roadside assistance. For full details, see the website.

Fuel & Spare Parts

Petrol stations, nearly all of which are self-service, are ubiquitous except in sparsely populated rural areas. Petrol is sold in litres.

Finding spare parts should not be a problem, especially in the cities, although availability depends on the age and model of your car. Be sure to have some sort of roadside-emergency-assistance plan in case your car breaks down.

Insurance

German law requires that all registered vehicles, including those brought in from abroad, carry third-party-liability insurance. You could face huge costs by driving uninsured or underinsured. Germans are very fussy about their cars, and even

nudging someone's bumper when jostling out of a tight parking space may well result in your having to pay for an entirely new one.

Normally private cars registered and insured in another European country do not require additional insurance, but do check this with your insurance provider before leaving home. Also keep a record of who to contact in case of a breakdown or accident.

When hiring a vehicle, make sure your contract includes adequate liability insurance at the very minimum. Rental agencies almost never include insurance that covers damage to the vehicle itself, called Collision Damage Waiver (CDW) or Loss Damage Waiver (LDW). It's optional, but driving without it is not recommended. Some credit-card companies cover CDW/LDW for a certain period if you charge the entire rental to your card; always confirm with your card issuer what it covers in Germany. Note that some local agencies may refuse to accept your credit-card coverage as proof of insurance.

Road Rules

Driving is on the right-hand side of the road and standard international signs are in use. If you're unfamiliar with these, pick up a pamphlet at your local motoring organisation or visit www.adac.de (search for 'traffic signs'). Obey the road rules and speed limits carefully.

Speed- and red-light cameras as well as radar traps are common and notices are sent to the car's registration address wherever that may be. If you're renting a car, the police will obtain your home address from the rental agency. There's a long list of fineable actions, including some perhaps surprising ones such as using abusive language or gestures and running out of petrol on the autobahn.

The usual speed limits are 50km/h on main city streets and 100km/h on highways, unless otherwise marked. Limits drop to 30km/h in residential streets. And yes, it's true: there really are no speed limits on autobahns... in theory. In fact, there are many stretches where slower speeds must be observed (near towns, road construction), so be sure to keep an eye out for those signs or risk getting ticketed. And, obviously, the higher the speed, the higher the fuel consumption and emissions.

Other important driving rules:

➡ The highest permissible blood-alcohol level for drivers is 0.05%, which for most people equates to one glass of wine or two small beers.

➡ Seat belts are mandatory for all passengers, including those in the back seat, and there's a €30 fine if you get caught not wearing one. If you're in an accident, not wearing a seat belt may invalidate your insurance. Children need a child seat if under four years and a seat cushion if under 12; they may not ride in the front until age 13.

➡ Motorcyclists must wear a helmet.

➡ Mobile phones may be used only if they are equipped with a hands-free kit or speakerphone.

➡ Pedestrians at crossings have absolute right of way over all motor vehicles.

➡ Always watch out for cyclists when turning right; they have the right of way.

➡ Right turns at a red light are only legal if there's a green arrow pointing to the right.

Hitching & Ride-Share

Hitching (*trampen*) is never entirely safe in any country,

and we don't recommend it. That said, in some rural areas in Germany that are poorly served by public transport – such as sections of the Alpine foothills and the Bavarian Forest – it is not uncommon to see people thumbing for a ride. If you do decide to hitch, understand that you are taking a small but potentially serious risk. Remember that it's safer to travel in pairs, and be sure to let someone know where you are planning to go. It's illegal to hitchhike on autobahns and from their entry or exit ramps.

A safer, inexpensive and eco-conscious form of travelling is ride-shares, where you travel as a passenger in a private car in exchange for some petrol money. Most arrangements are now set up via free online ride boards, such as www.blablacar.de, www.mitfahrzentrale.de and www.mitfahren.de. You can advertise a ride yourself or link up with a driver going to your destination.

Local Transport

Germany's cities and larger towns have efficient public-transport systems. Bigger cities, such as Berlin and Munich, integrate buses, trams, U-Bahn (underground, subway) trains and S-Bahn (suburban) trains into a single network.

Fares are determined by zones or time travelled, and sometimes by both. A multi-ticket strip (Streifenkarte or 4-Fahrtenkarte) or day pass (Tageskarte) generally offers better value than a single-ride ticket. Normally, tickets must be stamped upon boarding in order to be valid. Fines are levied if you're caught without a valid ticket.

Bicycle

Germans love to cycle, be it for errands, commuting, fitness or pleasure. Many cities have dedicated bicycle lanes, which must be used unless obstructed. There's no helmet law, not even for children, although using one is recommended, for obvious reasons. Bicycles must be equipped with a white light at the front, a red one at the back and yellow reflectors on the wheels and pedals.

Bus & Tram

Buses are a ubiquitous form of public transport and practically all towns have their own comprehensive network. Buses run at regular intervals, with restricted services in the evenings and at weekends. Some cities operate night buses along popular routes to get night owls safely home.

Occasionally, buses are supplemented by trams (Strassenbahn), which are usually faster because they travel on their own tracks, largely independent of other traffic. In city centres they sometimes run underground. Bus and tram drivers generally sell single tickets and day passes only.

S-Bahn

Metropolitan areas, such as Berlin and Munich, have a system of suburban trains called the S-Bahn. They are faster and cover a wider area than buses or trams but tend to be less frequent. S-Bahn lines are often linked to the national rail network and sometimes connect urban centres. Rail passes are generally valid on these services. Specific S-Bahn lines are abbreviated with 'S' followed by the number (eg S1, S7).

Taxi

Taxis are expensive and, given the excellent public-transport systems, not recommended unless you're in a real hurry. (They can actually be slower than trains or trams if you're stuck in traffic.) Cabs are metered and charged at a base rate (flag fall) plus a per-kilometre fee. These charges are fixed but vary from city to city. Some drivers charge extra for bulky luggage or night-time rides. It's rarely possible to flag down a taxi; more typical is to order one by phone (look up Taxiruf in the phone book) or board at a taxi rank. If you're at a hotel or restaurant, ask staff to call one for you. Taxis also often wait outside theatres or performance venues. Smartphone owners can order a taxi via the Mytaxi app (downloadable for free via iTunes or Google Play) in over 30 German cities.

Uber (www.uber.com), an app that allows private drivers to connect with potential passengers, is not widely used in Germany after a court ruled in May 2015 that the services UberPop and UberBlack violate German transportation laws. Uber reacted by creating UberX, which uses only professionally licensed drivers and is available in Düsseldorf, Frankfurt, Hamburg and Munich. Trip costs tend to be between 3% and 12% less than regular taxi fares. Exclusive to Berlin as of now is UberTaxi, which hooks passengers up with regular taxis. Normal rates apply.

U-Bahn

Underground (subway) trains are known as U-Bahn in Germany and are the fastest form of travel in big cities. Route maps are posted in all stations, and at many you'll be able to pick up a printed copy from the stationmaster or ticket office. The frequency of trains usually fluctuates with demand, meaning there are more trains during commuter rush hours than in the middle of the day. Tickets bought from vending machines must usually be validated before the start of your journey. Specific U-Bahn lines are abbreviated with 'U' followed by the number (eg U1, U7).

Train

Germany's rail system is operated almost entirely by Deutsche Bahn (www.bahn.com), with a variety of train types serving just about every corner of the country. The DB website has detailed information (in English and other languages), as well as a ticket-purchasing function with detailed instructions.

There is a growing number of routes operated by private companies but integrated into the DB network, such as the Ostdeutsche Eisenbahn in Saxony and the Bayerische Oberlandbahn in Bavaria.

Tickets may be bought using a credit card up to 10 minutes before departure at no surcharge. You will need to present a printout of your ticket, as well as the credit card used to buy it, to the conductor. Smartphone users can register with Deutsche Bahn and download the ticket via the free DB Navigator app.

Tickets are also available from vending machines and agents at the *Reisezentrum* (travel centre) in train stations. The latter charge a service fee but are useful if you need assistance with planning your itinerary (if necessary, ask for an English-speaking clerk).

Children under 15 travel for free if accompanied by at least one parent or grandparent. The only proviso is that the names of children aged between six and 14 must be registered on your ticket at the time of purchase. Children under six always travel free and without a ticket.

Smaller stations have only a few ticket windows and the smallest ones are equipped with vending machines only. English instructions are usually provided.

Tickets sold on board incur a surcharge and are not available on regional trains (RE, RB, IRE) or the S-Bahn. Agents, conductors and machines usually accept debit cards and major credit cards. With few exceptions (station unstaffed, vending machine broken), you will be fined if caught without a ticket.

Most train stations have coin-operated lockers *(Schliessfach)* costing from €1 to €4 per 24-hour period. Larger stations have staffed left-luggage offices *(Gepäck-aufbewahrung)*, which are a bit more expensive than lockers. If you leave your suitcase overnight, you'll be charged for two full days.

Reservations

➡ Seat reservations for long-distance travel are highly recommended, especially if you're travelling anytime on Friday, on a Sunday afternoon, during holiday periods or in summer. Choose from window or aisle seats, row or facing seats, or seats with a fixed table.

➡ Reservations are €4.50 (free if travelling 1st class) and can be made online and at ticket counters until 10 minutes before departure. You need to claim your seat within 15 minutes of boarding the train.

Classes

German trains have 1st- and 2nd-class cars, both of them modern and comfortable. If you're not too fussy, paying extra for 1st class is usually not worth it, except perhaps on busy travel days (Friday, Sunday afternoon and holidays), when 2nd-class cars can get very crowded. Seating is either in compartments of up to six people or in open-plan carriages with panoramic windows. On ICE trains you'll also enjoy reclining seats, tables, and audio systems in your armrest. Newer-generation ICE trains also have individual laptop outlets, mobile-phone reception in 1st class and, on some routes, wi-fi access.

Trains and stations are nonsmoking. ICE, IC and EC trains are air-conditioned and have a restaurant or self-service bistro.

Tickets

Standard, non-discounted train tickets tend to be quite

A PRIMER ON TRAIN TYPES

Here's the low-down on the alphabet soup of trains operated by Deutsche Bahn (DB):

➡ **InterCity Express (ICE)** Long-distance, high-speed trains that stop at major cities only and run at one- or two-hour intervals.

➡ **InterCity (IC), EuroCity (EC)** Long-distance trains that are fast, but slower than the ICE; also run at one- and two-hour intervals and stop in major cities. EC trains run to major cities in neighbouring countries.

➡ **InterRegio-Express (IRE)** Regional trains connecting cities with few intermediary stops.

➡ **City Night Line (CNL)** Night trains with sleeper cars and couchettes.

➡ **Regional Bahn (RB)** Local trains, mostly in rural areas, with frequent stops; the slowest in the system.

➡ **Regional Express (RE)** Local trains with limited stops that link rural areas with metropolitan centres and the S-Bahn.

➡ **S-Bahn** Local trains operating within a city and its suburban area.

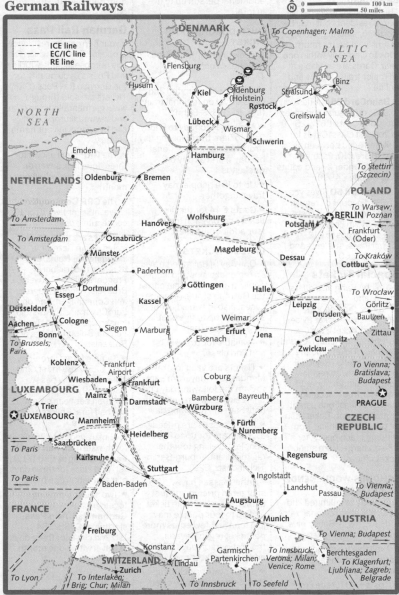

German Railways

expensive. On specific trains, a limited number of tickets is available at the discounted *Sparpreis* (saver fare), costing €29 to €99 in 2nd class and €49 to €149 in 1st. You need to book early or be lucky to snag one of these tickets, though. There's a €5 service charge if tickets are purchased by phone, from a travel agent or in the station ticket office. Other promotions, discounted tickets and special offers become available all the time. Check www.bahn.com for the latest deals.

BAHNCARD

The Bahncard is geared towards residents but may be worth considering if you plan extensive travel or return trips to Germany within one year. Cards are available at all major train stations and online.

➡ **BahnCard 25** Entitles you to 25% off regular and saver fares and costs €62/125 in 2nd/1st class. Cards for children aged between six and 18 are €10. Partners, students under 27 and adults over 60 pay €41/81.

➡ **BahnCard 50** Gives you a 50% discount on regular and saver fares and costs €255/515 in 2nd/1st class. The cost drops to €127/252 for partners, students and adults over 60.

Special Tickets

Deutsche Bahn also offers a trio of fabulous permanent rail deals: the *Schönes-Wochenende-Ticket* (Nice Weekend Ticket), the *Quer-durchs-Land-Ticket* (Around Germany Ticket) and the *Länder-Tickets* (Regional Tickets). As with regular tickets, children under 15 travel for free if accompanied by at least one parent or grandparent. Tickets can be purchased online, from vending machines or, for a €2 surcharge, from station ticket offices.

SCHÖNES-WOCHENENDE-TICKET

➡ One day of unlimited 2nd-class travel on regional trains (IRE, RE, RB, S-Bahn), plus local public transport.

➡ Available from midnight Saturday or Sunday until 3am the next day.

➡ Costs €40 for the first person and €4 for each additional person up to five in total.

QUER-DURCHS-LAND-TICKET

A weekday variation of the *Schönes-Wochenende-Ticket*.

➡ One day of unlimited 2nd-class travel on regional trains (IRE, RE, RB, S-Bahn).

➡ Available Monday to Friday 9am to 3am the following day (from midnight on national holidays) and all day on weekends.

➡ Up to five people may travel together.

➡ Costs €44 for the first ticket and €8 each for up to four additional tickets.

LÄNDER-TICKETS

➡ One day of unlimited travel on regional trains and local public transport within one of the German states (in some cases, also in two adjacent states) for up to five people travelling together.

➡ Available for travel in 1st and 2nd class.

➡ Tickets are valid for travel Monday to Friday from 9am to 3am the following day and on weekends from midnight until 3am the following day.

➡ Some passes are priced as a flat rate for up to five people travelling together (eg the Brandenburg-Berlin-Ticket costs €29).

➡ Other passes have staggered pricing: the first person buys the main ticket and up to four people may join for a just few euros more per ticket (eg in Bavaria, the first person pays €23; additional tickets cost €5).

➡ Some states, including Brandenburg-Berlin, offer cheaper *Nacht-Tickets* (night passes), usually valid from 6pm until 6am the following day.

German Rail Pass

If your permanent residence is outside Europe (which for this purpose includes Turkey and Russia), you qualify for the German Rail Pass (GRP). Tickets are sold through www.germanrailpasses.com and www.raileurope.com and by agents in your home country.

➡ The **GRP Flexi** allows for three, four, five, seven or 10 days of travel within one month.

➡ The **GRP Consecutive** is available for five, 10 or 15 consecutive days.

➡ Passes are valid on all trains within Germany, including ICE trains, and IC buses to Strasbourg, Prague, Krakow, Antwerp, Brussels, London, Zagreb and Copenhagen; and on EuroCity trains to Kufstein, Innsbruck, Bolzano, Trento, Verona, Bologna, Liège and Brussels.

➡ Sample fares: three-day pass €255/189 in 1st/2nd class; seven-day pass €363/269 in 1st/2nd class. Children between six and 11 pay half fare. Children under six travel free.

➡ Those aged 12 to 25 qualify for the **German Rail Youth Pass**, starting at €204/151 in 1st/2nd class for three days of travel within one month.

➡ Two adults travelling together can use the **German Rail Twin Pass**, starting at €382/284 in 1st/2nd class for three days of travel within one month.

Language

German belongs to the West Germanic language family, with English and Dutch as close relatives, and has around 100 million speakers. It is commonly divided into two forms – Low German (*Plattdeutsch*) and High German (*Hochdeutsch*). Low German is an umbrella term used for the dialects spoken in Northern Germany. High German is considered the standard form and is understood throughout German-speaking communities; it's also the variety used in this chapter.

German is easy for English speakers to pronounce because almost all of its sounds are also found in English. If you read our coloured pronunciation guides as if they were English, you'll have no problems being understood. Note that kh is like the 'ch' in 'Bach' or the Scottish 'loch' (pronounced at the back of the throat), r is also pronounced at the back of the throat (almost like a g, but with some friction), zh is pronounced as the 's' in 'measure', and ü as the 'ee' in 'see' but with rounded lips. The stressed syllables are indicated with italics.

BASICS

Hello.	Guten Tag.	goo·ten tahk
Goodbye.	Auf Wiedersehen.	owf vee·der·zay·en
Yes./No.	Ja./Nein.	yah/nain
Please.	Bitte.	bi·te
Thank you.	Danke.	dang·ke

WANT MORE?

For in-depth language information and handy phrases, check out Lonely Planet's *German Phrasebook*. You'll find them at **shop.lonelyplanet.com**, or you can buy Lonely Planet's iPhone phrasebooks at the Apple App Store.

You're welcome.	Bitte.	bi·te
Excuse me.	Entschuldigung.	ent·shul·di·gung
Sorry.	Entschuldigung.	ent·shul·di·gung

How are you?

Wie geht es Ihnen/dir? (pol/int)	vee gayt es ee·nen/deer

Fine. And you?

Danke, gut. Und Ihnen/dir? (pol/inf)	dang·ke goot unt ee·nen/deer

What's your name?

Wie ist Ihr Name? (pol)	vee ist eer nah·me
Wie heißt du? (inf)	vee haist doo

My name is ...

Mein Name ist ... (pol)	main nah·me ist ...
Ich heiße ... (inf)	ikh hai·se ...

Do you speak English?

Sprechen Sie Englisch? (pol)	shpre·khen zee eng·lish
Sprichst du Englisch? (inf)	shprikhst doo eng·lish

I don't understand.

Ich verstehe nicht.	ikh fer·shtay·e nikht

ACCOMMODATION

campsite	Campingplatz	kem·ping·plats
guesthouse	Pension	pahng·zyawn
hotel	Hotel	ho·tel
inn	Gasthof	gast·hawf
room in a private home	Privatzimmer	pri·vaht·tsi·mer
youth hostel	Jugend- herberge	yoo·gent· her·ber·ge

Do you have a ... room?	Haben Sie ein ...?	hah·ben zee ain ...
double	Doppelzimmer	do·pel·tsi·mer
single	Einzelzimmer	ain·tsel·tsi·mer
How much	Wie viel kostet	vee feel kos·tet

is it per ...?	es pro ...?	es praw ...
night	*Nacht*	nakht
person	*Person*	per·*zawn*

Is breakfast included?
Ist das Frühstück inklusive? — ist das *frü*·shtük in·kloo·*zee*·ve

DIRECTIONS

Where's ...?
Wo ist ...? — vaw ist ...

What's the address?
Wie ist die Adresse? — vee ist dee a·*dre*·se

How far is it?
Wie weit ist es? — vee vait ist es

Can you show me (on the map)?
Können Sie es mir (auf der Karte) zeigen? — *ker*·nen zee es meer (owf dair *kar*·te) *tsai*·gen

How can I get there?
Wie kann ich da hinkommen? — vee kan ikh dah *hin*·ko·men

Turn ...	*Biegen Sie ... ab.*	*bee*·gen zee ... ab
at the corner	*an der Ecke*	an dair *e*·ke
at the traffic lights	*bei der Ampel*	bai dair *am*·pel
left	*links*	lingks
right	*rechts*	rekhts

EATING & DRINKING

I'd like to reserve a table for ...	*Ich möchte einen Tisch für ... reservieren.*	ikh *merkh*·te *ai*·nen tish für ... re·zer·*vee*·ren
(eight) o'clock	*(acht) Uhr*	(akht) oor
(two) people	*(zwei) Personen*	(tsvai) per·*zaw*·nen

I'd like the menu, please.
Ich hätte gern die Speisekarte, bitte. — ikh *he*·te gern dee *shpai*·ze·kar·te *bi*·te

What would you recommend?
Was empfehlen Sie? — vas emp·*fay*·len zee

QUESTION WORDS

How?	*Wie?*	vee
What?	*Was?*	vas
When?	*Wann?*	van
Where?	*Wo?*	vaw
Who?	*Wer?*	vair
Why?	*Warum?*	va·*rum*

What's in that dish?
Was ist in diesem Gericht? — vas ist in *dee*·zem

I'm a vegetarian.
Ich bin Vegetarier/ Vegetarierin. (m/f) — ikh bin ve·ge·*tah*·ri·er/ ve·ge·*tah*·ri·e·rin

That was delicious.
Das hat hervorragend geschmeckt. — das hat her·*fawr*·rah·gent ge·*shmekt*

Cheers!
Prost! — prawst

Please bring the bill.
Bitte bringen Sie die Rechnung. — *bi*·te bring·en zee dee *rekh*·nung

Key Words

bar (pub)	*Kneipe*	*knai*·pe
bottle	*Flasche*	*fla*·she
bowl	*Schüssel*	*shü*·sel
breakfast	*Frühstück*	*frü*·shtük
cold	*kalt*	kalt
cup	*Tasse*	*ta*·se
daily special	*Gericht des Tages*	ge·*rikht* des *tah*·ges
delicatessen	*Feinkost-geschäft*	*fain*·kost·ge·sheft
desserts	*Nachspeisen*	*nahkh*·shpai·zen
dinner	*Abendessen*	*ah*·bent·e·sen
drink list	*Getränke-karte*	ge·*treng*·ke·kar·te
fork	*Gabel*	*gah*·bel
glass	*Glas*	glahs
grocery store	*Lebensmittel-laden*	*lay*·bens·mi·tel·lah·den
hot (warm)	*warm*	warm
knife	*Messer*	*me*·ser
lunch	*Mittagessen*	*mi*·tahk·e·sen
market	*Markt*	markt
plate	*Teller*	*te*·ler
restaurant	*Restaurant*	res·to·*rahng*
set menu	*Menü*	may·*nü*
spicy	*würzig*	*vür*·tsikh
spoon	*Löffel*	*ler*·fel
with/without	*mit/ohne*	mit/*aw*·ne

Meat & Fish

beef	*Rindfleisch*	*rint*·flaish
carp	*Karpfen*	*karp*·fen
fish	*Fisch*	fish
herring	*Hering*	*hay*·ring

lamb	*Lammfleisch*	*lam*·flaish
meat	*Fleisch*	flaish
pork	*Schweinefleisch*	shvai·ne·flaish
poultry	*Geflügelfleisch*	ge·*flü*·gel·flaish
salmon	*Lachs*	laks
sausage	*Wurst*	vurst
seafood	*Meeresfrüchte*	mair·res·frükh·te
shellfish	*Schaltiere*	shahl·tee·re
trout	*Forelle*	fo·re·le
veal	*Kalbfleisch*	kalp·flaish

Fruit & Vegetables

apple	*Apfel*	ap·fel
banana	*Banane*	ba·*nah*·ne
bean	*Bohne*	baw·ne
cabbage	*Kraut*	krowt
capsicum	*Paprika*	pap·ri·kah
carrot	*Mohrrübe*	mawr·rü·be
cucumber	*Gurke*	gur·ke
fruit	*Frucht/Obst*	frukht/awpst
grapes	*Weintrauben*	vain·trow·ben
lemon	*Zitrone*	tsi·*traw*·ne
lentil	*Linse*	lin·ze
lettuce	*Kopfsalat*	kopf·za·laht
mushroom	*Pilz*	pilts
nuts	*Nüsse*	nü·se
onion	*Zwiebel*	tsvee·bel
orange	*Orange*	o·*rahng*·zhe
pea	*Erbse*	erp·se
plum	*Pflaume*	pflow·me
potato	*Kartoffel*	kar·*to*·fel
spinach	*Spinat*	shpi·naht
strawberry	*Erdbeere*	ert·bair·re
tomato	*Tomate*	to·*mah*·te
vegetable	*Gemüse*	ge·*mü*·ze
watermelon	*Wasser-melone*	va·ser·me·law·ne

Other

bread	*Brot*	brawt
butter	*Butter*	bu·ter
cheese	*Käse*	kay·ze
egg/eggs	*Ei/Eier*	ai/ai·er
honey	*Honig*	haw·nikh
jam	*Marmelade*	mar·me·*lah*·de
pasta	*Nudeln*	noo·deln
pepper	*Pfeffer*	pfe·fer

NUMBERS

1	*eins*	ains
2	*zwei*	tsvai
3	*drei*	drai
4	*vier*	feer
5	*fünf*	fünf
6	*sechs*	zeks
7	*sieben*	zee·ben
8	*acht*	akht
9	*neun*	noyn
10	*zehn*	tsayn
20	*zwanzig*	tsvan·tsikh
30	*dreißig*	drai·tsikh
40	*vierzig*	feer·tsikh
50	*fünfzig*	fünf·tsikh
60	*sechzig*	zekh·tsikh
70	*siebzig*	zeep·tsikh
80	*achtzig*	akht·tsikh
90	*neunzig*	noyn·tsikh
100	*hundert*	hun·dert
1000	*tausend*	tow·sent

rice	*Reis*	rais
salt	*Salz*	zalts
soup	*Suppe*	zu·pe
sugar	*Zucker*	tsu·ker

Drinks

beer	*Bier*	beer
coffee	*Kaffee*	ka·fay
juice	*Saft*	zaft
milk	*Milch*	milkh
orange juice	*Orangensaft*	o·rang·zhen·zaft
red wine	*Rotwein*	rawt·vain
sparkling wine	*Sekt*	zekt
tea	*Tee*	tay
water	*Wasser*	va·ser
white wine	*Weißwein*	vais·vain

EMERGENCIES

Help! *Hilfe!*		hil·fe
Go away! *Gehen Sie weg!*		gay·en zee vek
Call the police! *Rufen Sie die Polizei!*		roo·fen zee dee po·li·tsai

Call a doctor!
Rufen Sie einen Arzt!   roo·fen zee ai·nen artst

Where are the toilets?
Wo ist die Toilette?   vo ist dee to·a·le·te

I'm lost.
Ich habe mich verirrt.   ikh hah·be mikh fer·irt

I'm sick.
Ich bin krank.   ikh bin krangk

It hurts here.
Es tut hier weh.   es toot heer vay

I'm allergic to ...
Ich bin allergisch   ikh bin a·lair·gish
gegen ...   gay·gen ...

SHOPPING & SERVICES

I'd like to buy ...
Ich möchte ... kaufen.   ikh merkh·te ... kow·fen

I'm just looking.
Ich schaue mich nur um.   ikh show·e mikh noor um

Can I look at it?
Können Sie mir   ker·nen zee es meer
zeigen?   tsai·gen

How much is this?
Wie viel kostet das?   vee feel kos·tet das

That's too expensive.
Das ist zu teuer.   das ist tsoo toy·er

Can you lower the price?
Können Sie mit dem   ker·nen zee mit dem
Preis heruntergehen?   prais he·run·ter·gay·en

There's a mistake in the bill.
Da ist ein Fehler   dah ist ain fay·ler
in der Rechnung.   in dair rekh·nung

ATM	*Geldautomat*	gelt·ow·to·maht
post office	*Postamt*	post·amt
tourist office	*Fremden-*	frem·den·
	verkehrsbüro	fer·kairs·bü·raw

TIME & DATES

What time is it? *Wie spät ist es?*   vee shpayt ist es

It's (10) o'clock. *Es ist (zehn) Uhr.*   es ist (tsayn) oor

At what time? *Um wie viel Uhr?*   um vee feel oor

At ... *Um ...*   um ...

morning	*Morgen*	mor·gen
afternoon	*Nachmittag*	nahkh·mi·tahk
evening	*Abend*	ah·bent

yesterday	*gestern*	ges·tern
today	*heute*	hoy·te
tomorrow	*morgen*	mor·gen

Monday	*Montag*	mawn·tahk
Tuesday	*Dienstag*	deens·tahk
Wednesday	*Mittwoch*	mit·vokh
Thursday	*Donnerstag*	do·ners·tahk
Friday	*Freitag*	frai·tahk
Saturday	*Samstag*	zams·tahk
Sunday	*Sonntag*	zon·tahk

January	*Januar*	yan·u·ahr
February	*Februar*	fay·bru·ahr
March	*März*	merts
April	*April*	a·pril
May	*Mai*	mai
June	*Juni*	yoo·ni
July	*Juli*	yoo·li
August	*August*	ow·gust
September	*September*	zep·tem·ber
October	*Oktober*	ok·taw·ber
November	*November*	no·vem·ber
December	*Dezember*	de·tsem·ber

TRANSPORT

Public Transport

boat	*Boot*	bawt
bus	*Bus*	bus
metro	*U-Bahn*	oo·bahn
plane	*Flugzeug*	flook·tsoyk
train	*Zug*	tsook

At what time's	*Wann fährt*	van fairt
the ... bus?	*der ... Bus?*	dair... bus
first	*erste*	ers·te
last	*letzte*	lets·te
A ... to (Berlin).	*Eine ... nach*	ai·ne ... nahkh
	(Berlin).	(ber·leen)
1st-class	*Fahrkarte*	fahr·kar·te
ticket	*erster Klasse*	ers·ter kla·se
2nd-class	*Fahrkarte*	fahr·kar·te
ticket	*zweiter Klasse*	tsvai·ter kla·se
one-way	*einfache*	ain·fa·khe
ticket	*Fahrkarte*	fahr·kar·te
return ticket	*Rückfahrkarte*	rük·fahr·kar·te

At what time does it arrive?
Wann kommt es an?   van komt es an

Is it a direct route?

Ist es eine direkte Verbindung?	*ist es ai·ne di·rek·te fer·bin·dung*	

Does it stop at (Freiburg)?
Hält es in (Freiburg)? — *helt es in (frai·boorg)*

What station is this?
Welcher Bahnhof ist das? — *vel·kher bahn·hawf ist das*

What's the next stop?
Welches ist der nächste Halt? — *vel·khes ist dair naykh·ste halt*

I want to get off here.
Ich möchte hier aussteigen. — *ikh merkh·te heer ows·shtai·gen*

Please tell me when we get to (Kiel).
Könnten Sie mir bitte sagen, wann wir in (Kiel) ankommen? — *kern·ten zee meer bi·te zah·gen van veer in (keel) an·ko·men*

Please take me to (this address).
Bitte bringen Sie mich zu (dieser Adresse). — *bi·te bring·en zee mikh tsoo (dee·zer a·dre·se)*

platform	*Bahnsteig*	*bahn·shtaik*
ticket office	*Fahrkarten-verkauf*	*fahr·kar·ten·fer·kowf*
timetable	*Fahrplan*	*fahr·plan*

Driving & Cycling

I'd like to hire a ...	*Ich mochte ein ... mieten.*	*ikh merkh·te ain ... mee·ten*
4WD	*Allrad-fahrzeug*	*al·raht·fahr·tsoyk*
bicycle	*Fahrrad*	*fahr·raht*
car	*Auto*	*ow·to*
motorbike	*Motorrad*	*maw·tor·raht*
How much	*Wie viel kostet*	*vee feel kos·tet*

is it per ...?	*es pro ...?*	*es praw ...*
day	*Tag*	*tahk*
week	*Woche*	*vo·khe*

bicycle pump	*Fahrradpumpe*	*fahr·raht·pum·pe*
child seat	*Kindersitz*	*kin·der·zits*
helmet	*Helm*	*helm*
petrol	*Benzin*	*ben·tseen*

Does this road go to ...?
Führt diese Straße nach ...? — *fürt dee·ze shtrah·se nahkh ...*

(How long) Can I park here?
(Wie lange) Kann ich hier parken? — *(vee lang·e) kan ikh heer par·ken*

Where's a petrol station?
Wo ist eine Tankstelle? — *vaw ist ai·ne tangk·shte·le*

I need a mechanic.
Ich brauche einen Mechaniker. — *Ikh brow·khe ai·nen me·khah·ni·ker*

My car/motorbike has broken down (at ...).
Ich habe (in ...) eine Panne mit meinem Auto/Motorrad. — *ikh hah·be (in ...) ai·ne pa·ne mit mai·nem ow·to/maw·tor·raht*

I've run out of petrol.
Ich habe kein Benzin mehr. — *ikh hah·be kain ben·tseen mair*

I have a flat tyre.
Ich habe eine Reifenpanne. — *Ikh hah·be ai·ne rai·fen·pa·ne*

Are there cycling paths?
Gibt es Fahrradwege? — *geept es fahr·raht·vay·ge*

Is there bicycle parking?
Gibt es Fahrrad-Parkplätze? — *geept es fahr·raht·park·ple·tse (pl) indicates plural*

GLOSSARY

(pl) indicates plural

Abtei – abbey
ADAC – Allgemeiner Deutscher Automobil Club; German Automobile Association
Allee – avenue
Altstadt – old town
Apotheke – pharmacy
Ärztehaus – medical clinic
Ärztlicher Notfalldienst – emergency medical service
Autobahn – motorway, freeway
Autofähre – car ferry

Bad – spa, bath
Bahnhof – train station
Bau – building
Bedienung – service; service charge
Berg – mountain
Besenwirtschaft – seasonal wine restaurant indicated by a broom above the doorway
Bibliothek – library
Bierkeller – cellar pub
Bierstube – traditional beer pub
BRD – Bundesrepublik Deutschland or, in English, FRG (Federal Republic of Germany); the name for Germany today; before reunification it applied to West Germany
Brücke – bridge
Brunnen – fountain, well
Bundesliga – Germany's premier football (soccer) league
Bundesrat – upper house of the German parliament
Bundestag – lower house of the German parliament
Burg – castle
Busbahnhof – bus station

CDU – Christlich Demokratische Union Deutschlands; Christian Democratic Union
Christkindlmarkt – Christmas market; also called *Weihnachtsmarkt*

CSU – Christlich-Soziale Union; Christian Social Union; Bavarian offshoot of CDU

DDR – Deutsche Demokratische Republik or, in English, GDR (German Democratic Republic); the name for former East Germany
Denkmal – memorial
Dirndl – traditional women's dress (Bavaria only)
Dom – cathedral
Dorf – village

Eiscafé – ice-cream parlour

Fahrplan – timetable
Fahrrad – bicycle
FDP – Freie Demokratische Partei; Free Democratic Party
Ferienwohnung, Ferienwohnungen (pl) – holiday flat or apartment
Fest – festival
Fleete – canals in Hamburg
Flohmarkt – flea market
Flughafen – airport
Forstweg – forestry track
FRG – see *BRD*

Garten – garden
Gasse – lane, alley
Gästehaus – guesthouse
Gaststätte, Gasthaus – informal restaurant, inn
GDR – see *DDR*
Gedenkstätte – memorial site
Gepäckaufbewahrung – left-luggage office

Hafen – harbour, port
Hauptbahnhof – central train station
Heide – heath
Hof, Höfe (pl) – courtyard
Höhle – cave
Hotel Garni – hotel without a restaurant that only serves breakfast

Imbiss – stand-up food stall; also called *Schnellimbiss*
Insel – island

Jugendherberge – youth hostel

Kanal – canal
Kapelle – chapel
Karte – ticket
Kartenvorverkauf – ticket booking office
Kino – cinema
Kirche – church
Kletterwand – climbing wall
Kloster – monastery, convent
Kneipe – pub
Konditorei – cake shop
KPD – Kommunistische Partei Deutschlands; German Communist Party
Krankenhaus – hospital
Kreuzgang – cloister
Kunst – art
Kurhaus – literally 'spa house', but usually a spa town's central building, used for events and often a casino
Kurtaxe – resort tax
Kurverwaltung – spa resort administration
Kurzentrum – spa centre

Land, Länder (pl) – state
Landtag – state parliament
Lederhosen – traditional leather trousers with braces (Bavaria only)
Lesbe, Lesben (pl) – lesbian (n)
lesbisch – lesbian (adj)

Markt – market; often used for *Marktplatz*
Marktplatz – marketplace or square; abbreviated to *Markt*
Mass – 1L tankard or stein of beer
Meer – sea
Mensa – university cafeteria

Mitwohnzentrale – accommodation-finding service for long-term stays

Münster – minster, large church, cathedral

Neustadt – new town

Nord – north

NSDAP – Nationalsozialistische Deutsche Arbeiterpartei; National Socialist German Workers' Party

Ost – east

Palais, Palast – palace, residential quarters of a castle

Paradies – literally 'paradise'; architectural term for a church vestibule or anteroom

Parkhaus – car park

Passage – shopping arcade

Pension, Pensionen (pl) – relatively cheap boarding house

Pfarrkirche – parish church

Platz – square

Putsch – revolt

Radwandern – bicycle touring

Radweg – bicycle path

Rathaus – town hall

Ratskeller – town hall restaurant

Reich – empire

Reisezentrum – travel centre in train or bus stations

Rundgang – tour, route

Saal, Säle (pl) – hall, room

Sammlung – collection

Säule – column, pillar

S-Bahn – suburban-metropolitan trains; Schnellbahn

Schatzkammer – treasury room

Schiff – ship

Schiffahrt – shipping, navigation

Schloss – palace, castle

Schnellimbiss - see *Imbiss*

schwul – gay (adj)

Schwuler, Schwule (pl) – gay (n)

SED – Sozialistische Einheitspartei Deutschlands; Socialist Unity Party

See – lake

Sesselbahn – chairlift

SPD – Sozialdemokratische Partei Deutschlands; Social Democratic Party

Stadt – city, town

Stehcafé – stand-up cafe

Strand – beach

Strasse – street; abbreviated to Str

Strausswirtschaft – seasonal wine pub indicated by wreath above the doorway

Süd – south

Tageskarte – daily menu; day ticket on public transport

Tal – valley

Teich – pond

Tor – gate

Trampen – hitchhike

Turm – tower

U-Bahn – underground train system

Ufer – bank (of river etc)

Verboten – forbidden

Verkehr – traffic

Verkehrsamt/Verkehrsverein – tourist office

Viertel – quarter, district

Wald – forest

Wattenmeer – tidal flats on the North Sea coast

Weg – way, path

Weihnachtsmarkt – see *Christkindlmarkt*

Weingut – wine-growing estate

Weinkeller – wine cellar

Weinprobe – wine tasting

Weinstube – traditional wine bar or tavern

Wende – 'change' of 1989, ie the fall of communism that led to the collapse of the GDR and German reunification

West – west

Wiese – meadow

Wurst – sausage

Zahnradbahn – cogwheel railway

Zimmer frei – rooms available

ZOB – Zentraler Omnibusbahnhof; central bus station**Imbiss** – stand-up food stall; also called *Schnellimbis*

Behind the Scenes

SEND US YOUR FEEDBACK

We love to hear from travellers – your comments keep us on our toes and help make our books better. Our well-travelled team reads every word on what you loved or loathed about this book. Although we cannot reply individually to your submissions, we always guarantee that your feedback goes straight to the appropriate authors, in time for the next edition. Each person who sends us information is thanked in the next edition – the most useful submissions are rewarded with a selection of digital PDF chapters.

Visit **lonelyplanet.com/contact** to submit your updates and suggestions or to ask for help. Our award-winning website also features inspirational travel stories, news and discussions.

Note: We may edit, reproduce and incorporate your comments in Lonely Planet products such as guidebooks, websites and digital products, so let us know if you don't want your comments reproduced or your name acknowledged. For a copy of our privacy policy visit lonelyplanet.com/privacy.

OUR READERS

Many thanks to the travellers who used the last edition and wrote to us with helpful hints, useful advice and interesting anecdotes:

Aaron Quesnel, Alessandra Furlan, Andy Jones, Bill Bowman, Chris Thompson, David Bourchier, David Lacy, David Thomas, Dennis Kerzig, Douglas McGarvey, Florian Wagner, Geert Brinkerink, Gisela Dahme, Jack Clancy, John Malone, Lukshmi Shanthakumar, Martin Hämmerle, Maximilian Benner, Niels van der Galiën, Roland Kitchen, Sabrina Bernhardt, Seda Melkumyan, Stuart Butchart, Tom Burke, Zeina Shukairy

AUTHOR THANKS

Andrea Schulte-Peevers

Big heartfelt thanks to the many wonderful people who've plied me with tips, insights, information, ideas and encouragement, including the following (in no particular order): Henrik Tidefjärd, Claudia Scheffler, Ubin Eoh, Frank Engster, Heiner & Claudia Schuster, Renate Freiling, Julia Ana Herchenbach, Johann Scharfe and, of course, David Peevers.

Kerry Christiani

A heartfelt *dankeschön* to friends and family in the Schwarzwald, especially Hans and Monika in Villingen and Anja at the Brickstone Hostel, Ulm. Big thanks to Claus Schäfer in Triberg for the interview. I'd also like to thank all the tourist board pros I met on the road and my Lonely Planet coauthors for being great to work with. Finally, thanks to my husband for his ongoing support and for introducing me to the Black Forest all those years ago.

Marc Di Duca

Huge thanks go to parents-in-law Mykola and Vira for looking after the boys while I was away. Also much gratitude goes to Oleksandr in Erding for night 'researching' the output of Bavaria's breweries, Andrea in Nuremberg and the staff at tourist offices across the region but in particular those in Coburg, Passau, Regensburg and Bayreuth.

Catherine Le Nevez

Vielen Dank first and foremost to Julian, and to all of the locals, fellow travellers and tourism professionals en route for insights, information and good times. Thanks especially to Steve in Frankfurt, Manuel and family in the Moselle Valley, and everyone in and around Heidelberg. Huge thanks too to Destination Editor Gemma Graham and the Germany team, and everyone at Lonely Planet. As ever, *merci encore* to my parents, brother, *belle-sœur* and *neveu*.

Tom Masters

Huge thanks to Thomas Beach, my main man in Leipzig. To Álvaro Rodríguez Martín for company in Saxon Switzerland and for not choking to death in that restaurant in Görlitz. Thanks also to Moritz Estermann, Marius Rauschenbach, Sadia Belhadi, KiKi Hahn and Mario Dzurila for their help with research.

Ryan Ver Berkmoes

Thanks to Claudia Stehle as always for taking me to the dark depths of Hamburg. Samuel L Bronkowitz gets his usual nod as does Andrea Schulte-Peevers who is reason enough to visit Germany (and a great Lonely Planet author). And my companions for tiny trains and big fun: Thoja von Uthmann, Oliver Naatz, Lutz Stöver and Anja Frauböse. Finally, my love amidst the ghosts of Berlin: Alexis Averbuck.

Benedict Walker

This work is dedicated to my aunty Bonnie (Anne Cook-Moore), who inspired me to become a writer and my Mum, Trish Walker, who taught me how to care and never stops believing 'I can do it'. To my new friends in Germany, particular, Lutz Zybtni, my amazing historian, and to Anna Cassastrova, Matthieu, Ruth, Kuba and Bryce and Moyfrid in Hannover: I'm so grateful for your friendship and support. I look forward to the next day we meet in your beautiful and inspiring country. Finally, to my friends at Lonley Planet, particularly to Gemma Graham for giving me this incredible opportunity, I remain forever filled with gratitude.

ACKNOWLEDGEMENTS

Climate map data adapted from Peel MC, Finlayson BL & McMahon TA (2007) 'Updated World Map of the Köppen-Geiger Climate Classification', Hydrology and Earth System Sciences, 11, 163344.

Cover photograph: View of Bacharach over Peterskirche/Brigitte Merz/Getty

THIS BOOK

This 8th edition of Lonely Planet's *Germany* guidebook was researched and written by Andrea Schulte-Peevers (coordinating author), Kerry Christiani, Marc Di Duca, Catherine Le Nevez, Tom Masters, Ryan Ver Berkmoes and Benedict Walker. The previous edition of this book was also written by Andrea, Kerry, Marc and Ryan, as well as Anthony Haywood and Daniel Robinson. This guidebook was commissioned in Lonely Planet's London office, and produced by the following:

Destination Editor Gemma Graham

Product Editors Elin Berglund, Bruce Evans

Senior Cartographer Valentina Kremenchutskaya

Book Designer Wendy Wright

Assisting Editors Susie Ashworth, Sarah Bailey, Judith Bamber, Pete Cruttenden, Carly Hall, Paul Harding, Anne Mulvaney, Sally O'Brien, Saralinda Turner

Assisting Cartographers Julie Dodkins, James Leversha, Julie Sheridan

Cover Researcher Naomi Parker

Thanks to Ryan Evans, Larissa Frost, Jouve India, Alison Ridgway, Lauren Wellicome, Tony Wheeler

Index

Map Pages **000**
Photo Pages **000**

NOTES

Map Legend

Sights

- Beach
- Bird Sanctuary
- Buddhist
- Castle/Palace
- Christian
- Confucian
- Hindu
- Islamic
- Jain
- Jewish
- Monument
- Museum/Gallery/Historic Building
- Ruin
- Shinto
- Sikh
- Taoist
- Winery/Vineyard
- Zoo/Wildlife Sanctuary
- Other Sight

Activities, Courses & Tours

- Bodysurfing
- Diving
- Canoeing/Kayaking
- Course/Tour
- Sento Hot Baths/Onsen
- Skiing
- Snorkelling
- Surfing
- Swimming/Pool
- Walking
- Windsurfing
- Other Activity

Sleeping

- Sleeping
- Camping

Eating

- Eating

Drinking & Nightlife

- Drinking & Nightlife
- Cafe

Entertainment

- Entertainment

Shopping

- Shopping

Information

- Bank
- Embassy/Consulate
- Hospital/Medical
- Internet
- Police
- Post Office
- Telephone
- Toilet
- Tourist Information
- Other Information

Geographic

- Beach
- Gate
- Hut/Shelter
- Lighthouse
- Lookout
- Mountain/Volcano
- Oasis
- Park
- Pass
- Picnic Area
- Waterfall

Population

- Capital (National)
- Capital (State/Province)
- City/Large Town
- Town/Village

Transport

- Airport
- Border crossing
- Bus
- Cable car/Funicular
- Cycling
- Ferry
- Metro station
- Monorail
- Parking
- Petrol station
- S-Bahn/S-train/Subway station
- Taxi
- T-bane/Tunnelbana station
- Train station/Railway
- Tram
- Tube station
- U-Bahn/Underground station
- Other Transport

Note: Not all symbols displayed above appear on the maps in this book

Routes

- Tollway
- Freeway
- Primary
- Secondary
- Tertiary
- Lane
- Unsealed road
- Road under construction
- Plaza/Mall
- Steps
- Tunnel
- Pedestrian overpass
- Walking Tour
- Walking Tour detour
- Path/Walking Trail

Boundaries

- International
- State/Province
- Disputed
- Regional/Suburb
- Marine Park
- Cliff
- Wall

Hydrography

- River, Creek
- Intermittent River
- Canal
- Water
- Dry/Salt/Intermittent Lake
- Reef

Areas

- Airport/Runway
- Beach/Desert
- Cemetery (Christian)
- Cemetery (Other)
- Glacier
- Mudflat
- Park/Forest
- Sight (Building)
- Sportsground
- Swamp/Mangrove

Tom Masters

Saxony Tom hails from London, but has lived in Berlin since 2009 and has travelled widely all over Germany in that time. During research for this book, he particularly enjoyed his time discovering Leipzig's secret life beyond the Altstadt, walking in Saxon Switzerland, the gorgeousness that is Görlitz and getting to know Dresden. More of Tom's work can be found at www.tommasters.net.

Ryan Ver Berkmoes

Cologne & Northern Rhineland, Hamburg & the North Ryan Ver Berkmoes once lived in Germany for three years, in Frankfurt, during which time he edited a magazine until he got a chance for a new career with Lonely Planet. One of his first jobs was working on Lonely Planet's Germany coverage. He loves smoked fish, which serves him well in the north, and beer, which serves him pretty well everywhere in Germany. Follow him at ryanverberkmoes.com and @ryanvb

Benedict Walker

Lower Saxony, Central Germany Currently hanging by the beach near his Mum, in hometown Newcastle, Ben is living his dreams, travelling the world for Lonely Planet. So far, Ben has co-written Lonely Planet's *Japan, Canada, Florida* and *Australia* guidebooks. This is his first time writing for the Germany team, soon to be followed with Vietnam. Otherwise, he's written and directed a play, toured Australia managing travel for rockstars and is an avid photographer toying with his original craft of film-making. He's an advocate of following your dreams – they can come true. For updates, see www.wordsandjourneys.com.

OUR STORY

A beat-up old car, a few dollars in the pocket and a sense of adventure. In 1972 that's all Tony and Maureen Wheeler needed for the trip of a lifetime – across Europe and Asia overland to Australia. It took several months, and at the end – broke but inspired – they sat at their kitchen table writing and stapling together their first travel guide, *Across Asia on the Cheap*. Within a week they'd sold 1500 copies. Lonely Planet was born.

Today, Lonely Planet has offices in Franklin, London, Melbourne, Oakland, Beijing and Delhi, with more than 600 staff and writers. We share Tony's belief that 'a great guidebook should do three things: inform, educate and amuse'.

OUR WRITERS

Andrea Schulte-Peevers

Coordinating author, Berlin, Around Belin Born and raised in Germany and educated in London and at UCLA, Andrea has travelled the distance to the moon and back in her visits to some 75 countries, but her favourite place in the world is still Berlin. She's written about her native country for two decades and authored or contributed to some 80 Lonely Planet titles, including all editions of this guide, the *Discover Germany* guide, the Berlin city guide and *Pocket Berlin*.

Read more about Andrea at:
https://auth.lonelyplanet.com/profiles/Andreaschultepeevers

Kerry Christiani

Stuttgart & the Black Forest Having lived for six years in the Black Forest, Kerry returned to this neck of the woods (her second home) to write her chapters. Summer hikes in the forest, bike rides on Lake Constance and going on the trail of Mozart and Maria in Salzburg kept her busy for this edition. She tweets @ kerrychristiani and lists her latest work at www.kerrychristiani.com. Kerry also wrote the Outdoors, Eat Like a Local, Travel with Children, Food & Drink and Landscapes & Wildlife chapters.

Read more about Kerry at:
https://auth.lonelyplanet.com/profiles/Kerrychristiani

Marc Di Duca

Munich, Bavaria A well-established travel-guide author, Marc has explored many corners of Germany over the last 25 years, but it's to the quirky variety and friendliness of Bavaria that he returns most willingly. When not hiking Alpine valleys, eating snowballs in Rothenburg ob der Tauber or brewery-hopping in Bamberg, he can be found in Sandwich, Kent, where he lives with his wife, Tanya, and their two sons.

Read more about Marc at:
https://auth.lonelyplanet.com/profiles/Madidu

Catherine Le Nevez

Frankfurt & Southern Rhineland Catherine's wanderlust kicked in when she first roadtripped across Europe – including Germany – aged four, and she's been roadtripping here ever since, completing her Doctorate of Creative Arts in Writing, Masters in Professional Writing, and post-grad qualifications in Editing and Publishing along the way. Catherine has worked as a freelance writer for many years and over the last decade-plus she's written scores of Lonely Planet guides and articles covering destinations all over Germany, Europe and beyond.

Read more about Catherine at:
http://auth.lonelyplanet.com/profiles/catherine_le_nevez

OVER PAGE | MORE WRITERS

Published by Lonely Planet Publications Pty Ltd
ADN 36 005 607 983
8th edition – March 2016
ISBN 978 1 74321 023 9
© Lonely Planet 2016   Photographs © as indicated 2016
10 9 8 7 6 5 4 3 2
Printed in Singapore

Although the authors and Lonely Planet have taken all reasonable care in preparing this book, we make no warranty about the accuracy or completeness of its content and, to the maximum extent permitted, disclaim all liability arising from its use.